A SORROW IN OUR HEART

The Life of Tecumseh

A SORROW IN OUR HEART

The Life of Tecumseh

Allan W. Eckert

This edition published in 1994 by SMITHMARK
Publishers, a division of U.S. Media Holdings, Inc.,
16 East 32nd Street, New York, NY 10016.

SMITHMARK books are available for bulk purchase
for sales promotion and premium use. For details write
or call the manager of special sales, SMITHMARK Publishers,
16 East 32nd Street, New York, NY 10016. (212) 532-6600.

This edition published by special arrangement with
W.S. Konecky Associates, Inc. and John Hawkins &
Associates, Inc., New York.

ISBN: 0-8317-5817-1

Printed in the United States of America

10 9 8 7 6 5 4 3 2

Maps designed by GDS/Jeffrey L. Ward
Maps based upon drawings provided by Allen W. Eckert

To the man whose life has
for so many years been intertwined with
the life of Tecumseh,

Marion N. Waggoner

. . . friend, companion and general manager of
the outdoor drama Tecumseh! . . .
this book is dedicated
with
appreciation and affection

When a white man kills an Indian in a fair fight it is called honorable, but when an Indian kills a white man in a fair fight it is called murder. When a white army battles Indians and wins it is called a great victory, but if they lose it is called a massacre and bigger armies are raised. If the Indian flees before the advance of such armies, when he tries to return he finds that white men are living where he lived. If he tries to fight off such armies, he is killed and the land is taken anyway. When an Indian is killed it is a great loss which leaves a gap in our people and a sorrow in our heart; when a white is killed, three or four others step up to take his place and there is no end to it. The white man seeks to conquer nature, to bend it to his will and to use it wastefully until it is all gone and then he simply moves on, leaving the waste behind him and looking for new places to take. The whole white race is a monster who is always hungry and what he eats is land.

**—Chiksika, elder brother of Tecumseh,
to Tecumseh, March 19, 1779.**

Maps or Diagrams

Acknowledgment

The author wishes to extend his sincere appreciation to fellow writer, historian, and friend, Phillip W. Hoffman, of Westlake Village, California, who is undoubtedly the foremost authority on the life of Simon Girty and whose assistance with certain aspects of research throughout the production of this work has been of considerable value; and whose constant cheerfulness and enthusiasm have been a mainstay during many a dark hour.

Author's Note

— 《 》 — Over the years much has been written about Tecumseh who, though never a chief in his own Shawnee tribe, rose to great heights through the power of his charisma, the strength of his humanity, and the scope of his dream of a great nation of Indians bound by a racial brotherhood that superseded the barriers of intertribal rivalries and hatreds.

A great body of mythology has grown around him, often clouding the wonderfully impressive facts of his life in a haze of misinformation. There is no need for that, since his character and accomplishments alone establish him as one of the finer human beings in recorded history.

It is the aim of the author, in presenting Tecumseh's life, to show how and why he became what he was. It is unworthy of him merely to bounce from major point to major point of his life and ignore or gloss over the minutiae of everyday life that molded him, guided him, and so decidedly influenced him. It is, therefore, my purpose in this book to meld in a continuous chronological flow, the details of childhood and family life—the warmth and humor, the pleasures and games, the love and sadnesses of everyday living—with the pervasive aspects of tribal culture and the irresistible press of outside events.

Author's Note

This is a biography, true, but is is more than merely that; it is what I choose to call *narrative biography,* in which the reader may, as with a good novel, feel himself drawn into the current of events and be able to identify closely with the characters. It is designed to be a book that utilizes all the better elements of the novel form, for excitement, pace, and continuity, yet at the same time remains reliable as an accurate depiction of the history it embraces. In this respect the author uses considerably more dialogue than one normally associates with strictly historical works. Such dialogue is not invented conversation but, rather, a form of painstakingly *reconstituted* dialogue that lies hidden in abundance in historical material. Such hidden dialogue is normally written as straight historical commentary, without direct quotes, but in it are couched the keywords that legitimately allow such information, if the effort is made, to be returned to vibrant and meaningful conversation that remains accurate to the intent and direction of what is occurring at any given time.

That the reader may better understand what is meant by keywords that point to hidden dialogue, it is only necessary to show here a brief paragraph as it actually appears in the original account. This following paragraph is one that appears in the great body of work (close to five hundred volumes of material) called the Draper Papers, housed in the Archives of the Wisconsin Historical Society Library at Madison. The paragraph, dealing with the frontiersman Captain Samuel Brady, appears on pages 298–299 of Volume 2 of the 33-volume series designated S, under the general title of Draper's Notes. By paying close attention to those phrases I have *specifically* italicized, the reader can easily see how the keywords show a hidden conversation that virtually cries out to be brought back from straight text to lively and accurate dialogue.

Brady, Francis McQuire, & their party went to the block house. Thomas Wells & another went ahead a short distance, to see. They discovered two young Indians, nearly grown, climbing trees.—these discovered the whites & made their escape. The Indian camp altogether numbered 10 Indians, the two young fellows, & two squaws. At the first alarm both of the squaws ran off, but one soon came back & surrendered herself. Joseph Edgington shot her—for which *Brady blamed him; thought it unkind & discreditable to make war upon women. Someone volunteered the remark that Edgington, when he shot, supposed he was shooting a warrior.* The thing was dropped, *that being deemed a good excuse.* This was after the affair or attack was over; but *Edgington privately declared he would kill any & every thing in the shape of an Indian whenever he could get the chance, from the size of his fist to any old gray-headed Indian, be they he or she.*

Obviously there is not only hidden dialogue in such a passage, but hidden emotions, thoughts and physical actions as well and these, of course, are the bits and pieces that, when properly and accurately reconstituted, form the flesh and blood that bring to life the bare bones of history.

The author has lived very closely with this man called Tecumseh for well over a quarter of a century. As a character, Tecumseh played a large role in the first of the six volumes of *The Winning of America* series, *The Frontiersmen,* and a somewhat smaller role in the fifth book of the series, *Gateway to Empire.* Research for the first took seven years, yet in the interval since that initial research began (in 1958), considerable new material has come to light. As a result, there will no doubt be a number of surprises in store for those who followed the activities of Tecumseh in those two books. In a few cases the author made use of material that later research proved to be either in error or exaggerated in the primary sources available at the time. Such errors, now discovered, have been pointed out in the amplification notes keyed to this present text.

In telling Tecumseh's story, the viewpoint taken in the writing was, of necessity, Tecumseh's. As such, we see him acting at any given time on the basis of what he knows or discovers through his own personal experience or contact with others. Thus, many of the amplification notes become quite important to the reader in understanding the machinations occurring coincidentally among the whites—their actions, correspondence, reports and the like, about which Tecumseh could have no knowledge until they impinged themselves upon him in the normal course of events. It is for this reason, more than in *The Winning of America* series, that the author recommends the reading of the notes where they are numerically indicated in the text; they are not *vital* to understanding, but they are a help.

Allan W. Eckert
Bellefontaine, Ohio
September 1991

Prologue

[March 9, 1768 — Wednesday]

— 《 》 — The man who stood silently, patiently, in the length-ening shadows at the water's edge was in no manner physically remarkable except, perhaps, for his eyes. There was a singular keenness about them, imbuing a quick and penetrating gaze that belied the passivity of his pose. As always, they missed little of his surroundings and nothing that moved. These were the eyes of Pucksinwah, war chief of the Shawnee nation.[1]

At the moment he was gazing across the pool, through the faint mist rising from the surface of the water, at the little half-face shelter erected several hours ago, listening intently for the sound that would ease his concern, but everything was still. He chose to take the silence as benign; had Methotasa's distress increased, someone would have emerged from the shelter and informed him. On the other hand, the absence of sound indicated the birth had not yet occurred. He had urged his wife to remain behind at their village, promising that he and his followers would return as swiftly as possible following the important council to be held at the capital city of the Shawnee tribe. She, however, insisted on coming along, certain there would be plenty of time for them to reach their destination well before her labor began. They had almost done so.

1

The large delegation of Kispokotha Shawnees had left their own village, Kispoko Town, on the Scioto River, some seventy miles southeast of here four days ago, taking their time on the easy trail leading to the tribe's principal village of Chalahgawtha.[2] There had been an early thaw and the snow that had cloaked the ground for a week or more was largely melted away. The procession they had made was a colorful one, almost everyone wrapped in his own brightly hued blanket or garbed in furs to ward off the chill. In the van were the foremost chiefs and some of the warriors astride horses, followed by more warriors afoot and then in succession by the old men, the women, and the children. Six hundred individuals, representing about two thirds of Kispoko Town's population, had elected to attend the grand council at Chalahgawtha and, as the sinuous file made its way northwestward, the air was filled with the laughter of the men, the almost incessant chattering and giggling of the women and the squeals and happy cries of the children, the latter rarely keeping to the path and covering half again the distance of each day's march by romping through woods and prairies, playing follow-the-leader and archery games, tag and mock battles as the procession moved.

On the first night they had camped on the rim of the north branch of Paint Creek and built their multitude of evening cookfires, with half a dozen or more family groups clustered about each of the fires, though with a great deal of intermingling occurring.[3] By early morning hours the temperature had plummeted to well below freezing and the wind whipped them unmercifully. Methotasa, still exhausted from the previous day's fifteen-mile walk, had begun showing signs of distress and, over her objections, Pucksinwah had bundled her well in blankets and placed her upon his own horse, which he led. The column of travelers was much more compacted this day and there was little straying or game playing by the children. Late in the afternoon they made their second camp about twelve miles from the first, along the main course of Paint Creek.[4] Numerous hasty shelters had been constructed in which the blanket-wrapped people huddled close together near the fires for mutual warmth. The weather had continued unpleasant yesterday, with several brief periods of snow pelting into their faces and camp last night had been made on the headwaters of a small stream about a dozen miles southeast of Chalahgawtha.[5]

This bitter cold snap broke during the night and by midmorning the temperature was well above freezing, the sky bright blue without a trace of clouds. In the early afternoon Methotasa's water had broken and her distress increased as labor pains struck. She did not complain and withstood them for some time as they endeavored to reach Chalahgawtha, now so close, but it was not to be. When within three good arrow flights of the town, as they were passing the spring and pool, it had become clear she could not travel or even be carried farther. Pucksinwah called a halt, summoned his second in command, Shemeneto—Black Snake—and directed him to lead their followers on the remaining march to Chalahgawtha. When he arrived, Shemeneto should report his chief's whereabouts, with the promise that Pucksinwah would arrive in time for the opening of the council at midday tomorrow. At the edge of this pool formed by the bubbling spring the shelter was quickly built.[6] Half a dozen women—midwives, referred to as aunts—stayed behind to assist Methotasa in the birth, and also remaining were the two older children of Pucksinwah and Methotasa, twelve-year-old Chiksika and ten-year-old Tecumapese.[7]

As much as Pucksinwah had wanted to reach Chalahgawtha today and spend this evening counciling with other chiefs in preparation for the beginning of the grand council tomorrow, his greater concern at this moment was with Methotasa. It was a difficult time for her, more so than with the previous births and he wondered if it was because ten years had passed since the birth of Tecumapese without another child being born. The war chief's features softened as he thought of his wife, remembering the first time he had ever seen her and how smitten he had been with her, despite the stress of the circumstances. Fifteen harvest moons had come and gone since then, yet the details were etched in his mind with indelible clarity. He had been a young man of twenty-six then, one of the best young warriors in the entire tribe, and he had been chosen by his fellows to lead a war party against the Cherokees living on the Shawnee River practically in the area where his own people had once lived and after whom the river had been named.[8]

It was here that they had met and, through Pucksinwah's skillful attack plan, defeated a much larger party of Cherokees at their village. Several Cherokee men had been killed and four taken captive along with a dozen women and children. Among these was a slim and very attractive girl of fifteen, who was captured by Oshashqua—Muskrat—the oldest member of their war party, who discovered her hiding in a pile of furs that were being bound into bundles for transport. This was Methotasa—A Turtle Laying Her Eggs in the Sand.[9]

The victorious Shawnees took the prisoners, as well as the furs and other village plunder, to their distant, well-hidden camp and that evening the four captive Cherokee warriors were tortured to death. Before that occurred, Pucksinwah, concerned especially for the terrified Methotasa, directed Oshashqua to take the women and children away from the camp and return with them in the morning. This was done and Pucksinwah remained solicitous of her comfort and safety on the return to Ohio. Oshashqua was of the Peckuwe sept and after their arrival, Methotasa, as his captive, was taken by him to his own village of Piqua Town on the Mad River.[10] There she was officially adopted by Oshashqua and his wife to take the place of their son, a young warrior who was killed on his very first raid against the Cherokees the year before. With this adoption she became part of the *Kahgilaywilani*—the Turtle *unsoma*.

Pucksinwah, in his own village of Kispoko Town, could not forget the attractive girl and, when not away leading frequent war raids into enemy territory, made occasional trips to see her at Oshashqua's house in Peckuwe Town. By the time she had been with the Shawnees for just over a year, he was paying much attention to her and at the next feast dance, in the late spring of 1755, she signified her acceptance of him by shyly slipping her bare hand into his and they were soon married.

Early the following summer Chiksika was born at Kispoko Town and, as Pucksinwah himself had done, spent his early boyhood playing games and learning the fundamentals of becoming a warrior on the broad plains of the Scioto Valley.[11] And this was also where, two years later, Tecumapese had been born.

A movement at the shelter broke Pucksinwah's reverie and his gaze sharpened. One of the aunts had emerged into the final rays of the setting sun and for a moment his pulse quickened, but she didn't head toward him. She merely stooped and picked up some of the firewood that Chiksika had been piling up outside the blanket-covered entryway and disappeared with it back into the shelter. Pucksinwah frowned faintly, again wishing that Methotasa had not insisted on making the trip and praying silently to Moneto and the Great Spirit to care for her now.

As he had done on several introspective moments recently, the war chief considered the wisdom of bringing another son into this turbulent world. That the babe to be born this day would be a boy, he had no doubt whatever. Somehow, with the prescience that he had always known—and that had saved him on innumerable occasions—he knew the child would be male. In his envisioning, however, there was no clear picture or feeling of how Methotasa would fare in this birth, and that worried him.

Chiksika stepped out of the woods with another large armload of firewood and headed for the shelter. Pucksinwah smiled as he watched. The boy was tall for his age and lean, yet well muscled and very sure in his movements. Already, in his games with the other boys, he was exhibiting impressive early signs of leadership. There was character and strength, and Pucksinwah was very proud of him. Yet, what lay in store for him and for his as yet unborn little brother in the years to come? Pucksinwah sighed and watched as Chiksika dropped his load on the pile and then listened carefully as one of the aunts stuck her head out past the blanket and said something to him. The boy nodded and set out again to seek a final load of firewood in the gathering twilight. The smile lingered on Pucksinwah's lips, but tinged now with a sense of sadness. There was a time when he would have cherished the vision of Chiksika's future and that of the little one to come—stalwart young men proud of their heritage as the fiercest and finest warriors among all the Indians, boldly making forays against enemy tribes in the Shawnee tradition, exhibiting great bravery and fighting skill coupled with keen intelligence, and returning home, as their father had done before them, with the well-deserved honors of war. But that was no longer the complete vision. Now there was a new and deadly element, more to be feared and reckoned with than any danger the Shawnees had ever faced in their history—the whites.

That was what this grand council at Chalahgawtha was all about; trying to decide what the Shawnees must do, as a nation, about the whites who were crossing the eastern mountains and spilling into this land of the Indians, bringing with them the ever more certain seeds of destruction. Individually these whites were as nothing, generally poor as fighting men because they had no training as warriors, largely cowardly and almost always deceitful, never a match for even half their number in Shawnee braves. Yet, these whites were armed with weapons infinitely superior to bows, knives, and war clubs; killing the Indians as well by the pestilences brought among them as by the drawing of blood, destroying without care the beasts and birds of forest and field that the Great Spirit had endowed to Her red children, cutting down stately woodlands and burning vast prairie expanses, damming free-running streams to build their mills for grinding grain and, worst of all, driving stakes into the breast of mother earth, building fences and setting apart, as their own, land that the Great Spirit had bestowed to all.

Pucksinwah's sudden shiver was inspired as much by his bleak thoughts as by the increasing coldness of the evening air. He stepped to a nearby log and sat upon it, tucking his blanket more snugly about himself. Since first the whites had come there had been troubles and with each passing year the problems had intensified. What a wonderful time it must have been before whites set foot in these lands and warfare was a clean and sharply defined, even joyful, intertribal matter. The Shawnee war chief remembered his own youth when the tribal historians spoke of those days long past, implanting the proud history of their tribe in the minds of the youngsters seated around the fire. Such tribal historians were carefully selected and intensively trained over a period of years with no other goal than to pass on to these rising generations that which was the truth of what was past, without embellishment, without amendment, without personal bias, always with incredible accuracy and, at the same time, instilling in their listeners a fierce and lasting pride in and for their own people. And the history of the Shawnees was indeed a colorful one.

Unlike virtually all the other tribes, which sank their roots in a specified territory and remained there, the Shawnees were astonishingly nomadic—traveling, warring, moving, pausing, then traveling again, red leaves drifting and eddying on the tide of time. More than this, they were extremely bellicose and not infrequently mercenary. They were a warrior race who reveled in the sheer joy of fighting and were masters in the art of warfare. They were frequently invited—and often temporarily accepted such invitations—by tribes of lesser war-making capabilities to settle among them, share in the bounty of their harvests and protect them if and when their enemies swooped down upon them, or even to launch their own raids into the territories of the foes of their hosts.

The history of the tribe, as relayed by the tribal historians to the wide-eyed listeners gathered around the fire, told many stories of great heroism and courage, tales of alliances and enmities, all becoming more focused, more detailed and more accurate the more modern they became. There were almost always good relations with such tribes as the Hurons and the Eries, the Sus-quehannocks and the Lenni Lenape and the Twightwees, along with many other tribes in the area of the western Great Lakes.[12] There were rarely good feelings, however, between them and the northeastern tribes—the Oneidas and Onondagas, the Mohawks and Senecas and Cayugas. So harshly did the Shawnees deal with them that they eventually banded themselves together in a confederation for self protection which some called Akonoshioni, meaning "the United People" and others called the Hodenosaunee, meaning "People of the Long House." But these names quickly gave way to a more common name, the Iroquois League—the Poisonous Snakes. Also called the Five Nations, the Iroquois became among the most avowed enemies of the Shawnees, jealous of their strength, mobility and skill in warfare. Their own reputation as a force powerful enough to face the Shawnees was augmented considerably when, while the majority of the Shawnees were away—some in the south, some in Missouri country and only a small number in the Ohio Valley—the Iroquois went to war against their powerful and numerous neighbors, the Hurons. The latter, because of their strength, numbers and pacific attitude, had long been respectfully referred to by other tribes as "grandfather," signifying wisdom and superiority.[13] Huron-Iroquois warfare was sporadic for nearly the entire first half of the last century, gradually intensifying when the new French settlers in the St. Lawrence Valley decided, at the behest of their proselytizing black-robed Jesuits, to support the Hurons. In so doing they acquired the enmity of the Iroquois. It was, so the tribal historians told Puck-sinwah and other listeners, in 1649 when something occurred that stretched the Iroquois reputation as fighters well beyond all reality and caused lasting ramifications for the Shawnees, who were not even involved. A large force of Iroquois warriors fought and defeated a considerably smaller party of Hurons. The surviving Hurons, being hotly pursued, took temporary refuge with an insignificant tribe called the Eries—the Cat People—who occupied a small pocket of territory near the southeastern end of the lake named after

them. When the Iroquois tracked the Hurons there and approached, the latter fled and escaped to their own people. The enraged Iroquois, instantly
retaliated against the virtually defenseless Eries, utterly destroyed their villages, then tracked down and murdered every man, woman and child until
the entire tribe was annihilated. It was hardly a great feat of warfare, yet it
substantially bolstered their reputation as wholly savage killers and the fear
evoked among neighboring tribes was practically unbounded. The Iroquois
relished the reputation and were delighted that now whole enemy villages
were precipitately abandoned when the cry was raised, "The Iroquois are
coming!" As if to cement their newfound notoriety, the Iroquois descended
on another small tribe, the benign Neutrals, to the north and west of them,
and similarly wiped them out. Once again the reputation of the Iroquois
expanded. Few outsiders seemed to notice that the boastful Iroquois were
sagacious enough to avoid any outright confrontation with the Hurons, or
their Shawnee and Delaware allies, unless the advantage for the Five Nations
was enormous.[14]

Prior to and throughout this period, the tribal historians related, the white
men came from across the great blue water to the east; from Spain first,
establishing themselves in northeastern Florida and then spreading out in exploratory parties wearing queer metal hats and chest plates and penetrating
quickly to the southern domain of the Shawnees along the river named for
them, the Suwannee. Then came the French and British, also in gigantic canoes
pushed by the wind, first planting settlements along the coast of the great
eastern water but quickly pushing inland and establishing contact with the
Indians, bringing with them a mixed blessing; tools, materials and weapons
that catapulted the Indians out of their primitive existence and into a modern
age and, in so doing, made them dependent upon the whites.

For the furs the Indians could trade to the whites they received in return
wonderful steel knives and hatchets, blankets, tools, fabrics, paint, clothing,
steel traps, condiments, cookware, spices, a variety of hardware, and the two
most important and society-altering items of all, liquor and guns. Invariably,
the liquor was gone almost immediately after it was received, with nothing
to show for it except the upset—and often mayhem—it caused, and the guns
were dependent upon the powder and lead they required.

Now the competition for the Indian trade became sharp between the
different white factions, especially between the British and French and evolved
into a vicious series of conflicts loosely called the Beaver Wars. Of those two
principal white factions, the British were far more deadly in their ultimate
goals. French traders closely intermingled with the Indians, quite often married
into their tribes and adopted their culture; but their trade goods were markedly
inferior to those the British had to offer, much higher priced and considerably
less abundant. The British traders, on the other hand, with their superb, highly

varied, seemingly endless supply of goods, could provide the Indians handily with everything they wanted, but they created more resentment among the natives in the process than did the French. British traders, even when among the tribes, largely kept to themselves, by and large considering them inferior races of ignorant savages incapable of social graces and subhuman in their sensitivity and emotions. They treated the Indians abominably in many circumstances, flagrantly cheated them in their dealings and supplied them with far too much liquor which, in effect, gave them nothing of lasting value for their work. Worst of all, the British traders served as the vanguard for a wave of settlers who followed and laid claim to Indian lands, without respect or regard to the beauties and intricacies of nature, raping the very land they took in their ravenous desire to possess.

Pucksinwah could still hear the tribal historians telling how this was only the beginning of the problem. The British committed themselves to a strong alliance with the Iroquois, believing that confederation's ridiculous claims of having been victorious in warfare over all enemies and accepting, without question, the Iroquois claim of being the most powerful body of Indians on the continent. When the English soon discovered that this belief was false, they deliberately set about convincing themselves and others that all other tribes were mere subjects of the Iroquois and bound by whatever decisions or treaties the Five Nations consummated. They did this primarily because they wanted to possess the land and its great natural wealth and they were quite willing to buy it from the Iroquois League, even though most often it was land the Iroquois neither owned nor controlled. And the Iroquois were more than willing to make a very good living by selling to the gullible whites any land they wanted, so long as it wasn't actual Iroquois territory. If these whites then became involved in disputes with the other tribes who hereditarily possessed the lands the Iroquois had sold, then that was their problem, although if the price was right, the Iroquois would lend the British their warrior strength to help back up their claims of having legally purchased the lands. Little wonder, then, that the injured tribes turned to the powerful, mercenary Shawnees as defenders of their own rights.

The whites, recognizing that the greatest danger they might have to face was the possibility of all red men uniting against them, considered it vital to foment bitter intertribal unrest, even between longtime allies, so that the entire frontier and the wilderness beyond was in a state of constant unrest and eruption. The cream of manhood of all the tribes was whittled away in the small and large conflicts that resulted and tribes that had once been powerful found themselves severely weakened and all the more dependent upon the whites they had initially welcomed and aided and who, while still squabbling for dominance in America, had now become virtually their masters.

There were those tribes who strove to stay neutral, but even they were not spared the devastating results of contact with the whites. Whole tribes, particularly those in the far eastern regions of the continent, were wiped out of existence by the diseases the whites brought among them—smallpox, measles, chicken pox, mumps, whooping cough, influenza, venereal diseases and even extremely virulent strains of the common cold.

In all this, the Shawnees occupied a unique position. They were fierce, dangerous, unpredictable, and essentially without land of their own to defend, quite willing to fight as mercenaries for this white faction or that, or for none, as the inclination struck them, often with different factions within their own tribe supporting different factions of the whites and yet, amazingly, never allowing these diverse alliances to become hot warfare among themselves. Their relations with the Five Nations remained consistently terrible, with the Iroquois strutting and boasting and claiming their superiority and the Shawnees, knowing they had nothing to prove, openly contemptuous of such claims and considering the greedy Iroquois as merely being "the running dogs of the British."

French relations with the tribes—excepting the Iroquois and their few allies—remained relatively good and these whites, recognizing exactly what the British were doing, began, in 1671, a concerted effort to thwart the British by taking formal possession of all the territory to the west and northwest of the Ohio River and, over the next half century, establishing numerous strategically located quasi-military fortifications and fur posts to back up their claims and successfully defend the rich fur trade. With these facilities in place, the grip the French now had on the western country to control the fur trade was peaceful, but very strong.

Actually beginning to believe their own reputation for ferocity and supremacy, the Iroquois began, in the 1680s, an effort to extend their actual occupied territory into the Ohio country. The Miamis, though currently the most powerful tribe in the northwest, suddenly found themselves in the maw of a dangerous pincers—being attacked on the west by their mortal enemies, the Sioux, and now threatened in the east by the Iroquois. In 1683 these Miamis asked the Shawnees for assistance. Accepting with alacrity, the Shawnees joined forces with the Miamis and some of that tribe's Delaware allies and, despite the Iroquois having superior weapons, easily beat back the invading war parties of the Five Nations. The Shawnees asked no immediate payment from the Miamis for helping, but it was a considerable favor owed them now that one day they would collect. The Iroquois, smarting under their humiliating repulsion, returned to their own Mohawk Valley and then blandly claimed to their British friends to have defeated all the western tribes, who were now their vassals, and all the territory involved where ownership might previously have been questionable, was now indisputably Iroquois territory and would the British care to buy any of it? Not even considering such a claim might be spurious, the British leaped at this golden opportunity and purchased a great deal.

Notwithstanding the French claims, the British now also made western claims of their own. Even while the western French posts were being built, the Great Father in England, King Charles II, granted a royal charter to William Penn for the whole region now called Pennsylvania, which was the territory of the Delawares, though claimed by the Iroquois. The Virginia colonial authorities proclaimed that their domain included all of the northwestern territory, extending westward through the Kan-tuck-kee region all the way to the Mississippi River and including the Illinois country.

As for the Shawnees, by this time they had grown very weary of the constant upheaval involved in all this political and territorial maneuvering, and most of those remaining in Pennsylvania migrated again in 1684. The majority, temporarily at peace with the powerful southern tribes, returned to the south. A smaller portion, however, about a thousand warriors, plus their families, under the leadership of Pucksinwah's grandfather, Opeththa—went west and settled on the Illinois River just above the mouth of the Vermilion, where René-Robert Cavalier de La Salle had built Fort St. Louis the previous year while the Shawnees were fighting off the Iroquois for the Miamis.[15] Glad for the protection the Shawnees would provide against would-be enemies, the Illinois tribes welcomed them warmly and La Salle himself, who had by this time visited more tribes than most whites even knew existed, was greatly impressed with them, writing in his reports to the governor of New France that, "I consider the Shawnees as the best, finest, most intelligent and most skilled warriors in America."

Opeththa had quickly become disenchanted with the Illinois country. Prairies were all well and good, but here there was too much of a good thing. The ground was too flat for their liking and instead of great forests, there were merely roughly circular groves of trees jutting upward like strange ships in a vast sea of grass. Most of the Shawnees began drifting off, some heading southward to join their kin on the Tombigbee or Savannah. Opeththa, with his most loyal core of warriors, remained on the Illinois for a while longer, until 1690, when a delegation of Delawares from the Susquehanna Valley came and, angered at living under the undeserved shadow of the Iroquois, implored the Shawnees to return to Pennsylvania. Undaunted by the possibility of again locking horns with the Iroquois, Opeththa agreed, but added that it might take a good while for them to get there, since they were planning to visit the Miamis on the way and might stay with them for half a year or so.

It took even longer. The Miamis, who still held claim to the lands north of the Ohio, had no villages left in the Muskingum, Scioto, and Little Miami River valleys and invited Opeththa and his remaining seventy-two warriors and their families to settle there as guests of the Miami. "We have been everywhere," Opeththa replied, "and can find no good land. Perhaps it is there. We will go to that place and stay for a while, but we have promised to rejoin our Delaware brothers on the Susquehanna. Should we find it not to our liking among them, then by and by we may return and accept your offer."

So Opeththa and his people went to the Scioto Valley, found the ground ideal for growing corn, pumpkins, beans, squash and whatever other vegetables they needed, found the streams filled with fish, and found a fairly good supply of deer and elk and turkey. Equally important, south of Ohio, across the river in the Kan-tuck-kee country there were large numbers of woods bison, deer, elk, bear and wolves. They remained here over a year and it was then, the tribal historians had told Pucksinwah and the others, just before resuming the journey to the Susquehanna, that Opeththa decided something that would eventually change the lives of the Shawnees for all time: he decided that one day he would address all the chiefs in Grand Council, saying to them that perhaps at last the Great Spirit had shown them where they were to sink their roots and end their eternal roving; a land that its owners, the Miamis, who owed them a great debt, might be convinced to give to them; a land that for once would be their very own and not just a place to occupy for a little while before moving on.

It was not until 1692 that Opeththa and his people arrived in the valley of the Susquehanna and were welcomed by the Delawares and Susquehannocks. Opeththa's new village was built on the lower Susquehanna and an uneasy peace was made with the British for purposes of trade. This relationship lasted for a few years until the jealous Iroquois finally sent surreptitious messages to the British that the Shawnees were strictly subjects of the Five Nations and that in any negotiations between British and Indians, only the Iroquois had any authority. To this the British fully agreed. With such a state of affairs existing, it was not long before Opeththa's people found out about the arrangement and relationships between the British and Shawnees degenerated even more.

Matters were not very good where the Shawnees in the south were concerned, either. By 1700 it was obvious to all the southern tribes that none of them could stand alone against the powerful Shawnees if that tribe decided to attack and so they did what the Five Nations had done long before: they bonded themselves together in an intertribal alliance—the Southern Confederacy—and, with their courage bolstered by the strength of their union, demanded that the Shawnees leave their lands. The Shawnees could have made an issue of it and gone to war against them and quite likely have won, but the fact of the matter was that they were once again experiencing itchy feet and were ready to emigrate back to the north. They agreed to leave, but warned that they would take their own time and the southern tribes would do well not to hurry them on their way. The Southern Confederacy nervously acquiesced and there began a gradual movement of the Shawnees northward over the next year until most had left the south and joined the growing population of Shawnees under Opeththa in east-central Pennsylvania.[16]

The influx of Shawnees set the Penn proprietors to worrying once again and so a major meeting, called the Great Elm Treaty, was held on April 23, 1701, at Kensington, close to Philadelphia. This treaty was between the Penns and the four principal Indian factions occupying the region of their royal charter—the Iroquois, the Delawares, the Susquehannocks and the Shawnees. It was, for a pleasant change, not a treaty for land acquisition, but one brought about by the Quakers under Penn in an effort to heal the rift that had so long existed between the Iroquois and the other three. Despite pessimism among the white enemies of the Quakers that such could ever be accomplished, amazingly enough a sort of peace was agreed to among the tribes and, while there were occasional minor differences after that, it lasted for over fifty years.

Eleven days after the Great Elm Treaty, another declaration of war was made between the French and English—this one called Queen Anne's War or the War of Spanish Succession. Its effect was not pronounced among the northern tribes but it caused severe rifts in the Southern Confederation and once again intertribal war raged there. One of the tribes deeply affected was the Tuscarawas of North Carolina. Having their fill of harassment from several neighboring tribes, including the Cherokees, they asked the Iroquois for permission to emigrate to New York and become part of the Iroquois League. The matter was deliberated in the League councils and at length, in 1710, the Tuscarawas were given admittance to the League, but only as the "children" or wards of the Oneidas, upon whose land they settled and without vote in the League Councils, being bound by whatever decisions the Oneidas made. Thus, the Iroquois League was no longer the Five Nations and would ever after be the Six Nations.

What was concerning the Shawnees under Opeththa now more than anything else was the disturbing influx of white settlers through the entire region east of the Susquehanna. In addition, trade with the English was badly souring. Since the land was the Delawares' and not their own to defend, little by little, splinter groups of Shawnees began breaking away and moving westward, into the Alleghenies and beyond, in the successive mountain ridges and valleys all the way to the confluence of the Monongahela and the Allegheny, where these two great rivers merged to form the broad and treacherous Ohio River. Even many of the Delawares, because of their own continuing trouble with the Iroquois and British, began following the Shawnees and settling near where they settled, mainly in the valleys of the Allegheny and the Beaver, though some, with permission of the Miamis, went as far west as the Muskingum valley, well beyond the reach of English settlers as well as the Iroquois.[17]

It was always at this stage of their narrations that the tribal historians seemed to draw themselves up with pride for what came next in the tribe's history. That occurred in the late summer of 1725 when a Grand Council of the Shawnees was held at the Peckuwe Shawnee village called Logstown, located at the mouth of Beaver River, twenty-two miles downstream on the Ohio from the confluence of the Allegheny and the Monongahela.[18] It was here that Opeththa addressed an audience of the most important chiefs and subchiefs of all five septs of the Shawnee tribe. He told them that his people were not content living on the Allegheny and that it was his conviction that the Ohio country was the very land promised to the tribe by the Great Spirit a hundred or more generations ago; the place where the Shawnees might ultimately settle and sink their roots and where they could finally end their nomadic lifestyle. Furthermore, it was land presently uninhabited, owned by Miamis who had already extended an invitation to the Shawnees to live upon it.

The members of the council deliberated on the matter and discussed it for many days. Some had lived there temporarily in the past and spoke highly of it, but all were concerned that it was land owned by the Miamis. As such, even if the Miamis had invited the Shawnees to live there, it would still be Miami land and therefore how could permanent roots be sunk? Shawnee honor would not permit them to simply take it, since the Miamis had always been their close friends and allies. No, they could not accept the kind invitation of the Miamis unless that tribe freely gave the land to them without restriction and to be forevermore the Shawnees' own territory. A delegation was thereupon selected to carry this decision to the Miamis at the head of the Maumee.

At practically this same moment in the principal Miami village of Pickawillany on the Great Miami River a remarkably related occurrence was in progress.[19] There, too, a council was being held to hear the words of their aged and greatly revered prophet, Michquala. The old man addressed the assemblage very gravely. The Miamis, he told them, with all their subtribes here represented—the Weas, Ouiatenons, Salamonies and Piankeshaws, the Mississinewas and Eel Rivers, the Atchatchakangouens, Pepicokias, Mengakonias and Kilatikas—represented over ten thousand warriors. Their territory extended in the east almost to the Pennsylvania country and in the south to the Ohio River, in the west to the Wabash River and even beyond that stream into a large portion of the Illinois country and in the north to the shores of Lake Michigan and across the southern Michigan country to Lake Erie. This made the Miamis perhaps the strongest tribe in this land. Yet, the very possession of so broad a territory would eventually cause their destruction, which not even their great strength could prevent, unless they took swift and drastic steps to prevent it. How would this destruction manifest itself? It would come in the form of the white man. Not the French, who had traded with them and lived among them for many years in harmony. Not the Spanish, who were too weak in this land to oppose even the French. No, nor even from the British, who were so demanding in their greed to possess the land and subjugate the tribes. The white man who would be such a danger would carry a long knife and he would lie, cheat, buy, promise, steal, and even gladly kill to take possession of these lands. He would be strong—powerful enough to defeat the other whites—and he would be a multitude as numberless as the leaves of the forest. Who was this white man that was so great a threat? He was the son of the English king. He was the colonist, who would turn against his own father, the British, and thrust him out of this land and back across the great water to the east from whence he came and then he would turn his attention to taking all the lands from the red men. He would come down the Ohio River in great numbers and he would come from the south in great numbers and the Ohio River would not be barrier enough to stop him, as he would cross over and strike at them until they were all dead or gone and the land was his to take. Great troubles would come upon the Miamis and the tribe must now search for a better barrier than the Ohio River between themselves and the white man who would come.

The speech had a great impact on the Miamis. They believed Michquala implicitly. The old prophet had spoken a truth they themselves could not see, but now that it was revealed to them they were greatly fearful and so they counciled many days trying to think of some way to thwart the tide of whites who would come against them as Michquala said. It was at this juncture that the Shawnee delegation from the Logstown Grand Council arrived among them. Their spokesmen addressed the Miamis at length, telling of their tribe's long, practically endless migrations; they spoke of the Miamis' kind offer to allow the Shawnees to settle as guests on the Ohio lands north of the big river; they thanked the Miamis for this kind and generous offer, but the Shawnees were no longer content to rest only a while in someone else's territory; the Great Spirit had directed them to find land, upon which to sink their roots permanently and this they would eventually do, somewhere, some time.

The Miamis went into hasty council and the answer seemed clear to all. Michquala had said they needed to find a better barrier than the Ohio River to protect them and their lands. What better barrier to place between themselves and the Ohio than the fiercest warrior tribe existing? Since the land would be devoured by whites if they did nothing, would it not be better to give it to their friends, the Shawnee, who then, by their very presence would prevent the whites from taking the land that was their own land? For once it did not take the chiefs long to reach a decision. The general council was reconvened and the Miamis addressed the Shawnees, telling them to go back and inform their people that if the Shawnees settle north of the Ohio, then the Miamis would give up all claim to those lands and they would belong to the Shawnees forever. The Shawnee delegation hastened back and there was great joy among them, for the Great Spirit had now shown the way. They accepted without delay and so now, for the first time in their remembered history, the Shawnees had their own land; land they could live upon, care for, protect and die for if it came to that.

In a very short time Shawnee villages had sprung up in many places in Ohio, especially in the valley of the Scioto River and its tributary, Paint Creek. Some were very small villages of only fifty or sixty individuals and others were quite large, such as Sinioto, also called Chalahgawtha, located at the mouth of the Scioto River where it empties into the Ohio. Among the first of the villages to be established was Kispoko Town, named after the Kispokotha sept, and situated on the west bank of the Scioto about seventy-five river miles upstream from its mouth. It was founded in the late summer of 1726 by Wawwaythi, the son of Opeththa and a war chief in his own right, and consisted of two hundred warriors of forty-five families.[20] And it was only mere weeks after the village was established that the first child was born here—the son of Wawwaythi and grandson of Opeththa—and he was named Pucksinwah.

Life was very good in the Ohio country for the Shawnees, the tribal historians went on, yet the old nomadic habits were hard to break. Different groups of Shawnees came and went over the years, some returning to Pennsylvania, some to northwestern Virginia on the upper waters of the Ohio or on the Kanawha, others to the south when there were periods of peace with the southern tribes. Through it all, however, there was no doubt that the Shawnees now considered Ohio as home and sooner or later they always came back and resumed residence here.

Pucksinwah was outstanding as a young warrior and became a favorite of the Kispokotha's principal war chief, Kawkawatchikay, who had succeeded Opeththa in the office after the latter's death in 1729. Pucksinwah accompanied many war parties against the southern tribes and was so utterly fearless in attacking, so bold in planning, and so considerate of his fellows that he soon ranked as the number three war chief after Kawkawatchikay and his second, Kishkalwa.

When Kawkawatchikay unexpectedly announced his intention of returning for a time to his old village, known as Shawnee Town, in the Wyoming Valley of Pennsylvania, a sizeable group of warriors and their families accompanied him.[21] Kishkalwa and Pucksinwah were of this number. They remained in Pennsylvania, closely associated with the Delawares for many years, living for a while at Kishkalwa, then at Tioga and at another time at Otsiningo.[22] Throughout this period Pucksinwah became skilled at political matters as well as warfare and was frequently a treaty negotiator with other tribes or with the whites and, with his knack for languages, often acted as interpreter.

Eventually Kawkawatchikay, old and tired, stepped down from his office as war chief and Kishkalwa, with the approval of all, succeeded him, with Pucksinwah as his second. After a number of councils, it was decided to return to Ohio. Pucksinwah was delighted, suddenly almost painfully aware of how much he missed his childhood home and determined never to live elsewhere again. They reestablished Kispoko Town at its original location and it was from there that, sometimes together and sometimes separately, Kishkalwa and Pucksinwah continued to lead many forays against the southern tribes.

Much had changed in Ohio during Pucksinwah's absence. During that period more Shawnees had come together to live as an organized tribe than at any time previously in their known history, and here they experienced a sense of security and belonging previously unknown to them. There were scores of Shawnee villages along such main rivers as the Muskingum, Scioto, Great Miami, Little Miami, and Mad. Two substantial villages were on the shore of the Ohio: Conedogwinit, which the British traders called the Upper Shawnee Town, was on the north bank opposite to and about three miles above the mouth of the Kanawha River; while the great sprawling Sinioto, also called Chalahgawtha—and referred to by traders as the Lower Shawnee Town—was at the mouth of the Scioto on the downstream side.

There were quite a number of trading posts throughout the wilderness now, mainly French but with ever more British traders establishing themselves among the tribes and caring little that the French considered this an invasion of their territory.[23] As for the Shawnees, they traded at their whim with both white factions, glad for the competition between the whites because it created better deals for them, but they did not allow any trading posts to be set up within their territory, preferring to go to the traders who were set up elsewhere among neighboring tribes. They had no objection, however, when John Findley descended the Ohio River in 1744, followed the Warrior Trail southward into the Kan-tuck-kee lands for some seventy miles before erecting a trading post on Elkhorn Creek and then spent a great deal of time traveling from village to village among the Shawnees in Ohio, making friends and providing goods the Shawnees wanted.[24] Another British trader who quickly made friends with the Shawnees and whom they liked very much was George Croghan, who traveled with an affable halfbreed French-Seneca as his interpreter, Andrew Montour. They had come to Ohio at the direction of the governor of Pennsylvania, Alexander Hamilton, with specific instructions to renew the chain of friendship with the Shawnees, Delawares and Wyandots on the Muskingum and to try to establish a trading arrangement with them. He did just that, so successfully and paying so much more than the French that within a few months large parties of Indians laden with beaver pelts were coming down from Canada and blandly passing the French fur post at the Indian village of Taranta, on western Lake Ontario, just to do business with him.[25] The French were greatly displeased. Traders such as Findley and Croghan provided a very real and necessary service and appeared to be no threat in and of themselves, but what bothered Pucksinwah considerably was that too often the English traders were followed by surveyors, land speculators and settlers.[26] Isolated log cabins were now showing up as far west of the Allegheny crest as the valleys of the Monongahela and the Youghiogheny in western Pennsylvania.

Though the French had proclaimed their exclusive right to trade among the tribes of the northwest, most of these tribes had never entered into any agreement giving them such exclusivity. In fact, the Miamis, impressed with better goods and lower prices offered by the British traders, in 1748 entered into a treaty of friendship and alliance with them and authorized British traders to enter their country and trade in it. The Shawnees applauded the Miami decision and praised that tribe's leaders for not being too closely stuck to any one group of whites, but they maintained their own ban against any trading posts being built in Shawnee territory.

Equally pleased was George Croghan who, accompanied as usual by Montour and also by Christopher Gist, an agent for the Ohio Company, came down the Ohio and stopped off at both Upper and Lower Shawnee Town to pay his respects and hand out some gifts. He and his party then went on, under friendly escort of the Shawnees, to the largest Miami town—the village of Pickawillany under Unemakemi, the tribe's principal chief, on the Great Miami River.[27] This was a good-sized village of over four hundred families and two thousand individuals. A series of councils ensued, presided over by Unemakemi and the second principal chief of the Miamis, a strong, rather ugly young man with direct gaze, whose name was Michikiniqua—Little Turtle. The upshot of the councils was that the Miamis accepted the gifts they brought and the British traders received permission to build a well-fortified trading post at Pickawillany. It was about this time that a party of four Ottawas showed up under the French flag and they, too, had presents for the Miamis as well as orders from the French that the tribe was not to trade with the British. Unemakemi—known to the French as Demoiselle, the Damselfly— merely laughed at them and then delivered an insulting speech for them to take back to the French authorities, along with the presents they had brought, which, aside from those he had scornfully thrown into the fire, he would not accept.

Again the displeasure of the French increased and everyone was certain that before too much longer a strong confrontation would be taking place between the French and English traders. Immediately after returning to Logstown, Croghan jubilantly continued back to the east with his news. In a short time he had come again to Logstown, not only with more gifts but with an official request from British authorities for permission to build a fort, which would be to the Indians' interest, at the junction of the Monongahela and the Allegheny. Coincidentally, the French were on hand with the same request, but they were refused and permission was granted to the English.

The French were by then extremely angry and a major war seemed to be shaping up between the whites. The Miamis immediately decided that if such a war became reality, they would not support either the French or the English, but remain neutral. What happened next did much to destroy the friendship that had existed between the French and the Miamis for so many years. On June 21, 1752, a party of Chippewas and Ottawas under the minor war chief, Pontiac, accompanied by the French agent Charles de Langlade and a troop of French soldiers, attacked Pickawillany by surprise, killed Chief Unemakemi in a very brutal manner, along with a number of others, took prisoner the party of English traders in the village at the time and killed one of them.[28] Michikiniqua, on the death of Unemakemi, became the new principal chief of the Miamis.

Almost immediately after the destruction of Pickawillany, Michikiniqua—Little Turtle—set his Miamis to constructing an even larger and much more impressive principal village, called Kekionga, at the confluence of the St. Joseph and St. Marys rivers. These two streams merged to form the Maumee River, which the English traders called the Miami of the Lake, since it flowed northeastward for just over a hundred miles before emptying into the far southwestern end of Lake Erie.[29]

Despite what the French had done and the strong Miami leanings toward the British, Pucksinwah was convinced that the latter represented a greater danger for all the Indians. Following the traders and surveyors over the mountains had been settlers, already establishing claims to land in the valleys of the Monongahela and the Youghiogheny, and he expressed his growing concern that the English "have very bad designs" against the Shawnees, adding that he thought it would not be long before they would be trying to do the same in the important Indian hunting grounds of Kan-tuck-kee, perhaps even into Ohio. He was determined to thwart any such attempts.

This was when Pucksinwah, then twenty-six, led the war party against the Cherokees that had resulted in the capture of Methotasa. And now, in the waning light of the day, Pucksinwah watched as Chiksika brought another armload of wood to the shelter where Methotasa lay in labor. One of the aunts emerged briefly and spoke to the twelve-year-old, who immediately set off around the upper end of the spring pool toward Pucksinwah.

"Not yet, father," Chiksika said as he approached, "but the aunt says it surely can't be too much longer."

Pucksinwah nodded and motioned for his son to sit beside him. Chiksika, clad in leathers and with no blanket, did so and Pucksinwah opened one side of his blanket and pulled the boy close beside him, wrapping him into the warmth. They sat silently together for a few minutes and then Chiksika looked up at his father. "It would have been a good thing if we had been able to reach Chalahgawtha today," he said.

Pucksinwah shook his head. "It was not to be, Chiksika, but we will be there tomorrow."

Chiksika considered this a moment, then asked, "How many will there be attending the grand council?"

A deep chuckle rumbled in Pucksinwah's chest. "More than you have ever seen together at any one time. Each of the other four septs will probably have at least as many people here as we. I have heard that Kikusgowlowa has come with even more."

Kikusgowlowa was chief of the Thawegila sept and of almost equal stature in the tribe to Hokolesqua—Cornstalk—who was chief of the Chalahgawthas. The Peckuwe sept was currently under Chief Wesecahnay—Black Beard—who was relatively new in his office and not well known outside his sept, and the Maykujays were under the venerable Chief Moluntha.[30]

Pucksinwah continued: "There will probably be close to three thousand men at the council and, counting all the women and children and old people such as ours who have come, along with all those who live at Chalahgawtha, altogether more than twelve thousand. Chalahgawtha will be very crowded."

"And what of Aquewelene? When does he come?" Aquewelene—literally Blanket Man—was the nickname the Shawnees used to refer to their favorite English trader, George Croghan.

"I am told he is already in Chalahgawtha, Chiksika. He shares the lodge of Chiungalla. We will first council among ourselves before he will be summoned. When he has said what he has come here to say, he will be sent on his way before our own council resumes to deliberate the matters he has presented."

Chiksika fell silent, thinking about this, and then spoke abruptly. "Are we going to have war with the English, father?"

"I don't know. We may. They continue forcing us toward it. We have been at peace with them now for three springs and we have abided by the treaty made on the Muskingum with their little general, Bouquet, but they continue to break that treaty and we cannot let them do so much longer. I think we will—" He broke off, looking toward the shelter, then stood up, pulling Chiksika to his feet beside him. "One of the aunts has come out. Run to her and tell her I am coming."

Chiksika nodded and sped away. Pucksinwah stretched and then followed at a walk, skirting the rim of the spring pool. When he reached them he found

19

that the aunt had not emerged from the shelter with any news, only to build
a fire outside for Pucksinwah and Chiksika and prepare them some food. She
picked up a flat piece of bark and disappeared for a moment into the shelter,
then reemerged with it heaped with glowing coals from the fire inside. These
she sprinkled on the dry grasses and twigs she had placed at the base of the
firewood she had previously stacked in a small cone and blew upon them until
they burst into flame and a good little cookfire was quickly going. As she
busied herself, making a stew of pieces of jerky and dried corn and beans and
other edibles tossed into a small pot half filled with water, she told them that
little had changed inside. Methotasa was still experiencing closely spaced labor
pains but without indication of the birth beginning yet. She was a garrulous
old woman and chattered on and on, more to Chiksika than to Pucksinwah,
who was lost in thought as he sat on the opposite side of the fire.

Vaguely Pucksinwah was aware that someone handed him a bowl of the
food when it was heated, but he ate mechanically, hardly tasting it and still
largely lost in the recesses of his own memories as the night closed about
them.

His reference to General Bouquet to Chiksika earlier had triggered more
memories of the turbulent decade that had followed his marriage to Methotasa.
It had been a difficult time for all and many important events had taken place,
not the least of which were two wars.

Sinioto—the Lower Shawnee Town—had remained the capital village of
the Shawnee nation until 1753 when torrential rains had caused floods of both
the Scioto and the Ohio and, while the inhabitants watched from the surrounding hills where they had gone for safety, flood waters nine feet deep had
carried away Sinioto. When they receded, the town was rebuilt, but this time
on the higher ground on the upstream side of the mouth of the Scioto.[31] It
was never quite the same. Sinioto still existed, but a new principal village, the
second Chalahgawtha, was built well upstream on the Scioto a few miles
downstream from the mouth of Paint Creek.[32]

To the east, the French ousted British traders from their posts on the
Allegheny and built three more forts to act as a further barrier to the incursions
of English trade into their claimed territory. The first of these, on Lake Erie,
was named after the peninsula upon which it was built, Fort Presque Isle; the
second, on the portage fifteen miles south near the headwaters of French Creek,
was named Fort Le Boeuf after the woods bison that roamed the forests; and
the third, Fort Machault—though more often called Fort Venango—another
sixty miles downstream at the mouth of French Creek where it entered the
Allegheny, at the site of the Seneca village of Venango, and, in the process,
taking possession of John Fraser's trading post built there two years previously
and capturing two English traders who were on hand, though not Fraser
himself.[33]

In a desperate effort to hold ground against the French, the British then began erecting a very strong fort at the confluence of the Monongahela and Allegheny, as Croghan had received permission for the British to do at Logstown Council four years previously. Before it could be finished, however, a French military force in April of 1754 swept in and captured it, completed the construction and named it Fort Duquesne.[34] The Virginians immediately mounted a force under Colonel George Washington and marched to recapture the place.

Pucksinwah was part of Kishkalwa's war party that attended the June 1754 council at Fort Duquesne called by its French commander, Captain Pierre de Contrecoeur. Pucksinwah had listened intently as the officer delivered a rousing address, telling them that France and England were now at war. He managed to convince the assembled Indians, including Delawares and Senecas as well as Shawnees, to unequivocally take up the hatchet against the English.[35] A short time later, the French and British armies met in the Battle of Fort Necessity at a place called Great Meadows where, after suffering about a hundred casualties, Washington surrendered. After signing the capitulation, Washington was allowed to lead his battered force back to Virginia. So began the French and Indian War.

Pucksinwah raised his head and looked around. The fire had burned down somewhat and the stars were very bright in the darkness of the sky. Chiksika had rolled himself up in a blanket next to the fire and was asleep, while the talkative aunt was nowhere to be seen and had evidently reentered the shelter. He gazed back at the fire and smiled faintly, not so much at the memory of his participation in the defeat of the English on that occasion but because soon after that he had returned home and then married Methotasa the following Planting Moon—May. Unfortunately, they had little time to spend together. A new call had come from Fort Duquesne that a much stronger British army was marching toward them and the French, now with only three hundred soldiers at Fort Duquesne, desperately needed the help of their Indian allies. The Indians of various tribes quickly returned. They ambushed the approaching enemy only ten miles from Fort Duquesne and decisively defeated the British force, killed 456 soldiers, mortally wounding their commander, General Edward Braddock in the process, and wounded another 421.[36] Their own losses were negligible—three officers killed and two wounded, twenty-seven soldiers and Indians killed and about the same number wounded. It was a great victory and Pucksinwah had been conspicuous and exemplary in his bravery and great fighting ability.[37]

Laden with their plunder of the battle, the Indian forces separated and Pucksinwah had returned immediately to Methotasa at Kispoko Town. However, fearing retaliation by the Virginians, the Shawnees had for the most part abandoned both Conedogwinit and Sinioto—the Upper and Lower Shawnee

Towns—and the majority of residents of those towns moved well up the Scioto among their tribesmen in the Pickaway Plains or much farther away, to the headwaters of the Mad River. Even Chalahgawtha, on the Scioto just below the mouth of Paint Creek, was deemed to be too exposed and its population abandoned the town and split into two groups and erected two other temporary towns, less vulnerable, while they decided on a location for the rebuilding of the tribal capital. One of these was some twelve or fifteen miles farther up the Scioto and the other was about fifteen miles northwest along Paint Creek and both were called Chalahgawtha. By the following spring, however, these villages were abandoned and their population drew together again and established the very large new principal town of Chalahgawtha on the Little Miami River. The Shawnee principal chief, Hokolesqua, moved his primary residence to Chalahgawtha, since the tribe's principal chief was expected to live in the capital village, but he continued to spend a great deal of his time in his own small village—Cornstalk's Town—along Scippo Creek on the Pickaway Plains.

Pucksinwah was home in Kispoko Town for only brief intervals in the year that followed and was not on hand when his first son, Chiksika, was born in the early spring of 1756. More often than not he was leading forays against British troops or against the isolated settlers that had oozed over the Alleghenies to take up a tenuous existence on Indian lands they had claimed and were determined to hold. From Pennsylvania to South Carolina, the frontier was afire with burning cabins, slaughtered livestock and butchered settlers.

Some of the Shawnees and Delawares still living along the Susquehanna met with the British Indian superintendent, William Johnson, and pledged to support the English in the war and, though they did so, there were no clashes between the opposing factions of Shawnees. This was not the first time different tribal factions had differing loyalties. Somehow each respected the other's decision and avoided direct confrontation in action.

The majority of the Iroquois had been vacillating in their loyalties but the severe Battle of Lake George and its associated Bloody Morning Scout right in their own front yard, with William Johnson's force defeating the French and Canadian Indians, convinced them to ally themselves to the British. Johnson extracted promises from all but the Cayugas that English forts should be built near their main towns, for their own protection, of course, from the French and hostile Indians.[38]

Johnson, aided by his new first deputy superintendent, George Croghan, seemed to be making headway toward getting the Shawnees, Delawares and Mingoes to do the same, but his efforts were quashed when the new colonial governor of Pennsylvania, Robert Hunter Morris, unilaterally declared war on them and offered bounties for their scalps. His action was followed up by a similar one from Governor Belcher of New Jersey.

Despite these drawbacks, in 1758 more groups of Shawnees made peace with the British and assisted them in expeditions against the Southern Indians, especially the Cherokees. And that summer was when Methotasa bore her second child, a daughter, and they named her Tecumapese—Shooting Star.

Pucksinwah was concerned for her future and that of two-year-old Chiksika. Despite the fact that the French were being victorious practically everywhere, Pucksinwah was experiencing portents that the English were going to emerge victorious in this war and that it might be wise to make a truce with them to at least prevent their march into Shawnee country. This belief was sharply bolstered when, the fall after Tecumapese was born, the British under General Forbes, after losing a battle in September, re-formed and marched against Fort Duquesne and took it, while the French fled without even a fight. Forbes ordered the place rebuilt, bigger, better, stronger and renamed Fort Pitt in honor of William Pitt, while the settlement outside the fort was called Pittsburgh. Most of the pro-French Indians in the area, disgusted at the actions of the French, turned and went home themselves. A few remained and negotiated a truce with the English and Pucksinwah was of this number.

But then, as if the British ousting of the French at the Forks of the Ohio had been a long awaited signal, almost immediately there began a marked influx of settlers into and over the Alleghenies, determined to get "their share" of the land while the getting was good. British authorities inveighed against such precipitate actions by individuals, but the words did little to prevent the inundation into the Delaware and Shawnee occupied lands between the crest of the mountains and the two great rivers that formed the Ohio, the Monongahela and the Allegheny. Some Shawnees and most of the Delawares were irate over the incursions and raiding parties went out frequently to kill or burn out settlers in the outlying areas west of the Susquehanna near the principal newer settlements called Carlisle and Shippensburg.

Nevertheless, the Shawnees in general council agreed that now there was little choice but to make peace and form an alliance with the British. With Kishkalwa and Pucksinwah as part of a Shawnee delegation, they responded to a major conference held by Croghan a few hundred yards up the Allegheny from Fort Pitt. The conference included eight major Indian nations, including the Shawnees, Delawares, Miamis, Ottawas, Cayugas, Senecas, Susquehannocks, and the splinter group of the Hurons who called themselves Wyandots. The Delawares and Shawnees, in solemn ceremony, recalled the war hatchet they had sent to the western tribes and, at the base of a large lone pine, buried it "that it may nevermore be found." They also promised, with this treaty of peace, to cease all raids against the settlers coming across the mountains, but the English had to promise as well that they would prohibit the whites from doing so and then enforce the ruling. Croghan promised that this would be seen to and that the only whites entering their country would be traders licensed through Sir William Johnson's Indian Department. He then told them that General Abercrombie had been recalled and that the new commander-in-chief of British forces in America was General Sir Jeffrey Amherst.

Pucksinwah stared at the remains of the fire, now no more than a small mound of glowing coals. So vividly did he remember the chill that had swept through him at Croghan's announcement that he shivered again now. It had been a valid presentiment. Amherst had turned out to be one of the worst things that had ever happened to the Indians. To begin with, he had openly and publicly announced that he considered all Indians to be subhuman savages that disgusted him beyond expression. Matters degenerated from that point.

When Quebec fell to the British in September 1759, it marked the beginning of the end of the conflict between the British and French in this theater of the war. One year later Montreal fell to the British and the French capitulated. All French posts in the region of the Great Lakes were to be surrendered to the British, making Canada and all its dependencies British Crown possessions. However, by the terms of the capitulation, this did not involve the French in Louisiana, who were morally bound to continue the war in progress and to do everything they could to promulgate bad feelings in the Indians toward the British until they were informed that an official French-English peace treaty had been signed. The result of this was that instead of surrendering their western Great Lakes posts, many of the French commanders merely abandoned them and led their garrisons to the Mississippi Valley to join the French garrisons in southwestern Illinois and farther downstream on the Mississippi. Fort de Chartres became, therefore, the closest significant French fortification to the new British holdings in the Northwest and in Canada.

Immediately following the French capitulation, the extension of the British trade with the western Indians was begun in earnest. Croghan and his new assistant, Alexander McKee, who had brought to Pittsburgh a large packhorse train of goods, followed the customary protocol of giving generous gifts to the Indians who visited, in the interest of a strong peaceful trade. But Croghan was soundly castigated by Amherst for such gifts, which Amherst, who understood almost nothing about trade and less about Indians, considered extravagant and unnecessary.

The Indians who had attended that treaty came away with more than gifts. On their way home a large number of the warriors died from smallpox. One of these was the Shawnee war chief, Kishkalwa, and with his death Pucksinwah had become chief of the Kispokotha sept. A short time later, in a major council held here at Chalahgawtha, Hokolesqua had extolled Pucksinwah for his outstanding bravery and heroism all through the war and, with approbation of the whole tribe, named him the new principal war chief of the Shawnee tribe, with the older Shemeneto—Black Snake—as his second. Pucksinwah was suffused with a wave of warmth in recalling the signal honor done him by his chief and his tribe. At age thirty-four, he was the youngest principal war chief the tribe had ever had, since the responsibility for such an office normally went to someone considerably older.

Within the next two years virtually all the Shawnees and Delawares remaining in Pennsylvania east of the mountains and a great many in the trans-Allegheny region had migrated west into Ohio and beyond, to the valleys of the Muskingum, Scioto, Great Miami, Mad, and Wabash. Following close behind were numerous traders who had obtained licenses from Sir William Johnson or George Croghan to engage in the Indian trade, including Richard Conner, Robert Callender, David Duncan, James Findley, Alexander Lowry, Michael Teaffe, Thomas Kenton, Hugh Crawford, John Hart, Alexander Henry, William Trent, and others, who quickly established posts at such places as Detroit, Sandusky, Kekionga, Wapatomica, Goschachgunk, Mackachack, Michilimackinac, La Baye, Ouiatenon, St. Joseph, Venango, Presque Isle, and Le Boeuf.[39] But, while licensed traders were now all throughout the Indian country, Amherst's trade restriction policies and high prices created extreme hardships for all the tribes. Very little ammunition could be traded, which left the Indians continually short of powder and lead or entirely without it, which limited their hunting and, in turn limited what they could bring in to trade for the goods they needed. Soon most of the tribes were reduced to near starvation, with no relief in sight.

Now the Indians everywhere in general and in the Detroit area in particular, were remembering what the Commandant of Detroit, Captain François de Bellestré, said to them in the general council of Indians he called before abandoning the post and heading for the Mississippi Valley. He had told them that the English would cheat them in trade and would make slaves of them by withholding the items they required for their survival. The Ottawa war chief, Pontiac, was among those who remembered only too well the commandant's parting words. "My children," he had told them gravely, "the English today overthrow your Father. As long as they have the upper hand, you will not have what you stand in need of, *but this will not last.*"

In the months following, French agents moved from village to village through the Indian country, pointing out the terrible conditions the Indians were now experiencing, encouraging them to take up the hatchet against the British and that if and when they did, they could count on the support of the French for the food and ammunition and other supplies they needed and, since there was still no official peace between the white adversaries, even the support of French military. The resentment against the English this created among the tribes was intensified by the fact of the continuing British occupation in their lands. The Shawnees and Delawares had given these whites permission to build a temporary fort at the forks of the Ohio in order to fight the French. With the ending of the war, they had expected Fort Pitt to be abandoned and the whites to withdraw east of the Alleghenies, except for traders. Instead of that, the forts all over the frontier were being strengthened and better garrisoned with seasoned soldiers and ever more settlers were moving westward beyond the Susquehanna. The Shawnees were especially unhappy when the news spread that Colonel Washington and other Virginians had received a royal grant of two and a half million acres in the Ohio Valley, running well downstream from Fort Pitt, and settlement of that area by whites, though not yet begun, was imminent.

The whites, or signs of their presence, were apt to be encountered almost anywhere now in the vastness of the wilderness woodlands. Late in 1760, Pucksinwah, returning from leading a small war party against the Cherokees in North Carolina, encountered a large party of whites and began approaching them making signs of peace, but without warning or cause they were shot at and forced to retreat with one of their number wounded in the leg. Farther away from the white-occupied areas and closer to home, his party came across some rocks that had been piled up in a circle as banking for a campfire and discovered strange deep carvings in a gigantic smooth-barked beech tree nearby:

D. BOON

CILLED A. BAR ON

TREE

IN THE

YEAR

1760[40]

The anger of the Indians increased when here and there individual Indians moving about on the frontier were killed by white hunters, traders or settlers. It started out when one was shot down at the Smyley Trading Post on the Salt Lake at Tuscarora in the Wyandot territory. Another was killed in Delaware country by Lieutenant Richard Piper of the Pennsylvania militia near Fort Ligonier. A third, along the Greenbrier River, was shot when he approached a party of whites dressing out a deer they had killed and told them they had no right to be entering or hunting upon Indian lands. As if these were signals opening the season on Indian killing, a rash of such occurrences began throughout the length of the frontier. Deputations of Indians complained to British officials about it and received promises that the guilty would be caught and punished, but they never were and the practice increased rather than slackened.

Soon there was war talk circulating widely among the Indians. In mid July of 1761, a deputation of two Seneca chiefs, Kyashuta and Teantoriance, arrived at Kispoko Town carrying twenty strings of war wampum and three large red wampum war belts. They said they had just come from councils among the Ottawas and Potawatomies at Detroit and at Sandusky in the Wyandot country.[41] The message they carried was for a war to be entered into against the English at their stations, both military and trading posts, throughout the territory of the western Indians. These proposals had been rejected by the general council at Detroit, but there were individual chiefs who had indicated acceptance of the idea in secret councils and one such was Pontiac. Pucksinwah, reminding the visiting Senecas that the Shawnees were now at peace with the English, according to the terms of the treaty entered into at Fort Pitt, had refused to accept the war belts, but sent the messengers on to see Hokolesqua at Chalahgawtha. Their reception there by the Shawnee principal chief was the same and, angry at being rebuffed, they went on, heading for the Miami tribe and the Illinois nations with the same message. It was clearly apparent that the seeds of discontent were sprouting. The alarm among the Indians increased when Major Henry Gladwin was sent to take command of the little garrison at Detroit and brought with him a small army of redcoats, the Sixtieth Regiment of Foot, along with some rangers and a company of artillerymen. This intensified in the minds of the Indians their grave need for the ammunition and other supplies being denied them by Amherst's policies and so they began taking matters into their own hands, confiscating such items and more wherever they could.[42]

Amherst's reaction was to even more sharply restrict the Indian trade, decrying the expenses of the Indian Department to satisfy what he termed "an insatiable and revolting race of beggars." He gave little countenance to the multitude of reports being forwarded to him by Croghan and Johnson that the Indians were now being treated abominably by the majority of whites on the frontiers, but especially by the traders, who swindled them, beat them, robbed, cheated, and otherwise maltreated them and met their entreaties with indifference, disrespect, neglect and insults. The murmurings among the tribes was becoming an angry rumble, since this was more evidence of precisely what the French had warned them would occur as soon as the English had a monopoly on Indian trade. In the Detroit area, Pontiac stepped up his angry tirades against the English in councils involving his own Ottawas and the Chippewas and Potawatomies, as well as the Hurons and their major splinter faction, the Wyandots. On the Pennsylvania frontier, a self-proclaimed Delaware prophet named Teedyscung, preaching a doctrine for the recovery of the lands taken from the Indians by the whites, was being taken very seri-ously.[43]

The deteriorating state of affairs was painfully apparent to Pucksinwah and Hokolesqua, who were among those Indian delegates summoned to a major council called at Lancaster by the governor of Pennsylvania, which included a number of the government's powerful Quaker faction, with George Croghan there in unofficial capacity, along with Andrew Montour. Also on hand among the 550 Indians in attendance were the Delaware prophet, Tee-dyscung, Chief Beaver of the same tribe, Seneca Chief Blue Cheeks, Michi-kiniqua of the Miamis, and the Oneida Chief Thomas King. The object of the council was to mollify the Indians but its effect was the opposite. The Quakers asked permission to establish government trading posts far to the west on the West Branch of the Susquehanna, "unmolested by Croghan and the military authorities," but Blue Cheeks violently opposed this as just one more effort of the whites to acquire Seneca lands. The Indians asked that Fort Augustus be "disbanded" but they were refused. Blue Cheeks was deliberately given more gifts than any other chief in attendance in the hope that this would cause jealousy among the other tribes of the Iroquois League and a permanent rift in that confederation, but what it resulted in was the assassination of that chief shortly after his return home. The Indian delegates left the council much dissatisfied, the Shawnees so much so that they scornfully threw away along-side the trail the presents that had been given to them.

By the autumn of 1762, Pontiac had succeeded in confederating the west-ern Great Lakes tribes under his leadership and secretly planned a simultaneous attack on all British installations the following spring, calling on warriors everywhere to fall upon the post nearest them as soon as runners brought word of his attack on Detroit. He added in his messages to the tribes that the great French father had promised to sustain them in such an outbreak.[44] Not all the tribes agreed to join under Pontiac's leadership, but the Shawnees promised to participate in the uprising, saying that they would strike Fort Pitt and posts farther east when the time came, as well as send warriors to Pontiac when he was ready, although not as many as they would have liked, since throughout the summer the tribe had suffered a terrible epidemic that had wiped out much of the population, including a great many fine young war-riors.[45]

Pontiac's War broke out when his forces attacked in the Detroit area and placed the fort there under siege. As runners spread the word, savage attacks occurred elsewhere in rapid succession. Fort Sandusky was taken with 27 killed, including all but one of the traders. Fort St. Joseph was next to fall, with 11 dead. They were followed by the destruction, with considerable loss of life, of Forts Miami, Ouiatenon, Michilimackinac, Presque Isle, Venango, and Le Boeuf. Fort Edward Augustus, formerly Fort La Baye at Green Bay, was abandoned and its garrison taken prisoner. Military convoys were hard hit. One, en route to Detroit, was struck at Point Pelee with 62 killed, all supplies lost and only 36 men escaping. Another, on the portage around Niagara Falls, was ambushed at Devil's Hole and 56 were killed, with only a single drummer boy escaping. At Detroit a detachment sent out from the besieged fort was struck hard and defeated in the Battle of Bloody Run, with 61 killed and wounded. Raiding parties swept through the frontiers of Pennsylvania, Maryland, and Virginia, causing much havoc and loss of life. Some 80 Shawnees under Hokolesqua ascended the Kanawha River and struck the new settlements that had sprung up at Muddy Creek, Greenbrier Valley, Jackson Valley, and the Shenandoah Valley. Delaware warriors under Chief Wolf wiped out the settlers in the Monongahela and Youghiogheny valleys. Pucksinwah's contingent of Shawnees, joined by Delawares, spread havoc through the river valleys of the Juniata, the Susquehanna, the Sherman, and Tuscaroras Creek and made sharp attacks against Forts Bedford and Ligonier. The Susquehannocks and Senecas fell upon and killed many of the Connecticut settlers in the Wyoming Valley.

Pucksinwah's Shawnees and some Delawares under Wolf then joined forces and placed Fort Pitt under a brief siege, that installation under command of Captain Simeon Ecuyer, who received an arrow wound in the leg. They broke off the attack when word came that an army of 460 soldiers led by Colonel Henry Bouquet was on the march against them from Fort Bedford. Pucksinwah immediately led his combined 95 Shawnee and Delaware warriors to Edge Hill, 26 miles to the east and set up an ambush. Through fighting cautiously from cover, rarely exposing themselves and making their shots count, they killed and wounded 8 British officers and 116 men. Bouquet was able to save his force from sure disaster only by effecting a clever counter-ambush, at which the Indians retreated. The attackers lost only 22 men, among them the Delaware chiefs Kittiskung and Wolf, yet Bouquet declared the two-day Battle of Bushy Run a victory for the whites and marched the rest of the way to Fort Pitt without further loss.

At Detroit, the siege lasted until October 30, when Pontiac, with all his appeals for French aid during the siege availing him nothing, was finally informed, as were all the participants on both sides, that France and England had made formal peace with the Treaty of Paris on February 10. Almost immediately abandoned by all his allies, Pontiac had no recourse but to lift the siege and withdraw to the Maumee Valley.[46]

On November 17, to the great joy of virtually everyone, General Amherst was recalled to London and General Thomas Gage was appointed British commander-in-chief in America.[47] Not only that, the British Board of Trade finally took the advice of Sir William Johnson and issued the Royal Proclamation of 1763, which created a hard and fast boundary between the whites and the Indians, making the crest of the Alleghenies the dividing line. According to the terminology of the Proclamation, . . . *everything west of the heads of the streams that ultimately empty into the Atlantic are to be, for the present and until our further pleasure be known, reserved for the tribes.* The white colonists would be required to stay east of this line and devote themselves to more fully developing the region between the coast and the Allegheny crest. This did not preclude trading, although very tight trading controls along the lines suggested by Sir William Johnson would be in effect, serving the dual purpose of giving English manufacturers an exclusive market for their goods among the Indians and requiring the Indians to remain west of the Proclamation line and continue to support the lucrative trade by selling their furs and skins only to agents of licensed British fur companies. Thus, any individual who wished to be in the fur trade was prohibited from it unless actually employed as an agent of a firm licensed by the British Board of Trade. The entrepreneurial traders, who had long been in business for themselves, howled with fury and frustration at the edict but, for the moment, could do little about it.

The ensuing winter and spring passed fairly quietly and, in June, a temporary truce was brought about between the western tribes and the English until a more permanent and binding peace treaty should be drawn up. Despite the fact that the French had stated they could not help the Indians against the English, a small flicker of hope remained alive that eventually these Frenchmen would again become strong enough to oppose the British and aid their red allies. This hope was bolstered by the news that a new French settlement was at this moment being made well up the Mississippi by Pierre Laclede and his party on the west side of the great river and about fifty miles upstream from Fort de Chartres. They were calling the place St. Louis.

In the months following Pontiac's collapsed uprising, Bouquet rebuilt his force and then, in October, 1764, marched into the Ohio country determined to cow the Indians. With neither food nor ammunition to sustain them in warring further with the British, and with no real hope of French aid, the tribes had no recourse but to sue for peace. Pucksinwah and Hokolesqua were among the delegation of chiefs that met Bouquet under a white flag at the mouth of Sandy Creek where it empties into the Tuscarawas River. Also present were Delaware chiefs Custaloga and Kitehi, known better to the whites as White Eyes and Turtle's Heart, along with Seneca Chief Kyashuta.

The Indians turned over eighteen prisoners but this in no measure satisfied Bouquet who gave them a severe tongue-lashing and threatened them with total destruction if they did not meet his demands. He then told them they had twelve days in which to meet him again downstream from here at the mouth of the Tuscarawas where it merged with the Walhonding to form the Muskingum River. There, at the Delaware capital village of Goschachgunk, at the time appointed, they must deliver up every man, woman, and child prisoner in their respective tribes, irrespective of whether or not such prisoners wished to be turned over, and each furnished by the Indians with a horse and clothing and provisions enough to get them to Fort Pitt. When this was done, Bouquet had admonished them, then he would tell them on what terms peace could be made.

The tribesmen hurried away, the Shawnee contingent pausing briefly at the easternmost Shawnee village, Wapatomica, directly across the head of the Muskingum River from Goschachgunk and warning their fellow tribesmen there to consider abandoning their village immediately and reestablishing somewhere farther west, since the present village might well be attacked and destroyed if trouble broke out at the next meeting with Bouquet.

Seated beside the dim coals of the campfire at the spring, Pucksinwah shook his head and grimaced. Surrendering the prisoners had been no easy task. In their tribe, as well as in others, many of the whites who had been captured had been adopted into the tribes and were fully accepted now as Indians. Many had married Indians and had since borne children who were Indian children. Most considered their lives as Indians much more desirable than as whites. The men could hunt and fish, gamble and join in the story telling, ramble at their content through the wilderness, play games and even join war parties and engage in combat against enemy tribes—all this in a manner they could never have done in their white society. The women, especially those who married into the tribe, found their lives fuller and better than they had been as white women, with husbands who generally treated them with kindness, respect and affection, never insulting them and rarely striking them unless truly deserving of it and, even then, more ceremonially than with vindictiveness or a desire to hurt; their cares and responsibilities were far less as Indians than as white women. And for the children, either those born to captive women or sired by captive men, or those captured and adopted into the tribe, theirs was a life scarcely less than idyllic, free of formal schooling, yet rich with education of other kinds; a life filled with games and laughter and close-knit love of family and community. Some captives, usually unadopted, who had refused to adjust to the Indian life and whose lives were made miserable by their own ill nature and its effect upon their captors, were happy to be liberated at last. But for by far the greater majority, what wrenching trauma it had been to be uprooted, removed from the arms of their loved ones and turned over to the whites to resume a life they no longer cared about or wished to have. Nevertheless, except for some individuals or families who had judiciously hidden in the woods until it would be safe to return to the villages, all prisoners were turned over to Bouquet at the head of the Muskingum. Day after day parties of Indians from all the tribes came in with them. Soon there were so many, with more coming all the time, that they could not properly be cared for and so a first contingent of 110 of them were sent to Fort Pitt under escort of Captain Abraham Buford and his company. Many more had been then been brought in until the final total was three hundred and ten.

Bouquet told them then that he could now accept their peace offerings with these provisions: each tribe must submit a delegation of chiefs as hostages—chiefs with the power to treat for their tribes, speaking for their nations in a binding manner, and that the tribes must be bound to support the promises that these chiefs would make. Among the Shawnees on hand, Catahecassa and Shemeneto—Black Hoof and Black Snake—volunteered, with the concurrence of Hokolesqua and Pucksinwah, to be the tribe's representative hostage chiefs. When they and the other delegate hostage chiefs, along with some 200 or more of their unpainted warriors, were ready to depart to confer with Sir William Johnson in making an official treaty of peace, Hokolesqua and Pucksinwah paused briefly to pay a final personal visit to Henry Bouquet. They both shook hands with him, but it was Hokolesqua who spoke.

"When you first came among us," the principal chief said, "you came with hatchet raised to strike us. We now take it from your hand and throw it to Moneto, that He may now do with it what shall seem good in His sight. We hope that you, who are a brave warrior, will take hold of the chain of friendship which we now extend to you. We, who are also brave warriors, will take hold as you do and, in pity for our women and children and our old people, we will think no more of war."

So ended the war and there was peace again in the land, although the official treaties were not fully formalized until after detailed formal councils between the hostage chiefs and Sir William Johnson the following summer, following which all those chiefs and their respective parties came home again.

Though the treaty had been made and there was no more fighting for the time being, the situation on the frontiers was not good. For the most part, the Royal Proclamation of 1763 was being ignored. With thousands of immigrants arriving regularly from England, Scotland, Wales, and Ireland, there was an even greater need to expand to the westward, to seek, as was their primary reason for coming to America, land of their own. They spilled over the Alleghenies in a steady flow, moving ever farther into the fertile valleys until each found the spot that particularly appealed to him and here he made his mark on boundary trees—tomahawk improvements, they were called— and claimed the land as his own.[48]

Trade was still tightly controlled and only licensed fur agents were able to pursue the practice without the very real fear of imprisonment. But the settlers, disorganized and with only their own needs and desires to consider, were as difficult to stop in their westward encroachment as mice scurrying through a cornfield. When Indian appeals to British officials failed in an effort to end the problem and oust the intruders, border raiding by small Indian war parties against the least protected settlers and settlements began again and quickly escalated. Thus far these raids had been carried out primarily by the Delawares and Senecas and the catch-all expatriate groups called Mingoes. But the situation was worsening and where, until recently, the Ohio lands had been spared, it took no great sense of presentiment to deduce that the whites were coming and that the Shawnees had to be ready, as a tribe, to deal with this eventuality. And that was the fundamental reason for the Grand Council scheduled to begin tomorrow in Chalahgawtha when the sun reached its highest point.

Pucksinwah sighed and picked up a small stick lying nearby and stirred the coals of the campfire. Momentarily they glowed more brightly and a single unburnt chunk of wood burst into flame, but the coals around it subsided to a dull orange-red again rather quickly.

"I'll put on some more wood, father."

Pucksinwah turned, smiling. Chiksika had already thrown off his blanket and was rising. "Has the baby been born yet?" he asked.

"Not yet, Chiksika. It is taking a long time."

The boy grunted an unintelligible response and walked to where he had piled the firewood and stooped to pick up some. At that moment there came the murmur of voices from the aunts inside the shelter. Father and son looked toward one another, barely visible to each other in the erratic light of the single burning chunk of wood but abruptly they were both illuminated much more and spun toward the source in time to see a huge brilliant meteor streak across the heavens from the north, passing directly over them in greenish-white incandescence. It was an awe-inspiring spectacle visible for fully twenty seconds, made all the more wondrous by the utter silence of its passage.

Chiksika gasped and Pucksinwah's mouth was agape, though he made no sound. Pucksinwah had often heard of such things before and had sometimes seen small meteors flash briefly in the sky, but never in his life anything so breathtaking as this. The tales of the old people flooded his mind: this meteor was The Panther—a powerful spirit passing over to the south, seeking a great hole for sleep. Every night, so the tales went, it passes somewhere over the earth to seek that lair in the south, though rarely witnessed. It was a very good sign.[49]

Practically on the tail of its passing, the sharp wail of a baby's cry erupted from within the shelter. Chiksika straightened and stepped to his father's side. He placed a hand on Pucksinwah's arm but was still too wonderstruck to speak. Pucksinwah pulled him close and put his arm around the boy's shoulders and they waited quietly and patiently, as tradition proclaimed they should.

The baby's cry quickly dwindled away and several minutes later one of the aunts came out grinning broadly, and told Pucksinwah he had a son. Pucksinwah nodded and stooped to enter the shelter, Chiksika at his heels.

Tecumapese was seated on the ground beside her mother and she smiled happily at her father and older brother. The giggling aunts filed outside leaving the family to themselves. Methotasa lay upon a large soft buffalo hide over a mat of cedar boughs. She was covered to her waist by a fine, very soft deer hide atop which was a trade blanket folded in half. Her breasts were swelled but not yet engorged with the milk that would soon come. Asleep in the crook of her arm was the infant, his skin now glistening faintly with the bear oil applied in a protective coating by the aunts.

As Pucksinwah knelt and placed a hand to his wife's cheek and looked at the baby, she smiled. He nodded approvingly and then told her of The Panther passing across the sky at the moment he was born, searching for its home in the south, and that, beyond question, it was the boy child's *unsoma*.[50]

By Shawnee custom, a male child is not named for ten days after his birth, nor a girl for twelve, in the belief that during that period an *unsoma*—an event worthy of notice, involving an animal of some kind—would occur which would suggest what Moneto or the Great Spirit wished the child's name to be. But this time there would be no need for waiting, for one of the most awe-inspiring signs of all had been given at the instant of birth and both parents knew that with such a coincident *unsoma* having occurred, there could be no other name for this boy child more significant than The Panther Passing Across.

Tecumseh![51]

Chapter 1

[March 14, 1768 — Monday]

— 《 》 — The infant Tecumseh was almost exactly twelve hours old when, five days ago, his father had strode through the expansive village of Chalahgawtha toward the council house, a fine red blanket draped over his shoulders. This was the largest of all the Shawnee villages, with over a thousand wegiwas, in each of which lived from one to three families.

Unlike most other Indian villages, which normally developed into a helter-skelter collection of dwellings placed wherever the individual wished, Chalahgawtha had a series of dwelling-free avenues radiating outward from a central clearing, in the center of which stood the largest, sturdiest and most permanent building, the *msi-kah-mi-qui* or council house.[52] Narrower curving avenues arced from one side of the village to the other and, in the blocks formed were the semipermanent dwellings called wegiwas, constructed of poles lashed to a framework of wood and covered over with broad strips of bark. In addition to over one thousand such dwellings, there were now many hundreds of the more portable tepees of the visiting Indians who had come for the general council, not only erected in every clear space between the wegiwas but extending well beyond the limits of these structures, leaving only the avenues open for travel.

35

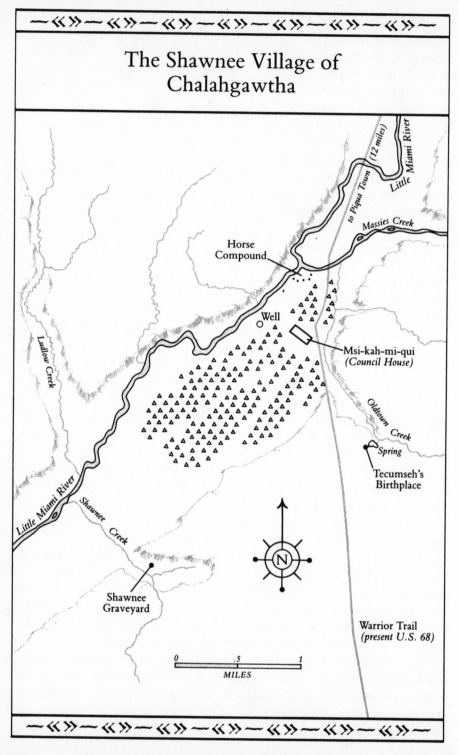

The Shawnee Village of Chalahgawtha

to Piqua Town (12 miles)

Little Miami River

Massies Creek

Horse Compound

Well

Ludlow Creek

Msi-kah-mi-qui
(Council House)

Oldtown Creek

Spring

Tecumseh's Birthplace

Little Miami River

Shawnee Creek

Shawnee Graveyard

N

Warrior Trail
(present U.S. 68)

0   .5   1
MILES

A faint bluish haze of smoke emanating from the multitude of cookfires filled the air and there was the persistent and pleasant sound of children squealing in play, dogs barking among the wegiwas, horses nickering in their pole corrals beyond the town limits and the continuous drone of a multitude of conversations. The avenue followed by Pucksinwah as he walked toward the *msi-kah-mi-qui* was the broadest of all and presently lined with people on both sides from the center of the town to its outermost limits, on hand to welcome their tribe's principal war chief. All had heard of the passage of the great meteor during the night and many had rushed outside in time to see it. Word had preceded Pucksinwah of the birth of his son coincident with the passage of such a great sign and the crowd lining the thoroughfare called phrases of greeting and congratulations as he passed, with the name *Tecumseh* frequently being uttered.

At first these people were mainly women, children, and the elderly, but the closer he came to the council house, the more young men and mature warriors were evident among them until, as he reached the expansive central clearing, the crowd was composed of hundreds of them, for whom there was not room enough in the *msi-kah-mi-qui,* large though it was.

The great council house was constructed of logs with a broad doorway hung with heavy buffalo hides in the center of each of three sides, with only the rear wall, looming above the expansive marsh, devoid of access. There were also numerous head–high window ports on each of the walls. The structure was fully one hundred twenty feet long and forty feet wide and the peak of its sloped roof perhaps twenty feet high and constructed of poles fastened side by side from peak to eave and then covered over first with overlapping bark shingles and then with a thin sod layer atop these to help anchor them in place.

At each of the three doors were stationed young men, filled with pride at the responsibility of their roles. Their task was to listen to the proceedings occurring within the council house and, at intervals, to move through the crowd outside, relaying the gist of what was transpiring inside.

A youth of about eighteen, who murmured a greeting as Pucksinwah approached, pulled aside the heavy buffalo skin at the doorway to allow him entry. For a moment Pucksinwah stood just inside, allowing his vision to adjust to the dimness and feeling the quickening of his pulse as he smelled the rich aroma of smoldering *kinnikinnick* from a multitude of pipes and began to recognize faces among the assembled chiefs and subchiefs, many of whom he had not seen for several years.[53] It would have been very dark inside the structure had it not been for the multitude of port holes covered over on the inside with *pahkapoomis*—the thin, stretched and dried and neatly sewn-together hairless skins of rabbits into which had been rubbed bear grease until they became translucent, allowing light to enter but warding off chilling drafts.

Five large smooth-barked beech logs stood as upright pillars about twenty feet apart inward from the center of each end wall, their tops V-notched to accept and anchor six slightly smaller beech logs that formed the main beams for supporting the roof. In each end wall, just below the beam, a large aperture allowed the movement of air through the structure and the escape of smoke from the smoldering *kinnikinnick* and the council fire. All four interior walls and the two main pillars had been decorated with numerous symbolic glyphs, geometric designs and renderings of animals.

Over two hundred men and some especially prominent women were seated on mats on the hard-packed earthen floor, arranged in essentially circular fashion and all facing toward the center where a fairly large council fire of tented logs had been built, now burned until black on the tops and glowing red-orange underneath, a wraithlike plume of blue-white smoke rising to escape through the ventilation apertures. Surrounding the fire was a ring of large, smoothly rounded river rocks in a circle some six feet in diameter. Beyond them was an open space about eight feet wide in which the various speakers would stand in their turn, allowing them to circle the council fire as they spoke so as to face and address the entire assemblage seated in concentric circles beyond. The first row of those in attendance was reserved for the ten most powerful and prestigious of the Shawnee chiefs. Hokolesqua—the great Cornstalk—principal chief of the Shawnee tribe as a whole and principal chief of the Chalahgawtha sept as well was there, with a vacant mat to his right where Pucksinwah was to sit. He nodded a greeting, along with others, as the war chief, having threaded his way through the assemblage, took his place.

Now began the first official act of the congress: the ritual passing of the pipes with great solemnity. Utter silence fell over the gathering as a young man entered from outside and approached the principal chief with two already lighted *calumets* that he handed in turn to Hokolesqua. Each was about three feet in length, its hickory stem painted and decorated with geometric figures and hung with strands of dyed rawhide, its hard, red-clay bowl carved with geometric symbols and figures of animals.[54] The chief drew once from the mouthpiece of the first, exhaled the smoke toward the council fire, then drew and exhaled again toward the ceiling. This pipe he handed to War Chief Pucksinwah on his right, principal chief of the Kispokothas. With the second *calumet* he did the same, this time handing it in turn to his left to Peace Chief Kikusgowlowa, principal chief of the Thawegilas. They, in their turn, puffed and passed the pipe on—Pucksinwah passing his right to the eldest and one of the most respected principal chiefs, Moluntha, of the Maykujays; Kikusgowlowa passing his left to Wesecahnay—Black Beard—principal chief of the Peckuwes. With the five principal chiefs having smoked, the pipes continued being passed, now to the second principal chiefs of each sept, seated in the same circle on the opposite side of the fire: Pucksinwah's going to Chiuxca—Black Stump—of the Peckuwes and Penegashega—Change of Feathers—of the Thawegilas, and Kikusgowlowa's going to Shemeneto—Black Snake—of the Kispokothas and Plukkemehnotee—Pluggy—of the Maykujays. Finally, both pipes ended in the hands of the second principal chief of the Chalahgaw-thas, Chiungalla—Black Fish—who performed the same smoking ritual with each that Hokolesqua had performed and handed them back to the warrior who had brought them. While this was occurring, the prevailing silence continued as numerous other ceremonial *calumets* were being passed among the other chiefs and subchiefs gathered here.[55]

As Hokolesqua came smoothly to his feet, all attention was upon him. He shrugged off his blanket, revealing that he was clad in simple but finely tanned doeskin leather leggins with a fringe running down each outseam and a similarly fringed blouse of the same material, belted at the waist and covering him halfway to the knees. His black hair, graying at the temples, was worn loose and shoulder length, without ornamentation. Around each upper arm and his right wrist he wore a band of beaten silver. His leggins were tucked into calf-high buffalo-hide moccasins crisscrossed with rawhide thong lacings and intricately decorated with tiny colorful beads and dyed porcupine quills. His only other adornment at this time was one of the greatest ornamental acquisitions any Indian could have—a necklace of forty upturned grizzly bear claws.[56]

Hokolesqua circled the council fire twice before speaking, his gaze sweeping across those seated before him. Then he began to speak and did not cease for over three hours. He discussed many matters of interest to the tribe as a whole, but concentrated most specifically on the encroachment of whites with resultant destruction of terrain, fish and game. They needed—*desperately* needed—the white man's trade, which had been cut drastically for so long, yet at the same time to open themselves to such trade was more often than not the precursor of other whites following who were *not* traders and who were universally intent upon claiming lands and driving the Indians out.

"How do we handle this situation?" Hokolesqua asked. "What do we do? The trader Croghan, whom we call Aquewelene, has come among us saying he bears news from the big man, Johnson, who is called Warraghiyagey by the Mohawks, of better trade being opened for us and is at this moment in the lodge of Chiungalla waiting to be heard.[57] Do we then hurt ourselves by telling him we do not want him or his English trade among us? Does Johnson's betterment of trade mean that we will benefit, or they, or both? Does it mean that in addition to the tools and goods we need, we will be provided with gunpowder and lead and new guns and men who can repair those that are broken? Or, as has happened all too often before, will better trade mean they are bringing the terrible firewater among us again to make us crazy men and muddy our minds so once again we can be cheated? If better trade is agreed to, does this mean that even more whites than now will come to cut open the breast of the earth, who is our mother, and burn her hair and chop off her limbs?"

There were numerous questions but very few answers as yet. When Hokolesqua finished speaking, Kikusgowlowa rose to speak and the thrust of his talk was to advocate leaving these lands behind and migrating once again beyond reach of the Englishmen going to lands the Spanish king had offered them on the west side of the grandmother of rivers, where that great stream—the Missitheepi—would act as a barrier against the English.

One by one others of the chiefs throughout the entire interior of the *msi-kah-mi-qui,* including Pucksinwah, arose and addressed the assembled chiefs, citing the pros and cons of both increased or decreased English trade. Put aside for the moment was Kikusgowlowa's advocacy of a tribal movement west of the Mississippi. Someday, perhaps, it might come to that and, though he obviously had more supporters now than the last time he broached the subject in council, Kikusgowlowa acceded to the will of the majority who had no wish to leave the land in which at last they had become so firmly entrenched.

Finally, about midday on the third day of the Grand Council, George Croghan was summoned to stand before the council fire and deliver his message from Sir William Johnson. There had been severe trade abuses in the past, he told them, and he would not insult their intelligence that such things might not occur again at the whim of unscrupulous traders, but Warraghiyagey had promised to do all in his power to open trade widely while at the same time maintaining strict control against such outrages. Heretofore trade had been solely in government hands, a monopoly that precluded healthy competitive trading and permitted only those traders in the actual employ of the king to bring goods among them. With the new trade Warraghiyagey was establishing, the business would be opened to anyone having the funds and means to open trade with the Shawnees and other Western tribes. He had heard, Croghan told them, of an inclination among the Shawnees to apply to the French or Spanish for what trade goods they needed, but said this was ill-advised and could only harm them, since neither power could fill their needs so well and so cheaply as could the English, and if the Shawnees were to try this, it would only strengthen the hands of those who opposed Warraghiyagey's efforts to bring about a healthy trade and lasting peace and could, in fact, totally cut off English trade with the Shawnees.

And what, Hokolesqua asked of Croghan in response, of the greatest hazard of all to the Shawnees if they accepted Warraghiyagey's offer—the threat of even more whites penetrating into their country? In this past year alone they had encountered two white men who had not only hunted extensively in the Kan-tuck-kee hunting grounds but who made marks on trees with their hatchets—marks that the Shawnees well knew were the first signs of whites claiming Indian lands.[58]

"They will be prohibited from doing that if Warraghiyagey's trade plan is accepted by you," Croghan replied.

Hokolesqua gave a low, bitter laugh. "We cannot believe that any such prohibition will stop them. Already the stinging flies that make sweet syrup are among us, meaning the whites who want our lands are not far behind. So what are we to do when—not if, but *when*—we find them taking our lands as their own?"

"There is only one thing for you to do when that occurs," Croghan replied simply. "You must then kill them."[59]

Croghan, after giving the Shawnees the large number of gifts he had brought for them, left Chalahgawtha late that afternoon to continue carrying Sir William Johnson's message of new trading practices to the Ottawas, Potawatomies, and Hurons near Detroit. Hokolesqua thanked him on behalf of the tribe for the gifts and assured him that when the Grand Council here concluded, he would send messengers to Croghan in Detroit with their decision.

For two more days the Grand Council continued, with the comments of Croghan carefully analyzed and the implications weighed. While they thought very highly of Croghan as an individual and respected Warraghiyagey as a champion for Indian causes, yet they knew the whites—especially the English—much too well to fully believe Croghan's sanguinary prospects. They tentatively agreed to accept the new increased trade proposal and sent runners with this word to Croghan at Detroit. At the same time, however, they sent appeals to the Spanish governor at St. Louis and the French captain commanding Fort de Chartres in the Illinois country for aid in the form of guns and ammunition to resist the advance of encroaching whites from the east.

In the early evening today, the council fire was extinguished and the Grand Council at Chalahgawtha came to a close. There was much revelry going on in the town, with singing and dancing and story-telling before the fires, but Pucksinwah and Chiksika did not participate. As they had done each night following adjournment of the day's councilling, they struck off at a quick pace toward the spring where Methotasa and Tecumapese, along with several of the aunts, were awaiting their return. In the morning they would be joined by the remainder of the Kispokotha delegation, who were spending the night here. Then all would return to Kispoko Town for festivities in celebration of the birth of their chief's new son, Tecumseh.

As they walked side by side, the twelve-year-old Chiksika slipped his hand into that of his father, comforted by the flow of affection he experienced from the contact.[60]

"Everybody," Chiksika remarked, "is saying that no matter what kind of trade we have with the whites, those traders will be followed by other white men who will try to take our lands. What then, father?"

"We will do as Aquewelene has advised, Chiksika," replied Pucksinwah. "We will kill them."

[February 9, 1771 — Saturday]

Just short of three years ago, Methotasa had stunned the Shawnee tribe by giving birth to Tecumseh at the very instant that a great celestial sign was occurring. Ten days ago—this time in her village of Kispoko Town on the Scioto—she had once again stunned the tribe with the culmination of her pregnancy, though this time eliciting at least as much an undercurrent of fear and dark mutterings as overt joy and congratulations.

It was near noon on the twenty-ninth day of January when Methotasa had gone into labor but some thirty difficult hours passed before she began giving birth in the early darkness on January 30 as the wind whistled shrill, eerie keenings through the chinks of the wegiwa and icy bits of wind-driven snow peppered the thin *pahkapoomis* covering the only window port. A tiny baby was born—a son—and followed, a short time later, by the birth of a second son. Then, incredibly to those in midwifery attendance, a *third* son was born! This final one emerged, kicking and jabbing and filling the wegiwa with squallings of greater volume than it seemed possible for such tiny lungs to produce.

Multiple births were not common among the Shawnees, but neither were they unknown. Twins were infrequently born, usually identical but occasionally not identical and somewhat more than half of these of opposite sexes. This birth of *triplets,* however, was unprecedented in the tribe.

Tecumseh, a toddler of almost three at the time of the birth of his triplet brothers, was little aware of the stir their arrival occasioned, just as he was essentially unaware of the significance of important events, political and martial, that had been occurring since his birth. The Illinois Confederation of tribes, for example, suspicious of the frequent visits of the once powerful Ottawa chief, Pontiac, to their lands and fearful that he would ultimately involve them in a war with the whites, arranged his assassination. The deed was executed only a few miles downstream from St. Louis, on the Illinois side of the Mississippi, in the Cahokia village in April 1769, when Tecumseh was only thirteen months old. Nor was Tecumseh cognizant of it when the coalition of northern tribes Pontiac once led against the British took great offense at the murder of their erstwhile commander and swept down into the Illinois country in murderous force and virtually annihilated all the tribes of the Illinois Confederation and occupied that territory—the Sacs and Foxes, Winnebagoes and Potawatomies firmly establishing themselves throughout the northern third of the Illinois country.[61]

Most disturbing to the Shawnees was a problem Tecumseh was still much too young to comprehend; the increase of whites into their territory due to the lifting of trade restrictions that Croghan had promised them. Some tribes who had agreed to allow trading posts or stores in their towns quickly found these villages becoming centers for transitory traders, many of whom, as the Shawnees had feared, were unscrupulous in their dealings. Equally, also as the Shawnees had feared, far too many of these traders relied on whiskey as a major factor in trade.

Along with the increased trade came an influx of whites roaming the woods and fields; not traders but, rather, adventurers, explorers, hunters, surveyors, and those who had fled to the wilderness to escape punishment for their crimes. Many of these were easily frightened away by simple confrontation, but others exhibited a remarkable persistence and refusal to be driven off. This was especially true of some of the whites who were penetrating into and exploring the hunting grounds of the Shawnees in the Kan-tuck-kee country. Recently a party of six such whites had even had the audacity to set up camps in that area and spent half a year exploring, hunting the game and trapping the fur animals that were rightfully the Shawnees'.[62] Two of these white hunters had finally been captured in their camp along the Psquawwe-theepi—Red River—by a Shawnee hunting party under the leadership of Amaghqua—Beaver—who, like Pucksinwah, had had considerable contact with the whites years earlier on the Pennsylvania frontier. Amaghqua, who had been nicknamed Captain Will by the whites, understood English well enough to converse brokenly in that tongue and he learned that their names were Daniel Boone and John Stuart and that one of the others was the trader the Shawnees had treated so kindly and allowed to enter their country provided he would only trade and not hunt or trap or try to settle there—John Findley. The game and furs the whites had accumulated were confiscated, along with their horses, and Boone and Stuart were held for seven days before being released with a stern warning and just enough supplies to sustain them on their return home.

"Now, brothers," Amaghqua had said upon setting them free, "you go home and stay there. Do not come here anymore. This is the Indians' hunting ground and all the animals, skins and furs are ours. If you are so foolish as to come here again, you can be sure the wasps and yellow jackets will sting you severely."

But the released men did not go home. Keeping out of sight, they had trailed Amaghqua's party, slipped into the Shawnee camp under cover of night and recovered several of their horses. Amaghqua was both impressed and angered at such audacity and immediately followed their trail, captured them again and reconfiscated the horses. During the night, however, Boone and Stuart managed to escape on foot and this time eluded Amaghqua's determined efforts to recapture and kill them.

When Amaghqua returned across the Ohio, word of his encounters with the whites quickly spread through all the Shawnee villages and with it the clear realization that such whites as Boone, Findley, and Stuart evidently could not be discouraged with kind treatment and stern warnings. It was time to follow the advice of Croghan.

Early the following spring, John Findley was again captured descending the Ohio and though he protested that he had only come to trade, they killed him. At about the same time another Shawnee party discovered that Boone and Stuart had come back into the Kan-tuck-kee hunting grounds and were again killing game. Stuart was overtaken and wounded with a gunshot, but he escaped and could not be found.[63] Though they made a determined effort to capture Boone, he earned their grudging respect and fear by besting them in woods lore, living in various caves and consistently managing to elude them while occasionally making phenomenally long shots to kill the Indians he encountered.

Far up the Spaylaywitheepi—the Ohio River—another manifestation of encroachment was occurring with frightening ramifications. Surveyors hired by wealthy land speculators in the east—George Washington being one of the latter, who had hired William Crawford, George Cox and Joseph Tomlinson for the task—were now moving downriver from Fort Pitt and surveying the best of the bottom lands on the east side of the Ohio River as far downstream as the mouths of Wheeling Creek and the Little Kanawha River. It was abundantly clear to the Indians that the scribbles these men made on paper and the marks they made on trees and rocks were the precursors of numerous other whites to follow. They were only too well aware of the reason why these surveyors and other whites were suddenly moving into the wilderness; that reason being the great council held in a New York fortification at the Mohawk River headwaters by Sir William Johnson in the fall of 1768, when Tecumseh was only six or seven months old, immediately known as the Fort Stanwix Treaty.

No previous treaty had ever been so devastating to the Shawnees and Cherokees in particular and to other tribes in only slightly lesser degree as the Fort Stanwix Treaty. The whites on hand, in addition to Johnson, included the governor of New Jersey, William Franklin, a large collection of self-important commissioners representing the colonies of New York, Virginia and Pennsylvania, and a swarm of hangers-on looking for anything of value they might snatch. By far the greater majority of the three thousand Indians attending were Iroquois, once again up to their old tricks of assuring the English colonists that they were the dominant tribe in America and that all other tribes were their vassals, living on lands belonging to the Iroquois League. There were a few uninvited Shawnees and Delawares on hand, who were treated with extreme rudeness and whose protests in regard to what was occurring were largely ignored. William Johnson, champion of the Indians, had indeed come through once again for the Indians—*his* Indians, the Iroquois.

In essence, it was agreed through the Fort Stanwix negotiations that the Indian/White boundary line established by the Royal Proclamation of 1763 as being the crest of the Appalachians should now be abolished, all the way from the St. Lawrence River southward to Tennessee. This meant that anyone who wished to do so could now legally cross westward over the mountains and begin claiming lands as their own—which only a hardy handful of frontiersmen had been doing illegally during the past four or five years—and that those wealthy land speculators could hire their own teams of surveyors to map and plat out the land, then advertise its availability and sell it to any buyer with the appropriate amount of funds.

In order for this to be done, it was necessary that the English colonists have legal title to all the territory from the Tennessee River northward to the Ohio—an area roughly comprising all of Tennessee, Kentucky and western Virginia. For this, the whites were willing to pay the sum of ten thousand pounds, to be proportionately distributed to the tribes who would, by the terms of this agreement, be dispossessed of their lands. The Iroquois speedily agreed and then claimed the whole ten thousand pounds bounty as their own, since all the territory was theirs, allegedly by right of conquest. Most of the whites on hand knew this was patently ridiculous, but they as speedily agreed so as to establish what they would hereafter regard as legal claim to the lands. It was a tremendous coup for the Iroquois who not only received an enormous profit by selling land to which they had no claim except by boast, but at the same time diverted white expansion from their own territory to the Ohio Valley, the rich Kan-tuck-kee hunting grounds, Tennessee, and that portion of Virginia westward of the Appalachian crest. Almost as an afterthought, the Iroquois—evidently with malicious glee at finding a way to avenge past humiliations by their old enemies, the Shawnees—ceded their alleged claim to the Ohio country to Dr. Thomas Walker, a land speculator who was the representative of the colonial governor of Virginia, Norborne Berkeley, the Baron de Botetourt.

The rage of the Shawnees when they learned of all this from their emissaries was as great as any ever harbored. Only one factor seemed to be in their favor. They still *occupied* the Ohio country and considered the Kan-tuck-kee hunting grounds as *their* domain and were resolved, to the very best of their ability, to fight off any white incursions into these territories.[64]

While such were matters quite beyond the comprehension of Tecumseh, he was nevertheless affected by them, seeing the warriors of his village ever more frequently arming themselves with bows and guns and heading out in small parties to hunt not only game in the wilds of Kan-tuck-kee, but a far more dangerous prey—the encroaching white man. Already the toddler was playing with a little bow made of a stick and a thin strand of rawhide and arrows formed from the straight stems of tall dried weeds. It was remarkable how quickly he grasped the knack of the draw and release and how soon he was sending his missiles whistling very close to his targets. The villagers, witnessing this activity in a little boy not yet three years old, agreed among themselves that he was destined to become a great hunter.

His uncommonly early ability with a bow was not the only aspect in which Tecumseh was noteworthy. Virtually from the time of his birth he rarely cried or whined or threw tantrums of any kind. Such behavior was distinctly frowned upon in the tribe and youngsters learned very early not to give vocal vent to anger, frustration or pain. Noisy outbursts on the part of a child were not only aggravating and a disgrace to the parents, they could often have grave consequences; a noisy child could easily ruin a hunt by frightening off game and, in times of hostilities, a wailing baby or whining toddler could direct an enemy to their location and result in disaster. Therefore, self-control *was* something they had to learn very early in life. Despite the imperativeness of learning it, no Shawnee infant or toddler was ever struck as a method to curtail its crying or other outbursts. Instead, from the very first days of their life they were taught the joys and rewards of being quiet and mannerly through the love and affection and close attendance of parents and siblings. If and when crying did occur, the babies were immediately scooped up and held gently in loving arms, tenderly rocked and soft sweet melodies sung to them, and they were fed well, usually long before there was any occasion for them to cry from hunger. Few Shawnee babies did not learn quickly and well the value of silence, but Tecumseh somehow seemed to know this innately and needed very little such training. One of his three new brothers, however, shrieked and cried almost continuously.

At the time the triplets were born, Tecumseh's father and brother, Pucksinwah and Chiksika, were absent from Kispoko Town. The war chief and his fifteen-year-old son were with a party hunting deer and buffalo across the Ohio River near the pooling bluish waters at a great salt lick called Pememo, which lay adjacent to the stream the Shawnees called Nepepimmatheepi—Salt

Seep River.[65] As usual in that productive vicinity, they had very good luck and returned to Kispoko Town three days after the birth, their horses laden with enough meat to last them the rest of the winter and well into spring.

Pucksinwah was astounded and pleased with the news that greeted him on his return—three new sons! He was also bemused by the even greater prestige that now came to him for having sired the triplets. Yet, among many of his tribesmen there was a disturbing sense of morbidity at the event. It was Penegashega—Change of Feathers—the second principal chief of the Tha-wegilas and foremost prophet and medicine man of the tribe, who said the multiple birth was an omen of grave portent for the Shawnees; that one of the trio of newborns—possibly two of them, and perhaps even all three—would bring disaster to their people. The shaman advocated they be killed during these first ten days, while they still had no identity and thus no crime would be committed.[66] Pucksinwah, however, despite considerable outside pressure to follow Penegashega's advice, steadfastly refused to do away with his newborn sons and today, on the prescribed tenth day following birth, the triplets were given their names and became actual people.

The boy who had been born first was called Kumskaka—A Cat that Flies in the Air—meaning the great horned owl. The second-born was named Sauwaseekau—A Door Opened. The third was the thinnest, smallest, darkest, and least attractive of the three. He was also the one who, from the very instant of birth, most often wailed without any perceivable reason, and so he was called Lowawluwaysica—He Makes a Loud Noise.[67]

[March 2, 1774 — Wednesday]

Tecumseh sat on the woven matting before the small fire in the wegiwa of Pucksinwah and continued to listen as his father went on with his account of what had occurred on his most recent journey. As always, he paid close attention to everything being said and yet, simultaneously, another part of his mind took in their surroundings, what was going on in the dwelling and, perhaps most importantly, his own feelings about this eventful day. He was very happy and relieved that his father had come home safely and pleased that he had awakened to be aware of it.

After an absence of ten days, Pucksinwah had returned home late last night and Tecumseh, hearing the murmur of conversation between his father and mother, awoke but did not stir under the warm buffalo skin that covered him. He could tell from Pucksinwah's voice that his father was weary and wondered what great adventures he must have had on the expedition, knowing as well that soon enough he would learn of them. His impulse had been to rise and join them, and he would have been welcome, but that would have been selfish and so he had remained motionless. His father and mother had embraced for a long moment, just standing there quietly in the dim light of the fire. Then Methotasa had quickly prepared food for her husband and skillfully rubbed his neck and shoulders as he ate.

Upon finishing, Pucksinwah moved silently to the sleeping area and paused at each form, in his usual ritual, to gently caress the heads of his children. Two of the three-year-old triplets stirred at his touch but did not awaken. Neither Chiksika nor Tecumapese moved as he touched them and as he came toward Tecumseh, the six-year-old feigned sleep. Pucksinwah squatted beside him and placed a hand on his cheek.

"You've been awake all this while, Tecumseh," he said softly.

Tecumseh opened his eyes. "I'm glad you're home, father."

Pucksinwah nodded, patting his son's cheek. "Tomorrow we will talk," he said as he straightened. "It is a very important day for all of us, but especially for Tecumapese."

It was obvious that Pucksinwah greatly loved Tecumseh and was deeply proud of him, as well he might be. At six years of age Tecumseh was exhibiting remarkably advanced traits in his agility and morality and most pertinently in his intelligence and leadership qualities. Other boys his age and even many somewhat older youngsters flocked to him wherever he was, unfailingly looking to him as their commander in the sports, games, and mock warfare in which they engaged. He now had a well-made bow of his own—small, to be sure, but fully capable of lethal result at short range—and through endless hours of practice he had become uncommonly skilled in its use. Already his prowess as a hunter was the talk of the Kispokothas; rarely did he set out into the surrounding fields and woods that he did not return with his buckskin pouch filled with squirrels, rabbits, quail or turkeys that he had downed. Along with keen marksmanship, he was developing the adjunctive skills so requisite for the good hunter or warrior—remarkable stealth in creeping close to prey before it could become aware of his presence, and a tracking ability already far beyond his years. To his keen eye, every broken twig, bent blade of grass, mark in the soil or stain in water had its own special meaning.

While he did much of this on his own, Tecumseh had superb tutors as well. From Pucksinwah and Chiksika and from Chaquiweshe and Blue Jacket, as well as from other members of this Shawnee community, he learned many things: the fundamentals and many advanced techniques of hunting, the bearing of his own wounds and how to treat them or the wounds of others with what nature provided, the elements of hand-to-hand fighting, the construction, care and use of not only bow and arrows but such weapons as knives, tomahawks, and war clubs. He had even been promised that soon he would be taught the use and care of firearms and, when deemed accomplished enough, would be given a gun, ball pouch and powderhorn of his very own.

Among the most important, if not the most dramatic, lessons he was learning were those from his father regarding the *strategy* of warfare. Pucksinwah strongly stressed the value of always making every effort to out-think an enemy—well before an engagement was begun, if that were possible—and never, under any circumstances, to underestimate his foe. There was great importance, the war chief told him gravely, especially when taken by surprise, in doing quickly, effectively, almost instinctively, what an enemy did not expect him to do, thereby throwing his adversary off balance for a few crucial moments and giving himself opportunity to seize the advantage and emerge victorious.

Sitting now by the wegiwa's perpetual fire as his father continued his relation, Tecumseh glanced over at his sixteen-year-old sister who was kneeling on a thickly furred robe and decided that pretty though she always was, she had never looked more radiantly beautiful than now. The Shawnees were as a rule a very handsome people but no other maiden in the village—perhaps in the tribe—was lovelier than she. Already she stood several inches taller than Methotasa, who was presently twisting her daughter's waist-long glossy black hair into a single thick braid that would fall down the middle of her back.

Tecumapese was clad in an extremely soft doeskin garment of simple shift design that could not hide her lithe figure nor conceal the fullness of her breasts. She wore plain, unadorned buckskin moccasins that she herself had made using skills learned from her mother. Quite remarkable similarity of features existed between Tecumseh and his sister and none who saw them together could ever doubt their relationship. Hers were somewhat more refined than his own, but there was that same broad forehead and high cheekbones that heightened the delicacy of her features. Her chin was straight and determined, her nose so well formed it might have been chiseled by a sculptor. Even the direct, penetrating gaze of their unusually large and expressive dark eyes seemed identical. While there was a close relationship among all the members of this family, that existing between Tecumseh and Tecumapese was something very special. She had always adored him and he her and now, as she glanced his way and saw him looking at her, she smiled widely, exposing the very white, evenly formed teeth that made her smile so engaging. He smiled back in the same way and gave a little nod, letting her know without words how happy he was for her this day.

Outside they could dimly hear the bustle and laughter as preparations were being made for this evening's feast and festivities, for this was the day

that Tecumapese would marry. Her husband-to-be was Chaquiweshe—the
Mink—a muscular, strong-featured twenty-year-old Kispokotha warrior
who, at this very moment, was seated on the opposite side of the fire from
Tecumseh, beside Chiksika.[68] Though Chiksika was two years younger, he
and Chaqui—as Chaquiweshe was familiarly known—had been the closest
companions ever since they were small boys. In early youth they had played
games, explored, studied nature's wonders, held mock battles and, as they
grew older, always went together on the seasonal hunting expeditions or
on forays against white settlements. The two young men were much alike—
well built, keen in their senses, swift in their reflexes and highly intelligent.
Both were utterly fearless in battle and had won many accolades for their
fighting skills. Seated now between Chaqui and Pucksinwah, Chiksika was
delighted. perhaps more than anyone else apart from Tecumapese, at the
prospect that this day Chaqui would become related to the family through
marriage.

In a far corner of the expansive wegiwa, the youngest members of the
family of Pucksinwah rolled about, playing and giggling on a pair of large
black bear skins. The three-year-old triplets were like puppies intent upon
their own activities and oblivious to practically anything else. If they understood anything their father was saying, it was not apparent. Sauwaseekau,
Kumskaka and Lowawluwaysica seemed to live in their own separate world,
eating, playing and sleeping together as if they were one identity.

Tecumseh returned his attention more directly to what his father was
saying. At age forty-eight, Pucksinwah was a man who emanated power and
strength. Renowned as one of the greatest warriors the tribe had ever produced,
his sagacity and battle skills against enemies was legendary and he was frequently compared to his outstanding grandfather, Opeththa, which was no
small honor of itself. It was said he had taken upwards of two hundred enemy
scalps in hand-to-hand combat and in all his battles had only once been slightly
wounded—when a Cherokee arrow clipped away a portion of his right earlobe.
The twenty-claw necklace he sometimes wore on ceremonial occasions was a
trophy of his one journey many years ago to the western mountains where,
so some exaggerated stories had it, he had leaped upon the back of a large
sow grizzly and, in a ferocious tussle, had dispatched her with nothing more
than his hunting knife.

A dominant personage in any gathering, Pucksinwah was an exceptionally
articulate speaker and always, as now, kept his audience riveted with his
narrations, easily able to imbue in listeners the excitement of the hunts and
battles in which he had participated and stirring their fascination with news
he had gathered from the world in which they lived. He had risen this morning
when the sun was only an hour high, strolled to the edge of the village where

he relieved himself in the special trench dug for that purpose, bathed in the icy waters of the nearby Little Miami River, and returned to his wegiwa to eat the hearty breakfast stew Methotasa had prepared and drink two cups of delicious hot chocolate she had prepared from the cocoa powder that was so important an item in the Indian trade. Finally, as his family had eagerly been waiting for him to do, Pucksinwah packed the bowl of his pipe with *kinni-kinnick,* lighted it with a glowing stick from the fire and, as customary, smoked in silence, obviously enjoying this interval of quiet to gather his thoughts before beginning his narration, at the same time heightening the anticipation of his listeners for what would come.

The only member of the household missing was Blue Jacket—Wehyah-pihehrsehnwah—the tall, dark-haired young man who had been adopted into Pucksinwah's family almost three years ago when he was a youth of seventeen and had been captured in western Virginia by a hunting party under Pucksinwah's leadership.[69]

The youth had wanted very much to become an Indian but he was not really prepared for the rigors this involved. On arrival at Kispoko Town, he was forced to run the gauntlet, in which, after a remarkably courageous effort to get through, he had been beaten into unconsciousness and required a fortnight of care to recover. As customary with adoptions, he had then been stripped and lavishly painted in various colors over his entire body. Pucksinwah recited an ancient Shawnee adoption liturgy ending with the words, "*Newecanetepa, weshemanitoo weshecatweloo, keweshelawaypa*"—The Great Spirit is the friend of the Indians; let us always do good. The youth was then led into the waters of the Scioto River by a trio of squaws who, when waist-deep, leaped upon him and pulled him under the surface. Scooping up handfuls of fine gravel and sand from the bottom, they had scrubbed him vigorously until no vestige of the paint remained. When they returned him to shore he was led to the *msi-kah-mi-qui* and there dressed in a fine blouse and leggins of buckskin liberally decorated with painted porcupine quills, ribbons, hanks of red hair and beads. His face was again painted, this time with considerable care, in lines and spots of bright colors, and a metal disk with an eagle feather affixed to it was attached to his hair. All this while, villagers had been filing into the *msi-kah-mi-qui* and taking seats on floor mats until finally the structure was densely packed. Pipes filled with *kinnikinnick* had been smoked by all present and when this was finished, Pucksinwah stood and placed a hand on the young man's shoulder, then spoke loudly enough for all present to hear.

"My son," he had said, "you are now flesh of our flesh and bone of our bone. By the ceremony performed this day, every drop of white blood was washed out of your veins. You are taken into the Shawnee Nation and initiated into a warrior sept. You are adopted into a great family and received with great seriousness and solemnity in the room and presence and place of a great man. After what has passed this day, you are now one of us by an old strong law and custom. My son, you have now nothing to fear—we here are under the same obligation to love, support and defend you, that we are to love and defend one another. Therefore, you are to consider yourself as one of our people and forevermore to be known and respected as Wehyahpihehrsehn-wah."

No captive the Shawnees had ever before adopted so quickly and completely adapted to the Shawnee way of life as Blue Jacket and his former life as a white quickly faded into mere dim memories. The Shawnee beliefs and customs—social, political, religious, and moral—became his own and within brief months he had become fluent in the Shawnee tongue. He had entered into the games, sports, labors and habits of his fellows with such a pronounced degree of cheerfulness, alacrity and respect for others that he had rapidly become very popular among all the Kispokothas and members of other Shawnee septs who met him.

Living in Pucksinwah's household, Blue Jacket had grown very close to the family members and over these past three years he and Chiksika, two years his junior, and Chaquiweshe, who was his own age, became virtually inseparable. But his greatest admiration and respect were reserved for Pucksinwah, who became far more a father to him than his own father had ever been. For his part, Pucksinwah spent many hours and days instructing Blue Jacket in all aspects of Shawnee life, especially the tribe's history, religion and culture.

"The Supreme Being of all things," Pucksinwah had told him, "is Moneto, who rules Yalakuquakumigigi [the Universe] and dispenses His blessings and favors to those who earn His good will, just as He brings unspeakable sorrow to those whose conduct merits His displeasure. Moneto is not to be mistaken for the Great Spirit, the ruler of destinies, who is subordinate to Him. The Great Spirit is known as *Inumsi Ilafewanu* and She is a grandmother who constantly weaves a great net called a *skemotah* which, when finished, will be lowered to the earth. All those who have proven themselves worthy will be gathered into its folds and taken to a world of great peace and happiness. At the same time an unspeakably terrible fate will overtake those not gathered up and the world will end. Good conduct always brings rewards, just as evil conduct brings misery and great sorrow.

"No one," the war chief had continued, "is forced to believe in these matters. Force is not necessary. We know them to be the truth. Morality is a fixed law, but each of us must be his own judge. From our earliest childhood it is instilled in our minds that deceitfulness among ourselves is a crime. We live according to our standards and principles and not for what others might think of us. Absolute honesty toward others of our tribe is the basis of character and the standards and rules of conduct are followed scrupulously. The foundation of all Shawnee intercourse is this: *Do not kill or injure your neighbor, for it is not him you injure, you injure yourself; but do good to him, therefore add to his days of happiness as you add to your own. Do not wrong your neighbor, nor hate him, for it is not him that you wrong—you wrong yourself; but love him, for Moneto loves him also, as He loves you."*

Blue Jacket learned that in the Shawnee tribe there was no such concept or institution as jail, but there were various punishments for misdeeds, determined by the gravity of the offense. The word of the chief was law and any persistent refusal to obey the unwritten code of honorable behavior was punishable by severe thrashing or even by death. Anyone who refused to manfully accept his just punishment was irrevocably ostracized from the tribe, to which death was infinitely preferable. Where women of the tribe were concerned, they were not excused from the same precepts of law that guided the men. One of the greatest crimes a woman could commit was *pockvano-madee-way*—gossip about people; meaning deliberate and malicious lying meant to cause harm, shame, humiliation or pain.

As for the Shawnee punishment of children, such a thing was virtually unknown. Punishments and threats were never used to make them obey. Instead, it was the child's pride that was appealed to in order to have him or her carry out the parents' wishes and it was a method that worked inordinately well. A parent who wanted to have an errand run or a chore taken care of only needed to say, in the presence of his children, what it was he wished and often with the comment added, "I wonder if there is a good child anywhere around who would do this." Normally there would then be a scramble among the children as they vied to fulfill the wish of mother or father. Praise from a parent or neighbor was a cherished reward and there was always community support in supplying such praise. It was not uncommon for anyone witnessing a child performing a task to wonder aloud "whose good child is this who does such a thing so nicely?" and, if told who the parent was, to exclaim, "My! Has so-and-so got such a good child as that?" In cases where a child did something bad, it was probably never done again, simply by the parent saying something like "Oh, how sad I am that my child has done this bad thing. I truly hope he will never do it again."

For Blue Jacket the most wonderful thing about life in the Shawnee tribe was the paradoxically patterned and lackadaisical lifestyle of everyday existence. The pattern was that consistently there was no pattern. They came and went as they chose without schedules of any kind, each doing what he chose, when and how he chose to do it. Yet somehow, almost unbelievably, the tasks necessary for ordinary survival got accomplished, simply because they *wanted* to do them and did so at their own time and pace. When not specifically involved in the major seasonal pursuits of hunting, sugar making, crop planting and harvesting or engaging in forays or actual war, the daily pursuits were largely hedonistic—hour after hour, from the time of early morning awakening until at least midnight or later, each day was a montage of sensual and artisanal satiation: they ate when they felt like it and however much or little; drank chocolate heavily sweetened with maple sugar; gambled for various stakes with dice or playing cards procured in abundance from traders; played games as simple as a form of mumblety-peg with their sheath knives or as complex as *Shequonurah*—meaning, simply, Stones—which was a sort of three-dimensional combination of chess, go and backgammon, played with multiple covered cups in layers and three sets of pebbles dyed red, black or white, a game requiring considerable strategy; they engaged in theatrical performances of highly dramatic or lightly musical foundation; strung beads; designed and fashioned ornaments; created strings and belts of wampum; sang lovely ballads solo or in groups, accompanied or *a cappella;* related, to individuals or audiences, stories of heroic exploits against man or beast and told tales of danger, mysticism, and the supernatural; they danced an almost endless variety of steps from leisurely to frantic; played sports such as one known simply as the Ball Game, which was similar to lacrosse but considerably more fiercely combative contests that could, on occasion, result in serious injury or even death; they strolled about the village as mummers in weird animal costumes, delighting in taking others by surprise and momentarily frightening them; knapped flint for arrow and spear heads and shaved shafts of wood for the same with knives or flint chips; they visited neighbors extensively to exchange news or stories or jokes or just idle talk, while at the same time participating in potluck meals at every stopping place; repaired guns and bows and worn-out tools; painted sagas of hunts and battles on long broad strips of skin that were rolled into tubes similar to papyrus; played with their children; carved figurines of wood or sculpted in clay; wrestled; engaged in practical jokes from the simplistic to the bizarre; played musical instruments such as horns, drums, a sort of pan-pipe, willow flutes, gourd rattles, a type of lute, harmonicas and even fiddles obtained in trade or raid. Not all these activities occurred at once, of course, or even on the same day, but they engaged in these and many more simply as the mood struck and for so long as it lasted.

Blue Jacket accepted the Shawnee customs and beliefs and pastimes unequivocally; he was now a Shawnee only and owed neither allegiance nor anything else to any other people, including the whites, except to return in kind the treatment received. And when he began going on forays against the white settlements with Pucksinwah, Chiksika, and Chaquiweshe, which he soon did, he attacked, slew, and scalped with as great vigor and determination as they. In fact, his absence from this gathering listening to Pucksinwah's relation was due to his presently being part of a war party under Shemeneto—Black Snake—which was scouring the Kan-tuck-kee hunting grounds for the white interlopers who had become so much more frequent over the past few years.

Pucksinwah's wegiwa was a noted focal point for collection and dissemination of news and frequently during this day visitors stopped by to listen to Pucksinwah, to have a bite to eat—since Methotasa's stewpot was always warm and its contents gladly shared—and perhaps to impart a bit of news before wandering off again to duties elsewhere. Now it was late in the afternoon and the war chief was still talking, his core of familial listeners every bit as avid to hear more as when he first began.

Virtually everything of moment that occurred east of the Mississippi came to Pucksinwah's attention and he possessed a phenomenal grasp of broad issues, situations and trends. Over the past three years those matters had become increasingly ominous. The Indian trade and the various traders involved in it were always subjects of keen interest and concern to the tribe.

A few of the traders—French and English alike—who traveled extensively through this vast country and established trading posts here and there, treated the Indians very well, were scrupulously fair and respected their customs and traditions. As a result they prospered and were well protected by the Indians they served. One of these was a French-Canadian named Peter Loramie, who established his post—called Loramie's Store—on a branch of the upper waters of the Great Miami River several miles from where Pickawillany had been—the old Miami village of Chief Unemakemi.[70] Another trader well favored by the Indians for his unfalteringly fair treatment of them was the Englishman William Burnett, who had first based his operations at Detroit but soon established one of the best trading posts east of the Mississippi at one of the largest Potawatomi villages, Topenebe's Town, on the St. Joseph River a few miles from the old French village of Petit Coeur de Cerf.[71] He quickly became very close friends with Chief Topenebe, who was among the most influential and powerful of Potawatomi chiefs, and firmly cemented his ties with the tribe when he married Topenebe's sister, Kawkeeme, after which the Potawatomies considered him one of their own.

For every good trader, however, there were a score or more who were wholly unscrupulous in their dealings with the tribes, and their numbers were increasing. Since the Fort Stanwix Treaty and the opening of trade to private enterprise, a bare trickle of entrepreneurial private traders into the wilderness had gradually turned into a flow and then into a veritable deluge. Just as the Indians had been so certain would happen, the traders were quickly followed by others—travelers, adventurers, explorers, opportunists, proselytizers of various religions, surveyors, land agents, speculators, and, more than anything else, an ominously growing number of ordinary settlers who were willing to undergo the tremendous risks involved in order to be among the first to snatch their share of the Indian lands.

Reports came to Pucksinwah from all over the northwest of these inroads, some amusing in the very audacity of the ventures, others tragic to the extreme in their consequences. There was the lone Frenchman named Medore Jennette who built a cabin on the Illinois River at the mouth of the Fox River and lived there undisturbed by anyone, delighting in serving as a guide to passing travelers on the Checagou Portage connecting Lake Michigan with the Illinois River and ultimately the Mississippi. There was the English trader of sorts named Peter Pond who started out with his party of men from Michilimackinac, crossed Lake Michigan by canoe to Green Bay, then traversed the upper Wisconsin area into the Minnesota country at the very time a small war had broken out between the Sioux and Chippewas. His party built cabins on a high bank of the Minnesota River where they remained all last winter and somehow got back to Michilimackinac mere weeks ago, not only with their scalps intact, but with a small fortune in animal skins purchased for practically nothing from the tribes visited.

A wry chuckle escaped Pucksinwah as he told of an Englishman named William Murray who fancied himself an empire builder and set himself up with a few other individuals as the Illinois Land Company. Last July this man Murray had met at Kaskaskia with several village chiefs from whom he was certain he had purchased an enormous segment of the Illinois country, from the Illinois River northward to the Wisconsin country, for the price of "five shillings to them in hand paid" plus some merchandise.

A bold—or perhaps stupid—settler named Adam Stroud came with his wife and seven children to the waters of the Elk River in western Virginia and sank in his roots for permanent residency. It was all too permanent for them. The nine Strouds were slain in one brief bloody attack by the Indians. Some time later, two brothers named Richards who came into that same area were similarly killed. Within mere weeks of one another the Potawatomies killed three British traders who attempted to cheat them—one in the southern Illinois country and two in the northern Indiana area. Then there were the four French-Canadian traders traveling on Lake Ontario with thirty large packs of fur skins, who landed to make camp and were waylaid by a party of Senecas who shot and killed them all and took their peltry.

But, Pucksinwah told his listeners, no matter how many of the settlers were slain or driven out, many times more that number were settling throughout the Ohio Valley and the valleys of most of that stream's major tributaries. A certain number, even when captured and driven out, were such skilled woodsmen that they matched the Shawnees themselves in this respect and some kept coming back despite threats and hardships. One of these was the man already several times captured and either set free or escaped—the one called Boone. He had returned, this time with his entire family and a number of companions, in several parties. A war party attacked two of these parties last fall, killing four in the first and, in the second, wounding two young men who they then tortured to death as a warning to the others. Daniel Boone's party, however, had turned the tables on the Shawnees by attacking them and killing one warrior and wounding another.[72] Boone and the surviving members of his party had fled south again and escaped, but Pucksinwah had no doubt they would be back to attempt sinking permanent roots there, since the marks the whites made on the trees this time were the same kind of marks Pucksinwah had often seen before, just before a new settlement of whites was established.

There was another frontiersman persistently showing up who, though very young, was very skilled in woods lore and had already escaped one Shawnee attack on his camp, in which one of his companions had been killed and their entire winter take of furs confiscated. That had occurred exactly a year ago and he had been observed on numerous occasions since but somehow always managed to evade capture. This powerful young giant was called Bahdler by his companions and Pucksinwah had no doubt they would be hearing and seeing much more of him.[73]

Numerous surveying parties streamed down the Ohio and among them came the party led by Captain Thomas Bullitt who had been dispatched by Virginia's relatively new colonial governor, a heavy-set, gray-haired man named John Murray, whose title was Lord Dunmore, to explore and survey the area in the vicinity of the stretch of rapids known as the Falls of the Ohio.[74]

Bullitt's party paused on their downstream passage long enough for Bullitt to travel swiftly up the Little Miami to Chalahgawtha to ask official permission from the Shawnees to perform this mission. Chief Chiungalla—Black Fish— was so bemused by the boldness of this lone white man striding into Chalahgawtha with no semblance of fear that permission was granted, with the proviso that they land and survey only on the south side of the Spaylaywitheepi, which the whites called the Ohio River. Bullitt agreed, returned to his party and they continued their downriver float toward the Falls. When they were near the mouth of the Great Miami River, the party split, one of the boats carrying five men landing on the Ohio shore and camping there. A party of Shawnees sent by Chiungalla to watch and make sure they lived up to Bullitt's promise, sent one of their number—a warrior named Peshewa—to tell them they were disobeying the restriction and must move over to the south shore of the river. One of the whites in the party, seeing the Shawnee coming, panicked, snatched up his rifle and shot Peshewa dead. Immediately the rest of the Shawnee party, shrieking with rage, swept down upon the whites and killed all five, then severely mutilated their bodies as a warning to others.

Pucksinwah could not deny that the Shawnees desperately needed a fair and equitable trade with the whites but, unfortunately, really good traders such as William Burnett and Peter Loramie were quite the exception. More often the traders, especially English ones, who came among the Indians treated them with behavior ranging from undisguised discourtesy to outright ugliness and brutality. The Indians suffered much of it with well-hidden but seething resentment, simply because they were so dependent upon the trade goods these men brought. But gradually their pride could no longer allow them to suffer such abuses and they began to retaliate. The Kickapoos, not dependent upon goods from either the British or French, were first to initiate such retaliation against the abusive or deceptive English traders who came among them, first by stealing horses and trade goods brought among them, finally by burning their trading posts and cabins and then by capturing and torturing to death those traders who continued their nefarious practices. Soon settlers establishing themselves near such posts as those at Cahokia, Kaskaskia, and Fort de Chartres were being killed in their cabins, their wives and children carried into captivity, their cabins burned and their Negro slaves mutilated or adopted into the tribe.[75] Eventually the Kickapoos, in parties of forty warriors each, began very effectively using boats to waylay travelers on the Ohio. Such Kickapoo retaliation for abusive treatment and fraudulent trading practices became a contagion that rapidly spread to the other tribes, especially the Potawatomies, but also including the Shawnees, who perhaps had the best reason for reacting. Would-be settlers had begun floating down the Ohio, intent upon settling along the south shore of that stream, and had discovered a new and grisly amusement to break the boredom of the long drift downstream; shooting at any Indian they saw along the Ohio shores. Most often they missed their aim, yet in half a hundred cases already they had hit the mark and either wounded or killed the Indian. When so many had been shot in this manner and over a dozen already killed, the Shawnees inaugurated a program of their own of attacking the rafts as they descended.

Incensed at such attacks by the Indians and wholly ignoring the fact that they were in direct retaliation for attacks by the whites, the British military commander in America, General Thomas Gage, ordered troops into readiness, began more direct retaliation against the "beastial savages" and advised Sir William Johnson of his step by writing:

> *Scarce a year passes that the Pouteatamies* [Potawatomies] *are not guilty of killing some of the traders and of course plundering their Effects, which it becomes absolutely necessary to put a stop to. . . .*

The suddenly increased flow of potential white settlers down the Ohio was the reason for the expedition from which Pucksinwah had just returned.

The Shawnees had gotten word that a large number of whites would soon be assembling on the Virginia bank of the Ohio at the mouth of Macatetheepi—Gunpowder River.[76] They meant to find out why and so it was Pucksinwah who had led a party of warriors there and studied the situation carefully from hiding. The ice cloaking the Ohio River was just beginning to break up at this time but was still thick enough in some areas for the Shawnee party to cross over unseen during the night. They found that several hundred whites had already gathered at the site where, a bit over a year ago, a settler named Ebenezer Zane had established a station that some people were calling Fort Zane and others were calling Wheeling. That station was not only still there, it was also still the farthest permanent white settlement downstream on the Ohio.

Though Pucksinwah observed that the majority of the men who gathered here at Wheeling carried guns, it was evident that they were not an army but merely a group of men brought together for another purpose. The war chief issued orders that no attack was to be made and that utter silence should be maintained while they studied the situation in an effort to determine what it all meant. Various officious white men were making speeches and numerous pieces of paper were being handed back and forth and scribbles made upon them. It took many hours of studying them before Pucksinwah finally began to fit the pieces of the puzzle together. Quite a number of the whites gathered here were Red Flag men, as the Shawnees called them—surveyors—and well equipped with a variety of surveying tools. A cold, sick anger had settled in Pucksinwah's breast with his realization that they were here to begin carving up this portion of the wilderness for the use of the white man.[77]

Unseen, Pucksinwah's party withdrew to the Ohio side of the river and just in time, for within hours of their passage, major blockages of ice began splitting free with a terrific booming and crashing noise. The spring break-up was occurring and now the river would be open for travel by anyone hardy enough to do so. Even as the Shawnees watched a little longer, a few small boatloads of these whites began descending the river. Traveling swiftly in a somewhat circuitous route, the Shawnees managed to entrap one of the boats that had become well separated from the others. Of the six men aboard they killed five, sparing only one who spoke a smattering of their tongue. This final man was questioned and in a difficult conversation with Pucksinwah, who understood more English than this man understood Shawnee, they learned that he was simply a hired laborer who had once worked the Indian trade but failed and that he was now merely a pole-carrier for the surveying team under their captain, John Floyd. Floyd, the captive said, was in one of the other boats, and that Floyd, too, was just an employee—the agent of Patrick Henry and Colonel George Washington, who were involved with the Ohio Land Company. Floyd's instructions from Washington were to survey and lay claim to about ten thousand acres of land lying not only on the Ohio side of the river, but also along the Scioto River in the very midst of Shawnee territory; the Scioto River, upon whose banks Pucksinwah's own Kispoko Town was located.

The man was terrified and Pucksinwah was sure he was telling the truth. Under further questioning he revealed that a man named Briscoe, leading a party of fifteen men in five canoes, had established a large camp on the Virginia side of the Ohio on a fine bottomland some six miles above the mouth of the Little Kanawha River and, while still just a temporary camp, he had announced that this was where he planned to establish a large permanent settlement.[78] He also said that a party of fourteen surveyors under two men named Lee and Wood had gone even farther down the Ohio to the mouth of the Big Sandy River, to which they had been guided by the big young frontiersman, Simon Butler, and that they had all claimed land there and built cabins.[79]

The intelligence infuriated Pucksinwah, but that wasn't the end of it. The badly frightened pole-carrier blurted out that the entire Wheeling Creek valley up to the forks had already been claimed by the four Zane brothers—Ebenezer, Silas, Andrew, and Jonathan—numerous members of the Zane family and that another party of men, eleven in all, under Captain Lewis Bonnet, who had originally planned to claim the land the Zanes got, had instead claimed a great quantity of the land along the main Wheeling Creek upstream from the Zanes' uppermost boundary at the forks.

Finally, the captive pole-carrier told them that the Ohio Valley between Fort Pitt and Wheeling was now alive with parties of frontiersmen and a whole string of supposedly permanent settlements were being established upstream on the Ohio from Wheeling—places with such names as Fish Creek Station, Cornwell's, Fish Creek Flat, Catfish Camp, and Little Shirtee, plus a number of others that as yet had not been given names. When the captive had at length fallen silent and it was evident he could supply no further information of value, Pucksinwah took out his knife. The pole-carrier's eyes bulged with apprehension, but the war chief merely cut away the rawhide thongs that had been used to bind his wrists and then spoke to him sternly.

"Go back to the Macatetheepi—the place you call Wheeling, where all these men met. Tell your friends what we have done here." He made a sweeping gesture across the bodies of the five who had been killed. "Tell them George Croghan told us to kill all Virginians found on the river. Tell them that from this time forward, this is what we will do. That includes all those who have made their marks on trees and carved up the land. Now go!"[80]

As the pole-carrier fled in great haste, Pucksinwah called his followers together, selected six of the most stalwart to stay with him and sent the remainder home to spread the alarming news of what they had discovered at

Macatetheepi—Wheeling. Of the six still with him, he sent two ahead as runners to Fort Pitt to alert Alexander McKee that they were coming for a conference to complain about the encroachments in the hunting grounds and, in fact, all over the territories of various tribes.

Alexander McKee, a principal deputy of Sir William Johnson in the Indian Department, was George Croghan's immediate superior and, along with Croghan, one of the few whites that had ever shown any sympathy to the Shawnees for their grievances. Fort Pitt, where McKee was headquartered, remained the center of British Indian trade in the west and collection point for the vast number of pelts brought in to be transshipped to the East and thence to Europe. A fur buyer with many years of experience in dealing with the Indians, McKee was not pleased with any prospect of interruption of the trade and that, plus the fact that he truly liked and admired the Shawnees, made him the most likely white man to help the tribe.

The Shawnee runners had paved the way well and Pucksinwah's delegation was received with warmth and kindness. McKee, reasonably fluent in the Shawnee tongue, welcomed them effusively, expressing his great pleasure at seeing Pucksinwah once again. He ordered food and drink for them all and then listened carefully to the war chief's litany of complaints, though it seemed apparent he knew in advance what they would be.

"Why," questioned McKee at one point, making a motion with his hand to indicate the six warriors with Pucksinwah, "are your young men running around with their hatchets?"

"Our warriors are every year more disappointed than the last in their success in the Kan-tuck-kee hunting ground," Pucksinwah replied. "They find the woods covered with white people. They look for the deer and elk and buffalo that are needed to feed their families and instead find rotted carcasses of these animals that the Maker of All has provided for the use of the Indians. They find the game animals slaughtered far beyond the need of those who kill them, many from which only a small part of the meat has been taken and the rest left to be eaten by *petweowas* and *sholees*.[81] One buffalo can feed a whole Indian family for more than a moon, yet we find many of them dead and only their tongues taken. We are angry that this should happen."

Alexander McKee sighed and shook his head. "I understand your anger and I am sorry, but in this matter there is nothing that I can personally do to give you any satisfaction. I can only promise to pass along to Sir William Johnson what you have told me and trust that he will meet with Lord Dunmore and attempt to satisfy your grievances. I ask only that you be patient and keep your young men quiet until a decision can be reached."

Pucksinwah nodded and the delegation soon afterwards left on their return to Kispoko Town. It was no more nor less than he had expected. Nor was it the only sign that terrible times were in store for the Shawnees and other northwestern tribes. Pucksinwah was painfully aware that another ominous indication of white tendrils tightening their grip on the northwestern country was evident in the British shipyards recently built at both ends of Lake Erie—one on Navy Island in the Niagara River, the other on the Detroit River—both busily constructing vessels specifically to control the upper Great Lakes. They were establishing a regular fleet of gunboats and the latest to be added was the forty-five-ton *Felicity* recently launched from the king's shipyard at Detroit. And Detroit itself had grown from a small fort and settlement in the midst of Indian villages to a city that now had a population of well over two thousand and was continuing to grow rapidly.[82]

The most disturbing intelligence Pucksinwah had to impart was that when they were halfway back to Kispoko Town runners had come to him with the fearful news that the Virginians, under Lord Dunmore, had initiated a program to raise a strong militia force, armed with the best that could be obtained in guns and swords, to invade the Ohio country and attack the Shawnees, using as an excuse the recent attacks made by the Indians against the surveyors entering their lands. These Virginia militia the Shawnees referred to as *Shemanese*—Long Knives—and there was no longer any doubt in Pucksinwah's mind that the Shawnees would soon be engaged in a hot war with them. Instead of going directly to Kispoko Town, he had detoured long enough to report the threat to Hokolesqua at his village on Scippo Creek.

The only hopeful sign in any of this was that at different times during his absence Pucksinwah had been approached and spoken to in secrecy by spokesmen for two different factions of white traders. One said he represented their Great Father, King George III, across the great sea, who was finding his children that he sent over to America to have become "unruly and disobedient" and it might be that these American colonists might try to separate themselves from their motherland and their father, the king. In such case, the king would be glad to provide the Shawnees with all they might need if they would ally themselves to him and take up the hatchet against these wayward children. The other, a representative of the Americans who were beginning to rebel against the strictures the Crown had placed on them, said there would almost certainly be a revolution very soon and if and when such a war broke out between the British king and his colonial subjects, would the Shawnees, if provided with the proper arms, equipment, supplies and sustenance, fight beside the Americans against the forces of the king? To each Pucksinwah had given no definite response, telling them truthfully that this was a matter only a Grand Council of the Shawnee tribe as a whole could decide, but told each spokesman he would be glad to carry the request back to his people for consideration. The vague hope in Pucksinwah's mind, seconded by Hokolesqua, was that such a possibility of war would indeed become a reality, which might result in the encroaching whites abandoning the frontiers in order to fight among themselves in the east.[83]

Pucksinwah had been talking for many hours but now he fell silent for a long moment. No one around the fire spoke or even moved and the only sound in the wegiwa was the faint whimpering of Lowawluwaysica in his sleep as he twitched and stirred in the throes of a bad dream. At last Pucksinwah shrugged and smiled slightly, attempting to cast off the aura of gloom that had settled on them all. The smile widened and his features softened as he glanced over to where his wife was carefully tying off the bottom of the long queue she had woven into their daughter's hair. His gaze moved along and settled on Chaquiweshe. Abruptly he leaned to his left, stretching his arm past Chiksika, and placed his hand on the shoulder of the young man who would so soon become his son-in-law.

"Today you become a member of our family, Chaqui," he said. "It is good. We welcome a son, brother, and husband. Before the first deep snow of winter, Tecumapese will bear you a son."

Exclamations of pleasure erupted from the family members at the pronouncement. Tecumseh let out an uncharacteristic yelp of joy and then grinned somewhat abashedly as all turned to look at him. He was very happy to hear the news and there was no doubt whatever in his mind, nor in the mind of any of the others, that what Pucksinwah had said was true. The war chief's gift for accurate prophecy was well known.

Chiksika gleefully thumped Chaqui on the back and Tecumapese scrambled to her feet and came around the fire to stand behind her father and place her arms lovingly around his neck. She leaned down and placed her cheek against the side of his head and said so softly that only Pucksinwah and Tecumseh heard her, "Thank you, father." Then she straightened and went to Chaqui and shyly took his hand, her eyes brimming with happiness.

Only two people in the wegiwa did not watch her as she did this. One was Pucksinwah who sat staring into the fire, his own eyes reflecting a deep, unspeakable sorrow. The other was Tecumseh who, watching his father, saw the sadness in his eyes. In that instant Tecumseh knew with unshakable certainty what his father knew—that Chaquiweshe would not live to see his own son.

[May 16, 1774 — Monday]

The seven Shawnees who had just emerged on the west shore after swimming their horses across the Ohio River paused to let their dripping animals blow and recover their strength after the exhausting quarter-mile swim. The youngest among them was the twenty-year-old Blue Jacket, who nimbly scrambled to his feet, standing high on the broad back of his horse. He cupped his eyes with both hands to shield his gaze and looked carefully up the river, then down, but saw no one crossing in pursuit. He then looked across the river to the point where they had entered it. The escort was still there on the far shore and one of the men—undoubtedly Croghan—raised his arm high in a wave, but neither Blue Jacket nor any of the others acknowledged it.

"No one following," he said as he dropped back astride his steed's back.

"Well enough," said Hokolesqua, his expression still very grim. "We've had our share of problems already." He switched his gaze to the wounded warrior, who was managing to sit reasonably erect but obviously in considerable pain. "Will you be able to continue the ride, Silverheels?" he asked. "We can easily make a carrier for you."

Silverheels, younger brother of the Shawnee principal chief, shook his head and grimaced faintly. Some fresh bright red blood was showing next to the older rusty stain of earlier bleeding on the river-soaked bandage that angled across his bare chest from the right shoulder. "No carrier, Hokolesqua," he replied. "I can ride. I've suffered worse."

Their sister, Nonhelema, a very muscular woman whose height of six and a half feet was taller than either of her brothers, nudged her horse closer and touched Silverheel's left arm with her fingertips, but spoke to Hokolesqua. "I'll be beside him if his strength fails. I won't let him fall."

"And I on the other side," spoke up Sheshepukwawala, the only other woman present, as she moved her own mount close on Silverheel's right.[84]

"With such protection, how could I fear anything?" A raspy chuckle escaped Silverheels but ended in a painful cough and a fleck of foamy blood appeared at one corner of his mouth.

"The horses are rested enough," said Pucksinwah, not caring to remain so near the whites any longer than necessary. "Let's go. Outhowwa Shokka, move out ahead of us and keep alert."

Yellow Hawk nodded, glanced reassuringly at Sheshe, as he called his wife, and thumped his heels into his horse's sides. The animal bolted up the steep bank and disappeared into the forest on the Mingo Trail which led to Goschachgunk.[85]

Pucksinwah reined his horse over beside Hokolesqua and then turned and looked at Blue Jacket. "Wehyahpihehrsehnwah, wait here for fifty breaths and then follow, staying well back. Stop often and listen. When you are positive no one is following, rejoin us. If, before that, you detect trouble, come up to us quickly so we can prepare for it."

Blue Jacket dipped his head and immediately began checking the load in his flintlock. He had held the gun high over his head during the crossing, but it paid to be sure. The lock was in good shape, the priming powder dry. When he looked up the five riders were just disappearing on the trail into the leafy canopy. Now that he was alone he let his expression reflect the anger seething in him over what had transpired. He had been sure something like this was going to happen and had been brash enough to say so, then was surprised when Hokolesqua agreed but said it was imperative that they make this one last effort for a reasonable peace before the frontier exploded around them.

Now the young warrior considered how this had all come about and his own unexpectedly pivotal role. The foray he had made with Shemeneto's party ten weeks ago, at the time Tecumapese and Chaquiweshe were married, had swept widely through the Kan-tuck-kee hunting grounds, from the mouth of Kantuckeetheepi to the great blue-water licks and then north on the Warrior Trail to the Spaylaywitheepi again.[86] They had found cold-ash remains of four different camps made by whites but no sign fresh enough to follow and, disappointingly, no trace of the persistent white hunter, Boone, whom they had hoped to encounter and capture or kill.

It had appeared their trip was in vain and they were rather dejected when, at the south shore of the Spaylaywitheepi near the great limestone bluffs, they spied some white surveyors busy at work and took them by surprise, capturing all without a shot being fired. They methodically destroyed all the surveying equipment, confiscated weapons and ammunition and then ordered them back into their canoes which were beached on the shore.

"You leave Kan-tuck-kee hunting ground forever," Shemeneto told them coldly in very broken English. "You never come back. We catch again, bones get dry white in sun. You go 'way. Now!"

The whites, obviously greatly relieved at not being kept captive, tortured or killed, paddled off upstream as fast as they could. The war party watched until the canoes disappeared around the first bend and then, laughing and joking at how frightened the whites had been, swam their horses across the Spaylaywitheepi and headed for home, their spirits greatly lifted.

Hardly had they returned to Kispoko Town when Blue Jacket was on his mount again, this time riding side by side with Pucksinwah as the war chief, with a score of escorting warriors, set off on an important state visit eastward. Pucksinwah had not invited Chiksika or Chaquiweshe to come along; this was the latter's time to be with his new wife and, as Methotasa had become ill, Chiksika was needed to look after Tecumseh while Tecumapese took care of her mother and the triplets. Pucksinwah was therefore pleased to have the company of his adopted son.

The man they were riding to see was one of the most widely known and respected of chiefs, revered by Indians and whites alike. He was a former Cayuga named Talgayeeta who, because of his strong pacifistic inclinations, had become expatriate to his own tribe and was now associated with the numerous dissociated Indians of various tribes living on the precarious white frontier and known collectively as Mingoes.[87] Some of the Mingoes were bellicose, but the majority followed the lead of Talgayeeta, whom they held in high esteem. He had long been a friend of the whites and was better known on the frontier and more often addressed by the secondary English name his father, Shikellimus, had given him than by his primary name. He was called Logan and his little village was near the mouth of Yellow Creek.[88]

Blue Jacket momentarily broke off his chain of thoughts and took a final look across the Ohio. Still no sign of pursuit, but that did not negate the possibility. He glanced up the river and shook his head faintly, realizing that this point where they had crossed was less than twenty miles below where he had first met the famed Talgayeeta. He sat quietly looking upstream a moment longer and then softly chirped his horse into movement, entering the woods some five or six minutes behind Hokolesqua's party. He kept alert, pausing frequently to listen for possible pursuit by hostile whites. Yet, at the same time, his mind replayed the tragic scenario of these past few weeks.

On their way eastward, Pucksinwah had told Blue Jacket that when Talgayeeta was first on his own as a young man, he had moved from Cayuga Lake to the valley of the Juniata River near where it flowed into the Susquehanna from the west. There he had built a good cabin and there he had met and married a beautiful young Shawnee woman, who had since died of the pox. Their years together, however, made him peculiarly sensitive to the problems of the Shawnees in regard to white encroachment. Talgayeeta, Pucksinwah had said, not only refused to take up arms against the whites during the French and Indian War or in the more recent war instigated by Pontiac, he did all in his power to smooth the troubled waters between whites and reds, his rhetoric in councils with the Indians and with the whites doing much to help end these crises earlier than might otherwise have occurred. He as frequently visited in homes of the whites as he did in dwellings of the Indians and always emanated such a sense of dignity, quiet strength and wisdom that one crusty old white trader seemed to have spoken for all when he remarked, "Logan is the best specimen of humanity I ever met with, either white or red."

Pucksinwah had hoped that, in view of Talgayeeta's relationship to the Shawnees through marriage, his appeals might convince this influential chief to encourage his Mingo companions and other red admirers to ally themselves to the Shawnees to fend off the invasion Lord Dunmore was preparing to launch into the Ohio country. Various Shawnee embassies had already been sent to all the tribes in the northwest, apprising them of the coming danger and urging them to unite with the Shawnees. No one truly believed Talgayeeta could be convinced to raise his voice and hand against the whites, but if there was anyone among the Shawnees who might be able to do so, Pucksinwah was that man.

So, in the middle of March they had met Talgayeeta in his little longhouse lodge on Yellow Creek and Talgayeeta had listened carefully to the impassioned plea of the Shawnee war chief. In concluding his remarks, Pucksinwah had said:

"The Shawnees can fight their own battles with the *Shemanese,* but your word, Talgayeeta, is needed to encourage other tribes and the Mingoes to stand fast and to stop—by battle, if necessary!—any whites crossing into the Ohio country. We Shawnees cannot and should not be expected to stand alone and guard the entire frontier against the flood of whites that will soon come, when it is for the benefit of all the tribes that this be done. *All* the tribes must do their part to help stem this flood and the word of Logan would sway many who would otherwise hold themselves apart from it."

Blue Jacket had never before heard so moving a discourse and was certain Talgayeeta could not resist its eloquence. And the chief was, in fact, quite impressed with what Pucksinwah had said. No single plea, however, could topple the foundation of nonviolence upon which his entire life had been rooted.

"Pucksinwah," he replied carefully, "you do me great honor coming here. The Shawnees are now and always have been my friends," he paused, then shook his head sadly and continued, "but never has Logan raised his hand against the whites; not even when some members of my own family fell in battles with them. There is no future in warring with a nation that has unlimited resources and more men by far than all the tribes together.

"Are not you Shawnees," he added reasonably, smiling faintly to take the sting out of his remark, "yourselves guilty of stealing horses and equipment from the whites on the border? Have you not, when occasion has prompted it, slain the whites? Consider your defiance of the whites: will it make their armies wither and die? Or will it instead cause immediate violent retribution against which no tribes can stand? You Shawnees are very proud and equally brave and your complaints against the whites are certainly justified. But can you not see how much better it would be to be guided by clear thought rather than blind emotion? Somehow, Pucksinwah, there must be a way in which white men and red men can live in harmony and peace. But such a goal can never be achieved without thoughtful restraint on both sides." He held out his hands, palms up, and shook his head. "No, Pucksinwah, return to your fellow chiefs and tell them that Logan will not raise either his hand or voice against the whites, but that I will send emissaries to them and ask of them the same restraint that I ask of the Indians."

Pucksinwah had sighed, realizing that there was no point in further argument. As he and his warriors prepared to leave, he addressed Talgayeeta a final time. "You are a wise man, Talgayeeta, but beware lest the Bad Spirit, Matchemenetoo, blind you to the inevitable and you one day find yourself in grave danger from the very white man you like so much. You, who call yourself Logan, heed this: there is not now, nor can there ever be, a true and equitable peace between Indian and white."

They had left Chief Logan's Yellow Creek village shortly after that and returned to the Scioto Valley. Pucksinwah, before reaching Kispoko Town and being reunited with his family, had stopped off at Hokolesqua's Town on Scippo Creek and reported to the principal chief details of his disappointing talk with Talgayeeta. But Hokolesqua's reaction had not been what he anticipated. The principal chief nodded slowly and finally said, "In spite of the provocation we have suffered, Pucksinwah, it may be that Talgayeeta is correct and that we must use restraint. If we do so and continue to negotiate with the whites, we may be able to come to an understanding with them that will allow us to avoid a war that, at best, would be devastating to us."

Pucksinwah managed to stifle a small groan of exasperation. "And so what do you wish us to do, then?" he asked. "My young warriors are eager to meet any force the *Shemanese* could send against us. They are confident they would win."

"No!" Hokolesqua said at once. "There will be no more fighting for now except in defense. We will keep our people on this side of the Spaylaywitheepi. We will stop our attacks on boats of the whites. Hunting parties may go out but, until directed otherwise, they are to stay on our side of the river. In the meanwhile we will send messengers to Croghan and McKee and any others who might help us negotiate a peace."

"These hunting parties that will go out on our side of the river," Pucksinwah said, "what are they to do if they encounter whites? Are they supposed to turn like frightened dogs and run off with tails between their legs? We are a warrior tribe and the Kispokothas a warrior sept. There are none more skilled. It is the purpose of our existence to meet any enemy bravely, even one who outnumbers us or has better weapons, and to defeat him."

"No," Hokolesqua repeated, "that must not be. Not now. We are not yet at war with the whites. They are preparing to come against us in such numbers and with such force that no tribe, however powerful and confident of its own strength, could stand against them. But, also, the children of the king are threatening to turn against their own father and if they do so, it must divert the threat they raise against us. We must stand clear of it and wait. Therefore, while there is still the slightest chance for it, we must attempt to negotiate a lasting peace that will reaffirm the Fort Stanwix Treaty and keep the Spaylaywitheepi as the boundary between them and us." Hokolesqua paused and then concluded. "But, no, our hunting parties that go out should not turn tail and run if they encounter whites. Instead they should approach these parties with signs of peace and greet the whites with courtesy and explain to them that it is against the treaty for them to be on our side of the river and they must turn back. If they do not go, we must appeal to their fathers to make them abide by the treaty and force those of their own people who disobey to return to where they belong.''

The majority of the older Shawnee chiefs met in council and agreed with Hokolesqua's reasoning. It was at least worth the effort. If it failed and no alternative remained, *then* there would be time to fight. And so, though there remained an undercurrent of disgruntlement throughout the tribe at this edict, the warriors for the most part obeyed. However, games involving combat and battle strategy, always popular among the boys of the tribe, now became the most engrossing pastime. Little Tecumseh was among those who increased practicing with his little bow so as to be ready for the war with the whites when it came, as he insisted it would.

The young men of the tribe, naturally hotheaded and yearning for the honors of war, bitterly resented being thwarted in their desire to fight the hated *Shemanese* and for the first time since Hokolesqua had become principal chief, there were murmurings against his decisions. Their reasoning, though simplistic, was undeniably sound: While the elders of the tribe waited for negotiations that might never occur—or have any real benefit to the tribe even if they did—whites were continuing to filter into the Kan-tuck-kee hunting grounds in ever greater numbers and even into the eastern hilly woodlands of the Ohio country.

In the weeks that followed, Chiksika, Chaquiweshe, and Blue Jacket were among the many young men who organized small hunting parties. Because of the proven hunting prowess of these three, each became a leader of his own party of hunters and these various parties vied with one another in the fields and woods.

This was the situation that existed when the deadly interrelated events of these past weeks had begun to transpire. Blue Jacket, still moving steadily on the trail of his chiefs and the wounded Silverheels, reined up once again and cocked his head as he listened. The terrain he was passing through now was all too familiar. Not many miles from here was where, as leader of one of the small hunting excursions, he had brought his party, which had consisted of only himself and two others. One was a barrel-chested, happy-go-lucky individual some years older than he whose name was Muga—the Bear. Not especially noted for his mental acuity, Muga was nevertheless a fairly good hunter who bore a broad scar across his right temple where, as an infant, he had been mauled by the animal after which he had been named. The other hunter of their party was largely untried: a seventeen-year-old named Aquewa Apetotha—Child in a Blanket.

They had been following a well-used game trail along Pipe Creek when Blue Jacket discovered a camp of two dozen disreputable-looking whites.[89] A surge of anger flooded him but he controlled himself and whispered to his companions to keep silent and they would detour around the camp and return to Kispokotha to report the presence of these whites to Pucksinwah.

Muga disagreed. "I think we should advance on the camp, as Hokolesqua has advised, showing we intend them no harm. Who knows what good might come of just such a simple meeting as this?" Aquewa Apetotha concurred.

Though his instincts shrieked mental warnings, Blue Jacket had at length acquiesced and the trio stepped out into full view in the clearing, their right hands raised in the gesture of peace. The men in the camp shouted hoarsely, scrambled for their guns and immediately began shooting. Both of Blue Jacket's companions were killed in those first moments and he himself had plunged back into the underbrush with the deadly sound of lead balls ripping through foliage around him and smacking into trees. Remembering Pucksinwah's often repeated advice to do the unexpected when surprised, he crouched and ran in a swift half-circle around the camp and was shortly peering into the clearing from behind a screen of brush. The scalp of Aquewa Apetotha, gripped in the hand of one of the men, was being shaken vigorously to free it of blood and a heavily bearded, rough-looking man was at this moment in the process of scalping Muga. The man came to his feet, bloody knife in one hand, scalp in the other, and triumphantly held it aloft for his companions to see, then went into his version of an Indian war dance but which was more reminiscent of an Irish jig.

Two other men, not previously seen, raced into the camp and an argument broke out. Though he could not clearly hear what they were saying, twice Blue Jacket heard one of the newcomers addressed as Colonel Cresap. He strained to hear better, cupping one ear toward the men and plugging the other with a finger. Only scattered words were spoken loudly enough for him to make them out, but they were enough—words such as ". . . Logan . . . Yeller Creek . . . kill 'em all . . ."[90]

He had fled then, silently as a forest fog, returning to where he and his companions had hobbled their horses. He had no trouble catching all three. Then, mounting his own and leading the other two, he rode as swiftly as possible to Talgayeeta's camp, but it was well after dark before he arrived. The chief remembered him, and made him welcome, calling for food and drink to be brought, but Blue Jacket shook his head and, apologizing for his rudeness, declared there was no time for that. The words had tumbled from him as he told what had occurred, ending with the apparent threat to Talgayeeta himself.

The chief looked concerned and was silent for a while, then shook his head sadly. "I am sorry, Wehyahpiherhsehnwah, for what you have gone through and about the death of your friends, but I think you must have misunderstood what those men said."

Blue Jacket's mouth fell open in amazement and he was about to protest, but Talgayeeta went on before he could speak. "You must realize, my young friend, that the whites have been the friends of Logan for many many years, just as the Indians have. They have often been welcomed here in my village and would have no reason to attack me or my people. I am sure you must be mistaken, but I will prepare myself in any event. I am indebted to you for coming to tell me. My home is yours. Food and bed will be prepared for you."

So angry that it was only with remarkable self-control Blue Jacket was able to reply at all, the young warrior shook his head and spoke in a strained voice. "I cannot stay. Pucksinwah must be told what has happened, as must the families of Muga and Aquewa Apetotha, so they may begin to mourn their loss and prepare for revenge." He could not help adding bitterly, "My own people will believe what I have to say."

Within moments he was mounted again and on his way back to Kispoko Town—hungry, thirsty, infinitely weary, but driven by a fury that would not let him rest, convinced that no matter what others might think of the chief called Logan, the man was a fool.

Blue Jacket momentarily shook the thoughts away and looked far ahead across the length of the extensive creek bottom he had just entered. The five riders were in sight about a quarter of a mile ahead of him and one of them, no doubt Silverheels, was being supported by a rider close beside him. Once again, Blue Jacket thought, bad news was on its way to Kispoko Town. There had been altogether too much of that lately. He remembered only too well how stunned the Shawnees had been by the sad news he had brought of the death of his companions and their anger, almost as strong as his own, at Talgayeeta's response.

Then another shock had come. It took a while for the news to reach them, but they finally learned that just three days after Blue Jacket's warning to Talgayeeta, a group of whites had ambushed a party of Indians from Talgayeeta's village and killed a large number of them, including all of the remaining relatives of that chief—his father, Shikellimus, his brother, his pregnant sister, and her husband. Then terrible atrocities had been committed upon their bodies.[91]

Three survivors of the ambush had summoned Talgayeeta to the scene, which was across the Ohio River from the mouth of Yellow Creek at a place called Baker's Bottom. When he saw with his own eyes what had happened, he had exploded with rage and instantly declared war against the whites, vowing he would not ground his tomahawk again until he had slain ten whites for every Indian who had been killed there. Then he abandoned his Yellow Creek village and sent all the women, children and elderly, with about half his warriors, to establish a new town within a few miles of Kispoko Town, not only so his warriors could aid the Shawnees, but so that the Shawnees could help protect his remaining people. With the warriors that had stayed beside him, he then launched a rampage of killing against the isolated frontier posts on the Ohio and Monongahela rivers and many of their tributaries.[92]

With the frontier teetering on the brink of all-out war, it was at this time, just a week ago, when a lone, unarmed white man had ridden into Hokolesqua's village under a flag of truce. His name was William Wood and he brought an urgent message from George Croghan, asking the Shawnee chief to come to Fort Pitt immediately to hold peace talks with Alexander McKee and himself and some other influential whites who were present. The Blanket Man's message had also discreetly suggested that instead of the usual large retinue of followers, Cornstalk be accompanied by only a few chiefs and perhaps some of the tribe's women, his reasoning being that the appearance of a large party of men at this delicate time might throw the whites in the neighborhood of Pittsburgh into a panic and problems could result.

Anxious to snatch this opportunity to possibly prevent major war from erupting, Hokolesqua had agreed to return with William Wood to Fort Pitt accompanied by no more than six others, including some influential women of the tribe. He had then made his selection of who was to go. That he picked War Chief Pucksinwah was fully expected and it was no surprise that he also selected his own younger brother and sister, Silverheels and Nonhelema. His choice of Outhowwa Shokka—Yellow Hawk—and the latter's wife Sheshepukwawala—Duck Eggs—as part of the delegation was quite reasonable, since Yellow Hawk, though not a chief, was noted for his intelligence and wisdom, and his wife, a close friend of Nonhelema, was the logical choice for another woman. No one, however, was more startled than Blue Jacket himself when he had been chosen by Hokolesqua as the final member of the delegation. At this announcement, Hokolesqua's nineteen-year-old son, Elinipsico, who had greatly wished to be included, shot a resentful glance at Blue Jacket. The latter met his friend's look directly and shook his head slightly, making a small gesture of incomprehension with his hands, but the reason why he was chosen was not long a mystery. His loyalty to the tribe and devotion to Pucksinwah and the war chief's family were well known, but he was included in this delegation primarily because of his knowledge of English. Yesterday, as they had approached Fort Pitt, he was instructed to speak only in the Shawnee tongue but to listen to the whites carefully without appearing to be doing so and to relay to Hokolesqua or Pucksinwah any useful information he heard or any suggestion of deception.

A considerable number of isolated posts and settlements newly established by the whites were now abandoned as a result of the increased killing on the frontier and the fear that war was imminent. The party encountered one such station just being abandoned as they passed and the men there, knowing

William Wood well and assured by him that this was a peace delegation, offered to escort Wood and the Shawnee delegation the remainder of the way to the fort so no unfortunate incidents might occur along the way. The offer was accepted. It was late afternoon when they finally reached the confluence of the Allegheny and Monongahela.

Hokolesqua and Pucksinwah were impressed at how remarkably Pittsburgh had grown since their last visit. This was no longer the tiny outpost it had been several years ago, but rather a substantial city of carefully laid out streets and several hundred cabins and well-constructed houses surrounding the fort, along with stores, taverns, trading posts, livery and blacksmith stables, and even a large boat-building establishment. With the influx of traders, trappers, and settlers deserting their outlying posts and settlements because of the fear of Indian war erupting, the city's population had increased to several thousand individuals and its hubbub and bustle were considerably aggravated by a rather hot controversy that had for some time been occurring here as well as in the east at Philadelphia and Williamsburg over whether Pittsburgh and Fort Pitt were to be considered as part of Pennsylvania or Virginia, with both sides vying vigorously and sometimes violently for dominance.

As they approached the fort, inside which were the quarters of both Croghan and McKee, their impromptu escort turned off and went about their own business. It would have been well if they had remained a little longer. A large group of ugly-tempered frontiersmen had gathered near the gate and as the seven Shawnees alighted from their horses, Blue Jacket hissed a warning, but it was too late. They were suddenly in the midst of a mob of several dozen angry frontiersmen and a wild melee broke out, which broke up only when Croghan rushed upon the scene with a pistol in each hand, one of which he fired into the air.

"Damn it, stop!" he shouted, his face suffused with anger. "Get away from these people. I'll shoot the next man who makes any move to harm them!"

There was little doubt that he meant it and the crowd fell back, muttering, but by then the damage was done. One of the Shawnees, Silverheels, with frothy red bubbles on his lips, lay gasping on the ground with two knife wounds, one in his right shoulder and the other deep in his chest. Hokolesqua stood over him, his expression reflecting his fury. Sheshepukwawa had dropped to her knees beside Silverheels and was already stuffing the chest wound with buzzard down from her pouch to staunch the flow of blood. The other four Shawnees, including Nonhelema, crouched in a circle around them, knives and tomahawks drawn.

The crowd was disbursed and profuse apologies made, but that was not enough. It was unconscionable that the principal chief of the Shawnees and his small party, having come here on a peace mission, should have been so insulted. Silverheels was treated by the fort surgeon, who dug out the saturated buzzard down, cleansed the wound and bandaged it, along with the one on Silverheels' shoulder. The surgeon pronounced the chest wound serious but not necessarily fatal if the man was well cared for. McKee said he would take them to the quarters that had been provided for them but Hokolesqua refused; they would not stay and there would no longer be any talk of peace. McKee understood and demanded that Captain John Connolly, as commanding officer of the militia in Fort Pitt, order a troop of his militia soldiers to escort the delegation back to where they would cross the Ohio on their way home. The canny Connolly agreed, realizing that by doing this as a "humanitarian gesture" it would help to quiet some of the voices being raised in accusation that he was the instigator of much of the border strife.

The party, well guarded, encamped for the night some fifteen miles west of Pittsburgh and, at the insistence of George Croghan, who had accompanied them, sentries were assigned to patrol the camp's perimeter all night.[93] The journey westward had resumed in early morning and, while several sour and muttering groups of frontiersmen passed them during the remaining twenty miles to the Ohio River opposite Mingo Bottoms, there had been no incidents. There Hokolesqua stiffly thanked Croghan for his help and the escort, coolly said good-bye and left without shaking hands, which Croghan considered a very bad sign. Then the seven Shawnees had swum their horses across the Spaylaywitheepi.

Now, having reached the western terminus of the long grassy bottomland he was following, Blue Jacket again stood on the back of his horse and looked carefully behind for several minutes. With a soft grunt of satisfaction, he dropped back down astride his mount and cantered into the woods to overtake the others, saddened that Silverheels had been wounded but otherwise not displeased that the hopes for peace had been shattered. The time was past due for the *Shemanese* to be taught that no longer would the Shawnees countenance their trespassing.[94]

[October 9, 1774 — Sunday]

In the pale light of a three-quarters moon, Pucksinwah could see the silhouetted form of Hokolesqua standing near the water's edge. Ever since this expedition began, the principal chief of the Shawnees had been in perpetual motion, overseeing all preparations, conferring with other Indian leaders, making certain that every possible advantage was being utilized. Now it was strange to see him standing motionless, staring over the silver-flecked waters of the

Spaylaywitheepi. Pucksinwah wondered what was passing through his chief's mind at this moment and experienced a wave of sympathy. Everything Hokolesqua had been doing these final days was against his own better judgment, yet he had been thrust into a position where he had no choice.

"He looks very lonely standing there like that, doesn't he father?"

The voice of Chiksika was barely a whisper in the darkness and Pucksinwah turned and placed an arm over his son's shoulders. He nodded and then realizing his nod could not be seen, replied as softly as Chiksika had spoken.

"The responsibility weighs heavily on him, Chiksika. It always does on a leader who is on the verge of sending his own men into a situation where many could be killed. He's a very brave man but, considering his own personal feelings, I suspect he would rather be almost anywhere else right now."

Chiksika was silent for a brief span and then he said, "You should have been the one commanding us here, father."

The war chief gave a small grunt of agreement. "Perhaps. But what Hokolesqua has so far done, I would have done no differently. I have only great respect for his leadership and if anyone can bring us to victory, he can."

A dark shape moved near and resolved itself into Blue Jacket. "All the canoes are in the water, Pucksinwah," his adopted son said quietly. "We're ready to cross."

"Good. Thank you, Wehyahpihehrsehnwah. I'll tell Hokolesqua." Pucksinwah stepped away and moved up beside the commander of the combined Indian forces and spoke, but his voice was too low for the two young men to hear.

Chiksika put the question to Blue Jacket that he had been reluctant to ask his father. "Are we going to defeat them?"

"Yes, I think so," Blue Jacket replied. "Either that or we'll die trying." He chuckled lightly at his own grim humor.

They fell silent and then Chiksika gave a little laugh of his own. "Tecumseh wanted very badly to come with us. Can you imagine him, six years old, in such a battle?"

"I think," Blue Jacket said, a smile in his voice, "he would probably do as well or better than some of those who have allied themselves to us. He's going to be a great warrior one day."

Hokolesqua and Pucksinwah passed close to them, heading toward where the others were now waiting for them. "Come along," the latter said. "It's time."

The events that had brought this force of about a thousand Indians to the banks of the Spaylaywitheepi in the middle of the night had moved along under their own momentum following the fracas at Fort Pitt when Silverheels had been stabbed. The younger brother of Hokolesqua had survived his wound and mended well and he was now among the warriors gathered here.

The reaction of the Shawnees to the enormous insult that had been perpetrated against their chief at that time was one of consummate outrage. Even those who had been the staunchest advocates of peace had finally admitted such treatment was intolerable. Hokolesqua had protested. He was grieved that his brother had been stabbed and shared their anger over such treatment to a peace delegation, but war with the *Shemanese,* he believed, would be a grave error. An insult had been received, yes, but better to suffer that sting than sacrifice the lives of their fine warriors, which was what a war would bring upon them.

"You know me well," he told them. "I have not become your chief by avoiding battle. But this time you must take a long, close look at what embarking into warfare against the whites can do to you. Destruction of our tribe is entirely possible. Heed my words! In this instance, would it not be better to swallow the insult, put aside our pride for once and resume peaceful negotiations with the whites? In the end result, far more would almost surely be accomplished in this way than by bloodshed."[95]

It was not to be. The tribe was aroused and for the first time since he had become their principal chief, Hokolesqua saw his advice overruled. In large measure this was due to three different occurrences—the fact that the worst threat to the Kan-tuck-kee hunting grounds had just been discovered, the desertion of a large number of Shawnees, and the unexpected stance that had been taken by Pucksinwah.

In the first instance, the newest threat to the hunting grounds south of the Spaylaywitheepi was not just some whites hunting, exploring or surveying there. This time what they found was a *fort,* seemingly sprung up overnight and obviously the first seed of actual white settlement.[96] The Shawnees were extremely upset about it and demanded of Hokolesqua permission to go there and destroy it, putting all its inhabitants to death. The chief did not overrule this possibility but he did get them to agree to wait for a while in view of what was developing on the upper Spaylaywitheepi frontier.

In the second matter, a group of the Thawegilas led by a faction of peace chiefs, though not including Kikusgowlowa, fearful of the army being raised to come against them and wanting no part of a war they felt the Shawnees could not win, simply packed up their belongings and, ignoring the jibes and insults from other members of the tribe for their weakness and fright, abandoned their tribe and the Ohio country and went to live among their former friends, the Creeks, along the headwaters of the Suwannee River in the swampy region the Creeks called Okefenokee—Land of Trembling Earth.

In the final matter, concerning Pucksinwah, for the first time in the memory of anyone in the tribe, he had not only failed to back up a decision by Hokolesqua, he had actively opposed it.

"Hokolesqua," he told them, "is my revered chief and also my friend. Yet now, as war chief of the tribe, I believe we have moved beyond the realm of negotiation and can only suffer by attempting more of it. There will be time enough to resume negotiations after we have confronted and bested the whites and can then negotiate from a position of strength rather than from a position of weakness and fear."

It made sense to the Shawnees and, by vote of the chiefs of all their septs and villages, they overruled the counsel of Hokolesqua and accepted that of Pucksinwah. Very quickly deputations of warriors had been selected and again dispatched to all the neighboring tribes, now no longer merely asking those tribes to ally themselves to the Shawnees for the coming war, but demanding it. The message of each delegation to the chiefs they visited was essentially the same: "We Shawnees stand between you and the whites and we mean to oppose them, which is to your benefit as well as to our own. But you must send warriors to aid us. We will not fight the *Shemanese* alone while you sit in the comfort of lodges and watch our blood being spilled for your benefit. Your choice is this; either send warriors to fight at our side or we will simply not fight at all, but pack up our goods and move well beyond the grandmother of rivers, leaving you then to face the white enemy on your own when he comes, which there is no doubt he will."

The alternative was strictly a bluff—the Shawnees would not willingly give up their country to anyone—but the adjoining tribes, well aware of the past migratory habits of the Shawnees, believed it. Yet, the Wyandots, Delawares, and Miamis remained reluctant to cast the final die that would irrevocably lock them in mortal combat with a foe who had all the advantage in numbers and weapons. Their spies continued to go out and gain whatever information they could concerning the enemy and watched his movements and they had become ever more uncomfortably aware of the extensive preparations being made by the Virginians.

Their fears were well founded. The first phase of Lord Dunmore's invasion plan was set in motion when Colonel Angus McDonald, with four hundred men, descended the Ohio by boat to the mouth of Captina Creek, where they landed and marched ninety miles through the Ohio wilderness to attack the Delawares at Goschachgunk and the Shawnees at Wapatomica.[97] Five miles from Goschachgunk they were ambushed by fifty warriors, primarily Shawnees. Two whites were killed and ten wounded, while the Indians escaped unscathed except for the slight wounding of one. The Shawnees and Delawares abandoned both towns before the army finally reached there, but the soldiers burned the deserted towns and destroyed the crops. The first tendril of Lord

Dunmore's War had reached well into the Shawnee heartland.[98] The loss of Wapatomica, the home village of Chief Kikusgowlowa of the Thawegilas, was not a great loss to the Shawnees. They had long been ready to abandon it when the time came, and without dallying had traveled about one hundred miles due west to establish a new town of Wapatomica on the headwaters of the Mad River only a few miles from Mackachack, the Maykujay Shawnee village of Chief Moluntha.[99] The effect of the McDonald expedition was to infuriate the Shawnees and turn many of those who supported Hokolesqua's inclination to sue for peace to instead demand retaliation.

Great numbers of whites from the east as well as from the frontiers had converged in answer to Lord Dunmore's proclamation—nineteen hundred at Fort Pitt and eleven hundred at Fort Union on the Greenbrier—and drilled regularly in preparation for their Ohio invasion. Quantities of supplies, new weapons and ammunition had been received from the east at both sites and very soon all this would be turned against the Indians. To the more northerly tribes, it was imperative that the Shawnees bear the brunt of these assaults and so, in the end, the Miamis, Wynadots, and Delawares agreed to help—but with two stipulations.

First, it must be their own decision how many warriors they would send to aid the Shawnees; when what was considered the proper number was agreed to among themselves, each of the three tribes would then send that number to assist. Secondly, *they* would have the choice of who was to be in command of the allied Indian forces, but agreed that it would definitely be a Shawnee.

The Shawnees accepted the stipulations and then were chagrined when the three tribes decided that the proper number of warriors to send would be one hundred each—a paltry three hundred to join the Shawnee warriors in facing perhaps ten times that many men Lord Dunmore was raising to come against them! In the second stipulation, naming who should be in command, the allied tribes dealt the Shawnees another surprise. Everyone had expected that Pucksinwah would be chosen or, if not he, then surely Shemeneto—Black Snake—or Chiungalla—Black Fish. Instead, it was Hokolesqua himself they selected to command.

The reasons for this were well considered: The three reluctant allies did not really believe the Indians could emerge victorious in a contest with the *Shemanese* and so they were anxious to hold to a minimum their possible loss of warriors and, in this same vein, while each was to be sending one hundred warriors, such warriors would not be the well-seasoned fighters of the tribes but, rather, hotheaded youths eager to fight but with very little practical war experience; and their choice of Hokolesqua as commander would unquestionably make it easy for the whites to place the entire blame on the Shawnees, since it wasn't just a mere war chief with some followers who had fought them, but the foremost chief of the nation, meaning he had support of the whole tribe. Thus, when the smoke of battle cleared and it was time for negotiations, the allied tribes could maintain that this had been a Shawnee affair, not theirs; they could not be held responsible simply because a few hot-bloods from their respective tribes had joined under the Shawnee banner to oppose the whites. In that way, whatever retribution the whites would have in mind to use in any resultant treaty with the Indians would be focused most pointedly at the Shawnees and not themselves.

So it had been. Spies sent out by the Shawnees soon reported that the majority of the southern wing of the army at Fort Union on the Greenbrier under Colonel Andrew Lewis, which numbered close to eleven hundred men, had begun to move and was heading for the mouth of Kanawhatheepi, where it was to rendezvous with the army under Lord Dunmore.[100] However, Lord Dunmore had not yet left Fort Pitt with his force of nineteen hundred men and it was apparent that Lewis would reach the rendezvous point considerably in advance of Dunmore's force. This was the first chink the Shawnee principal chief had detected in the armor of the *Shemanese* and Hokolesqua acted on it at once, sending runners to the allied tribes with word to immediately start their one hundred warriors each for the Indians' own predetermined rendezvous point with the Shawnees, at Yellow Hawk's village, on the Scioto River close to the mouth of Paint Creek. Ten of the best large canoes the Shawnees had, each capable of carrying ten men at a time, were put into top condition and readied for transport to the Spaylaywitheepi.

By the end of the first full week of October, the three hundred warriors of the Delawares, Miamis, and Wyandots, accompanied by a scattering of young battle-eager Ottawas and Potawatomies who had joined them just for the adventure, had reached the rendezvous and joined the near one hundred Mingoes under Talgayeeta and the core of the force, six hundred Shawnee warriors.[101] Hokolesqua addressed the assemblage at once, making one final effort to dissuade them.

"With all our warriors here gathered, we are a thousand strong. But think! The full force of the enemy is at least three men to our one and their weapons are newer and better. There is still time for us to send runners to them to talk of making peace. This is what my heart of hearts says we should do. I ask you one final time to think not of the glory of battle but of the future of our race. Give me your answer and I will abide by your wish: do we sue for peace or do we fight them?"

The cries of "Fight them! Fight them!" erupting amidst a wave of fierce war whoops was his answer. That very afternoon some spies came in and reported that Lord Dunmore's force, having the most men, had gone into motion and was rapidly descending the Spaylaywitheepi in a huge flotilla of canoes and rafts. At the present rate of travel of these two wings of the army, there would be, at best, only a day or two in which the wing under Colonel

Lewis—who had slightly more men than the Indians had—could be attacked before Lord Dunmore's force arrived to reinforce them and so the Indians must move into position without delay. With this information received, Hokolesqua made his final remark to the assemblage.

"We will attack the *Shemanese* under Colonel Lewis at once, but remember: Now there will be no turning back; now the seed of war has been planted and watered and already it sprouts. Whether it thrives and grows or is cut down remains yet to be seen."

At Hokolesqua's direction they quickly mounted horses and, with the ten canoes strapped and slung between two horses each, moved off southeastwardly on the War Trail that led directly to the mouth of the Kanawhatheepi, some sixty miles distant.[102] Here, having camped one night en route, they arrived late in the afternoon today, keeping well under cover as they approached the Spaylaywitheepi because their spies reported the Lewis army had already arrived and established a camp across the river, apparently there to await Lord Dunmore's arrival. The good news was that the *Shemanese* camp site was very poorly chosen for defense, since it was situated at the Kanawhatheepi mouth on a triangular piece of fairly open ground with the waters of the Spaylaywitheepi and Kanawhatheepi to the north and west, which would prohibit the army from retreating in those directions. To the east and south, forming the final side of the triangle, ran an arc of dense woodland all the way from the one river to the other, which would provide excellent cover for the attacking Indians. But something of a mystery had also developed. The Lewis army had evidently received word of a change in plans and had spent this entire day in a frenzy of raft-building, with preparations being made to break camp first thing in the morning and begin rafting across the Spaylaywitheepi.

The mystery was cleared up by the arrival of another party of spies from upstream. Lord Dunmore's force, they reported, had stopped at the mouth of the Hockhocking, sixty river miles upstream from this point, and there had built a small stockade. For some reason not known to them, Lord Dunmore had unexpectedly changed his plans and was no longer heading down the Spaylaywitheepi to rendezvous here with Lewis. Instead, he was marching up the Hockhocking to the point where his guides had told him he would intersect the major east-west Indian trail that led directly to the Pickaway Plains, which was now to be the new rendezvous point for him to meet Lewis. With this intelligence, Hokolesqua, conferring with Pucksinwah and other chiefs, refined his final plan for the forthcoming assault.

To avoid any chance of being accidentally detected by the Lewis army, Hokolesqua kept his warriors well back from the Spaylaywitheepi and, maintaining utmost silence, carefully moved his entire force through the woodlands to the mouth of a fair-sized creek with good access to the river, well hidden from the whites by a slight northward bend of the river and located three miles upstream from the mouth of the Kanawhatheepi.[103] Here, in the early evening hours, Hokolesqua issued orders for his Indians to make a cold camp— no fires—and see to their weapons, paint themselves for battle and then rest or sleep until the middle of the night. As was customary, the entire Indian force, which had eaten at last night's camp, would not eat again until after the battle had been fought, the belief being that the senses and reactions of the warrior were more acute on an empty stomach than on one that was full. At the midpoint of night, the canoes were to be quietly placed in the water and the crossing of the Spaylaywitheepi begun, each of the ten canoes carrying eight passengers at a time to the opposite shore—a total of ten to twelve round-trip crossings of each canoe in order to get the majority of the Indian force across. Horses and excess equipment were to be left here under guard of a mere handful of men. When the entire attack force had crossed, they would move stealthily into position while it was still dark, forming themselves on the forested perimeter of the triangle in which the Lewis army was camped. With the light of morning they would attack on Hokolesqua's signal, which would be given when the army was in the midst of breaking camp and the troops were least in readiness and with no real avenue for retreat open to them.

Now, in the deep of night, the time for their own crossing had arrived. The canoes had been quietly floated and were ready, each with two strong paddlers, to begin ferrying the warriors across. And it was not at all unexpected that Hokolesqua, Pucksinwah, Chiksika and Blue Jacket were among those in the first ten canoes to slip noiselessly away from the Ohio shore.

[October 10, 1774 — Monday]

They moved through the darkened woods with extreme care, allowing no brush to crackle, no twig to snap, no sound to escape their lips, progressing as much by feel as by sight, pausing often to listen and hearing only the throbbing of their own excited hearts. There was fear, vile and evil tasting, in some of them, but scarcely containable anticipation in most, filling them with a wildly atavistic desire to shatter the heavy silence with shrieks and screams. These were the near one thousand garishly painted warriors creeping slowly into their positions, fanning out over a wide arc until they were all but shoulder to shoulder across the forested base of a triangle whose apex was poorly named for this day's enterprise—Point Pleasant.

To their far right the waters of the broad Spaylaywitheepi hissed past with a murmur more imagined than heard, while to their left the Kanawha-theepi eddied with the faintest of gurgling as if in protest at the prospect of, in a few seconds more, losing its identity in the larger stream. Ahead of them lay more woodland, gradually thinning and then vanishing altogether as the ground itself narrowed to the point where the two great rivers converged. And at the heart of this point lay the blanketed mounds that were the slightly more than eight hundred militia soldiers Colonel Lewis had led down the Kanawhatheepi, their presence here and there punctuated by the muted red orange glow of embered campfires.

A portion of the Indians slipped into the waters of the Kanawhatheepi and swam quietly to the far side of that stream, directed by Hokolesqua to secrete themselves there and cut off any effort of the whites to escape across the narrower river. With rifles and bows, pistols and war clubs, spears and scalping knives, the principal body of Indians remained hidden in the woods awaiting the approaching dawn. It was at this juncture that nature took a hand, unexpectedly becoming an ally of the *Shemanese*. With insidious silence a fog crept in, mercurial in its habit, dense in one area, patchy in another, almost absent in yet another, swelling and fading, sliding ghostlike through the woods and over the rivers, at times wholly enshrouding large segments of recumbent militiamen and crouching warriors.

The Indians had approached no nearer the camp than about fifteen hundred yards, due not only to the thinning of protective forest cover but because a handful of scattered *Shemanese* sentries were walking perimeter patrol. The fog, which might mask the Indians to some extent, was of more benefit to the whites because it had been the plan of Hokolesqua, at his command, for the attackers to pour a withering fire into the camp. Now that advantage was negated by the Indians largely being unable to see their targets. With the dawn just becoming visible as a faint glow in the misty eastern sky, misfortune compounded itself with an unexpected occurrence.

Although Colonel Lewis had given the order that preparations for crossing the Ohio would begin at dawn, two of the militiamen arose just before that time and ambled together into the woods in the hope of bagging a turkey. They moved generally eastward in the edge of the wood flanking the Ohio River and, about a mile from the camp, misfortune played its third prank on the attackers. For the duration of about a dozen heartbeats, just as the pair neared the mouth of a small creek, the fickle fog broke apart and revealed to their stunned eyes a line of war-painted Indians facing in their direction and extending from the Ohio River shore on their left to out of sight in the misty forest on their right. A Shawnee warrior named Epinoosa flung up his rifle and shot, the report obscenely loud in the morning stillness, and one of the two men crumpled lifeless to the ground, a grape-sized lead ball having drilled through the center of his chest.[104]

The other man turned and fled, quickly disappearing into the mist that was once again closing in. The Indians could hear his terrified cries as he sprinted into the camp and the general hubbub that ensued as soldiers roused

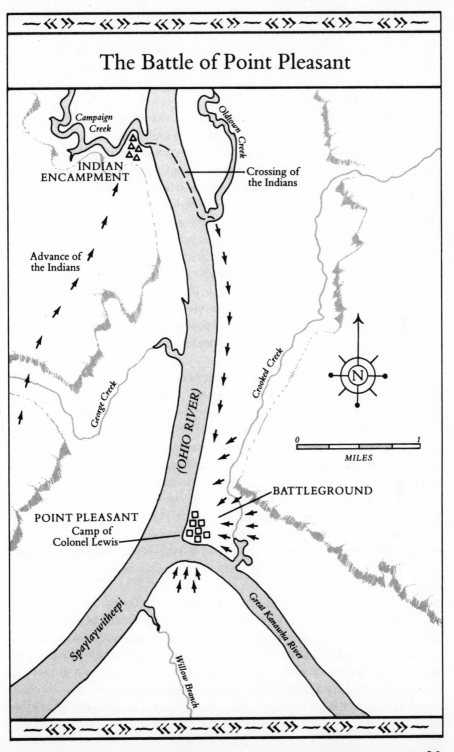

The Battle of Point Pleasant

from bedrolls and snatched their weapons. From one of the few tents that had been erected, a man emerged and conferred briefly with two others who had run up from an adjoining tent, one hastily buttoning a fine scarlet waistcoat. These two raced off, shouting orders which were relayed and in moments men were vaguely seen in the patchy mist forming themselves into three separate groups.[105]

As the commander's unit took its place in the center of the line and the entire three segments began marching forward into the woods, enough daylight, muted and gray, had evolved that now a sporadic firing was begun by the Indians closest to the Spaylaywitheepi and rapidly spread down the line all the way to the Kanawha. The heavy blue-white gunpowder smoke mingling with the fog made vision extremely poor. Despite less than adequate visibility, an early target was the man who wore the brilliant red waistcoat—Colonel Charles Lewis, the commander's brother. Rifles barked and he fell with a ball through his head, one of the first casualties.[106] On the other side of the line, close to the Ohio River, another principal officer—Colonel William Fleming—was severely wounded with a ball that passed through him just beneath the ribs.[107] A fierce and almost continuous shrieking from the Indians filled the air—a tactic well known and often used by the Shawnees to instill fear in opponents and thus produce uncontrollable panic and its resultant helplessness.

The shrieks, the screams, the blasting of weapons and hideous whiz-and-thunk of tomahawks and war clubs created a cacophony beyond belief and the layers of smoke in acrid screens stung the eyes until all the combatants wept hot tears that still could not clear their vision. The triple phalanx of militia held their ground for a while and then gave way, falling back beneath the power of the Indian attack, and Hokolesqua's warriors surged forward with increased howls. Overriding the incredible din, the powerful booming voice of Hokolesqua was raised in a stirring cry which he repeated over and over again up and down the line.

"Oui-shi-cat-to-oui! Oui-shi-cat-to-oui."[108]

Pucksinwah and Talgayeeta, too, were very active, not only in actual fighting but in passing back and forth in the Indian lines, encouraging the warriors.

With their lines crumbling, the militiamen began diving for cover behind anything available—logs, brush, standing trees, rocks, bodies of fallen friends, *anything* that would provide protection against the murderous barrage of gunfire directed at them. The advance of the Indians stopped and direct hand-to-hand conflict increased with more screaming, more groans and grunts and cursing and the ugly sound of viciously rent flesh and bone.

The whites gained a little ground, then lost it again, then held. Hokolesqua's warriors strove to force the *Shemanese* back and back, bunching them closer and closer together as they were forced to the apex of the triangle, thus making them ever more vulnerable through their very density as they lost ground. When the whites pushed back and the foot of the triangle from river to river lengthened, the lines of the Indians grew ever thinner, increasing their vulnerability. Thus, each side realized the desperate need to at least hold their ground and at best to push their adversaries back. With the cries of *"Oui-shi-cat-to-oui"* bolstering them, the Indians lunged again, recovering the ground they had momentarily lost, which now was littered with bodies and slickened into a scarlet mud. Time after time each side strove to thrust the other back to the point where they would be lost and time after time each side failed.

It remained a seesaw battle for an hour, then two, then three. Time lost all meaning and often simple survival became paramount. Exhaustion numbed limbs, searing smoke scalded tongues and throats and even the demonic cries of the warriors and the shouts and curses of the militia became slurred.

Though they had been involved in skirmishes on a number of occasions before, Blue Jacket, Chaquiweshe, and Chiksika were today engaging in their first actual battle and all three young Shawnees fought with a skill and execution that belied their inexperience. The three were close together when the fight broke out but gradually became separated as the melee continued. Chiksika's weapon of choice was a war club and he darted here and there in the line, swinging it with fierce accuracy, breaking the limbs and rib cages and skulls of the militiamen who swarmed around them in the murky area. Twice he felt a great surge of pride as he caught the gaze of his father upon him and saw the fierce approval in his eyes.

Blue Jacket had fired his flintlock only twice and then discarded it as ineffective and relied on his bow, smoothly releasing arrow after arrow with whining accuracy until his quiver was empty, then wading into the thickest of the combat with tomahawk in one hand, knife in the other, whirling and slashing with great effect. Seven times he left behind the bodies of those with whom he had grappled and whose scalps he had swiftly removed with triumphant screams and stuffed in his pouch before moving on. He was oblivious to the blood streaming down his own chest and back from a ball that had grazed his neck, giving him a nightmarish appearance that caused foes to quail and flee at his approach.

Chaquiweshe fought nearly as well, but only briefly before he was struck by a ball that ripped through his stomach and left him doubled over in agony for only an instant before a militiaman raced up and drove his knife through the young Shawnee's heart. The militiaman himself was downed in the act and strong hands picked up the body of Chaqui and carried it from the field and back to the canoes where it was transported across the river with a few other dead and wounded. Among them was Silverheels, his chest wound from the stabbing at Fort Pitt healed but his strength not fully recovered, who had fought near Hokolesqua until he collapsed with exhaustion. His giant sister, Nonhelema, bloodspattered from the soldiers she had been fighting, had scooped him up and cradled him childlike in her arms as she carried him all the way to the canoes.

Even as the battle raged, surging back and forth across its front in a swath some two hundred yards deep, another squad of the militia felled a number of small trees to form a breastwork of sorts and they and their fellows gradually made their way to it, took refuge behind it, strengthened it. The warriors plunged into it, ripped at it, tore through autumn ambered leaves and foliage as scarlet as the blood being shed. They breached the defense and drove their way into the whites and still the *Shemanese* resisted beyond the imaginings of their foes.

Just before noon, with the battle still raging furiously throughout the entire line, Chiksika and Pucksinwah happened to be fighting the enemy close to one another when a rifle ball struck Pucksinwah in the chest and slammed him to the ground. Instantly Chiksika raced to the spot, slung his father over his shoulder and stumbled as rapidly as possible toward the rear with him. When well away from the main fighting, he lay the war chief down beneath a large tree and began to plug the wound with buzzard down from his pouch, but Pucksinwah regained consciousness and shook his head.

"It's of no use," he whispered. "I am a dead man, as I knew I would be. . . . You are a good son, Chiksika. Promise me . . ." He broke off and grimaced.

"What, father? *Anything!* Promise you what?"

"Promise me that you will take care of Tecumseh. . . . Teach him to be a good warrior . . . a good man. Guide him in the right way. The little brothers, also. Provide . . . provide for the family. Promise me that you will never . . . make peace with the *Shemanese*. They wish only to devour us."

"I promise, father. Please, don't die." He cradled his father in his arms and wept, saying again, "Please, don't die."

There was no response. Pucksinwah was dead.

Chiksika sat holding him for a long while, then gathered him up once again and carried him the rest of the way to where the canoes were. A few other dead, along with several wounded, were in one canoe that two older Shawnees were just about ready to paddle across the river. Strong arms helped Chiksika gently lay Pucksinwah in the bottom of that canoe and he watched, his expression one of grim sorrow, as the canoe was thrust away from shore and the crossing begun. In a moment more he jerked his stained war club from his belt and set off at a lope toward the sounds of the distant battle.[109]

Time had become meaningless on the field of combat as the fighting persisted. Sometime earlier the fog had lifted, though none had noted exactly when, and the midpoint of day was already two hours into history, the afternoon harvest sun flaring through the coppery haze of a struggle that to its participants seemed destined to last until sunset on a never ending day. Hand-to-hand combat had slackened and gasping combatants moved apart as if by mutual agreement, regrouping, reassessing and resting while a sporadic firing continued across the length of the line from Spaylaywitheepi to Kanawhatheepi.

Suddenly came the booming voice of Hokolesqua with a new cry and, to the amazement and relief of the whites, his Indians began falling back, gradually, carefully, but unmistakably, carrying along with them the remainder of their dead and wounded, leaving not one of their own on the field.

Encouraged by the enemy's inexplicable withdrawal, the Virginians began to scramble through the breach in their impromptu defensive barricade to pursue, their throats already starting to swell with a blooming cry of victory, but their own commander intervened and ordered them back, fearful of a ruse of the Indians to lead them into an ambush from which few, if any, would emerge. It was a reaction Hokolesqua anticipated. Had it been a ruse, the bait would have been far more subtly presented.

This was no ruse, no trap, but neither was it precipitate flight. It was a deliberate, methodical, well-defended and very gradual withdrawal, with frequent pauses to hold for a while and then move again. There was very good reason for the withdrawal; runners had come with intelligence so imperative that they rushed headlong to Hokolesqua in the midst of the battlefield, dodging from tree to tree until they reached him. They imparted their news in gasping phrases: a reinforcement was coming for the *Shemanese;* half a thousand more Virginians descending the Kanawhatheepi and less than three hours away. Hokolesqua heard them out, expression initially grim, but then altering to the faintest of smiles. A short time, yes, but time enough to pull away in strength and dignity.[110]

A certain number of the whites followed for a half mile, then a mile, but the warning of their commander echoed in their minds and they grew afraid of the suspected ambush. They slowed and stopped and then picked their way back, confused and worried, past the multitude of bodies of their comrades and to their own lines, there to help shore up and improve a defensive barricade that should have been built days ago. When the final wisps of battle smoke thinned and dissipated in the later afternoon and early evening, not a single Indian, living or dead, remained on the field of combat.

As the final four canoes pushed into the current of the Spaylaywitheepi in the gathering dusk, Hokolesqua was in one of them, having refused to leave until all had crossed and, in his own leaving, facing rearward so that none could ever say he had turned his back in a contest with the *Shemanese.*[111]

Allan W. Eckert

[October 11, 1774 — Tuesday]

The Shawnees had continued moving after the crossing of the Spaylay-witheepi, Hokolesqua permitting no stopping until well into the night. They brought their dead with them, draped over the backs of their horses, except for Pucksinwah, who was held upright by Chiksika on the latter's horse, ankles tied beneath the belly of the horse, Chiksika behind and his father's back leaning against him, the whole world a hurtful blur to the young warrior as they rode. Blue Jacket switched with him at intervals to give him rest, but never for long; Chiksika needed the closeness, the final agonizing closeness that, however exhausting and emotionally wrenching, would end too soon.

Near the midpoint of night, the spies Hokolesqua had left temporarily behind caught up to them with word that the whites had firmly camped, with heavy guard; no one had crossed the river, no one had followed. At Hoko-lesqua's order they stopped to rest; some to gnaw on jerky and parched corn, some to nap; some to sit in small clusters in the darkness and relive the battle and the exploits and the anguish, some to bear the ache and throb of painful wounds, and some to ebb their lives away before the dawn . . . and one to simply sit propped against a tree in the darkness near a blanket-covered form that appeared to be merely asleep but was not.[112]

Those who chose to talk spoke more and more of reprisal upon them by the reinforced *Shemanese* and they fed upon the fear of one another. The army of Colonel Andrew Lewis, now with considerably more men than they, was behind them, soon to be snapping at their heels, and the army of Lord Dun-more, according to their spies, with considerably more men than they, was ahead of them, soon to be going for their throat. These armies were like wolves maneuvering and trapping prey between them. And, as with prey under such circumstances, immobilizing panic began taking root. In the morn-ing, refusing to meet the contemptuous gaze of Hokolesqua, the Delaware, Miami, and Wyandot factions mounted up and silently left for their own homes. The scattering of Ottawas and Potawatomies did the same, and then so did most of the Mingoes. Only twenty of Talgayeeta's followers stayed here with their chief called Logan, whose look of contempt for the deserters mirrored Hokolesqua's. The Shawnees resumed their journey home but now with the prevailing discussion among them being the need to sue for peace immediately, before it was too late, before they were destroyed by the whites.

There had been mixed sorrow and joy when the Shawnees returned to their Scioto Valley villages later this same day. Sorrow, intense and devas-tating, for those who had suffered loss and joy for those whose men had come home; but, overriding all, an uncharacteristic fear—the rooting of a contagion of panic planted by the warriors who had abandoned them and now watered by their own imagination. Hokolesqua could not believe this was occurring.

What had happened to Shawnee courage and strength? What had become of the Shawnees' abhorrence of fear and weakness?

Hokolesqua called for a council immediately. Now they were gathered before him and his face was set in stern, harsh lines as he looked out over the crowd and saw them subdued, almost cowed. These men in no way resembled the battle-hungry force they were less than a week ago when they had gathered in this very place to thrust aside his recommendation that they try to make peace.

The Shawnee chief's expression softened somewhat and he began speaking quietly but with his voice gradually rising in volume and intensity. "You fought well, my children," he told them, "and my heart sings the song of praise for your strength in battle, just as it sings the song of mourning for our brave warriors and chiefs who fell. Now I must ask you, was this all in vain? Many among you have already said to me, 'Let us now seek peace with the *Shemanese,* lest they come against us even more strongly.' My heart is filled with shame that my ears have heard these words. If it was peace you wanted, why did you not say so when I begged you to do so five days ago?

"What do we do now?" His words had become loud, filled with anger. "The *Shemanese* are coming upon us by two routes, far stronger than those we met alone, while we are weaker in the return of our brothers to their homes where they will be safe." He paused and the scathing contempt of his words overhung them as a palpable weight. "What do we do now?" he repeated. "Shall we turn out and fight them?"

No one stirred, no one replied. A massive embarrassment gripped them and they simply waited for him to go on which, after a moment more, he did: "Shall we now kill all our women and children and then fight them ourselves until we are all dead?"

Again the wordless silence in response and abruptly Hokolesqua changed before their eyes, the vital spark that drove him diminishing until all but gone. He reached to his belt and drew his tomahawk, streaked and stained with the blood of those he had slain. He held it high above his head for all to see and then threw it down so savagely that practically the entire head buried itself in the earth, shouting vehemently at the same time, "Since you are not inclined to fight, we will go and make peace!"

The cries of approval indicated it was what they wanted and messengers were sent at once to Lord Dunmore with proposals to council for this purpose. It was what Hokolesqua had so strongly advocated so short a time ago, but which now filled him with disgust and shame for his own people. The only thing that made it bearable was that if Lord Dunmore refused to accept their proposal for peace, Matthew Elliott—the trusted trader who had married a Shawnee woman and taken up residence in Hokolesqua's Town, and who had gone to Dunmore's bivouac, Camp Charlotte, in the Pickaway Plains, with the messengers—would hasten back to tell them. At that point they would launch an immediate attack on Lord Dunmore's force, then fall back across the Scioto and go into ambush to attack the whites again if they followed, and then they would fall back again to Chalahgawtha where they would stand their ground and fight to the end.

[October 27, 1774 — Thursday]

All but hidden by a light blanket wrapped tightly around him, Tecumseh sat in the shadowy corner of the wegiwa, knees drawn up, hands crossed on them, head down so his chin rested on the back of his hands. An immense sorrow enveloped him, as it had ever since the return of the Shawnee warriors to Kispoko Town on the second day following the battle at the Kanawhatheepi. Fifteen suns had come and gone since then and yet the devastating ache inside had abated little, if any. He had hardly eaten since then and there was a pronounced gauntness to his features now.

Methotasa and Tecumapese were suffering the same grief, yet seemed to be bearing up better under its burden than the little boy not yet seven years old. His mother and sister had suffered no less a shock than had the other women of the tribe who had lost loved ones and they had wept and mourned as much as others. Yet somehow they had seemed to find a reserve within from which to find the strength and resolve to carry on and to continue doing those things needing to be done. The pain remained, of course, deep in their eyes. Even now, as they performed their duties, they would still pause as their glances met and then move into one another's embrace to weep and mutually comfort.

Pucksinwah had been the core of their family and now he was gone, leaving a gap in their lives that could never truly be mended. All lightness had fled from Methotasa, her ready smile irretrievably gone. Tecumapese, though more resilient, had suffered a loss even greater—both a husband and a father. And she bore, as well, the knowledge that the child within her, now so close to being born, would never know his father, her beloved Chaqui. Chiksika and Blue Jacket, when present, were morose and short tempered, but both were away most of the time, several miles off toward the eastern end of the Pickaway Plains where Hokolesqua and the other chiefs were treating with the white father, Lord Dunmore. Only the triplets, now nearly four years old, were their usual selves. They had cried at first, though not so much from comprehension of loss as from fright at witnessing the woe of the rest of the family, but before long they were once again rolling about, tussling with one another, toddling in and out, eating and sleeping as they always had.

Now, in midafternoon, Methotasa was using a large smooth stick to stir the contents of a blackened pot suspended over the cookfire, while Tecumapese was wiping the hands and faces of the triplets with a cloth repeatedly dipped and wrung in a basin. Tecumseh paid no attention, nor did he look up when Blue Jacket and Chiksika shouldered aside the buffalo skin flap and entered.

Chiksika's sympathetic gaze touched the two women briefly, before boring into the shadows where Tecumseh sat hunched and silent. He strode to the boy and took him gently by the wrist. "Come with me, Tecumseh," he said, his tone forestalling any objection. To the others he said, "We will not be gone long. Blue Jacket will tell you what has happened."

Blue Jacket had already seated himself on one of the mats before the fire and Chiksika, without speaking further, guided his little brother out of the wegiwa and led him to the nearby bank of the Scioto, stopping before the large bare white log where the women often dried the clothes they had washed. There was a good bit of activity occurring in the village, but no one else was close by at the moment. He gripped Tecumseh under the arms and lifted him to a sitting position on the log and then raised one of his own legs high and straddled it, sitting so he was facing his brother. Leaning forward, he cupped the back of his brother's neck in one hand and pointed eastward with the other.

Across the river and over the great plain beyond, a long narrow dark line on the yellowed buffalo grasses was gradually being absorbed into the dim mass of the far distant forest. Not understanding its significance, the boy turned after a moment and looked at his older brother.

"Tecumseh," Chiksika said quietly, "that is the army of the whites heading for their own country. Hokolesqua and Nonhelema are escorting them as far as Hockhocking. The war is over. Today our chiefs made their marks on the treaty with the whites at the place where they were camped."

Chiksika nodded at the unspoken question in his little brother's eyes. "Yes, they're truly going away for good. The *Shemanese* have agreed that they will hereafter remain on their side of the Spaylaywitheepi. Our chiefs have agreed that the Shawnees will remain on their side of it. Hokolesqua told them that if the treaty is broken, it will be broken first by the whites. Only if they do not abide by their word given here will *we* then cross the river as well."[113] The manner in which Chiksika spoke said much that the words alone did not.

Tecumseh gave a small shake of his head. "You think it was a bad treaty for us." It was a statement, not a question.

Chiksika grunted derisively. "I think *any* treaty with them is bad. Our father said the *Shemanese* wanted only to devour our lands and I promised him I would never make a treaty with them."

"Then you promised for me as well, Chiksika," Tecumseh blurted. A spark of anger appeared in his eyes for just an instant. After a moment of quiet he spoke again. "Did Talgayeeta make peace with them?"

"He did not come to the treaty, but he sent a message saying he would war with them no more. Yes, Tecumseh, he made peace, but he gave up nothing to them."

There was bitterness in the little boy's words when he spoke again. "You think the *Shemanese* will cross the Spaylaywitheepi again, don't you?"

"I *know* it! Perhaps not for a while, but they will."

Tecumseh said nothing, his face becoming as expressionless as it had been in the wegiwa. Chiksika waited a moment and then, his hand still at his brother's nape, he tightened his grip a little and shook him.

"Tecumseh, no! *No!*" The boy's eyes refocused on him and Chiksika continued. "Listen to me, little brother, you must not go away from us again like this. All of our hearts are heavy. I loved our father as much as you and for longer. But Pucksinwah is gone, Tecumseh. Except for in our hearts, where he will always be, he is gone. He would not want you to do this. Can you believe that?"

The boy nodded and his voice was small. "Yes."

"Good. Then I have to tell you now what it was too painful to speak of before. He died in my arms, Tecumseh, but he talked to me before he died." Tecumseh sucked in a breath but Chiksika continued without pause. "He asked me to take care of the family and the little ones . . . and most specifically, Tecumseh, you. I promised what he asked: to take care of you and guide you in what is right and, most of all, Tecumseh, to teach you to be a good warrior, a good man. I intend to do that, all of it, to the best of my ability. But *you* have to help; *you* have to want it. Tecumseh, it was our father's dying wish."

A low moaning sound came from the little boy and then he whirled and threw himself into Chiksika's arms, the sounds evolving into heart-wrenching sobs. Chiksika smiled and gathered him in, leaned his cheek against the top of Tecumseh's head and suddenly his own shoulders were shuddering with silent sobs.

[December 2, 1774 — Friday]

The labor pains Tecumapese was undergoing now were very frequent and intense and she was glad her mother was beside her to help, although at the moment all Methotasa could do was pat the bulging stomach gently and murmur "Soon, Tecumapese, soon."

The young woman, naked and with only a fox-skin wrap over her shoulders for warmth, sat on a blanket with her back against the inner wall of the wegiwa, her knees drawn up and feet firmly planted and wide apart. This should have been a joyous occasion but there was little of gladness in the expression of either woman. Methotasa had become sharply unanimated and moved about doing her duties automatically but listlessly, the fact that they were no longer in Kispoko Town of little moment to her. Like her husband, Kispoko Town, by that name, no longer existed. Now it was the Village of Shemeneto—Black Snake's Town—and the powerfully built chief who had been Pucksinwah's second was now the tribe's war chief as well as the principal chief of the Kispokotha sept. But even Black Snake's Town, along with Hokolesqua's Town, Nonhelema's Town, Yellow Hawk's Town, and many—though not all—other smaller Shawnee villages along the Scioto River and Paint Creek and their tributaries would soon no longer exist. The manner in which the two wings of Lord Dunmore's army had closed upon them had made them decide to move considerably farther inland—a hundred miles or more to the northwest—to the upper waters of the Mad River and the Great Miami, in the vicinity where the Maykujay villages were already located and where Wapatomica had so recently been reestablished.

This wegiwa in which the two women now resided was much larger than the one that had been Pucksinwah's. This one was partitioned inside into separate quarters by hanging blankets and there was room enough inside for five resident families. This was the abode of Chiungalla—Black Fish—and it was situated close to the great *msi-kah-mi-qui* in the center of Chalahgawtha.

Chiksika, as the eldest son of Pucksinwah, had brought the entire family here—his mother and sister, his younger brother, Tecumseh, the near four-year-old triplets, along with their adopted brother, Blue Jacket—at the invitation of Chiungalla, less than two weeks after the *Shemanese* had returned to their own lands. Automatically, in accordance with the traditions of the tribe, the oversight and care of a fallen battle chief's family, because of his rank and service to the tribe, always became the responsibility of the second civil chief of the tribe—in this case Chiungalla—and so they had moved into his household, had become his wards and he their surrogate father. Just before arriving in Chalahgawtha, Chiksika had pointed out to Tecumseh, as they passed it, the spring beside which he had been born.

Chiungalla and Pucksinwah had been close friends for many years and so over the years the little family had come to know him reasonably well. They had all respected him highly and liked him well enough, but very quickly, now that they had become his charges, this liking developed into a deep and abiding warmth and devotion. The heavy-set chief of Chalahgawtha, soft spoken and wise, yet firm in the discharge of his duties, was deeply admired by his people and one of the most popular chiefs in the entire tribe. While Methotasa would still have no husband, her children would, in essence, have a father to help provide for the family's needs. It was a very sensible arrangement but, for the most part, Methotasa remained shrouded in her own personal grief, some vital spark within her having died along with Pucksinwah. She had never loved another man and she knew she never would again.

In the intervals between the now frequent and sharp, convulsive spasms of her labor, Tecumapese had been thinking a great deal about Chaquiweshe. His death in the battle at the mouth of the Kanawhatheepi had left an enormous gap in her life and, while she accepted with a certain degree of fatalism that he was gone and would never come back, there was a part of her that refused to accept this. Twice since the battle she had dreamed of him—dreams so clear, so filled with the vibrancy of him that she had awakened reaching out beside her, feeling for him, murmuring "Chaqui . . . Chaqui?" and wondering, when he was not there, why he had risen from their bed and gone out into the night. Then each time the real awakening followed and, with it, the pain, new and fresh once again and so great a burden for a girl who had not yet seen her seventeenth spring.

Often they had lain together in the night, talking about their child growing within her. Chaqui would sometimes put his ear against her stomach and hold imaginary conversations with his son, so serious and involved that at times Tecumapese would become convulsed with laughter and he would chide her for bouncing about so much. It was on one such occasion that they had considered what they would name their child. Shawnee parents normally waited the customary ten days before naming a son, but it wasn't prerequisite. After much discussion they had selected a name they both liked very much. That, of course, was assuming the baby was healthy and well formed and that Moneto did not send some kind of sign at the time of birth that would indicate He wished something different.

Tecumapese gasped as another labor pain struck and Methotasa, sitting beside her, reached out and patted her stomach again and murmured soothingly, but this time the contraction persisted and Methotasa knew the moment had come. Well experienced as a midwife, she now bade Tecumapese to squat on the blanket with her feet well apart and hold her hands in readiness to catch the infant that would in moments more be expelled. Drenched with perspiration but making very little sound except for sharp inhalations, Tecumapese did as Methotasa said, her mother's hands gripping her so she would not topple in her exertions. In a moment more, with a final great convulsive heave, the baby was ejected into her own hands. Methotasa immediately swabbed the blood and mucus from the tiny boy's face and used a strand of rawhide to tie the umbilicus close to the baby's belly before she cut it. At once Tecumapese took the child to her breast and guided a nipple into his mouth. There was no milk there yet, but the sense of security this provided was important for the child's well-being. Quickly Methotasa swabbed the rest of the infant clean, removed the placenta which now had also been expelled and cleansed her daughter's lower body and upper legs as well, then covered her first grandchild and the new mother with another blanket. Except for the faintest of whimpers, the baby had made no sound, comforted by the embrace of Tecumapese and the nipple. Neither mother nor daughter had remarked on the fact that the infant was a boy, as Pucksinwah had predicted. Neither had doubted for one moment that it would be.

Methotasa left momentarily then and when she returned she brought with her the six boys—Tecumseh, Chiksika, and Blue Jacket each holding one of the triplets in his arms. They stood at the foot of the blanket and smiled down at her. Tecumapese, smiling as well, momentarily moved the blanket aside so they could see the baby.

"You are now uncles," she told them. "Chiksika, Tecumseh, Wehyeh-pihehrsehnwah, Kumskaka, Sauwaseekau, Lowawluwaysica, this is your new nephew. His name is Spemica Lawba"—Big Horn. [114]

Chapter 2

— « » — In the nearly eighteen moons that Tecumseh had lived in Chalahgawtha he had changed considerably. He had grown tall for an eight-year-old, with an athletic frame, lean, solidly muscled, and erect in posture. He so excelled in sports, games, hunting and mock battles among boys his own age that it was virtually no contest for the others when he participated. As a result, far more frequently than the other boys, he joined in the activities of youngsters three or four years his senior and, within the framework of his physical limitations, even with them, he excelled. Over all the boys he exercised an extraordinary influence and was unqualifiedly their first choice as leader.

Mentally, he was uncommonly sharp, gathering and storing knowledge as if his mind were a sponge incapable of saturation. He constantly asked questions of his elders on virtually every conceivable subject that touched his life or theirs, his intense probing for information frequently causing a certain amount of discomfort among those he questioned when he found their replies lacking. Yet, he did not lord his accomplishments over others, exhibiting deference and sensitivity to his elders, concern and compassion to his fellows.

Because of his determination and willingness to practice interminably, Tecumseh had become an expert marksman with every weapon at his disposal that his arms were long enough and strong enough to control. That, combined with his pronounced stalking ability, largely taught him by Chiksika and Blue Jacket, had enabled him to become by far the best young hunter in Chalahgawtha. With a bow he almost never missed his target and had progressed to the point where, while in the midst of running, he could draw an arrow from his quiver, nock and draw and release with great facility, normally hitting any stationary target and, in the majority of tries, a moving target. Having become an accomplished rider, he could also shoot his bow very well from horseback, even when galloping. While he never had as much ammunition with which to practice as he wished, he had nevertheless become a fine marksman with a rifle and was now training himself to load and fire on the run, as he had heard certain frontiersmen, such as Boone, could do. He could throw a knife or tomahawk with considerable accuracy and had become formidable with a war club by dashing through a woods, wheeling and dodging, spinning and ducking as he struck at trees premarked by Chiksika or Blue Jacket.

Easily as proud of Tecumseh over these outstanding early accomplishments as his family was Chiungalla himself, who had two small daughters but no sons. The chief's daughters were a three-year-old and a newborn, respectively named Pommepesy and Pimmepesy. The seven members of Pucksinwah's family, including Blue Jacket, were still living in a separate quarter of his oversized lodge, called Chiksika's wegiwa, that had been partitioned off for their use. Though they were all still Chiungalla's charges, it was Tecumseh who was far and away his favorite and in whom the second principal chief took as much pride as if Tecumseh were his own flesh and blood. Frequently he spent long hours with the boy, just talking—discussing the politics and policies of the tribe, recounting the problems that had plagued them in their dealings with the whites from the very first contact, relating the stories of his own hunts and battles over the years. And from his exposure to Chiungalla, Tecumseh was learning a great deal about leadership.

It was from his beautiful and graceful sister, Tecumapese, now eighteen, that Tecumseh was taught good character and high morals. One of the more important attributes she instilled in him was the value of patience, irrespective to whatever endeavor it was applied in life. She taught him to respect and honor the aged and infirm and to help them whenever or wherever he could and especially to listen to what they had to say since, advanced in years as they were, they had experienced many things it would help him to know in years to come. Thus, revering the aged was already becoming an ingrained habit of his character. Closely related was respect for authority, not just with parents and chiefs but equally with those having won honors and stations in life not easily achieved. She stressed the need to pity those who were powerless or unfortunate, imbuing in him an abhorrence for cruelty which, whether perpetrated on man or beast, unfailingly degraded the one who did it. Honesty and truthfulness—to oneself as well as to others—was of utmost importance, for the man who lied, cheated or stole could never secure the most priceless possession of a Shawnee: honor among his fellows or in his own soul.

But while Tecumseh learned a great deal from a wide variety of mentors, it was from Chiksika that he learned the most. For his own part, Chiksika had grown to love Tecumseh deeply, much more than any of the triplets, who were now five. Two of those three—Sauwaseekau and Kumskaka—were just ordinary Shawnee children, not particularly distinctive in any way. The third, Lowawluwaysica, was notable only in a negative manner—for his bad temper, his persistent petulance, his almost total lack of a sense of humor, his innate rudeness and his overriding loudness. The only person he liked was Tecumseh, whom he tended to follow around whenever possible. For his part, Tecumseh treated all three of the triplets with kindness and concern, but he seemed to overextend himself with Lowawluwaysica because the little boy had no other real friend; everyone else just seemed to tolerate him, and not too well at that.

Over these nineteen months since the death of their father, Chiksika, in accordance with Pucksinwah's wishes, had dedicated himself to teaching Tecumseh all he could in all phases of Shawnee life. By word of mouth, since nothing was written, he taught his younger brother the codes, traditions and history of the tribe, not only impressing it into his memory so well he would not forget, but so definitively that he could repeat these matters verbatim, with nothing omitted, added or altered.

Chiksika was himself a very intelligent young man who had learned a great deal from his father as well as from others, so these were among the things he endeavored to impart to Tecumseh. He taught him to observe—not merely with his eyes but with all his senses in concert, each contributing its part to the whole for a fuller comprehension of what was being observed. He taught his brother how to bear pain in stoic silence, how to suffer loss with acceptance rather than depression, how to overcome fear in the face of danger, and how to be victorious without letting pride become his master. In matters of dialogue, he instructed Tecumseh in the necessity of studying the speaker closely as well as listening to his words, watching for the little nuances that themselves often spoke volumes—blinking eyes, a tongue flicked repeatedly over the lips, the rubbing together of fingertips or the shifting of position; all these things and a multitude of others often belied the uttered word. And, of major importance in all things, Tecumseh learned the great need for self-control, how not to be ruled by his passions.

Together Tecumseh and Chiksika roamed the woods and fields, swam in rivers and lakes, hunted the diminishing herds of woodlands buffalo, caught rock bass and sunfish and suckers in the smaller streams and fished in the large rivers for giant catfish and huge muskellunge.[115] Chiksika taught him the fundamentals of expert tracking, man and animal alike, reading volumes from the bent grasses and broken twigs and scratched earth, signs that indicated where an animal or man had been and where he was going, and not only how to track such prey but how to outmaneuver it by anticipating its movements. He showed Tecumseh how to build deadfalls and snares for game and how to trap the mink and otters, muskrats and beavers so important in the fur trade. And, because success or misfortune in the hunt or in battle might result from the vagaries of weather, he taught the boy how to read nature's abundant signs in this respect and use this knowledge to his best advantage.

"When dew is on the grass in the morning," Chiksika told him, "it will not rain during the day; when it is not there just after darkness has fallen, it will rain before morning. When birds fly low and silently, a bad storm is coming, and when the pigeon sits close to the trunk of the sapling during daytime, a great wind will soon blow. When the leaves of the maples turn over to show their underside, thunder and lightning will soon come. If the blackbirds flock together and start to fly south when summer is still with us, there will be much snow during the winter. When the swamp muskrat builds a low house of reeds and mud, the winter will be mild, but the larger and higher the house he builds, the worse the winter will be; and when he builds no house at all, but instead burrows beneath the ground, prepare for severe cold, for the waters of swamps and ponds and smaller streams will freeze to the bottom and even the great Spaylaywitheepi will freeze so that a horse may walk upon it."

He taught Tecumseh the art of swiftly building a half-face shelter, useful for several nights in succession in one locality, and how to build the more permanent wegiwa that was cool in summer and warm in winter, but that could be abandoned without great loss if the need arose. He showed his little brother how to find the plants that would cure him when he was ill, the herbs that could blunt the pain of a severe wound, and the wild fruits and nuts and roots that would sustain him when he was hungry.

It was when the Harvest Moon was full last autumn, just a year after the death of Pucksinwah, that Tecumseh had been summoned to Chief Chiungalla, whose quarters were at the opposite end of the long, spacious wegiwa. With solemn admonitions and instructions, the short but sturdy chief told the boy that he was now about to take the first step toward his approaching manhood— that it was time for him to prepare for his *Pawawka;* that is, to do those necessary things that would lead to his ultimate possession of some material object that would be his own personal means by which he could come into contact with both Moneto and the Great Spirit in times of need and from them receive power that might help him through his crisis.

"What you are about to do, Tecumseh," Chiungalla said, "is initiate yourself before Moneto and the Great Spirit as a proof of your worthiness for their consideration. You know, do you not, where the deep pool in the river is, over there?" The chief pointed to the west and slightly south.

Tecumseh knew the place well and nodded. "I have gone swimming there often, Father," he said, "in summer when the water is warm." The pool in question was a natural basin in the bed of the Little Miami River just a short distance downstream, where the water circled in a pleasant eddy about ten feet deep, though the rest of the stream rarely exceeded six feet in depth.

"You are to go to Chiksika's wegiwa now and remove all your clothing. Then run to that pool and leap in so that you are completely under water. When you come to the surface you are to leave the water at once and run back to your brother's quarters, where you will dry yourself and dress. Then return to me."

Tecumseh went to the partitioned section of the huge wegiwa where his own family lived, removed his clothing and, feeling self-conscious and foolish, ran naked to the river and leaped into the pool, gasping at the shock of the icy October sting of the water. He was trembling when he emerged and he ran back to the wegiwa even faster. He was no longer shivering when he presented himself to Chiungalla a short time later.

The chief smiled faintly and nodded. "It is a start," he said. "Now, each morning for ninety-nine more days—one hundred days in all—you will do this same thing immediately upon awakening each morning. You need not come to me each time. No one will force you to do this. No one will be watching to see if you do it. But you will know, as will Moneto and the Great Spirit. On the final day, you will come to me before you go to the river and I will tell you what you must do then."

Tecumseh faithfully performed the progressively more difficult ritual each morning as day by day winter came and intensified. Sometimes it even became necessary for him to first break the ice before he could make his plunge. The whole process had become a severe test of courage and endurance but he did not falter in his performance of it. He was, he knew, being disciplined in obedience and in respect for the command of his earthly father, to make himself worthy of being the recipient of the loving care and protection of Moneto and the Great Spirit.

On the morning of the final plunge in mid-January he presented himself to Chiungalla, who gripped his shoulders. "You have done well, Tecumseh," he told the boy, his manner grave, "and the time of your preparation is at an end. Now you must seek your *Pawawka* token. Today you are to do one final time as you have done for ninety-nine times before this. But today you must dive deeply, to the very bed of the river and you must close your hands over whatever they touch on the bottom. Do not look at what you have grasped in your hands. Leave the water and come directly to me with what you have found. Then we shall see."

He did so and in less than half an hour had returned, blue with the cold and shivering terribly, but his hands still clenched with what he had brought up from the bottom. The chief took one of his hands and pried it open and found there a waterlogged piece of twig and some gravel, all of which he cast aside. In the other there was some sand, a soggy blackened leaf and a chunk of white quartzite rock about the size of a pigeon's egg. Chiungalla's eyes lighted as he saw it and he held it up between his fingers, inspecting it closely. At length he gave an approving grunt and nodded.

"This, Tecumseh," he said, "is forever your *opawaka,* to be carried by you and used as an intermediary between yourself and the Great Spirit when you are in need of help and direction."

"But how do I use it, Father?" Tecumseh asked, perplexed.

Chiungalla smiled. "You will know the way when that time comes. Now go. You look very foolish standing there shivering because you have no clothes on."

For weeks Tecumseh had worked on the stone, laboriously chipping a groove all around it so that he could attach a cord to it and wear it around his neck. It was there now and he was sure that where it touched his skin, it imparted a warmth from within.

And now, at last, with the fundamentals of his little brother's initial training well learned, Chiksika knew it was time to begin the very serious business of advanced training for Tecumseh as a warrior. They were skills he would very soon need. With the Shawnees for the most part still scrupulously observing the agreement made with Lord Dunmore and remaining north and west of the Spaylaywitheepi, settlement by whites in the wilderness on the other side was increasing rapidly and becoming firmly entrenched.

In the Kentucky country, the roots of settlement were coming about as a direct result of the anger the Cherokees held for the Iroquois. That anger stemmed from the League's having sold the Cherokee lands in the Kentucky and Tennessee country to whites eight years ago at the Fort Stanwix Treaty council. When, not too long later, the Cherokees were approached by some whites wanting to buy that very land, a Cherokee faction sold it to them, including land almost all the way to the Spaylaywitheepi, which they had never owned or occupied to begin with.

The white man backing the land-buying scheme, the Shawnees had learned from traders, was a colonial attorney from North Carolina named Richard Henderson, who envisioned an empire of his own and hired men such as Daniel Boone, Hugh McGary and others to get it rooted.[116] Other developments were going on apace. As soon as the conflict with Lord Dunmore ended, a man called James Harrod had returned to the Kentucky country and reestablished the first settlement there—Harrodsburg, sometimes called Harrod's Town. John Floyd and Simon Kenton had also come back, Kenton under the alias of Butler. Boone had returned, leading more than thirty-five people through the Cumberland Gap, and Harrod was soon joined by families that left Boone and struck out on their own—the families of Hugh McGary, Richard Hogan, and Thomas Denton, along with their followers. Suddenly, especially beginning just over a year ago with the warming weather, the Kentucky country, so long the hunting ground of the Shawnees, was becoming overrun with whites. Very quickly other stations, as the whites called their forted settlements, were being established. Some twenty miles or so to the southeast of Harrodsburg a settlement was founded by Benjamin Logan and his party and called St. Asaph by him, but more often just called Logan's Fort by his men.[117]

On behalf of the Transylvania Land Company, the Shawnees' old nemesis, Boone, established a station near the big salt lick to which so much wildlife was attracted and they were calling it Boonesboro.[118] Thomas and John Hinkson established The Cedars, but which became better known as Hinkson's Fort, on the north bank of the South Fork of Licking River and, some fifteen miles west and a little south of that, George McClelland built McClelland's Station close to a wonderful spring of cold crystal water that bubbled up in such volume and so attractively that it was named Royal Spring and the station named after himself.[119]

Almost overnight, it seemed to the Shawnees, the Spaylaywitheepi had become a highway for emigrants coming into the wilderness and encroachment increased alarmingly. Great numbers of watercraft—well-built boats, ordinary canoes, huge oversized canoes, rafts, flatboats, keelboats, broadhorns, anything that would float and carry people and goods—were floating downstream and disgorging their contents on the shores opposite Shawnee territory . . . and sometimes on it.[120]

Chiksika and other Shawnees knew that it would only be a matter of time before a new conflict arose with these settlers, but by then it would be very difficult to drive them out. The forerunner of such conflict was already occurring as some of the more intrepid—or foolish—of the adventurers were ignoring the agreement made on the Pickaway Plains and crossing into the Ohio country again, especially on the upper Spaylaywitheepi, from Fort Randolph at the mouth of the Kanawha, where the Point Pleasant battle had been

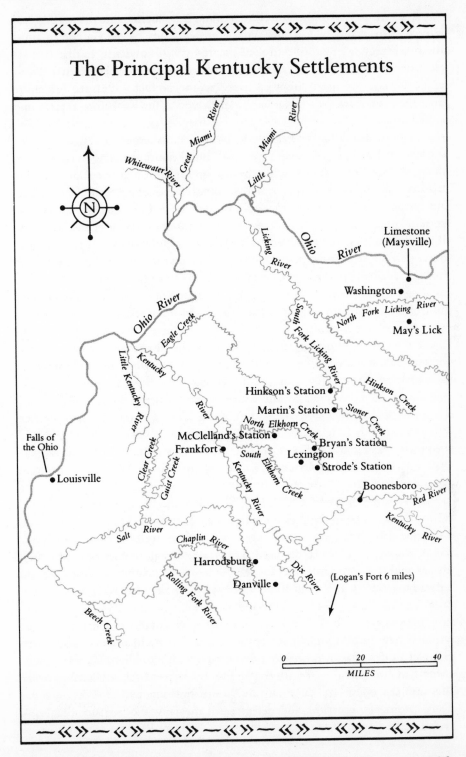

The Principal Kentucky Settlements

Whitewater River

Great Miami River

Little Miami River

Ohio River

Licking River

South Fork Licking River

Limestone (Maysville)

Washington

North Fork Licking River

May's Lick

Ohio River

Eagle Creek

Kentucky River

Little Kentucky River

Hinkson's Station

Hinkson Creek

Martin's Station

Stoner Creek

North Elkhorn Creek

McClelland's Station

Bryan's Station

Frankfort

South Elkhorn Creek

Lexington

Strode's Station

Falls of the Ohio

Clear Creek

Guist Creek

Kentucky River

Boonesboro

Red River

Louisville

Kentucky River

Salt River

Chaplin River

Dix River

Harrodsburg

(Logan's Fort 6 miles)

Danville

Rolling Fork River

Beech Creek

0	20	40

MILES

fought, all the way up to the Wheeling area and beyond. Settlements established before that brief war had grown with alarming speed. Wheeling and its surrounding area, for example, had many scores of new residents. In that area as well were some of the most rabidly Indian-hating whites on the frontier, who had begun now to make "hunting trips" across the Ohio, with the principal game they were seeking being any Indian who appeared before their gunsights.[121]

Chiksika and Blue Jacket, with Tecumseh listening in, discussed the problem of the whites. The war that had long been threatening between the far-off king and his white children in this land had broken out and the early hopes of the Indians that this would so involve the whites that they would have to draw back from the frontiers to support—or in some cases oppose— the revolution failed to materialize. To the contrary, now there were more whites than ever running around their country, with numerous British agents coming among the tribes to seek their aid in putting down the Americans rebelling against their king. The Shawnee chiefs had met in council with emissaries of the British—primarily the two British whites they knew best and trusted most, both of whom had married into the Shawnee tribe—Alexander McKee and Matthew Elliott. So far the chiefs, following the lead of Hokolesqua, unequivocally turned thumbs down on such an alliance, determined to live up to the terms of the agreement made with Lord Dunmore at the Pickaway Plains. But many of the younger warriors, furious at the infractions of the agreement by the whites and now being actively wooed by the British for alliance and actually encouraged to go after the Americans, were difficult to hold back. Only with the strongest of edicts, backed by chiefs in council, was Hokolesqua able to restrain the young braves eager for battle. Even then, now and again small parties of the Shawnees would cross the Spaylaywitheepi to spy on the activities of the whites.

Chiksika and Blue Jacket, through attending the Shawnee councils, were aware that, apart from the Pickaway Plains agreement, one of the reasons that their tribe was attempting to stay aloof from the contest between the whites was because their old and despised enemy, the Iroquois, had already made alliance with the British against the Americans and a Mohawk named Thayendanegea—whom the whites knew as Joseph Brant—had been named war chief. For the Shawnees to make the same kind of alliance, which was a tempting prospect, would in essence make them allies of the Iroquois, a concept extremely repugnant to the Shawnees as a whole. It would also be tantamount to a declaration of war against the *Shemanese,* with all its ramifications. The matter had come to a head with the large council held here at Chalahgawtha early during the last Heat Moon—July. Some three hundred fifty chiefs, subchiefs, prominent warriors and delegates of the five Shawnee septs had attended.

As usual, a variety of chiefs and prominent warriors had risen to speak and voiced their grievances about the whites—British and Americans alike—but the sentiment of the council attendees was about equally divided for peace or war. For the very first time Chiksika, in deference to his outstanding abilities as a young warrior, had been given leave to address the council more or less as a spokesman for the younger element among the warriors. He had experienced a strong flush of excitement and nervousness as he stood before the assemblage.

"I am Chiksika," he said, "son of War Chief Pucksinwah, chief of the Kispokothas, who died in the battle we fought nine moons ago where the Kanawhatheepi joins the Spaylaywitheepi. I carried him badly wounded from the field and he died a short time later in my arms." A lump had risen in his throat as the memories rushed back with great vividness and he paused a moment to collect himself, aided by momentarily meeting the gaze of Blue Jacket, who gravely nodded and then smiled faintly in encouragement. Chiksika moistened his lips and went on:

"One of the last things he said to me as he lay dying was this: 'Promise me you will never make peace with the *Shemanese*. They mean only to devour us.' That is exactly what they are doing now. As they are eating away the forests and game that belong to us in our hunting grounds, so next they will be devouring the very land upon which we live and using the bones of our fathers to pick their teeth. If we are to stop them at all, it must be now while they are still weak in their new settlements, not later when they have become big and strong by entirely devouring that which is ours. I speak for my companions as well as for myself and for the memory of my father when I say, let us strike them now!"

There were howls of approval, primarily from the younger warriors. Amid the uproar Chiksika returned to his place beside Blue Jacket experiencing a wonderful headiness at having been able to so move the emotions of his fellows with his words. Yet only a few minutes later the mood vanished because of the remarks that had been uttered by aged Chief Kikusgowlowa. This chief of the Thawegilas, though ill, had ridden his horse almost fifty miles south from Wapatomica to attend this council and he appeared very frail. In his youth and middle years he had been quite tall but now he was stooped and slight of frame and his long gray hair gleamed in the dimness.

"The septs have always been joined closely," he had said in his high and slightly tremulous voice, "in all important phases of Shawnee life, yet I tell you now that the Thawegilas have already seen their last war with the *Shemanese*. If once more the tomahawk is struck into the war post, the Thawegilas will leave the Shawnee nation and cross the great grandmother of rivers to the west, never to return."

It had been a brief and sobering delivery and those who advocated an all-out war against the *Shemanese* shifted uncomfortably and exchanged knowing glances. Hokolesqua, as principal chief of the tribe, had been the next to final speaker at that council, but the honor of speaking last had gone to Tecumseh's foster father, Chiungalla, because the council was being held in the *msi-kah-mi-qui* in Chalahgawtha, which was his village. Several other speakers had addressed the council after Kikusgowlowa's brief remarks and then came the most anticipated moment of the council as Hokolesqua stood and faced them.

"It is a bad time for us, yes," he said in opening, "and as your chief the fire in my breast wishes to burst forth in vengeance for those crimes that have been committed against us. I hold back in this desire for I have given my word, as have many of you here, that we will remain at peace."

There were some grunts of approbation but, intermingled among them, also a scattering of derisive cries impugning the principal chief's courage. Hokolesqua glared at the audience and an uneasy stillness once more settled over them. "Do not think," he said, his charged words hanging with implied threat in the semigloom of the council house, "now or ever, that Cornstalk so advises through fear, except fear our nation will perish. If once again we war with the *Shemanese,* it will be the beginning of our end. The white man is like the worm who, when cut in half, does not die but merely becomes two. For each one that is killed, two or three or even four rise to take his place."

He had let his gaze sweep across them for a long interval before resuming his talk with a reference to the agreement made with Lord Dunmore. "As the treaty last autumn opened the dam to let the whites down the river in a flood," he said, "so warfare against them will be opening the dam to permit them to flood our country here and take it from us. Yet, I have thought long on this and it comes to me that perhaps our young men are not so misguided in their anger. Perhaps it would be better in our hearts to die fighting for our rights and land than to live with insults of the whites in our ears and their heels on our necks."

Hokolesqua reached inside his blouse and extracted a folded paper which he snapped open with a flick of his hand and held high for all to see. "This is a speech," he said, "which has come to us from those who fought during the last Harvest Moon. They now invite us to Fort Pitt to confirm and ratify the peace agreement we made at that time with Lord Dunmore, so that it may be forever after a binding treaty. Though some of our young men have strayed from the agreement, we, as a tribe, have maintained our part of it, but the *Shemanese* have not. Because of that, it is not our wish to make our pledge any more binding."

With that he turned and tossed the paper into the council fire, his expression grim as it curled and burst into flame and then became black ash, while a great uproar filled the interior of the *msi-kah-mi-qui*. As the cries died away, he continued: "Though we will not put our hands to confirming a treaty that our hearts cannot accept because of injuries received, we must nevertheless not forget that our word was given to remain at peace and it is my wish that we continue to do so for now. As I have said, some of our young warriors with the blood running hot in their veins have crossed the Spaylaywitheepi and have killed some of those *Shemanese* who have settled there. This must not be, despite those provocations given us by which you retaliate."

He shook his head, exasperated, frustrated, and his voice imploring when he continued. "It is no easy matter to say we must not fight, just as it is no easy matter to bear the injuries being turned upon us. Yet it may be that if these injuries can be borne for a while, better relationships will come and we will be able to live with the whites as neighbors."

Many older members of the Thawegila, Maykujay, and Peckuwe septs had nodded their agreement with this observation, but Blue Jacket and Chiksika were among the faction—comprised mainly of Kispokothas and Chalahgawthas—who increased their murmurings of disgust and anger. Hokolesqua had let these impolite sounds run their course and when they finally faded away, he resumed:

"My young men are hard to hold and want to strike back when struck and it is not in my heart to tell them they are wrong. They are not wrong! But look deep into your hearts, each of you, and ask if any personal insult or injury is worth the destruction of our nation, which retaliation must surely bring."

There had been silence in the great room following this remark and after a moment Hokolesqua concluded with an announcement that took them by surprise. "A council is soon to be held by Cherokees in the Tennessee country to talk of opposing the *Shemanese*. I will go there and see if they will unite with us in such pursuit. Six summers ago they refused us when we asked this. Now the whites are settling among them as well and their hearts may have changed. If they will unite with us, then will I return with my hatchet raised and will recommend to all my chiefs that our whole nation declare war upon the whites. But until you learn further from me, I ask that you adhere to the agreements we made with the Dunmore on the Pickaway Plains."

There were sharp cries of approbation as he turned and moved back to his place beside Chiungalla and sat down. At the same time, Chiungalla had risen and stepped to the council fire. As a peace chief and second chief of the Chalahgawthas, it had been expected that he would agree with what the great Cornstalk had said, but Black Fish had never been known to toady to the opinion of even his own chief if it differed from what he felt or believed. With a gesture almost savage, he jabbed a stiff forefinger at the large roseate scar high on his right breast.

"This is my memory!" he said, the words deep and rumbling from that broad expanse of chest. "It tells me that no white man can be trusted at any time, any place."

There was a roar of approval, in which Chiksika and Blue Jacket joined with hearty cries.

"It tells me," Chiungalla went on, raising his voice to be heard over the din, which immediately subsided, "that when I accepted injury and insult from the white man, believing it would not happen again, it became worse than before. The Shawnee must live in dignity!"

Again a roar and again quickly hushed as he went on: "He must not only demand respect of others, white or Indian, but, even more important, he must retain his self-respect and he can never do this by turning his back on injury and insult. My memory," he tapped the scar again, "tells me this."

An approving murmur began to rise but he quelled it with an uplifted hand. He shook his head, saying, "I do not say we should make war, unless war is visited upon us, but I say we must protect ourselves. Hokolesqua has asked us to maintain the agreement made with Dunmore, but I say this: If our men are killed, *we* must kill. If our buffalo and elk are destroyed, then so must the cattle of the whites be destroyed and their horses taken away. If our woods are cut and our fields burned, then so must the cabins of the whites be burned. Only in this way will the *Shemanese* know that we will not allow our country to be ravished and they will think well on it before giving us further injury."

Despite the high feelings, that council had ended inconclusively and the fragile peace, such as it was, continued to prevail with only minor lapses occurring on each side as some whites entered into the Ohio country, others continued to shoot Indians from their boats while drifting downstream to claim Kentucky lands, and a handful of small Indian parties continued to cross the Spaylaywitheepi on brief hit-and-run attacks against individuals they found wandering alone or in small groups.

Some news that appeared good at first hearing had filtered to the Shawnees early last winter. The great land purchase made by Richard Henderson from the Cherokees for the Kentucky lands seemed to be collapsing. The governor of North Carolina had issued a proclamation declaring the purchase illegal, but that was a matter being contended. At first the Shawnees rejoiced, believing this would mean the settlements would be broken up and their people return to the east, but the joy was short-lived. While there might be no new colony— or country—named Transylvania, the settlers stayed on as free agents and only dug in their roots that much more deeply.

Tecumseh, listening to all these things being discussed by Chiksika and Blue Jacket, now shook his head, saying somewhat plaintively, "Doesn't anything *good* ever happen anymore?"

The young men laughed and Chiksika reached out and ruffled his little brother's hair. "It doesn't seem like it, does it Tecumseh? Let me see, I guess maybe there's one piece of good news you haven't heard yet."

"What," asked Tecumseh, brightening.

"Well, ever since Hokolesqua's big sister, Nonhelema, moved her village from the Scioto to where the Maykujays are, she has been courted by one of the chiefs there and word just got here that they have gotten married now."

"Who is the chief?" Tecumseh asked, wondering what Shawnee chief it might be who could manage a wife who was such a giant of a woman and so accustomed to dominance. Nonhelema was over six feet tall, very powerfully built, chief of her own village and long accustomed to being in command of warriors and had frequently led war parties.

"It is Moluntha," Chiksika replied, and then all three of them laughed heartily. Moluntha, eldest of all Shawnee chiefs and principal chief of the Maykujays, was gray-headed, frail, and eighty-four years old—hardly the image of anyone's idea of a mate for the robust and powerful Nonhelema, who was his cousin.

"Well," Tecumseh said, when their laughter finally died away, "our father always used to say that of all the Shawnee chiefs, he thought Moluntha had the most unquenchable spirit."

And once again the three burst into uncontrollable laughter.

[January 20, 1777 — Monday]

Tecumseh was still much too young to be permitted to attend a formal council meeting but he was nevertheless coming as close to doing so as he could. Chiungalla had called the council early this morning and both Chiksika and Blue Jacket, along with most of the other warriors in Chalahgawtha, had immediately repaired to the *msi-kah-mi-qui*. Tecumseh had donned his warmest garb, covered himself completely with a heavy buffalo robe and, as soon as all were inside, he had slipped up to the doorway and crouched there, fondling the *opawaka* token that hung from his neck.

It was so cold that occasionally branches in the distant woods cracked and snapped with loud reports and Tecumseh's breathing formed brief billowy clouds in the still air before his face as he tucked the robe tightly around himself. He freed one ear from its protective covering and, excited, strained to hear what was being said inside. What he was doing, he knew, would probably be frowned upon, but no one had said he couldn't and, anyway, as the best hunter and shooter among all the boys in Chalahgawtha, he already considered himself something of a warrior. After all, his tenth summer was approaching.

Inside, the voice of Chiungalla was audible, but this was not the warm, gentle voice Tecumseh was accustomed to from his foster father. It was harsh, cold, frightening him a little.

Chiungalla had begun by repeating some of the details of Hokolesqua's journey seven moons previously to the Cherokee council held at the place at the Tennessee River that the whites called Muscle Shoals. There, Hokolesqua had acted far more warlike than in his own councils here. He had stood before them while his attendant, Red Hawk, along with other aides unrolled and held up for all to see an enormous war belt of purple wampum, fully nine feet in length. Then the Shawnee chief had startled the entire gathering by pouring a pitcherful of vermilion dye over it, an act signifying not only war but an extremely bloody one. And when he spoke, his words had been very forceful:

"The Kan-tuck-kee lands upon which your tribe and mine have hunted together as brothers is now covered with the cabins and forts of the whites, who are like locusts eating the corn. The white men who come there, come as well into our land and yours, bringing with them guns and the determination to exterminate us all. They offer us little tokens which, if we take, we become indebted to them and soon they are saying the land is theirs because of what they have given us. They say we must live in peace with them, but the peace is to be on their terms and for their benefit. I tell you this: it is better for the red men to die like warriors than to diminish away by little bits. Now is the time to begin. If we fight like men, we may hope to enlarge our bounds. The Cherokees have a hatchet that was brought to you six summers past. Your brothers, the Shawnees, hope you will now take it up and use it immediately."

It had seemed evident that at this point in his talk, Hokolesqua had hoped to hear a rising of the war cry from those in attendance, but there was only stillness and he had grown angry. He had then snatched from Red Hawk's hands the end of the long war belt he was holding and lifted it high above his head.

"Heed!" he told them sharply. "If any nation shall refuse us now, we will hereafter consider them the common enemy of all red men and, when affairs with the *Shemanese* are settled, then we will fall upon such nations and destroy them!"

Despite the power of his talk, the Cherokees were divided. Only the most aggressive war chief, Dragging Canoe, accepted the belt for his faction, who now called themselves the Chickamauga, and promised his warriors would fight the encroaching whites.

Yet, Hokolesqua exasperated his own Shawnees, for when he came back home, he again strongly advocated maintaining the peace agreement made with Lord Dunmore. There were those who were beginning to think, Chiungalla told his listeners, that Hokolesqua was showing the indecisiveness and weakness of an old man, and those voices were saying perhaps it would be better if he stepped aside so his place might be taken by someone whose spine was straighter and stiffer.

At the doorway Tecumseh, still listening intently, shivered and changed position, exposing the other ear and covering the first, as it was now aching with the cold. He tried to tuck the buffalo robe more snugly around himself, but the bitter cold still seeped in, gripping, numbing. He thrust the discomfort out of his thoughts and listened more.

Chiungalla was now telling those assembled that over these past months the Shawnees were more and more being nudged to the point where they would have to retaliate in kind if they were to maintain their own self respect as warriors. Time and again along the Spaylaywitheepi, Mingoes, Wyandots, and Miamis were slipping across and raiding the settlements, stealing horses, killing cattle and sometimes people. Early on very little of this business was being done by the Shawnees, yet they were being blamed for it all and the whites were retaliating against them.

"This is why I have closed my eyes and stopped my ears," Chiungalla said, "when my young men here in Chalahgawtha have, in disobedience to the wishes of Hokolesqua, gone off to start doing the raids themselves against the whites, reasoning as young men will, why not, as they would be blamed in any event. I have not seen or heard them do this, for I have closed my eyes and stopped my ears. But now, because of those grave matters that have happened of late, I have opened my eyes and uncovered my ears and I knowingly and deliberately go against the will of the chiefs and encourage my young men to do these things all the more."

Chiungalla went on to warn them that they must not make the mistake of underestimating the fighting ability and cunning of some of the whites. While most were no match for the Indian, yet there were among them certain individuals who were as competent in woodland fighting in the Indian style as were the Indians themselves. One of these, he told them, was Boone. Time and again he had turned the tables on the Indians and so he must never be taken for granted. Another, the young giant, Bahd-ler, was every bit as skilled as Boone. And there were others.

"When you think you are very brave and skilled in fighting," he warned, "and believe you are a match for such men, think of some of the things they have done. Remember what this man Boone did in the last Heat Moon."

Tecumseh switched ears again, reaching up and vigorously rubbing the one just covered to ease the stinging. This weather was a mixed blessing: it kept people indoors and reduced the chances of his being observed eavesdropping here, but it was so cold! He leaned forward again, close to the heavy flap covering the council house doorway. Chiungalla was still speaking.

"Our great chief Hokolesqua," the words carried to Tecumseh well, "has told us that we must honor the agreement made with the *Shemanese* at the Chief Dunmore's camp. But now, as you know, one of our greatest chiefs— he who has for many years been among my best friends—has been killed and at last I am no longer willing to turn away."

There was no need for Chiungalla to elaborate on who the individual was. News of the death only a few weeks ago of Plukkemehnotee, second chief of the Maykujays—first under old Moluntha—had come as a severe shock to everyone and the story of how it happened was told over and over again.

To get at the root of it, one had to go back to last year during the Planting Moon—May. The rich frontier developer, Richard Henderson, was striving to preserve the personal empire that he had long been attempting to create in the Kan-tuck-kee hunting grounds of the Shawnees—a wilderness country that Virginia also claimed as her Fincastle lands by royal charter. That man, Henderson, Boone's employer, had assembled the hardy settlers at Boonesboro to establish their own government. But the settlers mistrusted him and soon held their own meeting at Harrodsburg, where they had selected two delegates to go to Williamsburg and petition the Assembly to include the Kan-tuck-kee area, now being called the Kentucky country, as a Virginia county in its own right and with its own elected representatives. More ominously for the Shawnees, the two men were also to procure from the government supplies of ammunition desperately needed by the settlers, plus a body of soldiers to protect the frontier.[122]

It was fully six moons later when those two men returned, this time on the upper Spaylaywitheepi with seven other men, floating downstream in three canoes.[123] A small party of Shemeneto's spies on the upper Spaylaywitheepi saw the party put ashore to camp and crept up to check on them. They overheard the men discussing their return to Kentucky and were astounded to discover they had with them a supply of ammunition large enough to start a war. Instantly they returned to their horses and thundered back to Kispoko Town to alert their chief.

Shemeneto considered it a very serious matter, certain that so large a supply of ammunition presaged an invasion of the Ohio country. It was urgent that they either capture or destroy the shipment before it reached its destination. He acted swiftly. Plukkemehnotee, a noted fighter of many years experience, was at that time visiting the Shawnee war chief and agreed to lead a war party by land while Shemeneto took another by water, in an effort to intercept the whites. Plukke's party of forty mounted warriors was to go overland to the place the whites were calling Limestone, just opposite where the prominent bluffs were on the Kentucky side, and waylay the party if Shemeneto's warriors failed to do so on the river.

Shemeneto and fifty of his warriors, in five large canoes, then set off down the Scioto to its mouth to ambush the white party when it passed. Hiding their canoes well up on shore, they waited and on the second morning the three canoes of the whites hove into view. They waited until the boats were passing the mouth of the Scioto and then began launching their own.

The whites, seeing what was happening, paddled furiously and got a good head start. The Shawnees had more men to paddle but their canoes were also much larger and heavier and so for a long while the two parties maintained about the same speed, separated from each other by several hundred yards. The day wore on and gradually the lighter canoes began to gain distance from their pursuers. By late in the afternoon and over twenty miles downstream from the mouth of the Scioto, the Shawnees had fallen about a mile behind. By late evening the fleeing whites were no longer in sight and Shemeneto reluctantly called off the pursuit, sending a runner by land to take this news to Chief Plukkemehnotee and tell him that Shemeneto was now relying on Plukke's party to be more successful than he.[124]

Plukke's party had made camp out of sight of the river and the chief had placed four men on watch. It was a cloudy night, very dark, and the lookouts saw nothing. They continued watching throughout the next morning without seeing anything, but late in the afternoon a runner from Shemeneto reached camp with word that the three canoes had outrun them and escaped. Practically on the heels of this, one of Plukke's lookouts, who had decided to check a little way downstream, came running back to report he had seen a canoe a quarter of a mile down, wedged in some branches projecting above the surface. Immediately Plukke realized what had happened. The whites had very quietly come ashore at Limestone at night, set their canoes adrift and took their precious cargo inland. They had a big head start, but it might be possible to catch them before they reached the settlements.

Plukke's party swam their horses over the river and immediately found signs where the white party had landed at the mouth of Limestone Creek and gone inland. By then it was nearly dark and too late to attempt tracking them, so Plukke allowed a large fire to be built in a deep niche in the rocks and they spent the night there drying their clothes, seeing to their horses and weapons and then resting. At dawn they took up the trail of the whites, following it to the closest of the settlements—Hinkson's Fort. The place was abandoned so Plukke, now sure they had not been in time to keep the ammunition from reaching the settlements, turned and went back to the Blue Licks. His warriors were cold and hungry and the horses needed rest and food, so he stopped, set up a hunting camp and spent the next three days letting the horses graze and replenishing their own meager food supplies with fresh game. At length a scout reported a small party of white horsemen approaching. They swiftly set up an ambush on the trail and the whites rode right into it.

At Plukke's command the Shawnees fired and two of the horsemen were killed outright, while another two lost control of their steeds and were thrown off. The remainder wheeled and galloped off at full speed, back the way they had come. The two dead were scalped and the other two taken captive. Within minutes Plukke had his warriors mounted and started in pursuit of those who had escaped.

They followed for some thirty miles but found the whites had managed to reach the fortified settlement called McClelland's Station and had taken refuge in its blockhouse. By then it was growing dark so they stayed out of sight, pulled back a distance to make camp and prepared to attack at dawn. With the very first light, Plukke led them in a direct frontal charge on the blockhouse, shooting at the structure as they neared it.

A volley of answering shots came from the gunports and four Indians fell. One was Plukkemehnotee, killed with two bullets through the chest. The Shawnees hesitated, scooped up their fallen and galloped out of range before stopping. The loss of their leader was a great blow, considered an omen of even greater tragedy ahead if they persisted. The whites were well protected and there was no way of knowing how many were inside. The warriors milled about indecisively for an hour just out of gun range and then they finally turned and left, heading for home.[125]

Outside the *msi-kah-mi-qui,* Tecumseh was now shivering so badly his chattering teeth made him fear he would be overheard and discovered. He knew he should get back to the wegiwa but what Chiungalla was saying inside held him in its magnetic grip.

"The death of Plukkemehnotee is an unspeakable affront to our tribe," the chief was saying, "and to me an act that cries in my heart for vengeance. It is a matter I mean to settle without delay. I wish for two hundred brave and experienced warriors to join me. I will lead them from this village to destroy every white settlement in our Kan-tuck-kee hunting grounds."

The growing murmur of assent and the scuffling sound as warriors came to their feet inside the council house sent Tecumseh scurrying away and back to the protection of the wegiwa. Later, thoroughly warmed by the fire, he thought about Chiungalla's final words in the council house and suddenly shivered again, but this time not from the cold.

[May 31, 1777 — Saturday]

Since the very beginning of this concerted onslaught against the Kentucky settlements, a great exultation had filled Chiksika, a sense of strength and power, pride, self-confidence, profound pleasure and nerve-tingling excitement. This, he thought, must be the very pinnacle of sensation that a warrior could achieve—every sense tuned to its greatest keenness, its highest pitch, imparting a conviction of indomitable presence.

He had mentioned it to Blue Jacket and was pleased to find his companion strongly shared the same feeling. Nor were they alone. From the very way they carried themselves as they rode—backs straight, chins high, eyes forward, bold, strong, arrogant, courageous—it was apparent that this same sensation was being experienced by most of those participating in the expedition.

"I think this must be the feeling my father tried to tell me about once, many years ago," Chiksika said meditatively. "He was very eloquent and yet, when I didn't understand what he meant, he couldn't seem to find the words to explain it to me. He tried, but finally gave it up and just said, 'One day, Chiksika, you will feel it too. Then you'll know.' I think now I know."

"If Pucksinwah couldn't express it," Blue Jacket replied, ducking beneath a low branch across the trail, "then I don't think anyone could. I feel it, as you do, but I don't think I could express it, except that I feel . . . well, somehow more *alive*."

The euphoria didn't fade. Day after day throughout the expedition it remained at a high level and not even the cold and uncomfortable business of swimming their horses across the Spaylaywitheepi—always the part that the majority most disliked—failed to dampen his spirits. That crossing was made close to the mouth of the Little Miami River and on the Kentucky side they followed the well-used trail that merged with the Warrior Trail about fifty miles south of the Spaylaywitheepi.[126] Chiungalla had immediately split his force in thirds, taking the center with a party of about seventy warriors, while the detachments flanked them at a distance of about half a mile. They had traveled about forty miles when the party on their left surprised a party of four whites making sugar in a camp they had established in a grove of maples. Three of the four were killed and scalped but one, though wounded, managed to escape, and the Indians got their weapons, horses and equipment.[127] Heartened by their success, the Shawnees continued south along the trail until, about seven miles north of the Warrior Trail, they reached Hinkson's Station. The place was still as it was when Plukke's party had found it over two moons ago—deserted and with no sign of recent occupancy. Here they had camped for a few days, giving the main body of warriors and their horses a good opportunity to rest while several ten-warrior parties were sent out by Chiungalla to reconnoiter the surrounding area in a radius of five or six miles.

On their third day there, Chiksika and Blue Jacket were with one such party being led by Chiungalla when they caught sight of a white man on horseback, galloping away on a trail leading westward. Ten other horses, saddled and with reins tied to bushes, were standing together just off the trail. The scouting party broke into sharp yips and cries and followed close behind Chiungalla, who was already thundering in pursuit. They passed the standing horses, which stamped about nervously, but only pursued the distant rider for about a hundred yards when Chiungalla brought them to a halt with an upraised hand.

"Something is peculiar here," he said. He led them back to the saddled horses, whose reins were loosened from their moorings and gripped by the warriors. Gentle chirpings soon quieted the nervous animals. Chiungalla looked the horses over carefully and then raised himself high and studied their surroundings. There was no real cover here, only a few scattered trees and more of this type of brush the horses had been tied to; certainly no place to take cover and make a stand, so where were the men? They had discussed the matter among themselves and concluded the white who escaped had been leading these horses and had merely paused here to rest or relieve himself. When he heard them coming he had simply abandoned the horses and fled for his life. Chiungalla, however, was concerned that this might indicate an army of whites somewhere in the area and that it would be wise to return to their camp. They did so, each of the warriors leading one of the saddled horses.[128]

Immediately upon reaching Hinkson's Station, Chiungalla had sent out riders to bring in the various scouting parties and preparations were made to break camp. Within an hour or so they were on their way, following the road the escaping rider had taken. It led to McClelland's Station, where Plukke-mehnotee had been killed, but that place, too, was abandoned. They set fire to the cabins and blockhouse and continued following the road, now leading in a southerly direction, toward Harrodsburg. Again Chiungalla had put out his flanking detachments, as well as sending out a number of smaller parties to scout the area toward Boonesboro. Blue Jacket and Chiksika were pleased to be riding under the command of so sagacious a leader.

In the forenoon of the following day, as they approached Harrodsburg, Chiungalla brought in the flankers, gave orders and the entire party, most on foot some still mounted, moved in on the settlement. The instant they heard a sentinel in the blockhouse cry out an alarm, they broke into a charge, shrieking their war cries. A deafening din of gunfire broke out, but with little effect. A few of Chiungalla's warriors suffered insignificant wounds and at least one of the defenders was hit and seen to fall. The attack swirled around the fort for more than an hour, still with no serious damage done by either side, but then Chiungalla drew his force back out of range as the skies became very heavy. A cold wind blew in, bringing with it tiny sharp snow crystals that peppered them like hail. Chiungalla sent in a few more waves of attackers but by late afternoon the weather had degenerated to a howling storm and he withdrew his force, leading his men westward a couple of miles to the Salt River where they established a camp and posted guards.

For weeks following this the camp was maintained, buffeted by a whole series of howling storms and subfreezing temperatures, with little respite between. Small raiding parties went out constantly to harass the settlements, but to little effect beyond occasionally wounding or killing a white. At last, after a sharp assault on Harrodsburg on March 28, they withdrew at Chiungalla's orders to the Blue Licks and established a strong camp.[129] Hunting parties were sent out to bring in meat, which they did in plenty, and when they were well rested, Chiungalla began sending out a multitude of small war parties ranging in size from four or five warriors to as many as twenty, to rove about in hit-and-run manner throughout the entire countryside, including the areas of Boonesboro and Harrodsburg. More and more they reported success as gradually the weather warmed into spring and as the settlers had to leave the protection of the forts to plow and plant. But every now and then such war parties also returned bearing with them warriors who had been wounded or killed in such encounters.

Toward the end of the Rain Moon—April—Chiungalla gathered his warriors together for another offensive, this time directed at Boonesboro. They surrounded the fort unseen during the night and lay in wait. Just after dawn the gate opened. Three men with rifles—one of them the young giant, Bahd-ler—posted themselves at the gate as guards and then two men came out, looked around carefully and moved out into the clearing. They began picking up any scattered twigs and branches that could be used as firewood. Chiungalla swiftly whispered a plan and a large number of his warriors moved into position, still under cover and unseen. When the two whites had their arms full and turned to go back to the fort, several Shawnees fired. One man fell and the other dropped his load and sprinted wildly for the gate some sixty yards distant.

Six warriors leaped from hiding in the nearest adjacent woods and rushed into the clearing toward the downed man, who was now trying to crawl to the fort. As they raced up, the warrior in the lead, Nenothtu—Warrior—drove his tomahawk into the settler's back, severing his spine. With a shriek of triumph he whipped out his knife and began removing the dead man's scalp.

The white warrior called Bahd-ler and the other two raced toward them and Bahd-ler fired as he ran, killing Nenothtu just as he straightened with the scalp in his hand. The other five warriors raced away, not toward the woods from which they had emerged, but down the length of the clearing. At the same moment Boone, leading ten others, dashed out of the fort in pursuit.

117

Bahd-ler, having reloaded as he ran, passed the bodies of Nenothtu and the settler with scarcely a glance. By this time Boone and his ten men were forty yards from the gate, all the whites believing this was only a small raiding party. It was then that Chiungalla gave the signal for the next phase of his plan. A horde of warriors burst from the woods and sprinted to get themselves between the Boone party and the gate.

Boone and his men slammed to a halt, realized they'd been duped and turned to run back. An approaching warrior dropped to one knee and took aim at Boone, but Bahd-ler, who had also spun around, snapped off a shot and the Shawnee screamed and then fell motionless. Chiksika and Blue Jacket were among the many who shot at Bahd-ler, but the man seemed under Moneto's protection, as no bullet struck him and he reloaded again in full run.

Now a scattering of supporting fire was coming from the fort and the running warriors were suddenly diving behind stumps or logs for cover. Bahd-ler shot another Shawnee, wounding him, and then amazingly reloaded a third time, still on the run. A warrior named Shequonur—The Rock—was among those who had taken refuge behind a stump and now, peering out from behind it, saw Boone approaching. He quickly aimed and fired and the ball struck Boone in the leg, breaking the bone and felling him. Dropping his gun, Shequonur leaped toward Boone, yanking out his tomahawk as he ran, raising it to deliver the finishing stroke, but the approaching Bahd-ler fired again. The ball tore through Shequonur's chest and the warrior dropped without a sound.

Even in the midst of all this frantic activity, many of the Shawnees paused to watch as the incredible Bahd-ler ran up to Boone, tossed his own gun aside and snatched up the wounded man into his arms as if he were a baby, then raced with him toward the gate. A pair of warriors gripping tomahawks sprinted to cut him off but Bahd-ler continued running toward them and then, unbelievably, as he came close and they raised their weapons to strike, he hurled Boone at them. Boone's body slammed into them, knocking both to the ground and stunning one. As the one tried to scramble up, Bahd-ler sank his own tomahawk in the warrior's head, killing him. He then scooped up Boone again, who was now unconscious, and, as the second warrior struggled to rise, incapacitated him with a mighty kick, then resumed his run with Boone to the fort, bullets whistling all around him and smacking into the logs of the gate as he entered. But he managed to get Boone inside and the gate was slammed shut.

Chiksika, frozen with amazement, had witnessed all this and now he remembered, as if the words were being newly spoken again, the admonishment to his warriors that Chiungalla had made in the council before this expedition was begun: *When you think you are very brave and skilled in fighting and believe you are a match for such men, think of some of the things they have done.*

Only now could he appreciate the wisdom of that utterance. How could the whites, usually so weak and unskilled in fighting, produce men like this giant warrior? And like Boone? The story of what Bahd-ler had done this day would be told for a long time to come around the council fires. And the warrior who could kill or capture such a man as this would gain a prestige that would remain with him all his days.

With the gate closed against them, Chiungalla placed the fort under siege and for three more days kept it surrounded and under sporadic fire. Then, at last, he withdrew with most of his warriors, leaving only a few behind to continue the harassment.

For the next moon they continued roving throughout the Kentucky country in numerous parties, attacking whenever and wherever they found anyone incautious enough to show himself. Only the man Bahd-ler seemed impervious and continued moving about, hunting game for the settlements and also actually hunting the warriors themselves as they hunted the whites—outrunning them, outshooting them, outwitting them.

Finally Chiungalla had assembled all his warriors at the Blue Licks camp. "We have been gone from our homes and our loved ones for almost four moons," he told them, "and now it is time we return. We will strike in force at two places and then, whether successful in destroying them or not, we will go home."

At dawn on the twenty-third day of the Planting Moon—May—they struck Boonesboro again, trading shots with those who fired back at them from the portholes, wounding several, but themselves suffering one warrior killed and another badly wounded. Early that night warriors slipped in close and tried to set the fort afire, but the fortifications had been constructed of greenwood and the fire would not catch. Later this same night they pulled away and by the light of morning on the twenty-fifth, no Indian remained in the vicinity of Boonesboro.

They had then gone again to Harrodsburg and observed it closely, unseen. The fort had been strengthened even more since their attack here and the guards were numerous and extremely alert. They watched for three days, waiting for an opportunity to rush and gain entry, but to no avail. And finally Chiungalla led them away, heading southeast on the road that connected Harrodsburg with Logan's Fort—St. Asaph—sixteen miles distant. There, in the dim light of dawn on the thirtieth, they watched from hiding as seven individuals—three carrying buckets hooked over the rifles on their shoulders, guarded by four men with rifles held at the ready—emerged from the gate to go the twenty or thirty yards to the cattle compound to milk the cows. Chiungalla gave the signal and a volley of shots broke out. When it was finished, all seven were dead.

Firing continued sporadically during the day and, from their concealment, the warriors killed all of the animals in the cattle compound. During the ensuing night six of the seven dead were scalped, the only one escaping this being a young woman whose upper body and head had been covered by a cow that fell upon her after being shot. When the party that scalped them came back they reported that three of the dead had been women clad in men's clothing. Chiungalla shook his head regretfully.

"It is a sorrow," he said, "that such should be. Those must be very bad men in there that they would expose their wives to such danger."[130]

The siege was maintained one more day without appreciable result and shortly after nightfall on this final day of the month, Chiungalla led his warriors away—all of them. It was time to go home.

So now, as they left the Kentucky settlements behind them, Chiksika still felt that glow of euphoria he had discussed with Blue Jacket as the expedition began. A good many settlers had been killed, along with virtually all their cattle, and over two hundred much-needed horses had been taken and were now in this procession heading for Chalahgawtha. The death of Chief Pluk-kemehnotee had certainly been fully avenged and perhaps now the whites would realize that the Shawnees could no longer step back and allow themselves to be injured in any way without sharp retaliation. And Chiksika grinned to himself as he thought about what pleasure there would be to sit at their fire and tell Tecumseh about all that had happened.

[August 8, 1777 — Friday]

It was one of the best and one of the worst times of Tecumseh's short life thus far.

"Tecumseh," Chiksika had said last evening as they sat before the fire, "tomorrow I am leading a small war party—eight of us—to try to strike one of the parties of whites coming down the Spaylaywitheepi. If you like, and if you'll promise to follow my orders, you may come along."

Tecumseh was momentarily speechless and then the words tumbled from him. "If I like? If I *like*? Of course I like! Oh, Chiksika, yes! I'll go. And I promise I'll do just as you say . . . everything you tell me!"

By tribal custom, Shawnee youths were not ordinarily invited to accompany a war party until they were at least twelve or thirteen years old, so it was little wonder that he, at age nine and a half, was overwhelmed. He had dreamed of this for so long!

Tecumapese, spooning freshly made succotash into a bowl for little Spem-ica Lawba, had looked up with a slight frown. "Don't you think he's still too young for that, Chiksika?" she said.

Her older brother grinned. "In years he's young, yes, but not in ability, Tecumapese. You know as well as I that he's better at hunting and in the war games than anybody else here his age and most of those who are much older. All he lacks is experience and it's time he starts getting some."

Tecumapese sighed, not convinced, yet relying on Chiksika's judgment. She looked at Tecumseh, smiling at the excitement in his eyes. "You stay very close to Chiksika, Tecumseh, and follow his instructions exactly. You must agree to that."

"I do! I will!"

In a flurry of activity he had spent the rest of the evening getting his equipment ready. He laid out his bow and checked its string, which he replaced with a new one; laid out all the arrows he had made and checked them over carefully, selecting the dozen best and filling his quiver with them; thoroughly checked his flintlock, powder horn, and shot pouch; honed a fine edge on his tomahawk and knife, though neither was dull; checked his medicine pouch to make sure it contained the wad of buzzard down for plugging wounds and the paints he would use to decorate his face and chest when they got there; checked everything twice and then spent a largely sleepless night as he waited for the dawn with the greatest anticipation that had ever filled him.

All the members of the party, Tecumseh excepted, were in their early twenties and all were simply dressed—six in usual summer hunting or war-making dress: sturdy buffalo-hide moccasins snugged and tied with rawhide at the ankle, a dun-colored trade shirt of calico or linen that was buttoned but not tucked in, a rawhide belt knotted in front through which a triple-folded piece of ocher-colored trade cloth had been passed so that it hung over the belt in the rear, passed through the legs snug and diaper-like against the crotch and again lapped over the belt in front, with the loose ends of the cloth hanging in a knee-length flap back and front. The three exceptions, Chiksika, Tecumseh, and a warrior named Wasegoboah—Stand Firm—had the same style of breech garb but their clouts were of finely tanned undecorated buckskin and all three wore open vests of similar hide.[131]

Five of the party, in keeping with a current fashion among the younger warriors, had shaved their heads except for a narrow brush of hair an inch or so high running from forehead to nape, plus a small patch of uncut hair just above and behind one ear, to which was attached one, two or sometimes three white-tipped eagle feathers angling back and downward to trail over the shoulder. Those with traditional shoulder-length unbraided hair wore head bands of green- or red-dyed cloth to keep their hair out of their eyes and to which similar feathers were attached. When not hunting or warring, this traditional-length hair, very black and shiny, was worn loose and ordinarily scrupulously combed.

All nine carried tomahawks and knives in their belts and medicine pouches slung diagonally over the shoulder. All had flintlock rifles, powderhorns, and shot pouches. Two, including Chiksika, had war clubs—an eighteen-inch length of skin from a cow's tail, split at one end so a rock the size of a goose egg could be inserted, then sewn closed with rawhide, soaked and dried so the skin stretched taut and tough over the rock; the other end cut in a loop to fit over the wrist so it would not slip from the grasp and be lost in battle. With the hand slipped through the loop and gripping the tubular tail section, it became a very facile, formidable weapon that could easily break an enemy's bones or crack his skull like an eggshell.

Chiksika rode in the lead as they left Chalahgawtha, with Wasegoboah and Tecumseh side by side directly behind him and the remaining six by twos behind them. Their plan was to strike the Spaylaywitheepi at the mouth of the Great Miami, so Chiksika led them westward for about fifteen miles until they encountered the Mad River less than a mile upstream from where it emptied into the Great Miami. From there they planned to follow the mother stream down its mouth, about seventy miles distant.

A pleasant open woodland lined the east shore where the two streams converged and they had progressed only half a mile below this point, talking and laughing, when Chiksika spied a white man's canoe drawn well up on shore and partially hidden under bushes. Instantly he twisted around to shout a warning and simultaneously a rifle shot shattered the stillness. Chiksika was slammed backwards off his horse and thudded to the ground.[132]

Wasegoboah snatched Tecumseh with one arm and leaped to the ground with him, shrieking for the others to take cover, which they were already doing, knowing that on their horses they were all too vulnerable. As the animals galloped off in fright, the Shawnees scrambled behind trees and logs, assessed the situation and at once began spreading out to encircle the spot where the powder smoke hung in the air.

Tecumseh was terrified. The bow still in his hand was broken, his arrows scattered, his gun stuck muzzle down in the ground. Wasegoboah had left him and was dodging toward the attackers, while no more than ten feet away lay Chiksika, motionless, but his eyes open and fixed on his little brother, his right side bathed in the scarlet of his own blood. A wave of sheer panic swept through the boy and he dropped his broken bow and fled, running back the way they had come. More shots sounded and lent speed to his flight. After several hundred feet he dived behind the trunk of a huge wind-fallen tree and cowered there, chest heaving and his whole body trembling uncontrollably.

After a moment more he heard war shrieks from his companions, punctuated with more shots. He reached up and clenched the white stone hanging

from the cord around his neck and immediately felt calmed. His *opawaka!*
"Please," he murmured, "don't let Chiksika die."

He released the stone and slithered down the river bank until close to the
water, then ran back in a crouch until he came to where the canoe was hidden.
Here he crept up the bank and found Chiksika was only a few feet away and
was greatly relieved to see him stirring. He scrambled close, gripped his
brother's left wrist and pulled him down the bank to the water's edge, then
ran back to the canoe and began pulling it toward the water.

"Tecumseh!"

It was Wasegoboah's voice and he looked up to see the young man and
two of the others at the top.

"They're dead, Tecumseh. There were only three. It's over." Wasegoboah
started down the bank. "Is Chiksika alive?"

"Yes, I'm alive."

Tecumseh spun around to find Chiksika coming up to a sitting position,
his left hand covering the wound on his right side. The boy ran toward
him, fighting back the tears of relief, but stopped short as Chiksika spoke
again, coldly.

"You ran, Tecumseh. In the face of an enemy, you turned and ran,
deserting your brothers."

The awfulness of the pronouncement crashed through Tecumseh's mind
with the impact of a physical blow. He opened his mouth to speak, but could
find no words. Wasegoboah stepped to his side and put a hand on his shoulder,
but it was to Chiksika that the warrior spoke.

"Tecumseh is still a very young boy, Chiksika, in his first combat. He
rode into an ambush. He saw his brother shot from his horse. He smelled
death in the air. He is only nine! Can you wonder that he felt fear and ran?
But, consider, Chiksika: he stopped, he came back to help, knowing he could
be—perhaps *would be*—killed. We have all felt fear at one time or another,
but to overcome it so quickly . . . *that,* my brother, is courage!"

Chiksika turned his gaze from Wasegoboah to Tecumseh and he looked
at him steadily for a time and then his expression softened. Slowly his lips
curled into a smile. "Wasegoboah is right, little brother. I apologize."

Tecumseh found his voice at last, and it was filled with self-condemnation.
"I ran," he said. "I'm sorry, Chiksika. I promise you, all of you," he glanced
at the others, then back at his brother, "I will never again run from an enemy
because I am afraid. Never."

The three dead men, two young and one older, were scalped. Their guns
and clothes were fairly new, hardly at all brush worn, and it was evident the
trio had been new to the frontier. No frontiersmen with any experience would
have attempted to ambush a party of well-armed Indians three times their own

number. That was stupidity, not bravery. And no experienced frontiersman could have missed killing Chiksika with a shot through the heart at such close range, instead of merely deeply gouging his right side, perhaps breaking a rib.[133]

Chiksika's wound was plugged and bound tight and by then three of the warriors had located all nine horses grazing in a small meadow less than a mile away and had little difficulty catching them. Never before had enemy whites come so close to Chalahgawtha before. Chiungalla should be told without delay. The expedition was canceled and they returned toward the village as rapidly as Chiksika's condition would allow.

As they rode, Tecumseh was silent and withdrawn. The others had clearly forgiven him for his panicky flight, but he had not forgiven himself. And he promised himself, as he had promised them, that never again would fear, however strong, cause him to flee in the face of an enemy. His hand had come up to his neck as he thought this and he was clutching his *opawaka*.

[October 10, 1777 — Friday]

The three Shawnees sat astride their horses on the Ohio River shore and stared across at the place where three years ago today the Battle of Point Pleasant had been fought. Now a fort stood there—Fort Randolph—with a sizeable scattering of settlers' cabins outside its picketed walls. The three included the principal chief of the tribe, Hokolesqua, his twenty-year-old son, Elinipsico, and the subchief, Red Hawk, who had long been Hokolesqua's foremost attendant.

"I still think this is all a big mistake, Hokolesqua," grumbled Red Hawk.

"You've made that very clear, Red Hawk. You don't have to cross with us if you don't want to. Nor you, Elinipsico," he added, glancing at his son. "This is my business, not yours. If you prefer, you can wait here until I return."

"I'm going with you, father," the young man said, though it was obvious he had his own misgivings.

"Oh, all right, let's do it then," Red Hawk said. He opened his pouch and removed a large square of folded white cloth and a length of rawhide thong. Shaking the cloth so it opened, he firmly tied one corner of it to the end of his spear and raised it as a flag of truce. Kneeing his horse forward to enter the water, he turned his head to look at the others as they followed and grumbled again, "I still think it's all a big mistake."

Hokolesqua did not reply, though he felt Red Hawk was probably correct. Hardly any of the chiefs in the tribe could understand why he deemed it necessary to warn the *Shemanese* that the Shawnees were attacking their settlements in the Kentucky country and on the upper Spaylaywitheepi. Hadn't that become abundantly clear, they asked, especially after the extensive expedition of Chiungalla against the Kentucky stations? To go to the *Shemanese* with such a message was, they argued, not only pointless, it could be downright dangerous. Yet, Hokolesqua's own honor and pride made it essential that he give the whites formal notice that it was no longer possible to hold the young men of his tribe in check and that the agreement made with Lord Dunmore three years previously could no longer be maintained.

Over the past year especially, matters had so degenerated that a virtual state of war existed with the Americans. Hordes of settlers had come down the Spaylaywitheepi and the Kentucky country had become overrun with them. Their initial tiny outposts had become strongly fortified settlements and were continuing to grow rapidly. The whites had broken the Pickaway Plains Treaty, if such it could be called, almost from the beginning. Incursions of armed whites into the Ohio country, especially along the upper Spaylaywitheepi in the vicinity of Wheeling, had now become so frequent that the Shawnees, in their own Ohio country, ran the risk of being shot from ambush any time they went hunting or had to travel from one place to another.

Hokolesqua's cherished hopes that his tribe could remain neutral in the present war of rebellion going on between the whites had all but vanished. As a testimonial to how things were changing, their Potawatomi allies in the Detroit area told them that toward the end of the summer following the Americans declaring their independence, the British commandant at Detroit, Lieutenant Governor Henry Hamilton, had met with them and the Hurons, the Ottawas, and the Chippewas. They had expected him to strongly urge them to attack the Americans on all frontiers. Instead, they found him very cool toward such an idea, though he did tell them the Crown expected their assistance and, during the talk, he took a peace belt that the Potawatomies had received from a pro-American faction of Delawares and very deliberately destroyed the peace emblem that had been woven into it. Yet, only six months later, during the past Hunger Moon—February—this same Hamilton was belatedly furious about the rebellion and was so eager for the Detroit area Indians to go out on raids against the Kentucky settlements to kill, destroy property and take prisoners, that he was offering them a bounty on scalps.[134]

Now Hokolesqua's own people were being supplied by the British at Detroit with arms and ammunition and many other things they needed that had for so long been scarce or absent. In return these redcoats expected the Shawnees to support their cause and make war against the king's enemies, his own American children, who had declared their independence from him.

So much had changed! And everything that occurred seemed so ominous. Where before only small parties of young Shawnee hotbloods were disobeying the tribal edict and crossing the Spaylaywitheepi to strike, and then most often just killing cattle or stealing horses, now they were actively searching out and killing anyone encountered. So frequent and harsh were the raids that one by one the Kentucky settlements were being abandoned, with some of their residents moving to the most strongly fortified ones and others returning to the East.

The death of Plukkemehnotee had ignited a fuse among the Shawnees that would not be extinguished and, while Hokolesqua was bitter about the fact that his own second in command of the tribe, Chiungalla, had led a major retaliatory expedition against the settlements without full tribal authorization, he could not deny that the expedition had been of value in thoroughly frightening the Kentucky settlers. By the beginning of the last Hunger Moon, only four stations were left—McClelland's, Logan's, Boonesboro, and Harrodsburg. Then McClelland's and Logan's were abandoned and only the two remained. Logan's had since been reoccupied but was very weak. Hokolesqua couldn't help but wonder if he had been wrong all along in insisting on maintaining the peace. Perhaps, had they struck the intruders with full force immediately from the beginning, the whites would never have gotten their toehold at all. Perhaps if the whole weight of Shawnee strength had joined with Chiungalla in his expedition instead of just two hundred, the entire Kentucky country would be clear of the whites now. Instead, just after the end of the Heat Moon a most ominous thing had occurred in the Kentucky country. The few warriors still hovering near Boonesboro and Harrodsburg had come back more than a little concerned. A white chief had arrived there at the head of a hundred men armed not only with new rifles, but with something different—long knives attached to the muzzle of each rifle. Even as they had watched from under cover, the warriors had seen these men practice with the weapons, shooting first at a suit filled with dried grasses and then immediately rushing at it and stabbing it through with hard jabs of the guns. It was impressive, to say the least.[135]

Hokolesqua shook his head to clear away the thoughts, not given to dwelling on what-ifs. He, as leader of the tribe, had given his word and a Shawnee's word was not given lightly, nor his promise easily broken. Now, with the whole frontier aflame and heating more with each passing day, the promise would be broken. How could it be maintained, now that the Wyandots had accepted the British war hatchet with such fervor?

Well supported with British arms and ammunition flowing to them from Detroit and Niagara, and even with British advisers traveling with them and sometimes adopting the dress of the Indians, the Wyandots at Upper Sandusky had launched a major offensive against the upper Spaylaywitheepi settlements.[136] It was effective, though not as much as it might have been had they acted in concert among themselves. Instead, nearing their objective, they had splintered apart in numerous small raiding parties and killed a good many isolated settlers, destroyed a lot of cabins and cattle and took scores of horses, but offensives against the stronger settlements had failed.

Wheeling had been attacked on the first day of September and placed under a siege that lasted two full days. Twenty-four whites were killed and half a dozen others wounded. Only one Wyandot was killed and another wounded.[137]

Twenty days later the same Wyandots, who had been watching the Wheeling area closely, observed a company of twenty-four men leave the fort and follow the Spaylaywitheepi downstream a dozen miles to the mouth of Grave Creek, where they camped for the night. Anticipating that the next morning the whites would move up the trail alongside Grave Creek, the Wyandots rigged an ambush at a place called the Narrows, where passage was very restricted between a high hill and the creek. Here they had strewn some trinkets on the ground as a bait. In the morning the company of men took the path and, as expected, stopped and clustered together when the trinkets were found. That was when the Indians opened fire, killing twenty-two of the twenty-four and again having only one of their own number killed.[138]

In addition to the attacks on Wheeling and at Grave Creek, the Wyandots, aided by many Mingoes and Delawares and a scattering of Shawnees, had hit isolated cabins and numerous tiny settlements in abundance all the way from the mouth of Yellow Creek down to Fort Randolph here at the mouth of the Kanawhatheepi, which Hokolesqua, Elinipsico, and Red Hawk were just now approaching. As a result, the whole area was in upheaval and many of the newer settlements such as Catfish Camp and Shepherd's Station had been abandoned or nearly so.

As the horses of the three Indians crossing the Spaylaywitheepi neared the Point Pleasant shore, a crowd of whites gathered but, at Red Hawk's vigorous waving of the white flag, no shots were fired and the trio was allowed to emerge from the water. They were immediately escorted by a squad of soldiers to the quarters of the Fort Randolph commander, Captain Matthew Arbuckle, who viewed them with suspicion and ill-concealed fear.

"Why have you come here, Cornstalk?" he asked.

Hokolesqua's command of English was reasonably good, but he spoke slowly and distinctly to be sure the officer understood him well. "I come with grave news. At the camp of Charlotte three years ago I gave my word as principal chief of the Shawnees that our tribe would keep the peace, would remain on our own side of the Spaylaywitheepi and refrain from retaliation if

grievances arose between my people and yours, but instead take those grievances to the white commanders and they would be smoothed. This was a talk-
treaty and papers were to be marked later at the Fort of Pitt, where the
Spaylaywitheepi begins. But because of the troubles that have risen, including
the war between your own people, this did not come about. We have been
injured in many ways by the whites since then and though we have brought
our grievances to the Fort of Pitt and discussed them at length, they have not
been smoothed and have only become worse."

Hokolesqua held Captain Arbuckle with a steady, steely gaze and continued. "Now I have come here to say to you that these grievances have
become too great to be borne. I can no longer restrain my young men from
joining the raiding parties encouraged by our friends, the British. I no longer
wish to restrain them. We have suffered much at the hands of the *Shemanese*
who have repeatedly broken the talk-treaty. Now there is a treaty no longer.
It is a matter of honor that we have come here to tell you this."

Captain Arbuckle arose from behind his desk and, without replying to
Hokolesqua's remarks, ordered the squad of soldiers to put them in confinement in a cabin which he designated, adding, "Apparently we're at war with
the Shawnees again. We'll hold these three hostage."

Angered at such treatment but unable to do anything about it, Hokolesqua
allowed himself and Elinipsico and Red Hawk—who looked at him accusingly—to be led to a single-room cabin in which there was a table and two
chairs, a large fireplace and a crude ladder leading up to a partial loft. In the
walls there were only three narrow slits as windows. The single door was
closed and bolted from the outside.

"I told you this was all a big mistake," Red Hawk commented bleakly.
He glanced up at the loft and then stooped and peered up the fireplace chimney.

"I do not regret that I came," Hokolesqua said calmly. "I regret only that
my son and my friend came with me, and that the whites have acted so
dishonorably."

Soon a disturbance was heard outside and through the slits they could see
Captain Arbuckle arguing with a large unruly group of armed men, saying
that the Indians were unarmed and official hostages and were not to be molested. Arbuckle, however, was shoved aside and the mob surged toward the
cabin.

Inside, Elinipsico began to scale the ladder to the tiny partial loft but
Hokolesqua called him to come back down, which he did. Hokolesqua placed
his hands on his son's shoulders. "My son," he said gently, "the Great Spirit
has seen fit that we should die together and has sent you to that end. It is Her
will, and She will gather us up, so let us submit."

Not inclined to such meek submission, Red Hawk leaped to the fireplace
and quickly scrambled up the chimney. He was no sooner out of sight than

the bolt was thrown and the door yanked open. The gap was immediately filled with a motley mixture of soldiers and frontiersmen armed with rifles. Hokolesqua, one arm over his son's shoulders, faced them without expression.

"By God," exclaimed their leader, Captain John Hall, "it *is* Cornstalk!" He brought his rifle to bear, as did Adam Barnes, Hugh Gailbreath, Malcolm McCoun, and William Roane, along with several others, and a barrage of shooting broke out. Even after Cornstalk and Elinipsico had fallen, others crowded to the door and shot into the bodies.

"Where the hell's the third one?" someone shouted and a search was begun, first up the loft and then the fireplace. The chimney had quickly narrowed and Red Hawk was braced fearfully as high up as he could go. It was not high enough. He kicked at the hands that reached for him but his ankles were grabbed and he was dragged, blackened with soot and shrieking, onto the cabin's hard-packed earthen floor where he was shot, tomahawked, and beaten with clubs and rifle butts until his form was hardly recognizable as human.

Such was the price of Shawnee honor.[139]

[February 8, 1778 — Sunday]

The wrath of the Shawnees at the murder of their principal chief, his son, and his chief attendant reverberated throughout the Shawnee nation. It was an act of war and if it was war the *Shemanese* wanted, they would now get it.

In a special council held in the great *msi-kah-mi-qui* in Chalahgawtha, Chiungalla—Black Fish—was confirmed by acclamation as the new principal chief of the tribe. His first official act in this role, after conferring lengthily with all the chiefs, was to declare that the Shawnee nation was now at war with the Americans. When he vowed immediate vengeance against the *Shemanese*, everyone suspected that this meant an expedition against the Kentucky settlements in the spring, since major expeditions undertaken during winter usually failed due to the hardships of a campaign under severe weather conditions. But when Chiungalla said immediate, he meant just that.

Normally, the Spaylaywitheepi did not freeze during the winter. Its volume and current speed were such that, while it might become a mass of floating platforms of ice broken off from along the shorelines or disgorged at the mouths of its tributaries, the bigger river itself stubbornly refused to freeze. It was only once every six or seven winters that the weather turned cold enough over a prolonged period of time for the Spaylaywitheepi to freeze so solidly that men and even horses could cross on the ice.

This was one of those winters.

Early in the Ice Moon—January—the temperature had plummeted to well below zero and remained there for more than a week. Even when a slight warming trend occurred, if such it could be called, the temperature stayed well below freezing day and night for over a month.

For the Shawnees, it presented an unexpected opportunity. Chiungalla's anger over the death of Hokolesqua was augmented by reports of a regular army having come to the Kentucky settlements. The force had soon gone away, but then returned. The chief decided this winter's solid freezing of the Spaylaywitheepi was an opportunity sent by Moneto Himself for them to check on this force, perhaps even engage it if it seemed weak enough. He called for warriors to join him on this expedition and, though the greater majority of Shawnee men were off at the hunting grounds, enough remained to raise a force of just over a hundred men, and they were joined by a few French traders from the upper Great Miami, including Peter Loramie.[140]

Chiungalla established his semipermanent base camp at a small but well-known salt lick just off the Warrior Trail, about a dozen miles after crossing the Spaylaywitheepi.[141] Had this been a hunting expedition, they would have stayed more to the canelands closer to the Spaylaywitheepi, since that was where the buffalo tended to spend the winter months rather than at the more open country of the licks. With a good camp made, he sent out half a dozen scouting parties of five men each, three of these separate groups led by Chiksika, Wasegoboah, and Blue Jacket. They fanned out in a broad semicircle, each party ranging over its area for a distance of some ten miles from the main camp.

Blue Jacket's party headed generally southwest, zigzagging back and forth across the Warrior Trail as they went, their eyes alternately scanning the snow-covered landscape far ahead for movement and the ground closer to them for any trace of tracks. It had begun snowing fairly hard an hour or so ago, so any tracks seen would be quite fresh. It was not tracks, however, that caught their attention when about three miles from camp.

Far ahead at the edge of a wood a large dark mound could been seen in the new snow and immediately they became intently alert. Blue Jacket led them into the skirt of woodlands close by and they stayed out of sight in its cover as they warily approached the object that had caught their attention. In ten minutes they discovered it to be a cow buffalo that had been killed, the meat dressed out and much of it taken away. There were very fresh tracks heading away toward the southwest.

Through the steadily falling snow, Blue Jacket studied the remains of the buffalo and the tracks briefly and nodded. "One man only," he said. "A single hunter."

"One *horse,* only, Wehyehpihehrsehnwah," corrected one of the warriors with him. "Could be two men on the same horse."

Blue Jacket shook his head. "One man only," he repeated. He pointed at the remains and then at the tracks. "Still plenty of meat on the carcass, but he cut away all his horse could carry, maybe four hundred pounds. He's not even riding, he's leading his horse."

The warrior took a closer look at the hoofprints and then smiled in a chagrined manner and nodded. Not completely obscured by the scuffing hoof-marks were the telltale tracks of a single man leading it.

"He's the hunter for a large party somewhere south of here," Blue Jacket went on. "Otherwise he would not have taken so much that he could not even ride his own horse. Not much snow in the tracks, either, so he can't be very far ahead. We'll try to overtake him before he gets to his camp."

He put his horse into a smart lope and the others followed in single file, the sound of their passage muffled by the hoof-deep snow. They followed the tracks over a knoll, through a woods on the other side and when they emerged from it, two miles or more from the carcass, their quarry was in view no more than a quarter-mile ahead. The horse's back was mounded with a load covered over with part of the buffalo hide and a sort of sling affair had been made to carry more of the meat trussed under the horse's belly.

At Blue Jacket's signal they broke into a gallop and had covered half the remaining distance before the man leading the horse turned and saw them. They could see him immediately jerk at the straps, trying to untie them. Failing, he reached for his knife to cut the thongs in order to dump the load and flee on horseback, but he couldn't seem to get his knife out of its sheath. Not wasting another instant and gripping his rifle in one hand, he raced off afoot.

The loaded horse was moving off at a walk and at a barked command from Blue Jacket as they passed it, one of the warriors veered off, caught up the animal's reins very easily and began following the others. The pursuers, yipping and yelling, were now close enough to send several shots at the running man and, at Blue Jacket's order, deliberately missing him and kicking up snow on either side as a warning for him to stop. When he didn't, Blue Jacket also snapped off a shot. The ball cut through one of the straps of the man's powder horn, leaving it dangling, and the runner, obviously realizing he could not escape, dodged behind a large tree. In a moment he reached around in front of the tree and leaned his rifle against it as a signal of surrender.

Whooping and laughing at their success, the Shawnees galloped up and dismounted. Blue Jacket quickly took the man's gun and ammunition and also discovered why he had been unable to free his mount of its load and try to escape on horseback. The straps he had used to tie the extra amount of meat to his horse's belly were not straps at all but, rather, broad strips of hide he had cut from the fresh buffalo skin and tied into tight knots—too tight to be quickly untied. When the white man had reached for his knife to cut these strips, he found the blade had frozen solidly to the sheath encasing it, and the haft of the knife was so greasy his hand just kept slipping off.

They discovered something else of great significance. The man who had surrendered held up his hand, palm foremost in a peace gesture and said, "How'd'ye do. My name is Dan'l Boone."[142]

The exhilaration that filled Blue Jacket as they took their captive back to Chiungalla's camp at the salt lick was almost too much to be borne. As leader of the party, as well as the one first to see Boone, touch him and disarm him, the credit—and the enormous prestige that must result—for capturing this enemy was Blue Jacket's alone, although custody and disposition of the captive was Chiungalla's, as leader of the expedition.

On the way back to the main camp, Blue Jacket questioned Boone, finding the use of English strange on his tongue after speaking virtually nothing but the Shawnee tongue for over six years and he frequently slipped into Shawnee idioms. This fact alone convinced Boone that Blue Jacket was merely an Indian who had learned English. When Blue Jacket asked where his party was located to which he was bringing the meat, Boone shook his head.

"No party," he said. "I am a hunter for the forts. This meat is for the many soldiers garrisoned now at all three forts."

Blue Jacket considered that this might be true, since the presence of the soldiers was known, but he was inclined to disbelieve, since it was unlikely a hunter was going to walk some forty or fifty miles to the nearest fort, Boonesboro, with a horseload of meat, especially when deer and elk could still be successfully hunted in much closer proximity to the forts.

At the main camp, following the incredible jubilation and awe evoked when Blue Jacket brought in his notorious captive, the truth was learned. Communication was no problem. Not only could Blue Jacket understand and be understood, Boone himself knew a smattering of Shawnee, plus Peter Loramie spoke English and Shawnee as well as French, and a black man named Pompey, who had escaped his white masters and joined the Shawnees was a tolerable interpreter. Finally, Chiungalla himself had learned a fair amount of English long ago from the traders who had stayed for prolonged periods in the Shawnee villages.

Warriors had gathered around to see at close range their legendary foe and to congratulate Blue Jacket on his stupendous achievement. Many came up and shook hands with Boone, including the one named Amaghqua—Captain Will—who, nine years earlier, had captured Boone twice and from whom Boone had once been released and once escaped. Among the Shawnees gathered around was the young warrior named Chiksika, whose party had just come in and who also had news of importance to impart to Chiungalla. They had roved toward Blue Licks and there, unseen, had spied upon a large party of whites—around thirty of them—who were in a semi-permanent camp and busily engaged in making salt.

Boone, who could not quite follow the rapid conversation, was now asked a question by the black Shawnee, Pompey. "My chief wants to know whose men those are at the Pememo."

"Pememo?"

Pompey nodded. "Yes, Pememo—Salt Spring, the big one on the Nepepimmatheepi.[143] The one you call Blue Licks."

Boone was silent a few seconds and then answered the question with a question. "How do you know there are any men there?"

"Our spies," replied Chiungalla for himself, "have been there and they have seen them."

Chiungalla watched Boone carefully and was pleased to see him accept this philosophically and then admit that, yes, they were his men. "We will go there tomorrow," Chiungalla said, "and kill them all."

Boone shook his partially upraised hand in negation. "Does that mean, then, that you have men you can afford to have killed? You will beat them, yes, with as many warriors as you have here, but they are well armed and will take many of you with them. Is this worth such a risk? Can you afford to have any of your warriors killed? Suppose you could have them all—and all that they have—without losing a man? Wouldn't that be better?"

"How could such a thing be accomplished?" asked Chiungalla.

"If you will promise me," Boone replied, "that you will not hurt them, nor make them run the gauntlet, I will go in to them in the morning and make them surrender themselves to you. They would be worth very much to you to sell as prisoners of war to your friends, the British, at Detroit."

Chiungalla pondered this a moment. The object of this expedition was retaliation for the murder of Hokolesqua, but what the man Boone was saying made sense. The Shawnees needed the aid of the British for a truly major offensive, which could not be undertaken until midsummer at the earliest. With the equipment and goods they could get by capturing this large party of salt makers, plus the reward they would get by surrendering the prisoners to Governor Hamilton in Detroit, they could prepare themselves for an offensive that would have every likelihood of crushing the Kentucky settlements.

The chief looked at Boone and then slowly nodded. "It is so agreed," he said, then added darkly, "but if you do not do as you say, or they refuse to do as you bid, then all will die—some in the gunfire as we fight and, for those who survive that, including you, death by torture, which is much worse."

"They will surrender, Black Fish," Boone said quietly, meaning it.

At close to noon the following day, the majority of the Indians arrived with Boone on the hill overlooking the salt spring. It was Sunday and no work was going on, the twenty-seven men in camp merely lazing about and some lying on their blankets atop the five or six inches of new snow of the previous day and soaking up the bright midday sun.[144] Not until the Indians had positioned themselves all around the camp unseen was Boone permitted to call out to them, explain that they were surrounded by Indians four times their own number and must surrender or be killed. Boone explained that he had received promises from the Indians that they would be well treated if they surrendered and neither tortured nor killed.

They surrendered and Chiungalla, by force of his will alone, managed to keep his warriors from exacting their vengeance for Hokolesqua upon them. That, he told them, would come a little later. What they would do now would pave the way to that end. With so many prisoners to oversee and the plunder acquired and needing to be carried—axes, kettles, tools, guns, food supplies, and salt already rendered—it was no longer practical to move against the settlements. He immediately turned the expedition back toward the Spaylay-witheepi and Chalahgawtha.

And, in honor of his great achievement in capturing Daniel Boone, Blue Jacket was permitted to ride beside Chiungalla at the head of the procession, all the way back to Chalahgawtha.[145]

[May 25, 1778 — Sunday]

Tecumseh was both excited and depressed; excited at the swirl of events occurring in and around Chalahgawtha and depressed because, due to his age, he was being largely excluded from the majority of it. All the boys of the huge village were agog with the war fever gripping the nation and Tecumseh was no exception. He so yearned to become a true warrior in his own right that it was almost a physical pain. His great fear was that the war would be all settled before he was able to become truly active as a warrior. Unlike the other boys, he was not satisfied in simply participating as a striker in the exciting gauntlet lines when prisoners were brought to the village.

In recent weeks a great influx had occurred in the number of prisoners being brought to Chalahgawtha. The majority of these, after being made to run the gauntlet, were sold to the British at Detroit. Some were adopted into families of Shawnees who took a special shine to them or who, in the Shawnee way, wanted an adopted son or daughter to take the place of a warrior in the family who had been killed. Now and again certain of the prisoners, deemed deserving of such a fate, were tortured to death in a diabolical manner.

In this latter respect, it bothered Tecumseh considerably, even touching him with a sense of guilt, that he so intensely disliked the atrocities perpetrated on some of the captives who had become marked for such a fate. Their prolonged agonies resulting from the variety of tortures they underwent, usually ending in being horribly burned at the stake, filled him with a sickening revulsion. While virtually everyone else hooted and howled and reacted with great glee at the plight of the prisoners and did all in their power to increase their agonies, Tecumseh held back and often went to Tecumapese and sat in the wegiwa with her, since she seemed to be the only other person in the village who shared or understood his feelings.

"You are only ten, Tecumseh," she told him, even while distant screams from the tortured could be heard, "and while you are a very brave boy, you are also sensitive, and it is hard for you to understand this. All throughout the history of our people it has been our tradition to torture prisoners who, because of the bad things they have done or because of circumstances, have been judged to deserve such treatment. It is said that by our doing this, the courage of the prisoner, as he dies, is taken into ourselves. Others may believe this, but I do not. I have never felt any braver because I watched a helpless prisoner die. While there are many Shawnee women and children who take part in these things, I do not, and there are a certain number of others like myself, and like you, who do not. And I have heard it said by other wives that many of the warriors do this not because they like it but because it is traditional to do so and they feel bound by those tribal traditions to participate."

"When I see it happen," Tecumseh admitted, "I want to shout at the others to stop, but I know they wouldn't and so all I can do then is take myself away. This makes me feel bad because I know I am expected to participate along with the others."

"The older you get, Tecumseh," Tecumapese said gently, hugging him close to her, "the more you will make your own decisions. In this, as in all other things throughout your life, you must do what your heart tells you is right, not what others tell you is expected."

The increase of prisoners being brought to Chalahgawtha had its onset just after the middle of the last Hunger Moon and Tecumseh had been on hand with all the others to welcome their chief and his returning warriors with all their plunder and prisoners. Word had swiftly gone through the village at the amazing feat Blue Jacket had accomplished with his capture of the famed Boone, word that just as swiftly spread to all the other Shawnee villages. There was disappointment among many, however, that the twenty-eight prisoners were not to run the gauntlet and none were to be tortured to death, but Tecumseh had been glad that such was the case.

Shortly after their arrival back here, Chiungalla, with a guard of forty warriors, escorted eleven of the prisoners to Detroit to sell them to the British. Boone was among those prisoners taken and Tecumseh thought they had seen the last of him, but when Chiungalla and his warriors returned six or seven weeks later, Boone returned with them. Chiungalla had taken a great liking to the captive on the trip from the Blue Licks to Chalahgawtha and this only increased during the trip to Detroit. By the time they reached there, though the British were very desirous of buying Boone, Chiungalla would not sell and announced his intention of adopting Boone into his family as his own son.[146]

While in Detroit, Chiungalla, on behalf of his tribe, formally accepted a war belt from Governor Hamilton and had lengthy discussions with him concerning the major invasion the Shawnees wanted to make this coming summer against the Kentucky settlements to once and for all destroy them. Hamilton had been much in favor of this and promised the support of the British in arms and ammunition and perhaps even soldiers and artillery with which to level the Kentucky forts. Such an invasion, however, could not possibly begin before August, at which time the British would rendezvous with the Shawnees on the Miami and go from there against the Kentucky settlements.

On his return, Chiungalla went far out of his way to visit the Wyandots at both Upper and Lower Sandusky and solicit their help in the campaign, then on to the villages of the Mingoes and Delawares in the valleys of the Huron and Sandusky rivers for the same purpose, then striking the headwaters of the Scioto and coming home by way of the Scioto villages at the Pickaway Plains. The Wyandots had been less than enthusiastic over the idea and had made no final commitment of warriors to the project. The Mingoes and Delawares were interested, but were so busy fighting off the incursions of whites from the upper Spaylaywitheepi that they could not promise for certain that they could or would supply warriors to meet at the planned rendezvous.

The presence of Boone with Chiungalla, as well as Blue Jacket, created great interest and Indians had come from miles in all directions to see them— to stand in awed contemplation before the frontiersman who had so often thwarted them, tricked them and outwitted them, and to gaze with unfeigned admiration at the captor, at this great young warrior, Blue Jacket, whose prestige had by now risen to such heights that his name was on the lips of every Indian in the West and Northwest.

The adoption of Boone into the family of Chiungalla was a festive affair that took place soon after their return to the village, in conjunction with several other adoptions, including another of the salt makers whom Chiungalla had decided to keep and adopt, Benjamin Kelly.[147] Boone was given the new name of Sheltowee, meaning Big Turtle, and from this point forward it was by this name that Chiungalla addressed him, though many of the other Shawnees still called him Boone.

Chiungalla had not remained in Chalahgawtha very long before he set off on a new expedition against the *Shemanese*—this time late in the Rain Moon and leading four hundred warriors, all Shawnees, from various villages on the

two Miami rivers, and the Mad and the Scioto, and this time very determined
to exact the deferred revenge for the murders of Hokolesqua and his two
companions. Aptly enough, the spearhead of the invasion was directed against
Fort Randolph at the mouth of the Kanawha, where the three Shawnees had
been killed.

At Chiungalla's direction a large portion of the warriors spread out in a
great semicircle on the south side of the Spaylaywitheepi, with Fort Randolph
as the core of its radius. Those well out from the fort attacked all settlements,
camps and isolated cabins they encountered and a great many settlers new to
the area were slain, their property taken, livestock killed and horses confiscated.
Those close to Fort Randolph at Point Pleasant attacked it with strength and
determination, but the defenses of the place had been greatly strengthened
following Hokolesqua's death, anticipating just such a retaliatory strike, and
these defenses held. A few individuals were killed on either side, but except
for bottling up the fort, little was accomplished and, after two weeks Chiungalla withdrew.

Having been thwarted at the fort, the rage of the Shawnees was fueled
by the fires of frustration and so now Chiungalla broke them into individual
small war parties with orders to swiftly range far and wide throughout the
entire Allegheny mountains frontier. They were to move swiftly and hit hard,
killing or capturing all whites encountered, being ever watchful on their back
trail for pursuit, taking all the plunder they could carry or load upon the horses
they found, and what they could not carry was to be destroyed. They were
to stay out so long as provisions and strength lasted, or until they had so much
plunder or captives that return was necessary, with instructions to all that in
any case they were to return by the end of the Heat Moon—July—to participate, with British help, in the invasion of Kentucky. Chiungalla himself was
returning immediately to Chalahgawtha to prepare for that invasion.

Practically overnight a wave of killing and property destruction swept
across the frontiers of Virginia and Pennsylvania such as had never before been
witnessed. Scores of whites were killed, then hundreds—rarely more than
eight or ten at a time—all over this broad sickle-shaped frontier. Like packs
of ravening wolves, these parties roved up the river valleys—up the Great and
Little Kanawhas, the Big Sandy and the New and the Greenbrier, the Monongahela and Allegheny and Youghiogheny, the Cheat and Kiskiminetas,
the Conemaugh and Loyalhanna, the Tug and the Elk and the Buckhannon,
and even into the great valleys of the Shenandoah and Susquehanna, now well
dotted with long-established farms.

Learning of the successes of this fiercely raging swarm of Shawnee war
parties, other tribes began to join in the general onslaught—Wyandots and
Delawares, Kickapoos and Potawatomies, Ottawas and Chippewas, and even
many of the Senecas. The war fever even touched the Iroquois and, enflamed

by British and Tories, a body of three hundred fifty warriors under the Mohawk Chief Thayendanegea—Joseph Brant—they fell upon the valley of the Cobbleskill some forty-five miles southwest of Albany and devastated it. In addition to many farm families, twenty-two Continentals, including their commander, were killed and scalped.

It was while most of the warriors were away on such raids that the commander at Fort Pitt, General Edward Hand, led a ragtag army of four hundred men out of the fort and into the Ohio wilderness on what he termed a "punitive expedition" meant to cow the unruly Indians and to capture a reported British and Indian supply depot on the Cuyahoga River. They marched all the way to the Tuscarawas without encountering anyone and Hand, growing more fearful by the moment, finally turned back without ever having reached his objective or even the Cuyahoga River. On their return they came upon a camp of Delawares less than fifty miles from Fort Pitt, all the men off on their winter's hunt. The camp was attacked at Hand's orders and they killed a small boy, two women and an old man and captured two other squaws. By the time they reached the safety of Fort Pitt again, Hand's cowardice was on everyone's lips and his abortive expedition already disparagingly being called the Squaw Campaign, so embarrassing Hand that he eventually resigned his western command and took post in the East. Before he did so, however, and only a fortnight after the abortive campaign ended, Alexander McKee and Matthew Elliott at Fort Pitt, along with the American interpreter there, Simon Girty, disgusted with the American army, defected to the British. Girty's brother, George, who had become a lieutenant in the Continental Army, heard the news of this and deserted from the army to join them. They all entered into British service in Detroit, in the Indian Department, where McKee was now in charge of that department and Simon Girty was serving as interpreter at two dollars per day. For the Shawnees, however, Hand's campaign served a good purpose; it brought the white threat virtually to the very doorstep of the Wyandots and now, realizing their own vulnerability and how great a threat the whites were to them, they were resolved to thwart any further incursions into their territory south of the Lake Erie shore.

With the return of the Shawnee war parties came scores of prisoners, men, women and children, some for sale to the British, some for adoption and many, as Tecumseh had feared, to suffer such long and agonizing tortures that they begged their captors to kill them and end their misery.

Among the earliest of the war parties to return to Chalahgawtha with captives, arriving near the end of the Planting Moon, was the one that had been placed under command of Chiksika, with Wasegoboah as second in command. Tecumseh, who was out at the eastern edge of the village, practicing with the new and much better bow he had built, was first to see them coming and he raced into the village spreading word of their approach. He ran directly to the wegiwa of Chiungalla and to the chief's quarters inside. As Chiungalla arose to go out to greet them, Tecumseh darted to his quarters at the other end of the huge wegiwa.

"Tecumapese!" he said, giving her a start. "Come on! Chiksika's war party is back. He's brought two captives that they caught. They're girls. Two young girls."

Tecumapese looked sharply at her brother. "You said Chiksika. What about Wasegoboah? Isn't he with them?"

"Oh, yes, he's with them. Come on!"

He tossed his bow and quiver onto his sleep mat and raced out, missing the look of relief that flooded Tecumapese's features at learning of Wasego-boah's return. Smiling, she put down the buckskin leggins she had been work-ing on and, with three-year-old Spemica Lawba, followed him out of the wegiwa, joined outside by her youngest brothers, the seven-year-old triplets, who had come running up from wherever they had been playing. Together they joined Tecumseh who was now standing close to Chiungalla near the council house.

Chiksika and Wasegoboah and the other five members of their party cantered up and stopped. The party had been followed by a noisy collection of yapping dogs, excited children, and quite a large portion of the town's remaining adult population. The two leaders of the party each had a small girl riding in front of him. They slid easily off their mounts and lowered the two wide-eyed girls to the ground. There was much laughter when the pair raced into each other's arms and stood fearfully together.

Chiungalla held up a hand, stilling the crowd, then welcoming the war-riors in their return and congratulating them for their evident successes. Swiftly Chiksika and Wasegoboah, with much good-natured interruption of each other and occasional interjections by others of the party, related their experiences.

Their own particular war party, initially twelve war-painted braves in six small canoes, had set off up the Kanawhatheepi, slightly miffed because three other parties had already preceded them up this stream and were out of sight. They paddled until dusk and then put ashore and made camp, resuming their journey at dawn. It was well into the afternoon when Chiksika, in the lead canoe abruptly raised a hand and the paddlers instantly froze. The canoes slowed and then began a drift back downstream with the current. Chiksika had partially raised himself and sniffed the air. A vagrant waft of breeze had brought a momentary scent of woodsmoke to his nostrils. It was gone as quickly as it had come but then another zephyr brought the scent again and his eyes scanned the eastern shoreline for its source. There had been no sign of visible smoke or habitation, but on the shoreline here was the mouth of an insignificant little feeder creek entering the river and Chiksika motioned for the party to maintain silence and put into it.

They slid into the mouth of the stream, which was fairly wide here but quickly narrowed where it made a sharp bend to the left only a few hundred yards upstream. They moved to this bend and eased around it, only to draw back immediately and put ashore at Chiksika's signals. He had seen a substantial cabin on a broad grassy bench twenty feet above the level of the stream.[148]

The warriors quickly spread out in the woods between themselves and the cabin and cautiously advanced. They saw two young girls, carrying a heavy wooden bucket between them, and a young man of about sixteen emerge from the cabin and talk for a moment. Then the young man went to a small corral and began mending a break in the rail fencing. The girls came closer to where Chiksika and Wasegoboah were hidden behind a screen of brush, walked directly to a sty and, with some grunting, began dumping slops into the hog trough.[149] It was at that moment that Chiksika and Wasegoboah had leaped from cover and snatched the girls from behind. Chiksika had managed to clap his hand over the mouth of the one, but Wasegoboah was not as fortunate and the girl in his grasp let out a chilling scream of mortal terror.

Instantly the pair had raced with their captives into the nearby heavier woods while, at the same time, more of their party emerged closer to the cabin and rushed upon it. Chiksika and Wasegoboah glimpsed a woman who had appeared in the doorway of the cabin, but then the woods closed in behind them and the two Shawnees continued their run toward where the canoes were beached, hearing the sound of a scream and shots behind them. The frightened girls, the younger one crying uncontrollably, were made to sit on the ground and were tightly bound at wrists and ankles. Chiksika stayed with them while Wasegoboah raced off.

Wasegoboah, returning to the cabin, found that the woman they had momentarily seen at the cabin door now lay on the ground seventy feet from the cabin, apparently dead, her head bloody and scalp gone. The young man who had been repairing the fence had somehow gotten into the cabin and was firing so frequently he evidently had two or more rifles. The warriors had taken cover and were occasionally shooting at the cabin but not risking exposure. Wasegoboah crept up behind the structure, tomahawk in hand, and sidled around until he could see the partially opened door with a rifle barrel protruding from it. The instant the gun was fired, the Shawnee leaped to the door, slammed his way in and grappled with the young man. Rolling and struggling, they fought their way to the outside, where Wasegoboah finally managed to sink his tomahawk into his opponent's neck, severely wounding him. The young white scrambled to his feet and managed to stagger a half dozen yards more before collapsing. Wasegoboah rushed up and dispatched him with a second tomahawk blow to the temple, then dropped to one knee, drew his knife and scalped him.

While this was occurring, other warriors entered the house and discovered two more girls, one younger and one older than the two who had been captured. The older girl fought them with an axe and wounded one of the warriors, but she was overcome and killed, as was the smaller one. Both were scalped.

By now more warriors had rushed up and, as Wasegoboah backed away with the scalp, three pounced upon the young man's body, stripped it of clothing and then hacked off the head with their tomahawks and kicked it a dozen feet away. The warriors inside the cabin were busy ransacking the place, setting aside anything of value that they wanted to take and dousing the entire interior of the cabin with lamp oil prior to setting it afire.

The terror of the two girl prisoners was magnified when Wasegoboah and the warriors who had taken the scalps of their mother, brother and sisters came near and shook the bloody hairpieces triumphantly in the air until Chiksika told them to stop and gave the order for the party to load all the plunder they could carry into the canoes and they would head for home. In under two hours from the first moment of their attack, having set the place on fire, they were on their way again, the canoes heavily laden with goods, themselves and their two captives. The one wounded warrior, who had been struck with the axe wielded by the older girl, was not severely injured and the wound had been bound up. It would soon heal and, all in all, they had had a very brief but quite successful campaign.[150]

Their return had been uneventful. They reached the Spaylaywitheepi without incident and made good time going down that stream, then paddled leisurely up the Sciototheepi until reaching Kispoko Town on the fourth day after the attack.[151] The captive girls were treated well there, but they were very much afraid of the Indians who thronged around them, touching their hair and clothing. They cringed from the burly, ugly Shemeneto when he strode up to them, but after looking at them without expression for a moment he suddenly grinned lopsidedly and the girls relaxed and, after a second or two, even smiled back. Shemeneto had laughed aloud and pointed at Margaret's blond hair and said, *"Matchsquathi Kisathoi."* Then he pointed at Elizabeth's dark hair and said, *"Matchsquathi Tebethto."*

At that everyone had laughed, clapped their hands and nodded in agreement. Seven members of the war party had remained in Kispoko Town and the remainder traded their canoes for seven horses—five to ride, two to carry plunder—and had ridden the remainder of the distance to Chalahgawtha, and here they were.

Now, with the two girls standing before him and obviously still a bit nervous but not really showing fear any longer, Chiungalla walked over and squatted in front of them. His smile was benevolent and it was plain to see that the girls were impressed equally with his presence and his garb. He wore beaded moccasins and fine doeskin leggins and a scarlet blanket hung over his shoulders. A string of upcurved bear claws was around his neck, each claw separated by inch-long cylinders of beaten silver, and his shoulder-length graying hair was unbound.

The sisters were taken considerably aback when he spoke to them in reasonably good English, his voice deep and warm and reassuring. "You have had a difficult time," he said, "and you are afraid, but you need not fear. We will not harm you. Since your family is no more, you will have a new family here. When you have rested and eaten, you will be taken to the river by the women and there your white blood will be washed away and you will be given new clothes and adopted. Since you were taken by Chiksika's party and Chiksika is my ward, you become a part of my family—the family of Chiungalla, the one you whites call Black Fish. You will be my adopted daughters. These," he indicated Pucksinwah's family, "will be your sister and brothers."

He pointed to the leader of the war party. "This one is Chiksika, who will be your eldest brother. Your sister," he inclined his head toward the attractive twenty-year-old woman, "is Tecumapese, who has with her your nephew, Spemica Lawba, who is three. This," he reached out and placed a hand on Tecumseh's shoulder, "is your brother, Tecumseh, who is about to enter his eleventh summer. And these, all of seven summers in the same birth, are your youngest brothers, Sauwaseekau, Lowawluwaysica and Kumskaka."

The older girl made a small curtsy and said in a firm voice showing no trace of fear, "My name is Margaret McKinzie and I am entering my eleventh summer. This is my sister, Elizabeth, who has eight summers."

Chiungalla shook his head and made a negative sound. "No," he replied. "Those are no longer your names. I am told Shemeneto has already given you new names. You are the fair one who smiles much, and so you are *Matchsquathi Kisathoi.*" He dipped his head toward the younger one and favored her with a smile. "This one who is dark and who smiles less is *Matchsquathi Tebethto.*"[152]

"Thank you," Margaret responded politely. "They are pretty names, but I do not know their meaning."

Chiungalla smiled. "*Matchsquathi Kisathoi* and *Matchsquathi Tebethto,*" he explained, "mean Little Sun and Little Moon."

Both girls smiled, pleased, and the surrounding crowd laughed and clapped their hands and chattered enthusiastically. Tecumseh took a step closer and touched Chiungalla's arm, who turned to face the boy inquiringly.

"Father," Tecumseh said, "please tell them that I will teach them Shawnee if they will teach me English."

Chiungalla grinned and relayed the remark in English and both Little Moon and Little Sun looked at Tecumseh somewhat shyly and then nodded.

[June 16, 1778 — Tuesday]

Sheltowee—Daniel Boone—had adapted well into his new Shawnee life as Chiungalla's adopted son and the principal chief was proud of him, proud of having so highly skilled a woodsman as part of his family. But, despite his pride, he had certain reservations about the sincerity of Sheltowee in fully accepting this new life. There was a thread of concern deep in his mind that Sheltowee, if given the opportunity, would run off and try to make it back to Kentucky to resume his life with the whites.

So strong was this feeling in Chiungalla initially that on several occasions secret watchers were posted and then Sheltowee left on his own to do one task or another, affording him that opportunity to make his break, if such was his intent. One such occasion came when Sheltowee came to him and asked if he could hobble his horse out in the prairie.

"Yes," Chiungalla replied, "after a little while." Chiungalla had then left him and posted several warriors out in the prairie to lie in the deep grass with their rifles and watch Sheltowee, and if he made any effort to leap on his horse and ride off, they were to shoot him. Then Chiungalla, about half an hour later, returned to his adopted son and told him to go ahead and do with his horse as he had requested.

Sheltowee led his horse out onto the prairie and for just an instant his eye caught the reflection of sunlight off a gunbarrel in the grass. He pretended not to have seen anything, casually hobbled his horse and then walked back toward the village, whistling a lilting tune as he went. This happened two or three times and Chiungalla was very pleased that Sheltowee not only had never shown any inclination to try to get away, but appeared not even to have considered such a prospect. So, in these over three moons that Sheltowee had been with them, Chiungalla had gradually eased off the restrictions.

His pride in Boone was engendered not only by the unfailing good humor of Sheltowee but as well in the speed with which the man had learned to converse with reasonable fluency in the Shawnee tongue and the remarkable dexterity he showed in the games, sports and competitions that were held. He was not the best wrestler at Chalahgawtha, but there were only a few who could pin him in their matches. In foot races he was very fleet and only a few of the Indians could beat him in a sprint and none in runs of a mile or more. In shooting at a mark, Sheltowee often lost, but Chiungalla was certain that he lost deliberately so as not to arouse jealousy in others. The chief was rightly convinced that in rifle marksmanship, his adopted son had no peer among his

Shawnee brothers; not only could he shoot well from a simple standing position, but even while on the run he rarely missed his mark. The warriors stood in awe of his ability to reload and fire while running, which none of them could emulate.[153] His keen hearing and eyesight were especially attuned to the woodlands and able to detect very quickly any movement or sound that was unusual. He took great amusement out of it when a practical joke was successfully perpetrated on him and was ingenious in devising such jokes to play on others, which were not always received with good grace by the victim but engendered much merriment among onlookers.

Through all this time he was with them, Boone was aware of the war planning going on and especially of the major offensive that was soon to be launched against Boonesboro. Some four hundred and fifty warriors had already gathered at Chalahgawtha and more were coming all the time. A sense of excitement was growing among them all and Boone realized it could not be long before their campaign began. When he had all the information about it he could get and the time was drawing near for the expedition to begin, he set about making final escape plans.

Nine days ago, when Chiksika, Wasegoboah and Blue Jacket were all away on raiding parties, he had been taken along with Chiungalla and his family, including Tecumseh and a number of warriors, to a salt lick on the bank of the Scioto some forty miles upstream from Kispoko Town.[154] They had spent three days making salt and had traveled two days on their way back to Chalahgawtha, Sheltowee's horse loaded with brass kettles, when they flushed a flock of turkeys, which flew to a distant grove of trees. Chiungalla, Tecumseh and the warriors galloped away after them, leaving Sheltowee with the women and children.

Deciding on the spur of the moment that he'd never have a better opportunity, Boone waited until the men disappeared into the woods and he began hearing shots, then took out his knife and cut the cords binding the kettles to his horse. They fell with a clatter and Chiungalla's wife ran up.[155]

"What are you doing, Sheltowee?" she demanded.

"Mother," Boone answered, "I am going home to see my wife."

"Oh, you must not! Chiungalla will be very angry."

She reached for the reins, but Boone pulled the horse away and broke into a gallop southward. Behind him he could hear Chiungalla's wife shrieking, but he was soon beyond hearing.

Chiungalla and the others came thundering back at her cries and quickly learned what had happened. The chief sent out six warriors to follow, and they trailed him for some distance but then came back. "He will get lost," one of them remarked hopefully to his chief.

Chiungalla shook his head sadly. "No, Sheltowee will not get lost. And we will not catch him. He knows he will die at the stake if we catch him again. No," he repeated, "we will not catch him. Sheltowee showed us only a little of what he is capable of doing."

"Then we will not see him again, father?" Tecumseh spoke up.

"I think we will see him again," Chiungalla replied slowly, "but only as an enemy, not as a son or brother. We will see him when we attack Boonesboro, which will be very soon."[156]

Chapter 3

— 《 》 —   Never before had Tecumseh seen Chiungalla so filled with rage and frustration as was the case now. If there had been one great lesson to be learned over these past weeks, the Shawnee principal chief had learned it only too well: the difference between the war-making techniques of the Shawnees and the British were so far apart that any effort to try to combine them became a self-defeating hurdle. It was a lesson that Tecumseh shared as well, since this was the first major Indian offensive in which he had been allowed to participate.

For all the buildup and preparation that had been involved in the operation, the final results could only be described as disappointing at best and, more appropriately, a fiasco. Chiungalla blamed himself as much as he blamed the whites who had accompanied the expedition; himself for acquiescing to their suggestions and demands and them for the fundamental stupidity of their ideas of how the campaign should be executed.

The foremost target of the invasion was Boonesboro. Not only was it the closest of the three remaining forts of the *Shemanese* in the Kentucky country, a more personal element had become involved with the escape of Sheltowee. A smoldering anger burned in the breast of Chiungalla for the manner in which his adopted son had betrayed confidence and trust. There were those among his people who insisted that Sheltowee had perished in the woods—that he could not possibly have made it back alone through a wilderness never before seen, but Chiungalla did not for an instant believe such arguments. He longed to recapture Sheltowee and make him pay the final price for his perfidy.

Tecumseh had been very concerned that, because of the panic that had gripped him a year ago on his first inclusion in a war party, a stigma had been attached to him and that it would be a long time, perhaps three or four more years, before he would again be included in any such venture. He was surprised, pleased and profoundly grateful, therefore, when Chiungalla had offhandedly announced that Tecumseh was to accompany this major expedition for the valuable experience it would give him. He must, however, Chiungalla warned, stay close to his brother and obey Chiksika implicitly. The only other young boys who had been included were several who were in their thirteenth or fourteenth summer. Quite a few other ten-year-olds looked on enviously as Tecumseh rode out with the party of four hundred forty warriors toward the rendezvous with the British on the Great Miami.

As they rode, Tecumseh and Chiksika talked of how much they missed Blue Jacket and wished he were along with them on this expedition. At the moment he was off leading raids against settlers in the area of Wheeling and Yellow Creek. That, however, was not what had taken him away from Chalahgawtha. A few months ago Weebinebe—Coldwater—the tribe's number one war chief under Shemeneto, had been killed by the fierce white rangers now making regular patrols through the upper Ohio River region. It was a tragic loss, and it was Shemeneto himself who had come to Chalahgawtha several months ago and asked Blue Jacket if he would accept the now vacant position as the tribe's second war chief. Blue Jacket was honored and had accepted with alacrity. Not unexpectedly, he had moved to Kispoko Town and, since then continued to increase his prestige in the tribe with the daring raids he led against the whites. But both Tecumseh and Chiksika—especially the latter, since the two had been such close friends—greatly missed his sharing their household. They had seen him only once since he left Chalahgawtha.

The rendezvous the brothers were now approaching, where the Mad River emptied into the Great Miami, was almost exactly on the spot where Chiksika's little war party had been ambushed last year, and Tecumseh had felt a resurgence of the shame he experienced on that occasion at having panicked. Chiksika, however, made no mention of it. There were other things to occupy their attention, not the least of which was that the rendezvous had been Chiungalla's first real disappointment of the campaign. Instead of being met with a small but respectable army of British soldiers equipped with fine weapons

including the great thunder guns that could blow apart the Kentucky fortifications, all that Governor Hamilton had sent from Detroit were thirteen men.
They included their commander, Captain Isador Chaine, who was half Wyandot, and his second in command, a French captain in the British service named
Duquesne, plus eleven men. Their rifles were only adequate, certainly not
much better than what the Shawnees had, and they had brought no artillery.

The second disappointment and perhaps the most crucial error of the
campaign occurred when they reached Blue Licks late in the afternoon on
Saturday, September 5. They had not been detected and Chiungalla's spies
had come in with encouraging intelligence: not only had Boonesboro become
lax in its preparedness for possible attack, with very often the main gate wide
open all day while residents went out to care for their gardens and cattle, but
a large percentage of its defenders, twenty-nine men, had ridden out under
Sheltowee some time ago and, though ten had come back, Sheltowee and the
others were still gone.[157] While Chiungalla had hoped to kill or capture Sheltowee, the able frontiersman's absence could be an advantage for the Shawnees.
Without his leadership or the support of his twenty men, the Boonesboro
defenders could not fight effectively and would undoubtedly make mistakes
Sheltowee would have avoided. It therefore became extremely important
to reach Boonesboro quickly and strike with complete surprise, perhaps
even gaining access through the main gate before it could be closed against
them.

The whites with Chiungalla's party, however, demurred. Captain Chaine
said his men were weary, needed rest and meant to have it, here at Blue Licks.
Further, they didn't want to attack the next day, either, since it was Sunday
and they had strong feelings against attacking on their Sabbath. Chiungalla
made the error of acceding to their argument.

"I would not," he had told them, "have you offend your God and so I
will tell my warriors they must rest here until the morrow has passed. On
the day after, we will begin our march against the fort of Sheltowee."[158]

On the following Monday, Chiungalla's force covered the remaining near
fifty miles to Boonesboro and were met by his spies who told him, to the
chagrin of all, that the Boone party had returned the preceding day, that the
fort had been shut tight against them and no less than fifty men were inside
to defend the place. At this news Chiungalla was for immediately canceling
the proposed strike against Boonesboro and instead hitting either Harrodsburg
or Logan's Fort, neither of which, so far as they knew, had any inkling of the
Shawnee presence. Once again he allowed himself to be argued out of this
decision by Captains Chaine and Duquesne, who were sure that if Chiungalla's
force surrounded Boonesboro and the next morning talked to its defender
under a flag, they could convince them that they were hopelessly outnumbered

and must surrender themselves and their fort or die. Though Chiungalla doubted it, he reluctantly agreed. That, Tecumseh realized now, had been the second major error.

Early next morning the Shawnees had surrounded the fort and Captains Chaine and Duquesne approached under a white flag. Guarded by six riflemen who remained at the gate and numerous others overlooking the wall above them, Boone came out alone and met them twenty yards from the fort. In a short while the two captains returned, smiling smugly, saying the ultimatum was delivered and the whites were evidently much afraid, especially at the threat that if they resisted their women and children would be massacred; that they did not wish blood spilled, and asked only for a delay until evening to discuss the matter among themselves, which the two British captains had granted. They were fully confident that, come evening, the entire fort would be theirs. Chiungalla, not believing this for an instant, stifled his rising anger. He commented to his chiefs that soldiers had strange ways of waging war and he would make some preparations of his own for the evening.

At the appointed time the two British officers, accompanied by Chiungalla, Catahecassa, Moluntha, Shemeneto, Wesecahnay, and fifteen other chiefs, all unarmed, strode into the far end of the clearing and began walking toward the fort. When sixty yards from the gate, the Indians stopped and the officers continued. Once again Boone came out to meet them, this time saying he thought their idea of his people surrendering was ridiculous and that they were determined to defend the fort so long as there was a soul inside who could still fire a gun.

Taken aback at the response, the officers moved a little distance away for a whispered conversation, then returned to Boone. "We do not wish you any harm here, Captain Boone," Chaine said. "We have a letter here from Governor Hamilton." He nodded to Duquesne who took out the letter and read aloud its proposal of the most favorable terms of surrender, provided the garrison would return to Detroit with the king's officers.

"Our orders from Governor Hamilton," Chaine added, after Duquesne finished, "were to take you people captive, not destroy you. Since you are determined to make this impossible, then we are authorized to offer a treaty of nonaggression between us."

"We'll agree to that," Boone replied promptly.

"Excellent," Chaine said, smiling cordially. "Such a treaty should be signed by the ten leading men of this fort—yourself and nine others. Captain Duquesne and I will sign the agreement as well, plus ten of the leading chiefs who are awaiting us there." He pointed. "Once the paper has been signed, we will have Chief Black Fish withdraw his forces."

Boone had nodded and returned to the fort. Within five minutes he returned, followed by nine men, all unarmed, joined the two officers and together they walked to where Chiungalla was waiting with his entourage. Behind them the gates of the fort were closed and its portholes and parapets bristled with guns. Chiungalla's expression was stony as they neared, but Boone seemed not to notice and walked up to him with a broad smile and shook his hand. "It is good to see you again, father," he said in Shawnee, "though the circumstances might be better."

"That is true, Sheltowee. It was a bad thing for you to do, to run off from us as you did. But that matter is past. Now we are here to sign the paper Captain Chaine has made out." He nodded to Chaine who took out the paper, unfolded it and handed it to Boone, along with a freshly dipped quill.

Boone barely glanced at it and then signed it on the top line of the broad signature spaces left at the bottom. One by one, with Duquesne dipping the quill between each signature into the small inkpot he held, the other nine whites signed their names.[159] Then Chiungalla and nine of his chiefs in succession made their marks on the paper. The paper and quill were returned to Chaine and then Shemeneto spoke up, saying that to make it binding, it was the custom for two Indians to shake the hands of every white man who had signed the treaty. Immediately two Shawnees approached each of the whites, hands extended, each preparing to take one of the white man's hands in both of his own. Forgetting that Boone understood the Shawnee tongue, Catahecassa—Black Hoof—said to the other Indians in a conversational tone, "Remember, as soon as you have their hands in your own, seize them tight and hold them." As Chiungalla took one of Boone's hands, the frontiersman spun and threw his adopted father to the ground and shouted, "Run for it! *Now!*"

In that instant all the whites were grappling with what few Indians had managed to snatch their hands. Boone ducked away from a tomahawk blow, throwing up a hand to ward it off. It struck the new leather hat he was wearing and slightly injured his head, and then his back, but it was largely just a glancing blow. He successfully jerked loose and raced for the fort, shouting for the gate to be opened. For a moment the Indians were shocked at seeing their chief down, thinking he had been shot by the rifles that had immediately barked from the fort. A number of the Indians who had emerged from the woods at a run were downed under the fusillade. Shemeneto, after a moment, cried out an order to shoot and a scattering of balls began kicking up the dirt close to the whites as they fled. A ball went through the shoulder of one of the men, but all ten had darted into the fort and the gate was closed and barred.[160]

With that a general firing had broken out on both sides. A small number of whites and a black slave were killed and a larger number of Shawnees. An attempt was made by Chiungalla's men to dig a tunnel into the fort, but this work was given up after a great deal of hard labor and more Shawnee deaths from sharpshooters in the fort. The firing had continued sporadically with only moderate effect for two more days and on the third night the disgruntled Chiungalla, favoring his right leg where a lead ball had furrowed deeply across his calf, announced that he was going to start home with about half the Indians, telling the remainder to stay and keep the whites in the fort occupied, but little by little over the ensuing days, for other parties to follow and come home.[161]

The siege of Boonesboro lasted for six additional days—a total of nine days—and at the end of that time, all the Shawnees had withdrawn. Tecumseh had been in the first large group that had gone away with Chiungalla and his incompetent British allies. When they parted with the latter at the same place where they had initially rendezvoused, Chiungalla sent the British on their way with an escort to Detroit, instructing the leader of that escort, a subchief named Coonahaw, to meet with Alexander McKee when he got there and explain how the British aid that had been sent was not only ineffective but decidedly detrimental. He was to ask McKee to relay this information to Governor Hamilton, along with assurances that the Shawnees were far from finished with the Kentucky whites and still meant to drive them out, but that they expected more and better assistance from their brothers, the British, for the next major assault.

There had been a bit of highly disconcerting news at Chalahgawtha on their return on September 14. Three nights before, Chiungalla was told, a short while after darkness had fallen, the fifty horses still in the fenced compound near where the smaller creek joined the Little Miami began to act up, snorting and whinnying, and then the dogs in the village began yapping and howling.[162] Suddenly there had come the crashing of gunfire and with it the noise of their horses galloping away into the night from the compound. At first they had thought they were under attack by a large party of whites, but that had not been the case. Careful investigation showed that there had evidently been only three whites involved, who had come there on three horses. Their hidden campsite was found the next morning and it was apparent they had been there a couple of days before turning the Shawnee horses loose after taking their pick of seven.

It had not been until the sun was straight up the following day that they managed to catch the scattered horses and get them back in their compound— except for the seven stolen. There were very few able warriors left in the village, since most had gone on the expedition with Chiungalla, but among those few was a cadaverous man of about forty named Bonah, who was in no way noted for his bravery or fighting ability and who had only one talent truly worthy of note. Bonah possessed an uncanny ability for tracking, and it had long been laughingly but admiringly said among his fellows that he could track the shadow of a butterfly that had flown across a pumpkin patch an hour before.

With four others of less than remarkable fighting skill, Bonah had set off on the first five horses recovered to track the enemy. With the whites having a full night's head start on such pursuit, the villagers had doubted he would overtake them before they reached and crossed the Spaylaywitheepi. Yet, just a matter of hours before Chiungalla's force returned, one of those who had gone with Bonah came back on a badly jaded horse and brought electrifying news. Through Bonah's phenomenal tracking ability, they had followed the devious trail all the way to the Spaylaywitheepi and there, on the north shore, had encountered the three whites.[163] They had captured one, killed another, and recovered all seven stolen horses, plus three others the whites had ridden. One of the whites had eluded them, but Bonah and the rest of his party were on their way back with the horses and their single prisoner and—this was the amazing part—the man he had captured was none other than the giant frontiersman who had for so long plagued them and eluded capture, Bahd-ler![164]

Late in the evening on the second day after Chiungalla and the majority of his warriors had returned to Chalahgawtha, a burst of whooping and hollering rose and word swept through the village that Bonah and his party were near with the recovered horses and the captive Bahd-ler. They had made camp a half-mile distant, as was customary when returning with an important prisoner who would have to run the gauntlet, and would bring him in early the following morning, thus giving the villagers ample opportunity to set up their gauntlet lines. The recovered horses had already been taken to the compound. Fresh clothing, food and certain necessaries requested by Bonah were sent.

In the morning, Bonah and his companions, resplendently clad in their finest clothing and most extravagant ornamentation, approached the quarter-mile long gauntlet. In his left hand Bonah carried upraised a spear gaily decorated with strips of colored ribbon and the scalp of the man they had killed attached to the top. In his right hand he gripped a length of rawhide, the other end a noose around Bahd-ler's neck, who also had his wrists bound behind him. The captive was barefoot and had been stripped of all clothing but trousers. As soon as they stopped at the head of the double line, even his trousers were taken. His face and bare chest were a mass of ugly bruises, scratches and deep gouges from treatment received before arriving here.[165]

The gauntlet was comprised of two lines of people, men and women of all ages and hordes of children, stretching all the way to the *msi-kah-mi-qui.* The two lines were facing each other eight or nine feet apart and everyone was armed with sticks, switches, clubs, rawhide straps, clumps of brambles, anything with which to lash out and strike the prisoner as he passed.

Tecumseh was in the line, as was Tecumapese, but more out of tradition than desire, each with a slender, supple willow switch. They had deliberately placed themselves within a hundred feet of the *msi-kah-mi-qui,* generally considered a poor spot because few gauntlet runners ever made it that far. Of course, by Shawnee law, if somehow the runner *did* manage to get there, then he was free of any further beating at this particular gauntlet.

Now, eight days after Bahd-ler's gauntlet, Tecumseh remembered the welling of admiration he had felt for this huge white man as his bonds had been cut away and he was impelled on his run by a hefty smack across the buttocks with a thick stick wielded by Bonah. How he had run! He had been pummeled severely at each step and his back had become crisscrossed by a network of bloody tracks. The pain was obviously great, yet no sound other than labored breathing had escaped him. He had almost made it to the council house and both Tecumseh and his sister had poised themselves to give him a token stroke as he passed, but twenty feet from them a warrior bearing a gnarled club stepped out in the middle of the gauntlet passage, blocking his way and prepared to smash him a mighty blow when he came within reach.

The incredible Bahd-ler had turned the tables by charging the warrior and striking him heavily with his balled fist, breaking his nose and knocking him senseless. The pause, however, was enough for several savage blows from others to strike him and he crumpled. Semiconscious, he was half-carried, half-dragged back to the starting point, given a drink and a ten-minute respite, then once again sent on his way through the gauntlet. Again, faltering badly, he had almost made it there when he suddenly lunged at a shrieking woman in the line, kicked her out of his way and attempted to run the remaining distance to the council house outside the lines.

A woman only a few yards from Tecumseh broke free and ran to cut him off, brandishing a hickory club. He tried to avoid her but was simply too weak and wobbly even to deflect the blow. It caught him on the nape and knocked him senseless. Immediately others crowded around and kept beating him until finally forced to desist by a command from Chiungalla.

In the eight days since then, the big frontiersman was nursed back to health until now he was in fairly good condition considering what he had been through. A short time ago he had been brought near the crowded *msi-kah-mi-qui* and tied in a sitting position to a stake, with Bonah standing guard close by. Ever more people were filing into the council house and sitting, many having come from as far away as the Scioto Valley or the upper Mad and Miami rivers. The fate of this young and powerful frontiersman who had so often beaten them at their own game, who had killed so many that had set out to kill him, had become a national matter and many voices had to be heard before it could be determined what should be done to him, and where.

A group of small children had gathered around and were teasing him unmercifully—jeering, kicking dust in his face, spitting on him, snickering at his discomfort. Tecumseh stood some distance apart, watching, disgusted by it. This man was an enemy, he knew, and deserved punishment for his crimes against the Shawnees; yet, at the same time he was uncomfortably aware that the Shawnee lives this man took had been taken in fair fight by armed enemies who sought to kill him. At no time had anyone ever accused him of torturing or humiliating anyone helpless and in his power. That such things should be happening to him now at the hands of the Shawnees embarrassed Tecumseh and made him feel ashamed of his own fellows.

One of the boys, a nice-looking youngster of twelve summers named Stand Under the Tree, approached the captive closely. He was noted for picking on younger boys, although he had long ago learned to stay clear of Tecumseh, preferring those who did not fight back. Now, standing over Bahd-ler, he dug a foul muçous glob from his own nostril and smeared it in the face and mouth of the bound man. Bahd-ler abruptly kicked, catching the boy full in the stomach, sending him sprawling and gasping for air. Tecumseh joined the other boys in their laughter. In a few moments the boy regained his breath and rushed off, only to return in less than two minutes with his mother. The woman was fat, ugly and evil tempered and she was carrying a blackberry branch studded with thorns, which she shook at Bahd-ler.

"You no kick Shawnee boy," she shrieked in English, then lashed him with the branch until his head and shoulders were bloody, stopping only when Bonah waved her away. The lanky warrior then untied the strand binding Bahd-ler to the stake and led him into the crowded council house. Tecumseh followed and crouched near the doorway to watch and listen. Perhaps Chiungalla would proclaim his wish to adopt this big young man, as he had Sheltowee. The tribe could do worse than have a man of such courage as an adopted son.

The frontiersman was taken close to the council fire ring and tied to one of the large beech trunk pillars. Some five hundred Shawnees had crowded inside the *msi-kah-mi-qui* and there was a general rumble of voices until Chiungalla entered and a stillness settled over them.

The chief's face was set in grim lines, not only because of the failure of his most recent expedition into Kentucky, but because spies had brought a variety of bad news: word that a white chief, whose name they had discovered was George Rogers Clark, had gathered nearly two hundred men on an island near the falls on the Spaylaywitheepi and had gone down the river. He had quickly made an agreement with three hundred Kickapoos, who swore to support him, and then had gone on to the Illinois country and, in swift succession, took the British posts at Kaskaskia and Cahokia. Worse yet, there was strong reason to believe that a large force of soldiers was being assembled at

Fort Pitt under a white chief named General Lachlan McIntosh, to lead a major invasion into Ohio against the Indians and it was presumed this meant specifically against the Shawnees.

The principal chief, limping slightly and using a staff to lean upon, walked up to the captive and pointed a finger at him and spoke in English, "You are the man the *Shemanese* call Bahd-ler, our great enemy. You have been stealing our horses?"

"I took seven horses from the Shawnees who have taken many times that number from the whites."

"Did Sheltowee, the man you call Captain Boone, tell you to steal our horses?"

"No. I did it by myself."

"Don't you know it's wrong to steal Indians' horses?"

The captive snorted derisively. "It is no more wrong than for you to come and steal our horses."

Chiungalla turned away a moment and then turned back. "The Shawnees have no cattle about their doors like the *Shemanese*. The buffalo are our cattle, but you come here and kill them. You have no business to kill Indians' cattle. Did you know that?"

"No, I did not. Did you know that the Shawnees have no business killing the white man's cattle?"

Chiungulla raised his staff and struck Bahd-ler a heavy blow over one shoulder, then followed up with a whole series of blows. Bahd-ler winced at the impacts but he made no sound. At length Chiungalla stopped and then walked over to stand between his two sitting subordinates, Catahecassa— Black Hoof—and Wesecahnay—Black Beard. He looked over the assembled Shawnees and spoke in a voice still tight with anger.

"I say the man Bahd-ler is guilty and vote he be declared *cuttahotha* and burned immediately here. How say the chiefs?"

One by one the chiefs rose and spoke their piece. There was much condemnation of Bahd-ler for penetrating to the very heart of the Shawnee Nation and humiliating them by stealing from them under their very noses, and there was great praise for the feat of Bonah in tracking and capturing the large and powerful enemy. Each chief concluded by casting his vote respecting the fate of the frontiersman and, with only four or five exceptions, each vote was for death at the stake. The only alteration in Chiungalla's suggestion was that since the whole Shawnee Nation had been affected by this man, then his death became a national concern, not a local one affecting only Chalahgawtha. Therefore, the execution should take place at the village most centrally located— Wapatomica—so the greatest number of Shawnees possible could attend. So it was agreed.

"Bonah," Chiungalla said, "to you goes the honor of taking this man you captured to Wapatomica. Select a party of good men to accompany you and prevent any attempt he might make to escape. Stop at each village along the way that a gauntlet may be run for the benefit of those who could not participate in the one that was held here, but do not let them kill him in these lines. He is to die at the stake in Wapatomica."

And at the doorway, though he could not fully understand why, since Bahd-ler was a great enemy of the Shawnees, a pervasive sadness filled Tecumseh.

[October 5, 1778 — Monday]

It took five days for news of the incident to reach Chalahgawtha and Tecumseh received it with oddly mixed emotions. He was overjoyed that Blue Jacket had again pulled off a feat that catapulted him into every Shawnee's conversation and talk was rife that one day he might become war chief of the tribe. At the same time, Tecumseh experienced a very real sense of sorrow that one of the bravest men he had ever encountered had met with what had to be, for him, so terribly unlucky a circumstance.

The incident had occurred on the first day of this Harvest Moon some forty miles north at Mackachack, principal village of the Maykujays, where Moluntha was chief, but actually had its beginning right here at Chalahgawtha on the day that Bonah, with the four warriors who had accompanied him, left this village with the white man who had been declared *cuttahotha*—Bahd-ler. The hapless captive had gone through a very difficult time on the journey. Barefoot and wearing only his ragged trousers, the frontiersman, his wrists bound behind him, had been pulled and jerked along behind their horses, tethered to a rawhide choke strap some thirty feet in length.[166] Every step of the way he had been severely tormented by Indians, mostly different groups of women and children who intercepted them to view this great enemy, each group following for a few miles. At every village encountered he again had to run the gauntlet, though his badly bruised and bleeding feet could scarcely carry him. Sometimes he made it through the line, but as often he was beaten unconscious. Each time his wounds were washed and medicated with considerable care and he was fed well and allowed to rest before journeying to the next town. Swarms of people came from the towns that were not on the route to Wapatomica—Buckangehela's Town, Stiahta's Town, McKee's Town, Mingo Town, Solomon's Town and Upper Sandusky—so they might get in their licks on him along the way.[167]

Despite the care given him at intervals, Bahd-ler was gradually weakening from the constant beatings and five days ago, as they had approached the head of the gauntlet line at Mackachack—also called Moluntha's Town—there had been quite a bit of betting going on among the warriors over whether he would make it through or not. The consensus was that he would not, since this line was close to half a mile long.

It was while they had stood waiting at the end of that line for the drum beat to sound at the council house that would start his run, that the amazing frontiersman took matters into his own hands. He burst into a run down the double line before the drum beat came and had run past fully thirty club wielders before they realized what was happening. He had then leaped directly at a squaw, who ducked down to get out of his way and he had cleared her by more than a foot and hit the ground running on the outside of the line. They had broken in pursuit at once but he was ahead of them and, with great strides, was quickly increasing his lead. There had been a confused tangle of men, women and children and by the time the most fleet among them had emerged out of the pack, Bahd-ler had a seventy-yard lead.

Though naked and barefoot, he raced with sustained speed and strength over, through and past a variety of obstacles—logs, rocks, erosion gullies and little creeks. At one point he leaped an erosion gully in the prairie that was fully fifteen feet wide and landed on the other side with a couple of feet to spare. Only one of his pursuers was able to leap it successfully, the others jumping down, running across and climbing up. By this time he had increased the distance between them to one hundred yards. Bonah was the single Indian who had leaped the gap, but neither his speed nor endurance were as great as Bahd-ler's and he was rapidly losing ground.

Bahd-ler had dashed into a half-mile wide prairie beyond the ditch, heading for a distant dark line of woodlands. He reached the woods and began using subterfuge to confuse his pursuers, running down little creeks, racing up slanting trees and leaping away from them far to one side, even occasionally climbing a tree and moving from one tree to another through the branches before descending many yards away and resuming his run.

At length he had come to a wide ravine between rolling hills and followed its course with that strong mile-eating lope he could maintain for hours if need be. The ravine ahead made a sharp turn left and he raced around the corner at full tilt, then slammed to a stop so suddenly that he fell, rolled over, regained his feet, and raced back the way he had come.

The reason was Blue Jacket. He, as second war chief under Shemeneto and leading six other Kispokotha horsemen, en route from Kispoko Town to Mackachack, was in the same broad ravine, and Bahd-ler had all but collided with Blue Jacket's horse. The Shawnees were as startled as the frontiersman, but immediately realized what was occurring and galloped in pursuit.

Bahd-ler, not wanting to run back into the hands of those chasing him afoot, turned from the ravine, scaled the bank and ran gasping for breath toward another island of trees a half mile distant. He was no more than a hundred feet from it when Blue Jacket overtook him, leaned forward and struck fiercely at Bahd-ler with his tomahawk. It was the pipe end rather than the blade of the tomahawk's head that hit Bahd-ler, the rounded end punching a section of bone its own three-quarter-inch diameter into his head, and he fell unconscious.

So Blue Jacket, who had gained renown with his capture of Boone, had now equalled that feat with his capture of the *cuttahotha*—Bahd-ler. Two of the greatest and most feared white frontiersmen, and Blue Jacket had captured both! And Tecumseh, who wished only the best for his good friend, nevertheless couldn't help feeling, deep inside, a pang of genuine regret that the incredibly courageous young frontiersman, Bahd-ler, had not succeeded in making the escape he so justly deserved.

[October 10, 1778 — Saturday]

While both Tecumseh and Chiksika had visited Mackachack several times in the past, this was the first time they had stayed in the beautiful village for any length of time. The rolling hills in this area were beautiful, well forested with trees now liberally daubed with the brilliant reds and yellows of autumn and separated from each other by equally lovely bottom lands covered with golden blankets of fine prairie grasses.

Moluntha had many long years ago selected this area for his village, locating it on a wonderful spring-fed stream that emptied into the Mad River only a mile distant.[168] That river itself differed greatly from all the other rivers in the Ohio country. The others were generally sluggish streams that drained broad areas of the country they passed through, becoming muddy torrents in the rainy season and only acquiring some degree of clarity late in the summer and autumn when rains were no longer so prevalent. The Mad River, however, was a stream fed by an abundance of large bubbling springs of crystal clear water and even in the rainiest of weather it did not become muddy like the others. Its bed was gravelly and its waters so sparkling clear that even in the deepest areas the bottom could clearly be seen, along with the fish they called *sharla*—trout—which existed in no other Ohio stream.

Four and a half miles to the north of Mackachack lay Wapatomica, the Thawegila village of Chief Kikusgowlowa, which, with its large *msi-kah-mi-qui* and well over five hundred wegiwas, was second only to Chalahgawtha in size and population and, because of its central location to all the other Shawnee villages, was becoming accepted as the capital of the nation.

Mackachack, on the other hand, had less than two hundred wegiwas and its council house was very small. Yet it was one of the most pleasant of all Shawnee villages and the brothers enjoyed being here. They had come to celebrate a very special wedding—that of their good friend and adopted brother, Blue Jacket, to the niece of Chief Moluntha, daughter of the younger brother of Moluntha, Wabete—the Elk.

Her name was Wabethe—the Swan—and Blue Jacket had met her for the first time within an hour of his capture of the escaping *cuttahotha*, Bahd-ler. The attraction between the young Kispoko chief and the Maykujay maiden had been instantaneous; she a tall, beautiful young woman of nineteen summers, her eyes large and dark and bold, her features finely chiseled with high cheekbones over smooth tan cheeks, her usually smiling mouth wide and set with very even and beautifully formed white teeth; he at age twenty-four, the dark-haired, tall, muscular, and very aristocratic appearing second war chief of the Shawnee Nation, whose courage and daring were already legendary in the tribe and who few even remembered anymore had been born a white and adopted into the tribe only six years before.

Blue Jacket had spent the remainder of that day of the capture as an honored guest in Moluntha's wegiwa and during those hours had scarcely been able to keep his eyes off her, nor she off him, even though Shawnee custom dictated that she lower her head and avert her eyes if their glances happened to meet. She had not done so, at least not immediately, looking at him instead for a long admiring moment with those deep bold eyes before smiling faintly and lowering her head.

Late the same evening a frolic dance had been held in which practically all the young unmarried men and women of the village, or who had come from elsewhere, had formed in a circle around the fire. The men lined up facing the circumference of the circle rather than the flames, each looking at the back of the man who stood several feet before him, while the women darted about to select their partners for the dance. Each man held his hands crossed behind his back and the woman who took a position behind him took his hands in hers, holding a cloth between them so their skin did not touch. But if the contact of hands was made without benefit of such a cloth, it was an acknowledgment of the woman's admiration and possible love for the warrior.

The shuffling dance, to the beat of a drum, the rattle of gravel-filled gourds and a peculiar melodic chant, then commenced and if the young woman who had grasped the man's hands without benefit of cloth pulled his hands up and bent her own head down to place her cheeks between his hands for a moment, it indicated she would consider him as a mate. If she took this one step further and turned her head first to left and then to right to press her tongue against his palms, then it was an avowal to become his wife if he would have her.

Blue Jacket had smiled when he glimpsed Wabethe run lightly to take a place behind him as the chant had begun and the shuffling forward movement commenced. His hands had been grasped by hers and there was no cloth between them. Before the line had made a half circle around the fire, she raised his hands behind him to her cheeks and before the first full circling had been completed her mouth had pressed to each palm in turn and he had exulted at the warmth of her tongue briefly touching each palm.

That had been ten days ago and tonight another dance—the wedding dance—would be held. If, during this ten-day interval since the frolic dance, the parties had not had a change of mind, by the time this dance was completed, those who had signified such intentions earlier would be husband and wife.

In the late afternoon today Chiksika and Tecumseh met with Blue Jacket and, along with Wasegoboah, who had also arrived and joined them, they strolled beside the beautiful stream. They talked as they walked, going over old times and exchanging news, the most immediate and interesting of which was what had occurred in regard to the condemned frontiersman, Bahd-ler.

Blue Jacket told them that after he had downed Bahd-ler with the blow from his tomahawk ten days ago, he had draped the unconscious frontiersman across his horse and rode with him into Mackachack, followed by the horsemen who had come with him. The gloom of depression that had settled over the Maykujay Shawnees at the escape of their prisoner turned to unparalleled joy and excitement as they saw Blue Jacket bring the captive back to them. Some, with gauntlet weapons still in their hands, ran up and began whipping and beating the unconscious frontiersman.

"I kicked at them and ordered them away," said Blue Jacket, "but they didn't want to give up, until Moluntha came up and ordered them to stop." Moluntha, he told them, had taken a position beside the horse, his gnarled old hand on the frontiersman's welted back, and his voice had been raspy in tone and harsh in content as he chided them.

"What kind of courage do my people have," he had asked them scornfully, "that they can beat a great enemy while he lies unconscious and helpless before them? What kind of respect do my people have for a man who can best them when his body is already weak with injury and pain? Do not make your kind ashamed of you. This is a man of mighty courage and strength. Since when does the Shawnee show his respect for such virtues in such manner?"

He had then pointed to his huge cousin-wife, Nonhelema, who stepped close to him. "Nonhelema," he told her, "take this brave white warrior to our wegiwa. Nurse him as you would your own son. He may now be dying, but yet nurse him well that he may survive. If he should live, I proclaim that another council of judgment will be held to determine whether or not the punishment he has already received at our hands is not payment enough for the theft of seven horses."

Bahd-ler had remained unconscious for two days, Blue Jacket told them, and then regained only a sort of semiconsciousness for the two days after that. That circular piece of bone that had been punched onto his brain by the pipe end of the tomahawk seemed to be holding him in some sort of daze. Yet, miraculously, on the fifth day of this Harvest Moon his mind cleared and by the end of the seventh day after being struck, he could sit up and even walk about some. His treatment by Nonhelema was excellent and his wounds began healing rapidly. Now it had been ten days and the prisoner, bound to a stake and guarded in one of the wegiwas, was deemed sufficiently recovered to undergo another judgment. Word of this had been sent to other chiefs, who would begin arriving tomorrow, and on the day after that, the council would be held. Would Chiksika and Wasegoboah stay over the extra two days to attend that council?

They both agreed they would and Blue Jacket said, *"Ouisah!"*—Good!— and then turned to Tecumseh. "I will get special permission from Moluntha for you to sit in the council house as well, Tecumseh."

The boy was overjoyed; the first time he would actually be allowed to attend a council! He was so excited by the prospect that he had difficulty concentrating on the remainder of the news that passed between the young men as they continued their walk.

First there was the matter of the three whites who had recently been sent by Hamilton, the British governor at Detroit, to take up residence with the Shawnees and get them more firmly committed to full alliance with the British in the continuing war of the revolution. One was their longtime champion at Fort Pitt who had finally defected from the Americans and gone to Detroit to serve the British, Alexander McKee. With his Shawnee wife, McKee had gone to her little village, now renamed McKee's Town, and settled there, though largely dividing his time between there and Detroit.[169] The second was Simon Girty, who settled in the Shawnee village that was immediately renamed Girty's Town and was located on the headwaters of the St. Marys River, thirty-eight miles northwest of Mackachack.[170] There he had been joined by his brother George, while another brother, James, had taken up residence with Mingoes in the village that had been rebuilt on the site of the old Delaware central village of Goschachgunk, from which raiding parties were going out frequently against the white settlements around the Wheeling area.

In other news a bit more disconcerting, Blue Jacket told them of two enemy whites who had recently excelled so much in Indian fighting that they bore close watching, as they might well turn out to be enemies as accomplished as Sheltowee or Bahd-ler. One was a man named Samuel Brady, a militia captain who had settled in or near the Washington, Pennsylvania, settlement and who had already killed numerous Indians, mostly Mingoes and Wyandots. The other was the daring leader of the whites, George Rogers Clark, who, with his very small, undisciplined army, had gone down the Spaylaywitheepi to the Illinois country and had taken Kaskaskia and Cahokia from the British. Where the latter were concerned, news of this bold move had infuriated the Hair Buyer—Governor Henry Hamilton—as well as causing him to fear that the Americans would ascend the Wabash, winning over the tribes on that stream prior to marching on Detroit itself. Hamilton had quickly raised a force of two hundred forty men and, leaving Detroit under command of a captain named Lernoult, was at this moment leading that force—augmented by other Indians en route to a total of about three hundred—toward the little post of Vincennes on the lower Wabash. That post, also called Fort Sackville, was under command of an American captain named Leonard Helm, and the Hair Buyer had no doubt whatever that he would force Helm to surrender his tiny command without resistance. Governor Hamilton was being escorted in his march by the Potawatomi chiefs Ashkinee, Nanaquiba, and Windigo—Man Eater—and had told those Indians he intended occupying Vincennes over the winter and then would strike Clark's army at Kaskaskia as soon as the weather broke next spring. He was, however, disappointed at having so few Kickapoo allies joining him. In answer to his complaints in this respect, Chief Mohinamba of the Kickapoos said that most of the Kickapoo warriors were then absent from the villages, having gone to their winter hunting grounds west of the Mississippi, but that "when they return in the spring, the Kickapoos will appear like mosquitoes and infest the Ohio frontier and all the rebel frontiers."[171]

By the time Blue Jacket had finished relating this, it had grown late, so the three men and the boy returned to Mackachack to rest and eat and, in Blue Jacket's case, to prepare for the wedding dance. It was fully dark an hour or two later when a large crowd of onlookers took seats on the ground in a broad oval before the fire that had been built in the principal clearing in the village. Tecumseh, Chiksika and Wasegoboah, at the chief's invitation, were to the left of the elderly Moluntha, while his wife and brother, Nonhelema and Wabete, were to his right.

The participants of the dance, twenty young men, including Blue Jacket, entered in single file, clad in striking costumes of the finest doeskin, which had been sun bleached almost white and well decorated with intricate beadwork, interwoven with feathers, shells, porcupine quills, and shiny brass baubles. They were barefoot, and those with long hair were wearing it loose to their shoulders and combed to a gloss that reflected the firelight. There was no ornamentation in their hair, nor in the short tufted hair of those eight or ten who had shaved their heads except for the crest and temple patch. None wore any kind of necklace, but all wore wide bracelets and upper arm bands of beaten silver as well as strands of painted shells about their ankles, which clinked in a melodious chorus as they walked.

A similar number of barefoot young women, including Wabethe, then entered the area, slipping at random through the seated guests and taking their places in a line some fifteen feet from the men, facing them, each positioning herself opposite the man of her choice. They, too, wore the superbly tanned and bleached doeskin, theirs in simple pullover shifts which covered them to their knees and were similarly adorned with beadwork, quills, brass and plumes. Their hair, also well combed, hung down their backs to their waistlines or even longer—one having hair that almost reached her ankles.

The men generally showed no expression but the women smiled boldly at them, eyes glittering with reflected firelight. Now and then they shook themselves so vigorously that their hair flared wildly and their young forms became pleasing contours momentarily outlined within their shifts. Every so often they stamped their feet, sometimes individually but most often in unison so that the clinking of shell anklets became a delightfully tinkling cadenced chorus.

Close to the fire sat a group of musicians with hand drums and rattles, along with a crude stringed instrument and a xylophonic arrangement of solid wooden cylinders depending from a cord. They now began a discordant and unconnected collection of sounds which quickly resolved themselves into a rhythmic pattern that became surprisingly melodious. An older man sitting in the circle surrounding the participants now rose and took a position at one end of the line, his motions timing themselves to the beat of the melody even before reaching his place. He immediately began a monotonous yet strangely compelling chant that fluctuated to the music:

"Ya ne no hoo wa no . . . ya ne no hoo wa no . . . ya ne no hoo wa no . . ."

The opposing lines of men and women began swaying with the weird tune and gradually inched toward one another until, when less than a foot separated them, the dancers themselves took up the chant in an alternating manner, first the soprano voices of the women, then a response by the deeper voices of the men. Some repeated the same meaningless words of the chanting, while others put words to the rhythm. Through all this they continued their forward motion until now separated by only an inch or so, all with their hands clasped behind them.

Wabethe, excited and her dancing eyes locked on Blue Jacket, chanted the first words to pass between them. Leaning forward so that her face was very close to his and her breasts were pressed against his broad chest, she sang softly, melodiously, in time with the chant, *"Psai-wi ne-noth-tu"*—Great warrior.

The whole line leaned the other way and now it was Blue Jacket who pressed himself against her, bending slightly at the waist and feeling the warmth of her breasts against him, the rich deep sounds rolling from his lips, *"U-le-thi e-qui-wa"*—Beautiful woman.

Back and forth they continued swaying in this manner, letting only their eyes and the touch of their bodies and the soft chantings convey their meanings.

"K-tch-o-ke-ma," she murmured. Great chief.

"Ke-sath-wa a lag-wa," he replied. You are sun and stars.

"Oui-shi e-shi-que-chi." Your face is filled with strength.

"U-le-thi oui-thai-ah." Your hair is lovely.

"Oui-sha t'kar-chi." Muscular legs.

"U-le-thi ski-she-quih." Pretty eyes.

Similar utterances were coming from all the other dancers, though none were saying exactly the same thing except for moments when they lapsed back into the same meaningless chant that had originated the dance. The result was a gripping murmur of sensual exchange as each of the dancers in turn whispered compliments in his or her own way. Wholly lost in themselves, the couples became oblivious to what was going on around them except the underlying musical rhythm and chant, hearing nothing of what other dancers said, not even those beside them, each couple lost in the importance of their own chantings and in the rising heat within them. The tempo picked up and the swaying quickened, with greater dips and pressures. Tiny beads of perspiration pearled themselves on Wabethe's upper lip and the firelight glinted in little sparkles from Blue Jacket's forehead.

"U-le-tha beh-quoi-tah," she murmured, pushing her stomach firmly against his. Your belly is handsome.

"Ah-quoi-teti beh-quoi-tah," he responded as they leaned the other way and he pushed back against her. And yours is warm.

"Cat-tu-oui ni-i-yah." Your body is perfect.

"Psai-wi uske-to-ma-ke." Your breasts are ripe melons.

"Ps' qui ah-quoi te-ti." Your blood runs hot.

"Qui-sah ki-te-hi." Your good heart is full of understanding.

Within just a few beats the tempo of the dance slowed, the dips becoming longer lasting and the body pressure stronger and more filled with passion. For the first time their hands came into play, gripping and holding the one bending backward to prevent a fall, both parties fondling and caressing as they straightened, only to bend the other way.

Now came the crucial moment of the dance; if either Wabethe or Blue Jacket remained silent or simply chanted *"Ouisah meni-e-de-luh"*—Good dance—they would part at the end of the dance and each go their own ways, without the embarrassment or perhaps humiliation of a plainly stated rejection.

But at this moment Blue Jacket leaned hard against Wabethe and his words were urgent. *"Ni haw-ku-nah-ga."* You are my wife.

164

"*Ni wy-she-an-a,*" Wabethe replied softly in his ear, smiling and resting her cheek against his. And you are my husband.[172]

[October 12, 1778 — Monday]

Tecumseh was appalled at how bruised and beaten the young frontiersman looked when he was led on a tether into the Mackachack council house by Bonah. Yet, worse than that was the sluggish manner in which he moved, as if having difficulty remembering how to place one foot before the other. There was a peculiar lack of expression on his face as well and an absence of the probing intelligence that had been in his eyes when he was a captive in Chalahgawtha.

As soon as Bonah had tied him to a center post and then squatted on his heels beside the captive, Moluntha came to his feet and a hush settled over those who had assembled. The Maykujay chief spoke only briefly, reiterating much of what Blue Jacket said he had told his people ten days ago: that this great enemy was also a man of great courage who now had run six gauntlets and suffered badly in each of them; that even in such condition he had the strength and courage to make an escape attempt from the very midst of the entire population of the village and had succeeded in it; that Moneto Himself, on the failure of the villagers to catch him, had decreed that the prisoner should not escape and had placed Blue Jacket in his path to cut him off and bring him down; that here was a young man who, in his estimation, had suffered more than enough for the theft of seven horses and, finally, that the Shawnees could greatly benefit by rescinding the stigma of *cuttahotha* and restoring him to the status of ordinary captive, so that he might then be adopted into the tribe and perhaps become as great a fighter *for* the Shawnees as he had been against them.

Other chiefs now rose and spoke, though none at great length, the consensus being that, despite his courage and recent suffering, so many harms had been done by this man against the Shawnees and so great was the threat he represented while he lived, that his death sentence should not be rescinded. In the end the majority ruled and Bahd-ler was reinstated as *cuttahotha*.

Moluntha rose at last and addressed the crowd in conclusion. "The chiefs have made known their wishes," he said slowly, sorrowfully. "Therefore, the *cuttahotha* will be marched at the rise of the sun tomorrow the remaining short journey to Wapatomica, where he will be executed in accordance with the judgment of the chiefs who met in council at Chalahgawtha."

At his gesture the prisoner was led away, still expressionless, still with that odd shuffling gait. A strangely subdued reaction prevailed among those in attendance as to what had occurred here. For his own part, Tecumseh again experienced a very unexpected but nonetheless strong welling of sympathy for the prisoner. He also could not help but wish that his own first council had been attended with matters in which he could have taken some measure of pride and satisfaction.

[January 20, 1779 — Wednesday]

Chiksika and Tecumseh were both on hand at Chalahgawtha when Bonah returned just as the sun was approaching the top of its rise today. A council was immediately scheduled in the *msi-kah-mi-qui* and Chiungalla sent criers running through the village to assemble all chiefs and warriors who wished to hear what had finally occurred in respect to their great enemy, Bahd-ler.

Over these past months Tecumseh had accompanied Chiksika on a number of swift raids against the Americans and had comported himself very well, earning the praise of his brother as well as others in the war party. Because of this he was accorded the privilege of warrior status and so, despite his young age, was permitted to enter the council house.

Bonah, even thinner than usual, had eaten and rested and now, unaccustomed to public speaking, stood before the assemblage nervously. He glanced at Chiungalla who signaled for him to begin. Bonah nodded and prefaced his remarks with an apology, saying there were some things he would go over that no doubt they already knew, but he would tell what had happened since he left Chalahgawtha with Bahd-ler as his captive four months earlier.

Quickly then the lanky warrior sketched in the details of the journey from Chalahgawtha to the reinstatement of the death penalty at Mackachack, all of which was well known by Tecumseh, but then, as Bonah continued with his relation of events since leaving Mackachack, the young Shawnee listened more closely. The belief held by many Shawnees that Bahd-ler was under the protection of Moneto was strengthened by what they now heard.

Bahd-ler, who seemed to have regained his senses considerably on the march to Wapatomica, had been required to run another gauntlet when they arrived there, but it had been a mild one compared to the others and he had run it with comparative ease and few additional injuries until just a few steps from the council house. At that time a squaw had stepped forward and struck him with a club over the healing tomahawk injury. He had recovered consciousness only to find that he was back at the head of the line and required to run it again—his eighth gauntlet run. This time he was unable to run so swiftly and was struck many times, but not on the head, and finally reached the sanctuary of the *msi-kah-mi-qui*. Despite his success, he was badly treated, stripped of clothing and staked spread-eagle on the ground while the women and children tormented him in a variety of ways for hours.

The Wapatomica Council held the next morning was merely to decide exactly *when* Bahd-ler should be put to death. The judgment was that this should take place at dawn, three days hence, at which time he would suffer the prolonged and hideous death at the stake.

On the morning scheduled for the execution a perversity of fate had once again intervened. Bahd-ler was painted black and readied for the stake when a party of a hundred twenty warriors returned from the upper Spaylaywitheepi, bringing with them eight prisoners from the Wheeling area. One of the members of the war party had turned out to be Simon Girty, with whom Bahd-ler had served in Dunmore's War. At that time they had become close friends and had made a blood-brother pact always to protect one another in all circumstances.

Girty had immediately addressed the Wapatomica Council with a lengthy, impassioned plea for the life of this man who was his blood-brother, recounting the many things they had gone through together, his speech extremely moving. The chiefs debated the matter at length and decided, since Simon Girty was such a good friend of theirs, and Bahd-ler such a good friend of his, that Bahd-ler was now declared *mattah cuttahotha*—not condemned—and that he would forthwith be adopted into the tribe.

Bahd-ler, Bonah went on, had been adopted by a Shawnee woman named Melassa Tequi—Sugar Tree—to take the place of her own son who had been killed in the attack on Boonesboro. The frontiersman had been given the Shawnee name of Psaiwiwuhkernekah Ptweowa—Great White Wolf. Bahd-ler had then, with Bonah still in tow, gone with his friend to Girty's Town, which was only a small collection of wegiwas and one cabin. They had stayed there briefly and then had traveled about the country together, going from town to town, and even met old chief Talgayeeta—Logan—who had a camp on the Scioto headwaters.[173] Girty and Bahd-ler had helped Talgayeeta build a cabin. Returning southward, they had just reached Solomon's Town when they were intercepted by the subchief Red Pole and four warriors.[174] Red Pole told them they had to return to Wapatomica immediately for an important council.

At Wapatomica it was learned that Bahd-ler had been recondemned to death because of a recent defeat the Shawnees had suffered in an attack on Logan's Fort, in which seven out of sixteen Shawnees in the war party had been killed. Red Pole had led the defeated party and he demanded Bahd-ler's death to avenge those deaths. Girty's renewed pleas had little effect except to anger the chiefs, but he did get them to change the place of execution to the Wyandot village of Upper Sandusky, as this would help cement alliance between the tribes and bring greater honor to the Shawnees. The suggestion was accepted and once again Bonah had led the *cuttahotha*, Bahd-ler, toward his execution at the Wyandot village forty-five miles northeast of Wapatomica.[175]

167

Bonah's temper had grown very short by this time. On their way to Upper Sandusky they had stopped to drink at a little rivulet near Solomon's Town. Bahd-ler had finished first, stepped across the rivulet and sat down. Furious at Bahd-ler's move without permission, Bonah leaped across after him and struck him with his war club, breaking the frontiersman's left arm just below the shoulder. Then he had forced him to continue on the march. No gauntlet was run at Solomon's Town, but just north of there they encountered an old man and woman chopping firewood. Their son had recently been killed by whites and the man, beside himself with rage, swung his axe at Bahd-ler's head. The frontiersman ducked away, but the blow hit him on the right shoulder, cutting a deep gash and breaking his collarbone. The old Shawnee was restrained and Bahd-ler was made to continue the march.

At Talgayeeta's camp, where they spent the night, Talgayeeta had his wife dress Bahd-ler's wounds. The former Cayuga told Bahd-ler he had a very influential friend at Upper Sandusky and would try to get him to help. On the second morning after that the march had continued toward Upper Sandusky. Ten miles from that destination a group of twenty Indian youths had galloped up and raced in circles around the party, venting shrill cries and then galloped off the way they had come. In another mile they came to where these young men and a dozen others had formed a thirty-yard gauntlet line in a clearing. Too weary and full of pain to care, the frontiersman had *walked* through the gauntlet, seemingly oblivious to the blows rained upon him. The youths were awe-struck and word spread that he was under the special protection of the Great Spirit and they raced off toward Upper Sandusky. Evidently because of what they said, there was no gauntlet to run at the big Wyandot village. He was simply scheduled to be burned at the stake at dawn.

At the next dawn, however, fate had again intervened. As Bahd-ler was being led to the stake, a severe rainstorm broke out, soaking the wood and kindling that had been laid and adding to the growing belief of his supernatural protection. The execution was postponed till the following morning.

That morning, however, a British officer of much influence among the Wyandots, Captain Peter Drouillard, uniformed in the full scarlet and gold of his rank, arrived and strongly urged that he be allowed to take the prisoner to Detroit for important questioning, after which he could be returned for the execution. The Wyandots agreed but said it was up to Bonah, since the *cuttahotha* was the Shawnee's prisoner. When Drouillard offered him a good reward to escort him and the prisoner to Detroit and then back here for the execution, Bonah had also agreed.[176]

At Detroit Bahd-ler's wounds were treated and after a considerable while Drouillard came to Bonah with word that the *cuttahotha* was too important to the British, for the information he had, to allow him to be executed. For Bonah's extra trouble he was given a large quantity of presents for himself and his fellow Shawnees. At that, Bonah had left the *cuttahotha* in Detroit and came back to Chalahgawtha, satisfied that he had done all he could do in the matter.

There were angry murmurings among many of those in attendance when Bonah finished his narration, but Tecumseh's voice was not among them. He was smiling faintly and inordinately pleased in his own heart that the incredible young frontiersman had escaped the death penalty. Such a man deserved only the honorable death of battle, not execution.[177]

[March 6, 1779 — Saturday]

The Shawnees considered themselves a proud and fearless people capable of standing bold and fending off whatever foe approached. They had never been given to flinching at shadows. Yet now a pervasive apprehension had begun gnawing at the entire tribe. It was as if a gigantic pincers was beginning to close around them, not yet in position, not yet touching them, not yet putting on any pressure, yet hovering in a way that caused them to begin looking over their shoulders more often and pausing to listen for sounds with ominous portent.

There were a number of reasons. First, the *Shemanese* war chief named McIntosh had assembled a force of fourteen hundred soldiers in the area of Fort Pitt. He then, in the fall, built a strong fort named Fort McIntosh after himself at the mouth of the Beaver River.[178] The Delawares, whose villages were closest, had immediately become alarmed and sent deputations to him at Fort McIntosh to sue for peace, but he turned them away, which alarmed them even more, and with good reason.[179] Three days following last Harvest Moon, he had marched into the Ohio country with twelve hundred of his soldiers and in a fortnight had reached the Tuscarawas River, some seventy miles into the territory of the Delawares and Wyandots, and there he had actually built an installation he called Fort Laurens.[180]

Only weeks ago, when a detail of eighteen soldiers left the fort, the Wyandots cut them off and killed all but two and now were concerned that their act would bring down upon them an even greater army of whites seeking vengeance. If that happened and the Wyandots were defeated and fled, there would be no obstacle remaining between the army and the Shawnees. The army could then swing around and attack them from both the east and the north. Simon Girty had been spying on them in the area of Fort McIntosh and Fort Pitt and was of the opinion that there would undoubtedly be some major attacks launched against the Ohio Indians as soon as the weather permitted.[181]

Far to the east, they had learned, another matter was shaping up that boded no good. George Washington had proposed to the Continental Congress that an expedition be set in motion to wipe out the Iroquois—not just an army to march in and do battle with them, but a huge ravaging force of five thousand soldiers that was to destroy every village and every vestige of stored food as well as growing crops.[182] If that expedition were successful, which the Shawnees did not wish for despite their acrimony toward the Iroquois, then wasn't it reasonable to assume that just such a force would soon be sent into the Shawnee territory with the same designs?

Then there was the matter of the Moravians. These Christian missionaries had moved into the valley of the Muskingum where they were having considerable success in converting the Delawares to Christianity and causing them to profess neutrality, but suspicions were strong that the missionaries themselves were spying on the surrounding Indians, including the Shawnees, and passing this intelligence to the Americans. One of the most prominent of the Delaware chiefs, Netawatwees, who had long been noted for his fighting ability, was one of those who had been converted and he had now taken the name of Abraham.[183] Where for a long while the only mission was the one called Lichtenau that had been established on the Muskingum just below Goschachgunk, now three new ones had just been set up on the Tuscarawas and given the names of Salem, Gnadenhutten, and Schoenbrun.[184] It was clear to the Shawnees that this missionary business was just one more means by which the whites were taking over the lands—and even the minds—of the Indians.

To the east and southeast, as well, the *Shemanese* continued to strengthen their hold on the Upper Ohio with new settlements and fortifications and banding together in little squads of men that brazenly slipped deep into the Ohio country to ambush the Mingoes and Delawares in their camps and sometimes within sight of their villages.

To the south the Kentuckians continued to strengthen their position, not only with improved fortifications but with greatly increasing numbers of men from the East. How long could it be before they were quite strong enough to mount an army and strike at Chalahgawtha and other villages?

Finally, and perhaps most frightening of all, there was the very real threat from the West, in the form of the white chief Clark, the *Shemanese* who had so handily taken Kaskaskia and Cahokia. When Governor Hamilton had, as expected, taken the little American fort called Sackville at Vincennes last November, the Shawnees were very pleased and were anticipating his attack on Clark in the spring. But now news had just been received that was devastating. This white chief Clark, with only one hundred twenty men, had marched overland for twenty days in the midst of winter—two hundred miles of half-frozen swamp and marshlands, often in icy water chest deep—and reached Vincennes undetected. Then, with these severely fatigued men, only nine days ago he had actually forced Governor Hamilton into unconditional surrender and had taken possession of Vincennes. Hamilton was now a prisoner, the Americans had control of both the Illinois *and* the Indiana countries, and numerous Indian delegations—Kickapoos, Potawatomies, Weas and others were said to be on their way to Vincennes to assure Clark that they wanted peace. If the *Shemanese* Clark were that good a commander, what would happen if he were to lead a decent-sized army against the Shawnees? It was a very disconcerting prospect.[185]

[March 19, 1779 — Friday]

Because of the many sessions spent at the feet of the tribal historians, sessions in which he listened as if mesmerized and retained what he heard with infallible accuracy, Tecumseh at eleven knew the Shawnee Nation's history as well, perhaps, as any other individual in the tribes. He was aware of the numerous times the tribe had migrated and of the scores of times where various factions had left from the main body for varying periods. But he was also most disturbingly aware that what was happening now had never occurred before in the tribe's history and was a matter of such grave consequence that it might well be the first real indication that the days of the Shawnees were numbered.

Over these past ten days, the Shawnee Nation had split irrevocably.

The elderly principal chief of the Thawegilas, Kikusgowlowa, had warned of it so many times in past councils that his cry of wolf had long ago lost its teeth and the only alarm most listeners felt when he rose to speak was that once again he would inveigh with his customary tiresome litany.

Never noted for brevity in oration nor for any pronounced degree of eloquence, Kikusgowlowa had, at the Shawnee Grand Council ten days ago, achieved near perfection in both respects. He had requested of Chiungalla that he be given the opportunity to speak first, since what he would say would have an important effect on all following talks. Perplexed and unsuspecting, Chiungalla had granted the boon.

Kikusgowlowa, leaning heavily on his staff, had taken his position before the council fire and from within a pouch slung at his side he removed a belt of wampum of which the Thawegilas had been custodians throughout the tribe's history. It was the Shawnee Unity Belt, three inches wide and five feet in length; a belt which, though rarely seen, was well known by all and revered as perhaps the single greatest Shawnee treasures. In the dead quiet that suddenly prevailed, he hung it from a loop at one end to a peg projecting from one of the principal pillars of the *msi-kah-mi-qui*. The belt was divided by color into five sections—from top to bottom, blue, white, green, yellow, and red, representative, in order, of the five Shawnee septs; Maykujays, Chalahgawthas, Peckuwes, Thawegilas, and Kispokothas.

Kikusgowlowa pulled more snugly around himself the old brown blanket draped over his shoulders and then he spoke in a voice that quavered—not from age but from emotion.

"I have come here to tell my Shawnee brothers that what has bound the five septs of our tribe so closely together since the dawn of our history is no more. For so long there have been those among us who have said that if once more our tribe raised the hatchet against the foe who could not be vanquished, we would sever those cords that have bound us in brotherhood. That time," he went on slowly, reaching inside his blanket and drawing out the old-fashioned wide-bladed tomahawk from his belt, "is upon us: the Shawnee hatchet is raised; the foe at which it strikes cannot be slain; the cords that have bound us are severed."

Amid a chorus of gasps he swung the tomahawk in a broad, backhanded arc that struck the belt slightly at a diagonal through the line of color change from white to green. The blade bit deeply into the post and stuck there and the lower three feet of the belt, severed, dropped to the earthen floor in a pile. The old chief stooped with a faint grunt and picked up the tricolored severed section and held it high, gripping it by the yellow in the middle and with the two loose ends of green and red hanging down limply on either side.

"As of this day and this moment, these three—the Thawegila, the Peckuwe and the Kispokotha—are forevermore cut apart from the Chalahgawtha and Maykujay. There can be no negotiation, no plea, no argument. It has all been said before now. It is done. In ten suns these three," he shook the belt section being held aloft, "will leave this land forever, never to return and no longer the brothers of those two who remain."

In these ten succeeding days there was scarcely a moment of inactivity as goods were packed, personal belongings gathered up and preparations made for the final separation. An immense national heartache filled the Shawnees and there was a pain beyond description in the eyes of them all, those departing as well as those remaining, for not only were the septs splitting, individual families were also being sundered as agreement among them could not be reached in respect to who should be followed.

The Shawnee Nation had been discussing what to do about the problem of the encroaching whites for so many years that it was difficult to pinpoint exactly when such talks began. Now, at last, the realization had come that there would never be a full accord reached among the five septs; those who advocated peace and adoption of the white man's ways were more than ever strongly convinced that this was the only means by which the Shawnee Nation could survive, especially in view of the American successes under George Rogers Clark against the British.

On the other hand, those who advocated war were equally convinced that life under white tyranny would be a life without honor, dignity, or self respect, to which death itself was infinitely preferable. For them it was not so great a surprise that the Thawegilas, noted for their pacifistic nature, had made the split. They were not even surprised that the Peckuwes had also done so, since they usually sided with the Thawegilas in matters of state. The great shock had been that the majority of the Kispokothas—the warrior sept of the Shawnees—had elected to go along. Shemeneto—Black Snake—had railed against his brother Kispokothas for their decision and attempted to sway them into remaining, but the decision had been made and there was, as Thawegila had said in the council, no argument that could make them remain. In the end, Shemeneto had refused to go and turned over his leadership of the Kispokothas to Outhowwa Shokka—Yellow Hawk—saying that he would never make peace with the *Shemanese*, nor would he be frightened out of his own land by them, but would stay on as war chief of those who remained and would move, with whatever of his people stayed with him, to the now being vacated Piqua Town a dozen miles north of Chalahgawtha.

Blue Jacket sided with his chief, declaring he would remain as well, as second war chief, but that he was moving among his wife's people, the May-kujays, and would establish a new village, to be called Blue Jacket's Town, eight miles north of Mackachack and four and a half miles northwest of Wapatomica.[186]

Chiksika and Wasegoboah refused to go with the Kispokothas and, of course, the remainder of Pucksinwah's family, with but one exception, stayed as well, remaining the wards of Chiungalla—Tecumapese, Tecumseh, Lo-wawluwaysica, Kumskaka, and Sauwaseekau. The single exception, which wrenched the hearts of these family members, was that their mother, Methotasa, had elected to go with her adopted people, the Peckuwes, turning over the care and raising of her four smallest children—Tecumseh and the eight-year-old triplets—to Tecumapese. Methotasa had never regained her full equilibrium after the death of Pucksinwah and Tecumapese had, in essence, been the female head of the family since then, so it was no great burden for the eldest daughter, but it was nevertheless a matter of deep sadness for all. Their adopted sisters, Kisathoi and Tebethto—the McKinzie sisters, Margaret and Elizabeth—were confused about the whole matter. It had been on the day after Kikusgowlowa had made his talk at the Grand Council that Kisathoi asked Tecumapese about it.

"Why is it, Tecumapese, that such a separation as this should occur, when it causes such sadness to everyone?"

Kisathoi had asked the question of Tecumapese because neither Chiksika nor Tecumseh were there. In fact the sisters rarely saw the two brothers lately, the reason being that ever since participating in Chiungalla's disappointing expedition against Boonesboro, Tecumseh had gone along with Chiksika on whatever raids he made against the whites. No longer even momentarily touched by the initial panic that had gripped him, Tecumseh was learning his battle skills well from his older brother, as well as on occasion from Wasegoboah and Blue Jacket. He had already taken several scalps and, though acknowledging that he yet had much to learn, he had become an asset on their forays, which was quite an accomplishment for an eleven-year-old, occurring at least two or three years before the time when Shawnee boys normally were introduced to actual warfare.

At the moment that Kisathoi had asked her question, she and Tebethto were sitting on either side of Tecumapese at the cookfire in the wegiwa, where Tecumapese had been showing them how to prepare a dish called *takuwah-nepi*.[187]

Tecumapese had paused in her instructions and hugged the pair close to her, one under each arm. "Because," she replied to Kisathoi's question, "there are those of us who feel very strongly about the land where our fathers lived and died and some who are equally willing to die to preserve it for our children. This means that they must fight to keep the white men out."

It had been some ten months since the two girls had been adopted into the tribe and into the family of Chiungalla and both girls, now thirteen and eleven, had adapted well to their new life. Both spoke the Shawnee language fluently, though in private they continued to speak in English, since Margaret was afraid if they did not do so, they would forget how. Over these months they had learned their fluency in the Shawnee tongue from Tecumseh and, in their sessions with him, long hours almost every day for many weeks, they had reciprocated by teaching Tecumseh to speak English so well that he could converse almost naturally with them in the tongue.

Most of all, the girls had come to love Tecumapese, who had become a mother to them, just as she had become so to Tecumseh and the triplet brothers. The girls received from her more care and tenderness and love than they had ever received from their own mother and it was from Tecumapese that they had learned so well the customs, social structure, and history of the tribe. Very frequently, when Tecumapese had other things to see to, they took care of her little son, Spemica Lawba, now five, who was a handsome and well-mannered little boy with dark inquisitive eyes and a ready smile. Tecumapese told them he looked much like his father, Chaquiweshe, who had been killed at the battle of Point Pleasant. Yet, at the same time there was some resemblance to Tecumseh in the boy and he had the same innate sense of politeness and friendliness about him that Tecumseh evinced.

Though the two sisters had come to know Chiksika well, he still tended to frighten them a little, mainly because he was a full grown and powerful young man who continued to fight against the whites and make raids against the settlers, as he had done against their own family. Nevertheless, in some perverse way they could not fully understand, they had come to share the pride that swelled in Tecumseh and Tecumapese when he returned in triumph from his forays. When Chiksika related the exploits of such raids as they sat around the fire in the late evening following such returns, they thrilled right along with the others in the accounts of narrow escapes, hand-to-hand combat, incidents of bravery, the taking of scalps as symbols of victory. They even shared in the sorrow when the death chant was sung for those warriors and chiefs who had lost their lives in such encounters.

Sitting with Tecumapese in the wegiwa, Kisathoi reached out and took away from Spemica Lawba the little burning twig the five-year-old had pulled from the fire and tossed it back where it belonged. Then she followed up on the comment Tecumapese had made in answer to her question.

"But why, in the first place," she persisted, "must men fight and kill each other for the land? There is so much of it! Surely there is enough that they could live together and share the woods and the fields and the rivers in peace, isn't there?"

Chiksika, Tecumseh and the triplets had entered the wegiwa just as Kisathoi had asked her question and Chiksika nodded at Tecumapese to go ahead and answer, the five brothers sitting down across the cookfire from her as she framed her reply. Spemica Lawba scrambled over to Tecumseh and happily snuggled up in his young uncle's lap.

"I often asked the same question when I was young," Tecumapese replied, smiling at her. "Sometimes I still do." She shrugged and sighed, giving a small smile to her brothers. For an instant she nibbled at her lip and then went on. "But I know now that it can never be. There are too many differences between us. Many times we have tried to live in peace with the whites, but even though treaties were made and hearts were in accord for this goal, it would not work."

"But why not?" Tebethto put in. "I don't understand why not, if it is what everyone wants."

"I will answer that, Little Moon," Chiksika had interjected, his expression and his eyes reflecting the sorrow that had taken residence in them all. "Our worlds are so different. The Indian lives with nature, accepting and using with care and restraint and love the blessings Moneto has given to all His children. We do not drive wooden posts into the breast of the mother earth to divide her into property as whites do, for we believe the earth belongs to all, to use wisely and well and equally. We hunt in woods and the prairies for the animals Moneto has placed there for our needs and we do not take more than we can use. Whites take all they want, not just what they need. I once counted the carcasses of seventy buffalo that had been killed near the Blue Licks and from which the only thing that was taken was the tongues, with the rest—meat and skin alike—left to rot."

Tecumseh was listening closely and he saw a shudder go through his older brother. Chiksika looked at him and there was no smile, no glint of happiness in his eyes, only a veil of frustration and sorrow. When he continued, he had forgotten about Tebethto and directed his remarks to Tecumseh. "The whites cut down the forests and burn the grasses in order to plant things Moneto did not intend to be here. While they are doing this, the animals they brought with them are allowed to wander and eat up the grasses and leaves belonging to the animals Moneto meant to be here. When we allow one white man to build his cabin, soon he has two, then ten, then more until there is little room left. By then the white man has forgotten the land is the Indians' and he has only been allowed to be there. Suddenly he looks upon the Indian as being an intruder on *his* land and tells the Indian he must move away to make room for more white men.

"When a white man kills an Indian in a fair fight, it is called honorable, but when an Indian kills a white man in a fair fight, it is called murder. When a white army battles Indians and wins, it is a great victory, but if they lose it is called a massacre and bigger armies are raised. If the Indian flees before the advance of such armies, when he tries to return he finds that white men are living where he lived. If he tries to fight off such armies, he is killed and the land is taken anyway. When an Indian is killed, it is a great loss which leaves a gap in our people and a sorrow in our heart; when a white is killed, three or four others step up to take his place and there is no end to it. The white man seeks to conquer nature, to bend it to his will and to use it wastefully until it is all gone and then he simply moves on, leaving the waste behind him and looking for new places to take. The whole white race is a monster who is always hungry and what he eats is land." He paused and shook his head and then glanced back at his sister and the two girls beside her, who were watching him soberly. "We Shawnees have long been divided among ourselves as to what path we should take, and because we have finally come to know that it is a difference between us that can never be resolved, we are doing today that which is the only thing left for us to do. Our tribe is splitting for all time and those of us who remain here will continue to try to find some way to stop the white wave that threatens to engulf us."

That discussion in the wegiwa had taken place over a week ago and since then the various chiefs had continued to weigh the pros and cons of leaving or staying behind. Catahecassa—Black Hoof—who was second principal chief of the Shawnees under Chiungalla, was one of those who was in a quandary about it for days. He very nearly concluded to go with those who were leaving but in the end had decided against it, knowing that one day he would rise to the post of principal chief of all who remained and the lure of such power was too much to resist. Catahecassa had always yearned for power.

Chiuxca—Black Stump—second chief of the Peckuwes, refused to accompany his sept, which was still under the leadership of Wesecahnay—Black Beard. He relinquished his position as second chief and resolved to live, with those few who would remain with him, at Piqua Town with Shemeneto and the meager residue of his Kispokothas.

Hardly any Thawegilas remained behind but among those who did was the second chief of the sept, the old chief medicine man and prophet of the tribe, Penegashega—Change of Feathers.

Now, with the final separation occurring, the heads of the three septs splitting away forever were Kikusgowlowa of the Thawegilas, Outhowwa Shokka—Yellow Hawk—of the Kispokothas, and Wesecahnay—Black Beard—of the Peckuwes. Following them were those who had given up in the struggle against the whites—nearly four thousand Shawnees from all five septs, including some twelve hundred from Chalahgawtha alone. What horses they had were being used as pack animals to transport their goods or to carry the aged or infirm. The remainder, comprising the majority, were to walk the long way to their destination.

Those participating in the exodus were being guided by their French trader friend, Peter Loramie, who shook hands with each of the remaining chiefs and wished them well, promising to return and to report on the journey after leading this departing faction to their new home west of the Mississippi. It would take them nearly a month to reach their new land, a grant of twenty-five square miles along Sugar Creek and Apple Creek near Cape Girardeau in the Missouri country.[188] Loramie had negotiated on behalf of the Shawnees with Spanish officials and had been heard sympathetically by Baron de Carondelet, who authorized the grant.

The final cleavage of the Shawnee Nation now took place and the remaining chiefs and only one hundred warriors left at Chalahgawtha watched in stoic silence as the long line of emigrants began moving off, seeking only the peace that they so greatly desired and leaving the Ohio country forever. Remaining to fight for the cherished Ohio territory, that had become their birthright, until the last warrior among them should leave his bones to bleach in the sun, were the broken remnants of the Chalahgawthas and Maykujays, a total of less than three thousand Shawnee men, women, and children. The ultimate result was that the Shawnees remaining, of which about only eight hundred fifty were effective warriors, now would have to face with greatly diminished strength an enemy whose own strength was increasing with frightening rapidity.

Tecumseh watched the exodus until the final individual vanished from view and in his breast, as in the hearts of all those who remained behind, there had lodged an encompassing sadness that would never leave and an emptiness the like of which, until now, was unknown in Shawnee history.[189]

[June 10, 1779 — Thursday]

Lowawluwaysica positively adored Tecumseh.

For the last-born of the triplets, now nine years old, the fact that he was fond of anyone was rather remarkable. He had no real friends, casual or close, and though he often played with his two triplet brothers, Sauwaseekau and Kumskaka, he held no great affection for them, tolerating them merely because they tended to submit with only mild protestation to his persistent bullying. He admired Chiksika but at the same time resented not only the pronounced warrior status he had achieved but also the discipline and training Chiksika endeavored to instill in him. He *did* like Tecumapese despite her frequent chiding of him for the multitude of things he did wrong, either deliberately or through ineptitude. It was only Tecumseh that he truly loved.

There was good reason. Tecumseh never looked at him with the faint distaste that so many others exhibited, nor was he ever scornful of Lowawluwaysica because the boy could not seem to excel in anything—not in sports, games, hunting, mock battles or anything else. Tecumseh was kind to him, constantly did favors for him without expecting reciprocation, complimented him on what few mild attributes he did possess and consistently bolstered his little brother's self-confidence. He treated the other two of the triplets in much the same way, but there was a sort of special empathy—or perhaps sympathy— that he held for Lowawluwaysica, simply because the lad was so signally incompetent in virtually all fields.

Lowawluwaysica brooded a great deal, rarely laughing unless it was at someone's misfortune. And, while only entering his tenth summer, he had already developed a pronounced fondness for alcohol and went to great lengths to satisfy his craving for it. If a trader left a jug or bottle or flask of whiskey unattended, Lowawluwaysica zeroed in on it with the determination of a bee after nectar, having canniness enough not to take the whole container, which loss would have been quickly detected, but hurriedly gulping as many mouthfuls as he could safely guzzle. When Chiksika and Tecumseh once came home with three half-kegs of whiskey they had taken as part of the plunder on an attack against whites rafting down the Spaylaywitheepi, Lowawluwaysica had pried open the bungs during the night, poured out into empty containers about a gallon from each and refilled the loss with water before replacing the bungs, then indulged himself for a week or more afterwards with surreptitious gulping from his hidden hoard. He had even shared some with Tecumseh, refusing to say where he had obtained it, and delighting that the raw whiskey made Tecumseh every bit as inebriated as it made him, though with a signal difference. Where Tecumseh became mellow and humorous and even silly with the effects of alcohol, Lowawluwaysica became surly, argumentative, often highly belligerent. In a very short time Tecumseh became as addicted to the fiery fluid as his younger brother and soon made it a priority on raids to watch for whiskey or rum amid the plunder and stash away what he could of it before it was seen by others, so that later, at Chalahgawtha, he and Lowawluwaysica could indulge their mutual habit.

Tecumseh did his best to instruct Lowawluwaysica in hunting skills, especially with bow and arrow, since he showed no affinity whatsoever for guns. Superb archer that he was, Tecumseh often withheld shooting at game they spotted so that Lowawluwaysica could have an opportunity at it. Occasionally the smaller boy would bag the quarry, at which Tecumseh would praise him highly on his improving skill.

What game the two did manage to down—largely rabbits, squirrels, woodchucks, raccoons, opossums, quail, ducks, smaller birds and occasional deer—was almost always, at Tecumseh's unwavering insistence, taken to the village and distributed among the aged men and women who were in need due to the absence of warriors in the family who were off on raids or who had been killed or injured. Tecumseh had quickly become a great favorite among the elderly, not only for his largess with the game he downed but because of his unflagging interest when they spoke for long hours of times past and of their own experiences. He assiduously absorbed their valuable comments on nature, woods lore, history, strategy of warfare, the making and use of various weapons and tools, plus a multitude of other matters.

While Tecumseh benefitted enormously from such contact with the tribe's elderly, and they from him, Lowawluwaysica exhibited impatience with their frailty, their slow speech and plodding ways due to the infirmities of age and retained to his own benefit very little of the valuable information they imparted, despite Tecumseh's cajoling that he pay closer attention.

Today was one of those days when Lowawluwaysica's failure to pay closer attention to the fundamentals of hunting brought tragic results. Tecumseh, with Lowawluwaysica trailing along, led a group of about a dozen boys into the fields to instruct them in bow hunting skills. One of the favorite forms of hunting for such tyros was shooting at *poi-ithakis*—passenger pigeons—as they flew past overhead, since even the worst shooters always managed to bring some down. The flocks were immense almost beyond description, oftentimes twenty or thirty birds in depth, a quarter-mile to a half-mile wide and sometimes taking actual days to pass, having as many as four or five million birds in a single flock.[190] Although these pigeons were around all summer, those huge flocks passed through only during the spring and autumn migrations, so their practice on this day was largely confined to four-legged game. They had let fly arrows at several rabbits and squirrels and had already bagged one rabbit, much to the pride of an eight-year-old for whom it was his first actual field hunting success. It was while they were crossing an extensive buffalo grass prairie that one of Tecumseh's triplet brothers, Sauwaseekau, who had been bringing up the rear, happened to glance upward and saw a large solitary crow flying past at a height of perhaps a hundred feet above them. As with the others of the party, he had an arrow nocked on his bowstring and ready for instant use, so he immediately pulled his bow to a full draw and released. The arrow missed the bird by only a few inches and continued upward to the highest point its velocity could carry it, then began its fall. The boy, seeing that the missile was going to come down in the midst of his companions, shouted an urgent warning.

"Illenalui peewahcah! Oshawkilcawni!"—Arrow coming down! Look out!

All the boys instantly crouched, bent their heads and covered them with their hands. The single exception was Lowawluwaysica, who either missed that vital lesson or failed to retain it. While the others ducked and covered themselves protectively, he looked up . . . just in time for the jagged, extremely sharp flint arrowhead to plunge into his right eye.

He dropped to his knees, screaming in pain, both hands cupped around the shaft, then rolled over onto his back, writhing and shrieking with the worst torment he had ever known. The other boys rushed to him and Tecumseh cradled his head in his lap and ordered the others to grip Lowawluwaysica's arms and legs and pin him firmly to prevent further injurious writhing. Ordering his brother to hold still, Tecumseh wrapped his left arm around Lowawluwaysica's head and pinned it firmly against his own chest. With care but firmness, he pulled the arrow free amid increased screaming from his brother. As the barbed flint arrowhead emerged, it brought with it a surprisingly small amount of blood but a mass of vitreous fluid and most of the collapsed eyeball. Sauwaseekau was devastated at what had happened and filled with an overwhelming sense of remorse.

They carried Lowawluwaysica, still writhing and screaming, to the wegiwa of the ancient Chalahgawtha medicine man and oracle, Assatakoma, who packed the largely empty eye socket with buzzard down to absorb whatever fluids were still seeping out and gravely put to words what everyone already knew—that Lowawluwaysica's right eye was forever gone. The weeping Sauwaseekau, who had been begging Lowawluwaysica's forgiveness every few seconds since the accident occurred was finally ordered by Assatakoma to be silent, that what had happened was what was meant to be and no words would change anything. After that Sauwaseekau became very withdrawn.

Tecumseh, for his part, though he knew it was not his fault, felt guilty about it, since he was the one who had led the party of youngsters out for their hunting lesson. As a result, he became even more solicitous of his injured brother's well-being—a fact that Lowawluwaysica, despite his love for Tecumseh, did not hesitate to use to his own fullest advantage.

[July 10, 1779 — Saturday]

For a long time the Shawnees had speculated on the possibility of the Kentuckians, as the settlers south of the Spaylaywitheepi were calling themselves, invading the Ohio country to attack a Shawnee stronghold. Chalahgawtha, being the closest village to the Ohio—only seventy-five miles down the Little Miami to its mouth—was considered the most likely target should such an attack occur.

Today speculation had become shattering reality.

Not much more than an hour before dawn a woman in one of the wegiwas awoke and went out to relieve herself. While squatted over the trench, sleepily hearing the rasp of katydids and chirp of crickets in the calm night air she heard something that wiped away all sleepiness with the effectiveness of icy water dashed in her face; the clink of metal and creak of leather that could only mean a horse or horses approaching—saddled horses. She raced silently back to the wegiwa and awoke her husband.

The warrior came outside, flintlock in hand, and listened intently, hearing nothing at first but then, from the direction of the Little Miami and slightly downstream, he heard the same sounds, followed by a distant faint commotion of someone falling over a log or branch in the darkness and then a barely heard expletive . . . in English.

"'*Shemanese!*" he shouted. *Shemanese!* Everyone up, it's an attack. *Shemanese!* Get up! Get up! Women to the council house—with the children. Get up! Everyone up!"

Immediately there was a great confusion of voices and running forms in the pale moonlight or silhouettes dashing past the few outdoor fires. Practically on the heels of the warning came shots from the woods; a few, at first, but quickly becoming a barrage, then settling down to an irregular constancy. The range from the riverine woods, where the shots were originating, to the village was too great for any degree of accuracy, but the air was filled with the hiss of passing balls and the thunk of many slamming into the wood of the wegiwas.[191]

The attack could not have come at a worse time for the Indians or a more propitious one for the whites. Three months earlier, before the tribe split, there might well have been a thousand warriors here. Even three nights ago there would have been at least one hundred and fifty warriors on hand to fight off the invaders, but two days earlier by far the greater majority of Chalah-gawtha's chiefs and warriors—over a hundred, all told—had left for a tribal council at Wapatomica. The result was that the village at this moment of the attack had a total of only twenty-four men and fifteen boys.

Tecumseh had jerked erect from his sleep at the first cries. Chiksika was one of those gone to Wapatomica, but Chiungalla was here, ill health having prevented his attending the council and the second principal chief Catahe-cassa—Black Hoof—having gone in his stead. At once, making sure Tecum-apese was awake and was gathering up the triplets, Spemica Lawba and the two adopted sisters to take them to the *msi-kah-mi-qui,* Tecumseh snatched up his rifle, horn and pouch, then his tomahawk and sprinted to the other end of the wegiwa to alert Chiungalla. The principal chief was already up and sending his wife and two daughters to the council house. He grasped his weapons and the two ran outside.

Answering shots were erupting from the village now, directed toward the gun flashes in the woods and there was still great confusion as women and children raced to the council house. The firing of the *Shemanese* had by now become merely sporadic shooting, but from the barrage of shots that had initially been sent into the village, Chiungalla knew the attackers had to number well over two hundred men. If such a force rushed the town and caught the warriors fighting in and about the flimsy wegiwas, there could be little doubt of the outcome—the Shawnees would be wiped out.

With dawn almost upon them, the only hope was to use the remaining darkness to get everyone into the sturdy *msi-kah-mi-qui* and a few of the closest wegiwas. He called out the order at once and the warriors quickly converged to the center of town.

Shortly after daylight, prepared to fight to the death in the council house, the Shawnees watched as the *Shemanese* left the woods and raced in a ragged wave to the outermost wegiwas of the village and disappeared among them. Some began reappearing with plunder in their grasp and curls of smoke rose as wegiwas were set ablaze. Chiungalla told his people to hold their fire.

"Their greed," he said, "will overcome their common sense. Let them take as they will. Let them burn as they will. They will come closer, believing we have not the strength to defend ourselves. Do not fire until I say, but have every gun in readiness. When it is time to fire, do not shoot at shadows. Pick your target and aim well."

By that time the soldiers had plundered and fired the outlying wegiwas and were now working within acceptable range of gunshot. Already they had collected quite an enormous amount of goods—blankets, fur robes, silver ornaments, kettles, implements, and some weapons.

"Now!" Chiungalla ordered.

Tecumseh was one of those who had been holding a bead on a particular soldier as he moved between the wegiwas. At Chiungalla's command he squeezed off his shot and was gratified to see the man knocked off his feet into a crumpled, motionless heap. Other Shawnees were firing, many with similar effectiveness. Incredibly, though the *Shemanese* became a little more cautious in how they were moving about, they continued to loot and burn and more of them fell under the Shawnee shooting from the *msi-kah-mi-qui*. By eight o'clock in the morning, ten of the invaders had been killed and no Shawnee was yet injured.

The Americans were fairly close to the council house now and Chiungalla and his people braced themselves for the onslaught that would be made against their sanctuary. Old Assatakoma began a loud but unintelligible monologue to the Great Spirit. Tecumseh licked his lips and felt to make sure his tomahawk was still safely in his belt. He reached up and gripped the *opawaka* hanging from his neck.

"Help my brothers and sisters," he murmured.

A rifle ball buzzed through one of the slit windows of the council house just as the subchief Red Pole was aiming his rifle, struck him on the forehead at the hairline and killed him instantly. Only a moment later another ball whipped through the gap in one doorway between the logs and the heavy buffalo skin flap—a tiny gap hardly wider than the diameter of the ball—and buried itself with a vicious smack high in the hip of Chiungalla, sending him tumbling to the hard-packed earth.

A short while later there was a lull in the firing and the sound of commands being given in English. Believing this to be the *Shemanese* chief's order to storm the council house, many of the warriors now took stances near the three large doorways of the *msi-kah-mi-qui,* tomahawks or war clubs in hand, prepared to meet that final charge, knowing they must die in the process. Several of the women had already begun singing the plaintive death chant. But the expected attack didn't come. What few whites were still visible were glimpsed only occasionally as they moved *away* and quickly became hidden by the smoke cloaking most of the village. Soon none could be seen at all.

After another half hour passed, a few warriors slipped out and were gone only a few minutes before returning to say the *Shemanese* had entirely withdrawn from the village and were now at the big horse compound by the creek, rounding up the many horses there. When it was still two hours before the sun had topped the sky, the warriors brought the welcome word that the *Shemanese* had gone, taking with them the loot they had plundered from the wegiwas and just under one hundred fifty horses.[192] However, at least two dozen other horses had managed to escape during the roundup and the oldest warrior present, Frog Hunter, a burly, scarred old veteran of many fights, took command and immediately ordered those escaped horses to be caught and a pursuit of the *Shemanese* begun, which he would lead.

Before long the horses that had broken free of the roundup, twenty-six of them, were captured and Tecumseh was one of those who rode out behind Frog Hunter in pursuit of the whites. Within eight miles they had caught up to them and, while there were far too many of the enemy to attack them with a charge, the Shawnees began a deadly sniping at them from under cover.[193]

As soldiers in the rear began dropping under this fire, the white chief stopped and pulled his force together in a defensive square, at which Frog Hunter moved his warriors back out of range. As soon as the whites began marching again, the Shawnees moved up and renewed their firing, killing more. Again the white chief stopped and formed the defensive square and again Frog Hunter pulled his men out of range. Five times in succession this same pattern occurred over the next eight miles until at last one of the lesser chiefs of the whites gathered together about a hundred men and charged the Indians. At this Frog Hunter ordered the pursuit ended and a return to Chalahgawtha.[194]

Arriving there, the Shawnees found that while many wegiwas had been burned, much of their goods taken, and 144 horses lost, there had been only two casualties—the death of Red Pole and the wounding of Chiungalla.[195] Runners were dispatched at once to Wapatomica to tell of the attack and get the Chalahgawtha warriors back here for protection as quickly as possible.

Tecumseh had immediately gone to the wegiwa and there found Tecumapese and the wife of Chiungalla tending the chief's wound. It was far more severe than at first believed. The lead ball had plunged into the principal chief's hip and struck the socket, causing it to virtually disintegrate, sending sharp slivers of bone through all the surrounding flesh. He was in great pain and as the glances of Tecumseh and his sister met, she shook her head faintly. The damage was extensive and irreparable.

Chiungalla, who had been lying with his eyes closed, opened them now and looked at Tecumseh and the ghost of a smile burned its way through the grimace of pain.

"You did well, Tecumseh," he whispered. "I am not dead yet and not for a while to come. I can hear the Great Spirit unfolding Her net, but She is doing so very slowly." He closed his eyes for so long that Tecumseh thought he had become unconscious, but then he opened them again, his gaze still on his young ward. "It cannot be more fitting," he said, "that when a great warrior dies, another great warrior appears. Pucksinwah would have been very proud of his son. You are a good warrior now, Tecumseh. One day you will be a great warrior.''

[September 15, 1779 — Wednesday]

The Great Spirit did indeed take a very long time in lowering Her net to take up Chiungalla.

Week after week and then moon following moon he lingered, gradually growing weaker, constantly in severe pain, yet lucid until very close to the end. On the third day following the attack on Chalahgawtha, Catahecassa—Black Hoof—second principal chief of the Shawnees, returned to the village with all the chiefs and warriors who had gone from here with him to the Wapatomica Grand Council. There was fierce anger burning in all of them that further intensified when they saw the charred remains of their town. All but the *msi-kah-mi-qui* and some eighty of the wegiwas closest to that structure had been burned. The dwellings could easily enough be replaced but that was not the case with the goods that had been taken or destroyed, especially the weapons, clothing, and cookware.

Catahecassa had come to see Chiungalla immediately on his return and Tecumseh, who had scarcely left his chief's side, moved respectfully away and stood quietly in a dim corner. The vague dislike he felt for the heavy-set second chief did not mirror itself in his expression except for a slight narrowing of his eyes. Catahecassa, unlike Chiungalla, was an essentially humorless man who took himself and his position very seriously. This became more than evident with his first words.

"Chiungalla," he said, "it is important at this time that our warriors have someone to look to for direction. A wound such as you have received will not allow you to carry on your office as the tribe needs, so it would be best to have a council called here immediately that I may lead our people in full authority."

Chiungalla regarded him steadily and when he spoke his voice was much stronger than it had been at any time since he was shot. "I am sure, Catahecassa, that you do think that would be best, but I must point out to you that what you see before you is not a corpse. Not yet."

"Oh," Catahecassa said hastily, "I didn't mean—"

"You meant exactly what you said," Chiungalla interrupted, "but no matter. In part you are correct; our people do need a leadership I cannot now provide. By my authority I place you in the position of principal chief *on a temporary basis* until we see what lies ahead. There will be time enough for a Grand Council to name who should be principal chief after me when my lungs have filled themselves a final time. Until then, I see, I hear, I speak, so you will discuss with me all matters having to do with our people. And you will keep me informed on all matters that are occurring where our problems with the whites are concerned."

Catahecassa's lips had become a thin line, but he merely nodded and said, "I will do as you say, of course, Chiungalla." He turned and left the wegiwa.

As soon as he left, the expressionless mask Chiungalla had worn dissolved into a grimace and he licked his lips. Tecumseh quickly brought him a cup of water, which he drank gratefully.

"Tecumseh," he said, his voice raspy with pain again, "I would like you to find Chiksika and ask him to come to me."

Tecumseh bobbed his head and dashed away and soon found his brother working with other warriors and some of the women, throwing the remaining charred wood of the wegiwas onto a large burning pile of similar material. In a short time the brothers were back with their chief and Chiungalla reached out a hand and gripped Chiksika's arm weakly.

"Chiksika," he said, "what I tell you now you must tell the other warriors here—Wasegoboah, Frog Hunter, all of them. It is important that I know what is happening around us. I want you and them to come to me here with news of any kind that they learn. They and you are to inquire of the other chiefs they see in other villages or wherever they find them, that they should tell you what is happening, that you may pass it to me. It is," he repeated, "important that I know. Also, the *Shemanese* have taken or destroyed much of what we need. War parties are to go out as often as they can into the Kentucky lands. They are to make every effort to take back whatever they can find of what was taken, and more. Especially they are to find weapons and horses to replace those we have lost. They must also kill the *Shemanese* at every opportunity. We must now hit them very hard for the injury they have given us."

So it began. For the remainder of the summer and into the Harvest Moon the war parties from Chalahgawtha, Tecumseh accompanying Chiksika on many of them, were in constant movement to and from Kentucky, causing havoc and terror wherever they went. Scores of new cabins were burnt, dozens of settlers were killed, injured, or captured. Strong demands were sent to the Detroit commander demanding that the British, who had so long begged them to take up the hatchet against the Americans, must now provide them with new and better weapons and ammunition and, most important, to provide troops and artillery to go with them against the forts in Kentucky.

Warriors and messengers came and went with great frequency, hardly a day passing when someone didn't arrive at the principal chief's wegiwa with news of the turmoil all around the Shawnee territory. From their own forays, from other chiefs and warriors and from traders and British agents, a great deal of news was brought to Chiungalla, most of it bad, but many good reports as well. Numerous horses were being taken from the Kentuckians and swum across the Spaylaywitheepi, and by the end of the two moons practically as many had been recovered as had been taken.

A large number of successful raids were being carried out against settlements and isolated settlers everywhere on the frontier, from the vicinity of Fort McIntosh at the mouth of Beaver River just below Pittsburgh all the way down to the Falls of the Spaylaywitheepi and beyond. Over a thousand new whites had settled in the Kentucky country during the past summer, most of them arriving by way of the Spaylaywitheepi. A great number of largely successful attacks were made against those hordes of whites coming downriver in rafts, canoes, and other boats of all description, including the huge craft called broadhorns, which could carry an amazing amount of goods, livestock, and people.

Especially helpful in these river attacks, the warriors reported, had been Tecumseh. Clad in white man's garb taken from other encounters, he would stand on the shore and call plaintively to passing boats for help, crying out to them that his family had been attacked and he was the only survivor. When they would put in to shore to pick him up they would run into a murderous ambush, usually with all members of the white party killed and scalped and the large quantity of goods they were transporting taken to the Shawnee villages.

By the end of summer Chalahgawtha had been restored to a near normal condition. While not all the burned wegiwas had been restored—and never would be, for many of those destroyed had been vacant since the splitting of the tribe—practically all their other losses in the Heat Moon attack by the *Shemanese* had been replaced with new and better goods. Chalahgawtha would never again be the great Shawnee center it had once been, but it was certainly a strong and populous village once again.

The news from Detroit was especially heartening. The British had been receptive to the demands of Chiungalla that they assist the Shawnees in future major attacks against the Kentuckians and had promised that plans were shaping up for a major offensive against the Kentucky forts the following spring. Best of all, they promised many well-armed troops of British soldiers and powerful artillery to accompany the Shawnees and that British Indian allies from other tribes, especially the Wyandots, Ottawas, and Delawares, would likely be joining the assault. In the meanwhile, their British friends would still be buying scalps and prisoners at Detroit.

Along with the reports came another chapter in the saga of the amazing Bahd-ler. The Great White Wolf, who was supposed to have been returned by the British to the Indians for his long-postponed execution, had escaped from Detroit well before Chalahgawtha was attacked and had made his way back on foot through the Indiana country, safely arriving at the new fort the Americans had just built at the Falls of the Spaylaywitheepi—Fort Nelson.[196] He was once again, just like the escaped Sheltowee, a most dangerous enemy. Tecumseh, secretly pleased that the remarkable frontiersman had really managed to get away after all, experienced a sudden very strong premonition that one day he would be facing the formidable Bahd-ler in mortal combat.

Despite the increased Shawnee attacks in Kentucky, ever more settlements were springing up, larger and stronger and the whole country was filling out with surveyors and land jobbers. Actual farms were being established and the settlements surrounding Harrodsburg and Logan's Fort were becoming towns. And a captive just brought in, who had been taken while descending the Spaylaywitheepi, told them that the Kentuckians now had a new father in the east—Governor Thomas Jefferson—who, the prisoner said, had moved the capital of the state from Williamsburg to Richmond.

And, speaking of new leadership, since word had reached Quebec that Lieutenant Governor Henry Hamilton had been sent in chains to the East to be imprisoned, a new commander for Detroit had been named. His name was Captain Arent de Peyster.

One warrior, who had spent some time with the Potawatomies came to Chiungalla with the report that a new trading post had been established by a white man named Gaurie on the river called Checagou just above its mouth at the southwestern end of Lake Michigan.[197] Not so many miles from there, at the southeastern end of Lake Michigan, another trading post had been established earlier in the year by a man named DuSable, who was the son of a French trader and a black slave woman, and who himself had married a Potawatomi woman named Gohna. He had visited the Checagou River area and thought it was so much better suited to a trading post that he had given up the one not long before established and now had built a much better one that was also on the Checagou River but much closer to its mouth than Gaurie's.[198]

Well to the east at Fort Laurens on the Tuscarawas, the one hundred fifty white soldiers garrisoned there under Colonel John Gibson had spent the whole of last winter in desperate need of food since expected provisions from Fort Pitt or Fort McIntosh had not arrived. One inadequate shipment of supplies under a white chief and fifteen soldiers had been forwarded in late January and reached Fort Laurens safely, but as they started their return, a party of Wyandots, Delawares, and Mingoes, led by Simon Girty, attacked them three miles from the fort, killed two and captured another carrying dispatches in his saddle bags, and the remainder were forced to flee back to Fort Laurens.[199] A large number of those Indians had gathered around the fort, bottling it up and continuing to try to pick off any soldiers who ventured outside and, at that time, the Indians anticipated that if they got some British help, they would soon be able to kill them all and destroy the fort. Girty and some of the Indians took the soldier they had captured to Detroit and Girty explained the Fort Laurens situation to the commander, telling him that the Wyandots at Sandusky, as well as other Indians, were prepared to attack but they needed ammunition. The Detroit commander promptly supplied them with food, ammunition and gifts and sent them, along with Captain Henry Bird, as an observer, back to do their mischief.

Hoping to starve the Fort Laurens garrison so much they would have to emerge, the Indians had been thwarted by the frontiersman Sam Brady, who was earning himself a reputation among the Wyandots and Delawares as fearful as that of Sheltowee and Bahd-ler among the Shawnees.

Brady had taken it upon himself to be the hunter for the troops and managed to supply them with fresh meat for a long while before the Indians were able to discover how he was doing so. The frontiersman would slip out of the fort under cover of night and go some miles away up the Tuscarawas to avoid being heard when he shot. He would then hunt until he had killed all the game he could manage and bring it to the river's edge. There he would make a raft with a hole in the center, pack the meat on the surface of the raft, cover it over well with brush and then shove it off. He would then enter the water himself despite very cold weather and water, dive under the raft and come up with his head through the center hole, so he was screened by the brush but could see out well enough to guide the raft from underneath. To the surrounding Indians it appeared to be only a pile of brush floating downstream and they paid no attention to it. Brady would float with the raft the several miles back to the fort where there was a curve in the river and the current swung the raft close to shore, always timing his arrival to be after nightfall. When he arrived he would wedge the raft firmly on the shore and then slip into the fort to get help carrying the meat inside.

The good news from that quarter, the messengers told Chiungalla, was that the Americans had finally decided that Fort Laurens was too remote to be properly supplied and was therefore untenable and so the entire garrison had been evacuated at the order of General McIntosh and had returned to Fort McIntosh and Fort Pitt. The abandoned fort had immediately been burned to the ground by the Indians, so now that area of the Ohio country, at least, was a little less threatened than before.

The most momentous news was that the Americans had put their expedition against the Iroquois into operation under a white chief named General John Sullivan and so devastating had it been to the Indians that for all intents and purposes the Iroquois League had ceased to exist.[200] As it began, the Mohawk chief, Thayendanegea—he whom the whites called Joseph Brant—

had tried to divert Sullivan by leading his warriors against an American settlement on the Delaware and the result was what was being called the Battle
of Minisink.[201] Thayendanegea had three warriors slain, but his party killed
forty-four Americans.

Sullivan had refused to be diverted, however, and his army of about five
thousand soldiers had swept northward from Pennsylvania into the New York
country and struck at the underbelly of the League. Under orders from George
Washington to destroy everything, Sullivan's force had reduced no less than
forty towns of the Iroquois—largely Senecas and Cayugas—to ashes, chopped
down thousands of acres of Indian orchards, destroyed more than one hundred
sixty thousand bushels of corn plus a commensurate amount of other vegetable
crops, all of which were to have been for the subsistence of the Iroquois over
the forthcoming winter and now they would surely starve and freeze.[202]

Chief Red Jacket of the Iroquois bitterly referred to George Washington
as Town Destroyer and said, "We are encircled, we are encompassed. We
stand, a small island in the bosom of the great waters. We are surrounded.
The Evil Spirit rides upon the wind. The waters are angry. They swell. They
press upon us and when the waves once settle over us, we shall disappear
forever. Who lives to mourn over us? No one! What marks our destruction?
Nothing! We are mingled with the earth and water and air."[203]

Several parties of warriors who had been skirmishing with the whites in
the area of the upper Spaylaywitheepi arrived at Chalahgawtha and reported
that in the first part of August, while the Iroquois in New York were occupied
with opposing General Sullivan, the commander of Fort Pitt, Colonel Daniel
Brodhead, had led his force of six hundred men up the Allegheny by land to
destroy the villages of the Munsee faction of the Delawares.[204] Captain Sam
Brady headed the advance troops of Brodhead's Expedition. They had discovered a war party of about sixty Indians, led by Chief Dehguswaygahent
of the Senecas and Chiefs Dayoosta and Natahgoah of the Delawares, descending the Allegheny in canoes to attack settlements in the area of Fort Pitt.
Brady had swiftly set up an ambush nine miles downstream from the village
of Conewago, at an island just over three miles below the mouth of the
Dagahshenodeago.[205] The unsuspecting Indians were caught in it and in a fierce
firing from the whites, Natahgoah and a prominent warrior named Hutgueote
managed to escape, but fifteen Indians were killed, including both Dehguswaygahent and Dayoosta, along with the prominent warriors named Dahgahswagaheh, Dahgahgahend and Gennehoon, plus fourteen others
wounded.[206] The war party had broken up and scattered and Brodhead's men
continued their advance to two small Delaware towns on the Kenjua Flat and,
a little farther upstream, the substantial Seneca village called Dunosahdahgah,
which was the village of the famed Chief Warhoyonehteh—Cornplanter.[207]
The whites found all three villages had been deserted at their approach—

Warhoyonehteh himself was fighting General Sullivan far to the east—and, after destroying five hundred acres of green corn and confiscating thirty horses, plundered the towns of a considerable quantity of traps and fur skins and finally burned all the dwellings. Brodhead's army then returned home.

Another Seneca chief, Gahgeote, just returned to the upper Allegheny after having fought Sullivan, discovered four of Brodhead's men who had become lost in the woods, pursued and killed them, then gathered up forty warriors and went far down the river to overtake the army and strike it from the rear, but he was too late, as the whites had already reached Fort Pitt.[208]

Chiungalla sighed at the ominous portents so rife in all these reports and it seemed that all will to fight off the inevitable had drained away from him. Tecumapese, Chiksika and Tecumseh were among those who were with their beloved chief in his final lucid moments.

"Perhaps . . ." Chiungalla's voice was barely a thready whisper and his eyes were on the brothers as he spoke, ". . . perhaps others will rise after me to continue the fight against this white-man foe whose numbers are endless and whose designs are implacable."

The principal chief of the Shawnees closed his eyes and rarely opened them up again, nor did he speak another word. Just before the first light of dawn three days ago, on the sixty-fourth day after receiving his wound, he quietly died.

Word of Chiungalla's death spread rapidly to all the Shawnee villages and from them all converged a swarm of chiefs and warriors, women, children and elderly upon Chalahgawtha. As they arrived they went directly to the *msi-kah-mi-qui* where the cold still form of Chiungalla, cleansed and groomed and wrapped in a fine new scarlet blanket, lay face up on a low platform. On the ground around the table and in the available spaces on its surface were a large number of items that had been brought by the mourners as tribute to their fallen chief: small belts of wampum, colorful ribbons, swaths of calico, wooden, bowls, small brass pans, fine new moccasins and vests and leggins, and a variety of food in small wooden boxes and drink in flasks. Beside him lay the four items that had been so important to him in life—on one side his knife in its sheath and his tomahawk, on the other his flintlock rifle and his pipe.

Those who had come wore simple clothing and no ornamentation, their hair loose, their faces daubed in lines and curves of indigo, ocher, and vermilion. Virtually all the males of an age above ten summers were smoking *kinnikinnick* in small pipes, from the stems of which hung teal feathers or ermine tails or both. Upon entering the council house, each person had stepped up to the bier and gazed for a moment at the one who had been their chief, their old, beloved, courageous leader, their trusted and revered counselor in all matters. Then each would move on in his turn, find an open place on the earthen floor and sit down. For hours they sat in this way, silent, smoking, grieving in harmony, but each bearing the grief within the solitude of his own heart.

Few chiefs in the history of the tribe had ever been loved so much by his people as Chiungalla.

In the two days before this, the young men of the village had spread out in the surrounding countryside and plied their hunting skills to the best of their ability and here, on mats upon the ground outside the *msi-kah-mi-qui* was the result of their efforts—a large accumulation of already partially cooked or fully prepared wild meats, fowls, and fish. There was the meat from twenty deer, three bears, a young buffalo, two elk, and a dozen raccoons; there were twenty ducks and twenty geese already roasted and fifty quail ready to be cooked; and there were scores of freshly caught fish, also ready to be spitted and cooked. On a broad fresh cloth were over a hundred round flat loaves of hard bread and a score or more of jugs, some filled with rusty-colored apple juice and others with *melassanepe,* a nectar of water and maple sugar. There was no alcohol in any form as it was strictly forbidden at a state funeral.

Tecumseh had been in charge of the hunters and now he was also in charge of the six other boys about his age who patrolled the perimeters of the food mats and kept the village dogs away. Numerous fires had been built and numerous kettles hung over them, from which vapors had already begun to rise, some with stews, some with ordinary water. A multitude of sticks sharpened on one end lay on a mat by themselves, ready for use for spitting whatever meat was chosen.

As the sun neared the tops of the trees to the west, Chiksika and seven other warriors, four to a side, passed four broad rawhide straps under the blanket-wrapped body. Each gripped one end of a strap and together they lifted the body and carried it without pause to the Shawnee graveyard two miles south beside a small creek.[209]

Immediately behind the bearers walked Chiungalla's family and then his wards and adopted children. Behind them came the chiefs and subchiefs, according to rank and led by Catahecassa. Blue Jacket was in this group. They were followed first by the warriors of Chalahgawtha and then those of other villages, then the women of Chalahgawtha, the women of other villages, and finally the children.

A grave had already been dug, two feet wide, seven feet in length and three and a half feet deep. At the bottom lay a split puncheon, while a similar one stood on edge along each of the long sides of the grave. Slowly and carefully the eight warriors lowered the body of their chief on its back onto the bottom puncheon and the straps pulled free. The last clothing he had worn in health was placed atop the body and his moccasins were cut into strips and pieces and placed with the clothing. Other than the body and these items, no weapons, food, mementos or anything else was put into the grave. A final puncheon brought from one side was laid over the body and the effect was now of a long, narrow, open-ended box in which the principal chief lay.

Removing a cloth bundle from his belt, Catahecassa now stepped to the grave and, as he did so, a thousand or more mourners joined in voicing the ululating, rather eerie sounds of the death chant—a melancholy, fluctuating tone embodying grief and despair. As the throbbing chant filled the evening air, Catahecassa reached into the little bag and, from his fingertips, sprinkled some of the contents over the top puncheon. This was the sacred tobacco called *nilu-famu* and, with the death chant continuing, Catahecassa moved slowly around the grave sprinkling the tobacco as he went. By the time he returned to his starting point, the pouch was empty and he dropped it onto the puncheon. With that the ritual was finished. Catahecassa turned and strode back toward the *msi-kah-mi-qui,* everyone but three following and continuing to chant until the council house was reached.

The three who had remained behind were Chiksika, Wasegoboah, and Blue Jacket. Not until the chanting was barely audible in the distance did the three, using their bare hands, begin to scoop the earth into the excavation. In half an hour, with the twilight deepening around them, they finished and rolled a smooth boulder the size of a pumpkin onto the foot of the grave. The three left immediately and walked directly to the nearby Little Miami River where they stripped off their clothing and discarded it. Wading into the stream, they scooped up sand and gravel in their hands and vigorously scrubbed themselves all over with it. Then they thrust fingers down their own throats, causing vomiting. Moving upstream a bit, they drank from the river until they could drink no more and then expelled that as well through forced regurgitation. All this was a purifying procedure, cleansing the individual inside and out. A bit farther upstream they found the fresh loincloths that had been placed there for them, put them on and jogged back to the village.

Quiet talking was occurring when the three warriors entered the *msi-kah-mi-qui,* as one by one, any on hand who had a special memory of or experience with Chiungalla and cared to share it, arose and spoke his piece in a conversational way. The women moved in and out with bowls of stew, with bark trays on which were heaped the game that had been roasted earlier or was still being roasted, or with jugs of the *melassanepe* nectar or apple juice, along with strips of smooth, thin bark that could be cut into sections and rolled into cone-shaped cups quite adequate as drinking vessels. No one present went hungry.

Throughout the entire night, not concluding till dawn streaked the eastern sky, the quiet discourses continued, bringing the listeners into a close affinity with their departed chief. While all still felt sadness at his demise, every person present also felt enriched by having shared with others a portion of an individual man's life that comprised a composite picture of a man of warmth, intelligence and great courage.

193

Allan W. Eckert

It was near dawn when Tecumseh became one of the last to rise and speak.

"I was luckier than most," he said. "I not only knew Chiungalla as chief but as foster father. I not only saw him in the village and in war parties, I lived in the same wegiwa with him. Of all the many lessons he taught me and the multitude of things he said, I remember best these words he spoke to me at the Blue Licks: 'Do not be bound by limits you place on yourself. It is only when you reach beyond what you think you can do that you will almost surely do far more than you thought you could.'"

Chapter 4

— ❮❯ — For a Shawnee lad only just past his twelfth summer, Tecumseh had become remarkably proficient as a young warrior. Largely this was due to Chiksika who, whenever it was possible to do so, took him along in the war parties he organized. Often these were forays engaged in no more than long-distance harassing of the whites in Kentucky or floating down the Spaylaywitheepi, perhaps resulting in a certain amount of plunder or horses taken, but little more. Occasionally, however, the skirmishes were more substantial, some involving combat at close quarters or even hand-to-hand fighting.

The rule of thumb for the tribe was that no Shawnee individual was expendable. The whites frequently went into fights fully expecting to have a certain number of men killed, but quickly filled these gaps with newcomers who kept arriving on the frontier in increasing numbers and, when need be, drafted into militia service. The Shawnees, however, chose their methods of fighting with great care, taking every possible precaution to avert the possibility of any warriors or chiefs being killed. When it did occur, the death was always greatly lamented, not only because of the high regard in which they held the lives of members of the tribe but because when a Shawnee fell, the gap it created in their defense remained so, as there was no reserve from which to draw. As a result, one of the more favored forms of fighting was to draw the enemy into an ambush so devastating that any who survived thought of little else than escape.

Because of his youth, Tecumseh had become especially valuable at luring river travelers into ambush and in the final weeks of the decade he had participated in several such actions. It was a role he found increasingly distasteful. Though most of the others in the war parties couldn't see it that way, he was growing uncomfortably aware of the great difference between luring a troop of armed men into an ambush and doing the same with river travelers who were so often families represented more by women and children than by men. It all came back to the philosophy that was growing in him with respect to the torture of prisoners; there was little that was admirable about taking the life of someone who was essentially defenseless.

Tecumseh was not displeased to see that where river travel was concerned, such travelers were growing very suspicious about anyone who hailed them from shore, especially from the Ohio side of the river. Some of the more experienced river boatmen, of which there were still only a mere handful, who piloted large rafts or broadhorns or flotillas of keelboats downriver had begun to react differently than the inexperienced river traveler. Such men now had taken to carrying on board a smaller craft, usually a light canoe big enough for only two or three adults. When hailed by an apparent lost child or woman or injured man, instead of putting the larger craft to shore immediately to pick up the unfortunate soul, they kept distant and instead launched the smaller boat with one or two armed men in it, approaching the individual on shore with extreme care. Some had even gotten to the point where they would not put in to the shore at all but approach only to within about a hundred yards and tell the distressed person that if he or she wished to be rescued they could blamed well swim out to the boat to be taken aboard. Nevertheless, there were few boatmen who were canny enough to take such precautions and an abundance who came to shore at once when an appeal was made.

Some ambushes were carried out with elaborate preparations if ample warning could be had that prospective victims were on the way. Such was the case less than a week after the death of Chiungalla when lookouts, who had been ranging far down the Spaylaywitheepi, galloped into Chalahgawtha with the news that just above the Falls and coming upstream at a slow but steady pace close to the Kentucky shore was a flotilla of five keelboats bearing about seventy men and what appeared to be a large shipment of ammunition.[210] The scouts had arrived as the Shawnees were holding an informal council with Matthew Elliott and two of the Girty brothers, Simon and George, who had been accompanied by a party of fifty Indians—Wyandots, Delawares, and Mingoes.[211] The purpose of the visit was to invite Catahecassa—the new Shawnee principal chief—and a delegation of his chiefs to attend an important council scheduled for the end of the Harvest Moon at Upper Sandusky. There, Elliott promised, Captain Henry Bird would be on hand with important news from Detroit. Now, however, the information about the supply flotilla took precedence and plans were made to intercept the boats. Considering the whites' rate of progress against the current, which scouts reported as being around ten miles per day, it was obvious they would have ample time to set up an effective ambush where the Licking River emptied into the Spaylaywitheepi.[212]

Eighty Shawnees joined the party, bringing the total to 130 warriors. Tecumseh went along, as Chiksika's shadow, and the entire force, with weapons ready, hid themselves in the rocks and heavy brush on both sides of the mouth of the Licking, the greater majority on the downstream side and all their canoes well hidden and ready to launch when the whites reached optimum position for the ambush.

A small, poorly made bark canoe was built as bait for the ambush and loaded in its center with several items taken in previous raids.[213] With warriors positioned, the "bait" canoe was placed for quick launching on the downriver side of the Licking at its mouth. In this way it was just out of sight of anyone coming upstream close to the Kentucky shore. Lookouts were positioned to give the signal for launching.

For days they waited before the keelboats finally hove into view close together from around the bend less than two miles downriver, but even this small distance would take several hours for them to traverse.[214] The boats were close to the Kentucky shore not only for protection but to minimize the amount of current they would have to buck. Eight or ten men on the shore side of each boat were poling the craft upriver, each pole man starting at the front of the boat, jabbing his long pole into the bottom and then "walking" the boat past the pole until he reached the stern. At that point he would jerk his pole out of the water and rapidly return with it to the bow to start the whole process over again. Two pole men on the river side of each craft continually pushed at the bottom to keep the boat fairly close to shore. It was rugged work and progress was slow, each boat moving along at the rate of only a mile or two per hour.

Timing was critical. If the bait canoe were launched too soon, it would take too long for the keelboats to reach the spot and if the Indians remained in the ambush area till then, it would arouse suspicion; if launched too late, they ran the risk of sharpshooters on the boats picking off the two Shawnees in the bark canoe. Keeping well hidden, the Indians waited for almost two hours until the keelboats were seventy yards distant. Then the lookout hidden high up the bluff gave a silent signal and the two Shawnees launched the bark canoe and began paddling clumsily out of the mouth of the Licking into the Spaylaywitheepi.

The two paddling Indians kept their heads turned away from the keelboats,

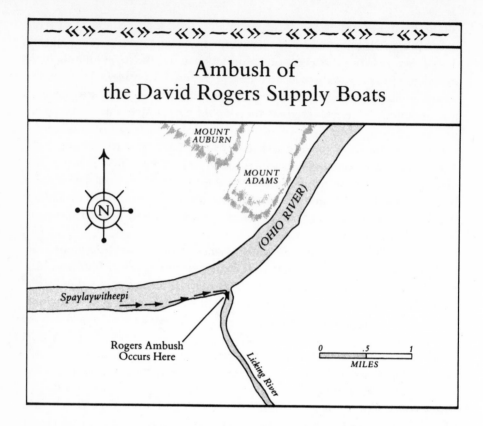

Ambush of the David Rogers Supply Boats

MOUNT AUBURN

MOUNT ADAMS

(OHIO RIVER)

Spaylaywitheepi

Rogers Ambush Occurs Here

Licking River

0   .5   1

MILES

as if looking upstream for any possible danger to appear. Not until they heard shouts from the keelboats, indicating they had been discovered, did they turn, startled, and look downstream. One pointed at the boats and then both began paddling furiously with their bark paddles, turning the clumsy little canoe back into the mouth of the Licking as if trying desperately to get away, but making very little progress.

There was a lot of excitement on the boats and one shot came toward the bark canoe, but was very wide of the mark. It was obvious that the boatmen saw exactly what they were supposed to see: a couple of Indians who had been on a raid in Kentucky and who had been caught in the act of trying to get back across the Ohio River with their plunder in that clumsy little bark boat that could hardly be paddled. The boatmen plied their poles with renewed vigor, knowing they had a good chance of overtaking the canoe or at least getting within reasonable shooting range of it.

The bark canoe slowly pulled out of sight of the boatmen into the Licking and the two Shawnees continued paddling up the tributary stream, protected by the very nearly half-circle bend of the point here. By the time the first of the keelboats reached the Licking's mouth and followed them into it and around the bend, now only a dozen feet from shore, the gap between them and the bark canoe had closed to about fifty yards. The two paddling Indians appeared to be tiring quickly, their frantic strokes not so powerful as at first. The boatmen began getting ready for some more accurate shooting.

Abruptly Simon Girty gave a bellowing cry and instantly a deafening barrage of shooting broke out while, simultaneously a half dozen canoes were launched from their hiding places and skimmed out into the mouth of the river behind four of the five keelboats to prevent their escape, missing only one that had fallen somewhat behind in the chase.[215] Only half the warriors had shot their rifles in that first volley and now these discarded the guns and drew their tomahawks. Under cover of the new firing that broke out from the remaining warriors, they burst from their hiding places, shrieking their war cries, and raced to the water's edge where they plunged into the stream, their leaps carrying them almost to the keelboats.

In the boats, all was confusion. The one craft that had fallen behind pulled well out into the Spaylaywitheepi and was moving off as quickly as possible. In the other four boats a score of men had already been killed in the first firing and more were dropping all the time. Panic embraced the whites and scarcely any shots were made toward the Indians. Some of the whites were leaping overboard from the river side of the boats, trying to swim with the current and quickly get out of range. Some of these were shot at by the Indians on the opposite side of the Licking's mouth or by those coming up from behind in the canoes. A handful of the whites who went overboard dove underwater and swam with the current, staying down until their lungs were bursting, then surfacing to gasp in a fresh breath and dive again. The warriors in the water on the shore side were already clambering into the keelboats, slashing furiously with their tomahawks. Only then did the gunfire from shore cease and those Indians rush out to aid their brothers.

It was all over in minutes. The one keelboat with its thirteen men that had eluded the trap was not pursued, but the four others had been pushed against the shore by the Indians, aided by the current, and wedged on a mud bar. Forty-five whites were killed, including their leader. Five men were captured by the Indians. Only seven of those who had leaped into the water managed to escape and more than half of those were wounded.[216]

Two warriors had been killed and three were slightly injured and the triumphant war party found that the boats contained a booty far beyond their expectations: a ton of gunpowder in forty 50-pound kegs, plus two tons of lead in bars, bullet molds, two boxes of new flintlock rifles, forty bales of new clothing, a chest filled with many thousands of dollars in Spanish silver, numerous kegs of rum and a wide variety of other goods.[217]

Although he had not done much more than shoot his rifle a couple of times, Tecumseh was more than pleased at having participated in one of the most successful ambushes ever accomplished on the Spaylaywitheepi.

[October 16, 1779 — Saturday]

Tecumseh and Lowawluwaysica were both well on their way to becoming drunk.

The gallon jug of rum that Tecumseh had surreptitiously taken as his share of the proceeds of the attack on the boats was what he felt he had earned as a participant. It was while others were busy with the prisoners in the gauntlet that he had filled the heavy crockery jug from one of the kegs that was taken as plunder, not even pouring back into the keg a like measure of water. Since he would claim no other part of the great amount of goods captured, he told himself, this was his just due.

He had hidden the jug under a pile of firewood in one of the many unoccupied wegiwas that had escaped last summer's burning. It was only a few hundred yards from the wegiwa that had once belonged to Chiungalla, but was now considered to be Chiksika's, since Chiungalla's widow, still grieving for her lost husband, had gone to live with her sister in Wapatomica. Chiksika and his four younger brothers, along with Tecumapese and her son, Spemica Lawba, as well as the adopted white girls, Kisathoi and Tebethto, all still lived together under that same roof.

As soon as the jug was concealed, Tecumseh had returned to the gauntlet line where four of the five prisoners had been stripped and made to run their grueling ordeal. The fifth had been taken northward by the Wyandots as they continued back to their villages. Tecumseh was not terribly disappointed to discover that he had come back just as the ritual had ended and everyone was chattering about how it had gone. Two of the captives had successfully made it to the *msi-kah-mi-qui* in the first mad dash; two others had fallen and been beaten insensible, one of whom was taken back to the head of the line for another run. He had made it to the council house on the second effort, though very much battered by the ordeal. The fourth prisoner, on his initial run, had faltered early, staggered, then crumpled under a rain of blows, and when they attempted to revive him for another run they found he was dead, his skull fractured by one particularly damaging blow. He was scalped and his body repeatedly struck with war clubs and tomahawks.

Among the excitedly milling Indians, Tecumseh found Lowawluwaysica, brandishing a stout stick and grinning happily at having been able to lay wood to three of the four men as they had stumbled by with whatever speed they could muster. But when Tecumseh whispered to his one-eyed brother about the rum he had cached, the nine-year-old had immediately tossed his club aside and insisted they go to the empty wegiwa and drink some.

Now they had been crouched here in the dimness for half an hour or more, vaguely hearing the anguished shrieks of the prisoners as the tortures at the stakes began. In a reversal of roles, since it was usually Lowawluwaysica whose disposition became progressively more sour with each swallow and Tecumseh who became mellow, this time Tecumseh became depressed and withdrawn the more he drank and Lowawluwaysica who became ebullient. The younger brother was torn between what he considered to be two of life's great pleasures—remaining here and drinking more, or returning to participate in the excitement of torturing an enemy to death. Logic dictated the answer: there was plenty of rum and Tecumseh certainly couldn't drink it all, so it would still be here later on; the prisoners, however, would soon be dead and so if he was to get his licks in at all, he had to do it now.

Lowawluwaysica was disappointed that Tecumseh declined joining him for the sport, but he merely shrugged and started away, calling over his shoulder he'd be back before long. He giggled and raced off, not so steady on his feet as when he entered the wegiwa, a dozen swigs of rum ago.

Tecumseh moved over near the broken-down doorway and sat on the ground, cradling the jug in his lap, able to see the Shawnee torturing occurring about half an arrow's flight distant. Two prisoners had been attached to individual stakes, each by a rawhide loop around the neck, the other end tied in a loop to the stake, permitting the captive to move in a circle up to five feet from the post.[218] At first there were shots and screams and laughter as black powder was shot into the skin at close range and sharpened sticks gouged the flesh. Little children and women raced up and lashed the captives viciously with slender switches that left terrible weals and sometimes broke the skin. One of the prisoners shrieked horribly as he lost an eye to a sharpened stick and another groaned and doubled over, falling to his knees as the result of a club rammed into his genitals. Sharp stones were thrown at the captives, bruising and cutting them, and some of the boys were using inadequate little bows to shoot arrows made of simple sharpened sticks into their bodies.

Then the fires were lighted in a ring of brush and firewood heaped all around each of the stakes at a distance of ten feet. The prisoners were not in the living fire, but they could not get away and their howlings grew worse and more frenzied as the flames grew. The heat on the inside of each circle became intense, singeing away the hair on their heads and bodies and causing the skin to redden and blister, then begin to blacken and shrivel. Heaps of hot coals were scooped up on pieces of bark and thrown at them, burning the flesh where they struck, then continuing to burn the bare feet that trod upon them. The prisoners ran in circles, stumbled, fell, crawled, regained their feet, shuffled aimlessly, screaming and begging, first for mercy and then for the peace of swift death to end their misery. But death at the stake was not designed to be swift for any captive. In several hours they would be dead, but it would indeed be at least a few hours first of indescribable hell.

Back in the deserted wegiwa, Tecumseh was finding that the rum was a big help. The more he drank, the less he was able to see clearly what was happening. The more he swallowed mouthfuls of the fiery liquid, the less he was able to hear the agonized cries and moans from the tortured. But at the same time he was also aware that, for some reason, he was unable to check the tears that continued to trickle down his cheeks.

[November 2, 1779 — Tuesday]

In his full dress uniform of scarlet, white, and gold, Captain Henry Bird made quite an impressive appearance as he stood before the assembled Indians in the council house at the Wyandot village of Upper Sandusky.[219] The British Indian Agent Alexander McKee was there, along with Simon and George Girty and their brother, Jim, who was just in from participating with the Wyandots and Mingoes on some successful upper Ohio River forays.

Everyone had heard, of course, of the wonderfully successful raid that had been pulled off on the Spaylaywitheepi against the supply boats coming upriver. The division of those supplies and gunpowder had provided the participants with a bounty they had not known for a considerable while. Now all the Indians, even that faction of the Wyandots that had for so long been advocating peace, were eager for the war to be stepped up and carried with vigor against the Kentuckians. It was what they had believed Captain Bird was here for—to promise British support for just such endeavors. They were not disappointed.

"Brothers," Captain Bird said, "I come bearing news of great moment to you. Our father across the eastern sea, King George, has become deeply concerned over how you have been treated by the Americans. He has wept over the burning of Chalahgawtha this past summer and the death of the great Shawnee chief, Black Fish, and he fears for the sanctity of your lands unless steps are taken to wipe out this threat.

"Brothers, my heart is glad that I am able to tell you now that Lieutenant General Frederick Haldimand, governor of Canada, upon instructions from the king, has authorized an invasion not only to crush the Kentucky forts, but also to force the Virginia frontier back east of the Allegheny Mountains."

There were great cries of pleasure and war whoops as the three Girty brothers, each in different tongues, interpreted the British officer's words. After a few moments Bird, smiling broadly, raised a hand and, as the hubbub faded, he continued:

"Such invasion, brothers, will not only regain for you your traditional hunting grounds south of the river, but it will prevent the western growth of American colonies—states, as they choose to rebelliously call themselves—now threatening your lands." Another favorable murmuring arose at this, but he went on without pause and it quickly faded. "My brothers, listen! My chief, Captain de Peyster, has empowered me to lead this invasion of the Kentucky lands and it will be an invasion the like of which this country has not heretofore witnessed. My chief will provide an army made up of British regular soldiers, Tories and officers from Detroit and green-coated rangers from Canada. The Kentucky forts are strong and have withstood attack before, but they will not be able to withstand *this* attack!"

The assembled Indians tensed, listening eagerly for the words they had so long waited to hear and, again, Bird did not disappoint them. "We will march against them not only with tomahawk and knife and flintlock, but with *cannons* as well—the great brass thunder guns that can knock down the wall of a fort with a single shot. For *this*, brothers, they have no defense!"

Again a wave of cheers and war whoops swelled and now became punctuated by cries of "When? *When?*"

"Brothers," Captain Bird concluded, "the winter season is upon us now and in the spring there is planting you must do so that your grain may grow for next winter's use. Therefore, the invasion will not start until the corn and melons and vegetables have been planted. Until that time, my chief will continue to buy scalps and prisoners from you at Detroit. And when the time comes to go, your friends beside me, Agent McKee and Simon Girty and his brothers, will come to you with the news and we wish for every warrior who can, to come along. The day of reckoning will be at hand for the *Shemanese!*"

The piercing shrieks and war cries that filled the council house were testimony enough that when the time came for the British to call upon them, they would be very ready to participate in the invasion of Kentucky.

[May 12, 1780 — Friday]

Lying on his mat in the darkened wegiwa, with only the coals of the cookfire shedding a vague illumination, Tecumseh could hear the others breathing heavily in their slumber and wished he were asleep as well. He was very tired from all the activity of the day that had stretched well into the night, yet sleep would not come for him. The reason, he knew, was because of the great loneliness filling him.

Tecumapese was gone.

It was only hours since she had been part of this household, yet her absence had, in this short time, created a gap he hadn't realized was possible. It was the first time in his life that there was not an overseeing woman sharing the wegiwa in which he lived and, because she had always been far more mother to him than sister, he could not help feeling forsaken.

It was not long after the raid on the boats last fall that Chiksika had called to Tecumseh to come walk with him and talk. The request had filled him with a slight unease, since normally Chiksika said whatever was on his mind in his usual forthright way. Tecumseh had wondered, at the time, if he had been found out in the matter of the rum and Chiksika did not want to scold him in front of the others. But that hadn't been the case at all. They had walked down by the Little Miami and stopped within sight of the very pool where Tecumseh had so long ago dived to the bottom for the *opawaka* which still hung about his neck.

"Tecumseh," his brother had said then, "I want you to know how proud of you I am. You are a fine young warrior, better by far than many who are older. It is a joy having you close to me on the raids we make, because I know I can depend on you." Chiksika blew out a little gust of air as if exasperated at himself at not coming to the point more directly. "It is for that very reason, because I can depend on you, that I have to tell you now that I will not be taking you with me on any more war parties until perhaps next spring or summer."

Tecumseh was nonplussed and because he did not know what to say, he had remained silent. Chiksika had put a hand to his shoulder and squeezed gently. "The Kentucky country is filling with whites as fast as we can count and I will be gone on raids a very great deal of the time. The point is, you are also a fine hunter and it is in that direction that you can be of most help now and you must take on a very important responsibility. For this winter you must become the hunter for our family. We have many mouths to feed— our three other brothers, plus Tecumapese, Spemica Lawba, Kisathoi, and Tebethto, as well as ourselves—that's nine people and you are really the only one to do this. In addition to us, there are many women in our village who have lost their men and it becomes our responsibility to try to help them as well, and the older ones, too, who cannot go out to hunt.

"This winter, little brother," he had gone on, "I will be back at intervals and will help when and as I can, but mainly it falls upon you to become the provider for our family and neighbors. I do promise you, though," he had laughed then, "that during those times I am at home, I will tell you in closest detail everything that has happened in my absence."

So it was that during this past severely cold and snowy winter, Tecumseh had put into almost daily practice the hunting skills he had learned.[220] He brought in to the village hundreds of rabbits, scores of turkeys, large numbers of grouse and squirrels, raccoons and opossums, and even, on three separate occasions, bear. Most often, however, he hunted deer and buffalo and when he came in, parties of women, along with other boys who could not hunt so well as he, would go to the places he directed them and bring in far more game than he alone could carry. In one day he killed seventeen deer and five buffalo. The women and the elderly praised him in the grandest terms, knowing that but for him, starvation and exposure would have taken a heavy toll, as it was doing among tribes all over the country.

Hardest hit of all, Chiksika reported on one of his nights at home, were the remnants of the Iroquois. With so many of their villages and practically all their crops destroyed by General Sullivan the preceding summer and autumn, many hundreds of them, weakened by hunger, had died of exposure.[221]

Despite the severity of the winter, hordes of whites kept moving into the Kentucky country and though war parties, like those led by Chiksika, struck at many of them and did a considerable damage, yet they kept coming. Now the Kentucky country was dotted with more than a dozen forts and all of those so crowded that settlements were springing up around them and isolated cabins being built in what seemed to be every favorable spot.[222] A major British-supported offensive against the settlements, Chiksika reported gloomily, was no longer just desirable, it was an absolute necessity; if the whites could not be driven out this coming year, chances were it would be the Shawnees and other tribes that would ultimately be driven out.

Several times, Chiksika related, he had seen their great enemy, Bahd-ler, moving from station to station, hunting for all the whites, helping to fight their battles, elusive as a shadow and, as always, strong as a bear and canny as a wolf. Sheltowee—Boone—he saw twice in the Boonesboro area where defenses had been greatly improved and were still being worked upon. They had managed to kill some of the whites there who became incautious, but there were always more ready and able to take their places.[223]

Chiksika had asked Tecumseh if their nine-year-old triplet brothers were helping with the work at home and Tecumseh hedged by saying they were doing the best they could. In the case of Sauwaseekau and Kumskaka, they *were* helping considerably, ranging far through the snows to gather up what firewood they could find for their own wegiwa and for their neighbors who needed help. And they did a wide variety of chores that Tecumapese laid out for them, but neither showed any real aptitude for hunting or even any zeal to become warriors.

Lowawluwaysica, on the other hand, was largely a shirker, doing as little as possible and, when put into a position where he really had to do a job, doing it poorly. It seemed incredible that Tecumseh and Lowawluwaysica, so closely related, could so greatly differ in almost every respect. Tecumseh, for example, was generally very quiet and unwaveringly thoughtful of his companions and the elderly in the village and very polite to other people. Lowawluwaysica was very noisy, boisterous, barely tolerated his elders and was

downright rude to companions and anyone younger. Tecumseh had a pronounced streak of modesty and when he spoke of his accomplishments, as it
was proper to do during the evening talk-times, he spoke of them truthfully
and always rather played down his remarkable exploits, as if embarrassed by
them. Lowawluwaysica, on the other hand, strutted about and boasted ex-
travagantly about the most insignificant of accomplishments.

The two boys differed greatly in physical appearance as well. Tecumseh
was tall, with a nice medium build for his age and pleasantly molded features.
Lowawluwaysica's features could never have been described as pleasant. Apart
from the sunken socket from his missing right eye, he was slightly bucktoothed
and his lips set in a perpetual grimace which, if anything, became uglier when
he cackled his shrill, irritating laughter. Yet, different though they were,
Lowawluwaysica doted on Tecumseh, and though he consistently failed at it,
the one-eyed boy just as consistently tried to emulate all that Tecumseh did.

Both Chiksika and Tecumapese had striven to instill in all the boys a deep
and abiding love for the truth, contempt for meanness and sordidness, fortitude
in suffering, and abiding courage in all circumstances. Their efforts were most
pronounced in Tecumseh, least so in Lowawluwaysica, who always teetered
on the very edge of censure from his elders because of his indifference in such
matters. He was slyly canny and uncommonly adept at concealing his petty
meanness and deceptions. As much as the love in him grew for Tecumseh,
so as well grew his envy for all Tecumseh did and was—a fact of which
Tecumseh was wholly ignorant. Even Chiksika failed to see the dichotomy.
But their twenty-two-year-old sister knew, and Lowawluwaysica knew he
could not deceive Tecumapese.

Thus, the very fact that this day had caused such a stirring of loneliness
in Tecumseh, was met with secret pleasure by Lowawluwaysica, who was
cunningly aware that he would find his life much easier without her around.
Tonight at the dance, Tecumapese, after just over five years a widow, had
become the wife of Wasegoboah. She was in his wegiwa this night and tomorrow would come for her possessions and move them out.

Tecumseh was happy for her and glad that such a good man and brave
warrior as Wasegoboah was her choice. Yet, lying in the darkness as he thought
of these things, Tecumseh wondered why every small happiness that came
along seemed to bear with it a nullifying sadness.

[June 22, 1780 — Thursday]

Chiksika rarely became angry and even on those infrequent occasions
when he did, the anger manifested itself most often in a narrowing of the eyes
and tightening of the lips, accompanied by stony silence. This time was dif-

ferent; this time Tecumseh was somewhat awed and even a bit frightened as he saw his steady older brother so infuriated that he slammed his tomahawk to the ground and raged loudly and long against a commander who not only had no stomach for war but who, because of what he was doing, had now placed the entire Shawnee tribe in severe jeopardy.

The anger was not limited to Chiksika. War Chief Shemeneto could scarcely be contained from taking out his wrath on the British commander, and Blue Jacket was hardly less infuriated. The entire force of warriors was similarly angry. Here and now, in their very grip, they had the first unqualified opportunity to actually wipe out every Kentucky fortification, station, and isolated cabin, and that grand opportunity was being discarded simply because of the qualms of one man—Captain Henry Bird.

There had been serious talk of killing Bird and getting on with it, but it was merely talk. Without the British commander and the force he commanded, and especially without the technology to use the artillery he had brought, the Indians would be no more effective against the Kentucky forts than on previous occasions. Everything had hinged on one British officer who, in the end, had turned out to be a man without spine.

It had all begun auspiciously enough. Tecumseh still reveled in the pride he felt when Chiksika had said that he, Tecumseh, was to be included in the forthcoming invasion of Kentucky. They, along with most of the warrior population of Chalahgawtha and other Shawnee villages, had moved off at once to meet Captain Bird who was at that moment approaching the rendezvous point at the mouth of the Mad River on the Great Miami. They arrived to find a large contingent of Shawnees from the villages along the Mad and upper Great Miami rivers had already assembled, totaling some 550 warriors.

As Captain Bird had promised last fall, he was coming not only with a full one hundred red-coated regular soldiers and an additional seventy green-coated Canadian Rangers, he was also bringing with him sufficient artillery to make a shambles of every fort in the Kentucky country.[224] It was with that force, including horses for the officers, that Captain Bird, accompanied by Alexander McKee and all three Girty brothers, had left Detroit several weeks earlier in a flotilla of boats that carried them down the Detroit River and across the western end of Lake Erie to the mouth of the Maumee, which they ascended to the Rapids, through which heavier boats could not traverse.[225] At this point the force had transferred to a great swarm of canoes and continued to follow the Maumee another forty-eight miles upstream to the mouth of the Auglaize, the officers riding their horses on shore and pacing the canoes.[226] There, expecting to rendezvous with about a hundred Indians from the southern Michigan and northern Ohio tribes, he was gratified to be met by over triple that number of war-painted warriors. The majority of the three hundred Indians who rendezvoused were Wyandots and Delawares, but also included a fair

number of Ottawas, Chippewas, Potawatomies and, at last, after much vac-
illation, a small number of Miamis. The latter tribe had finally begun to realize
that even the strong buffer zone of other tribes between them and the whites
might soon not be enough to insure their own protection.

Bird's force, now half a thousand strong with its augmentation by the
northern Indians, continued its journey, the multitude of canoes and a great
many more horsemen on shore following the Auglaize upstream to its headwaters to a point the Indians called Wapaghkonetta, where there was an eigh-
teen-mile portage trail moving east-southeast to connect with the headwaters
of the Great Miami. [227]

The force of about five hundred British, Canadians and Indians created
quite a stir when they arrived at the rendezvous at the mouth of the Mad
River. [228] Tecumseh was among the warriors who crowded around to see the
six pieces of artillery, the first ever seen by most of them. Even Catahecassa—
Black Hoof—moved close to inspect the thunder guns and nodded his approval. Five were French swivels, each carried on a single horse. The sixth
was the one that stirred the most interest and awe—a heavy brass cannon
mounted on a wheeled carriage and capable of shooting a single ball weighing
six pounds!

With the northern Indians that had joined him at the mouth of the Auglaize
and the multitude of Shawnees that had joined the procession as it moved
down the Great Miami to this rendezvous point, plus those already gathered
here under Catahecassa and Shemeneto, Captain Bird's entire force now
amounted to 1,250 men. They moved off at once and continued following the
Great Miami, both in the water in their multitude of canoes and on land on
horseback, down to its mouth at the Ohio River. [229] There was great excitement
and expectation among all the Indians. Spirits were extremely high and old
angers were rekindled in their hearts and minds, much to the irritation of
Captain Bird, as Jim and George Girty moved among them and reminded
them of their losses to the Americans in the past—Hokolesqua, Red Hawk,
Chiungalla, Pucksinwah, Shikellimus, Elinipsico, Plukkemehnotee, and many
others, calling them to avenge such irreplaceable losses. [230] And so vengeance
quickly became as much a driving factor on the expedition as the need to force
the Americans out. Never before had such an army been seen in this country
and never before had such a force been directed against the Kentucky settlements. Word had come of a buildup of military forces at Fort Nelson at the
Falls of the Ohio, so the projected first target was decided to be a considerable
distance from there, at Ruddell's Station on the Licking River, followed by
swift and devastating attacks in succession against such stations as Martin's,
Bryan's, Boonesboro, McAfee's, Logan's, Harrodsburg, Lexington, and finally Fort Nelson. Once all these were taken, the force could then move against

the American positions at Kaskaskia, Cahokia, and Vincennes to regain control of the West.[231]

The vast flotilla of canoes in the river and horsemen on the shores moved up the Ohio from the mouth of the Great Miami some twenty miles to opposite the mouth of the Licking on the Kentucky side, where all the horsemen swam their mounts across. The whole force then moved up the Licking until they reached the mouth of the South Fork of the Licking, where they finally stopped and erected a number of huts and tents to shelter their stores and baggage.[232] Leaving this camp and their canoes under a strong guard of both soldiers and Indians, they had then struck out overland, following the course of the South Fork for a while, then the dry bed of Snake Lick Creek, and finally reaching the river again and crossing it at a wide sweeping curve near the recently abandoned Boyd's Station. Here they had been forced to pause and fell trees to build a temporary ford over which to wheel the heavy cannon—logs tied together and first placed perpendicular to the current, then another layer of tied-together logs parallel to the current. The crossing was made without undue difficulty and they continued the march, their excitement rising the closer they came to Ruddell's Station. Without any further tree felling, they easily forded Raven Creek and Mill Creek and finally Gray's Run.[233] For another three or four miles they stayed on the southwest shore of the South Fork until they came to a fording place, where they crossed to the northeastern shore without incident.[234] It was under the first streakings of dawn that they had crept up the embankment below Ruddell's Station and it was here, at last that they had been discovered.

Tecumseh could remember very clearly the terrified cry of the guard on the wall of the fort as he shrieked out a warning to those within. The gate was already closed and within only a few minutes a hundred men were peering fearfully over the walls of the stockade, petrified at the sight of the six-pounder cannon being moved into position and loaded. The first incredibly loud boom of the cannon shook the very ground and on its heels came the heavy splintering smashing of wood as a whole section of the north blockhouse's outer wall was blown apart. The Indians grinned as they heard the screams of women and cries of men inside the fort. It was the culmination of a longtime dream of the Indians that such a weapon could be employed against these forts and now it lived up to their expectations. Against it, the Kentuckians forted here had no defense.

Almost immediately a white flag was raised and then the gate opened a little and several men emerged. Captain Bird and three of his officers cantered up to meet them and Bird wasted no time with conciliatory talk. He directed his remarks to the man who seemed to be in charge.

"I am Captain Henry Bird," he said brusquely, "and in the name of his majesty, King George the Third, I demand the immediate and unconditional surrender of this post. I take it you're in charge. Who are you?"

"My name," said their leader, "is John Ruddell. Actually my brother, Isaac, is in charge here but he was injured several days ago and cannot walk. I am temporarily taking his place."[235]

"Very good, sir. You have heard the demand for surrender. You have no choice. If you surrender your fort at once, your men will be taken prisoners of war and your women and children will be permitted to travel on their own to safety at the nearest place such can be found. If you refuse, your fort will be reduced by our artillery and all within will perish."

Ruddell hesitated only a moment before nodding and then turned and called out, "To all inside the fort, listen to me! This is John Ruddell. Ground your weapons and open the gate. I have surrendered the fort so that the women and children can take themselves to safety. This must be done at once!"

Within a few minutes the gates were thrown open, exposing a multitude of men and women clustered together fearfully, the rifles of the men stacked in several cones on the ground just inside the gate.[236] But Captain Bird had underestimated the rage of the Shawnees that had been fueled by the Girty brothers and the Indians, intent on massacre, abruptly burst into savage shrieks and raced inside with drawn war clubs and tomahawks, slashing left and right with abandon, downing every white they encountered without regard to age or gender. The carnage was terrible. Elizabeth Ruddell had her infant son yanked from her arms and thrown into a nearby fire and when she screamed and leaped to save him, she was struck on the forehead with a war club and fell unconscious.[237] John Ruddell hastened to their aid but he was tomahawked and his scalp taken.

During the melee, Chiksika snatched at a white youth madly dashing past and caught his wrist. The boy struggled furiously and Chiksika raised his tomahawk to strike, but at that moment Tecumseh ran up and gripped the boy from behind, pinning his arms to his sides.

"I'll take him, Chiksika," Tecumseh said.

Chiksika nodded, released his hold on the lad and sprinted away. Tecumseh, holding the boy tightly, spoke urgently in English in his captive's ear. "Don't fight. You will be killed if you do."

For a moment the boy, who was about Tecumseh's age, continued squirming to get free of Tecumseh's grip, but couldn't. "Holding you," Tecumseh said with a short laugh, "is like trying to hold on to a big fish. Now listen carefully. If you want to live, do not struggle anymore. I'll help you, but you must be quiet and stay with me wherever I go. Do you understand?"

The white youth nodded and relaxed and after a moment more Tecumseh released his hold and turned him around so they were face to face. Tecumseh smiled at him and repeated himself. "Stay with me. Do you promise?" The boy nodded and from that moment on closely followed Tecumseh wherever he went. By that time most of the slaughter had ended. In those first few moments around twenty of the Americans had been killed and there would have been more except for the intervention of Captain Bird.

Face pale and pinched with anger, he thrust himself between the horde of Indians and their intended victims and raised his arms, shouting at them to stop. So startled were they at this unexpected move on his part that they did indeed stop and stared at him.

"Chiefs!" he shouted, his eyes darting to various chiefs in turn and finally settling on Catahecassa. "What kind of warriors are these? What kind of men? How can you let them act this way against people who have laid down their arms and surrendered in good faith?" The scorn was heavy in his voice. "Is *this* the great bravery of the Indians that I have heard so much about? How much honor, Black Hoof, comes to a warrior when he butchers a baby and scalps a defenseless woman?"

Catahecassa nodded and ordered his men to stand back and, after a moment or two so did the chiefs of the Wyandots and other tribes. But though the indiscriminate mayhem ended, the killings were not yet completed. If these whites were to be taken prisoner, then the march of the army could not be hampered by those who were incapable of keeping up. The whites were gathered together, all of them, and again the tomahawks flew as a few of the too old, the ill, and the lame were executed where they stood and their scalps taken.[238]

When the carnage slackened and the survivors stood knotted in a cluster with their arms about one another, crying and moaning in their misery and fear, Captain Bird, obviously sickened by what had occurred, ordered them surrounded and protected by squads of his regulars. The Indians immediately turned their attention elsewhere and began systematically plundering the fort of everything conceivably of value to them, not the least of which was all the stacked rifles and the fair supply of ammunition. With his face set in hard, disgusted lines, Bird watched until they were finished and then sent McKee and the Girty brothers among them to call all the chiefs together for an immediate meeting.

"What I have seen here," he raged, not even opening his talk with the customary address of "Brothers," "has filled me with revulsion. This is not how a war is carried on! It was our intention to move next against Martin's Station, but there will be no more attacks *of any kind* if I do not get some promises from you chiefs right here and now."[239]

There was some grumbling and baleful looks from the chiefs as the words were interpreted, but Bird ignored them and went on: "I swear to you in the name of King George the Third and God Almighty Himself that if I do not get your unbreakable promise this moment that there will be no more massacres such as this, I will call off the entire invasion without delay and return with my men and artillery to Detroit. Give me your promises, here and now, or by God in heaven, we leave!"

The interpreted words sobered the chiefs considerably. All knew they had no chance whatever against the forts without the British and their artillery. As they stood momentarily mute before him, Captain Bird went on. "If you will give me your solemn word—*all of you!*—that all the prisoners, these," he pointed toward the clustered survivors, "and whatever others may fall into our hands, will be turned over to me to be taken to Detroit, and there will be no repetition of the shameful massacre your warriors have committed here, then we will go on to Martin's Station and take it. I, for my part, promise you that all plunder taken there, as here, will become your property. If that is not enough for you, then the invasion will be ended and we will separate from you and return to Detroit. Now, speak!"

One by one the chiefs spoke and each, though some with the greatest of reluctance, gave his word that there would be no further massacre of captives. At this, each of the prisoners was heavily loaded with plunder and the march begun for Martin's. Two of Captain Bird's lieutenants, with three of the captive settlers from Ruddell's, were sent ahead by Bird to demand the surrender of Martin's Station. They were instructed to give them Bird's word that there would be no massacre such as had occurred at Ruddell's unless they failed to surrender at once.

With no more choice than had been available at Ruddell's, Martin's Station surrendered without a shot being fired and its inhabitants—close to one hundred men, women and children—were taken prisoner. But with this acquisition, including all the plunder now gathered from Martin's, Captain Bird found himself on the horns of a dilemma. Buoyed by their successes, the Indians now very much wanted to move immediately against Bryan's Station, only twelve miles southwest, and Catahecassa volunteered enough of his warriors to strongly guard the captives while they were gone.[240] Bird, however, was virtually certain that if the suggestion were accepted, the nearly half a thousand prisoners would be butchered as soon as the army was out of earshot—a circumstance he simply could not allow. Nor could he reasonably diminish the strength of his own force by assigning troops to stay behind and guard them.[241]

Thus, less than two hours ago, Captain Bird had called the chiefs and principal warriors together and addressed them in the manner that had now left the entire Indian force so thoroughly frustrated and angry.

"We have done well," he told them. "The Americans have now seen what can happen to them in the face of British strength of arms and they will leave this country. You Indians have collected more plunder than you can carry and there are many prisoners to see to. Therefore, I am ending this campaign now and we are turning back to Ohio at once."

The dismay among the combined Indians was overwhelming. They now regarded Bird with the deepest of contempt, considering him a squeamish fool who wished to fight battles without shedding blood. But they could not force Captain Bird to fight if he refused to do so, nor could they carry on the attacks themselves without the support of the British and their artillery.

So now the short-lived invasion of Kentucky was over and they were on their way home. They had taken all the horses of the settlers, killed all their cattle, killed and scalped dozens of whites without the loss or even injury of any Indian, burned two major forts to the ground, taken close to five hundred prisoners and all the plunder those captives could possibly carry, and they should have been jubilant in their successes.

They were not.

"What happens now?" Tecumseh asked Chiksika. They were riding their horses side by side and the white boy was astride Tecumseh's horse as well, directly behind his young captor.

"Now?" Chiksika answered. "Now we pay the price for putting our trust in a soldier who turns out to be a woman. We have become the bee that has stung the bear. We have hurt the bear only a little and made him greatly angry and now the bear will do his utmost to squash the bee so that he will not be stung again."

Tecumseh thought about this a moment. "You think they will come against us again at Chalahgawtha?"

Chiksika nodded. "And more," he said bleakly.

[June 30, 1780 — Friday]

Within a few days of returning to Chalahgawtha, Chiksika adopted the white boy he and Tecumseh had caught, pleased with the way he had run the gauntlet on their arrival at the home village. A quarter-mile double line had been set up and the boy, who was very fleet, had raced through its course, dodging and swerving with remarkable agility and arrived at the *msi-kah-mi-qui* panting and grinning and very pleased with himself at having received only half a dozen minor blows on the way. It was a wonderful performance and his success had been cheered by the entire populace. Chiksika had commented admiringly, "He was as difficult to hit in the gauntlet line as it would be to catch a fish by hand in the river." Because of that, as well as the fact that Tecumseh had laughingly related how the boy had been as hard to hold on to as a big fish, they agreed to use that analogy as his new Shawnee name: Sinnanatha—Big Fish.

The boy, whose English name was Stephen Ruddell, was the brother of the baby boy who had been tossed into the fire and the son of the woman who had been knocked unconscious trying to save him. Despite such trauma, he had the resiliency to quickly adapt into his new life and, with their closeness in age—he was only six months younger—he and Tecumseh quickly became close companions. His brother, Abram Ruddell, four years younger, had been adopted into the family of another warrior here in Chalahgawtha and, though they saw one another often enough, there was no close association between them.[242]

Two prisoners had escaped on the way north and, with few exceptions, the large number of captives from Ruddell's and Martin's Stations had not even come to Chalahgawtha but had continued up the Great Miami with the force under Captain Bird, en route to Detroit.[243] There had been a pause at the mouth of the Mad River and a division of the spoils so the Shawnee factions could take their share with them. At such times there was often great hilarity as warriors donned women's petticoats and bonnets and did impromptu dances or otherwise clowned for the amusement of the group, but this time there had been none of that. A somber pall had settled over all of them and the knowledge was clear in every mind that the expedition, while successful, was sadly incomplete and would eventually, virtually without doubt, have terrible ramifications for them all. Not even the sotto voce assurances of the Girty brothers as they moved among the tribesmen that next time they would have a British commander with more stomach had the power to lift their gloom. The fact that the six-pounder cannon had been lost during the crossing of the Spaylaywitheepi was taken as an omen by many that dire things were to come.[244]

The only real solace the Shawnees could find was that they had destroyed two important forts and captured so many prisoners that it could not help but strike terror into the breasts of all the whites. Retaliate they might, but the warriors were all in agreement that an attack could not come this year, certainly not before next summer at the earliest, perhaps not till the summer after that. The Kentuckians were simply too feeble and too disorganized and there were almost no regular American soldiers there to spearhead any sort of attacks against them. An attack would come, eventually, they all agreed, but by then, perhaps, they themselves may have sufficiently strengthened themselves through good alliances with neighboring tribes as to successfully ward off whatever blow the *Shemanese* levied against them.

Chiksika and Tecumseh were delighted with Sinnanatha, who was eager to learn Shawnee ways and the Shawnee language. As Tecumseh had done and was still doing with Margaret and Elizabeth McKinzie—Kisathoi and Tebethto—the two boys taught one another, Tecumseh insisting that when they were in one another's presence, Sinnanatha speak only in Shawnee and himself only in English. The results were often comical in the extreme, but Tecumseh's grasp of the English language became better all the time and with it came a fuller understanding, though not approval, of the whites. Sinnanatha and the girls also taught Tecumseh good table manners, including how to hold and use utensils properly. All four of the youngsters got along very well together, and Tecumseh was pleased that Kisathoi and Tebethto had learned so well from Tecumapese that now, in her absence, they took over the household duties in Chiksika's wegiwa and performed them well.

It was not very long before Sinnanatha had become imbued with the Shawnee way of life and, as with Kisathoi and Tebethto, not only sympathized with the problems besetting the Shawnees but experienced a sense of guilt for the very real antagonism that bloomed in him toward his own white people for what they were doing to the Indians.

The four were all relatively close in age, but it was Tecumseh who seemed to be considerably older. He was always asking questions and searching for answers, not only from them but from many others in the tribe. He continued to spend much time with the older people, talking with them, listening to their stories, benefitting from the wisdom their years of experience had brought. His eyes had a searching quality that was sometimes disconcerting to others, as if he were probing far beyond their words and reaching deep into their very being to absorb what he found there. His memory was phenomenal and he seemed never to forget whatever was said to him or done in his presence. Progressively his quest for knowledge was swinging to abstract concepts and philosophies and he yearned for answers that quite often no one in the tribe could provide, a fact that caused unease in him and a desire to find somewhere the elusive answers.

The nine-year-old triplets continued to more or less live in their own little nine-year-old world. Lowawluwaysica was clearly the most intelligent of the three but equally the most devious and with the least admirable character traits and he was almost totally unlike the other two, both in temperament and appearance. Kumskaka had become a chubby, jolly boy, always in good humor and rather the comedian of the family, continually amusing the others with his outrageous antics and expressions. Sauwaseekau, on the other hand, was somber of nature, rarely smiling and almost never laughing aloud, taking all things with great seriousness. Seldom did he contribute anything to the talk-time fireside chats in the wegiwa, but he exhibited a special willingness to do practically anything for Lowawluwaysica, which was undoubtedly a form of atonement for having been the cause of the loss of the latter's eye a year ago. Lowawluwaysica did not hesitate to take outrageous advantage of his brother's willingness to atone.

When the weather was favorable, the language and discussion sessions among Tecumseh, Sinnanatha, Kisathoi and Tebethto took place outside, sometimes during walks along the river but more often below the low overhanging branches of a gigantic oak just a little southwest of the village. As they had begun to arrive there for one such session, the two girls got there first and settled themselves on the ground. Sinnanatha arrived next and sat near them, saying that Tecumseh would be coming along shortly, that he and Chiksika were talking at the moment. The three began holding a discussion of their own, in English, and talked about their respective backgrounds. The talk brought back to them memories of their true families and just as they glimpsed Tecumseh starting to come toward them, Kisathoi abruptly reverted for a moment to being Margaret McKinzie and her eyes filled with tears as she spoke.

"Elizabeth and I are not unhappy here. We love the family we've been adopted into. But we're always lonely for our real family. We know most of them are dead, but our father and brother Isaac may still be alive. If so, one day we'll be reunited. We miss them terribly. We love our father more than anyone else in the world and some day he'll come and take us away with him. It is all we live for and it *will* happen. But, if maybe it doesn't, then someday, when the conditions are just right, we'll simply walk away from here and become Margaret and Elizabeth McKinzie again, and then *we* will search for him."

They did not tell Tecumseh what they had been discussing when he reached them. He had news of his own to impart and was obviously excited by it. He sat down on the ground with them and rubbed his hands together happily.

"Chiksika and I are going on a journey," he announced.

"Where?" Tebethto asked excitedly, infected by his attitude.

"Westward," Tecumseh replied, "and probably northward, and maybe southward. Wherever the idea takes us. He says it is time I learn a little more about this great land beyond what I have seen here in Ohio and the little in the Kan-tuck-kee lands. He says it is time I see the Illinois country and the great grandmother of rivers and perhaps we will even be able to see our mother in the Missouri country."

"When are you going?" asked Kisathoi, somewhat worriedly. "And how long will you be gone? And what about us? What are we to do while you are both gone?"

Tecumseh shook his head. "I don't know when we will be back, but probably not for a couple of moons at least. Maybe more. Chiksika said there will be a lull in the fighting between us and the *Shemanese* now and this may be the last opportunity we have to take such a trip for a long time to come. In the meantime, he has arranged for you three and the triplets to stay with Tecumapese and Wasegoboah while we're gone."

"You didn't answer the first question," Tebethto said. "When are you and Chiksika leaving?"

"Tomorrow," Tecumseh replied, grinning broadly. "At the first light of day tomorrow."

[September 30, 1780 — Saturday]

The great journey of Chiksika and Tecumseh had come to an end and all the exhilaration of it, all the joy of seeing new lands and new people, hunting different game and experiencing the great breadth of the country that seemed to stretch away from them in natural beauty forever, had come to an end. Now they had returned to their tribe and found news and conditions worse than they could have imagined.

Tecumseh lay on his back in the stillness of the strange new wegiwa, the other members of the family asleep in the darkness close by. He unconsciously fondled the *opawaka* on the cord around his neck and wished that he, too, were asleep. But sleep eluded him and a montage of mental pictures filled his mind, of the journey that was ended, of the condition that was now and of the far less than hopeful prospects for the future.

There had been no time previously in Tecumseh's life when he had felt more alive or happier than he had throughout the whole of the wonderful trip with Chiksika. The exhilaration he had felt as they rode or walked together over the countryside was beyond expression. In his mind's ear he could still hear the gentle, musical voice of his older brother explaining various things about the wonders they saw and experienced—the streams, springs, lakes and hills, the individual great trees and the forests, the vast rippling prairies, the wildlife, and the heavens—and those hypnotic words had lulled him into a sort of trance in which he somehow became an actual part of each thing spoken of and as one with the whole of all things.

Despite the dreamy, drifting mesmerism it had induced in him, he nevertheless not only heard but remembered almost verbatim every word Chiksika had spoken to him and when he asked his frequent questions they were neither idle nor shallow and Chiksika was often hard put to answer. In many instances the older brother evinced astonishment at the perceptiveness of his little brother and of the probing nature of his mind, wondering at times why he had never thought to ask this or that himself, frequently mentally berating himself for his inability to provide the fullness of response Tecumseh was seeking. Over and over again Chiksika had experienced the weird sensation, induced by Tecumseh's questions and comments, that he were the younger and Tecumseh the elder.

They had ridden very far in their travels—far to the north and west to

217

the great blue body of water called *Miseken* by their northern brothers, the Potawatomies and Winnebagoes and Menominees, and then even farther north and west of that, out of the land of oaks and elms and hickories into the land of thousands of tiny gemlike lakes dotting great fresh-scented forests of pines and then to a still bigger blue sea of clear, cold, sweet water that was said to have no bottom.

They had traveled to the west then and came to a clear and cold and swift stream, smaller at this point by far than the Spaylaywitheepi, but which Chiksika said was the grandmother of rivers, the Missitheepi, who grew to such magnificent size that far downstream she devoured the Spaylaywitheepi and all other rivers. They followed her course southward for a long while, passing through the lands of the Foxes and Sacs and crossed over to the lands westward, into the country of the Mandans and Dakotahs and others of their Sioux relatives. They passed through the land of the peaceful Ioways and came to a great muddy river that tribe called *Missouritheepi,* which was at least equal to the Spaylaywitheepi. They did not cross this river, for to the south lay the territory of the fierce enemy of virtually all surrounding tribes, the Osages. They followed its northern shore eastward and came again to the grandmother of rivers, who nearly doubled her size as she devoured the *Missouritheepi.*

They followed the west shore of the larger river south again and after many days travel came to a place called Cape Girardeau by the French and Spaniards and where they visited a short time with that portion of their tribe that had split away almost a year and a half before. Old Chief Kikusgowlowa had died, but they saw many old friends and also their mother, Methotasa, who was living in some distant place in her mind that none other could enter and from which she emerged only briefly to greet them before taking refuge there again.

It was while they tarried there that Tecumseh had become silent and withdrawn, thinking of what they had seen thus far in their trip and of the great and wonderful goodness of Moneto to create a world of such variety and beauty for his Indian children. The very contemplation of these things brought numerous questions to his mind, some of which he had asked Chiksika, but the answers received had left him feeling largely dissatisfied. Why was it, for example, since Moneto was all-powerful, that he permitted the *Shemanese* to take the lands and lives of the Shawnees? Why were not all the Indian tribes one—the Shawnees and Wyandots, the Miamis and Potawatomies, Menominees and Sacs and Kickapoos and all the others they had seen, as well as the multitude of others stretching in all directions beyond—why were they not one people? Why did they fight each other instead of joining to oppose their common enemy? And, closer to home, why was it that the principal chief of the Shawnee Nation could only be a Chalahgawtha or a Thawegila? Why were he and Chiksika, as Kispokotha Shawnees, ineligible to become principal leaders of the tribe? Why was it that their own father, Pucksinwah, had been required to prove himself in battle time and again as a superb leader before his talents were recognized enough for him to become a chief, and even then only a secondary chief, a war chief, of the Shawnees?

When he put such questions to Chiksika, his brother sighed and tried to answer, knowing even as he told his little brother what he could, based on his own knowledge of the customs and traditions of the tribe, that Tecumseh would not be satisfied.

In the dimmest recesses of history, he told Tecumseh, according to their tribal historians, the Chalahgawthas had crossed a great icy sea to reach this land and here they encountered the Thawegilas. These two had vied for dominance in the tribe and, rather than engage in the destructiveness of war to settle the issue, they had devised a series of tests for the principal chiefs of both to perform. It took a long while and involved many bizarre occurrences but, in the end, it was decided that neither was the better, that they were equals and therefore the leader of the tribe must be an individual from one of these two septs only. No one ever contested that and the process had become one of the more fundamental and time-honored traditions of the tribe. So it remained to this very day.[245]

The tradition, though Tecumseh had heard it before, was fascinating, but to him it was also very unsatisfying and seemed manifestly unjust, since it precluded the Peckuwes, the Maykujays or the Kispokothas from ever providing a great Shawnee tribal leader. To Chiksika's profound shock, Tecumseh suggested, in what could only be considered as blasphemy, that a tradition, if found to be unjust, should be closely reexamined and perhaps its precepts revised if not suitable to the circumstances that exist at present, so long after the tradition was established. Chiksika pronounced that his ears had not heard what Tecumseh had said and warned that such a comment should not again pass his lips, *ever,* lest he wished to chance being ostracized from the tribe, to which any other fate was preferable.

At length they had left the Shawnee villages near Cape Girardeau and crossed the great river, traveling toward the rising sun through the land of the Kickapoos in the Illinois and Indiana countries and back at length, after an absence of three moons to what should have been a happy homecoming, but which had turned out to be a devastating view of a great scar of black ashes where the wegiwas and *msi-kah-mi-qui* of Chalahgawtha had been but were no longer. It was destruction far more complete than had been visited on the village fourteen months before.

With sickened hearts they hastened northward to the twelve-mile distant Piqua Town and found it similarly destroyed. They had then followed the Mad River upstream, encountering occasional individual Shawnees and even a couple of small war parties and learning from them what had happened, but not really stopping for long until they reached Blue Jacket's Town and sat with Wehyehpihehrsehnwah himself for many hours while he related the dreadful tidings of what had transpired during their absence.

The belief of the Shawnee warriors generally that the *Shemanese* were too weak and disorganized to mount an expedition against them for at least a year or two following the Shawnee expedition under Captain Bird had been wrong. Almost immediately the white chief who had captured Kaskaskia and Cahokia and Vincennes—George Rogers Clark—had mounted an army of over a thousand mounted men. These were largely not regular soldiers, of which there were only a very few, but instead they were the tough frontiersmen themselves from throughout the Kentucky country. Under Clark's leadership they had crossed the Spaylaywitheepi and arrowed directly to Chalahgawtha.[246]

Blue Jacket had shaken his head sorrowfully at the memory. Catahecassa, he said, had received word of the approach of the army in time enough to take steps to save his people, but it had been at great cost. The news had been brought to him by Simon Girty and his companion, the Kispokotha warrior named Red Snake, who had thundered into the village on lathered, snorting horses, and who had also said they had seen the dangerous frontiersman Bahdler with them.[247] With hardly more than a hundred warriors available in the village at the time, the Shawnee principal chief had realized the futility of attempting any sort of concerted defense in the town. There had been no time to waste and neither horses nor people enough to carry their goods to safety. In lieu of that, Catahecassa had ordered that all of the village's treasure, amounting to upwards of a ton of silver in the form of arm bands, gorgets, wristbands, medallions, rings, plates and bars of crude raw silver stock, be brought together and bound up in small rawhide bundles.[248] These and much more—kettles, utensils, weapons needing repair, and a multitude of other heavy objects— were similarly wrapped and the individual bundles were then passed hand-to-hand along a long line of the villagers, running all the way to the large bubbling spring in the marsh below the village. At that point each bundle in turn was thrown into the spring and disappeared into its depths to the bottom, twenty or thirty feet below, where they would be safe from being confiscated by the approaching army and could be recovered by the villagers when they returned.[249]

Blue Jacket told the brothers that as soon as this was accomplished, Catahecassa had ordered the warriors to set fire to every structure in Chalahgawtha, including the *msi-kah-mi-qui,* and all were afire when he led the Chalahgawthas away to Piqua Town on the Mad River, believing they would be safe there. They hadn't been. Catahecassa's hundred warriors had joined with the two hundred at Piqua Town and in a short time had been attacked there by Clark's army. There had been a very hot fight, but the defenders had been unable to hold against not only Clark's superior numbers but against his artillery.[250]

Twenty-six warriors, Blue Jacket told them sadly, had been killed and a dozen wounded, plus a great quantity of their crops destroyed. They had finally retreated to the Lower Piqua Town on the Great Miami, successfully taking off all of their women and children, all the wounded and half of their dead. No one seemed to know for certain how many of Clark's men had been killed, but the loss was not so great as the Shawnees'.[251]

All surviving residents of Piqua Town and Chalahgawtha, Blue Jacket told them, including their own family, were still at the Peckuwe towns on the Great Miami. These two towns, not many miles apart, had been largely empty since the Peckuwes moved to the Missouri country eighteen moons ago when the tribe split. Thus, the tiny Peckuwe population remaining in the Lower Piqua Town gave up the village entirely to the Chalahgawthas and had moved to the Upper Piqua Town, where refugees from the razed Piqua Town on the Mad River had joined them.[252]

Chiksika and Tecumseh, refusing with thanks Blue Jacket's offer to feed and house them if they liked, pushed on at once for the Lower Piqua Town and had found Tecumapese, Wasegoboah and the children there. There was joy at the reunion, but at the same time a pervading sadness at being reunited at such a place and under such conditions.[253]

The Lower Piqua Town, already renamed Chalahgawtha, was a safe place for their people for the time being, but neither Chiksika nor Tecumseh cared much for the terrain. It was flatter and less attractive than that in the valley of the Little Miami. The earth itself seemed less fertile and the springs were nowhere near so numerous, nor the game so abundant. Their hearts yearned for their own Chalahgawtha and others felt the same. Many of the warriors were talking about going back to the two towns and reestablishing them and firm plans were already being made to do just this; if not at once, then next spring when they could again plant their corn and vegetables and construct new wegiwas.

Wasegoboah had built a wegiwa of sorts for the family, but it was a rather sorry construction and so the whole family—including the triplets and Kisathoi, Tebethto, Sinnanatha, and even little Spemica Lawba—pitched in and quickly built a new one that was much better. But however good it was, it simply wasn't home and everyone knew it.

It was in this wegiwa that Tecumseh now lay awake with thoughts that kept slumber at bay. Abruptly he became aware of someone near and then the soft, close voice of Chiksika came. "You are troubled, brother. Tell me what is in your heart."

Tecumseh sat up in the darkness and reached out, placing a hand on

Chiksika's arm. "Today I heard a little girl from our village ask her mother why, if Moneto loved them, He allowed the *Shemanese* to kill her father and destroy her home and make her flee. Her mother hugged her and told her not to think of such things. But now *I* think of such things and now I ask *you*, Chiksika, if Moneto loves us as we love and respect Him, as well as the grain and animals and birds He provides for us, why then does He permit the white men to hunt us down? Why does He let them kill us? Why does he let them destroy our forests and our crops and our fields? Why does He hurt us so? *Why,* Chiksika?"

Chiksika patted his little brother's head and then hugged him to his chest for a long while, but he made no reply. He had none to make. He had asked these very questions of himself and did not know the answers.

[November 21, 1780 — Tuesday]

In being honored with his new full tribal warrior status at the age of only twelve and a half, Tecumseh had become one of the youngest Shawnees in the history of the tribe to receive such recognition; an accolade that brought him a surprising amount of prestige. By having achieved this rank, he was now able, if he so chose, to become the leader of war parties and hunting parties. In his shoulder-length glossy black hair, he could now wear the emblem of his rank, a single or double white-tipped eagle feather, affixed at the quill to a brass medallion and attached just over his ear, with the tips trailing downward over his shoulder. It was a symbol of rank he wore with pride and one which now permitted him to attend—and have a voice in—any council being held anywhere in the Shawnee Nation and, most particularly, the infrequent Grand Councils that were held involving matters of national concern among the Shawnees.

Chiksika was obviously very proud of his young brother, as were all the members of the family. Now it would be Tecumseh's decision, not his, as to whether the lad would accompany him on forays or major engagements against the enemy, or perhaps lead his own. And no longer would Tecumseh be required to be Chiksika's shadow when he went along; he could move independently where he wished, bound only by the obedience warriors of such a party were required to give its leader.

One of the things it permitted him to do was to visit a place he had long looked forward to seeing. For years he had heard intriguing stories about the extraordinary principal village of the Miami tribe, located to the north and west, where the waters of the St. Marys from the south and the St. Joseph from the north converged to form the Maumee—the village known far and wide as Kekionga.

A month ago he had gone there with Chiksika, Wasegoboah, and Blue Jacket, the four of them clad in fine garb and riding side by side on their excellent horses. Blue Jacket had been there a number of times, Chiksika a time or two and Wasegoboah and Tecumseh never, although he had listened closely as Chiksika had attempted to describe it to the family. However, Chiksika admitted that verbal description did little justice to so grand a village, which was actually more a true city than just an ordinary Indian village.

The name Kekionga meant The Glorious Gate and probably no more appropriate appellation could have been chosen. The Maumee River was formed here and flowed northeastward 132 miles to Lake Erie, providing access to Detroit and the Ottawa and Chippewa villages to the north of there, to the Wyandot villages along southern Lake Erie, and to the major routes by land or water to the ports and forts and centers of the East. Northward, up the St. Joseph, were many of the villages of the Potawatomies and Ottawas, while southward, up the St. Marys, were many of the smaller Miami villages. Like spokes radiating from a hub, several important portage routes gave direct access from Kekionga to a broad range of territory: a short portage to the north-northwest gave access to the headwaters of another, completely different river also called the St. Joseph, this one flowing northwest past the major trading center called St. Joseph that was operated by the famed and well-liked trader William Burnett.[254] Farther down that same stream, where it emptied into Lake Michigan, there was access to all the tribes to the north and west of that great body of water. To the northwest from Kekionga, another relatively easy portage connected with the headwaters of the Eel River, and down that stream were the numerous villages of the Eel River Miamis. A portage leading southwest from Kekionga connected to the Wabash River, which flowed westward and southward through the territory of the Wea branch of the Miami tribe, past the Tippecanoe villages and the important centers at Ouiatenon and Vincennes and finally into the Ohio River, with access at that point to the Illinois and western Kentucky country as well as the entire Mississippi Valley. And, of course, a journey down the Maumee and then up the Auglaize provided portage access to the Great Miami River, the western Ohio country and, ultimately, the Ohio River and the heart of Kentucky.

For Tecumseh, as well as his companions, Kekionga was the most cosmopolitan place ever encountered. A substantial percentage of its structures were permanent buildings—fine, well-built cabins of good size, some of them with spacious lofts and several main-floor rooms and a few even having their own fruit cellars. There were six or seven excellent trading posts, including another of those owned by William Burnett, offering a wider variety of goods than Tecumseh had ever seen gathered together in one place. Regular streets had been laid out and in front of the buildings facing the main central square, wide board sidewalks had been built so fine ladies from Detroit who visited here so frequently could pass from building to building during inclement weather and not get their flowing skirts muddied.

Many of the buildings had signs erected, identifying their purposes—some in French but the majority in English. There were stables for the horses that were ridden in by visitors, taverns for the thirsty, gambling rooms for those who wished to play at cards or dice, the wonderful trading posts ready and able to fill the needs of any Indian man or woman who came with the furs or leathers, sugar or lead, vegetables or grains to trade for the goods they wished to purchase. There was an official British government cabin where important closed-session meetings were often held with the chiefs resident here or visiting chiefs from other villages and tribes. A huge log building with a fine floor of close-fitted planking served the dual purpose of council hall and ballroom, with a spacious dais at one end where important chiefs and prestigious delegates could sit during councils and where musicians could be situated for the frequent balls that were held. Apart from the center of the town was another large, squat log building of many small rooms where certain women—most of them French or English, but with a scattering of Indian women as well—peddled their sexual favors to those who desired such services, all under the benevolent but stern direction of the tough old Frenchman, Monsieur Louis Duchamble and his heavy wife, Madame Josette, who was so domineering to everyone but her husband.

There were scores of residence cabins and hundreds of less permanent wegiwas and very temporary tepees, since many Indians from other tribes had also taken up residence here with the Miamis—a small number of Shawnees and larger numbers of Delawares, Wyandots, Potawatomies, and Ottawas. There was even an enclave of Cherokees at the western edge of the town.

Among the very finest of the dwellings was the residence of the principal chief of the Miamis, the powerful Michikiniqua—Little Turtle. It was a very spacious multiroom log structure with doors on three sides and windows with actual glass panes, fine furnishings that included well-crafted tables and chairs, sofa, feather-tick beds of such height it was necessary to step up on a small stool to climb into the bed proper, numerous shiny brass oil lamps with glass chimneys and shades upon which were painted pastoral scenes, well-made cupboards and sideboards and dry sinks, numerous framed pictures on the walls—artwork brought from Europe or executed by Canadian artisans—the largest wall mirrors many visitors had ever seen, fine china dishes and well-made glass goblets and crystal wine glasses and decanters, and, along one wall, a harpsichord that visitors with the skill to do so were urged to play. A dozen yards behind the house, with a narrow raised wooden sidewalk leading to it, was an excellent five-seater outhouse constructed of planking.

At age thirty-eight, Michikiniqua was one of the more impressive people Tecumseh had ever met, reminding him in some ways of his own father,

Pucksinwah. It wasn't that their appearance was so much alike but more the sense of a *presence* that they shared; a strength and controlled vitality, and a gaze that seemed capable of seeing far more than was immediately visible. Unlike Pucksinwah, however, Michikiniqua was a man who could never be described as handsome. His hawkish nose was too large for his face, his lips downcurved on one side into an expression of somewhat perpetual malevolence, his ears large and with enormous lobes, which had been pierced for pendants, a permanent hole through the nasal septum in which, on occasion, he hung metal or bone ornamentation, a long wide scar along his lower right jawline from chin almost to ear that was a memento of a slashing tomahawk wielded by Charles de Langlade during the fight where Chief Unemakemi had been killed and Pickawillany destroyed. He was not physically as large as Pucksinwah had been, but he was certainly as well built, with fine musculature in his broad chest, his arms and legs.

Michikiniqua had welcomed Blue Jacket warmly, having met him before and knowing of his great skill as a warrior. He remembered having met Chiksika once before and said with sincerity that he was pleased to see again the son of Pucksinwah. He shook hands gravely with Wasegoboah, his eyes reflecting approval of what he saw in the young man and then he had turned to Tecumseh, took his hand in both of his and looked at him steadily and expressionlessly for a somewhat discomfiting period before finally breaking into a lopsided smile and speaking.

"You have the eyes of your father," Michikiniqua said. "I see courage and determination behind them, as there were in his. You are very young for a warrior, but," he nodded his approval, "it is deserving that you be so. Great things will come of you."

Then he was gone and Tecumseh, rather dazed by the compliments, followed the others as they moved about through the hustle and bustle of Kekionga. There were a number of British soldiers here and an even greater number of British civilians, plus fully 150 Canadians, most of whom were in one way or another involved in the fur trade. There was also a large number of blacks, most of whom had been "liberated" on the frontiers in Virginia and Kentucky, only to find themselves in a not so different kind of servitude here.

By far the largest of the trading establishments was the William Burnett Trading Post, operated by his agents, since Burnett headquartered himself at his post far to the northwest on the St. Joseph. For Tecumseh, entering that trading post was like entering a dream world where everything one had ever thought about owning was available. The first thing noticeable was the aroma—a marvelous blend of the good scents of leather and perfumes, pickling brines and freshly ground coffee, rich hot chocolate and fur skins and tallow and waxes, dried fruits and fresh bread and lamp oil, tobacco, greenwood, biscuits, jerky and smoked hams and dried fish, fresh fruits and berries and vegetables; all combining into a never-to-be-forgotten aroma encountered nowhere else save in a well-stocked trading post.

At its center was a broad open space in the center of which stood a potbellied cast iron stove of the type that had been invented some thirty years earlier by Benjamin Franklin and now in wide use all over the frontier. There was a long bench with a slanting backrest and seven or eight chairs in a semicircle. This was the sociability center, where pipes were smoked, whiskey and rum were drunk, news and conversation was passed before, during, and after the trading. There were barrels and boxes and kegs and jugs and containers and sacks of different things, shelves and long tables and counters loaded with a magnificent array of all the items of merchandise that played so important a role in the lives of the Indians and upon which, in large measure, they had become so dependent.

Here there were bolts of cloth, clay pipes and cob pipes, hatchets and axes, sheath knives and tomahawks, shovels and picks, mattocks and augurs; here were reels of fine braided wire, strong and supple, for the making of snares and there were mounds of steel traps, some small enough to imprison the dainty leg of an ermine, others with fiercely toothed jaws and large enough to hold a mature grizzly—or practically sever the leg of the man unfortunate enough to accidentally step into one; here were kegs and large jugs of rum, flasks of brandy, good Madeira wines and bottles of cheap whiskey, all in direct flaunt of liquor trade regulations; here there were fish hooks and fishing lines and cord for making wampum belts and tiny colored beads with which to create their designs; here, too, were various pots and packets of paints—vermilion, white, ocher, indigo, black—for use by war parties to decorate their faces and bodies; there were large dark evil-looking sticks of twist tobacco, shredded tobacco in tins, chewing tobacco in bars and plugs and snuff of various qualities and flavors; there were mirrors of all kinds, framed and unframed, large and small, round and oval and square and rectangular; there were gewgaws and ornaments and medals of various sizes in brass and bronze and copper, and there was expensive jewelry and cheap bangles and baubles of glass and wire painted silver or gold; there was caulking gum and rolls of bark and heavy folded canvas sails; there were flags of different nations and flags with designs of no particular meaning and ribbons of various widths and lengths and colors; there were packets of paper and ink pots and quills and quill pens and quill knives, along with feathers and plumes from turkeys and eagles, swans and egrets and ostriches and peacocks, and varieties of smaller feathers in their natural coloration or dyed in lots of gaudy flamboyant hues; there were huge coils of hemp rope and large balls of cord and cones of twine and sewing threads of linen and cotton and silk in small spools; there were great curved needles for sewing hides as thick as buffalo and a variety of others down to tiny needles for fine detail work; there were half a dozen different sizes, weights, and colors of woolen blankets—one of the foremost items in the Indian trade—along with quantities of fabrics of broadcloth and Irish linen, wool and flannel and linsey-woolsey and striped cotton calico and plain cotton and even lovely delicate silks, along with the fine cotton material called swanskin and a much coarser cotton cloth known as onasburg; there were shoes and slippers and boots and moccasins; there were trousers and leggins and vests and blouses and petticoats, hats and bonnets and caps of all kinds, plain and decorated, common and fancy; brilliant scarlet jackets and coats trimmed in black, with shiny brass buttons and gold epaulets for distinguished chiefs, and ordinary woolen coats and jackets and longcoats in brown or green for warriors, plus a whole array of obsolete uniforms of the French and British and Dutch; there were bins of dried wheat and barley, corn and rice, oats, peas, beans and nuts; barrels of pickles and brined beef and pork, containers of tea and coffee, sugar and salt and pepper and a variety of spices and other herbs and condiments and shredded coconut, flour and lard and bear oil and goose grease; there were ear-bobs and brooches, bracelets and arm bands, gorgets and anklets, necklaces and combs made of basswood or silver, horn or tortoiseshell or ivory; there were platters and plates and flatware and utensils, cookware of all kinds from gigantic pots to tiny pans, in iron and brass and copper and tin; there were tightly sealed kegs of gunpowder—set well away from the stove—and bars of lead and bullet molds and lead balls of various sizes; there were gunworms and gunflints and ramrods, fine fusees and excellent muskets for important chiefs and ordinary serviceable flintlocks and cheap muskets for warriors; there were cedar shafts for arrow making and thicker shafts of hickory for spears; there were lengths of handpicked and trimmed osage for the making of bows and even some very expensive ready-made bows of fine yew from Europe; there were fire-making kits of flint and steel and punky tinder material; there were iron harpoon and fish spearheads, and bar iron and files and molten cloth, hammers and tongs, rosin and charcoal; there were tanned hides with or without fur; there were metal and wood and glass containers of a wide variety of sizes and shapes for a multitude of purposes; there were candles of tallow and wax and glass chimney hurricane lamps with fuel bowls of polished brass or dull pewter; there was borax and soap and perfumes and scented oils and tinctures and nostrums of many kinds—patent medicines packaged in boxes and phials and bottles; there was a wide array of books on a special shelf—Shakespeare, Plato, Aristotle, John Milton, Samuel Pepys, Benjamin Franklin, John Donne, Joseph Addison, Jonathan Swift, Izaak Walton and others and, of course, the Holy Bible. All these items and more—many more—were inside the trading post, while beneath it, for use later in the fall, was an enormous fruit cellar where large quantities of apples, pears, squash, pumpkins, cucumbers, beans, corn, and other harvested crops would be stored for trade throughout the winter. Outside, in the rear, a line of bark canoes leaned against the wall, along with a pair of small bateaux. Beyond them, in pens, were hogs and sheep and poultry. A long smokehouse was hung with a wonderful selection of meats—pork hams, venison hams, bear meat, beef, elk, moose, bison, turkeys, grouse, ducks, geese, swans, and crane. Henhouses with nest boxes provided abundant eggs, and in the stable yard adjoining were horses for sale or hire, for riding, plowing, pack-use, or other work. Finally, there was one other large log building, fifteen feet wide and sixty feet long with broad double doors in the middle and both ends, the interior of which was filled with the multitude of items packed and baled and boxed and barreled and ready for shipment to the East and much of it, eventually, to England—fine furs and skins and peltry of every description and type, well-tanned buckskin and elkhide, buffalo robes and great heavy bearskins, vast amounts of maple sugar in whole deerskin bags, fancy plumes, Indian costumes and native-made ornaments, dried fish and game meats, kegs of bear oil, and other items. Tecumseh was overwhelmed by it all and the other three had nearly to drag him away before he would leave.

Talk of the war was everywhere in Kekionga and great concern was being expressed among the Indians that the battle fever between the British and Americans was cooling and that peace talks were already in progress between them far across the sea in the great village called Paris. There were also murmurings that in these talks, that were expected to soon result in peace between them, the two white factions were dividing up the land of the Indians between themselves without consideration for the Indian inhabitants—and without any suggestion of Indian representation at the parlays.

It was this pervading concern that had inspired the visiting Shawnee foursome to leave Kekionga and move rapidly down the Maumee to the trail that led from the mouth of the Auglaize directly east to Lower Sandusky, where a significant council was in progress in which this very matter was being discussed by Alexander McKee.[255] Simon Girty was there, as was Matthew Elliott and Thayendanegea, the latter being honored for his continuing fighting against the Americans in the Mohawk Valley. Visitors from all tribes in the area were welcomed, though there were some raised eyebrows when Tecumseh entered behind Blue Jacket and Wasegoboah and with Chiksika at his side. But, seeing his warrior's headfeathers and the company he was with, they merely nodded approval and said nothing.

The council had begun twelve days before, at which time two oxen had been roasted and a great feast held, following which the ritual pipes had been smoked and the introductory remarks made by Chief Tarhe—The Crane—who was head of the peace faction of the Wyandots and in favor of peace in practically any manner. Other chiefs had then filled the days with their comments, including those made by Tarhe's bitter enemy, the Wyandot war chief, Pipe, who had been directing and often commanding so many forays against the whites on the upper Ohio River and who wished nothing more than to exterminate all the Americans.[256]

Now the council was winding down and McKee was preparing to deliver his concluding remarks and was carefully considering his choice of words. It had become only too clear to him through the comments of the chiefs that there was a strong—and increasing—suspicion among these Indians that the Americans and British were involved in secret negotiations concerning Indian lands; negotiations designed to keep the Indians in the dark while their lands were being divided among strangers. McKee had no idea how the news had slipped out to them and, true though it was, it had become his responsibility to allay those suspicions as much as possible and keep the Indians pro-British with promises and little else. Now he stood before them and waited as the shuffling, muttering and other sounds gradually died away and all eyes were directed to him.

"Brothers," he said, "I have heard your words and I know they are from your hearts, just as I hope you will know that mine are likewise. Part of what you have heard is true—that the war between the British and the rebellious Americans is ending.

"Brothers, it is also true what you have heard, that in the great French city of Paris across the great waters, these two are now starting to put their pens to paper in the signing of peace documents. But, brothers, what the bad birds have sung into your ears that is not true is that your friends, the British, are turning their backs on you. I know that many of you here believe this, but brothers, you are wrong to think so."

McKee paused a moment to let that soak in and to give the interpreters time to catch up, then held up his hand for a moment in a beneficent gesture before continuing: "Brothers, hear me! The treaty being made in Paris is not meant to deprive you of any extent of country, of which the right of soil belongs to you and is in yourselves as sole proprietors. It is important that you realize that your great father, the king, still acknowledges your happiness by his protection. He encourages you in your usual intercourse with trade and will continue to provide you with those things you need. You will receive guns and ammunition, knives and tomahawks, blankets and tobacco and hooks and whatever else you wish. The trading posts at the French Store and on the Maumee and St. Joseph and elsewhere will still provide your wants and you will still receive gifts from your great father, the king, at Niagara and Mackinac and Detroit. Hear me, brothers," McKee concluded loudly, "you have not been forsaken nor forgotten. You are still the children of your great father, the king, who loves you."

As the interpreters, who were keeping pace admirably, finished, the Indians nodded among themselves and an undercurrent of voices arose. The comments were essentially the same all over the council house. What McKee said was good; it was only their due. They had won the war with the Americans here in the West. Great damage had been inflicted upon the Kentucky settlements and, despite their recent brief crossing of the stream against Chalahgawtha and Piqua Town, the *Shemanese* were still south of the Ohio River. That the Americans were making any claims to their lands was ridiculous; the Indians here had never given either the French or British title to any of their lands—only permission to use little pieces of it temporarily, primarily to merely carry on the trade. There was no land in question that could be claimed to have been won by right of conquest.

One fact, above anything else had become clear to the Indians in attendance. Their support, if it be given to anyone, should be given only to the British. The Americans, like the British, brought goods among them, but it was quite clear that there was a difference, because it was much more than ordinary trading privileges the Americans wanted. They *expected* to purchase lands from the Indians and when they were refused, they moved themselves in and took the lands anyway and defied the Indians to do anything about it. So now, despite the fact that the British and Americans were apparently making peace between themselves, there was still a division between them and if the Indians were going to support any white faction hereafter, it would be the British.

Reading, as they always did, the allegory between what was said in council and what was actually meant, to them it was beyond doubt that Alexander McKee had just told them that while the war between the British and Americans might be coming to an end, it was a peace that was only temporary and that war would come again between them very soon. The war *would* come again! In the meanwhile the British would be supplying them with all the wherewithal they required to continue their harassment of those who would enter their country to steal their lands.

"What I derive from all this that McKee spoke," said Blue Jacket, as the four Shawnees rode southward toward their own villages, "is that when the time is right for them to do so, our British brothers will rise up and help us drive out the Americans. What do you think, Chiksika?"

"I think," said Tecumseh's older brother in a very measured way, "that that is exactly what McKee *wishes* us to think, but I am not so sure that I believe him. The British king would not be talking peace with the Americans if he thought he could defeat them. And if he does not think he can defeat the Americans now, when they are new and weak, how does he think he can defeat them later when they are stronger? Would he even *risk*, later on, raising his sword against the Americans again? *Wah!*" he said, voicing his strong negative. "I think not. What do I believe? I believe what my father said to me moments before he died—that the whites mean only to devour our lands and we should never make peace with them. He did not say just the British or the

French or the Americans—he said the *whites,* and they are *all* whites. *That* is what I believe and, for myself, I cannot look upon any agreement between the British and Americans as anything more than a clearing of the way for more taking of our lands. For my part, I will abide by what I promised my father—I will not make peace with them, now or ever."

"Nor I!" said Tecumseh.

[April 12, 1781 — Thursday]

No one in the war party had any inkling of the vow Tecumseh was this very moment making in his own mind. One or two among them, most particularly Chiksika and Wasegoboah, noted that the thirteen-year-old was rather morosely staying to himself and not engaging in the laughing banter and excited talk going on that was always a sort of release after an attack. Had they suffered the loss of one of their warriors, or even had one been injured, there might be just cause for his mood, but the attack had been a signal success, with all the near two score whites wiped out and not even a scratch to any warrior. Chiksika sighed, pushing away an impulse to go to his little brother's side and ask him what was wrong. No, Tecumseh was a warrior now and would justifiably resent it if Chiksika's effort was interpreted as overprotectiveness. Instead, he returned his attention to the others and joined in the recounting of the coup they had just pulled off at the Three Islands.

It had been a week ago yesterday that Shemeneto, at the suggestion of Chiksika and Wasegoboah, had organized the war party. Work had been progressing very well for weeks in the rebuilding of Chalahgawtha on the Little Miami and Piqua Town on the Mad, aided by the Kispokotha war chief and a good many of his people, and it was likely that before this moon was finished, they would be more or less abandoning the temporary Chalahgawtha at the Lower Piqua Town and moving back to their beloved Little Miami village site. But, unaccustomed to the hard work of reconstructing wegiwas and the far more difficult task of erecting a new *msi-kah-mi-qui,* Chiksika had finally declared it was time for a break from this labor and Wasegoboah and Tecumseh had immediately agreed. They had approached Shemeneto and suggested he lead an ambush party to Three Islands. The ugly old war chief's eyes had lighted and he burst into laughter and just that quickly the foray was born.

It had not been difficult to round up forty other young men to accompany them, with the object being to post themselves in hiding on the Three Islands in the midst of the Spaylaywitheepi and intercept the next party of whites they discovered descending. They were all quite sure it would not be a very long wait. Ever since the winter weather had broken a few weeks ago there

Allan W. Eckert

had been a veritable flood of boaters and rafters coming downstream to settle in the Kentucky lands.

The past winter had been difficult for the Shawnees. Clark's destruction of their corn crop and vegetables had left them severely in want. Without corn to parch or grind and without vegetables, especially yams and potatoes, their diet was badly imbalanced and the men were hard pressed to find game enough to keep them supplied with meat through the cold months. The temporary Chalahgawtha on the Great Miami was not much more than forty miles north and west of their burned-out village site, but the terrain was less hospitable, game less abundant, the winter seeming to be colder and simple existence tougher.

One thing that fueled them with determination, however, was the great resentment harbored against the Kentuckians for the hardships being suffered, where mere survival alone so taxed their strength and abilities that throughout the winter little energy remained to launch raids against the Kentucky settlements. In point of fact, the raids made early in the winter had been more instigated to secure food supplies from the whites than to destroy their forts and cabins. At the same time, throughout the fall and winter, work teams had journeyed regularly to the burned out Chalahgawtha, cleared away all the debris of the burnings and begun the job of restoration. The offered help of Shemeneto and his people had been gratefully accepted.

Shortly after the first of the year there was an increase in the number of war parties going out to strike at the Kentucky settlements, but it wasn't until the weather broke a few weeks ago that the workers at Chalahgawtha began splitting off in war parties, large and small, to slash with renewed savagery at the settlers throughout the Kentucky country and equally at the immigrants newly arriving from far up the Spaylaywitheepi.

The easiest and quite often most lucrative forays were those made against the river traffic, ambushes being simple to set up and whites drifting inexorably into them. The Indians had merely to ready themselves in their swift canoes and take cover in sheltered coves or creek mouths until the victims drifted to within inescapable range, then surge out and attack overwhelmingly. More often than not there were no white survivors. These easy victories helped restore the Shawnee confidence that had been so shaken the preceding August by Clark, who was since, the traders said, promoted to brigadier general. Ever since early March it had become relatively commonplace, with the upsurge of river traffic, for overturned canoes, demolished rafts and keelboats, and the bloated carcasses of livestock, as well as those of scalped and mutilated people, to be witnessed floating downstream in the Spaylaywitheepi's current.

It had not taken long for Ohio River travelers to become wise to the hazards awaiting them. They rarely drifted downstream alone anymore, nor was their drifting, as it had normally been before, in the center of the Spay-laywitheepi, where the current was most swift. Now they had begun to hug close to the Kentucky shore and bear the added days this caused in their journeys because of the more sluggish currents closer to shore. At least there they had a chance to quickly put to shore if an attack came and try to escape overland to the settlements or put up a more effective defense. Since this was the case, it now became sensible for the Shawnees in Shemeneto's party to set up the ambush as close to the Kentucky side as possible without actually being on the Kentucky side themselves and risking a surprise attack on their own party. The perfect answer was obviously the Three Islands. Instead of a quarter-mile to half-mile of water to traverse from the Ohio shore to reach the boats of the whites, from the uppermost island of the Three Islands, which was the one closest to the Kentucky shoreline, only a few hundred feet would separate them from their intended victims when the attack was launched.[257]

At Shemeneto's direction they had ridden their horses to the broad twisting creek mouth on the Ohio side just two and a half miles below the uppermost of the Three Islands. The preceding fall five large canoes had been hidden there by Shemeneto's warriors. They had not been sunk as usual but rather had been pulled into a tiny tributary less than two miles upstream and there dragged well up on shore, overturned atop their paddles and covered with brush.[258] The eight canoes were recovered in good shape and the horses left in a cold camp under guard of four warriors. Within a few hours the canoes and Indians were in position on the foremost island and the waiting began.

For three days they waited, their meager food supplies dwindling until, near noon today, just as Shemeneto had decided to give the order calling off the operation, two keelboats came into view around the bend less than three miles upstream, floating about thirty yards off the Kentucky shore. Instantly the war chief hissed his orders and all forty Shawnees slipped to their assigned canoes and hid with them. When the word was given, it would take only seconds to launch them all.

Within an hour after the first sighting, the two crowded boats were floating into the optimum range for ambush. A harsh shriek erupted from Shemeneto and instantly the canoes were launched, five men to each and all five paddling furiously. The keelboats were turned immediately toward the Kentucky shore and, amid the screaming of women, the men aboard wasted no time shooting at the attackers but bent their efforts to pole the two boats to an extensive sandbar along the shoreline as quickly as possible. But keelboats are sluggish at best and though they had at least a one-hundred-yard head start on their pursuers, they ground ashore only bare seconds before the Indian canoes.

Hoarse cries came from the men and continued screaming from the women and children, as they tumbled out of the boats and raced across the broad sandy strip toward the thirty-yard distant fringe of brush, trees, and rocks. The Shawnees surged after them, shooting most of the men before they reached cover and a good many of the women and children.

Tecumseh and another warrior sprinted after a husky man of about thirty who reached the rocks, dodged through them and began scrambling up the steep slope to the west. They followed, yipping and shrieking, all the way to the top, some thirty or forty feet over the river, all the while with the sounds of terrified screaming coming from below. They were rapidly closing the gap when the man, with a despairing look over his shoulder at them, veered and headed directly for the edge of the cliff. Without pause he leaped and just as he did so the warrior with Tecumseh threw his tomahawk. The blade caught the man in the right side of his back, burying itself deeply, and the man cried out in pain as he disappeared from sight. They heard the heavy splash of his hitting the water and ran to the cliff edge, peering over in time to see the ring of waves he caused quickly disappearing in the current, but of the man there was no trace. Satisfied that he could not survive, the pair turned and raced back down the hill, but by then all had been captured or killed.

Including the tomahawked man who had gone over the cliff, there had been sixteen men, twelve women, eight children, and three infants in the two boats. Now all were dead except two women with infants, a boy about six, and a girl about eight—all of them clustered together in a terror-stricken group—along with a man who had taken a ball in one calf and was now bound at ankles and wrists and sitting on the ground sobbing. Scattered around them were the thirty-one dead, some still being scalped, some still being mutilated.

Tecumseh stood back, his features set in harsh lines, while the warrior who had thrown the tomahawk jerked out his knife and leaped into the midst of the dead with the others and began repeatedly plunging his blade into their bodies. A wave of disgust filled Tecumseh. Women. Children. *Babies!* The whites were enemies, true, but what point to such totally barbaric acts against them even after they were dead? It simply made no sense to him. The sole consolation was that there were seven still alive, six of which, at least, would be taken back with them and probably sold to the British. The man . . . well, he was leg-wounded and could not walk, so his fate was sealed and Tecumseh steeled his mind to it.

What happened next was not according to Tecumseh's imagining. At a signal from Shemeneto the infants were ripped screaming from the arms of their mothers who, as they frantically strove to get them back, were toma-hawked and scalped. Then the neck of one infant was broken with a violent twist of the head and the other was gripped by one ankle, swung in a vicious circle and its head slammed against a large emergent rock.

The boy and girl who had been standing aghast at all this suddenly broke and ran, and the Shawnees, howling and laughing, quickly overtook them and brought them down with tomahawk blows and scalped them as well. Now only the wounded man remained. Shemeneto strode to him and gripped him by the hair, jerking him to his feet, but because of his wound he could not stand and he collapsed onto the hard-packed sand on his back, holding up his tied-together hands, moaning and begging.

Shemeneto regarded him contemptuously a moment, then kicked him very hard in the side and issued a stream of sharp commands. Immediately several warriors gripped the captive and began tearing off his trousers, cutting away his ankle bindings so they could free them. Another ran over and snatched one of the fallen push-poles from the keelboats and used his tomahawk to chop it into a four-foot length, then swiftly trimmed the chopped end to a rapidly tapered point. The blunted end was buried for half the length of the wood, leaving a firmly embedded two-foot-high stake projecting straight up in the air. A half-dozen warriors grabbed the white man who was now nude from the waist down, with his ankles retied together, and he wailed in terror and struggled weakly as they lifted and held him in a sitting position over the stake. He was lowered until the point touched his rectum and then in the midst of his begging and whimpering, he was dropped. The stake drove up through him and he gasped, but then made no further sound save for labored breathing as his heels scuffed and shoved at the ground. The struggling lasted for about ten minutes and then he died, his head lolling but his body held upright by the stake within.

At more directions from Shemeneto, the man's bindings were cut away, his legs bent, and his feet crossed in front of him so he appeared to be sitting Indian fashion. A blanket was tossed over his shoulders and wrapped snugly around his body, and then a battered, useless flintlock was placed across his knees and his hands placed upon it in a natural position. His head was moved so that his chin was nearly on his chest. Stepping back, the warriors surveyed their handiwork and then grinned widely as the others clapped their hands and shouted and laughed in approval. From a short distance away, the scene seemed to be an Indian guarding a scattering of bodies—an Indian who had fallen asleep on the job. Whatever whites came upon this scene would be quite a while figuring it out and approaching. The Shawnees howled with laughter at their wonderful joke.[259]

A short time later, all the plunder transferred to their own canoes, Shemeneto ordered the keelboats set afire and shoved adrift. And now, three hours later, they were back on their horses, returning toward Chalahgawtha, and Tecumseh, withdrawn and riding apart, still could feel the waves of revulsion in him over what had transpired. He was sickened and ashamed—ashamed of his people for their inhumanity, ashamed of his brother and Wasegoboah for laughing along with the others at the hideous atrocities and, most of all, ashamed of himself for watching it and saying nothing against it. Logically, he knew that whatever he might have said, the words of a thirteen-year-old would have had no weight among the seasoned warriors and would only have shamed his brother; logically, he knew that what was done had been done because the whites were their enemies and this was how, traditionally, enemies were treated; logically, he knew that these people, had they not been killed, would have been the very people who came to steal Shawnee lands and eject them from their own country. Logically, he knew these things.

Illogically though it might be, Tecumseh now lifted a hand and grasped his *opawaka* and made his silent vow: never again would he allow such barbaric brutality to occur in his presence, nor would he tolerate the company of anyone who participated in it, not even his own brother. He had held his tongue for the last time in this respect. Should anything even remotely like this occur again in his presence, he would speak out in the strongest possible terms against it, come what may.

This he vowed.

[January 3, 1782 — Thursday]

Under the glow of the large brass-bellied hurricane lamp on the desk in his quarters, the British Indian agent had, for the past few minutes, been using a small brush and black paint to mark eight large oilskin-wrapped packages on the floor before him. Each parcel was now directed to the attention of His Excellency, Frederick Haldimand, Governor of Canada.

Setting brush and pot aside, the agent removed the sheet of paper attached to each and carefully spread out all eight of them on his desk, arranged in the order in which they would best serve his needs. A rapid calculation of the figures on the sheets told him that within the eight packages were a total of 1,062 scalps that, after being received by Governor Haldimand, would be trans-shipped to King George III. They would be the proof to show His Royal Highness how falsified were the claims of George Washington and the American Congress that the expedition three years before of General Sullivan had broken the back of the Iroquois League in general and crushed the Senecas in particular.

Seating himself at the desk, he placed a sheet of fresh paper before himself, dipped his quill pen into the inkpot and began to write about the scalp shipment:

January 3d, 1782

May it please Your Excellency,

At the request of the Seneca Chiefs, I herewith send to Your Excellency, under the care of James Boyd, eight packages of scalps, cured, dried, hooped and painted with the Indian triumphal marks, of which the following is invoice and explanation.

No. 1. Containing 43 scalps of Congress soldiers, killed in different skirmishes; these are stretched on black hoops 4 inches in diameter; the inside of the skin painted red, with a small black spot to note their being killed by bullets. Also 62 of farmers killed in their homes; the hoops painted red, the skin painted brown, and marked with a hoe, a dark circle all around, to denote their being surprised in the night, and a black hatchet in the middle, signifying their being killed with that weapon.

No. 2. Containing 98 of farmers killed in their houses; hoops red, figure of a hoe to mark their profession, great white circle and sun, to show they were surprised in the daytime; a little red foot to show they stood upon their defence, and died fighting for their lives and families.

No. 3. Containing 97 of farmers; hoops green, to show they were killed in the fields; a large white circle with a little round mark on it for the sun, to show it was in the daytime, black bullet mark on some, and hatchet on others.

No. 4. Containing 102 of farmers, mixed of several of the marks above, only 18 marked with a little yellow flame, to denote their being of prisoners burned alive after being scalped, their nails pulled out by the roots, and other torments; one of these latter was supposed to be an American clergyman, his band being fixed to the hoop of his scalp. Most of the farmers appear by the hair to have been young or middle-aged men, there being but 67 very grey heads among them all; which made the service more essential.

No. 5. Containing 88 scalps of women, hair braided in the Indian fashion to show they were mothers, hoops blue, skin yellow ground with little red tadpoles to represent, by way of triumph, the tears of grief occasioned to their relations, a black scalping knife or hatchet at the bottom, to mark their being killed by those instruments; 17 others, very grey, black hoops, plain brown color, no marks but the short club or casse-tete, to show they were knocked down dead, or had their brains beat out.

No. 6. Containing 193 boy's [sic] scalps of various ages, small green hoops, whitish ground on the skin, with red tears in the middle, and black marks, knife, hatchet, or club as their death happened.

No. 7. Containing 211 girls [sic] scalps, big and little, small yellow hoops, white ground, tears, hatchet, club, scalping knife, &c.

No. 8. This package is a mixture of all the varieties above mentioned, to the number of 122, with a box of birch bark containing 29 little infant's [sic] scalps of various sizes, small white hoops, white ground, no tears, and only a little black knife in the middle, to show they were ripped out of their mother's [sic] bellies.[260]

[*April 25, 1782 — Thursday*]

In the spacious wegiwa the four Shawnees sat with blankets over their shoulders, the cookfire alone not quite enough to ward off the chill of the late cold snap that crept through the chinks and ran icy fingers up their backs. On their laps were pewter plates just handed to them by Wabethe, each heaped with *withsi-shekagosheke*—savory strips of dog meat that had been fried in a thin film of bear oil to a rich dark brown, along with an abundance of sliced onions, the dish filling the wegiwa with the wonderful aroma that had set their mouths to watering when they had entered a few minutes ago.

Chiksika picked up a piece of the meat from his plate and bit off a piece, then rolled his eyes. "If you weren't already married to him, Wabethe," he said, indicating Blue Jacket, "I would ask you to marry me. Would you consider two husbands?"

They all laughed and Wabethe smiled shyly, pleased at the compliment.

The light banter continued as they ate and two of them, Wasegoboah and Tecumseh, had second helpings. When they were finished and Wabethe had taken the plates away, all four lighted pipes and smoked in silence for a while, the taste of the aromatic *kinnikinnick* a pleasing finishing touch to the meal. Finally Blue Jacket set his pipe aside and, shaking his head sadly, said a single word that instantly dispelled all levity.

"Gnadenhutten."

Wasegoboah gently tapped his pipe bowl against one of the stones ringing the cookfire. "Sad," he murmured. "Very sad."

"I don't think Wingenund is so much disturbed about what happened to the Moravians as he makes out," Chiksika observed, his dislike for the Delaware chief apparent.

"Maybe not," Blue Jacket said, "but there's not much doubt he's going to use it any way he can to stir up the fires. And Pipe will help him. It's exactly what he's been looking for, something to set Tarhe back on his heels and swing the Wyandots over to the war fever he's been trying to promote."

The discussion continued long into the night, sometimes moving off at tangents but always eventually coming back to the fact of the massacre and what it boded for the future. It all had its beginnings shortly after the murder last fall of Talgayeeta. The old chief, whom the British still called Logan, had gone to Detroit to get liquor, to which he had become so addicted in recent years. When his wheedling request was flatly refused, he had become very angry. His eyes flashing with the fire that most had long thought burned out of him, Talgayeeta had snapped, "If the British won't give me what I want, maybe the Americans will. I'll go see Clark in Kentucky."

What worried British officials was whether or not Talgayeeta still carried enough influence with the Mingoes, as well as with his own Cayuga people and other tribes, that in going to the Americans as he threatened, he would pull them after him and away from British influence. It was a risk they did not relish. Logan was followed as he went south and just as he was approaching the very cabin that Bahd-ler and Girty had helped him build two years before, he had been murdered by a tomahawk blow from behind.

Shortly after that a delegation of four chiefs had visited the three Moravian towns on the Tuscarawas—Salem, Gnadenhutten, and Schoenbrun. The chiefs were Wingenund and Pimoacan of the Delawares, Pipe of the Wyandots, and Thayendanegea—Joseph Brant—of the Mohawks. Accompanying them had been Captain Matthew Elliott. They were all angry at the Moravian Delawares and especially at their leader, Abraham, a former minor chief named Neta-watwees before being proselytized. Though they had no absolute proof, they were sure the Moravians were spying upon them and passing information about their British-supported movements against the Americans on the upper Ohio.[261]

The visiting chiefs at first tried to coax Abraham to take his people from the three villages and move them to the Upper Sandusky area. When he politely refused, the coaxings became threats. Elliott, especially, lost his temper and berated Abraham and his Christianity soundly, winding up his tirade by saying, "You *must* take up residence on the Sandusky River. You have no choice. Go, or we will destroy your homes and your missions and you will all be killed on the spot."

Abraham had reluctantly given in. The ensuing winter had gone badly for the displaced Moravians, who suffered severe famine, while their parent tribe Delawares under Chief Wingenund and the Wyandots under Chief Pipe, along with other tribes in the vicinity had given them little help, being very busy themselves with their continuing attacks on the whites of the upper Ohio. After three unsuccessful visits to Detroit to plead for food for his people, Abraham had finally returned with news that he had been given permission to lead one hundred fifty of his Moravians back to their three towns on the Tuscarawas briefly, to try to glean some benefit from the corn crop left on its stalks the preceding fall and to gather up the meager stores of buried grains that were to be their planting seeds for the next season.

They returned there in early March and, while so engaged, a punitive force of Americans under Colonel David Williamson had shown up at Gna-denhutten.[262] By subterfuge, Williamson had not only gotten Abraham to instruct his people to give up their weapons as a show of good faith, but convinced him to send for those fifty of his people who had been left below at Salem. As soon as the latter arrived, all had their hands bound behind them and were herded into the two largest buildings in Gnadenhutten—the mission and large missionary's house beside it—with the men and boys in one and women in the other. Inside, they had been forced to sit on the floor and their ankles had been bound as well. There were two boys who managed to slip their bonds and escape.[263] They had raced off and warned those fifty who were still upstream at Schoenbrun that a massacre was occurring. At Gnadenhutten the 96 who were still bound—35 men, 27 women, and 34 children—beginning with Abraham himself, were systematically executed by being struck from behind with a huge cooper's mallet and their scalps taken off. When the deed was completed, Williamson had ordered both the church and the house burned with the bodies inside, which was done.[264]

Over the six weeks that had passed since then, word of the terrible massacre had reached every corner of the frontier, as well as all points east and reaction had been varied. The Kentucky settlers were shocked at such barbarism and the thought paramount in their minds was that when retaliation by the tribes came, as surely it must, it would reach out and engulf them as well. The settlers on the upper Ohio and in western Pennsylvania were somewhat shocked, but a surprising number contended that the redskins had "got what they deserved" and they even speculated on following up with another expedition of similar nature.

Word had come to the Shawnees that American leaders in the East had been deeply disturbed by the news but few accounts were published in the newspapers of what a truly cold-blooded, premeditated mass murder it had actually been and those newspapers mitigated the deed by referring to atrocities Indians had committed, especially those along the Ohio River of late. On the whole, their concerns were more with the peace negotiations going on in Paris that were bogging down, along with the multitude of problems at home in more firmly establishing the new federal government in the United States Congress that had only a year ago replaced the Continental Congress.

The Moravian missionaries were devastated and affixed blame to themselves for not remaining with their converts through their trials. At Detroit, the British were appalled, and proclaimed loudly against it, while continuing to make their shipments of scalps to the East. They also quickly saw the propaganda value inherent in the massacre to light even greater fires of resentment in the Indians against the Americans, adding the icing of benevolence to this cake by sending a company of redcoats to Upper Sandusky to escort the surviving Moravian Indians to a remote, quiet area where they could build a new village far from danger, along the banks of the Thames River in Ontario.

As for the Indians—the Delawares, Wyandots and Miamis, Ottawas, Chippewas, Potawatomies, Kickapoos, and others—all were furious, most of them in no way relating such a monstrous atrocity to their own atrocities, perpetrated on smaller numbers, perhaps, but no less gruesome. To them this only underlined the black character of the *Shemanese* and cemented their determination to annihilate such enemies whenever and wherever encountered.

Having discussed these matters well into the night, the four around the

fire in Blue Jacket's wegiwa fell silent until at last Tecumseh spoke up, directing
his remark to their host.

"In all this, what now are we going to do?"

Blue Jacket picked up his pipe and ran his fingers over the length of it,
then put it down again before answering. "I was not going to say anything
yet, since all plans are not fully made, but what you ask is a fair question and
deserves an answer. In a short time we will be sending runners to all the
Shawnee villages to prepare their young warriors for another major strike in
the Kan-tuck-kee country. I have been talking with our friend Girty. He says
we can expect no British assistance in such an enterprise—at least not in men—
as there has now been a cessation of hostilities between the Americans and
them while their peace talks continue across the eastern sea. However, he says
there will be some support given secretly in the form of gunpowder and
ammunition and other supplies. He further says that he has a plan for an attack
that may strike our *Shemanese* enemies very hard."

"What kind of plan?" Chiksika asked quickly.

Blue Jacket pursed his lips and hesitated, then faintly shrugged and went
on. "Girty has been impressed with the success of the ambushes that have
been carried out against them, mainly on the Spaylaywitheepi. He feels that
the *Shemanese* never seem to learn from such attacks and continue to blunder
into them. Now he thinks that another ambush should be laid, but this one
much larger and in a much different way."

"How?" Chiksika and Wasegoboah asked the question simultaneously.

"I will tell you the how, but not yet the where or when. What he plans
is to decoy a major force of the *Shemanese* on *land* into such an ambush, from
which few, if any, will escape. In this ambush he expects we will kill
hundreds."

Chapter 5

—《 》—　　The new council house at Chalahgawtha on the Little
Miami River was still not finished when the Grand
Council of the Northwestern Tribes was held there, so assembly took place
out of doors. The weather was good so there was no problem with that. Even
had the old *mis-kah-mi-qui* still stood here, however, it could not have contained
all the Indians who had come.

Simon Girty had brought with him not only some important chiefs of
the Wyandots and Delawares, he had brought along almost a hundred of their
warriors as well. For many, it was their first visit to Chalahgawtha since it
had been burned two years ago and then rebuilt this past spring and summer.
Remembering it as it had been in the days of its finest glory, they were sobered
by its appearance now.

The debris had long since been cleared away and there were forty or fifty
wegiwas, but of poor construction and scattered helter-skelter over the area
where there had once been broad avenues and neatly made dwellings. The
nearly completed council house was hardly a third the size of the previous
one, more solid than the wegiwas but certainly in no way comparable to the
initial council house that had been burned.

Perhaps one day Chalahgawtha would be built back to its former glory, but it was difficult to say when that might occur, especially since Shawnee energies were so largely directed at hit-and-run attacks against Kentuckians. What was being launched at this present council, however, was to be no minor raid. This was to be a strong invasion and, if all went according to plan, a crippling blow to the *Shemanese* south of the Spaylaywitheepi.

The basic plan of the invasion had been changed from its original design. It had begun under British Captain William Caldwell at the head of fifty redcoats and accompanied by Alexander McKee, who left Detroit with Thay-endanegea—Joseph Brant—and his followers, a total force near a thousand, the object being to hit the Wheeling area, but they were intercepted by Simon Girty with his news of a battle at Upper Sandusky.

Girty told them that an army of Americans had launched what they were proudly calling the Second Moravian Campaign, but that it had not been a federally approved or supported campaign. In fact, with the exception of its principal officers, who were "loaned" by Fort Pitt, the raggedy army had been comprised entirely of settlers from western Pennsylvania and that part of Virginia on the upper Ohio. Those settlers and their families, instead of becoming remorseful over the shameful mass murder of two-thirds of the Christianized Indians at Gnadenhutten, had quickly begun calling it a great victory and clamoring for another such invasion. Nearly five hundred men had volunteered for the second campaign, with its stated goal being to drive directly into the heart of the Wyandot and Delaware territory and wipe out the important villages of Upper and Lower Sandusky.

The 489 volunteers had rendezvoused on May 25 at the old Mingo Town in the broad bottomland on the west side of the Ohio where Cross Creek entered.[265] This was to be a "no mercy" campaign. The force was to move in rapidly, make its attack and dash back out before any sizeable force could be mounted against it, and with the unanimous resolution passed to instantly kill without mercy any Indian falling into their hands—warriors, chiefs, men, women, the elderly, children, or Christian Indians. Colonel William Crawford was elected commander, since he was much better liked than Colonel David Williamson, who had been in command at the Gnadenhutten Massacre. This army had speared toward the Wyandot villages and arrived on the Plains of Sandusky on June 7, where they marched directly into the ambush by nearly a thousand Indians.[266] The Americans retreated and this move quickly degenerated into an every-man-for-himself rout. Four warriors had met their death in the fight but over seventy of the whites had been killed and some thirty captured, including Colonel Crawford, who was sentenced to death at the stake.[267] Colonel Williamson managed to escape. Crawford suffered extensive grisly tortures for many hours before finally dying.[268]

This had all been good news to Caldwell's army, who were eager to follow up with a smashing attack on the upper Ohio. Girty, however, warned that the residue of the army, including Colonel Williamson, had made it back to the upper Ohio settlements, which were now alerted to their peril and would no doubt be waiting in defensive positions for just such a follow-up attack as Caldwell's force contemplated. To attack those forts when they were so prepared for it, Girty argued, was simply taking too great a risk and Girty had strongly advised taking the entire force and going instead against the whites in Kentucky. Caldwell thought Girty's idea made a lot of sense, so with his troops, McKee, Girty, and the remaining hundred of northern Indians had moved here to Chalahgawtha to hold council and get as many of the Shawnees as possible to join forces with them.

For ten days this Chalahgawtha Grand Council had been in session and many matters had been discussed, not the least of which was the major invasion the whites had launched from Forts Pitt and McIntosh against the Wyandots at Upper Sandusky and the decisive manner in which those whites had been whipped, simply because a very effective ambush had been used against them.

Girty's proposal now was that the Shawnees join them and they move in force to the Blue Licks area and there establish themselves out of sight for an ambush. Then, using less than half their force, they would move out against Bryan's Station, which, Girty had learned from a captive taken from there only a few weeks ago, was very weak.[269] It was part of the plan to observe the station and wait until two or three people were outside its gates before attacking, deliberately letting those outside get away so they could alert the men at the next nearest station, Lexington, six miles distant. The whites there would, virtually without doubt, mount a good-sized force to come against them. If the force were small, they would waylay it just before it reached the beleaguered station. If it were too large for that, which they would learn from the reports of their spies as soon as the force was on the move in their direction, the Indians would retreat toward the Blue Licks. Because of the size of the war party they were chasing, the whites would not be able to conceive that at least that many more would be waiting in ambush for them. At that point, Girty said, jerking out his tomahawk and slashing it through the air, they would spring the ambush, fall upon the Kentuckians and wipe them out.

The howls of approval and spontaneous war cries and breaking out of the war dance was immediate and, with the addition of the Shawnee warriors, the total force amounted to just over five hundred men. Even some of the very oldest of the warriors and chiefs—Moluntha, for instance, the Maykujay principal chief, who was 90 years old—had been so fired by Girty's words that they decided to go along. What had taken Caldwell so much by surprise and left him disgruntled was, apart from the Indians' unanimous affirmation of the plan, their equal affirmation of Simon Girty as their chosen leader for the enterprise. Caldwell had believed he would be in command but, with the unequivocal choice the Indians had made, he was left with few options: he could either let Girty have the command position, with the full weight of the Indians behind him, or turn his back on the whole campaign and return to Detroit, which he was loathe to do. In the end he had accepted the majority rule with poor grace.

"What do you think of the plan?" Tecumseh asked Chiksika, as they saw to their weapons and paints and prepared to move out.

"I think," Chiksika said, "there is probably no other man among us who understands the whites better than Girty and who can better judge their re-action. I wish we had two or three times the numbers we have. Since we don't, we will simply have to do our best with what we have. If anyone can successfully lure the Kan-tuck-kee whites into an ambush, he is the one. I think both of us can learn some good lessons by what Girty plans for us."

[August 19, 1782 — Monday]

Chiksika and Tecumseh were part of the decoy detachment of Indians who accompanied Captain William Caldwell against Bryan's Station. They had seen no sign of the pursuing whites yet, which was good, since this meant the Kentuckians had not seen them yet, either, and would be confident that the Indians they were following were unaware of the pursuit.

Now the waters of the Licking flowing past the Blue Licks were before them and they had started their crossing at the fording place. Tecumseh's mount began prancing about nervously at the water's edge and the fourteen-year-old warrior steadied the horse by patting its neck and murmuring some gentle words, then moved over beside Chiksika.

"Everything's gone according to plan so far, Tecumseh," Chiksika said as his younger brother came close. "Let's hope the rest will. Come on, we have to get across with the others."

Tecumseh nodded and pushed his mount forward into the water after Chiksika's. This was the only fording place nearby and one they had often used before, the bottom solid and the water, for the most part, only chest deep on the horses.[270] As he crossed, Tecumseh thought of what they had done thus far and was even more impressed than previously with the way things had worked out just as Simon Girty had said they would. Captain Caldwell had thought they would actually be able to take Bryan's Station and was disappointed that they had not penetrated the defenses. Girty, however, said that was not the point at all. The whole idea was to do something that would alert the Kentuckians and draw them into the web, and that was precisely what had been done.

After leaving Chalahgawtha and moving rapidly south, the combined force had made their crossing of the Spaylaywitheepi and moved directly to the Blue Licks undetected. There a little less than half of the Indian force—a total of 240 men, including Caldwell and his 50 redcoats—were dispatched to move against Bryan's. It was important, Girty said, for Caldwell to accompany the detachment to encourage the whites in their belief that it was the sole attacking force.

They had made the surprise assault on Bryan's Station on August 16, four days ago. Two men who had been out in the field raced off on foot to the southwest toward the six-mile-distant station of Lexington and, according to plan, no pursuit was made.[271] Eight spies were dispatched by Girty to follow them, keeping out of sight, to see that they gave the alarm as expected. Those spies, which included Tecumseh, were also to carefully watch the roads leading to and from Lexington.

Though the strike at Bryan's was a ploy, this did not mean no concerted attack was made. To the contrary, wave after wave of the attackers struck at the fort and Girty himself very nearly got killed during one of the attacks on the palisades. Everyone inside fought doggedly, even the women and children, and several Indians who carelessly let themselves become exposed to view were killed by sharpshooters inside the place, but so were some whites.[272] At one point an attempt was made to burn the place down with flaming arrows shot onto the roofs, but a man and two boys from inside the station prevented this by climbing out onto the roof and, amid bullets striking near them, tore off the burning shingles and threw them to the ground.[273] Those inside had seen their two men get away and knew they would be back with help soon, so they hung on and fought with grim determination. One of the defenders, a man named Reynolds, recognized Girty when the latter called out a demand for those in the fort to surrender. He refused, saying, "I know you, Girty! I'll tell you something—I've got a worthless dog who looks so much like you I call him Simon Girty." A volley of shots came at the heels of his cry and, though they missed him, one of the balls struck another of the defenders in the head and killed him. Two other men were shot at about the same time, one of them fatally.[274]

Outlying cabins and a small store were burned, while all the sheep, along with about one hundred head of cattle outside the station, were shot. The siege lasted all the remainder of that day, through the ensuing night and the entire following day.

Some of the spies, including Tecumseh, returned to Bryan's the next day with intelligence that shortly after the two escaped men arrived at Lexington, riders had galloped off in different directions for more help, while the remaining men at Lexington prepared to go to the rescue at Bryan's, which they knew could not hold out for very long.[275] Boonesboro was by far the closest of the stations appealed to for help and a force of ten mounted men arrived at Lexington from there very quickly. Within half an hour of their arrival, a party of forty men, including the ten from Boonesboro, headed for the relief of Bryan's. That was when Tecumseh and two others of the eight spies had left and galloped back to the attackers at Bryan's Station to report.

Immediately upon getting this information, Girty set up an ambush within his ambush and waited along the road leading from Lexington to Bryan's while the fight at the station continued. The rescue party soon came in view, but on hearing the sporadic firing at the fort they stopped. Then a detachment of seventeen split away and attempted to gallop directly into the fort. Girty and his men were ready and fired on them, killing one, wounding three, and causing the others, including those waiting on the road, to retreat back to Lexington.[276]

The siege at Bryan's continued until more spies came in with word that a large force of horsemen had arrived at Lexington and close to two hundred of them were, when the spies withdrew, preparing to move out against the Indians here.[277] With this intelligence, Girty broke off the siege and headed for Blue Licks, traveling fast, directly and making no effort to disguise their passage.

Now, just under twenty-four hours since then, they were crossing the Licking and three more of the spies left behind to watch caught up and reported that the pursuers were coming on hard, not more than seven or eight miles behind. The remainder of Girty's force immediately completed their crossing of the Licking and, following the previously laid out plan by their leader, traveled through the length of a deep ravine, gradually moving uphill, seeing no one, but knowing that more than two hundred fifty of their fellows were at this moment in hiding on the wooded slopes and atop the ridges on either side of them. They continued through the ravine and out the other end. A quarter-mile farther at the main camp, well hidden in a grove of trees, they left their horses and raced back on foot with their weapons to take their places with those hidden for the ambush.[278] One group of about forty was sent by Girty to a hilltop one hundred feet above the river where they were to show themselves, as if forming for battle, as a further encouragement for the whites to cross the river to attack. Girty himself was in hiding at the mouth of the ravine where the whites in pursuit would enter and it was he who would give the command to attack. No Indian was to move or betray his presence until Girty's signal.

All was in readiness and hardly fifteen minutes more had passed before the white pursuers galloped up to the south shore of the Licking and milled about there, looking across and pointing at the ground, at the river and at the north side at the far distant Indians forming up for a fight. A great deal of discussion was going on and evidently some hot arguing, as the sound of angry voices carried all the way across to those in hiding. At length, however, one very large individual reined apart from the group and set his horse to

The Blue Licks Ambush

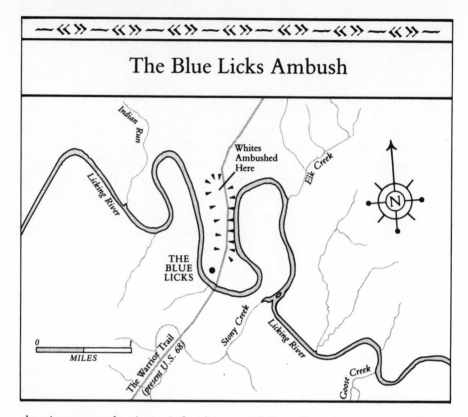

plunging across the river. A few began to follow him, then more and finally all of them. It was working and they were coming on![279]

The line of horsemen, three or four abreast, made the crossing and followed the tracks into the defile of the hills on the north side, their full force stretching out for a quarter-mile or more from front to rear. It was not until the hindmost were well within the mouth of the ravine that Girty stood to his full height and bellowed a mighty war cry. Instantly both sides of the ravine erupted in the echoing cry from half a thousand throats and an incredible barrage of gunfire broke out, the din added to by the screams of the horses and men receiving the gunfire. Every Kentuckian knew instantly they had ridden into an ambush and just as swiftly, fired back, dismounting and taking cover wherever possible, making a very decent stand for a force taken by such surprise. For ten minutes the fighting was furious and then, as they realized the futility of maintaining their stand, shrieked orders came to retreat and suddenly all the whites who were still capable of doing so were pouring out of the mouth of the ravine and back into the Licking—some on horseback, but most now on foot and most without weapons, having dropped their empty rifles when they turned and fled. Even while they were surging across the river, many were still picked off.

Seventy-two of the Kentuckians perished in the fight. Three Indians—two Shawnees and a Wyandot—had been killed and four others slightly injured. Upon reaching the south shore the retreaters continued running until all had disappeared over and beyond the hills to the south.[280]

The dead Kentuckians were stripped and scalped and many severely mutilated. A certain number of voices were now raised to mount up and go in pursuit of those who had escaped and who, much weaker now and at least half without weapons, could be wiped out as well, but both Caldwell and Girty knew the wisdom of being satisfied with their triumph and not risk turning it into disaster by pursuing and then finding themselves running into a large force of white reinforcements. Instead, he gave orders to finish their scalping, gather up all weapons and ammunition they could find, catch all the uninjured horses and kill those that were injured and then head immediately for Ohio.[281]

Now, as they trotted toward the Spaylaywitheepi, Chiksika with two scalps in his pouch and Tecumseh with one, the elder brother grinned. "Well, did you learn anything worthwhile in this fight, little brother?"

Tecumseh smiled back, fingering his *opawaka*. "I think I learned," he replied, "that even large parties of whites can be decoyed if good preparations are made. And I *know* I learned that I am glad Simon Girty is fighting with us and not against us."

[October 9, 1782 — Wednesday]

Chiksika, Tecumseh, and Wasegoboah, in their wegiwa in Chalahgawtha with the rest of the family, looked at one another as the voice of the crier came to them from outside, growing in volume, then diminishing as the crier moved on.

"All chiefs! All warriors! Come to the *msi-kah-mi-qui* at once for council. All chiefs! All warriors!"

They came to their feet immediately and Tecumapese, who had been telling stories to Spemica Lawba and the triplets, looked up at them, her expression worried. A call to council without previous notice, was ominous and the brief smile Wasegoboah gave her as the three left did little to relieve her apprehension.

The three filed into the council house and were surprised to see Blue Jacket sitting before the council fire between Catahecassa and that chief's principal attendant, Red Horse. The council house was alive with the buzz of muted conversations, everyone wondering what was going on, why Blue Jacket was here and why an unannounced council had been called. Many thought it had something to do with an attack made by Thayendanegea and his force, along

with the Wyandots, George Girty and some British troops, against the settlements on the upper Spaylaywitheepi. All had heard, of course, of how the
major settlement of Wheeling had been placed under siege and how, despite
the overwhelming odds on the part of the Indians, the fort had held out until
the siege was finally lifted after two days and two nights. Others were more
convinced that the council had been called because of some sort of imminent
danger from the *Shemanese,* and they were correct. The council house was
rapidly filling and within another ten minutes all had taken their seats on the
floor mats and prepared to light their pipes, but were halted in this when
Catahecassa abruptly stood and faced them.

"No pipes," he declared. "There is no time. There is grave news requiring
immediate action. Wehyehpihehrsehnwah will speak."

Catahecassa resumed his seat and Blue Jacket rose and faced the assemblage. In succinct manner he told them that he had received word that a large
force of whites under the dreaded George Rogers Clark had crossed the Spaylaywitheepi and was headed north. He had mounted his horse and headed that
way at once and encountered the army of over a thousand men where it had
made its camp, a few hours' ride south of here, where two creeks came
together.[282] Clad in white man's clothing, Blue Jacket went on, he had entered
the camp of the whites and learned their intentions. A detachment of 150
horsemen of the army had already split away, just after Blue Jacket arrived,
and was presently on its way under Colonel Logan to strike Lower Piqua and
Upper Piqua and possibly Mackachack and his own village.[283] The remainder,
under Clark and guided by none other than the one the Shawnees knew as
Bahd-ler, but whose real name was Simon Kenton, were on their way here,
to destroy the rebuilt Chalahgawtha and Piqua Town and then possibly move
farther north against Wapatomica.

"Catahecassa has told me," Blue Jacket went on, "that plans were being
made here to recover the goods that were hidden in the swamp spring the last
time Chalahgawtha was abandoned. It is a good thing that this was not done
yet, as this is part of what the whites are after in coming here. While I was
in their camp, I saw a General Order had been posted, tacked to a tree," he
reached into his pouch and removed a paper, which he unfolded, "and when
no one was looking I took it down and brought it away with me. I will read
it to you."

He held the paper up and read slowly, smoothly translating the English
to Shawnee. "It says, 'November 9, 1782. General Orders. As an action with
the enemy may be hourly expected, the officers are requested to pay the strictest
attention to their duty as suffering no man to quit his rank without leave, as
nothing is more dangerous than disorder. If fortunately any prisoner should
fall in our hands they are by no means to be put to death without leave, as it
will be attended with the immediate massacre of all our citizens that are in the

hands of the enemy and also deprive us of the advantage of exchanging for our own people. No person is to attempt to take any plunder until orders should issue for that purpose, under penalty of being punished for disobedience of orders and to have no share of such plunder himself. The officers in particular are requested to observe that the strictest notice be paid to this order, as much depends on it. All plunder taken is to be delivered to the quartermaster, to be divided among the different battalions in proportion to their numbers. Any person concealing plunder of any kind shall be considered as subject to the penalty of the above order.' And," Blue Jacket added, "it is signed, 'G. R. Clark.' As you can see, brothers, though not even here yet, they are already dividing up our goods among themselves.

"I have come to warn you," he went on, "that these *Shemanese,* over eight hundred of them, are only hours away on the move against you and there are not enough men here to oppose them. Once more Chalahgawtha— and Piqua Town as well—must be abandoned before they arrive. From here I will go to Piqua Town to alert them, and from there I will send messengers to Moluntha's Town, to Upper and Lower Piqua Towns, to Girty's Town and Solomon's Town and my own village. We will, for now, abandon all these towns in the face of the army's advance and we will converge at Wapatomica. It is there that we will hold fast and meet them with our full strength if they dare to come that far into our country. That is all I have to say. I must be gone."

Catahecassa stood and told all assembled to go to their wegiwas at once and gather up all they wished to take away with them, since anything left behind would be lost to the *Shemanese*. Fortunately, most of their grain was already buried in greased bearskin bags and would not be found, but whatever other grains they had in their wegiwas should be taken along and not left for the benefit of the whites. This time, he told them, the Chalahgawthas would not burn their own village, leaving that for the *Shemanese* to do, nor would they have time to gather up and take their cooking gear or the food presently being cooked.

"All such things are to be left as they are," Catahecassa told them. "It will help delay their pursuit of us and the longer we have to prepare to meet them, the greater our likelihood of success."

They all left the council house then and a few moments later Tecumseh watched Blue Jacket gallop off to the north toward Piqua Town, twelve miles distant. Standing at the outside corner of his wegiwa, he was in the shadow of it and almost without volition, his hand came up and grasped the *opawaka* hanging from the cord around his neck.

"Moneto," he whispered, "I call on you through this *opawaka* to help us. Let us escape without harm except to our wegiwas, which can always be built again. Spare our elders and our women and children and keep our warriors strong. Let not the *Shemanese* destroy them. And most of all, Moneto, spare my brother Chiksika, and my sister Tecumapese, and the members of our family. I, Tecumseh, ask this of you through the *opawaka* which I earned here."

Then he went inside the wegiwa to help the others with packing their belongings.

[October 28, 1782 — Monday]

A cold, implacable anger against the *Shemanese* had now lodged in the breast of Tecumseh. Because of what the army of Kentuckians under Clark and Logan had done, his people now had a very difficult winter ahead of them.

It had been an unusually bloodless campaign for both the Indians and the whites. Blue Jacket, who had taken over war command temporarily while Shemeneto was ill, had directed that the principal concern of the Shawnees at this point should not be to engage the enemy, but merely to keep themselves out of his reach, watch his movements closely and only if and when the *Shemanese* made an error and left themselves exposed and vulnerable would they attack.

That had not happened. Clark and Logan had both kept tight control over their men, maintaining a tight discipline and adherence to orders. The two advancing fronts of the whites had met virtually no resistance and succeeded in destroying a number of the Shawnee towns before returning to Kentucky. Their victory, however, though it would cause hardships for the Shawnees, was a hollow one at best. The towns they had encountered were abandoned and there was little they could do but burn down the structures and destroy what few supplies of goods and grains they could find.

Chalahgawtha had been destroyed again, shortly after Catahecassa had led them all away. But, as Catahecassa had said, leaving the village unburned and even food in the pots in the wegiwas helped delay the advance of the army, as they paused to devour all the victuals left behind and then lingered even longer to burn the town and its surrounding fields.[284]

Twelve miles to the north, at the rebuilt Piqua Town, the Shawnees retreating from Chalahgawtha had found their brothers there also packed up and ready to leave for Wapatomica and had joined them. Blue Jacket, at the head of half a hundred warriors, had come to aid more as a protective escort than anything else, since his force was nowhere near strong enough to oppose the more than ten-to-one odds Clark's wing of the army had over them. As the movement away from the Mad River Piqua Town began, Blue Jacket had given strict orders to all warriors to refrain from unnecessarily placing themselves in the front of the army's advance, telling them they could move along secretly on the flanks of the enemy to watch their movements, but not to get in front of them for any reason.

Blue Jacket himself had lingered to the last to make certain everyone was out of harm's way and was still at Piqua Town with one other warrior when, after the destruction of Chalahgawtha and its surroundings, Clark's army rode into the village. The warrior who was with Blue Jacket was Mesquetwee—Cloudy Day—who had painted his own face black as the result of a dream he had had the previous night, in which he had been killed by Clark's soldiers. Calmly prepared for this inevitability, he had chosen to remain and face their enemy to the last.

As the riders approached their hiding place in the rocks, Blue Jacket had grasped Mesquetwee's hand a final time. "You're sure you won't come away?" he asked.

Mesquetwee shook his head. "My dream has told me I must remain here and meet my fate. I will do so, but I will take at least one of the *Shemanese* with me."

Blue Jacket had nodded, understanding, squeezed the man's hand and ridden away unseen by the approaching force. Mesquetwee, armed with an old and much battered flintlock, along with tomahawk and knife, kept well hidden and watched them approach. He hoped to be able to bring down their chief, Clark, but did not know how he was supposed to recognize him, since he had never seen him. As the whites came closer, however, he saw two riding slightly apart and ahead of the others, one of whom he recognized as their great indestructible enemy, Bahd-ler—Simon Kenton.

The belief was now strong among the Shawnees that Kenton, who had survived so many ordeals and so many sentences of death in their hands, was under such special protection of Moneto that to strike him now would cause Moneto to become angry and turn His back upon the Shawnees. Thus, when Kenton rode up in the lead with another man beside him, Mesquetwee assumed the other man was General Clark and so, when he leveled his rifle and took aim, it was not at Kenton that he aimed but at the one he took to be Clark.

It was with satisfaction, when he squeezed off his shot, that Mesquetwee saw the man beside Kenton lurch and grasp himself as the bullet struck him. That man would have fallen from the saddle had not Kenton caught him and eased him to the ground. In just a moment Kenton and half a dozen others were spurring their horses toward where the shot had originated and, seeing them coming, Mesquetwee tossed his empty flintlock aside and drew his knife and tomahawk, facing the enemy with a devilish grin.

Several of the whites fired as they rode up to where he stood and Mesquetwee fell, dying from the wounds he received. He was still alive when Kenton came up to him and still wearing that peculiarly victorious smile when he gave a final shudder and died. One of the men who had fired scalped him and others took his weapons. There was no sign of anyone else around, so all went back to the main army, which was already engaged in burning the wegiwas and treating the wounded man.[285]

Blue Jacket, catching up to his people, first encountered Tecumseh and Sinnanatha coming toward him. The pair were pleased with themselves, reporting that they had killed two buffalo and had cut them up and the meat, much needed by the refugees, was ready to be picked up. When Blue Jacket asked where it was and was shown the spot, which was directly in the path of Clark's army, he became very angry with the two youths for disobeying orders to stay out of the front of the *Shemanese* and he jerked his ramrod from his rifle and gave both young men several hard whacks across their backs with it.

Both boys, Tecumseh in particular, were properly chagrined, knowing they deserved the punishment for disobeying orders. To atone, Tecumseh asked permission to take Sinnanatha with him and hunt for more meat for the refugees moving northward, saying they would go well ahead of them. Blue Jacket thought this was a very good idea and gave them instructions to bring down as much game as they could, since the Shawnees were going to need to cure every bit of meat it would be possible to get in order to help see them through the winter ahead. Other hunters, Blue Jacket told them, were out doing the same.

Tecumseh, armed only with bow and a quiverful of arrows, and Sinnanatha, with a flintlock, spurred their horses and soon had passed the line of refugees moving north. A dozen miles ahead of them, the two were crossing a long, narrow prairie when they heard the thunder of hooves and saw, at the far end of the grassland, a herd of buffalo appear, running hard directly toward them. The sight of dogs and Indian riders vaguely visible far beyond made them realize the herd was being chased by other Shawnee hunters.

A huge solitary oak stood in the prairie a dozen yards from them and the two went there at once and prepared to shoot as the animals passed. Sinnanatha checked the priming of his gun and Tecumseh emptied his quiver, laying out his entire supply of two dozen arrows on the ground beside the tree for instant access.

The buffalo herd split into two sections as it neared the big oak, passing on both sides at a full gallop. Sinnanatha fired and brought down the buffalo at which he had aimed. Tecumseh, smoothly nocking his arrows, drawing, aiming and releasing, shot arrow after arrow until the herd finally passed. When it was over, only five arrows remained unused, the other nineteen having been shot at the passing animals. Well beyond them, having fallen as they ran, were those buffalo that had been brought down. There were seventeen of them—the one killed by Sinnanatha and sixteen killed by Tecumseh. The arrows he had shot had driven themselves into their huge bodies almost to the fletching and in each case passing through the heart.

It was an outstanding feat of hunting and Tecumseh was much lauded for the accomplishment, not only by the hunters who had been driving the animals before them and had managed to down only a few, but by the entire group of refugees as they came upon the scene. A camp was made on the spot and all the animals dressed out, the meat cut in strips and fire dried, the hides kept for tanning, the horns for ornamentation and powder flasks and the soft organs—hearts, livers, kidneys, and brains—cooked for immediate consumption.[286]

Despite the success of the hunt and the accolades it brought him, Tecumseh was very dispirited by the destruction of their towns and the fact that the *Shemanese,* not satisfied with just burning them, had also set fire to the extremely dry prairie grasses and enormous raging fires had swept across the prairies and woodlands, killing much game and rendering the countryside unfit for habitation by man or beast for a long time to come.

War was war, the young Shawnee knew, and with it came the destruction not only of lives but of villages as well, but there was never any excuse, so far as he could see, for the wanton destruction of nature so often perpetrated by the whites. Tecumseh wondered how it was possible for any race of man to have so great a disregard for the natural bounty that Moneto had provided for all men. This was one of the major factors that so filled him with anger for the whites.

In addition to the destruction of Chalahgawtha, Clark had destroyed Piqua Town and two other small villages nearby, while the other wing of his army, under Colonel Logan, had destroyed both Lower Piqua Town and Upper Piqua Town, the French Store that had been reestablished by Peter Loramie on the creek named after him, and the smaller village of Pigeon Town, seven miles to the southwest where two streams converged.[287]

Seven villages had been destroyed with a remarkably small loss of life—one white and ten Indians—but with the destruction of a great deal of the countryside surrounding all seven villages. Fear and discouragement were constant companions of many of the Shawnees now, and, however regrettable, it was also understandable when, just after Clark's army returned to Kentucky, another faction of the Shawnees decided they had had enough of this continual harassment by the whites and had packed up their goods and moved west of the Mississippi to join the Shawnees that had gone there when the tribe split.

The only encouraging note this fall was the arrival of one hundred Cherokee warriors from the south, led by a war chief named Raven. At the behest of the British, they agreed to help the Shawnees for an undetermined time to come in fighting off the *Shemanese.* They were welcomed and established a village adjacent to the site of the Delaware village called Mingo Town.[288]

For his own part, Tecumseh was desolated and angry, all hope now gone that his beloved childhood home of Chalahgawtha, along the Little Miami River, would ever again be rebuilt.

[April 27, 1783 — Sunday]

The blouse and leggins of his buckskins considerably spattered with dried blood, Tecumseh stood somewhat apart from the others of Chiksika's war party and watched morosely the preparations being made to burn the prisoner to death.

The condemned man, a large individual of about thirty, had been stripped of all his clothing and bound with his back to the bare trunk of a long dead tree by a rawhide tug looped around his throat and looped as well around the tree. His hands had been tied tightly behind him also, but his feet remained unbound. He would be able to side-step around the tree, but not more than that. A large quantity of dry wood had been gathered and laid atop the circle of tinder material that had been placed six feet from the tree. The captive knew what was coming but said nothing, only glared defiantly at his captors.

This white man was the only survivor of a party of thirteen whites who had been discovered camping on the Ohio shore of the Spaylaywitheepi within a couple of miles of the mouth of the Scioto River. Chiksika's party, in temporary camp some distance away, had discovered the whites after hearing a solitary gunshot. Leaving their camp and horses under a guard of two warriors they crept up, taking their time and making no sound to betray their presence. It had taken them about half an hour to get into position for an attack. Unseen and unsuspected, the Shawnees observed the thirteen men in a small clearing at the bottom of a natural hollow some forty or fifty feet in diameter. The whites were lounging around a fire, talking and laughing and already starting to cook spitted venison from the deer one of them had killed, which was no doubt the shot the Shawnees had heard.

The campsite was poorly chosen because, though sufficiently hidden on the rim of a tiny creek entering the Spaylaywitheepi here, where their canoes had been drawn up, it had no decent avenue of escape. The slopes of the hollow were thick with trees and brush, allowing the attackers to stealthily surround the camp and move in to within thirty feet of them. Further, the whites were evidently very inexperienced since, while a couple of them had their rifles lying close beside them, most of the guns were leaning against rocky outcroppings several steps away.

Because of the danger of shooting one another across the clearing, Chiksika silently signed for his warriors to lay their guns aside and attack with

tomahawks and war clubs. With all his men poised, Chiksika bellowed fright-
eningly and the members of his party instantly leaped down upon them. The
fighting had been particularly hot and by far the most active and effective
warrior in the party was Tecumseh. With remarkable agility and daring he
had leaped about among the whites, swinging his war club with deadly accuracy and seeming to be everywhere at once, not only moving with tremendous grace and speed but apparently endowed with an ability to anticipate
his opponent's next move before it was made and thus himself strike more
effectively.

In the space of three minutes, all the whites were dead but one. The most
that any other warrior had slain was two, but Tecumseh had alone killed four
of the men and helped Chiksika in the dispatching of another. The bravery
and fierceness he had exhibited during the attack had been startling to behold
and was the talk of the entire camp when they arrived back there with their
prisoner. Not a warrior of the party had failed to approach and compliment
him as a "great young warrior." The fact that at age fifteen he had outshone
even the ablest warriors of the party was not only accepted without jealousy,
but with deep and warm approval. Chiksika was practically beside himself
with pride in his young brother. "I wish," he had said to Tecumseh while
they were on their way back to their camp, "that our father could have been
here to witness this. How proud of you he would have been, Tecumseh."

However, had it not been for his playing such an aggressive and prominent
role in the attack, the other members of the war party might have considered
it a very real sign of weakness that Tecumseh stood aside with disapproving
expression while preparations were being made for the death of the captive.
The circle of tinder and wood around the prisoner was lighted at several places
simultaneously and, as the flames quickly grew and threw out great heat, the
captive began to squirm and moan, sidestepping round and round the tree but
finding no relief from the searing heat. With long sticks, the warriors gradually
pushed the burning circle of material closer to the captive until finally his feet
and lower legs first became red, then blistered and peeled and finally blackened,
his genitalia similarly scorched and his pubic hair all singed away. Sobbing
and groaning and writhing in agony, he finally fell to his knees, then to his
side, as far as the loop about his neck would permit. At this, howling with
maniacal glee, the warriors used chunks of bark to scoop up and toss piles of
hot coals at him until he could move no more and was literally covered with
them. Even then the moaning continued, a forlorn cry of utter despair that
lasted for a long while until at last he fell silent and died.

Through it all, Tecumseh had watched, the familiar deep revulsion filling
him. And when at last the smoking body lay charred and lifeless, he could no
longer contain himself. As Red Horse jabbed at the blackened remains with

his spear to see if there were yet any sign of life, Tecumseh strode forward and snatched the long weapon away and threw it to one side.

Startled, Red Horse wheeled and faced him angrily. "What is wrong with you, Tecumseh? You tried to stop me! Why? Are you a woman, afraid of blood?"

Chiksika quickly stepped between them, his voice harsh and authoritative. "*Stop!* You fought well," he swept out his arm to include the others, "all of you. Now it is over. Would you kill one another after fighting side by side in battle?"

Red Horse, still furious, replied defiantly, "Yet Tecumseh tried to stop me. He is but a boy and he needs to be taught!"

"But not by you, Red Horse," Chiksika told him coldly. "*I* lead here, and *I* will decide who requires being taught. In this fight I saw my young brother fight better than I fought—better than *any* of you fought!"

Wasegoboah took a step toward them and stopped. "I would speak, Chiksika," he said.

"The husband of my sister has a wise head. Speak, Wasegoboah."

"Both you and Tecumseh are my friends," Wasegoboah said, speaking slowly and choosing his words carefully. "I have none better. But, equally, my eyes have seen him go against our traditions of war. It has always . . ."

"You see, Chiksika," Red Horse interrupted heatedly, "even Wasegoboah says it!"

Chiksika made a slashing movement with his hand, glaring. "Silence, Red Horse!" He turned and looked at his brother-in-law again. "Continue, Wasegoboah."

Wasegoboah licked his lips and bobbed his head once. "It has always been our way," he said, "to destroy any enemy who may fall into our hands, if we so wish. Am I to believe that my friend, Tecumseh, considers this to be wrong—especially when it is no less than the whites do to us?"

Chiksika considered this, then turned to face his brother. "The same question," he replied, "sits on my tongue. Tecumseh?"

Tecumseh looked from Chiksika to Wasegoboah, then back again. He shook his head and began turning away, speaking as he did so. "I have not yet put the words into my mouth, but they have long been in my heart."

Chiksika's sharp response stopped him in his tracks. "Do not turn your back to us!" As Tecumseh immediately faced him again, he continued, "What you have done here, Tecumseh, *must* be spoken of. If the words are in your heart, then you must open your heart to all of us. *Now!*"

Red Horse snorted contemptuously. "I do not wish to listen to a child speaking to men. You say he fought well, Chiksika." He turned his head and spat deliberately, then wiped his mouth with the back of his hand and continued, "That is no praise. Which of us did not? Since you wish him to *speak* as a man," he whipped his knife out of his belt and crouched, facing Tecumseh, "I would see how well he *fights* as a man!"

At the threat, Tecumseh had quickly gripped the haft of his own knife, but he did not draw it. After staring at Red Horse for a long moment, he dropped his hand. Red Horse gave a derisive little laugh and, straightening, began walking past him, saying, "And you call this *woman* your brother, Chiksika?"

With total unexpectedness, Tecumseh whirled, gripped the arm of Red Horse and twisted it, throwing him onto his back and in the same movement forcing the warrior's own knife blade against his throat. Red Horse, eyes wide, remained totally still and lay there breathing heavily, fully at the mercy of the young warrior. Tecumseh let him go and came to his feet, standing over the prostrate man.

"Now *I* will speak, Red Horse, and *you* will listen!" He looked around at the others who were watching the little drama intently. "You are my brothers—Chiksika by blood, but the rest of you in my heart. Brothers must speak from their hearts if love is to remain. Mine is heavy with what I have seen here. You will say that I am young and inexperienced in such matters, and you will be right, but I cannot keep from speaking. What I have seen here has made me sick and ashamed for you and for myself. What bravery, what courage, what strength is there in the torturing of a man unable to defend himself? Are we so unsure of ourselves that in order to prove our superiority, our own excellence, we must resort to something as disgusting and degrading as this?"

He sighed and shook his head and continued in a voice lowered but no less impassioned. "Hear me now, my older brothers, for I speak from my heart and my heart is heavy with shame and revulsion. Our dearly loved chief, Chiungalla, was strongly opposed to death at the stake, and in recent years I have come to understand why. Now I see that in the very act of committing it, we lower ourselves to something beneath animals, to something evil and hideous and revolting."

He paused and in the silence Wasegoboah spoke up. "What would you have us do, Tecumseh, when these whites slaughter the game we need to feed our families? Youth is in your words!"

Tecumseh turned his head toward him. "I will gladly," he said in a level, cold voice, "kill any foe in battle, but I will not be part of killing any man helpless in our grasp. I will not accept as friend, Wasegoboah, any man who will do this."

"He *was* our enemy," Chiksika interjected.

"Yes! And he deserved to die, but the death of a man, not a beast. We cannot call ourselves warriors if,'' he pointed to the blackened, smoking corpse, "we think of *this* as courage.''

He stopped and held out his hand to Red Horse, who finally took it and Tecumseh pulled him to his feet. Red Horse looked at the war party leader and said, "Chiksika, may I speak?" At Chiksika's nod, he faced Tecumseh again, but pointed one hand in the direction of the body. "Should we turn our backs when men like these enter our country and kill us, Tecumseh? You have not fought enough—or suffered enough—to speak as you do.''

Tecumseh held up a hand. "You speak from your heart, Red Horse, not from your mind, and your heart is angry. What do I know of suffering? The whites killed our father, Pucksinwah. They destroyed our villages. They forced us from the land we loved. I cannot stand aside and watch them do this. When they do, we must stop them. But I say to you, Red Horse, there is no *honor* in the torturing of *any* man.''

Tecumseh stepped a little closer to him and reached to his own belt and withdrew his knife. There was a sudden intake of breath among the onlookers, but the tension eased when he flipped the knife around, gripped the blade and extended the haft toward Red Horse.

"Take my knife. A moment ago you were angry enough to kill me. Take it now and pierce my heart if what I have said is not true.''

Red Horse put up both hands and shook his head, refusing to accept the knife and backing away. "No. I could not kill you in such a way.''

"Why not?" Tecumseh said. "Because there is no *honor* in it? What honor was there for us in his death? If the choice lies between tradition and honor,'' he looked around briefly, "who here would choose tradition? I do not and cannot believe Moneto could approve of such cowardice, of such desire to inflict unnecessary pain. An enemy he was, yes! Death he deserved, yes! But the death of a man, not that of a rat cornered and burned alive. How have we the right to call ourselves warriors, or even men, if we act in such manner?''

He resheathed his knife, looked at the blackened body, and then spoke in such a low voice that the others had to strain to hear him. "My heart is sick and heavy and what I have seen here will never be erased from my mind and I will never stop being ashamed of it. Young I may be. Inexperienced I may be. Yet this I can say with certainty: Never again will I take part in the torture like this of any living creature, man or animal. *Never!* Nor, as I have said, will I consider as friend any man who will allow himself to take part in so degrading a measure.''

For a considerable span of time there was silence and a very evident respect in the eyes of the others for this stripling warrior. Had anyone before ever heard such eloquence or such uncomfortable truth from one so young? When before had a fledgling warrior of only fifteen years shown his elders not only how to fight in battle but how to behave with humanity? At last Chiksika, who had been more than a little nonplussed at Tecumseh's outpouring, stepped to his brother's side and spoke softly, but loud enough for all to hear.

"What my little brother has said is truth," he began. "Who here among us, despite provocation, has not felt himself lowered and shamed to treat a human being—regardless of whether an enemy—like that!" He pointed an accusing finger at the grotesque body. "But who among us has had the courage to speak up and make us truly face the cowardice and shame of such an act? No man here today fought with greater skill or courage than Tecumseh and therefore his words must not be taken lightly. This I say to you: though he is not yet far beyond being a boy and I am a man twelve summers his elder, yet I am constantly learning from him and left feeling humble and unworthy in his presence. And this, too, I say to you now: that though he is a Kispokotha, yet will Tecumseh one day become the most powerful leader and greatest warrior the Shawnees have ever known!" He let his flashing gaze sweep across the men of his war party. "I therefore vow, here and now, that from this time forward I will never again take part in any such cruelty as this. Are there others here who will so vow?"

"I will vow the same!" It was Wasegoboah.

An older, slightly paunchy warrior with graying hair and only one eye stepped forward. "I, Frog Hunter," he said, "am the oldest here. The words of young Tecumseh have stirred me deeply. They are words wise beyond his years or yours or mine. He has won the respect and admiration of us all, and Shawnees everywhere will learn of his bravery this day, and of his wisdom. I gladly make the same vow."

One by one the others stepped forward and similarly made their vows and in Tecumseh there was a great welling of wonder and thankfulness and self-confidence. At last only one man remained who had not yet made the pledge—Red Horse, principal attendant of Chief Catahecassa. Now he stepped forward and finally reached out and placed a hand on Tecumseh's shoulder. His eyes rolled momentarily to the dead man, then back to lock on the young warrior before him.

"I am not sorry, Tecumseh," he said, "that he is dead, but I have become ashamed of *how* he died. I will continue to kill any white in battle, but I will torture no other prisoners. This I vow."

The heart of Chiksika swelled with pride in his little brother. He had no doubt whatever in the truth of what he had said of Tecumseh becoming a great leader. Was not Pucksinwah's family blessed with the ability to see— dimly, at times, but at other times clearly—events of importance in the future? And was not his young brother born under the momentous sign of the Panther Passing Across? There could be no question of it; Tecumseh was destined to become the greatest Shawnee leader the tribe had ever known.

[*November 5, 1783 — Wednesday*]

Waves of pain throbbed through Tecumseh and he clenched his jaws tightly to stifle the cries yearning to rip from his throat. In a daze he felt the strong hands of Chiksika lifting his head and cradling it and the soothing sounds his older brother was making seemed to help. But the grinding, searing pain came back again as the strong hands of others in the party lifted his lower body high enough to enable them to maneuver a blanket under him to use as a litter in which to carry him off.

He felt dissociated, slipping in and out of a dreamy state as much liquor-induced as caused by pain. Vaguely he was aware of being carried the mile or so back to their camp and, some time after that, the pain that exceeded all, as the others held him tightly under the arms while Chiksika gripped his leg firmly just below the knee and gave a sudden sharp pull that bloomed into a red explosion of agony in his mind, followed by blessed darkness.

He brought the pain back with him when he awoke and bore it with occasional grimace or sigh but with no other sound. The herbs Chiksika spooned into him helped deaden the pain but affected his sensibilities as well, making him lose track of the passage of time and finding himself reliving in his mind the things that had occurred since he and Chiksika had left the Ohio country on their second great journey.

What had prompted their journey came hardly a month after the occasion when Tecumseh had voiced his opposition to the torture of prisoners. As Frog Hunter had predicted, word of the young man's bravery and his remarkable eloquence had filtered into every corner of the Shawnee Nation and the subject of to torture or not to torture became a common topic of discussion. While many were for continuing the traditional practice, there were as many or even more who for the first time found the courage to speak out against that which they had so long disliked and had not dared to question because of tradition.

It was while the nation was still abuzz over this that a major council was held at Detroit and numerous Shawnees attended, Chiksika and Tecumseh among them, as well as Blue Jacket and Wasegoboah, all believing that it was for an announcement that the supplies they so badly needed had finally arrived and were to be distributed. Instead, they were addressed apologetically by both Alexander McKee, who was now in charge of the Indian Department in the West with the rank of colonel, and the Detroit commander, Captain Arent de Peyster, who told them that, regrettably, aid could not be extended to them as it had been in the past, that their father across the Great Water, the king, was asking them, through General Frederick Haldimand, to curtail, at least temporarily, any further fighting against the Virginians, that a true peace was very close to being made, not only in Paris between the British and the Americans, but between the Americans and the various tribes.[289] The war was winding down and should be completely ended by autumn and so it was most important during this delicate period that nothing occur to upset the balance.

Overnight, it seemed, hostilities along the entire length of the Ohio River virtually ceased as an uneasy, undeclared truce went into effect. But there were many rumors circulating that made the tribes, especially the Shawnees and Wyandots, extremely nervous. The first was that now the thoughts of the states would turn to development of the lands they claimed far to the west.[290] In the case of Virginia, it was said on good authority that there simply would not be enough lands south of the Ohio for that state to fulfill its bounty obligations to both Continental and state troops who had served with the promise of receiving land for service rather than hard money. Since Virginia had long before ceded to the United States Congress all its nebulous territorial claims to lands north and west of the Ohio River, the state quickly and successfully appealed to the federal government for the right of disposition to veterans of the over four-million-acre tract of land, to be called the Virginia Military Lands, in the very heart of the Ohio country.[291] These lands were to be given as military bounties to her veterans, both Continental and militia soldiers.

Were that not enough, it was being said that Connecticut was successfully reaffirming her claim to a bounty tract running deep inland from the south shore of Lake Erie, taking in three and a half million acres, and they were calling this tract the Western Reserve Lands.

These, of course, were all paper claims, since none of the land had been properly surveyed and, as Colonel Alexander McKee assured the collected Indians at Detroit, paper claims meant very little; it was possession that counted. But paper or not, these claims, which the Indians considered totally ridiculous, still made them very nervous.

With a tentative, fragile truce—if not an actual peace—in effect, Chiksika once again proposed he and Tecumseh take another extensive journey and Tecumseh eagerly agreed. Ten other Shawnees joined them and soon they had begun meandering their way westward and southward, visiting, as they had done before, a variety of tribes and villages, rekindling old friendships made on the first trip and making many more new ones on this.

They had visited the break-away portion of their tribe residing now on Apple Creek in the Cape Girardeau area west of the Mississippi. There they spent several weeks with their mother, who seemed a bit more in control of herself mentally than the last time they saw her. There was a lot of visiting with many friends and a seemingly endless supply of liquor to warm their stomachs, of which Chiksika partook in moderation and Tecumseh in con-

Allan W. Eckert

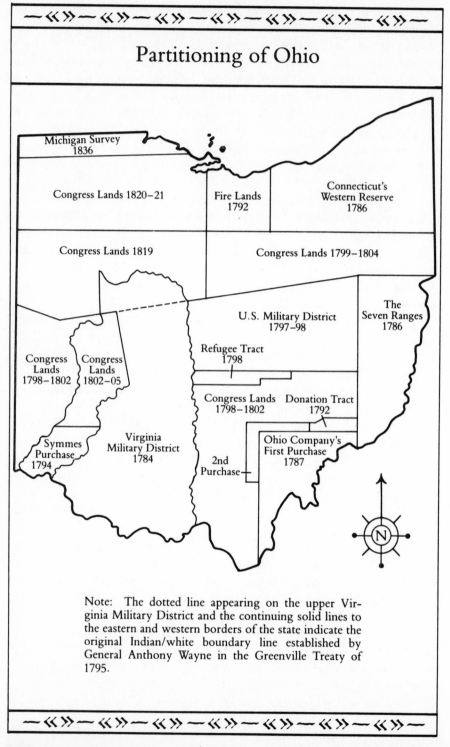

Partitioning of Ohio

Michigan Survey
1836

Congress Lands 1820–21

Fire Lands
1792

Connecticut's
Western Reserve
1786

Congress Lands 1819

Congress Lands 1799–1804

U.S. Military District
1797–98

The
Seven Ranges
1786

Refugee Tract
1798

Congress
Lands
1798–1802

Congress
Lands
1802–05

Congress Lands
1798–1802

Donation Tract
1792

Symmes
Purchase
1794

Virginia
Military District
1784

Ohio Company's
First Purchase
1787

2nd
Purchase

N

Note: The dotted line appearing on the upper Virginia Military District and the continuing solid lines to the eastern and western borders of the state indicate the original Indian/white boundary line established by General Anthony Wayne in the Greenville Treaty of 1795.

siderable excess. During the weeks spent there, Tecumseh was far more often drunk than sober, but no one seemed to mind—with the possible exception of Tecumseh himself—because he became so mellow and humorous when in his cups.

Upon leaving Cape Girardeau, they had recrossed the Mississippi and camped on the Illinois side for a few weeks, visiting the Kickapoos. It was while they were with them that word had come that the Treaty of Paris had been signed between the British and Americans. The war was over and the Americans had won their independence.[292] Despite that, the British at both Fort Niagara and Detroit were assuring the Indians that the *real* war between themselves and the Americans had only been put in abeyance and would flare again. British traders and agents also made it clear that while they could not overtly supply the tribes with the wherewithal to continue their struggle against American encroachment, they could and would do so covertly.

Another bit of news came to them that was met with considerable joy. Their dreaded enemy, General George Rogers Clark, had been relieved of command and his rank rescinded. On the whole, however, the Shawnees, and other Indians as well, were heartily disappointed with the results of the war. The Americans were more firmly entrenched than ever, still in possession of the upper Spaylaywitheepi and the Kentucky country, and more trouble was bound to come from these quarters sooner or later.

That was how matters stood when, ten days ago, the brothers and their party decided to move south and perhaps spend the winter with the Cherokees in warmer climes. They had crossed the Spaylaywitheepi at the southernmost tip of the Illinois country and began angling southeastward through the far western Kentucky country on the old Cherokee Trail.[293] It was as they came to the flatlands at the head of a substantial creek that they encountered a large herd of buffalo.[294]

Tecumseh, armed with bow and gun, made no effort to use them as other members of the party were preparing to do. He had been drinking fairly steadily from a large flask most of the morning and was now very tipsy. He shucked off both bow and quiver and thrust them, along with his rifle, at one of the young men who was riding beside him.

"Here, hold these!" he said.

Through simple reaction more than anything else, his companion took them and then, along with Chiksika and the others, watched with amazement and concern as Tecumseh galloped directly toward the massive plunging animals, pulling his knife from its sheath as he did so. He angled in on the thundering herd, guiding his horse along the outer edge and matching the speed of a good-sized bull. Gripping his knife crosswise in his teeth he crouched for an instant on his horse's back and then leaped onto the back of the bull buffalo, grasping his great shaggy mane with both hands and instantly locking his legs on both sides of the animal. The terrified bull snorted and rolled his eyes and ran even harder, angling a bit deeper into the galloping herd. Tecumseh released his grip with one hand and, still clinging to the mane with the other, his legs straining against the animal's sides, he snatched the knife out of his mouth and leaned far down over the great hump of the beast, attempting to plunge the blade deep into the throat and sever the jugular.

He missed.

The bull bellowed with pain and veered suddenly to the left. Tecumseh kept going straight, losing his knife and flying head over heels into the plunging throng. Fortunately he was still close enough to the edge of the herd that only a couple of animals struck him, bowling him over and sending him tumbling brokenly outside the edge of the pounding mass of flesh.

The others rode up at once, shooting their rifles to ward the herd away from trampling him even more. He was unconscious and two of the young men leaped off their horses and lifted his limp form, holding him up enough that Chiksika could grip him around the stomach from behind with one arm and ride off with him, hanging and flopping loosely.

Now, lying on the blanket in their camp and for the first time focusing more clearly on his brother, Tecumseh attempted a smile that was largely a failure. "I guess I shouldn't have done that," he said.

"No," Chiksika replied, "you shouldn't have. But, having done so, you shouldn't be alive, either. You'll live. You won't be walking for a good while, but you'll live."

"Is my leg broken?"

"Not your leg, your hip. The bone almost came through the skin." Chiksika looked at him steadily and there was no humor in his voice when he spoke. "You could very easily have been killed, Tecumseh. It is only through great good luck that you weren't. That was a very stupid thing to do."

Tecumseh nodded and then winced at the pain this simple movement caused. "It was the liquor, wasn't it?"

"Yes. It is bad. It robs us of good sense. It makes us do things that we are otherwise too smart to do, things dangerous to ourselves and to others."

"What do we do now, Chiksika?"

His older brother shrugged. "You will be a long time in healing. It will be necessary to bind you tightly so the bones will not pull apart while mending. So, we will have to make a permanent camp here and remain until you are well again. I will ask the others to help me build a good winter wegiwa. Then they can go if they want. I will stay with you." If there was any bitterness in him over the curtailment of their trip or the great amount of effort he would be put to in caring for Tecumseh while he healed, there was no indication of it in his voice.

They fell silent and Chiksika absently watched a murder of crows flying in ragged, ungainly pattern in the distance. At last Tecumseh spoke, but more to himself than to Chiksika.

"From this time forward," he vowed, "no liquid except water will ever again pass my lips."295

[May 22, 1784 — Saturday]

In the far western Kentucky country camp, Tecumseh was inside the wegiwa late in the afternoon when he heard some of the young men of their party suddenly begin talking excitedly outside. He quickly positioned the crude crutches under his arms and maneuvered himself out of the doorway with the skill of one who has long been accustomed to the use of such walking aids.

In the distance Chiksika, who had ridden off to hunt early this morning, was approaching and bringing with him not only some fresh meat—a good-sized deer draped over the horse's back directly in front of him—but another pair of riders, who were obviously Shawnees but not yet recognizable.

He waved at them but not until they had approached within twenty yards or so did he see that the two newcomers were the old warrior, Frog Hunter, and a Maykujay named Pyetta from Mackachack, who had been with them last fall but who had decided, after Tecumseh had broken his hip, to return to his own village for the winter rather than spending it here, but promising to come back in the spring. All crowded around and welcomed the two and before long they were sitting around the fire smoking their pipes and enjoying pleasant conversation.

Frog Hunter blew out a small puff of smoke and smiled at Tecumseh. "Well, Tecumseh, everyone has heard how you broke your hip. It is good to see you are moving about again. I take it you have not been wrestling with any bull buffaloes lately?"

Everyone laughed and Tecumseh, grinning, shook his head. "Not even cows or calves. I've given that up permanently," he glanced at Chiksika, "along with some other foolish things I was doing."

"There are not," Frog Hunter said, a note of respect creeping into his voice, "too many things you do that could be considered foolish. Those at home will be glad to hear you are mending well."

It was on a whim, Frog Hunter told them then, that he decided to accompany Pyetta to Chiksika's hunting camp for a visit. "I'm getting very old," he said, "and one day before too much longer, I will no longer be able to ride great distances. Pyetta's leaving to rejoin you was a good excuse for me to take a nice trip."

"What is the news from home, Frog Hunter?" Chiksika asked. "The war is not starting again, is it?"

The old warrior shook his head. "No. A few of our young men are still stealing horses in Kentucky and burning a few cabins, but there is no real war. In fact, war with the whites is as far away as I can remember it being and they have recently been sending speeches to us, asking that we meet with them to discuss a peace treaty."

Tecumseh's lips became a thin line and Chiksika frowned. "At what cost to us?" the older brother asked.

Frog Hunter shrugged. "Who knows? Land, no doubt, but no one has said that yet. Our chiefs received speeches from them and sent theirs back and eventually there will be a council."

"No good can come of it," Tecumseh said glumly. "There can never be peace between the Shawnees and the *Shemanese*."

"I agree," Chiksika added, "but we appreciate your bringing the news to us, Frog Hunter. Is there anything else worthy to tell?"

"Only that many new stations and cabins have been built in the Kentucky country since you left. There is now a large town on the south shore of the Spaylaywitheepi at the Falls—a place they call Louisville. Small stations elsewhere seem almost to spring up overnight. Even Bahd-ler—the one now called Simon Kenton—has built a new station on the small creek near the place they call Limestone. We have not yet moved against any of them. It is the feeling of Shemeneto and Blue Jacket that eventually we will, but even if we do, no one will go against the one made by Kenton. The Great Spirit has clearly shown us that it would be to our misfortune to disturb him there."[296]

They smoked some more then and talked casually about many things until Frog Hunter asked what their own plans were. At this Tecumseh said, "Let me reply to that, Chiksika."

He struggled to his feet, using his crutches and walked around the fire with them and then suddenly smiled. "I have a surprise for you, Chiksika. I will not need these anymore."

To the astonishment of the others he tossed one of the crutches into the fire, then the other, then walked around the fire again, this time unaided, limping a bit, but under his own unassisted power.

"I have been working on this for a long while," Tecumseh said. "For much too long—because of me—we have been held here, but no longer. To answer your question, Frog Hunter, we resume our trip to see our southern brothers as soon as possible. And we would be pleased if you would go along with us."

"I believe I will," Frog Hunter said.

[April 30, 1785 — Saturday]

After their absence from the tribe for only a month short of two years, it was a great pleasure for Chiksika and Tecumseh to be back among their own people and an even greater one to be reunited again with Tecumapese and Wasegoboah, with eleven-year-old Spemica Lawba and the triplets, who were now fourteen. They were presently all living in the substantial wegiwa Wasegoboah had built in Mackachack and, of course, the two older brothers had been welcomed to resume residence with them. They had accepted, preferring to live almost anywhere else besides the village in which the Shawnee principal chief, Catahecassa, lived.

A large percentage of the Chalahgawtha Shawnees were now living under Catahecassa at the village he had established on the upper waters of the Auglaize River, some thirty-five miles northwest of Wapatomica. Breaking from the custom of calling the principal village of the Chalahgawthas after the name of the sept, Catahecassa had somewhat self-servingly chosen to call the new village Catahecassa's Town. That name was not particularly in favor and the village was far better known by the name of the area where it was located. This was at the northwestern end of the portage from the Auglaize, which was in the Maumee River flowage, to the headwaters of the Great Miami, which was in the Ohio River flowage. The name of that portage was *Wapaughkonetta* and the village itself was now best known as Wapakoneta.

The two brothers had changed considerably during their absence, Chiksika, now twenty-nine, with a much more pronounced mature strength than when they had left and Tecumseh, now seventeen, tall, muscular, well formed—a superb example of a Shawnee warrior in young manhood. It was not the only way in which they had changed. Tecumseh still limped slightly but was no longer bothered much by the old hip injury and could ride or walk all day without undue discomfort. And Chiksika had become married to a Cherokee woman living in the village of Running Water, where she had only recently borne him a daughter.[297]

Both brothers had assisted the Cherokees in their continuing fights with the whites who persisted in encroaching into their territory and both were held in high esteem as warriors by their southern friends. Chiksika had even been asked to lead several Cherokee war parties on raids—a signal honor for someone not a member of the tribe. He also said he was planning to go back to Running Water sometime in the near future to get his wife and bring her and the baby back to Ohio with him.

All three of the triplets had been excited at the return of their older brothers, but Lowawluwaysica was especially pleased and immediately became again Tecumseh's shadow, doting on his every word or action and his hero worship all but comical in its intentness. Their young nephew, Spemica Lawba, was not far behind Lowawluwaysica in his admiration for Tecumseh and, unlike the one-eyed boy, for Chiksika as well. Kisathoi and Tebethto, now seventeen and fifteen respectively and in their seventh year with the Shawnees, had become attractive young maidens in the first bloom of womanhood and, though pleased at the return of the brothers, were suddenly very shy and retiring.

Sinnanatha, on the other hand, was quite vocal in his welcome of the pair and eager to tell them all about his new position in the tribe. Now seventeen, he had been selected as something of a neophyte priest, to serve in religious functions for his adopted family and, in this role, not required to go to war, though not prohibited from doing so if he chose. His duties included preparing offerings of thanks for the benefits received from Moneto, performing the ceremonial sacrifices of owls and white dogs and even the *fitlomugashee* ritual, which was the removal of the tongue of a bear that had been killed and the placing of it on the fire; if it curled up and twisted and crackled, this was regarded as an augury of a favorable hunt to come for the males in the household.

Tecumapese and Wasegoboah set about filling the brothers in on all important matters that had occurred in their country or affected it during their absence. Tecumseh and Chiksika were shocked to learn that the Kentucky country now boasted over forty-five thousand whites, the number increasing regularly. All remembered the words of Pucksinwah who had said that when a white man was killed two or three more stepped up to take his place and their numbers were endless, like the leaves in a forest.

"The Americans are claiming more and more land everywhere," Tecumapese told them. "While you were gone all that are left of the Six Nations held a large treaty council with the Americans at Fort Stanwix, in which they were compelled to give up what prisoners and Negroes they had and also made to sell the Americans practically all of their land. Red Jacket spoke on behalf of the tribes at that Fort Stanwix Treaty and he was very moving in what he said. Although many in the League have often called him cowardly and a peacemaker, it was he who stood at that council and demanded that they yield not an inch to the Americans and continue their fight against them, even without British support. He prophesied the gradual downfall of their people if they closed the treaty with the Americans and was very concerned for the honor of the Six Nations. At one place in the talks he rose up and said, 'Let us find a grave that will be a bloody labor for our enemies to dig, and it shall be a place where the traveler shall pause and think how gloriously we died.' "

"But they eventually wound up signing the treaty?" Chiksika asked.

"Yes," Wasegoboah spoke up, "they did so.[298] Now the Mohawks have gone permanently from the Mohawk River in New York. They, and others of the Six Nations who wish to join them, have been given a grant of land in Canada by the British General Haldimand. This is a broad stretch of land along the Ouise—what the British call Grand River—and extends six miles on either side of the river from its headwaters to its mouth at Lake Erie.[299]

"Also," he added, "in other matters, the great Miami chief we met in Kekionga, Michikiniqua, has adopted a white boy of about thirteen summers, captured on the Spaylaywitheepi some time ago and who lives with him now in his house in Kekionga. He has hair the color of a carrot, so Michikiniqua has named him Apekonit"—Wild Carrot.[300]

"Also," Tecumapese put in, "I'm sure you remember the white girl who was captured four years ago and adopted into the family of Leaning Tree— the one called Catherine Malotte? Well, our friend Simon Girty was smitten by her and just last month he asked permission to take her to Detroit to visit her mother and instead he married her at the mouth of the Detroit River."[301]

"In another matter," Wasegoboah went on, "the Delawares in our country have been increased in number a little bit by the arrival of their distant brethren who call themselves the Nanticokes, who had been living in the valley of the Susquehanna, but who have been forced away from there by the whites. They brought with them the bones of all their relatives and buried them in new graves here in Ohio."[302]

A particularly disturbing bit of news told to the brothers was that the Americans, in a strong force under command of an officer named Major John Doughty, had descended the Spaylaywitheepi and come ashore on the Ohio side at the mouth of the Muskingum and had just started construction there of a strong fort that was already being called Fort Harmar after Doughty's regimental commander, Josiah Harmar.[303] There was talk about moving against it and trying to destroy it, but so far it had all been talk. There could be no doubt, however, that this was a toehold on the Ohio country that the Americans meant to use as a launching place for further incursions into the Shawnee country.

The returned brothers had not yet seen Blue Jacket, who was in his own town eight miles north, but they would see him today, since Moluntha had exercised his prerogative as the eldest Shawnee chief and principal chief of the Maykujays to call a national council of the Shawnees to begin at noon this day at Wapatomica. Rumors were rife about what the council concerned, since there had been no official notification of topic. Some thought it might be to discuss the matter of the Kentuckians who, the chiefs here had recently learned, had met in their settlement of Danville to discuss separating from Virginia and creating their own state of Kentucky, giving as reasons their objection to Virginia taxes, their inability to adapt Virginia laws to the frontier, and the refusal of Virginia to permit pursuit of the Indians north of the Spaylaywitheepi.

The consensus, however, was that it had to do with the extremely disturbing news received just a week ago from the principal chief of the Delawares, Buckangehela, whose village was only ten miles west of Mackachack, where Stony Creek emptied into the Great Miami River. He had been summoned to attend treaty talks held on January 21 at Fort McIntosh at the mouth of Beaver River and on his return, he visited the Shawnees, who were called into an emergency council to hear what he had to say. He told them that the Wyandots had attended as well, and also to some degree the Ottawas and Chippewas. It was their first council with the American delegation, who called themselves the commissioners plenipotentiary of the United States of America. With them was a United States colonel, twenty other officers, eight hundred soldiers and sufficient artillery to make the chiefs shudder.

Buckangehela reported that the Fort McIntosh Treaty had not been a friendly one, and the chiefs in attendance had listened in stony silence to the arrogant, virtually belligerent statements of the commissioners, who all but bludgeoned them into signing away their lands, which the commissioners told them the Americans had won by right of conquest.

The commissioner who spoke, Buckangehela said, told them he would make the new boundary very clear to these assembled tribes so that there could be no misinterpretation that might result in future conflict. That boundary, he told them, was to start at the mouth of the river Cuyahoga and go upstream to the portage connecting it with the Tuscarawas Branch of the Muskingum, then down the Tuscarawas to the crossing place above where Fort Laurens had been, then directly westward to the portage between the Auglaize and Great Miami rivers, and then down the southeast side of the Great Miami to its mouth.[304]

The commissioner had then told the assembled tribes that east and south of this line was American territory and north and west of it was Indian territory and would belong to the assembled tribes. A few six-square-mile tracts had been set aside within the Indian portion for the United States government to establish trading posts upon.

The American commissioner, Buckangehela reported, was not at all concerned that the two-thirds of the Ohio country that this new boundary gave the Americans contained very little land claimed by any of the tribes represented at the Fort McIntosh treaty; that it was mostly territory belonging to the Shawnees, the Miamis, and some of the Mingoes. Yet, not one chief or representative of any of these three had been in attendance!

The Americans had taken some of their people hostage, Buckangehela had concluded, and so they had signed the treaty papers, knowing the Americans meant to get the land one way or another anyway.[305]

Consternation had been great, Chiksika and Tecumseh were told, when the Shawnees heard all this and they had immediately sent a speech to Colonel

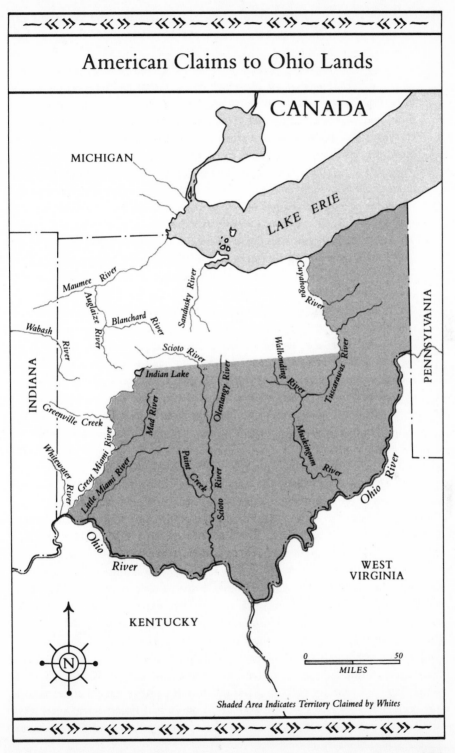

American Claims to Ohio Lands

CANADA

MICHIGAN

LAKE ERIE

Maumee River

Auglaize River

Blanchard River

Sandusky River

Cuyahoga River

Wabash River

INDIANA

Scioto River

Walhonding River

Tuscarawas River

PENNSYLVANIA

Indian Lake

Mad River

Olentangy River

Muskingum River

Greenville Creek

Whitewater River

Great Miami River

Little Miami River

Paint Creek

Scioto River

Ohio River

Ohio River

WEST VIRGINIA

KENTUCKY

N

0   50
MILES

Shaded Area Indicates Territory Claimed by Whites

Alexander McKee at Detroit demanding an explanation and they had not minced their words. In substance, what they had written to McKee was this:

> *Our friends the Delawares have told us the following, which we now pass on to you. "You, Colonel McKee, know very well that the Virginians called us to their Council, and we were obliged to go. They desired us to listen to them, and they told us they had beaten the English, the Six Nations and everybody they fought against, and we Delawares with the rest. They said the Great Spirit was on their side, by which they had gotten all our lands. They said to us, 'Your fathers, the English, gave us Americans all the land as far as the Mississippi and the big lakes. As we have beaten you, we have got all the country. If you had beaten us, it would have been the same case with us. We are as strong as a hickory tree that is not to be overpowered. We had no assistance in beating you, from either French or Spaniards. We have done it ourselves, as well as to all our other enemies. We are now the only people to be believed, and to us alone you must now listen. We are going to build a block house at Lower Sandusky, another at the Big Miami River, and then survey our lands and place people thereon. Then let us see who dare say any thing against it.' Father, this is what the Americans told us. We shall be glad to know from you whether it is true or not. If it is true, we shall soon be obliged to listen to them. We shall be glad to hear from you, and what news you may have from Quebec, as we expect the Americans upon us very soon. Father, we must now let you know that we are going to the Miamis. You are sensible we have long been in friendship with them, which we are now going to strengthen, after which we shall tell them what the Americans told us."*

The Shawnees had then, the brothers were informed, asked McKee for a meeting as soon as possible to discuss this great danger and what help the British were going to be to them when the trouble came with the Americans, as it was bound to do very soon. The Shawnee speech had been sent to McKee only those few days ago and as yet, of course, there had been no reply.

So, under the circumstances, it was reasonable to assume that this council that was being called today was to discuss this very serious matter. There were scores of horses of the visitors picketed nearby when Chiksika, Tecumseh, and Wasegoboah reached the center of Wapatomica and the *msi-kah-mi-qui* itself was already crowded, though the council had not yet officially begun. Moluntha was here, as was Catahecassa and the other sept chiefs and subchiefs. Shemeneto, though obviously unwell, had come from the new Kispoko Town, which had only recently been incorporated into the little village that heretofore had been called McKee's Town, some two and a half miles to the northwest of Wapatomica and halfway between that capital village and Blue Jacket's

Town. The ugly old war chief had lost a good bit of weight, causing his features to become drawn and his eyes sunken. The tribal doctors had given him every potion they knew and incanted over the strewn contents of their medicine bags, yet his illness persisted.

The brothers and Wasegoboah moved through the crowd, acknowledging with smiles and waves and passing words the welcome home remarks made by many of their fellows. Still, no one present seemed to have any really concrete idea of the reason this council had been called and so an expectant hush settled over the assemblage when a runner entered and whispered something in Moluntha's ear and then helped the old chief to his feet. A moment later Blue Jacket and a contingent of warriors from his village entered the council house and prepared to take seats on some of the few mats left open on the floor near the west wall.

"Wehyahpihehrsehnwah," the white-haired Moluntha said, his voice surprisingly strong and filled with authority, "you are to come here to sit for this council." He indicated a vacant mat on the floor beside his own and walked toward them. Nonhelema stood as Moluntha came back and helped ease her husband back into his seat on the mat beside her.

Obviously puzzled, Blue Jacket strode to the center, dipped his head respectfully at Moluntha and Catahecassa and sat down with legs bent and crossed at the ankles. Blue Jacket then caught a glimpse of Chiksika and Tecumseh and smiled broadly in silent greeting.

Pipes were lighted and passed, the smoking continuing until a vague blue-white haze filled the council house and the familiar and pleasant aroma of the *kinnikinnick* was everywhere. Not until all the pipes had been collected or laid aside did Catahecassa come to his feet and step to the fire, where he turned and faced the assembled chiefs, subchiefs, village chiefs and warriors.

"My children," he said, "we are come here for a most important matter. What will take place here today has never happened before and, I believe, will not again. It is a time of sadness and a time of rejoicing and I would ask our eldest chief to tell you of it."

Now it was he who reached down and took the skeletal hand of Moluntha and gently helped him rise, then resumed his own seat. Moluntha slowly let his gaze move two complete times across all those assembled before he spoke. He had become considerably more frail in these past two years the brothers had been gone and his face much more wrinkled, so much so that his eyes were all but hidden in the folds of loose skin. It seemed improbable that a voice still so strong could emerge from a frame so enfeebled.

"My children, what Catahecassa has told you is true. This is a day of sadness and rejoicing, but the rejoicing is the greater of the two and the sadness only aids in enriching the joy. You see before you one who is beginning his ninety-third summer. I am old and I grow weak. My eyes can no longer follow the flight of the pigeon nor my legs the trail of the deer. It is time for me to step aside as chief of the Maykujays and for this there must be a sadness in my heart and yours.

"It is my right," he went on, "not only as descending chief but as eldest of all the Shawnees, to select the warrior who will take my place. He must be the bravest of the brave, the boldest of the bold. But he must be more than this. He must know when to fight and when to withdraw. He must be able and willing to think first of his people and, if necessary, to lay down his life for them. He must be proven in battle and in leadership and he must have the respect and admiration of all his fellow tribesmen. He must be wise, yet able to use his wisdom without pride; cruel, if necessary, but not make cruelty his master or his pleasure; kind, but not let kindness become weakness.

"The man I have chosen has all these abilities and more. Only the principal chief could overrule this decision and Catahecassa has already told me he approves my choice. From this moment forward, the chief of the Maykujay Shawnees is the man who sits beside me now—Blue Jacket!"

Thus the special council ended and Tecumseh, Wasegoboah, and Chiksika were among those who crowded around to extend their heartiest and most sincere congratulations to Blue Jacket.

Now, an hour later, as the three rode back toward Mackachack in the early twilight, their pleasure at Blue Jacket's triumph dimmed and a pall of gloom cloaked them. The same thought was in the minds of all: the tendrils of the Americans were once again reaching out to encompass and destroy them and what brief period of relative peace they had enjoyed was rapidly coming to an end.

[June 10, 1785 — Friday]

The council held at Wapatomica was not in the *msi-kah-mi-qui* but, rather, out of doors and a large number of Indians besides the Shawnees had gathered to hear what Colonel Alexander McKee had to say.

There were many Wyandots here, including Pipe, Stiahta—better known to the whites as Roundhead—and Tarhe, The Crane. A sizeable faction of the Delawares were here under Chief Buckangehela and a smaller but rather more important delegation of chiefs of the Miamis led by none other than Michi-kiniqua himself.

"My brothers," McKee addressed them, "you are all greatly disturbed at the things that have been happening in and around your country and rightly so. You have even come to the point where you have accused your good friends, the British, of abandoning you and of giving away your country to the Americans in order to make peace with them.

"That is not true," he said, a note of anger coming into his voice, "but like all convincing lies, it is built on a bed of truth. We have just been through a long, difficult war with our rebellious children and your great father, the king, has felt it best that no more lives be lost at this time among his children, red or white. That is why he asks you now to no longer keep the hatchet raised against the Americans, but neither does he ask you to bury it; only that you keep it ready in your hand and that from time to time you sharpen it, so that when he is ready again to confront his rebellious children, you will also be ready.

"My brothers, in order for your great father, the king, to take compassion on his children and end this senseless bloodletting, he thought it best to make certain temporary concessions. He did make peace with the Americans in Paris, yes, and he did agree to a boundary line separating us in these lands, and he even agreed to give the Americans jurisdiction over their side of the boundary line, which is south of the line stretching through the middle of the four lakes—Ontario, Erie, Huron, and Superior. But while he agreed to their having jurisdiction, *he did not give them rights or title to the soil,* which is yours, as it always has been. Your great father simply does not wish another war at this time, which would only serve to disrupt you and displace your families and would only cause great hardships for his red children.

"My brothers, your great father, the king, has many swords in his pockets, but a large number of these have become dulled through overuse and now he must take the time to inspect each one and to sharpen it well so that when it is ready for use again, it will be deadly against his enemies. This will take some time, but you must have patience and have faith as well that your great father, the king, has not abandoned you. He cares deeply for you and wishes for you only that which is right and good and your just due. You must continue to have faith in him, just as he continues to have faith in you."

The speech went on for a long while, filled with doubletalk, vague promises and threats even more vague against the Americans, but with nothing concrete decided in any way except that their great father, the king, would continue to provide them with the gifts they needed to keep their bellies filled and the edge of their hatchets sharp.

There was a notable lack of response from the assembled Indians and when the council ended they went their own ways confused and gloomy, not entirely sure what it was that was said to them or what it meant; sure only that whatever else, the Americans were still moving into their lands and devouring them and that something *had* to be done to stop this, with or without the help of their great father, the king.

[January 31, 1786 — Tuesday]

Blue Jacket's party included himself, Chiksika, Tecumseh, Wasegoboah, and even old Chief Moluntha and his huge wife, Nonhelema, along with some others. They represented the Shawnee delegation that had come here to the mouth of the Great Miami to view firsthand the negotiations that were being conducted between the American commissioners and the band of three hundred pacifistic Shawnees who, without official tribal sanction, had been led here by the subchief Kekewapilethy—Tame Hawk.[306]

Furious at Kekewapilethy for his effrontery in taking tribal matters into his own hands, the smaller group of visiting Shawnees observed with silent anger the blockhouse—being called Fort Finney—that the whites had had the temerity to build here in the Ohio country, three-quarters of a mile above the river's mouth, under the guise that it was merely a temporary structure and would be dismantled when the treaty talks were concluded.

This Fort Finney Treaty talk was the result of what had all begun early last summer when delegations of Americans had started moving through Ohio, Indiana, and Michigan countries, inviting the various chiefs and delegates of their nations to attend the important treaty that was originally scheduled by them to begin the first day of the Harvest Moon at the Great Miami's mouth.

The fact that the Americans would not only select such a site for these talks, but arrange to hold them at a time when councils simply were not held because of harvesting, hunting, and other business requiring the tribes' attentions, indicated how little they understood or cared about the Indians in general.

Various American peace delegations had moved through the Northwest, visiting Shawnees, Miamis, Delawares, Wyandots, and other tribes, traveling in separate parties headed by Samuel Robertson, James Elliott, William Clark, and Daniel Rinkings. While uninvited, most emissaries had been received politely enough by the tribes, although there were a few occasions when they had been treated contemptuously and with considerable rudeness and once or twice with actual threat to their lives.

The general displeasure of the tribes was voiced at one of the councils held for these delegates at Lower Sandusky on September 20. Tarhe, as one of the more elder of the Wyandot chiefs, summed up what the tribes were all feeling:

"Brother Americans," he said with constrained politeness, "we acknowledge the receipt of your messages calling us to the mouth of the Big Miami River on the Ohio, to a treaty to be held there ten days from this date. When we consider that important business already transacted with you at Forts Stanwix and McIntosh has not yet had time to be made known and determined upon by those Nations concerned in it throughout this great country, we cannot help expressing that you have been too precipitate. Time must be allowed for the tribes to hold council among themselves to consider your proposals carefully. Such councils are essential to accomplish the desirable end of peace and make it permanent.

"We are equally surprised," Tarhe went on, his eyes hard and his tone cold, "that you seem to take no notice of the ancient council fires kindled by our forefathers, at which places *only* can the good works of peace be accommodated. When our business is fully settled and *we* are ready to meet you, then such meeting should be held at the place where our ancestors formerly met to settle matters tending to their welfare and happiness."

Tarhe had then gone on to say that the place where such counciling should be held was at the great council fire at Detroit. The American delegates, however, had no wish to hold such a meeting in proximity to the British, whom they suspected would sabotage their efforts among the tribes. They insisted that the general council should be held at the mouth of the Great Miami; but that, since the fort they were erecting there for that purpose was not yet completed, they would postpone the opening treaty talks for three months, till the first of January.

The American delegation had then left the Wyandot country and went to Wapatomica to inform the Shawnees of this same decision. Taken somewhat off balance by the appearance of this American delegation among them, the Shawnees agreed to hold council and listen to what they had to say. That was when, as the council convened, the self-important Shawnee subchief named Kekewapilethy—Tame Hawk—had asked permission to speak first. When this request was granted, he rose and, to the chagrin and irritation of the other Shawnees present, made a speech decidedly conciliatory toward the Americans. He strongly urged the young Shawnee warriors to leave off their raiding, to cease the killing and the stealing of horses that had been going on, and to have pity upon their own women and children by not hindering the good work of peace they were on here at this council. It was obvious that Kekewapilethy, who was generally considered to be an inconsequential chief with nothing of any great consequence between his ears, was very inclined to attend the proposed treaty talks and wished to grasp the American offerings of peace irrespective of at what cost. His speech had incurred such great displeasure among the other Shawnees in attendance that he left the council house in a rather apprehensively petulant way before the council was even finished.

Kekewapilethy's talk had been followed by a speech from another Shawnee subchief spokesman named Piteosawa, who spoke more truly the feelings of the tribe in general.

"Brothers of the Thirteen Fires," Piteosawa said coldly, "you sent speeches amongst us last year to invite us who are of one color to the council fire you kindled at Fort Stanwix, for the peace and other good things you said you had to offer us. Soon afterwards you kindled another council fire at Beaver River, at your Fort McIntosh, to which you also invited us, but to neither of which did we come because you had openly said you would keep some of our chiefs as hostages for the guarantee of our fidelity. But you ought to know this is not the way to make a good or lasting peace—to take our chiefs prisoners and come with soldiers at your backs. This cannot tend to general good between us.

"You now again," he went on, "invite us to another council fire at the mouth of the Great Miami. Your messengers have gone through several nations. But we are aware of your design to divide our councils. We are unanimous. And it is not right for you to kindle council fires among brush or nettles. Therefore, we now inform you that if you wish a council with all these many Indian nations, that at Detroit is the ancient council fire of our forefathers. *There* is the proper place. When we see you there, we will take your hand—but this cannot be sooner than next spring. We must have time to hear from other nations to the westward. Nothing is to be done by us but by general consent; we, the tribes of the Northwest, act and speak like one man."

It was in this vein that the council at Wapatomica continued and finally concluded. With that, the American delegation had gone on its way. It was not until late in the year, when word came to the Shawnee chiefs that Kekewapilethy and others had left their villages, that the truth came out. Catahecassa, Blue Jacket, and the others were thunderstruck when they investigated and discovered that before the American commissioners had left Wapatomica, Kekewapilethy had secretly gone to them on his own and promised to attend the planned treaty talks in January at the mouth of the Great Miami and that, on behalf of the Shawnee tribe, would be very agreeable to whatever was proposed.

That was where he was now and that was when Blue Jacket's party had left to come here to the mouth of the Great Miami to discover what was happening between Kekewapilethy and the American commissioners at Fort Finney. Now they had arrived and presented themselves to the American treaty commissioners plenipotentiary, Major General Samuel H. Parsons, Colonel Richard Butler, and George Rogers Clark, who regarded them with dark suspicion, while many of the whites in attendance were seen to grip their rifles more firmly and surreptitiously check their loads.

Blue Jacket, Chiksika and the others were escorted to where the talks were being held and were grudgingly invited to visit and observe, but were not considered as part of the Shawnee delegation already involved here and so had no right to speak. Insulted by such a restriction, yet not prepared for a full confrontation with the American troops and armed frontiersmen on hand, they had acquiesced. They were dumbfounded to discover that, despite earlier refusals to attend, there were official deputations here from the other northwestern tribes—Wyandots under Tarhe and Monakaduto, Delawares under Buckangehela, Pipe, Big Cat, and Awuncy, Chippewas under Wafrugahquealied, Ottawas under Nichefrewaw and Nichinesica, and Potawatomies under Nanimisea and Messquagoneke. And here, too, were the three hundred Shawnee pacifists that Kekewapilethy had brought with him, who were almost entirely women and children, bundled in skins and blankets against the January cold, but obviously suffering from it and just as obviously very hungry.

"How does Tame Hawk dare to bring those unfortunates with him and increase their misery?" Chiksika said angrily. "What does he hope to get out of this?"

"He wishes food and warm clothes for his people," Moluntha said mildly, "which is understandable, but better he should have applied to the rest of the tribe for them. It is a hard winter and none of us has much, but we would gladly have shared with him and them."

The talks were continuing and, in whispered discussions with chiefs and warriors who had been there from the beginning, they learned the essence of what had occurred thus far. When Kekewapilethy arrived with his three hundred hungry, cold, and weary followers, Colonel Richard Butler had ordered the firing of a military salute to honor them. He had then begun his talk with Kekewapilethy and when the subchief had proclaimed "All this land is ours," Butler had become very forceful in his remarks.

"We plainly tell you, Tame Hawk," he had said to Kekewapilethy, who cringed somewhat at the vehemence, "that this country belongs to the United States! Their blood has defended it and will forever protect it. Their proposals are liberal and just and you should be thankful for the forgiveness and offers of kindness of the United States." For the subchief's acceptance of the proposals, he added, he was prepared to offer peace and immediately give his tattered followers food and blankets.

Kekewapilethy had come prepared to negotiate and had been confident of his ability to do so to his own honor in the tribe. He had brought with him a black wampum belt, signifying war, and this he had then withdrawn from his pouch and placed on the table, saying, "You say you have goods for our women and children. You may keep your goods and give them to other nations. We will have none of them."

At this the three commissioners became angry and walked out and on their way, George Rogers Clark knocked the black wampum belt to the floor and stamped upon it. Having now given Tame Hawk a long period of time to reconsider, the commissioners returned and Butler told him his offer was as he had stated it and "you can take it or leave it, but the destruction of your women and children depends on your present choice."

All of Kekewapilethy's self-confidence had drained away at that point and he meekly gave in. Butler immediately ordered food distributed to the Shawnee's followers and presented him as well with enough whiskey for Kekewapilethy and the few adult males in his party to get drunk upon, which they did with gusto.

Now, with Blue Jacket's small party looking on, the talks were all but finished. The commissioners, with interpreters relaying their words to various factions almost simultaneously, went over the seven articles of the treaty step by step preparatory to signing.

The first article called for three hostages to be delivered up to the commissioners, to be held until all prisoners, white or black, taken during the late war, that were in the possession of the Shawnees and who had been taken by them or any other Indians living in their towns, were restored to the Americans.

Article Two stated that the Shawnees acknowledged the United States to be the sole and absolute sovereign of all the territory ceded to the Americans by the British at their treaty of peace.

Article Three required that if any Indians committed murder, robbery, or injury against any citizen of the States, the offenders were to be given up to the officer commanding the nearest United States post for trial and, in like manner, any white guilty of similar crimes against the Indians would similarly be punished according to the laws of the United States.

The fourth article called for the Shawnees to report any intelligence they gained of other tribes preparing to strike against the United States and that failure to do so would make them be considered as party to such measures and they would be punished accordingly.

Article Five stated that the United States granted peace to the Shawnees and received them into the favor and protection of the United States.

Article Six was one in which the wording was so confusing that none of the Indians on hand understood it, though they were encouraged in their *misunderstanding* of it. In its entirety, the article stated:

> *The United States do allot to the Shawanese Nation land within their Territory to live in and hunt upon, beginning at the south line of the lands allotted to the Wiandots and Dellawares, at the place where the main branch of the Great Miami intersects with said line, thence down the River Miamis to the fork of that River next below the old Fort which was taken by the French in the year 1752, thence due west to the River de la Pansé, then down that River to the River Wabash, beyond which line none of the citizens of the United States shall settle nor disturb the Shawanese in their settlements and possessions, and the Shawanese do relinquish to the United States all title or pretence of title they ever had on the lands east, west and south of the east, west and south lines before described.*

To all the Indians in attendance, this simply reaffirmed that the Shawnees would continue to live and hunt in their own Ohio territory, with the Ohio River being the border to the south and the territories of the Wyandots, Delawares, and Miamis being the border to the north. To the whites, it meant that the Shawnees had ceded *all* this land east of the Great Miami River to the United States.

Article Seven simply stated that if any citizen of the United States presumed to settle on the lands allotted to the Shawnees by this treaty, he would be put out of the protection of the United States.

While the commissioners were thus going over the articles of the treaty, Moluntha went to Kekewapilethy and sat with him an extended period, conversing. Blue Jacket and the others were certain he was upbraiding the subchief but then were startled when, as the commissioners finished, he came creakily to his feet and announced that he, as principal chief of the Maykujay Shawnees, and Kekewapilethy would be the principal treaty signers for the Shawnees.

"He has gone mad!" Wasegoboah whispered in amazed alarm to Blue Jacket, who nodded.

"Can't we stop him and Kekewapilethy?" Tecumseh asked, deeply concerned.

"We could and would, if it were necessary," Blue Jacket murmured, "but it is not. Neither of them represents the general council of the Shawnees and their names on the treaty will have no significance. Both will be reprimanded in council when we return, but for now we will let it be. The Americans have soldiers here and they are ready for trouble, which would certainly occur if we were to try that. Our party is too small and the weather too bad to launch an attack on them. But I tell you this, Tecumseh, I have never hated the Americans so much as I do this day. They *will* be destroyed. I will return here in the Green Moon, kill all the soldiers who remain and burn this fort which is such an insult to our dignity and intelligence."

One by one the chiefs came forward and made their marks on the treaty. As Moluntha prepared to do so, he made a comment to Commissioner Richard Butler, who nodded and took out a sheet of paper upon which he wrote something and gave it to the aged chief. Moluntha nodded, folded it and placed it in his pouch.

Why the chiefs of these other tribes were here and why they were signing the treaty made no sense to the visiting Shawnees under Blue Jacket. It was Shawnee territory, not theirs, that was the matter considered here. As the signing progressed, first by the Indians, then by the attesting whites and finally by the three commissioners plenipotentiary, Colonel Richard Butler became affable.[307] He chatted with the Indians through interpreters and never corrected their misunderstanding that the Ohio River was still the border between the Shawnees and the whites; in fact, when they remarked uneasily about the two forts the Americans had now built on their territory—this one and the one called Fort Harmar at the mouth of the Muskingum—he blandly reassured them that the purpose of those forts was not for invasion but as guard posts to turn back any whites who might attempt settling in Shawnee territory. He then remarked how delighted he was with the "new and everlasting friendship" sealed this day between the United States and the Shawnees, adding that "differences of opinion" between the two could now at last "be put aside for all time."

The paper which the doddering Moluntha had received from Colonel Butler, which he showed to Blue Jacket and his party with no small measure of pride, was merely a safe conduct pass, stating that the bearer, Moluntha, was one of the chiefs who had signed the Great Miami Treaty and that he and his people at Mackachack "had done all in their power to keep the Shawnee from going to war and said Moluntha is included among the friends of the United States, and is therefore in no wise to be molested." In addition to that paper, Moluntha had been presented with a written copy of the treaty.

As the visiting Shawnees mounted their horses to return to the north, all were dismayed at what Kekewapilethy had taken upon himself to do and even more disgusted and disheartened with the actions of the lovable old Moluntha who had for so long been held in respect by all and had become the ideal of so many young Shawnees. Now even Nonhelema, though she had said nothing against her husband, had her lips set in a grim line as she helped the old man mount up and then began riding close beside him, bringing up the rear of their little party.

As the ugly bastion called Fort Finney disappeared from view behind them, Chiksika muttered aloud, "At every contact with them I understand more fully than ever before why our father said never to make peace with the *Shemanese,* that they only mean to devour our land."

Tecumseh growled a sound of agreement and Blue Jacket looked at them both. "My adopted father, Pucksinwah, was one of the wisest men I ever knew." He rode for a moment longer in silence and then added, "For a long time we have been making little sidesteps toward a real war with the *Shemanese.* Today we have taken a great stride in that direction."

[February 9, 1786 — Thursday]

Because of his command of the English language, both written and verbal, this morning Tecumseh was summoned to the wegiwa of Moluntha and asked to write a letter to Alexander McKee in Detroit, which Moluntha would dictate. Tecumseh glanced at Nonhelema and she nodded faintly, so he sat on the stool before a short table and dipped the quill pen into the ink pot. Several sheets of paper were there and Tecumseh poised himself to write.

"I'm ready," he said quietly.

"To Colonel McKee," dictated Moluntha. "Father. Last fall the Americans, our brethren, called us to the Big Miami." He paused, waiting for the young warrior to catch up and when Tecumseh paused in his writing and looked up, he continued, stopping regularly to give the writer time. "When we arrived, in January, they told us they had something to communicate for our future welfare and that of our children after us. But, also, we heard nothing good from them. They told us that our father, the British king, had given us to them, with our lands likewise. Father, the commissioners assured us that everything in the articles that we now send you were agreeable to our best wishes and more generous than we could have expected from them. This induced us to sign the proposals, but we find that we have been ignorant of the real purport of them till we returned here. Our hostages, however, that were detained by them, have escaped and are come home safe. We inform you how they have deceived us, by telling us that the king of Great Britain had ceded the whole country to them. We were not sensible of the error we committed till our friend Elliott explained it to us. Father, we request you'll be strong and give us the best advice you are capable of in our present situation. You see, we never have been in more need of your friendship and good offices. We have been cheated by the Americans, who are still striving to work our destruction, and, without your assistance, they may be able to accomplish their end. You have too much wisdom not to be convinced of this truth as well as we are. We earnestly request you will consider, and send us a speedy answer. In the meantime, we salute you and remain your steady friends."

Helped by his big wife over to the table and onto the stool which Tecumseh now vacated, Moluntha sat down and, with Tecumseh's hand guiding his, laboriously signed his name at the bottom.[308]

[April 9, 1786 — Sunday]

The force of some two hundred Shawnees behind the leadership of Blue Jacket pulled up atop the high ridge and looked down at the turbulent yellowish floodwaters of the river well below them. Projecting above the surface and being battered by floating logs, branches, and even whole trees were just the very tops of the pickets and the roof of the crude installation that had been Fort Finney. Of the garrison that had been in occupancy up to three days ago, according to their spies, there was no sign.[309]

"Moneto," Chiksika murmured, "has spared us the task of wiping them out."

"And deprived us the pleasure," Tecumseh added.

"There will be others to take their places," Blue Jacket said, wheeling his horse around. "There always are. There always will be. And, in case you were thinking otherwise, Moneto will show us the task and provide us the pleasure—and the pain—far more than any of us really want. *That* I know!"

[October 21, 1786 — Saturday]

There could be no doubt that Tecumseh, now only four months from being nineteen, quite well epitomized what a young Shawnee warrior should be. He was neither uncommonly tall nor short, neither slim nor heavy. His physique was excellent, smoothly muscled without being muscle-bound. Walking, standing, or sitting, his posture was erect and his carriage graceful. Even more now than as a young boy, he was exceptionally agile and limber. All his features were well formed, nicely molded and not extreme in any way, his forehead broad but not bulbous, his nose strongly formed but not overly large or hooked or too straight. By far his most dominant external feature was his amazingly expressive eyes, able in an instant to change from gentle warmth to bright points of controlled anger, from sparkling gaiety to deep sorrow, from compassion to iron implacability. His mind, as always, was quick, incisive, questioning, retentive, facile, and inventive—a mind that immediately set him apart from most others with whom he came into contact.

He remained, as he had been for some time, the foremost hunter among all Shawnees. This was not merely because of great powers of endurance or other physical prowess but because he consistently used his brain to overcome obstacles that thwarted others or which they tried to batter down with brute force.

If there were questions to be asked, Tecumseh was invariably the one who asked them, always probing, seeking, reaching out ever farther for answers progressively more elusive. The questions put initially to Chiksika and Tecumapese were answered easily enough—questions to his elder brother in matters of warfare and politics, religion, tradition, and history; questions to his sister in matters of the heart and emotions, family, love, care, compassion, beauty, self-possession. But now he had gone far beyond the questions either Chiksika or Tecumapese were capable of answering. They could not respond to his earnest and often posed question of why Moneto, if he loved his red children, permitted them to suffer so terribly at the hands of the whites. They could formulate no answer to his query about what they could do—what *Indians* could do, individually and collectively—to curtail and repel the evils brought to their beautiful land by the whites. They could only shrug and remain mute when he asked them why, since the greatest peril facing *all* Indians was the white man, the Indians did not unite in a self-protective front to fend them off. Why did the Menominee fight the Fox and Chippewa fight the Sioux and Sac fight the Osage? Were they not, first of all, *Indians*? Were they not all children of Moneto?

The matters of the weeks just past troubled him tremendously and there was no one to whom he could turn for answers. He remembered with pride the wonderful courage and purpose with which they had mounted and ridden off toward the Wabash from the Maykujay villages—the cream of manhood from Mackachack, Pigeon Town, Blue Jacket's Town, Solomon's Town. With what fine and exalted hopes they had headed toward the rendezvous to unite in a strong, solid front with the Miamis, Potawatomies, Ottawas, Delawares, Kickapoos and Wyandots to face the army of eighteen hundred soldiers being led against the Wabash tribes by the great white warrior, Clark. With what shame did they arrive to find that instead of waging war, the man named Clark was speaking to them, humoring them, coddling them, convincing them of their foolishness in fighting for what they mistakenly thought were their rights, convincing them that the Americans wished no more land and no more strife from their red brothers.[310]

Tecumseh had been aghast to learn that his red brothers, after listening to the smooth-talking Clark, had finally declared for peace. First, and undoubtedly most important, it was the powerful and influential Michikiniqua who acquiesced to George Rogers Clark's proposals. Immediately the Miami chief had been supported by the chiefs of his subtribes, the Weas, Eel Rivers and Piankeshaws. The remaining Delawares and their kin, the Munsees, fell in with it. With that, the movement became a landslide and even the more warlike chiefs of the Potawatomies—Mtamins, Black Partridge, Topenebe, Nescotnemeg, Main Poche—had agreed to the proposals. By the time the Shawnees arrived, Tecumseh with them, it was all but over. Clark and his army had already departed in peace and headed back toward Kentucky on the Wabash Trail via Vincennes. The unstable coalition of tribes broke apart and scattered back to their own territories, so deep in the Northwest that they had little to fear from incursions of the whites, well protected as always by the buffer zone provided by the Shawnees. But for the Shawnees, there was no buffer zone.

So, the Shawnee warriors had turned around and rode dejectedly back to their own villages, only to find them destroyed, their wives and children prisoners of the whites. Or dead. Or missing. Among the dead, Moluntha; among the missing, Spemica Lawba, Kisathoi, and Tebethto. Tecumapese was there, coming tearfully into the embraces of Wasegoboah and Chiksika. And Tecumseh. She told them all she could of what she knew.

The first indication of any trouble had come fifteen days ago—on October 6. The village of Mackachack had seemed particularly empty, with so many

of the men gone—not only those who had gone with Shemeneto and Blue
Jacket on their respective raids against the *Shemanese* stations in Kentucky but
equally those that had gone with Chiksika, Wasegoboah and Tecumseh, including even the fifteen-year-old triplets and Sinnanatha, to join the confederation of Wabash tribes to oppose the invasion by Clark.[311] Remaining in the
village had been less than a dozen able-bodied men, along with the village's
women, children and elderly. And ninety-four-year-old Moluntha was there,
of course.

The sun had risen only a little over an hour before and Tecumapese had
been in their wegiwa, cooking little round loaves of corn bread, while the two
young women, Kisathoi, who was now eighteen, and Tebethto, sixteen, were
busy cutting and sewing pieces of well-tanned buckskin into garments. Spemica Lawba, who was twelve, was there as well and he was occupied in smooth-
ing a length of osage wood to make a bow. He had been distressed that he
had not been able to go along with the warriors to face Clark's army on the
Wabash.

Mackachack was still very quiet. Some of the women were passing to
and fro to the clear cool waters of the creek to fill bowls and jugs and basins
for the day's needs and some of the men were working outside at various
jobs, but the big task of continuing to harvest the corn from their extensive
fields around the village had not yet begun for the day. When the call for that
was sounded, virtually everyone would drop their present preoccupations and
join together for the community effort.

A dog had begun barking abruptly and then others joined in until there
was a furious din. Inside the wegiwa they could hear voices and a few shouts
and for an instant they stared at one another. Then they leaped to their feet
and rushed outside. The same thing was occurring elsewhere, with everyone
looking out over a prairie to the south. A white man was approaching at a
trot, holding aloft a stick to which was tied a white kerchief. Already the few
warriors in the village were moving out to meet him and a sense of tension
filled everyone.

The warriors had surrounded the white man and were attempting to
question him, but he could not understand them nor they him. In a few
moments one of the questioning warriors, named Anequoi—Squirrel—came
running back and did not stop until he reached Tecumapese.

"It is one of the *Shemanese*," he said, "with much to say, but we can't
understand him." He pointed at her son. "Spemica Lawba has learned much
of their tongue from Sinnanatha and these two," he indicated Kisathoi and
Tebethto, "and we need him to come and tell us what the man is saying."

Tecumapese had nodded and Spemica Lawba had sprinted away with the
warrior at once. The three women had watched as they reached the circle of
warriors and saw him talking with the white man, who gesticulated in an

agitated manner every once in a while. After a few moments another of the warriors, Wapeake—Cold Earth—moved surreptitiously behind and, without warning, buried his tomahawk in the man's head.[312] They scalped him, left him to lie where he fell and returned at a trot to the village, running immediately to Chief Moluntha. After a short time, as the hubbub in the village increased, Spemica Lawba returned.

"He was a bad man," he explained excitedly to his mother and adopted aunts. "He was part of an army coming here under the *Shemanese* chief called Colonel Logan. He ran away from them two nights ago and came here. He wanted silver for telling us. He was a bad man."

"An army, coming here?" Tecumapese had said.

Her son nodded. "And Chief Moluntha has ordered that everything be gathered up and packed for removal at once. He says that since the man deserted the army two evenings ago and came here as rapidly as he could, the army would be slower moving and probably could not possibly get here before tomorrow. But to be safe, he wants Mackachack to be abandoned before the sun is straight up today. We'll go to Wapatomica and maybe onward somewhere from there."

Tecumapese shuddered, remembering, and then told her husband and brothers that Moluntha had assumed, because the white man had been on foot, the whole army was as well, but they had not been. They were all mounted—about eight hundred of them—and they had moved very rapidly. Two hours before the sun was at its highest they had broken from cover and galloped to the attack, brandishing their long knives and rifles and making horrible screams and shrieks as they came.[313] There had been practically no resistance—a few shots sounding here and there as the few warriors tried to make a stand in the face of odds of about fifty to one. The warriors had no hope of winning, only possibly delaying the advance just a little to give their women and children time to escape. As for the latter, they fled screaming and scattering like so many quail bursting from cover.

Tecumapese said that at their own wegiwa, Kisathoi and Tebethto had been momentarily paralyzed. Spemica Lawba had disappeared and she herself, shrieking his name, had plunged into the heavy cover near the creek bank. The sisters, too, had found their legs and hand in hand they fled as fast as they had ever run, managing to reach the cover of a nearby island of woods.

The feeble resistance in Mackachack had been quickly overcome by the attackers. The handful of warriors, including Anequoi and Wapeake, had been killed in the first onslaught. One warrior, called Big Jim, who was running, was chased by an officer on horseback, but Big Jim whirled, fired his gun and shot the officer through the heart, killing him.[314] Big Jim was wounded at the same moment by someone else's shot, and he fell in the deep grass. While some soldiers gathered around their fallen officer, Big Jim quickly reloaded and as the men came toward him, he rose up and killed another. At this the other men poured a barrage of shots into him, killing him, and then rushed up and scalped him. Some of the women held their ground and tried to fight, but they had been cut down easily by the slashing swords. One white chief, leading the right wing, spurred his horse after a fleeing group of eight squaws, his sword held high.[315] As he overtook the heavyset middle-aged Sathea, he clove her skull with his blow and nearly lost his sword as she collapsed. He had found it necessary to brace his boot against her head and jerk hard in order to free his blade. With his balance regained, he had then galloped after the remaining seven and had chopped down six of them in succession, one of them being the seventeen-year-old Tima who had married the young warrior Petoui only three days before the war party had ridden out for the Wabash. The final woman, sister of subchief Red Horse, had stopped and whirled about, holding up a hand to fend off the blow. The white man's long knife had chopped off all four fingers and made a large gash on her scalp, but did not kill her. Other groups of women and children had by then ceased fleeing and had fallen to their knees screaming *"Mattah tshi! Mattah tshi!"*—Do not kill us!

Spemica Lawba had snatched up a tomahawk as the raiders swept in and raced toward the wegiwa of Chief Moluntha. He had heard his mother scream his name and looked back in time to see her plunge into the fringe of brush along the creek. As he had neared the chief's lodge in the center of Mackachack, he heard a horseman coming up at a gallop and ducked into a doorway and out of sight. At almost the same time Moluntha's voice was raised, shouting, *"Bahd-ler! Bahd-ler!"* The horseman was the great frontiersman who had once been their captive, Simon Kenton.

Moluntha had surrendered himself and his three wives to the big frontiersman.[316] Kenton, who had recognized Moluntha and remembered his kindness to him when he had been prisoner here, had accepted Moluntha's proffered tomahawk and had then ordered a group of eight privates who had galloped up to form a protective ring around the chief and his wives. Kenton had then moved off and returned moments later with the principal *Shemanese* chief, Logan, who was mounted on a chestnut mare. They had dismounted and the soldiers had opened their circle to let them enter. Moluntha had taken a paper out of his pouch and handed it to the white chief, smiling, bobbing his head and holding out his hand. Logan had shaken his hand and took the paper and read it. This was the safe conduct pass Moluntha had gotten at the Great Miami Treaty from Colonel Richard Butler. In his broken English, Moluntha had then said, "Moluntha surrenders himself and his wives into the hands of the great white chief Logan."

Logan took the skeletal hand and shook it and said, "You will not be harmed. Nor will your wives." He had then questioned the old chief briefly and Moluntha told him that all the Maykujay towns and Wapatomica were practically deserted, the warriors having gone to fight Clark. Logan, anticipating this, had nodded his head, turned and ordered the privates to surround Moluntha and his wives again, keeping them prisoners but not harming them. Then he and Kenton had ridden off.

Just a few minutes later three men rode up and dismounted, the one who was leading them looking very angry.[317] Moluntha had by this time lighted his pipe and, after taking a few puffs on it himself, was passing it around among the soldiers guarding him. The angry man and his two followers had shouldered their way through the guards and when Moluntha offered the pipe to him, the officer refused it and snarled a question at him.

"Were you at the Blue Licks battle?"

"Yes," Moluntha replied, "I was there."

"God damn you!" the officer shouted, his rage spilling over. "I'll give you Blue Licks pay!"

He had then jerked out his tomahawk and, before anyone could intervene, buried it to the handle in Moluntha's skull, killing him instantly. Moluntha fell with the safe conduct pass still clenched in his hand. Nonhelema had shrieked with rage and launched herself at the white man, but the guards leaped upon her and, with difficulty, brought her to the ground, subduing her.

Hardly had Moluntha fallen and Nonhelema been subdued than Logan and one of his officers returned and reined up, having witnessed everything from a short distance away. At the same time Spemica Lawba burst from the nearby wegiwa doorway with a cry of fury and raced to attack the man who had downed the old chief. One of the man's two followers snatched the boy around the waist as he passed.[318] Taking them by surprise with his unexpected strength and agility, Spemica Lawba had wrenched himself out of the grip, spun around and swung his tomahawk in a tight vicious arc. So extremely close was the blow to landing that it clipped off part of one of the man's eyebrows without breaking the skin. The man jerked back violently, stumbled and fell upon his back. Instantly Spemica Lawba was upon him, landing with bent knees in the man's solar plexus, driving out his wind with a great whoosh. Pinning the mans arms with his knees, Spemica Lawba raised his tomahawk for the killing blow. It had all happened with such swiftness that the others were initially stunned into immobility. Now the second follower snatched the boy's wrist, saving his friend's life and jerking the boy away fiercely, at the same time yanking the tomahawk out of his grip. Spemica Lawba spun again, fell, rolled over and shot back to a crouch, this time coming up with his knife in his hand. But now the others had shaken off their momentary paralysis and two more of the men grabbed his arms and held him. With the knife still in his hand he struggled violently, kicking toward their groins and butting with his head.

The great chief of the *Shemanese,* Tecumapese said, had then dismounted and made the soldiers release him and held out his hand to the boy and, after a moment of indecision, Spemica Lawba had surrendered his knife to him. Then the chief Logan and one of his foremost officers had turned and said many angry words to the man who had killed Moluntha and put him in custody of two of the others.[319] Bahd-ler, who came up a short while later, was so angry he had to be restrained from killing the man who had killed their old chief.

The battle, if such it could be called, was by then all over. Many had escaped in that first panicky exodus. Tecumapese had hidden under the over-hang of the creek bank and had not been found. The thirty-three women and children and a few old men taken prisoners, Spemica Lawba among them, were brought to a central place and the ten dead warriors and twelve others who had been killed, mostly women, were scalped. Three of the whites had been killed and three others wounded.[320] All the captives had been taken away with the army. Whether or not any of them were still alive, especially Spemica Lawba, Tecumapese did not know. Nor did she know what had become of the young women, Kisathoi and Tebethto—neither had been seen since the attack and they were presumed to have been found somewhere and captured or killed.[321]

The remainder of the army's campaign had been carried out without resistance, since those who had escaped from Mackachack had quickly fled to the other towns and warned them and they were abandoned when the army arrived. Army detachments had been sent out to the various towns and during the remainder of that day and the day following, thirteen Shawnee towns had been plundered and destroyed, including, besides Mackachack, Wapatomica and the nearby Kispoko Town and Blue Jacket's Town, Solomon's Town, Mingo Town, Mamacomink, Kekoko, Puckshanoses, Waccachalla, Pecowick, Wapakoneta, and Buckangehela's Town. In addition, all the Shawnee crops, just now ripened, were destroyed.[322]

The returned Shawnees, amidst the ruins of their villages and with their harvest destroyed, which was to carry them through the winter, faced a very bleak prospect. They were filled with fury at the death of old Moluntha who had been so revered in the tribe and, at the same time, Chiksika and Tecumseh sang praises for the courage of their nephew, Spemica Lawba, who had faced the whole army of eight hundred with only a tomahawk and a scalping knife. Tecumapese was proud of him as well, but more grief-stricken at the loss of her son.[323]

Now, with both Shemeneto and Blue Jacket having returned from their raids, the blanket-wrapped chiefs gathered around an outdoor council fire in gloomy session. Tecumseh listened closely to the words of Catahecassa and Shemeneto and the new chief of the Maykujays and second war chief under Shemeneto, Wehyehpihehrsehnwah—Blue Jacket. But what they said were only the words that had been said so many times before and there was little hope in any of them. For his own part, Tecumseh held his tongue, but he knew that somehow, some way, there had to be a means by which the advance of the whites could not only be checked, but by which they could be driven back and the lands restored that had been taken from the Shawnees and other tribes.

There had to be a way!

Chapter 6

[December 18, 1786 — Monday]

⚊ « » ⚊   This was the first truly international Indian council Tecumseh had ever attended and he could not help being impressed. It was being held in the sprawling Huron town called Sindathon's Village, which was named after its venerable old chief. While nowhere near so grand a village as was Kekionga, it was every bit as large, its layout so extensive that it occupied an area fully two miles square on the broad point of ground between the mouth of the Detroit River and the mouth of the Huron River, though its center was closer to the latter than the former. Here, in response to the urgent request from Sagoyewatha—the prominent Seneca chief known to the whites as Red Jacket—had assembled more than two thousand Indians from all directions. Each of the tribal delegations, though drawn together for this council, kept to itself, each forming its own enclave amidst the great assemblage, often viewing its neighbors with thinly masked suspicion or, in certain cases, actual hatred.

Here were not only the Senecas under the twenty-eight-year-old Sagoyewatha, who was clad in the broad-collared black greatcoat he customarily wore at this season, but also, near them, the Mohawks under Thayendanegea—Joseph Brant—his plucked head bare of all but a brushlike topknot at the crown, his lips turned faintly upward in that well-known perpetual sneering smile, his small glittery dark eyes missing nothing. Here were the Hurons under tall, gangly Sindathon and, near them, their offshoot tribe, the Wyandots, under Tarhe—The Crane—and the chunky little chief, Monakaduto—the Half King. The Potawatomies were here in large numbers, some seven hundred of them, under their chiefs Topenebe, Nanimisea, and Nescotnemeg, and the Ottawas under Nichinesica and their war chief, Oulamy. Here were the Chippewas, gathered under Wafrugahqealied, and their subtribe, the Missisaugi, under old Sekahos and Wabacumaga.[324] The Delawares and their subtribe, the Munsees, were here under Buckangehela and Pipe, and here as well were the two hundred forty Shawnees under Catahecassa, Shemeneto, and Blue Jacket, with Chiksika, Wasegoboah, and Tecumseh as part of the delegation.[325] And, so significantly, here also were the Miamis under Michikiniqua—Little Turtle—and, under the various chiefs and subchiefs, the six Miami subtribes—the Weas, the Piankeshaws, the Pepicokias, the Mengakonias, the Kalatikas, and the Ouiatenons, who were also known as the Atchatchakangouens.[326]

The Shawnees had come to this huge council from their new villages in territory allotted to them by the Miamis and Wyandots in the Maumee River flowage, some along the Auglaize, Little Auglaize, Blanchard, and Ottawa, but the majority on the Maumee—including the newest Chalahgawtha that had been established just a short distance upstream from the mouth of the Auglaize. The general movement of the Shawnees had been made easily enough, since so few of their possessions remained following the destruction by Logan's army and, while Tecumseh liked it better there than he had liked the Lower Piqua Town location, to his thinking it was not as nice as the Mackachack area and certainly couldn't compare to the Chalahgawtha site on the Little Miami.

The present council being held here in Sindathon's Town was the result of a series of belts and speeches that had passed between Sagoyewatha and the western tribes through the Wyandots. Over a year ago a confederacy of sorts had been set up among the tribes at his behest, patterned to some degree after the old Iroquois League, in which the good of one was the good of all and all were supposed to protect each other. But now that the real power of the Iroquois was gone, though there remained a certain degree of respect and deference for various individual chiefs of the Six Nations, the glue was not strong enough to make them bind together to the degree that they forgot old animosities. All the chiefs acknowledged that what Red Jacket had been saying over the past year or so was quite logical and very true, that they really did need to form a solid confederacy and protect each other, but logic and emotions conflicted and the old hatreds were too strong to wholly overcome. At the same time all were aware that they could not really depend on the British for help, even though there were some encouraging signs in this direction, including the fact that the British, in contravention to the Treaty of Paris, were beginning some very heavy reinforcements at the posts both at Detroit and Niagara.

It was over the past six or eight weeks that Red Jacket's exchange with the western tribes had become so urgent.

"Brothers and nephews," Red Jacket had said in his first speech, "you will remember that early last spring we lighted a council fire at Buffalo Creek, expecting that all our western brothers from every quarter would be present, but when we began to assemble at it, we found many of you absent. The business that we had then before us was a matter of such high importance to all of us of the same color that we thought it imprudent and too presumptuous to go on with it so long as one single representative should be absent. The business concerned the welfare of every Indian nation in our general confederacy.

"Brothers," the speech had continued, "as we were much disappointed in not having a full council at that time, we sent you a message that, with your concurrence, we would light another fire at Wapatomica Village, it being most central, but which soon afterwards met with the late unhappy disaster. Notwithstanding that we have been so often disappointed from different circumstances, we are still determined to deliver to you the opinions of the Five Nations on the present critical situation of affairs betwixt the Americans and the Indians.[327]

"Brothers and nephews, we beg of you to listen with particular attention to what we are now going to advance. I am sorry to observe that we have all acted imprudently since the peace was made with the Americans. In this observation we mean not to blame anyone in particular; it alludes to us all. We do not intend, however, to recapitulate our several misconducts, but now wish to adopt such measures for our future welfare as will seem prudent to us all.

"Brothers and nephews," Sagoyewatha went on, "when the English desired us to be quiet, we had a council at Sandusky in which it was agreed that, in matters of general concern to the Indians, we were to be of one mind and one council; that the different roads of our messengers should be kept open so that frequent intercourse might be carried on between us and, thus, that whatever place was pitched upon for the council fire, the readiest attendance might be given by us all. You may likewise remember that at that time an invitation was expected from the Americans, in which case it was agreed that our whole Confederacy should attend and that whatever we should agree to with them should be permanent.

"Some time after this, the expected invitation came to our quarter and we immediately let you know, but only *some* of your nations came. This created much confusion amongst the Five Nations, some of whom went to the Americans' council. The Americans very readily took advantage of this, and equally at some other small councils, and began to draw lines upon—and set boundaries in—the countries belonging to the different Indian nations. Some of the young warriors, being dissatisfied with this, were the first cause of fresh ruptures with the Americans."

A belt accompanying the speech was then given and the talk went on to reiterate what the confederacy they had formed was meant to be and to do and that the belt reaffirm this alliance. It was stressed that firm unanimity was essential for the future welfare and happiness of the various tribes. It was especially important, the message went on, that there should be no future separate councils, which could only serve to disunite the tribes.

At this point another belt had been presented—a large black one fully six feet long with representations of human figures hand in hand, along with a heart, signifying their brotherhood and that they were all of one heart. The belt was from the sachems of the Six Nations, who now added their speech, saying: "By this belt we unite all and bind all, particularly to the southward, leaving only a small opening to the westward for those nations of our own color who will, in time, become a further acquisition to our Confederacy; and we earnestly request that no nation will attempt to go out of this circle, as the opening is only intended to fill up the vacancy and not lessen what is already taken in." Here another belt was presented, large and white and with, at each extremity, a human hand held in position for grasping.

"We mean now," the sachems continued, "to inform you of our intentions in case of necessity. We mean to cross at Fort Erie.[328] Some of us are now in readiness on that side." A belt was presented and they went on: "We mean that all the belts we have now spoken upon shall proceed from this council fire to the different nations and then be returned to the Shawnees, as they live the most central."

The sachems had gone on to recount how the Indians had once been in control of the whole territory between where they now were and the Atlantic Ocean and the reason they were not so any longer was because of the lack of unanimity among them. They recalled that when the whites arrived they were at first viewed by the various tribes with awe and veneration, saying that all the Indians were "convinced that we were treating with beings like ourselves and who, through the unanimity they were prudent enough to preserve, had so much the superiority and, consequently, none of the divided efforts of our ancestors to oppose them had any effect. Therefore, let us profit by those things and be unanimous. Let us have a sense of our own value and if, after that, the Great Spirit wills that other colors should subdue us, let it be so— we then cannot reproach ourselves for misconduct."

The message, not yet finished, was so good and so to the core of things that Tecumseh, when he first heard it was stunned, because here were the Iroquois putting into words the thoughts that had been for so long lodged in his own heart and mind and the same thoughts with which he had so fruitlessly questioned Chiksika and Tecumapese. Yet, there was still some element missing, some fundamental *something* that failed to make the ideal become a reality and not even the wise men of the Iroquois had yet ascertained what it was.

The speech from the Iroquois sachems had gone on with the urgent need that there be among themselves no misunderstanding for what was being said. "If we make a war with any nation," they had gone on, "let it result from the great council fire. If we make peace, let it also proceed from our unanimous councils. But so long as we remain disunited, every inconvenience must attend us. The interests of any one nation should be the interests of us all. The welfare of the one should be the welfare of all the others!"

At this point a string of black wampum was presented denoting displeasure and the Iroquois sachems addressed the Wyandots directly. "Brothers, the Wyandots, you are the oldest brothers we have in this quarter but we have never yet been rightly able to distinguish your Fire-place. Whenever we, the Five Nations, came to you on private business, you introduced us to the English fire, when you should have had one under your own roofs. We, therefore, now brighten your fire that we may see it at a distance. If you look upon yourselves as a free people, you should keep up a fire of your own." Another small black belt was presented and the speech continued, "Since we have now brightened your council fire, we hope you will act accordingly where business is to be transacted at it. We shall attend if a fire is lighted on another place for that business. We ought all to attend. Also, we once more encourage you to be diligent on this point." Several strings were presented, denoting a change in subject. "We likewise desire the Wyandots and Delawares to look out for a place for the Shawnees to live, more to the westward, where they might settle afresh."

When the Wyandots sent their reply, Chief Tarhe had begun his message in a conciliatory tone, but all too quickly it degenerated to petty digs and fault finding that he was incapable of stifling. "Brothers of the Five Nations," he replied, "we have heard you deliver the sentiments of your war chiefs and sachems at this council fire, with three other Nations attending. We understand your meanings very fully and now return you thanks for your good speeches, by which you renew everything agreed upon at our council at Sandusky. We find all your sentiments very just and reasonable and that they tend very much to the interest and welfare of the Indians in general, for which reason we again thank you. I hope that at this present time everything will be accomplished that was intended. Everything would have remained in perfect tranquility long before now, but it was your fault it did not, because when you took the hatchet out of the hands of our warriors you did not bury it, but only set it to one side. We then covered it, but nevertheless the foolish young men took it up again. It is owing to that neglect on your part that we are now involved in the present troubles." To emphasize this criticism, a cluster of black strings was presented. "We have," Tarhe went on, "according to your desire, reestablished both the Shawnees and Delawares at the Glaize, so that you see we complied with all your requests.[329] We have likewise paid attention to the Fireplace which you recommended us to keep under our own roofs. We do now fix it at Sindathon's Village near the mouth of the River Detroit."

Answering for the Delawares was Chief Pipe who, with strings of wampum, replied: "Uncles of the Five Nations, we thank you for the speeches of your war chiefs and sachems. We understand them fully and consider them to be very much directed to the interests of the Indians in general and think it very reasonable that every sentence of them should be adhered to. We are exceedingly happy that your ideas are so well founded and give you hearty thanks." He then went on to comment favorably and in detail on every point the Five Nations had made.

Sagoyewatha was pleased with the reply of the Delawares but hardly with that from the Wyandots. Appearing in person with his delegation among them, he said in his response, "Nephews, the Delawares, we clearly understand your answer and thank you for your immediate reply, which you have given to the whole. We are happy that you, our nephews, are so well pleased and that you think what we have advanced is for the interest of us all."

To Tarhe, however, from whom he expected a great deal, Sagoyewatha became stern. "Brothers, the Wyandots," he said, "we are sorry that we are obliged to tell you in this pointed manner, that we are *not* satisfied with your answer. You seem not to make that ample reply that you *might* make, for there certainly must be more upon your minds than what you have let out. We, the Five Nations, are come this great distance to make our proposals and deliver our sentiments, which we thought for the best, and we should be sorry that any of our brothers here should be so lacking in generosity as not to explain themselves fully and give opinions on what we have said. We must *insist* upon it that you Wyandots will be more candid upon this occasion and let us know your *real* sentiments. If you have any better proposals or objections to make, we will be glad to have them. You are the oldest nation in this quarter and you *must* be sensible that the eyes of all the other nations are upon you. It cannot be otherwise than that your minds must be heavy laden with serious thoughts; it is surely expected! And you *cannot* be excused from speaking more fully on the present urgent occasion. How is it possible that you can have so little to say on a subject of such great importance to us all?" Here a black and white belt was presented.

Tarhe was contrite at the reprimand and he had immediately responded more to the satisfaction of the Seneca chief. "Brothers of the Five Nations, you were right when you told us we had not answered you fully. It is true, we did not, and the reason is there were only four nations present. I am determined now, however, to tell you more than I did before. In the first place, let us propose an exchange of prisoners. And let the Shawnees collect the whites amongst them in order to exchange for the prisoners which Colonel Logan took from them lately.

"In the next place," Tarhe continued, "we have now three scouting parties out to watch the movements of the Americans. If I find they mean to pass us, we intend, in accordance with your suggestions, to step on one side and let them do so. If, however, they mean to go to Detroit, we do not know what may happen then. And, if they mean to fall upon us, then I do not know how the warriors will react.

"You have now," he concluded, "brightened our fire and we shall keep it so. It burns quite fresh and the smoke of it reaches the skies. Therefore, this fall we will collect all nations 'round about and determine on something, good or bad, and then we will expect you will give your attendance also."

Those, then, had been the messages passed back and forth between the Iroquois and the western tribes that had led to this present international Grand Council taking place in Sindathon's Village here at the mouths of the Detroit and the Huron. Tecumseh was eager to hear what would be said, since so much of the preliminary talk had coincided with his own strong beliefs that some sort of a well-knit Indian coalition was essential if they were to stave off the continuing unbridled advance of the Americans. How could it be, Tecumseh wondered, that only a few short years ago the Shawnees had almost the whole of the Ohio country as theirs and now they had virtually none of it except that which had just been allotted to them by the Wyandots, Delawares, and Miamis in the valleys of the Auglaize and Maumee?

It was no surprise, as their sessions began, that Sagoyewatha had quickly been selected as chief spokesman to deliver the message to the American delegation in attendance. Thayendanegea had obviously wanted the role, but he was a far better war chief than he was orator, lacking the better skills of articulation to put his ideas across. Even he realized this and grudgingly backed off from the role in favor of Red Jacket.

Sagoyewatha, as was customary, began his message in a low key but gradually increased its volume and intensity. "To the Congress of the United States of America. Brothers of the thirteen United States of America, it is now more than three years since peace was made between the king of Great Britain and you, but we, the Indians, were disappointed, finding ourselves not included in that peace, according to our expectations. We thought that its conclusion would have promoted a friendship between the United States and Indians and we might enjoy that happiness that formerly existed between ourselves and our elder brothers, the British. We have received two very agreeable messages from the thirteen United States. We also received a message from the king, whose war we engaged in, desiring us to be quiet, which we accordingly complied with. During the time of this tranquility, we were deliberating the best method we could to form a lasting reconciliation with the thirteen United States. Plus at the same time, we thought that we were entering upon a reconciliation and friendship with a set of people born on the same continent with ourselves, certain that the quarrel that was between us was not of our own making. In the course of our councils, we believed we had hit upon an expedient that would promote a lasting peace between us."

A note of regret came into Sagoyewatha's voice as he continued. "Brothers, we are still of the same opinion as to the means which may reconcile us to each other. Although we had the best thought in mind during the before mentioned period, we are sorry to find that mischief has nevertheless occurred between you and us. We are still anxious to put our plan of accommodation into execution and we will briefly inform you of the means that seem to us to be most probable of affecting a firm and lasting peace and reconciliation.

"The first step toward this," he went on, his voice hardening now, "should be that all treaties carried on with the United States on our part should be with the general voice of the whole Confederacy and carried on in the most open manner, without any restraint on either side. And, especially as matters concerning the land are often the subject of our councils with you and a matter of the greatest importance and of general concern to us, in this case we hold it *indispensably necessary* that if *any* cessions of our lands should be made, it should be in the most public manner and by the united voice of the Confederacy—holding *all* partial treaties as void and of no effect.

"Brothers!" Sagoyewatha's voice became harsher, more accusatory. "We think it is owing to you—having managed everything your own way—that the tranquility between us, since the peace, has not lasted and the essential good has been followed by mischief and confusion. You kindled your council fires where *you* thought proper, without consulting *us,* at which you held separate treaties, and having entirely neglected our plan of having a General Conference with the different nations of the Confederacy. Had this plan happened, we have reason to believe everything would now have been settled between us in a most friendly manner. We did everything in our power at Fort Stanwix to induce you to follow this plan, as our real intentions were, at that very time, to promote peace and concord between us, that we might look upon each other as friends, having given you no cause or provocation to be otherwise." The stridency left his voice abruptly and he became more conciliatory. "Notwithstanding the mischief that has happened, we are still sincere in our wishes to have peace and tranquility established between us, earnestly hoping to find the same inclinations in you.

"Brothers," the conciliation became overt appeal, "we therefore wish you would take it in consideration and let us speak to you in the manner we proposed. Let us have a treaty with you early in the spring. Let us pursue reasonable steps. Let us meet halfway for our mutual convenience. We shall then bury in oblivion the misfortunes that have happened and meet each other on a footing of friendship.

"Brothers, we say let us meet halfway and let us pursue such steps as are becoming to upright and honest men. Until such time," again the hardness creeping back into his voice, "we beg that you will prevent your surveyors and other people coming upon our side of the Ohio River. We have told you before we wished to pursue just and equitable steps, and we are *determined* that they shall appear just and reasonable in the eyes of the world. *This* is the determination of all the chiefs of our Confederacy now assembled here, notwithstanding the accidents that have happened in our villages, even when in council, when several innocent chiefs were killed when absolutely engaged in promoting a peace with you, the thirteen United States. Although then interrupted, the chiefs here present still wish to meet you in the spring for the before mentioned good purpose, when we hope to speak to each other without either haughtiness or menace."

Sagoyewatha paused momentarily, catching himself, as if realizing he was bending too far for pride and self-respect to withstand. Again the character of his delivery changed as he became more clipped and definitive in his remarks to the Americans. "Brothers, we again request of you, in the most earnest manner, to order your surveyors and others that mark out lands, to cease from crossing the Ohio until we shall have spoken to you, because the mischief that has recently happened has originated in that quarter. We shall likewise prevent our people from going over until that time. It shall not be *our* fault if the plan we have suggested to you should not be carried into execution. Brothers, in that case, the event will be *very* precarious. And if fresh ruptures issue, we hope to be able to exculpate ourselves—and shall, *most assuredly, with our united force,* should we unfortunately be obliged to defend those rights and privileges which have been transmitted to us by our ancestors. And if we should, thereby, be reduced to misfortunes, the world will pity us when they think of the amicable proposals we now make to prevent the unnecessary effusion of blood. These are our thoughts and firm resolves and we earnestly desire that you will transmit to us, as soon as possible, your answer, be it what it may. This is done at our Confederate council fire at the Huron village near the mouth of the Detroit River, December eighteenth, seventeen hundred and eighty-five."

While all present at this council in Sindathon's Village marveled at the masterpiece of oratory by Sagoyewatha, Tecumseh brooded. The way the Seneca chief had begun, Tecumseh thought he was going to better develop the plan for a confederacy, but by the time the council was concluded, he had no doubt that it would fail, just as the others before it had failed.

Alone, of the Shawnees, Tecumseh had no newly elevated hopes that any of this would have beneficial result for Shawnees or, for that matter, for any of the tribes. He was now wholly convinced in his own mind that, irrespective of the platitudes they voiced, the United States did not want peace, that they did not want the Indians to have a confederacy or to meet them in their confederacy, and that their sole objective was to disunite, divide and then conquer them all. True, the Shawnees now had to go farther in order to reach out against the whites in Kentucky, but reaching out they were and they would continue to do so as they strove to take from the *Shemanese* whatever food supplies and goods they could to make up for those that Logan's army had destroyed, so that at least their people would be able to get through the winter without dying of famine and exposure.

No, so far as Tecumseh and many others of the Shawnees were concerned, despite Sagoyewatha's attempts to conciliate and mediate, the *Shemanese* would enjoy no lessening of the Shawnee raiders among them.[330]

[March 10, 1787 — Saturday]

The prisoner exchange was held on the day after Tecumseh's nineteenth birthday and what had started out with considerable apprehension and then evolved into a joyous affair had ultimately nosedived to a disaster that only served to strengthen Tecumseh's belief that the whites were not to be trusted at any time, *ever!*

It was Blue Jacket, acting on the suggestion made by the residue Iroquois and their new confederation of tribes at the recent Grand Council, who had been responsible for setting up a prisoner exchange involving the Shawnees. Simon Kenton had made similar efforts where the Kentuckians were concerned. The story of how it had all come about came out at the council held a dozen days ago at Blue Jacket's Town—the first general tribal council Blue Jacket had ever called. To the assembled chiefs and warriors he had related in meticulous detail what had transpired.

Following Grand Council advice at Sindathon's Village, Blue Jacket related, he had solitarily crossed the Spaylaywitheepi nearly opposite to the mouth of Limestone Creek and, skirting the Limestone settlement and traveling with great care to keep out of sight, he had gone some four miles inland to Kenton's Station on the stream the whites were calling Lawrence Creek. For nearly five hours he had watched the well-built redbrick structure that was Kenton's house until at last he was rewarded by seeing the frontiersman emerge, mount his horse and set off alone on the wagon road toward Limestone. No one else had been in sight and so, when Kenton was within forty yards of him, Blue Jacket had emerged from the cover where he was hiding, holding a white cloth high in one hand and his other hand upraised, palm forward, both as a sign of peace and to show Kenton he was unarmed.

Kenton had stopped with an exclamation and instantly brought his rifle to bear on Blue Jacket, but he hadn't fired—a reaction upon which Blue Jacket had risked his life. Slowly the frontiersman had lowered his rifle and asked the Shawnee who he was and what he wanted. That was the start of it. Blue Jacket had identified himself and then had calmly explained that the Shawnees were holding many whites from Kentucky as prisoners, just as the Kentuckians were holding many Shawnees they had captured. Could a prisoner exchange be arranged? Would the whites meet them in peace on the Spaylaywitheepi shore directly across from Limestone?[331] Would the whites bring their prisoners and promise peace and surrender them to the Shawnees if the Shawnees did the same with their white prisoners?

Kenton was very much taken with the idea and agreed, though he later told Blue Jacket that he had faced much opposition from settlers who had wanted to lay an ambush and kill the Shawnee party. Only the fact that the majority of prisoners on both sides would probably have been killed as a result swayed them from the idea. After quite a bit of negotiation it had been set up and today's exchange had been the result.

It had been a wary and suspicious two factions of people who had met each other at the designated site earlier today and many important figures on both sides had been present. With Blue Jacket was his superior as war chief, Shemeneto, and such subchiefs as Red Horse, Meouseka, King John, Captain Billy, and Petweowa—Captain Wolf—plus some sixty warriors, including Chiksika and Tecumseh. Among the whites with Kenton were Benjamin Logan, Robert Patterson, Benjamin Whiteman, Luther Calvin, Robert Todd, George Hany and their old formidable enemy Daniel Boone—Sheltowee— along with some sixty other frontiersmen and settlers.

There was considerable talk before the prisoners had been brought up— those of the Shawnees still held far back in the woods and those of the whites not yet having crossed the river. The speakers professed the need for peace in the country and spoke of friendship and of how the reds and whites needed to live together as brothers. It was largely talk that was merely politic and meant little. Everyone knew it, yet all participated because the matter of exchanging prisoners was foremost. Blue Jacket had whispered to Shemeneto that he was sure they would see some sort of white treachery before the day was done and the ugly old war chief had grunted knowingly. Tecumseh had felt sickened by the professions of friendship being exchanged and itched to draw his war club and charge among them. There were whites, such as Luther Calvin, who felt the same way and gripped their rifles menacingly while giving the Indians hard looks.

Blue Jacket and Shemeneto were especially vexed when one of their own subchiefs—King John, as he had named himself—had spoken. The head of a small Maykujay village with a population of sixty warriors and ninety women and children, he was one of those who had almost gone away westward when the tribe split and many times since then had expressed the wish that he had. Others wished it, too, Blue Jacket among them, since the man was a weakling who had never shown himself to be much of a warrior and caused more trouble among their people with his persistent whining about conditions than practically anyone else. When he spoke today, King John gravely told the whites that the Shawnees did indeed want peace and so desirous of this was he that, lest the warriors of his own village violate it, he planned to leave and join their brothers in the Missouri country immediately after this exchange and any of his people who wished to do so were welcome to accompany him. This was flagrant weakness in the face of an enemy and Blue Jacket, as well as Tecumseh and Chiksika and many others, felt shamed by it. However, it did help to ease the tensions prevailing between the two groups.

Somehow they had overcome the hurdles and the prisoners were finally brought forward and exchanged and there was much trauma involved. There were many whites among the Indians who did not *want* to be exchanged and ten, including Sinnanatha—Stephen Ruddell—who disliked the idea so much that he had hidden at the village and was unable to be found to be brought along. Similarly, among the whites there were a few Shawnee prisoners who had become accustomed to living with the whites and wanted to stay, among them the youth now known to them as Johnny Logan—Spemica Lawba. Many tears were shed, of sorrow as well as joy, but at last the exchange had been made.

Chiksika and Tecumseh were particularly upset when their nephew, Spemica Lawba, became very emotional in his departure from General Logan, wringing the older man's hand and embracing him and, worst of all, saying the words neither brother had ever expected to hear from the boy's lips. "Father," Spemica Lawba had said to the destroyer of his own village, "I will miss you and the others greatly, and I make this vow: to my white father I will always be Johnny Logan and I will never raise my hand against him or his army."

Nonhelema, very thin and drawn, was among the prisoners the whites returned, she having been kept in confinement the whole duration of her captivity because of the whites being uncomfortably aware of the warriorlike fighting ability of this huge and powerful woman.

A celebration had begun following the exchange. It had been a simple exchange, with no ransom in money or goods demanded by either side. A huge barbecue was begun with a couple of good beeves brought by the whites and two fine elk provided by the Shawnees. Indians and whites alike stacked their guns. More people crossed the river and dancing was begun.

The gaiety degenerated however when Luther Calvin recognized one of the Indian horses as having belonged to a settler named William McGinnis who had been killed in a raid not very long before. Immediately he swore he would get the animal "if I have to scalp every Injen here to get it!" It took the combined efforts of Boone, Kenton, and Blue Jacket to smooth matters, and the two whites known to the Indians as Bahd-ler and Sheltowee finally purchased the animal in question from Shemeneto for a keg of whiskey. However, the edge had been taken off the frolic and the whites started returning across the Spaylaywitheepi. The final three boats of the whites were only a hundred yards from the Ohio shore when it was discovered that Calvin and some of the other whites had earlier slipped away, overpowered the two guards where the Indian horses had been tied and had succeeded in stealing fourteen of them and swimming them across the river. The Shawnees howled with rage and a few shots were fired by the Indians at the final boats but they were ineffective and the whites in those boats paddled furiously and had quickly drawn themselves well out of range.

Now, returning with liberated friends and relatives toward their own villages, Tecumseh still felt turmoil boiling within him. He was deeply disturbed as Spemica Lawba chattered on and on about the family into which he had been adopted and the school he had attended and the wonderfully comfortable life he had led. How could his nephew have become so turned around in his thinking in so short a time? And Tecumseh wondered as well, as he had often wondered before, why it was that in any kind of civil dealings the Indians ever had with the whites, somehow it was the Indians who always wound up coming off second best.[332]

[October 3, 1787 — Wednesday]

Last March following the prisoner exchange, Tecumseh had felt that a new, all-out war with the *Shemanese* was so imminent that nothing could prevent its eruption and then, at the last moment, the threat abruptly eased when the Virginia government, acting on a directive from Congress, positively forbade any whites crossing over to the Ohio side of the Ohio River, under the strictest of penalties; similarly, Catahecassa, acting on the recommendation of the Confederacy of Western Tribes, forbade any war parties crossing the river to the Kentucky side to maraud. Ignoring the directives, Indians and whites alike continued to cross over and skirmishes did occur, but they were essentially minor events and the formal relationships between the red and white governments seemed to be in a sort of stasis.

In large measure this new atmosphere in the land had come about as the result of the major congressional action that was being called the Ordinance of 1787. Through this ordinance was officially established the gigantic tract of land called the Northwest Territory, embracing the land north and west of the Ohio River, clear to the Canadian border in the north and the Mississippi in the west.[333] By act of Congress, all this vast territory was established as a commonwealth—the first in the world whose organic law recognized every man as free and equal. It was an amazing document and so unique in its establishment that wherever posted, especially along the frontier, it was for weeks the single most important topic of discussion.[334]

Article Five of the ordinance was the one that caused no little degree of trepidation to ripple through the tribes presently residing within the bounds of the newly created Northwest Territory: in due time it was to be divided into no less than three states, nor more than five. The westernmost state in the Territory, eventually to be called Illinois, was to be bounded on the west by the Mississippi River, on the south by the Ohio River and on the east by the Wabash River as far upstream from its mouth as Vincennes and then, from there, on a line due north to the Canadian border. The middle state, eventually to be called Indiana, would also have the Ohio River as its southern boundary and its eastern boundary a line drawn from the western edge of the mouth of the Great Miami River due north to the Canadian border. Finally, the easternmost state, eventually to be known as Ohio, would take in the rest of that land to the east of the Indiana line and to the north and west of the Ohio River and the western border of Pennsylvania, northward to the Canadian border. The ordinance added, however, that Congress could "at its future discretion, form either one or two additional states [to be called Michigan and Wisconsin] in that part of the said Territory lying north of an east and west line drawn through the southerly bend or extreme of Lake Michigan."

What, if anything, encouraged the Indians most about the ordinance—and caused the Kentuckians to seethe with indignation—was found in Article Three of Section 14, which quite sanctimoniously declared in part:

> *The utmost good faith shall always be observed towards the Indians; their lands and property shall never be taken from them without their consent; and in their property, rights, and liberty they shall never be invaded or disturbed, unless in just and lawful wars authorized by Congress; but laws founded in justice and humanity shall, from time to time, be made, for preventing wrongs being done to them, and for preserving peace and friendship with them.*[335]

Paradoxically, another land office, to help process the influx of buyers flocking to the country, was opened at Louisville and was expressly created for receiving the locations and surveys made *north* of the Ohio River. It was very much needed by the whites, since literally thousands of land-hungry people were pouring down the Ohio River. The Virginia Legislature approved the layout of Limestone as a city on one hundred acres of land, "the property of John May and Simon Canton," and incorporated it as the city of Maysville.[336]

The Indians also learned that a white father had been named to be in charge of the land in which they lived. Congress, in establishing the various jurisdictions and territories within the Northwest Territory, had appointed as governor of the Ohio Territory an old-line soldier who had served an active role in the battles of Trenton and Princeton. He was a brigadier general named Arthur St. Clair, a Pennsylvanian.

There was more disturbing news for the tribes. Fort Harmar, at the mouth of the Muskingum, was now well established and so was the new Fort Finney directly across the Ohio River from Louisville in the Indiana territory. Close to Fort Harmar, construction was well under way on a very formidable, two-story walled fortification just east of the mouth of the Muskingum and this was being called Campus Martius.[337] There was a strong rumor afloat that from Fort Harmar, Colonel Josiah Harmar would, next spring or summer, launch a major United States Army offensive against the Shawnees.

That was just a rumor and rumors were always plentiful on the frontier. More to the moment at the present, suddenly and with but few exceptions, throughout the land there was a tenuous and uneasy peace, but a peace nonetheless. Chiksika immediately made plans to go see his wife in Tennessee and invited Tecumseh to go with him and Tecumseh had accepted with alacrity. However, the trip had been postponed because some April flooding of the Maumee had caused the evacuation of the new Chalahgawtha, just upstream on the Maumee from the mouth of the Auglaize. It was deemed pointless to rebuild it there, since future flooding would no doubt do the same thing and it was at this juncture that Catahecassa accepted an invitation from Michikiniqua of the Miamis to establish their newest Chalahgawtha at a location he designated close to Kekionga.

Everyone assisted in the move and the new village site, on high ground and situated pleasantly amidst a scattering of great oaks, elms, hickories, maples, and beeches, was located only three miles downstream from Kekionga on the north bank of the Maumee.[338] For the first time the Shawnees built a village that was comprised more of log cabins than of the transitory stick and bark structures called wegiwas. With the help of some of the British and Miamis from Kekionga, they soon had a first-rate village and one of a more permanent nature than ever before, with a small but very fine bubbling spring located within its midst.

The principal work of building the new Chalahgawtha was completed by the beginning of the Heat Moon and Tecumapese, Wasegoboah, the triplets, Spemica Lawba, and Sinnanatha moved in, with plenty of room left for Tecumseh and Chiksika when they should return. The trip Chiksika proposed had, over these weeks, evolved into plans for a trip as major as the first trip taken together, perhaps even more extensive than that and certainly longer in duration. As soon as the other members of the family were well ensconced in their large new cabin, Chiksika and Tecumseh mounted up, along with ten of their strong young friends who had wanted to go, and headed west, anticipating they would be gone for the better part of two years, perhaps even more.

Though initially Chiksika and Tecumseh had been inclined to take the sixteen-year-old triplets along with them, Sauwaseekau and Kumskaka showed little desire to be included in so extensive a trip. Lowawluwaysica, on the other hand, incorrectly assuming he was to be left behind, became repugnantly strident in demands to be taken along. Had he acted in a more pleasant manner, this probably would have occurred, but he became not only abusive, he also became—as he was increasingly these days—disgustingly drunk. As a result they did not take him, simply because of the problem they knew he would be to them throughout their travels. As Tecumseh himself succinctly put it to Chiksika, "We had enough troubles with a drunk on our last journey."

Though the ultimate destination was to be the village of Running Water where Chiksika's Cherokee wife and daughter were waiting, they reasoned that it would probably be at least a year before they arrived there. The small party headed directly west, but did not get terribly far on the first leg of their journey—actually only three miles, to Kekionga. Some of the young men of their party had not yet visited the nearby amazing Indian city in the wilderness and were delighted to stop there for a while. They amused themselves in various pursuits—visiting, gambling, engaging in sports and, of course, spending hours on end in the English trading posts where they closely viewed—and often coveted—the wondrous assortment of goods on display.

While this was occurring Chiksika and Tecumseh remained for a fortnight as guests of Michikiniqua in his wonderful house. Despite their disappointment the previous year when Michikiniqua had been first to accept the peace proposals by General Clark, they still had a great deal of respect for him and Tecumseh was especially impressed with—and talked with him for hours about—his ideas for a stronger confederacy of tribes to be formed to present a united defensive front against the encroaching whites. As guests in Michikiniqua's house, the Shawnee brothers were for the first time thrown into close association with the Miami chief's adopted son, Apekonit—William Wells—for whom they immediately formed a strong dislike.

The carrot-topped adopted Miami, who had been nicknamed Epiconyere, was not without considerable courage, but he was also a very nervous individual and this aspect of his character intensified whenever the discussion turned to war with the whites. At such times his eyes would blink rapidly and he would retreat into himself almost to the point of rudeness. When at last the brothers gathered up the other members of their party and left Kekionga to continue their journey westward, it was Tecumseh who turned to Chiksika and made a serious comment.

"I like Michikiniqua very much but I cannot say the same about Apekonit. Although he is Michikiniqua's adopted son and they are very close, one day we will find that he is our enemy and all that he has learned about us and our ways he will turn against us."

Chiksika had nodded, recognizing that this was another of Tecumseh's predictions, and his little brother's predictions always came to pass.

They had followed the Wabash River past the mouth of the Tippecanoe River to the village of Ouiatenon, where the old French fortification still stood and was being used as a sort of trading post.[339] Not caring particularly for this old village, the party only stayed a day and then went on, following the Indian trail that led northwestward to the Iroquois River, which they then followed downstream to its mouth at the Kankakee River. Here was Nescotnemeg's Town, a pleasant Potawatomi village of over a hundred large tepees. They spent a pleasant few days here and also at the village of the chief with the withered hand, Main Poche, some ten miles down the Kankakee. Farther yet down that river they came to where it joined the Des Plaines River to form the Illinois River and this much larger river they followed for some thirty miles downstream until they came to the Potawatomi village called Pimitoui on the north bank.[340]

It was in Pimitoui that a youth of about sixteen became entranced by Chiksika and Tecumseh and attached himself to them. He was a very powerfully built young man named Chaubenee—Coal Burner. About five feet nine inches tall and weighing at least two hundred pounds, he was greatly muscled and there seemed not to be an ounce of fat on his entire body.[341] This young man clung with great concentration to every word uttered by the brothers, begging them, when they fell silent, for more stories of their past battles with the *Shemanese*—whom his own people called *Chemokemon*—and urging them on to greater details about their journeys together. His face was round and friendly, and he laughed often. Although this was a Potawatomi village, the young Indian was not Potawatomi by birth. His father was an Ottawa named Opawana and his mother a Seneca. He himself had been born in a village on the Maumee River.[342]

Chaubenee had been brought to the Illinois country at an early age by his parents, to live here at Pimitoui under old Chief Spotka, who was also known by the name of Hanokula. His father, Opawana, who had fought beside Pontiac at the siege of Detroit in 1763, had several times accompanied Pontiac to the Illinois country. He had also helped avenge the assassination of Pontiac at the hands of the Illinois Confederacy. He had liked the area and, years later, came back to live here, not at all discomfited by the fact that Pimitoui was a Potawatomi village.

At present, Opawana's sons, Chaubenee and Mukonse—Little Bear—who was two years younger, were thought of more as Potawatomi than as Ottawa. Should either marry a Potawatomi woman—which was likely in Chaubenee's case, since he was in love with Canoku, daughter of Chief Spotka—they would then, in actuality, become Potawatomi.[343] Chaubenee's little brother also became an instant admirer of Chiksika and Tecumseh, though not with quite the degree of hero worship as evinced by Chaubenee. When, after a visit of several weeks there, the Shawnee party had finally left Pimitoui, still heading west, Chaubenee begged permission to go along but the decision went against him.

"You have not thought on it enough yet, Chaubenee," Chiksika told him. "There are many hardships we will face, especially over the winter, and it is altogether possible that we will aid our friends, the Sacs, against the Osages. If so, there would be grave danger. Think on it longer and if, when we return here, which we plan on doing, you are still of a mind to join us, we will welcome you."

So they had left the disappointed youth behind and moved on, stopping here and there and moving northwestward until at last they reached Saukenuk, the principal Sac village located on the Rock River very close to its mouth at the Mississippi.[344] They had been heartily welcomed by the Sacs who, having just finished the harvest, were preparing to go on their annual winter hunt. The crops had been cleaned and packed for storage—great strings of crabapples had been sun dried, pouches filled with dried grains or vegetable seeds for next year's planting; all these food goods were packed into well-greased skin bags that were themselves wrapped in bark and buried in specially located holes that were then carefully disguised so no one else would find them. When this work was done and the harvest feast—the largest and most boisterous of the year—was completed, a full tribal council had been called and hunting areas allotted for the coming winter. The visiting Shawnees eagerly accepted their invitation to come along.

It was today that the village crier had walked about through Saukenuk calling that this was the day of departure. Within a few hours the various hunting parties were filing away and, with one of them, headed for the country of the Dakotah Sioux, were Chiksika, Tecumseh, and their ten Shawnee followers.

"It is just as well, Chiksika," Tecumseh confided as they rode out with their hosts, "that no attacks on the Osages were planned this season by our friends, the Sacs. You would have wanted to go along, I know, but I could not have done so." He hesitated and then corrected himself. "I *would* not have done so. And because I would not, I would be thought of as a coward."

"I would not think of you as a coward, little brother," Chiksika replied slowly. "Not for that or anything else. I know you too well for that. But I think you have a reason beyond what others might think. Will you share it with me?"

Tecumseh nodded. "I will join any tribe fighting against the whites, who are our great enemy," he said, "but I will not put my hand to the killing of Indians by Indians, no matter what tribe. We are a people and should not kill each other. If we do not realize that, how can we hope to stand against the whites?"

[September 17, 1788 — Tuesday]

The many months the Shawnee party under Chiksika had spent with the Sacs had been a wonderful interlude for them all. It had not only given them, Tecumseh in particular, the opportunity to share firsthand in the activities of a culture different in many respects from their own, but had also provided them an opportunity to be away from war with the whites and to experience what Indian life must really have been like for their own people through the seasons before the problems with the whites arose.

From Saukenuk last fall they had ridden to the great grasslands of the Dakotahs to the north and west, where the terrain was virtually devoid of trees and one could see for miles to an unbroken horizon. Often the great prairies were dotted with bison herds so vast that they blanketed the terrain with their hundreds of thousands of forms. For weeks they remained on horseback, pursuing the bison in a thunder of confusion, stalking the elk and dainty pronghorns, cutting the meat into strips and drying it on racks over smoky fires for a food source to last them well over the winter and, all the while, keeping a close eye out for the much feared war parties of the Sioux.

As the bitterness of winter arrived in earnest, hunting ceased and they moved northeastward to the pine forests where trapping began, using steel traps purchased from the traders as well as constructing deadfalls and setting snares. The days were spent in checking the traps, removing their catches of mink, otter, beaver, marten, and muskrat, baiting and resetting the traps, snares, and deadfalls, skinning the fur animals that had been caught and, finally, toward the end of winter, congregating with their bales of fur skins at the trading posts to barter their catch for the guns and goods they needed and wanted.

They had then moved farther east to the great groves of maples where the trees were tapped and the sap boiled until rendered down to the brown sugar that was always such a valuable item in the trade as well as for their own consumption. By then the Planting Moon was approaching and the various parties from all over had converged once again at Saukenuk and the other permanent Sac villages. Here the various families busied themselves opening the caches where the foods and seeds and supplies had been buried the previous fall. A portion of the preserved harvest of last fall—dried corn and beans and the seeds of pumpkin, squash, and sunflower—were ground into meals for bread and various dishes. Great kettles of stew in which these and other ingredients were tossed, along with large quantities of jerked and dried meats from their hunting, bubbled constantly over the fires in their lodges and the families relaxed, gorging themselves and smoking their pipes as they alternately told their own stories and listened to the stories of others, boasting of their hunts or their raids into enemy country and many of them imbibing the liquor procured from traders.

Soon the women and children trooped out with their hoes to the gardens and fields, using the seeds that were set aside for planting this year's crop. Most of the fields went unprotected, but sometimes a garden area would be enclosed with a flimsy fencing of sapling poles to keep out the deer and bison and occasional elk.

Feasting and dancing had followed the planting—a sort of going away festivity, since immediately afterwards the males of the tribe again split into various parties and moved out. Some of the groups headed westward through the Iowa country to the area of the Council Bluffs, where hunting was good for elk and buffalo and where the excitement of the hunt was spiced with the element of danger from possible attack by raiding parties of Osages. Others, including the group Chiksika and his party accompanied, went up the Mississippi to the region of Apple River where the Sac and Fox mines were located and where they dug and smelted lead ore. Their methods were crude but by mid-July they had made close to four thousand pounds of pure metal in misshapen pigs, these to be used in barter with traders and with other tribes. It was close to the Apple River lead mines, but on the opposite side of the Mississippi, that the Sacs and Foxes had just given to the trader Julien Dubuque, as a mark of respect and affection, a large piece of land containing lead mines.[345] While they were gone to their hunting and mining, the women, children, and elderly who had remained at the villages tended to the crops, fished, and sundried or smoked their catches, gathered great armloads of reeds to be woven into mats upon which they would sleep and eat, gathered bark to form into boxes and sewed skins together to make pouches, these items to be used as the parcels in which to bury the food and supplies to sustain them over the winter. Somehow there never seemed to be time enough to do all that needed to be done or all that they wanted to do.

Converging on the home villages again, the Sacs and their brother tribe, the Foxes, engaged in a series of feasts and dances, participated in wedding ceremonies, repaired bows and guns, made arrow shafts, chipped flint heads for arrows and spears, continued to cultivate crops and attended various coun-

cils. Horse racing was very popular, as was the violent sport of lacrosse, played
on a grassy field upwards of three hundred yards in length—a sort of modified
mayhem where blood flowed freely, eyes were blackened, teeth knocked out,
arms and legs—and sometimes heads—broken. The Sacs and Foxes were great
gamblers and Chiksika and Tecumseh and their fellow Shawnees watched
closely, intrigued not only by the intensity of the sports but by the fervor of
the betting, where almost anything could be a prize—guns, bows, arrows,
tomahawks, horses, blankets, liquor. The most furiously played games were
those competitions involving teams of visiting Winnebagoes, Potawatomies,
Menominees, Iowas, and Chippewas, where team spirit became nationalistic
and passions reached high pitches.

Now, at last, as harvest time began again, Chiksika and his party bade
their hosts farewell and set off, following the west shore of the Mississippi
northward all the way up to the village of Wabasha, chief of the woodland
Sioux, just downstream from the mouth of the Chippewa River.[346] They were
greeted warmly, treated well, presented with gifts of food and invited to return.

They returned down the east side of the Mississippi, stopping at several
villages of the Menominee and Winnebago and finally at the village called
Prairie du Chien, where there had long been a large British trading post. Here
they visited briefly with Winnebagoes who had gathered for prewinter trading,
then moved directly eastward to the principal Winnebago villages at Four
Lakes.[347] By the time they reached the mouth of the Milwackie at Lake Michigan, where Chief Siggenauk of the Potawatomies had his villages, the weather
had begun turning cold.[348] Again they were received with honors and spent
enjoyable hours listening to Siggenauk's stories and striving to remain polite
when urged that the Shawnees should make peace with the Americans, since
he was sure it was those whites who would eventually become the only power
in this vast country.[349]

The ride down the southwestern shore of Lake Michigan was delightful
and they spent three days at the tiny trading post in the place the Indians called
Checagou.[350] They traded at Jean Baptiste DuSable's small, well-equipped
trading post and visited with Potawatomi Chief Black Partridge in his village
close by, finding him a man of very pleasant disposition who consistently
wore a gold crescent ornament dangling from his nostrils. At their departure,
they moved southward across the Checagou Portage to the Des Plaines River
and followed it downstream to where it met the Kankakee and formed the
Illinois River. From there it was not too many miles downstream to the village
of Pimitoui.

It was when within sight of Pimitoui, while they moved along casually,
talking as they rode, that Chiksika remarked on how much Tecumseh had
changed in the past few years.

"There are great things in store for you, little brother," he said. "I see you as becoming a very important man."

Tecumseh grinned. Chiksika was almost as widely known for his prophetic abilities as their father had been. Tecumseh, too, had considerable prophetic skill, though not yet so much recognized for it as was Chiksika.

A joyous cry reached them and a distant rider came galloping up, waving his arms and hooting wildly. Long before they could make out the features of the newcomer, the very size of him left no doubt as to his identity. Chaubenee thundered up, wild with excitement at their return, full of questions about where they had gone, what they had done and what they had seen. Finally he asked, "Where are you going now?"

"First to the Missouri country to see our mother," Tecumseh replied, "at Cape Girardeau, then far to the south to where Chiksika's wife and daughter are in the Cherokee village of Running Water."

Chiksika spoke. "Last year when we were here you wished to go with us. I told you to think on it more. Have you done so?"

Chaubenee nodded gravely. "I still wish to go with you."

"Then you will."

In the morning they rode out on the trail heading south, Chaubenee happily astride the horse given to him by his elderly father, Opawana. Though Chaubenee greatly liked both of the brothers, it was to Tecumseh that he was most drawn, possibly because they were closer in age, possibly because there was about Tecumseh a personal magnetism that was all but overpowering, yet most difficult to assess. Wherever Tecumseh happened to be, Chaubenee was sure to be close at hand.

It was a friendship both young men felt sure would last for a very long time.

[April 13, 1789 — Monday]

When the dozen warriors led by Chiksika had arrived in the Cape Girardeau area a little over a week after leaving Pimitoui, they were welcomed by many old friends in the Apple Creek village of the absentee Shawnees, but the person they had come specifically to see was not there. The mother of Chiksika and Tecumseh, they were told, had left her village west of the Mississippi several months before with several young Shawnee men who had offered to escort her on the journey. Methotasa, who had not been too mentally competent for some time, had suddenly seemed perfectly normal and had expressed a strong desire to see her family—not the one in Ohio, but the one she had not seen since she was a maiden and had been kidnapped from them by the Shawnees—the Cherokees. She had realized her father was dead, but she had hoped to find her mother and sisters if possible.

Chiksika thought he might know where to find her, having heard on numerous occasions as a boy the story of her capture by the war party of which Pucksinwah had been a part. They had decided to stay in the Kispokotha village at Apple Creek to rest a few days before moving along on her trail. If Chiksika's calculations were correct, she would be at a village not far from Running Water where his wife and daughter were. The few days, however, had turned into weeks when a severe early snowstorm struck and travel was out of the question until there was a thaw.

When the thaw did come, the thirteen set off, following the same route they had followed when they last visited here. Another storm overtook them when they reached the area where Tecumseh had broken his hip just over four years ago and so they rebuilt the remains of that old camp and stayed there for some six weeks, hunting and enjoying their camaraderie, continuing to find their new friend, Chaubenee, an asset to their party. He was a good hunter, a brave warrior, and an able story teller, regaling them with recountings of incidents filled with humor and adventure. When at last the weather broke again, they moved on.

In the Tennessee country they had quickly teamed up with a party of Cherokees, by whom they were welcomed and invited to join their strikes against the whites now so rapidly filling their country. The Shawnees were glad to do so and it was not long before word was going all through the Cherokee country of this party of young warriors who were so skilled in fighting and seemed not to know the meaning of fear. Tecumseh quickly earned fame among them when he exhibited phenomenal bravery in the face of overwhelming odds on one occasion in particular.

The incident occurred when their party had split, Tecumseh and about half the Shawnees with a party of about the same number of Cherokees had moved around one side of a great valley, while Chiksika and Chaubenee, along with the rest of the Shawnees and a similar number of Cherokee warriors went around the other. Camp was made by the party Tecumseh was accompanying and the entire group of six Shawnees and seven Cherokees was preparing its evening meal at the edge of a cane brake when, without warning, they were suddenly attacked by a party of forty whites. Instead of fleeing, Tecumseh shrieked commands that held the group together and then led them in a shattering charge so unexpected and unnerving to the whites that they broke and fled. Two of the whites had been killed and not a single Indian injured and so word of this exploit also surged through the Cherokee Nation and Tecumseh's stature among them became even greater.

They had finally come to the village where Methotasa had located her relatives, only to learn from them that just a few weeks earlier she had died, having been taken ill from the rigors and privations of her winter journey, but at least having had the joy of a reunion with her long lost family before beginning to sink. After several days of being virtually comatose, A Turtle Laying Her Eggs in the Sand had finally regained consciousness long enough to clearly say the word "Pucksinwah!" and then she had died. The brothers and their companions had stayed with her relations for a while, helping them with their struggles against the whites, all the members of the northern party showing such dash and courage that soon delegations of Cherokees were coming by from all over to ask them to join in their hunts and raids. Tecumseh especially continued growing in their esteem because of the unparalleled courage he displayed in every encounter and the charmed life he seemed to lead.

At Running Water Chiksika was finally reunited with his Cherokee wife and their daughter, now five years old, who were living with the parents of Chiksika's wife. It was a pleasant reunion and they had settled in for a nice stay. Throughout February and March and into April they had remained with the Cherokees and they had come to like them very much. Tecumseh, in particular, during their stays with the Miamis and Potawatomies, Sacs and Kickapoos, Sioux and Winnebagoes, Kickapoos and Cherokees, absorbed a great deal of the culture of each, which differed so widely. At the same time he came to the reinforced realization that, though tribes were different in many of their habits and customs, yet the people themselves were basically similar, irrespective of tribe or race or the way in which they worshipped. They were all humans and they all had human desires and needs that were essentially alike, differing only in degree from one individual to another. Each had the fundamental cravings to love and be loved, fears to overcome, ambitions to attempt fulfilling and basic human values to be nurtured.

One night, as they were in camp with their Cherokee hosts, preparing for a raid on the morrow against a particularly aggravating little settlement of whites from which considerable trouble had been emanating, Chiksika had suddenly come up to where Tecumseh and Chaubenee were putting their gear in readiness. He stopped near Tecumseh and then unexpectedly reached out and placed his hand on his younger brother's shoulder, his expression quite sober.

"Something has come to me, little brother," he said, "that I would rather not share with you, but must. Tecumseh, what I say now will come to be."

Chaubenee had stopped what he was doing and was watching the brothers curiously. A presentiment of his own abruptly chilled Tecumseh's heart, but he only nodded and said nothing and Chiksika continued: "Just as our father knew that he would die in that battle against the *Shemanese* where the Kanawhatheepi and Spaylaywitheepi meet, so I know that I will die tomorrow during our little battle. When the sun is at its highest, then will a bullet from the whites strike me here," he placed a fingertip to his forehead, "and my life will be ended. But do not let the others falter. Lead them on with attack at once and they will emerge victorious."

Tecumseh and Chaubenee both were stunned and Chaubenee began to speak but Chiksika held up a hand, cutting him off, and continued to speak slowly, intensely. "Tecumseh, listen to me. You must carry on for our people and become for them a leader. You will do this, I know. I have looked ahead and seen you not as the chief of the Shawnees but as the greatest and most powerful leader the Indians have ever known. I have seen you journey to far lands—to where we have gone together and far beyond—and I have watched you bring together under your hand a brotherhood of Indians such as has never before been known. This I tell you. This I know to be true."

Tecumseh was so upset over Chiksika's prediction of his own death that he could not speak, but he vowed in his heart to remain close to his brother's side throughout the engagement and he could see that Chaubenee was prepared to do the same. And so they had. The fight with the whites, begun in the forenoon, was a hot one. Three times the Cherokees charged, supported by the Shawnees under the thirty-two-year-old Chiksika, and three times they had been forced to take cover, but not before taking their toll of the whites each time.

The Cherokee chief had no desire to sacrifice his men, but he was also convinced that the flimsy fortification in which the whites had taken refuge would fall to them with one more charge. Pulling up well out of effective range of the whites, he assembled his force behind him for that final charge. It was at this moment that Chiksika reached out and placed a hand over Tecumseh's and squeezed it. He indicated a straight hickory sapling and the sun above it. There was almost no shadow of the tree's trunk, since the sun was at its zenith.

"Happy am I, little brother," Chiksika said softly, "to fall in battle and not die in a wegiwa like an old woman, to which I would prefer the carrion birds to pick my bones."[351]

The two brothers, riding side by side, with Chaubenee directly behind them, moved to join the others. There was a heavy thunking sound and Tecumseh spun in his saddle to see Chiksika beginning to fall, a hole nearly the diameter of his thumb in the middle of his brother's forehead. Then came the sound of the distant shot which, though fired from far beyond any effective range, had accidentally found its mark.

Tecumseh caught Chiksika before he fell, then lowered him to Chaubenee, who had leaped from his horse. Tecumseh raised his war club—the weapon Chiksika had given him as a gift long ago—and shouted to the Cherokees to follow him in the final charge. They would not. Shocked at what had happened, they considered it an omen and began to withdraw.

Tecumseh dismounted and knelt beside his brother. Shaking off Chaubenee's help, he picked up the man, cradling him in his arms. His cheeks were wet and he did not hear what Chaubenee was saying, nor feel Chaubenee's comforting hand on his back. All he felt was a monumental heaviness in his own heart.[352]

[October 11, 1790 — Monday]

It was almost exactly two years since Chaubenee had joined the party of Shawnees under Chiksika and over that passage of time his initial adulation for Tecumseh had in no manner diminished. To the contrary, it was now stronger than ever and it was obvious that the bond that had developed between the two was deeply rooted and very permanent. Part of this bonding had been due to their sharing in the great sorrow engendered by Chiksika's untimely death, but it went far beyond that. They had become as close as brothers, perhaps closer, especially on the part of Chaubenee. The young Potawatomi had become virtually a disciple of Tecumseh, but then so, too, had the remaining ten Shawnees in their little party.

Both Tecumseh and Chaubenee had changed considerably in this interval. Chaubenee, at nineteen, had grown about an inch taller, but was still relatively short—a broad oaken block of a young man, possessing great strength, a quick and retentive mind, almost perpetual good humor, and still a great deal of his happy-go-lucky boyishness.

Tecumseh, at twenty-two, was quite obviously no longer a boy in any respect. His bearing, his speech, his entire appearance exuded the aura of a man in full possession of himself, a man with strong lines of character engraved on his face by the sorrow he had borne and the danger he had overcome.

All eleven members of their party adored him and had unqualified faith in him. They had learned to act so swiftly and so unwaveringly on his instructions that a mere conversational suggestion was, to them, as deserving of obedience as the harshly barked command of a military leader to his subordinates. Such fidelity was by no means misplaced. Tecumseh's abilities, his strength of character, his courage and wisdom had continued to keep him in the forefront of the talk among the Cherokees.

That Tecumseh had taken over leadership of their little band following Chiksika's death was so natural, so foregone a conclusion, that there had been no necessity of engaging in a vote of confidence. Their confidence in him had been instilled a long time ago; who else among them could possibly have offered so much? Yet it was Tecumseh himself who was not entirely sure of his ability to become the leader Chiksika had predicted he would be. If, in fact, it were true, then he would have to put himself to the test to become satisfied in his own mind and heart that he was worthy of such responsibility.

With Chaubenee constantly and fearlessly at his side, Tecumseh began a period of pitting himself against overwhelming odds, assessing the strengths and weaknesses of an enemy with remarkable speed and accuracy, directing his followers in every fight in a manner that always gave them the greatest edge for success and the least for jeopardy. Time after time, in conjunction with the Cherokees, he attacked forces far superior to their own in numbers and weaponry and time after time emerged victorious. Always considering themselves the best fighters in the world, the Cherokees were awestruck by Tecumseh's abilities and not much less by those of his handful of followers, especially Chaubenee, before whom powerful enemies fled in terror or were slain. While most of the Cherokee chiefs were considerably older and more experienced than Tecumseh, they were soon clamoring to fall in under his leadership, seeing in him something more than any of them possessed—an intangible, indescribable aura that set him apart as a leader to follow anywhere at any time, even against seemingly invincible odds.

The women of the Cherokee tribe were immediately and overwhelmingly smitten by Tecumseh and quite a few made it clear that they loved him and wished to become his wife. There were none that he loved but, because it was expected of him and Chaubenee and the ten Shawnee warriors in his command, he accepted the gift of a lovely Cherokee maiden to cook for him, attend to his needs and satisfy his carnal cravings. She was, in every respect except for the ritual of marriage, his wife, and though it was a pleasant preoccupation to have her in this role, he did not love her as she came to love him. He treated her with gentle kindness while, at the same time, making it unmistakably clear that the day would come when he would ride off for good and would not be taking her with him when he did so.[353]

Chaubenee followed Tecumseh's lead, remaining true in his heart to Canoku back in Pimitoui, yet enjoying cohabitation with the maiden who had been presented to him. She cared for him a great deal, saw to his needs and comfort and twice, when he was slightly wounded, nursed him back to fitness. His foremost devotion, however, was reserved for the brother of Chiksika.

Tecumseh's fame as an indomitable warrior quickly spread throughout the other southern tribes and deputations of Chikasaws, Choctaws and Creeks came to see this incredible young man. Some even followed him in battle and always came away marveling at his fighting ability, his fearlessness and his unflagging concern for his followers and so further word of him spread among their own peoples. Nor was there any need to embellish their tales.

Here Tecumseh led a party consisting only of Chaubenee, two of his Shawnees and two Cherokee warriors against a well-armed mounted party of sixteen whites, slaying all but two who escaped to carry the news back to the whites of this new demon chief who had appeared on the scene and who advanced and was victorious when every circumstance dictated he should have suffered terrible defeat. There he charged down upon a party of eight whites all by himself, his fierce shrieks and hideously painted features momentarily paralyzing them with fear—four of them falling in succession under his skill-fully wielded war club before the others dropped their weapons and fled in abject panic. He helped to lead the stinging defeat of a large force of whites on Lookout Mountain, and another time he led Chaubenee and his band of ten Shawnees, with only one Cherokee along, in a fierce rush against a new settlement, killing every man, destroying the buildings, and taking more than twenty women and children prisoners, whom he turned over to the Cherokees. Tecumseh had never killed or hurt a woman or child and even went out of his way to make certain that others fighting under his leadership did not do so.

The story the Cherokees loved to tell about him had its genesis on the night when, as he lay on a buffalo skin before a small campfire with eight of his men—Chaubenee, three Shawnees, and four Cherokees ranged around the blaze—his amazingly acute senses suddenly warned him that a large force was surrounding them and would attack in moments. In a conversational tone he told the others what the situation was and warned them to stay where they were until he made his move and then to rush a certain segment of the circle drawn about them. He then sat up, stretched and yawned and casually came to his feet. Leaning over as if to straighten the buffalo pelt upon which he had been lying, he suddenly flung it over the fire so that in an instant all light was blacked out. In an irresistible rush the warriors smashed through the ring of thirty white men as if their enemy had been made of paper and left behind them the bodies of five of their attackers, themselves losing only a few personal items. But that was not enough for Tecumseh. Traveling swiftly in a semi-circle, he led them back in a shrieking charge from the opposite side of the party of whites who now, certain that they themselves were the ones who had become surrounded, panicked and fled in a complete rout of totally de-moralized men, leaving another seven of their number dead upon the ground.

No less than six times Chaubenee's life had been saved through Te-cumseh's uncanny knack for assessing any situation in an instant and acting immediately in a manner geared to swing the scales of advantage in his own favor. Three different times his camp was attacked by surprise in the night and each time he not only fought back with such ferocity that his attackers retreated, but not once was any man in his command seriously injured.

The fame of Tecumseh and Chaubenee and the ten Shawnee followers had grown phenomenally and soon Indians throughout the south were clam-oring for him to join them and lead their war parties against the whites. But at last, having proven himself to his own satisfaction, Tecumseh's thoughts turned to home. Often he would move apart from the others just after dawn and stand solitarily on some knoll, looking eastward toward the sun just clearing the horizon, knowing that the same sun was at this very moment bathing in its new glow that land along the Little Miami River that he loved so much—a land he missed more than anyone suspected. He and his party had finally said their farewells, promising to someday return for a visit, and headed north again. They passed the place where Chiksika was buried and tarried there a day before moving on and coming at last, on this day, to the point where even the mighty Spaylaywitheepi became swallowed up in the greater waters of the grandmother of rivers.

Not long after crossing over, the trail split, part continuing northward and another part moving off to the northeast, toward the far distant Wabash. It was here and now that the Shawnees parted from Chaubenee.

After murmuring a few words and shaking hands with each man in turn, Chaubenee at last stood with Tecumseh and they gripped each other's wrists, the eyes of both damp at the parting.

"We will meet again, Chaubenee," Tecumseh promised. "I tell you this not as a hope, but as a truth. I know it will come to be. There is much for us together in the future."

Chaubenee nodded, pleased to hear this but no less distressed at the parting. "I will always follow you, Tecumseh," he vowed. "When you call, wherever I am and no matter where you are, I will come at once. What you wish me to do, I will do without question. You are now, and you will always be, my chief as well as my friend."

[November 6, 1790 — Saturday]

An impromptu council of welcome had been called three days ago in Chalahgawtha along the north bank of the Maumee within an hour of Tecumseh's return with his band of ten warriors. Everyone marveled at how much he and those who had accompanied him had changed. They had been gone for some three years and over that period word of the party had filtered back to the tribe, first their extensive travels and then their growing renown as a fighting force in the South. Tecumseh's fame had grown in his own tribe during his absence almost as much as it had among the southern tribes.

It was Catahecassa—Black Hoof—who, standing before the council fire with Tecumseh beside him, formally welcomed him back. No great affection had ever existed between the two and there was none there now, yet Catahecassa was sincere in his remarks. He placed his gnarled hands on the young warrior's shoulders and a small smile touched his lips as he spoke in a voice that carried to every ear in the crowded council house.

"Moneto has been kind to bring you back safely to your people," he said. "You went away from us little more than a boy and you have returned a man, with the stories of your exploits among our southern brothers preceding you. It is well. You have shown the Cherokees that the Shawnee remains a great warrior and your nation is well pleased with you. All of your people grieve with you over the death of Chiksika, who was also a good man and a fine warrior, and I speak for all of the Shawnees when I say welcome home Tecumseh."

There was much Tecumseh could have said, since the words welled within him, but with the simple eloquence for which he was already noted, he placed his own hands on Catahecassa's shoulders and summed up his feelings in four earnest words.

"My heart is filled."

It was later that same day, when a much smaller number of close friends among the chiefs and warriors, along with their wives and even some of the older children, gathered in an informal group in the large main room of Blue Jacket's house, one of the structures that had miraculously escaped the recent destruction that had swept Kekionga and its adjacent villages. There they listened to Tecumseh tell of his travels and battles and, in turn, passed along to him information of what had occurred among them and throughout the Ohio country during his absence. Tecumapese was there, of course, still saddened over the death of Chiksika, which they had all heard about long before, and over the death of Methotasa, that they had not heard about, but their sorrow was overshadowed by the joy of having Tecumseh home again. Wasegoboah was with her, of course, as was Spemica Lawba, who had become a fine-looking sixteen-year-old bearing a great resemblance to his uncle Tecumseh at that age. Here, too, were Lowawluwaysica, Kumskaka, and Sauwaseekau, the nineteen-year-old triplets listening with fascination to every word uttered by their older brother and very proud of him. And, of course, Blue Jacket was here, along with his wife, Wabethe, and their son, Little Blue Jacket, now eleven years old. Blue Jacket had made it a special point, in a brief private meeting between them, to greet Tecumseh with great warmth and to commiserate over the loss of Chiksika and Methotasa.

There was a rich sense of closeness among them all and the mood-shifts as they moved from topic to topic were reflected in their reactions. There was a great deal of merriment and laughter and, along with it, moments of heartfelt sorrow. Food was served at intervals and the talking went on and on for much longer than any had anticipated at the beginning. With only occasional breaks to sleep and take care of personal needs, the talking continued for three days.

An important thing that had occurred, which now filled Tecumseh with considerable satisfaction, leavened with an element of sorrow, was that Blue Jacket, in addition to being principal chief of the Maykujays, was now also the first war chief of the Shawnee Nation, old ugly Shemeneto finally having succumbed the preceding year to the illness that had so long plagued him.

Blue Jacket had also experienced a couple of narrow escapes the spring following Tecumseh's departure, when he had first been wounded and later captured by the whites during a raid into Kentucky. The wounding had occurred as he stood on a rock overlooking the Spaylaywitheepi and watching from nearly a half-mile distance more boats of white immigrants heading for settlement in Kentucky. Those in the boats had seen him, too, and puffs of smoke had come from their rifles as they snapped off shots at him, but he had had little fear because the distance was so great. Then, incredibly one of the balls had found its mark, plunging into his side with a tremendous blow. He had plugged the wound with buzzard down and managed to get onto his horse and head for home, but remembering little of the long trip, only that he fell unconscious as he entered the village. Wabethe had probed and found the bullet and removed it, cleansed the wound and cared for him and he had recovered quickly. Then, a few weeks later, a horse-stealing raid had been launched to go into Kentucky and Blue Jacket, though still weak, had insisted on going along. His party of fifteen warriors had crossed the Spaylaywitheepi, followed the Warrior Trail south and quickly managed to seize thirty horses in the neighborhood of the relatively new Strode's Station just north of Boonesboro.[354] They drove them back to the Spaylaywitheepi and his warriors swam them across five miles upstream from Maysville at Cabin Creek. Blue Jacket, still weak from his wound, had needed to rest and told the others to drive the horses to their village and he would soon follow. Unwilling to leave him alone, two warriors had remained with him and made a small camp.

Later that evening, without warning, a dozen whites had attacked them and killed the two warriors in the first firing. Blue Jacket had tried to escape but a horseman overtook him and hit him over the head with his rifle barrel, stunning him, and he was forced to surrender. They had bound him and taken him to Maysville, where they had stayed in Boone's cabin one night. In succession they had stopped briefly in Washington, May's Lick, Millersburg, and Stockton's Station and, on the third night, reached Strode's Station where Blue Jacket had been bound hand and foot and tied to a post in a cabin. With considerable effort he had managed to free himself from the post but was still bound at the wrists and ankles. He had silently hopped past his sleeping guard and gotten outside. There he hopped away in the darkness, covering quite a distance before pausing to rest. He was able, by bending over and using his teeth to bite through the cords, to free himself of the ankle bonds but could not get rid of the wrist bonds behind his back. Without wasting further time trying to do so, he had then set off at an easy run and reached Strode's Station. There he stole a horse, mounted it with some difficulty and had finally made it back home.

Immigration to Kentucky by whites from the East had continued apace for all the time Tecumseh had been absent, and there were now so many white people in Kentucky that the Shawnees had generally given up hope of ever forcing them out. Tecumseh was not of the same opinion and believed that somehow there had to be a way to make this flood reverse itself.

Blue Jacket told Tecumseh and his other listeners around the fire that the alliance of tribes that had included the residue Iroquois and the Western Confederacy, had continued trying to deal with the whites but had little success, the whites seeming determined to look for any excuse to keep from meeting the unified body of Indians in reasonable council. In an effort to bend as much as humanly possible in an effort to appease the land greed of the Americans and avert the new war that seemed to be shaping up, the Indian confederation had, as a body, offered to give the Americans total ownership of approximately one-quarter of Ohio—an enormous tract that split Ohio from north to south in its eastern quadrant—but since the Americans considered, by right of the fraudulent treaty made at Fort Finney, that they already owned it, Arthur St. Clair, governor of the Ohio Territory, rejected it with a speech that not only refused the offer, but which was more accusatory, inflammatory, and threatening than anything else.

In the midst of all this negotiating that seemed to accomplish nothing beyond causing frustration, Blue Jacket remarked that the whites had been surging ahead with their encroachments. New settlements were everywhere and one of particular note was established across the Spaylaywitheepi from the mouth of the Licking and was being called Losantiville.[355] Also, Governor St. Clair had drawn some invisible lines in the Ohio Territory which took in about half of all of the Ohio country and he was calling the land enclosed within those lines Washington County, which, Blue Jacket said with controlled anger, could only be viewed as the same type of first step the whites always took when they began carving up the land in little pieces.

St. Clair had, in December of 1788, Blue Jacket went on, held treaty talks with some of the Indians. These talks had gone on for days and days but accomplished virtually nothing except the airing of old grievances and the same charges and countercharges in regard to ownership of the lands. It became obvious to all the Indians that the sole purpose of St. Clair in holding the Fort Harmar treaty talks was to create insurmountable dissension among the tribes. Later this was confirmed when interpreter spies had passed on word to the chiefs that St. Clair was so sure he had accomplished this goal that his report to authorities in the East described the Treaty of Fort Harmar as a great success and that it had broken the Indian Confederacy.

Gradually, however, the United States, very weak at first, was gaining in strength and its new government establishing laws and directives by which its citizens would live and prosper. A year ago January, in the first session of the United States Congress, which replaced the Congress of the Confederation of States, the Ohio Territory was given a permanent status among the states of the Union, which opened the door to eventual statehood for Ohio. And not long after that, in April 1789, the Destroyer of Towns and great enemy of the Indians, George Washington, had been inaugurated as president of the United States.[356]

Blue Jacket told Tecumseh that over these past three years he and Michikiniqua had become fairly close friends and often, in Kekionga, discussed the continuing problem of the land-hungry Americans. For the first time, Michikiniqua had begun expressing fears that the remoteness of Kekionga and the other Miami villages was no longer so great as to insure it would not be attacked by Americans and even the multitude of British there were having similar apprehensions. Blue Jacket, remembering well the time that he, along with Chiksika, Wasegoboah, and Tecumseh, had visited Kekionga, said that those British living in and operating businesses there had helped make the sprawling Indian city an even greater metropolis than it had been during that visit. To be entirely accurate, it was actually a whole collection of villages closely adjacent to one another. The Chalahgawtha that had been established three miles down the Maumee from Michikiniqua's residence was only one of more than a dozen major Indian enclaves that were part of the whole. In addition to a good many Americans who had abandoned their own people and were now living there, Kekionga also now had a population of over one hundred fifty permanent residents from Canada, mainly British but with a number of French as well. Great balls were still held regularly, along with a variety of sporting events and gambling, to say nothing of the enormous amount of trade engaged in there.

With the failure of anything being accomplished by the talks with the United States through St. Clair, and the encroachment of whites north of the Ohio moving into full speed, Blue Jacket said that Shawnee raids against these settlements were increased. The results had been predictable. As soon as the new settlements at the mouths of the Muskingum, Scioto, Little Miami, and Great Miami were struck—with nine whites killed at the settlements now being called Losantiville, Columbia, and Symmes City—the white settlers began erecting a series of block houses of their own in these settlements apart from the government. Purportedly to aid in such defense of the inhabitants, but in actuality more as a launching pad for expeditions against the Shawnees, Miamis, and other Indians to the north, a new and very strong fortification was built a year ago last summer at Losantiville and named Fort Washington.[357] It had not taken long for the government to begin preparing to use the fort for its real purpose. Last December, with the fort all but completed, General Harmar had left Fort Harmar and moved down the Ohio with three hundred federal troops and occupied it.[358] Shortly afterwards, Blue Jacket said, very alarming news had flashed through all the tribes and there was no doubt as to the validity of it. Colonel Alexander McKee, at Detroit, was the one who passed it on to the Indians, telling them that the British commander in Detroit, Major Patrick Murray, had received a letter from Governor Arthur St. Clair. The Ohio governor had written to him as a warning that a major offensive was being planned to use, under command of General Harmar, the militias of Virginia, Pennsylvania, and Kentucky, in addition to regulars, to crush the Northwestern tribes. However, St. Clair had added, President Washington was concerned lest the British at Detroit misconstrue this as an invasion against them and a war between the whites be reignited, and so had ordered him to write this letter. The final paragraph of the letter had made it quite clear, beyond any misunderstanding, what was afoot:

> *The expedition about to be undertaken is not intended against the post you have the honor to command, nor any other place at present in possession of the troops of his Britannic Majesty, but is on foot with the sole design of humbling and chastising some of the savage tribes, whose depredations have become intolerable and whose cruelties have of late become an outrage, not only to the people of America, but to humanity.*[359]

In his naivete, St. Clair had asked Murray to keep the American designs secret from the Indians. It was at this point, Blue Jacket said, that the British had informed them what was happening and, at the same time, quietly reinstituted their previous arrangement of paying the Indians fifty dollars for each American scalp and one hundred dollars for each living prisoner. But what had been of most concern when the contents of that letter were revealed, Blue Jacket related, was the objective at which General Harmar would direct his force.

The target was to be Kekionga.

It was during last January, Blue Jacket continued in his narration of events, that Governor St. Clair himself had come to Losantiville and was quartered at Fort Washington. The day after his arrival, St. Clair had drawn some more invisible lines in Ohio and created another county, called Hamilton, and he had also prevailed upon the proprietors of Losantiville to change the name of the settlement to Cincinnati.[360]

In response to the growing number of forays being made by Kentuckians against the Indians in Ohio, the Shawnees increased their own attacks against the Kentucky settlements early in the year and by February's end had killed thirty-three more settlers. That figure at one time would have been a major disaster to the Kentuckians—now it was hardly a drop in the bucket. But the Kentuckians had protested greatly when Virginia Governor Beverly Randolph issued a reinforced directive forbidding Kentuckians to enter into the territory of the United States on the north side of the Ohio or to make raids against the Indians living there.

Although the constant attacking and counterattacking between Indians and whites was no matter for levity, once in a while an incident occurred that, in the retelling, grew more and more humorous. One of these, that still brought a chuckle rumbling out of Blue Jacket's chest, was an incident that had occurred just at the end of the last Rain Moon on the Kentucky side of the Spaylay-witheepi not quite a mile below the mouth of the Kanawhatheepi. In this instance, Blue Jacket, leading half a dozen warriors, spied a lone white man hunting on the high bluffs overlooking the Spaylaywitheepi. He was a small man, short and slight, probably weighing not much more than a hundred pounds, and had seen them about the same time they saw him. Immediately the race was on.

The Indians had closed in on the man who found himself coming to one of the higher bluffs with nothing else ahead except open space and the broad river about one hundred fifty feet below and at least that far distant from the bluff. The man had looked around wildly, but there was no avenue of escape. He had again looked over the edge anxiously and just as Blue Jacket's party was racing the last few yards to capture him, he tossed his rifle far out and down and then, incredibly, leaped after it.

The Shawnees reached the edge an instant later, just in time to see the falling man plummet into the uppermost branches of an enormous buckeye tree, about fifty feet high and the top of which was fully sixty feet below the top of the bluff. Though its branches had swollen buds upon them, the tree had not yet leafed out. Its branches, normally very brittle, were relatively limber with the flowing sap of spring and as he plunged through them, the uppermost branches bent with his weight, some of them breaking. The deeper into the tree he fell, the thicker the branches and the more that were snapping as he struck them. Some were as much as two or three inches thick. Blue Jacket laughed aloud in his reminiscence. "It was like a series of guns going off, and this white man, he just kept pop-pop-popping through the branches until he hit the ground below the tree, which was growing on a broad ledge. We were sure he was killed, but he got up and jumped to a lower ledge, then to a lower one at least fifteen or eighteen feet below that, then down two more smaller ones, and the last we saw him, he had scooped up his rifle as he ran past it and disappeared into some woods."[361]

Everyone on hand as Blue Jacket finished telling that particular incident broke into laughter and applause, but they quickly sobered as he continued with his narration, which now moved into areas considerably more serious. The Shawnee war chief reported that Governor St. Clair, alarmed by the increasing attacks being made by Indians and believing that the British had kept secret from their red allies the proposed invasion against them, sent messengers to them during the last week of that same month, professing peace and inviting them to meet with him to discuss their grievances, so that such matters could be resolved and they could live in friendship. The hypocrisy behind the messages was so flagrant that the messengers had been fortunate indeed to get away with their scalps still intact.

Even while the peace emissaries were still out, General Harmar had led a preliminary excursion toward the Scioto Valley to look for Indians.[362] They had scoured the country toward the Scioto and had found some camps, but the Indians, knowing of their approach, slipped away well in advance of the army's arrival. One group of fourteen of Harmar's men, however, found the trail of some Indians and, behind the tracking abilities of one of Colonel Charles Scott's volunteers, followed it and came up on four Shawnee warriors, all of whom they killed simultaneously.[363] All four, Blue Jacket said, were very young and inexperienced and had paid the price, to the sorrow of the nation, of not finding a well-experienced warrior to lead them.

Ever since first learning from the Detroit British about the planned strike against Kekionga, both Blue Jacket and Michikiniqua had kept spies hovering around Fort Washington to observe preparations and report. They had also sent an urgent request to their allies to the north and west to aid them when the time came. The Potawatomies had immediately responded that they would be on hand to assist and proclaimed that if and when Harmar should show up with his army, their own women would chase the soldiers away with switches. By last August the intelligence from their spies showed that Harmar had gathered a force of just under fifteen hundred men who were drilling regularly and that posted general orders indicated they would begin their march against Kekionga in September.

The Indian leaders, Blue Jacket went on, were gathered at Miamitown, formerly called the New French Store, adjacent to Kekionga, when word arrived that Harmar's force had started their march, bringing with them three pieces of artillery.[364] But, with both the Wyandots and Delawares inclined, at the moment, toward peace, there had not been the turnout of Indian allies that had been hoped for. There were just over one hundred Indians who assembled, largely Shawnees and Miamis, but with a scattering of Potawatomies. The Indians themselves had been fearful at the smallness of their own number when compared with the force of nearly fifteen hundred coming toward them under Harmar. Even the arrival of half a hundred Ottawas in response to the appeal for help did little to raise the hopes of the Indians.[365] One hundred fifty Indians against odds of better than nine to one did not inspire visions of victory.

With Harmar's army well on the march toward them, the combined Indian force had selected Blue Jacket and Michikiniqua as coleaders in the coming confrontation and all the whites—British, French, and American turncoats— who were at Kekionga were warned to leave the area until the danger was past. The greater part of Kekionga was then set afire. Many of the rebuilt

Shawnee towns, such as Mackachack, Blue Jacket's Town, Wapatomica, and
Wapakoneta were similarly evacuated and burned, the women and children
transported to temporary camps on the headwaters of the Elkhart River.

Among those who left Kekionga was Michikiniqua's daughter, Wanagapeth—A Sweet Breeze—who was now the wife of his adopted son, Apekonit. The latter had elected to stay behind and fight with his adopted father,
who was also his father-in-law. With considerable trepidation, the defenders
waited while their spies reported that the American army was coming ever
closer.[366] While they waited, Michikiniqua and Blue Jacket went over strategy
of how best to oppose the Americans. They decided, in view of their far fewer
numbers, to remain out of sight, let the Harmar army think everyone had fled
in the face of such danger and then attack when his defenses were lowered
enough to create a vulnerability of which they could take advantage.

Unobserved themselves and now joined by Simon Girty, who rode a
black stallion and wore a scarlet cape, they watched as the army entered
Chalahgawtha and camped there.[367] They watched as the army entered Miamitown and destroyed the abandoned trading post of John Kinzie after looting
it of all they wanted.[368] They watched as the army burned virtually all the
buildings the Indians themselves had not burned during their evacuation.[369]
They watched as great portions of their cornfields were chopped down, stacked
and burned and some fifteen thousand bushels of stored corn were destroyed,
along with a large quantity of vegetables.[370] They watched and waited for a
blunder to be made by Harmar and they were finally rewarded.

While the main army was still camped at Chalahgawtha, the American
general unnecessarily split his force, sending out a detachment of around two
hundred of his men.[371] The Indian spies brought word of this at once to their
commanders and in swift order an ambush was set up where the Indian trail
passed through heavy brush in the Eel River bottom. Without having sent
out a forward guard or flankers the detachment marched directly into it. The
Indian force, screeching and screaming and sending in a deafening barrage of
shots, seemed to be a larger force than it actually was and the Americans
became demoralized and retreated, leaving seventy men dead on the scene.[372]
The Indians fully expected, Blue Jacket went on, that as soon as the survivors
reached Harmar's main force, the entire white army would immediately return
to the scene bristling for a major engagement. Instead, wholly unexpectedly,
Harmar put them into a retreat.

After eight miles the retreat stopped and, during the night, another detachment was sent out, this time a body of 360 regulars and militia.[373] This
detachment of the army, upon reaching Kekionga in the morning, split into
four parties and moved into different quarters of the town. It was another
mistake. The Indians could not have stood up against an attack by the whole
force, but against the split detachment they had not hesitated. They struck

again, hitting all four sections of it and parlayed their good fortune into a second victory even more substantial than the first. With Blue Jacket and Michikiniqua leading charges, they had swept down upon them in an assault so devastating in its intensity that the detachment fell apart and could not recover. The skirmishing lasted three hours and one hundred thirteen Americans were killed in this second ambush. What little resistance was offered was as quickly beaten down and the survivors fled back to the army with the news.[374]

Incredibly, Blue Jacket went on, though Harmar's force still outnumbered the Indians by a vast margin and most of his men were fresh and had not yet even fired their rifles, the white chief lifted his skirts and ran. Blue Jacket said at this point he was all for following up the demoralized army and wiping them out, especially since another contingent of Indian allies had just arrived— one hundred fifty Sacs and Foxes—but there were other chiefs who were more cautious and recommended restraint, fearful for their women and children in hiding, and their view prevailed.

This time Harmar's army retreated all the way back to Fort Washington, leaving a total of 183 dead behind him, of which 75 were regulars.[375] At the beginning of the general retreat, much of the army's equipment was discarded along the way, so that their trail was littered with such debris.

A total of twenty-seven warriors had been killed outright and eighteen wounded, three of whom later died.[376] Nevertheless, the victory had been a great and heady elixir for all the Indians, including those who had not participated. Only two Indians had been captured—a warrior who was taken back to Fort Washington and later released, and a girl eleven years old who was a Maykujay named Pskipahcah Ouiskelotha—Bluebird—found by the soldiers as she was hiding in one of the ransacked villages adjoining Kekionga.[377]

With great jubilation, Blue Jacket concluded his narration, the Indians gathered up among themselves the supplies, weapons and ammunition that had been left behind in the precipitate haste of the retreating army, including a large number of packhorses, and the taste of victory was very sweet in all their mouths.

That a force of only one hundred fifty Indians could attack—and defeat!— an army of nearly fifteen hundred was news that had swept throughout the Northwest in these two weeks that had passed since then and there was clear indication that the next time a call was issued to the Indian allies it would be answered by thousands, not just a paltry handful.

The relation of all these matters had lasted well into the third night following Tecumseh's return and now, with the stories told, most of the visitors had drifted away and the only ones remaining with Blue Jacket and Wabethe in their house were Tecumseh, Wasegoboah, and Spemica Lawba.

"I very much regret that I was not here to fight beside you and Michikiniqua," Tecumseh said, breaking the silence that had settled over them for the past few minutes, during which he had packed and lighted his pipe. "Had I any idea how serious the situation had become, I would have come back from the Cherokees long before now."[378]

"I regret it as well, Tecumseh," Blue Jacket replied. "There is no doubt we could have used you."

"You have become a very great leader among us, Blue Jacket," Tecumseh said. "Among all the Indians now, in fact, and justly so. It was a very fine victory and I commend you for your leadership. No chief we have ever had could have done better."

Blue Jacket smiled, acknowledging the compliment with pleasure. He, too, lighted his pipe with a glowing twig from the fire and then he faced Tecumseh again, his countenance serious. "I have my own thoughts about it, Tecumseh," he said, "but I would like to have yours. Do you think they will come again?"

Peripherally, Tecumseh saw that his nephew was looking at him intently, but he kept his eyes on Blue Jacket. "I think, Wehyehpihehrsehnwah," he responded, "that the Americans will not long sit still in view of what the Shawnees and the other tribes have now done to them. I think that not only will they return, but that they will come with a larger and much stronger army than before, and perhaps a better leader."

"I hope they don't!" blurted Spemica Lawba, then dropped his eyes for having the temerity to speak without being recognized.

"We *all* hope they don't," Blue Jacket responded dryly, "but our reasons may differ. Would it be because you lived with them for some time that you now wish they would not attack again?"

The youth raised his head and looked at the chief directly, a faintly smoldering defiance in his eyes. "I do not hate them," he said. "I wish they would stay where they are and we where we are and that there could be peace between us. They are not all bad people."

Tecumseh was smiling in faint amusement. "No people," he put in, "are all bad, Spemica Lawba, just as none are all good. From what you have told us, the General Logan who took you is a good man. But he is also the one who last destroyed our Chalahgawtha at the Little Miami and the other towns as well. It was his men who killed Chief Moluntha and so many of our women." He shrugged. "I do not know if he wishes our land, but the *Shemanese* mostly do and we must oppose this."

Spemica Lawba nodded miserably. "I understand that, but I do not want to fight against General Logan. I have told him I would never do so."

"It was a promise you should not have made," Blue Jacket retorted, an edge to his words.

"But one," Tecumseh said, speaking to the chief, "that a person of honor would have made; that you would have made, Blue Jacket, or I, under similar circumstances." He let his eyes shift to his nephew. "I hope the time may never come when you will encounter him in war."

There was another lapse in the conversation following this and then Tecumseh spoke again, this time to Blue Jacket. "You leave in the morning?"

The chief of the Maykujays nodded. "I will meet with the Detroit commandant. If we are to successfully oppose the next army the *Shemanese* send against us, we will need help from the British."

[December 13, 1790 — Monday]

Tecumseh studied Blue Jacket as the Maykujay principal chief wolfed down the large bowl of rich, meaty stew Wabethe had ladled out for him, noting especially his haggard appearance. The Shawnee war chief was only thirty-six, he knew, yet he appeared older this night, his eyes somewhat sunken and his cheeks hollow. The past months had been very hard on him and he had been in almost perpetual motion, which had not ended with the retreat of General Harmar back to Fort Washington. The trip on horseback through the unseasonably bitter weather of this early winter to Detroit and back had played its part in sapping his energy.

"I want nothing more," his first words were, after he had warmly greeted Wabethe, "than to fill my belly with your good food and then sleep for a week."

Despite the comment, he had immediately sent for Tecumseh, to go over with him what had taken place in the meeting with the Detroit commandant, Major Patrick Murray. Tecumseh had come at once, eager to hear the details of Blue Jacket's trip to Detroit, but he waited in polite silence while the war chief finished his meal, declining with thanks Wabethe's invitation that he have something to eat.

Blue Jacket, upon finishing, arose and went to a corner of the room where he rummaged in some baggage and came back with two items—a rather large flat rectangular box of finely fitted and beautifully polished wood and an excellent British sword in a scabbard—both of which he presented to Tecumseh with a smile.

"These, my good friend, are for you. Two sets of each," he indicated the box and the sword, "were presented to me by some traders in Detroit. One set was for me to keep, the other for me to give to the worthiest chief or warrior I knew. I know of none more worthy than you, Tecumseh, so these are yours."

Deeply moved by both Blue Jacket's compliment and generosity, Tecumseh slowly drew the sword from its elaborately engraved scabbard, noting instantly its fine balance and quality steel blade. "Thank you, dear friend," he said softly. "I will wear it with pride and wield it against our enemies."

"Exactly what I had in mind," Blue Jacket replied with a low laugh. "Now, take a look inside the box."

Tecumseh unlatched the two polished brass snaps and swung up the hinged lid. His jaw dropped and his eyes widened. Inside, lying in fitted red velvet beds, were two matched flintlock pistols with over-and-under ten-inch barrels, each pistol with double hammers and triggers. The barrels and breeches were ornate with delicately engraved scrollwork and on each appeared the neatly printed words, *H. W. Mortimer, London*. Tecumseh was so overwhelmed he could not speak.

"I trust you'll use those in the same way," Blue Jacket said casually, loading his pipe with tobacco from a fine suede drawstring pouch. "I'm told they are very accurate up to about fifty feet. Now, before you get carried away any more than you already seem to be, let's talk about my trip to Detroit."

He lighted his pipe and began relating his story. The trip to and from Detroit, he told Tecumseh, had been unremarkable except for the cold, from which he had suffered considerably.

"As soon as I got there," Blue Jacket went on, "I went to see Alexander McKee. Simon Girty was with him. We talked for a while and then McKee left for a time. When he came back he had a squad of soldiers with him who actually saluted me and then we were escorted with much ceremony to the quarters of Major Murray. Girty came along as well, although McKee had told Major Murray that I spoke English very well and no interpreter would be necessary. McKee had told the major that it was believed I was initially a white who had been captured and adopted into the tribe. Major Murray was impressed with my words and said I spoke English marvelously well, but it was obvious he didn't believe an adopted white could achieve the rank I have in the tribe.

"I had determined from the beginning to talk to him very directly, as the English talk, without the metaphors we use so much in our councils, because this tends to confuse the English. He had heard about our defeat of Harmar's army, of course, and was very pleased by it and said he had no doubt the king would also be happy to learn of it. When he had finished saying all he meant to say at the beginning, I started off by telling him that we fully expected a major retaliatory expedition against us by the Americans next summer and, while we would undoubtedly have an increase of Indian allies helping us, if we were to face them with strength, we were going to require help from the British.

"What I said to him next, Tecumseh," Blue Jacket continued, "was very blunt and I think it disconcerted him a good bit. I said to him, 'Major Murray, whether or not you are willing to admit it, you are dependent upon us for the continuation of the trade you enjoy in the Northwest. We, the Shawnees,' I told him, 'are closest to the Americans and bear the brunt of every move they make in the Ohio country. The Miamis are next and they are under Michikiniqua—the one you call Little Turtle—and they sometimes help us to fend off the *Shemanese*. The Potawatomies are next, but they are far from the Americans. They have suffered few losses to themselves and are only halfway in their help to us. Some bands support us, such as those near Detroit and those on the St. Joseph, but others prefer to remain aloof. We continue to ask their help but do not know if we will get it. Whether or not we do, help from you *must* be given or the British—and their trade—will be eliminated from the Northwest.' "

Tecumseh smiled as his host paused and remarked, "I can well see why he would have found what you said to be disconcerting. What did he say?"

"He said he was impressed and that the same thoughts had been expressed to him in different words by a committee of the merchants and traders of Detroit."[379]

Major Murray, Blue Jacket went on, said the Detroit merchants told him theirs was a business dependent on Northwest commerce and which brought to British coffers over a hundred and fifty thousand pounds annually. They were very upset, he said, over the fact that a number of their trading posts—Kinzie's at Miamitown, Burnett's, Wharton's, Fitzsimmon's, and some others—had already been destroyed by the Americans at considerable loss. They acknowledged that Kinzie was already building a new post at the mouth of the Auglaize and that Burnett had gone to his other post on the St. Joseph, but they told him that was not the point. The point was their businesses were obviously now in jeopardy from further strikes by the Americans, which they were sure would be coming soon. The invasion by General Harmar, despite the fact that we had defeated him, alarmed those traders a great deal.

"I then said this to him," Blue Jacket said, after taking a couple of puffs on his pipe, "I said, 'You British have given us some guns and ammunition and supplies of food and blankets and fabrics. But what we need most is support by men. Armies! Give us soldiers and officers and artillery. Support *us,* just as you wish us to support your interests in our territory.' I finished by standing up and saying to him very forcefully, 'This I can say, Major Murray. If you do *not* help us, then we will be forced to abandon our homes and withdraw beyond the Mississippi.' "

"And his reaction to that?" Tecumseh prompted.

"He stood up also and then he walked back and forth for some time before he finally stopped in front of me. He told me he was in a very difficult position, because he had no authority to commit British forces to such an end, yet, at the same time, that he was painfully aware of the urgent need to do so. He also was very apprehensive that if he did do so, it could easily provoke a new war with the Americans and, he pointed out, on a more personal level, it could be the ruination of his military career.

"Finally," Blue Jacket said, setting his pipe aside, "he said to me these words: 'Chief Blue Jacket, you *must* protect the barrier between the Americans and the red people, and you must *not* forsake the trade that links us together in amity and interest. I have the utmost sympathy for the position and needs of the Shawnees in this matter and I commend you for the brilliant defense you made of your country. I will give you whatever support it is in my power to give and I will relay your words to your great father, the king, for his consideration and direction. You have stated your right to the country you are defending. You are the best judges of the rights by which you hold your lands. Your country, you say, has not been given away. You cannot then be blamable in being unanimous to defend it.' "

Blue Jacket shook his head as if trying to clear it. "All at once he was talking, as the whites so often do, without saying anything and only making those who listen to them become confused. So I stopped him, and I told him I had but one further thing to tell him before I left and that he should pay great attention to it. This is what I said: 'Your words circle like soaring birds which never land. I will try to catch them and take them back for my people to hear. I will take the weapons and ammunition you have given us and those they will understand. We will wait to see what *your* great father, the king, has to say. And we *expect* he will help his Indian children as they have helped him.' "

Blue Jacket expelled a great gust of air and shook his head again. "I don't know if what I said to him is going to make any difference. The British do not want to fight another war with the Americans, at least not now, so they say."

Tecumseh touched his friend's arm. "What you said to him will have a very strong effect, Blue Jacket. I know it. They may not wish to light the fires of another war, but even more, they do not wish to lose the trade here that is the foundation of all they have and do in this country. They *will* help."

Later, lying near the fire in the temporary wegiwa he and Wasegoboah and the triplets had built, Tecumseh stared into the embers, sleep elusive. He briefly touched his *opawaka*. Yes, the British would help the Indians. They really had no other choice.

He lay quietly for a moment, thinking appreciatively of the fine weapons Blue Jacket had given him. After a while he suddenly smiled in the dimness, thinking of the messenger who had stopped by earlier this day. He had come from the West and among the pieces of news he had imparted was that the warrior Chaubenee, who had gone with Tecumseh and Chiksika to the South, had been received home in Pimitoui with great honors. Two days after his

return from the South, he had married Canoku and the following week there
had been a feast in his honor, attended not only by all from his own village
but from Potawatomi villages very distant. Black Partridge and a band from
the Chicago area came, as did young Chief Gomo from Peoria Lake and
Nescotnemeg from the Kankakee River. Word of his exploits beside Tecumseh
among the Cherokees had long preceded him and he was afforded great respect.
A council had been held and speaker after speaker had risen to extol the courage
of their son who had gone away a boy and returned home not just a man,
but as a warrior among warriors. Old Chief Spotka—Hanokula—had been
last to speak and the words he said had been most important.

"I have always been a warrior," the messenger had quoted the elderly
chief as having said, "and in my youth I won great honors and excelled beyond
those with whom I lived and for this I was finally made a chief. At that time
I said that when a warrior rose among us who was as I was then, to him I
would give over my chieftainship. Chaubenee is such a one—not only as I
was then, but even more. From this day forward, he is your chief."

Tecumseh's smile broadened as he remembered the messenger's final
words. "Although he was born an Ottawa, Chaubenee is now fully a Potawatomi and he is also, at nineteen summers, the youngest chief any Potawatomi village has ever had."

[March 19, 1791 — Tuesday]

Throughout the past winter the Shawnees had stepped up their attacks in
the Ohio Valley, striking hard and mercilessly against the settlers wherever
possible. Rumors continually swept through the nation that a massive assault
was being planned against the Northwestern tribes, but no definite information
was forthcoming. There was some gratification to be had in the fact that,
while General Harmar had managed to survive charges of military incom-
petence, his reputation had been utterly ruined and his career in the army
finished.[380]

Thus far the response from the British at Detroit was less than heartening.
As both Alexander McKee and Simon Girty informed the Shawnees, considerable correspondence had been passing between the authorities there and the
governor-general of Canada, Sir Guy Carleton, who had recently been created
the first Baron Dorchester. The upshot was that the British were now talking
up a peace offensive rather than aiding their red allies in a war, a fact which
became clear in the council called at Detroit in early January.

McKee and Matthew Elliott presided at the council and it was Elliott who
laid out the plan: On behalf of the tribes, the British, who were having difficulties with France at the moment and were disinclined to open another war

with the Americans at present, would serve in an intermediary function with the Americans and make strong efforts to firmly establish a permanent and irrevocable boundary between the Americans and the Indians that would limit American encroachment westward only so far as the Muskingum River and northward only to the Ohio River. Such a proposal was nothing new but this time there was a twist—there would be no infringement of the boundary by the Americans because the British would guarantee its inviolability; they would, if the Americans crossed the boundary, immediately come to full aid of the Indians.

The Indians went away from the council uncommitted to such an arrangement and largely disgruntled despite the presents they had received of basic necessities, along with arms and ammunition. Long experience had taught them the *Shemanese* were no respecters of boundaries and the only sure way of keeping them out of Indian territory was to destroy them when they entered and, equally, to destroy the settlements and fortified stations that were the launching points for such incursions. In the meanwhile, the British increased the number of agents moving about through the Indian territory and promised a continuing supply of the weapons and ammunition they needed to continue their raids and oppose, if it became necessary, a future expedition against them.

On January 10, Blue Jacket, with Simon Girty beside him, led a party of some three hundred Shawnees, Miamis, Delawares, and Potawatomies against one of the newest of the settlements on the Ohio side of the river, Dunlap's Station, which was located eighteen miles northwest of Cincinnati. Though it was a well-fortified place with a little garrison of a dozen federal soldiers commanded by Lieutenant Jacob Kingsbury and they put up a gallant defense, the Indians would probably have taken the place except for an enemy they could not combat, the weather. In only a matter of hours the temperature had plummeted from just below freezing to well below zero and the attackers suffered badly from it. When it was learned that a reinforcement of nearly a hundred soldiers was on the way from Fort Washington, the attack was broken off, but not before a settler who had been captured was tied to a tree and tortured to death as a warning to the whites who watched helplessly from the fort.[381]

At close to the same time a party of forty Indians, mostly Shawnees but with a few Ottawas and Kickapoos, surprised the new Big Bottom Settlement, twenty-four miles up the Muskingum from Marietta and Fort Harmar.[382] Three weeks after its establishment in mid-December, while the men were still in the process of completing the construction, the Indians broke in so suddenly that not a gun was fired in defense and within mere minutes fourteen whites were killed—eleven men, two children and a woman. Three men were taken prisoner and three others escaped.

As soon as early thaws opened river travel again, another great influx of settlers began floating down the Ohio on rafts and in boats built at shipyards in the Pittsburgh area. In a very short time more new settlements sprang up in both Kentucky and Ohio. A substantial blockhouse was built on one island of the Three Islands area and garrisoned to thwart Indian attacks so frequently launched from them. Close by the Three Islands Blockhouse, on the Ohio shore, the town of Manchester was quickly established and its numerous cabins surrounded by strong pickets set in the ground and a blockhouse built at each of the angles.

In direct reaction to the influx, Indian attacks against the boats again became frequent. Tecumseh was very prominent in leading a number of these attacks close to the mouth of the Scioto and once again was on hand when the attackers tied a captive man to a tree and began laying out the ring of firewood to torture him to death.

Tecumseh, now wearing the British sword and the brace of pistols he had received from Blue Jacket, stepped up in front of the prisoner before the fire could be lighted and faced the Shawnees ringed about. His eyes were hard and his voice cold. "Most, if not all of you," he said, "know my feelings against the torture of prisoners. I ask that you refrain from doing what you are planning to do here. It is by such acts that we are called savages or barbarians. To kill this man in such a way," he pointed at the ring of firewood, "is cowardice."

Though the prisoner could not understand the words being said, he recognized that this Indian was trying to help him and a spark of hope was kindled in his eyes.

"*We* captured this white, Tecumseh," said one of the warriors, "not *you*. A prisoner is private property, for those who caught him to do with as they please. This one is to die," he said adamantly, "in the way we have chosen."

Their gazes remained locked for a moment and then, with one fluid movement, Tecumseh pulled one of the pistols from his belt, turned and shot the captive through the head. As the white man slumped in death, still held up by his bindings, Tecumseh turned back toward the others, who were stunned by what had occurred. He replaced the pistol in his belt and regarded them a moment in stony silence, then calmly walked away without a further word. Since then, he was pleased to note, there had been another decrease in the torturing to death of prisoners.

The first substantial indication to reach the tribe that an expedition was being organized to come against them was when word was brought that the various county lieutenants in Kentucky were calling for volunteers to join a late summer campaign to be headed by none other than Governor Arthur St. Clair himself. Spies were sent out to learn everything possible about such plans, but it was from Alexander McKee that they learned the most. British spies in governmental offices among the Americans had forwarded to Quebec,

Montreal, Niagara, and Detroit the disturbing intelligence they had gleaned.

The American president had been very humiliated over what had happened to the First Army of the United States under General Harmar and had decided something *had* to be done. He had taken the matter to Congress who had given him what amounted to a free hand to take care of the situation, appropriating over three hundred thousand dollars to finance the campaign. The president had thereupon conferred with the Secretary of War Henry Knox and they had selected their friend, the former Revolutionary War General St. Clair, to don the military mantle once again, organize a massive campaign to strike deep into the heartland of the Indians, engage and defeat the tribes where necessary and cow the remainder into total submission to the United States of America.

The explicit orders, as best could be determined, were that St. Clair was to at once start building an army—a new one and good one—of approximately twenty-five hundred men and to train it very well to both fight and obey. He was then, with this force, to march to the site of Harmar's defeat at Kekionga, where he was to establish a large fort capable of withstanding the concerted attack of whatever number of Indians might conceivably come against it. In addition, as he progressed along his route from Fort Washington to the head of the Maumee, he was to build a series of intermediary forts, their purpose being in part to serve as repository for equipment and supplies necessary to his march, but primarily to intimidate the Indians.

St. Clair had already informed each county lieutenant in Kentucky what his requisitions of men would be and that these men were to be placed in a state of readiness to come to St. Clair as soon as he should call for them.

So at last the rumors circulating for so long among tribes in the Northwest had become reality: full-scale war with the United States of America.

Chapter 7

[May 17, 1791 — Tuesday]

— ⟪ ⟫ — Only two days ago Tecumseh, high on one of the great hills overlooking the Cincinnati and Fort Washington area, had pulled open the fine brass telescope to its full length and peered through it at the activity taking place well below his party on the north shore of the Spaylaywitheepi. Never before had he seen so many rafts and boats at one time. There must have been upwards of two hundred of them, perhaps even more, and each loaded with cattle, horses, hogs, and most of all men— many in uniform but the majority in simple garb of settler or frontiersman. At that moment it had been impossible to say exactly how many men, but surely no less than a thousand. This was the army that had left Pittsburgh seventeen days ago; the army of Governor-General Arthur St. Clair; the army of the United States, that was supposed to move against the Northwestern tribes sometime this coming summer to avenge the humiliation that had been meted out to General Harmar.

Tecumseh was not impressed.

The very lackadaisical manner in which most of the men had disembarked on the makeshift wharfs that comprised the Cincinnati waterfront underlined the lack of discipline prevalent among them. Considering the number and severity of attacks the Indians had been launching against river travel this spring, it was almost inconceivable that they would be so careless and it made Tecumseh feel that if this were the type of army that would be coming against them, then there might yet be hope.

Word had come to Blue Jacket and Michikiniqua shortly after the force left Pittsburgh, and at the same time numerous other parties were dispatched to various areas of the Spaylaywitheepi to increase the attacks and disrupt the continuing influx of settlers. Tecumseh was placed in charge of the spying operations made on the army, with his brother-in-law, Wasegoboah, as his second in command. Now, the initial spying completed, Tecumseh left Wasegoboah in charge and repaired at once to the major camp of the Miamis and Shawnees on the Scioto River.

Those Indians had been very busy during the time Tecumseh, Wasegoboah, and the others had been engaged in their spying. On March 19 an attack had been made against a party of 35 men making their way upriver—14 aboard a flatboat carrying baggage and provisions and 21 men on the Ohio shore keeping pace. When they reached the mouth of the Scioto and gathered together for the ferrying across of the men on foot, an ambush was sprung. A devastating barrage of gunfire erupted that, in the first few moments, killed all but three of the party on shore, while two of the rowers in the boat were killed and another wounded.[383] The very next day, at the mouth of Tygart's Creek on the Kentucky side well above the mouth of the Scioto, another boat was fired into from ambush by a party of Miamis as it came close to shore and of 21 men aboard, 18 were killed.[384]

Blue Jacket himself had led one of the parties striking those traveling by water, finding that no matter how often the ruse of using whites to lure passing parties to shore had worked, the whites simply didn't seem able to resist. This was proven four days after the attack at the mouth of the Scioto when a large boat was spotted coming downstream. Two whites that had been taken prisoner were forced to decoy the boat ashore, in which were thirteen men and two women. Those in the boat were very suspicious of the two men who appeared on shore and pleaded to be taken aboard, saying that their party had been ambushed and they were the only survivors. After some penetrating questioning from a distance, those in the boat were finally convinced they were truly whites in distress and not Indians and the boat came shoreward. It had no sooner landed and been tied to a half-buried chunk of driftwood than the shots rang out and all fifteen aboard the boat were killed.[385]

Even when boaters of different parties joined together to protect one another with their increased strength, it was not much help. Such was the case the very next day—March 24—when a three-boat party was attacked six or seven miles above the mouth of the Scioto. Warned upstream of the hazards of traveling downstream alone, the larger party of seven families in a big keelboat was joined by a smaller boat containing two families and then, shortly after, were joined by yet another boat of medium size containing sixteen people, including the boat's commander and his wife and their twelve children, down to the age of five, plus a couple of young men who had joined them. These three boats were attacked by three large canoes of Indians—twenty or more per craft. The small boat and larger boat managed to get away with three dead aboard and five wounded, but having killed five Indians. The medium-sized boat, with sixteen aboard, was captured. Unfortunately for them, the man in command was recognized by the Indians to be Jacob Greathouse, the man who, in the spring of 1774, had butchered the entire family of Talgayeeta—Chief Logan—at Yellow Creek. For years the story had been told around the campfires of how Greathouse, after killing Shikellimus, the father of Talgayeeta, and the other men of his party, had then shot and stripped the pregnant sister of Talgayeeta and hung her by her wrists. Then, while she was still alive, they had slit open her belly and left her to die with the unborn infant dangling from her. For such a man and his family, a special punishment was reserved. The two young men and twelve children were lashed to trees, burned about the feet and legs and then beaten to death with willow switches. Jacob Greathouse and his wife, however, had each been stripped and tethered to different saplings with a loop running from neck to tree. Their bellies had been opened just above the pubic hair and the entrails severed, with the loose end of each tied to the sapling. The two had then been prodded around their individual trees so that their entrails pulled out and wound around the trunks. The wife of Greathouse had not survived long, dying before her insides were half unwound. Greathouse, however, had stumbled along until his entire intestines and stomach had been pulled free before he died. Both had then had hot coals stuffed into the body cavity. All in the party had been scalped.[386]

At almost exactly the same time, a party of Potawatomies boldly killed and scalped two whites who were discovered hunting directly across from Cincinnati near the mouth of the Licking—the sound of the shots easily carrying across the river to those in the town and fort.

Throughout the length of the Ohio River, from well below Louisville all the way up to Pittsburgh and even on the Allegheny and Monongahela above that place, similar attacks of terrible consequence were occurring, on settlers as well as river travelers, with the most prevalent attacks occurring in the vicinity of Cincinnati, Maysville, Three Islands, Point Pleasant, Marietta, and Wheeling. It was one of the bloodiest springs on record, yet the whites kept coming.

Now, Tecumseh reported the first intelligence of his spying ventures to Blue Jacket and Michikiniqua. He described the arrival of St. Clair's largely undisciplined army at Fort Washington, along with several other things his men had learned—among them, that on March 25 an order had come down from Virginia Governor Randolph directing the county lieutenants of the far

western Virginia counties to discharge any troops that may have been embodied under the authority of Virginia, as now the defense of the western
frontier had, by presidential order, become the responsibility of the United
States Army. However, only a month later, these same western counties were
sent orders to inaugurate a draft system to engage men in the armed service
under such leaders as Charles Scott, Benjamin Logan, John Brown, Harry
Innes, and Isaac Shelby, such men to be held ready to join the campaign of
St. Clair when he was ready for them. Tecumseh also reported that he had
seen some artillery being unloaded from the boats that had arrived at Cincinnati.

Blue Jacket and Michikiniqua were not pleased with the news, but they
were with the manner in which Tecumseh had gathered it. The two chiefs
decided it was time to get back to the Maumee River and get their own force
embodied, with whatever British aid was going to be made available, to meet
St. Clair's force before it could reach the Maumee and destroy the new villages
that had been established downriver from what was left of Kekionga all the
way to the mouth of the Auglaize. They ordered the majority of their men
to remain out along the Spaylaywitheepi and continue attacking river travelers
and settlements until word was brought to them to rejoin the main body, at
which they were to cease all attacks along the river and repair at once to the
Maumee.

Now, as Blue Jacket and Michikiniqua and a small number of their principal men headed for the Maumee themselves, Tecumseh joined them and laid
out an idea for their approval in regard to continued spying on St. Clair's
army.

"Where our own forces will gather, and where you will be," Tecumseh
told them, "will be a long distance away from where St. Clair's army is—
close to two hundred miles—and it will take a long time for the news I have
gathered to reach you. Such delays could be very dangerous and I have an
idea for getting the information to you much faster."

Both chiefs looked very interested and Michikiniqua said, "Tell us, Tecumseh."

"When we get to Kekionga," Tecumseh replied, "assign to me a total of
fifty men, each with a good horse. Three of these men and their horses I
would leave in Kekionga and the rest I would take with me when I return to
spy on St. Clair at Fort Washington. Twenty miles south of here, I would
direct three more of those men to make a camp and remain there in readiness.
Then each twenty miles after that I would do the same thing. When I reached
the vicinity of Fort Washington, I would still have twenty men left with me
to spread out and do the spying, while behind us will be ten camps of three
men each, ready and waiting. Each day I would dispatch a single rider northward with the information gathered over the last full day. He would ride as

speedily as possible to the closest camp north and relay the information to one of the men there, who would then, in turn, ride as rapidly to the next camp. This would continue until at last the final rider would reach here and give you the news. This would mean that in less than one day, the information I have gathered of St. Clair would reach you. Soon after the rider relayed from me reaches you at the Maumee, you would dispatch one of the three riders from here to follow the same route south, also at good speed, with whatever messages or instructions you may have for me, he also to stop at the first camp south and relay his word from you to another rider with a fresh horse. In this way, constantly having men moving on fresh horses, our line of communication could be kept open and very swift, with each man and horse having three days of rest between each hard ride."387

Michikiniqua and Blue Jacket, who had been looking at the twenty-three-year-old warrior intently as he spoke, now looked at one another, each seeing the glint of instant approval in the other's eyes.

"Tecumseh," Blue Jacket said, his voice reflecting the awe his young friend had inspired in him, "you never cease to amaze me. It is an excellent idea and we will see to it at once when we get home."

[June 29, 1791 — Wednesday]

The system set up by Tecumseh to relay intelligence of the enemy to the chiefs at the Maumee was working wonderfully well. No untoward incidents had occurred and a steady stream of information from his corps of roving spies, relayed to the chiefs, was keeping them well posted on St. Clair's preparations for his campaign. Thus far the news had been very encouraging.

St. Clair had assembled some fourteen hundred men by this time, with another thousand or a little more scheduled to be coming soon, both from the Kentucky settlements and from points up the Ohio River all the way to Fort Pitt. The encouraging data was not the manpower but that the army was sorely in need of supplies that had not yet come, and if they did not come very soon the expedition, scheduled to start on the first day of August, would have to be postponed.

News relayed back to Tecumseh had not been of any real significance until today. It was late afternoon when the lathered horse of one of his riders from the north galloped into their camp high on the wooded hills well back from the fort and settlement.388 The whites farther down the Spaylaywitheepi at Louisville had successfully pulled off a well-engineered subterfuge against the Wabash River villages but now, despite the initial victory it gave the whites, it was working to the advantage of the tribes.

Having gathered a force of seven hundred Kentuckians, Brigadier General

Charles Scott and his second in command, Lieutenant Colonel James Wilkinson, had left Louisville on May 23 on a march northwest against the villages of the Kickapoos, Weas, and Piankeshaws on the Wabash River, planning on going as far as the mouth of Eel River, where the large village of Kethlipecanunk was located, and destroying all the villages along the way, including Ouiatenon.[389]

The subterfuge had come about evidently as a result of their remembering how neatly Colonel Logan's army had wiped out the Shawnee villages when Clark had moved his force against the upper Wabash tribes and the Shawnee warriors had gone to aid the Miamis, leaving their own villages unprotected. Following this idea, Scott and Wilkinson had sent out a dozen pet Indians to tell the Indians of the Wabash villages that St. Clair's army was on the move against the Maumee villages and help was needed immediately.[390] The idea being, of course, to get the warriors of these villages they planned to hit well out of the way.

The plan had worked wonderfully. As soon as notified that St. Clair was on his move, the warriors fitted themselves out with the weapons and supplies, painted themselves for war and set off for the Maumee. By the time they got there and found nothing occurring or even apt to occur for quite some time, the army of Kentuckians was entering and ravaging the towns of the Kickapoos and those of the Miami subtribes, the Weas and Piankeshaws.[391]

At his temporary headquarters in Ouiatenon, Scott had sent a speech to the Piankeshaws and Weas, demanding they surrender or be destroyed. Those still there had no choice but to obey. With the killing of thirty-two men—primarily very young or very old warriors—and the destruction of six towns, along with their food supplies as well as their growing crops, and having taken fifty-eight women and children as captives, Scott immediately turned his army around and beat a hasty retreat to Louisville.

The whites were jubilant with their victory but what little they gained, Tecumseh was informed in the message from Blue Jacket, was offset by the fact that so great was the fury of the returning warriors that those who had only been halfheartedly supporting the growing coalition to oppose St. Clair, now became devoted to doing so, and those among the tribe, as well as the neighboring Kickapoos and Potawatomies who had been advocating making peace with the Americans, now had done a complete turnabout and were vowing full support. This was true as well with the elements among the Wyandot, Ottawa, and Chippewa tribes that had been inclined toward peace. With this change, it appeared quite likely that instead of having only 1,200 to 1,500 warriors with which to attack St. Clair, the combined Indian force would wind up having 2,000 or 3,000. Now even the Indian women, generally peaceably inclined, were clamoring for war against St. Clair to such an extent that many were preparing to join the army of Indians when it was formed and go along with it. Toward this end, as well, the message went on, an embassy of two Wyandot chiefs, Tayauendottoontraw and Tsoondoweno, had been sent to the Southern tribes to ask them to join the growing alliance of northern tribes opposed to the Americans.[392]

"As for the victory of the whites," the messenger quoted Blue Jacket as saying in conclusion, "is a victory really a victory if it does you more harm than good?"

[September 1, 1791 — Thursday]

When Tecumseh observed the detachment of some five hundred soldiers moving out of Fort Washington to the west a month ago, he was concerned enough to send a special messenger riding northward with the news. The fact that those soldiers had marched on a course directly westward was perplexing. The most obvious destinations seemed to be either Louisville or Vincennes, but more likely the former than the latter, since Indian attacks on the Spaylaywitheepi below the Falls had been causing considerable alarm among the Louisville residents.

Word had come back from Michikiniqua and Blue Jacket by the end of the second day after his message was sent, telling him it was believed that the force was, indeed, going to bolster Louisville and to continue his close observation of St. Clair's army at Fort Washington. As matters turned out, not until today, however, did he learn that his initial apprehensions had been correct. The force had been under command of Lieutenant Colonel James Wilkinson and had moved westward only as far as the White River, at which it struck north, reached the Wabash just a few miles above the mouth of Eel River, crossed it and continued northeast where, at Eel River, he fell upon the village of Kenapacomaqua.[393] There Wilkinson's detachment killed six Miami warriors, two women and a child. Two soldiers were killed, one wounded. The village was destroyed. Without spending too much more time in enemy territory, Wilkinson had terminated his hit-and-run raid and brought his army back to safety at Louisville.

Some other news Blue Jacket sent from the north was encouraging. Canada had just been split by the British into two major districts, to be called Upper Canada and Lower Canada. That portion east of the Great Lakes was now Lower Canada, while the remainder was Upper Canada and its new British lieutenant governor was thirty-nine-year-old Colonel John Graves Simcoe. All indications were that he was concerned about the welfare of the tribes and wanted to help them. To this end, he had already ordered construction of a fort at the foot of the Maumee Rapids, a dozen miles up the Maumee from Lake Erie; an installation to be named Fort Miamis after the tribe at its headwaters and after the fact that the Indians called the river the Miami of the Lake. This fort was to be built close to the ruins of the old French Fort Miamis. The combined Indian tribes were overjoyed at what appeared to be tangible proof that the British meant to actively support them in the major action shaping up.[394]

As a sort of counterpoint to that action was the council that Colonel Alexander McKee had just held with the combined tribes on the Maumee, where he had urged them to make peace with the United States, even to the point of offering his services as mediator between them and the Americans. It was clear that he had little belief they would go for such a proposal, but he had been ordered to make the offer, since the British home office was growing ever more anxious, with the growth of such a significant Indian force on the Maumee, that when and if a major battle came, the British would unwillingly become involved in it.

"We have good reason not to trust the Americans," Tecumseh said in his reply, "but I am by no means convinced we do not have a sufficiency of cause to mistrust the British as well. Their past actions have shown us that they do only that which most supports their own aims and desires. They say they are our friends, but sometimes one must watch friends even more closely than enemies."

[October 22, 1791 — Saturday]

There had been some belief expressed among the Indians that since the expedition had been so long delayed due to essential supplies not coming, it would be postponed until the following spring. St. Clair had expected to have a full complement of three thousand men and all necessary supplies relayed from Fort Pitt in plenty of time for a summer invasion. As September began this had not occurred and he still found himself with less than half the men he required and practically no supplies.[395] Despite this, he was under considerable pressure and felt his reputation was on the line; so, while he railed at the fact that he hadn't enough men and the quartermaster corps were a pack of fools, he also made it very clear that he was not going to cancel this operation for any reason. Time after time the target date for expected departure came and went without either his supplies or reinforcements arriving. At last he announced that he would put his expedition in motion on September 17. The closer the time came to that date, the more daring Tecumseh became in his spying activities and the more nervous he made Wasegoboah because of it.

Donning *Shemanese* clothing taken in previous raids and concealing his long black hair beneath a wide-brimmed leather hat, Tecumseh had entered Cincinnati and walked the streets as casually as if he were a resident, pausing as they did here and there to read the notices posted on walls and occasionally greeting a passer-by with a "Good morning" or "Good afternoon." Four different times he actually entered Fort Washington proper.

The first time he decided to enter the bastion he had seen soldiers and citizens passing back and forth through the gate. When he finally attempted it himself, he had merely fallen in behind one such group and had approached the sentries at the wide open gate, his heart hammering wildly inside his breast, though outwardly he was very calm. One of the guards had given him a searching look but he had merely smiled broadly, tossed a little wave that was half salute and said, "Scout." The sentry had smiled back and waved him in.

Moving determinedly from point to point within the fort, as if he were on special errands, Tecumseh was able to inspect the entire installation closely, even pausing to read carefully the General Orders that had been posted. He watched soldiers drilling on the parade ground and eavesdropped on conversations by pausing to tie a shoe or read a paper he carried in his hand to make it appear he was about official business.[396]

By the time he was in Cincinnati for the sixth time and in Fort Washington itself for the fourth time, the sentries at the gate had become so accustomed to seeing him that they scarcely paid any attention. The quantity—and quality—of the information he gathered was little short of amazing and, at the end of each day, back in his camp, he would send another rider on his way with the intelligence.

The disreputable face of the army did not seem of great concern to St. Clair. Tecumseh's lips had curled in scorn when he read the posted General Order that said the army would emerge victorious from any encounter with the savages because, *it has been proved that savages, if violently attacked, will always break and give away; and once broke, for the want of discipline, will never rally . . .* The matter of the lack of supplies for the army was something St. Clair considered to be far more serious and intelligence of which was of the utmost importance to the Indian leaders. Tecumseh meticulously reported how private contractors were showing up in large numbers, trying to sell their inferior goods at greatly inflated prices and St. Clair was still holding out against them despite his army's need, feeling sure the supplies requisitioned to him should arrive from Fort Pitt momentarily. But they did not.[397]

When Tecumseh learned that the line of march was not going to follow the route Harmar had taken through old Chalahgawtha on the Little Miami, he quickly sent word northward and had his relay camps moved westward to be close to where St. Clair would pass. The posted lines of march and lines of battle had indicated that the force leaving here would strike out just a little west of due north and continue on that line until the Great Miami River was reached. From there, all indications were that it would go straight north rather than to follow the Indian trail along the bank of the Great Miami.

On September 17, St. Clair grimly left behind instructions that when the anticipated supplies arrived they should be forwarded on to him at once. He then, with Major General Richard Butler as his second in command, marched his army out of Fort Washington and past scores of cheering Cincinnati spectators, which included Tecumseh, who closely noted the numbers of troops and their arms.[398] St. Clair had expected to have a force made up of no less than four-fifths regular United States Army troops. Instead, he was leaving with only 700 regulars, including both officers and men, and 690 very unhappy militia draftees from Kentucky.[399] Besides the 1,400 troops, some 400 civilians were following behind, primarily wives and children of the soldiers and a large number of prostitutes out for a killing of their own. He also had with him eight pieces of field artillery.[400]

Tecumseh had slipped away then and raced to his camp where one of the messengers was sent off at once with word of the army's departure, its strength and arms. Then, with the others, he had followed the army, keeping well out of sight.

Twenty-three miles out of Cincinnati, at a good fording place of the Great Miami River, General St. Clair called a halt, established a camp in an adjacent high prairie and ordered the erection of a strong installation to be called Fort Hamilton.[401] Tecumseh's messengers from the first relay camp north of Cincinnati had by this time joined him and as soon as a camp was established several miles from the army in a well-secluded grove, he sent a messenger out with instructions to the next relay team to keep out of the army's way and the next relay rider to continue toward the Maumee with the news.

The messengers who had arrived brought good news. On the day before the army left Fort Washington, a major council of the allied Indian nations had convened at the mouth of the Auglaize on a broad prairie overlooking the Maumee and adjacent to the trading post that John Kinzie established after the destruction of his store at Kekionga. To aid the Indians, Kinzie—called Shawneeawkee by the Indians—donated most of the supplies he had on hand, a gift the Indians, especially Tecumseh, vowed not to forget. In a unanimity almost unknown to the Indian nations, intertribal disputes had been put aside and all were in accord with the need to act together in what needed to be done.

The accord, however, had not extended to the British in the matter that counted most—manpower. Represented by Indian Agents Alexander McKee and Matthew Elliott, and with Simon Girty also on hand, the British reluctantly agreed to provide arms, ammunition, and gunpowder, as well as three British liaison men as unofficial observers, consultants, and advisers, but they assiduously refused to publicly involve themselves, stating that if they did so,

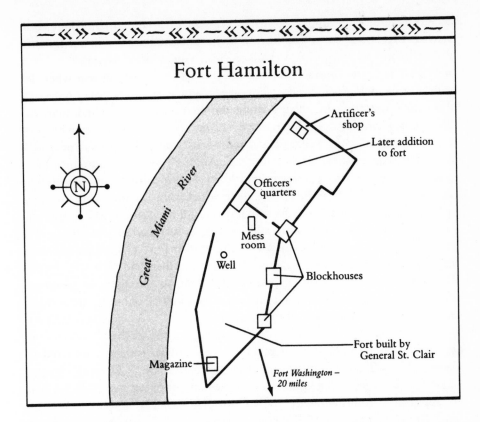

Fort Hamilton

the Americans could and would use that as an excuse to march against Detroit which, if they took it, would leave the Indians out on a limb.

The principal business the Indians had at this council was to select their battle leaders for the coming affray and pledge their warriors and chiefs totally to that end. The foremost discussion had dealt with who was to be in general command of the Indian force and for some time it was balanced between Blue Jacket of the Shawnees and Michikiniqua of the Miamis. It was an impasse that was finally resolved by the fact that since the Miami and Shawnee had worked so well together against Harmar's troops the preceding year, they should do so again now. Michikiniqua should have the top command, but Blue Jacket would act virtually as a cocommander, though in matters involving highest authority decision, he would be second in command, followed in turn by Tarhe of the Wyandots and Pipe of the Delawares. Wawpawwawqua— White Loon—would lead the Mohawks and Weas. So it went, down the line through the Ottawas and Chippewas, who had come from as far away as Michilimackinac, Winnebagoes from as far distant as the valley of the Wisconsin River, Sacs and Foxes from the valleys of the Rock and Mississippi rivers, Potawatomies from the areas of Checagou, Milwackie, Peoria Lake,

351

and from along the Illinois, Fox, Des Plaines, St. Joseph, and Elkhart river valleys, Kickapoos from the central and southern Illinois country and the valleys of the mid Wabash, Vermilion, and Sangamon rivers, Piankeshaws and Weas from the middle and upper valleys of the Wabash and from the valleys of the Eel, Mississinewa, Tippecanoe, and Salamonie rivers, Delawares from their scattering of villages along the Tuscarawas, upper Muskingum, Walhonding, White, and Whitewater rivers, some Senecas and Mohawks from the Grand River country of Ontario, and a scattering of Mingoes from wherever their transitory camps were located. Among this most unusual convergence of warriors was a contingent of forty Potawatomies who had shown up under the leadership of a young village chief from Pimitoui named Chaubenee who was very anxious to be reunited with his good friend Tecumseh.

It was Girty, the messenger told Tecumseh, who had brought the crowd of nearly three thousand Indians screaming to their feet. The influential white man stood before them a long quiet moment and then said, in a far carrying voice, that never before had he seen so great and so courageous a gathering of Indians. Then he had reached into his pocket and pulled out a large white egg, holding it up high for all to see.

"This," he went on loudly, dramatically, "represents the whites coming toward us, while my fingers encircling it represent our brotherhood of Indians here. What will be the outcome when they meet? *See!*" He had abruptly tightened and turned the egg into a crushed and dripping mass and the roar of approval from his audience was an awesome sound to hear.

The new commander of the allied Indian forces, Michikiniqua, was the final speaker, the messenger had reported. His talk may not have been so dramatic as Girty's, but it was no less inspiring.

Tecumseh and his men continued their spying but with Tecumseh, because of his command of English, doing the most and taking the greatest risks, usually entering the camp before dawn, spending the day watching, moving about and watching construction of the fort. He also listened closely to the growing complaints of the men as their initial lack of morale degenerated to black depression and rebelliousness, largely because their commander refused to share the very limited army rations with the camp followers. As soon as the new fort was all but completed and officially named, the general set his army in motion again, moving north, leaving behind twenty men to garrison the new Fort Hamilton. It was at this point that approximately half of the camp followers gave up on the venture and set off on their return to Cincinnati. Once again, Tecumseh set his own messenger into motion, but at a pace far more swift than the army's.

The events that began yesterday morning, continued during last night and culminated this morning were occurrences that threw a whole new light on matters, greatly elating Tecumseh and his followers and causing a considerable change in plans. Early yesterday morning, when the army had reached a point forty-four miles north of Fort Hamilton, St. Clair had ordered another stop and the construction of another fort, this one close to where two inconsequential streams converged.[402] No one in the entire army was considered exempt from the work and all the soldiers and officers, including even St. Clair himself, set about erecting the structure. With only ten men short of fourteen hundred busy cutting timbers, trimming them, digging, sinking the palings, and other requisite work, a serviceable fortification was completed by nightfall and officially named Fort Jefferson.[403]

During the night the disgruntlement of the drafted militia manifested itself most strongly when three hundred of them, by prearranged signal, quietly arose, collected their gear and supplies and slipped out of camp. As soon as they were beyond hearing, they raced away at top speed. In the morning, when news of the mass desertion was brought to St. Clair, he was beside himself with fury, not only at their desertion but at the fact that they had taken such quantities of the meager supplies meant for this expedition and his even greater fear that they would encounter and plunder the supply train he expected to be coming after him. He had immediately ordered a detachment of 140 regulars under Major John Hamtramck to pursue them.[404] Then, leaving Fort Jefferson with 20 men to serve as its garrison, he pushed his force to the north again, with his original strength of near 1,400 dwindled at this point to a total of only 920.[405]

Now, giving instructions to Wasegoboah and leaving the spies in his charge, Tecumseh mounted his own horse. "This time," he told them, "*I* will carry the news!"

[October 26, 1791 — Wednesday]

"My brothers!" Michikiniqua said, his voice carrying well in the crisp autumn air to the ears of all the many chiefs and warriors in attendance. "Only a short time ago our British brother, Simon Girty, told us that he has seen many armies of brave warriors before, but never one so great nor so courageous as you who are gathered here. To that I would add, never one so determined to crush the whites who invade our lands and take away our women and children."

Michikiniqua paused to let the roar of response to his words die away and then continued. "In these many weeks past we have sent out eyes to watch the movements of the *Shemanese* chief called St. Clair. Because of the courage and skill of the young Shawnee warrior, Tecumseh, son of Pucksinwah, we have known each move of the *Shemanese* and of their strengths and weaknesses. The protective hand of the Great Spirit has covered Tecumseh, for he walked among them, read their words and listened to their secret meetings without detection. He sent runners flying to us with all he learned and we have been able to plan to meet the enemy where it will best serve us.

"Now," Michikiniqua continued, "Tecumseh has flown to us himself with the best words yet brought. He sits among us, there," he pointed toward the Shawnee contingent, "with his chiefs, Catahecassa and Wehyehpihehrsehnwah, and I would ask him to stand before you and tell what he has learned and what we should do now, with which I am in full agreement."

Michikiniqua turned and walked toward the Shawnees and Tecumseh, seated between the principal chief and war chief, came lithely to his feet. The Miami chief gripped his hand and wrist with his own hands and Tecumseh accepted the honor with pleasure. He escorted Michikiniqua back to his seat beside Apekonit and then faced the largest audience he had ever addressed.

There was an aura of strength in his bearing and power in his words and his listeners were transfixed. Chaubenee, seated with his own contingent of Potawatomies, had felt it often and now once again experienced that overwhelming surge of admiration that this twenty-three-year-old Shawnee evoked. Others who had never seen or heard of him before seemed similarly affected.

"Brothers! I bring news that will be short in telling, but immensely important in its meaning. The *Shemanese* general, St. Clair, was preparing to bring a force against us of three thousand soldiers, both bluecoats and soldiers from across the Spaylaywitheepi. But his chiefs far to the east have failed him and when he left Fort Washington, where the Spaylaywitheepi makes its northern bend, he had less than half the soldiers planned. His supplies failed to reach him and so he marched with only half enough and his men are hungry and cold and discouraged. He built two forts and had to leave men to guard them. Then, in the middle of the night, three hundred of his white chickens flew away and so he sent nearly half that many bluecoats to chase them and bring them back and continued his own march north. He is now very weak, with just over nine hundred men—only a third part of the number of warriors assembled here."

Tecumseh paused as an excited murmur rippled through the crowd, then spoke again as it died. "Brothers! The bluecoats he sent to chase those who fled from him may come back. The hundreds of other soldiers he has expected may arrive at Fort Washington with the supplies and all these may be sent on to him. But they could not reach him as quickly as we! They move slowly, even when in haste, and if we ride against him now—this day!—we will find him still weak, still hungry and without defense, camping at the place on the trail where the Wabash can be leaped across by a horse. We cannot afford to wait until they reach the place where the warriors under Michikiniqua and Wehyehpihehrsehnwah defeated them during the last Harvest Moon. By then his belly may be filled and his weak arms strengthened. No! Brothers, we must move to cut him off, *now!*"

The Indians leaped to their feet shrieking war cries and roaring approval to what Tecumseh had said. A sense of wild elation, controlled but overwhelming, flooded Tecumseh in the realization that the words from his own mouth had evoked such a response in so many. The *power* of it! There was a little more talk after that, but not much. Blue Jacket had shaken his hand warmly and congratulated him for the skill, daring and ingenuity he had shown in all his spying endeavors. Catahecassa, however, not only said no word of praise, he merely looked at Tecumseh somewhat balefully, then turned and walked away. For the very first time Tecumseh detected in his chief something he'd never noticed before but which evidently had been growing for some time—*resentment*. That and something else, even more elusive, but which finally came to him: resentment and just the faintest trace of *jealousy*. But why on earth, Tecumseh wondered, would the principal chief of the Shawnees, the most powerful man in the tribe, harbor resentment and jealousy for *him*? He had no idea, but it was certainly something to think about.

Within four hours, their faces garishly painted in red and white, yellow and black and blue, the entire Indian force set out for the headwaters of the Wabash.

Beside Tecumseh rode Chaubenee, who looked over at his friend and grinned. "I told you I would come any time you needed me," he said.

Tecumseh grinned back at his burly young friend. "I had no doubt you would. I have heard that you are now married to Canoku," he said, "and that you have become chief of your village. You have done well."

Chaubenee's grin widened in pleasure at the words, looked around at the vast army of mounted Indians and then back at Tecumseh. His words were simple and sincere. "You have done very well yourself, my brother."

[November 3, 1791 — Thursday]

Two days ago the Indians, some three thousand strong, had established their cold camp, without fire and without food, hardly three miles north of the headwaters of the Wabash, observing great care in keeping themselves from being detected. The fast was upon them now and they would not eat again until the battle had been fought. But confidence filled their bellies and the fervor of war heated their blood and warmed them. A general feeling of keen anticipation prevailed among all the tribesmen and morale was very high.

The site recommended by Tecumseh had been selected now for the attack. If, as predicted by Tecumseh, the force of soldiers approaching in midafternoon went into camp when they reached the thirty-foot-wide stream that was the upper Wabash, then they would strike it at dawn tomorrow. If, however, they crossed the stream and continued to approach, the attack would be made later this afternoon while the force was engaged in the difficult business of fording the stream.

Tecumseh's spies, sent by Wasegoboah, had brought them the latest happenings with the force of whites moving against them: After leaving Fort Jefferson, St. Clair's army had continued marching northward, hampered by an abundance of cold, miserable rain that soaked the earth so that as the army passed across, it became a veritable sea of muck, particularly for the artillery carriages. The worse the weather became, the more St. Clair's own condition and disposition deteriorated, the gout paining him so terribly that at intervals he had to be carried on a litter.

Forward observers had reported an increase in Indian sign on the ground they were crossing and catching occasional glimpses of Indians but not in numbers enough to cause any real concern. Now, having traveled some twenty-eight miles since leaving Fort Jefferson and a faint new snow coating the ground as lightly as a hoar frost, word came to the commander that the van of the army was approaching a stream believed to be the headwaters of the St. Marys River and that, while only some thirty feet wide, it would present certain difficulties in crossing.[406] Did the general mean to cross it yet this day? No, the general did not. The army would collect during the remainder of the afternoon on the higher ground that formed a plateau lightly timbered with oak, ash, and hickory south of the stream and get a decent night's rest for the crossing first thing tomorrow.

Over this piece of ground the encampment was spread in two lines, some seventy feet apart with four pieces of cannon in the center of each line. At his orders, however, a leading detachment under Lieutenant Colonel Oldham, consisting of about two hundred fifty Kentucky militia and a company of rangers were to cross the stream and advance across the three-hundred-yard-wide bottom land on the other side of the stream, and continue to the top of a slight rise about a quarter-mile distant before making camp.[407] Because the army was infinitely weary from its day's march, even though they had traveled hardly eight miles, St. Clair made the decision to postpone the erection of any kind of defensive fortification until the morrow. It was precisely the point where Tecumseh had said they would be encountered and the first time most of the warriors had experienced Tecumseh's prophetic ability. They were greatly impressed, even awed.

Wasegoboah himself came in and reported that always before when they had stopped for the night in dangerous territory, the army had immediately erected breastworks from logs and branches in case of an unexpected attack. This time they had not done so. They had not even moved what wagons they had with them into a line behind which they could take cover. The wagons merely stood where they had stopped, in helter-skelter pattern. The soldiers had literally dropped in their tracks, entirely fatigued, in their two marching lines an arrow flight apart. Some built small fires, but most merely curled up to sleep, their bellies empty. Again—another ripple of wonder spread throughout the Indian encampment—Tecumseh's prediction had come to pass: the army of *Shemanese* was weak, cold, hungry and *without defense*!

So auspicious were the signs that many of the warriors, especially the Sacs, Winnebagoes and Kickapoos, wished to leap to the attack immediately, but Michikiniqua and Blue Jacket stayed them. "We must wait," Blue Jacket said, "until the dawn. We are so many that if we try to attack them in the dark of night, we will hurt one another even as we try to hurt the enemy. Beyond this, at dawn the *Shemanese* will be coldest and in least command of their wits and their confusion will become our ally."

Wasegoboah reported that when the *Shemanese* commander failed to send out reconnoitering parties to scout the area for several miles ahead, the militia commanders decided to do so on their own and several scouting parties had been sent out from the company of rangers. It was as dusk created a pall over the area that one of the rangers, Private Robert Branshaw, returned in some haste to the forward detachment and reported to Colonel Oldham that he had discovered tracks in the new snow that was falling and had followed them until he spotted a small Indian camp a mile or so ahead. Unknowingly, what he had detected were Wasegoboah's men.

"I figure," Branshaw told the colonel, "that it's nothing much more than a scouting party sent out by the main body of the Indians to spy on us and maybe get a scalp or two if they can do so without any big risk."

Though Oldham agreed this was likely and immediately sent Branshaw back to keep an eye on it, he nevertheless neglected to report the sighting to the general. It was well known to Oldham and the other officers that St. Clair's gout had been particularly troublesome to him this day and, as a result, his temper was on hair trigger. No one cared to further trouble him and run the risk of feeling the effect of that temper.

As darkness closed in, the Indian force moved in closer and, at a point about three-quarters of a mile from the enemy, split their line and began moving carefully around the outermost limits of the whites to encircle them as much as possible. By the wee hours of the morning they had completed this encirclement except for the farthest south arc of the circle along the route the army had advanced upon, purposely leaving this gap to avoid detection should a detachment come up to join St. Clair from the south, or messengers be sent back in that direction by the general. With the encirclement completed, word was quietly passed and the Indians gradually crept inward, tightening the circle until they were no more than a quarter mile from St. Clair's army and themselves still undetected.

The stage was set.[408]

[November 4, 1791 — Friday]

The skies had cleared only an hour or so ago and, as the first gray streaks of dawn laced the eastern darkness like cold fingers, the three thousand Indians under Michikiniqua and Blue Jacket braced themselves for the assault against St. Clair's army, awaiting only the cry from Michikiniqua that would galvanize them into action. Their bodies ached with the cold of crouching under their buffalo robes through the night on the army's perimeter, yearned with the need for movement to loosen stiffened limbs and send hot blood racing to their extremities. The discomfort had been heightened by the fall of two to three inches of heavy snow earlier during the night.

For a little while some two hours ago it had seemed that the battle would break out prematurely. A small squad of soldiers had come toward the Indian lines, the several men visible only as barely perceptible darker shadows against the snow. They had paused and held a murmured conversation and then abruptly raised their rifles and a few shots rang out. With remarkable discipline, the Indians had stayed hidden and as abruptly as it had begun, the firing had ceased. The soldiers clustered together a little longer and then turned and went back to the camp, which they had awakened with their shooting. Conversations were vaguely heard and voices calling, "All's well," and the camp gradually slipped back into its somnolescence.[409] While the incident could have upset the attack plans, it didn't and, in fact, turned out to work to the Indians' advantage. Having had one false alarm, the whites would not be quite so quick to respond when the next alarm—the real one—came. Also, it helped to snap many Indians out of the quasi-stupor they had fallen into while waiting for the attack signal to be given.

Now, with the threads of dawn lighting the east and objects just becoming discernible, sound and movement began coming from St. Clair's camp. The commanding general was walking among his men, long-knife in hand, issuing orders relayed by officers and the soldiers were beginning to rise. Still the Indians held their place, waiting. The soldiers were formed in their units and held so for a while as their commander spoke and then as subordinate officers spoke after him.[410] For many long minutes they were held in their formations and then, at last, with the sky becoming progressively brighter, they were dismissed.

The Indians watched as the men went back to bedrolls or tents, freshly primed their weapons and loaded the cannon. With these matters finished, the troops began building small campfires and preparing breakfast, some going to the edge of the stream to scoop up containers of water. It was while they were busiest in these pursuits and the naked branches of trees now etched distinct webwork patterns against the sky that the signal came.

"HAAAaaaaaaaaahhh!"

The shriek of Michikiniqua's voice broke the eerie stillness on one side of the encirclement and the voice of Blue Jacket picked up the cry on the other side. In that instant the entire Indian force erupted in a cacophony of hideous cries and plunged to the attack. The forward guard, north of the stream, was encountered first. Totally demoralized, scarcely without firing a shot, they dropped their weapons and fled back toward the main body of the army, in mere moments splashing through the icy waters of the narrow Wabash, their own chaotic screams of pure terror a contagion that afflicted the entire army, throwing it into a state of fatal confusion.

As the charging Indians neared the stream, the Americans, responding to the screamed commands of their officers, rallied and momentarily checked the charge with a hot fire, but only momentarily. The answering fire from the Indians was directed at the line and caused staggering losses among the soldiers.

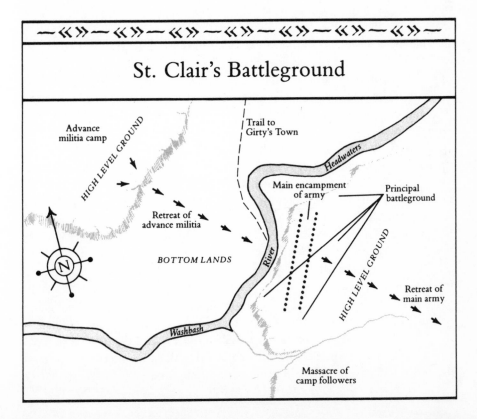

St. Clair's Battleground

Advance
militia camp

HIGH LEVEL GROUND

Trail to
Girty's Town

Headwaters

Main encampment
of army

Principal
battleground

Retreat of
advance militia

BOTTOM LANDS

River

N

HIGH LEVEL GROUND

Retreat of
main army

Washbash

Massacre of
camp followers

The circle of attackers was tightening, many warriors already darting about among the confused troops with slashing tomahawks.

Colonel George Gibson, commander of the artillery, tried desperately to rally his men, shouting "Fight them! Fight them! I'd rather die ten thousand deaths than let these savages take this field!" In that instant a bullet severed his spine. Captain Ford, artillery officer, though dangerously wounded, took up where Gibson had left off. "Stand by your guns!" he screamed at the artillery crews. "Die like men, not like cowards!" His own death came only a minute later. Other officers took up screaming for the artillery to fire, but now it was discovered to their horror that the cannon powder was defective and would not properly ignite. Only two of the big guns went off, neither doing any serious damage. Immediately the Indians attacked the artillerists with their greatest weight of firepower, flintlocks blasting in a staccato din lasting several minutes. As it died away, all the artillerymen and their officers lay dead or dying.

General St. Clair called for his horse and even as he was mounting, the animal was struck by a ball and killed. So were two others in succession. In exasperation he hobbled painfully off afoot and even in their panic, the soldiers were startled to see him racing back and forth among them in the hottest areas of fire, calling upon them to be steady, to hold their ground, to aim well, to make every shot count. While giving these orders, a lead ball barely grazed the side of his head and took away a lock of his scraggly gray hair.

The Indians now rushed both flanks of the army simultaneously and were opposed in counterattack by Major General Richard Butler on the right and Major William Clark on the left, both of whom were momentarily successful in repulsing the Indians. Within a few more seconds, however, Clark died with a tomahawk blade in his heart and Butler, dazed and leaning against a tree, was dying, having been struck by four bullets. Two of his three remaining men snatched him and half dragged, half carried him to the surgeon's tent, where Dr. Edward Grassen immediately began tending his wounds. An Ottawa plunged into the tent, shot the doctor with a pistol and then began trying to take Butler's scalp. Dr. Grassen in his dying moments, managed to reach his gun and shot the Indian dead. Moments later both he and Butler were also dead.[411]

Blue Jacket seemed to be everywhere at once. Fifteen men had already fallen to his gun and tomahawk and fifteen fresh scalps were wadded together in his pouch.[412] He was a veritable demon in his speed and savagery and many soldiers who saw him coming simply threw down their weapons and fled.

St. Clair's glance fell on Colonel William Darke and the general shouted at him to lead a bayonet charge. Darke swiftly rallied his men and executed the order with great spirit. In a moment, seeing one of his officers, Major

360

Fowler, in imminent danger of being tomahawked, Darke raced up brandishing his sword and beheaded the Indian who was about to strike.

St. Clair had hurried on and found Lieutenant Colonel Oldham, commander of the forward guard, now here in the midst of the army and standing wide-eyed beside a tree. The general ordered him to rally his men and lead an attack similar to Darke's, but Oldham merely turned fearful eyes on him, shook his head and said, "Damn it, that's suicide! I won't do it!"

Hardly had the words been spoken when a bullet tore away the whole rear of his skull and he pitched to the ground, dead. St. Clair simply turned and himself rallied Oldham's men and led a bayonet charge against the Indians' left, momentarily repulsing them. Twice more in succession he led similar attacks and while men dropped everywhere about him, he remained unscathed.

Chaubenee stayed as near Tecumseh as he could, determined to protect him from any unseen danger approaching, but he had difficulty keeping up. Armed only with war club and scalping knife, the young Shawnee was an incredible fighting machine, downing soldier after soldier with his smashing blows, leaping with abandon from one clash to another in vicious hand-to-hand battle. The meaty smacks of clubs and tomahawks against flesh, the cries of the injured and dying, the frenzied screams of plunging horses and the overwhelming din of thousands of screeching Indians was a crescendo beyond description. Chaubenee realized abruptly he had become separated from Tecumseh and devoted his whole attention to killing others and staying alive.

St. Clair, hardly able to walk anymore, was still moving about. He came upon a half-dozen privates standing in a cluster, weeping. Drawing his pistol, he pointed it at them. "Get back into the fight," he ordered harshly, "or by God I will shoot you dead where you stand!" The men scattered. Other groups, however, similarly paralyzed with fear, weaponless and bewildered, were simply mowed down by the Indians.

At last St. Clair's legs gave out and, no longer able to walk, he was scrabbling about on hands and knees, still calling orders and begging someone to get him a horse so he could properly direct his men. At last a frightened and recalcitrant packhorse was found and St. Clair was lifted astride the animal's back. Though he could hardly coax it into anything more than a walk, at least the general was mobile again. It didn't seem to make much difference. His orders were repeatedly being disobeyed or ignored, by regulars as well as militia. The entire army of St. Clair was in total disruption and in terrible straits, with the problems intensifying every second.

Some soldiers were still trying to fire the eight cannon, but without success. In addition to the powder being so defective it would hardly ignite, it had been packed in mislabeled kegs marked "For the Infantry." Boxes marked "Flints" were found to contain gunlocks. Confusion and panic increased and men were running in circles, crying, or standing slack-jawed in the paralysis of fear, watching the approach of death. Nor was it only the soldiers who were being killed. The wives and children and prostitutes that had been following the army were also cut down. Many were running back and forth, wringing their hands and screaming, some were running southward as fast as they could, while others stood transfixed or dropped to their knees and began to pray. A great number sobbed and groaned in each other's arms and some had fallen in faints. The Indians rushed among them with flailing tomahawks, war clubs and knives and, in the end, only three individuals of the over two hundred managed to escape.[413] The snow underfoot everywhere had become a scarlet slush and bodies were sprawled like jackstraws.

As he darted about, Ensign John Whistler caught a glimpse of the slaughter of the camp followers and murmured a brief prayer of thanks that he had not allowed Annie and the children to come along. Even as he thought this, a tomahawk swung at his head missed its mark and laid open his shoulder to the bone, wedging there. As the warrior struggled to jerk it loose, the officer brought his pistol up under the man's chin and fired, not even looking as the Indian went down, only surging away as best he could with the tomahawk still embedded in his shoulder.

The red-haired Apekonit had been given the responsibility by Michikiniqua to lead three hundred Miamis in a drive against the eight cannon to silence them, and it had been his attack that was so effective, with all the big guns now in Indian possession. He triumphantly carried this news to Michikiniqua and then stayed close to his adopted father, twice killing soldiers who would have slain the Indian commander had he not been there.

With prearranged calls, Michikiniqua and Blue Jacket—both splattered with blood but no drop of it their own—drew the Indians into another attack force and again the Indians simultaneously struck both flanks and the rear with redoubled energy and the soldiers before them were mowed down in windrows, as if struck by a great scythe.

Of the British on hand with the Indians, only Simon Girty took part in the actual fighting, clad and painted like an Indian and unrecognizable as anything else by the Americans and already with six men having fallen to his gun and tomahawk.[414]

Incredibly, for over three hours the battle had been fought and well over half the army was dead or dying. The whites remaining who were capable of fighting clustered near their commander in the middle of the encampment, desperately trying to hide behind overturned wagons, dead horses or even the bodies of their own companions. For them there was now only one hope remaining if they were to avoid an absolute massacre and St. Clair, still on the packhorse, knew what it was. He cupped his mouth and bellowed out the order for retreat and the whole of the surviving whites capable of doing so turned and rushed en masse, breaking through the weakest part of the Indian lines, where the warriors had spread themselves thin trying to close off the rear. The order to retreat had reignited the panic and soldiers dropped their rifles, threw off their greatcoats to make better speed and ran with the breath of the devil at their heels, the retreat having become an absolute rout. Wounded companions were left behind, still vainly trying to hold their own while the retreaters ran into one another, pushed each other aside, stumbled over fallen comrades and continued running. The Indians fired into the fleeing pack and scores more were dropped, but their companions continued running.

The Indians did not pursue, under orders of Michikiniqua, who had runners quickly pass the word, "You must be satisfied—you have killed enough!" Together he and Blue Jacket held the warriors at the scene of battle and gradually the din faded.[415] Sporadic firing and the screams of the dying being scalped or tomahawked continued for a considerable while, but by noon it was all over. No living whites were left on the battlefield and those few who had escaped had long since disappeared.[416]

The scalping began in earnest then. Some of the warriors had scalped as they downed their foes, but others, such as Tecumseh and Chaubenee had simply struck and struck again, moving on instantly once a foe was downed. A great horde of Indian women who had remained hidden in the woods during the battle now emerged and joined in the bloody business of scalping and then helped to gather up the weapons and supplies that had belonged to the dead or were discarded by those who had fled. Bodies were stripped of shoes and clothing and left naked and bare-skulled on the stained snow. The eight cannon, too large to be taken away in the deep snow and muck were carefully hidden— some in a deep hole in the Wabash—for safekeeping and later recovery for possible use against their former owners.[417]

A careful search was ordered by Michikiniqua for any dead or wounded Indians. A total of sixty-six were found dead and tenderly wrapped in shrouding made of the army's abandoned tent canvas. These were tied to horses, to be brought back to their villages or to be buried in a place well away from here. Incredibly, only nine Indians had been wounded and, of these, only one seemed likely to die.

By midafternoon, the Indian force was moving off, horses staggering under the weight of plunder that had been recovered, mainly weapons. Late in the day the skies became a dark gray and deepened into a gloomy twilight. A new snowfall began, mercifully coating the red mire with fresh white and covering the ghastly, grotesquely contorted remains of 832 dead American soldiers and camp followers.[418]

[*December 31, 1791 — Saturday*]

The year ended in a more gratifying manner for the Shawnees than had any year in recent memory. The inspiring defeat of General St. Clair's army had not only boosted their self-confidence immeasurably, their portion of the plunder from the battlefield helped provide the wherewithal that would see them through the forthcoming winter. Additionally, one of the most joyous immediate results was that the influx of immigrants coming down the Spaylaywitheepi had ground to a virtual standstill.

The Indians, soon after division of spoils, broke up into separate factions and returned home by different routes, bearing with them a multitude of stories that would be told and retold in the councils and around the cook-fires for months and years to come. Never before in the history of any of these tribes had there been so inspiring a victory and such a rejuvenation of hope that perhaps there was yet strength and determination enough within the Indians to drive the whites out of the Indian lands.

It was with considerable sadness on both their parts that Tecumseh and Chaubenee bade each other farewell, with Tecumseh reiterating his previously made assertion that there was still to be much for them together in the future. Within a fortnight following the battle, Tecumseh had led a party of thirty young warriors toward the Spaylaywitheepi and engaged in a series of hard strikes against new settlements north of that stream and attacks on individual encroachers.

Among those who fell victim to such attacks were some of the more experienced frontiersmen who mistakenly felt that the Indians, content with their victory, would be inclined to spend the winter in the comfort of their own abodes far to the north. Two such individuals, who had for the past five years run their traplines without interference along what was called Locust Creek, almost directly across the Ohio River from Maysville, did not count on the tracking ability of Tecumseh and pushed their luck one season too often. Tecumseh's sharp gaze, picking up vestiges of their trail that others of his party had missed, followed it up and, when they came upon the pair in their well-hidden camp and in the act of skinning out their day's catch of muskrats, the two were slain and their entire store of pelts taken, as well as their goods.[419]

In another instance, a party of whites hunting along the Great Miami River not far from Fort Hamilton, detected smoke and carefully followed it up. Undetected, they discovered Tecumseh's hunting camp. Taking position to give themselves the best advantage, they fired on the Indians gathered around the campfire cooking their meal. Two warriors were slightly wounded and the whites, expecting the Indians to plunge away in terror, were totally taken aback when Tecumseh led a shrieking charge directly at them. Two of the whites were killed and scalped and the remainder scattered and considered themselves very fortunate to finally make it back to Fort Hamilton individually.

At the same time that he was hunting and tracking down enemies, Tecumseh was continuing to pick up whatever information he could. He learned, for example, that St. Clair, when he left Fort Washington to go to Philadelphia to explain his defeat to the president, had put a capable officer of the regulars, David Zeigler, newly promoted to the rank of major, in charge of the fort.[420] Less than a month later, however, Colonel James Wilkinson supplanted Major Zeigler as commander of Fort Washington, and the day after Wilkinson took command, he ordered the construction of a new fort between Fort Hamilton and Fort Jefferson, to be named Fort St. Clair.[421] A good engineer, Major John Gano, was placed in charge of the construction and assisting him was an eager young ensign who had arrived at Fort Washington only a few days too late to be included in the St. Clair expedition. He was a likeable young man who had personally been appointed to his rank by George Washington and whose late father, Benjamin Harrison, had been one of the signers of the Declaration of Independence. A headstrong young man who had quit medical school in favor of a military career, his name was William Henry Harrison. When Tecumseh heard the name, his eyes widened and a tiny shiver raced down his back as so often occurred when he was experiencing a presentiment. Unconsciously, his hand came up and cupped the *opawaka* dangling from his neck.

[April 11, 1792 — Wednesday]

As customary when forming a war party, Tecumseh made a very strong point of instructing those who elected to follow him that he expected—no, *demanded*—instant and unquestioning obedience to any command he might give, no matter how strange or out of place it seemed to be. Anyone, he always added, who did not like that idea or felt himself incapable of acting instantaneously on Tecumseh's order had no place in his party. Occasionally someone would drop out, but far more often those who wished to ride in a Tecumseh war party were eager to do precisely as he asked.

Such had been the case with this present party of sixty warriors who, ten days ago, had volunteered to accompany him on a horse-stealing expedition in Kentucky. Sinnanatha had elected to go along this time and all were young men like themselves with the exception of Chiuxca and Frog Hunter, both of whom were many years his senior. Frog Hunter was one of the oldest active warriors in the tribe. Chiuxca, on the other hand, was principal chief of the Peckuwes and that he would even consider going along in a subordinate role to Tecumseh was little short of amazing. It was Chiuxca himself, however, who explained his reasons.

"For a good many years now, Tecumseh," he said, chuckling, "I've heard—and believe—the stories of your skill in practically everything. But, while I believe, I really want to see for myself. You don't mind, do you?"

"Not at all," Tecumseh replied. "I'm very honored."

"And, like the others," Chiuxca added, now laughing aloud, "I pledge to follow your orders exactly and instantly."

So they had set out, Tecumseh in the lead on his large powerful black gelding and the others following, bringing along with them, at Chiuxca's suggestion, three of the large marquee tents that had been part of the plunder at St. Clair's defeat. "I may want to go along, Tecumseh," Chiuxca explained, "but that doesn't mean I want to sleep out on the open ground during the Rain Moon. I'm a little too old to enjoy that. We can bring them along on three of my packhorses."

The big tents, each capable of sleeping twenty, had turned out to be a welcome addition. During seven of the ten nights they had been gone, rain had fallen, three of the times in torrents. The tents had kept them dry and comfortable. They did not, however, take them across the Spaylaywitheepi with them, but left them and the packhorses under guard of two men in a small camp a half-mile from the river.

The raids on the three settlements had gone very well. Their aim was to steal sixty good horses, one per man, which was the maximum they could safely handle and retain if a pursuit were mounted. Skirting both Maysville and Washington, which they planned to hit on the return trip, they had struck first at May's Lick, eight miles south of Washington. Just after darkness had fallen they crept to the large fenced lot where twenty-two horses were being kept. Cooing softly to calm the animals and feeding them nuggets of maple sugar to make them more tractable, they had very quietly blindfolded the animals one by one with strips of blanketing tied over their eyes and then haltered each with lengths of rope with which to lead them away. It was a lark. Without anyone in the station being any the wiser, they walked all twenty-two horses away to where the others of the party were waiting and then mounted their own and led the stolen horses behind, maintaining silence until they were more than a mile distant from the station.

It was close to midnight when they approached Washington, four miles southwest of Maysville and only one cabin showed a light. They stopped a quarter mile distant and while the others waited, Tecumseh slipped away on foot to reconnoiter. In twenty minutes he returned. "Thirty-four of them," he whispered, "in a lot behind the third and fourth cabins. I want thirty-five men with me, two to bring their rifles in case of trouble."

Within another five minutes, carrying their blanket strips, ropes and sugar packs, they were on their way, creeping along carefully behind their leader. The horses here were a little more skittish and it took longer to quietly calm them, then get the blindfolds and halters in place. They were just walking the last of them out of the fenced lot when a small dog came bounding toward them yapping furiously. Two other dogs near the cabins took up the commotion, barking loudly.

The solitary light in the one cabin went out and a door opened. "Who the hell's out there?" demanded a gruff voice in the darkness.

One of the two warriors with rifles brought his gun up and sent a shot crashing toward the cabin. They heard the door slam and loud voices from there and elsewhere and hied away quickly. An instant later there were more shots—many more—this time from several of the cabins and the balls could be heard clipping through leaves and branches and thumping into tree trunks, but neither men nor horses were struck.

The others were ready and waiting, weapons out and prepared to charge in to help if necessary. It wasn't. Mounting their own horses, they led the captive animals away at a good pace and Tecumseh gave the order that they would forego trying to get any others at Maysville now. It was too risky and there was likely to be a pursuit mounted.

They swam the animals across the Spaylaywitheepi ten miles below Maysville and returned to their little camp, picked up the two men and horses left there and continued heading northward.[422] Throughout the remainder of the night they traveled at a fast pace, not slowing to a more normal progress until sunrise.

They stopped then to eat but not to rest, chatting and laughing among themselves and very pleased with their haul of fifty-six good horses. When they resumed leading the horses northward, their pace was very easy and in the middle of the afternoon, when a buildup of heavy clouds betokened rain before too long, they decided to stop and set up camp. At this point they were about forty miles north of where they had crossed the Spaylaywitheepi and they were much less apprehensive about the possibility of encountering any parties of whites.

The site chosen to set up their night's camp was on the east bank of the East Fork of the Little Miami River. At this point a small creek emptied into the river from the east and formed an elevated triangular flat some thirty feet over the pleasant crystal clear waters of East Fork. Here they began to set up the three marquee tents.[423] Several of the young men were belling and hobbling the horses to release them in an adjacent meadow to the east where they could graze on the new emerald green grasses.

While this was going on and, with a few hours of daylight remaining, Tecumseh asked for someone to range back several miles on their backtrail to make sure they were not being pursued. It wasn't likely, but Tecumseh rarely neglected taking such precautions and it amused him to see the approval in Chiuxca's eyes as he made his request. Frog Hunter volunteered for the job and, since the old warrior's own horse had already been hobbled, Tecumseh offered him his own large black gelding. He was well aware that Frog Hunter greatly admired the big black but would never have presumed asking to ride it. Now that warrior grinned and nodded and in moments was riding back the way they had come, the little bell that had already been hung about the horse's neck tinkling faintly.

While camp was still being set up, Tecumseh and Sinnanatha elected to get some meat for the party and set out afoot, taking only their bows with them. Within half an hour Tecumseh had brought down two fine fat deer. The pair draped the animals over their shoulders and carried them back to camp where they were quickly dressed out, spitted and cooked over the camp-fire. Tecumseh was a little concerned that Frog Hunter was not back yet but, knowing well the old warrior's sagaciousness, convinced himself he was all right and would return soon. They had no sooner begun to eat than the rain began pelting down and the party split into thirds and retired into the three big tents. The heavy rain lasted only a short while, then tapered off to a more gentle rainfall. Everyone in the party was weary, having traveled a long way and with no sleep the previous night so, by the time the rain stopped completely, a couple of hours after darkness had fallen, most of the Indians were asleep.

Several of the younger men in the party were assigned to rebuild the rain-dampened fire and keep it going through the night so Frog Hunter would have no difficulty locating them on his return. To get the fire going well again, they spread out and collected dry dead branches still on standing trees, since the scattering of wood on the ground was too saturated to burn well. Once the fire was nicely going again, some of the heavier chunks of wood that had been taken inside one of the tents to keep it dry were brought out and soon a good overnight fire was going again that would require only occasional refueling.

Near midnight a fire tender arose, glanced out and saw that the fire had burned down quite a bit. He picked up a couple of good-sized chunks of the dry wood, took them outside and placed them on the coals. In moments the flames were licking over them and lighting the darkness. He stood there a moment watching and was just about to return to the tent when the shot came.

The lead ball caught the young warrior in the back, severed his spine, smashed through his heart and erupted from his chest, sending him flopping lifeless to the ground beside the fire. Other shots came then, twenty or more, in a sporadic manner and on the heels of the blasts Tecumseh erupted from the tent he was in, war club gripped in his right hand.

"Attack!" he shouted, plunging toward where the shots had originated.

"*Attack!* They are few!" In only a few bounds he was among the attackers who were frantically trying to reload. The first swing of his club crushed the skull of one of the whites, dropping him where he stood. The others scattered like quail into the darkness. [424]

Other warriors were tumbling out of the tents now, rallying to Tecumseh's cries and a general firing broke out, directed toward the sounds of men thrashing away through the underbrush. Sinnanatha, clutching his rifle, glimpsed the bulk of a huge man before him, thrust the muzzle of his rifle directly into the center of his chest and pulled the trigger. The gun misfired as a squib and the ball barely made it out of the barrel of the gun. Both men, shaken, darted off in opposite directions. [425]

The general gunfire had little effect other than to spur the whites into a frantic effort to get away fast. The big frontiersman whom Sinnanatha had almost killed raised his voice in a great bellow—"Scatter!"—and scatter they did.

The Shawnees did not pursue. There would be no possibility whatever of trailing their attackers until daylight. In this present moonless dark it would be pointless and extremely dangerous to even attempt to do so, but Tecumseh immediately set up a ring of guards to watch and listen for anyone returning, then assessed the damage to themselves. Considering that they had been taken wholly by surprise and a good many shots had been fired into the tents, their loss was minimal. Apart from the young warrior who had been killed at the fire and Frog Hunter, who they now assumed was either dead or captured, only one other warrior in the tents had been killed. Three others had been slightly wounded but were in good shape.

Tecumseh felt grudging admiration for whoever led the party of whites. He had selected his method and time of attack well and was obviously very bold to hit so much larger a party than his own and thought ahead enough to have the leeway of half a night's head start if pursuit of them was to be launched. It was the type of audacity Tecumseh would have exhibited and the type of plan he would have made had the circumstances been reversed.

In the ominous stillness that had settled over the camp now, Chiuxca, Tecumseh, and some of the other leading men of the party met in council and discussed what they should do. Should they follow in the morning and perhaps overtake and kill or capture some of the whites, or would they be walking into an ambush if they did so? Suppose these men had been merely the advance scouting party of another army like Harmar's or St. Clair's?

Prudence ruled and it was decided to break camp at once and head north. Chiuxca praised Tecumseh for his coolness and ferocity under fire and was not surprised when Tecumseh turned leadership of the party over to him and said he was going to take only a dozen men from the group and, in the morning, see if they could find Frog Hunter and rescue him, if possible, as well as search for some of the attackers. If there was a larger force, they would spy on it and learn its intentions.[426]

The tents were struck and packed away and the hobbled horses were rounded up, found easily in the darkness by the tinkling of their neck bells, and tethered individually behind the mounted warriors who were ready to head north. Thirteen were left for the party who remained behind. Tecumseh and his dozen men, including Sinnanatha, saw them off in the darkness and then retired to a nearby defensible hollow and crouched there in readiness until dawn, the horses tied up close by.

Just as soon as it was light enough, they were on their way, following their own backtrail that Frog Hunter had taken the previous afternoon. In just over two miles they heard the stamping and snorting of horses and moved up stealthily. In a few minutes they discovered the twenty-four tied-up mounts of the whites and were encouraged. That they had not returned for the animals meant three important things: first, that they were not part of a larger party or they would have returned here in the darkness and ridden back to their companions; second, that their leader was shrewd enough to realize that had they returned here to get the horses, they could easily be followed and over-taken and that they had a much greater likelihood of escaping if they remained afoot and scattered; third, that since the black gelding was not here, it meant one of the men must have returned to this place and taken it and, if so, his fresh tracks following last night's rain would be easy enough to locate and follow.

Tecumseh ranged out farther and circled. In a few moments he uttered an exclamation. Not only had he discovered the fresh trail of one man leading a horse, but a distinctive indentation in the rear right hoofmark identified it as Tecumseh's treasured black gelding. Ordering Sinnanatha and two other warriors to accompany him and the remainder to stay and hobble the horses of the whites and let them graze, he took up the trail at a rapid pace, following it as it angled to the southwest. Within half a mile the footprints of the man disappeared, indicating he had mounted the gelding and was now riding.

Fifteen miles from where they had found the horses of the whites, Tecumseh suddenly stopped and held up a hand, both stopping and silencing his followers. He lifted his head and his nostrils flared as he sniffed the air to catch again the elusive scent that had made him stop so abruptly. There! It came to him again; the faint but unmistakable aroma of cooking bacon. Through hand signals, Tecumseh had them tie their horses out of sight in a small hollow and then follow him as he let his keen nose lead them through the woodland to the source of the scent.

Several hundred yards later they entered a clearing and saw, only forty feet ahead, a small redheaded white man crouched by his little campfire, gnawing on a greasy, smoke-blackened chunk of bacon rind. The gelding was tied to a sapling a dozen feet from him. The man saw them in the same instant, dropped the bacon and snatched up his rifle, then ran as fast as he could.

The shortness of the little man's legs betrayed him and he could not match the speed of his pursuers. The instant he realized they were overtaking him, he stopped, wheeled about and leveled his rifle at them. Sinnanatha and the other two warriors immediately darted behind trees, but not Tecumseh, who put on a burst of speed and, as the man's greasy hands slid and fumbled for an instant on the gun, threw himself upon him and bowled him over, the gun going off into the air as it flew from his grasp.

The little redheaded man was no match for Tecumseh and in an instant was on his back with Tecumseh's knife poised at his throat. The white ceased all struggles and, after a moment, Tecumseh pulled him to his feet and tied his hands behind him. They then led him back to the man's camp and untied the black gelding. Tecumseh patted the animal's nose and let it nuzzle his hand before leaping to its back. Forcing the prisoner along, they returned to where their own horses were tied and lifted the white man onto the back of the horse Tecumseh had ridden here.

On the way back to the others at the abandoned camp of the whites, Tecumseh questioned the man in English and discovered that his name was Alexander McIntyre. He was at first disinclined to talk much but, at Tecumseh's evident admiration for the boldness of the attack and his curiosity as to who their leader had been, he admitted that it was Simon Kenton. At first Tecumseh frowned but then, remembering, brightened.

"You mean the man who was called Bahd-ler, who was once our prisoner?"

"That's the one," McIntyre replied.

"Bahd-ler!" Tecumseh said, nodding, then smiled. "I am pleased that it was such a great warrior as the *cuttahotha* who did this. He is a worthy enemy and someday I will meet him again. Soon, I think."

"Get ready to die if you do," the red-haired man said sourly.

Tecumseh asked then about Frog Hunter and was dismayed to learn that he had been killed and the body hidden, but that before dying had told them that his leader was Tecumseh, who would soon be coming to avenge him. He added that they had been trailing the horse thieves all the way from where they had crossed the Ohio below Maysville and had eventually heard the tinkling of the horse's bell coming their way and they had hidden. Kenton, he said, had wanted to take the approaching Indian alive but one of his party— a man named Neil Washburn—had shot and killed him. At Tecumseh's probing, McIntyre said he really wasn't sure where Washburn had hid the body and doubted that he could find the spot.

McIntyre went on to say that then Kenton and Washburn had scouted ahead on foot, following the dead Indian's backtrail and had found and spied on the camp of the Indians from under cover. They had been watching, he said, when the rain came and all the Indians had taken shelter in the tents. That was when Kenton had decided to surprise the camp in the middle of the night. Since the party of the whites was only about a third as large as the Shawnee party, Kenton had given them instructions to surround the camp and, at his signal to all fire simultaneously into the tents while at the same time setting up a great chorus of yelling, to make the Indians think they were being attacked by many more than were there and perhaps panic them into flight.

"Prob'ly would've worked, too," McIntyre went on, " 'cept Luther Calvin got all excited when that buck came out to feed the fire and he shot before the others. Then, when us others shot, it was scattered and didn't sound so much like a big party as Kenton meant for it to. That's when he yelled at us to scatter and we did. Me, I figgered I'd hie back to where we left the horses and take that nice black horse for myself. Reckon now I shouldn't've did that."

After that they rode in silence the remainder of the way to where the others were waiting, who hooted with delight as they caught sight of Tecumseh's party returning with the black horse and white prisoner. Despite Tecumseh's earlier assurances to the contrary, these warriors had been worried that the whites would return for their horses and attack them. Relief was in their voices now and they chattered like excited children as McIntyre was tied to a tree. Was there nothing this Tecumseh couldn't do?

However, when Tecumseh now ordered them to round up the somewhat scattered horses, their fear returned. Suppose, they said, the *Shemanese* had crept up in the woods and were waiting for them to split up? Why not just leave the horses and go home?

Tecumseh snorted. "What frightened sparrows! I see here no future leaders of the Shawnees. Stay together and tremble, if you like. I will get the horses."

He started away and Sinnanatha joined him. The others were chagrined, but the fear in them was stronger than the shame and they remained where they were. In a moment Tecumseh and Sinnanatha had disappeared into the woods. Their job wasn't easy. Although the hobbles did not let the horses move very rapidly, they had spread out considerably to find graze in these woods and it took the better part of an hour to locate and gather them and lead them back. They were unprepared for the sight that met them on their return.

From a pole stuck in the ground in the center of the trail, the scalpless head of Alexander McIntyre stared sightlessly at them. On another pole close by, his still dripping heart was impaled. Arms and legs had been hacked off and his body cut in two just below the rib cage and these six grotesque pieces were hung with rawhide strips from tree limbs overhanging the trail.

Tecumseh's gaze went one by one over the pieces and by the time he looked back at his men his expression had become one of great rage. When he spoke his voice was low, almost a hiss, trembling with the anger that filled it.

"Cowards! Rabbits! You are not Shawnees. No! You are not even men. You are worse than the carrion birds. You disgust me with your cruelty. Are your hearts so weak? Is there no room in them for pity? Are you so afraid of your enemy that you must kill and mutilate him when he is tied and helpless in your grasp? Is this what our chiefs have taught you of courage? To destroy the weak or those unable to defend themselves? This is not courage. No! This is cowardice of the worst kind. I am ashamed for you. I am ashamed *of* you. And I am most of all ashamed that you are of my people!"

As if struck by physical blows, the warriors winced at the words. They could not hold Tecumseh's cold gaze, nor could they speak, knowing what he said was true. Tecumseh stared at them in silence for a long while and finally spoke again, his voice less outraged but even colder than before.

"We will go home now, where you will be safe from enemies, whether they are bound or not. All of you but Sinnanatha will ride behind me at all times that I will not have to look upon you. It will be our last ride together. I will not bear the company of cowards."[427]

[July 1, 1792 — Sunday]

By far the greater majority of the Shawnees as well as other tribesmen were still riding high in the belief that the United States had been so thoroughly trounced at St. Clair's Defeat that no further military onslaughts would be mounted against them. The very fact that for months the country had been overrun by peace emissaries from the United States government seemed to be the proof of this contention and Catahecassa, principal chief of the Shawnees, was loud in proclaiming that his tribe had finally won in the long struggle against the *Shemanese* and that now it would only be a matter of time until a firm and binding treaty could be made that would protect the Shawnees and other tribes, along with their remaining lands, for all time.

Among those who put no faith whatsoever in these assertions were three of the most influential Indians in the Northwest Territory—Michikiniqua, Blue Jacket and Tecumseh. Time after time the three had sat together—usually in Michikiniqua's new house in the rebuilt Kekionga—and discussed the matter, always coming to the same inevitable conclusion: that the United States government had not yet mounted another invasion against them simply because it was not yet ready, financially or militarily, to undertake such an effort.

Admittedly, ever since the defeat of St. Clair there had been a great lull

in the conflict between Shawnees and Kentuckians, as well as between Pennsylvanians and Wyandots, and stronger efforts were being made by the whites
to enforce the edicts against any white parties entering the lands north and
west of the Ohio River.

Through their informational grapevine with the British at Detroit, the
tribes had learned the details of the government's investigation into the causes
of St. Clair's devastating failure. It had taken exactly three moons for the army
to return to the site of St. Clair's Defeat under Lieutenant Colonel James
Wilkinson to bury the dead Americans still littering the ground at the battle
site on the Wabash headwaters. With a strong party from Fort Washington,
Wilkinson had arrived at the site on February 4, gathered from the deep snow
what dead they could easily locate—which was only seventy-eight frozen
corpses and included none of the camp followers—and buried them in a common grave, then quickly left with what few muskets and pieces of artillery
equipment they could find.[428]

Three weeks later, St. Clair had been exonerated by Congress. Hundreds
of witnesses had been questioned and much deliberation taken to come up
with the investigation's bottom line, which was that St. Clair "was not justly
liable to much censure, if any."[429]

In the matter of the peace offensive the United States appeared to be
taking from its new seat of government, Washington, District of Columbia,
the six emissaries sent out at different times had all been looked upon as spies
and all had been killed. Yet so determined was the government that it refused
to take offense at this and instead simply hired some more emissaries, including
some Iroquois, to carry the next proposals and they were presently wandering
about the country.

On the first day of June, just one moon ago, Kentucky had finally severed
itself from Virginia and became a state in its own right among the United
States and, in the Sheaf of Wheat Tavern in Lexington, a log structure temporarily being used as a statehouse, the new state legislature had met for its
first session and elected as governor, by common consent, Isaac Shelby.

The news imparted to the Indians by their British friends that caused the
greatest undercurrent of trepidation, however, was that the American government was gradually rebuilding its military strength and was determined
not to make the mistakes that had been prevalent previously—most particularly
not to send out politically selected generals to lead inexperienced armies recruited from civilian communities. The need was great for a strong commander
of proven military leadership capabilities and a strong army of well-disciplined
regular soldiers.

Toward this end, in which President Washington was in full accord, the
chief executive drew up a list of twenty possible candidates for the position

of commanding general and submitted the list to his cabinet for comment. There was a great deal of discussion as one by one, for a variety of causes, the names fell by the wayside until at last only one remained and he was considered as being no prize.

The individual in question had commanded a Pennsylvania battalion during the Revolution and had risen to the rank of brigadier general through his services, rendered successively at the battles of Brandywine, Paoli, Monmouth, Valley Forge, Stony Point, and, finally, Yorktown. Though he had never been honored previously with an independent command of his own, he had proven himself to be a man who believed in strict discipline among the troops and who had shown himself to be prudent and dependable under all circumstances, as well as being somewhat of a thinker with a good grasp of military strategy. On the negative side of the ledger, he was a drinker, a womanizer, a man with an irritable disposition who did not get along well with fellow officers, a man excessively vain, a man who, like St. Clair, was overweight and suffered chronically from gout. His record as a businessman following the Revolution was not at all inspiring. He had made faulty business ventures in Pennsylvania that left him practically destitute and then had purchased a plantation in Georgia and moved there, only to very quickly go bankrupt. With creditors hounding him, he turned to politics and won the Georgia race for a seat in the United States House of Representatives, only to have that election overturned because of fraud. So unsure was Washington, even after selecting this man, he wrote that he was "never more embarrassed making any appointment" and only hoped that "time, reflection, good advice and, above all, a due sense of the importance of the trust which is committed to him will correct his foibles, or cast a shade over them."

Bestowing upon him the rank of major general and placing him in command of the United States military in the West, President George Washington had, this past April, named as the successor to Arthur St. Clair, the officer who had won such unflattering sobriquets as Mad Anthony and Dandy Tony— Anthony Wayne.

The Indians knew nothing of him but they were not pleased about the new western military commander when Alexander McKee quoted to them a single paragraph from a letter written by the British minister to the United States, George Hammond, to the lieutenant governor of Upper Canada, General John Graves Simcoe, which said:

> *General Wayne is unquestionably the most active, vigilant, and enterprising Officer in the American Service, and will be tempted to use every exertion to justify the expectations of his countrymen and to efface the Stain which the late defeat has cast upon American Arms.*

Now the news had just reached the tribes that fully justified the apprehensions of Michikiniqua, Blue Jacket and Tecumseh. Mindful of the fact that with the destruction of St. Clair's army, the total number of United States regulars in the West was down to only 750 officers and men, the United States Congress had not hesitated very much in appropriating, last month, the sum of $1,026,477.05 to raise, pay, and equip a new United States Army of five thousand regulars, of which an adequate proportion was to be assigned to Major General Wayne and his second-in-command, the newly promoted Brigadier General James Wilkinson, for an expedition against the Indians of the Northwest. Wayne had immediately moved his headquarters to Fort Pitt to begin amassing a force of twenty-five hundred men to be called the Legion of the United States.

Yet there were mixed signals that still had a good part of the Indian population of the Northwest very confused. On the one hand General Wayne was initiating a build-up of troops eventually destined, so it was believed, to come against them. On the other, Wayne himself had just issued a letter that very neatly undercut any plan the new State of Kentucky may have been harboring, now that it was no longer controlled by Virginia, to move against the Indians. That letter, now well posted throughout the frontier, stated in its entirety:

Head Quarters, Pittsburgh, June 23, 1792

Sir,

The President of the United States has thought it proper to endeavor to come to some explanation with the hostile Indians in order to lead to such measures as will, eventually, be productive of a General Peace. In the interim, and until the effects of those overtures are known, it would be highly improper that any hostile attempts should be made against any of the Indian towns or settlements, however laudable that kind of zeal and enterprise may be in due time and season.

I am therefore ordered by the President, and I do hereby, in his name, most solemnly forbid and restrain any attempts being made against any of the Indian towns until the result of the aforesaid overtures for peace are known; but this restraint does not extend to prohibit the severest punishment against all hostile parties of Indians who may be found hovering upon the frontiers. You will, therefore, govern yourself accordingly.

I am, with much esteem and regard, Sir,
Your most ob'. Hum'. Servant,
Ant'. Wayne
Major General and Commander in Chief of

the Army of the United States

To the Lieutenant of
the County of Mason

So, what did it all mean? Was there to be peace or was there to be war? Almost all the Indians were confused, but not Michikiniqua, Blue Jacket, and Tecumseh. With unshakable certainty, they *knew*.

War!

[December 31, 1792 — Monday]

George Washington's peace overtures among the Shawnees and other Northwestern tribes continued to come to exactly nothing. The Indians had been over this ground before and, burned as they had been with the so-called peace overtures at Fort Stanwix, Fort McIntosh, and Fort Finney, they were extremely wary. In the majority of cases, the Indians simply refused to even discuss possible negotiations. In those cases where they did hear out the emissary, the proposals evoked nothing but scorn. What fools did the *Shemanese* think the Indians were? How many times in the past had they listened to such proposals? How many times had they agreed, only to find themselves pushed farther back, their land taken, their game destroyed?

One of the delegations sent by the United States to propose terms of peace had, as its principal speaker, none other than Seneca Chief Sagoyewatha—Red Jacket. His appearance in such a role greatly angered the Northwestern tribes. In the proposal he delivered, which was patently ridiculous and demeaning in what it offered, he concluded with an earnest appeal.

"If the Americans are indeed prepared to make such a generous offer," Sagoyewatha said, "then you who are assembled here should not be too proud-spirited and reject it, lest the Great Spirit should become angry with you."

Tecumseh was on hand at the council and yearned to have the opportunity to reply to Sagoyewatha, but he was not called upon. An old Thawegila Shawnee orator, Messquakenoe, who had often served as spokesman for the tribe on such occasions, had been selected to respond on behalf of all the assembled tribes and his reply was neither tactful nor charitable.

"Brother," said Messquakenoe in a much less than brotherly tone of voice, "how do you dare to come before us and tell us what we should or should not do? How do you dare to speak on behalf of the Americans, who not many moons since, were your avowed enemies and who ejected you from your lands? How do you dare to presume to speak on behalf of the Great Spirit as if you were Her prophet and Her voice?

"Brother," Messquakenoe went on inexorably, "where have you been? It is well known among us all that over the past five summers, while we western nations have been fighting against the *Shemanese,* the Six Nations have been notably absent. You Iroquois have always been an untrustworthy people and you seem to have become even more so since you have been seduced by the Americans and made to cower with your tails between your legs."

A murmur of approval rumbled through the assembled Indians and Tecumseh was among the many who were pleased and impressed with the remarks. When the undercurrent of voices had finally run its course, Messquakenoe continued.

"Brother, why would you think that we here would even consider any offer made to us by the treacherous *Shemanese*? The Shawnee, the Miami and the other allied tribes here represented have, within the space of one year, twice defeated large armies of them who have foolishly marched against us. Should we, then, be the ones to meekly accept an offer from them that they *might* agree to, if we first commit ourselves to peace? No! But we who are assembled here are reasonable people and if the *Shemanese* are so desirous of peace as they say, then we *might* offer terms to them."

Sagoyewatha's jaw was set in a hard line and his expression was stony as he listened to the insults being heaped upon his own people and the Americans whom he presently represented. After a long delay, during which the primary chiefs met and discussed what terms they could offer to the Americans, Messquakenoe delivered the terms that had been drafted.

"Brother," he said, "take back to your American friends and protectors these words we now put into your ears . . . *Our* terms are these: *all* of the lands to the north and the west of the Spaylaywitheepi, which is called Ohio River by others, is ours forever. The Americans who are already in place in this land must withdraw. The Shawnees must, since it is their land upon which these white cabins and forts have been erected, be paid for this intrusion and they must also be paid for their former hunting grounds of the Kan-tuck-kee, which have been illegally occupied by the *Shemanese* and ruined by them as a hunting ground. That is what must be done. If the Americans wish to accept these conditions and have the peace which they loudly but not genuinely profess, then the Miami, Shawnee, Wyandot and Delaware tribes and their allies will be willing to receive the official representatives of the United States next summer. That is all we have to say. There is no more."

Sagoyewatha retired with his delegation and considered. When he finally made his reply, his horns were withdrawn and his manner conciliatory. "Brothers of the tribes here assembled," he said, "now that your feelings have been clearly explained, I understand and agree with them and I will inform the Americans of what you have said and of the offer you have made."[430]

Even while such matters were occurring, the State of Connecticut, cavalierly disregarding the continuing Indian peril and certainly with no consideration for many Wyandot villages in the area, gave 500,000 acres of the western portion of her Western Reserve claim for the benefit of citizens who had suffered from the British during the American Revolution. This grant of 781 square miles was to be distributed among the 1,870 residents of nine Connecticut towns who had "suffered by fire" and for that reason the tract was being called The Fire Lands.

Tecumseh and Blue Jacket continued to lead attacks against river travelers, settlers and troop movements, separately or together, gradually building up the reserve of Shawnee supplies with the plunder taken and knowing that all the talk, all the political maneuverings, and the professions of wanting peace were nothing more than camouflage to cover the slow but strong and thorough building of his invasionary army by General Anthony Wayne on the upper Ohio—an army all the Indians expected to move against them as soon as the warmer weather came next spring.

Michikiniqua and Blue Jacket joined forces again late in the year in a brief but harsh attack against a United States Army supply train returning from Fort Jefferson to Fort Hamilton. The supply train consisted of one hundred packhorses being escorted by a similar number of mounted Kentucky riflemen under Captain John Adair. Their ambush occurred on November 6 at a place called the Forty Foot Pitch, located just seven miles east of Fort St. Clair.[431] Fourteen soldiers were killed and the valuable string of American horses was captured.

It was from Simon Girty that the Shawnees garnered the most reliable information in respect to what General Wayne was doing. He did a considerable amount of spying on that front by disguising himself as an old Frenchman and mixing with the officers who frequented Duncan's Tavern and other such establishments in Pittsburgh. Little he had to report was of an encouraging nature. Wayne was whipping his army into a better and more disciplined fighting force than had ever before been seen on the American frontier, keeping them constantly busy with drilling, learning maneuvers, keeping their arms and equipment clean and in good working order, instructing them endlessly in shooting and reloading, in proper order on the march and, most of all, teaching them to obey the orders of their superior officers without question and, in so doing, instilling them with a fear and respect for military discipline that Wayne felt was the absolute core of any good army.

Wayne, Girty told them, frequently had men publicly whipped for infractions of orders or duties, with minor offenses such as laziness, uncleanliness or not being properly in uniform bringing a penalty of twenty lashes and more serious offenses—insubordination, drinking on duty, striking an officer, sleeping on duty, leaving one's post without permission, dereliction of duty—bringing the harsh punishment of one hundred lashes.

Wayne considered desertion the most serious offense and his army was plagued by it during the first weeks at Fort Pitt. He quickly curtailed it by having a firing squad execute any deserters who were caught. By the time seven such executions had occurred, desertion was no longer a serious problem.[432]

Another matter Girty reported was that General Wayne's own aide-de-camp, Captain Ballard Smith, had incurred his commander's wrath through drinking to excess and was relieved of his duties and another young officer, an ensign, promoted to lieutenant and assigned to the slot Ballard had occupied, and that this young, serious-minded officer was named William Henry Harrison. And once again, hearing this name caused a chill of presentiment to momentarily and disconcertingly touch Tecumseh.

Girty further reported that by this time Wayne had raised a thousand troops whom he continued to train rigorously and, to make it more difficult to get whiskey or to contract venereal diseases, he had moved his force away from Pittsburgh, establishing a new camp he called Legionville, twenty-two miles downstream on a high bluff overlooking the Ohio some seven miles above the mouth of Beaver River.

Most disturbing of all, Wayne was listening to people who knew the Indians—guides, scouts, missionaries, rangers, anyone who had experience with them and could give him information that would permit him to gain an insight into their strengths and weaknesses and how best they could be defeated. No other western commander had ever done that before, and this fact alone about Wayne disturbed Tecumseh considerably. The information Wayne assimilated appeared to have convinced him he could whip the Indians at any time and in any place.[433]

Never before, Girty warned, had the Americans had an officer in command who was so dedicated to performing to the utmost the task laid out for him. This was a commander who would not allow himself to be egged into any combat for which he was not fully prepared, but that when he finally did take the field, he was apt to be indomitable. In this respect, Girty strongly believed, in opposition to most of the tribes, that Wayne, who had not struck at them this year, would not strike at them next year, either, as he would still be gathering his strength and intelligence; but that the year following, 1794, he was apt to make a strike from which the tribes could never recover.

Blue Jacket did not put too much credence in this, but Michikiniqua did.

So, too, did Tecumseh.

[December 31, 1793 — Tuesday]

Many things had occurred over this past year that were upsetting to Tecumseh and the majority of the Indians in the Northwest Territory, but none so much as the fact that the white feather had been shown by Michikiniqua. In the face of the continuing buildup of the army under Major General Anthony Wayne and with a great confrontation ever more imminent, the allied tribes had again turned to Michikiniqua and Blue Jacket to be cocommanders of the combined Indian force when the conflict came. That was when the ripple of shock spread throughout the land.

Michikiniqua refused.

The Miami principal chief explained that he did not think it at all wise to oppose Wayne and that the tribes should make very strong efforts, while there was still the opportunity to do so, to come to some kind of peaceable terms with the Americans.

There was more than ample reason for this most influential of all chiefs in the Northwest Territory to take such a stand. As Girty had predicted, the expected invasion by Wayne's army had not occurred this year and the continued intelligence provided by Tecumseh and his spies underlined in every report the sense that in Wayne the Indians would be facing an extremely formidable foe.

As had been the case with St. Clair's army, Tecumseh had been assigned by Blue Jacket, much to the disapproval of Catahecassa, to spy on Wayne, evaluate his preparations and progress and report his findings frequently. For many months, at far more risk to himself and his men than had been the case at Fort Washington, Tecumseh had been doing just that.

Throughout the winter and into early spring he had studied Wayne, but not able this time to enter the actual camp of the army, called Legionville, because of the extremely tight security that the general had established. Relying more heavily than ever on the brass telescope he carried in his pouch, Tecumseh watched for interminable hours and days and weeks the activities occurring there: watched as Wayne issued rounds of blank ammunition and had segments of his force dress themselves as Indians and try to surprise other segments of his uniformed force; watched as endless hours of drilling occurred in which the soldiers practiced and perfected not only their method of march but their skills in shooting, in hand-to-hand combat, in bayonet charges, in sham battles with blank cartridges, and other offensive tactics; watched as week by week the flotilla of boats being constructed grew larger until at last the entire Spaylaywitheepi shoreline for a mile on either side of Legionville was lined with boats drawn up and ready to be launched; watched as artillerymen practiced their shooting, the thunderous reports of the big guns rumbling and echoing

through the surrounding hills and the balls of these weapons ever more accurately striking their targets and demolishing them. [434]

Tecumseh was still watching when, on the tenth day of the Rain Moon,
with the Spaylaywitheepi well free of ice and open to navigation, the entire
army of twenty-five hundred men abandoned Legionville and embarked on
their journey downstream. Keeping himself and his men well out of sight, he
followed on shore as the incredible flotilla—the largest ever seen on any river
west of the Alleghenies—passed downstream.

Tecumseh was still on hand, pacing the troops when they finally arrived
at Fort Washington and there were soon joined by the eight hundred mounted
volunteers General Charles Scott had raised in Kentucky. [435] Since there was
nowhere near enough room for them all within the confines of the fort, a
huge campground was established nearby on the only level section available,
from which all trees and stumps were immediately removed by energetic work
details. Since it was the only suitable ground anywhere nearby, Wayne named
the camp Hobson's Choice and immediately set his now more experienced
and disciplined troops to training the Kentucky volunteers. He also met with
the huge man he was told was the most remarkable scout, spy, and Indian
fighter on the entire American frontier—Simon Kenton—and quickly made
him a major in command of the army's spies.

Throughout the remainder of spring and summer and into the autumn,
as Tecumseh had continued his spying, Wayne continued to build and train
his army. Tecumseh had been aware, of course, that the preceding June,
Michikiniqua's adopted son, the redheaded Apekonit, had, with Michikiniqua's sad and reluctant approval, said farewell to him and returned to the
whites, resuming his name of William Wells. Now part of the disturbing
intelligence that Tecumseh was passing on to Blue Jacket and the tribes included
the fact that William Wells had presented himself to Wayne and, with his
expertise in regard to the Miamis and other tribes, offered to serve as a spy
and interpreter and had been given a field commission by Wayne as a captain.
It gave Tecumseh no great satisfaction to know that his long-ago prediction
that one day Apekonit would use his knowledge of the Indians against them
had obviously come to pass.

On the twentieth day of the Harvest Moon, Wayne had finally put his
force into motion and marched to Fort Hamilton, camping on the same ground
where Tecumseh had observed St. Clair's army in its camp two years earlier. [436]
The general, however, had been in no way content to remain at Fort Hamilton
and left there almost immediately, marched his force first to Fort St. Clair and
then on to Fort Jefferson, where they arrived on October 26. [437] Finding that
installation much too small and ill placed for defensive measures, he had
immediately pushed his troops on another six miles and began construction

of a much better installation, which he named Fort Greenville after his friend and fellow officer of the Revolution, General Nathanael Greene.

Wayne's war preparations did not prevent his continuing to send out peace proposals to the tribes. A dozen men or more were dispatched under flags of truce to the tribes, giving the tribes a choice of accepting peace or suffering annihilation.[438] These emissaries were no more successful than those from Washington had been. But even with those messengers scorned, the combined Indians and their British friends were growing increasingly apprehensive over the looming battle with Wayne's army.

Where the watching of Wayne's army was concerned, the job of Tecumseh and his team of warriors and messengers was made considerably more difficult by the rangings of Kenton's company of spies, who spread out in all directions, having occasional skirmishes with the Indians, taking back a number of prisoners to be questioned by Wayne and killing about as many Indians as were captured. Kenton was eager to get on with the expedition, but when Wayne announced, with the completion of Fort Greenville just a fortnight ago, that this was to be the army's winter headquarters and that the march would not be resumed until next summer, the big frontiersman became disgruntled and depressed.

To combat this, Wayne detached Kenton and his mounted spies with a force of three hundred unmounted men under Major Robert McMahon, who was also spoiling for a fight, directing them to "go out toward Lake Erie until you find something to fight."

As soon as their march began and their direction noted, Tecumseh galloped off to the Shawnee villages at the mouth of the Auglaize and notified Blue Jacket. At once the war chief sent out a call for warriors and by the time the army detachment began moving down the Auglaize, an ambush had been laid with a thousand warriors ready and waiting for them. Once again, as on so many occasions in the past, the gread Bahd-ler thwarted them.

Ranging far ahead with a handful of his scouts, Kenton found enough Indian sign toward the lower Auglaize to convince him they were heading into a trap. His party galloped back to Major McMahon's plodding footsoldier force at once and reported their find. In a short while afterwards, the detachment of whites, much to the frustration of the Shawnees, turned around and marched back to Fort Greenville.[439]

During their absence, General Wayne had begun construction of another fort—this one at the site of St. Clair's Defeat. They had arrived there just a week ago, on Christmas day. The next day was spent in gathering the bones remaining above ground, including some six hundred human skulls, and burying them. One of the captured Indians—captured by none other than Captain William Wells and Lieutenant Robert McClennan—had been turned over to

General Wayne for questioning and, at the insistence of Wells that he do so, had revealed where the four six-pounder cannon were hidden that had been taken in St. Clair's Defeat—two under a large log and two in the Wabash. A search was made and the artillery was found, recovered and sent back to Fort Greenville. The new fort was named Fort Recovery and on its completion two companies—one of riflemen and one of artillerymen, consisting of 150 men—were left to garrison it while the rest returned to Fort Greenville. On his arrival, Wayne was saluted by the recovered cannon that had been cleaned and remounted on gun carriages.

So, with such extensive and carefully controlled plans being made by Wayne for his forthcoming expedition against them, the refusal of Michikiniqua to again assume the mantle of overall leadership of the Indians was both a great shock and worriment. At once there came charges from some of the other chiefs that Michikiniqua was becoming old and tired and turning into a coward. Michikiniqua refused to accept the bait. Instead, at the council where these accusations were hurled, he simply raised his hands for silence and then spoke calmly but very solemnly.

"We have beaten the enemy twice under separate commanders," he told them. "We cannot expect the same good fortune always. The Americans are now led by a chief who never sleeps. The night and the day are alike to him, and during all the time that he has been marching on our villages, notwithstanding the watchfulness of our young men, we have never been able to surprise him. Think well of it. There is something whispers to me that it would be prudent to listen to his offers of peace."

The discussion, of which Tecumseh was a part, continued after Michikiniqua's remarks but it was obvious that now, although the Miami chief bowed to their will and said he would fight if that was their desire, he would not be commander-in-chief. The force of combined Indians now needed a man well proven in warfare and leadership, a man of strength, cunning and ferocity, who had the respect not only of his own tribe but of *all* the Northwestern tribes. They had just such a man.

Unanimously, Blue Jacket was selected as commander-in-chief of the Indian forces.

[July 2, 1794 — Wednesday]

His countenance as grim as that of all the other Indians arriving now at the mouth of the Auglaize, Tecumseh wished there was some way, something he could say or do, that would miraculously heal the rift that had so unexpectedly developed between the Shawnees and their northern allies. How could it be that their combined move against the *Shemanese* at Fort Recovery that had started out so well, suddenly took on the proportions of a disaster, with twenty Indians killed?

Blame placing was easy enough. The Ottawas and Chippewas and, to a lesser degree, the Potawatomies were obviously at fault, yet they refused to see it that way, reacting emotionally rather than reasonably, and themselves pointing the finger of blame at the Shawnees generally and at Blue Jacket specifically. Now, at the worst possible time, when General Wayne was poised to strike them, there was the very real likelihood that when they reached Chalahgawtha in just a short while, their northern allies would abandon them permanently.

Tecumseh shook his head, thinking back over the events of these past few months that had ultimately led them to this crisis. Matters had continued looking reasonably good for the Indians throughout last winter, especially with their British friends becoming less and less covert in their support and in their declarations against the United States. On the tenth day of the Hunger Moon, Lord Dorchester—Guy Carleton—at a council held in Quebec, railed at the Americans, telling the assembled Indians that the United States were a greedy and untrustworthy nation spoiling for a fight in order to take more Indian lands and to disrupt the interests of His Majesty in the process, which was evident from General Wayne's army so closely approaching the western British posts. He was angered with the Americans as well for their growing ties with the French, for whom the British harbored only contempt and hatred and he was equally upset over the disputes the British were having with the Americans in regard to maritime rights. And he had also said the words that the tribesmen had been longing to hear ever since the conclusion of the Revolutionary War. The Americans, Lord Dorchester said, needed to be taught a very strong lesson for their imperialistic insolence. "Children," he added, "from the manner in which the people of the United States push on, and act, and talk on this side, and from what I learn of their conduct towards the sea, I shall not be surprised if we are at war with the United States in the course of a year."[440]

Upper Canada Lieutenant Governor John Simcoe quickly ordered the beefing up of defenses at Fort Miamis, at the Maumee Rapids, including not only strengthening the garrison but also the installation of some artillery pieces there.[441] So convinced were the Shawnees and other tribes that he was, with these actions, committing the British to actual physical aid for the Indians when they should clash with Wayne's army, that a decision was made among the chiefs to fall back from Wayne's advance until they were in the vicinity of Fort Miamis and there make their stand. And the Potawatomies on the St. Joseph and Tippecanoe rivers, who were being swayed by the American peace proposals, which would cost them nothing so far as their own territory was concerned, did an about-face and recommitted themselves to the anti-American tribal alliance. All the Indians were clearly envisioning the redcoats boiling out of Fort Miamis to help their Indian allies and the thought gave them much comfort. Even the gentle warning to them from Alexander McKee that they should not bank too highly on British succor unless a British-American war were actually declared failed to dash their expectations.[442]

Another good piece of news that had filtered to them was that their long-time nemesis, Simon Kenton, in command of the spy company of General Wayne's army had become very sick during the winter and had resigned from his commission and gone back to Kentucky.[443] Further, General Wayne was having trouble getting his requisite supplies through, as much because of difficulties with civilian contractors as from the Indians and was forced to postpone his anticipated resumed march in the middle of the Rain Moon until the supply matters could be resolved.[444]

At the beginning of the Planting Moon, Blue Jacket had sent out messengers to the allied tribes, telling them it was time to assemble at the mouth of the Auglaize and prepare to meet Wayne's army. The response had been swift and in a few weeks some twelve hundred warriors had gathered there, with more coming all the time, but they were disappointed to find that Wayne's army was still holed up in its series of newly constructed forts stretching from Fort Washington to Fort Recovery.

Contingents of Ottawas and Chippewas from the Michigan country came, along with Potawatomies from the St. Joseph River in the southwestern Michigan area, as well as other Potawatomi factions from the Indiana and Illinois country. Among those who came, Tecumseh was delighted to see, was a contingent of more than one hundred Potawatomies from Pimitoui under his good friend Chaubenee. They had a joyful reunion and Chaubenee said he was prepared to stay with Tecumseh until the crisis was resolved, but unless the American rabbits came out of their holes, he wasn't sure how long he could keep his warriors waiting before they tired and started drifting away toward Illinois. Other chiefs were voicing the same sentiments. The single factor that helped prevent this was that the British at Fort Miamis were being very generous in their distribution of gifts to the Indians who were assembling, especially in equipping them very well for war.

When word came in June that General Wayne was making preparations to march out against them from Greenville, the boredom of the Indians ended and they quickly painted themselves for war and, with Blue Jacket at their head, the twelve hundred warriors headed toward Fort Recovery, where they hoped to intercept the Americans. There was great disappointment when they arrived in the Fort Recovery area late on June 29 and discovered that Wayne was still at Greenville, and this disappointment was increased when they learned that a large supply train of twelve hundred barrels of flour under military escort of 140 soldiers had come out of Fort Greenville and safely reached Fort Recovery only a few hours before the Indians themselves got there.[445]

Tecumseh's spies, however, reported to him with encouraging news that he immediately passed on to Blue Jacket: though the supply train of three hundred packhorses had successfully made it into Fort Recovery with their supplies, this same escort was preparing to lead the three hundred load-free packhorses back to Greenville first thing in the morning and there were excellent prospects for a good ambush. The Shawnees had been experiencing the need to replenish their supply of horses in recent months and so the addition of three hundred good horses to the Indian force would be very welcome indeed.

Blue Jacket immediately planned such an attack. The whites were as yet unaware of the presence of the Indian force in the darkness beyond the walls and Blue Jacket's plan, discussed in a hidden council more than a mile away, was to make no move against the fort itself, which was too strong for them to attack, but to wait until the train of empty packhorses had been led far enough away in the morning that they could be cut off with no chance of getting back to the safety of the fort. Specifically, the Shawnees, Miamis, Delawares and some of the Potawatomies would make a surprise attack on the military escort with the horses, kill as many of the escorting soldiers as possible in the first onslaught and then concentrate on catching all the horses. At the same time, the Ottawas and Chippewas, along with some others of the Potawatomies and a few Wyandots, would remain hidden close to the fort and not show themselves until the fight at the packhorse train broke out. At this point, it was almost certain that a company of soldiers from the fort would come out to try to assist those being attacked. The Ottawas and Chippewas, keeping out of range of the guns in the fort, were to wait until the rescuers passed and then charge in behind them and cut off any attempt by them to retreat back into the fort.

Well hidden, the two Indian forces waited as dawn broke and then the sunrise came. At seven o'clock the gates were opened and the unloaded packhorses emerged, and though the return escort was not the 140 soldiers that had brought the supplies here, there were still a large number of soldiers herding the horses. Fully expecting that the gates of the fort would be closed as soon as the last of them exited, the contingent of Ottawas, Chippewas, and Potawatomies were delighted to see that they were left open and immediately made plans of their own to strike at the fort itself and try to gain entry instead of keeping out of range following the plan Blue Jacket had laid out.

Just as the packhorse escort reached the heavy woodland a mile from the fort, Blue Jacket screamed his war cry and the Indians burst from cover, themselves shrieking and shooting as they charged. Close to half the escort fell, killed or wounded, under the first onslaught, and the terrified packhorses galloped off, away from the fort, with the majority of Blue Jacket's contingent in hot pursuit, quickly disappearing from sight of the fort.

Back closer to the fort, the second Indian contingent charged out, racing toward the stockade and practically collided with fifty mounted dragoons galloping out to the rescue of the escort. With the path still open, some survivors of the packhorse escort were already dodging through the turmoil and streaking back into the fort. The mounted soldiers wheeled to thunder back inside and collided with a hundred infantrymen on their way to help. In the resultant confusion four of the five officers and a great many of the soldiers were killed by the gunfire of the approaching Indians.[446] As soon as the survivors were safely inside, the gates were slammed shut and barred only moments before the Indians got there. A withering fire broke out as the soldiers inside fired from blockhouses and over the walls. In that deadly rain of bullets, fully a score of the attackers were killed, plus a great number wounded.[447]

The Indians pulled back, continuing to fire at the fort but without any appreciable effect, expecting Blue Jacket's contingent to reinforce them at once. But Blue Jacket's warriors were still pursing the horses and far from the fort now, believing that, as had been planned, the other force had cut off a rescue effort and were now mowing them down, along with the survivors of the initial attack on the packhorse escort.

All the horses were captured and the exultant Indians under Blue Jacket finally came back with the animals. They were stunned to discover that the other force had accomplished nothing and had lost twenty warriors in their abortive effort. Arguments erupted between the two Indian contingents, the Ottawas and Chippewas, demanding to know why Blue Jacket's force had abandoned them and not come to their aid and bluntly accusing them of cowardice. Blue Jacket angrily countered by pointing out that had they not disobeyed his orders, none of them would have been killed at all, and that they had been foolish not to adhere to the original plan to which they had agreed. When the Ottawas and Chippewas demanded the captured horses, Blue Jacket refused, saying their disobedience of orders merited them no reward.

Throughout the day, as a desultory firing was maintained against the fort, the arguing continued between Indian factions and when finally the siege ended at nightfall and the Indians moved away a few miles to camp for the night, the rift remained between them and they camped apart from each other. Even when the move began the following morning back toward the mouth of the Auglaize, the two factions kept to themselves with occasional angry words exchanged and resentments running high.

"It is our warriors who died," the Ottawa and Chippewa chiefs said bitterly, "while it is you who get the horses which rightfully belong to us."

"Your losses," retorted Blue Jacket, "are the result of your own disobedience to orders, which jeopardized the whole affair. Because of that, you have no right to anything."

Now, in sullen silence, an icy wall of bitterness between them, the two groups following the Auglaize had reached the Maumee and what Tecumseh feared would happen occurred. A small delegation of chiefs of the Ottawas and Chippewas angrily confronted Blue Jacket.

"We are no longer a part of you," their spokesman said tightly. "We return to our homes now and leave you to face the Americans, when they come, on your own. We will no longer help you."

Grimly, the Blue Jacket contingent watched in silence as the irate Ottawas and Chippewas and the St. Joseph River Potawatomies moved off. They represented close to half of the entire allied Indian force gathered here and this was a severe loss that they could not afford, but which they were helpless to prevent. Worse yet, it was a foregone conclusion that as those Indians returned to the north, they would turn back others of their people who were still on their way here to help fight the Americans.

Tecumseh and Chaubenee moved up to where Blue Jacket was standing and it was Chaubenee who spoke.

"The northern Potawatomies have abandoned you," he told Blue Jacket, "and they should not have done so. My Potawatomies from the West do not support this action. What they did was wrong. They *know* it was wrong and they are angry at themselves but they direct this anger at you instead. It may be, when they have had time to cool their minds and hearts, they will return. But it also may be they will never return."

"I do not believe they will come back," Blue Jacket said glumly, his eyes still on the departing warriors. "What this now means is that General Wayne will strike us with two thousand of his regular soldiers and another sixteen hundred Kentucky men on horses and we must face them with only six hundred."[448]

Chapter 8

[August 19, 1794 — Tuesday]

— 《 》 — Fallen Timbers.

That was the name of this place where the Indians had made their encampment and where, on the morrow, the long-expected confrontations with the army of General Anthony Wayne would take place. The ground here favored the type of fighting the Indians preferred, with more than ample cover—a quarter-mile wide and mile-and-a-half long jumble of broken and fallen trees that had become a blight on the landscape last spring when a tornado had raged through the forest and snapped great gnarled limbs and trunks as if they had been mere twigs. The tribes, since then, had called this place Fallen Timbers, and if there were any place at all where they might stand a chance against the military force that would attack them, it was here.[449]

Having fallen silent now, Tecumseh and Blue Jacket, along with Chaubenee and Wasegoboah and a few other chiefs and warriors, sat off to themselves on one edge of this large encampment on the north side of the Maumee River, the red-orange coals of the fire flaring every once in a while when touched by a vagrant breeze. There was really no more to say; the die was cast and it was simply a matter of waiting.

The little group had discussed strategy for many hours and though none were fully satisfied with what had been adopted as the final plan of action, there was really no alternative. If worse came to worst, as they had to admit might well occur, the recourse at that point would be to fall back downstream the two miles to Fort Miamis and take refuge there within the confines of the bastion, protected by her artillery and British troops.

Colonel Alexander McKee and Captains William Caldwell and Matthew Elliott, along with other British officers and agents, including Simon Girty, had cautioned them not to expect full British aid in the initial onslaught, pointing out that though relations were strained between them and the Americans, there had as yet been no actual declaration of war and no orders giving them authority to give active support. By the same token, however, the Indians were informed that protection could not be interpreted as active support and every intimation had been given that should the Indians have to fall back from the force opposing them, such British protection would be forthcoming and Fort Miamis would be their haven.

Normally the Indians would have been keyed up on the eve of battle, but this time there was a definite pall overhanging the encampment—a sense, if not of gloom, then certainly of vague underlying apprehension among the two thousand allied Indians gathered. For his own part, Tecumseh was nowhere nearly so convinced as Blue Jacket that they could place any reliance on the half hundred or so British who were in the encampment with them now. He stared soberly into the embers, considering the events that had brought them to this place and time.

All the villages along the entire length of the Maumee had now been abandoned, the women and children and elderly sent northward into the Michigan country, safely out of reach of Wayne's force, yet the structures and fields of corn and vegetables left untended were very likely to be destroyed if the Indians did not pull off an overwhelming victory. Earlier, having been warned by Chaubenee and his Potawatomies that Wayne's force, descending the Auglaize, was only six miles distant and approaching rapidly, even the trader Shawneeawkee—John Kinzie—had abandoned his big trading post at the mouth of the Auglaize. With the help of the Potawatomies, in exchange for some goods, what Kinzie had that could be carried back to Detroit with him had been loaded on the limited number of packhorses and into the seven bateaux he had available. Shortly after he left, a cloud of smoke had risen and drifted off above the trees, giving indication that for the second time a Kinzie trading post had been put to the torch by the Americans.

This had all come about when, at long last, General Wayne had finally, at 8 A.M. on July 28, marched his army of 3,800 men northward out of Greenville, the 2,200 Legion regulars taking the lead and the 1,600 Kentuckians under General Scott bringing up the rear. That first day's march had taken the army twelve miles, to the headwaters of the Stillwater River, where camp was made on the south side of the stream for the night.[450]

The army had marched on the next morning, moving rapidly, and passed Fort Recovery, under salute of its guns by noon. A half mile after crossing the upper Wabash, Wayne had called a halt to give the lagging baggage train time to catch up, which took so long that camp was finally made on that site for the night. The following day—July 30—marching northward along the Wabash, they had reached the mouth of Beaver Creek, a tributary of the Wabash. Here the ground was so marshy that Wayne halted the army and paused for two days while his engineers constructed a good bridge as well as a small fortification, which was named Fort Adams.[451] While this work was going on, Wayne sent a body of his engineer corps, under heavy guard, to continue clearing a road for the army to the St. Marys River, another sixteen miles north. This was where the army camped on the night of August 1 and began construction of Fort Randolph.[452] Here, while Wayne rested in his tent, workers chopped down a large beech close by that, when it fell, crashed onto Wayne's tent and very nearly killed the general, badly dazing him with a severe head blow and causing considerable injury to his body, multiple bruises and internal bleeding that lasted for days afterwards.[453] It was while they were busy erecting the fort here that Tecumseh was dismayed to see the army joined by another contingent of militia—eight hundred mounted men from the south.[454]

Tecumseh immediately sent messengers to the war chief that Wayne's force was now forty-four-hundred strong and this had caused Blue Jacket to send out additional messengers to the adjoining tribes, including the Potawatomies, Ottawas, and Chippewas who had left in a huff after the attack on Fort Recovery. He warned them of Wayne's advance and that they, too, would be imperiled if the army wasn't stopped, reminding them of their glorious victory over St. Clair and begging them to put their petty anger aside and send their warriors to him at once. Yet, only a small portion of those who had shown up to fight against St. Clair came now and at this point Blue Jacket's whole force amounted to only a thousand. It was obvious that the size of Wayne's army and Michikiniqua's refusal to take command of the Indians had made them very wary.

Tecumseh had continued spying on the Americans, following closely and, when they stopped, had watched each evening as the vigilant Wayne, leaving nothing to chance, set his men to work at once in felling trees and building a breastwork of logs six hundred feet square. Tecumseh had approached so near that through his brass telescope he was able to closely study Wayne and his young aide, William Henry Harrison, as they sat together and talked at the campfire before their tent.[455] William Wells, formerly Apekonit, was another who kept coming and going, appearing before General Wayne frequently with intelligence about the Indian forces. One day, Tecumseh knew, Michikiniqua's former adopted son would pay dearly for this perfidy. Though Wayne was their enemy, Tecumseh could not help being very impressed with all the general's precautions and the large number of sentries that he posted to patrol the camp perimeter throughout the night. Here was a calculating foe, indeed, and the words came back to mind that Michikiniqua had uttered that the Americans were now led by a general who never sleeps.

Michikiniqua made a hurried trip to Detroit and was received very cordially by its new commander, Colonel Richard England. The combined Indians, Michikiniqua told him, desperately needed help from the British now, and he wanted at least twenty British regulars and two pieces of field artillery. England responded courteously enough but evasively, without having promised Michikiniqua anything and by the time the latter left, he was convinced the British would provide them with little, if any, assistance. It was not the kind of news Blue Jacket wanted to hear. Yet, he was gratified only a couple of days ago by the arrival of Captain Matthew Elliott from Detroit at the head of a packhorse train well laden with food and other supplies and escorted by two hundred Ottawas under Chief Kinjoino, which now raised his total force to twelve hundred.

On the fourth day of August, before the work on Fort Randolph was finished, Wayne ordered the march resumed, leaving the place garrisoned by forty invalid soldiers and under command of Captain Thomas Underwood, who was himself sick. The army struck off in a northeasterly direction and soon encountered a muddy stream which Wayne's guides told him was a tributary of the Auglaize, which they followed downstream, Tecumseh pacing them all the way, until at last they came to the Auglaize twelve miles above where it emptied into the Maumee.[456]

When Tecumseh's messengers reached Blue Jacket with word of this, the Indian commander ordered all the women, children and elderly in the Miami and Shawnee villages in the vicinity of the Auglaize River mouth to leave at once for the Michigan country. As soon as they were well away, he led his own warriors some sixty miles down the Maumee and made a temporary encampment along the rapids at a place the old French traders had called Roche de Boeuf, a broad clearing on shore adjacent to a small island of very craggy rocks rising from the water to a considerable height, with its summit covered by a growth of cedar.[457]

With Tecumseh still observing, Wayne marched his army down the remaining distance of the Auglaize to its mouth, passing through and destroying great tracts of vegetables under cultivation and hundreds upon hundreds of acres of corn just becoming fully eared. At once he sent out detachments to burn all the villages in the area as well as the Kinzie Trading Post and immediately began erecting, in the triangular point of ground between the Maumee and Auglaize, a new and very substantial fort. Even before it was finished, while he was standing with General Scott looking over the construction of blockhouses, pickets, fascines and ditches, Wayne grunted in approval.

"It pleases me greatly," he commented, "to build this fort in the very midst of this grand emporium of the hostile Indians of the West. When it is finished, I defy the English, Indians, and all the devils in Hell to take it!"

"Then call it Fort Defiance," Scott remarked, and Wayne did so. [458]

From this point Wayne sent word to the tribes via a squaw and an old Indian man captured in one of the villages, making one final offer to talk peace. The chiefs held a council and now, becoming keyed up for the approaching fight, had voted against it. There were a couple of good reasons, the first being that only a short time ago a reinforcement of a hundred British regulars had arrived at Fort Miamis and they took this to mean that the British there were building up their own strength for the coming confrontation. Second, there had come very encouraging word that the British Captain William Caldwell was on his way with 53 men of the Detroit militia and 800 Chippewas newly arrived from the Saginaw area. Those militiamen were to report to Fort Miamis and the Chippewas would be joining Blue Jacket's force in a day or two, raising his total to 2,000 warriors. So, while it certainly didn't make the opposing forces equal, it helped and the vote had gone against any peace talks. Better to wait and see what happened at the confrontation.

The Chippewas had arrived two days later. While there was still a barrier of resentment between them and the Shawnees, at least both sides agreed to put personal feelings in abeyance for the time being in order to face together the greater foe.

After remaining at the mouth of the Auglaize for a week, Wayne had put his army on the move again on August 15, down the north side of the Maumee and had moved as far downstream as the village of Chief Snake, where they camped for the night under heavy guard. [459] The next day the army marched another ten miles downstream, their progress slowed by steep ravines through which it was extremely difficult to pull the wagons and gun carriages. [460] The day before yesterday the army had marched fourteen miles and camped for the night at the head of the rapids, which put them only ten miles from the main Indian encampment at Roche de Boeuf. [461]

It was at this point that Blue Jacket, shortly after Tecumseh rejoined the main party of Indians, decided to break camp and move downstream some three miles to the area of Fallen Timbers, not only for the protection it would give them but for its proximity to Fort Miamis. It was fully expected that the next day Wayne would march the final distance to them and the battle would be engaged and so the night before last the Indians had gone into their traditional pre-battle fast. It was here they waited while the army moved again yesterday, August 18, but instead of going right past the position at Roche de Boeuf that the Indians had vacated, the army stopped to camp there. That meant the Indians would continue their fast an extra day, but this was no great hardship and there was no doubt in the minds of any of the Indians that the battle would be fought on the morrow.

General Wayne had turned out to be even more sagacious than they had realized. Aware that the fast had begun and that the Indians were waiting in the area of the Fallen Timbers, the commanding general had deliberately held his position all of today, taking advantage of the delay to throw up a small bastion called Fort Deposit in which to store all the baggage not needed in the actual combat.

So now it was late at night and to the small group of Indians sitting about the remains of the campfire, it appeared that both Moneto and the Great Spirit had turned their heads away from their red children. With the battle sure to take place tomorrow, not only were they facing a powerful enemy well over twice their own number, they were light-headed and weakened from the fast that had lasted much longer than anticipated and was not yet ended. And, as a final touch of irony, now the skies opened and a veritable deluge of rain engulfed them.

[August 20, 1794 — Wednesday]

At long last, some thirty-three months after St. Clair's Defeat, the United States Army under Major General Anthony Wayne marched into the major battle the Indians had been expecting ever since that event—the Battle of Fallen Timbers.

The Americans, well over four thousand strong, had risen to the reveille drum at dawn and after a little more than an hour of preparation, had formed their battle lines, but due to a sudden heavy shower that struck, the march out of camp was postponed from 6 A.M. for one hour. At exactly 7 A.M., the army moved out of its encampment at Roche de Boeuf and followed the Maumee portage trail downstream toward the Fallen Timbers area, which began four miles below their camp and where the two thousand Indians under command of Blue Jacket awaited them.[462]

The heavy thunderstorm that raged during the night had eased by this time to a steady moderate rain. Crouched among the jumble of fallen trees and branches, their carefully applied war paint now streaked and smeared and giving them an even more frightening appearance than when first applied, the Indians watched and waited. Blue Jacket was in the front center of the Indians, while Tecumseh and the nineteen-year-old triplets, Sauwaseekau, Kumskaka, and Lowawluwaysica, along with Sinnanatha, Wasegoboah, and Chaubenee close by, were on the left between the portage trail and the river. At intervals

Blue Jacket sent runners, including Tecumseh, back to Fort Miamis to ask when the soldiers were going to join them behind the breastwork of fallen trees. The replies were consistently evasive. The Indians were told to have patience and not to worry, that the support was there and would become available when it was really necessary. In the meanwhile, they had already been provided with about half a hundred of Captain William Caldwell's Canadians dressed and painted as Indians to assist them.

The rain had thoroughly chilled the Indians, as compared to the American soldiers who had been dry and relatively comfortable in their tents. Now, in small groups at first, then in larger numbers, the Indians left the Fallen Timbers area and went to the temporary campground a half mile below where some British were serving hot soup and gills of rum and broke their self-imposed fast. By the time word came that Wayne's army was on the move toward them, the force crouched amid the fallen timbers had dwindled from two thousand to around thirteen hundred.

Spies had brought word to General Wayne of the disposition of the Indians and now, as he approached the Fallen Timbers area at close to 9 A.M., he put his strategic talents to their best use. Leading his army into that tract of fallen timber was apt to be suicide and so he quickly formulated his plan. Splitting off a section of his force, he ordered it to move to the left out of sight of the river and the main army and to advance at that point parallel to the trail and to stop and wait as soon as the Fallen Timbers area came into sight. When they had moved ahead for a sufficient length of time and were out of sight, Wayne started a battalion of the mounted riflemen down the portage trail. His plan was to use the same ruse strategy against the Indians as had so often been used to great effect by the Indians against the whites. The mounted battalion was to move forward on the trail as if they were the advance of the whole army until attacked, which would no doubt occur as they approached or entered the area of fallen timbers. At this point they were to put up a brief fight and then, in apparent fear and confusion, turn and flee back the way they had come, hopefully drawing the Indians out of the dense cover after them. As soon as a sizeable number of the attackers had boiled out of their cover in pursuit, the hidden left wing of the army, at the sound of the drumrolls, would drive to the attack and attempt to turn the right flank of the enemy and encircle it, while the main army suddenly surged ahead and engaged the enemy on ground far more advantageous to the army for a fight.

Among the downed timber, the Indians watched as what appeared to be the head of the army, a four-abreast column of mounted men with rifles, came into view at a light trot with banners waving. They slowed to a walk as they neared the forward edge of the fallen timbers, as if reluctant to enter the area, but entered it nonetheless. Half a hundred of the horsemen had entered the fallen timbers area when Blue Jacket shrieked his attack cry and in an instant shot with bows and guns and then surged from hiding with war clubs and tomahawks. The mounted men fought back briefly, emptying their rifles toward whatever attackers they could see, milling and turning and finally breaking in disorder and starting to gallop back the way they had come, the Indians in hot pursuit.[463]

The maneuver would have worked perfectly except for one thing: the drumroll signal for the army's left wing to drive to the attack and encircle the exposed enemy could not be heard, not only largely drowned out by the gunfire, but also considerably muted and muffled because of the continuing rainfall. After several moments of chasing the fleeing soldiers, Tecumseh spied the main body of the army in an overwhelming mass surging forward to meet the mounted battalion and he shrieked a warning that was passed down the line to Blue Jacket and the others. The Indians stopped and turned back and finally the army's left wing began to move, but by then too late and the Indians for the most part made it back into the tangled timberland. Several shots were lobbed into the timber after the Indians—first shells and then cannister and grape shot—but without much effect due to the density of the cover.[464] It was at this point that Lowawluwaysica slipped away and was seen no more for several days.[465]

Now, with the battle engaged, the army of Wayne continued to surge forward. The artillery shooting was stopped and the Legionnaire foot soldiers raced into the timber with fixed bayonets, where a very hot fight ensued.[466] The Indians held their ground well at first and both sides suffered considerable loss as the fighting moved from tree to tree, log to log. Among the first to fall of the Indians, with a bullet through his brain, was one of the triplets, Sauwaseekau, who had been fighting close beside Kumskaka and Sinnanatha.[467] Before long, however, the sheer weight of numbers in favor of the whites began forcing the Indians back. Yard by agonizing yard they fell away with the army pressing them hard until at last, an hour after the battle had begun, they were beginning to emerge from the other end of the area of fallen timber and at this point Blue Jacket issued the order for retreat to Fort Miamis.[468]

In a rush, leaving a score or more of their number dead or dying amid the jumble of timber, the Indians sped in a disorganized mass the remaining three miles to Fort Miamis and called for the British regulars to come out and assist them as promised. The gates stayed closed. The Indians, Tecumseh among them, clustered in front of the gates and pounded upon them with their fists, demanding entry and the protection of the interior of the fort before the Americans should hove onto the scene.

The gates remained closed.

"My orders," the fort commander, Major William Campbell called to them self-consciously, "instruct me to do nothing more than safeguard the integrity of this fort."

Tecumseh drew apart from the others, sickened and enraged by the actuality of what he had all along suspected might occur, his fury fueled all the more over the death of his brother, Sauwaseekau, and knowing this was an example of British treachery he would never forget and not soon, if ever, forgive. The British looked over the walls and out of the portholes at them clustered below but continued to refuse any support, offensive or defensive. Blue Jacket, no less frustrated and angry, realizing that their white allies were throwing them to the wolves, finally gave the word to disperse and the Indians fled past the fort, past the small encampment of Indians a half mile below it and well beyond, scattering as they fled. The Battle of Fallen Timbers was over and the Americans were clearly victorious.

Later—much later—Alexander McKee and Simon Girty showed up in the night at the temporary camp the Shawnees had set up at the mouth of Swan Creek, knowingly risking their lives, considering the anger of the Shawnees for what they considered to be the treachery of their British brothers. The pair spoke long and hard, attempting to assuage them, pointing out that the British officer commanding Fort Miamis, Major William Campbell, had refused to open the gates to them on the grounds that the Americans would have considered this an act of war and would undoubtedly have attacked. And, since the Americans had artillery with them and a vastly greater number of troops than the less than two hundred redcoats within the fort, they could not have withstood the attack.

Tecumseh listened in stony silence as the Indian agent and the interpreter made these explanations and then went on to tell what had happened when the Americans arrived at Fort Miamis, which they had shortly after the disappearance of the Indians.

The British had themselves later learned that General Wayne had written authorization from President Washington via the secretary of war to "attack and demolish the British fort of Miami" if he so chose but, though it had been touch and go for a while, he had declined to expose his men to the necessary deaths it would have entailed to effect this.

What happened was that the Americans came into view in full strength with trumpets sounding and drums beating and assessed the scene immediately, realized the Indians were gone and then, under Wayne's orders, methodically destroyed all the grain and vegetables growing around the fort and burned down all the buildings surrounding it, including the small trading post there owned by Alexander McKee. The effrontery of it had caused the watching garrison to literally groan in frustration.[469]

Wayne and his second in command, General Wilkinson, along with several other officers, including Wayne's aide, Lieutenant William Henry Harrison, had then boldly ridden their horses within eighty yards of the walls and in plain sight. So angered were the regulars inside the fort that one officer, a captain, grabbed a torch and attempted to apply it to a cannon pointed directly at the American officers and was restrained only by Major Campbell himself threatening to run him through with his sword if he didn't desist. The captain desisted and the commander then had him placed under arrest.

Major Campbell himself, however, McKee went on, was practically as furious as the captain over Wayne's actions and sent him a note protesting the general's near approach to a post belonging to His Majesty's troops, declaring that he knew of no war existing between Britain and America, adding that so near an approach could not be again permitted and he would be fired on if he attempted it. Wayne, in return, had fired off two sharp replies, asserting that Fort Miamis had been built in contravention to the Treaty of Paris and ordering the British to get out of American territory—specifically, to leave Fort Miamis at once and retire to the next nearest British post. Major Campbell responded with the brief but firm note that he should certainly remain where he was until he was ordered to evacuate the place by the authority who placed him there, or the fortune of war compelled him to surrender it. Wayne at this point very seriously considered a strike at the fort but finally decided against it, deciding that at the moment his laurels were such that it would be wise for him to quit while he was ahead.

To Blue Jacket and the other chiefs who appeared before him, McKee remained very apologetic for the lack of active British participation in the affair and urged the Indians, with Wayne already having destroyed many of the villages and crops and certain to do more of the same on his return up the Maumee, to make their winter camp here at the mouth of Swan Creek just a mile or so upstream from Lake Erie's Maumee Bay. If they did so, he promised, they would be supplied with food and clothing throughout the winter.[470]

The number of killed on both sides was not great for a conflict involving such numbers, largely because the greater part of the battle had been fought among fallen timbers and far more bullets lodged in intervening tree trunks, branches, and logs than in flesh.[471] Nevertheless, the victory belonged to General Wayne's army and the Indians were more crushed and despondent than ever before. For the first time, without any reservation, the Indians realized that the Americans were now the dominant force in their country and the knowledge was appalling.[472]

[December 31, 1794 — Wednesday]

Tecumseh was not truly reclusive, but these days he had become very close to it. The good nature, the humor and the lightness that had always been hallmarks of his character seemed to be gone. Now, more often than not, he sat by himself in the dim confines of his own wegiwa in the tiny village he had established only a few weeks ago on Deer Creek. He had visibly aged over the past few months and appeared to be considerably older than his twenty-six years. It was what he had seen and heard and experienced that had caused these changes in him since the Battle of Fallen Timbers.

Immediately following the battle numerous chiefs, at different times and on their own—for the benefit of themselves or their villages or their own tribes and with no consideration whatsoever for the Confederacy of tribes they had begun calling the Seven Nations—had gone to General Wayne and sued for peace. They hadn't represented all the Indians, of course, and there had been many, like himself, who had no desire to make any kind of peace with the whites. They, like him, had been fully prepared to continue the struggle against the whites. Even after the American dead had been buried with honors and the wounded loaded on litters to be taken to Fort Defiance, some sniping had continued on the army during its return upriver and several soldiers were killed or wounded.[473]

Despite such incidents, the ingrained superstitions of the various tribesmen had been deeply touched by the Battle of Fallen Timbers. That Moneto and the Great Spirit had turned their faces from the Indians at the battle was now, in the uneasy minds of so many of the Indians, no longer an uncomfortable possibility but rather something that the majority of them truly believed.

The influx of individuals, small groups and whole tribal delegations to see General Wayne, to surrender unconditionally and beg for peace at his terms, had been staggering. The whites considered it to be nothing more than the brilliance of Wayne in the field and the decisiveness with which he had brought his army against the tribes at Fallen Timbers that had so thoroughly cowed the tribes, not understanding how deeply rooted and fundamental to tribal beliefs and policies their superstitions were.

In his return from Fallen Timbers to his headquarters at Fort Greenville, Wayne had continued to show the power and indomitability of the United States. He had sent out detachments on either side of the Maumee as he moved back toward Fort Defiance, giving them orders to destroy every village, every trading post or home belonging to British agents or traders, every cornfield, every plot of vegetables in a swath some ten miles wide and fifty miles long, and they had done so. The smoke that arose signaling the accomplishment of this was not just the smoke of the burned buildings that dissipated in the atmosphere, but equally the hopes and dreams of the Indians.

At Fort Defiance, which Wayne's army reached on August 27, the general detached a large portion of his force up the Auglaize to return southward toward Greenville and Fort Washington, bearing with them dispatches and many of the more mobile wounded.

On September 14, with fortification improvements being made on Fort Defiance and the more seriously wounded being well cared for, Wayne had set his army in motion again and continued up the Maumee to where it was formed by the St. Joseph and St. Marys rivers and there, on September 22, had his engineers begin to build, on the site of the once great village of Kekionga, a very large, strong fortification. It was completed on October 22 and Colonel John Hamtramck named as its commanding officer, and Hamtramck, in turn, in honor of the commander-in-chief, promptly fired over one hundred fifty rounds in salute, led three rousing cheers and named the new installation Fort Wayne.

Here the Indian delegations continued coming to General Wayne to sue for peace. In this respect, William Wells, for his valuable spying services against the Indians who had long nurtured him, was given permission to establish a large farm in the area and here he was quickly joined by his wife, Wanagapeth— A Sweet Breeze—who was Michikiniqua's daughter. Because of Wells's long association and considerable knowledge of the Miami tribe and its divisions, as well as other tribes of the area, Wayne appointed him temporary government agent, justice of the peace, and interpreter at Fort Wayne and told him he would recommend to authorities back east that he be officially installed as the United States Indian agent for this district.

Soon after this Wayne had returned to Greenville as the army's winter quarters and even there the Indian delegations from as far distant as the Sacs on the Mississippi had continued coming to him, asking peace. To them all his response was the same: he would grant them a temporary peace, but all were to appear at Greenville for a great treaty council next June to conclude a permanent, binding, and unbreakable treaty of peace between the United States government and all the Northwestern tribes. In the meanwhile, to show their good faith in the petitions for peace, they were to begin, at once, to bring to Greenville and turn over to him any and all prisoners in their hands, whether they had been formally adopted into the tribes or not. Only then could and would the new boundary lines be established and forever afterwards the various tribes live in peace and brotherhood with the whites.

The exchange of prisoners that forthwith occurred and was continuing at this time, was entered into with alacrity by the tribes now so anxious to please and mollify General Wayne. Even longtime adoptees such as Stephen Ruddell—Sinnanatha—and his brother, Abram, who had been with the Shawnees for fourteen years, were surrendered to the American general.[474] There was not one general prisoner exchange at a given time, but over the weeks and months that followed, from the end of the Battle of Fallen Timbers to the end of the great council at Greenville, prisoners were regularly being brought in to be exchanged. This, as much as anything, finally convinced the Kentucky settlers that peace had truly come at last and that now a man could chop his wood or pasture his cattle and horses without fear of being robbed or killed by Indians. For the very first time since settlers had first begun descending the Ohio River, attacks on the boats and rafts of the immigrants had entirely ceased. Land development in both Kentucky and Ohio boomed as never before. Among those who benefitted from the cessation of Ohio River attacks were a large number of French citizens who had been duped out of their life savings in a fraudulent land deal touted in France, wherein settlers would receive large parcels of land in the beautiful Ohio Valley close to where Marietta—named after Marie Antoinette, of course—had been laid out. They had arrived to find their real-estate dreams were a bubble that had burst, and though some had settled in the area of Gallipolis, a little downstream and across the Ohio from Point Pleasant, even those claims had been lost due to disputed titles. The United States government thereupon took pity on them and donated a tract of just over twenty-five thousand acres to the French sufferers of the land fraud; this parcel of land, dubbed the French Grant, bordering the north shore of the Ohio for some eighteen miles between the mouths of the Big Sandy and Scioto Rivers.[475]

Far northward, along the south shore of Lake Erie, the remainder of the Western Reserve Lands east of the Cuyahoga River had been sold by the Connecticut Legislature to the Connecticut Land Company and steps were already under way to have the entire three-million-acre plot surveyed into townships of five square miles each and settlement begun without delay.

As for Tecumseh, he sat in on council after council of the Shawnees held by Catahecassa and consistently argued against making any sort of peace treaty with the Americans. Catahecassa just as determinedly stated that it was his wish and demand that the other chiefs support him in making peace on behalf of the entire tribe with General Wayne. Tempers had become very short and the discussions heated, Tecumseh declaring that he would *never* make peace with the treacherous whites and berating Catahecassa for his willingness to do so. Tecumseh was supported in his contentions by a small but strong and devoted clique of followers but, despite this, the odds were against him. Not only had Catahecassa been peaceably inclined all along, but the disaster at Fallen Timbers had made by far the majority of the Shawnee chiefs side with the principal chief.

"I cannot lend my support to such a decision!" Tecumseh said during his concluding heated exchange with Catahecassa. "Whether or not you can see it, or will believe it, I tell you that there is no doubt that the Americans continue to want—and will continue to take!—Shawnee lands and the lands of other tribes so long as it remains to be taken. I will *not* attend the treaty General Wayne has called. I will *never* make peace with the Americans. This is the land of our fathers, the land where their bones are buried and whose graves we should defend to our last breaths. That is what I intend to do."

"*No,* Tecumseh," Catahecassa replied angrily. "You must not! You *can-*

not, since the Shawnee council has now made its decision and you are bound by the decisions of this council. If you continue to make war against the whites, they will hold us responsible as a tribe and cause further trouble for us all."

Tecumseh shook his head and his words emerged as brittle and cold as chunks of ice. "If I cannot, as a Shawnee, protect the lands I love, the lands so many of our people have fought and died for, then I will do so on my own. I, and any of those who are of like mind with me, cannot stay here, which would mean that we agree and support such a decision, which we do not. We will go away from here and make our own village apart from you and we will wait and see what shall occur. If, in fact, Catahecassa, you and the other Shawnee chiefs put your names to such a treaty of peace with the Americans, we will then forever sever ourselves from the tribe."

There was a great gasp from among the assemblage at this declaration and an angry rumbling arose. Blue Jacket was one of the chiefs who came to Tecumseh and asked him to reconsider, but Tecumseh remained adamant. "You are my friend, Blue Jacket. You will always be so. But this is a matter that goes beyond friendships. Catahecassa and the other chiefs are wrong in their decision to make peace next summer with the Americans and if you agree with him and them, then you, too, Blue Jacket, are wrong and it is a decision you and they will live to regret."

It had been a traumatic council and immediately after its conclusion, Tecumseh had packed up his meager goods and left. With him went Wasegoboah, Tecumapese, Kumskaka, Lowawluwaysica, and several others who supported him and, disenchanted with Shawnee tribal leadership under Catahecassa, were willing to give up everything in their belief in him.[476]

They had immediately moved southward, the sixteen of them, and as they came into the vicinity of the upper Mad River, not many miles from where Mackachack and Wapatomica and Blue Jacket's Town and all the other Shawnee villages had been located, an incident occurred that was thought very significant by the followers. Here, along the headwaters of Deer Creek, not terribly far from where a similar incident had occurred so long ago when Clark had invaded their country, Tecumseh in one morning's hunt with bow and arrows, downed sixteen buffalo in succession, exactly as he had done on that day twelve years ago.[477] The meat was sliced and smoked and jerked to help sustain them through the winter and the hides tanned to keep them warm. And since game seemed to still be plentiful in this area, the decision was made to establish their little temporary Deer Creek Village and spend the winter hunting and surviving as best they could while they waited to see what would happen at the great council at Greenville next summer.

It was Lowawluwaysica who came up with an idea geared to help pull

Tecumseh out of the emotional slump he had been suffering since the defeat at Fallen Timbers. In recent years there had been little opportunity for games or the competitions that the Shawnees so much enjoyed and very quickly all the males of the village fell into the spirit of it and encouraged Tecumseh to participate, which he finally, with some reluctance, agreed to do. The competition was to be a three-day deer hunt, using only bow and arrows, with each hunter dressing, skinning, and hanging his take at the close of each day, the meat to be picked up by the women after the hunt and brought back to the village for a feast and for curing into jerky. Word of the projected hunting competition spread and soon men from other villages were coming to take part in it and a sense of happy excitement filled them all at the prospect of at last having a good hunt where they needn't fear running afoul of hostile whites.

At the end of the three-day hunt, the men brought in the proofs of their skill—the hides of the animals they had killed. Many of the warriors brought in three or four skins apiece and a fair number had killed five or six. Perhaps a dozen had taken ten each and three men had each downed twelve. Tecumseh returned pulling a makeshift sledge of bark behind him, on which were tied the hides of the deer he had killed—a total of thirty of them.

It was the custom at the feast following the hunt for each man to tell of his own experiences and there was much laughter and admiration as one after another they told their tales. When it came to be Tecumseh's turn, a respectful silence fell over them all and they clung to his every word. Unlike the boastful way in which those who had preceded him told of their exploits, Tecumseh spoke softly, simply and with an appealing eloquence that captured his audience completely and left them marveling at his oratorical abilities as much as over his hunting skill. Once again the news of the great prowess of Tecumseh filtered throughout the Indian nations. And a glow of pride and expectation filled Lowawluwaysica. One day, he was sure, the time would come for his older brother to take up the reins of leadership and when that time came, he was certain to have many followers. And, thought his one-eyed brother, at his right hand would be Lowawluwaysica.

However, despite the therapeutic benefit of the hunting competition and the pleasure in the accolades that followed, Tecumseh remained depressed and pessimistic about what lay ahead for all the Indians.

[May 1, 1795 — Friday]

If there lingered any trace of hope among the Indians with Tecumseh or elsewhere that the British would finally rise and thrust the Americans out of the Northwest, it was dashed when word swept through the tribes of the new treaty of peace with the United States that the American special envoy, John Jay, had negotiated with the British in London. That treaty had been signed last November 19, and though it covered many aspects of international trade and other matters, the provision that struck home with the Northwestern Indians most directly dealt with the strong British posts at Mackinac, Detroit, and Niagara.

The grave nebulosity in the Treaty of Paris over eleven years ago that had enabled the British to so disruptively retain their hold on these vital western posts in American territory had finally been resolved by the astute Mr. Jay. By the new terms to which the British had agreed, *all* British posts anywhere in the territory of the United States would be evacuated by the first day of June next year.[478] At councils held with the Indians in the Detroit area, assurances were quickly given by the British that this did not mean they were actually leaving. In point of fact, they said, they were only moving across the Detroit River to Canada where, at Amherstburg, hardly fifteen miles from Detroit, they were building a very large fort, much bigger and better than the Detroit fort, and calling it Fort Malden. From here, they promised, they would continue to provide the Indians with the gifts and annuities and supplies they were accustomed to receiving. The explanations and plans did little to instill any rejuvenation of confidence in the Indians for the British.

In the Deer Creek Village, Lowawluwaysica, utilizing the Indian medicine training he had been receiving from the old Shawnee medicine man, Penegashega—Change of Feathers—now carried with him wherever he went a pouch filled with herbs, bits of bone, symbolic and mystical objects, and other paraphernalia and passed himself off as the village doctor. He had even learned a number of the healing chants from old Penegashega and used them now in treating those afflicted with illness. In the majority of cases the patients got better, though they no doubt would have done the same without any treatment. For payment of his services, the one-eyed youngest brother of Tecumseh most often, when it was available, would take liquor in lieu of anything else. As always, in everything he did, Lowawluwaysica constantly looked for shortcuts to success. Most often he did not find them and relied then on his inherent weasellike craftiness to carry him through and remaining, as in the majority of his undertakings, abysmally average and taking refuge in his close blood relationship to Tecumseh. Where Tecumseh declined to boast very much of his own accomplishments, Lowawluwaysica would boast all the louder on his behalf and there was certainly much to boast about.

At twenty-seven Tecumseh was a most formidable warrior, an unparalleled hunter and tracker, a remarkable tactician and logician, a gifted linguist in English as well as in a number of Indian dialects, and most definitely an accomplished leader of men. He continued to be temperate, never again having tasted alcohol in any form following his pledge to Chiksika eleven years earlier. He had become even more strongly handsome with the character lines that time and experience had etched on his features and he remained, in most circumstances, very gentle and good-natured. The only avenue in which he seemed to do less than excel was in his choice of a mate.

Shortly after the Deer Creek Village was established, an attractive, slender and strong young woman of twenty-three summers decided that Tecumseh needed a wife. Named Mohnetohse, she was the daughter of one of the older Peckuwe warriors among them. With her naturally aggressive way she impinged herself upon his life and it came as a surprise to no one when she and Tecumseh were soon married. As a married woman, however, her character changed considerably—or, more likely, revealed its true nature—and she became domineering, accusatory, berative, and demanding, constantly railing at Tecumseh and finding fault in all he did. Were it not that she was pregnant, no one in the village had any doubt he would have sent her away long before now.[479]

News had come to the Deer Creek Village over the past few months that General Wayne, still quartered at Fort Greenville, was continually being visited by chiefs declaring for peace. Most disheartening was the fact that two such chiefs were Blue Jacket and Michikiniqua, who visited with Wayne before the winter was quite over. After that visit, Wayne had magnanimously sent word to the displaced Shawnees under Catahecassa, as well as to other Indians, that if they wished to do so, they could resettle, at least temporarily, at their old village sites, provided they remained peaceful and quiet. As a result, Catahecassa had returned to the site of Wapakoneta and had reestablished the principal village of the Shawnees there, reinstituting the name Wapakoneta. Blue Jacket's Town had also been reestablished when the war chief returned there, and Wapatomica was being rebuilt with a good *msi-kah-mi-qui,* but the nearby ruins of Mackachack, McKee's Town, and others remained uninhabited. Numerous other small new villages of both Shawnee and Miami Indians similarly were springing up again in the valleys of the Maumee, Auglaize, Blanchard, Ottawa, and Little Auglaize. Another surprise came with news that Michikiniqua, accepting the commanding general's invitation, had reestablished a moderate-sized village at the Kekionga site quite close to Fort Wayne. Also, though Chief Five Medals of the St. Joseph River Potawatomies had made an armistice with Wayne and had agreed to attend the Greenville council, the Milwackie and Illinois River Potawatomies under young Siggenauk and Chaubenee were following Tecumseh's lead and not committing themselves to anything.

[September 22, 1795 — Tuesday]

That the war chief of the Shawnees should specifically pay a visit to Tecumseh at his Deer Creek Village and spend long hours explaining to him all details of the Greenville Treaty, so recently concluded, was a real honor. It underlined the level of prestige Tecumseh now had among the Indians even though he was himself, in the eyes of Shawnee chiefs, still merely a warrior.

Blue Jacket had arrived this morning with a contingent of chiefs and warriors that included Chiuxca, Chaubenee, Spemica Lawba, and a bright, seventeen-year-old half-breed Potawatomi named Sauganash, whom the English called Billy Caldwell.[480]

Tecumseh had been overjoyed to see his old friends once again, warmly shaking hands with Blue Jacket and Chiuxca, embracing his nephew, Spemica Lawba, enfolding his huge friend Chaubenee in a great bear hug, and cordially greeting young Sauganash. The latter gazed at him with something almost akin to reverence and it was clear that he was as smitten by Tecumseh in this first meeting as Chaubenee had been those years ago.

Laden with pots and dishes heaped with good food, Wasegoboah and Tecumapese had joined them, along with Kumskaka and Lowawluwaysica, and all had eaten heartily at Tecumseh's table, smoked their pipes and spent the first hour or so in pleasant reminiscences and in the sharing of news of less than monumental significance, saving the most important matter of discussion—the Greenville Treaty—for last.

Because he was a stranger in their midst and more than a little over-awed at being included in this august company at the insistence of Chaubenee, Sauganash was invited to speak first and tell them something of his background. A sinewy but well-built young man of erect posture and animated expression, he was embarrassed at first but quickly warmed to the matter and spoke swiftly, succinctly, and very intelligently. His father, he said, was an Irishman who was a great admirer of both Blue Jacket and Tecumseh and was the officer who had brought the fifty-three Canadians from Detroit who, dressed and painted as Indians, had fought under Blue Jacket at the Battle of Fallen Timbers.

As he continued with his narration, it was apparent to everyone present that Sauganash was an extremely nimble-minded and accomplished young man with a keen memory, a well-developed sense of humor and considerable education. He had been born in Canada in 1778 just across the river from Detroit and at an early age had been presented by his father to the Jesuits in Detroit to be educated. Possessed of a pronounced flair for languages, he spoke English and French fluently and could read and write in both languages equally well. In addition to his own native Potawatomi, he spoke seven other Indian languages and many dialects within those languages. He was skilled in mathematics and geography and had begun learning cartography when he left the Jesuits to be on his own, not in full accord with the Catholic beliefs of his mentors, which were so in variance with his tribal religious beliefs. His Potawatomi name was Tequitoh—Straight Tree—but practically everyone addressed or referred to him by his nickname, Sauganash—The Englishman. From Chaubenee he had heard a great deal about Blue Jacket and Tecumseh and both, along with Chaubenee, had more or less become his personal heroes.

They welcomed him with genuine warmth to their inner circle, if such it could be called, and then went on to other matters. Spemica Lawba was next to speak and the twenty-year-old proudly announced that he had just gotten married. In the same prisoner exchange with General Wayne that had restored Sinnanatha and his brother, Abram, to the whites, was a young Shawnee woman who had been captured by the whites during the Harmar expedition against Kekionga and now, at age sixteen, had been restored to her tribe. Her name was Pskipahcah Ouiskelotha—Bluebird—and they had taken one look at each other and had instantly fallen in love. They had quickly gotten married and were very happy together.

The talk continued, each present contributing whatever he knew that was of interest or importance. Tecumseh related that he was no longer married to Mohnetohse; that she had given birth to a son they had named Mahyawwekawpawe seven weeks ago but had neglected the child badly; her ill behavior toward himself was something Tecumseh could overlook, but neglect of his son was another matter. He had invoked the ancient Shawnee marital law, taken the infant boy away from her and put him in the care of Tecumapese and then ordered Mohnetohse away from him forever, sending her back in disgrace to her parents—an action by Tecumseh that had been lauded by the others of his village.

Other pieces of incidental news followed:

General Wayne's aide during the Fallen Timbers campaign, Lieutenant William Henry Harrison, had been promoted to captain and was now in command of Fort Washington, and Harrison had just married a young woman named Anna Symmes, daughter of the territorial judge and land speculator, Benjamin Symmes . . . adjacent Cincinnati was growing rapidly, now with well over a hundred cabins, ten large brick houses, business establishments that included stores, bakeries, blacksmith and livery stables and a population, exclusive of the garrison, exceeding five hundred . . . similar startling growth throughout Ohio, with the great new influx of whites constructing houses, churches, schools, even whole villages . . . the Potawatomies, as well as being the most numerous of the Northwestern tribes, continued to be the most fractioned, with dissension among them very strong, now mainly because

those tribal divisions in the East—those on the Elkhart River under Onaxa,
the upper St. Joseph under Wapeme, the lower St. Joseph under Topenebe—
had benefitted far more in treaty payments and annuities than those farther
west—those on Peoria Lake under Gomo, on the Milwackie under Siggenauk,
at Checagou under Black Partridge, on the Kankakee under Nescotnemeg,
and on the Illinois under Chaubenee . . . an army colonel, John Johnston, who
had struck up a rapport with Catahecassa and established a federal trading post
at Wapakoneta, had since been named Indian agent to the Shawnees and would
be at Fort Wayne with William Wells—Apekonit—who was now officially
agent to the Miamis . . . John Conner, whom the Shawnees especially favored
as an unusually honest trader had established a new trading post on the Whitewater River[481] . . . Topenebe—Sits Quietly—the chief of the St. Joseph Potawatomies, had now so ascended in power that he was as close to a principal
chief of the sprawling nations as any chief had ever been . . . that while a
general peace had settled over the Northwest since the Battle of Fallen Timbers,
there had still been scattered outbreaks of violence, most particularly in the
area of the southern Illinois country. The Kickapoos attacked groups of settlers
here and there, wiping out the entire family of Samuel Chew, destroying
another settler and his wife and their thirteen Negro slaves, and attacking
white individuals wherever they found them. A band of Kickapoos had been
captured by the whites and falsely accused of being the perpetrators of those
attacks. White authorities refused to listen and herded them toward Cahokia
where they were to be incarcerated until trial could be held, but they were
waylaid by an angry mob of whites from Bellville and all the captive Indians
killed. This had caused Governor St. Clair to issue a stern proclamation against
any white person entering Indian territory to insult, injure, or kill any Indian,
which mollified the Kickapoos somewhat but did nothing to enhance St. Clair's
greatly diminished popularity among the whites. . . .

At last, well into the night but with none of those on hand willing to
stop, they had exhausted all the other news except the matter of the Greenville
Treaty and it was here that Blue Jacket took over and told, as best he could,
what had transpired there.

The council fire, supposed to have been ignited on the first day of June,
had not actually been lighted until June 15 due to the slowness of many of the
delegates in arriving and so the first days had been filled with eating and
drinking and visiting among those gathering.

In his opening talk to them, Blue Jacket said, Wayne had said, "I have
cleared the ground of all brush and rubbish, and have opened roads to the
east, the west, the north, and the south, that all your nations may come in
safety and with ease to meet me. The ground on which this council house
stands is unstained with blood and is as pure as the heart of General Washington, the great chief of America, and of his great council; as pure as my

heart, which now wishes for nothing so much as peace and brotherly love. The heavens are bright, the roads are open, we will rest in peace and love and wait the arrival of our brothers. In the interim we will have a little refreshment, to wash the dust from our throats. We will, on this happy occasion, be merry without passing the bounds of temperance and sobriety. We will now cover up the council fire and keep it alive till the remainder of the different tribes assemble and form a full meeting and representation."

Teteboxti, most ancient of the Delaware chiefs, had responded to Wayne, saying, "All my people shall be informed of the commencement of our friendship and they will rejoice in it and I hope it will never end."

Day after day, week after week more delegates arrived—each greeted by General Wayne and receiving peace belts in solemn ceremony—until finally, by the middle of the Heat Moon, all were present who were expected and the actual council began.

The Delawares, Blue Jacket told Tecumseh, had constituted the largest single Indian contingent present, numbering 381 individuals and led by Buckangehela, Teteboxti and Peketelemund. The 240 Potawatomies present were represented by a large number of chiefs that included New Corn, Asimethe, Gizes, Topenebe, Five Medals, White Pigeon, Siggenauk, Chaubenee, Nescotnemeg and Gomo among others. 180 Wyandots were there under Chiefs Tarhe, Pipe and Stiahta, 143 Shawnees under Catahecassa, Chiuxca and Blue Jacket and 73 Miamis under Michikiniqua, which included 22 Eel River Miamis under Chief LeGris and a dozen other Weas and Piankeshaws under the leadership of Chief Reyntwoco. 46 Chippewas were there under Chiefs Massas and Bad Bird and the 45 Ottawas attending were led by Chief Augooshaway. 10 Kickapoos and Kaskaskias had arrived under Chief Keeahah. The Sacs and Foxes, though invited to attend, had refused.

The Indians were all impressed with how Wayne conducted himself and the treaty, allowing plenty of time for the ritual smoking of the *calumets* and then, when discussions began, allowing ample time for each matter to be interpreted, discussed and debated, moving slowly, methodically, having prepared himself well with strings and belts of wampum, which he displayed and distributed as his points were made.[482] Wayne had distributed no liquor to the Indians, so all were soberly clear-minded as matters progressed. To each of the principal chiefs in attendance, Wayne had presented a large brass medallion, on one side of which was a raised profile of George Washington and the other side exhibiting whites and Indians shaking hands. The medallions were strung on loops of brass chain or brightly colored ribbons, to be worn about the neck if the owner chose.

Blue Jacket, Chaubenee, and Sauganash had all personally met the general's assistant, William Henry Harrison, and were impressed with him. A British agent, John Askin, Jr., clad as an Indian, was discovered attempting to subvert the Indians and get them to insist on their sovereignty, and Wayne, when he learned of it from William Wells, had the man arrested and confined until after the treaty was signed, certified, and distributed.

The greatest initial difficulty was with the Potawatomies. By their form of tribal government, there was virtually no real central government among them and each of the tribe's branches—and even many individual villages—acted autonomously and so the chiefs of each branch or even individual village chiefs had to be negotiated with separately, which, in most cases, was not possible. Some 240 Potawatomies had attended but, while this was the largest representation by any single tribe, they mainly represented those factions along the St. Joseph, Tippecanoe, Elkhart, and Huron rivers and, with the exception of Siggenauk, Chaubenee, Nescotnemeg, and Gomo, most of the western factions were largely unrepresented. [483]

Indian delegates continued straggling in even after the preliminaries had begun and in all cases Wayne had carefully gone over with them what had already been discussed so they were apprised of all things. [484] At last, however, all the Indians had arrived who were going to come—a total of 1,100 chiefs and delegates representing 12 tribes of the Northwest Territory.

Blue Jacket, with the others here talking with Tecumseh fully agreeing with what he said, described General Wayne as the best treaty commissioner any of the chiefs had ever seen. He was at all times gentle with the Indians in attendance, treating them with courteous firmness. He did not, as they had expected him to do, start out by reiterating the claim that the United States were the absolute owners of all the territory east of the Mississippi, in consequence of the 1783 Treaty of Paris. [485] Instead, he had stated to the tribes that they were to have free and exclusive use of all lands not specifically ceded by them to the United States. At the same time, he told them that in their signing of the treaty the tribes were acknowledging they were under the sole protection of the United States and the United States alone had exclusive right to preemption of such land in subsequent treaties. He assured them, as well, that by the terms of the treaty, if any white man should unjustly kill an Indian, that man should be apprehended by the whites and turned over to the Indians for punishment, and vice versa. Since always before the whites had claimed the right to punish both Indians and whites—usually the former and rarely the latter for such infractions—the chiefs were very impressed with this provision. [486]

The cession of Indian lands to the United States was the crux of the entire treaty. In trade for land, the Indians in effect purchased peace and annuities—a peace they now felt assured would be lasting—and they also, in effect, purchased the right to their own territory within the new boundaries; a right they felt assured at last would never be infringed upon.

General Wayne had told them, Blue Jacket related, that the new treaty being made at Greenville was to be based, in large measure—with some

revisions, which were to be explained—on the boundary lines established by
the Fort McIntosh Treaty on January 21, 1785. The biggest single land cession
involved the Ohio Territory. Although the Indians would retain hunting and
fishing privileges throughout the entire Ohio area, there was a definite dividing
line between Indian and white territories established in this treaty and he had
read it carefully to them, explaining in detail so they would understand its
significance.

Blue Jacket pulled out a piece of paper from his pouch and handed it to
Sauganash, telling him to read it aloud, which he did:

> *The general boundary line between the lands of the United States and the*
> *lands of the said Indian tribes shall begin at the mouth of the Cuyahoga*
> *River and run thence up the same to the Portage between that and the*
> *Tuscarawas branch of the Muskingum, thence down that branch to the*
> *crossing place above Fort Laurens, thence westerly to a fork of the branch*
> *of the Great Miami River running into the Ohio, at or near which stood*
> *Loramie's Store and where commenced the Portage between the Miami of*
> *the Ohio and St. Marys River, which is a branch of the Miami which runs*
> *into Lake Erie; thence a westerly course to Fort Recovery, which stands on*
> *a branch of the Wabash; thence southerly in a direct line to the Ohio, so as*
> *to intersect that river opposite the mouth of the Kentucky or Cuttawa River.*[487]

In addition, Blue Jacket went on, when Sauganash finished and handed
the paper back to him, General Wayne had told them that the United States
would require the cession of sixteen tracts of land within the Indian territory
for government reservations.[488] Each of the tracts was considered important
in the extreme to the United States, not only for the opening of Indian trade
to the Americans, but for the establishment of forts within the Indian territory
from which to distribute annuities and regulate the trade.[489] At this point, Blue
Jacket related, some of the chiefs had objected, but not enough of them and
it was only too clear to all in attendance—Indians and whites alike—that the
Indians were tired of war, tired of disputed boundaries, tired of being caught
in the pincers of two opposing white powers—and so the majority had prevailed and the land cessions were agreed to, in the belief that now they could
hunt and fish in peace, enjoy a peaceful trade, and raise their crops and families
in peace.[490]

With all negotiating finished, the ninety-one various chiefs had made their
marks on the treaty. Michikiniqua was last of the Indians to sign and had
declared, as he did so, that he would also be last to break the agreement.
General Wayne then signed it, along with some of his officers and the official
governmental witnesses. On August 7 the signed treaties had been exchanged

and Chief Tarhe of the Wyandots—the respected "grandfathers" of the other Northwestern tribes—was given custodianship of an official transcript on behalf of the assembled tribes.

Blue Jacket concluded by saying that in his farewell address, General Wayne had solemnly said to them, "I now fervently pray to the Great Spirit that the peace now established may be permanent and that it now holds us together in the bonds of friendship until time shall be no more. I also pray that the Great Spirit above may enlighten your minds and open your eyes to your true happiness, that your children may learn to cultivate the earth and enjoy the fruits of peace and industry."[491]

A silence fell over the group when Blue Jacket finished and both Chiuxca and Blue Jacket loaded fresh tobacco into their pipes and lighted them. Spemica Lawba and Sauganash studied the expressions of their elders but said nothing. At last Blue Jacket, blowing out a puff of blue-white smoke, spoke to Tecumseh.

"Your refusal to attend the Greenville Treaty, my friend, caused a reaction that may surprise you. Those who attended—many of them—felt coerced to come and appeared there begrudgingly, but because of the strength of General Wayne and fearing his wrath if they did not attend, they came. But what they talked about a great deal before the true negotiations began was that you, Tecumseh, had shown the courage to stay away; that you had stated you would never make peace with the whites. They see in you that piece of themselves that they had hidden away. Many of them, especially the younger chiefs and warriors, are greatly impressed with you and that you even had courage enough to temporarily pull away from your own tribe to support your view. They see you now as a champion of the rights of the Indian and one who refuses to bend under the ill wind from the whites. They see you, Tecumseh, as the one among all who holds true to the Indian standard of self-esteem and dignity and you have suddenly risen greatly in prestige in their hearts and minds. Only a few were upset at your stand, most of all Chief Catahecassa, who feels you have personally insulted him."

Tecumseh's expression was grim when he replied. "I am sorry he feels that way, since an insult to him was not intended. I stated only that I could not make peace with the whites and could not live with those who did. What I had feared would happen *has* happened: we have entirely lost, by the terms of the treaty, practically all in Ohio that was our own. Even the land of this little village where we now sit has been signed away and we no longer have any right to be here."

The bitterness in his voice became heavier as he went on. "My people and I will remain here until we have completed the harvest we have already begun of our corn and vegetables. Then we will move away."

"But to where, Uncle?" interjected Spemica Lawba. "Catahecassa cannot allow you to return to our villages now. He says this would raise ill feelings and dissension among our people."

Tecumseh looked at his nephew sorrowfully, regretting that his sister's son was so willing to accept the dictates of the whites. "When I left the tribe," he replied slowly, "and took these people with me, I told Catahecassa that if he and the other Shawnee chiefs should put their names to the treaty, our temporary severance from the tribe would become permanent. That has now taken place. I would not return to the villages even were I welcome, because I could not live with what is in my heart and mind and still abide by the leadership of Catahecassa. Our chief has been a satisfactory chief since the death of Chiungalla, but he is weary of war and thinks he is best serving our people by ceding lands instead of lives." He shrugged faintly. "Perhaps he is correct, but I cannot live with that. This is—*was*—our land and it is here that the bones of our fathers and our fathers' fathers are buried, and if we cannot protect what is ours, what is left to us? No, Spemica Lawba," he went on, shaking his head slowly, "I will not return to our villages. I will go above the treaty line on the Great Miami, but in a village of my own making, and perhaps not for long.

"Wehyehpihehrsehnwah," he said, turning to Blue Jacket, "it has been good seeing you again. And you, Chiuxca. And my good friend, Chaubenee, and our new young friend, Sauganash. Though the news has been painful, I thank you for bringing it."

Tecumseh stood and walked to the doorway of the wegiwa and heard the whistling of a chilling wind beyond the buffalo-hide flap. He stood with his back to the others but they said nothing, knowing he was not yet finished with what he had to say. When he turned back to them he looked no less grim and his voice was laced with a determination as chilling as the wind outside.

"Only this do I have left to say: my heart is a stone, heavy with sadness for my people; cold in the knowledge that no treaty will keep the whites out of our small lands that we are now left with; hard with the determination to resist for so long as I live and breathe. Now we are weak and many of our people are afraid. But hear me: a single twig breaks easily, but the bundle of twigs is strong. Someday I will embrace our brother tribes and draw them into a bundle and together we will win our country back from the whites."

Blue Jacket studied him with a piercing gaze and then finally nodded. "I think maybe you will," he said softly.

"When you do," Chaubenee said, rising and walking to Tecumseh, "I will be where long ago I vowed always to be—at your side."

"As will I," put in Wasegoboah.

"And I," echoed Sauganash.

[October 7, 1796 — Friday]

Tecumseh, astride the large chestnut mare he was riding these days, splashed across the Little Miami River at the knee-high fording place and continued forward the remaining few yards until he came to the edge of the riverine woods, from which he emerged a few yards and brought his horse to a halt. He sat high, looking back and forth slowly until satisfied that there were no whites or signs of their construction present. Then he put the mare in motion again, crossing the marshy lowland to the rise and then following it on firmer ground toward where the great Chalahgawtha *msi-kah-mi-qui* had once stood.

His eyes studied the ground as the horse moved and he saw traces of what had once been here—an occasional arrowhead, a shard of pottery, a bit of rotted buckskin, a rusted tomahawk head with the broken shaft still attached, a corn-grinding stone, a hide scraper—the bits and pieces of a life and a people now gone from here. An encompassing sadness cloaked him as he continued following the ridge to where the council house had been.

So different, so changed, so terrible! He looked out over the expanse of dun-colored weeds covering ground that once harbored a great village and expansive fields of corn and a proud and numerous people. Now, far less numerous, those people were gone, most far to the north and some, such as those of his own village, far to the west and north. He thought of the Deer Creek Village where for seventeen months he had anchored the people who had followed him when they separated from the tribe. They had stayed there through last winter, hunting, talking, surviving.

There, before the first snowfall, Tecumseh had married a second time, not because he had fallen in love but because he had needed someone to care for his household, someone to cook for him, someone to fill his carnal needs, someone to care for his son, Mahyawwekawpawe, and relieve Tecumapese of that responsibility, and he had married her because he had been so urged by his followers to take another wife to bear him children and set an example for his people.

Mamate was a few years older than he, the widow of a warrior who had been killed during a raid in Kentucky almost two years before, and a woman of limited intelligence who loved him no more than he loved her, but who needed him as well as someone who could provide her a home, bring in the meat of his hunting and fishing, protect her and, perhaps, give her what her first husband had not—a child.

It had been with a surprising lack of emotion that he greeted the news of her pregnancy late last year. As the harshness of winter lost its grip on the land, they had abandoned the Deer Creek Village and moved back to where he had lived on the upper Great Miami in what had been Lower Piqua Town and was changed to Chalahgawtha. They had planted fields of corn and plots of vegetables, but Tecumseh had not liked the area any more this time than he had the first.

The year had thus far been extraordinarily quiet, with few reports of difficulties between the Indians and whites filtering to Tecumseh's ears. The one significant occurrence was that finally, late in the spring, the British gave up their posts in United States territory to the Americans. At Fort Niagara, the redcoats withdrew across the Niagara River into Ontario and redistributed themselves in Fort Erie and Fort George. At Mackinac Island, the British withdrew to a new fort they had erected on St. Joseph Island in the North Channel at the mouth of the St. Marys River where it empties into Lake Huron. Of more immediate concern to the Northwestern tribes, Fort Miamis was abandoned entirely and its garrison, along with the one at Detroit, moved, as British officials had promised, into their new western headquarters, Fort Malden at Amherstburg. This was a bigger and better installation than the fort fifteen miles away at Detroit, but it was also less conveniently located, being separated now from the Northwestern tribes by the broad, swift strait called the Detroit River which connected the upper Great Lakes with Lake Erie.

The relinquishment of Detroit to the Americans had occurred on July 11. A force under General Wayne had come to Detroit from the mouth of the Maumee in the fifty-ton sloop, *Detroit,* accompanied by eleven large bateaux, but the general had become so ill with his gout that he had been unable to participate in the transference ceremonies.[492] This duty was taken over by an advance detachment of sixty-five soldiers under Captain Moses Porter who accepted possession of Detroit and the fort from Colonel Richard England.[493] A proclamation had then been issued to the citizens of Detroit that all who wished to remain were welcome to do so, but that in order to stay they had to renounce their British citizenship and pledge allegiance to the United States of America, at which they would become American citizens. Many had crossed the river with the British troops, but quite a few remained and took the pledge, with the trader John Kinzie among the latter. The only unexpected event was when Simon Girty, astride his horse on the King's Wharf, shook his fist at the approaching Americans and hurled verbal abuse at them. When a squad of soldiers was sent to apprehend him and put him in the guardhouse, he waited until they were close and then spurred his horse into a gigantic leap off the wharf and into the river. As the horse rose to the surface with the rider still on its back, Girty waved his hat wildly at the astonished soldiers and shouted "Hurrah for King George!" and then swam his horse all the way over to the Canadian side of the river.

Back in Ohio at just about this same time, Tecumseh's wife had become ill and failed steadily. When the baby was born, near the end of August, Mamate was so weak that soon afterward she died in the night. The infant boy, whom Tecumseh had named Naythawaynah—A Panther Seizing Its Prey—survived and now both the two-month-old boy and his fourteen-month-old brother were being well cared for by Tecumapese, who looked upon the responsibility with pleasure, for she loved children and she loved Tecumseh dearly.[494] As Tecumseh had grown in prestige among the warriors of the nation, so too had Tecumapese, now thirty-eight, achieved great stature among the women of the tribe, who looked upon her as tribal mother, perhaps the greatest distinction a Shawnee woman could acquire.

Shortly after their relocation to the Great Miami, while Tecumseh was wandering alone along the banks of the Whitewater River in the Indiana country, not far from where that stream was joined by its East Fork, he found a location that appealed to him because of a vague resemblance to the Little Miami River location that he so loved. As soon as the corn and vegetables were harvested, the Great Miami Village was abandoned and a new one established at the new site and called the Whitewater Village.[495]

This was where they were situated now, not very far from where the American John Conner was operating his trading post, but still Tecumseh was not satisfied with the location. Sometimes with his medicine-man brother, Lowawluwaysica, but more often alone, he would mount his horse and journey the sixty miles eastward in order to roam through the countryside he loved more than any other—the area surrounding the site of the long ago abandoned and destroyed Chalahgawtha.

Now, a lonely figure astride his horse, standing next to where a fire-blackened chunk of cornerpost still marked the former location of the *msi-kah-mi-qui*, he continued to let his eyes guide his memory to what had been. There, in the distance, was where he had been born. Here, close at hand, was where, as a boy, he had wrestled and played games with other Shawnee youngsters. There, in the deep pool of Little Miami River, was where he had won the *opawaka* that he still wore about his neck. Here was where he had lived so happily in a wegiwa with Chiksika. And there was the trail along which they had borne the body of their beloved Chief Chiungalla for burial.

With the eyes he had used twenty years earlier, Tecumseh now saw the great expanse of wegiwas that had comprised the village of Chalahgawtha and the huge impressive *msi-kah-mi-qui* that had been its core. With those same eyes he saw the bustle of hundreds of people—proud, carefree, happy people—as they tended their crops, tanned their fur skins and hides, knapped their arrowheads and sat about their fires telling the wonderful stories of life here long and long ago.

The scene blurred and misted and an overwhelming sadness arose in him, bringing with it the determination that somehow, in some way and at some time, the Shawnees *must* reclaim this land that they so dearly loved and that was so rightfully theirs.

[June 1, 1798 — Friday]

It was at Tecumseh's lodge in the Whitewater Village along the Whitewater River of Indiana Territory, that Spemica Lawba was reunited with his family for the first time since that visit to Tecumseh at the Deer Creek Village shortly after the Greenville Treaty was signed. No one questioned why he had come, since that would have been exceedingly impolite, and he had been heartily welcomed by all, especially his mother, and he had accepted with alacrity when Tecumapese invited him to join them for the dinner just being served. Seated around the large rectangular table, at the head of which sat Tecumseh, there were, in addition to Tecumapese and her husband, Wasegoboah, Spemica Lawba's other uncles, Kumskaka and Lowawluwaysica. Tecumseh's sons, Mahyawwekawpawe and Naythawaynah, now aged three and two respectively, were both asleep on a bed along one wall.

They had eaten well and now, having finished their pipes, it was time they talked, as was customary, about the events of the recent past. They spoke of the fact that Chaubenee and his wife, Canoku, had left her father's village of Pimitoui on the Illinois River and had now established a new town of their own, called Chaubenee's Village, beside a beautiful prairie island twenty-five miles to the north.[496]

The casual talking continued. Spemica Lawba proudly announced that he was now a father. Pskipahcah Ouiskelotha—Bluebird—had a few months ago given birth to a beautiful daughter whom they had named Psquawwe Sisqui—Red Leaf—because on the eleventh day after her birth, while she lay asleep, a bright red maple leaf, caught by the fingers of a breeze, had drifted down and landed lightly in the middle of her forehead without even awakening her. All were very pleased to hear of the birth and heartily approved of the name selected.

They spoke next of Simon Girty, whose eyesight had begun to fail, and who had also become such a drunk that his wife, Catherine, after thirteen years of putting up with it and his unkindness toward her, had finally left him.

The news that Spemica Lawba brought of Blue Jacket was one of the lighter moments of their discussion and left all of them greatly amused. There were few things in the temperament of the Shawnees that appealed to them more, in the vein of humor, than a well-engineered practical joke. And, as

Spemica Lawba put it, no other practical joke in Shawnee memory had been more involved or better executed than that which Blue Jacket had pulled off on a small group of whites.

One of the prevailing puzzles among the pioneers was the question of where the Shawnees mined the silver they used so extensively in ornamentation. All the settlers were convinced that the tribe had a fantastic source of it somewhere, since even the most destitute Shawnee warrior seemed to have an ample supply of fine hand-beaten armbands, necklaces, bracelets, medallions and other objects of the purest quality silver, and the prevalent belief among the settlers was that the man who could find this hoard would undoubtedly stake his claim on a small piece of land that would ultimately be worth millions of dollars.

Frequently individual Shawnees had been pressed, in friendly discussions, to reveal the source, but they adamantly refused to even discuss the matter. But recently a particularly avaricious Kentuckian named Jonathan Flack had come to Blue Jacket's Town and spent several months there and in the war chief's hunting camp trying to induce him to divulge the location, all the while continuing to jack up the value of what he would give in return for such information. He even established a combine of backers who called themselves The Blue Jacket Mining Company.

A long period of negotiation ensued in respect to how much would be paid. When payment was finally made—a number of horses, a great deal of goods, and a large amount of cash, all of which Blue Jacket turned over to his people—he hesitantly told them the location. The mines, he said, were in Kentucky, along the Red River tributary of the Kentucky River. The information stunned them. No wonder no one had ever been able to find the source: tradition among the whites had it that the fabulous mines were located somewhere in the vicinity of old Chalahgawtha, most likely in the deep glen to the northeast a few miles.[497]

With Blue Jacket guiding them, the party had then gone to that area in Kentucky, which Blue Jacket told them was "a very sacred place" and he required seclusion to purify and humble himself through fasting and thus appease the Great Spirit so as to get Her permission to disclose the whereabouts of the mines.

After much time passed, Blue Jacket returned and the search began. However, unable to find the right area, he blamed the dimming of his own eyes with age. He suggested that the men of The Blue Jacket Mining Company should wait there and he would return home and send his son, Little Blue Jacket, whose eyes were clear and who also knew the location of the mines. The whites had agreed readily. Blue Jacket and Wabethe departed and the whites waited . . . and waited . . . They were still waiting when, two hundred miles to the north, word spread throughout the Shawnee Nation of the great practical joke and Shawnees everywhere, as they discussed it, howled with glee.[498]

There were other matters of interest. Tecumseh learned that not only had the appointment of William Wells as Indian agent to the Miamis been confirmed, but that there had been a reconciliation of sorts between him and his adopted father, Michikiniqua, and the two of them had even gone east together as part of a delegation and had met the new Great Father of the United States, John Adams.[499] Tecumseh was also informed that Wells and Michikiniqua's daughter, Wanagapeth, now had three children named Etonah, Penezaquah, and Tonon, but who had been baptized as James, Rebekah, and William Wayne Wells.

The talk about Wells put a chill to the warm and friendly discussion at the table and it was apparent that casual talking was finished and it was time for Spemica Lawba to state his purpose in coming. It was Tecumseh who broached the subject.

"My heart wants to believe," he said slowly, a trace of wistfulness in his voice, "that you have come to join us, but my mind says this is not so and that you wish only for us to return to Wapakoneta and live again under Catahecassa."

The twenty-three-year-old shifted uneasily but continued to meet his uncle's gaze directly. He grunted an assent and added, "As always, your mind sees the truth. I have been sent by our chief to ask that you and those who follow you," he let his eyes slide across those present, "return to your people."

"Catahecassa is *your* chief, nephew!" Lowawluwaysica spoke up harshly, the empty eyesocket deep with shadow and disturbingly malevolent, combining with his unpleasant features in a macabre mask. "He is no longer ours. We are no longer Shawnees. We—"

Tecumseh raised a hand and cut him off, his lips tightening. He turned back to Spemica Lawba. "The words of your uncle are sharply spoken," he said, "but they are nevertheless true. You know that all of us here—and those who have followed us—cannot agree with Catahecassa that the Greenville Treaty is binding upon us all and that we must bury the hatchet forever. Though I may not have admired him, I had always respected Catahecassa as chief and so it came as a hard blow to learn that he really believes the *Shemanese* will live up to the agreement. It is why we drifted apart; why others clung to me who felt as I did, that our troubles with the *Shemanese* are not ended. They want ever more of what is ours, while we wish to have returned to us that of ours which the *Shemanese* have already taken. How does one come to agreement with they who have burned our villages, killed and imprisoned our people, driven us off our ancestral lands and driven wedges among us to divide us? How does one come to agreement with they who sit at this moment on land stolen from us? We cannot. We step aside now because we are weak, but such will not always be. One day we will be in a position to negotiate from strength, not from weakness, and when that time comes we will rightfully claim that which was taken away."

He lapsed into silence and for a considerable period no one spoke. Spemica Lawba was on the verge of doing so, but then held his tongue as his mother began to speak softly, a great sadness in her voice. "Tecumseh," she said, "does not always speak what is in his heart if he feels it will serve no good purpose, but since I am your mother, I will put to words what he has left unsaid. It is a difficult enough burden to bear for me—for *us!*—to know that you have chosen to remain with Catahecassa on the Auglaize rather than with us, who are your first blood. It is much worse, much more difficult to understand, when little birds whisper in our ears that you serve with and for the *Shemanese;* that you carry the words of the soldier Harrison at Fort Washington as his messenger; that you have become the friend of the one who was known as Apekonit, who turned away from his father, Michikiniqua, to aid the *Shemanese* in their last battle against us.[500] These things are true, Spemica Lawba?"

For the first time her son averted his eyes, lowered his head slightly and nodded. In a moment he looked up at her and misery was evident in his expression, intermingled with a trace of defiance. "It is true. But not *all* of the *Shemanese* are bad. Many, such as he who gave me the name of Johnny Logan, are good men who wish nothing to which they are not entitled." He transferred his gaze to Tecumseh. "See what has happened to us. Once we were so strong that the *Shemanese* begged us for favors. Now, while they have increased to a strength we never knew, we have weakened steadily. More than half our people remaining after Fallen Timbers have separated and live now far west of the Missitheepi . . . or with you. Those who remain see the choices they have only too clearly: oppose the *Shemanese* and die . . . to no purpose, or else accept the terms of the agreement we have made with them, even though they may not be the best for us, and live with them, accepting what little there is for us to accept, rather than lose everything. *That* is what Catahecassa has asked me to express to you." His tone became imploring. "Tecumseh, for your sake and for the sake of our tribe, which needs your strength, come back to us."

Tecumseh shook his head and his voice was gentle but firm. "It is not possible, Spemica Lawba. We are where we are. Our course is set. By ourselves we cannot hope to recover what we have lost, what others have lost and are still losing. Now others are beginning to feel that stab of the white man which has pierced us for so long. Some are beginning to listen. Soon many others will do so also and, when they do, then we will begin to have the *strength* to talk to the Americans."

"So you will remain here until then?"

Again Tecumseh shook his head. "We leave here soon," he said. "Buck-angehela moved his Delaware village to White River after his town was destroyed.[501] Now he has come to us and asked us to come and reside among his people where they are still situated to the north and west of here. They have opened their hearts and arms to us, as our own Shawnees will not. They ask us to come and live with them, hunt with them, reside in peace with them. They have asked us, should the time come when it be necessary, if we will lead them against any enemy who might threaten them. We have told them that we will."

[June 7, 1799 — Friday]

Tecumseh as a warrior had first come to the attention of other tribes beyond the Shawnees when, during his extensive stay among the Cherokees, he had left them awed at his courage, strategy and fighting prowess. He had first gained some intertribal recognition for his intelligence, perspicacity, and prophetic abilities when he had addressed the confederated tribes in respect to his spying activities on the United States Army just prior to their tremendous victory at St. Clair's Defeat. Now he had begun to rise into greater prominence among the various tribes of the Northwestern Territory due to the forceful and disturbing truths he was uttering and the riveting eloquence with which he delivered them.

Suddenly Wyandots and Kickapoos, Ottawas and Chippewas and Potawatomies were asking among themselves, who was this man who was suddenly gripping them by the hair of their heads and making them open their eyes to what was truly occurring around them? Who was this man of such conviction that he stood as the only voice of his tribe crying out against the Greenville Treaty? Who was this man of such courage and of such belief in his own views that he chose to stand alone, incurring the anger and enmity of all his chiefs, and separate himself from his own nation rather than submit to what he felt was intrinsically wrong? Who was this man who, by his words alone, was making all of them *think*?

Tecumseh himself seemed to take a deep delight in addressing audiences, depending not on flagrant gestures or blatant emotionalism to hold them, but saying simply and well what was in his heart and expressing it in such manner that each listener was inclined to remark to himself, "That is how I have felt inside but I have never been able to say it."

At this open-air council being held now at the place where the east-west trail from Deer Creek to Lower Piqua crossed the trail that headed north to Blue Jacket's Town, he addressed an audience of seventy, mostly Ottawas and

Wyandots.[502] He had been speaking for well over an hour, drawing a comparison of what this country had been to what it was now and the word pictures he used touched them deeply.

He reminded them that where before there had been no Americans in the country of the Great Lakes except by their permission, now they were on the Cuyahoga, on the Maumee, on the Detroit, on the Wabash, on the island where the three Great Lakes came together far to the north. "Where they are able to place a toe," he told them, "soon after they are stamping their feet and making the earth tremble. Now they are building their great ships at the Niagara and at Detroit and where are these ships to go?[503] Can we for one moment believe that such ships are meant only, as they say, to move between Buffalo and Detroit? No! Soon they will be seen in the farthest reaches of the lakes of Huron and Michigan and Superior. And will the white men on those ships be content to stay on them and merely look at the beauty of the land that lies beyond?

"Now," he went on, "even the whites who were the first to move into this area are moving onward to open new areas far beyond us. Among these is Sheltowee—Daniel Boone—who has left Kentucky behind and is now settling with his family across the Mississippi in Missouri country and what will happen next? It is well known to us that when one white like that moves in, others soon follow. What will happen there is what has already happened here. *Think!* Where the great village of Kekionga stood there is now an American fort and many *Shemanese*. Where the great village of Chalahgawtha stood there are now settlers and farms, as there are all over my country and yours.[504]

"My brothers," he told them in conclusion, "how can our people continue to deceive themselves with their foolish belief in the supposed strength of the white chief Wayne's treaty signed at his fort of Greenville? The only difference between this treaty and the hundreds before it is the boundary line. Each time we have been told, 'This, Indian brother, is the last treaty, the one that will be honored by red men and white men alike for all time.' Such lies make the vomit burn in my throat. This is *not* the last treaty. There will be another. And another after that. And others to follow. And each time it will be the Indians, your people and mine, who will be pushed back, not the whites. *Think!* When was the last treaty that the whites ever conceded ground to us that was not already ours to begin with? At this very moment an hour's easy ride to the south is the newest of the white settlements.[505] The cold spring there that has always flowed for us, now satisfies the whites living in the fourteen cabins they have built by it.[506] Soon other whites will come and build. And will all of these be content to stay behind Wayne's boundary? On my tongue is the harsh laughter of mockery. How does the white man consider his red brother? The answer has always been clear: he does not believe the red man sufficiently good to live. Think on this, brothers. Put aside your anger.

423

Put aside your fear. Put aside your vain hopes. *Think!* Think without prejudice of what I have said here and it will become as clear to you as it is to me why the very leaves of the forest drop tears of pity on us as we walk beneath. And after you think on it, remember this: any child can snap with ease the single hair from a horse's tail, but not the strongest man, not the wildest stallion, can break the rope woven of those same hairs."

[May 21, 1800 — Wednesday]

Tecumseh was one of the many hundreds of Indians who had made this trip to the great clearing a mile south of Amherstburg and sixteen miles from Detroit. Here, in the vicinity of the fine farm that had many years ago been established by Alexander McKee, the long-delayed Death Dance was held in honor of their friend and protector, McKee, who had died a year ago January.

Simon Girty had come from his farm a few miles farther south and Matthew Elliott, McKee's successor in the Indian Department, was there, along with McKee's son, Thomas, and a large number of officers and soldiers from Fort Malden, plus a whole corps of green-coated Canadian Militia.

A great feast had been held first and then this was followed by the slow, intricate, methodical Death Dance in which more than two hundred Indians participated and that continued without pause for two full days and nights. This was an honor that had never before been bestowed upon a white man and only rarely for chiefs or warriors of uncommonly great distinction.

Alexander McKee had been their friend and their protector and he was sorely missed.[507]

[January 1, 1801 — Thursday]

As the second hand of time passed midnight and made its first click into the nineteenth century, seven men and one woman were seated around the table in a sturdy log cabin in Buckangehela's Town on the White River sixty miles due west of Greenville. The cabin, situated on a little knoll a few yards from the river, was set somewhat apart from the twenty other abodes—cabins and wegiwas alike—in the Delaware village. In those other lodges were upwards of two hundred Delawares and some one hundred Shawnees sleeping peacefully, wholly unaware of the momentous meeting occurring so close at hand.

The heavy cloud cover of yesterday had cleared away and the night was very clear, the stars a myriad of diamond bits against the deep midnight dark. A knee-deep blanket of new snow covered the earth around the cabin and the only movement in the vicinity was the faintly wavering column of smoke emerging from the stone chimney and rising almost straight upward in the calm night air.

Inside the cabin the seven who listened closely to the one who spoke were very aware that what was occurring here, at this moment, would undoubtedly affect every person, Indian or white, in the entire Northwest Territory.

The two who had come the farthest had arrived yesterday within hours of each other, one from the northern Illinois country, the other from the vicinity of Detroit. Chaubenee and Sauganash were deeply honored to have been included in this gathering. Approaching thirty now, Chaubenee, seated to Tecumseh's right, was still the short, powerfully built individual he had been as a younger man, stocky and broadly barrel-chested, and his unlined round face still as open and friendly as it had always been, its lack of lines imparting a look of innocence that belied the wide experience he had and the many life-and-death struggles in which he had engaged. Sauganash, on the other hand, now nearing twenty-three, had lost his boyishness and had become a fine figure of an Indian, tall, lean and hard, his intelligent eyes above the slightly hawkish nose alive with the fire of undimmed youthful idealism. He was seated next to Chaubenee.

The two had come here at the express invitation of Tecumseh, as had Stiahta—Roundhead—from his village on the Scioto headwaters southwest of Upper Sandusky. He sat at the foot of the table, and the apparel he wore indicated that he continued to be one of the most appearance-conscious individuals in the Wyandot tribe. His hair, still dark but beginning to show strands of gray, was braided in two thick, glossy queues that hung down over his shoulders to near midbreast of the intricately beaded and frilled buckskin blouse he wore. A thick rope, around which had been sewn the skin of a timber rattlesnake, served as his belt, its ends terminating in golden tassels. His trousers were soft but heavy elkhide, loose to the knee and snugly fitted to the shank, and around his hips, snugged under the belt, he wore a half-skirt of buffalo skin, hair side inward, to protect him against cold and to pad his rump on a long-distance ride. In a corner of the room lay his hat, a muskrat fur tricorne from which projected toward the rear a single broad tailfeather of a turkey gobbler, its trailing end black and fringed with white.

Tecumseh was at the head of the table and to his left sat his sister, Tecumapese, now in her forty-third year and still a strikingly handsome woman with loose black hair combed shiny and hanging to her waist. Her features were firm and unblemished, so cleanly chiseled she might have been sculpted beneath the skilled hands of a Michelangelo. That she, a woman, should be included here was not unexpected. Her intelligence and sensitivity were such that she had become the only person from whom Tecumseh would unreservedly accept advice and counsel. She was clad in the simple soft doeskin shift she always favored, the one she was wearing now dyed to a deep rich mahogany color. Beside her sat Wasegoboah, not only her husband, two years older than she, but with the possible exception of Chaubenee, Tecumseh's closest friend. It had become axiomatic that wherever Tecumseh was, there too would be found Wasegoboah—a pillar of strength and dependability upon whom Tecumseh relied without reservation.

The remaining two of the group, seated across from one another to left and right of Stiahta, were Tecumseh's two remaining triplet brothers, Kumskaka and Lowawluwaysica, who were only a month away from being thirty. Kumskaka still bore a faint resemblance to their elder brother Chiksika, who had been killed in Tennessee so long ago. He was a quiet man and, though he had never particularly excelled as warrior or leader, he was unalterably devoted to Tecumseh and had become, of his own volition, something of an official bodyguard to him.

Finally, there was Lowawluwaysica, who resembled no one in the cabin, not even his triplet brother. He was not really thin, yet his features were hatchetlike, with the nose sharply beaked, the cheekbones relatively high and the cheeks themselves hollow. One of his ears had a lobe half again as long as the other and when he smiled, his thin lips crooked up on the right but down on the left. Over his empty eyesocket he had recently begun wearing a black eye patch that had been presented to him by the trader John Conner.[508] In character he remained as he had always been—high-strung, nervous, and unusually irritable. His rare, explosive laughter, most often elicited from someone else's discomfort than because of humor, was a shrill and grating cackle with a witchlike quality. He was swift to accuse unjustifiably, swift to take offense at imagined slights, and very susceptible to bursts of blind rage. He longed for renown in his own right and, secretly convinced in his own mind that he would never acquire it, he clung ever closer to Tecumseh and basked in the reflected glow of his older brother's growing prestige.

This very private council in the cabin had begun not long after nightfall, after bellies had been filled, bladders emptied and pipes smoked. It was then that Tecumseh had begun to speak, not in oration but rather in a quiet conversational tone. It had not taken long for his audience of seven to realize that what they were hearing was apt to affect the remainder of their lives, along with a great many other people.

He had begun by touching on occurrences, most of them ominous, of the past eighteen months that directly or indirectly affected them all. In defiance to the Greenville Treaty, cabins of whites had begun popping up at random in many areas north of the boundary line set by that treaty, in the guaranteed inviolate Indian lands and the same was occurring in the southern portions of both Illinois and Indiana. Nine months ago, in March, the United States had begun allocating portions of the former Western Reserve Lands in Ohio as bounties to American soldiers who had fought in the Revolution, and by the end of April over a thousand new settlers were sinking new roots just south of Lake Erie. Sawmills had been built and seven hundred miles of new roads had been cut through the virgin land to connect the various settlements. During that same month of April the Americans had established another frontier fort well north of the Greenville Treaty line. Erected near the mouth of the Maumee, it was named Fort Industry.[509]

A short while later, the young officer who had been the aide of General Wayne and then the commander of Fort Washington and had moved on to become the secretary of the Northwest Territory and one of its two delegates in Congress—William Henry Harrison—had risen in Congress Hall and introduced a bill proposing that Congress divide the Northwest Territory into two parts—one to be officially the Ohio Territory, which was already poised on the brink of statehood, and the other to be the remainder of the west and north.[510] Last May 7 that division had formally occurred and the new boundary followed the line that had been drawn for the western edge of the Greenville Treaty boundary, from the mouth of the Kentucky River directly to Fort Recovery and now from there directly north to the Canadian Territorial line. Everything westward to the Mississippi River was now the Indiana Territory, with the seat of government at Vincennes on the Wabash. President John Adams had then appointed a governor to this vast Indiana Territory, giving that individual such powers as had never before been bestowed upon any individual, civilian or military, since the organization of the United States, making him a virtual king of the territory, responsible only to the president and even that only to a relatively minor degree.[511] That chosen individual was able at will to enact any law and he held within his grasp the power of life and death over anyone within the territory, Indian or white. And, Tecumseh pointed out gravely, that individual had been given the power to treat with the Indians in any manner he saw fit on behalf of the United States. Amazingly, the appointee—a tall, gaunt man with brooding eyes and somber countenance beneath a shock of unruly rust-colored hair—was only twenty-seven years old.

His name was William Henry Harrison.

Even as he spoke the name, Tecumseh's expression tightened, as if he were containing only with great effort a vast hatred for this man, laced with a wariness that seemed to border on fear. Tecumseh's listeners looked at one another wonderingly. How was it that such a reaction could occur in him at the mere mention of the young white man's name? What was there about him, seen by Tecumseh, that was hidden from them? They didn't know, but an ominous chill rippled through them as he continued.

"All during the past summer," he said, "and into the fall and winter and even now, this Harrison has been establishing himself at Vincennes, building a great house such as this land has never seen and from which he intends to run our lives—mine, yours, the lives of all Indians." His voice became lower, abruptly filled with a huskiness that shocked them. "He is aided by many, but three in particular who can do us great harm. One of these," he glanced to his right, "is a village chief of your own Potawatomi tribe, Chaubenee. His name is Winnemac and his lips are always at the ear of Harrison.[512] Harrison listens! He learned this from the soldier he served at Fallen Timbers—General Wayne; learned to listen and to heed the advice of those who have been more intimate with the enemy than he. In this he admits humility and in that humility there is great strength. Few leaders ever acquire such ability, but those who do accomplish many things."

Chaubenee nodded. "I know Winnemac," he said, "though not well. I have *heard* more of him than I know of my own witness. I am told that he considers himself to be more than he is; that he craves power over all the Potawatomi, which he will never get, not so long as we have such chiefs as Topenebe, Onoxa, Pinequa, Gomo, Siggenauk, and Black Partridge."

"And Chaubenee," Tecumseh reminded softly, smiling.

"You said three could do us harm, brother," interjected Lowawluwaysica. "Who are the other two?"

A fleeting frown touched Tecumseh's face as he looked at his one-eyed brother, then stared into the dying fire. As if it were a command, Lowawluwaysica scrambled to his feet and moved into a shadowed recess of the cabin, returning in a moment with an armload of medium-sized branch sections and a dry, barkless log about the length of his lower leg. He quickly positioned the branch sections across the glowing coals in the stone fireplace and then laid the log atop them and resumed his seat. In a moment the branches burst into flame and licked at the log, crackling cheerily. Still, Tecumseh looked into the fire wordlessly, as if seeking a vision. Lowawluwaysica fidgeted and seemed about to speak again, but held his tongue as Tecumseh went on.

"Another is he who was once white, then Indian, now white again; he whom we knew as Apekonit, or sometimes Epiconyare," there was contempt in his voice as he spat out the word, for Epiconyare meant brave and loyal, "but who is now William Wells and who has become agent to the Miamis for the Americans. He learned much from his father, Michikiniqua, and from the Miamis, until he began to be afraid of their future and returned to the protection of the whites. He knows about us and our ways and now he, too, tells Harrison much and performs many tasks for him which he pretends are for our benefit. Michikiniqua believes him, but I do not."

He paused again and when, after a moment, he did not continue, Tecumapese rolled her eyes toward him and spoke the words he seemed reluctant to say. "And the third," she said tonelessly, "is my son and your nephew, Spemica Lawba."

Tecumseh nodded. "Yes. Because of the kindness of one man among the *Shemanese,* he has turned his heart from us. He remains in Wapakoneta with Catahecassa and Pskipahcah Ouiskelotha and the child she has borne him, but he journeys often to Vincennes and Harrison has already come to rely heavily on him for many things, among which is convincing Catahecassa that he must keep the Shawnees in place and quiet." Bitterness laced the words.

"Harrison sees too clearly for one with eyes so young," he went on, "and his eyes are set upon even more distant things which will affect all of us."

For the first time since the pipes had been finished, Stiahta spoke up. "Your eyes are clear, Tecumseh, and they see farther and deeper. If they did not, we would not be here this night. Since you came to this village you have been thinking, and before that you thought on the Whitewater River, and even before that, on the Great Miami and at Deer Creek, it is said that you thought deeply. All of these thoughts of yours have now come together; if they had not, you would not have summoned us. Now it is time for those thoughts of yours to become words for our ears. Will you give them to us?"

Tecumseh smiled at him. "You know my heart very well, Grandfather." The smile vanished as rapidly as it had appeared. "Yes, it is time for thoughts to become words. I have a plan. I have thought on it for many seasons. I have altered it many times to fit conditions as they have changed. Now there is little more changing that can be done and as the thoughts become words, the words must then become actions."

He came to his feet in a fluid movement, the blanket that had been over his shoulders falling softly onto his chair. He wore heavy buckskin leggins and a long-sleeved blouse of the same material which, untucked, fell nearly to his knees. Thick, high-topped elkhide moccasins encased his feet and were laced with rawhide up his calves. A necklace of downcurved bear claws separated by inch-long cylinders of silver around his neck—a gift from Michikiniqua almost a decade ago following St. Clair's Defeat, the claws being trophies of Michikiniqua's hunts and symbols of strength, and the silver dividers having been purchased from Shawneeawkee, the silversmith and former English trader, when he had his trading post at Miamitown on the Maumee close to Kekionga.

A change had come over Tecumseh, something sensed rather than seen, and all who were present felt it strongly. He did not look at any of them, nor at the fire. His gaze was steady and straight ahead and what he saw was not within the cabin. And when he spoke, it was with a different timbre, filled with vision and hope and at times crackling with contained excitement that affected them all.

"What I see," he began, "may take ten or twelve summers of great effort to bring about, but I can do it. I *will* do so! Should my plan ripen into success— and it *must!*—the *Shemanese* will be driven back, not only across the Spaylaywitheepi, but even beyond the mountains that first greet the morning sun.

"Given equal arms and equal numbers, no force of white men can stand before us. How many times have mere handfuls of Indians driven back greatly superior white forces? How few times have we ourselves been defeated by them, and then only through their greater numbers and stronger weapons? Our victory over the general called Harmar showed what a small force of Indians could do to a larger *Shemanese* army. Our victory over the general called St. Clair showed what a large Indian force could do to a smaller *Shemanese* army, even though it had cannons and better rifles and had only to hold and defend, not attack.

"Beginning in the Rain Moon," he went on, "I will begin drawing the tribes together, but not in a confederation. Past confederations, such as those that were formed under Pontiac and Thayendanegea and even Michikiniqua, eventually failed. There were two reasons for such failure: their leadership eventually fell apart and the confederacies were not united strongly enough in the first instance to overcome the tribal hatreds that existed among them."

Tecumseh shook his head faintly. "No. They were doomed from the beginning. That is not what I will make. Mine will be a union not of five or six tribes loosely brought together to fight a common enemy. That is not enough. I will do much more. With the help of Moneto and the gifts he has given me—the abilities to see and speak and convince—I will ride far and visit many. I will draw on the experience I gained at the side of Chiksika as we visited so many different tribes and learned much of their history, their traditions and their problems with the whites. I will take my time and convince the tribes of the necessity of joining together without hatred between them to gnaw at them and eventually destroy them. I will tell them these things in such a manner that they will stamp their feet and clap their hands and shout, and they will chafe at any delay in forming the union. One by one I will draw together and interweave in a single force the warriors of fifty or more different tribes. When at last we confront the whites, it will not be with just a few thousand warriors. No! It will be with a single unified body of *fifty thousand* warriors!"

His listeners caught their breaths at the vision and the grip of Wasego-boah's hand on his wife's elbow nearly paralyzed Tecumapese's arm. Chaubenee's and Sauganash's eyes were glinting and Stiahta's mouth had fallen open. Kumskaka stared at his older brother rapturously and Lowawluwaysica was literally trembling with his excitement, his small teeth glinting in a savage, crooked grin.

"With such a force," Tecumseh continued, "we may have no need greater than showing ourselves to gain what we wish. I hope we will not *have* to fight. No more Indians must be killed needlessly. White leaders will recognize our power and for once it will be they who must give in to our terms. And our demands will be that they withdraw from our country and return eastward of the mountains. If possible, we will avoid war, but if it comes to war, we will not turn aside!

"The travels I made as a boy with Chiksika and later as a man," he went on, the fervor of his talk lessening slightly, "showed me the strength of various tribes. They are strong, very strong, all of them . . . as individuals! Against the whites, as individual tribes, they are nevertheless too weak. Even in small confederations, with each still retaining its own tribal form and its own leadership, they could not oppose the whites for long, though they were stronger and could hold their own for a while. But in the union I foresee, where they will be joined as *brothers,* without regard to tribe, all under a single strong leadership against the most deadly foe in any of our histories, that enemy will be swept away as the autumn leaves before the wind that springs from the West!

"I will start my unification of the Indians with fifty tribes. There are more than that, many more, and once they see the value of the strength of our union, they will all hasten to join us. From the Northeast there will be the Iroquois—Mohawks, Oneidas, Cayugas, Onondagas, Senecas, and their nephews, the Tuscarawas. From our own country there will be Wyandots and Potawatomies and Delawares and Miamis and the children of the Miamis—Weas and Eel Rivers and Piankeshaws. There will be the Kickapoos and the few Kaskaskias who remain. And there will be our own Shawnees, who will see at last the values to which they are now blinded. From the north I will collect the fathers of the Wyandots, the Hurons, along with the Ottawas and Chippewas and the children of the Chippewas, the Mississaugies. From the Northwest, the Menominees and Winnebagoes, the Mandans and Dakotahs. In the far west I will draw together the Sacs and their brothers, the Foxes, and from beyond the Mississippi, the Iowas and Sioux, the Omahas, the Cheyennes, the Poncas and Pawnees and Comanches, the Otoes and Missouris, the Osages and Kansas and Ouichitas.

"That is not all!" He lifted his arm arrow-straight and pointed. "From the Southwest will come the Quapaws and Yazoos, the Caddos and Hasinais and Kitchais and Tawakonias." He moved his arm. "From the south, our good friends the Cherokees, and their neighbors, the Choctaws and Chickasaws, the Alabamas and Biloxies and Upper Creeks. And from the Southeast, those warriors who remain of the Santees and Catawbas, and the Lower Creeks and their brothers, the Seminoles."

Lowawluwaysica had suddenly frowned and opened his mouth to speak, but Tecumseh slashed his arm sideways through the air and cut him off. "Think not that they will not come. They will! With the gift of prophecy that Moneto has given me—as he gave it to my father and my brother who died in my arms—I will give them more than merely words. I will give them signs in which to believe. I will call upon their honor, their pride, their religion, their superstitions. Every argument, every force I can bring to bear, I will do so without hesitation.

"You here will help me," he said, his gaze sweeping across them, his burning eyes holding them transfixed. "Each of you will have a contribution to give to make this plan ripen and come to fruit. Each of you will pass along to your own people and to others the *need* for them to join us if they are to survive. Stiahta will do it with his influence and strength, Chaubenee and Sauganash with their passion, Wasegoboah and Tecumapese and Kumskaka with their persuasion and conviction that it remains our only course for survival, and Lowawluwaysica will put to good use his obvious talents—the ability to agitate, to anger, to stir to a fury against the *Shemanese* the thoughts of every Indian.

"We will form a new village and it will not be the village of a tribe nor of several tribes. It will be a village of *Indians*! We will not be Shawnees nor Potawatomies nor Wyandots nor Cherokees nor Sioux. We will be *Indians*, all of us! It will happen, but it will not happen easily or quickly. As I told you in the beginning, it will take ten or twelve years of very great effort to bring about. But I tell you again, it *will* happen! With some of the tribes we must move slowly, carefully, gradually gaining their confidence, their trust, their respect, and their willingness to follow. With other tribes it will go swiftly, with only a word or two needed for the war belts to begin circulating and the tomahawks to be struck into the war posts.

"Now," he added, his voice dropping, "what is most important of all: while this is going on, *they must not show it*! They must abide by their treaties at all costs. They must, when the time comes—as come it will!—overlook infringement of their rights by the whites. They must profess a peaceable intent in all things until we are ready. If there is any possibility of accomplishing our aims without warfare, then this must be the course we follow. But, war or not, it will be done. And the facts of what we are doing must be kept from the whites. No outsider must *ever* be allowed to sit in on the councils and those who might feel they have a right to sit in but are against us—those such as Spemica Lawba and Winnemac and William Wells—must be denied.

"We ourselves, all of us, must faithfully and honestly and forever bury whatever past insults and hostilities and animosities have risen between us and each of us, as individuals, must treat every other, regardless of his tribe, as no less than a fellow Indian fighting at his side for the same cause.

"In the village we will establish, and for the new race of *Indians* we will create, we must set up strong guides and codes that will enable us to reach the important goal we seek. We must *absolutely* cease the drinking of alcohol in any form, for it is through this firewater that our brains and our wills and our purpose are destroyed. Though our pipes may still be filled with *kinni-*

kinnick, we must stop our smoking of the tall green weed which brings strange dreams and weaknesses that could defeat us.[513] We must, politely but firmly, break whatever alliances presently exist between us and the whites—be they Americans, British, French, or Spanish. We must encourage our Indians to accept from the whites anything of value they wish to offer in the form of gratuities or annuities, but they must join no white force to fight another white force, for in that direction lies ruin. With past alliances, Indians have been used, manipulated like tools, to promote only the welfare of one white faction over another. Let the whites fight among themselves if they wish. It will weaken them. But let not any Indian bind himself to any white man or white cause or white ideal.

"There will be occasions when we must temporarily swallow our pride, and this will be one of the greater difficulties to overcome. At such times, if necessary, we must fall back when the *Shemanese* nudge us. We must turn our cheeks and pretend to be rabbits, and under no pretext must we take up the hatchet against the whites until—and unless!—there is no other choice, and then not until I myself give the sign. Later I will say what sign this will be, but I tell you now it will be a sign that will come to all tribes the same day and at the same time.

"Finally," he concluded, "when the period of waiting and building and growing is over, we will demand the return of our lands. With such a great unified force to give power to our demand, there is every reason to hope and believe the whites will leave our lands peaceably. But if they will not, then I will give the signal. If and when this unmistakable sign is given, our irresistible wave of warriors will wash across the face of the land to drown every white man who has not the sense to flee east of the mountains to the East."

Chapter 9

—《 》— The four mounted Indians emerged from the water on the west side of the Wabash a few miles north of Vincennes and rode their horses up the low muddy embankment, not pausing until they reached the top of a knoll covered with the brilliant emerald green of new grasses and a scattering of large hardwood trees just coming into full leaf.

The air was sweet and fresh following last night's light rain and was now redolent of rich moist earth and the fragrance of the flowers and other new growths of spring. In the distance a great flock of passenger pigeons flew in a vast, undulating flock, dipping and rising as they continued northward toward their distant breeding grounds and, from the perspective of the Indians, appearing to be an odd, low hanging stream of dark smoke. Closer at hand, among the widely separated oaks and elms and hickories, the flickers were voicing the hammer blows of their courtship songs, intermingled with a background chorus of hundreds of other trillings and rolls and whistlings from the multitude of thrushes and warblers, wrens and finches, meadowlarks, bobolinks, robins, and red-winged blackbirds, all establishing territories, selecting mates and setting up housekeeping. In the near distance ahead across the prairie a small herd of buffalo moved slowly southwestward, the handful of great massively shouldered bulls in the lead turning their heads now and again to look warily at the men on horses. An unseen squirrel not far away barked angrily at the intrusion or possibly at the pair of red-tailed hawks overhead engaged in the wild gyrations of a nuptial flight.

It was a perfectly glorious spring morning, the whole world of nature seeming fresh and clean and unsullied, free of cares and vibrantly alive. Tecumseh's broad chest expanded as he inhaled deeply and looked at his three companions, smiling.

"Well, my friends," he said, chuckling lightly, "does it feel good to be back in Indian country again?"

It took an instant for Chaubenee, Sauganash, and Stiahta to get his drift, but when they realized his meaning they burst into hoots of laughter. It was the same sort of laughter that had rocked Indians throughout the entire Northwest when word had flashed through their villages of the tremendous coup that Tecumseh had pulled off in his vast practical joke that overshadowed even the silver mine hoax perpetrated four years ago by Blue Jacket. This time it had involved a white man well known to most, by reputation if not by personal contact.

The matter had occurred just over a month ago when Tecumseh was in the final stages of preparation for a major journey to speak of his grand plan to other tribes. With total unexpectedness, the white frontiersman Simon Kenton—who was still referred to by many as *Cuttahotha* or Bahd-ler—had boldly ridden all by himself into the White River Village and asked to speak with Tecumseh. Surprised at the effrontery, despite the fact that peace still prevailed, Tecumseh had listened to a proposal Kenton made and it hadn't taken long to realize that here was a man who had largely taken leave of his senses.

Simon Kenton had led countless daring expeditions against the Shawnees in their own territory; had been captured and condemned to death at the stake; had successfully run more gauntlets than any other captive in their history and had miraculously escaped his fate time and again, until he had escaped them entirely and left behind the belief that he was under the protection of Moneto; he, with Blue Jacket, had engineered the great prisoner exchange on the north bank of the Spaylaywitheepi and he was the man who had, so daringly and with so few men, attacked the camp of Tecumseh on the East Fork of the Little Miami River; who, along with Boone and Brady and a select few others, had won the greatest fear—and respect—of the Indians.

Yet here was this formidable giant of a man asking Tecumseh to sell him an enormous tract of land in the Indiana Territory. It was established practice among the tribes not to physically harm insane people, who were believed to be under the special protection of the Great Spirit, but there was no prohibition of taking the fullest advantage of any situation in which such individuals were involved. And there was marvelous opportunity for taking just such advantage in this case.[514]

As Kenton laid out his proposal, his peculiar reasoning became clear. Here was a man who had claimed hundreds of thousands of acres of land in the Kentucky country and who had lost a great portion of it through overlapping land claims by those who came later and were more astute in the legal matters of filing claims. Now, though he had become very wealthy in those land dealings, practically all his Kentucky claims were gone, along with all his Ohio holdings obtained in the Symmes Purchase. In recent years he had been claiming and developing Ohio lands in the settlement areas the whites were calling Springfield and Urbana, but he was no longer content with little bits and pieces.[515] He envisioned an empire all his own, recalling how Richard Henderson, in his Watauga Treaty with the Cherokees, had bought all of Kentucky to establish a separate country called Transylvania. Even though Virginia had promptly invalidated Henderson's title, at least he had been permitted to keep a sizeable portion of his claim. In considering this, Kenton had thought at length in regard to what Indian or Indians he should engage in a treaty to effect his purpose and eventually decided upon the Shawnee who had gained so much recognition in recent years among all the Indians—Tecumseh.

To this end Kenton produced a paper written up for him by a man named Abey Clark, in which Kenton agreed to give Tecumseh and his Indians a large amount of cash money along with "considerable goods and provisions," including the promise to "pay more money or goods as long as grass grows and water runs." In exchange, Tecumseh was to give Kenton all of the land lying between the Wabash and the Great Miami rivers—an area close to five thousand square miles.[516]

It was, of course, prohibited by the United States Congress for private individuals to treat with the Indians in the matter of land—a fact well known to both Kenton and Tecumseh. But the frontiersman had visions of pulling it off and Tecumseh looked upon the whole thing as a great joke. Had Kenton proposed buying the moon from him, he would have sold him that as well. There was more to it than just the amusement value of a great practical joke; here was an opportunity to be paid in some degree for the Kentucky and Ohio lands that had been stolen from the Indians. The funds and goods Kenton proposed as payment would alleviate a great deal of suffering the Indians had been experiencing. Finally, it was quite in keeping with Tecumseh's directive for Indians to take anything the whites might offer.

Tecumseh accepted the deal.

Word of it spread rapidly through the tribes and the Indians rocked with glee over this tremendous joke and gratefully benefitted from their share.[517]

Once again, for pulling off so tremendous a coup against their great enemy, Tecumseh's prestige among the tribes had soared.

"Yes, Tecumseh," said Chaubenee, looking back eastward across the Wabash at Kenton's Land, as it was now jokingly called, "it is wonderful to be back in Indian country again. We all missed it greatly."

Again the four burst into laughter. It was in this pleasant frame of mind that they put their heels to their horses and headed northwest into the prairie country on the first leg of a journey that would take them to the councils of every tribe as far north as the Canadian border and then eastward over the top of Lake Michigan, then southward again across the broad Mackinac Strait and down through the Michigan country.

The prime objective was for these three to learn from Tecumseh on this trip. They were to study him closely as he spoke, paying close attention to his delivery, the structure of his talks and how each speech, though identical in basic content, was subtly revised to have special appeal and specific meaning to the particular group he was addressing. Most of all they were to learn the basic doctrine that he was bringing to the many villages and tribes because when at last they parted, these three would continue spreading Tecumseh's doctrine throughout their own countries, solidifying what Tecumseh had begun, converting as many as possible to these precepts, sending on as many as would volunteer, to join Tecumseh at the White River Village and become part of his core of strength. It was what he had already dispatched Lowawluwaysica to do among the Shawnees, Delawares, and Miamis of their own country.

[November 14, 1802 — Sunday]

As much as Chaubenee, Stiahta, and Sauganash expected at the onset of their journey that Tecumseh would be forceful in talks to the Illinois, Wisconsin, and Michigan country tribes, they were hardly prepared for the amazing response he had elicited.

The four of them had traveled a long way. After crossing the Wabash just north of Vincennes, they had gone first to the Kickapoos in the central Illinois country and then had moved about among the widely scattered factions of the Potawatomi north of there. The journey had carried them in a wide sweep then, first to the west all the way to the Mississippi and far to the north and then back eastward to the Michigan country. Following his well-received talks to the Kickapoos and Potawatomies, Tecumseh had spoken to the Sacs and Foxes, the Winnebagoes and Mandans and Menominees, the Chippewas and Ottawas, the Hurons and their children, the Wyandots.

Allan W. Eckert

Everywhere they had gone this dynamic speaker who was their leader had driven home the messages that history should have taught the tribes but that somehow they had largely missed. He had urged, cajoled, reasoned, speaking to small gatherings and large, putting across as forcefully as he could the elements of his great plan and what it would mean to all Indians when finally it came to fruition. He was messianic in his impassioned speeches but not in his message, for what he brought them was not a message of salvation for the soul but one they could better grasp and embrace—a mesmerizing message of survival and reclamation, a message pointing out with piercing incisiveness what the Indians had lost to the whites, what was presently being taken by these intruders and what the tribes yet stood to lose if the wave of whites *everywhere* was not stopped and pushed back. He was the right man at the right time and he touched them deeply, fundamentally, because they were a restless, unhappy, displaced people who had been pushed and shoved beyond endurance. They were a people ready for change and he brought it to them; a people in whom he caused a resurgence of what most of them had lost— *hope!* He offered them the hope that there really might be a way to regain what had been lost, to recover that which had been taken, to reoccupy that which was gone.

Within himself Tecumseh felt a great exaltation as he saw how his words caught and held his listeners; how easily, with the proper turn of a phrase, he could stir in them the basic emotions of anger and hate, love, pleasure, regret and sorrow, fear and hope and *unity!* Each time he began to speak he was never really sure exactly what he would say, but then the words would come to him, rolling fluently from his tongue and never failing to stir deeply all who heard. And his followers noted carefully how his message to each group was always the same and yet always different, tailored to drive home his points within the framework of that particular group's own experience with the whites.

By the time they had reached the mouth of the Maumee, Tecumseh was the talk of the Indian nations and some two score eager young men had attached themselves to him. Here, at the Maumee, they were parting for now, and Tecumseh was entrusting the three original members of his party, plus another ten of the most devoted who had become followers, to carry his message with them to every tribe and every village they encountered.

The content and direction of Tecumseh's talks had very well indeed set the pattern for these disciples, who were now quite ready to go out on their own to extract promises from the various tribes and recruit ever more active followers. As for Tecumseh himself, he would go home to rest for a while and then move on again to other tribes in other directions.

His was a journey that had only just begun.

438

[December 31, 1802 — Friday]

Tecumseh sat smoking quietly in the dimness of his White River Village cabin, hearing the soft breathing of his woman deep in slumber in the bed along one wall.[518] In the flickering light of the fire he thought of the meeting held at this very place one year ago and of events that had occurred during the year that had not touched him but that had been brought to his ears.

The year was ending with the peace continuing between Indians and whites, but not so smoothly as previously. There were additional indications of encroachment occurring in territory guaranteed to the Indians by the Greenville Treaty and there was a slight rise in killings, especially at the hands of the Kickapoos.

He was very disturbed at the news that the white governor of this Indiana Territory, William Henry Harrison, aided by Spemica Lawba, William Wells, and Winnemac, had visited a great many chiefs of the Potawatomi and Miami villages, feeling them out in regard to whether they would sell a large segment of their territory. The very fact that he would approach individual village chiefs on such business rather than a general tribal council indicated he was attempting to drive wedges between various tribal factions and it was something that would have to be watched carefully.

Harrison had also held council with certain chiefs of the Miamis, Potawatomies, and Kickapoos at Vincennes last September to distribute annuities. At that council, held beneath the great arbors at his opulent estate called Grouseland, he encouraged the Indians, who were complaining about the great decline in game animals, to turn their interests to farming instead of hunting; a prospect distinctly demeaning to those Indians there represented, who were hunters by tradition and culture and considered agriculture as strictly work for women and children. Harrison had made his suggestion, it was said, after receiving numerous complaints from white citizens whose livestock was disappearing and who angrily reported that the Indians had taken to "shooting deer with bells on their necks."[519]

Michikiniqua, who had attended that Vincennes council, had requested that Fort Wayne, which was more centrally located to the Indians, be made the new annuities distribution center with William Wells as agent in charge. He also asked that government suppress the trade in liquor that was increasing alarmingly, saying, "It is a fatal poison among the tribes."[520] Liquor, increasingly a refuge from a world grown much too complex, was causing great disruption in the tribes, especially among families who, under its influence, quarreled bitterly among themselves or with neighbors. It fogged reason and resulted in things being said, fights being held, lands being sold, and treaties being made that should never have occurred had the participants been in a sober state of mind.[521]

This was a problem Tecumseh encountered in respect to Lowawluwaysica. Except for one truly outstanding idea conceived during Tecumseh's six-month absence, his one-eyed brother had failed miserably in his appointed task. Tecumseh, on his return to the White River Village, was extremely disappointed in the signal lack of success Lowawluwaysica had experienced; not one village, group or even individual among the Shawnees had been swayed enough by the things he had said to them to throw in with Tecumseh. Nor had anyone from among the Delaware and Wyandot villages. Whisperings had come to Tecumseh that his brother had spent the past summer wandering from village to village, as he had been directed to do, but that his principal aim at each seemed, more than anything else, to find out who had liquor and then try to wheedle some for himself.

The single point that kept Lowawluwaysica's efforts from having been a thorough failure was an idea spawned in him because of an incident he witnessed last Planting Moon while in Catahecassa's village of Wapakoneta. Catahecassa had just returned from visiting the great white father in Washington when a small body of Delawares had, with permission of the Shawnee chief, taken up temporary residence there under a minor chief named Amaghqua—Beaver. This Delaware chief, for some reason unknown to Lowawluwaysica, was accused of witchcraft. The charge had been made by the foremost medicine man, mystic, and prophet of the Delawares, Kulaquati, who had met with a tribal council, and Amaghqua had been sentenced to death.

There was no appealing such a decision, and Amaghqua had resigned himself to his fate. When the time came for the execution to be carried out, Lowawluwaysica told Tecumseh, Amaghqua had dressed himself in fine clothing, embraced his wife and little son and then, flanked by a pair of husky Delaware warriors, had walked casually toward a little rise at the edge of the village. A large number of Shawnees, including Lowawluwaysica, along with some other Delawares, gathered to witness the execution.

Amaghqua had quietly and calmly bade farewell to several people he knew, then stepped a pace or two away and turned his back to his guards and faced the setting sun. One guard removed a war club from his belt, raised it high and brought it down on the top of the chief's head in a blow so savage that it crushed the whole top of Amaghqua's skull. The execution had been that quick and simple.

Lowawluwaysica said he had thought a great deal about what he had witnessed and suddenly a most provocative idea had struck him. Among the Shawnees, in a position equivalent to the Delaware prophet and mystic Kulaquati, was their own medicine man, Penegashega, now well into his nineties and the oldest individual in the tribe. He was a man, as Tecumseh well knew, who could not only cure illnesses, invoke secret spells, and display, to some degree, the ability of a seer or prophet, but a man whose sense of sociological values was such that he was expected to perform as tribal conscience and moral reformer among the Shawnees. As such—and as so graphically witnessed in the case of Kulaquati—he could wield enormous power that, on occasion, rivaled or possibly even superseded that of the principal chief.

Penegashega was very frail and must certainly die before long and a new medicine man prophet selected to replace him. It was not a matter of mere succession. This extremely influential post was awarded by the Shawnee Council on review of self-assertions by Shawnees who exhibited the best qualifications for the job. Selection normally became one of the minor doctors or medicine men of the tribe who had been tutored by the medicine man who had died. Lowawluwaysica was one of those.

Suppose, suggested Lowawluwaysica, he and Tecumseh were to combine their talents—he providing the medical knowledge and innate craftiness required by the office and Tecumseh providing prophecy. In scores of incidents it had already been proved that Tecumseh was a far better prophet than Penegashega. In the privacy of their own quarters, Tecumseh could give Lowawluwaysica the prophecies to advance as his own among the people. It would be natural then, when Penegashega died, for Lowawluwaysica to step into the exalted office, from which he could wield great power as the tribe's prophet and conscience. His voice thereupon added to Tecumseh's would provide just that much more impetus in encouraging their own people and perhaps even those from other tribes to embrace Tecumseh's plan. The one adjunct of his idea that Lowawluwaysica did not mention to Tecumseh was that if they encountered any really serious opposition to Tecumseh's plan, perhaps a few executions for witchcraft could relieve the problem. It was exciting food for thought.

Tecumseh was definitely intrigued by the idea and so now, as he had been doing ever since Lowawluwaysica first made the proposal, and as he would continue to do until he left in spring to visit more tribes, Tecumseh carefully rehearsed his younger brother in the prophecies he was to make to various Shawnees during his absence.

[December 10, 1804 — Monday]

At no time previously had Tecumseh felt so physically exhausted as now. Three days ago he had finally returned to the White River Village practically in a state of collapse. He had turned his horse over to a warrior for care and stumbled into his cabin. Hot food prepared by his woman was in the kettles overhanging the fire but he had been too weary even to eat. He had fallen into bed and was almost instantly asleep. For thirty hours he scarcely moved.

At last he had risen, wolfed down a huge meal of meat-rich stew and then flopped onto the bed again and slept another six hours.

Now, slept out but still not really rested, he lay staring at the cabin's rough loft over his head but seeing nothing, his vision turned inward and his mind filled with a jumbled montage of images of the travels he had made, the chiefs and warriors he had met, the speeches made, the seemingly never-ending rides through all kinds of weather. So many places seen, so many things done, yet so many places still to visit to do those things remaining undone.

Was it really nearly two years since he had first given Lowawluwaysica the prophecies that he was to voice as if they were his own? In an odd intertangling of time, it seemed like only a few weeks ago, while at the same time as if it had occurred in some dim and distant recess of the past.

In the spring of that year, 1803, just as Tecumseh was preparing to ride out toward the northeast to spread his word among the greatly disrupted tribes in upper New York and beyond, an incident occurred that underlined how his own prestige had increased. Ohio had officially become a state on February 19, with the village of Chillicothe as its capital, located on the site where the great Chalahgawtha of the Shawnees had been situated, on the Scioto near the mouth of Paint Creek. Less than two months later a settler named Thomas Herrod, whose cabin was only a few miles from the new capital, was found shot dead and scalped. The white populace had become alarmed that this betokened a new outbreak of Indian violence. A trio of ne'er-do-well whites had in turn waylaid and murdered a friendly old Shawnee living in the area named Wawwilaway who, before dying, managed to shoot one of his assailants dead and club another unconscious with a rifle butt.

Fearing this would spark retaliation by the Shawnees, the whites around the capital appealed to their new governor, Dr. Edward Tiffin, for help. Tiffin immediately dispatched a message to the most prominent and influential Indian he knew of—Tecumseh—begging him to come and assure the citizens at Chillicothe that a new Indian war was not imminent.

Tecumseh went there immediately and for over two hours addressed a crowd of about five hundred—practically the entire population of the new capital. He allayed their fears, saying that the Indians were abiding by the peace made at Greenville and that none of his people had killed the settler Herrod, nor had they any idea who had done so. It was sad, he continued, that Wawwilaway had been killed, but the old warrior had shown true Shawnee courage and died bravely and there was no movement afoot by the Indians to retaliate in any way. He urged the whole matter be dropped and the whites and Indians left to go about their separate business at peace.[522]

While in the Chillicothe area, a bit of news had come to Tecumseh that was simultaneously disturbing and encouraging. The disturbing part was that

Michikiniqua had, at the urgings of William Wells and the Potawatomi village Chief Winnemac, negotiated at Vincennes with William Henry Harrison last October to sell a sizeable tract of Indiana land. But when negotiations were completed—and this was the encouraging part—Michikiniqua had second thoughts and refused to sign the land sale treaty. Despite his refusal, the deal went through, signed by Potawatomies, even though it was Miami territory. This had angered Michikiniqua and now it seemed he might reverse his stance and swing his weight, and his tribe's, behind Tecumseh.[523]

Immediately after that Chillicothe speech, Tecumseh had set out on his delayed journey, moving rapidly to the Northeast and spreading his message as he passed through western Pennsylvania and throughout upper New York and well into Canada.[524] He brought his message to the remnant bands of Delawares and Susquehannocks, Senecas, Cayugas, Oneidas, and Onondagas, and their adopted nephews, the Tuscarawas. He spoke to bands of the Mohawks and Caughnawagas and Abnakis, and, as he moved northwestward up the Ottawa and Nipissing rivers, to the Mississaugies and Tionontaties, the Amikwas and Noquets.

He had returned late in the season, half frozen and weary beyond measure, but had rested little. The prophecies he had given Lowawluwaysica to pass along to the people had been relayed, but in garbled fashion because Lowawluwaysica was frequently very drunk and got many of the events mixed up. Those prophecies that had indeed come to pass were sloughed off by most as good guesses about inconsequential matters. Though a few listeners were impressed, the majority were not, not so much because of the words but because of the repugnant personality who presented them. Once again Tecumseh had sat with his brother for hours and days going over predictions for the coming year.

By late in the Wind Moon Tecumseh was on the move again, visiting first the Miami subtribe villages along the mid-Wabash and Tippecanoe and then the Potawatomies farther to the west, including a quick visit with Chaubenee, who led him to the Checagou River to see a new American fort close to where the river emptied into Lake Michigan. Only recently completed, it was named Fort Dearborn, and the settlement growing up around it was being called Chicago.[525] Before moving on, having viewed it with quiet anger, Tecumseh said in a cold voice to Chaubenee, "One day I will destroy this place."

Chaubenee and Tecumseh parted soon afterwards and by July Tecumseh was far up the Mississippi, first in the country of the Mandans and then westward among the Dakotahs, which was a subtribe of the Sioux, and then to the various branches of the Santee division of that mighty Nadouessioux nation—as the Sioux tribe was called by the whites—including the Sisseton and Wahpeton, the Wahpekute and the Mdewkanton.

They welcomed him warmly and Tecumseh was pleased, remembering only too well that when he first started these journeys he had been unknown among many of the tribes and had often met with suspicion, only gradually winning those people over with his eloquence. Now it had become rare for him to reach any area where his fame as a speaker had not preceded him, as it had here in the Minnesota country. Never before had any other Indian traveled so far among so many different peoples nor become so widely known and respected and influential.

The message he delivered covered all the ground of his grand plan and more. He spoke to them of the persistent treachery of the whites and of the hollowness of their promises and treaties. If, he warned, the Nadouessioux were not willing to become red brothers all—*Indians,* not red men of different tribes—then they must fall separately, defeated or uprooted, scattered and lost. Attempting to make peace with the whites would avail them no more than it had ever done for other tribes and likely even less, for the whites would then treat them as animals. Ultimately, they would live in misery, wallowing in filth and becoming foggy-brained from white man's liquor as the only way to cope with their situation, themselves and their families starving, disease ridden, and utterly despondent. Even should the great plan be adopted by them and fail—which he did not believe would happen—was not an honorable death in the field of battle preferable by far to *that*?

Wherever he went, Tecumseh continued to gear his talks most pertinently to the specific tribe being addressed. So it was when, early in the Heat Moon, he visited the Wahpeton Sioux on the stream French traders named St. Peters River. The first place he had spoken here was in the village of Chief Pineshow.[526]

The Nadouessioux are a great and numerous nation, he had told them, and, among the Wahpetons and other divisions of that nation, they are intensely proud of their heritage and jealous of their country and rightly so. Long had the stories been told in their tepees and before their council fires of the troubles brought by the white men upon the Indians east of the grandmother of rivers. No matter whether the Indians had offered peace or waged war, they were eventually pushed back out of their lands. The times it had happened were too many to number. Had they not all been decimated—some even wiped out—by the white man's diseases and the weak remainder pushed back? Were not all of them *still* being pushed back?

The Nadouessioux must peel back the husks from their eyes and see what was coming. No longer was the grandmother of rivers a barrier to hold back the white flood. No! Until the year before there had come only a few scattered Americans among them, mainly trappers and traders, alone and in small parties, weak and fearful, coming in peace, they said, to trap and trade and no more, just as they had told the tribes to the east when first they penetrated deeply into Indian country. But now the great white chief Jefferson had bought from the French, who had no just title to it, all this land and more and would soon be coming to claim it—land that belonged to the Nadouessioux! At that very moment he had told them, as the Wahpeton Sioux were aware, a large force of whites under the young Captains William Clark and Meriwether Lewis was moving to the upper reaches of the Missouri to find their way across the great mountains to the west and reach the western sea.[527]

And heed well this fact: the young Captain William Clark was the brother of the white chief George Rogers Clark, who had helped take the Ohio lands from the Indians! Other whites would follow. More trappers and traders, then missionaries, then surveyors, and finally the flood of settlers. It was always thus. Thirty summers ago the lands of the Shawnees had seen the same; and though they had fought, yet they had seen their game destroyed, their forests leveled, their prairies burned, their lands taken, their villages ruined, their warriors killed. And now the Kentucky country and the Ohio country had become part of the Seventeen Fires—individual States in the constantly spreading Union of the whites.

So it would happen here. Not *might* happen. *Would* happen. Unless the union of the Indians became too strong for the whites, unless the Indians here and everywhere else put aside their own disagreements and realize that we are all brothers—just as the different white races have made themselves all brothers in their Union—then there would never be strength enough to hold back the white tide. He was not appealing to them to become part of an alliance nor even a confederacy. Those had been tried and though they may have had some temporary successes, they had eventually failed. No, what he was establishing was an *amalgamation*—a thrusting aside of jealousies and mistrust and hatreds, and the forging of one people—*Indians*—who were first and foremost faithful to each other in every respect and unified as a single body, removed from all nationalistic rivalries.

Already many tribes were agreeable and holding themselves in readiness to mold themselves into this one great family of *Indians* when the time came. The number was growing constantly and in a few more years there would be fifty tribes or maybe a hundred or more, all joined into one brotherhood to hold and protect what is theirs against the most terrible enemy any of them had ever faced. What he needed to know now was, when the time came, would the Sioux, like the others, take up their weapons and link arms and hearts in perpetual brotherhood with *Indians* from all directions?

And the Sioux had said they would.

He had gone on, westward and southward, in a loop that carried him through the country of the Omahas and Iowas and they, too, listened in awe to this man who, with his stirring words, could rebuild hopes, redeem dignity, instill self-respect, and rekindle flagging courage. When, ever, had such a man been before? When, ever, such a glorious dream?

And so at last he had come home again as winter began to scratch its bitter bony fingers across the landscape. What greeted him was another deeply troubling item of news. The white man lately being considered by Tecumseh as the most dangerous individual foe of the red man, William Henry Harrison, had just perpetrated another fraud against the Indians—in this instance the Sacs and Foxes and, to a lesser degree, the Iowas and Winnebagoes—and this time involving a gigantic chunk of land in the Mississippi Valley, taking in much of northwestern Illinois, a piece of southwestern Wisconsin, and a slice of northeastern Missouri. At St. Louis William Henry Harrison had, on November 3, conspired with his agents to get five minor Sac chiefs drunk and then coerced them into signing a treaty in which, for a payment of some twenty-two hundred dollars in goods and a one-thousand-dollar annuity, they sold to the United States this tract of land totaling fifty-one *million* acres![528]

Now, still lying on his bed in the cabin, Tecumseh sighed, as much from frustration as from the weariness. His job was such a very long way from being finished. There were still the tribes of the far west and southwest, the south and the southeast to visit and convince, despite the great bitterness existing between so many of them. And not all of the tribes of the east and north and northwest had agreed to his plan. He was convinced that sooner or later they would—especially as they learned of Governor Harrison's latest theft of Indian lands—but he and his followers would have to visit them again and perhaps again, opening their eyes to their fate if they did not accept his plan, making them see that there were, in the end, but two choices—survival or destruction. He planned to visit once again all the tribes that had refused and this time he would then flood them with arguments and prophecies that were even more convincing.

[August 26, 1805 — Monday]

The greatest disappointment for Tecumseh was occurring in his own homeland Ohio, the region that had been set aside for Lowawluwaysica to cover and draw the tribes together. His younger brother still had not been very successful. The predictions Tecumseh had given him to relay at intervals as his own to the Indians had come true and Lowawluwaysica had gained a certain amount of esteem as a prophet, but he had not persuaded them, not even his brother Shawnees, to embrace Tecumseh's plan.

Apart from Lowawluwaysica's persistent problem with intemperance, the principal reason for his failure lay in the two chiefs of the Shawnees and Miamis—Catahecassa and Michikiniqua. Both intensely disliked and mistrusted Lowawluwaysica and had advised their people against taking him at

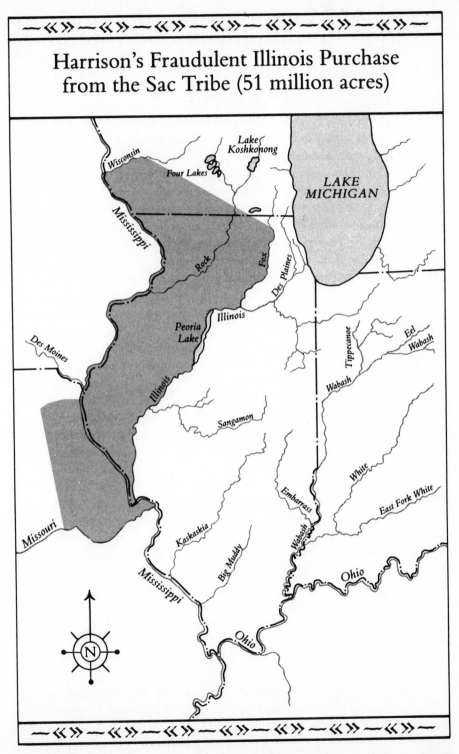

Harrison's Fraudulent Illinois Purchase from the Sac Tribe (51 million acres)

all seriously. Both were especially opposed to adopting Tecumseh's plan, which they publicly considered as being dishonorable in view of the treaty signed at Greenville. Even Blue Jacket, who had long been Tecumseh's good friend and admirer, was not fully convinced it was the proper thing to do. But the more compelling reason behind their opposition, particularly in the case of Catahecassa, was the fact that those chiefs—and many of the older Shawnees—were angry at what seemed to be Tecumseh's effort to usurp Catahecassa's authority in the tribe—aspiring to the post of principal chief for which, by Shawnee law and tradition, he was not qualified—and his grandiose effort to become the number one man of a great coalition of Indians and, in the process, arrogating control of the varied tribal chiefs as well.

A great many tribes were already keenly receptive of Tecumseh's message, his grand plan—some tentatively, others reasonably firmly—all of them tee-tering now in the balance, all of them sending their eyes to watch what would happen next; all of them wondering in their private conversations why it should be that so many distant tribes were able to see the wisdom and power behind the words of this man Tecumseh and yet the tribes in his own land, including even the very tribe from which he had sprung, not yet declaring themselves in support of his great plan.

It was time, Tecumseh knew, to move more directly here; time to gain the respect and confidence of all the Delawares, Miamis and Wyandots, in Ohio; and time, most of all, to gain the support of the Shawnees. If Lowaw-luwaysica could not do it by himself, then it was time for Tecumseh to put in abeyance further trips to other tribes and concentrate on the people close to home. How could they expect other tribes to pledge their allegiance to this great amalgamation if the leaders of the movement could not even convince their own people to accept it?

More than with any of the others of his devoted followers, Tecumseh spent time with Lowawluwaysica, instructing him in great detail about what to say and even how to say it. He gave his brother a number of new and even more significant prophecies to memorize and, when the time was right, to pass on to those concerned. That was his brother's job—to convince the *people*. As for the chiefs, evidently that was up to Tecumseh himself. He would speak to each one quietly, individually, in the privacy of each chief's wegiwa. It would not be an easy matter; serious rifts had developed between himself and many of the chiefs who were so jealous of their rank and prestige, and these must somehow be overcome. They must somehow be made to realize the imperativeness of putting aside their own personal pride and ambitions in order to best serve their own people.

Then, when matters seemed at their lowest ebb, an extremely fortunate event occurred for the brothers. It came to pass shortly after Tecumseh said farewell to Buckangehela and his Delawares at the White River Village and led his followers back to Ohio. A new village was quickly set up at Greenville and, while his followers were settling in, Tecumseh and Lowawluwaysica and a handful of others had begun making their rounds of all the Shawnee villages, Tecumseh talking to the chiefs and his brother to the people. But because of Catahecassa's continued strong opposition, they were generally given short shrift.

The turning point had come when the pair arrived at the Shawnee village of Tawa on the Auglaize River. That arrival took place as the village was suffering an epidemic of a particularly virulent stomach sickness.[529] One of its first victims was the most esteemed of Shawnee prophets and medicine men, Penegashega—Change of Feathers—who had collapsed two days previously and who had died within hours of the arrival of the brothers. At once Tecumseh and his small group of followers had held a hurried conference in private and Tecumseh spoke to Lowawluwaysica with greater intensity than he had previously displayed.

"This is a bad sickness that has struck our Shawnee brothers," he said, "and it is not yet over. More than twenty have been afflicted by it and already Penegashega has died. What is yet to come provides us with an opportunity we must not let pass by. Lowawluwaysica, I want you to assemble the warriors of this village—all of them, including those who are sick—and you are to tell them you have had a vision. In this vision, you will say, you have seen three more men die of the sickness, but that by the end of five days, those others now afflicted will be getting well again, because you will cast the sickness from them. You will tell them that the three who are yet to die are men who are evil, men engaged in witchcraft, and they will die because you, Lowawluwaysica, will not save them because of what they are and what they do. You will also tell them that at the end of that time, when these things have come to pass and they have witnessed your truth and ability, you will speak to them again with a very important message. Do you understand?"

Lowawluwaysica nodded, but there was something about his response, some slight hesitation, that caused Tecumseh to place his hand on his brother's head and look into his one good eye with a stare so intense, so penetrating, that it was frightening. Lowawluwaysica began to tremble and tried to look away.

"Look into my eyes and do not let your own stray," Tecumseh had commanded. "Hear and remember what I say to you now." He had then repeated, virtually word for word, the instructions and predictions just given.

It had all come about precisely as Tecumseh had prophesied: the three men had died and the others recovered. Practically all of the population of the village had then assembled to hear what else this remarkable Lowawluwaysica had promised to say. The ugly, one-eyed Shawnee's remarks had been brief and to the letter of what Tecumseh had coached him to say: that the sickness, which had been a manifestation of witchcraft, had been terminated through Lowawluwaysica's own powerful spells; that it had been caused by the three men who were last to die and that they had died because Lowawluwaysica had turned upon them that same sickness which they had loosed on others, as just punishment for their deed; that the full moon had just occurred and that on the day following the next full moon, at Tecumseh's Village at Greenville, he would deliver a major speech of extreme importance to every Shawnee; that all these people present here listening to him now should carry word of this to all the Shawnee villages and urge in the strongest possible terms that every Shawnee who could walk or ride be on hand at Greenville when he, Lowawluwaysica, would make that speech.530

Word of the amazing and prophetic occurrence had flashed to every village of the tribe and to the tribes beyond. There was an indefinable sense of something terribly important pending and while none could explain it, everyone felt it, and a great number of Shawnees prepared to hear what was to be said . . . and so also did a considerable number of Wyandots, Delawares, Miamis, and Potawatomies.

[September 22, 1805 — Sunday]

It was the day before yesterday when Chaubenee and Sauganash caught sight of Tecumseh's Village for the first time and they had reined in their horses and just stared for a moment. By way of the Indian news grapevine they had known, of course, that their leader had selected a site near the old fort, but knowing it and actually seeing it were two different things.531

Chaubenee had shaken his head in wondering admiration and then chuckled. "Leave it to Tecumseh," he had said, "to do something like this."

Sauganash had agreed with a short grunt, adding, "As usual, he always seems to do the unexpected."

It had been with something akin to malicious satisfaction that Tecumseh had, this past summer, built his new cabin and established the new village named after himself virtually in the shadow of the southwest wall of Fort Greenville.532 His very audacity had positively delighted his followers and Indians as far distant as the upper Michigan country and the Wisconsin area and in the Mississippi Valley, who smiled and nodded sagely when told of it, the significance of such temerity not lost on them and amused but not at all surprised that this bold leader had so insultingly flaunted the might of the Americans by establishing his village adjacent to the very structure that had been the western headquarters of Major General Anthony Wayne. The fact that the fort was no longer occupied, having been decommissioned, made no difference—the symbolism still remained.

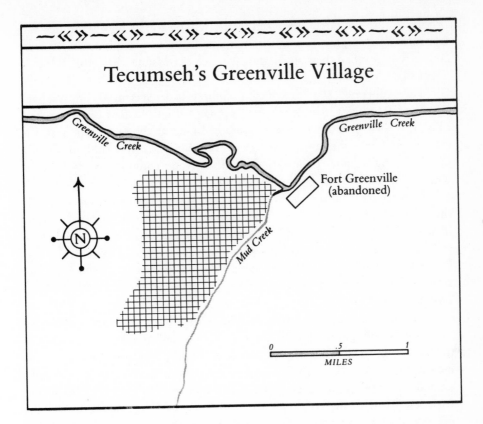

The citizens of the town of Greenville, that had grown much over these dozen years since the fort was built, took no pleasure in having the Indians so close, especially with the frequent comings and goings of parties of "foreign" Indians who came to hear Tecumseh's words whenever he returned from his trips. Their complaints and petitions to the Ohio governor and other officials had thus far had little effect in eliminating the problem.

Governor Edward Tiffin's response had been predictable: by the letter of the Greenville Treaty, the Indians were perhaps intruding, yet it had been General Wayne himself who had invited the reestablishment of any of the old villages of theirs that the Indians wished to resettle. The governor acknowledged that although this site chosen by Tecumseh had once, in the far distant past, supported a tiny village of perhaps a dozen wegiwas, his action, the Greenville citizens felt, greatly stretched the intent of Wayne's generous and unfortunate invitation. Yet, the governor had replied, how could they compel Tecumseh and his people to evacuate this new village if they did not also force a similar evacuation of Wapatomica, Wapakoneta, Blue Jacket's Town, Roundhead's Village, and the many other sites that had been reoccupied by Shawnees, Delawares, and Wyandots since the Greenville Treaty? Were the citizens in

Greenville and elsewhere, he asked, really willing to risk another Indian war that such a peremptory act of ejection was liable to precipitate? They were not, so they muffled their anger and, as much as possible, their fear. But they didn't like it one bit.

The deliberateness with which Tecumseh had selected the site was well calculated. He knew that while such presence might at first cause a certain amount of discomfiture to the citizens, it would at the same time instill in them a quite opposite sense of security, even though largely subliminal: with the village right under their eye, the Indians really couldn't do any mischief without the citizens being immediately aware of preparations. Imparting such a sense of security among the whites was integral to Tecumseh's plan; had he chosen a distant or hidden site, the arrival and departure of so many visiting Indians, which could not long have gone unnoticed, would have caused much greater suspicions and trepidation. Obviously, there would initially be some unrest but he also knew that the longer the village was here and the more accustomed the citizenry became to seeing the Indians, the less they would be concerned.

As Chaubenee and Sauganash had kneed their horses forward and entered Tecumseh's Village, they were impressed and pleased with the number of followers who had gathered, the cluster of cabins, wegiwas, and tepees indicating there must be four hundred or more who were resident.[533] A substantial number of those on hand here were people that Sauganash and Chaubenee had themselves recruited in the area of Lake Michigan over the past two years following that first year of traveling with Tecumseh. Combined with all those who had come to hear the special message that was to be given tomorrow, there had to be close to a thousand Indians on hand, the greater majority of them Shawnee. The air was thick with the smoke of the many cookfires and the two horsemen had picked their way with care through the crowd toward the cabin that was pointed out to them as Tecumseh's, which was closest to the confluence of the two little creeks. A young man with a good arm could easily have thrown a stone from in front of that cabin across the smaller creek and hit the wall of the fort.

"Could you have imagined all this," Chaubenee had asked his companion, gesturing at the people and buildings, "on that fine spring day three years ago when we first set out with Tecumseh?"

Sauganash had hesitated and then replied, "I think so, Chaubenee. I really expected it would happen. I didn't anticipate it would be here, so close to Fort Greenville, but I was sure of it. Just as I'm sure there will be a great many more coming all the time."

Their reunion with the man to whom they had sworn their devotion and allegiance had filled all three with great satisfaction. Throughout the rest of that day and all of yesterday they and the others who made up the elite inner council of which Tecumseh was unquestionably the leader, listened with admiration as he recounted his travels to distant tribes over these past years. Wasegoboah and Tecumapese were on hand, of course, as was Stiahta of the Wyandots, resplendent, as usual, in his garb and ornamentation. Here were Lowawluwaysica and Kumskaka and here, too, was Skesh—formerly Oskesh—a Potawatomi chief originally recruited by Chaubenee, who seemed to have been as completely won over to Tecumseh as Chaubenee and Sauganash before him.[534]

The group had clung with fascination to the words of Tecumseh as he told them not only of his progress, but equally of his failures in some areas. While already he had more tribes verbally aligned behind him than any other Indian leader had ever gathered, yet he admitted they were not enough and, though he had traveled incredible distances, he told them he would have to travel even farther and work even harder if the grand plan were ever to come to fruition. There were still those many nations to the south with whom he had to meet and whom he had to convince to accept his precepts, and this would take much time. By the same token there were a number of tribes to the north and west who had initially rejected his ideas, but he was convinced he could swing them to his support with further visits, especially in view of the fact that at this very moment not only had the exploratory expedition of Lewis and Clark penetrated far to the west, another one—that of a Captain Zebulon Pike—was moving far up the Mississippi into the Minnesota country. Both of these expeditions were tangible proof of the peril he had warned those tribes about and undoubtedly a vanguard opening the way for a great deluge of whites to follow. That must not happen, and to those tribes he would return with stronger arguments and more convincing prophecies, but those matters had been put aside for the moment with the necessity of attending to the problems of strengthening his coalition closer to home.[535]

The great meeting, Tecumseh had said, that was to be held on the morrow was crucial to their interests and he then, in the presence of the others, instructed Lowawluwaysica in great detail about what he was to say and even the manner in which he was to say it. Even much later, when the others departed, Tecumseh and Lowawluwaysica had remained behind and continued to talk.

Last night had been the full moon, and now they were all assembled, close to a thousand people seated on the ground in a broad semicircle before the empty wagon that had been drawn up for Lowawluwaysica to stand upon so he would be visible to all and his words carry well. A number of whites from Greenville, curious and decidedly nervous, approached and stood well to the rear, held back by their fear from moving in any closer.

Tecumseh and his principal lieutenants sat together to one side as Lo-wawluwaysica moved to the front of the assemblage, mounted the wagon and stood facing them on its flat bed. The murmuring of the crowd slowly died away and, as it did so, Chaubenee, who disliked his leader's one-eyed brother and doubted he could carry this off, leaned toward Tecumseh and whispered.

"Will he be able to do this, Tecumseh? Can he make them believe?"

Tecumseh smiled. "Watch, my friend. Those of the Tawa village already believe, as do many who have come. Those who do not yet believe will be caught up. During the night, while you and the others slept, I stayed up with him and talked to him. He knows well now what he is to say and how he is to say it. Listen!"

Before them, Lowawluwaysica raised his hands and the last of the murmurings stilled.

"Hear me, brothers!"

Chaubenee, who had never heard Lowawluwaysica speak publicly, marveled at the strength of his voice and it was evident that others were having the same reaction.

"You have witnessed my powers of prophecy in the past," he went on. "The things I have said would be have come to pass. And some of you have seen the three die as I predicted they would, and you have witnessed the miracles I have performed in casting out the sickness that threatened your own lives.

"You have known me by the name of Lowawluwaysica, but no longer! From this day forward I shall be known to all men as Tenskwatawa—One With Open Mouth—and my mouth will be open with words which will lead you to a better life, to better health, to a better future![536] Penegashega the Prophet is dead. I say to you now that henceforth *I* am your Prophet and there is none other who qualifies, none other who can do for you what I can do. Do you wish me to take this high office?"

He had begun his talk slowly, with some hesitation, as if unsure of himself, but his words had picked up pace and vibrancy and now he had become more animated, more in control. He paused after his question and Chaubenee grinned as he watched the speaker, with a crafty glint in his eye, cup a hand behind each ear in an exaggerated stance of listening. There was a roar of approval from the crowd and Tecumapese reached out and squeezed Tecumseh's wrist.

"*That* is our little brother?" she murmured wonderingly.

The man who now called himself Tenskwatawa waited until the cries died away and then, his eyes glinting and a faint smile creasing his thin lips, he began to speak again. "I *am* Tenskwatawa, and my people call on me to serve them as Prophet. But such must first be approved by the Shawnee Council. Since those wise men are among us today and since our Prophet is dead and there is little time to waste in lengthy discussion, I call on them now, here and at this moment, to say whether or not I am the Shawnee Prophet!"

Tecumseh's nod was so imperceptible that it was scarcely visible, but Chaubenee saw it and knew that this was exactly as he had planned it, calculated to take the old Shawnee Council members in attendance by surprise and without opportunity to confer and gather opposition strength, if such would have been their intention. It was a brilliant maneuver and Chaubenee shared the exultation that swept their little group as one by one Tenskwatawa pointed at the Shawnee Council members, called their names and demanded response. Even though there was momentary hesitation among a few, all finally nodded.

They had done it! Just as Tecumseh had said they would. Tenskwatawa was officially the new Shawnee Prophet.

Now the speaker raised his arms to still the excited talking that had risen among his listeners, then resumed speaking. At considerable length he went over the points Tecumseh had instructed him to make. He was, he told them, truly a prophet, given to see into the future without need of such superstitious paraphernalia as bits of bone and tiny smooth stones and little pouches of fine sand to sprinkle and spread in strange designs on a piece of cured skin, such as Penegashega had needed. The use of such, he told them, was itself a form of witchcraft—evil sorcery that depended upon supplication to the Devil, Matchemenetoo, rather than to the Great Spirit or Moneto.

"I will lead you away from such evil beliefs!" he cried. "I tell you that those who practice such medicine are themselves possessed and will not go to the good Afterworld, nor will they ever see Moneto. Those who have such medicine bags must throw them away, because where once they were good, now they have lost their virtue and such pouches have become the places where Matchemenetoo rests when he is not up to mischief.[537]

"Listen, my brothers!" he thundered with increased vehemence. "On the day that Penegashega died, I went up into the clouds and the first place I came to was the dwelling of Matchemenetoo; here I saw all who had died as drunkards, with flames of fire issuing from their mouths."

A sudden whispering rippled through the crowd and Tenskwatawa smiled, knowing the reason, as he let it run its course. He was himself a heavy drinker and few among the Shawnees here assembled had not frequently seen him almost blind with the effects of liquor, staggering and reeling toward his wegiwa to fall on his bed mat and sleep it away.

"Yes!" His single word exploded like a gunshot and again snatched their attention. "Yes," he repeated, "previous to this revelation I myself drank, but this has so frightened me that I will *never* drink again, and I say to you gathered here that neither must you drink." He continued expounding in this vein for a considerable while and then abruptly switched to another topic and spoke earnestly, forcefully.

"Brothers! We are Indians! We must keep our women from marrying white men. This is one of the great causes of unhappiness and the means by which white men have long tried to destroy the pure strain of Indian blood. The blood of Indian woman and white man must nevermore be allowed to mix, under threat of the most severe penalty!"

Chaubenee glanced at Sauganash and saw that he, son of an English father and Potawatomi mother, was frowning and a muscle was twitching in his cheek. Tecumseh saw it, too, and leaned far over to pat his knee and reassure him as Tenskwatawa went on without pause. Only Tecumseh, of all those who comprised his inner circle, was not flabbergasted at the extraordinary scope and depth of the speech as it continued for over three hours, or amazed at the transformation that had occurred in the formerly inept Lowawluwaysica, now a very domineering speaker who called himself Tenskwatawa, The Prophet!

Chaubenee, Sauganash, Stiahta, Skesh, Kumskaka, Wasegoboah, and even Tecumapese, who knew him best, listened with fascination as the one-eyed speaker propounded on the matters they had so often heard from Tecumseh, but which Tenskwatawa now delivered as his own and, in the process, held the entire audience spellbound. He emphasized the importance of all Indians everywhere in this land becoming one people, united to common goals—just as those people who were first of all Americans were comprised of English, French, Spanish, Irish, Scots, German, and other races. He told them that the property of one Indian must become the property of all Indians, each Indian working for the common good of all. He told them that it was the duty of the young at all times to cherish and support those who were old and infirm; that new forms of dress, especially the wearing of white man's clothing, were detestable practices that had to end—no Indian should wear woolen or linen or cotton material made by the whites but, instead, they must return to the ways of their fathers and dress in the skins of animals; that they must return to the habits of their fathers and their fathers before them and reject the habits they had learned from the white men. Since Moneto had created the buffalo, elk, deer, and other wild creatures for their use, it was wrong to eat the flesh of hogs, cattle or sheep, and it was equally wrong to eat bread made of white man's wheat flour when their own bread was the flour ground from Indian corn.

"You must believe," he said, in a voice filled with passion, "that the Indian race—not just this tribe or that, but *the whole Indian race*—is superior to any other race on earth, for this is true! Now that I am your Prophet, we have embarked on the trail that will show our superiority to the entire world. Hear what I say! No Indian who believes in the power and protectiveness of Moneto and has confidence in himself and his Indian brothers need *ever* look to any man of another race for help. We do not need help, as the whites would have us believe. They have tried every means in their power to make us dependent upon them and upon those things they can provide for us, but the fathers of our fathers lived well without such things and so must we. We have allowed the white man to lead us away from our own beliefs and traditions. Now we must go back to them. We must return to a greater respect and admiration for Moneto and for the many gifts and blessings he has bestowed upon us all."

He stopped with a dramatic pause and his arm stretched straight out from his shoulder as he pointed to Fort Greenville and, as he continued, his voice was heavy with bitterness. "Behold those pale faces! Gone, but *not* gone, and the war talks of your old chiefs and the land talks of your old counsellors will not save us. The old village chiefs and others who receive money for our land which they have sold are mad. They are drunk! The young warriors and hunters and the women and children will be cheated out of their lands, more than already. I see it! If you allow the white skins to make roads through your country, they will soon erect more forts like this, *everywhere*. Awake! Dig up your tomahawk, because the time is close at hand when we must give it the color of the sun spirit when he first rises in fiery wrath out of the great eastern sea.

"When I went into the clouds, my own Good Spirit, Naanteena, appeared to me. Listen! Hear what my Good Spirit has imparted to me and gifted me with. Brothers, give heed! Women, remember what I say! Naanteena is the Good Spirit of my destiny and has given me the vision to behold, long before the time of it, what shall come to pass, and She has shown me a fearful sign of destruction that threatens our race. Naanteena has caused me to behold the pale-faced warriors destroying our forests and muddying our clear waters, and I have seen rivers swollen with the blood of the red people. This I was directed to impart to you by that Good Spirit, who said you must awaken, arouse and assemble in council, which is where we now find ourselves. And when that had come to pass, Naanteena told me, as it has now done, then will all the red people know that I am their Prophet!"

His voice dropped and his listeners automatically leaned forward and listened more intently so as not to miss a word of what he was saying. "The Great Spirit has revealed to me why it has been, in the past, that no matter whether we lost battles or won them, it has always been the Indian who has found himself on the side where lands and crops and lives have been lost, and the Great Spirit has shown me how all this can be changed.

"As I take on the duties as Prophet—as I begin a life of devotion to the cause and principles of the Indian people—this now I say to you: a tremendous power has been given to me by the Great Spirit to confound our enemies, to cure all diseases and to prevent death from sickness or on the battlefield. I am your Prophet—Tenskwatawa!"

The entire audience was deeply moved by what this dramatic speaker was saying. Rarely had they ever heard such impassioned speaking. Tecumseh's noddings became more evident as the various points were made and he was impressed and pleased that his little brother so mesmerized his listeners. The only area thus far in which he had been surprised was the name change to Tenskwatawa, but he thought it was very timely and he fully approved.

Chaubenee, for his part, was overwhelmed by the change that had been wrought in the self-proclaimed Prophet; a change that seemed to be visibly occurring even as he spoke. Tecumseh's brother was still the unpleasant ugly man who was devoid of any of the dignity or noble characteristics the leader himself possessed so abundantly. This one-eyed man was, Chaubenee knew, still not a brave or truthful man, or one above cruelty if he could benefit by it. He had not lost his feral cunning nor his showy smartness. Yet somehow—and Chaubenee could not fathom how it had occurred—on this day the man who now called himself Tenskwatawa was possessed of powers of persuasiveness and plausibility entirely equal to those of Tecumseh himself. Perhaps, Chaubenee mused, closer to the truth than even he suspected, perhaps it was because on this day, at this time and place, Tenskwatawa had not only believed in what he was saying, he believed in *himself,* possibly for the first time in his life.

Chaubenee still did not like Tenskwatawa, but he admitted to himself that he was greatly impressed, and he knew the others were, also. He promised himself he would use some of The Prophet's rhetoric—which was initially Tecumseh's, of course—in his own talks to Indian groups whom he yet hoped to convince to espouse Tecumseh's cause and join him.

During the body of his speech, Tenskwatawa had referred to Tecumseh frequently. Now, in his concluding remarks, he told his listeners that this place, Tecumseh's Village, was not a Shawnee village, but rather an *Indian* village, and all who believed in him, Tenskwatawa, as The Prophet, and in Tecumseh as the man who would lead them to greater glory than they had ever known before, were welcome to come here to live.[538]

With great satisfaction, Tecumseh and the members of his inner council saw now that far more would be joining them than they had at first believed.

[March 20, 1806 — Thursday]

With so many Indians from among the Northwestern tribes now being attracted to Greenville to hear the preachings of Tenskwatawa as The Prophet, and with so many whites in such close proximity, it had become clear to Tecumseh that two matters would have to be taken care of quickly. First, it was vital that he reveal to these Indians the nature of his grand plan of amalgamation of all the tribes as simply Indian and reveal to them the long-range objective of taking all this country back from the whites. Second, it was imperative that they continue for absolutely as long as it was possible to do so, to keep this matter secret from the whites.

It was obvious that they could not hold a war council of that nature at Tecumseh's Village or even in its close vicinity without the whites of Greenville becoming aware of what was going on, resulting in premature exposure of the grand plan. With this in mind, Tecumseh considered where such a council might best be held. It had to be a location easily accessible to the Indians and yet not in any of their villages, since there was still great opposition among the Indians in Ohio toward Tecumseh and should a war council be held in any of those villages, word of it would quickly reach the white authorities.

At length Tecumseh settled on a place he knew close to where Buckangehela's Town had once been located. That town had been situated on the point where the stream named after Buckangehela emptied into the Great Miami; Tecumseh set up his hidden village—actually more of a camp—a mile and a half from there. A half-mile down the Great Miami was the mouth of another stream called Stony Creek, and it was a full mile upstream on this little Stony Creek, on a high bench of land west of the creek, where the hidden camp called Stony Creek Village was established.

There was good reason for this, since whites living in the area frequently followed the trail paralleling the larger river's course and also plied its waters with small boats. They did not, however, go upstream on Stony Creek, so it should be a fairly secure location. This, then, was where the hidden village was established during the winter and where the two major war councils were held.[539]

The first Stony Creek Council had been held in the middle of the Hunger Moon and had lasted for ten days, attended by some seven hundred warriors from among the Shawnees, Delawares, and Miamis. Great care was taken to turn back any whites who came into the area and to carefully screen the Indians themselves who came to attend, turning away those who were known to be strongly in favor of the whites and in maintaining the Greenville Treaty.

The second Stony Creek Council, just concluded and equally as long, had seen almost a thousand warriors in attendance, including many from the same tribes, plus a number of Wyandots and Ottawas and a scattering of Chippewas and Potawatomies. The fervor was high at both war councils and the war dances held with great enthusiasm, complete with paint and feathers and, at intervals, decorated tomahawks being sunk into the war posts that had been set up. Full commitment to the plan had not been officially given by any of the tribes who attended, yet Tecumseh felt assured that he now held a good grip on them and they would respond when the call was made.

Tecumseh had known that eventually the whites must realize that something peculiar was in the wind. It couldn't be helped. He also knew that they might consider the signs they detected as evidence of uprising. That, too, was

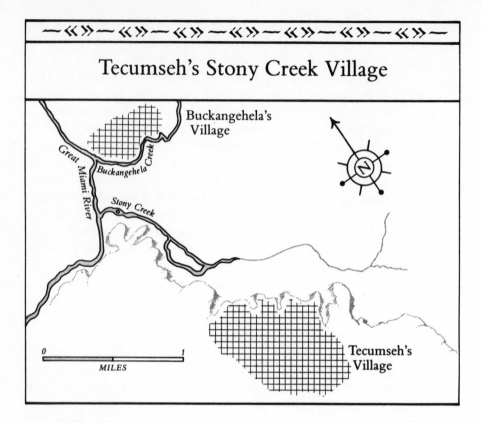

unavoidable. The important thing was that they not find out the details of the grand plan. When it was reported to him that during the eighth day of the first council, two whites had been turned away who were trying to see what was going on and that one of these two had been Simon Kenton, he fully expected some sort of repercussion. It was not long in coming.[540] One of the whites—the militia officer named Thomas Moore—had returned on February 21 with a letter from the governor that Tecumseh had read with more amusement than alarm, very pleased that it had been Moore who delivered it and not Kenton, who would have recognized him. Moore was strongly under the impression that Tecumseh was the principal chief of all the Shawnees and Tecumseh had not disabused him of the notion. The letter Moore delivered to him from the governor had said:

> *To the Principal Chiefs of the Shawnee Indians*
>
> *Friends and Brothers*
>
>   *I have received information from our respectable white brothers settled on the waters of the Mad River, that from the hostile appearances manifested*

*amongst our Red Brothers they have cause to be alarmed, and some of them
are leaving their homes and requesting assistance to protect them. I cannot
believe that our Red Brothers will be so far lost to a sense of their duty and
best interests as to entertain a desire to disturb the peace and friendship which
so happily subsists between them and us; on our part we sincerely wish to
brighten up the chain of peace and friendship in token of which I herewith
present you a fine white belt—but as our people are distressed to know your
determinations—and as I wish to quiet their fears, and to prevent our people
from injuring our Red brethren, I do request that you will expressly state to
our respectable Major Moore, who will present you with this letter, if you
have any cause of complaint against our people. If you have, make it known
to me, and if you have not I shall then be able to prevent any serious
consequences that might otherwise happen both to you and to us. In hopes
that the Great Spirit will incline your hearts and the hearts of your people
to peace, I remain your friend,*

*Edward Tiffin, Governor of
the State of Ohio*

*Chillicothe
February 19th, 1806*

As soon as he had accepted the wampum belt and finished reading the
speech, Tecumseh had told Major Moore to return home, that no attack would
be made on any white settlement, and to tell Governor Tiffin that he would
receive a letter from the Shawnees in one moon.

He had smiled as Moore rode off and then went right ahead with the
plans for the second council to be held here at the Stony Creek. The vague
worry that had touched him since the whites first came here and tried to enter
the council was now alleviated; the possibility of hostilities breaking out prematurely because of this was now put at rest. The whole chain of events had,
in fact, provided him with an unexpected opportunity to imbue the white
government with a reestablished sense of security. The governor was clearly
under the impression that the council was being held strictly by Shawnees and
by waiting a month to respond, it had not only given them ample opportunity
to hold the second council here, it would undoubtedly also make the governor
think that the letter was the result of a long and careful deliberation by the
full Shawnee Council. This was the first opportunity Tecumseh had ever had
to repay in kind the many devious and deceitful messages the Shawnees had
received over the years from the whites. It was very pleasant to be, for once,
on the giving rather than the receiving end of such a document. He felt no
pang of guilt over what he wrote now as the "official" response to Governor
Tiffin and, while his command of written English was perhaps not as pro-

nounced as might be desired, it would certainly put across very well the
assurances he wished to convey. He now wrote:

Friend and Brother

*Never a speech was received with more joy than yours handed to us by
Major Moore. We were all in great trouble at that time for the sake of your
people, and we would not account for it, for we were entirely innocent of
what they wanted to impute on our nation, was absolutely out of our knowledge.*

*We have immediately return our prayers to the Great Spirit above, for
you, and will never forgotten your goodness towards us, and we thanks him
for having given us such a good and wise man. We were very much please
of one part of your speech saying you didn't believe that we wished to cause
any disturbance with the white people. No be well assured it was never our
intention, nor never will be in our part. We have more things of more
important than that to mind, which is believe in God. We will tell you what
was our intention when we were blame incorrectly. We had got all our young
men and young women together to try to larn them good things, to worship
the Great God above us and to fixt ourselves in a good place for to raiz
shanty full grain for our women and children. We thought we were doing
well, particularly when it was requested by our Father Jefferson to do so and
expected to be safe or protected by all our brothers, the white people of the
United States, but to our sorry and great surprise, we were interrupted and
all the people of Mad River or about were preparing to come against us to
destroy the whole of us. Upon foolish lies that bad people had told them.
So that our women are all in fears. And we do not know what to do for to
secure them in a peaceable place that we might have happy with all our
neighbors. We believe that some of the principal men are to easy belonging
of the Militia Department. Good men should be appointed, particularly those
that wish not to have a war of us, and that they may keep peace and not to
make a great noise without foundation. We beg you may publish the contrary
of this bad news to all your people that for the future we might not be
disturbed any more and that you may punish those bad men that wish to
break the chain of friendship that ties our hands together. Four our good
chain will always be bright on our side. We have no more to say at present,
only to assure you of our sincerity towards you and beg you may continue
to do as good and that you may have along life in great prosperity and
happiness and we may love one another like to brothers out to do.*

*from your friends
the Shawnees*[541]

[April 28, 1806 — Monday]

This was the third day Tecumseh and Tenskwatawa had spent in their old cabin in the White River Village of Buckangehela and they were preparing to continue their journey back to Greenville when they heard the sounds of voices and people approaching the cabin. The brothers stepped outside, then stopped and waited when they saw their old Delaware friend Buckangehela and his second, Chief Peketelemund, approaching with a small group of their people. In his hand Buckangehela held a sheet of paper. The group stopped a dozen feet from the brothers and Buckangehela held up the paper, which was obviously a letter, and started to speak, but Tecumseh held up a hand, stopping him.

"Who is it that I only partly see behind my Delaware friends?"

Spemica Lawba, standing between a white officer and Peketelemund, stepped forward.[542] "I greet my uncles with respect and friendship," he said. "I came here to deliver to Chief Buckangehela, and to translate for him, a letter from Governor Harrison. I had looked forward to seeing you." His eyes shifted briefly beyond them to the open cabin door, then back to them. "I had also hoped to see my mother, when I learned that she had been traveling with you. I have not seen her for too long."

"Tecumapese was with us," Tecumseh said evenly, no semblance of warmth in his voice. "She continued back to our village at Greenville when Tenskwatawa and I came here." He looked at his nephew steadily. "My eyes are glad to see you; my heart is not, since it knows you come here as an agent of one whose aim is to harm the Indians."

"Indians and whites can live in peace, Tecumseh." Spemica Lawba spoke softly, without rancor. At age thirty-two he had finally begun to lose his ingenuous boyish appearance.

"You are incorrect, nephew," Tecumseh said, an edge of sharpness coming into his voice. "Indians and whites can *never* live in peace. They can only live close to one another if the Indian does what the white man wishes and moves aside when the white man stretches. All our history and that of other tribes has shown this to be true." He shifted his eyes to Buckangehela. "What has the white beaver written to you?"

Buckangehela stepped forward and handed him the letter. "Spemica Lawba will read it to you," he said, "as he did for me."

Tecumseh shook his head. "I will read it myself, aloud, so you may see if what was translated to you is what I find."

Spemica Lawba, hurt and resentful, spoke up before he could do so. "Uncle," he said, "I have read the letter truly and fairly to Chief Buckangehela and his people, and you will see that the governor is not pleased with the things my uncle Tenskwatawa has been doing and saying."

That came as no surprise to Tecumseh, who himself had not been pleased with some of the things Tenskwatawa had done since he became the Shawnee Prophet. Foremost among these had been the brutal witch hunt that was inaugurated by his little brother.

During the winter the trails leading to Greenville had been choked with transients as more than two thousand Indians had come to see and hear the great Prophet who had risen in their midst. Tenskwatawa, vain and deceptive though he was, apparently really believed in the benefits to be gained by what he preached. He believed—and declared—that the moral precepts of all the tribes, but especially the Shawnees, had slipped during the years of association with the whites and it was up to him to lead them back: to abolish whiskey drinking and female promiscuity and intermarriage with whites, to stop arguing among themselves and treat all kinsmen with respect and kindness, to show respect for authority, to provide food and shelter to widows and orphans and the elderly and, in fact, anyone not able to care for himself, to use guns for defense or war but to hunt only with spears and arrows, to return to stone and wooden tools and pottery vessels of their own manufacture for cooking and drinking, and, most of all, to abolish witchcraft and severely punish those found engaged in it.

There were, among the Northwestern tribes, a good many—particularly among the established chiefs and subchiefs—who were resentful of Tenskwatawa's leap into prominence and authority and the influence he held over their people, and angry over the way they had been so unexpectedly forced into giving their approval of Tenskwatawa as Prophet without lengthy councilling beforehand. Others found the idea of abdicating their heritage as members of a proud tribe and adopting a new status as simply Indians, without heritage or tradition or intertribal enmity, to be abhorrent. Some—Catahecassa, Tarhe and Michikiniqua in particular—were loud in their dununciation of both Tenskwatawa and Tecumseh as dangerous rebels within their midst. Such resistance was gaining a strong foothold at a time when Tecumseh was absent, visiting the Potawatomies. Tenskwatawa decided on a tactic designed to make others think twice before becoming too vocal in their opposition: he would inaugurate something of an inquisition, slowly at first, to see what the reaction would be, but then more vigorously if it went well.

In his speeches, Tenskwatawa then took to becoming very angry, shouting tirades of verbal abuse at those who, thinking only of themselves, would stand in the way of all their brother Indians. He proclaimed that such people were possessed by evil spirits that had to be destroyed and was delighted when there arose a general muttering of agreement among his listeners.

An elderly, childless widow of a Delaware subchief was the first to be executed as the result of Tenskwatawa's accusations. Knowing that she always carried a medicine bag containing various charms and amulets, Tenskwatawa, without prior warning, accused her of being a witch and declared that she ought to be burned to death for her crime. Voices rose in support of the contention and later the same day the old woman was taken by a dozen warriors of her own tribe, bound, placed atop a large pile of wood and burned to death. No one voiced anything except approbation for ridding the tribe of this witch.

The following day Tenskwatawa had gone further. He accused the ancient Delaware Chief Teteboxti with similar witchcraft and ordered his execution. Tenskwatawa recalled only too well how Teteboxti, after Fallen Timbers, had been one of the first to rush to General Wayne to beg for mercy and was among the first to sign the treaty of peace. At once resigned to his fate, Teteboxti arrayed himself in his finest clothing and then even assisted in the erection of his own pyre. At this point, to many who were wavering in acceptance of The Prophet's true ability, this was a distinctly convincing display. They admired the benevolence of The Prophet who took pity on the white-haired old chief and allowed him to be killed first by a tomahawk blow before being burned. The same fate befell Teteboxti's nephew, a warrior who had taken the name Billy Patterson.

The next victim of Tenskwatawa's inquisition was a Wyandot who, as a Christian convert, called himself Joshua, and who was alleged to commune frequently with a huge bird fond of devouring humans. Once again no word of protest was raised against what was happening, lest the protester himself be accused of being possessed by evil spirits and ordered executed. The Prophet, buoyed by the power he suddenly possessed, now even made journeys to several neighboring villages and pointed out others who were supposedly possessed and these, after he left, were burned by the inhabitants. Invited by Buckangehela to return to the White River Village and several other villages nearby to "purify" them, Tenskwatawa went there and quickly pointed out five women as practitioners of evil sorcery and all five were promptly executed. The first of these was an old hag of a woman named Coltos, who was slowly roasted over several days and who, under the excruciating pain, admitted that she owned a medicine bag in which she kept powerful amulets that gave her the power of flight. At Upper Sandusky, however, Tenskwatawa encountered some opposition. Invited there by some Wyandots of the Porcupine clan, Tenskwatawa identified four women of the tribe as witches and suggested the villagers, for their own safety, execute them. Chief Tarhe, infuriated at his audacity, ordered him away and managed to prevent the execution of the women.

Tecumseh was finally informed of what was going on during his absence and, appalled at what Tenskwatawa was doing, he had hurried back to Greenville and made him stop, aware that while Tenskwatawa's witch hunt was certainly tending to muffle overt opposition to them both, at the same time it was instilling deep resentments that would eventually alienate the tribes and turn the Indian populace against them beyond recovery.

For the first time the British Indian Department was beginning to take serious note of the brothers and was shrewd enough to deduce that Tecumseh was undoubtedly the real leader of the two and would be a very important ally when, as seemed increasingly likely these days, actual warfare resumed between themselves and the Americans. An Indian agent named Frederick Fisher, the trading partner of Matthew Elliott, was dispatched by the deputy superintendent of Indian Affairs, William Claus, to Tecumseh with gifts and promises and ordered to remain with him under guise of being a trader to allay any suspicions the Americans might entertain of official British attempts to establish alliance.

News of these witchcraft executions had caused a strong reaction in Governor Harrison, which he had unleashed verbally during the visit of a delegation of Delawares to Vincennes on the first day of the Rain Moon. That delegation, under Chief Peketelemund, had told Harrison that while they had not formally accepted the spiritual leadership of Tenskwatawa, the Delawares were strongly inclined in that direction because of the amazing ability he continued exhibiting in his prophecies. Which was when, Peketelemund had told Buckangehela and Tecumseh earlier, Harrison had reacted so strongly.

"The Prophet be damned!" Harrison had stormed. "This man you speak of as The Prophet has no more prophetic ability than I. You have been misled! Your people should all know of this. You say he tells you that those who deal in magic and witchcraft should be burned at the stake. By what right does he pretend to be God among you? By what foolishness do you and your chief, Buckangehela, accept what he says without proof? Are you such mindless children as that?"

It was at that point that he had invited the Delaware delegation to refresh themselves with the food and drink he was providing there at his imposing Grouseland estate, while he composed a letter to be taken to Buckangehela for the entire Delaware tribe, determined, as he put it to Spemica Lawba— who he consistently addressed as Johnny Logan and who he considered to be one of his best agents among the Indians—to write words to be circulated among the Indians that would, once and for all, put the quietus to The Prophet's growing influence. He was not unaware of the recent growing rumblings of hostility among the Indians toward the Americans and he was convinced in his own mind that The Prophet was no more than a pawn for the British at Amherstburg. Consistently more reports were coming in of British agitation among the tribes; their tendrils, usually in the guise of traders, stretching deep into the more remote recesses of the Northwest: here a trader decried desecration of Indian burial grounds by the Americans, there a trader stirred resentment over the expeditions of Pike up the Mississippi and Lewis and Clark up the Missouri, and apparently everywhere these traders were stirring up hatred in the minds of the Indians for Harrison personally, depicting him as a land-ravenous monster. Added to that was the sudden appearance of the self-proclaimed Shawnee Prophet and the alarming number of Indians who were being strongly influenced by what he was telling them, which, of itself, Harrison considered to be only one more indication that this so-called Prophet was being used by the British.

A year ago the likelihood of another war between the British and Americans was so implausible as to be laughable. Now the smell of it was in the air and, as British and American relations continued growing more strained, war talk was everywhere and once again the old fears were enveloping the land.

Harrison had made it no secret that he was very glad Thomas Jefferson had been reelected and had begun his second term last year with George Clinton as his new vice-president to replace the erratic Aaron Burr, and that Jefferson had retained Henry Dearborn as secretary of war. Jefferson now had enough experience with Indians to perceive, with a minimum of data, that a serious situation was developing in the Northwest and to this end the president had, last January, personally addressed the chiefs of the Sacs, Foxes, and Potawatomies, telling them: "Our nation is numerous and strong, but we wish to be just to all and particularly to be kind and useful to our red children. We are establishing government factories among you as rapidly as possible to supply you with goods in exchange for the fur pelts you bring. We do this as a favor to you, for we wish no profit in this business. My Children, we are strong; we are numerous as the stars in the heavens, and we are all gunmen, yet we live in peace and friendship with all nations."

It had been at that point, Tecumseh knew, that Harrison had received orders from President Jefferson to try to divert the Indian attachment to the British by paying them higher prices for their furs and selling trade goods to them much more cheaply than the British could afford to do. And Tecumseh was also amusedly aware that the British had turned the tables on the Americans by sending parties of Indians to buy American goods from the traders and return with them to Amherstburg, where the British would buy them from the Indians at a price cheaper than it was for them to bring the same items from England. It was also with some relief that Tecumseh knew Harrison was, these days, concerning himself very little with what was occurring at Detroit and in the Michigan country, that responsibility having been taken out of his hands by the establishment, a bit over a year ago, of the Michigan Territory, with Detroit as its capital and a man named William Hull, who resigned his Massachusetts state senatorship to accept the appointment, as its governor.

Harrison remained the single biggest individual threat for the Indians. Obviously, he wanted to keep matters on a very even keel while he continued seeking peaceful land cessions from the Indians. His phenomenal success with the St. Louis Treaty, purchasing 51 million acres for next to nothing had clearly prompted him to attempt to duplicate it with minor chiefs among the Potawatomies, Miamis, and Delawares in the Indiana country and he was being unfortunately successful, largely through the efforts of the self-important little chief of the Potawatomies, Winnemac, along with the group of minor Miami and Potawatomi chiefs Winnemac seemed to have no trouble controlling.

Tecumseh had been furious when he learned about the quiet little arrangements Harrison had made through Winnemac and the minor chiefs for the purchase of Indiana lands that those chiefs had neither right nor authority to sell. Harrison and the president had no qualms at buying from them at ridiculously low prices and then quickly getting such purchases ratified by the Congress with undue haste and practically without question. These were all chickens that would undoubtedly one day come to roost, just as the fraudulent purchase from the Sacs would, but by then it would be too late to do anything about it. And, of course, interspersed with the fraudulent or at least highly unethical land deals Harrison was engaging in were the purchases he was making that were quite legal and ethical, such as the land cession he had gotten from the Piankeshaws last December when they sold the remainder of their Illinois lands to him.

Harrison had also evinced a great deal of nervousness, Tecumseh knew, about the two secret councils of the Indians that Tecumseh had held at his Stony Creek Village in February and March. No doubt he had become alert when word had been brought to him that not only no whites had been allowed to attend those councils but that even Indians known to have American sympathies were turned away. It was, so far as Tecumseh knew, the first that Harrison had ever heard The Prophet had a brother and that his name was Tecumseh, who was merely a warrior, not a chief, and it was quite apparent that Harrison still firmly believed that Tenskwatawa was the leader of the breakaway faction from the Shawnees that was inspiring such unrest among so many tribes. This was precisely as Tecumseh wanted it to be and the reason why he had allowed Tenskwatawa to step into the light of notoriety while he himself remained largely unknown to the whites; the longer he could keep Harrison from recognizing where the power lay, the more that could be accomplished before steps were mounted to balk him—as they assuredly would be once the facts were realized. Harrison was not so convinced as Governor Tiffin that the secret councils had been simply innocuous Indian affairs of a strictly tribal nature.

At any rate, Harrison was determined to thwart The Prophet in what seemed to him to be that individual's efforts to use tribal superstitions to stampede the Indians into warfare, which, Spemica Lawba said, was the reason for the letter he had written that Tecumseh held in his hand.

" 'My Children,' " Tecumseh now read aloud, smoothly translating it into the Shawnee tongue, " 'my heart is filled with grief and my eyes are dissolved in tears at the news which has reached me. You have been celebrated for your wisdom above all the tribes of red people who inhabit this great island. Your fame as warriors has extended to the remotest nations, and the wisdom of your chiefs has gained you the appellation of grandfathers from all the neighboring tribes.' " Tecumseh shook his head at this and looked up at the others to say, "So much for how well this Governor Harrison knows and understands us, since he mistakes the Delawares for Wyandots![543] But let me continue with what the white chief has to say: 'From what cause, then, does it proceed that you have departed from the wise counsels of your fathers and covered yourselves with guilt? My Children, tread back the steps you have taken and endeavor to regain the straight road you have abandoned. The dark, crooked and thorny one which you are now pursuing will certainly lead you to endless woe and misery. But who is this pretended prophet who dares speak in the name of the great Creator? Examine him. Is he more wise and virtuous than you are yourselves, that he should be selected to convey to you the orders of your God? Demand of him some proofs at least of his being the messenger of the Deity.' "

Tenskwatawa's eyes widened and he looked somewhat stricken, but he quickly masked his dismay with a scowl as Tecumseh continued reading aloud.

" 'If God had really empowered him, He has doubtless authorized him to perform miracles that he may be known and received as a prophet. If he is really a prophet, ask him to cause the sun to stand still or the moon to alter its course, the rivers to cease to flow, or the dead to rise from their graves. If he does these things, you may believe he has been sent from God.' "

Tecumseh paused and glanced at Tenskwatawa who was still scowling, but in whose eyes his brother could detect a flicker of panic. Tecumseh shook his head almost imperceptibly and returned his attention to the letter and continued to read. " 'He tells you that the Great Spirit commands you to punish with death those who deal in magic, and that he is authorized to point them out. Wretched delusion! Is then the Master of Life obliged to appoint mortal man to punish those who offend Him? Has He not the thunder and the power of nature at His command? And could He not sweep away from the earth a whole nation with one motion of His arm? My Children, do not believe that the great and good Creator of Mankind has directed you to destroy your own flesh; and do not doubt that if you pursue this abominable wickedness His vengeance will overtake and crush you.

" 'The above is addressed to you in the name of the Seventeen Fires. I now speak to you from myself, as a friend who wishes nothing more sincerely than to see you prosperous and happy. Clear your eyes, I beseech you, from the mist which surrounds them. No longer be imposed on by the arts of an imposter. Drive him from your town, and let peace and harmony prevail amongst you. Let your poor old men and women sleep in quietness, and banish from their minds the dreadful idea of being burnt alive by their own friends and countrymen. I charge you to stop your bloody career; and if you value the friendship of your Great Father, the President—if you wish to preserve the good opinion of the Seventeen Fires—let me hear by the return of the bearer that you have determined to follow my advice. Your friend and adviser, William Henry Harrison, Governor, Indiana Territory.'

"So, there we have it," Tecumseh said mildly, folding the letter and handing it back to Buckangehela. He glanced at Spemica Lawba and Peketelemund and then back at Buckangehela and finally at his brother, his eyes conveying a message to Tenskwatawa that was understood. As Tecumseh stepped back to stand beside his brother, Tenskwatawa spoke.

"Let the messengers rest and eat. I will retire to my place and meditate on this and see what direction, if any, I shall receive from the Great Spirit on this matter."

Tenskwatawa, with a show of haughtiness, turned and reentered the cabin and Tecumseh followed him. Inside, however, the assumed airs evaporated and he dissolved into open fear.

"What do we do, brother?" he asked tremulously. "This could throw down all we have built."

Tecumseh shook his head disappointedly. "After all this time, Tenskwatawa, do you still not believe that I can foretell what will occur, just as our brother Chiksika could, and our father Pucksinwah before him? You have been giving the people the predictions that I gave you to give to them, so how can you not believe what you, above all others, know to be true?" He sighed. "Come, sit with me, and we will prepare your reply."

Ten minutes short of an hour later the brothers emerged, Tenskwatawa once again with the hauteur of The Prophet and ordering that all the villagers be assembled at once. When they had done so, Tenskwatawa addressed them in a voice that was strong but laced with heavy bitterness. He denounced the whites generally and Harrison in particular, saying that the fact Harrison addressed the Delawares as grandfathers among the tribes was clear evidence that he knew not whereof he spoke and that he, Tenskwatawa, had nothing but scorn for any Indian who believed what white men said or wrote. He told them that during the past hour he had conferred with the Great Spirit and that She was angry and would give them a sign.

"The white beaver, Harrison," he went on, "said that you should ask me, if I am really a prophet, to cause the sun to stand still and that if I can do this, then you can believe that I have been sent from God. Those are his words, not mine! Therefore, listen now to what I have to say: Fifty days from this day there will be no cloud in the sky. Yet, when the sun has reached its highest point, at that moment will the Great Spirit take it into Her hand and hide it from us. The darkness of night will thereupon cover us and the stars will shine round about us. The birds will go to roost and the night creatures will awaken and stir. Then you will know, *beyond further doubt,* as the white chief Harrison has said, that your Prophet has been sent to you from Moneto.''[544]

[June 17, 1806 — Tuesday]

In Wapakoneta, Blue Jacket's Town, Wapatomica, Upper Sandusky, Tecumseh's Village, and numerous other Indian villages throughout Ohio, this was a day long anticipated, and late in the forenoon Indians everywhere stopped what they were doing indoors and came outside to stand or sit as individuals or in large and small groups. This was the fiftieth day—the day when, on acceptance of the challenge issued by William Henry Harrison, The Prophet had said the Great Spirit would grasp the sun in Her hand and turn the day into night. Word of the challenge and its acceptance had spread to virtually every village and so now they waited and watched.

At precisely noon there was an eclipse of the sun.

In the fields and forests confused birds went to roost and many nocturnal animals roused and began stirring about. Stars of the first and second magnitude became visible, along with some of the planets. The darkness lasted for varying periods and its totality stretched from the southern shore of Lake Michigan in the north to near Cincinnati in the south. Over Greenville, which was near the center of the totality, the darkness lasted for close to seven minutes, plus extended intervals of waxing and waning dimness before and after. In the Indian villages there was consternation and fear and many of the Indians rushed indoors again and hid, awed and deeply moved by such an occurrence, convinced now more than ever of the tremendous power of Tenskwatawa and his validity as The Prophet.

At Fort Wayne, Indian Agent William Wells stepped outside the door of his house, looked upward and muttered, "Damn! There'll be hell to pay now."

In Chaubenee's Village on Indian Creek, sixty-five miles west and south of Chicago, Sauganash, who was visiting, murmured the single word, "Tecumseh," and Chaubenee nodded, for they knew.

In Vincennes, Governor William Henry Harrison was furious at having been bested at his own game and wondered aloud from whom Tenskwatawa had gotten advance knowledge of the solar eclipse.

At Greenville, where Tenskwatawa stood with close to a thousand Indians encircling him at a respectable distance, this man who called himself The Prophet raised his arms and cried out in a far-carrying voice during the awed hush that had settled over them. "Behold! Did I not prophesy truly? The Great Spirit has grasped the sun and darkness has shrouded the earth!"

In his cabin a short distance away, Tecumseh sat quietly in the darkness, smiling, neither surprised nor awed.

And throughout the Indian nations of the Northwest there arose a new and deeper respect for—and fear of—the prophet who had arisen among the Shawnees. To their immense relief, the darkness passed and the full brightness of a sunny, cloudless day returned. Before nightfall, a thousand Indians and more had begun preparations for a pilgrimage to Greenville to see and hear this great man who commanded even the sun.

[May 18, 1808 — Wednesday]

Tecumseh, Chaubenee, and Sauganash and their three young companions reined up their horses and looked back at the panorama stretching out before and slightly below them. Along the banks of this great river several hundred people were busily engaged in the construction of a very large and very important village—a village wholly devoid of tribal affiliations; a large community that was simply a village of *Indians,* united in a brotherhood that superseded the boundaries of sect, sept, clan or tribe.

This was the new capital of the *Indian* nation.

"It is going to be the most important village ever built!" Sauganash exclaimed enthusiastically.

"A great village," Chaubenee said, and the three young men bobbed their heads in agreement.

Tecumseh nodded as well, feeling they were correct, yet knowing there was a great deal still to be done before it could reach their expectations. He reined his horse around and said, "Let's go, my friends. We have a long ride ahead."

There were two principal reasons why Tecumseh had finally come to the decision to move his village far away from Greenville, far away from Ohio and far away from the whites. The first was because of the sharply increased apprehensions among the whites over their presence and the incidents that had occurred that raised the specter of a new Indian war in the brewing. The second was because there was simply not room enough any longer, nor food supplies enough, especially game, in the Greenville area to support them, despite the fact that Tecumseh's Village had expanded to include sixty permanent log cabins, over one hundred each of wegiwas and tepees, plus a large *msi-kah-mi-qui* 150 feet long and 35 feet in width.[545] Besides, away from the whites they would no longer have to be so constrained in their actions and utterances as they were at Greenville.

It was now nearly two years since the great solar eclipse had occurred and in that interval there had been many changes and many occurrences that dictated the wisdom of such a move.

The increase in The Prophet's influence and prestige following the eclipse had been phenomenal and long lasting, as was the fear that had been instilled by the short-lived witch hunt that Tenskwatawa had initiated. While The Prophet continued his preachings in Tecumseh's Village and his recruiting among the neighboring tribes, Tecumseh continued making his journeys to more distant tribes, continued to press upon them recognition of the jeopardy they were in, the hazard posed by the encroaching whites and the paramount need for all red men to think of themselves as brother Indians and not merely as tribesmen. Sometimes he made these journeys alone, but more often with a cadre of his principal lieutenants—Wasegoboah, Chaubenee, Stiahta, Sauganash, Metea, and occasionally Tecumapese—as well as a contingent of ten to twenty warriors. Metea was a Potawatomi subchief who had taken the place of Skesh, whom Tecumseh had sent away when it was discovered that he was one of those Potawatomies who, along with Winnemac, had sold Wabash River lands belonging to the Miamis to Harrison. The strong American garrisons established in the forts at Chicago, Detroit, Mackinac, and St. Louis added graphic emphasis to his warnings.

Opposition by chiefs of various tribes, though not quite so vigorous as before, still continued to thwart them, those chiefs having no intention of becoming subservient to The Prophet or surrendering their leadership to Tecumseh. Others balked on a more personal level. Main Poche of the Potawatomies, for example, though he sympathized with Tecumseh's determination to eventually confront the whites and agreed to side with him when he did so, remained a fiery chief who had no intention of curtailing his own warring against enemy tribes such as the Osages, nor any intention of considering them as brother Indians.[546] His fathers, and their fathers before them, had fought these enemies and he was determined to do the same so long as he had the breath to do so. Nor had he any sympathy with Tenskwatawa's new doctrine; he had no intention of curtailing or even diminishing his consumption of liquor, which he loved and drank in great quantities.

"The Great Spirit has often told me," Main Poche declared, rubbing his chin with the congenitally deformed stub of his left hand, "that if I ever refrained from going to war against my Indian enemies, or refrained from drinking, I would then become nothing more than a common man in my nation. I have never been just a common man and have no intention of becoming one."

The British secret agent in the guise of a trader, Frederick Fisher, had established a reasonably close rapport with Tenskwatawa at Greenville, largely because of the frequent goods he turned over to the Shawnee brothers, outwardly appearing to be items traded for but in actuality gifts from the British Indian Department to maintain what might be a very beneficial association with these expatriate Shawnees gaining so much influence among all the Indians.

"With the Americans so nervous about you people being here," Fisher said one day to Tenskwatawa, "aren't you worried about them clamping down on you to make you move back into your own territory?"

An ugly smile had creased Tenskwatawa's crooked lips. He tapped his own chest with a stiff forefinger and replied, "I do not worry about anything the Americans might do. I can bring darkness between the Americans and us; more, I can bring the very sun under my feet! What white man can do this?"

He picked up a wooden bowl and tossed its watery contents to one side in a spray. "I can overthrow the Americans as easily as this. Do you want to know how much I care for Americans?"

Before Fisher could reply, The Prophet bent over at the waist and slapped a palm to his behind and at this same moment discharged an enormous and noisy blast of intestinal gas.

"That," he said, breaking into cackling laughter, "is how much I care for Americans."

When Governor Tiffin resigned his office in March 1807 to become a United States senator, Thomas Kirker had become acting governor and Kirker immediately made no bones about being very nervous about the Indian situation. Learning that The Prophet had made a series of inflammatory speeches in the Detroit area and that now a great many Indians from tribes that Kirker himself had never even heard of were showing up around Greenville to hear more of the mystic's strange preaching and, further, that more than a score of Indians in opposition to the Shawnee brothers had been accused by Tenskwatawa of witchcraft and executed by their own people, Kirker's nervousness became distinct alarm.

Most of the whites in Ohio were beginning to expect that a war would break out soon—if not with the Indians, then with the British. Everyone had heard how the British warship *Leopard* had fired upon the American frigate *Chesapeake* on the Virginia coast, boarded her and kidnapped some of her crew; that English agents were known to be moving in large numbers among the Indians, inciting them to join forces with them against the Americans.[547]

Only recently the whites in Ohio had begun passing resolutions of loyalty and forwarding them to Governor Kirker. When Tenskwatawa addressed a group of northern Indians who had gathered at Yellow Springs, just south of Springfield, a frontier militiaman named Ben Whiteman had spied upon them and then rushed to Kirker and suggested that there be a general calling out of the militia at once. Aware that there was obviously some kind of trouble brewing at Greenville, Kirker had not called up the militia but he did appoint a delegation from the Shaker Society at Lebanon to attend some of The Prophet's speeches and report their feelings about the Shawnee mystic and what possible threat he and Tecumseh represented to the white population of Ohio.[548]

One of the newer and more active converts to Tenskwatawa's doctrine was a loud-voiced Ottawa named Kekoonshartha—Trout—who, Tecumseh was pleased to see, immediately on his return to northern Michigan, began spreading word of both The Prophet's theology and Tecumseh's grand plan, warning his own people and the neighboring Chippewas that the end of the world was near and that when it occurred the only ones who would survive would be those who now became faithful followers of the Shawnee brothers, along with a certain number of dead that he, Kekoonshartha, would raise up because of their previous good life.[549]

The present move away from Greenville would have taken place a year earlier, had it not been for the meddling of the Indian agent at Fort Wayne, William Wells. It had been in the middle of the Rain Moon just over a year ago when, without official authorization, Wells sent a former adopted Shawnee, Anthony Shane, with a message to Tecumseh and Tenskwatawa, ordering them to come to Fort Wayne to receive a message he would deliver to them from their great father, the president of the United States.

Tecumseh impaled Shane with his sharp gaze and said in a voice that brooked no argument, "Go back to Fort Wayne and tell Captain Wells that Tecumseh has no father who is called president of the United States. The sun is my father; the moon is my mother. I know none other. Tell Captain Wells that my fire is kindled on the spot appointed by the Great Spirit above and that if he has anything to communicate to me, *he* must come *here*. I shall expect him in six days from this time. Tell Captain Wells he will be received in safety and a council held with many Indians in attendance."

Wells, knowing of the witchcraft executions and fearful for his life if he showed up, despite Tecumseh's assurance of safety, declined coming to Greenville and instead sent Shane back again with another message stating with poorly disguised arrogance that Tecumseh, Tenskwatawa and their followers were illegally settled at Greenville and, as they had showed considerable disrespect for the government of the United States, they were ordered to "move from that place and off the land of the United States immediately," since it was now American land in accordance with the Greenville Treaty and that once they did so, moving beyond the boundaries agreed upon at the treaty, assistance would be given them by the government until they were established in their new home. The message ended with Wells instructing them to love the Americans and obey the orders of American officials.

The many Indians who had gathered at Greenville to hear what Wells in person had to say were greatly angered when he failed to show up, which they took to be a slight against themselves and an indication of cowardice. Tecumseh had read the second message aloud and with undisguised contempt. He then commented at length to Shane on the mistreatment of the Indians by the whites and directed Shane to go back and tell Wells that it was the Indian lands that had been taken and were still being encroached upon.

"These lands are ours," he went on. "No one has a right to remove us, because we were the first owners. Moneto has appointed this place for us on which to light our fires, and here we will remain. As to boundaries, the Master of Life knows none, nor will he acknowledge any. Nor will his red people acknowledge any. If the president of the Seventeen Fires has anything more to say to me, he must send a man of note as his messenger. I will hold no further intercourse with Captain Wells."

So, instead of leaving Greenville as initially planned, during the early summer of 1807, the move had been put off for a year so that there could be no possible suggestion that Tecumseh and his people had left because of any fear of William Wells or his representations, official or otherwise, on behalf of the United States government.

It was shortly after the Wells matter, toward the end of the Rain Moon, when an incident occurred that caused great apprehension among the whites and resulted in Governor Kirker finally calling up the Ohio militia—20 companies from 5 different militia brigades, totaling 1,865 men. A settler named Thomas Bowyer was killed and scalped as he worked in his field a few miles west of Urbana.[550] Once again settlers from outlying areas flocked to Springfield to take refuge from the supposed Indian uprising and many wives and children were sent back to Kentucky for safety.

Initially, Catahecassa blamed the death on Tecumseh's followers and Tecumseh countered by saying it was done by Catahecassa's people to stir white resentments against him and his people. Both were asked by whites to attend a council near Kenton's Mill in Springfield to settle the matter.

In accordance with a plan previously agreed to, the one hundred seventy Indians under eighty-six-year-old Catahecassa, and accompanied by Blue Jacket and Captain John, left their tomahawks with Major Thomas Moore in Urbana and carried only their rifles. It was agreed that when they arrived at the council ground in Springfield, all armed men not taking part in the talks should stand well away in the rear, each on his own side, while the whites and chiefs, none of them carrying weapons, should advance to the center and speak.

Tecumseh and the 130 Indians of his party, including Stiahta and Wasegoboah, came via a different route, not passing through Urbana, and arrived with both guns and tomahawks. At the insistence of the whites who were in charge—which included Simon Kenton, Benjamin Whiteman, William Ward, James McPherson, and Thomas Moore—all the Indians, including Catahecassa's, stacked their arms to one side. The single exception was Tecumseh, who refused to surrender his pipe tomahawk and said, with chilling humor, "I may want to use one end or the other of it before the day is out."

At this juncture Parson James Pinchard approached Tecumseh with a dirty, long-stemmed clay pipe and suggested that if he wanted to smoke for peace, he could use this. Tecumseh took it and gave Pinchard such a penetrating stare that the frightened little man backed off hastily. Smiling faintly, Tecumseh gingerly sniffed the bowl of the pipe, wrinkled his nose in a ludicrously distasteful expression and pitched the pipe over his head and far into a patch of briars. Both the Indians and whites had howled with laughter and the tension was considerably eased.

Among the whites who greeted Tecumseh was Simon Kenton, who shook hands with him in a friendly manner. Tecumseh grinned and said loudly in English, "Are there any white men on hand here who would like to buy Indiana?" Again a burst of riotous laughter.

Kenton grinned shamefacedly. When the laughter faded, he replied loudly, "If there are, I'll sell it to 'em, since I already bought it!" A third wave of laughter swept the crowd.

Indicating Benjamin Whiteman, who was commander of the militia and in uniform on this occasion, Tecumseh asked Kenton, "Who is this general?"

"This is Ben Whiteman," Kenton replied. "He was a member of my party that night when we attacked your camp on East Fork fifteen years ago."

Tecumseh, remembering well the night when he had killed the white attacker whose name, he had just learned, was Sam Barr, now looked over Whiteman in a speculative way, his face largely expressionless but his eyes twinkling.

"Are you," he said to Whiteman, "a big man?"

Whiteman was taken somewhat aback at the question but, after a moment's hesitation, he answered, "Yes."

"Well," said Tecumseh, "I am a better man than you."

"That is yet to be tried," Whiteman retorted, a slight edge to his voice.

"Oh no," Tecumseh said, breaking into his grin again and stepping up to the militia general. He slapped Whiteman's shoulder in a friendly way and continued, "I whipped you when we were boys. Maybe I'll do it again."

More laughter broke out and Whiteman had the grace to join in. With that the council had begun in a pleasant mood. Still, everyone was prepared for trouble to erupt when one or the other of the two principal Indians accused his opposite of the murder. And so it had, when Tecumseh stepped up to Catahecassa, placed his hand on the chief's shoulder and said, "This is the man who committed the murder."

It took the rest of the day and most of the next to bring the council back to even keel, many hours of haranguing having caused considerable anger on both sides. On the third day, however, it was Tecumseh who spoke first and he surprised everyone.

"I have no knowledge," he said, "of who killed and scalped the settler. I am also certain that Chief Catahecassa has no knowledge of it, either."

Catahecassa was obviously very pleased at the remark and agreed to it. The council continued, discussing where the murder had been committed, how it had been perpetrated and all known circumstances involved. It turned out that Bowyer, working about a hundred yards from his cabin at dusk, had been shot through the body by three balls virtually simultaneously. When his wife peered out of the cabin fearfully, she saw Indians in the act of scalping him. She and another woman ran for help and when they came back with it, the body was found face down, scalped and tomahawked and with two rattles, a hank of hair and a bow and arrows lying across his back.

Tecumseh asked that these Indian items be brought forward for examination and, when they were, it became obvious that they were not of Shawnee construction but appeared to be either Ottawa or Chippewa. The conclusion of the council was that the murder had evidently been committed by a roving party of Indians foreign to the area and that both Catahecassa and Tecumseh were to be held blameless.

Tecumseh then said he would try to ease the fears of the whites who were concerned about his village at Greenville and the number of Indians who kept arriving and departing. He launched into a lengthy and forceful discourse about how he and his brother Tenskwatawa were hoping to uplift the Shawness and the Indians of other nations with their doctrine. When at length the council broke up, Blue Jacket, looking older than his fifty-three years, came to Tecumseh and gripped his arm warmly.

"We have not seen one another in much too long, Tecumseh," he said. "My heart is happy that my eyes have looked upon you again and that my ears have heard your words. Without turning my back on my chief, I will do whatever it is in my power to do to help you."

Tecumseh nodded, thankful for the words. "And mine is filled with pleasure, as well," he said quietly, "to see again my old friend."[551]

Governor Kirker had sent General Thomas Worthington and Colonel

Duncan McArthur to invite Tecumseh and other Ohio Indian leaders to come to the Ohio capital city, Chillicothe, for a banquet in their honor and perhaps to assure the citizens there that an Indian war was not imminent, as so many still feared. They agreed to come and in a short while they—Tecumseh, Blue Jacket, Stiahta, and the Delaware Chief Panther of the Unami sect of his tribe— were attending the record-breaking mass meeting presided over by the governor.

Tecumseh gave a moving address in English that lasted for nearly three hours and during which he was compellingly able, magnetic, and convincing, holding his entire audience spellbound. Worthington and McArthur had already submitted a report to the governor that was entirely favorable to The Prophet's program, with no evidence having turned up that it was a covert war movement. With that report and the personal assurance of Tecumseh that the Indians desired to live in peace with the whites, the unrest and hostile feelings abated. Governor Kirker ordered the discharge of the militia that had been called up and the hundreds of whites who listened to Tecumseh's eloquent speech with close attention returned to their homes relieved of their fears that another Indian war was impending.[552]

Following the official ceremonies, Tecumseh, Blue Jacket, Stiahta, and Panther were invited to a formal dinner at Adena, the palatial mansion of one of the peace commissioners, General Thomas Worthington.[553] They accepted and were duly impressed when, after a ride to the top of a rather steep hill, they saw before them the most elegant dwelling any of them had ever seen, overlooking the great Scioto Valley, the expanse of the present capital city of Chillicothe and the area where the old Shawnee capital of Chalahgawtha had been located, as well as the first of the impressive range of great Ohio hills to the east.[554]

A brand new structure and, in fact, not entirely completed, Adena was a huge dwelling of fine, flowing, modern architecture and filled with the most exquisite of colonial furnishings and art. On the great table was a magnificent array of foods shipped in from the East or all the way from Europe and place settings of the finest china, crystal, and silver. Concerned that the red guests not be offended in any way whatever, guests and servants alike were instructed on manners and protocol.[555]

Impressively polite and formally clad servants moved discreetly among the guests with silver trays, passing around dainty cups filled with wonderfully aromatic coffee. In the course of their doing so, cups were given to Tecumseh, Stiahta, and Blue Jacket, but Panther was inadvertently overlooked.

As soon as the server moved off, Panther's three companions began a rapid exchange with him in the Shawnee tongue, which so startled the guests that all stopped to watch and listen. Panther was very obviously taken aback and his responses, which the white guests only heard as a rapid-fire gibberish, quickly became heated and his eyes flashed with apparent anger that greatly alarmed the whites, who thought the slight that had evidently so agitated their red guests would result in bloodshed.

What was actually occurring was an *unsoma* joke—in which Tecumseh, Roundhead, and Blue Jacket immediately insulted Panther's *unsoma*—his sept symbol or totem creature—as being an animal so slow and stupid it could not even find the coffee, and quickly dubbing him "the coffeeless chief." And, as required by the traditional ritual of *unsoma* bantering, Panther had to retaliate with jibes of his own, as if in anger, but meant to be insults against their *unsoma* that were even worse.

It might have continued but Tecumseh suddenly noted the great consternation of the guests and broke it off, apologizing to their hosts and the guests that what had been going on was simply a form of Indian humor. The guests then all laughed, but far more from relief than from humor. Throughout the remainder of the affair, Mrs. Worthington paid lavish attention to Panther and his coffee cup never became empty.

In leaving, and in appreciation for the kindness and hospitality shown to them, Tecumseh presented as a gift to the Worthingtons, on behalf of himself and his three companions, a fine ceremonial tomahawk.[556]

Tecumseh returned to Greenville after the council with Governor Kirker at Chillicothe to find that during his absence Governor Harrison had sent a messenger, their old trader acquaintance John Conner, to Greenville with a message to be delivered to the chiefs and head men there. That message denounced Tenskwatawa as charlatan and fool, suggested that other Shawnees drive him away. When Conner arrived and found Tecumseh gone, he didn't know what to do except obey what Tenskwatawa told him to do—deliver it to Tenskwatawa himself.

Conner, Tenskwatawa told Tecumseh, obviously suddenly fearing for his life, had read the whole of Harrison's message, translating it into Shawnee. Tenskwatawa smiled wryly.

"You would have been proud of me, brother," he said. "I heard him out calmly and just as calmly told him the governor's accusations were untrue and he should go back and tell Harrison he can rest assured that it was the least of our ideas to make disturbances and that we would rather try to stop such things than encourage them. Conner went away relieved . . . and very fast."

Tecumseh smiled. "You did well, little brother. Well, indeed."

It was a few weeks later that Main Poche of the Potawatomies had arrived at Greenville and stayed with the brothers for several weeks. While he still refused to support Tecumseh's idea of tribal amalgamation in its entirety, he admitted there was great merit to it and, apart from giving up his alcohol and becoming cozy with the Osages, he would fully support Tecumseh in it. He then made the suggestion, as Tecumseh realized now upon retrospection, that was to change everything.

"Tecumseh," he had said, "you know that you cannot remain here much longer. How will you feed all your people? Where will you place them? How soon will it be before one finds it impossible to stop the waggling of a tongue loosened by liquor and tells the whites what your plans truly are? Now, consider this. My people have lands where no one lives at the moment, at the place where the Tippecanoe and the Wabash come together. There you would be far away from the Americans, who could not come against you without great effort, great expense and long advance warning. There you would find plenty of game for the bellies of all your followers and more. There you would find room to grow all the corn and vegetables you could possibly need. There you would be far removed from the jealousies of your own tribal chiefs, who hate and fear you. And, Tecumseh, there you would be much closer to the tribes in Illinois and Michigan and Wisconsin, and they closer to you when the time came for them to assemble under your arm."

When he stopped, the silence stretched out between them for a long while and then at last Tecumseh raised his head and met Main Poche's glance directly. "We will come," he said quietly. "It will take time to prepare, but we will be there in time to plant the corn next spring."

That simply the plans had been made. Gradually, over the winter, the Indians who had come to be converted to Tenskwatawa's theology drifted away back to their home villages, the admonition of Tecumseh in their ears that when they returned to him, it should be not to Greenville, but to the village where the Tippecanoe met the Wabash.

Late in the winter, toward the end of the Hunger Moon, Tecumseh was brought some news that made him despise William Wells more than ever. The Fort Wayne Indian agent had suggested to Harrison that a trap be set to catch Tecumseh and Tenskwatawa and imprison them to prevent further unrest among the Indians. Harrison, Tecumseh was told, had flatly refused the notion, telling Wells that such an act would undoubtedly do more than anything else to unite the tribes and cause an outbreak of war. And so, while Tecumseh's dislike of Wells increased, his respect for the sagacity of Harrison increased as well. Here, Tecumseh knew, was an enemy altogether too smart; the kind who, when and if he made his move, would do so only when the odds, *all of them,* were in his own favor.

As the winter dwindled away, all the residents of Tecumseh's Village at Greenville packed everything they owned in preparation for the move to the mouth of the Tippecanoe. Tecumseh directed that they would emigrate to their new location in two parties—Tecumseh himself to lead the mounted warriors and a number of packhorses by land and move swiftly to the area where the Tippecanoe flowed into the Wabash and there to scout the area and select the site best suited for their new village; Tenskwatawa, in charge of the major part of the baggage and equipment and at the head of all the women and children and elderly, was to lead his party afoot the twenty-one miles along the Northwest Trail to the Mississinewa River headwaters.[557] Here they would construct canoes and rafts, load all the baggage and gear into these craft and float down the Mississinewa to where it emptied into the Wabash, then down the Wabash the remaining fifty miles to where they would rejoin Tecumseh at the Tippecanoe.[558]

As soon as word of the emigration of Tecumseh and his close to half a thousand people reached the Miamis, there was considerable consternation among them. They had not been informed beforehand of the move and knew nothing of the destination. Michikiniqua and other Miami chiefs were immediately fearful that they meant to settle somewhere near Fort Wayne and there subvert the young Miami warriors to their anti-American views in opposition to the Greenville Treaty, to which Michikiniqua adhered rigidly. They held a council at Fort Wayne and then Michikiniqua, leading a party of warriors on horseback, struck off to the south, intercepting Tenskwatawa's party while still building canoes and rafts at the Mississinewa headwaters.

"Tenskwatawa," Michikiniqua said coldly, when he confronted The Prophet, "you are warned not to settle your people on the waters of the Wabash. This is the only warning you will receive. If you disobey it, we will swoop down upon you and destroy you and I will personally see that your scalp hangs in my lodge."

At one time Tenskwatawa would have quailed before such a comment from the great chief who had led the Indians in the defeat of St. Clair. In those intervening years, however, Michikiniqua had lost a great deal of his influence with other tribes, while at the same time Tenskwatawa had significantly grown in stature and power and, especially, self-assurance.

"You, Michikiniqua," he retorted, "have no authority to direct me to do or not do anything. I am guided and directed by a much higher authority than you. The Master of Life has directed me to move my people to the Tippecanoe and there to build my village and this is what I will do. All the other tribes of the West have agreed to meet us there and if a white man should put his foot over the boundary line, our warriors will easily put him back where he should be."

Tenskwatawa saw that the expression of Michikiniqua was now pinched and strained and it pleased him to be facing down the once great war chief. "You should be ashamed of yourself," he went on, "for continuing to cling to the Americans while such of them as your own adopted son, Apekonit, and Governor Harrison steal your land from beneath your very nose by dealing with little chiefs who should be under your control but are no longer. Go home, Michikiniqua, and get your own house in order."

Angry, but at the same time not willing to punish Tenskwatawa for his insolence and thereby decidedly risk raising the ire of Tecumseh and his considerable following of warriors and chiefs, Michikiniqua wheeled his horse about and galloped back toward Fort Wayne, his warriors at his heels. For his own part, Tenskwatawa grinned and felt giddy at having emerged on top in the confrontation. He had shamed and humbled Michikiniqua and knew that word of what had transpired would quickly spread among the Indians, enhancing his own reputation and at the same time diminishing Michikiniqua's. He was proud of himself and knew Tecumseh would be pleased at how he had handled the situation.

Tecumseh *was* pleased when he learned of it, during the last week of April when the contingent under his brother arrived at the mouth of the Tippecanoe, but at the same time he was saddened over the loss of stature of the chief for whom he had always harbored such great admiration.

The site that had been selected by Tecumseh for the new village that was to be called Tippecanoe was on good high ground on the north bank overlooking the Wabash just over two and a half miles downstream from where the Tippecanoe entered.[559] Starting from scratch rather than rebuilding or adding to an existing village, Tecumseh was able to direct construction along lines that differed considerably from the lackadaisical and generally haphazard manner in which Indian villages were generally formed. Here he established regular lots symmetrically spaced on the north bank of the river, with several rows of good strong cabins and more temporary wegiwas to be built upon them. Beyond them and farther from the river, at opposite ends of the principal village layout, was where three very large buildings were to be situated. The first of these was, in essence, a great hotel to be called the House of Strangers, constructed of logs and bark and designed specifically for the use of the many transient Indians expected to converge here in time to come. It was situated on a low shelf of ground facing the river. The other two large buildings were at the opposite end of the village site, situated on high prairie ground and surrounded by more cabins and wegiwas. One of these was to be a huge building that was to be the *msi-kah-mi-qui*—a long, spacious log structure with room for at least five hundred people to assemble for general councils. Close to this was the third building, also large, though somewhat smaller than the council house. This structure, also of logs and bark, was to be Tenskwatawa's medicine lodge—a place where he could meditate as well as a veritable temple in which he would be high priest and address Indian pilgrims who came to hear his theological and sociological messages.

Shortly after the Planting Moon began, Chaubenee and Sauganash arrived

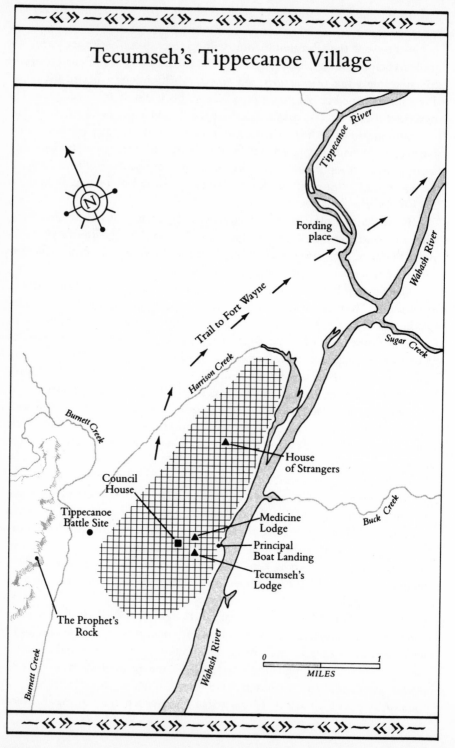

Tecumseh's Tippecanoe Village

Tippecanoe River

Fording place

Wabash River

Trail to Fort Wayne

Harrison Creek

Sugar Creek

Burnett Creek

House of Strangers

Council House

Buck Creek

Tippecanoe Battle Site

Medicine Lodge

Principal Boat Landing

Tecumseh's Lodge

The Prophet's Rock

Burnett Creek

Wabash River

0   1

MILES

from the Illinois country, bringing with them the pleasing news that by far the greater majority of the Indians they had addressed were presently very inclined toward the amalgamation and awaiting word of what they were next to do. The pair thought the new village location was excellent and were glad it was so far away from the Americans, whose proximity at Greenville had always made them very nervous. It was a warm and happy reunion of the three and they had talked of many things well into the night.

By the end of two weeks of concentrated work by practically everyone, the village was shaping up nicely and some, because of the large medicine lodge, were calling it Prophetstown, while others, the majority, simply referred to it as Tippecanoe. It had the promise of becoming a very fine village indeed.

It was late yesterday afternoon when a Fox Indian, acting as a runner, arrived with a message he said was for The Prophet from the deputy superintendent of Indian affairs at Amherstburg, William Claus. He was brought to the Shawnee brothers and told them that similar couriers had been dispatched to all the chiefs throughout the Northwest. He was himself going on to Ouiatenon as soon as he left here. All were being invited to come immediately to Amherstburg to discuss the current problems with the Americans—those affecting the British as well as those affecting the Indians. Abundant supplies would be distributed to everyone and important messages from British officials would be delivered in respect to the military and political situation. Claus had been particularly desirous of Tenskwatawa's presence, the runner said.

"Tenskwatawa will not be leaving here," Tecumseh told the Fox messenger, "but I will come with a few of my people. We thank you for the words you have brought. Food and bed will be furnished to you, that you may have a full belly and rest before continuing to Ouiatenon. I and those who will accompany me will leave in the morning."

Tenskwatawa was at first very upset that he was not to be included in the trip to Amherstburg, but Tecumseh convinced him how important it was that he remain here, not only to oversee the continuing construction of the village, but because it was crucial he be on hand as new Indians arrived here to see The Prophet. Tecumseh sat for long hours after that with Tenskwatawa, giving him instructions on what was to be his first important mission from this place: once the village was near completion, Tenskwatawa was to frame a conciliatory message which he was to send by special delegation on the 175-mile trip down the Wabash to Vincennes. The message was to be for Governor William Henry Harrison and its primary purpose was to assuage any fears he and the other whites might have concerning the establishment of the new village and its purpose. In his message, Tenskwatawa was to be in no way insulting or haughty. It was not yet time to offend this great enemy in any way. Tenskwatawa promised to do as Tecumseh directed.

In the forenoon of this eighteenth day of the Planting Moon, Tecumseh, Chaubenee, Sauganash, and three husky young warriors mounted their horses and headed away. They had hardly gone a quarter-mile beyond the current limits of the village when they abruptly reined up as a group of a dozen Indians came into sight on the trail ahead. The six waited and as the riders drew nearer Tecumseh recognized them as some chiefs of the Delawares and Miamis who, during councils, had been especially vocal in their opposition to his plan. As they drew their horses to a stop some twenty feet away he greeted them without warmth and asked what they wanted.

"We have come to see Tenskwatawa," one of them replied.

"He was ordered by Michikiniqua," put in another, "not to try to put down his roots anywhere on the Wabash. Word came to us that he had and now," he tilted his head toward the village, "we see that he has. We are here to tell him he cannot stay."

"You will speak to me, not to him," Tecumseh told them, his words clipped and brittle. "I am in charge here. I selected the spot where this village would be, at the invitation of our friends, the Potawatomies, whose country this is. Turn your horses around and leave."

"How do you dare—"

Tecumseh cut him off with a harsh exclamation. "Dogs! Cowards! Those who love the Americans and sell them Indian lands are not welcome here. Return to Michikiniqua and tell him to send no more of the likes of you to us." He rested his hand lightly on the war club in his belt and his narrowed eyes were dangerous as he continued. "You are very fortunate. We give you leave to return, if you do so immediately. If any more come here who are of your mind, their widows and orphans will mourn. Get away from here now while you are still able to do so. *Go!*"

Their expressions tight with anger, the chiefs wheeled about and put their horses into a gallop and were quickly lost behind the trees in the direction from which they had come. Tecumseh turned and looked at his companions and saw that their hands, too, were on their weapons. His features softened and then he smiled, shaking his head ruefully.

"With rabbits like that leading them, little wonder we have not drawn more of their tribes into our fold. They will not come back, nor will any others appear here from them. Let's move on."

He chirped his horse into movement and his five companions, themselves smiling now and more relaxed, fell in with him. Chaubenee and Sauganash on either side, the three warriors slightly behind. Sauganash turned his head and gave Tecumseh a long, speculative look. When Tecumseh glanced at him he posed the question that was on his mind.

"What would we have done, Tecumseh, if they had defied you and tried to enter the village?"

"We would then," Tecumseh replied in a matter of fact manner, "have found it necessary to go a little distance out of our way, to Fort Wayne, in order to deliver their bodies to Michikiniqua."

A short time later the six paused to look back at the construction continuing on the new Indian capital called Tippecanoe, well behind and slightly below them. After a moment they turned and resumed their 200-mile journey to Amherstburg.

Chapter 10

—《 》— All in all, Tecumseh was quite pleased with the way matters were progressing with the whites, both British and Americans. His own meetings with ranking British officials in Amherstburg had produced some unexpectedly good results and he was more than gratified at the way Tenskwatawa had handled himself in regard to William Henry Harrison at Vincennes. The important thing now was to continue to improve the advantages that had been gained.

On his arrival at Amherstburg on June 8 with Chaubenee, Sauganash, and the three warriors from Tippecanoe, he had been impressed to find some fifteen hundred chiefs and warriors from all over the Northwest assembled here already and more had arrived after him. He had met immediately with old Matthew Elliott, who was delighted to see him again. Elliott had a very fine home called The Point, which was located a mile down the east bank of the Detroit River from Amherstburg and Fort Malden. The agent explained that his superior, William Claus, the deputy Indian supervisor, was not presently at Amherstburg but due momentarily. He invited Tecumseh to stay with him while he was to be at Amherstburg and Tecumseh politely declined, saying that he could not sleep indoors in a bed while his companions were camping outside. Elliott agreed, but then suggested that Tecumseh and his four men, instead of camping out of doors, use the nice dry comfortable loft over the granary on his property and to this Tecumseh assented. He and his companions also ate numerous times at the sumptuous table set by Elliott's wife.

During this interval Tecumseh also visited at Simon Girty's farm, along with a Huron named Split Log, who was an old friend of Girty's. They found the fifty-seven-year-old man, who had been such a fierce fighter in previous times, to be rapidly losing his eyesight and no longer the athletic and powerful woodsman he once had been. These days Girty took his greatest enjoyment in excessive drinking, his faithful old horse almost every day carrying him the few miles into Amherstburg to his favorite tavern and every evening bringing him home while his inebriated owner dozed in the saddle.

Claus arrived on June 11 and Tecumseh immediately went into conference with him. The Indian supervisor had evidently been briefed that Tecumseh was the head of a new, powerful, and rapidly growing coalition of tribes that appeared to be stronger and more widespread than any such organization had been in the past. With this strongly in mind, Claus showed considerable deference to him. The very fact that, before meeting with any others of the multitude of chiefs on hand, he spent three full hours with Tecumseh, was clear indication of the extent to which the Shawnee's influence had expanded and added that much more to Tecumseh's prestige by giving him such preferential treatment.

Among the first things Tecumseh made clear was that he would not participate in any councils that included Catahecassa, who was on hand with many of his people, or Michikiniqua or, for that matter, any other chief who was supporting the American presence in their lands. Such chiefs and their followers, he said in a very imperious manner, he considered to be American dogs.[560] This strong and immediate display of anti-Americanism pleased Claus highly and made him determined that Tecumseh should meet and talk with Sir James Craig's Upper Canadian deputy governor-general, Francis Gore, who would be arriving here to personally address the Indians in about a month.

In their private conversations, Claus admitted to Tecumseh that it was altogether likely that within the next two or three years the British would again be at war with the Americans. In such an event, one of the key regions of the contest would be the Northwest. In this respect it was most important for Tecumseh to meet and talk with General Gore. Tecumseh agreed to wait but said he would not stay at Elliott's place for that length of time, nor even in Amherstburg. The majority of the Indians who had gathered were across the river in Michigan and that was where Tecumseh planned to camp and spend this interval talking to the various Indian leaders and turning as many as possible that were remaining aloof and neutral toward support of his amalgamation.

This was what he had done, he and his few men, along with Stiahta, who had now joined them, staying in a wegiwa provided for him by Chief Walk in the Water of the Wyandots. The quarters were in the village of Maguaga, which was not very far upstream from the large Wyandot village and old French settlement of Brownstown, which was itself on the west bank of the river close to the upper end of Grosse Island. In the month that followed, hardly an hour of any day passed when Tecumseh was not speaking earnestly to individual chiefs or small groups of them or addressing various small councils that were called to which warriors as well as chiefs were invited. What he discovered was that while a fair percentage of the Indians did not want to associate at all with the pro-American faction primarily under Catahecassa, Michikiniqua, and Tarhe, yet neither were they willing to wholly commit themselves to support of Tecumseh's plan. Foremost among these hold-offs were the Hurons and their Wyandot branch who were adopting a wait-and-see attitude. Tecumseh felt confident that when the time came and they fully realized the strength and size of his amalgamation, they would throw aside their neutrality and join him.

Immediately upon his arrival at Amherstburg, Francis Gore was informed about Tecumseh, including the suspicion now so strong among the British agents here that, while it was The Prophet they had been hearing so much about and whom they had assumed was the power among the Northwestern Indians, evidently it was Tecumseh, who was so much more a commanding figure and leader, who was really the one in charge. Gore determined to meet privately with him immediately following his talk.

The council with the tribes, held on the broad council grounds adjacent to Fort Malden, commenced on the eleventh day of the Heat Moon. It was a trick, the deputy governor-general privately said to Elliott, to get Indians to commit themselves to alliance in a war that might not even occur and, if it did, was still several years away, while at the same time attempting to keep any American spies present from returning to their leaders with word that the British were preparing for such a war.

"I am sure, my children," Gore told them, while Elliott interpreted, "that it is quite unnecessary for me to call to your remembrance the faithful assurance with which the king, your father, has so uniformly complied with all his engagements and promises made to your forefathers and yourselves in former times. Nothing is required of you in return for your great father's benevolence and religious regard to his promises but a renewal and faithful observance of the engagements made by your ancestors and yourselves. I will not offend you by entertaining the smallest doubt of your readiness on all occasions, when called upon, to prove your affectionate attachment for the king, your great father. I came not to invite you to take up the hatchet, but I wish to put you on your guard against any attempt that may be made by any enemy to disturb the peace of your country."

That set the tenor for the remainder of his talk, which was a multitude of words signifying virtually nothing. Tecumseh was contemptuous with the lack of commitment in the talk and with the manner in which the deputy governor-general walked a thin edge between rejecting the Indians and embracing them. So pronounced was their disappointment in the talk they had waited so long to hear that were it not for the presents so lavishly distributed to those in attendance, there could well have been difficulty.

Immediately upon adjournment of the general council, Gore sent for Tecumseh and they had their private talk. Pompous though Gore may have been, he was no fool and quickly discovered that here before him was no savage one step up from barbarism, who would smilingly accept mealy-mouthed utterances so long as they were accompanied by liquor or a gift. Having been apprised of the current size of Tecumseh's coalition of tribes and its constantly growing potential, as well as its far-reaching aspects, not only in the Northwest but in virtually all directions, Gore was keenly desirous of privately engaging Tecumseh in an alliance with the British. But, while Tecumseh concurred in Gore's assessment that the Americans were a great threat to both the British and the Indians, he was not willing to commit himself and his people to any such alliance. Not yet, at any rate. With disconcerting directness he told the deputy governor-general that he did not trust the British and this distrust was reinforced when officials like Gore attempted to make the Indians believe the British had always lived up to their promises. He reminded Gore how, at the Battle of Fallen Timbers, the British had broken their promises and turned their backs on their Indian allies when they were in their greatest distress and imploring Major Campbell at Fort Miamis to help them or at least provide refuge. Both had been refused and, as a result, many fine chiefs and warriors had died—including Tecumseh's own brother Sauwaseekau—who might be alive this day if the British had lived up to their promises. With such a record behind them, was it any wonder Tecumseh did not trust them as allies?

As their talk continued, however, the chill between them dissipated and at length, for the first time to any white person, Tecumseh revealed the incredible scope of the coalition of tribes he was amalgamating and what their objective would be insofar as the Americans were concerned. For these reasons, Tecumseh had gone on, unless the British were willing to commit themselves in a very significant manner to him and his people in respect to arms, ammunition, artillery, food, clothing, and other supplies in abundance, as well as a strong army of soldiers, he would hold his Indians apart and uninvolved in any forthcoming dispute between the British and Americans.

Impressed by the ultimatum and fascinated by this, the most commanding and powerful Indian leader he had ever encountered, Gore realized more than ever the importance of having Tecumseh in his stable, so to speak. At the same time, he knew he could not possibly commit the government to such demands. However, he felt strongly that there was the good possibility, in view of Tecumseh's hatred for the Americans and his desire to recover what they had taken from his people, that by concerted wooing of Tecumseh and The Prophet with frequent and abundant gifts of necessaries from the British larder, they could be brought into alignment for the Crown when the war ultimately broke out, as he was sure it would. To this end he did commit the British government to send to Tippecanoe at once, and at intervals thereafter, generous supplies of food and ammunition.

Before leaving for Tippecanoe the third week in July, Tecumseh had a final meeting with Gore, who shook his hand warmly and Tecumseh reiterated his stance a final time in respect to the growing friction between the British and Americans.

"Our intention," he said, "is not to take part in such quarrels. However, if the Americans encroach further on our lands, we are resolved to strike. If at such time the king should be in earnest and appear in sufficient strength, we will hold fast to him."

Now Tecumseh, having left Chaubenee and Sauganash in Michigan to continue visiting various chiefs with his message on their way home, had returned to Tippecanoe and was more than pleased with what he found. Some forty cabins had been built in his absence and there were twice that many wegiwas and a large number of quonsets and tepees. Tenskwatawa's medicine lodge had been completed and both the House of Strangers and the *msi-kah-mi-qui* were nearing that point. New arrivals of Indians had increased the resident population from just over four hundred when he left to near six hundred now, plus the constant coming and going of transients who had made the pilgrimage to hear The Prophet speak and gravely listen to his predictions.

He was especially proud of Tenskwatawa in the way he had carried out the directions for contact with William Henry Harrison at Vincennes. As instructed, not long after Tecumseh's departure for Amherstburg, Tenskwatawa had sent a carefully coached delegation down the Wabash to Vincennes, where his message had been delivered to the Indiana Territory governor.

In essence the message from Tenskwatawa, if not actually obsequious then certainly ironic, said: My followers and I have moved our village to near the mouth of the Tippecanoe so as to no longer disrupt the good citizens of Greenville and, equally, to be closer to Governor Harrison as a demonstration not only of our pacific nature but also to enjoy the benefits of his protection; that despite what malicious songs about them may have been sung in the governor's ear by some bad birds, their wish was only for peace and serenity and the opportunity to worship Moneto as Indian tradition dictated and not disturb any whites in the process of doing so; that he had communed with the Great Spirit, who had specifically instructed him not to raise the tomahawk against the Americans, but instead to mind their own business, grow their own vegetables and corn and see to the health and welfare of their women and children and ancient ones; that it was his prime desire to live in peace with Harrison and his people; that a great many travelers from far distant lands had come to hear him speak the words put into his mouth by the Great Spirit, but that there were so many of them that they were always suffering from hunger and a lack of the most necessary supplies and that they would most gratefully accept whatever provisions Harrison, in the goodness of his heart, might send to ease their suffering; that once the crop they had planted this spring could be harvested, their hunger would be abolished, but until then the hollow bellies of their people cried in anguished want; that once all the crops were doing well and there was opportunity for him to get away for a little while from his duties, he would himself come down the Wabash on a special trip just to visit the governor and assure him in person of his sincerity and good intentions.[561]

The supplies given by Harrison had helped a great deal in providing for the villagers at Tippecanoe and Tecumseh not only heartily approved of how the whole matter had been handled, he now instructed Tenskwatawa on what to say and how to act when he visited Harrison later in the summer. As for Tecumseh himself, it was time for another major trip. He was going to visit Main Poche in Illinois and perhaps Gomo as well and, when finished counciling with those Potawatomi chiefs, he would see the Kickapoos in the southern Illinois country and then cross the Mississippi to visit their brother Shawnees there and perhaps even get them to espouse his plan. After that, who knew?

Perhaps the Osages.

[January 29, 1809 — Sunday]

Outside the cabin a bitter wind whipped and shrilled, moaning as if in sympathy with the speaker, occasionally sucking great drafts of air up the chimney with a prolonged booming sound and causing the embers to flicker and dance with renewed life. The hurricane lamp on the table, set to its brightest, caused magnified shadows of the men to loom with dark malevolence against the smooth gray logs that comprised the walls.

For more than two hours Tecumseh had been addressing the men seated around the table in this cabin in Upper Sandusky. Here were a dozen of the most influential men of the Wyandot tribe, including their principal chief, Tarhe—The Crane—and they had been paying close attention to what he said. It was clear, though, from the glances they kept shooting at Tarhe, that unless Tecumseh convinced that individual, the whole effort would be pointless;

obviously, they were all, with the single exception of Stiahta, going to follow in the direction their chief indicated.

He had told them of the delegation sent at his direction by Tenskwatawa from Tippecanoe to Harrison and the good results it had brought. Then he had spoken of his visit to the Illinois tribes the previous summer and how the Potawatomies and Kickapoos had largely accepted his plan. He had gone on, he said, to visit the Osages but here had to admit he had been turned back by warriors of that tribe who were at that moment engaged in warfare with a large mixed-tribe war party from east of the Mississippi and they wanted nothing to do with those tribes in any way.

He had then, Tecumseh told them, gone on to visit the Shawnees in Missouri who had so long ago split away from the main body of the tribe, believing the Mississippi River would prove to be an impassible barrier between them and the encroaching whites. Now they were finding that the big river was no barrier after all and even though they were well isolated in their villages along Apple Creek in the Cape Girardeau area, yet whites were beginning to come into that area and claim lands—among them none other than the great frontiersman, Simon Kenton, who at one time had been sentenced to be executed right in this very town of Upper Sandusky.[562] Tecumseh said he had told his brother Shawnees there that this was history repeating itself: just as Kenton had, by claiming Kentucky lands, paved the way for the invasion of Ohio across the Spaylaywitheepi, so he was now paving the way across the Mississippi for the invasion of the Missouri country by his claiming of lands there. The Apple Creek Shawnees had finally begun to see that Tecumseh had been correct in his warnings and they were seriously counciling over whether or not they should join his struggle or flee still farther to the west. Tecumseh said he also had found that witchcraft trials were occurring among his absentee brothers—over the period of the preceding year some fifty had been accused and executed—and he prevailed upon them to stop such practices, which they had agreed to do.

As soon as he returned to his own village on the Wabash after that, Tecumseh went on, he had found that not only had Tenskwatawa's personal journey down the Wabash to visit Harrison at Vincennes gone very well, but that Tippecanoe had continued to grow in his absence, with close to eight hundred permanent residents and about that many more who were transients, from among whom many more were constantly joining him.

Because he felt it was important to know exactly how matters stood in regard to Harrison, he related to these Wyandot chiefs full details of the visit Tenskwatawa and a large crowd of his followers paid last August to Vincennes. His brother, he said, had spent two weeks there and had met with Harrison numerous times during that period. The impression Tenskwatawa had given to Harrison was that he had nothing to hide from the governor and even the

governor's Indian friends who were on hand told Harrison that the speeches
Tenskwatawa was giving to him now were no different in delivery or intent
than those he had been giving for years, and that the topic he touched upon
most often and most earnestly was the great evil that resulted both from war
and from the intemperate use of liquor. It was, Tecumseh said, during Tenskwatawa's final meeting with Harrison before returning home that he had,
with great sincerity, made this speech:

" 'Father, it is three years since I first began that system of religion which
I now practice. The white people and some of the Indians were against me,
but I had no other intention but to introduce among the Indians those good
principles of religion which the white people profess. I was spoken badly of
by the white people, who reproached me with misleading the Indians, but I
defy them to say that I did anything amiss.'

"My brother," Tecumseh went on, "then said to Harrison: 'Father, I was
told you intended to hang me. When I heard this I intended to remember it
and tell my father when I went to see him and relate the truth. I heard, when
I settled on the Wabash, that my father, the governor, had declared that all
the land between Vincennes and Fort Wayne was the property of the Seventeen
Fires. I also heard that you wanted to know, my father, whether I was God
or man, and that you said if I was the former, I should not steal horses. I
heard this from Mr. Wells, but I believe it originated with himself.'

"Then," Tecumseh went on, "my brother then told him: 'The Great
Spirit told me to tell the Indians that he had made them and made the world;
that he had placed them on it to do good and not evil. I told all the redskins
that the way they were in was not good and that they ought to abandon it;
that we ought to consider ourselves as one man, but we ought to live agreeably
to our several customs, the red people after their mode and the white people
after theirs; particularly that the red people should not drink whiskey, that it
was not made for them but for the white people who knew how to use it and
that it is the cause of all the mischiefs which the Indians suffer, and that they
must follow the directions of the Moneto and we must listen to Him, as it
was He that made us; determine to listen to nothing that is bad; do not take
up the tomahawk, should it be offered by the British or by the *Shemanese;* do
not meddle with anything that does not belong to you, but mind your business
and cultivate the ground, that your women and children may have enough to
live on.'

"Tenskwatawa then told him," Tecumseh continued, "these things: 'I
now inform you that it is our intention to live in peace with our father and
his people forever. My father, I have informed you what we mean to do, and
I call the Great Spirit to witness the truth of my declaration. The religion
which I have established for the last three years has been attended by all the
different tribes of Indians in this part of the world. Those Indians were once

495

different people; they are now but one; they are all determined to practice what I have communicated to them, that has come immediately from the Great Spirit through me.

" 'Brother, I speak to you as a warrior. You are one. But let us lay aside this character and attend to the care of our children, that they may live in comfort and peace. We desire that you will join us for the preservation of both red and white people. Formerly, when we lived in ignorance, we were foolish, but now, since we listen to the Great Spirit, we are happy.'

"My brother then finished this talk with Harrison," Tecumseh said, "by saying to him: 'I have listened to what you have said to us. You have promised to assist us. I now request you, in behalf of all the red people, to use your exertions to prevent the sale of liquor to us. We are all well pleased to hear you say that you will endeavor to promote our happiness. We give you every assurance that we will follow the dictates of the Great Spirit. We are also pleased with the attention you have shown us. Also with the good intentions of our father the president. If you give us a few articles, such as needles, flints, hoes, gunpowder, and the like, we will take the animals that afford us meat with powder and ball.'

"Those were the things, brothers," Tecumseh said, "that my brother, Tenskwatawa told to Governor Harrison, who was very impressed with what he said and provided him with all those things he asked for and more.[563] Why then should it be that if his words can soothe the mind of our greatest enemy, yet they seem to have no power to move you? Why is it you should be content to live at the whim of another race who, if and when they wish it, will wipe you away as if you are but a fly buzzing before one's face? Do you not remember what you once had? Do you not recall your pride? Do you not remember that your fathers gave their lives for these lands and are here buried? Here is an oppportunity to bring back what was, to live again as men and to be able to look into your own eyes in the mirror-glass without shame. Why, then, do you not take it? Why do you so strongly oppose us, your own people, who wish only for you what is good and just, and cling to those who would and will destroy you?"

Tecumseh looked at the men sitting silently at the table and he seemed to deflate a little, as if some elemental hope had just wheezed away. He sighed and concluded his long talk as he had concluded other talks to chiefs of other tribes:

"There is game in plenty around our Tippecanoe village. There is room for all and more. There are rich fields for the growing of corn and vegetables and the streams are filled with fish. We live again as our fathers and theirs before them lived, free from the influence of the whites. Will you not come live with us as Indians, where the good of one is the good of all?"

What he did not tell them was that last summer's corn crop at Tippecanoe had largely failed, primarily because everyone was so busy listening to the preachings of Tenskwatawa and visiting among themselves, with no one want-ing to do the work. Besides, the packhorse loads of supplies Harrison had sent to Tippecanoe created the impression of there being no real necessity for the hard work of farming if food was there for the asking. But there were a great many mouths to feed and the food Harrison sent was soon depleted and no more forthcoming. Because of a particularly cold and snowy winter, game was scarce everywhere and so famine struck hard at Tippecanoe and a large number of Ottawas and Chippewas began drifting away to their home villages with the comment that maybe they would return to Tippecanoe . . . but maybe not. These were matters Tecumseh did not mention because he con-sidered them temporary concerns that would pass when a little more attention was paid to them.

Nor did he tell them of the subtle changes that had taken place in Tens-kwatawa himself—changes Tecumseh sensed that nagged at him a little, yet which he more or less pushed aside as being of minor importance. In point of fact, they were not at all unimportant. In Tenskwatawa's eyes, Tecumseh was still a great leader, a great war chief, personifying for other Indians a wide range of admirable characteristics. But in The Prophet's eyes, his brother was no longer quite the *absolute* leader Tenskwatawa had long considered him to be. Who was it, he asked himself, that these people came to the Prophet's Town to see and hear? Who was it who gave them a strong religion? Who was it who kept them from the vices of theft and drunkenness and promiscuity with whites? Who was it who foretold for them the future? Yes! It was Tens-kwatawa, not Tecumseh. Let his elder brother, if he wished, continue to believe that The Prophet was his man, controlled and ordered by him. Let Tecumseh continue to give the prophecies for him to pass on to their people; were not these prophecies merely verification of the events he had already foreseen in his own mind? He was indeed the greatest Prophet ever known to the Indians and he would, in time, lead his people to the restoration of all that they had lost at the hands of the whites. Tecumseh was right—they did not need the British to help them. They would overcome by themselves and, when the time came, they would know that it was The Prophet, not his brother, who was the guiding and redeeming factor for all the Indians. Tenskwatawa needed the help of no man. He was supreme, invincible, second only to Moneto Himself. *He was The Prophet!*

These, however, were matters within the mind of Tenskwatawa and Tecumseh was largely ignorant of them, involved as he was in the rigors of trying to reach and sway those who continued to balk at joining him in his great dream of a unified Indian nation; just as he was trying to reach and sway these dozen men before him who controlled their tribe.

Those at the table remained silent for a long while when Tecumseh fin-ished talking. At length Tarhe, staring at the lamp on the table and not looking at Tecumseh, began to speak, but his words were directed at the other chiefs, not to Tecumseh.

"Beware," he said, "of the dreams that this man places in your mind with his words. I tell you that Tecumseh and his brother, who calls himself The Prophet, wish only to lure you to their village for their own purposes. I say we must wait and see. *If* things are as Tecumseh says they are at Tippecanoe, and we learn of this from others, then we may consider joining them there. But for now our place is here."

Stiahta caught Tecumseh's eye and gave a negligible shake of his head and in that instant Tecumseh knew that it was quite likely that for so long as Tarhe was their principal chief, the Wyandots would not join him.

[July 13, 1809 — Thursday]

The smell of war was in the air.

Day by day the signs of its approach had been increasing, and Tecumseh was hard pressed to prevent the Indians from leaping into a premature renewal of hostilities against the Americans.

Just after his failure to convince Tarhe's Wyandots to join his own people at Tippecanoe, Tecumseh returned home to find a mixed blessing. An epidemic had struck in his absence and many of his followers had died. Most affected had been the Ottawas and Chippewas, who placed the blame on Tecumseh and a large portion of them gathered up their things and returned to their own Michigan villages. Tecumseh was sorry to see them go, but was sure they would come back and, in the meanwhile, their leaving had helped ease the critical food shortage.

On the heels of that he received word that the Sacs, Foxes, and Kickapoos in the Illinois country had become sharply concerned over the sudden increase of whites in their land. A new fort—Fort Madison—had been built on the *west* bank of the Mississippi in Iowa country, in the territory of the Sacs, Foxes, and Ioways, and already the Sacs were sniping at it at intervals from under cover.[564] Accompanied by Sauganash, who had now become his personal aide and secretary, Tecumseh rushed there and went into immediate council with the Sacs in their principal village of Saukenuk at the mouth of the Rock River. They must, he told them, restrain themselves and have patience; if one or two or a handful of tribes attacked the Americans before the appointed time, it could only result in disaster for the tribes involved and for the grand plan in general. If necessary, they must hold their anger and their pride in check and turn the other cheek, devoting themselves to keeping their entire energies in reserve for that great wave of retaliation from the Indian amalgamation that would drive the whites forever from their lands. Grudgingly, the Sacs agreed to try to cool the tempers of their young warriors, but warned that they might not be successful.

Tecumseh and Sauganash moved eastward from there and visited Chaubenee, finding him just on the verge of heading out to recruit in the villages along the west shore of Lake Michigan all the way up to Green Bay, primarily Potawatomies in the lower area and Winnebagoes farther north. They spent a good bit of time in the village of Black Partridge, close to Chicago, and visited briefly with their old trader friend John Kinzie. He had now set up a substantial trading post there, having purchased and improved the post that was first established by DuSable. Chicago itself had grown much, spreading out around Fort Dearborn. There they were joined by one of Chaubenee's most reliable converts to Tecumseh's cause, Chechepinqua, a halfbreed like Sauganash, his father a Scot and his mother Ottawa, and who was known among the whites as Alexander Robinson. Several councils were held in Black Partridge's Town and a few other villages in the area, but their visit was kept secret from the whites.

At what had been Milwackie and was now being called Milwaukee, they held very successful councils with the younger Siggenauk, who was now chief and had become very influential in the area and who, unlike his father, the elder Siggenauk, despised the Americans and yearned for the time when Tecumseh would give the word for Chicago and Fort Dearborn to be attacked.

By the time they reached Green Bay, half a hundred new recruits had already been sent on their way to Tippecanoe. There were dozens of Winnebago villages in the area of Green Bay, Lake Winnebago and the Fox River here, but what plans the four had for addressing councils were interrupted when a mounted messenger brought news to Tecumseh of a very serious nature. His own brother, Tenskwatawa, was engaging in war talk with the Indians gathered under him at Tippecanoe, actively urging that they strike Vincennes in force and destroy it. As a result of this, some of the Indians already at Tippecanoe—especially Ottawas, Chippewas and Potawatomies— were becoming alarmed and returning to their own villages, while other tribes and individuals who had been on the verge of joining the Tippecanoe assemblage were holding off. So far had Tenskwatawa carried his plan that some five hundred of the more bellicose Tippecanoe Indians had descended the Wabash in canoes and set up a camp within fifty miles of Vincennes. From that point they were spying on Harrison to see if the time was propitious to launch an attack. Furious, Tecumseh left Chaubenee and Chechepinqua to carry on the work and he and Sauganash had returned to Tippecanoe with all haste.

Tecumseh was dismayed when he saw Tenskwatawa and the changes that had come over his little brother. The Prophet walked now with a pompous strut, wore furs and feathers and frills that set him apart, painted his face and body and limbs in grotesque ways and had removed the black patch that covered his empty eye socket and placed into the hole a round white stone upon which had been painted a hideous glaring eye. Tecumseh saw at once how those of the village tended to avoid his younger brother and he sensed their fear. When he demanded to know what was going on, Tenskwatawa merely smiled in a peculiar manner and explained that the superstitions of the people went deep, that they expected their Prophet to be different, not as one of them, and that what Tecumseh saw in them as fear was a respectful awe, which was to be anticipated of those who were in the presence of one whom they believed to be the chosen of the Great Spirit.

At once Tecumseh went into private council with Tenskwatawa, casti- gating him for his ambition, ordering him to get rid of his flamboyant cos- tuming and imperious manner, warning him to follow orders or he would soon be answering to Tecumseh himself in a manner he would not find pleas- ant.

The current problem was compounded when it was learned that William Wells had also received detailed reports from his spies about Tenskwatawa's war preparations and utterances. Wells had immediately sent word to Governor Harrison that, according to the reports he had received, The Prophet had required the Indians at Tippecanoe to take up arms against the government, not only to exterminate Vincennes but also the settlements along the Ohio River. The Prophet, Wells had gone on in his report, was telling his followers that this was the order of the Great Spirit, who threatened destruction to those who disobeyed.

Tecumseh had instantly sent runners to the five hundred camped far down the Wabash with orders to return to Tippecanoe at once, which they did, their own spies having just returned from Vincennes with word that Harrison had gotten wind of what was occurring and had organized two companies of volunteer militia, now garrisoned at Fort Knox, just three miles above Vin- cennes.

The principal reason for all this unrest was because of the newest land acquisition Harrison had pulled off during the spring. At that time he had met in Greenville with a select few peaceable chiefs of the Miami tribe and its Eel River branch, along with a handful of Delawares and Potawatomies.[565] Not surprisingly, Winnemac had played a major role in choreographing the entire thing. For what could only be described as a token payment—$7,000 worth of goods and an annuity of $1,750—Harrison had gotten them to make their marks on a treaty which irrevocably transferred to the United States a three- million-acre tract of land lying east of the Wabash River—land upon which more than half a dozen tribes were presently living, a tract which began at a point twenty-one miles north of Vincennes and extended north and west, with its northern boundary hardly more than a few miles from Tippecanoe, then moved southeastward three-fourths of the way across the Indiana country.

At the finalizing treaty council in Fort Wayne, Harrison had called out, asking if all the Indians were present who were considered to have any claim on this land. He had been assured they were. Even though not true—and he knew it wasn't—the Fort Wayne Treaty was nevertheless signed and another great chunk of land was gobbled up by the United States.[566]

This latest land deal greatly angered Tecumseh but it also worked to his advantage. The land Harrison had gotten was the home of a great many Miamis and Delawares who had not as yet espoused Tecumseh's cause and who had felt safe where they were located. Now, generally without their knowledge or participation, their lands had been sold out from under them and they realized only too well that what Tecumseh had been saying all along was true and so they now moved to Tippecanoe.

Tecumseh, too, was greatly angered at Harrison's move and he planned to call the governor to account for it, but not yet; the time was not propitious for him to make an issue of it. In fact, it was more important now to allay as much as possible the governor's suspicions that an uprising was forming. To this end, Tecumseh ordered his brother to go down to Vincennes with a small party and convince Harrison that his fears were misdirected.

Tenskwatawa, along with forty of his men, paddled down to Vincennes under a flag of truce and there he and Harrison conferred at length, this time Harrison stern and gruff and Tenskwatawa meekly denying that he or Tecumseh had any part in the suspected plan. Following the instructions Tecumseh had given him at their village, Tenskwatawa claimed that the plot was entirely confined to the tribes of the Mississippi and Illinois rivers and that it was he, The Prophet, who had made his influence known and prevailed upon them to put aside their warlike ideas. Harrison was not convinced.[567]

Somehow, open conflict had been avoided, but suspicion continued to be the watchword. The United States, under its new president, James Madison, continued to be suspicious of the British, Harrison continued to be suspicious of Tecumseh and Tenskwatawa, many Indian chiefs continued to be suspicious of the amalgamation of tribes, Tecumseh continued to be suspicious of growing insubordination in his brother, the settlers everywhere continued to be suspicious of all Indians, and Tenskwatawa continued to be suspicious of everything and everybody.

Tecumseh was deeply disappointed in what Tenskwatawa had been doing in his recent absences, realizing that his younger brother had done far more to alienate the tribes of the Northwest than to assist in drawing them into the amalgamation. His talk of an attack on Vincennes and the wrath of the Great Spirit to descend upon those who did not join in this enterprise had sent a very real stab of apprehension through all these tribes. It was a maddening development that would now require Tecumseh to once again visit those who

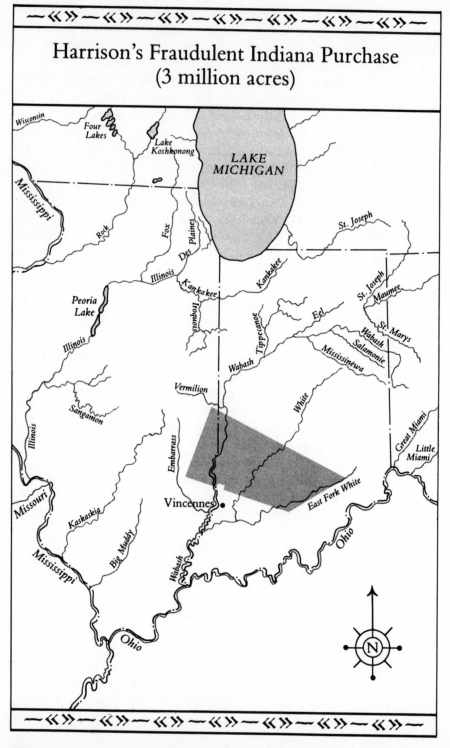

Harrison's Fraudulent Indiana Purchase
(3 million acres)

had bolted and attempt to convince them that they had truly misconstrued what was occurring.

[December 31, 1809 — Sunday]

Tecumseh!

The name was spoken in fearful whispers and bold cries. It spread across the land, through the forests and prairies, on the lakes and rivers, in wegiwas and quonsets and tepees. It was repeated in log cabins and brick mansions, in open-air councils and echoing legislative halls. It brought hope and it brought fright; it evoked anger and inspired devotion. It was on the tongues of a vast multitude who had never seen him nor heard him speak and it was on the tongues of an incredible number who had. Never before had an Indian of any tribe been so well known, or an Indian so well known, actually so little known.

Tecumseh! A warrior. Not even a chief. A man, but not an ordinary man: one with a vision, a dream, and a voice—a voice that could touch the masses powerfully, a voice that caused hearts to swell with pride, that filled bodies with dignity and minds with determination, a voice that instilled into cowed Indians the wonder and glory of restored belief in themselves.

Tecumseh! He was everywhere and nowhere: a wraith, a phantom presence, appearing, then gone, only to appear somewhere else. From the vast pine forests of Minnesota to the misted blue slopes of Tennessee, from the head of the St. Lawrence to the mouth of the Ohio, from cloaking hardwood forests of the Susquehanna to grassy hills of middle Missouri, they knew him.

Tecumseh! Wherever he spoke, large crowds assembled to listen. He did not shout, yet his strong words carried well to every ear. He did not coax or wheedle or beseech; he explained and he reasoned. He gave them his vision, his dream of one people, *Indians,* united in a bond that no outside power could rend asunder and before which all enemies would quail. He did not threaten nor coerce nor demand; he illustrated—sketching in verbal pictures the irresistible encroachment of the whites.

Tecumseh!

This is what he told them: that the first white man came with timid contact and fawning obedience and great desire for nothing more than to be of help, often in the form of benevolent men in flowing black robes or unsmiling men in dark clothing with white collars, sometimes in the form of sturdy men whose eyes saw great distances ahead and who wished no more than to cross that mountain or follow this river; then came the men with sun-darkened skin, carrying gifts of marvelous things we red men never had, which they would trade for the furs of the animals given so abundantly by the Moneto to His red children, and soon the animals were no longer so plentiful and the men with sun-darkened skins would move on; then would come the men whose skins had seen little sun and who had eyes that squinted and could not look directly into the eyes of another, men who marked this tree and that rock and this creek and that river and who made many marks on white paper, and these men brought even greater gifts to us and the promise of more, in exchange for just a little piece of land here and another little piece there, and for all these wonderful things they held in promise, all that was necessary was to make a mark on a piece of paper; then would come the flood of men of all kinds, bringing with them large families of women and children and dreams somehow always bigger than capabilities, and these men said that a tiny piece of the small piece of land belonged to them and they could do with it as they wished and so they cut down its forests and burned its grasses and ripped open its belly with great heavy blades drawn by powerful oxen; and when these little pieces of land—no longer places where we Indians could roam and hunt and fish as we always had—were filled with the white people and dotted with the ugly log houses in the midst of the devastation they had created, then again would come the men in robes and the farseeing men and the sun-darkened men with gifts and the men with papers to be marked and they all moved deeper and deeper into the land; and then, when it was enough and there should be no more and we Indians turned them back, then came the men who all dressed in the same clothes and who all moved at the same time to the same drumbeat and who all had harsh cold eyes and long cold swords and hard cold hearts and what they could not get by trade or by gifts or by treaty, they then took by blood, killing our men and taking away our women and our children and desecrating the graves of our fathers and letting their herds of animals eat what the wild animals needed, so there were no more of them left when it was time to hunt them and feed our families; and fences barred our way and fish could no longer swim up our streams and lay their eggs, for their way was barred by dams the whites had built to run the wheels of their mills and grind their flour; and when the little war would be over, it would be of no matter who won or who lost, for it always became such that the boundary between white man and red was invariably farther toward the setting sun; and always they promised—*and promise still!*—they are friends who wished only peace. Yes, we killed them, but for each who fell there were two or three or ten or one hundred who appeared to take his place and the lone warrior or the lone village or the lone tribe could not stem them; and even when two or three or five or ten tribes came together to try to hold them back, they were not enough. Yes, the tribes have warred against one another and there are great hurts that go back to times that none of us can remember, though we still war with one another over them; and this, brothers, is our weakness. Knowing our weakness, we know as well the seeds of our strength, for each of us is such a seed and our strength is all of us together, as one, for only in this way can we turn aside, turn away, stop and drive back the white flood that will forever drown us if we do not. It can be done! It should be done! Brothers, *it must be done!* This—and much more—is what Tecumseh told them.

Most were convinced; some were not. Many came with him; many more did not, but of those who did not, most stood ready to come when the sign eventually appeared that he told them would come. Many others—those who had stood aloof as a disguise for their fear—would come flocking along, once it all began, to reap the benefits of what they had let others construct for them.

Tecumseh had returned to Tippecanoe a short time ago, gratified to learn that not only had this year's harvest of corn been exceptionally good, a large shipment of much-needed British goods from Amherstburg had just been delivered in secrecy by special agents of the Crown. With the agents had come the Sac chief, Elk Hawk, bearing in even greater secrecy a wampum belt and speech from the British which he delivered in private to the brothers. It said:

> *Brothers. You will keep all your people that you now have with you in readiness. Your Great Father who lives over the great waters is about quarreling with the Big Knives. You will collect as many Indians from the westward of your country as you possibly can. You will tell the Big Knives that you and your people are inclined for peace, that you don't wish for war; and should the Big Knives ask you to council, go and council with them, but by all means collect as many Indians as you possibly can at your town, and I shall always communicate to you the words of your Great Father who lives on the other side of the great waters. If you are in want of anything, come here and all your wants will be supplied. Your brothers, the Sakies [Sacs] cannot come and live with you; it is too far and it is better that they should remain on the Mississippi, where they will have enough to do in case of a war between your British Father and the Big Knives.*

Tecumseh was greatly pleased with the message. Thus far, at least, Gore was honoring the promises he had made at Amherstburg. It was a good start.

Tecumseh also found that his disciplining of Tenskwatawa for his rash actions early in the summer had brought some good results. William Wells was having bad times; his wife, Wanagapeth, had died, and he himself, though still evidently serving as a spy for Harrison, had been replaced at Fort Wayne as Indian agent by his political opponent and bitter enemy, John Johnston, an immigrant from Ireland. Tenskwatawa, taking advantage of the situation, had journeyed to Fort Wayne with several horses stolen from the whites, which he turned over to the new Indian agent, telling him that they had been brought to Tippecanoe by hostile Indians and had been confiscated by him and were now being returned with apologies. At the same time he told Johnston that the reports Wells had made of a supposed uprising had been lies told merely for the purpose of stirring up trouble. Johnston had been impressed with Tenskwatawa's apparent sincerity and told Governor Harrison this in his report.

Now, at year's end, Tecumseh had time for a brief rest before once again he would set out for the Illinois country with Sauganash to confer with Chaubenee and, with them, to put more words, fresh words, strong words into the ears of those who controlled so many others but who would still not commit themselves and their people to what they had yet to realize remained their final hope.

Before he would embark on this next journey, however, there were important things to be done. He summoned Tenskwatawa and talked to him at length, giving him a number of very strict orders that his brother was warned to obey to the letter. Foremost among these was the preparation of what he was to designate as sacred slabs.

Tecumseh opened one of two sealed bales he had brought back with him on a packhorse from his last trip and showed Tenskwatawa the contents— fifty slats of red cedar wood, each of them thirteen and one-half inches long and three-eighths of an inch thick, one inch wide at the base and tapering to one-half inch wide at the rounded top. Tenskwatawa was to retire into abolute seclusion with these pieces of wood and carve each into a replica of the sacred slab he now showed his brother that had already been carved into the design required. When Tenskwatawa was finished with the task, he was to assemble all the Indians, show them the slabs and tell them that he had made them under the direction of the Great Spirit. The directions for carving the sacred slabs were explicit.

Each slab was to be carved, on one side only, with the same symbols. These symbols were to have a double meaning—one to tell any curious whites who might see them, the other to be the true meaning. For the whites, these were to be described as heavenly sticks—symbols which would guide them to the happy Afterlife. The public interpretation of the symbols, reading from bottom to top were *family*, which was the most important factor in everyday Indian life, the *earth* upon which they lived, followed by the principal features of the earth: *water, lightning, trees, the four corners of the earth, corn, fowl and the animals of earth and air, all plant life, the sun, the blue sky* and all of these having to be experienced and understood before the *people* could reach the uppermost symbol, *Heaven.*

The actual meaning of this symbolism, however, was considerably different and much more menacing. It was for *all the Indians on both sides of the Mississippi River* to come in a *straight direction* toward the rendezvous point at *lightning speed* with their *weapons;* coming from *all directions,* leaving behind the *tending of corn* or *storing of grain* to become *united* when the *great sign of trembling earth* was given so that *all the tribes* might, in *one movement,* by peace-

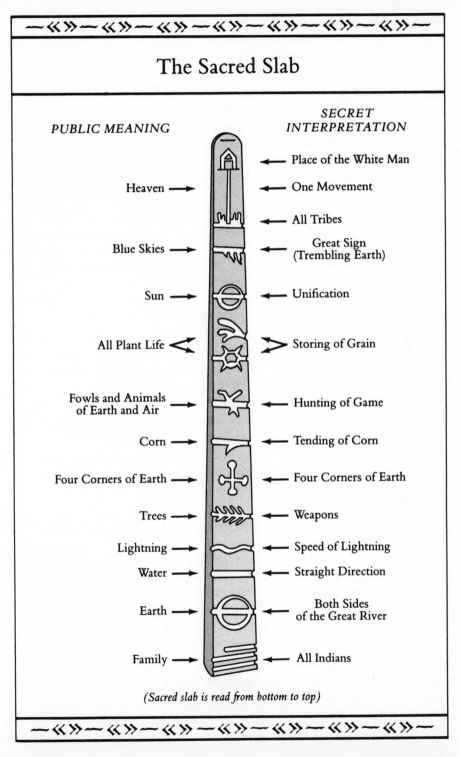

The Sacred Slab

PUBLIC MEANING		SECRET INTERPRETATION
		Place of the White Man
Heaven →		One Movement
		All Tribes
Blue Skies →		Great Sign (Trembling Earth)
Sun →		Unification
All Plant Life →		Storing of Grain
Fowls and Animals of Earth and Air →		Hunting of Game
Corn →		Tending of Corn
Four Corners of Earth →		Four Corners of Earth
Trees →		Weapons
Lightning →		Speed of Lightning
Water →		Straight Direction
Earth →		Both Sides of the Great River
Family →		All Indians

(Sacred slab is read from bottom to top)

able means if possible but by warfare if necessary, take over the *place of the whites* which had been usurped from them.[568]

The slabs, Tecumseh told Tenskwatawa, must all be finished during the next month, since they had to be delivered by runners during the Hunger Moon and each must be accompanied by a bundle of special sticks. He opened the second bale and showed Tenskwatawa the sticks stained red with vermilion—each stick a quarter-inch square and fifteen inches long, twenty-one such sticks to a bundle, each of the bundles tied with a length of rawhide tug, and fifty of these bundles.

Thirty of these bundles, each accompanied by one of the slabs, were to be delivered during the Hunger Moon to the principal chiefs of the thirty major tribes of the West, Northwest, North, Northeast, and East. The remainder, along with their slabs, would be taken by Tecumseh himself when he went to visit the Southern tribes, perhaps during this coming year but more likely in the year to follow. Each of the red sticks was to represent one moon. Each runner, as he delivered the bundle and slab entrusted to him to the specific chief, would instruct that chief as to its meaning, both public and private, and that he should, beginning with the next moon—the Wind Moon—throw away one of the sticks at each full moon until only one stick remained. Then they were to begin a nightly vigil, watching the sky for the sign of Tecumseh— the Panther Passing Across. When they observed this great celestial body sear its way across the night sky from east to west in a brilliant streak of greenish fire, they were to immediately cut the final stick into thirty pieces. Each night thereafter, one of these pieces was to be burned and when no more remained, then would come to all at the same time the great sign that Tecumseh had been telling them would occur and which they would not fail to recognize— a great and powerful trembling of the very earth itself.[569]

[June 26, 1810 — Tuesday]

Tecumseh was extremely pleased with how matters had gone at Wapakoneta and at how the influence of Catahecassa had slipped so badly in recent months that he had been unable to prevent Tecumseh from speaking his mind with great effect in the center circle of Shawnee capital village.

It had not been a formal council at Wapakoneta, but that hadn't mattered. His message had been heard loud and clear by the majority of the chiefs and villagers and it would remain with them for a long while. Now, with that distasteful business behind him, a sudden flush of exhilaration suffusing him, Tecumseh was en route with Chaubenee and Sauganash to see his old friend, the Shawnee war chief, Blue Jacket, who had sent word that he knew now that he had been wrong and that he and his followers were at last ready to throw their full weight behind Tecumseh and participate in his grand plan. Wehyehpihehrsehnwah, Tecumseh knew, would now be especially interested in hearing the details of Tecumseh's most recent activities.

The antipathy for Harrison among the tribes had continued to grow as a result of the governor's deceitful and unethical purchase of the three million acres of Indiana Territory land, but it was not confined to Harrison alone. The tribesmen were equally angry with those Indians who had participated in the treaty, especially Michikiniqua, Five Medals, and Winnemac. In the case of Michikiniqua they tended to excuse what he had done because of his ill health and the fact that he had obviously not been mentally competent. Five Medals, however, became the brunt of a great deal of criticism and Winnemac had gone into hiding on learning that he had been marked for assassination for his major role in swindling his own and neighboring tribes.

There was a rise in the number of confrontations between Indians and whites throughout the Indiana and Illinois frontier and these caused the festering friction between the races to become ever more aggravated. Tecumseh was gratified to learn that Harrison was having his hands full keeping a lid on tensions in the Vincennes area and seemed as inclined as Tecumseh himself to prevent the precipitate outbreak of hostilities.

With the coming of spring and warmer weather, the recruiting efforts of Tecumseh and his lieutenants had begun showing dividends. A constant flow of Indians of various tribes converged on Tippecanoe from all directions. Among them, from the Illinois country, was Main Poche and his Potawatomies, along with several bodies of Kickapoos from the valleys of the Sangamon and Vermilion. There was an increase in the numbers of Delawares, Potawatomies, and Miamis as well, mainly young warriors who remained incensed over what their chiefs had done at the Fort Wayne treaty and who openly declared that they considered Michikiniqua to be "contemptible beyond description." With all these new arrivals, the resident population of Tippecanoe was now approaching a thousand and the village itself extended for fully two miles along the north bank of the Wabash below the mouth of the Tippecanoe. In addition, there was a constant flow in and out of visiting parties of Indians who were still coming in large numbers, now just as much to listen to Tecumseh speak of his grand plan as to hear the preachings of Tenskwatawa. Among these, unexpectedly, were close to two hundred fifty Sacs and Foxes from northwestern Illinois and southwestern Wisconsin, who stayed at Tippecanoe for a fortnight before moving on to Amherstburg.[570]

For Tecumseh there was a certain amount of gratification that these days a very definite wave of alarm was rising among the settlers along the frontier everywhere because of him. Fear was being evinced over what this powerful Indian leader, Tecumseh, was planning to do. Waves of disturbing rumors that an Indian confederacy of unbelievable size was being molded by Tecumseh to be launched against the whites throbbed along the frontier from St. Louis to Vincennes and the new Ohio capital of Zanesville, as well as being echoed in legislative meetings in the Kentucky capital of Frankfort and even in Washington, D.C.

Tecumseh's spies had informed him that William Henry Harrison had dispatched a messenger to Catahecassa at Wapakoneta, praising the Shawnee principal chief for his continued wisdom and strength in refusing to listen to the preachments of Tenskwatawa and the rumored warmongering of Tecumseh. He reiterated his warning of the terrible destruction that would inevitably fall upon the red men if they once again raised the hatchet against Americans. The messengers said that old Catahecassa had been extremely pleased with the governor's praise and had returned the messenger with a reaffirmation of his friendship under the terms of the Greenville Treaty. It was upon receipt of this news that Tecumseh had determined to once again pay a visit to Wapakoneta because, despite Catahecassa's declaration, word had come that a large number of his followers who had heretofore been so devoted, had become disenchanted with his leadership. Among those dissidents—and Tecumseh's pulse had raced when he heard of it—was Blue Jacket, who had publicly announced that he was now quite ready to join forces with Tecumseh.

That was not the end of the good news that had reached Tecumseh. Harrison, learning that a large council of Indians not allied to Tecumseh had assembled at Topenebe's Town on the St. Joseph, had sent an appeal to the assembled chiefs through the pro-American contingent of Delawares, exhorting them to remain untainted by the influence of the Shawnee brothers, pointing out again, in less than tactful terms, the destruction that would come to them if they took up the hatchet against the whites. He had then made a serious error by adding in his message that if war between the Americans and the hostile Indians did break out, the friendly Indians would be in grave danger because the whites would be unable to distinguish between friendly Indian and foe.

The Wyandots, who were attending that meeting in large numbers under Chief Tarhe, had taken great umbrage at this, considering it to be tantamount to a declaration of war. He was also very angry that recently the United States government had failed to pay some annuities that were due and had failed to deliver supplies that had been promised. Not only that, were not white settlers, in defiance of the Greenville Treaty and just as Tecumseh had predicted they would, at this moment spilling into the valley of the Sandusky River and erecting their cabins in the heart of the Wyandot country? So Tarhe, who carried so much weight with all the Northwestern Indians, had reversed his decision to stand apart. The Wyandots as a whole vowed their allegiance to Tecumseh and vowed equally to adopt the principles being taught by The

Prophet. As Tecumseh knew would happen if once the Wyandots could be won over, almost overnight the attitude of the remaining reluctant chiefs— with the exception of the embittered Catahecassa—changed. If their revered "grandfathers," the Wyandots, venerated through all time for their talents, vigor, and wisdom, were adopting the new doctrine, might it not be sensible for all of them to do the same? Not all did, but more did than did not.

Among those few who refused to follow Tarhe's lead was the Wyandot chief Leatherlips, who had stalked away from the council in anger, followed by his own people, and returned to his village in Ohio. Then Stiahta came to the forefront. Leatherlips was one of the minor chiefs known to have attended Harrison's three-million-acre land grab at Fort Wayne and had been given lavish presents at the time. In a council of the Wyandot chiefs, held at Stiahta's demand, Leatherlips was found guilty of treason and witchcraft and was sentenced to be executed.

Stiahta had headed the party of five executioners who went immediately to Leatherlips's Village on the Scioto, ten miles above the little settlement of Franklinton.[571] Upon their arrival a council was held and Stiahta spoke with heat and bitterness of any chief who should so ignore the cause of his followers and fellow men. Leatherlips was permitted to reply in his own defense but it came as no surprise to anyone when, after two hours of deliberation, the death penalty was upheld. In a ritualistic ceremony involving prayers and the death chant, Leatherlips was executed with four tomahawk blows to the head and then buried in a shallow grave.

Word of the execution had spread quickly and that, along with the fact that the Wyandots had truly adopted the principles of Tecumseh and Tenskwatawa caused the unallied tribes and chiefs to reassess their postures. Perhaps the Wyandots were right. Were not the Wyandots a wise and proud tribe? Were they not the keepers of the original copy of the Treaty of Greenville? Had they not been custodians of the war belt that had once united so many tribes into one confederation? And had they not admitted in open council with Tenskwatawa that they were tired of the white-man situation and looked upon everything that had been done since the Treaty of Greenville as nothing? Most of all, had they not, just recently, publicly and proudly announced their acceptance of Tecumseh's grand plan? Perhaps they, too, should join this great amalgamation of Tecumseh's.

Having agreed to turn over to The Prophet the war belt of which they had so long been custodians, a large segment of the Wyandot population had then joined together in a huge party to carry the belt to Tippecanoe. On the way they stopped and held a council with Michikiniqua and the other Miami chiefs, showed them the great belt and reproached them for having united with the whites against their red brothers in the matter of the land sale, which they now all declared was illegal and not binding. The Miamis were so impressed that they immediately joined in the procession and, because the parent tribe had been so swayed, the Eel River Miamis joined them as well.

Grosble, the principal chief of the Piankeshaw Miamis, was so disturbed at all this that he immediately broke up his villages and began a migration westward of the Mississippi, dispatching a messenger as he left to Harrison and informing him that within a thirty-mile radius of Tippecanoe there were now encamped over three thousand warriors; that all were carrying on a great deal of secret counciling and there was much talk that simultaneous attacks were to be made on Vincennes, St. Louis, Kaskaskia, Chicago, Fort Wayne, and Detroit.

Harrison had evidently not believed this because, while Tecumseh was at Wapakoneta, a messenger had arrived from The Prophet with news that Harrison had sent a boatload of salt up the Wabash—part of the annuities for the Kickapoos. As the boat reached Tippecanoe a couple of weeks ago, Tenskwatawa stopped it. The Kickapoos in the village believed the salt was a partial payment for the land deal Harrison had made at Fort Wayne, to which they were violently opposed, and so they refused it. Tenskwatawa had not hurt the men who had brought it but he had ordered the crew to leave it on the shore while they continued upstream. By the time they came back, he told them, Tecumseh would no doubt have returned. Tecumseh had chuckled when he heard the news, approving what Tenskwatawa had done.

At Wapakoneta, Tecumseh had found there was still bitter opposition from the eighty-eight-year-old Catahecassa, who refused even to go into council with him and told Tecumseh insultingly that if he had anything to say, he could say it right here where they were standing, in the center circle of the town with all the villagers gathered around them.

Standing off to one side, Chaubenee felt his own insides churn at the rude and offensive words and manner of Catahecassa. He leaned over to Sauganash, who was holding the reins of his own horse and Tecumseh's in one hand, and spoke in a harsh undertone.

"I don't understand it, Sauganash. The more cause Tecumseh has for anger, the less he submits to it. If I were up there," he tilted his head toward the front of the assemblage, "I'd burn off their ears with my words."

"Which is why," Sauganash pointed out to his great barrel-chested friend, "Tecumseh is a warrior who leads and we are chiefs who follow . . . and gladly!"

Catahecassa reached into his blouse, removed a folded piece of paper, held it up flauntingly. He then opened it and extended the paper toward Tecumseh in his skeletal hand. Tecumseh took it, read it swiftly and then himself held it up for all to see.

"This," he said loudly, "is a letter Chief Catahecassa has shown me with pride. It is from the white devil, Harrison, who praises Catahecassa for his peaceful disposition and friendliness toward the Americans." He spoke the words as if they were an epithet and then, in a wholly unexpected movement, abruptly crumpled the paper, stepped to a nearby fire and tossed it onto the coals, where it stretched, browned and then burst into flames. There was a startled gasp from the onlookers.

"So much for praise from our greatest enemy! If your Governor Harrison were here," Tecumseh said, his voice brittle with scorn, "I would serve him in the same way." He swiveled his head, letting his gaze sweep across the chiefs and warriors standing around them. "You, above all, are my people— my own Shawnee brothers. Can you people not see," he asked them, "that the whites are deceiving you? For my part, I will never put any confidence in them. Look around you. How well have you been treated by them? How much have you gained by the treaties you have signed in the absence of those who wished to save our land? As to you chiefs here who sold land to the white chief Harrison, what words I have of you my mouth is too ashamed to speak. Dogs and skunks have not so little mind as those who did this. If only I had been here, not one inch of our land would he have bought. And every Indian who has put his thumb to it should have his thumbs cut off!"

Without one further word, Tecumseh had stalked away, mounted the horse Sauganash was holding for him and led his small party away on the road leading southeastward toward Blue Jacket's Town, thirty miles distant. .

Now, as they approached Blue Jacket's cabin, Tecumseh realized by the somber attitude of the Shawnees who had watched his passage into the village in utter silence that something was very wrong. It did not take long to find out what.

Blue Jacket had died.[572]

[July 3, 1810 — Tuesday]

Tecumseh, Chaubenee, and Sauganash, with their small party of warriors, turned their horses over to some young men at Tippecanoe and, along with Tenskwatawa, walked to the riverbank to inspect the eight barrels of salt that had been left there by the crew of boatmen. A great number of the Indians of this huge village had followed along and now lined the banks behind them. The French-Canadian trader Michael Brouillette moved up close to them as Tecumseh kicked at one of the barrels.

"What will you do with it, Tecumseh?" he asked.

Tecumseh did not respond, looking beyond him upriver at the flatboat that had just come into view and was being poled toward them. The villagers started raising a cry but ceased as Tecumseh raised his hand. There was an anticipatory tension in the air.

It took nearly half an hour before the large boat finally scraped ashore and several of the crew members alighted, one of whom was obviously the captain of the craft. Tecumseh pointed at the barrels and spoke to the captain coldly, in English.

"Load these back on your boat. They do not belong here. The Kickapoos who are here refuse to accept them and we know that if they did, your Governor Harrison would consider them as payment for the lands he has stolen."

The captain shrugged and summoned the remainder of his crew. Planks were laid from the gunwale to shore as a ramp and one by one the heavy barrels were rolled aboard while the Indians looked on. When they were finished and before all the crew got back aboard, Tecumseh stepped up and, with both hands, grasped one of the men by the hair of his head and shook him violently.

"Are you an American spy?" he demanded. When the frightened man said nothing, Tecumseh thrust him away, then repeated his act and his question with another. Again there was no response, but now the captain, angered, stepped up to intervene. Tecumseh spun and shook him just as violently as he had done the others.

"You!" he said. "You are an American spy? In this place, we kill American spies."

The captain jerked himself free and took a couple of steps backward, holding up a hand, his momentary courage puddled into fear, his eyes shifting nervously from Tecumseh to the swarm of Indians gathered on the slope. "Stop!" he said. He looked at Tecumseh. "Why are you doing this? We are not spies. We are not even Americans! We are Frenchmen—Creoles. These others know little English. We have done nothing wrong. We were only hired by Governor Harrison to bring up the salt and other goods."

"You and those who work with you," Tecumseh said, "get back aboard your boat and leave this place. Go back to Governor Harrison and tell him Tecumseh says we know of his tricks and are not taken in by them!"

The man scrambled back aboard the boat and was starting to give the order to shove off when Tecumseh stopped him with a word. "Wait!"

Tecumseh turned to look at Brouillette, gaze narrowed and features hard. "I said we kill American spies here. You, American dog," he pointed at the trader, "are such a spy."

Michael Brouillette, shook his head and opened his mouth to protest but Tecumseh cut him off. "Do not deny it! Did you think we were so stupid that we did not know from the very day you arrived that you were a spy sent among us by Harrison?"

Brouillette paled and licked his lips.

"What you saw here, what you heard, what you learned—all these were only the things that we *let* you see and hear and learn. We will not kill you this time, but if you come back here again, perhaps we will. Get on the boat and go back to your master. Do not take any of the goods you brought with you. They are our payment for tolerating your presence and for releasing you unharmed. Tell this to Harrison and tell him as well not to be so foolish as to send any more spies among us."

Michael Brouillette nodded and, without a word, boarded the flatboat. Within moments they were on their way back to Vincennes.[573]

[July 14, 1810 — Saturday]

In his lodge at Tippecanoe, Tecumseh silently read the letter just handed to him by Joseph Barron, special messenger from Governor William Henry Harrison.

Barron, his face streaked with runnels of perspiration that had little to do with the heat of this day, licked his lips and waited nervously. In view of what had occurred these past couple of weeks, his nervousness was justified. The Indians had become very bold lately, brazenly stealing horses from the settlers along the Wabash, occasionally within sight of Vincennes.

The return of the badly frightened Michael Brouillette and the crew of the annuities boat had created quite a stir in Vincennes and greatly irritated Harrison, who once again had grumbled aloud his wish that the federal troops from Pittsburgh would soon arrive. At once, upon hearing Brouillette's report, Harrison had sent another French Creole, Toussaint Dubois, to directly confront The Prophet and ask him what his intentions were, as well as to gather any other information he could.

Dubois had been received coolly and Tenskwatawa had told him only that he had no hostile intentions toward the United States and he was here simply because the Great Spirit had told him to gather Indians at this place and that was what he was doing. Dubois had suggested Tenskwatawa come with a delegation and meet with Harrison at Vincennes to discuss the situation, but The Prophet shook his head and answered bluntly.

"The last time I visited Governor Harrison at Vincennes, I was badly treated. I have no wish to be insulted again."

When Dubois had then inquired why the salt shipment had not been accepted, Tenskwatawa refused to answer the question and merely suggested to Dubois that he leave, which the Creole was prudent enough to do without argument.

Now had come this third man from Harrison and there had been good reason for his nervousness. Some distance outside the village he had been met by a large party of warriors who, with rather frightening yells and hoots, had led him to a huge chair before The Prophet's medicine lodge and in which Tenskwatawa sat with his face screwed into an ugly scowl, his wife, Gimewane, seated on the ground to the right of the chair.[574]

Barron had been left standing alone in front of The Prophet at a distance of about ten feet, while Tenskwatawa simply stared at him for two or three minutes without sign of recognition, though he knew Barron quite well. At last The Prophet came to his feet and addressed the white man angrily.

"For what purpose do you come here? Brouillette was here; he was a spy. Dubois was here; he was a spy. Now *you* have come. You, too, are a spy." Tenskwatawa raised his right arm at an angle and pointed a finger at the ground at Barron's feet. "There is your grave. Look on it."

Joseph Barron had begun to tremble and it was at that juncture that Tecumseh strode out of a large cabin nearby, tossed an impatient glance at his brother and then walked up to within a couple of feet of Barron, greeting him coldly.

"Your life is in no danger," he went on, "but what is your reason for coming here. Speak!"

"I have been sent here by Governor Harrison," Barron replied, holding up a sealed envelope. "He has written a message to The Prophet, which he has requested that I read to him."

Tecumseh held out his hand and Barron, with a furtive glance at Tenskwatawa, handed it to the elder brother. Tecumseh glanced at the envelope and then back at the messenger. "Come," he said, leading him into his cabin, unaware of the resentment flashing in his brother's eyes. They moved to the table, where Tecumseh sat down and indicated the chair opposite. Barron bobbed his head and sat down, sweat still glistening on his cheeks and forehead.

Tecumseh sliced open the envelope with his knife, removed and unfolded the paper inside and read:

William Henry Harrison, Governor and
Commander-in-Chief of the Territory of Indiana,
to the Shawnee Chief and the Indians
assembled at Tippecanoe:

> *Notwithstanding the improper language which you have used towards me,*
> *I will endeavor to open your eyes to your true interests. Notwithstanding*
> *what white men have told you, I am not your personal enemy. . . . Although*
> *I must say that you are an enemy to the Seventeen Fires, and that you have*
> *used the greatest exertion to lead them astray. In this you have been in some*
> *manner successful; as I am told they are ready to raise the tomahawk against*

their father, yet their father, notwithstanding his anger at their folly, is full of goodness, and is always ready to receive into his arms those of his children who are willing to repent, acknowledge their fault, and ask his forgiveness.

There is yet but little harm done, which may be easily repaired. The chain of friendship which united the whites with the Indians may be renewed, and be as strong as ever. A great deal of that work depends on you—the destiny of those who are under your direction depends upon the choice you make of the two roads which are before you. The one is large, open and pleasant, and leads to peace, security, and happiness; the other, on the contrary, is narrow and crooked, and leads to misery and ruin. Don't deceive yourselves; do not believe that all nations of Indians are able to resist the force of the Seventeen Fires. I know your warriors are brave, but ours are not less so. But what can a few warriors do against the innumerable warriors of the Seventeen Fires? Our blue-coats are more numerous than you can count; our hunters are like the leaves of the forest, or the grains of sand on the Wabash. Do you think that the red-coats can protect you; they are not able to protect themselves. They do not think of going to war with us. If they did, you would in a few moons see our flags wave over all the forts of Canada. What reason have you to complain of the Seventeen Fires? Have they taken anything from you? Have they ever violated the treaties made with the red men? You say they have purchased lands from those who have no right to sell them. Show that this is true and the land will be instantly restored. Show us the rightful owners. I have full power to arrange this business; but if you would rather carry your complaints before your great father, the President, you shall be indulged. I will immediately take means to send you, with those chiefs you may choose, to the city where your father lives. Everything necessary shall be prepared for your journey, and means taken for your safe return.

Tecumseh folded the letter and returned it to its envelope, then looked up to find Barron watching him apprehensively. He smiled faintly to put the man at ease and spoke softly.

"Moneto said He gave this great island to His red children. He placed the whites on the other side of the big water. They were not content with their own, but came to take ours from us. They have driven us from the sea to the lakes. We can go no farther. They have taken upon themselves to say this tract belongs to the Miamis, this to the Delawares, and so on. But the Great Spirit intended it to be the common property of all the tribes. Nor can it be sold without the consent of all. Our father tells us that we have no business on the Wabash, that the land belongs to other tribes, but the Great Spirit ordered us to come here and we shall stay."

He paused, thinking, then placed a finger on the envelope before him and looked up at Joseph Barron again. "Harrison," he said. "I have never met him, but I remember seeing him as a young man sitting beside his General Wayne."

He stopped again, thinking briefly of that long-ago day sixteen years earlier when he had looked into General Anthony Wayne's camp with his brass telescope and observed the young officer seated beside his general—the young officer who had now become the most important white man in the West and the deadliest individual foe of the Indians.

"I have never troubled the white men much," Tecumseh continued at length, "but now I will go to Vincennes and show the governor that he has been listening to bad men when he is told that we are meditating war against the Seventeen Fires. As Governor Harrison is eager for peace, so also are we, and I will be glad to talk and try to work out our difficulties. Tenskwatawa will not be coming. I will be the one to council with Governor Harrison, but he must know that there is one thing on which we will talk that I will not bend. The Treaty of Fort Wayne must be set aside, as the land belongs to all the red people, not to a few cowardly old chiefs who have placed their thumbs to that paper. I will come to Vincennes. Since it is a peace mission, I will arrive there in one moon with some thirty of my principal men . . ." He stopped, considering, then after a moment went on, "and probably a hundred of my young men who are fond of attending upon such occasions."[575]

[August 15, 1810 — Wednesday]

"You are a liar!"

Directed at William Henry Harrison, the words burst like pistol shots from Tecumseh. His eyes, cold, hard, implacable, were locked on the governor and he continued harshly, "Everything you have said is false! The Indians have been cheated and imposed upon by you and the Seventeen Fires. Nothing you have said—before, or now at this council—can be trusted. You lie and you cheat!"

The words were indicative of the tenor of everything that had occurred here in Vincennes since the council began this morning on the grounds of Grouseland, the governor's mansion.[576]

It had all begun last Sunday—August 12—when Tecumseh and his party of eighty followers, the faces and bare chests and backs of all painted in garish streaks and swirls and dots of red, blue, white, and yellow, had arrived in canoes and, after being stopped briefly for inspection by Captain George Floyd at Fort Knox, had made camp along the riverbank two miles downstream from that fort and a mile upstream from the Grouseland Estate.[577]

Messages had passed back and forth between Harrison and Tecumseh—carried by Harrison's interpreters, none other than Stephen Ruddell, formerly Sinnanatha, and Spemica Lawba—during Monday and Tuesday, August 13 and 14, setting up the schedule and guidelines for the council. Tecumseh instructed his men as to their behavior and how they should appear at his warning signal should trouble break out, while Harrison alerted his own forces in the same way and instructed his commissioners and witnesses to be on hand for the start of the council an hour after sunrise.

This morning, after instructing his men to leave their rifles in camp but to wear blankets about themselves, beneath which they were to have such weapons as knives, tomahawks and war clubs, Tecumseh led them on foot to the Grouseland Estate. In accordance with the governor's request, he left all but eleven of his followers at the fringe of woodland, some seven hundred feet away from the council portico adjacent to the mansion, telling them to spread out and remain in place until the council began and then, if necessary, to gradually move in closer until they were within hearing of his voice. Then, accompanied by Chaubenee, Sauganash, Stiahta, Wasegoboah, and Metea as his lieutenants, and chiefs of the Kickapoo, Ottawa, Wyandot, Miami, Potawatomi, and Winnebago tribes, Tecumseh followed the curving road through the estate gardens until he was among the arbors some forty yards from the mansion itself, where he stopped.

Harrison had ordered benches and chairs set up under the broad roof of the columned portico, where they would be shaded from the sun or, if the occasion arose, protected from the rain. There Harrison was waiting, along with the judges of the Territorial Supreme Court, his military aides, including General Gibson and Major Joseph McCormick, along with Captains William Whitlock and George Floyd. There was also an honor guard platoon of seventeen United States Army regulars under command of Lieutenant Jennings and a sergeant, all resplendent in their finest uniforms. Close to Harrison were Joseph Barron, Stephen Ruddell, Spemica Lawba, and Winnemac. A large number of prominent citizens of Vincennes were close by and, standing back from the portico a respectful distance, some 200 or 300 ordinary civilian spectators had also gathered.

As soon as Tecumseh stopped, Harrison sent Joseph Barron to discover what was the matter. Barron approached and stopped a dozen feet away, dipped his head and smiled.

"It is with pleasure that I greet you, and those who are with you, on behalf of Governor Harrison. The governor would like you to come to the portico for the council, where seats have been arranged."

"I do not care to talk with a roof above us," Tecumseh replied. "Tell your chief I prefer the council to be held here, where I stand."

Barron had returned at once to Governor Harrison with the message and Harrison, if displeased, masked it well and acquiesced, immediately walking forward to meet Tecumseh.

"I think having our meeting in the open will be pleasant," he told Tecumseh. "I will order the chairs and benches brought here so that I can offer proper seats to my honored guests, since it is the order of your great father in Washington that you be shown every courtesy."

"My father?" Tecumseh said. He shook his head and pointed upward. "The sun is my father; the earth is my mother, who nourishes me, and on her bosom I will recline."

So saying, he issued a command and his followers arranged themselves comfortably on the grass and waited while chairs and benches were brought and the entire group at the portico moved to the new location.[578] A table was brought as well, behind which was placed an armchair for the governor, flanked by ordinary chairs for his aides and interpreters. At length, all were seated—Tecumseh's men, the chiefs and his lieutenants, sitting cross-legged on the ground behind where he remained standing some twenty feet from the table.

Tecumseh's eyes hardened on seeing Spemica Lawba and his own former adopted brother, Sinnanatha, along with Winnemac, close to the governor. The latter two lowered their eyes when he looked at them but Spemica Lawba met his gaze directly.

Governor Harrison formally welcomed his Indian guests to the council and then, through interpretation by Spemica Lawba, invited his principal guest to speak first. Tecumseh nodded and began at once, speaking in the Shawnee tongue, not in English, in which he could not have been as expressive as he wished. At the same time Spemica Lawba rose and stood between them, slightly to one side.

"It is not with pleasure that I find you here, nephew," Tecumseh said, speaking in the Shawnee tongue.

Spemica Lawba's gaze narrowed but he replied politely. "I have been asked to interpret, uncle. You know I will truthfully interpret what is said."

Tecumseh nodded. "Yes, I know that. So now I will speak to your master." He turned his attention to Harrison and spoke directly to him, still in the Shawnee language. For some two hours he discussed instance after instance of the perfidy of the whites in their dealings with the Indians, of treaties made and broken, of Indians constantly losing to the Americans the land of their fathers and those before them. He said he did not know if he could ever be friends with the United States in view of the cold-blooded murder of the principal chief of the Shawnees, Cornstalk, along with his son and his aide, who had come on a mission of peace to Fort Randolph but had been put into a room from which they could not escape and then, wholly defenseless, had been shot down; or in view of the cold-blooded butchery committed on nearly a hundred similarly defenseless Moravian Indians by the Americans at the Gnadenhutten Massacre; or in view of the cold-blooded murder of the venerable Chief Moluntha who was tomahawked to death after having surrendered to the Americans.[579] At last, however, he finally came to the matters more directly related to this council.

"Brother," he said, "I wish you to listen to me well. As I think you do not clearly understand what I before said to you, I will explain it again." As it had been up until now, so swift was Spemica Lawba's interpretation that he finished only a few beats after Tecumseh, who continued without pause. "Brother, since peace was made, you have killed some of the Shawnees, Winnebagoes, Delawares, and Miamis and you have taken our lands from us and I do not see how we can remain at peace if you continue to do so. *You* try to force the red people to do some injury. It is *you* that are pushing them on to do some mischief. You endeavor to make distinctions: you wish to prevent the Indians doing as we wish them—to unite and let them consider their lands as the common property of the whole; you take tribes aside and advise them not to come into this measure; and until our design is accomplished, we do not wish to accept your invitation to go and see the president."

He paused to allow the interpreter to catch up and, when Spemica Lawba stopped speaking, continued. "The reason I tell you this: you want, by your distinction of Indian tribes in allotting to each a particular tract of land, to make them war with each other. *You* never see the *Indian* come, do you, and endeavor to make the white people do so? You are continually driving the red people; when, at last, you will drive them into the Great Lake, where they can't either stand or walk.

"Brother, you ought to know what you are doing with the Indians. Perhaps it is by direction of the president to make those distinctions. It is a very bad thing and we do not like it. It is true that I, with the help of my brother, Tenskwatawa, who is The Prophet, and many others, have organized a combination of all the Indian tribes in this quarter to put a stop to the encroachments of the white people and to establish a principle that the lands should be considered common property and none sold without the consent of all. Since my residence at Tippecanoe, we have endeavored to level all distinctions—to destroy village chiefs, by whom all mischief is done. It is they who sell our lands to the Americans. Our object is to let our affairs be transacted by warriors.

"Brother, this land that was sold and the goods that were given for it were only done by a few. The treaty was afterwards brought here and the Weas were induced to give their consent, because of their small numbers. The treaty at Fort Wayne was made through the threats of Winnemac . . ." He glared at the Potawatomi village chief, who averted his eyes, "but in the future we are prepared to punish those chiefs who may come forward to propose to sell the land." Tecumseh looked back at Harrison and, as Spemica Lawba caught up, added, "If you continue to purchase them, it will produce war among the different tribes and, at last, I do not know what the consequences will be to the white people."

Tecumseh turned and caught the eye of Sauganash, who immediately stood and held aloft the letter that Harrison had sent to Tecumseh a month ago. He turned slowly in a circle with it and, when all had seen it, refolded it and sat down again. Tecumseh addressed Harrison anew.

"Brother, I was glad to hear your speech. You said if we could show you that the land was sold by people who had no right to sell, you would restore it." He pointed a level finger at Winnemac. "Those that did sell did not own it . . .[580] These tribes set up a claim, but," he let his pointing arm swing in the direction of his camp, "the tribes with me will not agree with their claim." He paused for several heartbeats then added in an ominous tone, "If the land is not restored to us, you will see, when we return to our homes, how it will be settled.

"Hear me!" The two words came like rifle shots and Harrison jerked in surprise, then scowled, angry with himself for starting as he had. "We shall have," Tecumseh continued, "a great council at which all the tribes will be present, when we shall show to those who sold that they had no right to the claim that they set up." Again his stare impaled Winnemac. "And you will see what will be done to those chiefs that did sell land to you."

Tecumseh clenched his hand and put his fist to his chest. "I am not alone in this determination; it is the determination of all the warriors and red people that listen to me. I now wish *you*," his gaze flashed to Harrison, "to listen to me. If you do not, it will appear as if you wished to kill all the chiefs that sold you the land. I tell you so because I am authorized by all the tribes to do so. *I* am the head of them all! I am a warrior and all the warriors will meet together in two or three moons from this. Then I will call for those chiefs that sold you the land and shall know what to do with them. If you do not restore the land, you will have a hand in killing them!"

Winnemac blanched. This was no longer a vague threat and he was very much afraid. At this point Tecumseh broke off in a tirade against Winnemac in the Potawatomi tongue that was so swift and abusive that the interpreters were lost and the official recorder could not write, but Winnemac understood only too well and his fear increased almost to the point of panic.

At last Tecumseh had paused and, in the silence that fell, the whites shifted uncomfortably in their seats and the white spectators looked at one another fearfully. Some commissioners put their heads together and began whispering. They stopped at a gesture from Harrison, who then nodded at Tecumseh to go on.

"Brother," the Shawnee said, in a less frigid tone, "do not believe that I came here to get presents from you. If you offer us any, we will not take them. By our taking goods from you, you will hereafter say that with them you purchased another piece of land from us."

As Spemica Lawba interpreted, Harrison's cheeks and neck reddened and again he frowned at this involuntary reaction to Tecumseh's words that had hit home so pointedly. He was looking at Tecumseh with a different expression than when they first met, as if suddenly realizing that here was no ordinary Indian; that here was a man of great intelligence and power who might well turn out to be the most dangerous threat he had ever faced.

"It has been the object of both myself and my brother," Tecumseh was continuing, "to prevent the lands being sold. Should you not return the land, it will occasion us to call a great council that will meet at the Huron village, where the council fire has already been lighted, at which those who sold the lands shall be called and shall suffer for their conduct."

His voice now softened a little, a subtle plea for reason on the governor's part. "Brother, I wish you would take pity on the red people and do what I have requested. If you will not give up the land and do cross the boundary of your present settlement, it will be very hard and produce great troubles among us.

"How," he asked, first slapping his hands to his thighs and then raising his arms as if in supplication, "how can we have confidence in the white people? When Jesus Christ came on the earth, you killed and nailed him on a cross. You thought he was dead, but you were mistaken. You have Shakers among you and you laugh and make light of their worship. Everything I have said to you is the truth. The Great Spirit has inspired me and I speak nothing but the truth to you."

Tecumseh studied Harrison as he continued to sit with his hands on the table before him, but the governor's face was a mask in which he could read nothing and Tecumseh suddenly experienced the feeling that no matter what words were used on this man, in the end it would make no difference to him. And so, though he had planned on talking much longer, going over past treaties and the consistent breaking thereof by the whites, he realized it was pointless and he now concluded his remarks quickly.

"Brother, I hope you will confess that you ought not to have listened to those bad birds who bring you bad news. I have declared myself freely to you and if any explanations should be required from our town, send a man who can speak to us. If you think it proper to give us any presents—and *we* can be convinced they are given through friendship alone—we will accept them. As we intend to hold our council in the Huron village that is near the British, we may probably make them a visit; but should they offer us powder and tomahawk, we will take the powder and refuse the tomahawk.[581] I wish you,

Brother, to consider everything I have said as true and that it is the sentiment of all the red people that listen to me."

Tecumseh stood in place until Spemica Lawba had finished, then he nodded to Harrison, turned and stepped back to his lieutenants, where he sat down on the ground in the place that had been kept open for him in their midst.

Now Harrison came to his feet and began to speak, again with Spemica Lawba making the reverse interpretation. He said it was ridiculous to declare that the Indians were all one people; if the Great Spirit had meant this to be true, why then had they been given different tongues? He said the lands along the Wabash had belonged to the Miamis and the United States had bought the land from them for a further annuity, as in previous purchases of smaller tracts, the benefit of which the Miamis had for a long time experienced in the promptness with which the United States had paid them. These Miamis, he said, had acted in their own best interest in selling the lands and Tecumseh, as a Shawnee, and the other Indians at Tippecanoe, who had come from a distant country, were not justified in attempting to control the Miamis in the disposal of their own land. He turned to sit down and allow time for the interpretation, but Tecumseh had understood the words. It became one of the rare occasions of his life when he lost his temper. He leaped to his feet and shouted loudly in the Shawnee tongue, savagely gesticulating as he did so.

"*You are a liar!* Everything you have said is false! The Indians have been cheated and imposed upon by you and by the Seventeen Fires. Nothing you have said—before, or now at this council—can be trusted. You lie and you cheat!"

Still facing away from Tecumseh, Harrison had stiffened. To one side, Winnemac had bent over and was attempting to prime his pistol without being seen. General Gibson spoke curtly to Lieutenant Jennings, "These fellows intend mischief. Bring up the guard," and the young officer sprinted away. Instantly the five Indians who were Tecumseh's lieutenants, tomahawks appearing in their hands as if by magic, sprang to their feet in a semicircle behind him and stepped up to enclose him in their midst. Harrison jerked his dress sword from its scabbard with a vicious metallic swish. Beside him, Captain Floyd drew his dagger and Winnemac cocked the big curved hammer on the pistol with a loud ominous click. Many of the spectators were picking up pieces of firewood to use as clubs or showing other weapons and the Reverend Winans, Methodist minister, ran to the door of the governor's house, where he snatched up a rifle leaning there and stood ready to defend the governor's family. The instant Tecumseh saw Harrison draw his sword, he issued a shrill, far-carrying cry and instantly the remainder of his warriors leaped into view and stood ready with their weapons. At this many of the citizens panicked and raced away, knocking down a post and rail fence some fifty yards distant in their panicky exodus.

Time seemed balanced on razor edge and the sudden silence was broken only by the sound of running feet as Lieutenant Jennings and the guard came dashing up holding rifles at ready. The governor stayed them and everyone else with an upraised hand and then looked at Spemica Lawba.

"What did Tecumseh say, Johnny?"

Spemica Lawba repeated accurately in English what Tecumseh had said and, as he spoke, the governor's expression changed to one of tightly controlled anger. When the interpretation was finished, Harrison, his gaze locked on Tecumseh all the while, said bleakly, "You are a bad man for interrupting our deliberations in such a manner. I will have no further communication with you. You and your people may go in safety, since you have come under my protection to the council fire, but you must leave immediately."

Tecumseh, having also stayed his own people with an upraised hand, signaled them now to join him and they moved away quickly and returned to camp. By the time they got there Tecumseh had cooled off considerably and now regretted losing control and thus giving Harrison exactly the sort of edge he was looking for to bring war down upon them. It was still too soon for such a war to begin; it would damage the grand plan that had been so many years in preparation. He realized he would have to make amends.

"Wasegoboah," he said, calling his brother-in-law to him, "return there under a flag and seek out your wife's son. Tell him that I ask him to come to me at the first light of day tomorrow."

[August 16, 1810 — Thursday]

"Uncle?"

Tecumseh, who had been staring into the coals, looked up and saw his nephew silhouetted against the early morning sun, clad in white man's shirt and trousers but wearing moccasins and a knife sheathed at his belt. Tecumseh came to his feet and faced him within arm's reach, then dipped his head once in faint greeting.

"I tell you first, Spemica Lawba," he said, "that your mother is well. She is with Tenskwatawa and Kumskaka at Tippecanoe."

"I am glad she is well," Spemica Lawba replied. He said nothing further, waiting.

"I wish you to carry to Governor Harrison my words of regret over what took place yesterday. Tell him I ask that the council be reconvened, that I may explain why I acted as I did. Assure him that no direct threat was intended against himself or the whites attending and that such an action will not happen again."

"I will do as you ask," he said, then turned to leave.

"Spemica Lawba!" The command stopped him and when he looked back Tecumseh went on. "We miss you—your mother and your uncles and Wasegoboah. It is not too late for you and Pskipahcah Ouiskelotha to return to us."

A faint smile touched Spemica Lawba. "I thank you. Pskipahcah Ouiskelotha is in the village of our chief, Catahecassa, where she cares for our daughter and two sons. She remains loyal to her chief, as do I. He *is* my chief and I will remain loyal to his wishes. Only if he should agree to join you— or you should come back to us—can we again be together."

"Catahecassa will not. I cannot."

"Then it is sad," Spemica Lawba said softly.

"Yes," Tecumseh agreed, "it is sad." Abruptly he held out his hand and, surprised, his nephew gripped it in both of his, then turned and trotted back toward Grouseland.

In less than an hour it was Sinnanatha who returned with word that Governor Harrison had agreed to another council and this time when Tecumseh and his lieutenants arrived he saw that all the whites were armed, but he made no issue of it. He simply faced Harrison and the governor spoke without preamble.

"Do you intend to prevent the survey on the land on the Wabash?" He looked past Tecumseh at the various chiefs.

Cool and dignified now, Tecumseh replied softly. "I alone am the acknowledged head of all the Indians and I am determined that the old boundary shall continue."

Still Harrison's gaze remained on the Indians behind him with unspoken question. At Tecumseh's nod to them, one by one they rose, identified themselves and their tribe, acknowledged that they had accepted Tecumseh, who had united them all, as their leader and stated their intention to support him in whatever course he took. Stiahta was last to speak and, as he finished, Harrison looked back at Tecumseh.

"If they follow you," he said threateningly, "how many of the Kickapoos and other tribes present do you think will then continue to receive their annuities?"

"Brother," Tecumseh replied, contempt heavy in his voice, "when you speak to me of annuities, I look at the land and pity the women and children. I am authorized to say that they will not *accept* them! They want to save that piece of land. We do not wish *you* to take it. It is small enough for our purposes. If you *do* take it," he added, just as threateningly as Harrison had spoken, "you must blame yourself as the cause of trouble between us and the tribes who sold it to you. *I want the present boundary line to continue!* Should you cross it, I assure you it will be productive of bad consequences."

Harrison considered this for a long quiet moment and then nodded. "Since you have been candid in acknowledging your intentions, I would be so, too. I will send the president a faithful statement of what you have said in disputing the claim to the lands in question. I will tell you what the president's answer is when I receive it. However, I am sure the president will never admit these lands to be the property of any other than those tribes who have occupied them since the white people came to America. Since we have come to title of them by fair purchase, then *I* am sure that these titles will be protected and supported by the sword. I hereby adjourn this council."

Taken aback, Tecumseh watched as he turned and walked to the mansion. An ugly feeling filled Tecumseh that he had initiated events he was powerless to control and that were gaining their own momentum. Deep in thought, he walked slowly to the camp, his followers close behind and not intruding on his contemplation. After their arrival there, as Tecumseh kept to himself, the four score Indians of his party sat or moved about in an uncertain way, wondering what was next.

[August 17, 1810 — Friday]

In the early light of the new day, preparations were being made by the Indians, at Tecumseh's direction, to break up the camp and return to Tippecanoe when a commotion of voices rose and Tecumseh looked about to find its cause. A lone man was approaching them on the road that led to Grouseland.

It was William Henry Harrison.

An instant sharp command from Tecumseh nipped any thought of harming the governor and Tecumseh, alone, strode out to meet him. Obviously it had been the governor's turn to have overnight second thoughts. The two enemies shook hands politely and it was Harrison who spoke first.

"Are your intentions really as you stated them in council?"

"They are," Tecumseh replied. "It would be only with great reluctance that I would make war upon the United States, since I have no complaint against them except their illegal purchases of Indian lands from those who had no right to sell them. I am anxious to be at peace with the Americans and if you will prevail upon the president to give up the land in question and agree never again to make a treaty without the consent of all the tribes, I will be your faithful ally and assist you in all your wars against the British. I know that the British are always urging us to war for their own advantages; certainly not for the good of the red man. They urge us to attack the Americans as one might set a dog to fight. I would rather be a friend of the Seventeen Fires. However, if the president does not comply with my terms, I will be obliged to take the other side."

Harrison sighed. "I will tell the president of your propositions. But, again, I say there is not the least probability that he will accede to your terms."

"Well," Tecumseh said, nodding gravely, "as the great white chief is to determine the matter, I hope the Great Spirit will put enough sense in his head to induce him to direct you to give up this land. It is true, he is so far off he will not be injured by the war; he may sit in the town and drink his wine, while you and I will have to fight it out."

And Harrison could only nod.

[January 12, 1811 — Saturday]

"When, Tecumseh?" Tenskwatawa demanded, wheeling around from where he was standing in front of the big fireplace. "When, *if ever,* are we going to do what you keep telling all the tribes we will do—push the Americans out of our lands?"

Tecumseh regarded his brother steadily, again irritated by the younger man's chronic impatience and persistently unpleasant disposition. Once again he considered, as he had done so many times in the past, the wisdom of removing him from power as The Prophet and replacing him with someone steadier and more dependable, such as Wasegoboah or Chaubenee or Stiahta.

It was undeniable that hardly anyone liked Tenskwatawa. They feared him, true enough, and some even respected him—or at least the power he represented—but there was no one who really *liked* him, not even Tecumapese, who had always been more forgiving of his failings than anyone else.

Even while he considered such a change, Tecumseh knew in his own heart he would not do it and there were a variety of good reasons. Foremost among these was the fact that with his grand plan just beginning to come to its culmination, it would at best set everything back at least a year; at worst, conceivably cause irreparable damage to the whole amalgamation.

Apart from the fact that Tenskwatawa would be devastated and his sole purpose in life taken away, none of those it would be desirable to have in the position was at this time really able to take on the responsibility. Stiahta, with his broad influence and bluff likability, as well as his prestige as a warrior chief, was probably the most appropriate candidate, yet he had his own villages to oversee and was more embroiled than ever at the moment with the power struggle occurring among the Wyandots and Hurons. If he let down his guard for more than a moment, his power and influence were liable to be usurped.

Chaubenee was a personal favorite as a possibility, but the Potawatomi chief, too, had a demanding responsibility among the Potawatomi in Illinois and his principal political adversary, Gomo, would like nothing better than to overthrow him and recapture under his own leadership so much of the

Illinois Valley authority that Chaubenee had whittled away from him. Besides, Chaubenee had his own family to consider, from whom he had already been absent a great deal because of aiding Tecumseh. His wife, Canoku, had grown enormously fat, now weighing over four hundred pounds and Chaubenee had just taken as a second wife a Kickapoo woman named Cebebaqua—Sleep-walker.[582]

That left Wasegoboah, who, though lacking in imagination and leadership qualities, was nevertheless a man who, with proper direction, could handle the responsibility reasonably well. He had been among Tecumseh's closest friends since childhood and yet now he was devastated by his loss of Tecumapese. The two had been having problems in recent years, the origin of which Tecumseh did not know, that had erupted in some severe quarrels. The matter had become so serious during the harvest last fall that Wasegoboah, in his anger, had invoked the Shawnee divorce ritual and told her to leave. She had, and when Wasegoboah, in a day or two, had second thoughts and sought to bring her back, she had refused to come. They had fought more over it until finally, in an effort to give both a chance to review matters with clearer minds, it had been Tecumseh who had stepped in and suggested that his sister leave Tippecanoe and stay for a few months—perhaps over the winter—with friends among the Shawnees along Apple Creek in the Missouri country. She had snatched at the idea and within two days was gone . . . and Wasegoboah had been deeply depressed ever since. Tecumseh had decided he would bring her back with him next time he went there and perhaps by then time would have resolved their difficulties. In the meanwhile, however, Wasegoboah was in no mental state to take on any new responsibilities.

No, the only thing to do was to leave matters as they were and keep the recalcitrant Tenskwatawa in check as much as possible, especially since everything would be put into motion by the end of this year. The prospects for success were looking better all the time, especially where the far western and northwestern tribes were concerned. His visit to them following last summer's council at Vincennes with Governor Harrison had brought very good results. He had ridden to those tribes with Sauganash at his side and an enthusiastic polyglot party of forty warriors from Tippecanoe at his heels. The Kickapoos and Potawatomies were now almost entirely behind him, as were the Iowas and Menominees and a fair number of the Sioux, Mandans, and Winnebagoes. Best of all, the Sacs and Foxes were now committed to come to him under one of their more powerful war chiefs, Makataimeshekiakiak—Black Hawk—despite opposition from his nemesis, the younger but very influential peace chief, Keokuk.[583]

As the summer of 1810 had dwindled away into autumn, Tecumseh, still at the head of his party of young warriors, but which had now been augmented in their travels by 120 others who wished to follow him back to Tippecanoe, had found himself back again in Amherstburg. The party of 160, including thirty-three women and children, was comprised of Potawatomies, Ottawas, Sacs and Winnebagoes and had made quite an impression not only at Amherstburg but as they had passed Detroit.

Upon his arrival at these places, Tecumseh was gratified to find that his prominence among the British was exceptionally increased, and they now unequivocally considered him the most important of all the Northwestern Indians and, as such, the most important to curry to their own favor. They openly referred to him as the supreme commander of the Northwestern tribes. And, while Tecumseh did not really want to form an alliance with the British, realistically he knew that without being heavily and continuously supplied by them, the projected move against the Americans could not possibly succeed. What he had hoped to do, in going to Amherstburg, was to get the British to commit themselves to that sort of support without expecting a blanket commitment by him of solid alliance of the tribes when action against the United States was initiated. It was no longer much of a question of *if* the British and Americans would war again, but exactly *when*. All indications were that it would not be much longer—surely by late summer of 1812.

In his talks with Matthew Elliott, Tecumseh had been very candid. "I have come here," he told the old Indian agent, "with the intention of informing you that we have not forgotten—we can *never* forget!—what passed between you Englishmen and our ancestors, and also to let you know our present determination. The warriors have taken all their chiefs and turned their faces toward you, never again to look at the Americans. And we, the warriors, now manage the affairs of our nation; and we sit at or near the borders where the contest will begin. You, Father, have nourished us and raised us up from childhood. We are now men and think ourselves capable of defending our country, in which case you have given us active assistance and always advice. We are now determined to defend it ourselves and, after raising you on your feet, leave you behind; but," he added firmly, "expecting you will push toward us what may be necessary to supply our wants." Tecumseh also told him that his next major trip would be the last—that in the summer to come he would visit the Southern tribes and gather them into his amalgam. "By the time I visit you again," he told Elliott, "the business will be done."

With Sir James Craig terminally ill at Quebec and Sir George Prevost poised to succeed him with Sir George Drummond as his second, Elliott had not bothered to trouble them greatly with extensive details about what was occurring and, essentially on his own authority, made a lavish distribution of gifts to Tecumseh's Indians—weapons, gunpowder, blankets, food, and other supplies—and promised there would be plenty more to come for so long as they would need it.

At the same time a major council of Indians had been convened on the west side of the Detroit River at Brownstown and Tecumseh had intended to attend it until he learned it had been called by William Hull, the governor of Michigan Territory, and was packed primarily by such pro-American Indians as Catahecassa, Walk in the Water, and others who had consistently opposed Tecumseh and railed against this amalgamation.

In his address to the assemblage at Brownstown, Hull had attacked Tecumseh viciously and informed them what he had learned from Harrison: that Tecumseh had, at the Vincennes Council, boldly asserted that he alone was the leader of all the Northwestern tribes, which, as Hull had expected, angered the pro-American Indians considerably, but, as Hull had *not* anticipated, frightened them considerably as well.[584]

Over dinner at his big house, The Point, Elliott told Tecumseh an interesting account about Main Poche. The chief with the deformed hand had come here several weeks ago at the head of a war party to pick up ammunition and supplies for the small expedition he was leading against the Osages. While they smoked their after-dinner pipes, the Potawatomi had told him of a visit just concluded with Governor William Henry Harrison, who had summoned him to Vincennes.[585]

Plying Main Poche heavily with liquor, Harrison tried to bribe the chief into selling land to him, first with the promise of gifts and then, when that failed, compounded the mistake by subtly threatening the Potawatomies with the might of the army. It was at that point that Main Poche had had enough and came to his feet glowering, unfeigned menace in his voice. "You think us fools!" he had told Harrison. "Can you truly think that we believe to the last little bit what sort of games you play with us? Do you think we do not see how you are trying to divide us? You try to entice us with liquor and gifts to forget about our people, our lands, our heritage. You astonish me with your talk! Whenever you do wrong, there is nothing said or done; but when *we* do anything, you immediately take us and tie us by the neck with a rope. You warn us by asking what will become of our women and children if there is a war. On the other hand, what will become of *your* women and children? It is best to avoid war!"

Tecumseh had been delighted to hear that Main Poche had resisted Harrison's enticements and had even denounced Harrison for his deceptiveness, word of which, he knew, would quickly pass among the tribes and further strengthen the warnings he himself had been making about Harrison.

On his return to Tippecanoe, which now was so populous it had the appearance of a small city, Tecumseh had been informed by Tenskwatawa that only a month earlier, in late October, Michael Brouillette had shown up again, sent by Governor Harrison to see Tecumseh. In his brother's absence, Tenskwatawa had taken the message, which was that the president had not yet replied to Tecumseh's speech at Vincennes. Tenskwatawa assured his brother that he had treated Brouillette politely, but had once more warned that there would be grave ramifications, if any attempt were made by the Americans to survey or place settlers upon any part of the three million acres claimed in the Fort Wayne Treaty.

Tecumseh's reflection on all these matters was broken when a hand gripped his shoulder and he looked up to find Tenskwatawa standing over him, reiterating his query.

"Just exactly *when* are you planning to push the Americans out of our lands?"

Tecumseh sighed. "You, Tenskwatawa," he said, pushing his brother's hand away, "should know the answer to that better than anyone. Did you not carve the slabs and see to their delivery, with the red sticks, to all the chiefs? The wait will not be much longer, so push impatience aside. Come summer I will visit the Cherokees and Creeks and other Southern tribes. My business with them will take that summer only and when I return, all will be done and then, Tenskwatawa, *then* it will be time."

"And are we assured of British support for it?" Tenskwatawa persisted.

The faint jingle of buckles and bits reached them, along with the snorting and stamping of horses and both men looked at each other and then moved to the door and looked out. Tenskwatawa's final question now required no answer. A huge pack train had just arrived from the British at Amherstburg carrying enough blankets, food, medications and other supplies to keep the entire large population of Tippecanoe very comfortable throughout the remainder of this relatively gentle winter.

[July 9, 1811 — Tuesday]

As Tecumseh began to get affairs in order at Tippecanoe for his absence while visiting the Southern tribes on this final major journey, he considered the things that had occurred this past spring and what possible effect they might have.

While normally he did not approve of anything William Wells did, he had to admit that the former adopted son of Michikiniqua had acted well in preventing a massacre at Fort Wayne that might have ignited the entire frontier much too prematurely. In March a party of Potawatomies under a brutish chief named Peesotum had held a dance in a large marquee tent outside Fort Wayne that most of the prominent citizens and their families had attended.[586] The plan had been for a sudden attack to be launched on the whites in the midst of the dance. Wells, who was still justice of the peace, recognized the signs and, at the risk of his own life, had nipped the plan in the bud, humiliating Peesotum in the process and earning his undying enmity. Tecumseh, who had been on his way to Amherstburg at the time with a large contingent of his warriors, heard about it and went out of his way to see Wells and thank him for his timely intervention. Wells had waved off the thanks and countered with an accusation that some of the Kickapoos at Tippecanoe had been killing settlers in the southern Illinois country, south of the Kaskaskia River and the Big Muddy as well as stealing horses and cattle, and he wanted the perpetrators surrendered to him.

Tecumseh had denied any knowledge of it but did admit there were some stolen horses in Tippecanoe that he would have returned to Wells on his return there. "Do not, however," he added, "take this as a weakening on our part. It is not. We have found some surveyors sent out by Harrison into the Fort Wayne Treaty land. We could easily have killed them, but we were kind and did not and only sent them back to Harrison with a warning. We will not be so generous with those he sends out next. I am wholly and completely determined to resist the encroachments these whites are making beyond the boundaries into Indian country."

"Those are dreams, not plans," Wells commented dourly. "They will never come to pass."

"You will see the contrary, Apekonit," Tecumseh had replied with some heat, "if you are lucky and live long enough."

Continuing his journey, Tecumseh arrived at Amherstburg to discover that Main Poche was there, recovering from a wound so severe it had nearly killed him. He and his mixed-bag war party of 170 Potawatomies, Kickapoos, Sacs, and Foxes had penetrated the Osage country in Missouri late last fall and quickly encountered an Osage hunting party. They had killed five of the Osages and taken a prisoner but, during the fight a bullet had passed through Main Poche's chest, barely nicking his heart. The wound was so severe that Main Poche could neither walk nor ride and had been carried to the Missouri River and floated down to the St. Charles area near St. Louis, where he had spent the remainder of the winter. As soon as travel was reasonable in the spring, he had been taken the rest of the way here to Fort Malden where he was now recuperating well under the care of the post surgeon. Nevertheless, it would still be a considerable while before he would be well enough to hunt or make war.

In a major council held with the British at Fort Malden, Tecumseh informed them that as soon as he returned from the South, he would be ready to present his ultimatum to the Americans. This took the British authorities somewhat aback.

"Be not in too much of a hurry, Tecumseh," he was told, "as your great father, the king, has not yet finally determined to fight the Americans." They leavened his disappointment, however, with assurances that such conflict could not be very far off and when at last the British regained control of North

America, the boundary line between Indians and whites would once again be set at the Ohio River. They also provided him with thirty packhorse loads of ammunition to take back to Tippecanoe with him.

In the midst of his preparations for his forthcoming extensive trip to the Southern tribes, Tecumseh was interrupted by the arrival at Tippecanoe of a fully uniformed officer of the United States Army.[587]

Arriving in a large canoe paddled by four Frenchmen hired at Vincennes, Captain Walter Wilson successfully masked his nervousness at the hoard of whooping Indians who converged on the Wabash River bank as the bow of his trim craft scraped ashore among the multitude of Indian canoes beached here. In a carefully memorized sentence in the Shawnee tongue he said in a firm voice, "I come bearing a message from Governor Harrison for your chief, Tecumseh." There were some head-bobbings and a chorus of talking and he was escorted up the broad quarter-mile path to the level benchland some sixty feet above the river.

Captain Wilson had expected Tippecanoe to be a substantial village but was quite unprepared for the real size of this great Indian metropolis stretching out to the right for some two miles. The size of the huge House of Strangers, which alone now housed over three hundred Indians, as well as the enormous council house and the adjacent medicine lodge, awed him and he swiftly estimated their size, as well as the scope of the entire village with its hundreds of wegiwas, quonsets, and tepees, to report these matters to Governor Harrison on his return—assuming, of course, that he would return at all. There had been no guarantees, when he volunteered ten days earlier for the risky task, as to what his reception would be when he arrived in the stronghold of the enemy.

There was no doubt whatever in his mind, as he was led to an oversized cabin not far from the council house that the imposing Indian standing on the small stoop, though he wore very little decoration or insignia of rank, was the great Tecumseh, about whom he had heard so much since his arrival at Vincennes with Colonel Charles Boyd's regiment from Pittsburgh.

"Who are you and why are you here?" Tecumseh asked.

Mentally breathing a sigh of relief that the man spoke English, the officer snapped to attention. "Sir," he said crisply, "I am Captain Walter Wilson of the Fourth Regiment of the United States Army. I have come bearing a message from Governor William Henry Harrison for Chief Tecumseh. Are you he?"

"I am Tecumseh. Please enter." In the Shawnee tongue he thanked the villagers for bringing the soldier to him, adding they could go about their business now as he conferred with him.

Tecumseh's thoughts were racing. He was certain this officer's visit was as a direct result of the recent confiscation earlier this month that, as he put it, "my foolish brother, Tenskwatawa," had perpetrated in his absence. An-

other salt shipment had been sent up the Wabash by Harrison for the Miamis
and Kickapoos. Despite Tecumseh's admonition to Tenskwatawa before he
left for Amherstburg that his brother avoid doing anything that would anger
Harrison, when the flatboat came ashore at Tippecanoe to drop off several
barrels of salt for the Kickapoos who were there, Tenskwatawa had ordered
that the entire shipment, including other goods as well as the salt, be seized.
The captain of the boat was the same Creole who had been intercepted the
previous year and when he protested, Tenskwatawa reminded him that the
entire earlier salt shipment had been refused and was sent back. This, he said,
only restored to them what was rightfully theirs. Besides, the salt and other
goods were sorely needed, Tenskwatawa indiscreetly boasted, because he had
two thousand warriors to provide for here in Tippecanoe and Tecumseh would
soon be back from the lakes with a good many more.

Inside, at Tecumseh's gesture, they seated themselves at the table and
Tecumseh asked his woman to bring them coffee and a plate of food for their
guest. Since it would not be seemly to plunge at once into the business that
had brought the officer here, Tecumseh engaged him in cordial conversation
while they sipped coffee and the visitor gratefully ate the food placed before
him. Tecumseh had nodded approvingly when the young man asked that his
French paddlers at the boat be provided with victuals, if this were not too
great an imposition. At Tecumseh's request to her, his woman left the cabin
to see to it.

After having talked of many things, Tecumseh finally opened the door
for the business at hand. "You say you have brought a message to me from
Governor Harrison."

"Yes, sir." He reached into his blouse and removed a packet wrapped in
oilskin. From it he extracted a letter and, poised to open it, looked at Tecumseh.
"If you like, I will be pleased to read it to you."

Tecumseh smiled and extended his arm. "Thank you, Captain Wilson,"
he said, "but I will read it for myself."

Wilson nodded and handed him the letter and then sat quietly as Tecumseh
opened it, unfolded the pages, saw that it was written in the distinctive hand
of William Henry Harrison, addressed to himself and Tenskwatawa and dated
June 17 at Vincennes. He read:

> BROTHERS: *Listen to me. I speak to you about matters of importance to both
> the white people and yourselves; open your ears, therefore, and attend to
> what I shall say. Brothers, this is the third year that all white people in this
> country have been alarmed at your proceedings, you threaten us with war;
> you invite all the tribes to the north and west of you to join against us.*
>
> *Brothers, your warriors who have lately been here deny this, but I have
> received information from every direction; the tribes on the Mississippi have*

sent me word that you intended to murder me, and then to commence a war upon our people. I have also received the speech you sent to the Potawatomies and others to join you for that purpose; but if I had no other evidence of your hostility to us, your seizing the salt I lately sent up the Wabash is sufficient. Brothers, our citizens are alarmed, and my warriors are preparing themselves, not to strike you, but to defend themselves and their women and children. You shall not surprise us as you expect to do; you are about to undertake a very rash act. As a friend, I advise you to consider well of it; a little reflection may save us a great deal of trouble and prevent much mischief; it is not yet too late.

Brothers, what can be the inducement for you to undertake an enterprise when there is so little probability of success? Do you really think that the handful of men that you have about you are able to contend with the Seventeen Fires, or even that the whole of the tribes united could contend against the Kentucky Fire alone? Brothers, I am myself of the Long Knife Fire.[588] As soon as they hear my voice you will see them pouring forth their swarms of hunting-shirt men, as numerous as the mosquitoes on the shores of the Wabash. Brothers, take care of their stings. Brothers, it is not our wish to hurt you; if we did, we certainly have the power to do it. Look at the number of our warriors to the east of you, above and below the Great Miami; to the south, on both sides of the Ohio, and below you also. You are brave men, but what could you do against such a multitude?—but we wish to live in peace and happiness.

Brothers, the citizens of this country are alarmed. They must be satisfied that you have no design to do them mischief, or they will not lay aside their arms. You have also insulted the government of the United States by seizing the salt that was intended for other tribes; satisfaction must be given for that also. Brothers, you talk of coming to see me, attended by all your young men; this, however, must not be so. If your intentions are good, you have need to bring but a few of your young men with you. I must be plain with you; I will not suffer you to come into our settlements with such a force.

Brothers, if you wish to satisfy us that your intentions are good, follow the advice I have given you before; that is, that one or both of you should visit the President of the United States and lay your grievances before him. He will treat you well, listen to what you say, and if you can show him that you have been injured, you will receive justice. If you will follow my advice in this respect it will convince the citizens of this country and myself that you have no design to attack them.

Brothers, with respect to the land that was purchased. . . . I can enter into no negotiations with you on that subject; the affair is in the hands of the President. If you wish to go and see him, I will supply you with the means.

Brothers, the person who delivers this is one of my war officers. He is a man in whom I have entire confidence. Whatever he says to you, although it may not be contained in this paper, you may believe comes from me.

My friend Tecumseh, the bearer is a good man and a brave warrior. I hope you will treat him well. You are yourself a warrior, and all such should have esteem for each other.

William Henry Harrison, Governor
Cmdr In Chief, Indiana Territory

Tecumseh looked up, pushing the paper to one side on the table. Captain Wilson was watching him closely and Tecumseh smiled faintly. Yes, this one was a good warrior; ever watchful.

"Your chief speaks highly of you," Tecumseh said, tilting his head toward the letter. "He seems to fear that we might harm you. You may rest assured, no harm whatsoever will come to you or the men with you. You will not mind waiting while I write a reply to Governor Harrison?"

"Thank you, sir." Wilson smiled in return. "No, sir, I won't mind waiting at all. If I may say so, sir, ever since I first met you, I have had no fear that you would harm me."

Tecumseh now grinned broadly. "Now I thank you. Warriors such as we sometimes learn it is safer to trust the word of an enemy than that of a friend. I will write the letter now."

From a little stand nearby, Tecumseh brought an ink pot, paper and several freshly trimmed quill pens. He sat quietly a moment, considering what he would say. He was not pleased with the fact that this would now cause him to postpone for several weeks the southern trip that he had been planning to begin within a week. Yet, equally, there could be some advantages inherent in another council with Harrison before he left.

Without another glance at his guest, he dipped one of the pens and began writing swiftly.

Brother: I give you a few words until I will be with you myself. Brother, at Vincennes, I wish you to listen to me whilst I send you a few words, and I hope they will ease your heart. I know how you look on your young men and young women and children with pity, to see them so alarmed. Brother, I wish you now to examine what you have from me. I hope it will be a satisfaction to you, if your intentions are like mine, to wash away all these bad stories that have been circulated. I will be with you myself in eighteen days from this day.

Brother, we cannot say what will become of us, as the Great Spirit has the management of us all at Her will. I may be there before the time, and

may not be there until the day. I hope that when we come together all these
bad tales will be settled. By this I hope that our young men, young women
and children will be easy. I wish you, brother, to let them know when I
come to Vincennes and see you, all will be settled in peace and happiness.
Brother, these are only a few words to let you know that I will be with you
myself; and when I am with you, I can inform you better. Brother, if I find
I can be with you in less than eighteen days, I will send one of my young
men before me to let you know the time I will be with you.

Tecumseh

Putting his quill to one side, Tecumseh blew on the paper until he was
satisfied the ink was dry, then folded it and handed it to Captain Wilson.

"You may tell your chief, my young friend," he said, "what I did not
say in the letter—that although I will come to visit him as he requests, it will
not be with a few men only, which would be most unseemly. As he knows,
it is the way of all the tribes when an important council is held, for a large
number of people to come with their chiefs. However, so as not to arouse the
fears of his white people at so many coming, I will include a number of our
women so they will see we come in peace."[589]

[July 30, 1811 — Tuesday]

Tecumseh's second council with William Henry Harrison at the Grouseland Estate in Vincennes opened with somewhat less drama than that of the
previous year, but hardly with less tension, despite the fact that the governor
had mustered eight hundred federal troops for the occasion.

Determined that he would not lose his temper this time, no matter how
much the governor might lie or twist things to suit his purposes, Tecumseh
was also faced with combating the specter of fear haunting his people the closer
the time came to leave Tippecanoe for the council. They were haunted not
only because their spies had brought word of how greatly strengthened Harrison was with reinforcements from both the East and from Kentucky, but
also because his force was fairly bristling with artillery.[590]

In an effort to allay these fears, Tecumseh had called a council in Tippecanoe on the eve of their departure and addressed them in a steady, reassuring
voice.

"My friends," he told them, "this night the spirits of our fathers are
listening to our deliberations, and shall it be said by distant nations, whose
eyes are now on us, that we were met here with an army of *Shemanese* and
got frightened of them, broke up our league and scattered off like cowards?

Or shall it be said that after having matured our plans and about to strike in defense of our homes and hunting grounds, we were intimidated into compliance with the terms of the intruder and wampum, by his holding out to us the hand of peace and friendship, and with the other pointing to his forces? Who is there among you, here, now, around the council fire, that would withdraw from our league and go backwards like the crawfish? By being united and all of one mind, we might prevent what is left of our country from passing into the hands of the white man and, in time, other nations will join us. Rouse up your drooping spirits, my friends!"

It had helped and it was with generally high spirits that, at sunrise the following morning those who were traveling down the Wabash in canoes—which was the majority of the three hundred accompanying him to the council, including thirty women—had embarked downstream. However, the twenty chiefs and warriors who would accompany Tecumseh to the South still waited nearby on their horses—six Shawnees, six Kickapoos, three Potawatomies, two Wyandots, and one each of the Winnebago, Ottawa and Chippewa tribes. Chaubenee was there, holding the reins of Tecumseh's horse, as was Jim Blue Jacket, formerly Little Blue Jacket, the son of his old friend who had died last year. Here, too, was Seekaboo, minor prophet from Wapakoneta, who had at last broken with Catahecassa and joined Tecumseh and whose fluency in the tongues of the Southern tribes made him a valuable asset.[591]

Now, with the sun not yet an hour high, those who were remaining here at Tippecanoe—some twenty-three hundred warriors, women, and children—stood quietly at a respectful distance, as Tecumseh talked earnestly with his younger brother in front of the medicine lodge, from which the pair had just emerged. Tecumseh placed his hands on Tenskwatawa's shoulders and his instructions were explicit.

"Everything in Tippecanoe and among our people is being left in trust with you, Tenskwatawa," he said. "You must continue to give your message to them, soothe their minds and keep the fires in their breasts in check until I return. It is of the utmost importance at this stage that the peace be maintained. Within another five moons we will be strong enough to stand by ourselves and make our demands. The great sign will come then and this will be the turning point of the fortunes of all the Indians on this great island."

He looked at his younger brother steadily, the niggling of a lingering concern in his mind. He was only too well aware of Tenskwatawa's volatile nature and rash tendencies. He dropped his hands and looked around at the many Indians still left here.

"It is most imperative," he continued, "that between now and then, no open hostilities *of any kind* break out between us and the whites. Harrison is a very shrewd man who reads us too well. He has now heard many whispers of our plan but he does not know it all. In Vincennes, when we talk, I will tell him only what he already knows from his spies, but he is very shrewd and his own senses will tell him something is in the wind beyond what has been said. He will grasp any excuse to open actual war with us.

"I will give us a good margin by making him believe he has more time than he has. I will say that I will not be returning from the South until next spring is far advanced. But you know, as I have told you, that what is to happen will be before the winter is truly upon us.

"Tenskwatawa," he said, his tone becoming stern, "it is in my mind that Governor Harrison *will* attempt something in my absence to make you act foolishly. *This must not happen!* If it becomes necessary for you to make concessions for the sake of maintaining the peace, *make them!* If it becomes necessary to take insult and swallow pride, then such *must* be done. More than anything else, if Harrison should set his army in motion toward you, you are to get out of the way; scatter, disappear into the forest. If he attempts to destroy Tippecanoe, abandon it, move away and let him have his will. Tippecanoe can be rebuilt. Our union, if it becomes ruptured, cannot. Do you fully understand?"

Tenskwatawa smiled and nodded. Tecumseh regarded him silently for a long moment and then he, too, nodded. "Moneto be with you," he said.

Turning, he moved quickly to the horsemen and mounted. The assembled villagers were watching him closely and he stretched out both arms and repeated himself in a loud voice.

"Moneto be with you all!"

A loud chorus of cheers and yips and yells broke out as he put his horse in motion then and the others fell in behind him. Within a few minutes they had disappeared from sight along the woodland trail bordering the river.

Tenskwatawa, smiling, turned and reentered the medicine lodge. For the first time at such a departure, Tecumseh had not given him any prophecies to pass along to the people. It was just as well—Tenskwatawa had forecasts of his own to make and he didn't need Tecumseh's help to see the future.

He was The Prophet!

It had not taken Tecumseh's mounted party very long to overtake the much larger party in canoes and pace them along the shoreline. There had been no untoward events on the journey and three days ago they had set up camp in the same place they had camped the year before, on the Wabash River bank a mile above Grouseland and two miles below Fort Knox. The days since then had been filled with almost continuous counciling. Hundreds of troops were moving about Vincennes and Tecumseh sent word to Harrison saying that if so many soldiers armed with rifles were going to attend the council, then he would order that all his warriors carry firearms as well. Harrison replied that only a small number of dragoons would have firearms, whereupon Tecumseh ordered his men to leave their guns in camp, but to take with them their bows and arrows as well as tomahawks or war clubs.

The council had been scheduled to begin the day before yesterday and everyone involved had met at the council ground a short distance from the Grouseland mansion, but a heavy thunderstorm had begun and the council was called off for the day, to begin tomorrow. The spirit of the Indians dropped at this, they considering the storm was a very bad omen and that the Great Spirit, weeping upon the council, had shown displeasure.

Yesterday morning they tried it again and, accompanied by 180 of his men, Tecumseh walked to the same open ground where the council last year was held. At his hand signal, the warriors and chiefs sat down on the ground in a broad semicircle behind him.

As before the whites had arranged themselves on either side and behind where Governor Harrison sat behind a table, flanked by commissioners and interpreters and a substantial armed guard of soldiers off to one side. Among the Indians and whites alike, there was more than the usual solemnity that accompanied such a council and Harrison in particular evinced irritation at the large number of men who had accompanied Tecumseh.[592]

Without delay and with little finesse, Harrison opened the council and this time he elected to speak first. He referred at once to the alleged murder of two whites in the Illinois country and the considerable alarm Tecumseh had occasioned by coming to Vincennes with so many of his people. To Tecumseh this was an insult and his features hardened; by rights he should have been attended by six hundred. Not noticing, Harrison moved on, promising to listen to anything Tecumseh or his chiefs might have to say about the land purchase made with the Fort Wayne Treaty, but he would enter into no negotiations about it since, as he had explained in his letter, the matter was in the hands of the president. He then brought up the problem of the salt shipment that had been seized by Tenskwatawa and demanded an explanation.

Sarcasm was heavy in Tecumseh's voice as he rose and replied. "The salt that was taken was taken in my absence, just as the salt that was refused the previous year was stopped from going upriver in my absence. It seems to me that it is impossible to please the governor. Last year you were angry because the salt was refused and this year you are just as much displeased that it was taken!"

It was all he had to say on the subject and Governor Harrison, obviously angry, adjourned the meeting until the following day.

When the council reconvened at noon today, Wawpawwawqua—White Loon—chief of the Weas, opened the proceedings with a speech lasting several hours, detailing the many treaties made by Harrison with various Indians, clearly exposing the great deceit that had been used on the part of the whites in dividing the tribes, dealing with minor chiefs and illegally gaining cessions of land.

When at last Wawpawwawqua finished and resumed his place with the others, Harrison immediately changed the subject with no comment whatever on what had just been said, thereby delivering the Wea chief a substantial insult. Instead, the governor had addressed Tecumseh, asking him to turn over for prosecution by the whites the two Potawatomies who had slain the two white men, saying that if Tecumseh did so, it would show the governor that he was sincere in his professions of friendship.

Tecumseh's reply was strained. At considerable length he told Harrison that he had taken great pains to unite the Northwestern Indian tribes under himself and the whites were unnecessarily alarmed at this. Had not the United States, he asked, set the example itself by establishing a union of Seventeen Fires? The Indians did not complain of this, he said. Why then should the whites feel justified in complaining when the Indians united? Was it not as fair for one as for the other? As for the Potawatomies Harrison asked for, Tecumseh would not deliver them up. The two whites who died had not been murdered; they had been executed, bringing the fate upon themselves by shooting two Weas without provocation and while those whites themselves were trespassing in Indian country. He added that he had long since set the whites an example of forgiveness of injuries and that now they ought to imitate him.

"We have said enough here," Tecumseh said abruptly, weary of this council that was going nowhere and accomplishing nothing. "You yourself have said the heart of the problem between us is in the hands of your president. There is, then, no further point in speaking with you. Soon after this council is concluded, I will leave this country for a long visit with the tribes to the South to ask them to become a part of our Indian union. After visiting them, I will visit the Osage tribe and return home by the Missouri when the spring is well advanced. A great number of Indians will be coming back to settle at Tippecanoe with us. We will make them welcome. But the land you falsely purchased on the Wabash is our finest hunting ground and we will need it to secure food for these people. I hope that nothing will be done by the whites toward settling this hunting ground before my return. The affairs of the tribes in the Northwest are in my hands and I give you assurance that you need have no fear of war breaking our during my absence; nothing will be done without me; I will dispatch messengers in every direction to prevent them from doing any mischief and to remain quiet until my return next spring. At that time, when our union is complete, then I will be ready to visit the president and settle all difficulties with him."

By this time night had fallen and the moon was up. Entirely displeased with the way the council had gone, Governor Harrison closed it on a sharp warning note. He pointed to the celestial orb and spoke grimly.

"The moon you see would sooner fall to the ground than the president would suffer his people to be murdered with impunity, and I will put petticoats on my soldiers sooner than give up a country I have bought fairly from its true owners!"[593]

Chapter 11

—《 》— The reaction among the Southern tribes to the message brought to them by Tecumseh and his deputation from the North ranged from wild enthusiasm for his grand plan, especially among the young warriors, to outright belligerence and threats against him, especially among the older chiefs or mingoes, as they referred to their rank. Each of the tribes visited was presented with a sacred slab and a bundle of red sticks, but where the stick bundles had once been large, they had eventually become very small. His fame had greatly preceded him and even in the most remote of villages the word of his visiting and talking to the tribes of the South dominated conversation, engendering large measures of hope and fear, happiness and trepidation.

Even among those who feared him and were filled with apprehension for what disaster he might bring down upon them, there were few who could not relate to his influence and power or who failed to be stirred by the visions he ignited with his dream of a great amalgamation of tribes in which all Indians were brothers united against a common and indisputably deadly foe. In almost constant motion, he had visited the Choctaws, Chickasaws, and Cherokees, the Biloxis, Creeks, Alabamas and Seminoles, the Calusas, Santees, Yazoos, Natchez, Tawakonias, and the Caddos.

Tecumseh and his men had moved southward swiftly after the futile council at Vincennes, crossing the Spaylaywitheepi near the mouth of the Wabash, arrowing through Kentucky and Tennessee without more than overnight pauses until they crossed the great Tennessee River close to where the Chickasaw halfbreed chief, George Colbert, had established a ferry.[594] Colbert, who had personally gained much in his contact with the whites, had no desire to see this position jeopardized by Tecumseh and so, while overtly welcoming Tecumseh and agreeably summoning Chickasaw chiefs to attend a major council to hear the Shawnee, at the same time he covertly did all in his power to undermine Tecumseh and turn the tribe against him.

The Chickasaws had assembled quickly and listened to his message and, though they treated him and his men with respect, they would not commit themselves to him, remembering all too painfully that for hundreds of years their people had warred against the Northern tribes and they could not conceive of embracing them now as brothers. But, while they did not accept his plan, they were moved by his eloquence and provided him a mounted escort of their own warriors to lead him to whatever villages he wished to visit.

They stopped and visited a number of villages as they traveled southwestward, following the trail that flanked the north bank of the Buttahatchee to where it flowed into the Tombigbee and there crossed that larger stream to the sprawling Choctaw village called Red Pepper's Town on the Oktibbeha River.[595] They were hospitably met by Chief Red Pepper, who directed them to a nearby place to set up their camp for the night. He also generously provided the party with food and whiskey enough for each of them to have a healthy drink. There were no drinkers among Tecumseh's party, however, and so their Chickasaw escort gladly drank up the entire amount and became drunk and abusive toward the Chocktaws—to such an extent that Tecumseh was forced to order his men to disarm their escort and tie them up to prevent a fight from breaking out. During much of the night Tecumseh conferred with Red Pepper, finding him to be a pacific chief who was obviously concerned at the scope of Tecumseh's plan and felt he should talk with a tribal authority much more powerful than he. In the morning, after Tecumseh released the bound Chickasaws and sent them on their way back home, Red Pepper provided a new escort and directed them to take Tecumseh's party to the village of the Chocktaw war mingo, Mashulatubbe.[596]

Mashulatubbe was a large, powerful man who welcomed the Northern delegation warmly and quickly became highly enthusiastic as Seekaboo interpreted Tecumseh's remarks. He thought the idea of the Indian amalgamation was inspired and immediately provided additional men to guide the Northern Indians to nearby towns while he sent runners with word to all mingoes to come at once to attend a major council at his village.

In a remarkably short time several hundred Choctaws had assembled at

Mashulatubbe's Village and Tecumseh's followers had elected to make a dramatic appearance. They entered the council and all but Tecumseh were clad only in buckskin breechclouts and leggins that were fringed and profusely beaded and all their heads were shaved except for a short, broad, brushlike band of upraised hair from above the forehead back over the top of the head to the nape and there evolving into a queue hanging down the back into which had been interwoven hawk feathers. Tecumseh had merely donned a simple undecorated buckskin blouse almost to his knees and similar leggins and he wore a scarlet flannel head band over which was a narrow silver band, with his hair loose to the shoulders below it and a single pure white feather with scarlet end attached above his forehead and angled slightly backward. On their upper arms they wore beaten silver armbands and a few had crescent-shaped silver gorgets hanging from their necks. Some of the warriors had painted a bright red semicircular line beneath their eyes, with a red spot at each temple and a larger circle of solid red centered on the chest.

With Seekaboo skillfully interpreting, Tecumseh told the respectful listeners what had occurred in the North—the gradual whittling away of Indian lands and the forcing of the tribes ever back.[597]

"Have we not," he asked them, "for years had before our eyes a sample of their designs, and are they not sufficient harbingers of their future determination?" He continued in this vein for a while and then arrowed in on the methods of the whites. "They are," he said, "a people fond of innovations, quick to contrive and quick to put their schemes into effectual execution, no matter how great and wrong the injury to us, while we are content to preserve what we already have. Their designs are to enlarge their possessions by taking yours."

No single tribe or even a small union would be able to stop this process, he went on with his warning, as history had so well proven. "Before the palefaces came among us," he said, "we enjoyed the happiness of unbounded freedom and were acquainted with neither riches nor wants, nor with oppression. How is it now? Wants and oppressions are our lot, for are we not controlled in everything, and dare we move without asking them, by your leave? Are we not being stripped, day by day, of the little that remains of our ancient liberty? Do they not even now kick and strike us as they do their black-faces? How long will it be before they will tie us to a post and whip us and make us labor for them in their cornfields, as they do them?

"Shall we calmly wait until they become so numerous that we will no longer be able to resist oppression? The white usurpation of our common country must be stopped or we, its rightful owners, will be forever destroyed and wiped out as a race of people. Will we wait to be destroyed in our turn, without making an effort worthy of our race? Shall we give up our homes, our country, bequeathed to us by the Great Spirit, the graves of our dead and everything that is dear to us, without a struggle? I know you will cry with me, Never! Never! Then let us, by unity of action, destroy them all—which we can now do—or drive them back whence they came. War or extermination is now our only choice. Let us form one body, one heart, and defend—to the last warrior!—our country, our homes, our liberty and the graves of our fathers."

He told them how now, to end this once and for all, all the Northern tribes had put aside their personal enmities and joined as brother *Indians* against the white scourge. The Chocktaws, he told them, had not yet suffered so badly at the hands of the whites, but they soon would; they had one of the most beautiful lands he had ever seen anywhere and it was a spear to his heart to know that eventually it must all become the possession of the whites.[598] Were the Chocktaws willing for this to happen? Would they, as so many of the Northern tribes had fruitlessly done, try on their own to fend off the white invasion when it came? Or would they simply bow before the whites and back away? Or were they warriors who would stand up for their rights and, realizing the great power of the whites, pledge themselves to the Indian brotherhood to effectively combat the white menace?

Here, at last, Tecumseh encountered strong resistance. The principal mingo of the Choctaws was Pushmataha, and he was greatly displeased at this Shawnee so brashly entering the territory of his people and causing unrest with such speeches.[599] His response to Tecumseh was harsh and insulting.

"We Choctaws have no need to demand peace with the whites," he said. "We are already at peace with them and they do not bother us, nor we them. It would be foolish beyond measure for us to send off our young men to fight in Northern battles which are not our business. It would be foolish as well for our young men here to rise against those with whom we are at peace." He pointed at Tecumseh and his voice became hard, accusatory. "I know your history well. You have always been a troublemaker. When you have found yourself unable to pick a quarrel with the white man, you have stirred up strife between different tribes of your own race. Not only that, you are a monarch and unyielding tyrant within your own domain; every Shawnee man, woman and child must bow in humble submission to your imperious will!"

The charges were so undeserving and so false that Tecumseh was stunned at first and then greatly angered. How could they not see that the whites would soon push them quite as hard as they pushed the Northern tribes? How could they fail to see the significance of the Northern tribes, many of who had been intensely bitter enemies over many generations, now melded together to fight the foe who threatened them all? Could they truly believe that the troubles between Indians and whites in the North were due to the Indians picking the fights? How could they not understand the significance of the whites having pushed the Indians of the North back so far that they were virtually extinct in the lands east of the mountains and being pushed to that point east of the Mississippi?

Pushmataha, however, had gone on doggedly. "You do not have our sympathy," he said, "nor can you expect our support. As for Mashulatubbe and his young warriors whose blood is hot for war, I say this: if any of you foolishly go off to join Tecumseh's fight against the whites or rise up here to strike down the whites who neighbor us, you will be considered as traitors to your own nation and, when you return, you will be put to death for having disobeyed the restrictions here laid before you."

So cowed were the Choctaw mingoes that none, not even Mashulatubbe, rose to dispute him and Tecumseh, realizing the pointlessness of trying to balk Pushmataha here, left the council with his men and shortly afterwards went to other major Indian centers in the region, such as Mokalusha and Chunky.[600]

Pushmataha, not satisfied, continued to dog Tecumseh's party in the days following and at every place where Tecumseh made major address, refuted them immediately after the talk and continued to threaten execution to any who should rise to help Tecumseh in his plan. In exasperation, the Northern delegation finally turned eastward and southward, out of the country of the Choctaws into that of the Creeks and Muscogees, then the Seminoles and Yemasees and Apalachicolas, then back westward again along the great blue gulf to the Biloxies and Alabamas and northward along the Mississippi to the Yazoos and Natchez. His greatest disappointment came as he was visiting the Creeks, when a deputation of Cherokees came to see him. Planning to visit the Cherokees next, he greeted them warmly, but they refused to shake hands with him and delivered the speech of their chief, Stonahajo, who said they were at peace with the whites and determined to stay so and, in no uncertain terms, warned Tecumseh and his party not to come into Cherokee territory at all or they would certainly be slain at once.[601]

His words to the remaining Southern tribes were far more incendiary than those he had so long used in the North. Then he had felt that there would be room for negotiation with the president when such a strong opposing force should merely rear itself before him and state its demands. Now, with the unbending words of Harrison still in his ears and convinced that what had to be won by the Indians could only be achieved through actual warfare, he was no longer so strongly suggesting that they bargain through a peaceful show of strength.

There existed, among many of the well-established leaders, what he had encountered in Pushmataha—a great jealousy that this foreign Indian should come among them and threaten the dissolution of their own power with his message and their antagonism came to the surface in a variety of ways. Some would gladly have assassinated him except that they truly feared repercussions from those he had brought with him, those he had united in the North, and even their own people, since many were so mesmerized by the dream of glory he was instilling in them.

Chief Little Prince of the Lower Creeks and Big Warrior of the Upper Creeks were two of those who seethed with indignation at this stranger from the North who came among them and so swayed his older people and fired up their young warriors with his elocution and common sense.[602] Big Warrior, who did not dare to refuse Tecumseh the right to address a national council, was nevertheless not at all pleased when Tecumseh and his party, accompanied by an escort of nineteen Choctaws and forty-seven Cherokees, arrived to speak in Big Warrior's own principal village of Tuckabatchee at the confluence of the Tallapoosa and Coosa Rivers.[603] Chiefs and their deputations had arrived all day long on the day set for the talk and Tecumseh, to make sure everyone had arrived who was coming, held off beginning his address until midnight. Then, before a large council fire under the stars, he began, as usual, tracing the Indian and white relationship over the years.

"Accursed be the race," he added, his voice crackling with indignation and reaching every ear in the large assemblage, "that has seized our country and made women of our warriors! Wipe away the mists that have clouded your vision and look about you at what the whites have done. It is not yet as much as has touched us who are your Northern brothers, but I promise you it will be as much and more in a little while. They have seized your land bit by bit, as they have done ours, until those of you who remain are cramped in a little area where there is hardly room to breathe. Their axes have felled your greatest trees and their saws have cut into little pieces the forests that have stood in their path. They have corrupted your little chiefs, as they have corrupted ours, with whiskey and cheap gifts that are soon gone and with nothing to show for it. They have defiled your women and they have trampled upon the graves of your dead. You—and we!—have stood back everywhere and let this occur and our fathers, from their graves, reproach us as slaves and cowards. I hear them now in the wailing winds!"

He cupped a hand behind his ear and listened, as did the crowd who faced him, and such was the power of his suggestion that though the air was calm, they, like him, heard the sighing moan of a breeze that was not, and in it the anguish of all those who had died at the hands of the whites.

"Who," he went on, dropping his hand and speaking more harshly, "are these white people that we should so fear them? Are they warriors as good as we? No! How have they taken so much of what is ours? They have done this by taking advantage of the angers and hurts we red men have so long held against one another. They have encouraged us to dissent more among ourselves, to hate and fear our neighbor tribes, knowing that what they could not possibly take from the whole, they can easily take from the pieces. We must put those pieces back together and put aside those former hurts and pains and angers that have existed between us and bury them as if they never were. Who are these whites who have so skillfully learned our great weakness and have used it to manipulate us to their own benefit? I will tell you who they are: they are merely men, no more. Hear me, my brothers! They cannot run fast and this makes them good marks at which to shoot, as they are only men! Our fathers have killed many of them. We are the sons of our fathers! We are not women! We can—and we *must*—stain the earth red with their blood."[604]

On the heels of his talk the air was rent by the howls and shrieks of the warriors as they raised their tomahawks high and slashed them wildly through the air. But Big Warrior himself had listened with a disapproving frown no matter how earnestly and convincingly Tecumseh had spoken. The Creek chief remained unmoved and, despite the evident enthusiasm of the warriors, refused to pledge the cooperation of his people. Tecumseh was now heartily tired of the shortsightedness of so many of the chiefs of these Southern tribes and he let his gaze sweep across the multitude assembled before him and finally settle on Big Warrior. There was more than just a mere thread of scorn in his voice as he pointed at the chief and spoke.

"Your blood is white! You accept into your ears but not into your heart the words I bring you. You, like many of the others, have accepted the sticks and the wampum and you have even touched the hatchet at your belt, yet I know you do not mean to fight and I know the reason: you do not believe I have been sent by the Great Spirit. But you *shall* know. When the time comes for all these things to come together, then will I stamp my foot to the ground and awaken our great mother earth who will at last stretch her great muscles at the desecration she has so long borne from the whites and your ears will be filled with the rumble and roar of her anger. She will cause your houses to fall to the ground and the bones of every man to tremble with the trembling of the ground. Your water jugs will crack and fall apart and great trees will lean and fall, though there be no wind. And when she thus reveals to you her inner heart, then must you drop your mattocks and your fish scrapers and pick up your hatchets to rise with one mind and one heart against those whites who have so defiled her."

Chief Big Warrior was finally impressed in spite of himself and he agreed that he and his people would so rise up, if and when the great sign of which he spoke occurred, and Tecumseh was pleased, because he knew it would come. He was equally gratified when Josiah Francis, an English-Creek halfbreed, along with several of his cohorts, became so involved with the new doctrine of the Northern tribes that they became disciples of the movement in the South and promised to continue to promote it here even after Tecumseh was gone. They spoke, Tecumseh learned, for a sizeable segment of the Creeks.

It was late in the Harvest Moon that Tecumseh and his original party, with the exception of Seekaboo, who was staying with the Creeks to continue Tecumseh's message there, headed northwestward to the Mississippi. Tecumseh was not happy with how his message had been received by the Southern tribes. Many of the young men would undoubtedly rise against the whites in the South when the great sign came and others would head north to join them at Tippecanoe, but for the most part the mission had failed and he was depressed because of it.

They encountered the Mississippi at the mouth of Nonconnah Creek and crossed in canoes provided by Chief Chucalissa, whose village was nearby, herding the riderless horses across with them.[605] Up through the Arkansas country they traveled, still angling northwestward until, in the southern Missouri country, under a sign of peace, they came to the first of the Osage villages. They were met with suspicion and fear and quickly surrounded by an ominously silent and sullen group of Osages. When their object was made known, they were escorted to a larger village, called Tanwakanwakaghe, almost three full days' journey, where a major council was being held.[606]

It was a tense situation. Here was a party made up of Indians from east of the Mississippi—the same tribes who so often came against them in war parties, the same man who had come to them once before under the sign of peace and had been turned back. This time they listened as Tecumseh spoke stirringly, finally telling them to open their eyes to the inroads that white traders and hunters were already making in their midst.

"Brothers," he told them, "the white men are not friends to the Indians. At first they only asked for land sufficient for a wegiwa. Now nothing will satisfy them but the whole of our hunting grounds, from the rising to the setting sun.

"Brothers, the white men despise and cheat the Indians; they abuse and insult them and they do not think the red men sufficiently good to live.

"If you do not unite with us," he went on, "they will first destroy us and then you will fall easy prey to them. The whites have destroyed many nations of red men because they were not united, because they were not friends to each other.

"Brothers," Tecumseh concluded, "the red men all wish for peace, but where white people are there is no peace for the Indian except in the bosom of our Mother Earth."

Though his message was well received and there were strong murmurings of approval, the Osages eventually declined; too many tribes had come against them in the past and built up powerful enmities that could not be ended with but a few words. It was a good thing, what this man Tecumseh was proposing, but it simply wasn't possible yet. One day, perhaps, but not yet.

The Osages provided them with an escort and safe passage back toward the Mississippi, leaving them at last at the headwaters of the St. Francis River and returning to their own people. Tecumseh and his party went on, traveling leisurely, still heading southeastward, stopping to hunt occasionally. Eventually, by the end of the second week in November, they had reached the Shawnee villages on Apple Creek near Cape Girardeau.

The season was well advanced by now, with early winter winds and snow sweeping across the hills and woodlands and so here they settled down to visit among the villages of the Shawnees who had so long ago separated from those who had remained behind in the Ohio country. And it was here that Tecumseh, looking for his sister, was informed that Tecumapese had not long ago left here, that she had become enamored of a French trader named Francis Maisonville and had taken up living with him as his woman somewhere to the south of here, forty or fifty or sixty miles to the distant, rumored to be in a lonely cabin in the woods close to a small stream. She had not been seen since, but the Frenchman she was with was known to be seen at intervals in the white settlement called New Madrid.

Angry that Tecumapese not only had turned away from Wasegoboah but had even turned her back on her own people and taken up with a white man, Tecumseh set out alone to find her and bring her back.

[November 16, 1811 — Saturday]

On this clear and crisp night at close to midnight, the sky a blanket of bright stars undiminished in their brilliance by the presence of the moon, an enormous meteor entered Earth's atmosphere somewhere over the center of the great range of Rocky Mountains to the west, traveling from west to east. The buffeting of the atmosphere caused it to burst into a myriad of small pieces and three very large ones. The small pieces were quickly consumed in the fire of friction, but the three large pieces, spreading out from one another, flared into intense greenish white fire as they scored the dark heavens over the south, central, and northern parts of eastern North America.

The vigils being kept by the various small groups that had been assigned to the task, ever since the next to final red stick had been discarded at the last full moon, were now rewarded: in southern Canada from far west of the great Lake-of-the-Woods to the falls of Niagara they saw it; in the Missouri country and the Territories of Illinois and Indiana, and in Ohio and Pennsylvania and

New York they saw it; in the areas of Mississippi and Tennessee, Alabama and Georgia and Florida they saw it. They stared in awe at the sign of the Panther Passing Across, some of them feeling gratified at the realization of the prediction, others deeply afraid. Some of those who saw it snapped the final red stick across a knee and cast it into the fire and retired to the darkness of their abodes and prayed to their personal spirits or the Great Spirit Herself. The greater majority, however, carefully marked and cut the final red stick into thirty equal pieces, knowing that from this night forward one of these pieces would be dropped into the fire and burned.

And then they waited.

[December 16, 1811 — Monday]

Tecumseh had finally found Tecumapese.

After a long and fruitless search he had finally entered New Madrid and asked questions of the men he met there, most of whom, until he spoke to them, simply ignored him, as they ignored other Indians wandering about. Even the majority of those he spoke with shrugged, having heard of the trader named Maisonville, but not knowing where his cabin was located. No one had any idea who he was and when he spoke to them in English, merely presumed he was one of the Indians who frequented the trading posts, looking for handouts of whiskey. One of the men told him that Maisonville was off in Osage country to the west and probably wouldn't be back for another couple of weeks. At last, however, in a small trading post in the little town, the proprietor knew where Maisonville's cabin was located and gave him directions.

The cabin was hardly two miles from the New Madrid settlement, but well hidden in a small creek valley. Bundled up in his heavy buffalo coat, Tecumseh might have been the trader himself coming home late in the afternoon today and, when he unceremoniously opened the door and walked in, Tecumapese thought it was her man and was greatly shocked to discover her brother.

She had called his name, rushed to him and embraced him, bubbling with questions. Where had he come from? How had he found her? The flow of questions and the joy she expressed however, were short lived. Sternly, Tecumseh told her she had no business leaving her own people and taking up with a white man, which was wholly contrary to the teaching now so prevalent among their people. Her place, he told her, was with the Indians and especially with Wasegoboah, who was so lost without her. Tecumapese told him she no longer loved Wasegoboah, nor he her; that she had met and fallen in love with Maisonville and where he was, there she would be. They were planning to get married.

Tecumseh refused to hear such things and told her to gather her possessions and dress warmly, that he was taking her back to Apple Creek. Though he would not, he said, force her to return to Wasegoboah, since that was her decision, she could not, however, live with a white man and must return to the Shawnees. At first she argued but quickly realized it was in vain and she meekly did as he bade.

They had headed back toward Apple Creek at once but were hardly ten miles from New Madrid and, in the twilight, had just established their camp for the night when two riders came into view. Tecumseh and Tecumapese watched them come, recognizing even from a distance in the dimness that the pair were Indians. They were not, however, prepared for who they were and were amazed and delighted to see, as they came close, that they were two of Tecumseh's principal lieutenants from Tippecanoe: the Wyandot war chief Stiahta—he whom the whites called Roundhead—and the Potawatomi sub-chief name Metea.

The pair rode as if with a great weight on their shoulders, but Tecumseh could see the weight they bore lay within their hearts and their minds and that their mission was a grave one. Nevertheless, he welcomed them to the fire and, while they ate, Stiahta and Metea told of their search for Tecumseh, which had begun thirty-eight days before.

The two Indians had traveled day by day through Indiana and Kentucky and Tennessee, their pace slow, methodical, their nightly stops early and their morning departures late—men reluctant to move on, yet driven by duty and love to do so. Their minds told them to hasten, but the lead in their hearts had taken precedence and slowed them. Bit by bit they had unraveled his trail, following it into Georgia and Florida, then westward into Alabama and Mississippi. At length the trail grew dim as they were told that Tecumseh and his party had left the South and headed for the Mississippi and someone had been heard to say that they would visit the Osages and perhaps some other tribes in the West after that, but that before returning to their own country, they would visit among the Shawnee villages at Apple Creek in the region of Cape Girardeau, and so, wary about entering the Osage country, that was where they had headed.

Arriving there they found Tecumseh had been at the Apple Creek villages but was now searching for Tecumapese somewhere to the south in the vicinity of the New Madrid settlement. So, they left and came this way and here they were, reunited at last.

Tecumseh nodded and reached out, placing his hand on Stiahta's arm. "We will smoke," he said, "and then you will tell me the bad news that has brought you to me."

It had all started, Stiahta related, when seven young warriors—two Shawnees, two Kickapoos and one each Eel River Miami, Potawatomi and Wyandot—had come to Tenskwatawa and asked his permission to move down the Wabash to the white settlements and steal a horse apiece. Tenskwatawa had granted them permission and used the opportunity to proclaim to the others at Tippecanoe that this was wonderful proof of how individual Indians from different tribes could work together and depend upon each other as brothers, and The Prophet had also predicted that the raid would be entirely successful.

It was. In five days the seven had returned riding their stolen horses and boasting of their prowess and how they had taken the horses from beneath the very noses of the whites, almost as if they were invisible.

The Prophet had been very pleased but that pleasure hadn't lasted long. The very next afternoon a party of fifteen armed whites rode into the village, having followed the tracks the horse thieves had left. They demanded from Tenskwatawa the return of the seven horses and Tenskwatawa, somewhat disconcerted at their appearance, agreed and tried to laugh the whole thing off as just a prank played on the whites by some of his young men. The whites had not been amused and they rode off grim-faced, leading their seven recovered horses.

Tenskwatawa had retired into the medicine lodge and when he emerged an hour later he was frowning and announced that he had received a vision from the Great Spirit, who had informed him that the seven horses were rightfully the property of the Indians and that if a large party would go in pursuit of them to take them back, no harm would befall them. Within a few minutes fifty warriors had galloped off on the mission.

Shortly after midnight the party returned, jubilant at their coup. Acting on The Prophet's prediction that they would not be harmed, when they saw the flickering light of the white men's camp, they had boldly ridden in, kept the whites at bay with leveled rifles and took not only the seven horses, but the fifteen that the whites had been riding and told them to go back where they belonged and never to return to Tippecanoe if they valued their lives. No shots had been fired and no lives lost. The Tippecanoe Indians were now more than ever convinced that, with the Great Spirit behind them and The Prophet to guide them, nothing was impossible.

A few weeks later, however, spies had come in to Tippecanoe with disturbing news. An army of about a thousand men, with William Henry Harrison himself in their lead, had marched out of Vincennes and were headed this way.[607] Tenskwatawa had sent spies back to continue watching Harrison and they returned with word that the Indiana Territory governor had stopped and built a fort that was called Fort Harrison.[608] Tenskwatawa had then called a major council and told the Tippecanoe villagers that if Harrison continued moving his army toward Tippecanoe, they would have no choice but to attack that army and defeat it. There had been a great deal of opposition at first, spearheaded by Wasegoboah, but Tenskwatawa had threatened him with death if he persisted and Wasegoboah had backed away. Many of the two thousand Tippecanoe Indians had gone to their home villages to visit during the absence of Tecumseh and so at this time the total warrior force was only 350 Indians and Tenskwatawa had told those who remained that he had received directions from the Great Spirit and assurances that when they attacked, they had no need to fear the whites, that the bullets of the whites would pass through them without harming them.[609] Tenskwatawa also told them that he would mount a high rock nearby and there he would direct their fighting and beat his drum and so long as they heard the sound of his drum, they must continue to fight until the whites were all dead.[610] The Tippecanoe Indians had then held a series of war dances lasting several nights and while these were occurring, one of Tenskwatawa's spies shot one of Harrison's sentries and seriously wounded him.

A packhorse train of supplies had been delivered to Harrison's army and the next day—October 28—Harrison had put his army on the move again, electing to use the trail on the northwest side of the river, which was longer than the trail on the southeast side of the river, but which avoided the dense woods that the narrower southeast trail went through, along which Harrison evidently thought the Indians would ambush him. However, after following the northwest trail for a while, Harrison had abruptly crossed his army over the river and followed the southeast trail.

On the night of November 5, Harrison had encamped within ten miles of Tippecanoe. He had placed some interpreters at the front of his force and as they moved closer the next day and started to get glimpses of Indians, he directed them to call out invitations for the Indians to come in and submit without having to resort to battle, but the Indians had responded only with hoots and insulting gestures.

Finally, late that afternoon of November 6, Tenskwatawa sent three Indian messengers to Harrison to inquire why Harrison was approaching them with an army; they said that the Indians wished only for peace and wanted to treat with him for it. Harrison had considered this and agreed to treat with the Indians in the morning. He told Tenskwatawa's men he would move ahead a little more toward Tippecanoe until he found a good camping place. However, as he came nearer to the village the terrain changed and, to accommodate, he had changed the order in which his troops were marching. The maneuver startled the Indians, who thought he was going into battle formation, but when a deputation confronted him he denied this and said he had no intention of attacking.

The army had finally found a good camping place a bit more than a half-mile from Tippecanoe and a strong guard was set up to patrol the camp's perimeter.[611]

Tenskwatawa's plan, Stiahta said, was revealed to all the Indians in a war council held just after nightfall. A delegation of chiefs were to go the next morning, as planned, to Harrison's council and there they would agree to all the proposals. They were then to retire a short distance away to where the warriors were in hiding—all except for two Winnebagoes, who had volunteered to stay behind close to Harrison and, as soon as the chiefs reached safety, they were to yank out their tomahawks and assassinate Harrison, which would initiate the battle.

Tenskwatawa had changed this plan, Stiahta told Tecumseh, but without explanation. The night had been especially dark, with heavily overcast skies and soon a cold drizzle had set in. A large number of the Tippecanoe Indians were clustered around as The Prophet emerged from the medicine lodge. Tenskwatawa had painted a circle of solid white, three inches in diameter, over the empty eye socket, and wore a scarlet turban around his head. A thick braid of his hair hung down behind his left ear, held together at the end by a cylinder of silver. Dangling from his ears were huge silver earrings—one in the shape of a five-pointed star and the other a crescent—around his neck was a large silver gorget upon which rested a necklace of upturned bear claws. A pair of scarlet sashes, anchored front and rear, crossed his chest and back in a broad **X** and tied snugly around his neck was a hip-length cape of ermine. His wrists were encircled by at least a dozen bracelets of silver, brass, and beads and his buckskin blouse and leggins were flamboyantly decorated in geographic designs with painted porcupine quills.

He had stood before them for a long moment and then abruptly raised his arms and seemed to go into some kind of a trance, his body and arms jerking in strange movements while he muttered mysterious words. After an interval, he had suddenly jerked to awareness, as if coming awake and raised his arms for silence.

"We cannot wait!" he shouted. "We must attack first, while it is still dark. White men cannot fight in the dark. The Great Spirit has talked to me and said half of the white chief's army is now dead and the other half is crazy. Their eyes will be clouded by the darkness of night, while my warriors will be able to see as if under the bright sun of daylight. It will be a small matter to finish them off with our tomahawks. We will strike them before dawn."

The Indians began moving into position about four o'clock in the morning, but Harrison had awakened his men well before dawn and it was still before daylight when one of the perimeter guards saw an Indian creeping up and shot him.

The full attack of the Indians had broken out then, with Wawpawwawqua and Stone Eater leading the warriors and the Battle of Tippecanoe was under way. Harrison's guard had given way at the first onslaught, but within moments they rallied, extinguished their campfires and had their guns primed. The darkness was so complete that it was virtually necessary to feel with outstretched hand the person encountered to determine whether he was friend or enemy. Throughout this terrifying two hours of the battle came the distant drumbeats and weird cries, along with a war song, from Tenskwatawa, perched atop the promontory of rocks nearby.

Soon a runner came up to Tenskwatawa and informed him that Indians were indeed falling and dying in the most natural way. The Prophet had simply shaken his head in annoyance and cupped his mouth and shrieked, "Fight on! It will take a little while for the prophecy to be fulfilled. Fight on!" He then broke into his weird chant again, accompanied by the drumbeats and his warriors fought with renewed frenzy, abandoning their usual mode of fighting from cover and rushing into the open to attack in hand-to-hand combat, directly into the bayonets of the soldiers.

As dawn came, however, the cold morning light revealed that there were dead Indians all around and Tenskwatawa was no longer chanting, no longer beating his drum. The Americans had suffered 188 casualties, of which 62 soldiers were dead, but 38 Indians had also been killed.[612] Several Indians gave sharp cries and within a few minutes all the attacking force of Indians had melted out of sight in the surrounding woods. The Battle of Tippecanoe was over. The Indians continued to Tippecanoe, snatched up what possessions they could and abandoned the town, retiring to a camp about ten miles distant on Wildcat Creek.

During the day Harrison's army had secured its perimeter, buried dead and treated the wounded. On the next day they burned Tippecanoe and a lot of equipment as well as five thousand bushels of corn and beans. Most of the Indians, watching this from the woods, now dispersed very much afraid, returning to their own villages to get out of the way of harm.[613] Hardly two hundred warriors remained of the many who had been at Tippecanoe and word was quickly spreading to the tribes of what had happened. The following day after the battle, Stiahta said, he and Metea had set out to locate Tecumseh.

Tecumseh's face was set in harsh hard lines. All the work, all the effort, all the influence and power built up over so many years, all the hopes of so many Indians—all devastated by his one-eyed brother's stupidity and desperate grab for power. He sat quietly, staring into the fire, a hollowness within him that was gradually filling with rage. The relation of events had taken a long time. Midnight had come and gone just moments ago.

"What of Tenskwatawa?" he asked tightly.

"We have him," Metea spoke up. "He tried to slip away but we caught him. Many wanted to kill him at once, but Wasegoboah stayed them. He told them to wait until your return, that it was up to you to determine what should happen to the one who called himself The Prophet.''

Tecumseh nodded slowly. "We will go in the morning, back to Apple River, where we will leave Tecumapese.[614] Then we will return to Tippecanoe and see what can be done to salvage our union, and what will be done to Tenskwatawa.''

But their departure was somewhat delayed. Among the tribes in all directions from them, it was the thirtieth night after the great sign of the Panther Passing Across and many of the chiefs had just finished tossing into the fire the thirtieth and final section of the last of the red sticks and now they waited.

Only a few moments after Tecumseh's remark in the camp close to New Madrid, the earth bucked and rocked and lurched beneath them amid a grinding, crashing, thundering roar beyond anything any of them had ever before heard or felt, slamming them to the ground at the epicenter of a gigantic earthquake.

Around them, dozens, scores, hundreds of trees snapped and fell, adding this crescendo of noise to continuing din. The concentric shock waves of unbelievable magnitude spread out in all directions and the land continued to buck and heave as if it had suddenly become viscous. Here, where the Ohio River met the Mississippi, where Kentucky, Illinois, Missouri, Arkansas, and Tennessee came together within mere miles, fantastic splits appeared in the ground and huge tracts of land were swallowed up.[615] Directly across the Mississippi from New Madrid and only a few miles away from the river, near the border of Kentucky and Tennessee, a monstrous section of ground sank as if stepped upon and mashed down by some gigantic foot and water from subterranean sources gushed forth in fantastic volume and quickly filled the huge depression.[616] The whole midsection of the Mississippi River writhed and heaved and tremendous bluffs toppled and fell thunderingly into the muddy waters. Entire sections of land were inundated and others that were riverbed were left high in the air. The grandmother of rivers herself turned and flowed backward for a long while, swirling, hissing, churning, sending gigantic washes of water smashing across the land. At length, when it had all settled down, the entire face of the land in the New Madrid area had been changed.

In Kentucky and Tennessee, in Arkansas and Missouri, in the Illinois and Indiana Territories, settlers were thrown from their beds and heard the timbers of their cabins wrenched apart, watched their chimney bricks and stones crumble into heaps of debris masked in choking clouds of dust. Bridges snapped and tumbled into rivers and creeks. Glass shattered, fences and barns collapsed, fires broke out. Along steep ravines the cliffsides slipped and filled their chasms and new ones formed in gigantic splits and the air was filled with a deafening roar.

Everywhere birds were roused from their roosts with screeches of fright and flapping of wings. Cattle and horses bellowed and kicked, lost their footing and tumbled to the ground where they rolled about, unable to regain their footing.

To the west, whole herds of buffalo were knocked down, rose, fell again, scrambled to their feet and stampeded in abject panic through the prairie lands, their bellowing an echo of the grinding earth; the ground vibrated rapidly and sent vast clouds of choking dust into the air.

To the south, the entire northern shoreline of the Gulf of Mexico was agitated; whole forests fell in incredible tangles; the ground in Alabama and Mississippi trembled and vibrated in the midst of deep powerful groaning from within the earth and, in Creek, Choctaw, and Chickasaw villages, water jugs split and the buildings cracked and fell and on the lips of many who fled into the open was said, with great awe, a single word—"Tecumseh!"

To the south and east pines whipped and lashed and lakes emptied of their water and indentations appeared and were filled with muddy water in great turmoil, while the jolting of the earth was felt by residents of the coastal city of Charleston, South Carolina, over six hundred miles distant.

To the south and west tremendous boulders broke loose on hills and bluffs and carved tremendous swaths as they crashed through the trees and brush to the bottoms. Rapidly rushing streams stopped, eddied, some going abruptly dry and the fish that had lived in them flopped on the muddy or rocky beds.

Far to the east, some seven hundred miles distant, President James Madison awakened from a deep sleep and wondered about the cause of the deep muted rumbling sound.

In all of the Great Lakes, but especially Lake Michigan and Lake Erie, the waters danced and great waves broke on the shorelines, though the wind was negligible. In Detroit, Chicago, Cleveland, Cincinnati, Pittsburgh, Louisville, Vincennes, Kaskaskia, and St. Louis, as well as numerous small towns and settlements, damage occurred ranging from mild to severe. Throughout the whole northwestern country tree branches broke with sharp snaps and there was a fierce grinding sound that set teeth on edge and reached to the very marrow of the bones.

Such was the great earthquake that struck at New Madrid and was felt to greater or lesser degree for almost a thousand miles in all directions; such was the earthquake that had occurred where no one could possibly have anticipated or predicted that one would occur except, perhaps, said a multitude throughout the land, a Shawnee whose name was Tecumseh.[617]

[January 2, 1812 — Thursday]

Tecumseh is coming!

The news swept through the Wildcat Creek encampment with the speed of a freshening breeze and Indians poured from the twenty or more wegiwas and tepees and stood waiting, blankets of fur robes wrapped tightly about themselves against the chill.

From the distant woodland on a small trail that came from the southwest, eight riders appeared, Tecumseh, flanked by Sauganash and Chaubenee, leading this residue of his party that had left Vincennes with him. They had ridden a great distance and the newly acquired weight in their hearts was a greater burden by far than any that might have been strapped to their backs. Only hours ago they had ridden through the blackened remains of what had been Tippecanoe, the residue of ash and charred timbers bearing mute testimony to what had occurred. Yet, now they rode erect and there was about their approach a peculiar silence that became contagious to the waiting group. As they rode into the encampment, the near two hundred who stood waiting parted to accept them. There were no words of greeting, no smiles of pleasure or relief. All took their cue from Tecumseh, whose face was set in hard lines and whose eyes smoldered with controlled fury. It was before Wasegoboah that Tecumseh reined up his horse and those with him stopped as well. He dismounted, as did they, surrendering their horses to young warriors who approached from the crowd. The four words Tecumseh spoke surprised no one.

"Take me to Tenskwatawa."

Wasegoboah nodded and led them toward a wegiwa somewhat larger than the others. The structure could not hold them all and those who were unable to get in simply stood and waited, still as silently, outside its entrance. Inside, a post had been erected in the middle of the earthen floor and bound to it, his wrists tied behind him with rawhide tugs, was Tenskwatawa.

The one-eyed man cringed and a repugnant whimpering sound escaped him when he saw in the dimness that his brother had returned. None of those who had squeezed into the wegiwa believed that Tenskwatawa had any more than mere moments left to live and this belief was reinforced as Tecumseh, approaching the prisoner, slid his razor-edged knife from its belt sheath.

Tenskwatawa's whimpering evolved into a mournful wail and the front of his leggins began suddenly darkening as a bladder he could no longer control discharged its contents. He slid to the ground when his knees, equally out of control, collapsed beneath him and his head hung, his face hidden by the scraggle of dirtied hair. It was this hair that Tecumseh reached out and snatched, his expression one of loathing. He jerked his brother's head back savagely, exposing the vulnerable throat and placing the edge of his blade against it. He moved it slightly and a trickle of scarlet blood slid down Tenskwatawa's neck, staining his collar. The wailing ceased, replaced by a gurgling, blubbering sound. Tecumseh spoke then, softly, yet his utterly cold voice clearly audible to all, freezing the breath in every chest.

"It would be a favor to you, Tenskwatawa, were I to let my hand have its way. But I will not kill you. That would be too easy, too honorable a fate."

He took the blade away from his brother's throat and cut away the bonds. Slowly, unbelievingly, still fearful, Tenskwatawa came to his feet as his older brother returned his knife to its sheath. Tecumseh's hands suddenly shot out and gripped the hair at Tenskwatawa's temples and he shook him so violently that his nose began to bleed. Tenskwatawa wailed again, certain that his scalp was being ripped away and his neck broken. Then Tecumseh threw him away. Tenskwatawa sprawled to the ground and began scrambling on all fours to escape. Instantly several warriors jerked knives or tomahawks from their waistbands, but a harsh order from Wasegoboah stayed them.

"Stop! Do not interfere. What Tecumseh plans for his brother is his concern only. No one has more right to say what should be done," he spat out the words contemptuously, "with the one who called himself a prophet!"

Tecumseh had followed up and again gripped Tenskwatawa by the hair, pinning his body to the ground with one knee and jerking Tenskwatawa's head back so his eyes were forced to meet the glare of Tecumseh's. There was no vestige of warmth in the latter and his voice was intense and utterly implacable.

"In one day, Tenskwatawa—*in one day!*—you have destroyed what I have taken over ten summers to build and which now can never be rebuilt. In one day you have destroyed the hopes of *all* Indians. You are a liar, a cheat, a fool filled with the lust for power. You are no longer The Prophet. You are no longer a Shawnee, nor even an Indian! You are dishonored as no man has ever before been dishonored." His voice dropped, becoming even more frightening. "I will not kill you, but your death begins this day and it will be years in coming, for each day you will die a little more. From this time forward you will live with scorn and disgust, with the hatred and distrust of all men. You will be without family or friends. You will be without a people and you will live the rest of your miserable life scorned by those you sought to rule and who now despise you. From this day forward you will be all alone and when, at last, death becomes final for you, no living creature will mourn." He paused, then thrust the head away from him. "Go! I am finished with you!"

Devastated, Tenskwatawa let his gaze move across those watching, but now they averted their eyes from him as a creature beneath contempt. With the aspect of a craven dog that had been severely whipped, the once Prophet slunk from the wegiwa and disappeared outside. In the silence that filled the interior, Tecumseh now moved among his people, quietly grasping their hands in turn, his features gradually softening. In this way he greeted them, embracing some, such as Wasegoboah, who were closest to his heart.

"Tecumseh," Wasegoboah murmured, deeply moved as Tecumseh gripped his shoulders, then his hands, "our hearts are full—filled with sorrow for what has happened, filled with regret that we failed you, yet filled with joy at your return. Few of us are left, but those who stayed and those who have returned and those who will yet come back to support you, remain loyal in every way, even unto death."

In turn, Stiahta, Chaubenee, and Sauganash reaffirmed aloud the vow that each had spoken on the way here: that they and whatever warriors they controlled would stay with Tecumseh and fight beside him until, if necessary, they were no more.

"We await only your word," Black Partridge added. "Whether we are with you or on the shores of Lake Michigan, you have only to whisper and we will do as you require."

When the greetings were finished, Tecumseh immediately called a council of all present. A large fire was built and then he talked for a long while of those things that had occurred on their trip to the South and the West. "As we passed through Tippecanoe on our return," he said, his voice now slightly tremulous with the emotion he could not entirely contain, "I stood upon the ashes of my own home, whose flames had gone up to Moneto, and there I summoned the spirits of the warriors who had fallen. And as I snuffed up the smell of their blood from the ground, I swore once more eternal hatred—the hatred of an avenger! Now I am here among you and my grief is great."

There would, he went on, now no longer be enough who would come, despite the great sign that had been given to them, to enable his grand plan to succeed. It had been wiped away. Now only one recourse lay before them, though it was what he had long discoursed against. They would have to throw their weight, such as it was, behind the British and aid them in destroying the Americans. Perhaps many of the Indians who had initially panicked when they learned of Tippecanoe would yet return to the amalgamation, but on this they could not depend. Strong efforts must be made to reassure those who had not wholly turned their backs, those who wavered. All those assembled here would, therefore, tomorrow mount their horse and disperse to their own villages and relate what had occurred here, assuring their own people that all was not lost, that with the union of all tribes they could still regain what had been taken from them and safeguard that which remained to them. They were to spread the word that though The Prophet had failed them, Tecumseh would not, that he was now rebuilding the village of Tippecanoe. Those who yet believed in Tecumseh and the future of the Indian race were to take up their weapons and strike out for the original site of their convergence, Tippecanoe, and from there he would lead them to the British fort called Malden at Amherstburg.

[April 10, 1812 — Friday]

Tippecanoe was again a functioning village. It was nowhere near so large and extensive as it had once been, nor were the House of Strangers and the great medicine lodge any longer in existence, but dozens of wegiwas had been built and a few cabins and even a makeshift *msi-kah-mi-qui* that could accommodate several hundred in council.

Tecumseh had thrown his entire energies, shortly after his return, into causing Tippecanoe to rise phoenixlike from its ashes and become a symbol to the scattered Indians of a rebirth in the hope and dream that he had so long instilled in them. In February he had sent out numerous runners in all directions inviting the dispersed warriors to return. Many Indians had already converged here as a result of the great sign of the earthquake and its jarring aftershocks— not so many as Tecumseh had once anticipated, but neither so few as he had feared immediately after his return.

Close to a thousand had come back and more were returning all the time. There was no longer a resident prophet, nor would there be one, Tecumseh averred, and what bound them to each other now must be solely the desire to stand, in the protection of their land, against the Americans. Despite his initial fury directed at Tenskwatawa and his more or less sending him into exile, yet he had finally relented and let the cowed shell of a man return to Tippecanoe with them—no longer in a position of authority, no longer trusted but nevertheless one who, under close supervision, might be of some small benefit to the Indian cause. And Tenskwatawa, his delusions of grandeur forever erased, was now pathetically eager to do anything to please.

While many of those who had abandoned Tecumseh did not now return, this did not necessarily mean that they had totally turned away from him or the ideals he had fired within them. They might yet return to him, some conceded, and they might not. In the interval, since full-scale war was indubitably shaping up, why not make the most of it where they were?

So, all over the frontier, from Mississippi and Alabama and Tennessee to the central and upper Mississippi Valley and eastward to Ohio, minor instances of hostile outbreaks occurred. At first these were isolated cases—the theft of horses here, the burning of a cabin there, a small herd of cows shot to death with bows and arrows elsewhere. Once again settlers fell into the habit of carrying their rifles or shotguns with them into their fields and once again the specter of fear overshadowed them all. Soon enough the minor annoyances became attacks on the whites themselves, modestly begun and quietly executed by the meaty thunk of a tomahawk or the muted thud of a war club, with the thrust of a knife or the whirring whine of an arrow.

A settler was killed near Springfield, Ohio, and then another only a short distance away near Urbana. A soldier at Fort Recovery who had gone out to hunt was found four days later spread-eagled and scalped. A lone rider near Greenville was brought down with a single arrow from an unseen archer. Three men following the Detroit Trace were captured near Fort Defiance, tied to trees and used for knife-throwing contests and then scalped and beheaded. Kickapoo attacks in similar manner escalated in central and southern Illinois, while alarms were constant among those fearing the Potawatomies in the regions of Chicago and Milwaukee.[618]

Less than a month after his return, Tecumseh had received a message from Harrison in which the governor held out to the Indians the offer of amnesty and a repeat of his proposal to escort Tecumseh and his brother— assuming them still to be in power—to go to Washington as part of a delegation of Indian leaders to confer with the president, but in which the brothers would be forbidden to serve as delegation leaders. To maintain the shaky communication and provide Harrison no excuse for another march against them, Tecumseh responded politely, making no comment in regard to the offer of amnesty but accepting the offer to go see the president, stating however, that this would have to wait for summer, after the corn was planted.

At Tippecanoe the winter had been difficult but they had survived. Stores of grain that had been successfully hidden away from Harrison's army were recovered and helped sustain them, and their survival through the remainder of the winter was assured when Tecumseh made a quick trip to Amherstburg and acquired, with Matthew Elliott's aid, a welcome packhorse train of food supplies and ammunition from the British stores at Fort Malden.[619]

In March Tecumseh had again sent messages to Catahecassa and his people at Wapakoneta and Blue Jacket's Town and Wapatomica, asking them to come and take up residence at Tippecanoe, but the messages went unanswered, the silence indicative of the continued enmity harbored by Catahecassa against him to such extent that the Shawnee principal chief was making offers to the Americans to have Tecumseh assassinated for them.[620] At about the same time the Hurons under Walk in the Water had sent Tecumseh a white wampum belt and the request that he turn aside from the way of war and make peace with the Americans who were in their lands and beyond uprooting, but though Tecumseh met with some of the chiefs at Fort Wayne, he refused to accept the offers and, in fact, convinced some of their number to rejoin him.

Now, in the midst of Harrison talking peace to the tribes, Tecumseh had received news that he viewed as the first truly significant act on the part of the Americans to instigate the outbreak of war on the western frontier. With an urgency not previously manifested, William Henry Harrison was authorized to take command of all troops in the Indiana and Illinois Territories and even to call upon the Kentucky Militia for assistance if necessary. President Madison had summoned the Michigan Territory governor, William Hull, and former Secretary of War Henry Dearborn, to Washington. Dearborn was appointed to the rank of major general and named commander-in-chief of the entire United States Army. Hull was given the rank of brigadier general and placed in command of the Northwestern Department of the Army. It was the orders to Hull that most directly affected Tecumseh and his warriors.

General William Hull was to raise a Northwestern Army of twelve hundred men, assemble them at Urbana, Ohio, and from there he was to cut a road northward through the wilderness for 175 miles to Detroit. In the process of doing so, he was ordered to cow the Indians along the way into neutrality, convince the British at Amherstburg that they could not depend on Indian support, establish his army at Detroit and immediately launch an invasion into Canada to capture Fort Malden and Amherstburg. Obviously, with last fall's destruction of Tippecanoe, they no longer considered Tecumseh and his men to be a viable threat.

They were wrong.

[June 18, 1812 — Thursday]

War!

The fragile thread of peace, frayed and worn by years of international friction, had at last snapped and today the United States of America formally declared war on Great Britain.

There were many reasons, not the least of which was the agitation by British agents and traders among the tribes on the frontier, who continually fanned the flames of resentment and hatred for wrongs done to them by the Americans; traders and agents who also supplied the Indians with guns, ammunition and other goods. More prominent as a reason, however, was the annoying policy of the Royal Navy to board American ships and impress American seamen into British service under the claim that they were deserters. Some seven thousand men had already been conscripted in this way and, were that not enough, under the British Orders in Council, which had been established to prevent American ships from dealing with France, some four hundred Yankee ships had been confiscated on the Atlantic, on occasion within sight of the American mainland. All these matters and more had generated a situation that simply could no longer be tolerated.

Immediately upon the declaration the militias were called up of the eighteen states of the Union—including Louisiana, which had become the eighteenth on April 30. American doves in the political scene, of which there had been a considerable decline of late, screamed foul and pointed out that the Constitution did not provide for Congress calling out the militia to support a war of America's own declaration, but only to execute the laws of the Union, suppress insurrections, and repel invasions. The hawks, in their exultation, had no trouble drowning out these doves. At the War Mess, where he first heard the news along with other hawks, Henry Clay leaped and pronked about in his interpretation of a Shawnee war dance, while throughout the East church bells rang, cannon boomed, rockets were fired and glory-seeking, adventurous young men hastened to enlist in the army.

Not too surprisingly, one of Thomas Jefferson's first reactions was to think of land acquisition and he jubilantly wrote to a friend:

> *upon the whole I have known of no war entered into under more favorable circumstances. . . . We . . . shall strip Great Britain of all her possessions on this continent.*

While the news of the declaration of the War of 1812 swept through the East with record speed, it was considerably more delayed on the frontiers where communications were, at best, slow and undependable. No one there had any inkling as yet that war had been declared, including General William Hull and the twenty-two hundred men he was currently marching toward Detroit.[621]

Although Hull had certain qualifications for his position as Michigan Territorial governor, from which duties he was presently officially excused, with pay, he was quite probably the worst possible choice that could have been made for a frontier commanding general. Though he had once been a lieutenant colonel, from the beginning his role as a general had the aspect of a comedy of errors which, had it not been so potentially disastrous, would have been laughable. Discipline, from the highest ranking officers to the lowest privates, was sorely lacking. This was compounded by the fact that the election of officers among the militia, which made up the bulk of his army, had caused great dissension. It bothered Hull not at all that his own regular army second-in-command, Lieutenant Colonel James Miller, was outranked by three elected militia colonels, Duncan McArthur, James Findley, and Lewis Cass. Hull had gathered his militia force at three Ohio locations—Cincinnati, Dayton and Urbana—and the whole business had all the earmarks of a road show of performers, complete with parades, supposedly inspirational speeches that were nothing more than meaningless rhetoric, clownish performances, and a string of easily preventable accidents and errors.

Hull, not caring a whit about the ugly murmurings of nepotism, had early on named his own son, Captain Abraham F. Hull, as his principal aide-de-camp, conveniently overlooking the fact that the young officer was unreliable, hotheaded, a fuzzy-thinker, and only occasionally sober. The general himself, fifty-eight years old and paunchy, strutted about with pompous posturings and occasional speeches notable more for their bombast than anything else. Three days ago, just prior to setting his troops in motion northward from Urbana, Hull, in his stentorian voice, addressed his troops.

"In marching through a wilderness," he intoned, "memorable for savage barbarity, you will remember the causes by which the barbarity has been heretofore excited. In viewing the ground stained with the blood of your fellow citizens, it will be impossible to suppress your feelings of indignation. Passing by the ruins of a fortress erected in our territory by a foreign nation, in times of profound peace, and for the express purpose of exciting the savages to hostility and supplying them with the means of conducting a barbarous war, must remind you of that system of oppression and injustice which that nation has continually practiced, and which the spirit of an indignant people can no longer endure."

Not entirely sure exactly what he said, the troops cheered nevertheless, and Hull, followed by a coterie of regular and militia officers, set his horse into a walk to review the paraded troops. It didn't last long: Captain Abraham Hull's horse, frightened by the racket of fife and drum, reared and pawed the air, very nearly dumping its inebriated rider before turning and galloping off in the wrong direction amid howls of laughter from the troops. Then it was the general's turn. His horse abruptly became intractable and began spinning about in tight circles. In succession the commanding general lost his hat, his stirrups, his balance and his dignity, dropped the reins and snatched the horse's mane in terror and somehow managed to stay on its back until it calmed down.

The force was put into motion and in a few miles, close to where the ruins of the old Shawnee town of Mackachack were still visible, began to ford the Mad River which, at this point, was about fifteen feet wide and stony-bottomed.[622] Young Captain Hull, still reeling in his saddle from the effects of overindulging before the march began, was clad in his finest uniform. Taking it upon himself to show the troops the way a gallant mounted officer crossed such a stream, he spurred his horse forward into the river. Resenting the hard jab of the spurs, his steed took a great leap from the bank, landed in three feet of water and planted all four feet solidly and stopped.

Captain Hull did not.

To the extreme merriment of the troops, the commanding general's son was catapulted high over the horse's head and executed a quite commendable but wholly unintentional midair somersault, then landed in a sitting position in the water, with just the top of his head showing and his fine cocked hat jauntily floating away with the current.

The inauspicious march continued, the troops evincing little concern that the whole American frontier these days was abroil with hostility and wilderness travel was highly hazardous at best and ambushes frequent; that settlers near Fort Dearborn had recently been killed, as had some forty others already this spring near Vincennes, Kaskaskia, and elsewhere in the territories of Illinois and Indiana.

Only the day before yesterday, guided now by some friendly Miamis and Shawnees—one of the latter being Spemica Lawba—the procession had reached the Scioto River headwaters and paused long enough on the south bank to build a couple of blockhouses, each twenty by forty feet, connected by a stockade and enclosing a half-acre of ground, close to where old Talgayeeta—Chief Logan—had made his final home. They named it Fort McArthur after the militia colonel who directed the construction.[623]

The comedy of errors continued, but now with more tragic results. Last night one of Colonel McArthur's men, Private Peter Vassar, on guard duty, sipped too frequently from his canteen, which held whiskey, not water. Becoming drowsy, he decided it wouldn't hurt if he took just a brief nap beneath a tree. His alcohol-stimulated mind produced a nightmare of fiercely attacking Indians and Vassar, jerking erect, snatched up his rifle and instantly shot the first thing he saw moving, which happened to be his fellow sentry, Private Joseph England. Vassar was held for future court-martial, and England, shot through the chest, managed to survive but was finished on this campaign.[624]

And on this day of the declaration of the War of 1812 . . .

. . . while the supreme commander of the American Army, Major General Henry Dearborn, gorged himself on rich food in a Boston restaurant;

. . . while Illinois Territory Governor Ninian Edwards was glumly announcing to his constituency that "We have no security from these Indians," and that more attacks would occur;

. . . while Tecumseh, with Chaubenee at his side and en route to Amherstburg with three hundred warriors, paused for four days of conferences with Fort Wayne agent Benjamin Stickney;[625]

. . . while Main Poche, at Amherstburg, counciled with Matthew Elliott and awaited the arrival of Tecumseh to provide their assembled warriors with arms and ammunition from the British, in order to strike the approaching army of William Hull;

. . . while the British at Amherstburg placed a reward of one hundred fifty dollars on the scalp of Tecumseh's nephew, Spemica Lawba, who was now serving as a guide and spy for Hull's army;

. . . while messengers on swift horses were speedily bearing urgent messages to all British commanders in Canada, informing them of the American declaration of war . . .

. . . while all this was occurring, someone in Washington suggested that it might be a good idea to inform General Hull that war had been declared . . .

. . . and someone else agreed and wrote out the necessary advisories and orders and directed that they be dispatched to General Hull at once . . .

. . . and someone else dispatched them to General Hull in an ordinary envelope that found its way into an ordinary leather mail pouch that found its way into an ordinary mail-packet shipment bound for Buffalo, Cleveland, and Detroit.

And, if not lost en route, as ordinary mail sometimes was, delivery of the envelope to the addressee might be accomplished . . .

. . . in due time.

[July 3, 1812 — Friday]

It was on his arrival at Amherstburg today that Tecumseh first learned, with considerable gratification, of the American declaration of war against the British and the fact that their army, under General Hull, was presently on the march in this direction. He immediately stated that he and his followers were allies to the British in this conflict and just as quickly gathered about him the parties of his warriors who had been sent here earlier by him. He informed them of the news and then added, "Let them come then! I hear them and see them in the South and in the East, like the autumn leaves rolling and rustling in the breeze. It is well. Shall Tecumseh tremble? Shall they say he hated the white man and feared him? No! The mountains and the plains which the Great Spirit gave are behind and around me. I too, have my warriors and here— where we were born and where we will die, on the Scioto, on the Wabash, on the broad waters of the North—my voice shall be heard!"

In preparation for this eventuality of war, but to avoid raising suspicions with large movements of his warriors, for several weeks prior to this time Tecumseh had been sending, from Tippecanoe, small parties of twenty to forty warriors toward the Detroit area, instructed to make camps and hold themselves in readiness there for his arrival. All this had been as a direct result of the secret message he had received six weeks earlier at the Mississinewa Council.

Held at the village of Chief Shetoon on the Wabash at the mouth of the Mississinewa River, it had been a major council of the tribes still opposed to Tecumseh and wishing to remain neutral in case war should break out between the Americans and British.[626] Among the over six hundred Indians who had attended were the staunchly neutral chiefs, Michikiniqua of the Miamis and

Five Medals of the Potawatomies, along with William Wells. Though himself not invited, Tecumseh had shown up and quickly became the butt of open council condemnation from the pacific tribes for his agitation among them against the Americans. One of his principal accusers was the Wyandot mixed-blood chief, Isador Chaine from Flat Rock—across the Detroit River from Fort Malden—who berated him soundly for such activities.[627]

Tecumseh had admitted in his reply that the recent Battle of Tippecanoe was "an unfortunate transaction," adding, "and had I been at home, there would have been no blood shed. But since my return we have communicated with the Americans and the matter is now settled between us and Governor Harrison, so there remains no point in any further recriminations about it." Spying Winnemac in attendance, Tecumseh's retort had become more barbed. "We defy a living creature to say we ever advised anyone, directly or indirectly, to make war on our white brothers. It has constantly been our misfortune," his gaze impaled Winnemac, "to have our views misrepresented to our white brethren. This has been done by pretended chiefs of the Potawatomies, who also are in the habit of selling land that did not belong to them."

Later, however, in a private meeting between them, Isador Chaine had revealed to Tecumseh that he came as a secret agent from Matthew Elliott. He passed to Tecumseh a black war belt from Elliott, along with the British agent's advisory that war with the Americans was imminent and he was requesting that Tecumseh start surreptitiously sending his warriors from Tippecanoe to Amherstburg and himself come as soon as possible to obtain guns and ammunition to be distributed among his allies.

It had been pleasant for Tecumseh, on his arrival at Amherstburg, to find his old friend Main Poche. The chief with the withered hand, however, was in a glum frame of mind due to a message he had just received from the Illinois River Potawatomies. Shortly after his arrival here he had sent them war belts of black wampum and asked them to join him at Fort Malden, but the reply just received was a polite refusal, that they themselves every day expected to be attacked by the Americans and must stay and defend their villages.

This was Tecumseh's third day here and ever since his arrival he had been involved in a number of councils with British officials and, at their behest, had also visited the Indians on the west side of the river around Brownstown, who were largely Hurons, who now were adopting the name of their southern faction, the Wyandots. Elliott had pointed out to Tecumseh that those Indians were in a pivotal position that made their alliance vital to both British and Americans. Though proclaiming their neutrality, should they swing to American alliance, it could create all sorts of problems, so it was important to win them, if possible, to British support. If done, the communication and supply route between Detroit and Ohio, following the arrival of Hull's army, could easily be interrupted.

However, though Tecumseh and Stiahta worked very hard to get the northern Wyandots to join them against the Americans, their efforts at a major council held here at Fort Malden were largely spurned. Because of the strong influence held by Walk in the Water among the former Hurons, Tecumseh asked him what part he and his warriors expected to play in the war.

"Why do we hesitate about siding with the British in this fight?" Walk in the Water replied. "Listen and I will tell you. My people have tasted the bitter dregs of war. Some of our most distinguished chiefs and many of our warriors were slain in the Battle of Fallen Timbers, where the British broke their promise and gave us no support. We who are the Hurons and Wyandots suffered more than any other tribe at that time and so now we think it best to remain entirely neutral and take no part in what is to come."

His reply raised a distinct commotion among other tribes represented at the council. Most vociferous were the Chippewas, whose spokesman stood and pointed an accusing finger at Walk in the Water. "You are a Yankee! You are a woman! You are afraid to fight. Why don't you go home and spend the rest of your days carrying babies around on your back, since that seems to be what you are best suited for. You are—"

"Hold!" It was Stiahta who interrupted and now came to the defense. "How do you dare to insult one whose former strength as a warrior is so well known? You have heard what Walk in the Water has stated. It is true. We did suffer severely at Fallen Timbers and, while I personally support Tecumseh and the British, I don't wonder that my northern Wyandot brothers hesitate about engaging in further warfare. As for you Shawnees and Delawares here gathered, I know you will fight, but as for you blustering Chippewas, you are no braves! You are merely camp followers. At Wayne's fight you stayed well out of harm's way and merely crept in after the fighting and stripped and plundered the dead that we Wyandots had killed!"

Among the Wyandot chiefs who had been present was Tarhe who, like so many others as a result of the Battle of Tippecanoe, had rescinded his alliance with Tecumseh and returned to a neutral stance. He had become very angry at Stiahta's public declarations in support of Tecumseh and the British and the enthusiastic war dance that had followed the Fort Malden council. Immediately after their return to Brownstown, Tarhe summoned the chiefs and, ignoring Stiahta's defense of Walk in the Water, he maneuvered the Wyandot Council into removing Stiahta from his post as tribal war chief and replacing him with a puppet chief named George Punch.

Now Tecumseh was surprised when a deputation of Wyandots from Chiefs Walk in the Water, Tarhe, and Between the Logs came to him, bearing an invitation of their own for Tecumseh to visit their council and hear the reasons why they wished to remain aloof from the British and American conflict. Tecumseh, irked both at the action against Stiahta and that the Wyandots should be so shortsighted as to where their best interests lay in the long run, now replied in a way that left no room for negotiation.

"No!" he said. "I will not attend. I have taken sides with the king, my father, and I will suffer my bones to lay and bleach upon this shore before I will recross that stream to join in any council of neutrality."

[July 5, 1812 — Sunday]

With the arrival at Amherstburg early today of three hundred Sacs from Saukenuk at the mouth of the Rock River in the Illinois, Tecumseh's warrior force totaled just over a thousand but more should be coming very soon. He had just finished sending runners to all the chiefs who had pledged their support to congregate at once at this place. To those he knew were going to carry on anti-American operations in their own areas, he also sent explicit instructions.

The message he had sent to the Potawatomies in the Chicago area was a good example. The message was carried by Wapeme—White Pigeon—who had left here early this morning. He was first to go to Nescotnemeg on the Kankakee and the message was this: The time has come. The Americans have declared war against the British. Many kegs of gunpowder and sacks filled with lead ball are on their way to you at this moment from the British at this place. It had been agreed between Tecumseh and Nescotnemeg earlier that it was the latter's place to plan the attack that was to be made on Fort Dearborn; that it was previously agreed it was Siggenauk's place to lead that attack; that Nescotnemeg would be joined by the warriors under Black Partridge from the Chicago area, his brother Waubansee from the Fox River, and Naunongee from the Calumet area; finally, that the attack should occur as previously agreed, in the middle of the next moon—August.

Now, as Tecumseh watched from a distance the lumbering column that was the army of General William Hull approaching the southern edge of Detroit, he was impressed with its size but not with its demeanor. The force moved in a sloppy manner accompanied by a lot of noise, conversation, horseplay and laughter. It was obviously made up primarily of young men who were wholly inexperienced in warfare and, as such, were likely to break and panic quickly under the stress of being attacked.

Ever since the Hull army had reached the Maumee, Tecumseh's spies had watched it closely and reported to him regularly. What they said about its movement and its officers underlined the basic weaknesses under which it labored and the major errors it committed. The army had camped opposite the old Fallen Timbers battlefield, rested there a day and then had moved down to the ruins of the old British installation, Fort Miamis, at the foot of the Maumee Rapids. Here, at the uppermost point of the navigable waters of the river they had found a trader named Captain Luther Chapin who owned the little schooner *Cuyahoga* which he plied frequently between this point and Detroit.

Hull immediately had what he thought to be an inspirational idea; he would hire Captain Chapin to transport to Detroit for him all of the army's excess baggage, entrenching tools, all the army's musical instruments and the men who played them, three soldiers' wives who had tagged along and the paymaster, Lewis Dent. Some thirty officers and men who were incapacitated due to illness would accompany the schooner in an open boat under command of Second Lieutenant George Gooding, whose wife was aboard the schooner. The officer placed in charge of packing the baggage aboard the *Cuyahoga* was General Hull's son.

Relatively sober on this particular day, Abraham Hull had executed his father's orders quickly and efficiently and then, in an effort to show his initiative, he also carefully packed in the general's trunks all of his father's papers, orders, notes, correspondence, accounts and field reports. He also included the up-to-date muster roles for the whole army, company by company, made out that very day. All these and the remainder of the baggage put aboard the *Cuyahoga* were placed under the direct charge of the assistant quartermaster general, William Beall.

It was at this point that a delegation of officers, with Captain James McPherson of Cincinnati as its spokesman, suggested to the commander that it was altogether possible that war had been declared by now and since the British navy controlled Lake Erie and the *Cuyahoga* would also have to pass directly in front of Fort Malden at Amherstburg, there might be problems.

General Hull had sniffed and responded frostily, "Had war been declared, I assure you I would have been informed of it by now. No, gentlemen, you are shying at shadows. The *Cuyahoga* will be awaiting us at the Detroit wharf when we arrive."

Even as Hull was discussing the matter with his officers, somewhat over three hundred miles to the north British Indian agent and trader Robert Dickson and the 135 Indians—Sioux, Menominee, Chippewa, Sac, Winnebago and Ottawa—he had brought with him from the Wisconsin country arrived at St. Joseph Island at the Straits of Mackinac and reported to the British commander, Captain Charles Roberts. They immediately began active preparations for an assault on Fort Mackinac as soon as they should learn of war being declared. Swift Menominee runners were sent to Amherstburg to advise of the readiness to the north; all that was needed for their attack to be launched was an order from the British commander, Major General Isaac Brock, to that effect.

At this very moment, twenty miles away from Hull's camp, a young Cleveland lawyer named Charles Shaler was riding as rapidly as possible toward the Maumee, desperately hoping to intercept Hull there. Word of the declaration of war had reached there and, with it, an imperative message from the War Department. Finally realizing its error, the War Department urged that an ordinary letter en route to Hull be located and sped on its way by express. Much to the disapproval of the postmaster, the Cleveland mail was pawed through until the final mail packet bound for Detroit was opened and sifted through and the letter found. Immediately Shaler was on his way with it. But by then, Hull, too, was on his way, having set his army in motion around the west shore of Lake Erie toward Detroit.

Shaler arrived at the Maumee, his horse bug-eyed and gasping with exhaustion, to find a detachment of twenty-five soldiers under Lieutenant Davidson busily building a small blockhouse but Hull and his army gone on. So was the schooner *Cuyahoga*. Shaler groaned and, despite the exhaustion of his mount, galloped into the night on the army's trail. It was not until 2 A.M. on July 2 that Shaler finally urged his plodding steed into General Hull's camp and immediately repaired to the general's tent with his momentous news. Hull summoned his officers, informed them of the declaration of war and ordered them to keep it from their men for the time being. He quickly sent a party of men off to locate a boat and try to overtake and warn the *Cuyahoga*. In the process, he forgot to relay information about the declaration of war to Fort Mackinac, Fort Dearborn, and Fort Wayne.

The news had reached Hull too late. Long before this the British knew of the war being declared and they were ready. A lookout with a powerful telescope had been stationed by the Fort Malden commander, Lieutenant Colonel Thomas Bligh St. George, to watch for any American ships. Early in the day the *Cuyahoga* was spotted as she entered the Detroit River, her American flag fluttering jauntily in the lake breeze. St. George immediately dispatched a well-seasoned twenty-nine-year-old French-Canadian, Frederic Rolette, to intercept her. It was a good choice. Rolette, a member of the Provincial Marines, had served in sea battles under a great teacher—Horatio Nelson. He was a veteran of the battles of Trafalgar and the Nile, had been wounded five times and managed to survive. Now he immediately gathered six of his men, armed them with swords and pistols, then set out in a small boat on an interception course. Several canoes filled with Tecumseh's Indians followed.

Unaware of the war in progress, the troops in the *Cuyahoga* and the accompanying open boat made no effort to stop their approach, considering them a welcoming party. Lieutenant Rolette fired one shot from his pistol and boarded the *Cuyahoga* without resistance, informed Captain Chapin and his crew and passengers of the declaration of war, replaced the American flag with the Union Jack and took his prize into Amherstburg without contest, adding the final ignominy of forcing the American band aboard to play "God Save the King" all the way to shore.

Tecumseh was at the head of the more than five hundred Indians who crowded the shores to whoop and shriek their delight at this first evidence they had seen of the British actually warring against the Americans, as had for so long been promised. Tecumseh himself was grinning broadly. It had happened at last! The British were committed beyond recall.

Not until later, however, did Lieutenant Colonel St. George realize just what a prize he had taken—when a search of the ship turned up General Hull's up-to-date rosters, war plans and correspondence. Yet, William Hull was not the only commander who made serious errors: St. George was so badly rattled that an American force of over two thousand men was across the river from him—his own little garrison consisting of only three hundred men of the Forty-first Regiment and a single company of artillery—that he completely overlooked sending word of it, or the captured Hull papers, to his commander, General Brock, at York.

Before dawn Tecumseh, Stiahta, Chaubenee, and Main Poche each took separate parties of warriors across the river and spread out to continue observing Hull's army. Between dawn and sunrise Hull put his men into movement again and was dumbfounded when word was brought to him that the *Cuyahoga* had been taken. So adversely was he affected that it was as if a tomahawk had buried itself in his stomach; whatever self-confidence he had flushed away as water away from a squeezed sponge.

Only a few hours later, far to the north, Captain Charlies Roberts on St. Joseph Island received word of the outbreak of war, brought from Amherstburg by canoe as speedily as possible by fur trader Toussaint Pothier. Roberts immediately put his men on alert and, to augment Dickson's Indians, raised an additional force of 140 French-Canadian voyageurs. All that remained was for permission to come from General Brock for them to make a surprise assault on the American Fort Mackinac, under command of Lieutenant Porter Hanks, who was still ignorant of the war.

Yesterday, as Tecumseh and his Indians had continued to watch unobserved, Hull's army reached the Huron River and went into camp as his engineers set about constructing a bridge for their passage.[628] It was during the evening that a sober and much deflated General William Hull announced to his troops that the United States had declared war upon the British, which brought cheers from the throats of many of his soldiers, only a handful giving any thought at all to the *Cuyahoga* and her possible fate.

Today, once again in motion, the army crossed over the new bridge and passed the large Wyandot village at Brownstown and Walk in the Water's smaller village of Maguaga.[629] Tecumseh was furious with the way Walk in the Water and his people flocked out of their homes to greet the Americans as they passed. Late in the day the army reached Spring Wells at the southern edge of Detroit, and here they went into camp, from which the houses of Detroit's twelve hundred residents could be seen. Charles Shaler had to walk the last few hundred feet into the camp when his horse finally dropped dead beneath him.

Tecumseh now sent runners to his other parties and with the exception of a few left to spy on the army, all retired to Amherstburg, prepared to set up ambushes against the Americans, who were expected to cross the Detroit River on the morrow.

[July 19, 1812 — Sunday]

The first real engagement of the war on the western front was coming to a close and Tecumseh was reasonably well pleased with how his warriors had handled themselves. There was an edge of disappointment in the knowledge, however, that while the enemy had felt their sting, he was not badly hurt. They *had* prevented Americans from advancing on Fort Malden, however, and that was the matter that most concerned Lieutenant Colonel St. George.

Tecumseh was sure they would not come back here, at least not right away, but reluctant to leave anything to chance, he left a dozen good men to guard the remains of the bridge and a pair of his swiftest runners to bring the news immediately if somehow the Americans did actually try it again.

As he returned with his men to the fort he considered the strange things that had been occurring since the Hull army reached Detroit. He was confused by things General Hull did and even more by the things that the American commander didn't do. Hull had moved his force of twenty-two hundred men into the fort at Detroit and took command of the establishment from Captain John Whistler, adding his garrison to the strength of the army, which brought the total number of his force close to twenty-five hundred. So, here was an enemy with the power to have stormed—and *taken*—Fort Malden at almost any time during the past two weeks, yet he hadn't done so. It just didn't make sense.

Instead of launching his army across the river immediately after a good night's rest, Hull had instead sent a single officer bearing a white flag down the river in a small boat to the Amherstburg wharf. He had been surrounded by soldiers, Indians and citizens immediately upon landing but showed no fear.

"I am Colonel Lewis Cass," he had said firmly, "and I have come to see the commanding officer of Fort Malden."

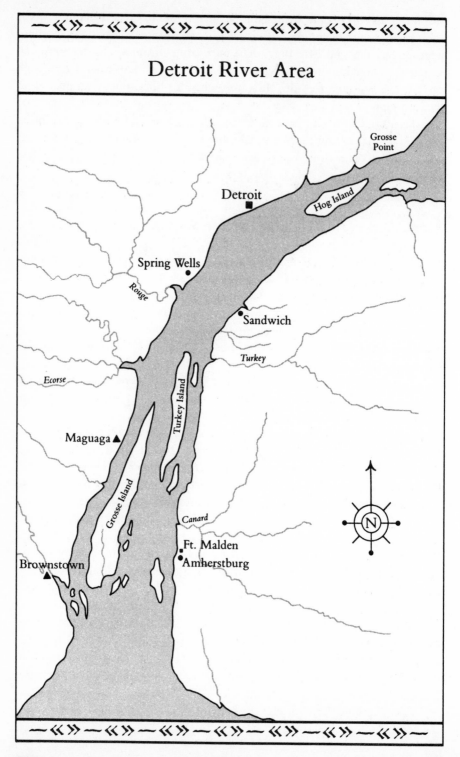

Detroit River Area

Everyone had been certain he was bearing a demand by Hull that the garrison surrender before the unnecessary effusion of blood—the usual type of surrender demand, which would, of course, be haughtily rejected—but that hadn't been the case at all. When he was escorted to the headquarters office of Lieutenant Colonel Thomas Bligh St. George, the message he bore from General Hull carried a politely worded demand that he give up the *Cuyahoga* and the Americans taken with her . . . along with the baggage that had been aboard. In just as polite a response, St. George, although inwardly quaking at the size of the enemy force across the river, in essence told General Hull to go straight to hell and sent Cass back with the message.

Tecumseh was summoned and asked if it was true that large numbers of his Indians had been having second thoughts and abandoning him. Tecumseh admitted that a good many had been listening to the encouragements of Walk in the Water and had crossed over and were staying at Maguaga, but that he felt sure that espousal of a neutral stance was only a temporary thing and they would be soon returning to him. In fact, many already had. Aware of the problem long before St. George was, Tecumseh, Stiahta, Chaubenee, Sauganash, and Main Poche had all crossed the river only the day before and councilled with Walk in the Water.

"We cannot force you to join with us if that is not your wish," Tecumseh told Walk in the Water. "Nor would we seek to prevent your advocating neutrality among your own people. But from this time forward, at the risk of incurring our wrath against you, do so no longer among those of other tribes."

Walk in the Water had acquiesced and had even promised that he himself and his people would remain neutral only so long as they saw it was to their own best interests to do so but that, if in some miraculous manner, Tecumseh's force emerged victorious in the open conflicts that were sure to come against the superior American force, he would then think of this as a sign from the Great Spirit that it was time to reconsider his stance and perhaps throw in with Tecumseh. "But, for the sake of my people," he added, "I cannot do that yet."

That was reasonably satisfactory for the time being and, as Tecumseh informed St. George, some of the Indians who had left him had come back, but his numbers were still far fewer than he wished. He reminded St. George, however, that it was not only his own Indians who had pulled away and the Fort Malden commander had better stop the desertions among his own soldiers.

St. George had nodded. It was only too true. Though his three hundred regulars remained staunch in their duty, he was beset with mass desertions among his eight hundred militia and the knowledge was heavy within him that there was no way he could hold out in the event of a full-scale attack by

Hull's army. It was at this juncture, his thoughts nudged back into focus by the Hull demand carried to him by Cass, that St. George realized he had better inform General Brock of the appearance of the American army here. He did so, at the same time forwarding to his commander the captured Hull documents.

That same day General Hull, too, had finally realized he had neglected to inform the commanders of the forts under his jurisdiction—Mackinac, Wayne, and Dearborn—of the fact that a state of war existed and ordered them to get their forts into a defensive state at once. But, though he dictated the messages, he left no instructions for the immediate dispatch of the notifications by express to the posts in question and so, for now, the orders continued to rest in their pouches in Detroit.

The following day, July 7, five pieces of artillery from the fort at Detroit were rolled into position at Spring Wells and began a bombardment of Sandwich, the settlement directly across the river on the Canadian side.[630] The town was already largely abandoned and no lives were lost and little real damage done. Hull's troops, who had thought this was prelude to their mass crossing in invasionary force were disappointed. The bombardment petered out and the army continued sitting where it was.

Similar disappointment was experienced the next day on St. Joseph Island by the large force of Indians and militia being held in readiness there to attack Fort Mackinac, when a dispatch arrived with directions to hold still and await further orders.

Tecumseh seeing the hesitation of Hull could not immediately understand it, but ordered his several dozen warriors who were watching the fort to move in closer, remaining out of effective rifle range but showing themselves frequently in different sectors to let the Americans know they would be facing a sizeable Indian force if they left the safety of the fort. The ploy worked far better than Tecumseh had any right to hope. Though not yet fully apparent even to his own troops, William Hull was absolutely terrified of Indians and, with the rumors circulating that Tecumseh had many thousands of Indians poised to attack, the American commander magnified the scattered sightings of Indians into a monumental savage force waiting to pounce upon them.

For six days Hull, in essence, sat on his hands, doing nothing while the impatience of his troops increased and became dissatisfied mutterings. In this interval he held several inconsequential councils with small groups of Indians who presented themselves professing peaceful intentions, including Chief Walk in the Water, but he did not really believe them and, when they offered to support the Americans, he rejected them. The old American brig *Adams* in the Detroit shipyard was in need of extensive repairs, so a crew was put to work on this, but the unfamiliar labors went slowly. Hull also gave in somewhat to the growing pressure from his increasingly impatient officers and dispatched an express to Ohio Governor Return J. Meigs at Chillicothe, again the Ohio capital, asking him to send supplies immediately. At the same time, as the result of a conference with his principal field officers, Hull agreed to invade Canada.

For the first time Tecumseh had experienced a certain measure of respect for the American force for the surprise they had pulled off. Word had been brought to him by his spies on July 11 that first more artillery had been rolled into position at Spring Wells, then a number of small boats had been moved into position there for use and, finally, late in the day, an entire regiment under Colonel McArthur had marched the short distance downstream to Spring Wells and was held there.

Tecumseh had immediately notified the Fort Malden commander and withdrew all his warriors from the American side. Supported by a small number of French-Canadian militia, Tecumseh carefully positioned his force in a major ambush setup along the road leading from Sandwich, southward to Fort Malden, fourteen miles distant, expecting the invasion to take place about dawn or shortly thereafter. The ambush was set at the place where dense woodland and brush came close to the road at the bridge over Turkey Creek, five miles south of Sandwich.

The troop movement to Spring Wells had all been a stratagem that had worked perfectly. While Tecumseh's force patiently waited for the crossing to begin in the early morning, it was already occurring all through the night of July 11 and into the wee hours of the morning of July 12 five miles above the fort, at the lower end of Hog Island.[631] There, observing the strictest silence in its maneuver, most of the remainder of the army crossed in a flotilla of small boats, wholly without opposition and not even observed until it entered Sandwich from the north.

When it was finally discovered that the Hull army was, well before dawn, already occupying Sandwich, Tecumseh was chagrined at being so neatly duped. At the same time he admired the skill with which the crossing had been made, the first real sign that the American officers had given of more than mediocre tactical acumen. He rode back at once in the predawn darkness to Fort Malden and informed the commandant.

Lieutenant Colonel Thomas Bligh St. George blanched at the news. Full-scale attack on the fort now seemed imminent. There was, however, a nearby natural barrier that could be put to benefit; three miles north of Fort Malden the Canard River emptied into the Detroit. The river was unfordable, almost one hundred feet wide, very deep and with extremely muddy shores. There was only one crossing, the River Road bridge—a strong wooden structure twelve feet wide. Loathe to destroy that bridge entirely and hamper his own access to the area north of it, St. George ordered a large crew of men out at once to remove all the planking that formed the roadway, leaving only the sleeper beams, over which two single files of men could cross but horses, artillery, supply wagons and the like could not. Then, in the fringe of timber along the road a hundred yards south of the bridge he set up a small battery of artillery supported by forty British regulars. The nearest fording place of the Canard, and not a good one at all, was more than a mile upstream through dense forest and almost impenetrable brush; the only decent one was fully five miles upstream.

General Hull had himself been in the last boat to leave the American side and when it touched ashore on the Canadian side he announced grandly, "The critical moment draws near!" The town of Sandwich was found to be all but deserted and Hull set up his headquarters in the new brick home of Georgian architecture that had recently been built by the French-Canadian militia colonel Jean Baptiste Baby. The American force geared itself for an immediate thrust down the River Road to Fort Malden, but once again Hull vacillated and held them in place.

With the sunrise, Hull issued a strongly worded proclamation advising the populace of Sandwich to return to their homes without fear, but also warning that any white man found fighting beside the Indians would be destroyed.

The next day a force of forty men under Captain Henry Ulry was sent southward along the River Road to reconnoiter toward Fort Malden and came running back after a while with news that they had discovered where Tecumseh's Indians had lain in ambush close to the Turkey Creek bridge. They were not prepared for the wave of terror that washed through Hull at this intelligence, causing him to become pale and perspire. For the first time his officers began to realize the truth; that their commander was more afraid of a force of twenty or thirty Indians in ambush than a force of fifty times that many enemy soldiers facing him directly. Though there were at this time no more than fifteen hundred Indians in the whole Detroit and Amherstburg area, including women and children, the rumors that had been haunting him all along—that Tecumseh was backed by a force of between five and ten thousand Indians from tribes all over the continent—now had become fact to him, virtually smothering him.

The proclamation Hull had issued had, to the dismay of St. George and Tecumseh, caused numerous Canadian residents, many of whom were emigrants from the United States, to take advantage of the amnesty offered and go back across the river to Detroit. What was much worse, it also caused half of the French-Canadian militia to desert and struck fear into the hearts of some of the Indians, notably the Mississaugi branch of the Chippewas. A body of some two hundred of them the very next day abandoned Tecumseh and struck out northeastward for the Thames River and points east. This defection and the threat of others possible in the days ahead caused Tecumseh to replan some of his strategy.

Several days ago he had sent a message to Tenskwatawa telling him to take the Tippecanoe warriors and go to Fort Wayne, where word of the war declaration would not yet have reached and, professing friendship for the whites, he was to collect from the Indian agent the twelve horseloads of ammunition that had been promised by him to the Tippecanoe Indians for peaceful use in hunting. Now, however, fearing that the British and Indians here at Amherstburg were going to have to stay on the defensive instead of mounting an offensive as he had hoped, Tecumseh realized that Tippecanoe would be in grave jeopardy of another attack from the south by Harrison as soon as news of the war declaration reached there. He therefore immediately had a large red war belt prepared, on which was symbolized the great broad ax of the king of England, and sent Sauganash with it to intercept Tenskwatawa at Fort Wayne with important orders: Tenskwatawa was to get away from Fort Wayne immediately, return to Tippecanoe and at once on arrival send all the women and children to the west. Under a strong escort of Winnebagoes, they were to go to the village of Kauraykawsawkaw—White Crow—and other Winnebago villages on the Rock River in Illinois and the Four Lakes area in Wisconsin. As soon as they were safely away, Tenskwatawa was to lead the remaining warriors down the Wabash and attack Vincennes. If they failed to capture the town in one stroke, they were to make a swift retreat, not to Tippecanoe, which should then be abandoned, but westward after their families and where, eventually, Tecumseh would rejoin them to continue the fight against the whites. He had no further fear Tenskwatawa would not follow these orders to the letter.

The defection by the body of Mississaugi Chippewas had not gone unnoticed by the Americans. Hull's scouts reported to him on July 14 the movement of the body of Indians toward the Thames and the general was almost pathetically relieved that at least one portion of the Indians was moving away, for whatever purpose. He then grudgingly acquiesced to the strong request of Colonel McArthur, whose regiment had now also crossed the river, that he be allowed to pursue those Indians with a large detachment of his own men, supported by Colonel Findley's rifle corps. While they were never able to overtake the Indians, they did find and loot considerable stockpiles of British supplies along the Thames, including two hundred barrels of flour, four hundred new blankets and a good number of arms and ammunition. They had then confiscated enough boats to transport the captured goods back to Sandwich via Lake St. Clair.

Far to the north, Captain Charles Roberts finally received orders from

General Brock to attempt to seize Fort Mackinac from the Americans. Traveling in a flotilla of canoes, he led his force of six hundred Indians, soldiers, and traders under cover of darkness to Mackinac Island, surrounded the fort unseen and in the first light of morning sent in a demand for its surrender. Having heard nothing yet of war being declared and totally unprepared, Lieutenant Porter Hanks surrendered his garrison of sixty-one men and himself without a shot being fired.[632]

On the Detroit River, still more time passed without much of anything happening while Hull remained locked in place at Sandwich. This lack of activity had begun to have serious implications among the Indians, who were beginning to fear now that the Americans were simply waiting for yet more American soldiers to join them, though they hardly needed such a reinforcement. In addition, word had just been received from Fort Wayne that was particularly unsettling to the Indians.

William Wells had called for the Indians of the Wabash and Maumee—especially the Potawatomies—to assemble at Fort Wayne for a council at which, at the orders of Governor Harrison, he would provide them with gifts in abundance; some whiskey as well as a great deal of food and gifts of blankets, clothing and other supplies, including even a small amount of gunpowder and lead for their hunting. The council was for a dual purpose; a continuance of placation of the Indians in regard to the land matters and, more pertinently, to woo them away from the British and Tecumseh.

The council fire had been lighted and Wells waited. Twenty-five hundred Indians had been expected, mostly Potawatomies, but only two hundred fifty Indians had arrived and none were of that tribe. Instead, they were Miamis led by Wells's former Indian father, Michikiniqua, now seventy and so severely ailing from gout that he could not walk and had been carried to the council on a litter. In the midst of their waiting for the others to arrive, Michikiniqua had suddenly sat bolt upright and his eyes blazed as he pointed a trembling finger at something none but he could see, and then fell back.

Michikiniqua—Little Turtle—was dead.

To the Indians in the Detroit area, it made no difference whether or not they had been in favor of Michikiniqua's pacific policies; his death was mourned by all, including Tecumseh. It was at this point that a large number of those Indians who were camped with Tecumseh near the Canard River bridge, weary of the waiting, returned to either their larger and more permanent camp to the south of Fort Malden or crossed the Detroit River to the villages there.

Tecumseh, left near the bridge with no more than eighty warriors, had a difficult time keeping their spirits buoyed and preventing additional desertions. That was why he was gratified when finally, two days ago, a company of soldiers under thirty-year-old Captain Josiah Snelling moved south from

Sandwich and occupied the tiny French settlement called Petit Cote, a mile above the Canard River bridge. They had expected the force to continue its march to the bridge, but it had not.

The following day—yesterday—Colonel McArthur had convinced General Hull to let him advance with a force of 150 men down the River Road toward Fort Malden, to relieve Captain Snelling and reconnoiter closer to the enemy.[633] Hull ordered him, however, not to attempt to cross the Canard River nor to go within reach of the twenty-gun British ship *Queen Charlotte,* lying at anchor in the Detroit River off the mouth of the Canard.

Tecumseh's spies reported the movement at once and the defensive post at the southern end of the River Road bridge was put on alert and strengthened, the 40 regulars now supported by 25 dragoons and 150 Canadian militia, plus Tecumseh's 80 men now on hand. Not knowing whether the American troop movement was just a detachment or the first wave of the whole enemy force, Tecumseh ordered all his warriors to return to the south side of the river and take cover in the woods. He, along with Stiahta and Main Poche, rifles in hand, scaled the battery to watch.

Before long the Americans came into view several hundred yards away north of the river. They halted and the three Indian leaders could see them observing through telescopes the remains of the bridge and defenses beyond. Ridiculously, though far beyond rifle range, the American riflemen fired a volley of shots toward them, but none of the balls even came close. Tecumseh called to his men not to fire or expose themselves until the enemy came to the river's edge. It didn't happen. The riflemen reloaded and fired another volley, just as ineffectually.

Tecumseh looked at his companions and grinned. "I'm going across to see if I can tease them into coming closer."

Main Poche and Stiahta looked at each other and nodded and Stiahta replied, "Not alone, you're not. Let's go."

The three Indians trotted the hundred yards to the bridge and ran with sure strides across the foot-wide sleeper beams to its north end, then trotted abreast on the road toward the enemy. Balls began kicking up the dirt around them but they continued approaching until about 50 yards beyond the bridge and now within 150 yards of their foes, where they finally stopped.

"Fire," Tecumseh said, "and then run back."

The three fired almost simultaneously toward the Americans and drew another volley toward themselves. They turned and began running back with balls whizzing all around them, Tecumseh sprinting into the lead, with Stiahta not far behind and Main Poche, bigger and heavier, bringing up the rear. A lead ball struck the latter in the neck and sent him sprawling loose-jointed to the ground where he lay unmoving.

Tecumseh, reaching the bridge, stopped and turned to let his companions pass across and realized at the same time that Main Poche was down. "Take this," he cried at Stiahta, tossing his rifle at him, "and get across." Stiahta snatched the gun in midair without losing stride and sped across the sleeper beams.

Tecumseh raced back toward Main Poche, but had not gotten halfway there when the wounded man raised himself, came groggily to his feet and staggered toward Tecumseh. When they met, Tecumseh put Main Poche's arm over his shoulder and ran as best he could with him back to the bridge. Stiahta had returned, without the rifles, to the north end and together, before and behind their wounded companion, they helped him across.

The wound was not serious, the ball having passed cleanly through the neck muscle behind and below his left ear, missing the spine by only a fraction of an inch. All this while the American riflemen fired volley after volley for another half hour, but never budged a foot closer. Finally they turned and moved back out of sight toward Petit Cote.

As soon as they were out of sight, Tecumseh selected thirty of his men and led them across the bridge and to a clump of brush and trees close to where the Americans had stood and fired, between the road and the Detroit River. Here they took cover and waited. Soon two American officers—Colonel McArthur and Adjutant Puthuff—with telescopes came back toward them astride horses, evidently to study the situation further. They would have ridden into the ambush neatly, but several overanxious warriors fired too early and the officers turned their mounts and fled. They, in turn, were met by the detachment rushing to their rescue. A hurried conference was held among them and then the whole force marched directly toward the brush where Tecumseh's Indians were hiding. This time the Indians continued firing until the Americans were not much over a hundred yards distant and it became obvious they were not going to be deterred from the advance. Unwilling to risk his warriors' lives in trying to hold the position, Tecumseh ordered them back across the bridge.

The Americans did continue their advance until they came to the river's edge, at which a general firing broke out again from both sides, but badly directed and without effect. Colonel McArthur's horse was shot out from under him with a bullet through its forehead and three American soldiers were wounded.

Late in the afternoon the Americans withdrew back toward Petit Cote and immediately Tecumseh led his entire Indian force in pursuit, firing at them frequently and detaching a small party to circle around in the woods to the east and try to come up on their rear. When the American detachment stopped, faced about and returned the fire in volley, all the Indians except Tecumseh flopped flat to the ground to avoid being hit. Tecumseh simply waited a moment as the balls buzzed viciously around him.

The Americans, running short of ammunition, had evidently seen the Indian party trying to slip around behind so this time when they resumed their march they did not stop at Petit Cote but continued back toward Sandwich until, about sunset, they crossed the Turkey Creek bridge, where they were reinforced by Colonel Cass's regiment with a six-pounder cannon, and here they camped.

Tecumseh withdrew his warriors south of the Canard again and by the following morning, today, the defenses at the south end of the bridge had been greatly augmented by more Indians—bringing Tecumseh's force here now to 150 warriors—as well as more troops and more field pieces. It was well this was done, since the Americans, themselves reinforced by another regiment, returned in the forenoon with artillery. They were held at bay a considerable distance away and lobbed a few shots back with their own six-pounder, but eventually gave up and retreated back to Sandwich.

Everything seemed to be in a state of stasis at the moment and now, as Tecumseh approached Fort Malden again, he had to admit to himself he had no idea what was coming next.

[July 29, 1812 — Wednesday]

Chaubenee and Sauganash were in the council house in the village of Black Partridge on the Des Plaines River not very far from Chicago and Fort Dearborn. They had been sent here by Tecumseh on very fast horses on a mission with two principal objectives. First, to spread the news to the Potawatomies and Winnebagoes in the area of Chicago, Milwaukee, and the Rock River of the fall of Fort Mackinac to the British, largely because of the assistance of the Menominees, Ottawas, and Chippewas.

Tecumseh had been informed of Mackinac's fall a day before the British at Amherstburg learned of it and two days before General Hull was himself so shattered by the news. It had been this electrifying news that had suddenly had the effect of cementing the tribes together in a stronger force under Tecumseh. The long wavering Walk in the Water was only one of the chiefs who crossed the Detroit River and threw their lot to Tecumseh and in a very short time his warrior force at Amherstburg of less than seven hundred had doubled in size and was still growing.

General Hull's actions—or lack of them—continued to perplex Tecumseh and the British. The skirmish at the Canard River bridge, while relatively minor and resulting in no clear victory for anyone, had nevertheless shown the Americans that with a concerted attack the bridge could easily enough be taken and that bridge was the entire key to taking Amherstburg and Fort Malden and wresting control from the British of this whole sector of Upper Canada. Hull's officers had beleaguered him with the fact that there was no other practicable way for the army to approach the British stronghold; no other place within ten or fifteen miles where the horses could pull the heavy artillery across without becoming hopelessly mired—artillery that could quickly shatter the British bastion and bring the redcoats to their knees. With the sleepers of the bridge still firmly in place, once the infantry pushed the defenders back, new planking could quickly be laid across, opening the way to their triumph.

But Hull had unexpectedly rejected the idea, drew his troops back to Sandwich and then confounded and alarmed his own force by placing Colonel McArthur in charge there and himself returning across the river to Detroit, with no indication given when, or if, he would return.[634]

Grave murmurings regarding the courage of the general, or his lack of it, were rampant and they grew when it became known that one of General Hull's aides, Captain James Brown, had slipped away to Fort Malden under a flag of truce and later he had returned and refused to explain his actions.[635]

Tecumseh's spies continued to watch the army closely, moving back and forth in small groups and large parties along a path parallel to but less used than the River Road, running between the Petit Cote settlement and Sandwich. Soon they reported to Tecumseh that the Americans had discovered the path and a detachment under Major James Denny had been sent out and was setting up an ambush for the Indians along that path just north of Petit Cote. In a well-planned and executed countermove, Tecumseh set up his own ambush and, with himself and the neck-bandaged Main Poche leading them, surprised the Americans and forced them to retire after a brief skirmish that left six of the American soldiers dead and two wounded. The detachment might well have been annihilated had it not been for the timely arrival of some Ohio Militia reinforcements.[636]

Word had just come to Tecumseh from his spies that a large American supply train consisting of 150 packhorses loaded with flour, food, and other goods, along with a herd of 300 head of beef cattle, was observed moving northward, escorted by close to 100 Ohio white men, and was at this time just north of the Maumee Rapids, evidently bound for General Hull's army.[637]

Tecumseh's eyes glittered and he immediately made plans for its reception. Not wishing to deplete his force here in proximity to Hull's army and Amherstburg, he sent the spies back to continue watching the supply train and give him ample warning of its approach. They would ambush it between Frenchtown, on the River Raisin, and Detroit. With that plan fixed, he conferred with Lieutenant Colonel St. George at Fort Malden. Then, with twenty-three of his warriors and accompanied by Matthew Elliott's son Alexander, he crossed the Detroit by canoe and established a camp near Brownstown.

Five days after his departure from Sandwich, General Hull had come back across the river, looking less harried and a bit more in control of himself as he reestablished himself in the fortification built around the brick home of a Mr. Gowie, which was named Fort Gowie. There had been a quickening of pulses among the troops when it seemed that Hull was on the verge of issuing some strong offensive orders.

That was when everything changed with the arrival of a ship on the Detroit River, coming from upstream and flying the British colors. She was brought about by a shot across her bow and a few minutes later a substantial group of American soldiers and civilians were disembarking. The leader, Lieutenant Porter Hanks immediately informed General Hull of his unconditional surrender of Fort Mackinac to a large force of British and Indians.

All the fears of Indians that Hull had been holding at bay with great effort instantly came crashing down on him. His eyes became glass, his jaw dropped and he swayed to such extent that some thought he was on the verge of fainting. Not even realizing he was speaking aloud, he murmured, "Dear God, the whole northern horde of Indians will be let loose upon us." In a daze he reeled back to his headquarters and secluded himself there and the hopes of his troops to be set loose on an offensive began oozing away.

On the heels of this news came more to shatter his confidence. Tecumseh's forces had successfully cut off the communication and supply lines between Detroit and Fort Dearborn and there were whisperings that a major attack was in the works for the western allies of Tecumseh to attack that Chicago fort very soon.

The most important message from Tecumseh that had brought Chaubenee and Sauganash to the Chicago area, however, was to reaffirm to the assemblage of chiefs here in Black Partridge's village the validity of what Tecumseh had predicted much earlier and was still predicting: that Detroit would fall and the American Army would be lost in the middle of August and that the attack on Fort Dearborn should still be launched, as planned, to coincide with that. It was Tecumseh's suggestion that the Potawatomies in that whole region at the southern end of Lake Michigan, acting with what would seem to be peaceable intent, should begin moving into Chicago five or six days prior to that, setting up their lodges close to the fort and carrying on normal activities to allay fears.

Immediately all this information was relayed by swift riders to Siggenauk at Milwaukee, Mawgehset—Big Foot—at Lake Geneva, the Winnebago chiefs Karamone, Mackraragah, Kauraykawsawkaw, Sansamani, and Shawonoe on the Upper Rock River, to Gomo at Peoria Lake, to Nescotnemeg on the

Kankakee and Naunongee on the Calumet. By tomorrow night war dances would be occurring.

Chaubenee and Sauganash, upon leaving the council, immediately rode boldly into Chicago and stopped briefly at Fort Dearborn to pay their respects to a nervous Captain Nathan Heald, who came out to meet them. They talked for a short while and then the two Indians crossed over the Chicago River and went to the home and trading post of John Kinzie. That visit was the second principal objective of this mission Tecumseh had sent them on; Kinzie had always shown himself to be a good friend of the Indians, had helped them immeasurably and at great expense to himself prior to the Battle of Fallen Timbers, and so efforts must be taken, in a very subtle way, to try to prevent any harm coming to him and his family when the attack occurred here.

They found Kinzie at his store and greeted him with genuine friendliness, as they had for so many years. He made them very welcome, fed them a good meal and afterwards smoked with them and sipped brandy. It was Chaubenee who finally came to the point.

"Shawneeawkee," he said, addressing him by the name the Indians had given him, "Sauganash and I are your friends and we are concerned for you and your family—for their health and well-being. It might be wise for you and your family very soon to take a trip for your health. You are always working very hard here. Your women and children should have some time with you when you are not concerned with work and you can devote yourself to them. Yes, it would be very wise for you to take a trip."

The trader looked at them sharply and he was silent for a little while. "Perhaps," he said at last, "my friends are right. It might be well for our health to take such a trip as you suggest. Maybe we will do it when autumn comes and traveling is more pleasant. But," he added, and his voice hardened, "I could not leave here until at least then."

Chaubenee and Sauganash regarded him steadily for an extended time and then reached out in turn and shook hands with the trader. At the door of the trading post, as they were leaving, Sauganash paused a moment and looked back at the trader.

"Think well, Shawneeawkee, on what my brother Chaubenee has told you this day."

Then they were gone, heading back to rejoin Tecumseh.

[August 4, 1812 — Tuesday]

During the forenoon today a party of Tecumseh's Indians came into his camp near Brownstown with a mounted messenger they had captured bearing a dispatch pouch and headed south at a rapid gait. Tecumseh questioned the man but he refused to answer, nor even give his name.

He didn't have to. In the pouch was a letter from General Hull to a Captain H. Brush who, it quickly became clear, was the officer bringing the supply train north from Ohio. Hull's message informed Brush that it was known that Tecumseh and a number of his Indians were back on the west side of the Detroit and it was believed they meant to intercept the supply train. Brush was informed that Major Thomas Van Horne had been dispatched at the head of a detachment of 150 infantrymen to ferry his men across the Detroit River and then march to join the supply train in the vicinity of Frenchtown and escort them back to Detroit. That force, Hull wrote, would be a while in arriving since a good many of the men were on foot.

At once Tecumseh sent a message to St. George, explaining the situation and asking for a reinforcement. He considered sending for some additional warriors of his own, too, but then decided against it; they were needed more on the other side of the river in case Hull should launch a sudden full-scale surprise attack against Fort Malden. At the moment he had with him seventy-four warriors and, while waiting for a response from the Fort Malden commander, he sent three of his men, mounted on good horses, northward to spy on the American detachment's movements. At the same time he placed forty-five under Stiahta to move south and set up an ambush north of Frenchtown to hit the supply train shortly after it left River Raisin.

The sun was nearly setting when word was brought to him that the American detachment, wearied from the time-consuming river crossing and the short march that followed, had gone into camp for the night at the mouth of the Ecorse River only a few miles north of their camp. A short time later a British military detachment sent by St. George arrived at Tecumseh's camp—forty militiamen under Major Adam Muir—having crossed the Detroit River in canoes. Since the Americans had stopped their march for the day, Muir's detachment went into camp with Tecumseh, close to Brownstown, prepared to engage the enemy in the morning.

Tecumseh conferred with Major Muir and they considered the situation carefully. When the Americans resumed their march in the morning, they would move southward on the main road. That road, however, just after passing Walk in the Water's abandoned village of Maguaga, split around a large cornfield. There was no way of knowing for certain which fork they would take. Tecumseh's plan was adopted. Main Poche and a dozen of the remaining warriors would remain with Muir and set up an ambush along the west road close to where they were camped here near Brownstown, which was the road the detachment was most likely to take. That road, half a mile above where the two roads again converged, crossed a small creek where there was plenty of cover for a good ambush. Tecumseh and the remaining dozen Indians would move farther north, close to the fork, and set up an ambush along the smaller east road, which was closer to the river. They would all move into position an hour before dawn.

With everything set, Tecumseh turned to Main Poche and their remaining twenty-four warriors and smiled broadly.

"Get your weapons in readiness," he said. "Tomorrow morning we will spill the first real American blood of this war."

Chapter 12

[August 5, 1812 — Wednesday]

— ❮ ❯ —   "They're coming, Tecumseh!"

Tecumseh, just preparing his men to leave camp with an hour to go before dawn arrived, was surprised at the words of his spy who had ridden up. The warrior was excited and his horse lathered from the hard gallop all the way from the Ecorse River. The words tumbled from the warrior as he went on.

"They've sent out a small advance party first—twenty men—a mile or so ahead, but the rest are following."[638]

Tecumseh immediately alerted Major Muir and Main Poche to get their ambush in order and set off at top speed with his own dozen men for the advanced position he was taking on the east road. In a short time he arrived there and got his men into hiding in the shoulder-high corn. Aware that thirteen Indians hardly made up a strong force, Tecumseh's orders were explicit: if the party came down this road, they would fire simultaneously at it and then, while confusion reigned among the Americans, eleven of the warriors would melt away into the cornfield and move at high speed back to their main force while Tecumseh and Jim Blue Jacket would keep under cover and see what developed.[639]

It was light enough to see reasonably well by the time the advance party reached the fork. Tecumseh watched the distant men closely as they paused there briefly and then was not surprised when the party moved off on the west fork. Three of the men, however, split off and started down the smaller river road toward them. Within ten minutes they walked into the ambush and at Tecumseh's signal, everyone fired. All three went down, dead when they hit the ground.[640] The Indians burst from cover, scalped all three and just as quickly vanished, already hearing sounds of the major part of the party running toward the scene.

From a screen of brush closer to the Detroit River, Tecumseh and Jim Blue Jacket watched as the other section of the party appeared back at the fork in the road, watched as they pointed toward the bodies lying on the east road and raced up to them. The Americans looked around fearfully and their leader studied the ground carefully. Then they picked up the bodies and started back toward the army with them. Tecumseh and Jim Blue Jacket paced them in hiding and watched when, as they reached Maguaga, they hid the bodies under some large pieces of bark and then left the road and continued moving north through cover toward the main detachment, which they encountered in only a few minutes.

"They will probably all turn and run back to the army," Jim Blue Jacket whispered.

Tecumseh shook his head. "I don't think so. I saw the one study the ground closely. He knows we were only a few. I think they'll continue. The question is, will they now take the east road or the west?"

Even as they watched a trio of riders who were French farmers and evidently from the Frenchtown vicinity of River Raisin, came cantering up and stopped. They talked with the commander for a while with considerable excitement and gesticulation, but finally continued on their way toward Detroit, while the detachment, at full alert and weapons ready, resumed their march toward the south.[641]

Tecumseh and Jim Blue Jacket watched intently as the detachment approached the fork in the road and Tecumseh murmured "Good!" when, without hesitation, they took the west road leading toward the ambush. Immediately the pair moved completely out of sight, regained the east road and ran at full speed back to the main ambush where the latest news was passed and everyone gotten into position and out of sight.

The place for the ambush was well chosen. Just north of Brownstown the road narrowed considerably where it crossed the small creek. The margin of the creek and the sides of the road for a considerable distance in both directions were cloaked with heavy brush and undergrowth. All of Major Muir's militia and the majority of the Indians were south of the creek, but some of the latter had also taken positions well hidden in the brush along the road north of the creek.

Not until the head of the detachment had reached the south side of the creek did the shrieking signal erupt from Tecumseh and a tremendous burst of gunfire break out, accompanied by ear-piercing screams from every Indian throat. The soldiers, their minds already filled with fear and by the image of the thousands of Indians that General Hull was sure were around Detroit, instantly panicked. They dropped their weapons, their packs, and the dispatch packet and fled.

Van Horne and his officers tried to rally the men into a stand but to little avail. A few, who had retained their weapons, stopped and fired at the attackers, but then immediately fled again. Early in the action Tecumseh, stained war club in hand, was slightly wounded when a bullet creased his thigh and caused a lot of bleeding but not much damage, and he hardly noticed as he fought on.[642] A short distance from him Jim Blue Jacket leaped up and pulled a mounted officer from his horse and killed him with a tomahawk blow. An instant later, while he was scalping the man, another officer thundered past and all but beheaded the Shawnee with a slashing stroke of his saber.

The remnants of the American detachment straggled back into their Ecorse River camp of the night before with seventy of their number missing, twenty wounded and seventeen left dead at the scene of the ambush. The wounded were sent the rest of the way up to Detroit by boat and the remainder regrouped and returned there afoot, still terrified at what they were already calling the Battle of Brownstown, although calling it a battle was rather stretching the point.

Tecumseh's force did not pursue them for any great distance, content with the victory thus far and not willing to push their luck. All the dead at the battlefield were scalped and stripped and their bodies impaled on poles set up along the road, there to serve as a warning for others who might come along. One young soldier, captured by Main Poche, was being held by some Indian women who had been part of the force and his fate hung in balance until four warriors came up carrying the nearly beheaded body of Jim Blue Jacket. Furious, Main Poche gave a signal and two of the women drove their knives into the soldier, one in his neck, the other in his side. As he screamed and began to fall, Main Poche buried a tomahawk in his head.[643]

Tecumseh met with Major Muir, who was now preparing his men to move back to Fort Malden, and suggested they remain in place, stating that he was sure another American detachment would come soon, probably larger than the first. They would want to collect and bury their dead and there was still the matter of the supply convoy, which would almost certainly not come closer unless provided with an escort.

Muir considered this and nodded. He sent off a report to the Fort Malden commander with the good news of their victory here and a request for more troops to meet the expected second American detachment.

"And now," Tecumseh said, "we wait. And watch."

[August 9, 1812 — Sunday]

Although saddened at the loss of Jim Blue Jacket, Tecumseh had been very pleased, the day after the Battle of Brownstown, with the return of Chaubenee and Sauganash and with the assurances they brought that the Indians in the Chicago area were poised to strike the Americans in Fort Dearborn and its surroundings. He listened with approval to their report on how Nescotnemeg's plan was drawn, at the readiness of Siggenauk and his people to help carry it out on the fifteenth day of August, and at the fact that Black Partridge was already moving his people adjacent to the fort under the guise of friendship. He was less than pleased, however, that John Kinzie had told them that he would not leave Chicago before autumn.

Kinzie, though now an American citizen, was the only British individual to live up to his promises to the Indians at the time of the Battle of Fallen Timbers and to help the Indians far beyond what was expected, and Tecumseh simply could not abandon him and his family now to an uncertain fate. There was little doubt in his mind that once the attack at Chicago began in earnest, the killing of Americans there would become general and the Kinzie family was in extreme jeopardy; the Indians who knew him would not harm him, but not all who were coming to share in the attack knew him. Even though Chaubenee and Sauganash had just returned from that place, there was little choice but to send them back to take more definitive steps for rescue of the entire Kinzie family. With their great influence among the Potawatomies, who would be the most numerous tribe on hand for the attack, Chaubenee and Sauganash were perhaps the only ones who could prevent their deaths and get them away.

"It would be a great sadness," he told them finally, "if Shawneeawkee or his family came to harm. On good horses, how long will you need to arrive at Chicago?"

"We took six days," Sauganash replied, "getting from there to here, but with good fresh horses we could easily make it in five days maximum, probably less."

Tecumseh nodded. "Good," he said. "Then you will leave here the evening of the third day from now, when there will be more good news to carry to the chiefs there from here."

When they asked him what he meant by "more good news from here," Tecumseh only smiled enigmatically and told them they would see.

During the four days that had followed the Battle of Brownstown, the British detachment remained in place, their initial enthusiasm gradually diminishing when the expected American detachment did not show up as anticipated. The number of British here had increased to near four hundred through the militia reinforcement sent by Lieutenant Colonel St. George, but the inactivity took its toll and, with their rations all but depleted, Adam Muir finally gave up and was just getting his force back into their boats for the return to Fort Malden when Tecumseh had galloped up and stopped them.

"It is as I told you it would be," he said. "Another detachment of Americans is coming. It is larger and better armed than the first, but I have a plan."

He outlined his strategy and Major Adam Muir readily agreed to it. The odds were in favor of the Americans—six hundred American soldiers, including an artillery unit, against Muir's four hundred militia and Tecumseh's Indians, which now numbered seventy here—but the plan was so boldly conceived that they could not resist and they moved quickly to the point where Tecumseh planned the ambush.[644] This time it would occur close to Maguaga. The Muir militia could hide in a ravine that the road crossed, and Tecumseh's warriors would hide farther north in a cornfield flanking the road on the east. At the prearranged signal a volley would be fired, followed by an immediate rush of the British soldiers with bayonets fixed and a simultaneous rush on the rear of the American detachment by warriors on both sides with war clubs and tomahawks.

It had occurred precisely as Tecumseh had said. It was a beastly hot day and the American force moved slowly. At close to four o'clock in the afternoon today, while passing Walk in the Water's abandoned Wyandot village of Maguaga, the detachment of Lieutenant Colonel James Miller filed past the spot where the bodies of the three men earlier killed lay bloated beneath covering bark which hid the presence of the bodies but none of their stench.[645] The detachment was within a half mile of the same spot where McCulloch had been ambushed and certainly where no one among the Americans conceived that an ambush would recur.

But it did.

Tecumseh gave the signal and there was immediate chaos as the Battle of Maguaga broke out. American lines faltered, broke, reformed and broke again. Men were falling all around and within minutes the gunsmoke turned the battlefield into a nightmarish world of fearsome shadowy human shapes unidentifiable as friend or foe beyond twenty feet. A segment of the Potawatomies who got on the west side of the road and were driven back by a determined rush of some Americans, abruptly turned and raced back toward the British lines. The British, in the belief that all of Tecumseh's force was on the east side of the road, thought the movement toward them was Americans coming and fired at them and the Potawatomies returned the fire, resulting in momentary confusion before the matter was straightened out.

Within minutes Major Muir took two bullets, one through the shoulder and another through the leg, but he kept on fighting and shouting his commands. The American Ensign John Whistler, Jr., son of the former Fort Dearborn commander, received a severe wound when a ball slammed through his rib cage on the right side.[646] A ball nipped the right earlobe of Chaubenee and another neatly clipped away an eagle feather being worn by Sauganash on the right side of his head. Tecumseh was in the thick of the fighting at all times, swinging his war club with deadly effectiveness, the slight wound in his thigh from the skirmish four days earlier forgotten. He was not touched this time.

Despite the advantage of the surprise attack and the initial faltering of the Americans, the British and Indians were gradually pushed back and finally gave way. The Americans pursued them two miles toward Brownstown but, with evening approaching, they were finally recalled. The battle statistics were interesting. Two Indians had been killed and six wounded. The British had six dead, twenty-one wounded, including Major Muir. And among the Americans—who held the field at the end of the contest and therefore claimed victory in the battle—there were eighteen dead and sixty-four wounded.[647] The mission to reach the supply train at River Raisin and escort it the remainder of the way to Detroit was abandoned as Miller ordered his men to establish a heavily guarded camp here at Maguaga and he then sent a message requesting a reinforcement from Hull.[648]

Major Muir led his men to the river and began the ferrying of his force across in bateaux and canoes.[649] Tecumseh called Chaubenee and Sauganash to him and embraced the pair. "Go now," he said. "Tell our Potawatomi friends of our two good fights here and find our friend there in Chicago and keep him and his family from harm. Return to me as soon as you can."

Walk in the Water, who had fought with the Indians, once again had second thoughts and now abandoned Tecumseh and, with his Wyandots, resumed his former neutral stance. Tecumseh ignored it and, leaving only a skeletal force of his own warriors on the Michigan side of the river to continue spying, he and the bulk of his warriors paddled across the river after Muir's force and, on arrival, was met by Matthew Elliott.

"There is good news here, Tecumseh," the Indian agent told him. "The commanding general is on his way here with a good reinforcement from Niagara. We expect him very soon."

[August 14, 1812 — Friday]

Tecumseh had been prepared to dislike Major General Isaac Brock as simply another of the pompous governor-generals the British seemed to favor, but he was pleasantly surprised. Here was no strutting dandy of an officer inflated with his own importance; this was a man with the eye and attitude of a warrior, a white chief who missed nothing, who listened and who thought. Tecumseh was more than a little impressed.

At age forty-three—only a year younger than Tecumseh—Isaac Brock was a physically huge man, three inches over six feet tall, having broad shoulders and hips and close to two hundred fifty pounds. A professional soldier thrown as well into the role of Canadian governor, instead of the other way around, Brock had previously given outstanding service in the Napoleonic wars, where he was noted as an imaginative, aggressive, and virtually fearless commander. As a memento of one of his previous campaigns, his left eye was permanently closed and he was also lame and walked with the assistance of a cane, but the afflictions seemed to have no effect on his capabilities.

Most important where Tecumseh and his followers were concerned, Brock greatly sympathized with the plight of the western tribes and had long been a very vocal advocate of the prospect for establishment of a separate and inviolate Indian territory in the Northwest. He strongly believed that, for their services in behalf of the king, it behooved the British to guarantee them such a territory of their own and never to renege on that guarantee.

Brock had been marshaling his forces to meet the American forces assembling for a major campaign in the Niagara area, but the reports from Fort Malden had disturbed him considerably, especially when he learned the American general had invaded Canada and established a headquarters at Sandwich, from which he could with ease cut off and capture Fort Malden and Amherstburg and then overrun that whole section of Upper Canada. If that occurred, as Matthew Elliott was warning in his dispatches, the Indian allies of the British would simply disappear.

With matters moving slowly in the Niagara area, Brock had finally come to the conclusion he could risk taking a force of some four hundred soldiers—a quarter of them regulars—along with sixty Iroquois who had attached themselves to him, and rush to Amherstburg for a quick campaign, then return to Niagara before anything of moment occurred there. Accordingly, on August 8 he had loaded this force into ten large bateaux and yesterday, late in the evening, had arrived here at Amherstburg.

Good news had met Brock on his arrival. He had already been informed of the two abortive missions by the Americans to get their supply train in, thwarted largely because of the actions of Tecumseh and his Indian force. Now, even more encouragingly, he learned that only the day before yesterday, General Hull had abandoned his foothold in Canada and retreated back across the Detroit River into the American fort and it was obvious that he was greatly upset over the loss of Fort Mackinac and the fights that occurred at Brownstown and Maguaga and, even more, feared that a great horde of Indians was gradually surrounding him.[650]

What impressed Tecumseh immediately about Brock was his response to the welcome he received on his arrival at the Amherstburg wharf. Under the light of hundreds of torches, Canadian citizens and militiamen cheered wildly and some five hundred Indians under Tecumseh began enthusiastically discharging their guns in the air. Brock had immediately ordered that this be stopped, since it was a wasteful use of ammunition that could be better employed against the Americans. Further, Brock had wasted no time sending Matthew Elliott to bring Tecumseh to him to confer on what measures were required now against Hull.

Tecumseh appeared at once, apologized for his warriors' misuse of ammunition and promised it would not happen again. The general and the Indian leader assessed one another carefully and both were impressed with what they saw. Brock had heard a great deal about Tecumseh and now meeting him, seeing the commanding way he carried himself and his lack of the usual accoutrement of the self-important Indian chief, he was also quite impressed.[651]

General Brock promised to give a general address to the assembled Indians first thing in the morning, and that is what he did today, brief and to the point, telling the nearly one thousand Indians who had gathered that he had been sent by their great father across the waters, the king of England, to drive the Americans from Detroit and as far south as it was necessary to push them. He proclaimed Tecumseh a renowned fighter and great leader and acknowledged him as "the general of the Indians."[652]

Tecumseh, in a public show of honor to Brock, appeared wearing more ornamentation than was his custom—his feet clad in moccasins richly decorated in patterns of dyed porcupine quills and, over his simple fringed buckskin jacket and trousers, a ceremonial pipe wedged in his belt and a multicolored string of wampum around his neck, along with a large silver pendant medallion of King George III. A double-quill eagle-feather headdress at his right temple trailed back and down over his shoulder and his hair was held in place by a vermilion band of fabric over which was a narrower silver band. He also wore a nose piece on this occasion—a trio of tiny silver crowns depending from his nasal septum.

As soon as Brock finished his brief talk, Tecumseh stepped forward and said, in response, "We, your Indian allies, are overjoyed that our father beyond the great salt lake, the king, has at length awoke from his long sleep and permitted his warriors to come to the assistance of his red children. The

Americans suddenly came against us with a great force when I was absent and destroyed our village and slew our warriors. They came to us hungry and then cut off the hands of our brothers who gave them corn. We gave them rivers of fish and they poisoned our springs. We gave them forest-clad mountains and valleys full of game and in return, what did they give our warriors and our women? Rum! And trinkets! And a grave! We, on our part, are willing to shed the last drop of blood in the service of our father, the king."

Then Tecumseh and Brock, along with several of the former's chiefs and the latter's staff officers, met in private to more thoroughly probe the matter of what should now be undertaken.[653]

Letters from Hull to the secretary of war and other officials in the East had been confiscated when couriers were captured. A close study of what they contained showed clearly that Hull was a badly frightened commander whose enemy was much greater in his mind than in reality and this was a factor they could use against him to advantage. By promoting the impression that there were an enormous number of Indians on hand, that General Brock had arrived with a major war force from the East, and that a devastating blow was being organized against Hull, it was believed the American general might buckle under his own fears. A strong move, Brock said, should be made against Hull without delay and this is exactly what they would do.

Greatly admiring the initiative Brock was taking, Tecumseh turned to Elliott and murmured, "Hooo-eee, *this* is a man!"

The British general then said what he really needed was a good map of Detroit and the fort. Immediately Tecumseh drew a map for him of such quality and exactitude that it might have been rendered by an accomplished cartographer. Again, Brock was extremely impressed with the capabilities of the Indian leader.

Brock then brought up a matter of some concern to him. Assuming they could indeed frighten Hull into surrender, would Tecumseh be able to control his warriors sufficiently so there would be no rushing in of a mob of drunken Indians to perpetrate a general massacre? This *must,* the British general insisted, be a matter prohibited beforehand and without possibility of breach—he would not tolerate any such savagery to occur, either directed against the American soldiers or against the civilians in Detroit itself.

"My warriors have already given me their pledge," Tecumseh replied. "They will not taste any liquor until the Americans are beaten, and, as for their abusing or killing any of the Americans once they have surrendered, I give you my pledge that such will not occur. No! I despise them too much to meddle with them."

Brock nodded, pleased, and immediately put the Fort Malden garrison into motion, along with the reinforcement that he had brought, moving them up the river road, over the quickly repaired Canard River bridge to Sandwich.

They were unopposed, and even a skeletal force that Hull had left at Fort Gowie was withdrawn by Hull almost immediately upon Brock starting his movement.[654]

[August 15, 1812 — Saturday]

Tecumseh listened carefully to what General Brock was saying, the sound of the commander's voice occasionally drowned out by the earth-vibrating thunder of the artillery firing.

Since late afternoon the bombardment of the Detroit fort had been under way and though a few shells were lobbed back by the American artillerists, they were largely misdirected and fell short or were from cannon too small to do any significant damage.

The fight had broken out following this morning's demand sent to Hull by Brock that he surrender. The message had been taken across the river by two of Brock's aides, Colonel Robert McDonald of the Canadian Militia and Captain Glegg of the Forty-ninth British Foot. The two British officers were conducted blindfolded to a house and held there, with the blinds drawn, while the message they bore was transmitted to General Hull and his reply awaited. In his message General Brock had written:

> *It is far from my intention to enter into a war of extermination, but you must be aware that the numerous body of Indians who have attached themselves to my troops will be beyond my command once the contest commences.*

Brock, of course, did not expect Hull to surrender immediately, nor was he concerned that Tecumseh's warriors would massacre the Americans. In the former instance, a certain show of resistance was requisite on the part of Hull lest the specter of cowardice and collusion rise up to haunt him more than was already occurring.[655] In the latter instance, Brock already had—and trusted—the assurances by Tecumseh that the Indians would be restrained from a general massacre, but the likelihood was merely stated to add more fuel to the fires of fear within Hull in respect to the Indians and to demoralize him beyond any thought of more than passive resistance.

Hull's reply was greatly delayed, much to the impatience of the waiting British officers, but it was finally delivered. In his reply, Hull refused to capitulate and added that he was: "prepared to meet any force which may be at your disposal, and any consequences which may result from any exertion of it you may think proper to make."

Now, as the desultory bombardment diminished and then faded away entirely with the deepening of twilight, Tecumseh listened carefully as Brock outlined his plan: he wanted Tecumseh and his warriors to cross over the Detroit unseen during the night and surround the Detroit village. When, in the morning, the British army began its crossing to assault the fort, Tecumseh and his warriors would enter the town from the north and west and effectively prevent resistance from the American inhabitants. Tecumseh thought it was a good plan and agreed.

General Brock looked at Tecumseh speculatively for a long moment and then deliberately removed the broad scarlet sash he was wearing and presented it to him. "A token," he murmured, "of my respect for a very brave man and trusted ally."

Pleased, Tecumseh accepted the gift and wrapped it about himself. General Brock smacked his hands together once in approval, his face wreathed in a great smile, and Tecumseh dipped his head in grave acknowledgement of the unprecedented honor bestowed upon him by the most accomplished British war chief he had ever encountered.

Half an hour later, Tecumseh was standing before the fire and addressing his warriors in their camp, explaining what they were to do this night and in the morning. In closing his talk, his voice became stern and his manner almost frightening.

"I tell you one final time, my brothers," he said, "that in what lies ahead you may defend yourselves if the need arises, but it should not arise. You are to take the Americans prisoners as you encounter them, but you are in no way to abuse them. Neither are you to kill any except that it be in the need of saving your own lives. Any who do not obey completely in this respect will ultimately answer to me and, I assure you, to their sorrow."

He then strode up to Stiahta, who had just returned from where his party to the south had been waiting to ambush the supply train. Removing from around himself the scarlet sash that had been presented to him by Brock, Tecumseh in turn presented it to the big Wyandot chief.

"You have fought more than I in your career," he told Stiahta simply, "so I cannot wear such a distinction where you would see it, and I will not wear anything that all should not see. You are more deserving of it than I, so it is yours."

And Stiahta was even more proud to receive it from Tecumseh than Tecumseh had been in getting it from General Brock.

[August 16, 1812 — Sunday]

During the three hours following midnight, Tecumseh and seven hundred of his warriors—wearing only breechclouts and moccasins and flamboyantly painted for war—silently crossed the river in relays in a swarm of canoes. Over the next hour or so they positioned themselves along the perimeter of Detroit.

Tecumseh passed the word for the warriors to keep themselves well hidden until the word should be given and then he himself took a position close to the river and watched in the breaking light of dawn for the crossing of the main British army to begin. The wait was not long. Just before sunrise a small armada of boats pushed out from the Canadian shore well below Detroit and began moving across. Tecumseh grinned and ran to the top of a knoll where he cupped his mouth and issued the wailing, keening cry that was the signal for the warriors to move.

Boldly, yet not unduly exposing themselves to possible gunfire, the warriors entered the town from north and west, filling the air with their raucous shrieks and quickly terrifying the civilian residents beyond description. Yet there was no resistance. The residents kept hidden behind locked doors or stood in their doorways or gathered in little frightened groups, but no one fired a weapon or offered resistance, not even when warriors darted into the homes and pawed through their belongings, snatched up hot biscuits or breads or other breakfast foods in their passage and crammed their mouths full with one hand while gripping the tomahawk or war club in the other.

Within the fort General Hull was alerted of their coming and instantly summoned his officers on the double, all the while mumbling to himself and talking in an inchoate manner about "savages numerous beyond example" and "red devils" who were "more greedy of violence . . . than the Vikings or Huns." It was apparent to all the officers who assembled that he had been drinking heavily throughout much of the night in order to get into the state he was in. His eyes rolled wildly and spittle drooled from his mouth corners and at one point he was heard to cry out, "My God, what will I do with these women and children?"

Hardly had a discussion begun among them in assessment of their situation—not the least of which was the swarm of Indians moving into the town and in this direction—when there was a screaming whine and a cannonball lobbed from across the river smashed into the general's personal quarters, very nearly hitting his daughter and her children. Other balls followed and one smashed into a store where Lieutenant Porter Hanks was standing and all but cut him in two, killing him instantly. Hull came and looked at the remains and tobacco juice leaked from his mouth, dribbled off his chin and stained his shirt front. Pale and wobbly, he turned away and returned to his quarters.

Within moments loud cheers rose from the British army under General Brock, now assembling with six pieces of light artillery just south of the fort, and the shrieking of the advancing Indians turned into cries of jubilation. Inside the fort, a white bedsheet was hoisted. General Hull, to the utmost anguish of his officers and men, was signaling surrender.

Some while later Hull sent a messenger to General Brock asking for terms and at noon General Brock and Tecumseh rode side by side through the streets of Detroit to formally accept the capitulation. Brock was clad in scarlet coat and cocked hat adorned with plumes and was quite an impressive figure, but Tecumseh himself wore only a blue breechclout and red leggins and moccasins without adornment, yet somehow he looked every bit as splendid as the British general beside him.

General Hull was brought before them and Brock looked at him contemptuously, but his voice remained level when he spoke.

"If your men attempt to escape or complain of their treatment," Brock told him, "I cannot be answerable for the consequences, but if they remain quiet and orderly, they shall shortly be released and no harm shall befall them."

The American troops were then ordered to assemble on the parade ground and there piled up their rifles, swords, pistols, knives, cartridge boxes, and the like; the men themselves were finally led off and placed under guard in the citadel. As Tecumseh had promised Brock, no massacre occurred and no prisoners were tortured, only some horses and goods were taken here and there throughout the town as spoils of war. Hull's surrender included not only himself, his officers, his men and the fort, but also the detachment of over three hundred fifty men under Colonels Duncan McArthur and Lewis Cass that had gone to locate and escort the supply convoy under Captain Brush at River Raisin.[656] The American flag in the fort was lowered and the British standard raised in its stead and with that, Detroit was once again in British hands.

[August 17, 1812 — Monday]

Summoned late yesterday by General Brock, Tecumseh had listened while the British officer gave him instructions in respect to the Henry Brush supply convoy that had been waiting all this while at Frenchtown.

"I sent Matthew Elliott to Frenchtown to speak to Captain Henry Brush who, as you know, received permission from the citizens there to build a small fortification and where he has been sitting waiting for an escort from General Hull. In my name Colonel Elliott demanded his surrender and the surrender of his supply train, but this was refused. Now I wish you and your warriors to accompany my detachment under Major Peter Chambers and go there to take the Americans prisoner if possible and confiscate their goods."

Selecting Stiahta and his Wyandots to go with him, Tecumseh and his Indians, mounted on good horses, had galloped off to River Raisin. The Americans and their supply train, however, were gone, having left to return to Ohio immediately after Elliott's departure. Stiahta's Wyandots, who had missed out on all the activities at Detroit while they lay in wait for the supply train or its escort, were furious and now they took out their wrath on the French residents of the town for having allowed the Americans sanctuary there and even encouraged their building of the small stockade and blockhouse. That structure was set afire and the houses of the Frenchmen were pillaged. Most of the residents submitted meekly to the indignity and two who protested and tried to protect their goods were killed.

Tecumseh and Stiahta were displeased with these actions and ordered them stopped and a pursuit of the American supply train launched. Captain Brush, however, had too much of a head start. They followed his trail all the way to the Maumee, where they found another blockhouse the Americans had built and burned it as well. At this point, however, considering further pursuit pointless, Tecumseh called it off and they returned to Detroit, satisfied that the Americans were no longer a force in this area from the Maumee northward.

[December 31, 1812 — Thursday]

Tecumseh stared into the fire unseeingly, the weight of depression blanketing him more completely than the heavy buffalo robe that enshrouded him as he sat here in the unfamiliar surroundings, the keening of the cold night wind outside echoing the coldness that filled his mind and gripped his heart.

Tenskwatawa, sitting close by, said nothing, knowing full well the futility of attempting to engage his older brother in conversation when he was in such a mood, yet not entirely able to understand why Tecumseh had locked himself away from everyone. There had been a few setbacks, yes, but, so far as Tenskwatawa himself could see, the good things that had occurred since the beginning of the war far outweighed the bad. He had no way of knowing that at this time and this place, the hopes and dreams of the man who had envisioned a glorious Indian nation were shriveling as inevitably as the shriveling of autumn leaves and, as with the leaves themselves, drifting away into nothingness.

A montage played itself out across his mind's eye and in his mind's ear, a flickering of the sights and sounds of all the many things that had occurred since the surrender of Detroit; their sum total becoming the road leading him only to this ultimate despair and pointing the way only to ultimate defeat.

The great success at Detroit had been followed by an even more complete one at Chicago. Chaubenee and Sauganash had returned at last from their mission and reported to Tecumseh the details of what had occurred. Even though the actual initial plan had to be altered due to the evacuation of Fort Dearborn under orders its commanding officer had received from General Hull, the attack had taken place and entirely with the anticipated results.

Practically all the residents of Chicago had taken refuge within the walls of Fort Dearborn and, had they remained there and defended the place, it was unlikely that the attack of the Indians, however concerted it was, could have taken the place. But the orders received by Captain Nathan Heald had directed him to give to the Indians all the stores in the fort, destroy the ammunition and whiskey and evacuate, and that is what he did.

At exactly nine o'clock in the morning on August 15—the day before the capitulation of Detroit—the gates to Fort Dearborn were thrown open and the entire American military and civilian population filed out in the beginning of a march that was to take them to Fort Wayne. 109 individuals filed out, escorted by a party of 27 friendly Miami Indians that had been sent by the Fort Wayne commander under Captain William Wells.[657]

It had taken fully five minutes for the entire column to clear the gates of the fort and as soon as they were away a great many of the waiting Indians poured in and began looting the place, expecting to find among the stores that were left the large supply of ammunition and whiskey known to be within the fort. Their rage was extreme at finding it had all been destroyed by being dumped into a well.

The procession had now stretched out to some three hundred yards in length from its van to its rear, following the Indian trail that led southward and then eastward along the curving shore of Lake Michigan, filing between the lake on their left and a line of high sand dunes on their right.

The mounted escort of Miamis, well in advance, discovered an ambush set up to hit the file and attempted to dissuade the attackers but were ordered to clear out or themselves fall with the whites. The Miamis thundered away. Realizing they were about to be attacked, Captain Heald ordered his file to close up, directed his men into a fighting posture and charged toward the Indians hidden behind the dunes—a gallant but futile effort. The fight broke at 9:30 A.M. about a mile and a half south of the fort and it became a massacre in which eighty-six Americans were killed.[658] William Wells—Apekonit—was among those who had been killed, his heart ripped from his chest after he had fallen and devoured raw by his enemies. But, Chaubenee and Sauganash told Tecumseh, though they themselves had arrived after the massacre, having been delayed by a severe storm en route, they had found the Kinzie family being held captive and had managed to prevent their being killed.

The victory of the Indians at Chicago was complete and that, combined with the capitulation of Detroit had sent a flush of exultation throughout all the tribes. Many of the Indians who had been pro-American now became neutral or switched their allegiance entirely to the British, along with those who had maintained neutrality all along.

With Hull's army taken so abysmally, the entire frontier—Michigan, Ohio, Indiana, Illinois, even Missouri—erupted in an orgy of bloody skirmishes and, at last, the warriors of the Miami tribe had joined Tecumseh practically en masse. Nor were they the only ones. Sacs came, too, and so did more of the Winnebagoes, Potawatomies, and Ottawas, as well as scattered bands from the Sioux, Cherokee, and the Upper and Lower Creeks.[659] The smell of victory was in the nostrils of the Indians, and the intertribal amalgamation, so severely damaged by the ambitious Tenskwatawa, began gradually re-forming. Import councils were being held everywhere and now the words of Tecumseh were being as revered as though they had been uttered by Moneto.

Tecumseh, riding the crest of his reborn fame and influence, was abruptly constantly on the move and had addressed many of the councils. The principal obstacles, he said, now left standing between them and their regaining complete control of the Ohio and Indiana countries were Fort Harrison on the Wabash and Fort Wayne at the head of the Maumee. Therefore, the Potawatomies and Ottawas, led by Tecumseh and aided by the British, would capture Fort Wayne, which was presently under command of Captain Oscar Rhea. And, instead of attacking Vincennes, as previously planned, Tenskwatawa would join, if not lead, the Tippecanoe Indians—largely Kickapoos, Winnebagoes, and Miamis—against Fort Harrison, which was presently under command of a young captain named Zachary Taylor.[660]

For the Americans in Michigan, the situation had become horrible. Despite Tecumseh's explicit instructions, in his absence the Indians committed all sorts of depredations and tortures and fear was a rampaging monster that prowled the frontier. The British moved southward from Detroit and Amherstburg and ensconced themselves at Frenchtown on the River Raisin to command the land approach to Detroit.

Yet, despite these triumphs for the Indians and British, there were still some Indian factions, such as the Shawnees under Catahecassa, who did not change their stance.

The American rank and file who had been captured at Detroit were subsequently paroled, with the proviso that they not again lift arms against the British or Indians in this present war, and sent back to Ohio; the governor-general and staff officers held for further questioning and ultimate prisoner exchange. The reaction of the American citizens and government to Hull was one of great antipathy and steps were taken at once for him to be tried by court-martial on charges of cowardice and treason as soon as he should be released. But, to Tecumseh's dismay, the reaction generally among the American populace was not despair but an incredibly aroused spirit of patriotism. The whole country, but especially the frontier area, was aroused with an enthusiasm for retaliation and revenge that was electric. Calls to arms were hailed with rapture by the white inhabitants and men capable of bearing arms vied with each other over who should be first to enlist, all of them everywhere placing their trust in the liberality of Congress for future indemnification for their services. Kentucky, Ohio, Virginia, Maryland, and Pennsylvania all poured forth their eager young men by the thousands. By August 25, only nine days after Hull's surrender, 4,000 men, armed and equipped, assembled at Urbana alone. The city and county of Baltimore proposed to raise, by itself, an entire regiment, and Virginia sent out 1,500 men, for whom the ladies of Richmond made knapsacks and tents. On the spur of the moment, 1,800 Kentuckians marched from Newport on the Ohio River, and the United States congressman from Kentucky, Colonel Richard M. Johnson, proposed to raise 500 mounted men and lead them to Detroit. A battle lust reminiscent of when the frontier was in their own backyard swept the Kentuckians and in a short time Kentucky alone had provided over 6,000 men for various posts on the frontier. Kentucky Governor Shelby appointed William Henry Harrison to have command of all troops raised by his state and bestowed upon him the rank of brevet major general. Not to be outdone and somewhat chagrined that Kentucky had gotten the jump on matters, the federal government quickly commissioned Harrison as a brigadier general of the United States Army. Since now, with Hull's surrender, it was necessary to name a new commander of the re-forming Northwestern Army, everyone naturally assumed the choice would be Harrison; after all, his defeat of the Tippecanoe Indians less than a year ago was still a matter of great national pride.

The federal government, however, with inexplicable stubbornness and a seeming inability to learn from past mistakes, chose instead James Winchester, another old-line soldier—with political connections—who had been a captain during the Revolution. For the past three decades Winchester had been in retirement on his Tennessee farm and what military skills he may have possessed as a young officer were now decidedly diminished; he was, on the whole, not much better a choice for the top command than Hull had been. When the military learned of his appointment with the rank of major general, their laments were loud and long, since Winchester embodied just about everything they detested in a leader; he was old, fat, stubborn, overbearing and exceedingly pompous. Worse, he knew little of strategy, was very dense, refused to listen to any officer subordinate to him and was unbearably dictatorial. It was only with the greatest of difficulty and effort that Harrison—

who, as something of an afterthought, had been placed second in command—was able to keep his own men from deserting when they learned Winchester was the new commander-in-chief.

When word reached Harrison from Captain Zachary Taylor at Fort Harrison that Indians were gathering around both his post and Fort Wayne and attack seemed imminent, Harrison instructed Taylor to hold on as best he could and himself took over the twenty-two hundred troops Winchester had assembled at Fort Washington in Cincinnati and led them toward Fort Wayne.

Tecumseh learned that his nephew, Spemica Lawba, after successfully guiding the messenger from the Ohio militia colonels at Detroit to Governor Meigs in Ohio, had then gone at once to Harrison and was first to inform him of the surrender of Hull. And when Harrison marched out of Cincinnati en route to Fort Wayne, he sent ahead of him Spemica Lawba and his companion, Bright Horn, along with army scout William Oliver, with word for Captain Rhea to defend as best he could, that help was coming.

The attacks upon Fort Harrison and Fort Wayne began simultaneously on September 3, but they shouldn't have. Tecumseh had told the Indians to wait, especially in the attack on Fort Wayne, until he could be there to direct matters and be backed up by British soldiers and artillery. But the Indians, flushed with the success of the war thus far in their favor, hadn't waited. Similar attacks at about this same time were made on schedule by the Sacs and Winnebagoes on the Mississippi against Fort Madison and Fort Belle Vue.

At Fort Harrison, Zachary Taylor had a garrison of only fifty men, of whom a third were sick, and when a body of Miami, Kickapoo and Winnebago warriors came with their women and children and asked admittance to hold council, that they were desperately in need of food, he refused them entry. Food was lowered over the walls to them, but he stubbornly refused to open the gate. The next day the Indians set fire to one of the blockhouses that made up a part of the walls. As a section burned away and left a gap in the wall, upwards of a hundred Indians lying in wait fired their weapons through it and then charged. Taylor held them off with gunfire from his own troops and then directed construction of a breastwork of logs over the gap. It served the purpose and though the Indians hovered about for eight days longer, they could not break the defenses and went away angry and frustrated.[661] The Winnebagoes who participated in the attack were so upset at its failure that they set out from there directly for their own villages in northern Illinois and southern Wisconsin, thus preventing Tenskwatawa from sending the women and children in Tippecanoe along with them. Disheartened by the failed attack and fearful of what Tecumseh's reaction would be, Tenskwatawa left the main body of Indians and returned to Tippecanoe alone. The remainder of the war party, now essentially Kickapoos and Miamis, took out their wrath a short time later at a settlement of whites on Pigeon Roost Creek, a branch of White River, where they massacred twenty-one men, women, and children.

At Fort Wayne, things had not gone much better. The fort itself was sturdily constructed and had a garrison of seventy men, but it had one grievous flaw—its commander. Captain Oscar Rhea was a man very much inclined to heavy drinking.

It was Five Medals and Winnemac who, now having conveniently changed sides and espousing Tecumseh's cause, opened the attack on the fort too early.[662] Much burning of buildings in the surrounding town took place, but the Fort Wayne garrison remained behind the closed gates. The Indians had then devised a clever plan for entry. A large concentration of warriors— upwards of six hundred—were hidden in a semicircle around two sides of the fort. Then Winnemac, who was well known there, along with four other chiefs, including Five Medals, Chappien, Blackbird, and Aubenaw—Look Back—openly approached, all of them draped in blankets, and asked to be permitted inside to discuss a peace proposal. The idea was that when Captain Rhea had gathered his officers together, they would suddenly pull the hidden pistols from under their blankets and kill the three lieutenants, sparing only Rhea himself. Because of his predilection for drink, they believed he was a weak man and that once his officers were dead and his own life threatened, he would agree to open the gates and surrender the fort.

It all went as planned and they were just about to enter the fort when Spemica Lawba, Bright Horn, and William Oliver rode up. Knowing them to be scouts for the army and that Harrison could not be far behind, Winnemac sullenly shook hands with the trio and said he decided not to talk peace after all. With that all five of the chiefs turned and walked back into the woods and immediately a heavy firing broke out and the three newcomers ducked inside. A hurried conference was held and it was felt the fort might be taken if someone did not get word to Harrison right away to set his march toward them into full speed. Spemica Lawba and Bright Horn volunteered to go. At a break in the firing they thundered out on their horses and galloped past the enemy lines, barely ahead of the Indians who were converging. As the garrison, watching over the walls, cheered them on, Spemica Lawba waved, let out a triumphant yell of his own and disappeared. The two reached Harrison in good time with the urgent news.

The attackers continued firing at the fort, several times setting the walls afire with flaming arrows. Captain Rhea told his men it was time to surrender and would have done so except that Lieutenant Joseph Curtis threatened to put him to death if he made the suggestion again, relieved him of duty and placed him in confinement for drunkenness.[663] Lieutenant Curtis then furnished every man able to shoot with several stands of loaded weapons and ordered them to hold off firing until the enemy, believing them to be out of ammunition, came close. It worked well. The Indians made a concerted rush but fell back under the withering fire, leaving eighteen dead warriors on the ground.

Just before Harrison's army reached the fort on September 12, the Indians attempted one last trick. First they built several great fires at a distance so that the billowing smoke might lead the forted soldiers to think a battle was in progress. Then, in great disorder and acting the part of a routed force, they fled past the gate. The object was to draw the garrison out in pursuit and lead it straight into a trap, but the men inside were content to stay put and await Harrison. With that the siege was lifted and the enemy disappeared. Harrison arrived the next day and immediately sent out detachments and caused great destruction among the villages within two days' march.

All this occurred while Tecumseh was at Fort Malden striving, without a great deal of success, to get the new commander there to provide substantial support—both men and artillery—for the projected attacks against Fort Wayne and Fort Harrison. General Brock and Tecumseh, following Detroit's capitulation, had spent a considerable amount of time together discussing the war and strategy insofar as this western front was concerned. They dined together often and a genuine friendship developed between them, each recognizing the other as an outstanding leader of men.[664]

That pleasant association with General Brock had ended abruptly, however, when the British commander was alerted that the Americans were about to strike on the Niagara frontier. He regretfully bade adieu to Tecumseh and set off for there, leaving as the new commander of the British troops in the west a self-important colonel named Henry Proctor.

Short and squat, with a low and heavy brow, Proctor was an adequate officer but one greatly concerned with protecting his own image among his superiors. Relatively new to the frontier, he had no great love of—and little use for—the Indians, considering them, on the whole, to be more of a nuisance than an asset. As a result, no real rapport with Tecumseh or any of the other Indian leaders was ever developed by him. Yet, with the specific instructions of General Brock in his ears that he was to cooperate with and aid Tecumseh in further moves against the Americans, he did so, but only with the greatest reluctance.

It hadn't helped the relationship between the British officer and the Indian leader when Tecumseh caused Proctor to back down and lose face. Only a day or so after the departure of Brock, Tecumseh was approached by a comely young French woman whom he recognized as the daughter of Hubert LaCroix, a well-established trader of Detroit.[665] He and LaCroix, who was an employee of the North West Fur Company, had formed a friendship of sorts over the years. They had not, however, seen one another much of late, since LaCroix was among those citizens of Sandwich and Detroit who had taken advantage of the amnesty offered by Hull on his arrival there and declared themselves for American citizenship. Now Mademoiselle LaCroix begged Tecumseh for his help, saying that her father had been arrested by soldiers sent by Colonel Proctor and had been taken away in chains. His friendship with Tecumseh was known and so, to prevent a scene, the captive was secreted aboard a vessel at the Detroit wharf, to be sent with other prisoners to the Citadel at Quebec. Tecumseh immediately went to the British headquarters and strode into the office of Colonel Proctor.

"Are you," he asked peremptorily, "holding prisoner aboard one of your ships my friend, Hubert LaCroix?"

Irritated at the Indian's presumptive manner, Proctor drew himself up and was about to respond with a denial when Tecumseh spoke again.

"I warn you," he said grimly, "if I ever detect you in a falsehood, I and my Indians will immediately abandon you."

Having no desire to be known among his superiors as the man who lost the Indians to the British as allies, Proctor grudgingly nodded. "Yes," he said, "he is being held prisoner. We believe him to be a spy."

"He is no spy!" Tecumseh retorted. "He is a trader and he is my friend. I want him released and given his freedom at once."

The two men stared at one another for a long moment and then it was Proctor who averted his eyes. He sighed and swiftly wrote out an order, which he blotted and handed to Tecumseh. "Take this to the captain of the vessel," he said, "and your friend LaCroix will be released."

Tecumseh took the paper and did not look at it until he was well away from headquarters. When he did so, his lips curved in a satisfied smile. The order was brief in the extreme:

Sir:—The King of the Woods wishes for the release of LaCroix and he is to be set at liberty at once.

H. Proctor, Col., Cmmdt.

With such a start to their association, there was little love lost between Tecumseh and the new British commandant, but this disturbed Tecumseh not at all and in no way diminished his persistent demands for the material assistance that had been promised by General Brock for the attacks on the American frontier posts. The British soldiers would provide a foundation of morale for the Indians who, constantly seeing them, would know that the might of the great king of England was behind them in their efforts. On the other hand, the artillery, Tecumseh knew, was absolutely vital to their ends. No matter how many Indians he had behind him, they would not be able to breach the walls of these strong forts without the explosive power of the great guns.

At last Proctor had acquiesced to the demands and authorized Major Adam Muir to go by boat the next morning with three cannon and a force of 250 regulars and militia and join Tecumseh's force at the mouth of the Maumee. The Indians were elated and that night they held a great war dance just outside the walls of Fort Malden. In the morning Muir's force set off by boat and the Indians by land, Tecumseh and three trusted chiefs—Stiahta, Main Poche, and Split Log—leading eight hundred warriors.

The rendezvous at the mouth of the Maumee was accomplished without mishap and the united force moved up the Maumee to the foot of the Rapids. Here the cannon were unloaded and the troops disembarked and the movement upstream continued along the portage road on the northwest side of the river. They moved along steadily and soon passed the mouth of the Auglaize and the old Fort Defiance, still standing but abandoned and in a great state of disrepair. They were not more than a dozen miles above that point when a series of messengers arrived with unsettling news. The first told of the attack on Fort Harrison and its failure; that Tenskwatawa, abandoned by the Winnebagoes, had returned to Tippecanoe and was still there with all the women and children and only a small number of warriors to protect them. The second messenger told of the equally premature attack on Fort Wayne and its failure and the fact that General Harrison had arrived there with a force of twenty-two hundred men. The third runner brought the disturbing news that another American general, James Winchester, had arrived at Fort Wayne and seemed to have taken control of that army away from Harrison and was at this moment leading about a third of that force—some eight hundred men—down the Maumee toward them. He could conceivably reach them within a day and a half.[666]

Major Muir balked at once. His little force could hardly attack such a major American force, he said, not even with the help of the Indians, and he was not prepared to give the enemy an opportunity to capture his artillery. Tecumseh and Stiahta scoffed. This American army, according to their spies, was similar to other such armies they had faced—disorganized, lacking in discipline and easily thrown into panic—and they urged moving upstream and setting up an ambush immediately.

Muir agreed to halt where they were and dig in and defend themselves but Tecumseh shook his head. The place where they were was not suitable for setting up an ambush and they had to move upstream farther to where there were narrow defiles and paths flanked by dense woodland. Runners brought further word that Winchester's force had gone into camp only eight miles upstream and Muir, fearing that the Americans would try to outflank him under the cover of night, fell back to the mouth of the Auglaize and made preparations to meet the Americans there.

Now the Indians began getting a very bad feeling about what might lie ahead for them. A large number of the Ottawas and Chippewas melted away into the forest during the move back to the Auglaize and never showed up again. With their diminished force, Tecumseh and Stiahta councilated on where best to strike the enemy, but they could not reach an agreement and once more Muir put his own small force into movement and retreated even farther down the Maumee. Still greatly fearful of losing his artillery to the Americans, he ordered the big guns taken back to the boats at the foot of the rapids and loaded aboard.

By this time Tecumseh and his chiefs were angry and frustrated. The desertion of their own warriors, the loss of the cannon, which they considered essential, and the lackluster behavior of Major Muir with his constant retreats was considerably diminishing the fire in the remaining warriors for any kind of confrontation at this time with the greatly superior American force. While Tecumseh and Stiahta were still strongly for attacking the enemy, new word was brought that the Americans had stopped only briefly at the mouth of the Auglaize and built a temporary fortification there, then had continued downstream and now were but two miles away.[667] At that point Muir showed the white feather. He ordered a general retreat of his men back down the river and, with no support at all, Tecumseh's remaining force had no alternative but to follow.

Upon reaching their boats, the British force boarded with unseemly haste and embarked at once for the lake and Fort Malden. The expedition was a total failure. The Indians continued to watch Winchester's army until it reached the Maumee Rapids and there, with the weather steadily worsening, it suddenly stopped and set up a more permanent camp, which was evidently to be the winter quarters of the army. With that, the fears that Winchester would continue moving against the Indian villages in the Detroit area were put aside and Tecumseh led his Indians back to their own main encampment near Fort Malden. There, deprived of an early winter hunt to provide themselves with meat for the remainder of the frigid season, the Indians were forced to beg for food and blankets from Colonel Proctor to hold them over, presumably until the campaigns began again the following spring.

A shock awaited them on their arrival—news that contributed greatly to Tecumseh's plunge into the depths of depression. A fierce little battle had taken place on October 13 at a place called Queenston on the Niagara Peninsula. American forces under General Henry Dearborn had streamed across the Niagara River and invaded Canada at that point and the British had met the attack head on and had thrown it back. During the engagement, however,

Major General Isaac Brock had been killed. The loss of the British commander who had become his friend hit Tecumseh very hard and, were that not enough, Brock's successor as the British commander-in-chief of British western military operations turned out to be Henry Proctor, now promoted to brigadier general.

There was a second big surprise awaiting Tecumseh at Amherstburg—his brother Tenskwatawa. Contritely and repeatedly stressing that it was not his fault, the one-eyed former Prophet related to Tecumseh details of the abortive attack on Fort Harrison and his abandonment by the Winnebagoes. Because of that, he explained, with no one to act as their guide or escort, there had been no way to send the women and children at Tippecanoe to the Winnebago villages in the Wisconsin country. He had, however, as directed by Tecumseh, abandoned Tippecanoe, hid all remaining food stores in the nearby woods and established a new, much smaller village in the northwestern Indiana country, about halfway between the Tippecanoe and Lake Michigan.[668]

The big problem was, however, Tenskwatawa went on, their remaining people—about three hundred of them, primarily the old and lame as well as women and children—had very little food, even including the goods still hidden near Tippecanoe, and it was necessary to get some from the British here at Amherstburg if they were not to suffer a severe famine before spring.

Tecumseh and Main Poche presented themselves to General Proctor and counciled with him for a time, with British food provisions being the principal topic of conversation. Proctor had considerable stores of food but with the large number of hungry Indians that were on hand, it would be very trying to feed them all over the whole winter. The season was well advanced, he said, with any kind of winter campaign by the Americans seemingly out of the question, so it would probably be better if the majority of the Indians returned to their own home villages and then reassembled here next spring when the major American campaign would no doubt be reignited. To this end, Proctor said, he would give Tecumseh enough food to sustain his people in the new village for the winter, provided they supplemented it by hunting whenever they could and he would also provide ammunition to help them in this pursuit.

It seemed reasonable enough and Tecumseh accepted the offer. A council of the Indians in the encampment south of Fort Malden was held and Tecumseh instructed them that, if they wished, they could go home for the remainder of the winter, but they must be sure to be back here again as soon as the weather broke in spring. A great many left. And finally, early in December, escorted by Main Poche and a party of his Potawatomies, Tecumseh and Tenskwatawa set off for their new Kankakee village with a sizeable quantity of supplies. The majority of Indians now remaining in the vicinity of Detroit were the resident Wyandots.

The new village was cold, unfamiliar and certainly not home, but it was a haven for them and their people for the winter. Since they were on a main Indian trail, news filtered to them at irregular intervals and little of it was encouraging. They learned that in the Illinois country an expedition against the Kickapoos had been launched in October by Illinois Governor Ninian Edwards and Colonel Russell. With the force of over three hundred fifty men they penetrated deep into the interior regions of the country, following the Sangamon and the Sabine Fork, and finally coming to Peoria Lake. A major engagement had taken place in which three towns were burned, an immense quantity of goods plundered, great stores of corn and other food supplies destroyed, some thirty Indians killed, near that many wounded and four taken prisoner. Among the Americans, no one was killed and only four men wounded, just one dangerously. It was a great victory for the Americans and a severe blow to the Kickapoos.

More bad news reached them. In mid-November a party of twelve hundred Kentuckians led by General Samuel Hopkins rampaged their way up the Wabash all the way to Tippecanoe, destroying every Indian village encountered. The final village destroyed was Tippecanoe. The militia also stumbled upon the hidden stores of food in the adjacent forest and confiscated everything. They paid dearly for it, however. A party of warriors returning to get some of the food discovered them, crept up and killed eighteen before they were themselves driven away.

There was yet worse news to come. Harrison, thwarted in his idea of continuing the winter campaign into the Michigan country, early in December sent out a hit-and-run expedition of six hundred militia men under Colonel John Campbell to locate and burn the villages of the remaining refugee Miamis. These were the Miamis who had been driven away from the Fort Wayne area and forced to make their temporary villages, which were little more than camps, near the mouth of the Mississinewa. Only about one hundred Miami warriors remained but, with nowhere else to go, they held their ground at the village called Silver Hill and fought desperately to protect their families. Silver Hill and two other villages were destroyed. Fifty warriors had been killed and a like number of women and children had been taken prisoner. As a final degradation, the bodies of the dead were thrown into the river.

The Miami tribe, for all intents and purposes, was extinguished.

Finally, one last piece of sad news to bring to a close what, despite the fall of Detroit and Chicago, Tecumseh considered to be one of the worst years of his life. The news was brought by the Shawnee named Bright Horn, companion of Spemica Lawba, who was his fellow scout spy for General Harrison.

Bright Horn said that in the third week of November, he and Spemica Lawba, along with their friend Otter, grandnephew of Catahecassa, had been dispatched by General Harrison on a spying mission to the Maumee Rapids.

They had discovered Tecumseh's force of enemy Indians and British in disturbing numbers and had returned at once to the new Fort Winchester, close to the ruins of Fort Defiance, and reported their discovery to General Winchester. The fort's second in command, a Kentucky militia major named Samuel Price, who knew nothing of Spemica Lawba's long dedicated service to the United States, who despised Indians generally and who had no foundation for such an allegation, accused Spemica Lawba of lying and treachery. Deeply stung, Spemica Lawba was determined to prove his loyalty to the Americans. The next day he and Bright Horn and Otter returned toward the Rapids. They encountered, killed, and scalped the opportunist Potawatomi chief Winnemac and also the British Indian agent Alexander Elliott, son of Matthew Elliott. In the process, however, Spemica Lawba was shot through the body. He was carried back to Fort Winchester where he lingered until November 25, and then he died.[669]

So now the year was ended and Tecumseh sat hunched beneath a buffalo robe in a cold wegiwa, in a strange village that was home but not home, staring unseeingly into a fire that generated no warmth, and he was deeply, deeply depressed.

[April 9, 1813 — Friday]

"Tecumseh is here! He's come back. Tecumseh is here!"

The words swept through the great Indian encampment in the Detroit area and within mere minutes every wegiwa and cabin, every quonset and tepee had disgorged its occupants until some fifteen hundred throats echoed the cries and added their own in a surge of intense jubilation.

Flanked by Chaubenee and Stiahta, Tecumseh never looked better than he did today on his arrival in the Detroit area, followed by a thousand warriors. He sat tall and straight in his saddle and there was once again that look about him of a man whose eyes were on distant horizons invisible to his companions. He exuded strength and confidence and a welling of gladness rose within him as he smiled and raised one arm high in greeting and then, after a moment, the other, as if in benediction.

"They are ready for the war to begin again, Tecumseh," said Chaubenee. "They needed to see you for the fuse to be lighted."

"They'll have their war," Tecumseh replied, "very soon." He looked from his heavy-set companion on his right to the elegantly dressed Wyandot on his left. "Chaubenee. Stiahta. The first thing we have to do is see General Proctor and build a little fire under him for what needs to be done."

"Then let's not waste any time," Stiahta said. He looked at Tecumseh steadily and then added, "It is good to have you back, Tecumseh."

Tecumseh regarded him steadily and then the faintest suggestion of a smile tilted his lips and he dipped his head slightly in acknowledgment, knowing it was not the physical presence here at this moment that Stiahta meant. He was referring to the individual he had visited at the beginning of the Hunger Moon; the individual he found in the depths of black depression and who required firm nudging to thrust him up and out of the pit of despair in which he had been mired.

On that first day of the Hunger Moon—February—Stiahta had come to him at the new village on the Kankakee, bringing with him the electric jolt of news that Tecumseh so sorely needed to snap the mood that had enshrouded him for a month. It had taken many hours of sitting before the fire, talking and smoking and talking again for Stiahta to relate the remarkable thing that had happened at a time of year when no such thing could or should have been anticipated—the Battle of Frenchtown.

Stiahta related that General Proctor had directed a British and Indian force to take post in Frenchtown on River Raisin for the winter, there to keep watch and give early warning in case of any sign of the Americans moving against them. Frenchtown was a community largely made up of well-to-do farmers who were noted for the fine fruits and vegetables they raised. The British detachment that lodged itself there on Proctor's order was under command of Major John Reynolds and consisted of two companies of Canadian volunteers commanded by Captains Paul Maisonville and Matthew Elliott, the latter being the remaining son of the Indian agent, Colonel Matthew Elliott. They also had with them part of an artillery company. The Indian contingent consisted of slightly less than four hundred warriors under Stiahta, who was in command of all the Indians during Tecumseh's absence, with Walk in the Water, who had once again changed sides, acting as his second, and with Sauganash as his aide.

It had been early in January, Stiahta related, that a deputation of residents of Frenchtown slipped away and went to General Winchester at the foot of the Maumee Rapids to ask for his help. These Frenchmen, Stiahta said, complained to Winchester that they were being oppressed by the British and Indians who had taken post in their town. Stiahta had grinned at this point in his relation, telling Tecumseh that while they had no intention of harming the French residents, they did have to have food and other supplies and the only way to get it was to confiscate it from those residents, who had plenty.

Later interrogation of prisoners, Stiahta went on, revealed that the Frenchtown delegation told Winchester that their stores of food and drink were regularly being pillaged to fill the appetites of the unwanted guests and, unless a stop was put to it quickly, the residents themselves would be undergoing famine before the end of winter. Further, with supplies getting scarce and the residents growing considerably less willing to surrender their goods, they had been threatened with having their town burned to the ground around them if they didn't comply and themselves carried off as prisoners.

Frenchtown was only thirty-six miles away from his own camp and Winchester decided that he had just been presented with a golden opportunity. He could march there, drive out the British and Indians and occupy the town in considerably greater comfort than here and use that as the launching point for next spring's campaign. With an immediate march, there would not even be the hazard of his men getting wet and thereby suffering exposure, since the winter to that point had been so intensely cold that Lake Erie was covered with a solid blanket of ice no less than three feet thick. Even the Detroit River, which most years stayed open because of its swift current, was so solidly frozen that horses pulling heavy sledges safely moved over its surface.

Though Winchester's orders from General Harrison were to stay in place at the foot of the Maumee Rapids, he reasoned that pulling off a coup such as this would undoubtedly make the president and the secretary of war realize what a mistake they had made in promoting Harrison to the commanding position over him. So, on the night of January 16, Winchester held a consultation with his field officers and a course of action was agreed upon. Winchester split his force, retaining three hundred eighty men with himself as a reserve at the Rapids and, early in the morning on January 17, sent out 420 men under militia Lieutenant Colonel William Lewis to "liberate" Frenchtown.[670]

The detachment moved out with alacrity, knowing that once they got to Frenchtown they would no longer be outside in the bitter elements but in snug homes with warm fireplaces. With the movement well in motion, Winchester finally sent an express to Harrison, not asking for permission but simply telling him about what he had done. Then, deciding Lewis needed more strength, Winchester sent out an additional 100 men under Lieutenant Colonel John Allen to overtake the Lewis detachment and join it.

The first day's march carried Lewis and his men down the river to Maumee Bay and they camped at the mouth of Swan Creek. Within an hour after stopping, they were joined by Allen's detachment of one hundred. Allen became second in command, with Majors Ben Graves and George Madison as support officers. Late that night another Frenchtown resident—a man named Day—came to their camp and gave them specific information about the strength and position of the British and Indians at the town and warned that Colonel Elliott was expected there sometime on the eighteenth with a considerable reinforcement of both Canadians and Indians.

Early the following morning Lewis had put his detachment into movement and soon met more of the Frenchtown inhabitants moving toward the south. They were questioned as to what kind of artillery Major Reynolds had there and the reply made Lewis grin: "They have two pieces about large enough to kill a mouse."

Lewis pressed on, sometimes moving on land, sometimes on the ice of Lake Erie. Upon reaching the River Raisin well below the town, they marched up its frozen surface and when only three miles from the town, Lewis deployed his troops in battle formation and the order he had written the night before to bolster their spirits and fire their determination was read to them. They then moved on and as they came in sight of the town at three o'clock in the afternoon, they received fire from the British and the battle was on.

The Americans put up a very good fight, Stiahta admitted, and it was quite a hot battle that raged back and forth for some three hours. The Americans finally drove the British and Indians out and took the town, but only at the cost of a dozen of their soldiers killed and fifty-five wounded. We, Stiahta said sorrowfully, had fifty-five killed, almost all Canadian militia, and about the same number wounded.

The repulsed British and Indians, exhausted by the battle, camped some miles away and tended to their wounded. In the morning they resumed their movement and reached Fort Malden by midday. With grudging praise, Stiahta related that General Proctor had leaped into action with uncharacteristic swiftness and brilliance. The remainder of the day and night of the nineteenth were spent in mounting and preparing a strong retaliatory force, which was to move out first thing the morning of the twentieth. Stiahta, Walk in the Water and Sauganash had circulated among the villages, alerting all the Indians as to what had occurred and gathering warriors to assemble at Fort Malden for the main thrust.

Immediately following the battle, Lewis had fortified his position in the town and sent an express rider back to the Maumee Rapids with the news of their victory and occupation of Frenchtown. General Winchester, elated by the news, sent off an express of his own to Harrison, relaying the news and stating that he was immediately sending another detachment of two hundred men to Frenchtown under Colonel Wells and that he himself would follow as soon as this message was sent, leaving a little force of only eighty men at the Maumee Rapids camp.

With a good horse beneath him and Peter Navarre of Frenchtown as his guide, Winchester arrived at River Raisin village on the morning of January 20, well ahead of Colonel Wells's detachment, which arrived later in the day. While, contrary to their expectations, the troops camped outdoors around the old stockade on the north side of the river, Winchester established his headquarters in the comfortable house of Francis Navarre, father of his guide, on the south side of the river.

Early in the morning on the twentieth Proctor assembled his force at Fort Malden and, with Lieutenant Colonel St. George as his second, set them in motion—five hundred troops made up of regulars and militia, with half a dozen three-pounder cannon, plus eight hundred Indians under Stiahta. A small company of regulars were left to occupy the fort and the procession proceeded across the river.[671]

Proctor's march that day covered about half the distance to Frenchtown before going into camp for the night. Early on the twenty-first the march was resumed and spies for the Americans watched and then raced back to Frenchtown and reported the British and Indian approach to Winchester. Other spies continued their observations and were gratified to see the Proctor force stop and go into camp for the night at Stony Creek, five miles distant from Frenchtown. This, too, was reported to Winchester, who alerted his men to prepare themselves for attack sometime during the following day.

Proctor's bag of tricks was not empty. Soon after full darkness was over them, a number of men were selected to keep the fires burning throughout the night to give the impression the army was still camped here and then, under cover of darkness, Proctor led almost the whole of his force to within about seventy yards of the town and positioned his men and artillery for a full-scale attack before dawn.

At 5 A.M., well before daylight, on January 22, the British and Indians struck in a devastating attack that took the Americans entirely by surprise, the noise of the battle punctuated by the heavy booming of the 6 three-inch guns and the blasting of their explosive shells. So suddenly and unexpectedly was the attack made that the Americans had no chance of forming themselves advantageously. Greatly frightened, a number of Winchester's men, including the general himself, tried to flee and were cut down by the Indians under Stiahta; fifty of these were killed and scalped and most of the remainder captured, Winchester among them. The captured American general, along with Colonel Lewis, was taken in the protective custody of Stiahta and, by a circuitous route, brought to the rear of the British lines, where he was subsequently confronted by General Proctor.[672]

Despite inferior numbers, the Americans still in the town lay down a withering fire and held the more exposed enemy at bay, even doing some damage; Proctor's second in command, Lieutenant Colonel St. George, was among the British who were killed. At length Proctor directed Winchester to order his men to surrender or he would demolish the entire town around them with his artillery, set the rubble afire and then permit the Indians to destroy all who survived. Winchester capitulated, but the troops, now being commanded by Major Madison, would not lay down their arms until they received promises from Proctor himself that their wounded would be cared for and safely brought to Detroit or Amherstburg as soon as possible and that all of them would get protection from the Indians. Proctor gave his word.

About a score of Americans, as well as Peter Navarre and his brother, had managed to escape and were making their way toward Harrison as rapidly as possible. Meanwhile at Frenchtown, gathering up his own wounded and the six hundred unwounded American prisoners, Proctor set out for Fort Malden, taking General Winchester with him. His promises of protection for those who surrendered were worthless. He left just one British officer behind to protect the two hundred wounded Americans still in the town under Indian guard.

There was no stopping what happened next, Stiahta explained to Tecumseh. With the heat of battle still strong within them, the Indians waited until Proctor's force was out of sight and then held a council on what should be done. Though a quarter of a century had passed since the Gnadenhutten Massacre had occurred, it was not forgotten and it was decided in council that here was a chance to take in full measure the long-postponed vengeance. The one hundred American wounded who were ambulatory were assembled outside and the two houses containing about half that many bedridden wounded were put to the torch. The screams of those inside were horrible and some who attempted to crawl out were felled or forced back with rifle fire.

When the roasting of the hundred was finished, the Indians set off toward Fort Malden with the remaining wounded, most of them poorly dressed and many even shoeless. All but a small handful of these wounded gave out on the march and, as each collapsed or fell behind, a tomahawk blow to the skull ended the misery and he was scalped and left on the ice. Some eighty prisoners were massacred in this manner before Stiahta and the British officer left in charge were able to stop the slaughter.[673]

At one point, Stiahta said, Sauganash made a strong attempt to prevent any further butchery of the prisoners. Leading a group of Indians, he had caught up with a squad of twenty-five Americans floundering on foot through deep snow and trying to escape. They were surrounded and several were tomahawked before Sauganash managed to prevail on them not to harm the others. At the same time he took under his care a tall American officer who said he was Major Ben Graves from Kentucky. Sauganash turned to the other Indians of his party and said, "Stop the killing! We'll take these fellows prisoners."

At that moment Graves jerked out a knife from under his coat and leaped at Sauganash.[674] A nearby Potawatomi named Fox shouted, "Look out, Sauganash, he's going to stab you!"

Sauganash spun around and tried to jump back to evade the blade being leveled at him, but his heel caught against a sapling and he fell. Before he could recover, Graves leaped upon him and drove his knife deeply into Sauganash's neck behind his windpipe. Sauganash reached up and gripped the blade, cutting his hand badly as he held it to keep his attacker from twisting it or slicing it out of him. By then Fox had reached them and he thrust his pistol against Graves's head and jerked the trigger, killing the major instantly. Black Partridge, who was one of the Indian party, shrieked out "Kill every one of the dogs!" and so they did.

"And Sauganash?" Tecumseh had asked anxiously.

"He will recover. The knife was carefully pulled out and Colonel Elliott put him in a bed on a sleigh and took him to his father at Fort Malden, where he was getting good care when I left there."

Even as Stiahta had narrated the details of the events at River Raisin, Tecumseh had felt a lift in his spirits, a flow of adrenaline, a wish that he had been on hand. He realized that despite the setbacks and sorrows that had been suffered, it was nevertheless the Americans in this war who were suffering major defeat after defeat and he was needed to help his red brothers. The cloying depression that had so long been plaguing him began draining away. When the Wyandot chief had finished, they smoked again in silence for a while and finally Tecumseh had reached out and placed his hand on the shoulder of his friend.

"Stiahta, tomorrow I will begin another trip to visit one final time the tribes to the west. I will stop at Chaubenee's Town and get him to come along, but will you come with me as well?"

Stiahta had grinned broadly. "I had hoped you would ask me. Yes, of course I will."

And so, leaving Tenskwatawa in charge of the village, they had gone off and, soon picking up Chaubenee, had spent the whole of February and March visiting the villages throughout the Illinois country. They had gone as far as the Mississippi on the west, the Sangamon on the south and the Wisconsin on the north, gathering up followers as they rode until now, at last, they had returned to the Detroit area, prepared to resume the struggle against the Americans.

Within a few hours Tecumseh was in council with General Proctor. With him were Chaubenee, Stiahta, Wasegoboah, Walk in the Water and—to Tecumseh's great joy—Sauganash, on the side of whose neck could be clearly seen the still-healing scar from the blade that had nearly ended his life.

General Proctor, Tecumseh found, seemed more sure of himself than previously and, through Matthew Elliott, who was in attendance as interpreter, spoke to them far more respectfully than on former occasions. It was apparent that he had come to the conclusion that his Indian allies were more than merely a horde of ignorant savages. His address to them was polite and conciliatory and, even though the death of his commander had lifted him to his own present position of command, he seemed genuinely regretful over the passing of General Brock.

The British general mentioned in passing that he had been informed by Colonel Elliott that, at the end of January, the principal chief of the Shawnees, Catahecassa, had been the victim of an assassination attempt. Details were sketchy but it seemed that Catahecassa had paid a visit to the American General George Tupper at Fort McArthur and while they smoked the *calumet* together in the general's tent, someone had shot through the canvas and struck Catahecassa in the head. It had not killed Catahecassa, but he was an old man and his recuperation would take a long while.[675]

He also informed them that the American officers taken prisoner at the capitulation at Detroit, including General Hull, had been among others returned to the Americans in a prisoner exchange eleven weeks ago.

Of primary concern to Tecumseh and the chiefs, as well as to Matthew Elliott, was the need, without much delay, to get the assembled three thousand Indians actively involved in a campaign. If they were not quickly employed, they would grow bored and begin drifting off, either to hunt or to mount small raiding parties of their own for hit-and-run attacks against the Americans. While many of the Indians were intensely loyal to Tecumseh and would remain no matter what, at least as many were young warriors from far distant tribes for whom all this was a bit of a lark and helped to fill their traditional need to seek out and engage enemies to win laurels of heroism for themselves among their own people. There was also the lure of acquiring plunder as a result of such fights. If held in place too long, they would ultimately begin seeking these things on their own.

Proctor nodded understandingly and to this end he had some interesting and intriguing information of his own to impart. William Henry Harrison, upon learning of Winchester's disobedience of orders and the resultant disaster, had been beside himself with fury. News of the River Raisin affair had spread quickly throughout the country and Harrison was quickly besieged with demands to move against the British here at Fort Malden as swiftly as possible. Great numbers of volunteers, primarily from Virginia and Pennsylvania, were arriving for such service, intent upon avenging their dead countrymen. More were also expected from Kentucky and Ohio as soon as they could be raised.[676] By mid-February Harrison had accumulated an army of eighteen hundred men at Fort Wayne and he led them down the Maumee, refurbished Fort Defiance and then progressed farther downstream and began construction of a new major frontier fort. This latter installation, still under construction, was being called Fort Meigs after the Ohio governor. It was a large installation, its upright log walls enclosing an area of over nine acres and it was being built on the south side of the Maumee River at the foot of the Rapids, just a short distance upstream from where old Fort Miamis had been located.

The taking of that fort and its destruction, Proctor went on, should be considered a major objective and he was agreeable to committing his entire energies, resources and forces toward that end so long as he had the unswerving assurance of help from his Indian allies in that endeavor. Fort Meigs, he went on, if allowed to be completed, would create a serious danger to the British and Indian interests in this quarter. It would provide Harrison the only reasonable access to Lake Erie and the only feasible installation from which to launch a major invasion against Canada. If the fort could be destroyed and Harrison's force driven off, it was probable that American plans to take and occupy Michigan and northern Ohio would be terminated by the federal government as being simply too expensive, too dangerous and too logistically impracticable. That possibility was further enhanced by the fact that Lieutenant Robert Barclay, who had acquired much acclaim for his steadiness and heroism at the Battle of Trafalgar, had been appointed commodore of the entire British fleet on Lake Erie and would quickly destroy any ships the Americans might attempt to launch on the lake.[677]

Tecumseh and his advisers were strongly taken by the idea and, without demur among any of them, agreed to support the British fully in the operation. Proctor nodded, pleased, and said he would start preparations at once—as the Indians should also do—and that they should be able to put the operation in motion in about a fortnight.

Before adjourning there was another matter Tecumseh had to bring up. Their good friend and brother, General Brock, had promised them that if, as he was confident would occur, the British emerged victorious over the Americans in this present war, that all the territory north and west of the Ohio River would revert to the Indians as their own absolute territory beyond any white claim. Now, however, General Brock was dead and the Indians needed reassurance: was this still going to be the case and was the king going to honor the commitment Brock had made to them?

This was a delicate matter for Proctor. He was quite sure that the king would never hold to such agreement and yet, if he told that to these Indians, there was a very real possibility that they would end their alliance and walk away.

"It is not for me," he said, "to speak for His Majesty in this matter, since I am not privy to what prior arrangements may have been made between him and General Brock. This I will commit myself to, however: if matters work out as we hope, then I can assure you that all of the country north of the Maumee River, including the whole of the Michigan country, will be set aside and guaranteed to the tribes as their own territory, permanently and inviolately.

"What is more, Tecumseh," he added, looking at him directly, "should we be able to capture William Henry Harrison, he will be turned over to you personally to be used by you as a hostage or in any other way you see fit."

[April 29, 1813 — Thursday]

Tecumseh and Henry Proctor emerged from the trees into a small clearing and looked outward at the vista spread before them directly to the south. The wooded slopes continued steeply downward, angling two hundred feet south to the bottomland fifty feet below and that level bottom extended for another two hundred yards to the Maumee River. The river itself was six hundred feet wide at this point, spreading out flatly from its long passage down the Rapids, the foot of which was directly before them. In a situation remarkably similar to their own position, a bottomland on the south side of the river extended two hundred yards to a slope every bit as steep as their own and rising to a broad treeless plateau the same height above the river as they were themselves. Exactly three thousand feet from where they sat on their horses was the nearly completed American installation that had been rising here for the past ten or twelve weeks.

Fort Meigs.

From this distance they could see men moving about on the ramparts and in the blockhouses and even as they watched there was a sudden soundless puff of white smoke from behind the stockade walls. Instants later there was a brief high-pitched whining sound and then a heavy thud and small explosion as a cannonball struck the slope some thirty feet below them and forty feet to their right. Their horses shied and at the same moment came the delayed reverberating roar of the cannon itself.

The men brought their dancing horses under control and Tecumseh nodded as he patted his mount's neck soothingly. "Our Americans are already showing their teeth," he said evenly, "but their aim needs improvement."

"Captain," Proctor said, swiveling around in the saddle and addressing one of his artillery officers behind them, "erect the final emplacement here. Two embrasures. Twenty-four and six. Plenty of earth and logs."

Tecumseh nodded again. This, then, would be the sixth and final artillery emplacement, with one of the great twenty-four-pound cannons and a six-pounder. The other two in the battery on this side of the river were already under construction just to the west, each with a big six-pounder wheeled cannon and a howitzer, one emplacement two hundred feet distant and another some two hundred feet beyond that. A second battery, with three similar emplacements—one with another twenty-four-pounder, one with a three-pounder, one with a howitzer and all three with mortars—was presently being prepared on the south side of the river, well protected in a forest fringe eastward and slightly south of Fort Meigs, but only some four hundred yards distant.[678]

Despite the destructive power the nine pieces of artillery represented, Tecumseh had his doubts over how effective they would be against the strong

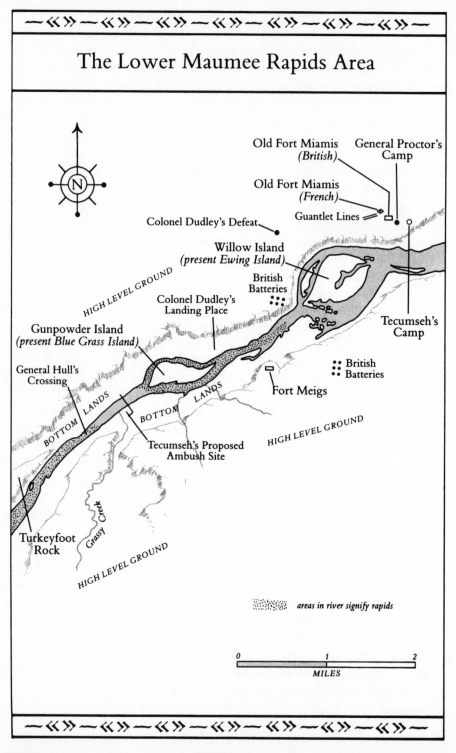

The Lower Maumee Rapids Area

Old Fort Miamis *(British)*

General Proctor's Camp

Old Fort Miamis *(French)*

Colonel Dudley's Defeat

Guantlet Lines

Willow Island *(present Ewing Island)*

British Batteries

Colonel Dudley's Landing Place

HIGH LEVEL GROUND

Tecumseh's Camp

Gunpowder Island *(present Blue Grass Island)*

General Hull's Crossing

British Batteries

Fort Meigs

BOTTOM LANDS

BOTTOM LANDS

HIGH LEVEL GROUND

Tecumseh's Proposed Ambush Site

Turkeyfoot Rock

Grassy Creek

HIGH LEVEL GROUND

▒▒ *areas in river signify rapids*

0   1   2

MILES

fort General Harrison had erected here. He had similar doubts, Proctor's assurances aside, that they would ever be able to breach those strong stockaded walls and any thought of setting them afire was pointless, since all the timber used was greenwood—sap-filled and essentially fire resistant—from the trees that had stood on the plateau.

There was within him, however, a sense of gratification that his most deadly foe was within those walls and now, at long last, he and William Henry Harrison were about to meet in actual battle.[679] With it there was the certain knowledge that while the direct frontal attack of the British might well keep the Americans bottled up, it would require subterfuge, neatly executed, on the part of his own Indian forces to get the Americans into a situation where they could be defeated. The problem would be to keep the interest of his warriors from flagging. A prolonged siege was not the Indian idea of war.

These past five days since leaving Amherstburg had been busy ones indeed. Each in their own way, the British and American forces had made extensive preparations for this present campaign. General Proctor had equipped and drilled the thousand men he was bringing along, half of whom were regulars and the remainder Canadian militia, and he had made arrangements with Commodore Barclay to transport all these men, their equipment, artillery, supplies and even a number of horses, in the British fleet from the Amherstburg wharf, taking them across the western end of Lake Erie, into Maumee Bay, and then finally upriver in two shallow-drafted gunboats as far as navigation was possible, to near the foot of the Rapids.[680]

Tecumseh's force—the thousand warriors who would be accompanying him—spent those preparatory days sharpening their weapons, seeing to their guns, refilling their paint pots and preparing their pouches with the staple rations of jerky and parched corn that would see them through many days. Night after night councils were held, pipes smoked and the war dances were staged before huge fires as the warriors worked themselves up to a high pitch of excitement.

At last the time for departure had come. On April 24 the military troops and supplies were all loaded aboard Barclay's flotilla and set off on the water journey. At the same time Tecumseh's thousand warriors, war-painted and bristling with a variety of weapons, set off on horseback, Tecumseh in the lead, flanked by Stiahta and Main Poche on his right and Chaubenee, Sauganash, and Wasegoboah on his left, and the horde of other chiefs and warriors strung out behind six abreast in a wavering snakelike column. Another two hundred warriors, largely Wyandots, were already in the area of Fort Meigs, keeping a close watch on the enemy and Tecumseh's force would unite with them on their arrival. Leaving at the same time as Barclay's flotilla, the thousand mounted Indians had followed the western fringe of the lake toward the rendezvous point at the mouth of Swan Creek.

It was here, where the water was still quite deep, that Barclay's larger ships were put to anchor the day before yesterday and all the artillery and its ammunition and the remainder of the most pertinent supplies were loaded aboard the two gunboats. Tecumseh and his warriors arrived just as sturdy polemen began the final push of these bulky craft the three and a half miles upstream to the landing place adjacent to and just below the ruins of old Fort Miamis. The troops marched along the north shore on the road that led to the fort and an adjacent campground was prepared, in the center of which was General Proctor's headquarters marquee.

Sight of the old Fort Miamis ruins early yesterday morning had brought unpleasant memories back to Tecumseh and many others of the older Indians here who had participated in the Battle of Fallen Timbers; the fort whose gates had been shut against them in their hour of need by the British inside. That, Tecumseh was determined, would never happen again.

Almost immediately on their arrival, Tecumseh with his lieutenants and Proctor with his aides and artillery officers had gone upstream another mile and a half beyond the British camp and reconnoitered the entire area around Fort Meigs, selecting the sites for the artillery batteries to be constructed and getting the work started on them, then discussing strategy. Proctor's artillery officers were confident that though Harrison's stockaded walls might provide protection initially, they would not be able to hold long against continuous battering by the cannon. Further, explosive cannonballs—which Tecumseh called "double-balls"—lobbed in high looping trajectories and falling within the palisade would burst upon impact and send a deadly spray of metal fragments and lead shot in all directions with devastating results for those inside. Tecumseh and his warriors, it was planned, would hover all around the fort as close as possible and lay down a continuous harassing fire which would prevent those inside from fleeing. At the same time, they would keep watch for expected reinforcements and cut them off.

Several times during this period of planning and placement, as they had become exposed to view from the fort, rifle fire broke out as random shots were sent their way; the distance far too great for any effectiveness, yet as a warning that they had better not approach any closer.

It was while they studied the various sites for the artillery emplacements that a number of Tecumseh's young men climbed surrounding trees and unleashed a peppering of rifle fire toward the fort. When these warriors descended from their lofty perches, they informed Tecumseh and Proctor that a great deal of digging was going on inside the walls of the expansive stockade along the lines of tents. Two young officers with telescopes were then sent up the trees to take a look and they returned confirming the report and adding that an entire latticework of trenches was being dug. Proctor was disgruntled at the news; with the near one thousand Americans taking cover in these trenches, the explosive British cannonballs would have limited success when they struck inside the fort.[681]

There was need for haste in getting the British batteries into operating condition. Spies had brought word that a reinforcement of twelve hundred American soldiers—Kentucky militia—were on their way to Fort Meigs and were at this point no more than four days away. It was obvious that Harrison would remain tightly holed up in Fort Meigs in a strictly defensive posture until their arrival and then, thus strengthened, would undoubtedly begin his own offensive with his total of troops about equaling the total number of British and Indians combined.

Tecumseh's Indians had established their principal encampment in the broad field directly east of the Fort Miamis ruins and Proctor's encampment, but only a small number of the warriors were there at any one time during the daylight hours.[682] Preliminary contact between the enemies brought some moments of jubilation to the warriors and equally some moments of anger or frustration. Early on, four Ottawa boys, the oldest of which was only fourteen, ambushed an American party carrying dispatches to Fort Meigs. No one was killed, but the Americans dropped their pouches and fled and the boys recovered them and brought them to Tecumseh. None of the documents were of any real value strategically, but all the Indians whooped with glee at these four boys having routed a strong party of full-grown men.

The majority of the Indians spread out widely staying well clear of the fort but surrounding it and watching for the occasional scouting patrols sent out by Harrison, hoping to cut them off and bring them down. The popping of rifle fire had been sporadic but almost constant since their arrival here and there had already been several tragic incidents, one of which had been especially infuriating because it involved Indian against Indian.

Tecumseh was not at all pleased to learn from his spies that there were a number of pro-American Indians—mainly Catahecassa's Shawnees—inside the fort with Harrison and even less happy when, during one of their relatively close approaches to the walls, the booming voice of one of these Indians came to them from over the top of the wall; a voice that Tecumseh at once recognized as that belonging to his old friend of many years before, Chiuxca.[683]

"Hooo-eee!" Chiuxca cried and, speaking in the Shawnee tongue, continued, "There are a heap of Americans here and more coming. Better clear out, or they will have all your scalps!"

A burst of rifle fire from Tecumseh's warriors cut off the taunts, but many of the warriors were very angry that the chief who had once been so prominent in the fights against the *Shemanese* had now so completely allied himself to them. A short time later, Chiuxca added injury to insult. Carrying a rifle and a pistol, he slipped out of the fort and dodged from stump to stump in the area that had been cleared of trees for construction of the fort. Close to the fringe of woodland and two hundred yards from the fort, he crouched behind a tall forked stump and waited. Soon a pair of Tecumseh's warriors came by, slipping through the forest fringe and pausing occasionally to look at the fort. When they were no more than thirty feet from him Chiuxca suddenly gobbled like a turkey and both men stopped and looked. Chiuxca put a lead ball through the head of one and, as the other charged at him shrieking, he calmly leveled his pistol and shot him through the heart at a distance of ten feet. Then he scalped them both and came back to the fort grinning broadly and with his bloody trophies dangling from his belt.

First blood had been drawn in what was the beginning of the Siege of Fort Meigs.

The Indians were swift in retaliation. One Potawatomi warrior noted as a fine marksman climbed with his rifle to the top of a tall tree, from which he could see over the stockade walls. He saw two men standing close together and aimed carefully at the larger of the pair and fired. The distance was almost two hundred yards, yet he was gratified to see one of them flop to the ground with the loose-jointed flaccidity of death.

Continuing their retaliation, late in the evening a party of bold Winnebagoes and Kickapoos, under a covering fire by their fellows in the woods, slipped in right to the walls of the fort and, at an attached fenced lot, killed a large number of hogs and cows being held there temporarily. They also stampeded the dozen or so horses.

Now, with General Proctor having just ordered the twenty-four-pounder and six-pounder in this emplacement, they prepared to leave when there was a second puff of smoke at the fort and again the brief whine as the projectile came in. This time, however, it struck the ground no more than four or five feet away and sent a great shower of dirt and debris over them and they all lurched away into the covering woodland immediately on their frightened horses.

With sunset not far distant, Proctor and his officers returned to their camp and Tecumseh and his men went to theirs, where Tecumseh immediately assembled the chiefs and spoke to them of a plan that required their agreement. They listened carefully and then one by one agreed to his proposal. Tecumseh then summoned Sauganash and Chaubenee and with them and a few warriors accompanying him, moved down to the river and crossed it. They rode northward through the woods until they came to the broad clearing around Fort Meigs. They then followed the fringe of woodland around the fort at a distance of nearly two hundred yards until they came to a place where an erosion gully appeared before them, coming from the direction of the fort. Its sides were high enough that a single man on foot, keeping low, could follow it without exposing himself until within perhaps eighty or ninety yards of the walls.

Tecumseh grunted in satisfaction and stopped his horse and dismounted. His followers did the same.

"Sauganash," Tecumseh said, "take out now the writing materials you carry in your saddle pouch and write the words I give you."

Sauganash nodded, extracted paper, pen and ink pot from his saddle bag, straddled a smooth, barkless log and placed the materials before him, ready to write.

"To Governor Harrison," Tecumseh dictated. "We are enemies and we are met here to oppose one another at last. Why should not we, who are the leaders, settle the matter between us alone, so that the blood of our fine young men need not be shed in the fight which presents itself? Meet me in combat on a neutral ground of your choice and with whatever weapon is your choice, or even with none, and I will have the same, or none, and we will then fight this matter out between us until one of us is dead. He who triumphs will then hold this ground and he who has been beaten, his people will immediately return home and remain quiet ever after. My chiefs are in agreement on this head. We are men. Let us meet like men. Let us fight like men. Let us spare our people. I await your answer. Swing a lantern above the gate if you accept. I will be watching and I will then come and meet you for the contest. Tecumseh."

As soon as the ink from Sauganash's pen was dry, Tecumseh took the paper and folded it into a flat strip two inches wide. Selecting an arrow from the quiver of one of the warriors with them, he wrapped it snugly around the shaft just behind the chipped flint head and tied it tightly in place with a thin strand of rawhide. Then, borrowing the warrior's bow he said, "Wait," and, in the gathering twilight, moved off in a crouch in the gully toward the fort. When as close as he could get, he suddenly stood erect, pulled the bow to full draw and sent the arrow off in a high arcing trajectory. It whirred through the calm evening air, passed well over the wall and disappeared behind it.

Voices were raised and a shot was fired, plucking up a clump of dirt close to Tecumseh's feet. He ducked back down into the gully and raced back as more shots came, but without effect. His followers were grinning as he returned to them and together they rode to a spot where they could see the gate and there they stopped and waited.

Three hours later, when no response was given, they returned to their own camp.[684]

[May 4, 1812 — Tuesday]

"No! I will *not* permit it. You, Tecumseh, agreed before we ever came here that you would abide by my wishes as commanding general. I hold you to that promise now."

Tecumseh regarded Proctor steadily, knowing the general was making a grave error in his dogmatic refusal, yet unable to budge him; at the same time bound to honor the promise he had made at Fort Malden. But that such an opportunity as this to deliver a deadly blow to the enemy should be allowed to slip through their grasp was galling.

"I will live up to my promise," he said tightly, his voice laced with frustration, "but mark what I say, you will come to regret this."

Tecumseh had for the most part approved of Proctor's actions to this point, even though they had not been as effective as he had anticipated. He recalled the wild jubilation and cries of excitement that had swept the entire Indian force when, on the first day of the Planting Moon the British batteries were finally completed and the bombardment of Fort Meigs was begun.

Actually, there had been some minor firing by the British the night before, but not from the batteries. One of the broad, heavy gunboats was towed upstream past the half-mile wide and three-quarter-mile long Willow Island and anchored in midriver.[685] From a howitzer mounted on her deck a total of thirty shots were fired at the fort over the course of the night but with virtually no effect and, in the light of morning it withdrew before the American artillery could be brought to bear on it.

At 10 A.M. that day, the first British battery became fully functional and the bombardment began with shot afer shot being fired and the Maumee Valley reverberating with the deep-throated thunder of the twenty-four-pounder. Tecumseh's warriors expected the stockade walls would quickly tumble down, but such was not the case. The sappy wood of which the pickets were constructed bowed and bent with the impacts but they did not shatter to smithereens as would have the timbers of a long-established fort whose uprights had fully dried and become brittle. The great balls striking the walls would simply rip through, making holes as big as themselves or a little larger and then burying themselves ineffectually in the long mounds of earth formed by the Grand Traverse and the Little Traverse, which were extensive, interconnecting trenches dug inside the fort at Harrison's order.

Soon other British guns joined in the bombardment, some of the balls continuing to be directed at the stockading, others lofted high to arc down within the palisade. A few Americans were killed—including one who had his head carried away by a cannonball—and a few were injured but, for the volume of shots fired, the results were very poor indeed.[686]

In an effort to salve the disappointment of his followers, Tecumseh told the warriors that the Americans were like timid groundhogs who hid in their holes at the first sign of trouble and he continued to send out parties to patrol the perimeters and scour the surrounding countryside. There were brief skirmishes here and there with American patrols that were sent out and, early in the action, a noted Winnebago chief, Spotted Arm, was severely wounded and put out of action for some time to come.[687] A few Americans were wounded when they crept down to the river to fill buckets and other containers with water for those in the fort, the well being dug inside not yet completed.

There was return fire from the American guns, but only at extended and irregular intervals, indicating to the British artillerists that the enemy probably had only a very limited supply of cannon ammunition and were conserving it.[688]

For the first three full days—and often at night as well—the guns of the British thundered and roared. This morning, however, the guns remained silent and Tecumseh and his Indians watched as an officer from Proctor, splendidly clad in his scarlet coat, white trousers, and black boots, put ashore in a canoe on the south side of the river under a white flag and, a parade of one, marched fearlessly to the gate of Fort Meigs. This was Major Peter Chambers of the Forty-first Regiment, who carried a demand from Proctor for Harrison to surrender in order to spare the effusion of blood.

He was allowed to enter and was inside for hardly more than ten minutes when the gate was opened and he returned to his canoe, his gait hardly as firm and commanding as it had been on his approach. Tecumseh was with General Proctor when Major Chambers reported to him and there was a sense of dismay in his report. Upon entering the fort, he related, he had expected to see extensive damage and many dead and wounded as a result of the three-day bombardment. He saw nothing of the kind. A handful of men were wearing bandages over slight wounds, but no one seemed incapacitated and there was no sign whatever of bodies.[689]

Major Chambers said that he was led to the grand battery position where General Harrison was standing and, after a proper salute and greeting, he delivered General Proctor's message. Harrison listened to his words, smiling mirthlessly and then had replied, "The demand, under present circumstances, is a most extraordinary one. As General Proctor did not send me a summons to surrender on his first arrival, I had supposed he believed me determined to do my duty. His present message indicates an opinion of me that I am at a loss to account for."

Chambers related that he was at once apologetic and replied, "Sir, General Proctor would never think of saying anything to wound your feelings. The character of General Harrison as an officer is well known. General Proctor's force is very respectable and there is, with him, a larger body of Indians than has ever before been embodied."

General Harrison's response to that, Major Chambers said, had been brusque to the point of rudeness. He had said, "I believe I have a very correct idea of General Proctor's force. It is not such to create the least apprehension for the result of the contest, whatever shape he may be pleased hereafter to give it."

The American general had then beckoned to one of his officers to show the British officer out but had made one final remark that Chambers was directed to pass on to General Proctor. "Assure the general, however," Harrison had said, "that he will never have this post *surrendered* to him upon any terms. Should it fall into his hands, it will be in a manner calculated to do him more honor, and to give him larger claims upon the gratitude of his government, than any capitulation could possibly do."

Major Chambers had hesitated a moment in his relation and then added, "General Proctor, sir, as soon as the gate closed behind me, there was a tremendous cheer raised from the men inside."

It was late tonight when a trio of Tecumseh's spies came to him with important news from up the Maumee River. It had been known for the past three days that an American force of some twelve hundred men had arrived at Fort Defiance, but now that force had embarked from there in a large number of small boats and was presently descending the Rapids toward Fort Meigs.[690] Unable to negotiate the rough rocky water in the darkness, they had stopped and made camp some three miles above Fort Meigs. They would undoubtedly continue their journey first thing in the morning.

Tecumseh was immediately excited at the prospect and he quickly formulated a plan. A half mile above Fort Meigs was a large island the Indians called Macate Menethi—Gunpowder Island—so called because trader John Kinzie had once hidden a number of kegs of gunpowder there just prior to the Battle of Fallen Timbers.[691] At the uppermost point of that island there was a three-quarter-mile stretch of river without rapids which extended upstream to a point adjacent to where the Battle of Fallen Timbers had been fought. Coming off the rapids above, the boats of the whites would slow considerably in their passage through this stretch of calm water. The river was less than two hundred yards wide at this point and Tecumseh knew that under the cover of darkness this night he could secrete his entire force of warriors on the brushy banks along both sides of this stretch and neatly ambush the flotilla when it was well into the calm water and floating smoothly. At this point the warriors would themselves be protected by good cover and from five to ten feet above the river level, shooting at a slightly downward angle at the boats and therefore not endangering their fellows on opposite sides of the river. Cramped and badly exposed in the crowded boats, the enemy would be extremely vulnerable; any who escaped the first firing by flinging themselves into the water could easily be picked off as they attempted to swim to safety. If the ambush was well timed—and there was no reason why it should not be—they stood a good chance of wiping out the entire reinforcement in a matter of minutes.

636

Tecumseh went to Proctor's camp immediately and refused to be put off when informed that the commander had retired and should not be disturbed. He demanded that the general be awakened at once to hear what he had to say. Reluctantly this was done and Proctor, disheveled from sleep, was in a foul mood when the Indian leader was brought before him. Sleepy and irascible he listened to what Tecumseh had to say but was already shaking his head before the plan was fully outlined.

"No," he said, "I cannot allow it. If the absence of your warriors was detected by General Harrison, my batteries would become vulnerable to attack and could be overrun. Also, if for some reason your attack should fail and the Americans turn the tables on you, which they might well do since they have a larger force, I would then be without my Indian allies to continue the attack against Fort Meigs. The risks are too great. The same object you hope for can better be achieved by preparing the artillery to fire against the boats when they arrive at the fort in the morning, so the answer is no."

Tecumseh, unbelieving at this adamant stance of Proctor against such an opportunity, continued to argue his points, speaking rapidly and with growing agitation, suspecting that more than anything else, Proctor did not wish to let the Indians achieve such a great victory while his own army was apart from the action. But the more he argued for it, the greater Proctor's obstinacy became until finally the general put up his hands, cutting Tecumseh off in midsentence.

"No! I will *not* permit it. You, Tecumseh, agreed before we ever came here that you would abide by my wishes as commanding general. I hold you to that promise now."

Tecumseh regarded General Proctor steadily and when, at length, he replied, his words were icy. "I will live up to my promise, but mark what I say, you will come to regret this."[692]

[May 5, 1813 — Wednesday]

Shortly after dawn the word was brought to Tecumseh in his encampment that a large detachment of American soldiers was just then leaving Fort Meigs and marching slowly toward the southeast, advancing against and apparently intent upon silencing the battery of guns there.

Tecumseh immediately roused his men. Several hundred were directed to take a position in the woods to the west of the battery on the north side of the river, with instructions to harass the boats of the reinforcing Americans when they should appear. Several hundred more he directed to cross the river at this point and move up the south side to strike and, if possible cut off the retreat of the American detachment presently marching against the south battery.

Tecumseh, mounting his fine dappled gray mare, then went to the adjacent camp of General Proctor and found him already preparing to march across the river with a troop of soldiers, having also received word of the threat to the south battery. He informed the British commander that he had already sent a large number of his warriors to engage them and attempt to cut them off and, though the general did not say so directly, there was an air of "I told you so" about him in regard to this unexpected American move against his guns—an unspoken accusation that had Tecumseh's Indians not been available, the gun emplacements would surely be lost. Mounting his horse, the general was joined by several of his mounted regular officers and Colonel Matthew Elliott. All of them, Tecumseh included, descended the steep slope to the river, crossed over to the south side and hastened toward the battery.

A lot of small-arms fighting was going on there when they arrived, but they were relieved to find that the battery was still in the hands of the British who, along with the Indians, were putting up a stiff resistance. Clouds of gunsmoke wafted among the trees making visibility difficult and, as a result, a great deal of the fighting was becoming hand-to-hand combat, with a considerable amount of shrieking from the Indians and hoarse cries from the whites, interspersed with occasional thunderous blasts from the larger cannon and the harsher thumping booms of the mortars being fired. Vaguely heard as a background noise to the immediate din was the distant popping of rifles from across the river, which Tecumseh assumed to be his warriors harassing the reinforcements arriving by boat.

For over three hours the fight continued, with the Americans gradually losing ground and falling back toward Fort Meigs. Then a warrior on foot came racing up with paralyzing news. The flotilla of boats had never shown up as expected, but suddenly the Indians on the wooded slopes west of the north battery had been rushed by an overwhelming force of Americans on foot under a colonel named William Dudley.[693] Taken by surprise, the Indians had been forced back and the Americans had driven them on. The British artillerists and their guards in the north battery had been unable to retard the American advance and had eventually been forced to abandon the three emplacements. The entire battery had easily fallen into the hands of the American detachment and at once all the cannon had been spiked so they were rendered incapable of being fired. Then the Americans had continued pursuing the Indians in a moving battle to the northeast.[694] They had penetrated more than a mile beyond the battery and had come dangerously close to the camps of the British and Indians when the Indians had suddenly become strongly reinforced by more Indians from their camp and the American drive was halted and had begun to fall back.[695]

Tecumseh instantly deduced what had happened. The Americans had landed their boats before coming in sight of the fort and had marched on foot on the north side of the river in an apparently successful effort to silence the British guns. With a shrill, distinctive cry, Tecumseh halted his warriors in their gradual pressing of the American detachment which, so abruptly relieved, turned at once and hastened back toward the fort. Leaving a small portion of his warriors here to protect the battery, Tecumseh led the rest in a wide swing through the woodland around the south side of Fort Meigs and returned to the river a half-mile upstream from the fort. They were in time to see the tail-end of an American detachment that had evidently landed on the south side of the river just disappearing into the fort.

Tecumseh and his warriors crossed the river not far below the foot of Macate Menethi and within moments encountered the beached boats of the American detachment that had landed on the north side. Those boats lay drawn up on shore for five hundred yards or so downstream and, even as they looked in that direction, they saw a sizeable number of Americans, weaponless and in complete terrified rout, racing toward the nearest of the boats.[696] Tecumseh sent his warriors running to cut them off.

The Americans arrived first—some of them—and in frantic haste leaped into the boats and pushed off. About one hundred fifty of them managed to get clear and cross over, but a great many more were intercepted on the shore or emerging from the wooded slopes. The fighting became very general and extremely one-sided since the majority of the Americans spilling out of the woods had no weapons and, gripped by panic, were fleeing for their lives. Scores of them were downed under tomahawks and war clubs as Tecumseh's warriors gradually pushed their way toward where the battery was located.

After a long while another runner appeared, caught sight of Tecumseh on his horse and raced up to him. In broken sentences he gasped out the latest intelligence. The Americans who had landed and spiked the artillery had continued in pursuit of the fleeing British and Indians in a tree-to-tree battle that at first moved rapidly but gradually slowed as the Americans met more and more resistance from the Indians, the latter gradually being reinforced by more of their fellows from the encampment. Soon the American command had been heard to shout the order to retreat and the soldiers had simply thrown down their weapons and fled. A fair amount had eluded them, but the greater majority had been cut off in the area of the battery. A great many had been killed and the remainder had surrendered. Those who had surrendered to the British were herded toward the remains of old Fort Miamis and held there under guard in an old cattle yard of sorts. Those who were captured by the Indians were stripped of all clothing and forced to march, considerably abused along the way, to the same place where, by then, a gauntlet line had been formed. It was no mere gauntlet of switches and sticks and clubs. The Indians in the line were armed with tomahawks, war clubs, swords and bayonetted guns. A considerable number of the captives were not making it through the line into the fort and bodies were all over the place. Worse yet, those Americans who had managed to get inside the ruined fort to supposed safety, were being stabbed, bludgeoned, and tomahawked to death by a mob of Indians who had clambered over the broken-down walls, led by a party of Chippewas under Chief Normee, who was not honoring the sanctuary that should have been theirs on successfully running the gauntlet.

Tecumseh drove his heels into his horse's sides and sent her galloping through the woods, upslope past the battery and toward the Fort Miamis ruins. There was a scattering of bodies at first, then dozens and finally scores, most of them nude, scalped and mutilated.

One of the dead was Colonel William Dudley, who had been killed only a short while before. Dudley was being brought to the old fort when they passed a British officer in the company of some of his soldiers and a group of garishly painted Chippewa Indians and the American colonel, upon seeing him, asked urgently, "Are you General Proctor?"

Proctor looked at him without expression and answered, "Yes, I am."

"Then," Dudley said, "as commander of this force of Americans who have surrendered themselves into your hands, I claim your protection."

Proctor regarded him contemptuously for a moment and then, without a word, turned his back and walked away toward the old fort, followed by his soldiers. Immediately the chief of this party of Chippewas stepped forward and buried his tomahawk in Dudley's head, drew out his knife and scalped him and then slit open his chest and cut out his heart and held it up.

"Now your heart can see brave men!" he said. He tossed the bloody organ to a nearby warrior, who tore out a bite with his teeth, then passed it to others who did the same.[697]

Approaching the old fort, Tecumseh saw the gauntlet lines, twenty to thirty feet apart and one hundred and fifty yards in length, with bodies of Americans littering the whole way, while some prisoners were still being made to run through and having tomahawks or war clubs thrown at them or being shot at during their passage.[698] He galloped through the lines, shouting orders for the Indians to desist. Two other horses approaching from the direction of the British encampment caught his eye and he saw that one was ridden by Sauganash and the other by Matthew Elliott, who was brandishing his sword as he galloped to the scene. All three reached the fort's crumbled gate at about the same moment, galloped inside and then leaped off their horses.

The interior of the old fort contained about a quarter acre of ground and about eighty Americans were sitting huddled together below an earthen embankment in a sort of pen overgrown with grass, most of them without clothing and continually trying to move into the center of their cluster as individuals on the perimeter were singled out and being tomahawked or stabbed by the Chippewas and other war-painted Indians crowded around them.[699] A number of British soldiers were standing around but only one made any attempt to help the Americans and was himself shot down by an Indian for his interference.[700] After that the other British soldiers refrained from any further interfering with the Indians. Off to one side stood General Proctor, intently watching and making no effort to stop the slaughter.[701]

Sauganash immediately began berating the blood-bespattered Chippewas, Chief Normee in particular, for their cowardice, two of the Indians at that moment preparing to kill a quailing American, one gripping him by the hair and the other ready to drive his knife into him.

Tecumseh shouldered past his lieutenant, his face dark with rage, and his war club gripped in his hand. He strode to the clustered prisoners and knocked aside the black-painted Chippewa who was gripping the prisoner's hair and turned to the other and ordered him to stop. Instead, the knife-wielding Chippewa, concentric red and black circles painted around his eyes, thrust his blade into the prisoner's heart, killing him. Tecumseh lunged forward and struck the Indian a crushing blow on the head with his war club and the offending Chippewa fell, lifeless.[702]

Then Tecumseh spun around and again shouted at the others to stop, which they did, falling back in confusion and shock at seeing their Indian commander down one of their own tribesmen.

"Now you want to kill all these prisoners, do you?" Tecumseh continued. A few voices among the Indians answered affirmatively and Tecumseh looked fiercely toward them. He held up his blood-stained war club threateningly and replied, "Then you must kill me first and then you can do as you please. Maybe some of you will die in the effort."

The surrounding Indians became silent and after a moment Tecumseh thrust his club back into his belt and continued addressing them scathingly. "Did we not direct in council that prisoners at our mercy were not to be tortured or slain? Did we not acknowledge that such cruelty was the act of frightened men? Where is your bravery now? What has become of my warriors? You are to fight in battle to desperation, but you are never to redden your hands in the blood of prisoners!"

He paused and his glance fell on General Proctor who was staring at him. Tecumseh pointed a finger at him accusingly.

"Why have you allowed your prisoners to be killed in cold blood?" he demanded.

"Sir," replied Proctor, "your Indians cannot be commanded."

"Not by cowards," Tecumseh told him coldly. "Take these prisoners to a place where they will be safe."

Proctor made no move to do so and in a moment Tecumseh's lip curled contemptuously. "Begone!" he said. "You are unfit to command. Go and put on petticoats."

The two men stared at each other with naked malice for fully half a minute before Proctor turned and walked away without a word. By this time Chief Normee and his Chippewas had slunk away and Tecumseh now placed the remaining American prisoners under guard of a group of his more trusted warriors and ordered all the others to return with him now to where the real fighting was going on and where brave men, not cowards, were needed.[703]

Taking his cue from Tecumseh, Matthew Elliott also was doing all he could to curtail the butchery in what the prisoners called the bull pen, since they had been taken there like cattle brought to slaughter. The old Indian agent, in his fury, struck several of the offending Chippewas across the face with the flat of his sword and growled, "You damned cowardly souls. All you are fit for is plunder."[704]

As soon as Tecumseh departed with his Indians, Elliott called the British soldiers together who had been standing about watching and ordered them to take the remaining prisoners at once to the boats and put them on board and to then guard them and prevent any further such attacks. Word was to be passed immediately that other Americans still being caught in the woods, of which there were a great many, were to be taken to the river's edge and held there.

The Americans inside the ruins of old Fort Miamis were now ordered to their feet and, some being carried or aided in walking by their companions, 155 were led to the river and finally placed in relative safety on the boats. On the adjacent shore, almost 200 other prisoners were gathered who had been taken elsewhere in the woods. All of these prisoners, aboard the boats and on shore, huddled together and tried not to think of their 300 fellow Americans lying dead in the old fort and on the forested slopes above them.[705]

[May 9, 1813 — Sunday]

Day by day following the destruction of Colonel Dudley's detachment, Tecumseh could see that it was not going to be possible to hold his warriors in place at Fort Meigs. As individuals, small groups and large parties, they began drawing away, the Potawatomies first and then the Ottawas and Chippewas. So far as they were concerned, it was all over and the victory was already theirs. Harrison might still be inside the walls of Fort Meigs, but they were little concerned about that, convinced that he would have no recourse now but to withdraw up the Maumee Valley with his tail between his legs.

They had drawn his fangs.

More than anything else, the various warriors were keenly disappointed in the big guns of the British and their lack of effectiveness in battering down the Fort Meigs walls. Even the Canadian militia were disappointed in the fact that with artillery like that, the American fortification continued to stand. The only reason why more of the Indians had not gone away immediately was that they were scouring the woods, locating the plunder they felt was rightfully theirs—the guns that had been dropped, the packs filled with food and ammunition, the unexpected bonus that Dudley's captured boats provided, loaded as they were with provisions, clothing and other supplies.

On the morning of May 6 the prisoners, miserable in their cramped quarters aboard the boats but nonetheless thankful they were still alive after the harrowing events of the day before, were moved down to the mouth of the Maumee. Those who were injured and unable to walk were taken down by boat and the remainder marched in a sorrowful procession down the trail that followed the northwest bank. The marchers and the boats then had continued to follow the lake shore eastward to the mouth of the Vermilion River, where there was a new American settlement.[706] Here they were paroled and left to find their own way home, with the officers being given the instruments of parole for themselves and their men, in which it was stipulated that they were not to fight again, so long as this war lasted, against Britain or her allies—the term allies including the Indians. Settlers in the area helped them as they could, but their own means were meager.

At the foot of the Rapids, the big guns that had been spiked by Dudley's detachment were unable to be repaired on the scene as the spikes were wedged into the vents beyond extraction until specialized tools could be used at Fort Malden to make the artillery again usable. On May 7 Tecumseh had met with Proctor in an encounter overhung with chill and demanded that the British troops accept more of the brunt of the fighting.

"If the Americans wish to fight like groundhogs from their holes," he told Proctor, "then the Indians will fight like beavers and gradually chew down his walls or tunnel under them, but we must have the help of your soldiers."

Proctor, however, was coming to the conclusion that it was not feasible to continue the siege any longer. With the power of his artillery all but gone, he deemed it would be essentially worthless to continue bottling up Fort Meigs. Already about half of the Indians and his militia were gone, with the remainder threatening to follow. It was time, they said, to get the spring plowing and planting done and they could not afford to neglect such matters that were the basis of their livelihood and the welfare of their families.

Yesterday, then, the big guns had been pulled away from their moorings in the batteries and reloaded aboard the boats, along with the majority of the army's supplies and equipment remaining. Early this morning the entire British army withdrew and started back to Fort Malden. Tecumseh and his remaining warriors had no choice but to follow.

The Siege of Fort Meigs had ended.[707]

Chapter 13

— ⟨⟨ ⟩⟩ — The antipathy between Tecumseh and Brigadier General
Henry Proctor continued to grow following the return
to Amherstburg. Tecumseh was not concerned with masking the contempt
he felt for the British commander for his actions—or lack of them—at the
massacre of Colonel Dudley's men and Proctor was angry at the Indian leader
for his intractability and inability to grasp what Proctor considered to be the
strategies of modern warfare. He was also irritated that Tecumseh and his
Indian force continued to press for precipitate action against the Americans
still ensconced at Fort Meigs.

Tecumseh had been gratified, on their return, to find that a considerable
number of the Indians he had recruited from far away tribes had shown up.
A number of Sioux had come, and Menominees under their prominent war
chief, Oppomishshah—White Elk.[708] There was a return, as well, of more of
the Winnebagoes, Potawatomies, and Kickapoos. Several parties of Sac, Fox,
and Iowa had come from the Mississippi Valley, as had a scattering of Creeks
and Alabamas, and even a few Chickasaws and Choctaws. All had heard of
and were encouraged by the capture of the two American armies—Hull's and
Winchester's—and of the fall of Mackinac, Detroit and Chicago and the victory

against Harrison's force at Fort Meigs. The most significant number—a single body of some six hundred warriors, mainly Ottawas and Chippewas—had come streaming down from the area of Michilimackinac and other areas of the north, led by the British trader Robert Dickson. These were in large measure the Indians who had been involved in the capture of Fort Mackinac and, oddly enough, instead of being incensed, they were quite impressed with the stories of the way Tecumseh had balked Chief Normee and his men at the massacre.

By late June Tecumseh's warrior force camped south of Detroit and in the Amherstburg area totaled some thirty-six hundred, all of whom were eager for action and not content to sit too long doing nothing. Many of these arriving Indians had taken up temporary residence along the Ecorse River, the River Rouge, and in the village Tecumseh had established on the banks of the Huron River near its mouth, just across the Detroit River and slightly downstream from Amherstburg.

The inactivity bothered Tecumseh even more than the others. The knowledge was painfully in his mind that while others might consider the Siege of Fort Meigs as having been a victory, he did not. Harrison's army was still there, still being strengthened and still posing a most viable threat. Tecumseh in no way underestimated Harrison and knew that he would move to strike as soon as possible. New American forts were being established—including even, to Tecumseh's disgust, a headquarters Harrison had now established right among the pro-American Wyandots under Tarhe at Upper Sandusky—and Tecumseh was convinced if they did not strike soon, the Americans would quickly be strong enough to discard the present defensive stance in favor of an offensive.[709]

To add to the need for immediate action of some kind, spies had come to Tecumseh with very disturbing news. Up until now the American government had refused to accept the services of any of the tribes as allies, preferring them merely to remain neutral and not support Tecumseh in his endeavors and only using a small number as scouts and guides. Now, however, it was discovered that William Henry Harrison had finally convinced the government of the efficacy of letting him use Indians as offensive allies wherever possible. When grudging permission had finally been granted, Harrison had immediately held council with the neutral Shawnees, Delawares, Senecas, and Wyandots.

"It is time," Harrison told them in his speech at Upper Sandusky, "for all the neutral Indians to take up with one side or the other in the war being waged. General Proctor has sent a message to me in which he said he will trade his American prisoners for the Indians friendly to the United States. This looks as though General Proctor has received some hint that you are willing to take up the tomahawk against the United States.

"Your father, the president," he added firmly, "wants no false friends. You must either prove your friendship by moving far into the interior or else by joining me in the war."

The assembled chiefs, Tecumseh's spies reported, had included Buck-angehela of the Delawares and Chiuxca, the latter acting in the stead of the still-recuperating Catahecassa, and they had quickly held a private council and then reconvened with Harrison and it was Tarhe, principal chief of the Wyan-dots, who gave their reply.

"We have been waiting many moons," Tarhe had told Harrison gravely, "for an invitation to fight for the Americans. I speak for all the tribes present when I profess our friendship. We have agreed, without any dissension, to join you."

Harrison had obviously been very pleased and replied, "I will let you know when you are wanted. But you must conform to our mode of warfare. You are not to kill defenseless prisoners, old men, women or children. General Proctor, I have been told, has promised to deliver me into the hands of Te-cumseh if I am captured. Now, if I can succeed in taking Proctor, you shall have him for your prisoner, provided you will treat him as a squaw and only put petticoats on him, for he must be a coward who would kill a defenseless prisoner."

Tecumseh, after delivering this intelligence, held strained meetings with Proctor in which he tried to put across just how much of a threat Harrison represented. Though Proctor did not disagree with the Indian leader's assessment, he complained that he was not now in a proper state of preparedness to march against them. For one thing, he was having great difficulty in sup-plying the gathered Indians with the food they required. His own supply lines, he said, were presently interrupted on Lake Erie by the British warships being forced to patrol the waters of the middle and eastern southern portions of Lake Erie along its southern shore, where warships were being fitted out by young Oliver Hazard Perry. Without the crucial supplies being denied him, he was incapable of mounting an attack force. Control of Lake Erie, Proctor argued, was becoming a crucial issue. He envisioned Harrison's army being loaded aboard these ships of Perry's and transported across the lake well east of Amherstburg, then spreading out to surround and cut off Fort Malden from all contact with the rest of Canada.

Perry's men, according to Proctor's spies, were not only continuing to outfit ships at Buffalo but had also established a shipyard in the protected bay at Presque Isle adjacent to the American settlement of Erie on the Pennsylvania shore.[710] Further, some of the ships were finding safe mooring near the mouth of the Sandusky River in Sandusky Bay. Only eight miles above the bay, on the lower Sandusky River, a little post called Fort Stephenson had been erected on the road between Upper Sandusky and Lower Sandusky. Proctor suggested that Tecumseh lead out a force of his Indians and attack Fort Stephenson and the American settlements in the area and, if successful there, move against the American positions of the southern Lake Erie shore east of there, especially those at the mouth of the Vermilion River and at Cleveland and most particularly the shipyard at Presque Isle, which was known to be quite weakly defended. Tecumseh balked at that idea. He was still rankled by the fact that Harrison had held Fort Meigs against their determined assault in May and, more than anything else at the moment, he wished to see that post, which he considered the most advantageous to the enemy, reduced to ashes. Proctor protested that, without the support of Commodore Barclay's ships on Lake Erie, he would not be able to transport his bigger guns there again, but Tecumseh brushed this aside as inconsequential, arguing that the big guns had not had much effect in the first place and that he, Tecumseh, had a plan whereby the Americans would be drawn out of their fort and could then be destroyed.

Proctor was in a dilemma. The proposed attack against Fort Meigs, he felt, was not likely to accomplish anything. Yet, at the same time, his Indian allies in the Amherstburg area were too demanding on his stores and were suffering hunger and, if held here much longer without being fed, would begin to desert him. Reluctantly then, he agreed to another Fort Meigs campaign, knowing that once in the field the Indians would at least be able to supplement their meager food rations from him with hunting of their own to bring in meat. Proctor added, however, that if the plan Tecumseh had for taking Fort Meigs should fail, then his own army would pull its support of Tecumseh away from there and move without any further delay to the Sandusky River to turn its attention on attacking and destroying Fort Stephenson.

Pleased, Tecumseh now returned to his village on the Huron and assembled in his own wegiwa those who were closest to him: Chaubenee, Sauganash, Stiahta, Wasegoboah, Tenskwatawa, and a few others. Stiahta, the dandy as always, arrived with the long feather of a peacock affixed to his headband and clad in the scarlet coat of a British officer, the sash Tecumseh had given him wrapped around him, and a fine sword in scabbard buckled to his waistband, but wearing beneath the coat no shirt or trousers, only a blue breechclout and decorated moccasins.

Tecumseh greeted them all in turn and, after they had eaten and smoked, he addressed them quietly, telling them of Proctor's agreement to another Fort Meigs attack and that the Indians must now be brought into a state of readiness, as the expedition would be launched in three days. There was considerable excitement at the news and as it died away, Tecumseh spoke again, even more softly, his indefinable tone immediately causing them concern.

"What we begin now," he concluded, "is the beginning of the end. In one way or another, this present war will be finished for all of us in three moons. At the end of that time I will finally leave you forever, as it is the intention of the Great Spirit to grasp me in Her net." He held up a hand, cutting off their dismayed reaction, and went on. "My being killed does not mean that the Indians cannot accomplish their objective. With strength and courage and perseverance, we must push on. It is my hope only that before the end becomes final for me, I may personally kill him who has been, and remains, our greatest enemy, William Henry Harrison."

[July 27, 1813 — Tuesday]

The ruse Tecumseh had so well devised to draw the Americans out of Fort Meigs utterly failed.

"Now what do we do, Tecumseh?" Chaubenee asked, trying to keep the deep disappointment out of his voice. He had been every bit as sure as Tecumseh that the plan would work.

"We go with General Proctor's army," Tecumseh said, "and see what he plans to do in this attack he wishes against Fort Stephenson."

The bitterness was heavy in him that the second Siege of Fort Meigs had ended in such failure, still hardly able to believe that the elaborate artifice had not worked. It had all seemed so grand a deception from the very beginning and all the Indians in their preliminary war councils at his village of the Huron River had embraced the idea enthusiastically from his very first proposal of it.

They had all left the Amherstburg area on July 15: one thousand Canadian militia and British regulars in a number of very small gunboats accompanied by a great armada of canoes in which were Robert Dickson and the majority of the six hundred northern Indians he had brought—largely the Menominees, Ottawas, and Chippewas. Tecumseh and the remainder of the Indians—the Potawatomies and Winnebagoes, Kickapoos and Delawares, Shawnees and Wyandots—again going by land around the western end of Lake Erie. The whole force amounted to over four thousand and there had been a great air of eager expectation among them all when they set off, leaving only a skeleton force to guard Fort Malden, along with five hundred warriors remaining behind to help in that protection as well as to guard the Indian camps and their women and children.

The majority had arrived at the foot of the Maumee Rapids late on July 19 and the remainder the next day and the separate British and Indian camps were set up adjacent to each other as before and on the same ground close to the ruins of the old Fort Miamis. Initial reconnaissance of Fort Meigs showed it had been strengthened considerably since the first siege had been lifted in

May. Observers reported that its garrison had been increased by reinforcements and now numbered fifteen hundred men. Numerous new artillery emplacements had been made in the fort's walls and the army inside seemed very ready for any kind of assault the enemy might bring against them. Damage caused by the British artillery during the first siege in May had been largely repaired, a few new traverses had been dug, a better wharfing accommodation had been constructed on the rim of the Maumee and the ground surrounding the fort for two hundred yards had been cleared of all logs and other debris that might be used as cover by attacking Indians. Even most of the numerous stumps that had been sticking up all over these fields had been burned and only blackened spots of ashy ground indicated where they had been. The American fort's commander was taking no chances.

The Indians, with a few British along, went to the old battery sites and found them essentially as they had left them. From these, especially the former emplacement sites on the south side of the river, they sent a hail of small-arms fire toward the fort with little effectiveness and causing the Americans to retaliate by lobbing cannonballs their way, which forced them to scramble away quickly.[711]

Minor ineffective small-arms fire had been continued against Fort Meigs by both Proctor's men and several hundred of Tecumseh's Indians the remainder of this day and the next. At one point a party of Tecumseh's men surprised some nine American soldiers, part of a picket guard, within three hundred yards of the fort, killed six of them, took three prisoners and drove off half a dozen yoke of oxen and some horses, all to the great joy of the Indians, who took this early success as a favorable sign.

This was followed, however, by an encounter not so successful. Intent upon the fort, the Indians did not notice the approach of a party of twenty-six American soldiers, who had come from the Portage Block House on the Auglaize River.[712] Creeping up as close as they could get without being observed, the little detachment suddenly burst from its cover and daringly raced toward the fort as bullets whizzed all around them. Soldiers in the fort quickly realized what was occurring and began shooting over the ramparts to lay down a covering fire for their arriving fellows. With the exception of having only one man killed and two horses lost, the detachment made it safely into the fort, whose gates were briefly swung open to admit them. In this action Tecumseh's left earlobe was barely nicked by a bullet that broke the skin and caused some bleeding, but which was insignificant as a wound. During the night of July 22, the Indians staged a great war dance, with the sounds of the drums and the shrieking and chanting carrying faintly to the American fort.

Then, early on July 23, the firing by British and Indians ceased and, in view of the American soldiers watching over the ramparts, Tecumseh led eight hundred of his warriors up the road that paralleled the Maumee River and disappeared from sight.[713] The supposition was strong that Indians were on their way to attack little Fort Winchester at the mouth of the Auglaize.[714]

About 2 P.M. that day, a detachment of some two hundred men was sent out from Fort Meigs to the edge of the woods to circle around and try to determine whether the British were erecting any batteries unseen by those in the fort and also to bring in the bodies of the pickets who had been killed.[715] They made no discoveries but were eventually detected themselves by a party of four Indians who fired on them and then fled to give the alarm. Three hundred British and Indians were immediately sent out to try to cut them off, but they were too late, the detachment having made it back into the safety of the fort by then.

Two days later—on July 25—the whole British force was detected by the Americans in the process of breaking up their camp near old Fort Miamis and moving across the Maumee to its southeastern side, where they established a new camp behind a well-screened point of woods.[716]

Dickson's northern Indians had remained with the British, keeping out of sight of the Americans, and the remainder of the Indians Tecumseh had not taken with him on the apparant move toward Fort Winchester—a total of some sixteen hundred warriors—split their force in half. Eight hundred placed themselves in well-concealed ambush on both sides of the road leading to Lower Sandusky. The other eight hundred took a widely circuitous route around Fort Meigs to the south, out of sight of the fort, to rejoin Tecumseh's force camped a few miles away to the west. They brought with them, as Tecumseh had instructed, every piece of American uniform that had been taken from their captives.

When the new arrivals got to him, Tecumseh distributed the American coats and hats, shirts and trousers and dressed his warriors in them. Then, on July 26, giving them their final instructions, he led his original force of eight hundred back toward Fort Meigs, with the Indians disguised as Americans following several hundred yards behind.[717] When within hearing of Fort Meigs, both Indian forces began firing their weapons, screaming and shouting and Tecumseh's force soon appeared in view of the fort as if in retreat, running eastward and pausing every now and then to reload and fire their weapons back at their supposed pursuers. The disguised Indians came into view, firing toward the retreating party, acting much as the American forces acted in similar circumstances and driving the Indians before them from tree to tree and stump to stump. Realism was added by several of the pursued Indians screaming as if injured and limping or dragging themselves off and others, falling as if shot dead, were scooped up and carried off by their companions. The whole demonstration lasted over an hour, with sometimes the Indians gaining ground and pushing the "soldiers" back and at other times the Indians being pushed

back. It was all quite a show and, to many in the fort, extremely convincing.[718]
The Indians being "chased" disappeared from view on the road leading toward
Lower Sandusky and so too, very gradually, did the pursuing "soldiers." As
soon as they were out of sight of the fort and still shrieking and firing their
guns, the sixteen hundred took their places with the party waiting in ambush.
But the soldiers in Fort Meigs stayed put and Tecumseh, disgusted and discouraged, finally had to admit the ruse had failed.

In the midst of a heavy thunderstorm that suddenly crashed over them,
they rejoined Proctor and his army and the remainder of the Indians. Tecumseh
counciled with the British general in his headquarters marquee throughout
most of the next day and Proctor, sensing the foul mood Tecumseh was
experiencing, wisely refrained from any scornful looks or I-told-you-so utterances. He merely firmed up the plans for what the army would do now
and announced that the Siege of Fort Meigs would be lifted by noon the next
day.

"Now what do we do, Tecumseh?" Chaubenee asked.

"We go with General Proctor's army," Tecumseh replied bitterly, "and
see what he plans to do in this attack he wishes against Fort Stephenson."

[August 11, 1813 — Wednesday]

Tecumseh, with Chaubenee, Sauganash, and Stiahta close to him, looked
across this expansive village of his close to the mouth of the Huron River and
shook his head sorrowfully. In the week since their return here, close to a
third of Tecumseh's entire Indian force had deserted him. In them all had been
the sure knowledge that Harrison would soon be leading his army here and
they had no intention of being on hand for such a confrontation.

Tecumseh was not surprised at the desertions, fully expecting them considering what had occurred in the attack on Fort Stephenson, but saddened
by them nonetheless and determined that if the fortunes of the Indians did not
soon take a very definite upswing, he would hold a council of those remaining
and urge they all return to their homes and consider this war lost.

Fort Stephenson had been the pivotal point.

There, in only a few disastrous minutes, the entire course of matters had
been drastically altered. It had all seemed to be such a simple matter when
they arrived on August 1 and viewed from a short distance the little fort lying
before them: a tiny log stockade with two blockhouses—on north and west
sides—and only 170 defenders inside, the structure itself surrounded by a
moatlike ditch and in the midst of a two- or three-acre clearing that had formed
by the felling of the surrounding trees to build it. How could it have had any

hope of standing against a besieging force of British and Indians with some twenty-five times as many men?

Immediately after lifting the second Siege of Fort Meigs, Proctor and his army had descended the Maumee River and Maumee Bay to Lake Erie and followed the shoreline of Lake Erie to Sandusky Bay. They had then moved up the Sandusky River, where they joined Tecumseh's force, which had come here overland and were already waiting.

Proctor was gratified to learn from his scouts that there was no other American force anywhere in the vicinity that was strong enough to launch a counteroffensive against them and he was quite positive that the little fort would quickly fall before the sheer weight of numbers against them.[719] He considered the plucking of this little plum to be important strategically because, when it fell and his army occupied it, they would then have outflanked the Americans at Fort Meigs and Fort Winchester and discouraged any plans afoot to move against Amherstburg and Fort Malden.

His hope, at the onset, was that the little installation could be taken with only a small demonstration of their power. Its commander, Major George Croghan, was scarcely more than a boy—a twenty-one-year-old major of the United States Army's Seventeenth Infantry with extremely limited experience in any kind of fighting.[720]

With this in mind, General Proctor, shortly after their arrival, started a bombardment of the stockade with his few light artillery pieces aboard the gunboats and his five-and-a-half-inch howitzer on shore. He also sent in a couple of sorties of his men to attack the walls.

Young Croghan, however, directing his men to quite a spirited defense of the place, succeeded in beating back the sorties and suffered little damage of any consequence from the bombardment. A few times during the course of the morning the Americans fired a shot from their single piece of artillery, a six-pounder, but those shots were not terribly effective and simply convinced the enemy that the defenders were very short of cannon ammunition. Disgruntled at the show of resistance, Proctor continued the same activity until midafternoon, when he called a cease-fire and sent in, under a flag of truce, his demand that the fort surrender.

The flag was carried by two men—the British Indian agent Matthew Elliott and Major Peter Chambers, the latter being the same officer who had unsuccessfully carried the surrender demand to Harrison at the first Siege of Fort Meigs. They were met outside the stockade by Major Croghan's spokesman, Ensign Edmund Shipp. After the usual polite introductions were observed, Chambers got down to business.

"I am instructed, sir," he said, "by General Proctor, to demand the surrender of this fort. The general is most anxious to spare the effusion of human blood, which he cannot do should he be under the necessity of reducing it by the powerful force of artillery, regulars, and Indians under his command."

"And I, sir," Ensign Shipp replied evenly, "am instructed to advise you that the commandant and garrison of this fort are determined to defend it to the last extremity. No force, sir, however great, can induce us to surrender. You may advise your commander that we are resolved to maintain our post or bury ourselves in its ruin."

"Oh, don't be stupid!" Elliott interjected sharply. "There is an immense body of Indians here and if we succeed in taking your fort, *which we will,* they will not be able to be restrained from murdering the whole garrison." When Ensign Shipp merely looked at him without reply, the Indian agent angrily smacked his fist into his palm and added, "You are a fine young man. I pity your situation. For God's sake, surrender and prevent the terrible slaughter that must follow resistance."

"Gentlemen," Ensign Shipp's voice shook just slightly, "when—and *if*— the fort is taken, there will be none to massacre. It will not be given up while a man is able to resist."

At this moment a Potawatomi who had crept up in a nearby erosion gully, raced up behind Shipp and attempted to wrest away the sword scabbarded at the young officer's side. At once Elliott, with an oath, thrust the warrior away and sharply ordered him to behave himself. The warrior stalked off in apparent anger.

Shipp was quite certain the incident with the Potawatomi was nothing but a carefully contrived scare scene. He reached out, shook the hand of Elliott, saluted Major Chambers and walked back into the fort. Chambers and Elliott looked at one another and then returned to Proctor. A short time later the bombardment had resumed, though with little more effect than initially.

The attack broke off with nightfall, but Proctor determined to resume it again in the morning. In retrospect, it was easy enough for Proctor and his men to deduce what happened during the night. Because the British artillery fire had been concentrated toward the northwest angle of the fort, Major Croghan had correctly guessed that this was where a concentrated attack would occur. In preparation, he had moved his single cannon to a blockhouse where it could command this angle and the ditch before it. Then he masked the embrasure so it would not be evident from the outside that the big gun was there. He loaded the cannon with half a charge of powder and a double load of grapeshot.

Shortly after dawn Proctor opened up again, this time with his six-pounder artillery, and continued firing for several hours without very satisfactory effect. Smoke from the battle hung in a heavy fog all around the fort, causing eyes to water and sharply reducing visibility. It was near 5 P.M. when Proctor, frustrated and angry, had ordered a full-scale charge at the northwest angle, the British Forty-first leading the way under Lieutenant Colonel Short and supported in their rear by Indians, mainly Dickson's warriors. At the same time, Tecumseh's warriors were continuing to pour rifle fire into the other side of the fort to keep the Americans busy. Carrying ladders and a large number of axes, the charging force reached the surrounding ditch and leaped into it, fairly well hidden by the dense smoke. At once they positioned their ladders and began chopping quickly into the timbers. Others, clustered closely together, were standing ready to leap into the gap and pour into the fort to overwhelm the defenders as soon as a large hole was created.

In the embrasure looking down the length of the ditch, Croghan had been ready. At his signal the masking of the embrasure was taken away and the six-pounder thundered out its devastating charge, mowing down the men in the ditch as if they had been struck by a gigantic scythe.

Chief Big Thunder, son of the Sioux war chief Little Crow, took a lead ball through his cheeks and teeth but managed to dash away to safety. Spotted Arm, the Winnebago war chief, just recovered from his previous wound, had his arm severely wounded when a ball of grapeshot passed through it and shattered the bone.[721] Lieutenant Colonel Short, severely wounded through the thigh, staggered to his feet and attempted to raise a white handkerchief in surrender, but the cannon had been hurriedly reloaded and a second charge of the vicious grapeshot killed a great many more, including Short, who took several of the shot through his chest. Major Adam Muir, second in command, with most of the men falling dead around him, himself fell and feigned death until he could scramble away unobserved.

Those of the British and Indians in the ditch who could do so, pulled themselves out and ran or staggered or crawled back toward their own lines, while their fellows laid down covering fire to aid them. Proctor ordered a retreat to the boats. After full darkness had fallen, squads were sent back to the fort and recovered as many of the dead and wounded as they could safely carry away, which were loaded aboard the waiting gunboats.[722] With precipitate haste, the flotilla set off downstream for the return to Amherstburg, so reduced in number that there were insufficient men to handle all the gunboats and one of them, loaded with camp equipment, had to be left behind. While they moved downstream, Tecumseh and his warriors, stunned at the reversed fortunes, themselves melted away to the west to return home overland.

One hundred British had been killed and there were large numbers of wounded who managed to escape. About thirty Indians were wounded, but none of them mortally. In the entire siege, the Americans had only one man killed and seven wounded.[723]

A large number of Tecumseh's followers, especially those factions that had suffered the most injury, abandoned him long before they reached the Huron River again—primarily the Sac and Fox, the Winnegaboes and Menominees, and about half the Chippewas—all vowing never again to fight with or for the British.

So now, looking over the remaining two thousand warriors still with him at the Huron River village, Chaubenee, Sauganash, and Stiahta with him, Tecumseh shook his head sorrowfully.

"Our British allies are led by a general who is not only weak and cowardly, but who has now become very much afraid. I do not know what he will do when Harrison soon attempts to come knocking on his door, but I fear that whatever he does it will be that which is best for him and with little thought for us. Very soon I will have to confront him and learn what he expects of us . . . and tell him what we expect of him."

[August 26, 1813 — Thursday]

"Why," Tecumseh asked pointedly, "have you been standing for so long with your hands tied behind you?"

Brigadier General Henry Proctor, who at that moment was pacing with his hands locked behind his back, brought them forward self-consciously, though he knew Tecumseh was not referring to his immediate stance. He moved about in apparent discomfort, seemingly unable to stand still for very long; a man beset by insurmountable problems and fears.

"For the moment, Tecumseh," he said, irked that he was put in the position of having to try to explain grand strategy to a savage, "the war has moved out of our hands and what happens now neither I nor you have any control over. It is a naval matter now which, though I will attempt to explain it to you, Indians cannot be expected to understand, and, whether we like it or not, we have no choice but to wait and see."

What Proctor was referring to was the British fleet under Commodore Robert Barclay, which now lay at anchor in the mouth of the Detroit River, poised to move into action against the American fleet under Commodore Oliver Hazard Perry that had recently left their safe shelters and moved into the waters of western Lake Erie—seemingly a group of floating ducks defying a family of eagles waiting to pounce.[724]

Immediately upon the appearance of the American fleet heading westward along Lake Erie's shore, Barclay had sailed to the Detroit River anchorage, having insufficient arms, supplies and manpower among his six ships to engage the enemy at that moment. As soon as possible, Proctor went on, Commodore Barclay's fleet would be properly readied for battle and would handily demolish the American fleet. When that happened, the Americans would be deprived of the means they were relying upon of crossing Lake Erie to attack them here at Amherstburg. This would mean that Harrison's army would have to come by foot, marching around Lake Erie and becoming, in the process, vulnerable to attacks by Tecumseh's warriors and Proctor's army, in the type of fighting they did not know and understand. They would not have a fort to retreat to, nor holes to hide in as they had at Fort Meigs, and would be forced to stand and fight as armies should.

In the meanwhile, the American ships that for the past two days had been hovering and circling in the visible distance on that lake in an insulting challenge to Barclay to come out and fight, would have to wait a little longer.[725] Proctor said he was aware that Tecumseh and many of his Indians had paddled over to Bois Blanc Island to watch the American ships and had been deeply disappointed in their expectations that the British fleet would come out to engage them. Much as Barclay had wished to make this kind of response, Proctor told him, he could not. The big problem at the moment and the reason why there was delay, was a shortage of British manpower on this front. With the loss of so many of his regulars at the Fort Stephenson fight, Proctor was himself dangerously in need of reinforcements. For these he had already sent two urgent messages to Governor-general Sir George Prevost, yet the requisite men and supplies had not come.[726]

Now, Proctor said, he would send a third request and, to the best of his abilities of persuasion, he would entreat Prevost to send the help so desperately needed. In the meanwhile, he would continue in his efforts to convert some of his soldiers into sailors to aid Barclay.

The reinforcement required was not just for himself, he added, but for Commodore Barclay as well, who was so short of able seamen that he could not properly operate and control his fleet. Proctor had been finding it necessary to deplete his own meager ranks to assign soldiers to act as temporary seamen for Barclay, but that was not the proper answer; they could help in the maintenance and sailing of the ships, but when it came time for an engagement, their lack of naval fighting methods could prove to be more of a liability than an asset.

So far as armament went, what artillery Proctor could spare had already been taken from Fort Malden and mounted on the decks of Barclay's ships. Apart from that, Proctor concluded, for the moment there was nothing to do but stand and wait—as Tecumseh had put it, with hands tied behind—for the additional help that was needed. As soon as it arrived, he promised, Barclay would sail out to meet and utterly destroy the annoying American fleet under Perry.

Tecumseh believed little of what Proctor told him these days, but this time he believed the general was telling the truth. The problem was that his own people were still deserting him, not only because of the humiliating defeat at Fort Stephenson, where a little boy in a little house successfully defied the might of the combined British and Indians, but even more these days because of the inactivity, with which warriors ready to fight had never had patience.

Realizing that Proctor had finished his explanations, Tecumseh nodded. "I will," he said, "go now and tell my people that you English are making ready your great war canoes to seek out and destroy the Americans. That they will understand and it will hold them in place for a little longer."

As soon as Tecumseh left, Proctor wrote the letter he promised he would, but he now had little real hope there would be any favorable response.[727]

[September 18, 1813 — Saturday]

Tecumseh stared at the British commander, forcing himself with remarkable self-control, considering the circumstances, to still the trembling of absolute fury that gripped him. He knew Proctor was afraid of him but he was also sure that the general was unaware of how very close he was to death at this instant.

How much he was tempted!

In one quick movement, Tecumseh knew, he could jerk out his war club and crush the skull of this miserable excuse of a human being before him and, with a continuation of the same movement, similarly knock out the brains of Matthew Elliott, standing nervously a few feet away, for his complicity in the enormous deceit that they had perpetrated against him and his people.

This very instant, in the general's private office in Fort Malden, they had come to the culmination of the events that had begun nine days earlier when Commodore Barclay's fleet had finally weighed anchor and left the mouth of the Detroit River to pursue and destroy the little fleet of American ships that had been taunting them.

The long-awaited reinforcement from Sir George Prevost had come at last and a paltry one it was indeed. A measly detachment of forty seamen had arrived on September 9 and, with them, a note from Prevost instructing Proctor that immediately on their arrival they should be placed aboard the ships and Captain Barclay "should make his appearance on the Lake to meet the enemy." As for the other help Proctor had so urgently requested, Prevost's comment was both ridiculous and galling. He wrote:

> *The ordnance and naval stores you require must be taken from the enemy, whose resources must become yours; I am much mistaken if you do not find Captain Barclay well disposed to play that game.*

So, with little more at his disposal to fight with than hope and determination, Barclay had sailed his six-vessel fleet out of the mouth of the Detroit River that same day in search of Perry's, which had now disappeared. The sailing of the ships, all with battle flags raised and all freshly painted in orange and black, with acres of sail bellied out in the gentle breeze, was quite a colorful spectacle and heralded by the cheers of the soldiers and Indians who lined the banks. The sleek little 70-ton schooner *Chippewa* led the pack, followed by the newly rerigged 490-ton ship *Detroit*. In succession followed the 180-ton brig *General Hunter,* the 400-ton ship *Queen Charlotte,* the 230-ton schooner *Lady Prevost* and the 90-ton sloop *Little Belt.*

Just before noon the next day—September 10—the Indians had all been very excited when the distant rumbling thunder of big guns was heard and everyone knew Barclay had found and engaged Perry's fleet. Many of the Indians climbed the highest trees to try to see what was occurring, but the battle was too far distant, though some claimed to have seen smoke.[728]

Tecumseh and his warriors waited for the victorious Barclay to come sailing back into view. When he did not show up by dark, they decided he had simply anchored his fleet to rest, make repairs or do whatever else needed to be done and would probably arrive the next day. The next day, however, came and went with no sign of the ships. And the next.[729]

Tecumseh sensed something very ominous in the wind and this feeling was bolstered when, on August 13, word was brought to him by some warriors that they had seen General Proctor at Fort Malden and described him as appearing melancholy and that they had seen soldiers assembling trunks, packing cases and empty barrels. Requesting to see Proctor himself, Tecumseh was told that the commander was temporarily indisposed and seeing no one. He immediately sought out Matthew Elliott and demanded to know what was going on. Elliott hedged but covered it by telling Tecumseh he must assemble all his people for a grand council to be held in five days, on September 18, at which time General Proctor himself would make some very important remarks about what they were going to do in regard to General Harrison.

Not pleased with the response, Tecumseh nevertheless assembled runners and sent them out to the various chiefs and subchiefs, directing them all, with their warriors, to be certain to attend the planned council where Proctor would speak to them and where Tecumseh himself had some very important words for Proctor that involved them all.

In the evening of that day he dined with several British officers and their wives in Amherstburg—an engagement that had been planned for some time— and during which he hoped to learn more about what was going on. The dinner conversation, however, carefully skirted such matters except at one point when an officer momentarily slipped and mentioned that in the days ahead, as they confronted Harrison, Tecumseh and his warriors might not find the general always doing exactly as they wished.

Tecumseh, on hearing this, delicately wiped his mouth with his napkin and rose. He thanked his hosts and hostesses for the dinner and then walked to the door, where he turned back and made a final remark. "General Proctor," he said in a voice laced with menace, "had better take heed how he opposes the wishes of his red brothers, lest tomahawk and scalping knife become his lot."

Near noon on the following day—September 14—Tecumseh received word that soldiers at the fort were beginning to take things apart.[730] He went there immediately and saw the dismantling work under way and confronted the officer in charge.

"What are you doing?" he asked.

"We are following specific orders from General Proctor," was the reply, "which we are at liberty to divulge to no one."

Tecumseh's instant anger was so threatening that the engineers ceased working, withdrew a short distance away to hold a private conference and then sent one of their number running to headquarters to inform Proctor and get further instructions. Matthew Elliott was in Proctor's office at the time and Proctor stormed that he was not accountable to Tecumseh and had "a perfect right to give any secret orders I think proper."

Elliott immediately counseled treading with care. "You cannot continue to withhold information from them this way," he told the general. "If you try to do so, they might cut the wampum belt and no man can answer for the consequences."

Suddenly apprehensive, Proctor settled down. He was silent for a moment as he stood with his hands clasped behind him, his head bowed in thought. Then he looked up at Elliott and said, "You go to Tecumseh now, Colonel, and express to him my apologies. Tell him that due to the press of very important business that I cannot put off, it is simply not possible for me to speak to him in person at this time. However, tell him that I will hold a private meeting with him—you there, too, of course—immediately following the general council on Saturday and at that time I will explain all, listen carefully to all he has to say and answer any questions he may raise."[731]

Elliott returned at once to Tecumseh and apologetically delivered the message. Tecumseh, though still angry, accepted with remarkably good grace what Elliott told him and returned to his people.[732]

For the next three days none of the Indians saw General Proctor anywhere, though the dismantling and packing at Fort Malden continued unabated, with crews even working through the night and it was apparent, even to the most obtuse, that preparations were being made for a full-scale evacuation.

It was a bright, sunny morning today when the council convened in the Amherstburg municipal council hall, where similar councils had been held with the Indians for well over a score of years. The building was jammed with chiefs and warriors, while other warriors filled the street and square outside, along with wives and children, waiting to learn what was said.

Proctor, surrounded by a number of his officers and a platoon of armed guards, appeared very nervous and this apprehension abated very little during the pipe-smoking ritual. When at last the preliminaries were over and he stood to address them, a heavy silence fell over the assemblage. He had seen where Tecumseh, his features fixed in a scowl, was seated with his principal chiefs and aides—Chaubenee, Stiahta, Sauganash, Wasegoboah, and a few others—but his glance had slid away quickly and he did not look toward them again as he delivered his brief talk and interpreters swiftly and accurately did their job.

In clipped words and short sentences he came immediately to the point, saying that it was with the utmost regret that he had to tell them that a major invasion of Canada by the Americans would undoubtedly begin within the next week and that this circumstance had made it become necessary for the British army here to prepare to abandon and burn Fort Malden and strategically withdraw a short distance to the Thames River where, if a proper place and time could be found, he would make his stand against the Americans, assuming they would be rash enough to follow him. He added, as well, that he did not have, nor had he ever harbored, any thought of abandoning his courageous Indian allies and wished them to continue with him to the place where it was thought best to turn and face their common enemy.

The reaction to his words was at first a stunned silence and then an angrier outburst than had ever before been witnessed in this great hall. Tecumseh's expression had become set in hard harsh lines and his eyes flickered dangerously, his hand resting on the head of his war club at his belt. The announcement had not caught very many by surprise, since the packing going on at the fort clearly indicated some such thing was in the works, but the actual utterance of it as a fact by the commanding general brought forth all the long pent-up rage they had harbored for him and for the British for so long a time. Here once again, as always seemed to happen at a time of great crisis—as had happened at Fallen Timbers and other places—the British were showing the white feather and looking to the preservation of their own skins as the matter of first and foremost importance.

It took a long time for the tumult to die away and it only did so completely when Tecumseh rose and held out his arms for silence, then stooped and picked up a broad belt of wampum at its midpoint, with both ends hanging nearly to the floor. One of Proctor's aides—his own private interpreter assigned to a chair beside him—sat at a desk, pen poised to write swiftly and capture every word uttered.[733] Time seemed balanced on a knife edge as Tecumseh looked across those gathered here and then locked his gaze on Proctor. He spoke directly to the general and, though he did not shout or even seem to raise his voice, his words were clearly heard in every ear.

"Father," he began, "listen to your children! You have them all before you. The war before this, our British father gave the hatchet to his red children when our old chiefs were alive. They are now all dead. In that war our father was thrown on his back by the Americans, and our father took them by the hand without our knowledge, and we are afraid our father will do so again this time. Summer before last, when I came forward with my red brethren and was ready to take up the hatchet in favor of our British father, we were told not to be in a hurry, that he had not yet determined to fight the Americans.

"*Listen!* When war was declared, our father stood up and gave us the tomahawk and told us that he was ready to strike the Americans, that he wanted our aid and that he would certainly get our lands back which the Americans had taken from us.

"*Listen!* You told us at that time to bring forward our families to this place and we did so. And you promised to take care of them and they should want for nothing while the men would go and fight the enemy; that we need not trouble ourselves about the enemy's garrisons, that we knew nothing about them and that our father would attend to that part of the business. You also told your red children that you would take good care of your garrison here, which made our hearts glad.

"*Listen!* When we were last at the Rapids it is true we gave you little assistance. It is hard to fight people who live like groundhogs."

As he continued without pause, a note of sarcasm crept into his voice and his eyes remained unwaveringly on Proctor. "Father, *listen!* Our fleet has gone out. We know they have fought. We have heard the great guns. But we know nothing of what has happened to our father with one arm. Our ships have gone one way and we are very much astonished to see our father tying everything up and preparing to run the other without letting his children know what his intentions are. You always told us to remain here and take care of our lands. It made our hearts glad to hear that was your wish. Our great father, the king, is the head and *you* represent him."

The sarcasm deepened into words ripe with contempt and insult. "You always told us you would never draw your foot off British ground, but now, Father, we see that you are drawing back and we are sorry to see our father doing so without seeing the enemy. We must compare our father's conduct to a fat dog that carries its tail on its back but, when affrighted, drops it between his legs and runs off."

There was a great deal of laughter at this utterance, but neither Tecumseh nor Proctor were smiling.

"Father, *listen!* The Americans have not yet defeated us by land. Neither are we sure they have done so by water. We therefore wish to remain here and fight our enemy should they make their appearance. If they beat us, we will then retreat with our father.

"At the Battle of the Rapids last war, the Americans certainly defeated us. And when we returned to our father's fort at that place, the gates were shut against us. We were afraid that it would now be the case but, instead of that, we now see our British father preparing to march out of his garrison."

Tecumseh's words lost their harshness and became an entreaty: "Father, you have got the arms and ammunition which our great father sent to his children. If you have an idea of going away, give them to us and you may go and welcome! For us, our lives are in the hands of the Great Spirit. We are determined to defend our lands and, if it be Her will, we wish to leave our bones upon them."

Tecumseh's speech was concluded and the council broke up, and Proctor was suddenly very glad that he had told Matthew Elliott to invite Tecumseh to a private council after this one. Had that not been the case, he was convinced that he would have been killed where he stood and all his guards and officers with him. As Tecumseh finished speaking the Indians erupted in a frenzied chorus of hoots and screeches, many raising tomahawks or knives or war clubs and brandishing them until Elliott stood high and in stentorian voice ordered them to put away their weapons and behave. They did so, but even then the actions of the Indians, the looks they gave him, the way they continued fingering their belt weapons and the gestures they made with their hands all signified clearly to Proctor that without the staying hand of Tecumseh, now raised in his protection, nothing could have prevented their rage from erupting into mayhem.

Surrounded by the guards and officers, Proctor, Tecumseh, and Elliott left the council and rode in strained silence in a carriage the short distance to Fort Malden. There, instructing the officers and guards who had accompanied them on horseback to remain outside, Proctor led Tecumseh and Elliott into his private office and closed the door. He offered Tecumseh a seat but the Indian shook his head and responded with a question.

"What has happened to our one-armed chief and his ships? *Give me the truth!*"

Proctor blanched and locked his hands behind his back so their trembling would not be seen. He cleared his throat, licked his lips and then told Tecumseh everything that had been withheld from him: that Commodore Barclay had been defeated in the great Battle of Lake Erie; that the entire British fleet on those waters had been captured by the Americans; that Commodore Perry was presently completing the repairs necessary on those ships and his own; that General Harrison, with his army, grown now to near eight thousand men, was assembled on the shore and ready to board those ships, as soon as they were ready, and be transported here to attack Amherstburg and Fort Malden and continue his invasion of Canada from this point.

Now Tecumseh stared at the British commander, forcing himself with remarkable self-control, considering the circumstances, to still the trembling of absolute fury that gripped him. He knew Proctor was very much afraid of him but he was also sure that the general was unaware of how very close he was to death at this instant.

How much he was tempted!

In one quick movement, Tecumseh knew, he could jerk out his war club and crush the skull of this miserable excuse of a human being before him and, with a continuation of the same movement, similarly knock out the brains of Matthew Elliott, standing nervously only a few feet away, for his complicity in the enormous deceit perpetrated against him and his people.

Proctor and Elliott both seemed to become aware simultaneously of the imminent danger but for once the general said the exact right thing at the exact right time. Dropping his hands to his sides he took one step closer to Tecumseh, so that now they were only an arm's length apart.

"It is in your mind to kill me," he said, amazingly calm in his delivery, "and I stand before you ready to receive the blow; but if you do so, you will be doing yourself and your people a great disservice. If you hear me out, you will better understand why I have done as I have."

Tecumseh relaxed slightly and the nod he gave was barely perceptible. "I will hear you," he said, "but first I will say what it is in my heart to say and you will listen."

Proctor nodded, again moistening his lips with the tip of his tongue. Both he and Elliott, who now moved to a nearby chair and sat down, were perspiring.

"You say," Tecumseh began, addressing his remarks to Proctor, "that Harrison is preparing to come over the lake to attack us here. Why, then, do you prepare to run before you have even seen the flash of his sword in the sunlight? It is not a good thing to run before the shadow he throws. I propose this: you stay here at the fort with your proper soldiers and prepare your defenses and stand ready to hold and fight if he should come. Give me the militia and with them and my own people, we will meet Harrison where he will no doubt try to land, four miles below Amherstburg. We will strike him before he lands and as he lands and after he lands. The Detroit River will redden with their blood. If they continue in spite of us, we will fall back and fight them foot by foot and tree by tree and Fort Malden should be maintained to the last. For the Indians, whose land this is, I say this; we will not give up the fight against Harrison and sooner or later all that will be left of us is our bones. It is better that we leave our bones in the lands of our fathers than in lands that know us not and where we are strangers." He paused, then added, "Now that you have heard me, say what it is that you have to say."

Proctor began, sometimes aided by comments from Elliott, but mostly alone. He spread out on his desk maps of their whole area that were better executed and more accurate than any Tecumseh had ever before seen. There was, he said, every likelihood that in landing his invasionary force, Harrison would come ashore not only frontally, below Amherstburg, but equally with a flanking movement somewhere between the mouth of the Detroit River and Point Pelee. At the same time, his mounted Kentuckians, of which he was known to have some four thousand, were to be sent by land around the lake to Detroit and cross there.[734] These flanking forces uniting, British and Indians alike would be boxed in with no means of escape, and that included the women and children. Once they were wiped out, Harrison would then have access to overrun all of Upper Canada virtually without opposition.

Tecumseh shook his head, unimpressed. He looked from Proctor to Elliott and back again. "I am in the company of cowards," he said, "who fear the very wind that brings scent of an enemy."[735]

Proctor refused to take umbrage. He was not finished. If, when he was, Tecumseh still cared to deem him a coward, then that was his choice. Tecumseh considered this and then nodded for him to continue.

Those things alone, Proctor went on, that he had just spoken of, would not prevent their making a brave stand and, as Tecumseh said, leaving their bones to whiten on this land. But how pointless it would be to endeavor to make such a stand when there was absolutely *no* chance of pulling victory from defeat. The American fleet was now in absolute control of Lake Erie, meaning that no shipments of supplies or provisions could be expected. At this very moment they were all but out of food of any kind, no convoys having been able to get through because of the blockade Perry had earlier set up on the lake. Their artillery was all but gone, most of it having been placed aboard the ships of Barclay's fleet and now in possession of the Americans. Even ammunition for small arms was extremely limited—enough to defend their rear as they retreated to a place more advantageous to themselves to make a stand, a place where the enemy was wholly unfamiliar with the ground, where there would be the kind of cover best suited to the Indian mode of fighting, where supplies could reach them with greater facility from the East and where Harrison's own supply lines would stretch to the breaking point.

Referring again to the map, Proctor went on. What he proposed was the abandonment of this area that was impossible for them to hold; the Indian women and children in the Amherstburg area to be sent ahead of the army's retreat to safety; the army taking what artillery remained and withdrawing in orderly fashion some sixty miles eastward, first along the southern shore of Lake St. Clair to the mouth of the Thames River, then up that river beyond the head of navigable waters and thus beyond the reach of Perry's ships; the Indians to bring up the rear and, if necessary, engaging in skirmishes as tactics of a delaying action to give the army time to find and fortify a good position and get artillery and men in place to meet Harrison in full battle, if he should be foolish enough to follow them so far.[736]

In this way, Proctor concluded, the Indians would be given an opportunity to fight Harrison with a good chance of winning which, if they did, would go a long way toward ultimately restoring to them their lost lands. Was that not more sensible than needlessly being boxed in here and giving up their lives and their land for nothing?

Grudgingly, Tecumseh had been swayed by the reasonableness of the argument. He was too much of a strategist himself not to recognize the validity of what Proctor had said. He had no qualms against leaving his bones as a final symbol of his struggle against the white encroachment, but the logic was there—why should defending Amherstburg and Fort Malden be considered the final battleground? If there was even the remotest chance of striking in a manner that might turn the tables and regain to the Indians the initiative, was it not worth that effort? Was that not what he himself had spoken for all along?

"I agree," he said at last. "For myself, I agree. Whether or not the other chiefs will do so is something only they can answer. I will council with them and present to them what you have told me. Then we will see what will be."

[September 20, 1813 — Monday]

In Tecumseh's Huron River village the council fire caused flickering shadows of the thirty-eight assembled chiefs to weave and dance on the inner walls of the large wegiwa. Here were the remaining most powerful chiefs and subchiefs of all the various tribal factions that had come here to fight under his leadership—all the Northwestern tribes and a scattering of those from much greater distances, such as the Sioux and the Iowa, the Creek and Alabama, the Chickasaw, Omaha, Caughnawaga, and Tionontati and Noquet. These thirty-eight chiefs represented the near twenty-five hundred warriors still under Tecumseh's command.

Pipes had all been smoked and for the past hour they had been listening closely as Tecumseh told them of his private visit with Henry Proctor and Matthew Elliott, relating to them practically verbatim what had been said to him and what his response had been. At last he finished describing that meeting and he regarded them in silence for a long while. None spoke, knowing he was not finished and that what he had yet to say was probably more important to them than what had already been said.

"My brothers, my friends," Tecumseh went on at last, "you have heard what was said between the English general and me. Now you must hear what is in my heart to say. Though I have told him I will follow his wishes in what lies ahead, I spoke only for myself and not for you. That is what you here must now decide and I must speak the truth to you as I see it in my heart and in my mind.

"My brothers, my friends, I have long said that so long as one of you has the mind to continue this struggle, that I would not leave you. That was my word to you and I will honor that word. My home is on the battlefield and I have no fear of death. Yet, I would here and now dissuade you from continuing this struggle. I see ahead no glory, no victory, only pain and suffering, despair and ultimate defeat. What was once our dream to do and what we might once have done is now no longer possible to us. I have seen it! We are at last finished and must soon, like the leaves of this season, blow away and scatter before the powerful wind of the Americans. I now relieve you of your vows and promises and advise you to take your warriors and go home while there is yet time."

One by one, throughout the night, the chiefs rose and spoke in response. Many remained incensed at the deception Proctor had perpetrated upon them and were primed to abandon him anyway, the words of Tecumseh adding only impetus to their inclinations. More than half soberly accepted the relief Tecumseh offered and said they would collect their warriors in the morning and head back to their own territories, their own tribes, their villages, their homes and their families. Most significant among these was Main Poche who, always the realist, recognized the truth in what Tecumseh had said and the futility of continuing the struggle at this point. Walk in the Water, who had vacillated between the British and the Americans all through the war thus far, made his final choice now and said he would leave.[737]

There were a number, however, who remained adamant for continuing the struggle. Among these were the chiefs of the Sioux and Chippewa in particular, who spoke at length and were strong in their desire to honor their word that they had given to their British father and said that they would remain and fight and that they expected Tecumseh to continue to lead them as he had promised he would.

There were some who, because of the words spoken by those two, felt their own pride stung and agreed that they, too, would stay and fight. Also remaining was a faction of thirty of the young Creeks who had so believed in Tecumseh's message given in the South that they now referred to themselves as the Red Sticks, after the calendar sticks Tecumseh had presented to the tribes.

And then there were those who were the stalwarts and who remained as strongly devoted to Tecumseh himself as to the cause that bound them. Chaubenee and Stiahta were among the last to speak and their words were alike. Stiahta vowed his continued faith in Tecumseh and their cause and said he would never leave Tecumseh's side.

Chaubenee raised his great bulk from the mat upon which he sat and faced Tecumseh directly. "You are my leader, Tecumseh," he said. "Since I was very young I have believed in you and followed you and I will continue to do so now. But even more than being my leader, you are my friend. I have none closer and, for as long as one or the other of us should remain alive, I will never leave you."

[September 27, 1813 — Monday]

The lone horseman sat on his mount at the southernmost tip of Canadian land where the Detroit River flowed into the expanse of Lake Erie. It was late afternoon and Tecumseh had been here by himself for many hours and now his vigil was at last rewarded.

Far in the distance over the water to the south he saw a large number of dark specks appearing on the horizon and with surprising speed they quickly resolved themselves into ships he knew to be the American fleet under Commodore Oliver Hazard Perry—a little armada carrying on its decks, as well as in the smaller boats being escorted, the nearly eight thousand men who made up the Western army of the United States under command of Major General William Henry Harrison.[738]

They would, Tecumseh knew, find little of value or use awaiting them when they put to shore. Five days earlier, having shipped most of his remaining supplies to Sandwich, General Proctor had instructed his men to burn the shipyards at Amherstburg. The following day—September 23—he issued the same orders for the destruction of Fort Malden and several other governmental buildings and in a short time they were all being devoured by hungry flames. The remains of the British army and its Indian allies filed away to the north, to Sandwich where they camped to more fully prepare themselves for the movement ahead. Last in the file to cross the Canard River bridge were five horsemen—Tecumseh, Chaubenee, Wasegoboah, Sauganash and Stiahta—who stopped at the north end of the bridge and looked back. In the crisp early autumn air lead-colored smoke continued to boil up in a billowing plume from the burning structures three miles below and it was a melancholy sight.

"My brothers," Tecumseh said softly, "I feel well assured that we shall never return."

The camp at Sandwich had been broken at dawn this morning and they left, heading eastward. The two thousand women and children, Indians and whites alike, and other noncombatants were well in front. Proctor's neat army column, now almost devoid of supporting Canadian militia, followed and marched eastward on the road skirting the southern shore of Lake St. Clair, flanked and followed by all the warriors who remained of Tecumseh's force, slightly less than a thousand—some mounted but most on foot.

Only Tecumseh stayed behind, a sense of sadness gripping him as he watched the departure toward the Thames River. He had continued watching until they disappeared from sight in the sparse woodlands and then reined his horse around and cantered back southward to the mouth of the Detroit.

Now he was on the beach there, sometimes moving back and forth along the shoreline, other times merely sitting still on his mount and continuing to watch as the American ships and smaller boats came ever closer. There were sixteen major vessels and eighty open boats. At length he could clearly make out the fluttering of pennants, the waving of battle flags, the jagged scars of the recent Battle of Lake Erie and even the figures of men on deck observing him through telescopes.

When at last he was satisfied with his assessment of their numbers and strength he reined his horse around and, in a proud and unhurried manner, trotted away to the north to overtake his retreating fellows.[739]

[October 4, 1813 — Monday]

Tecumseh stood up and instantly the circle of eleven intimates who sat on logs drawn up around the campfire close to him on the bank of the Thames broke off their conversations and came to a respectful silence, their eyes on him. The silence stretched out, but the fact that he did not speak immediately did not surprise them. He often paused before letting the words leave his tongue and, somehow, it always seemed that the longer the pause, the more significant the words that eventually came.

A brief burst of distant laughter reached them from the main Indian encampment, but they paid no attention to it, continuing to watch their leader closely. Tecumseh looked to his left first and then let his own gaze move slowly across them, touching and briefly stopping on each man, imparting something of himself in each meeting of eyes. Here was his good friend Stiahta—Roundhead—the rock of a man who had so long supported him in every way, even relinquishing his role as Wyandot war chief to remain faithful.[740] Beside Stiahta sat the powerful Potawatomi Black Partridge—Mkedepoke—who had been so instrumental in the taking of Chicago. Next was Tecumseh's trusted lieutenant, advisor and confidant, Sauganash, and there, beside him, the squat, ugly Black Hawk—Makataimeshekiakiak—of the Sacs, the war chief's plucked head glistening baldly in the firelight. Sitting very erectly to his left was the headstrong and short-tempered Winnebago war chief, Carrymaunee, and then Waubansee, another war chief of the Potawatomi. Here sat his oldest friend and former husband of his sister, Wasegoboah, staunch and faithful as always.[741] Next was his Chippewa companion, the war chief Ooshawanoo, with his younger brother, Little Pine, beside him. There was Naiwash, the dependable but always surly Ottawa chief, and, finally, to Tecumseh's right, his closest and dearest friend for so many years, Chaubenee, of the Potawatomi.

Tecumseh turned his gaze now to the fire. He looked into it for a few seconds and continued looking at it as he began to speak, his voice so low at first that several leaned forward to better hear him.

"My brothers, my dear friends, hear me well. Tomorrow we go into our final battle with the Americans. In this battle I will be killed."

There was a sharp intake of breaths and consternation reflected in the faces of everyone present. All began talking at once and Tecumseh did not stop them, considering instead the matters that had occurred to bring them to this time and place.

Though Tecumseh had been last to leave the area of Amherstburg, it had not taken him long to overtake the retreating Proctor. Shortly after that they had reached the mouth of the Thames and began following it upstream. Tecumseh had been uncharacteristically impatient in his desire to find a suitable place to make their stand. Time after time as they passed locations that would afford them certain advantages, Tecumseh pointed them out to the British general and they discussed them, but Proctor always found something he did not like and they moved on. Finally, after two days and half a dozen such stops they came, on October 3, to Dalson's Farm, a place on the south bank of the Thames where a substantial fordable tributary called McGregor's Creek emptied into the larger river and there was a large mill nearby. This time when Tecumseh suggested it as a proper place to fight, Proctor agreed.

"It is a good place," Tecumseh commented to Matthew Elliott, pleased that a decision had at last been made. "When I look at these two streams they remind me of the place where the Tippecanoe enters the Wabash in our home country."

After a short while, however, Proctor, out of sight of the Indians, reconsidered and let his fears get the best of him. Without consulting Tecumseh, he put his army in motion again. When, late in the day, Tecumseh, accompanied by some of his warriors and Elliott, went to discuss strategy with him, he found only a few pieces of abandoned artillery that had been deliberately rendered useless and some discarded baggage. His fury was ignited.

"What," he asked Elliott harshly, "is taking this other man away?"

Elliott knew the answer, as did Tecumseh—simple fear—but the agent simply shrugged and said, "I don't know."

Word began circulating among the Indians that Proctor had abandoned them and Tenskwatawa, who had been traveling ahead with some of the noncombatants, returned at this juncture, saying Proctor was obviously fleeing and adding meaningfully, "I would like to strip him of his uniform."

Some of the Indians began seriously discussing overtaking Proctor and killing him and they even threw such baleful looks at Elliott that the agent became decidedly fearful for his own life. He at once sent word to the retreating army that the wrath of the Indians would soon become uncontrollable, with drastic results for the British, if the Indians were not provided with some explanation for the continued retreat. As a final line in his message, Elliott wrote: *"I will not, by God, sacrifice myself!"*

Thoroughly disgusted now and hungering for the action long denied him, Tecumseh sent the majority of his Indians ahead with instructions to cross the Thames to the north bank on the trail of the army and after a mile or so make a camp, where he and those who now remained with him would join them after darkness had fallen. He had decided to stay here south of the Thames and on the east side of McGregor's Creek with about two hundred of his warriors for a preliminary skirmish with the enemy. Matthew Elliott stayed with them. The bridge they had crossed over McGregor's Creek was then burned to impede the pursuing army's progress and they took position hidden in the brush. They hadn't long to wait.[742] The vanguard of Harrison's army appeared—a thousand mounted Kentuckians—and, finding the bridge destroyed, started to ford the creek but the fire from the hidden Indians broke out and became so hot that they had to withdraw to cover on their side. The fight lasted two hours, until nightfall made it too dark to continue the contest, but casualties were very light on both sides. Two of the Indians were killed in the fight and a small number wounded, including Tecumseh, whose left arm close to the shoulder had been creased by a bullet.[743]

Tecumseh had continued to hold his Indians on the ground until ten small artillery pieces were brought up and then he ordered his party to follow him to the camp that had been set up along the Thames by the other warriors. During the course of this movement news was brought that Proctor had finally stopped near a Delaware Moravian Indian town—the same Moravian Indians who so many years ago had fled Ohio following the Gnadenhutten Massacre. The news came a bit late; the persistent retreating of the British and the swift pursuit of the Americans had demoralized many of the Indians and during this interval quite a number more abandoned Tecumseh, including the Sioux and many of the Chippewas who had been so adamant about Tecumseh's remaining with them to lead them in the fight.

In the morning—October 4—advance troops from Harrison were again closing on them and some minor instances of firing occurred. Tecumseh broke camp and, with the exception of a small number of warriors left to spy on Harrison's movements, put the remaining warriors of his party—now numbering only about five hundred—into movement, waiting until every man of his party was out of danger before following. Despite the anger he was showing in regard to Proctor, Tecumseh seemed actually to be rather enjoying being engaged again in serious fighting and with the knowledge that there was more to come.[744]

The Indians had set up their camp along the Thames and now, well into the night, Tecumseh had just uttered the prediction of his own death on the morrow. He continued looking into the fire until the concerned voices around him dwindled away into uneasy silence and then he finally looked up at them again.

"You are my friends, my people," he said, his voice still as low as when he made the shattering announcement a few moments ago. "I love you too well to see you sacrificed in an unequal contest from which no good can result. I would dissuade you from fighting this fight, encourage you to leave now, this night, for there is no victory ahead, only sorrow. Yet, time after time, even until tonight, you have made known to me that it is your desire to fight the Americans here and so I am willing to go with my people and be guided by their wishes."

Tecumseh then began to remove every sign of rank that he wore: a large medal bearing the likeness of King George III, a pair of bracelets, a necklace of downcurved bear claws separated by silver cylinders and, finally, even his two-feathered headband. These he set to one side where his personal weapons were collected beside his blanket and mat. There, one by one he took up the weapons that he had previously laid out: the fine sword that had been presented to him by General Brock on that officer's departure from Amherstburg for Niagara, the tomahawk that Chiksika had so long ago given him, the pair of Mortimer pistols given to him by Blue Jacket, the fine flintlock rifle that had been given to him by John Kinzie before the Battle of Fallen Timbers.

He passed them out in turn, first shaking the man's hand and then giving him the item he wished him to have—the sword to Chaubenee, telling him with a faint smile, "Wield it well; it brings death to enemies!"; the tomahawk to Black Hawk; one of the pistols to Sauganash, the other to Stiahta; finally, the rifle to Wasegoboah.[745]

Each accepted his gift with gratitude but equally with great sorrow, for it underlined the reality of the prediction Tecumseh had just made. Turning again to Wasegoboah, who was still holding the flintlock almost reverently, Tecumseh reached out and slid the ramrod from its shaft below the barrel. He extended it to Wasegoboah who, puzzled, accepted it in his free hand.

"Wasegoboah," Tecumseh said, "if it is possible for you to do so, keep close to me when we engage in our battle tomorrow. When you see me fall, fight your way to my side and strike my body four times with this rod. If you will do so, I will then arise and, with my life renewed and charmed against further harm, will lead you to victory. But should I fall," and now his eyes left Wasegoboah and passed over the others, "and this cannot be done, then retreat at once, for further fighting will be useless."

With a sense of awe in his voice, Wasegoboah promised he would stay close and that when Tecumseh should fall, he would come to his side at once and strike the four blows as directed. Not one of the Indians present had any doubt that if Tecumseh did fall and his body was struck with the rod, he would arise as he had indicated. They had long ago learned to accept the mysterious predictions from their leader without question. After all, had they not always come true?[746]

"As for me," Tecumseh concluded, his hand upon the war club in his belt, "I keep only my war club, which my brother Chiksika gave to me when I was a boy and with which I have slain many enemies. I have but one ambition remaining—that I may meet Harrison face to face tomorrow and let the last victim of this club be him."

[October 5, 1813 — Tuesday]

Shortly after dawn Tecumseh called to his warriors to prepare to move out of their overnight camp. He wore plain, smoked buckskin trousers and a simple knee-length blouse of similar soft leather snugged at the waist with a narrow but very fine and intricately beaded belt, in which his war club was wedged. On his feet were low-cut sturdy buffalo-hide moccasins, and he also wore a narrow headband of dark red cloth knotted at the rear. There was nothing about him, except his demeanor, to suggest that he was anything but just another warrior—as he had always considered himself to be.

Within mere minutes he put his warriors into movement after the British who were waiting for him, so messengers had said last night, at the Moravian town.[747] Always cautious, Tecumseh led his men in a circuitous route, well away from the road and far out into the woods, lest the Americans had somehow slipped past them in the night and set a trap for them to fall into along the road.

When they finally reached the Moravian town late in the morning, they were astonished to find Proctor had moved out, not on another retreat but this time back along the road in the direction of the camp Tecumseh and his men had earlier vacated. Four of the five pieces of artillery left in British possession had been left under a small guard of soldiers in the Moravian town and Proctor had gone back down the road to the west, taking only one six-pounder cannon with him.[748] Following his trace downriver at top speed, they came up with the British army in about two miles and Tecumseh sought out Proctor immediately, accusing him sharply of the worst kind of cowardice.

"We have had enough of your lifting of your skirts and running away," he stormed. "I demand that you stop here and now to hold battle. If you retreat one step farther, my warriors will desert you and leave you to face Harrison by yourselves."

Proctor reluctantly agreed, terrified at the prospect of the Indians abandoning him now when Harrison was already crouching to spring at their throats, and he hurriedly told Tecumseh he had selected this as the place for the battle. Tecumseh inspected the site carefully and though it was not the sort of location he would have chosen, he was not entirely displeased with it.[749] At this point, just having the army stopping and preparing for battle was the most encouraging thing. The army had been following a carriage road and the location selected by Proctor had natural impediments on both sides. On the south side of the road they were following was the Thames River, wide and deep and not fordable anywhere nearby. On the other side of the road was a long narrow strip of swampy thicket. Beyond this was an equally narrow strip of dry woodland which again, on its north, quickly gave way to another extensive swampy ground and tangled undergrowth—a place where concerted forward progress by Harrison's army would be greatly impeded. The strip of dry woodland formed a sort of east-west isthmus and, other than the road itself, was the only place anywhere nearby that would permit reasonable passage by the pursuing Americans.

It was a place relatively well situated for a strong defensive stand; a place in which to fight . . . and perhaps to die.[750]

The British force—now a total of six hundred men, including what Canadian militia remained—took position in two lines to command the road approach, their single cannon positioned right in the middle of the road. Proctor seemed very apprehensive when word came that Harrison's force had forded the Thames and was now on the north side with them and rapidly heading their way. Tecumseh, noting the general's nervousness, said reassuringly to him, "Father, tell your men to be firm and all will be well." He then moved out and, with his five hundred warriors, took position on the dry isthmus of timberland as well as some in the marsh itself on both sides and on the higher ground to the east. They ensconced themselves well in hollows and thickets, behind logs and whole uprooted trees. Tecumseh and his closest companions took position in the heavy timber on the dry isthmus.

Everyone—British and Indians alike—knew that they were greatly outnumbered; even though Harrison had left many of his men at Detroit, at Sandwich and at various locations along the way during the pursuit, he still had at least three thousand men—a thousand of them well mounted—and two pieces of artillery in his pursuing force.

Sauganash was close beside Tecumseh and, having seen the British position, he shook his head and commented sourly that he thought they would get little help from the British in this fight. "They are just like sheep," he said, "with their wool tangled and fastened in the bushes. And as fearful. They can't fight. The Americans will brush them all away like chaff before the wind. It makes no difference, though, Tecumseh, for whatever the British do, I will stand by you to the last. I pledge myself not to run till you set me the example."

Now they waited, and in a little while a runner arrived saying the general wished to see Tecumseh. Informing his fellows that he would return quickly, Tecumseh went to the British and found Proctor well to the rear of his army with a group of his officers and Matthew Elliott. It was evident with Proctor's first words that Elliott had suggested he make some conciliatory gestures toward Tecumseh or risk losing him and his warriors.

"Tecumseh," Proctor said, "I wish you to look at how I have placed my troops and see if you think they might better be deployed."

Tecumseh inspected the two lines of troops and soon came back. "They are too thickly posted," he said. "They will be exposed to the enemy's rifle fire and their lives thrown away to no advantage. Spread them out more and especially encourage those at the big gun to have stout hearts, since the enemy will push strongest at that gun to silence it."

Before he left Proctor to return to his position, Tecumseh walked down the line of officers and shook the hand of each, murmuring words of encouragement. Then he returned to his fellows in the woods.[751] His favorites were seated on logs, awaiting the American advance and calmly smoking when Tecumseh rejoined them. Sauganash immediately came to him and spoke worriedly, addressing him with the respectful term which he often used, even though at age thirty-five he was only ten years younger than Tecumseh.

"My father, what are we to do? Shall we fight the Americans?"

Tecumseh nodded. "Yes, my son, very soon we will be in their smoke." He paused reflectively and then made a decision he knew would save his friend's life. "But right now you are wanted by the general. You are to wait with him and bring any message he has for me. Go."

Sauganash nodded and sprinted away. Tecumseh and his fellows continued smoking their pipes and chatting. Then a very strange thing occurred. Though there was no sound of a shot, all heard the buzzing whine of a bullet and Tecumseh, standing, grunted and grabbed the left side of his chest and staggered.

Instantly Chaubenee was on his feet and came to him with great concern. "Tecumseh, are you hit?"

Tecumseh took his hand away. There was no sign of any injury and in a moment he straightened, the sudden pain having entirely left him. He shook his head. "It is *Matchemeneto* and a bad sign."

The others were as shaken by the occurrence as Tecumseh and urged him at once to leave and they would remain behind and do the fighting, but again Tecumseh shook his head and said, "No, I can't think of such an act."[752]

By this time it was approaching midafternoon and the first indication Tecumseh and his Indians had that the Americans were upon them was when they heard the blare of distant tin bugles sounding the charge for the Battle of the Thames and then a lot of muted rifle fire and shouting from the direction of the British lines. It lasted for only a few minutes and the Indians immediately sprang into their positions and got ready.[753]

An eerie silence stretched out for some time after that, with occasional distant shots and barely heard voices. Then there came a sound of crashing brush closer to them to the west and rapidly coming their way. An advance force of about twenty horsemen burst into view and were met by a withering hail of fire from the Indians and several of the riders were killed. The advance was followed by a larger force of about one hundred forty more and a major engagement broke out.[754] One of those to fall, within the very first minutes, was a finely clad horseman, obviously a commander, on a white horse. Both he and his horse were severely wounded, the horse falling partially atop him.[755]

Wasegoboah, who was evidently one of those who had brought the horseman down, burst from cover and rushed toward the wounded and pinned American with tomahawk raised. Before he could strike, however, he was killed by a bullet through his brain.[756] A heated firing broke out, driving other Indians back for the moment and several soldiers came rushing to their commander's aid. The horse had taken seven bullets, the worst of which was a great wound in its side that was steadily streaming blood, but they managed to get the animal back on its feet and then placed their fallen officer on the horse and steadied him as they led it out of sight toward the rear.[757] Gradually, in a fight lasting over an hour, the Indians forced the attackers back, but then more Americans came up and the Indians began losing ground.

Throughout the fighting the voice of Tecumseh was heard shouting "Be brave! Be strong! Be brave!"

Tecumseh leaped from cover to cover, swinging his war club violently at each encounter, Chaubenee, Black Hawk, and Stiahta hanging close. At one point, growing overheated with the exertions and encumbered by the long buckskin blouse he was wearing, Tecumseh paused long enough to jerk it off and toss it aside and continue fighting bare-chested. Instants later, a gray-haired man riding a white horse charged into view and the Indians, taking him to be an officer, fired off a number of shots at him and brought him down at the feet of another soldier's horse, which shied nervously.[758]

Stiahta, in his resplendent battle costume, was one of the Indians who had fired, sprang forward and rushed up in an attempt to scalp the fallen man. The other rider, who was obviously an officer, slashed at him with his sword, but Stiahta evaded the blows and continued trying to get the scalp. At this point another soldier came running up, dropped to his knee and took aim under the belly of the officer's horse and shot Stiahta dead.[759]

At this point the whites, stopped by the heavy firing of the Indians, took cover momentarily, while the Indians also fell back slightly and crouched behind trees and logs, watching for an opportunity to shoot. Somehow during the fighting Tecumseh's war club had been wrenched from his hand and was lost and now, no longer within range of hand-to-hand combat, Tecumseh snatched up the rifle and tomahawk of a warrior who had been killed close to him. Peering out from behind a tree, Tecumseh saw a soldier scrambling along the ground toward the dead gray-haired man. He and others shot at the soldier but none of the shots found the mark. The soldier reached the body, snatched up the dead man's rifle and shot pouch and scrambled back to his own lines, shots still whizzing about him but all missing.[760] In a few minutes that same soldier, along with five or six others, began moving to their right and, in the process, spreading out and getting somewhat closer to Tecumseh's position, but still too much hidden for him to get off a decent shot. With Chaubenee following behind, Tecumseh sprang up and dodged from tree to tree until he had a reasonable opportunity at the partially exposed lead soldier, who was the one who had recovered the gun of the gray-haired man. Standing beside a huge old dead tree, he began to level his gun and at that instant another soldier slightly more to his right stepped into full view and shrieked a warning.

"Look out, King! An Indian is aiming at you!"[761]

Tecumseh spun in a quarter-turn and pointed his rifle at the fully exposed man and as he did so the soldier to his left brought up the gray-haired man's gun and fired. The range was short and the two heavy lead balls slammed into Tecumseh's left side about an inch apart and a half-inch below his left nipple and angled through his heart, slamming him motionless to the ground on his stomach.

Tecumseh was dead.

The voice of the private who shot him was raised in a triumphant cry, "I've killed one damned yaller Indian booger!"

Chaubenee and other Indians immediately fired a furious volley, forcing the whites to scramble back further into the deep cover and Chaubenee rushed to where Tecumseh lay and checked him.[762] There was no doubt whatever that he was dead and instantly Chaubenee threw back his head and shrieked the far-carrying death-cry, following it with equally booming words.

"Tecumseh is dead! Retreat! Retreat!"

The words were picked up and relayed over and over throughout the whole body of Indians. All the warriors had been instructed that if the cry was lifted that Tecumseh was dead, they were instantly to break off all fighting and, seeing to their own personal safety, to flee at top speed. They did so.[763]

Within mere minutes the Indians had melted away and a weird stillness settled over the battlefield.[764] They had lost the war. They had lost their homelands. They had lost their cause.

They had lost Tecumseh![765]

Amplification
Notes

1. Pucksinwah (pronounced Puck-SIN-wah) has also been variously spelled Pucksinwa, Puk-shinwa, Puckeshinewah, and Pooksehnwe. In nickname form, which the Shawnees frequently used, it was Pucksonotha, Paxinosa or Puckshenose. Most past and current Shawnee tribal references to him use the preferred spelling of Pucksinwah.

2. Chalahgawtha (pronounced Chuh-LAH-guh-thuh), more familiarly known at present as Chillicothe, was the capital village of the Shawnee tribe and was located on the east side of the Little Miami River just below the mouth of Massies Creek, in present Greene Co, O., at the site of present Oldtown, three miles north on U.S. 68 of the county seat of Xenia. A certain degree of confusion exists, however, as to location of the village since, at different times, there were no less than seven Shawnee villages in Ohio that went by this same name. The reason for this was that it was customary, though not a rule, for the principal town of each Shawnee sept (or clan) to be named after the sept. Sometimes such a village would have an alternate name, but would also be referred to by the sept name. The particular village in question here was actually the fifth of the seven known Ohio towns called Chalahgawtha (or Chillicothe.) These seven Chalahgaw-thas, in order of their existence, were: (1) the village also known as Sinioto or, as the English traders called it, Lower Shawnee Town, located at the mouth of the Scioto (pronounced Sy-OH-toe) River where it empties into the Ohio River on the site of the present Scioto County seat, Portsmouth; (2) on the site of present Chillicothe, seat of present Ross Co., and stretching three miles northward, all the way to the site of the present community of Hopetown; (3) near the present town of Westfall in Pickaway Co., on the southwest side of Big Darby Creek a short distance above its mouth at the Scioto River, four miles northwest from the present county seat of Circleville and extending for more than a mile along the creek; (4) on the east bank of the North Fork of Paint Creek 10 miles northwest of present Chillicothe, on the site of the present town of Frankfort; (5) the village at Oldtown, Greene Co., O., described at the beginning of this note; (6) on the Great Miami River near the site of the present Miami County seat of Piqua (although this town later, when the Chalahgawtha sept moved farther north, was taken over by the Peckuwe sept again and renamed after that sept and the name corrupted to the present Piqua); and (7) on the Maumee River in Defiance Co., about a mile upstream from the present county seat of Defiance. Kispoko Town, principal village of the Kispokotha sept of the Shawnee tribe, was at this time located on the west bank of Scioto River, just a bit over eight miles downstream from present Circleville, not far from the present village of Yellow Bud in Ross Co. At this time Kispoko Town had a population of around 900 individuals, while Chalahgawtha (No. 5) had a population of about 5,000.

3. This first night's camp was made just west of where the present counties of Fayette, Ross and Pickaway converge.

4. This second camp was located at approximately the site of the present Fayette Co. village of Eber.

5. The third camp was made on the site of the Greene Co. village of Jamestown.

6. The spring and its pond are now part of the fish hatchery system on the grounds of the District Six headquarters of the Ohio Division of Wildlife, Xenia.

7. Chiksika (pronounced Chik-SIK-uh, sometimes spelled Cheeksekah or Chiksekau) was also nicknamed Pepquannahek, meaning Gunshot. At least one account states that Chiksika was born in the village of Kishkalwa on the west side of the Susquehanna River opposite present Harrisburg. That, however, is an error. Most of the Kispokothas, including Wawwaythi, the father of Pucksinwah, had by that time left the Susquehanna Valley and founded Kispoko Town in Ohio, and that both Chiksika and their daughter, Tecumapese (also known as Menewaulakoosee), two years younger than Chiksika, were born at the same Kispoko Town where their father had been born. It should be mentioned here that at least one account (Elizabeth F. Ellet's *Pioneer Women of the West,* Porter & Coates, N.Y., 1852, Arno Press, 1972; pp. 156–157) states that at the time of the birth of Tecumseh, Pucksinwah had an eight-year-old boy named Richard Sparks living in his family whom he had captured in western Pennsylvania four years previously and had adopted into his family. Since no other account the author has encountered corroborates this and no further information about him or when and under what circumstances he left the family of Pucksinwah has been discovered, the Ellet account is considered too unsupported to include here.

8. The Shawnee River of that time is the present Cumberland River and the Cherokee villages in question were located in the vicinity of present Nashville, Tenn.

9. Methotasa (pronounced Meth-oh-TAH-suh and also appearing in some accounts as Methotase, Methoataske or Methoatase) was a Cherokee, which is in variance to the author's statement in his earlier work, *The Frontiersmen* (Little, Brown, 1967; Bantam, 1970), that she was a full-blooded Shawnee. There was some hint of either Creek or Cherokee lineage in the initial research, but at that time it could not be substantiated and the weight of evidence seemed to favor strictly Shawnee lineage. However, in the continued research over more than a quarter-century, data has been unearthed that Methotasa was, indisputably, Cherokee, and captured in the circumstances portrayed in this present work. The identity of her parents, however, remains a mystery, although it is possible that her father was one of those slain by the attacking Shawnee war party.

10. Piqua Town was located on the Mad River of Ohio, about five miles west of present Springfield in Clark Co., O., at the site of present George Rogers Clark State Park.

11. These plains, essentially oval in shape and comprised at that time of thick buffalo grass growing on unusually rich soil, have their southern extremity at the Scioto River where it is crossed by the Ross-Pickaway county line, several miles north of present Chillicothe, O., and extend in a swath averaging some 3 miles wide in a northeastward direction some 7.5 miles to about 2 miles due east of Circleville. They have come to be known as the Pickaway Plains; they and Pickaway County being named after the Peckuwe sept of the Shawnee tribe.

12. The Lenni Lenape, meaning The People, were subsequently renamed by the English who called them the Delawares after the river along which they resided, which itself had been named after their colonial Virginia Gov. Baron Thomas West, known as the third Lord De la Warr or, less formally, simply Lord Delaware. The Twightwees became much more familiar as the Miami Indians, although the name they called themselves (and as they were referred to by the earliest French, Spanish, and English explorers and traders) was Twightwee, an onomatopoeic word for the cry of the sandhill crane.

13. The Hurons at this time numbered over 30,000 individuals, which was about twice as many as the constituent five tribes of the Iroquois League, and occupied the area of western Lake Ontario, the eastern end and southern shores of Lake Erie, the entire Niagara River region, northwestern Pennsylvania, northern Ohio, and southeastern Michigan.

14. The Delawares at this time numbered about 10,000 individuals and had their principal village near the site of present Germantown, close to Philadelphia, Pa., as well as numerous others in the Susquehanna, Lehigh, Schuylkill, Hudson, Wyoming, and Delaware valleys, and in present Delaware, New Jersey, Manhattan Island, and Ohio. Their principal chief was Tamanend, who was more familiarly called Tammany and from whom derives Tammany Hall.

15. Opeththa is often spelled Opessa in the early documents. He was about thirty-two years old at the time he led his followers to the Illinois River.

16. More often than not the accounts of the friction between the Shawnees and the Southern tribes state that the Shawnees were driven out of the territory by those tribes, just as similar accounts state that the Shawnees were driven out of Pennsylvania by the Iroquois. These statements, normally written from information received by the tribes opposing the Shawnees who wished to present themselves in a favorable light, appear to be gross exaggerations or outright falsehoods. So far as the author has been able to ascertain, there was never a single case where any opposing faction actually *drove* the Shawnees out of a region. That the Shawnees were sometimes requested to leave there is no doubt, and most often they did so, but only at their own leisure and convenience, never because force was brought to bear, never in haste and never because they were being pursued.

17. Greater details of the pressures brought to bear on the Delawares by both the Iroquois League and the British can be found in the author's *Wilderness Empire* (Little, Brown, 1969; Bantam, 1971).

18. Logstown—so called by the whites after the large number of permanent log cabins, rather than temporary wegiwas the Indians had built—was situated on the site of present West Bridgewater in Beaver Co., Pa. While it was initially established by the Peckuwe sept of the Shawnees, after several years it became a village made up largely of Delawares. Some time after that it became a Mingo town, its population then consisting largely of tribal breakaway groups of Shawnees, Senecas, Delawares, Cayugas, and smaller numbers of Hurons, Mohegans, and Mohawks, plus a fair number of traders. Logstown was known by a variety of names over the years, including Peckuwe Town, Mingo Town, Shinga's Town, Shingo's Town, Beaver Town, and Shenango. At the time that Opeththa addressed the council of chiefs here, the village was called Peckuwe Town and comprised of 74 cabins and at least three trading posts.

19. Pickawillany, the principal village of the Miami tribe at that juncture, was located on the banks of the Great Miami River on the site of the present city of Piqua, Miami Co., O.

20. Little is recorded about the life of the father of Pucksinwah, Wawwaythi, except that he was about thirty years old at the time of Pucksinwah's birth and that he was also known by the names of Lawpkaway, Loyparcowah, and Opeththa's son. No information has been discovered relative to the identity of his wife, Pucksinwah's mother.

21. Shawnee Town was located on the Susquehanna River some sixty miles above where the West Branch of the Susquehanna emptied into the main river. It was situated on the north bank of the river at this point, five miles downstream from present Wilkes-Barre, on the site of the present town of Plymouth, Luzern Co., Pa.

22. Kishkalwa was located at the mouth of Conodoguinet Creek opposite present Harrisburg and near present West Fairview, Cumberland Co. Tioga was located at the mouth of the Tioga River where it enters the Susquehanna about five miles south of the New York border, near the present city of Sayre in Bradford Co., Pa. Otsiningo was located on the Susquehanna at the mouth of the Chenango River at the site of present Binghamton in Broome Co., N.Y.

23. In 1746 it was reported to the governor of New France, the Marquis de La Galissoniere, that 300 or more English traders were crossing the Alleghenies and penetrating the vast region under French control, with some of these traders going as far to the west as to trade with the Osages in the Missouri country west of the Mississippi, and active consideration was given as to what measures could be employed to remove them.

24. The trading post erected by Findley was situated on the site of the present city of Lexington in Fayette Co., Ky. This was the first structure ever built by whites in Kentucky. There is a tradition, probably apocryphal, that the first trade goods he brought were packed in hay for protection and he threw this hay away as he unwrapped the goods at his post. The hay was in seed and these seeds took root and grew and, so the tradition claims, this was the start of the bluegrass of Kentucky.

25. The French fur post at the village of Taranta, when taken over by the British in 1760, was renamed York. It was on the site of the present city of Toronto.

26. In 1742 John Fraser (sometimes erroneously spelled Frazier) crossed the Alleghenies and settled not far from present Pittsburgh on the Monongahela River at the site of the present city of Braddock, Allegheny Co. In so doing he became the first permanent white settler west of the Alleghenies. He was only a vanguard. In 1748 the Ohio Company, organized by wealthy planters in Virginia and Maryland, with Thomas Lee (president of the Virginia Council and acting governor of the Dominion of Virginia) as its president, received from King George II a grant of 500,000 acres in Virginia *west of the Alleghenies* and thereby opening the gates to settlement of Indian territory. Lee at this time somewhat revises the already expansive area claimed by Virginia with his proclamation that the Virginia boundaries are now "the Atlantic on the east, North Carolina on the south, the Potomac on the north, and the Great South Sea (Pacific Ocean) on the west, including California" (since California at this time is thought to be an island). At once they sent out the experienced frontiersman Christopher Gist to make a survey down the Ohio River as far as the Falls (adjacent to present Louisville). Simultaneously they sent another distinguished frontiersman, Thomas Cresap, with Delaware Chief Nemacolin to chart out a road from the eastern Pennsylvania settlements, over the mountains and all the way to the lands claimed by the Ohio Company, this road to be called the Nemacolin Trail. Cresap had arrived in Maryland from England in 1717 and had soon become very prominent on the Appalachian border. In 1734 he served as a captain in the Maryland Militia and this military title stuck with him the remainder of his life. Lee also authorized a party under Dr. James Walker and John Lewis, who represented the Loyal Company, to survey an additional 800,000 acres beyond the southwestern Alleghenies. In doing so, Walker discovered a large natural gap in the mountains providing easy access to the Kentucky wilderness, and the Shawnee River. He promptly named them both after the current prime minister of England, the Duke of Cumberland—hence, Cumberland Gap and the Cumberland River.

27. Chief Unemakemi, powerful principal chief of the Miamis and all the subtribes of the Miami confederation, was known to the French traders as Demoiselle, meaning Damselfly, and to the English traders as Old Britain.

28. Full details of the death of Unemakemi and destruction of Pickawillany can be found in the author's *Wilderness Empire* (Little, Brown, 1969; Bantam, 1971).

29. Kekionga, the new capital of the Miami tribe and its confederation, was located in the center of the present city of Ft. Wayne, in Allen Co., Ind. The Maumee River was, for a considerable while, called the Omee by the Indians of the area. It empties into Lake Erie at the site of present Toledo, Ohio. White settlers often called the Maumee River the Miami of the Lake, thus distinguishing it from the other two Miami Rivers, the Great Miami and the Little Miami, which flow southward and empty into the Ohio River on either side of present Cincinnati, Hamilton Co., O.

30. Each of the five Shawnee septs or clans had a particular function to the tribe as a whole. The Chalahgawtha and Thawegila septs were basically in charge of political matters that affected the tribe as a whole, as well as with the relationships the Shawnees had with other tribes, and it was from one of these two septs that the principal leaders of the tribe were always chosen; by tradition, no leader of the other three clans was eligible to become principal chief of the tribe. In addition, it was usually from both of these septs that those who would be tribal historians were chosen and trained. Broadly speaking, the Thawegilas were essentially the Southern Shawnees, while the Chalahgawthas were the Northern Shawnees, though there was always much intermingling between them. Variant spellings for the Thawegila sept include Sawakola, Sawokla, Sawokli, Assiwakala, Swickly, and Sewickley. The Chalahgawtha sept name had the least number of variant spellings, becoming most commonly known as Chillicothe. So far as the other three septs were concerned, the Maykujays were in charge of matters pertaining to health and medicine—the doctors or medicine men of the tribe—although their duties sometimes overlapped with those of the Peckuwe sept, who were in charge of spiritual matters—the worship of Moneto, the Great Spirit, and the lesser deities or spirits in their religion and mythology. Variant spellings for the Maykujay sept include Maquck, Mequck, Muquck, Macqueechaick, Mackachak, Mecquachake, Machachach, Macqueechek, and Maykujayki. The English derivation, presently used in the area of Logan Co., O., where the sept's principal town was located, is Mac-o-chee. The Peckuwe sept was also written as Piqua and Pickaway (both of these still in use in Miami Co. and Ross Co., O.) as well as Peckuwetha, Pequea, Pechoquealin, Pecquealin, and (erroneously) Pickawillany. Finally, the Kispokotha sept was the warrior clan, largely providing the warriors and war chiefs of the nation and whose principal chief, though never eligible to become principal chief of the tribe, was next in power and prestige to the nation's principal chief. Its variant spellings included Kispougo, Kiuspocotha, Kiskapooke, Kispoke, and Kispugoki. The chief of each sept was autonomous in matters pertaining to his own sept, but under the direction of the nation's principal chief in matters pertaining to the tribe as a whole. However, except for the designation as principal chief of the nation, most of these demarcations were very flexible, as for example in later years when an adopted Maykujay brave who was named Wehyehpihehrsehnwah (pronounced WAY-yeh-PEH-air-SANE-wah)—Blue Jacket—became war chief of the entire tribe and Pucksinwah's son, Lowawluwaysica (pronounced Low-WAH-loo-WAY-sick-ah, and later known as Tenskwatawa), who was, of course, of the Kispokotha sept, became medicine man and prophet.

31. The rebuilt Sinioto (Lower Shawnee Town) was relocated from its original location, on the west side of the mouth of the Scioto, to the higher ground close to the east side of the mouth of that stream, facing onto the Ohio River on the site of the western edge of the present city of Portsmouth, Scioto Co., O.

32. This second Ohio Chalahgawtha (Chillicothe) was located on the site of the present Ross Co. city of Chillicothe and extended from the north bank of the river, about where the Bridge Street bridge is located, northward along the base of the hills (roughly following present Bridge Street, U.S. 23) to the site of the present little community of Hopewell. The larger hills just east of these foothills are the small mountains depicted on the Ohio State Seal, the largest ones being named Mount Logan, Mountain Eyes, Bunker Hill, Rocky Knob, Sand Hill, Bald Hill, and Sugarloaf. The outdoor drama *Tecumseh!*, written by the author, has been produced every summer there since 1973, under the auspices of the Scioto Society, in the expansive, 11-stage Sugarloaf Mountain Amphitheater built halfway up the south slope of Sugarloaf.

33. Ft. Presque Isle was located at the site of the present city of Erie in Erie Co., Pa. Ft. Le Boeuf, also in Erie Co., was located along present U.S. 19 just north of the present town of Waterford, at the site of the Ft. Le Boeuf Memorial. Ft. Machault (Ft. Venango) was located in Venango Co., Pa., on the site of the present city of Franklin.

34. On the site of present Pittsburgh, Allegheny Co., Pa., near the east end of the Ft. Pitt Bridge.

35. Though Contrecoeur told the Indians that the French and English were at war, and in effect they were, no formal declaration of the French and Indian War was made until May 18, 1756, when England declared against France, who responded with their own war declaration the following June 9.

36. This battle, afterwards known as Braddock's Defeat, took place along the north bank of the Monongahela in the present Pittsburgh suburb of Braddock.

37. The Battle of Lake George and Bloody Morning Scout (September 1755) as well as details of the Ft. Necessity Campaign and Braddock's Defeat and all the frontier battles and events of the French and Indian War are covered in much greater detail in *Wilderness Empire.*

38. Sir William Johnson was greatly criticized and opposed for these efforts and Benjamin Franklin was among those who suspected that the Iroquois were privately encouraging the Shawnees, Delawares and Mingoes to attack the frontiers. The irate Franklin told the Pennsylvania Assembly, "I regard the application made through Sir William Johnson to these nations to procure us peace as the most unfortunate step we ever took. During Sir William's negotiations, Pennsylvania's hands will be tied while her people are being butchered. In short, I do not believe we shall ever have a firm peace with the Indians till we have well drubbed them all."

39. Wapatomica, farthest east of the Ohio Shawnee villages, was at this time located at the confluence of the Walhonding and Tuscarawas Rivers, where they join to form the Muskingum, directly across the river from the principal Delaware village of Goschachgunk, which later became corrupted to Coshocton, with the Coshocton County seat presently located there. Later, Wapatomica was moved to the Mad River, a few miles northeast of Mackachack, which was located a mile east of present West Liberty in Logan Co., O. Though the French had destroyed both Ft. Le Boeuf and Ft. Venango when they abandoned them, installations at these locations were rebuilt by the British by this time.

40. In a letter written by Dr. G. M. Ramsey, of Mecklenburg, Knox Co., Tenn., to historian Lyman Copeland Draper in January 1848, the former wrote that he found this inscription, still legible on the beech tree and that the entire inscription measured about 15 by 20 inches. This date is some years earlier than that usually recorded as the time when Daniel Boone, then living in the Yadkin Valley of North Carolina, first started exploring the Tennessee and Kentucky areas. Ramsey reported to Draper that evidence of Boone's camp was still there nearby and was situated in the center of fine hunting grounds and that he would try to get for Draper an engraving or plate made of the inscription and would send him a copy. However, there is no evidence that he ever followed up in this project.

41. The Iroquois were angry with the British for not removing their forts, as promised, after the war with the French had ended, but the evidence suggests that the war belts carried to the western tribes by the Senecas was not a measure approved of by the Iroquois League in general and that the Senecas acted unilaterally in this measure. Kyashuta was also known as Guyashuta and Guyachiouton, while Teantoriance was also called Tahaiadoris.

42. Col. Henry Bouquet, commanding at Ft. Pitt, wrote to Amherst on June 30, 1761, that Indian relations had badly degenerated and that, with the exception of the Delawares, the behavior of the Indians was becoming intolerable, with horse theft an epidemic and soldiers and traders alike being robbed by the Indians.

43. Learning of these meetings and being warned by Sir William Johnson and George Croghan of the very real possibility of open hostilities, Amherst scoffed at the Indians being any kind of threat and issued orders that if they did commit hostilities, then they "*. . . must not only expect the severest retaliation, but the destruction of all their nations, for I am firmly resolved, whenever they give me occasion, to extirpate them root and branch.*"

44. Croghan, hearing whispers of the plan by Pontiac, immediately relayed the information to Amherst, who sneeringly discounted it, writing in return, "*I look upon the intelligence you receive of the French stirring up the western Indians of little consequence, as it is not in their power to hurt us.*"

45. The malady that caused such a multitude of Shawnee deaths in the summer and early autumn of 1762 was not positively identified but is believed to have been a particularly virulent strain of measles contracted from English traders. Disease brought by whites (who were largely immune due to centuries of exposure to them in Europe) devastated great numbers of Indians, who had no immunity at all to the variety of poxes, fevers and other viral and bacterial maladies the whites spread. In some instances whole tribes were wiped out by such scourges as measles, smallpox, cholera, influenza, mumps and whooping cough. Many Indians who survived the contagions and fled westward carried the germs with them and infected tribes that as yet had not even had any contact with the whites. A broad general estimate based on circumstantial evidence and anecdotal accounts indicates that in the century beginning in 1600, about 50 percent of the Indian population of all tribes east of the Mississippi were killed by diseases introduced by the colonists from Europe.

46. Full details of Pontiac's War, the Amherst policies and incidents that led to it, and subsequent events, are chronicled in the author's *The Conquerors* (Little, Brown, 1970; Bantam, 1981)

47. The moment that the Ft. Pitt commander, Capt. Simeon Ecuyer, learned of Amherst being recalled, he sat down and wrote to Bouquet: "What universal cries of joy and what bumpers of Madeira are drunk to his prompt departure!"

48. A great many of the colonial officials in America were now beginning to chafe at English home rule and were especially incensed over the 1763 Proclamation. Some, such as George Washington, were stripped of previous grants due to the proclamation. Washington lost the 2.5-million-acre grant he and others had received in the Ohio Valley in 1760 and he spoke for the other land speculators when he angrily wrote to one of them: "I can never look upon that proclamation in any other light (but I say this between ourselves) than as a temporary expedient to quiet the minds of the Indians." Benjamin Franklin was no less perturbed by it, considering the proclamation as nothing more than an economic maneuver to benefit a few at the expense of both the colonists and the Indians. As he stated it in his 1766 address to the British House of Commons: "The trade with the Indians, though carried on in America, is not an American interest. The people of America are chiefly farmers and planters; scarce anything that they raise or produce is an article of commerce with the Indians. The Indian trade is a British interest: it is carried on with British manufactures, for the profit of British merchants and manufacturers."

49. While many historians have tended to treat the supposed incident of this celestial phenomenon as apocryphal, Shawnee tradition is unshakably firm in fixing the date of Tecumseh's birth as coincident with the instant of the passage of a rather spectacular meteor, which appeared at the northeastern horizon and passed across the heavens in a searing greenish-white flash, to disappear below the horizon in the southwest. A close study of the available written history and folklore of adjacent tribes indicates that what appears to have been this same meteor was witnessed by such tribes as the Tadosac, the western (but not the eastern) Penobscot, the Lake St. John and Cree Indians, the westernmost Iroquois League tribes (the Seneca, Cayuga, and Onondaga, but not the far more easterly Oneida or Mohawk), the Huron and Delaware, the Miami and its eastern subtribes, but not the Weas or other more westerly ones, and not the Kickapoo or Illinois tribes. It was also seen by the Cherokee, Chickasaw, and Choctaw tribes, but not the Osage, Alabama, or Quapaw. What this indicates is that the meteor apparently first entered the atmosphere and became visible somewhere over the St. Lawrence River, probably close to its mouth, and passed southeastward in an approximate line over such modern landmarks as the cities of Quebec and Montreal, Lake Ontario, Buffalo, northeastern to southcentral Lake Erie, Cleveland, Columbus, Cincinnati, Louisville and Memphis, but evidently burned out before reaching Houston. In consultation on March 5–6, 1990, with Dr. Stephen Dick and Professor LeRoy Daggett, astronomical phenomena experts of the U.S. Naval Observatory in Washington, D.C., the author was informed that while accurate records are available for the past advent of comets and eclipses, both lunar and solar, there is no catalog of sightings of meteors and only scant cataloging of meteorites (which are meteors that strike the earth before burning out) and that the majority of meteor and meteorite reports are those that occurred in the newspapers and periodicals of the time or in the private journals, diaries and correspondence of witnesses to the events. The year of Tecumseh's birth is established by the fact that he was six years old when his father was killed at the Battle of Point Pleasant, on October 10, 1774, and 12 years old when Stephen Ruddell, just six months younger, was captured and adopted into the family of Tecumseh and who subsequently wrote much of their association and described, in the process, their closeness in age. Regarding the precise date of Tecumseh's birth, that of March 9 is admittedly open to question and should not be accepted as absolute. However, it is not a date merely selected at random but, rather, based on a comment made to the author in personal conversation with the late Arthur Rollett, then principal chief of the Shawnees, in which he stated that tribal tradition holds that Tecumseh was born the ninth day following the Hunger Moon (February). This would, therefore, strongly suggest (though by no means prove) that both the birth of Tecumseh and the passage of the meteor occurred on the night of March 9, 1768.

50. The *unsoma,* explained simplistically, is a sort of good luck symbol by which the individual is guided and blessed throughout his or her life. More definitively explained, it is a sort of intramural social symbol within the tribe only. By Shawnee traditional belief, the *unsoma* is the good genius of an attendant spirit, which is animal in form, but which may be represented by some other significant sign—as in the case of the meteor of Tecumseh's birth, which is traditionally the panther. This *unsoma* is represented, in one way or another, in the name ultimately given to the child. There are six basic divisions of *unsoma,* which are: 1. The *Msaywaywilanoi,* meaning the horse-man, but the group comprised of all animals with hooves; 2. The *Patahginaythilani,* meaning the rabbit-man, comprised of rabbits, hares, squirrels, mice, chipmunks, and similar animals; 3. The *Kahgilaywilani,* meaning the turtle-man, comprised of all forms of turtles and tortoises and sometimes lizards, snakes, frogs, toads, and allied creatures; 4. The *Palawilani,* meaning the bird-man, and comprised of all feathered creatures; 5. The *Theypodewilani,* meaning the bear-man, and comprised of all animals with oblong feet, such as bears, raccoons, opossums, skunks, mink, otters, and other such creatures; 6. The *Patakuthidaywilani,* meaning cat-man, and including all round-footed animals such as any members of the cat or dog families or other round-footed species. This *unsoma* was Tecumseh's, and also Tecumapese's, since it included the panther, also known as cougar, puma, or mountain lion. Once an *unsoma* is established for an infant, it is then the child's obligation, according to Shawnee custom, throughout the remainder of his life, to defend this good-luck genius against any and all disparagement occurring in social banter by those belonging to other *unsoma* divisions, and equally to defend all other persons belonging to the same *unsoma* as his own classification from such disparagement. It becomes a matter of considerable amusement and social sparring during visits among the Shawnees to engage in defaming one another's *unsoma* while, at the same time, protecting their own. It is most often engaged in during times of pleasant relaxation, as at mealtimes or when groups are gathered about the evening fires for the telling of stories, exploits, or news. This business of attacking another's *unsoma* is always done in a sense of friendly jibing and to be retaliated with similar repartee. The jibes must be taken with good composure and given with the highest degree of humor possible, the retorts to such jibing must be similarly in a humorous vein, and at no time are the remarks to be taken or given as an actual offense. But apart from the joviality, the *unsoma* is very seriously taken by the individual as his good luck symbol for the rest of his life and anything in his vicinity that affects such a symbol advantageously or adversely is taken as a premonitory as to what the individual's own lot will be in the events that immediately follow. Thus, if before a skirmish or battle, a hawk is seen to capture and kill a rabbit, then the individual with the bird-man *unsoma* can look forward to good luck, and the one with the rabbit-man *unsoma* can expect ill fortune, in the struggle to follow.

51. Tecumseh's name has variously been spelled Tekumfi, Tikumfa, Tecumtha, Tikomfi, and Tekamthi, but the most commonly accepted form is Tecumseh. It should also be noted here that Elizabeth Ellet, in *Pioneer Women of the West,* states on pp. 156–157 that a four-year-old boy named Richard Sparks was captured by the Shawnees in Kentucky in 1764 and adopted into the Pucksinwah family, where he was still living and age eight at the time of the birth of Tecumseh, but without further mention of him after this time. No other source examined by the author makes any mention of this and the authenticity of the report is in doubt, especially since there were no white settlers in the Kentucky area in 1764 and, in fact, only one or two very daring white frontiersmen had ventured into that area prior to 1771. Undoubtedly such a boy of this name could have been captured on Shawnee forays in Pennsylvania or Virginia, but without further substantive source material, the author is inclined to consider the report as being in error.

52. *Msi-qua-mi-qui* is pronounced em-SEE-kaa-MEE-kwee. This council house at the Chalah-gawtha on the Little Miami River was, so far as can be determined, the largest such structure the Shawnees had ever erected in any of their villages.

53. *Kinnikinnick* (pronounced KIN–ny–kin–NICK) was a pungent blend of specially dried leaves, the blend often becoming very individualistic, but the principal ingredients being leaves of the red willow (osier) and sumac and often with the addition of dried bearberry and shredded dogwood bark. With the advent of greater white contact and Indian trade, ordinary smoking tobacco from the plant called *tabac,* which grew abundantly in the wild from the Kan-tuck-kee region southward, was often mixed with the blend because of its constant and slow-burning attributes. The fragrance was strong but not unpleasant. Occasionally, for ritualistic purposes, especially among the tribal medicine men and seers, small amounts of crushed dried marijuana were added, but it was not a constituent of the normal *kinnikinnick* mixure. Marijuana at this time was very abundant as a wild plant throughout the present Midwest. So far as the author's research has determined, marijuana had never been grown by the Indians as a crop, though *tabac* (tobacco) was, especially among the Cherokees, Creeks, and Alabamas.

54. The hardened red clay of which the bowl and part of the stem of the *calumet* was carved was of a material obtained in trade by the Shawnees from the tribes of the Ouisconsing (Wisconsin) country, primarily the Winnebagoes and Menominees. This clay was a fine-grained, compact, partially metamorphosed material commonly called pipestone or catlinite today. It was quarried by the Indians from 16-inch beds occurring in only two known locations then, beneath heavy deposits of quartzite rock, which had to be pried away to expose the clay. When first removed, usually cut out in rectangular blocks about four inches square and a foot and a half in length, the red clay was reasonably malleable and could easily be carved with steel blades into figures and patterns adorning the bowl. Much was carved immediately but often the purchasing tribes wished to have clean material to carve themselves, so the blocks were packed inside cloth packages kept moist to prevent drying and traded to other tribes as raw material. Pipes smoked by the general assemblage were normally noncarved (or lightly carved) bowls of the dried and hardened red clay. The main ceremonial pipes, however, were very intricately carved, not only on the bowls but sometimes on the stem section as well and were heat treated by continually passing the fashioned bowl slowly through a living flame (but not holding it in the flame for any lengthy period) until it had thoroughly dried and cured to a very hard consistency and brick-red color. Such *calumets* were very valuable and highly prized by the tribes who owned them and were painstakingly protected. Most ordinary ceremonial pipestone pipes, when fitted with hollowed stems of carved hickory, were about two feet in length. The larger principal ritual pipes were usually about three feet long.

55. Pronunciation of the names of these ten foremost chiefs of the Shawnees is as follows: Hokolesqua is Ho-ko-LESS-kwa.(In some accounts he is also called Keightughgua, pronounced kay-TUH-gwa.) Pucksinwah is Puck-SIN-wah. Kikusgowlowa is KEE-cuss-GOW-low-wah. Moluntha is Moe-LUN-tha. Wesecahnay is Wes-see-CAH-nay. Chiuxca is Chee-UX-cah. Penegashega is Pen-nee-gah-SHEE-gah. Shemeneto is She-mee-NEE-too. Plukkemehnotee is PLUCK-kee-mee-NO-tee. Chiungalla is Chee-un-GAH-lah.

56. The grizzly bear claw necklace was perhaps the foremost symbol of any warrior's prowess and, as such, was the most prized ornamentation. It could neither be traded for nor purchased and could be obtained in only two ways—both extremely dangerous. Such claw necklaces normally came in 20-claw or 40-claw versions and were made of the enormous yellow-striped claws of the grizzly bear—20 claws to one bear—and were far more than merely beautiful and impressive ornamentation. The first of the two ways of procuring such a necklace was for the warrior to journey very far to the western mountains, through extremely dangerous enemy Indian territory, and there to track down and kill one or two grizzlies—usually with only spear and knife—and then return home with the claws to be fashioned into a necklace. The second means was equally dangerous. This entailed long periods of spying on the village of an enemy tribe—usually Arapahoes, Crows, Blackfeet, Cheyennes, Rees, or Sioux—until such vigilance was rewarded by sight of a warrior or chief wearing such a necklace; then watching him until he could be confronted and fought to the death in hand-to-hand combat and the necklace taken—or be killed in the attempt. More often than not, warriors who embarked on such perilous self-imposed missions were never heard of again. Thus, the prestige imparted in the owning of such an ornamentation was extremely high.

57. Sir William Johnson, baronet, superintendent of the Northern and Western Indian Affairs, had been adopted into the Mohawk tribe and had been given the name Warraghiyagey (pronounced WAR-uh-hee-YAY-gee, the "g" in the final syllable hard).

58. The two whites alluded to by Hokolesqua were John Findley and Daniel Boone. Findley had come down the Ohio by raft and landed on the Kentucky shore, where he met with Shawnee hunting parties and, though held prisoner, was well treated by them, even to the point of traveling inland with them and hunting along the Kentucky River, before finally slipping away from them and escaping through the Cumberland Gap into the Yadkin Valley of North Carolina. That was where he encountered his companion of Braddok's Defeat, Boone. Findley told Boone of his travels through the Kentucky country and painted such glowing pictures of the fertility and beauty of the land and its abundance of game that Boone entered that country and spent an entire winter hunting a broad range of country around a camp he had established adjacent to a salt spring in the vicinity of present Prestonburg, Ky. Traces of his presence had been found by the Indians and a party of Shawnees had been sent to drive him out but found his camp deserted when they arrived only a few weeks before the council at Chalahgawtha. Boone, having safely returned home, immediately set about planning another and more extensive incursion into the Kentucky country, this time to be guided by Findley and taking four other adventurous young men along with them.

59. The "stinging flies that make sweet syrup" spoken of by Hokolesqua were honeybees, which were unknown in North America until settlers brought them over from Europe. They increased and spread rapidly and the white encroachment seemed almost to keep pace with them. Thus, it quickly became axiomatic among the tribes that when the white man's "stinging flies" were seen establishing themselves in hives built in hollow trees and rock crannies, it would not be long at all before the white men themselves showed up to claim the land. Although Croghan later denied he ever advocated that the Shawnees kill encroaching whites, no less than five Shawnee chiefs, interviewed on separate occasions, ascribed this comment to George Croghan in the Chalahgawtha Grand Council of 1768.

60. Hand-holding was a very common physical expression of affection among the Shawnees, and not limited to family members. Very often grown men who were close friends would walk hand in hand, much to the amusement of white settlers witnessing this practice for the first time.

61. Greater details of the assassination of Pontiac and the resultant annihilation of the Illinois Confederation of tribes in retribution by the combined Ottawa, Chippewa, Potawatomi, Sac, Fox, Winnebago, and Menominee tribes, along with subsequent events, are chronicled in the author's *Gateway to Empire* (Little, Brown, 1983; Bantam, 1984).

62. This party of six was led by Daniel Boone, whose imagination had been fired by further details of Kentucky he had learned from his old acquaintance John Findley. Getting Stuart's promise to guide him to the Warrior's Trail and deeper into Kentucky, Boone received financial backing from the wealthy land developer Richard Henderson, a lawyer who had just become an associate justice of the North Carolina Superior Court. Boone's party set off on May 1, 1769. In addition to Boone himself and Findley, the party included Boone's brother-in-law John Stuart, Joseph Holden, James Moncey (whose name is also spelled Mooney and Money in various accounts) and William Cool (spelled Cooley in some accounts). A second party, led by Boone's brother, Squire Boone, joined them later with more supplies. Boone was enthralled with the country and its abundant game and later reported that "buffalo were more frequent than I have seen cattle in the settlements, browsing on the leaves of cane, or cropping the herbage on those extensive plains." When the rest of his party returned to North Carolina, Boone stayed on to continue his hunting and exploration. In December he was rejoined by Stuart, his brother, Squire, and some of the others, and they decided to hunt and trap in pairs through the winter. It was on December 23 that Boone and Stuart, hunting together, were captured by the Shawnee party under Amaghqua, whom they called Captain Will, and held until December 29 before being released. The pair, having stolen their horses back from the Indians were trailed and captured again, but this time escaped and returned to their Station Creek camp, found it abandoned and their partners gone and so they made their way back to North Carolina, where they found the others of their party preparing to return and rescue them.

63. Boone, his brother, Squire, John Stuart, and a man named Alex Neely, undaunted by the previous encounters with the Shawnees, had returned to Kentucky in the spring of 1770. For a while they hunted in pairs but later Stuart and Boone, though in the same camp, decided to hunt alone. That was when the Shawnees encountered Stuart and shot him. Stuart was severely wounded, the bullet breaking his arm and severing a major artery. He took refuge from the pursuing Indians in a hollow sycamore tree and there he died from loss of blood. It was not until five years later that his bones were found by Boone in the hollow tree.

64. The *Pennsylvania Gazette* for August 9, 1770, reported that as of that date, upwards of thirty white families of settlers in the area of western Virginia had been slain by marauding Indians, primarily Shawnees.

65. This great salt lick was formed by several gigantic salt springs at the site of present Blue Licks, Ky., along the present Licking River, and was a great attraction for animals, especially ruminants, for many miles around. Because of the abundance of game in its vicinity, it was a choice hunting site for the Indians and later for the whites. As Kentucky became settled, the area adjacent to the Blue Licks evolved into a resort town called Blue Lick Springs, where thousands flocked to soak in the supposedly healing waters. This lasted until 1896 when, overnight, the springs mysteriously stopped flowing and have never flowed since. Of the once bustling village established there, very little now remains.

66. The ten-day customary waiting period for the naming of children was rooted in more than merely waiting for a sign from the Great Spirit to indicate what the offspring's name should be. Until a name was given, the Shawnee child had no identity and thus, if he died during this critical period of life, the body was merely disposed of without formal burial and there was little if any grief; it was as if the child had never existed. By the same token, if there was some factor about the infant which suggested a bad, difficult, or dependent life ahead—such as severe deformity, paralysis, seemingly incurable illness or similar malady—the infant could be dispatched by the parents during this first ten-day nonentity period without any onus of a crime having been committed.

67. Kumskaka—pronounced Come-SKAH-kuh—was also known as Elkskwatawa—pronounced Elks-kwah-TAH-wah—meaning in the first version, A Fire That Is Moved From Place To Place, and in the second version, A Cat That Flies Through The Air, and in the third version, Star Over The Great Water. These alternate names confused some historians who mistakenly believed they designated two or three different people and thus attributed Pucksinwah with having six or seven sons instead of five. No reason has been discovered by the author for the second-born infant to have been named Sauwaseekau—A Door Opened. The third born of the triplets, Lowawluwaysica (spelled Lalawethika in some sources), in his adult years (as many other Indians did when a significant event occurred in their lives) changed his name, as will be seen. Historian R. David Edmunds, in his volume entitled *Tecumseh and the Quest for Indian Leadership* (Little, Brown; Boston, 1984), states (p. 19) that a second daughter, name not provided, was born to Methoataske (Methotasa) subsequent to the birth of Tecumapese and prior to the birth of Tecumseh, and that a third daughter, named Nehaaeemo, was born about two years after Tecumseh, but Edmunds provides no specific source references for these contentions. The author has not only found no verification of these supposed younger sisters of Tecumapese being born, he has discovered no mention of them or their lives in any of the multitude of accounts examined on

Shawnee history generally and the family life of Pucksinwah and Methotasa in particular, and the author therefore fails to place credence in the claims.

68. There is some evidence that suggests Chaquiweshe (pronounced CHOCK-kee-WEE-she) might have been the son of Shemeneto—Black Snake—who was second chief of the Kispokotha sept. Chaquiweshe was also known as Peleo—The Turkey.

69. Wehyahpihehrsehnwah, meaning Blue Jacket, was actually Marmaduke Van Swearingen, who had long yearned to lead the Indian life and gladly welcomed his own capture when he was taken by the Pucksinwah hunting party on June 5, 1771, along Cherry Creek near his family's frontier residence on the site of what is now the city of Richwood in eastern Nicholas Co., almost on the border of Greenbrier Co., in West Virginia. He had been named after the blue sleeveless hunting shirt he was wearing when captured. Greater details in respect to Blue Jacket and his life with the Shawnees may be found in the author's volume entitled *The Frontiersmen* as well as in his young adult novel entitled *Blue Jacket: War Chief of the Shawnees* (Little, Brown, 1969).

70. Peter (Pierre Louis) Loramie's "store" was situated on present Loramie Creek some fifteen miles upstream from its mouth at the Great Miami, near the dam of present Lake Loramie and only a short distance eastward from the site of the present Shelby Co. town of Ft. Loramie, O. Loramie was born in Lachine, Canada, on the St. Lawrence, in March 1748.

71. Burnett's post was located in present Berrien Co., Mich., on the site of the present city of Niles. The principal villages of the Potawatomies at this time were situated on the sites of the present cities of Milwaukee in Wisconsin, St. Joseph, Niles, Three Rivers, and Kalamazoo in Michigan, Elkhart, South Bend, Mishawaka, Michigan City and Gary in Indiana, and Chicago, Des Plaines, Elgin, Aurora, Kankakee, Joliet, Morris, Ottawa, La Salle, Peru, and Peoria in Illinois.

72. The two young men, both 17 years old, who were first shot through the hips and then tortured to death in a most gruesome manner, were Henry Russell and Daniel Boone's eldest son, James. The attack occurred in the Powell Valley on the Red River in Powell Co., less than 20 miles southeast of Lexington, Ky.

73. This was Simon Kenton, who at this time was traveling under the alias of Simon Butler because he erroneously thought he had killed a rival in a fight they had in the northeastern section of present Fauquier Co., Va. Kenton and two companions, William Strader and George Yeager, had established a camp on Elk River close to its mouth—site of present Charleston, W.Va.—and were there when the Shawnees attacked them and killed George Yeager. Strader and Kenton escaped. Strader returned to the East but Kenton stayed on in the wilderness to become one of the most skilled frontiersmen in American history. Greater details of his entire life, including this incident, can be found in *The Frontiersmen*.

74. The Falls of the Ohio was a widely recognized landmark comprised of a stretch of relatively steep rapids and dangerous navigation on the Ohio River adjacent to the site of present Louisville in Jefferson Co., Ky.

75. Ft. de Chartres had been established by the French more than half a century ago, in 1722, on the east bank of the Mississippi five miles upstream from present Prairie du Rocher, Ill., just north of the mouth of the Kaskaskia River, but was formally turned over to the English by the terms of the Treaty of Paris in 1760. The French continued to occupy it, however, under Capt. Louis St. Ange de Bellerive until 1765 when he relinquished it to British Capt. James Sterling and withdrew his meager complement of troops to St. Louis. Sterling immediately renamed it Ft. Cavendish, but no one seemed to like that name and the French name for the installation continued to be used.

76. The stream that the Shawnees called Macatetheepi—meaning Gunpowder River—is the present Wheeling Creek, the mouth of which is at the site of the present city of Wheeling in Ohio Co., W.Va.

77. The gathering at the mouth of Wheeling Creek was an indirect outgrowth of the 1768 Ft. Stanwix rescission of the Royal Proclamation of 1763, removing Indian trade from governmental monopoly. It was more directly the result of a public announcement made by Virginia's governor, John Murray, Earl of Dunmore (he succeeded Virginia Gov. Berkeley in 1771), who stated that he would begin, at the mouth of Wheeling Creek on the date indicated, to issue patents for land on *both* sides of the Ohio River. The majority of the whites who showed up were not would-be settlers but rather agents of land speculators in the East, along with employees of these agents. Both George Rogers Clark and William Crawford were on hand as agents for the Ohio Land Company that had been formed by a combine of well-known and quite wealthy Virginians, including George Washington, and their instructions were to look for at least 200,000 acres of good bottom land in the Ohio Valley, which would then be platted into lots and sold to prospective settlers. One of the few on hand acting for his own individual interests was a man named Michael Cresap (son of Thomas Cresap, who had helped found the Ohio Company in 1748–49), who had earlier failed in the fur trade. Subsequent to that, in 1771, Cresap, at age 29, had made improvements in the area of Wheeling at the location called Round Bottom (but Cresap's heirs were subsequently ousted because surveys showed the land had earlier been claimed by George Washington). Now he was planning to go 150 miles downstream on the Ohio and claim a substantial parcel of land close to the mouth of the Great Kanawha River (site of present Point Pleasant, W.Va.) and there establish an important outpost settlement. Kanawha is pronounced Kuh-NAH-whuh. The Shawnee name for the river is Kanawhatheepi—Kuh-NAH-whuh-THEEE-pee.

78. The Briscoe in question was Dr. John Briscoe who, the preceding March, had established the camp on the site of present Boaz, W.Va.

79. This was the party under the command of Hancock Lee and Dr. John Wood, who had descended the Ohio in May 1773, stopped briefly at Briscoe's Camp above the mouth of the Little Kanawha, where they had been joined by Simon Kenton (alias Butler) and continued down to the mouth of the Big Sandy River, which is the dividing line between present West Virginia and Kentucky. The land they claimed and the cabins they built at that site were on the ground now occupied by the city of Catlettsburg, W.Va.

80. This surveyor, his name not recorded, managed to get back to the Wheeling area and reported to authorities there what had occurred. Some days later Dr. John Connolly, the rather despotic frontiersman whom Lord Dunmore had appointed Virginia's magistrate of western Pennsylvania, issued a public letter stating that it was not only the right but the duty of all frontiersmen and settlers in the area to take up their weapons and avenge the insults the Shawnees had given them. Connolly, who had been born at Wright's Ferry in Pennsylvania in 1743, had spent considerable time among the Indians. As a young man he was a medical officer in the Pennsylvania Militia from 1762 until 1764 and had subsequently gone to the Illinois country where he studied Indian languages in Kaskaskia for three years. In 1770 he had returned up the Ohio River to Ft. Pitt and practiced medicine in Pittsburgh until 1772, when he received a grant of Kentucky land from Lord Dunmore and subsequently became his agent in land speculation and other matters. In 1772 he had been appointed a captain in the Virginia Militia as well as magistrate for the district of West Augusta and was instrumental in causing much of the friction existing between Pennsylvanians and Virginians when he prevented Pennsylvania traders from dealing with the Indians while at the same time promoting Virginia trade with them. He also imposed a very stiff fur tax on Pittsburgh traders.

81. *Petweowas* means wolves; *sholees* means vultures.

82. The first Detroit census had been taken the preceding November by Justice of the Peace Philip Dejean and indicated the following: Male population above 10 years old, 758; Children under 10 years old, 524; Slaves, 85; Oxen, 473; Cows, 609; Heifers, 412; Sheep, 628; Hogs, 1,067; Houses, 280; Barns, 157; Acres under cultivation, 2,602.

83. Already many American colonists had come to the conclusion that a war of revolution was inevitable if their human rights were not to be entirely smothered. The collision between Bostonians and the soldiers of the king on King Street (now State Street) in Boston on March 5, 1770, seemed to be the igniting match to this pending conflagration. Matters were not helped when, on July 18, 1772, Lord Dunmore, perturbed at the growing antagonism of the colonists and their overt dissatisfaction with English rule, issued an order dissolving the right of assembly "because of its expression of revolutionary sentiment."

84. Nonhelema (pronounced NON-hel-LEE-muh), because of her great size, strength and proven fighting ability, had come to be known among the frontier whites as The Grenadier Squaw. She was the chief of her own small village which was directly across Scippo Creek from Hokolesqua's village on the Pickaway Plains. Sheshepukwawala (pronounced SHESH-ee-puck-WAHL-luh and meaning Duck Eggs) lived with her husband, Yellow Hawk—Outhowwa Shokka (pronounced ooo-THOU-wuh SHOCK-kuh)—in the residue village of what had been the second Chalahgawtha in Ohio, located on the Scioto close to the mouth of Paint Creek at the site of present Chillicothe, Ross Co., O. Most of the population had long ago moved to the present Chalahgawtha on the Little Miami River.

85. The Mingo Trail was a long-used Indian path which ran from the present town of Mingo Junction, just below Steubenville, in Jefferson Co., O., to present Cadiz, county seat of Harrison Co., near which it reached the headwaters of the Tuscarawas River, then followed that river through the sites of present Urichsville, Gnadenhutten, and Newcomerstown to the Delaware principal village of Goschachgunk, which was located on the site of the present county seat of Coshocton in the county of the same name. This was where the Walhonding and Tuscarawas rivers converge to form the Muskingum. The Shawnee village of Wapatomica was located directly across the Muskingum from Goschachgunk and a good trail led from there directly to the Pickaway Plains and the Shawnee villages at that place, which were collectively known as the Scioto villages.

86. The sweep Shemeneto's war party made on this occasion entered Kentucky at the mouth of the Kentucky River—site of present Prestonville, Carroll Co.—and followed that river upstream to the mouth of Elkhorn Creek in Franklin Co. several miles north of the present capital city of Frankfort, then up the Elkhorn to where it was crossed by the Warrior Trail in present Fayette Co. just northeast of present Lexington. Here they left the creek and followed the Warrior Trail, which is essentially the route of present U.S. 68, moving northeast to the Blue Licks on Licking River, sweeping the area in a wide radius around the salt springs, then following the Warrior Trail northeastward again until they reached and crossed the Ohio River at the site of Maysville—formerly Limestone—in present Mason Co.

87. His name is pronounced Tall-gah-YEE-tuh. Though some sources suggest he was a Seneca, he was actually a Cayuga.

88. The village of Chief Logan (Talgayeeta) was generally called Logan's Town and was located only a bit over a mile downstream from present Wellsville, Ohio, on the north bank of Yellow Creek about a half mile upstream from its mouth, where a commercial campground is presently located. Logan's father, Shikellimus (pronounced Sheh-KELL-im-muss) had himself long been very close to the whites and many years ago, well before Talgayeeta was born, when his village was on the shores of Cayuga Lake in New York, the dwelling of Shikellimus offered warmth, food, and good companionship to any who stopped by, white or red. It was in the course of his being so generous a host that Shikellimus had met James Logan, an intimate of William Penn and the founder of Philadelphia's Loganian Library. A strong friendship developed between James Logan and Shikellimus and when the wife of Shikellimus bore him a son, Talgayetta became the son's Cayuga name, but Logan (some say John Logan) was the alternate name bestowed in honor of the friend of Shikellimus. Talgayeeta grew into manhood with the same sense of generosity and hospitality his father possessed and an even greater utopian desire to see the development of lasting peace between the red and white races. As a result, his little longhouse on Yellow Creek had become famed as a safe stop for weary and hungry travelers.

89. The camp had been established close to the mouth of Pipe Creek in present Jefferson Co., O., a few hundred yards from the Ohio River and in the vicinity of the present city of Steubenville.

90. This ambush appears to have had its genesis with a proclamation made at Ft. Pitt a few weeks earlier by the megalomanic Dr. John Connolly, whom Lord Dunmore had appointed as his agent for Virginia there. Connolly, who despised the Indians, thought nothing of fabricating supposed attacks by the Indians on the frontier settlements (some such *had* occurred, of course, but not in the numbers or severity Connolly broadcast). Connolly's aim was to instigate a war with the Indians whereby they could be justifiably attacked in force and driven from their lands, which could then be claimed by Lord Dunmore and himself, along with select others, for settlement rights. At this juncture Connolly learned that a party of Shawnees had just captured several members of John Floyd's surveying team and had destroyed all their surveying equipment and then, without physically harming the surveyors, had sent them on their way with a warning never to come back. Coincidentally, at practically the same time, a war party of Cherokees had attacked a party of Pennsylvania traders on the Ohio River, killing one and wounding two others. Connolly deliberately changed these reports so as to make the party of Shawnees guilty of both incidents. He then issued his inflammatory statement encouraging parties of frontiersmen to attack and kill the Shawnees whenever and wherever encountered. This was, in essence, an unauthorized declaration of war. It caused the desired reaction among the border people, especially the ruffian type. Michael Cresap's reaction when he heard the Connolly pronouncement, only the day before the attack on Blue Jacket's little hunting party, remarked, "I am well pleased with it and will put every Indian I meet on the river to death!" The two men who came into the camp immediately after the two Indians were killed were Cresap and his companion, 21-year-old George Rogers Clark, the latter almost beside himself with rage at the killing of the two Indians, which he termed "brutal, savage, senseless killings." When Cresap's men hotly proposed the idea of going to the Yellow Creek village of Logan and killing all the Indians there, Cresap and Clark vetoed the notion, since Logan was known to them both as a staunch friend of the whites. However, a short while later they met the Jacob Greathouse party on the Ohio River, coming upstream from Briscoe's where they had met the surveying party under Capt. James Harrod, who had been sent by Lord Dunmore to complete the surveying activities in the Kan-tuck-kee country that had been begun by the Capt. Thomas Bullitt party. It was then that Cresap told the Greathouse party about the two Shawnees his men had killed and of the location of Logan's village, in no way aware of the use to which Greathouse would put the information.

91. The party of quasi-criminal frontiersmen who ambushed and killed the family of Logan (for greater details of which, see *The Frontiersmen*) was not the party led by Michael Cresap, whose party had murdered Muga and Aquewa Apetotha, although for a long while Cresap was blamed, not only by Logan but by many of the frontiersmen themselves. The word eventually got around, however, that the brutal attack had been made by a party of one Jacob Greathouse (some sources call him Michael Greathouse), elder brother of Capt. Daniel Greathouse who was then stationed at Ft. Pitt. Reaction among the whites to the massacre of Shikellimus, his family and other members of his party, was generally received with shock and revulsion in the East. Charles Lee decried it as "a black, impious piece of work," and Thomas Jefferson deemed it "inhuman and indecent." Even Virginia governor John Murray—Lord Dunmore—who had little feeling of compassion toward the Indians, agreed that the act was "marked with an extraordinary degree of cruelty and inhumanity." However much the authorities expressed shock and horror over the incident, no official action was ever taken to apprehend the offenders or to recompense Logan for the loss of his entire family. Capt. Michael Cresap not long after this was commissioned by the Maryland Assembly to recruit troops for the Continental Army and returned to the East for the performance of that duty. He died in New York City on October 18 (some accounts say it was October 25), 1775, at the age of 33.

92. The reaction among the settlers to these attacks was swift; most of them abandoned their places and flocked into either Ft. Pitt or the substantial settlement called Washington—on the site of the present city of that name, which is the Washington County seat. Pioneer Gilbert Simpson who, in exchange for some land on which to settle, was building a flour mill for George Washington on the Youghiogheny, wrote a letter to Washington saying, in part:

> *The country at this time is in great confusion, the Indians declaring war against us. I suppose there have been broken up and gone off at least 500 families within one week past, but I am determined to stand to the last or lose my life with what I have. There have been two or three skirmishes with whites and Indians. There have been 19 Indians killed, and one wounded—all*

> *between the Mingo Town and Pittsburgh, and I believe it has been the white people's fault altogether.*

but that figure of 19 Indians killed evidently meaning the Indians killed by both the ambush by Cresap's men and the atrocity perpetrated by the Jacob Greathouse party. Further information of the massacre by the Greathouse party was sent in another letter to Washington by his old friend, Valentine Crawford, who had settled on Jacob's Creek at this time. Valentine wrote, in part:

> *. . . and on Saturday last [April 30] about 12 o'clock, there was one Greathouse and about 20 men fell on a party of Indians at the mouth of Yellow Creek, and killed ten of them [actually thirteen] and brought away one child a prisoner, which is now at my brother William Crawford's. This alarm has made the people move from over the Monongahela, off Shirtee and Raccoon [creeks] as fast as you ever saw them move in the year 1756 or '57 in Frederick County, Virginia. There were more than one thousand people crossed the Monongahela in one day at three ferries not one mile apart.*

93. This camp was apparently made in the vicinity of the present town of Tyre near the western edge of Allegheny County.

94. A few otherwise reliable sources state that the delegation was attacked on its way home and "several Shawnee chiefs killed and scalped," but this is evidently an error of confusing the deaths of Muga and Aquewa Apetotha (the Bear, and Child in a Blanket) as being related to the delegation. Neither were chiefs, nor were they part of the delegation, and no further attack was made on Hokolesqua's party as it returned home.

95. It was at about this time that, with the assistance of an English trader, Hokolesqua wrote to Alexander McKee, absolving him and George Croghan of any blame connected with the attack on the Shawnee delegation at Ft. Pitt. He went on, in regard to the rapidly escalating encroachment of whites, to ask MeKee *"to present our good Intentions to the Governors of Virginia and Pennsylvania, and request that a stop may be put to such Doings in the Future . . . I have with great Trouble prevailed upon the foolish People among us to sit still and do no harm till we see whether it is the intention of the white people in general to fall upon us . . ."* It was just after this that Sir William Johnson, super-intendent of Indians, died at his home in the Mohawk Valley of New York while in the midst of a council with the Iroquois.

96. The fort was actually a small group of permanent buildings enclosed by a stockade that had been erected by a party under surveyor James Harrod. This was the first permanent settlement in Kentucky and was located several miles from the Kentucky River close to the east bank of Salt River, on the site now occupied by Harrodsburg in present Mercer County. Boone and Stoner, who had been sent along different routes by Lord Dunmore to warn the surveyors in Kentucky to return home, met each other there and together founded the Harrodsburg settlement. The pair immediately registered themselves as settlers there and each confirmed his claim by building a cabin. Then, heeding the warning from Lord Dunmore, the settlement was temporarily abandoned and the settlers and surveyors returned east.

97. The landing was on June 9, 1774, at the site of the present village of Powhatan Point in Belmont Co., O., occurring the day before Lord Dunmore, on behalf of the Virginia Colony, formally declared war on the Shawnees. McDonald's rank as colonel was brevet; he was actually a major.

98. The entire brief campaign of Col. Angus McDonald accomplished little of value except to expose the cowardice of the commander, who consistently traveled far in the rear and who, at the first sound of gunfire, dived behind a log and cowered there until the skirmish ended. Simon Kenton participated in this campaign, along with his new friend, Ensign Simon Girty, who slightly wounded the single injured Indian by executing a phenomenally long shot.

99. Wapatomica (which means Capital Town) was relocated in present Logan Co., O., on a slight elevation a few hundred yards west of the upper Mad River, four and a half miles southeast of the present county seat of Bellefontaine, two miles south of present Zanesfield, and six miles northeast of present West Liberty. The land where it was located was first settled by Samuel

McCulloch, earlier a Wheeling area settler, and for many years has been part of the farm owned by a family named Sidesinger. Moluntha's Village (or Moluntha's Town), also called Mackachack, was located on the north side of present Mac-o-chee Creek a mile east of the present town of West Liberty and four and a half miles south of Wapatomica.

100. Actually, only a little over eight hundred men moved out with Col. Andrew Lewis. For reasons not quite clear now, Col. Lewis had to leave three hundred men behind when the march was begun, but Lewis ordered Col. John Christie to follow him with these men, along with as many additional enlistees as he could get, and to rejoin Lewis as soon as possible. The force under Col. Lewis—none of them, including officers, having any manner of uniform (as was also the case with Lord Dunmore's wing of the army)—had a long and difficult march, laid out specifically by Lord Dunmore, over largely unmapped wilderness, moving first down the Greenbrier River to where it converged with the Bluestone River to form the New River, then down the New to its confluence with the Great Kanawha and finally down that stream to the rendezvous point at its mouth on the Ohio River at the site of the present city of Point Pleasant, in present Mason Co., W.Va. It was an extremely rigorous march that took nineteen days to complete. Considerable friction existed between Lewis, who supported the views of those calling for separation from England, and Lord Dunmore who was a king's man through and through. There were many in the Lewis wing who believed, with considerable justification, that Lord Dunmore wished to discredit Lewis and his colonial militiamen and had deliberately ordered them to follow this route in an effort to foment dissatisfaction, dissent, and desertion among his ranks. That, however, did not occur.

101. It was reported that by this time, nearly half a year after his entire family had been murdered by the Greathouse party, Talgayeeta (Chief Logan) had fulfilled his vow of taking ten white scalps for each member of the party that had been killed, and that one of these victims was allegedly the famed early frontiersman named David Duncan, who disappears from the pages of history during this period.

102. This War Trail was later used as a trace by the whites to lay out the course of the present old U.S. 35 from present Xenia, Greene Co., O., to Gallipolis, Gallia Co., O., then paralleling the Ohio River in an upstream direction for three miles to exactly opposite the mouth of the Great Kanawha and present Point Pleasant, W.Va.

103. The creek in question here is not, as some accounts contend, the present George Creek, which enters the Ohio from the north also, but which is quite small and visible from the mouth of the Kanawha. The larger creek, where Hokolesqua's force rested and crossed, is the present Campaign Creek (named after the Shawnee activity there at this time), exactly three miles above the Kanawha mouth and at the southern edge of the little village of present Addison, Ohio, and Hokolesqua's Indians took position for the river crossing on a fairly broad bottom at the mouth of Campaign Creek precisely where it is crossed by present Ohio State Route 7.

104. These two men were apparently James Robertson and a man identified only as Hickman, the latter being the one who was killed, although one account (found faulty in numerous other respects) says the second man was named Valentine Sevier and that both men fired at the Indians (not true, neither man did) and that both escaped back to the camp to give the alarm. The creek where they first discovered the Indians, often misidentified as present Oldtown Creek some two and a half miles up the Ohio from the Kanawha, was actually an arm of present Crooked Creek which empties into the Ohio two thousand yards above the mouth of the Kanawha.

105. Pvt. Robertson had run directly to the tent of Col. Andrew Lewis and reported what occurred. A general alarm was sounded and the commander's two regimental commanders—his brother, Col. Charles Lewis, and Col. William Fleming (misspelled as Flemming in some accounts)—were directed to form their companies; Charles Lewis to position his so it covered a third of the distance from the Kanawha toward the Ohio, Fleming to place his a third of the distance from the Ohio toward the Kanawha, and Andrew Lewis would take the center with his men, all three segments to advance as soon as so formed. Lewis also set a squad of men to work hastily building a breastwork of logs and dead branches in the area and to fell trees at this time for the same purpose.

106. One early decidedly romantic account states that Charles Lewis, after being mortally wounded "yet was able to walk back after receiving the wound into his own tent, where he expired. He was met on the way by the commander-in-chief, his brother, Colonel Andrew Lewis, who remarked to him, 'I expected something fatal would befall you.' To which the wounded officer calmly replied, 'It is the fate of war.' " That he would be able to walk back to his tent after such a wound, to say nothing of going out of his way to get to the middle of the line and pause for a calm, stilted, and decidedly fatalistic exchange with his brother in the midst of the first moments of a severe pitched battle is, of course, suspect to say the least. In this same vein, a monumental number of such romantic fancies surround virtually all the major events (and many minor ones) transpiring up to and through the War of 1812, all of them penned as the absolute truth, frequently as alleged eyewitness reports, but the majority false or badly distorted and thus doing considerable damage to historical verity.

107. William Fleming, 45, commanded the Botetourt Regiment in this battle. A Scot who had attended the University of Edinburgh, he had come to Virginia in 1755 and, during the French and Indian War, served as an ensign in Col. George Washington's regiment. He recovered from the wound received at Point Pleasant and in 1776 became county lieutenant of Botetourt Co., then served in the Virginia Legislature 1777–1779, was on the Virginia Council in 1780 and was acting Virginia governor for the first twelve days in June 1781.

108. Pronounced WEE-shee-cah-TOO-wee, meaning "Be strong!" One account asserts that Cornstalk made these utterances while riding a great white horse back and forth along the Indian line, but this is more romanticizing; all the horses were left on the Ohio side of the river. The same account, attributed to trader William McCulloch, states that "Cornstalk tomahawked a Mingo chief who showed signs of cowardice" and elsewhere in the same account identifies the supposedly slain Mingo as Chief Elinipsico. The author has found no reference anywhere to a chief of that name among the Mingoes and, in fact, the only Elinipsico encountered in over a quarter-century of research is Hokolesqua's own nineteen-year-old son, who was participating in this battle, his first, but was not killed, so this account is deemed spurious.

109. There is a prevailing myth concerning the death of Pucksinwah that states he did not die at the Battle of Point Pleasant at all, but was murdered by a party of white hunters from Kentucky in the region of the Shawnee village called Piqua Town on the Mad River (just west of present Springfield, Ohio; see Note 10) and that each year on the anniversary of his death, Methotasa and Tecumseh would make a pilgrimage to his grave. All that is pure fiction.

110. The approaching troops were the reinforcement from Ft. Union under Col. John Christie, who was bringing not only the three hundred militia troops he had been left with there, but an additional two hundred he had managed to gather in the interval following the army's departure three weeks earlier. They arrived at Point Pleasant about 5 P.M. (although some reports say 8 P.M.).

111. Because of the withdrawal of the Indians, leaving the whites in possession of the battleground, most historians record this Battle of Point Pleasant as a victory for Col. Lewis's force. If so, it was pyrrhic victory at best. A few contend that the battle resulted in a draw, with neither side clearly victorious. Yet, in the final analysis, statistics alone seem to indicate that the Indians emerged the victors. Among the whites, a total of 75 men had been killed, including half their commissioned officers, and another 140 injured, with 88 of these beyond any futher fighting capabilities in the campaign. Many early accounts give the Indian dead as numbering "around three hundred," attributing this figure to that same trader, William McCulloch, who, it appears, related many fictions as truths. In actuality, the Indians had lost 22 men—14 killed on the battlefield and 8 others who died of their wounds over the next several days. Their total in non-mortally wounded was a mere 18. Thus, the day had ended with a total of 215 casualties for the whites and 40 for the Indians—a ratio of over five to one.

112. It has been stated in some accounts that the Shawnee dead, including Pucksinwah, were buried on the north side of the Ohio River immediately after the crossing. That is not true.

Shawnee dead were brought home for burial if at all possible; only when circumstances made it impossible to do so would they be buried close to where they fell, most often only temporarily and later to be disinterred and brought back for more formal burial in the Shawnee burial grounds.

113. Though several Indians spoke at the treaty talks, Hokolesqua (Cornstalk) was principal speaker and made a very favorable impression on those who heard him, exemplified in a letter subsequently written by Col. John Wilson, who said:

> . . . *When Cornstalk arose to speak he was in no wise confused or daunted, but spoke in a distinct and audible voice, without stammering or repetition, and with peculiar emphasis. His looks, while addressing Dunmore, were truly grand and majestic, yet graceful and attractive. I have heard the finest orators in Virginia—Patrick Henry and Richard Henry Lee—but never have I heard one whose powers of delivery surpassed those of Cornstalk.*

Other details of Dunmore's War, from the instigation of the affair to the Camp Charlotte Treaty may be found in the author's *The Frontiersmen*. Lord Dunmore exacted promises from the eighteen Shawnees who attended the peace talks that not only would they remain on their own side of the river so long as the whites did the same but that they would also cease molesting boats of the whites that were traveling on the Ohio River, that they would return the horses and goods they had taken from the white settlements as well as the white prisoners that they had and, finally, that the Shawnees would no longer hunt in the Kan-tuck-kee hunting grounds. In exchange for this, whites would be strictly forbidden to set foot on the Shawnee side of the Ohio River. Further, the Shawnees gave over to Lord Dunmore four minor chiefs who were to be hostages as insurance for the faithful perpetration of the treaty by the Shawnees (but these four, who were taken to Williamsburg, escaped the following year when the revolution broke out and returned to their people). It should be noted here that no actual documentation of the treaty itself exists today, but evidence from the letters, journals and logs of the time by those associated with it agree in substance with the provisions here outlined. Some accounts, written at the time and believed to be accurate, indicate that this was not a treaty at all but merely a provisional agreement and that a formal treaty along the same lines was to be consummated at Ft. Pitt the following spring, but that never occurred and that therefore the Camp Charlotte agreement was not binding on either side.

114. The name is pronounced SPEM-ih-cuh LAW-buh. This name has been interpreted by some as Bright Horn, but Big Horn is correct. In the early documents there are several accounts concerning the parentage of Spemica Lawba which are confusing and do not jibe with the other existing data from numerous sources. These few accounts all appear to derive from a brief comment in a letter written in September 1845 to historian Lyman Draper [see Draper Manuscripts DD-YY-1/44], in which one Robert Remick (also spelled once as Renick) states that his father, Joshua, married Tecumseh's elder sister, Tecumapese, and that Joshua Remick was the father of Spemica Lawba. No substantiation for the claim or even any kind of *post facto* supportive evidence can be located and the author strongly doubts its authenticity, considering it to be only one more of the many fabrications involving Tecumseh and his family.

115. Catfish and muskellunge in excess of one hundred pounds were very common at this time in the Ohio River and its major tributaries, and as late as 1840 a muskellunge weighing just under one hundred pounds was caught at the mouth of the Muskingum River.

116. Richard Henderson had been born in Hanover Co., Va., in 1735, but his family had moved to North Carolina when he was seven and he had been there ever since. He had studied law and was admitted to the North Carolina bar. In 1764 he had become acquainted with Daniel Boone and his imagination was fired by the stories Boone told of the vast rich Kentucky lands so plentiful with game. He immediately organized Richard Henderson and Company and then later the Louisa Company, which evolved into the Transylvania Land Company. His dealings with the Cherokees involved the sale of twenty million acres, which Henderson planned to become the fourteenth colony—perhaps even a separate country of his own named the Republic of Transylvania, in which the developers would retain large tracts for themselves and sell the rest to prospective settlers, charging a perpetual quit-rent for every acre sold and retaining special rights in the government of the region. Henderson's partners in this endeavor were David, Thomas, and

Nathaniel Hart, John Williams, James Hogg, Leonard Hendley Bullock, John Lutterell, and William Johnston. By Christmas of 1774, Henderson was publicly advertising the Kentucky lands for settlement, while Boone was spending much of his time going back and forth between Henderson and the Cherokees as negotiator. The deal was made final at Watauga (present Sycamore Shoals, near the junction of the Watauga and Holston Rivers in northeastern Tenn.) in January 1775 with 1,200 Cherokees on hand, to whom was paid $10,000 in goods and guns. Boone started laying out the Wilderness Road from North Carolina through the Cumberland Gap to the site of Boonesboro in March, and Henderson's company took possession of the land on April 20, 1775. There were some Indian attacks at this time, but these were primarily by Cherokees who had been opposed to the sale of these lands to Henderson.

117. Later, when concerted attack by the Indians on this fort failed, the place was called Standing Fort—a name eventually corrupted into the name of the present city on the site, Stanford, Ky.

118. No city developed where Boonesboro was established and it is now the site of Fort Boonesboro State Park some 20 miles southeast of Lexington. Vast numbers of animals traditionally came to the various Kentucky licks to satisfy their craving for salt by licking the rocks and drinking the brackish water at such sites. Simon Kenton, in May of 1775, counted 1,100 buffalo in single file going to the Blue Licks and an immense number of others in the surrounding hills.

119. Hinkson's (sometimes spelled Hinkston's) Station was located on the north bank of the South Fork of the Licking River, three miles below present Ruddell's Mills, almost on the Nicholas/Harrison county line and about a half mile in a straight course below the mouth of Townsend Creek, some 20 miles (in a straight line) northeast of present Lexington. Hinkson's Station was also variously known at different times as Hinkson's Fort, The Cedars, Ruddell's Fort, and Ruddell's Station. McClelland's Station, 15 miles east-northeast of Hinkson's Station, evolved into the present city of Georgetown, 12 miles north by north-northwest of Lexington. Robert Patterson was camped at an especially beautiful spot on Elkhorn Creek and planning to build a station on the site when he learned of the Battle of Lexington and he determined then and there to name his settlement the same—now present Lexington, Ky.

120. For some time one of the most popular forms of transportation for the more affluent would-be settlers going down the Ohio with all their worldly goods was an enormous flat-decked raft upon which would actually be built a large cabin for them and their families, storage sheds for their goods, and even fenced corrals for their livestock. Upon arriving at the preselected destination, everything would be dismantled, including even the boat itself, and the lumber then used to build cabins and fortifications on the land. Thus, they were not only comfortable accommodations for the long trip downstream, they were actually floating, virtually ready-made prefabricated settlements.

121. William Croghan, at this time in Ft. Pitt, noted that the population in that area was far more concerned with Indian fighting than with the issues of the Revolutionary War, observing that: "The country talks of nothing but killing Indians and taking possession of their lands." Peter Parchment was one of these Indian haters who killed them wherever he could. Finding one friendly Indian sitting intoxicated on the bank of the Allegheny just above Pittsburgh one day in the spring of 1775, he crept up and buried his tomahawk in the man's skull and threw his body into the river. Not long after this he found another near the same place, killed him in the same way and stuffed the body into a hollow tree.

122. That first legislative assembly in Kentucky was held at Boonesboro on May 23, 1776, and was presided over by Richard Henderson. Delegates from each of the settlements had come, representing a constituency of 150 people, and the proceedings were opened with a prayer by the Reverend John Leythe. As a skilled lawyer and politician, Henderson explained the true republican principal of government, telling them that the only legitimate source of political power was to be found in the will of the people. As he put it:

> *If any doubts remain among you with respect to the force and efficiency of whatever laws you now or hereafter make, be pleased to consider that all power is originally in the people. Make it their interest, therefore, by impartial and beneficent laws and you will be sure of their inclination to see them enforced.*

The legislature continued in session for three days and it became obvious that Henderson, if he could not create the colony he wanted, wished to have the Kentucky country become a part of North Carolina, with himself still in a strong and manipulative position. This did not sit well with the majority, who were Virginians, and in their own meeting at Harrodsburg on June 6, they selected George Rogers Clark and John Gabriel Jones as delegates to petition the Virginia Assembly to create Kentucky County out of this wilderness. A complete list of those who were present at this latter meeting does not seem to have been preserved, but among those in attendance in addition to Jones and Clark were: William Bartel, Daniel Boone, Squire Boone, Joseph Crockett, Jacob Drennon, Richard Durett, John Floyd, James Gerrard, Pierre Girault, Michael Goodnight, Willis Green, David Hathaway, Charles Hazlipp, John Hinkson, George Jameson, Simon Kenton (Butler), Samuel Lacasagne, Henry Lee, Benjamin Logan, Gabriel Madison, John McClelland, Sam McDowell, George Mutern, John Niblack, Robert Patterson, Isaac Shelby, Michael Stoner, Levi Todd, Daniel Trabue, Abraham Venable, and James Wilkinson.

123. The mission of George Rogers Clark and John Gabriel Jones to Williamsburg had been successful only after considerable problems. They had arrived just as the summer session of the Virginia Assembly had adjourned and so had immediately gone to see Gov. Patrick Henry. The chief executive was sympathetic but said he did not have authority to issue arms and ammunition or call out troops to defend the far distant and nebulously defined Fincastle Co., especially with the country at war and all men and supplies needed to fight the British. He agreed, however, that the frontier needed defending and should have military support from Virginia, but there were further difficulties; Henderson was gaining support in having his Transylvania project legalized and if that occurred, no Virginia help of any kind could be sent. After much discussion and planning, Gov. Henry took Clark and Jones to the state's executive council and added his voice to theirs in plea. The executive council, less than enthusiastic, said there was no way to help unless Henderson's project was quashed and Kentucky became a separate Virginia county with its own elected representatives. The two men retorted that they were already legally elected representatives and if Virginia would not help, they would seek aid from Pennsylvania or North Carolina—a prospect intolerable to the council. Finally, on August 23, a decision was made: the two men would be given a quarter ton of gunpowder and sufficient lead, and in return they would remain in Williamsburg for the reconvening of the Assembly in fall and if they could succeed in having Henderson's purchase declared illegal and the new county of Kentucky formed, perhaps actual military aid could also be sent. The pair stayed on and in the fall made their plea to the Assembly. The matter was considered and then put to committee, with a vote to be made before Christmas. With that, the pair set off for Ft. Pitt where their precious authorized requisition for ammunition was to be filled. There they received the lead and five hundred pounds of gunpowder, hired seven men to help, put it into their canoes and headed for Kentucky.

124. Clark and Jones had gained the advantage but they were close to total exhaustion and, even though the Indians were no longer in sight, believed they were still being pursued. They came to the Three Islands just after dark and hastily put ashore there. (These three large islands were 35 miles downstream from the Scioto River mouth and opposite present Manchester, Ohio.) As quickly as possible they hid the powder and lead in five different locations, then set off again in the canoes. Ten miles farther downstream, at the mouth of Limestone Creek, they put to shore, set their canoes adrift and struck out overland for help at Hinkson's Station, some forty miles southwest.

125. Clark and Jones and their seven men had arrived at Hinkson's Station only to find it nearly deserted. They immediately struck out for McClelland's Station (present Georgetown, Ky.) where they hoped to find enough men to help them retrieve the ammunition. But most of the men of McClelland's were on a hunting trip, so Clark left Jones there with five men and continued southward toward Harrodsburg for help. Soon after Clark's departure, the hunting party from McClelland's returned and, when Jones explained the situation, they decided to head out on their own to see if they could recover the precious powder and lead. It was as they reached the Blue Licks that they were ambushed by the Shawnees under Plukke (called Pluggy by the whites). In the meanwhile, Clark, moving south, met the huge young frontiersman, Simon Kenton (Butler), en route, explained the situation and they hurried on to Harrodsburg together. A meeting was called and when the problem was laid out to them, thirty men volunteered to help recover the powder and lead. Quite soon Simon was leading them back toward McClelland's. They were met by George McClelland who told them of the ambush and the loss of John Gabriel Jones and settler William Graden, plus the capture of two others, including Clark's nephew. Those who had escaped the ambush and returned to McClelland's believed the Indians were close behind and would soon attack the station. The Kenton party rushed to McClelland's and quickly evacuated the women and children back to Harrodsburg, with most of the volunteer men escorting them. A core of about eighteen men remained to meet Pluggy's attack. As that attack came and the Indians, firing their rifles, charged the blockhouse, one of their first shots freakishly went through a niche in the logs and killed George McClelland. They watched as the Indians picked up their fallen chief, lingered for a while and then rode off. After making sure the Indians were really gone, the ammunition hidden on the Three Islands was recovered and brought to the settlements, along with exciting news that had just been brought downriver by a messenger: on December 6 the Virginia Assembly had declared the Transylvania land purchase illegal and officially created Kentucky Co., that county having the same boundaries as the State of Kentucky today.

126. The crossing of the Ohio River was made in the vicinity of present Ft. Thomas, Ky., and the trail followed southward essentially following the route of present U.S. 27, that trail merging with the great Warrior Trail at the site of present city of Paris, Bourbon Co., Ky.

127. No identity of the three sugar makers who were killed or the one who escaped has been located, only the fact that the wounded man managed to get away in the heavy brush and traveled three days afoot—having covered some fifty miles—before finally staggering into Harrodsburg on March 6, 1777, and collapsing. Only five days earlier a commission had arrived at Harrodsburg appointing George Rogers Clark a major and placing him in command of the entire Kentucky County and responsible for the defense of the western frontier, directing him to appoint officers for the first militia of Kentucky. He immediately appointed Daniel Boone, John Todd, and James Harrod as captains, Joe Lindsay as commissary, and Silas Harlan, Simon Butler (Kenton), Benjamin Linn, Samuel Moore, and Thomas Brooks as spies.

128. The rider who escaped was Michael Stoner. The other horses belonged to the rest of the party sent out from Harrodsburg under John Haggin (a resident of Hinkson's Fort who had taken refuge at Harrodsburg) and guarded by Simon Kenton (Butler) as well as Michael Stoner. Their mission was to get the flax that had been harvested and left at Hinkson's Station. This so-called flax was actually the steeped (or rotted) and beaten four-foot stems of nettle, the strands of which could be spun into a sort of strong linen or, when combined with buffalo wool, spun into a very strong and serviceable heavy cloth. The other ten men, including Kenton, were off their horses when they heard the Indians approaching and had time only to dive off the road and into the cover of the bushes an instant before the Indians came into view. Fuller details of this encounter and the white perspective of ensuing matters involving the attacks of the Shawnees under Chief Black Fish against the Kentucky settlements may be found in *The Frontiersmen*.

129. The whites inside Harrodsburg were overjoyed at the withdrawal of Black Fish—Chiungalla—and his Shawnees, though some felt it was only a respite before another attack, as before. Benjamin Logan, however, was so certain the Shawnees had withdrawn for good this time that he left Harrodsburg with his fourteen men and their families, and returned to his abandoned St. Asaph settlement to reoccupy it.

130. Many of the chroniclers of this incident make a strong point of stressing that three of the seven killed here were unarmed women, thus further blackening the reputation of the Indians. Few have pointed out, however, that all three women were dressed in men's clothing—this was so any skulking Indians might believe the fort had more men than there actually were—and, further, that the women carried their milk buckets on a stick held over their shoulder like a rifle, again, to make any watchers believe there was abundant firepower in the fort.

131. Wasegoboah is pronounced WAH-see-go-BOW-uh. The literal translation, Stand Firm, is usually thought by chroniclers to denote courage; actually it has nothing to do with courage and refers, immodestly to our concepts, to the genitalia.

132. The Great Miami and Mad Rivers converge in the center of the present city of Dayton, Ohio, and this attack occurred on the northern edge of the present downtown district, approximately adjacent to the site of the Dayton YMCA at Ludlow and Monument streets.

133. There is no positive evidence as to the identity of these three men but there is good reason to believe they were Nathaniel and Robert Larkin, brothers, and an older man known only as William (or Williams), all three of whom had appeared several weeks earlier at Pittsburgh from the East, presumably Philadelphia, bought a canoe and boasted that they were "going on an excursion to hunt some wild Indians." They set off down the Ohio, stopped briefly at Wheeling and Ft. Randolph and were never heard of again. At least one report suggests that the white party was made up of Andrew Johnson and 11 men whom he led to within five miles of Chalahgawtha prior to July of 1778, but this is discounted because the time frame is incorrect—the Johnson scout occurring almost a year later—and too many details of that latter incident do not jibe with the known facts of this described encounter, including Johnson's own report on his return that they made the entire trip into Indian country undetected.

134. Gov. Hamilton at Detroit was seeking aid not only from the Indians but from the white traders and settlers throughout the Michigan area, from Detroit all the way to Michilimackinac. In line with this, on June 24, 1777, he issued the following proclamation:

> *By virtue of the power and authority to me given by his Excellency, Sir Guy Carleton, Knight of the Bath, Governor of the Province of Quebec, General & Commander-in-Chief, &c., &c., &c.:*
>
> *I do assure all such as are inclined to withdraw themselves from the tyranny and oppression of the rebel committees, and take refuge in this settlement, or any of the posts commanded by his Majesty's officers, shall be humanely treated, shall be lodged and victualled, and such as come off in arms and shall use them in defence of his Majesty against rebels and traitors till the extinction of this rebellion, shall receive pay adequate to their former stations in the rebel service, and all common men who shall serve during that period shall receive his Majesty's bounty of two hundred acres of land.*
>
> *Given under my hand and seal*
>
>

Henry Hamilton

Lt. Governor & Superintendent
>
>
> *God Save the King!*

135. The "white chief" leading the company of 100 soldiers was Col. John Bowman, who had been commissioned for this service by the governor of Virginia, Patrick Henry, and the Virginia Council, who had requisitioned troops for such service from Col. George Washington, commander of the Continental Army of the United States. So far as can be ascertained, this was the first appearance of bayonets west of the Alleghenies. Since the Indian threat appeared to have passed by the time the troops arrived, they stayed only a short time before returning to the East. About the same time, a friend of Daniel Boone, Bailey Smith, arrived with 40 to 50 mounted riflemen he had raised in North Carolina. They, too, in the face of no apparent threat, remained only a short time. The departure of all the troops left Kentucky with only 105 able-bodied men to defend the three forts still existing there—65 at Harrodsburg, 22 at Boonesboro, and 15 at St. Asaph (Logan's Fort). When word of this weakness filtered back to Virginia, Bowman was reprimanded and ordered back to Kentucky with his troops.

136. Lower Sandusky was initially located on the south shore of Sandusky Bay in present Erie Co. on the site of the present city of Sandusky, Ohio, but later on moved to the site of present Fremont, O., in Sandusky Co. Upper Sandusky was located in what is now Wyandot Co., just east of the site of the present city of Upper Sandusky, Ohio.

137. This siege of Wheeling, now generally known as the First Siege of Wheeling, occurred at a time when only nine able-bodied men were at the fort. However, a company of 24 border guards under Capt. Samuel Mason happened to be on one of the regular tours for the protection of the frontier. They had begun their tour at the settlement of Washington (present Washington, Pa.) and as they neared Wheeling they were decoyed into an ambush in which 20 whites were killed and two of the four who escaped were seriously wounded. Four other whites, not connected with Capt. Mason's company, were killed in proximity to Wheeling.

138. The mouth of Grave Creek is the site of present Moundsville, Marshall Co., W.Va. The attack, variously known as the Grave Creek Massacre or Foreman's Defeat, was against a company of 24 men led by Capt. William Foreman, which had left Wheeling to see if there was any sign of Indians still in the area. A small settlement had been at the mouth of Grave Creek but had been abandoned prior to the attack on Wheeling. Foreman's company camped overnight at or near the deserted blockhouse of the Grave Creek Settlement and had progressed up the trail along Grave Creek the morning of September 22 despite warnings by Capt. William Linn, who suspected an ambush. Linn, who refused to go into the Narrows with the marchers, was one of the few who escaped death. All the dead of the Foreman Defeat were buried in a common grave four days after the ambush.

139. There are a wide variety of disparate accounts of this incident which are, in the main, similar but which vary widely in the details. As best as the author can reconstruct the matter, it appears that Capt. James Hall (whose title was not military, but one bestowed by his followers) and several of his men had, some time before (anywhere from a week prior to this incident to the day of it, but most often the day before), crossed the Ohio River (some accounts say the Kanawha) to hunt. Two of his hunters encountered two Indians (some accounts say ambushed by them) and in the resultant skirmish, one of the two whites (a man named Gilmore) was killed. When the survivors returned to the settlement adjacent to Ft. Randolph and learned of the incarceration of the three Indians, they raised a group of "enraged soldiers" and, resolved on revenge, headed for the cabin where the Indians were being held prisoner. The fort commander, Capt. Matthew Arbuckle, is said to have attempted to talk them out of this, but was brushed aside and the murderous deed followed. In Hokolesqua's body alone there were nine (some say seven or eight, some eleven) bullet holes, and the other two were similarly riddled and also clubbed repeatedly after death. Red Hawk, in some accounts, is described as a Delaware chief, but this is incorrect. Just over five months later, on March 27, 1778, the Virginia Council issued a notice for the arrest of five of the identified perpetrators, Hugh Gailbreath, Adam Barnes, Malcolm McCoun, William Roan, and their leader, James Hall, offering a reward of $200 for Hall, $150 for McCoun, and $100 each for the others, charging them with being "deeply concerned and perpetrating the atrocities & barbarous murder of the Shawanese Indians on the 10th of November [October] last at Fort Randolph, as appears from sundry depositions transmitted to the governor." There seems to be no record of any of these five ever having been arrested or tried for their crime. Sixty-three years later, in 1841, while excavations were being made at Point Pleasant for a street, the remains of three men were found, believed to be those of Cornstalk, Elinipsico and Red Hawk. The account states that "the bones were much broken and jammed as if by blows, & five or six balls also found among them." These bones were buried in the yard of the Mason County Court House.

140. Estimates of the number of Indians on this expedition range from 100 to 140; the number of 102 is mentioned by two different men who observed the party and this seems to be an accurate figure, though slightly contradicted by Boone's statement which declares there were 118 Indians. In addition the Frenchmen who accompanied the party numbered at least four and possibly six. It is also suspected, but not provable, that several British agents were among the Indians, perhaps themselves in Indian garb.

141. This salt lick was a highly favored hunting camp that the Shawnees had used for many decades while traveling to or from the South or simply as a destination hunting camp. The salt springs here were not as large as those at Blue Licks, but they were significant and often visited by herds of woodlands bison as well as elk and deer. The place is the present site of the town of May's Lick in Mason Co., Ky.

142. The typical greeting of "How do you do," shortened in the vernacular to "How'd'ye do," (or even "How'ja-do") was a very difficult expression for the Indians to articulate and, in their usual manner of simplifying difficult names or expressions, they shortened it to just the first word, which is where the Indian greeting of "How!" originated—a greeting often thought hackneyed or trite or even a "Hollywood" creation. It was an expression very widely used among Indians greeting whites at this time and later. Details of Boone's capture and subsequent events were faithfully recorded verbatim by his son Nathan who, in turn, gave them to historian Lyman C. Draper when the latter interviewed him at his home in Missouri 73 years later.

143. Nepepimmatheepi is pronounced NEE-pee-PEE-muh-THEEE-pee.

144. The party of salt makers had originally been 30 men, plus Boone as hunter to supply meat for them, but a few days previously three men had been sent back—one each to the three settlements—with the salt that had been thus far made. So many men were needed because the salt was made by boiling the waters of the spring in ten-gallon kettles over a dozen or more large fires and the job of keeping the fires stoked with wood was a major operation. It required the boiling down of a dozen kettles of water to produce one gallon of salt, with the end product to be equally divided among the three remaining forts in Kentucky. It was a white, fine-grained salt and, because of the quality of the nitre in it, especially useful for the preservation of meat brought in by the hunters. Boone reported that Simon Kenton had visited the salt camp only the day before this incident and passed along the news of the day, primarily that the hardy frontiersman Jacob Drennon, friend of both of them, had been killed by Indians near Boonesboro just after the salt party had left there and that George Rogers Clark had gotten the support of the Virginia government in a plan to lead an expedition against the British installations at Kaskaskia and Cahokia in the Illinois country and was to collect his men on Corn Island at the Falls of the Ohio.

145. Chiungalla lived up to his word and the captives were not mistreated or forced to run a gauntlet (though Boone did have to run the gauntlet because he had not included himself in the leniency agreement, but it was a token gauntlet at best and he was not hurt). The prisoners were made to carry most of the plunder. Everyone suffered severely from the cold and many of the Indians and prisoners alike had their ears, toes, fingertips, and noses frozen before reaching Chalahgawtha.

146. While they were in Detroit, Gov. Hamilton asked Chiungalla's permission to talk to Boone and to keep the frontiersman overnight and return him the following morning. Chiungalla agreed and Boone was brought to Hamilton. Hamilton questioned Boone extensively about the state of affairs in Kentucky, its troops and defenses and what he knew of the progress of the war in the East. Boone answered truthfully in those matters where he knew Hamilton had the information or could get it, but made up some rather far-fetched exaggerations about other matters in an effort to convince Hamilton that the Kentuckians were stronger and better fortified than was actually the case. After having dined Boone and giving him a comfortable bed for the night, the next morning Hamilton ordered the King's Commissary to furnish Boone with a horse, saddle, bridle, and blanket, which was done, and also with a quantity of silver ornaments for him to use as currency while with the Indians. Because this was witnessed by other prisoners, some of whom made it back to Kentucky and reported what had occurred, the feeling became prevalent that Boone, in getting the salt makers to surrender without a fight and in conferring with Hamilton and receiving gifts from him, was in collusion with the enemy—both Indian and English—and the feelings of some ran very high against him.

147. Boone, now well aware that a plan was underfoot for the major invasion of the Kentucky country, and still being very closely watched himself, decided it would be to the best interest of the Kentuckians and to himself to cheerfully go along with the adoption and bide his time, gaining the confidence of the Shawnees and learning as much as possible of their plans until such time as he could be quite sure of effecting his escape, and then go and warn the Kentucky settlements and help them get defenses in order to meet the proposed attack. (The author used much of this information, as well as the trial data of Boone's subsequent court-martial for treason as the basis for his novel *The Court-martial of Daniel Boone* [Little, Brown, 1973; Bantam, 1987] in which the facts are accurate but some of the dialogue and action was fictionalized to provide continuity and drama.) Benjamin Kenny, who was a minister of the Gospel, unfortunately was not of a literary bent and therefore little was preserved concerning his adoption into and four-year stay with the family of Chiungalla. It is recorded that the Reverend Kelly called Tecumseh by the name of Tecumseh-keh and fraternized considerably with him, though in what respect and to what extent is not known. Unfortunately, as well, although Boone was residing in the same wegiwa as Tecumseh, he later commented very little about the boy except to say "I run with him and found him a fine companion."

148. This was the cabin of Moredock McKinzie (spelled McKenzie or McKensey in many accounts), who had found this little pocket of isolation and settled on it three years ago with his wife, Jemima (called Erina in some accounts), and their six children—Isaac, Henley, Sallie, Margaret, Elizabeth, and Mary Ann. McKinzie had first come into this country as a soldier in Lord Dunmore's War, serving under the command of Col. Andrew Lewis. He had paid close attention to this wild new country as they descended the Greenbrier, New, and Kanawha in succession and was enthralled with what he saw, determining then that if he survived, he would come back and find a place to settle in this region. He had indeed survived the Battle of Point Pleasant and, true to his vow, he had come back, did some preliminary exploring and then found this site for his cabin. It was just enough off the beaten path of the Kanawha that travelers, unless they knew its location, simply passed it by, unaware it was even there.

149. The young man was 20-year-old Henley McKinzie. Their mother, Jemima, was in the cabin at this time preparing a stew. Their father, Moredock McKinzie, and his 20-year-old son, Isaac, had gone early in the morning to try to recover their horses which had escaped from their corral through a break in the fence the preceding night and were at this moment about five miles away.

150. Moredock McKinzie and his son, Isaac, did not arrive back at the still burning remains of their cabin until near midnight. They found that Mrs. Jemima McKinzie, though suffering severe tomahawk wounds to head and breast and her scalp taken, was still alive, though unconscious. They found Henley also, dead, and feared the four girls were in the burning cabin, but Mrs. McKinzie recovered consciousness for only a moment before she died, just long enough to tell her husband that two of their four daughters had been kidnapped. Greater details of the McKinzie family, the attack by the Indians and Moredock McKinzie's years-long search for his daughters may be found in the author's *Gateway to Empire* (Little, Brown, 1983; Bantam, 1984).

151. Sciototheepi (the Scioto River) is pronounced sy-OH-toe-THEEE-pee.

152. Matchsquathi is pronounced match-SKWAH-theee. Kisathoi (sometimes spelled Kisahthoi) and Tebethto are pronounced kih-thuh-THOY and tee-BETH-toe.

153. The process of reloading and firing a flintlock rifle while on the run was no small feat and one which only a relatively few frontiersmen ever mastered, among them Simon Kenton, Samuel Brady, Lewis Wetzel, Jacob Drennon, and, of course, Boone. It involved pouring the correct amount of gunpowder into the small muzzle hole of the gun from a powder horn or powder flask, then dropping in a lead ball, then freeing the ramrod from its holder and inserting this into the muzzle hole and ramming the charge down firmly, replacing the ramrod in its holder, and finally, without spilling it, pouring another small bit of powder into the pan to create the flash that would ignite the gunpowder in the breech when the flint struck steel and sparked. There is no record of any Indian ever having mastered the technique, though quite a few tried, including Tecumseh.

154. This salt lick was very rich in good quality salt and, when not in use, was hidden by a large engraved stone that was rolled over on top of it. It was located in the present Columbus, Ohio, suburb of Upper Arlington and is believed to have been covered by the waters of the Griggs Reservoir when the Julian Griggs Dam was built there.

155. The author has never encountered any description of or name for the woman who was the wife of Black Fish—Chiungalla. The same is true for the two sons he is reported to have had, which causes the author to believe he had no sons at all, since the sons of a principal chief were usually quite prominent simply because of the relationship.

156. In making his escape, Boone rode his horse very hard through the remaining few hours of daylight and then throughout the night. By ten o'clock the following morning, his horse gave out and could travel no farther, so Boone removed the saddle, bridle, and saddle blanket and hung them over a low tree limb (not in a hollow tree as some accounts have contended) and continued on foot, moving rapidly and backtracking often to confuse possible pursuers. Late that day he came to the Ohio River (apparently just a little above present Maysville) and quickly found a couple of standing dead tree trunks with their bases rotted. These he pushed over, dragged them to the river and tied them together with grape vines as a makeshift raft and swam across the Ohio, pushing the raft before him and resting on it often. Once across he traveled at a steady but easier pace and made nighttime camps. Having traveled about 150 miles, he arrived at Boonesboro late in the day on June 20, four days after his escape. He was welcomed back with some reservation and was soon arrested and charged with several counts of treason and confined, while the intelligence he brought back concerning the projected invasion by the Shawnees was regarded with suspicion by many. In his subsequent trial, in which he defended himself, he was acquitted of all charges and promoted to the rank of major in the county militia.

157. Boone, on his return to Boonesboro, had alerted the settlements that a major attack was imminent and defenses were immediately improved. When the attack did not come by mid-July as he expected and still had not occurred by early August, he decided that it had been called off and so he raised a party of twenty-nine men, including himself and Simon Kenton, and led them off on an expedition planned to go into the Ohio country toward Paint Creek and the Scioto villages. They had gotten only as far as the Blue Licks, however, when ten of their party got cold feet and returned to Boonesboro. Boone and Kenton and the remaining seventeen went on and crossed the Ohio.

158. Had they moved on at once, as Black Fish had been inclined to do, chances are good they would have successfully infested Boonesboro. As it was, that very evening, shortly after nightfall, Boone and sixteen of his eighteen men, returning from their Paint Creek expedition, detected the Indians camped at Blue Licks, realized their intentions and made a wide detour around them, arriving at Boonesboro with the alarm well before the war party showed up. The two men missing from those under Boone were Simon Kenton (Butler) and Alexander Montgomery, who had remained behind a little longer in the Ohio country. Boone's expedition had been rather successful. Kenton had scouted ahead to the vicinity of Yellow Hawk's village at the confluence of Paint Creek and the Scioto River (the former Chalahgawtha village) but had been discovered by an old man and boy from that village riding the same horse. As they charged at him, Kenton killed both with the same shot. He was then pursued by a few others, but Boone and his remaining seventeen men showed up and drove them off. The boy who had been mortally wounded had told Kenton before he died that most of their young men were away with Chiungalla to attack Boonesboro, so now Boone said they had to head back there immediately. Kenton and Montgomery elected to stay behind a few hours and try to steal some of the horses from the village. At great risk they had managed to do this and, with the four horses taken from the village, one of which they recognized as having been stolen from Benjamin Logan and the other three also from Logan's Fort, they too had returned to Kentucky and passed by Chiungalla's camp some six hours after Boone. They, however, did not go to Boonesboro but directly to Logan's Fort with the recovered horses from there. Greater details of this Boone and Kenton expedition may be found in *The Frontiersmen*.

159. Among the other nine who signed with Boone were his brother, Squire, Flanders Callaway, Samuel Callaway and Maj. Smith. Boone had warned the others inside to be prepared for anything and to be ready to fire if treachery were detected and open and shut the gate quickly if they were forced to make a run for it, which he expected would occur.

160. The wounded man was Squire Boone, brother of Daniel, and some historians contend that the ball that struck him came from the fort, not from the Indians.

161. Statistics concerning killed and wounded are sketchy and widely varied depending on whose report is considered. The most accurate figures seem to be two whites killed and about eight wounded, while the Indians suffered about 34 killed and about 20 wounded.

162. The disturbance took place in the early night of September 11, about the time Chiungalla's force was making camp at the Blue Licks on their first night's return from Boonesboro. The Chalahgawtha horse compound was located about forty yards upstream on Massies Creek from where it empties into the Little Miami River, along the east bank almost directly opposite the present principal buildings of the Xenia Water Works, and some 850 feet downstream from where present U.S. 68 crosses Massies Creek.

163. When Simon Kenton and Alexander Montgomery had bypassed Boonesboro on their way back from the Paint Creek expedition, they had gone directly to Logan's Fort to deliver the four horses from there that they had recovered from Yellow Hawk's village. On their arrival they found the frontier commander there, Col. John Bowman. Their intention had been to immediately return to Boonesboro, but Bowman told the pair they were now under his exclusive command and he was sending them, along with a young man named George Clarke (not George Rogers Clark), on an important mission—to spy on the principal Shawnee village of Chalahgawtha, the location of which Boone had told Simon. The two experienced frontiersmen had been intrigued by the idea and improvised on it, deciding to make it a horse-stealing operation as well. They had taken a supply of salt and halters to aid in the project. They had made it to Chalahgawtha undetected and spied on the place for two days and a night before attempting to get the horses. Using the salt liberally to calm the horses, they quietly put bridles on seven—the maximum number they thought they could lead and still outdistance pursuit—and it was just about then that something spooked the horses and the uproar began. They had quickly pulled down a section of the fencing and shot their guns to scatter all but the seven horses they were taking and in that way delay pursuit while the Indians had to wait till the next day to round up the horses and begin that pursuit. Bonah's tracking ability was indeed prodigious. Kenton had gone to great effort to throw off would-be trackers by backtracking, traveling up or down each little stream they encountered before leaving it and using other stratagems, but Bonah was not fooled. He and his four warriors followed the devious trail unerringly on a course that led them, using present landmarks, down the Little Miami River to Morrow, up Todds Fork a quarter-mile, up one of its north flowing tributaries for a mile, then on a fairly straight line south by south-southeast (with occasional quarter-mile moves up or down small creeks) through present Butlerville, Pleasant Plain, Modest, Monterey, and Williamsburg, where they crossed the East Fork of the Little Miami, then southeast through New Harmony, Locust Ridge, and Shiloh to Newhope, where they struck White Oak Creek and followed it down to about where Georgetown is, then east to the Warrior Trail (present U.S. 68) on which they went southeast through Redoak and Logan's Gap, striking the Ohio River shore at about where Ripley is now located.

164. The party of Simon Kenton (alias Butler and called Bahd-ler by the Indians) had reached the Ohio in ample time to escape, but when they got there the wind was high enough to cause whitecaps, the river itself was swollen and full of floating driftwood from recent storms upstream and though they made numerous attempts, they could not get the horses to swim across. While they were in this dilemma, the Bonah party caught up to them. Simon saw them first and tried to shoot the leader but his gun misfired and he was seen, pursued and caught. He was tied to a tree and then Montgomery showed up at a distance and shot at the Indians, missed and was himself pursued, caught and instantly killed and scalped. George Clarke got away by slipping into the Ohio and kicking his way across while clinging to a log. Only the recognition of Kenton as the greatly feared Bahd-ler saved his life for the moment, as such a renowned enemy had to be taken to their chief. Full details of this incident and Kenton's captivity may be found in *The Frontiersmen*.

165. Each night since his capture, Kenton had been forced to lie spread-eagled on the ground on his back, his wrists and ankles tied to trees or stakes and a pole laid across his neck and attached to each wrist, plus a rawhide halter snugged around his neck and tied to a tree behind him. In such a position he suffered much torment from flies, ants, and mosquitoes. On the first morning after his capture he had been placed facing backwards on the most unruly of the horses they had taken, his ankles tied under the horse's belly and a short rawhide cord tied from around his neck to around the horse's neck. Then the horse had been suddenly whipped across the rump to make it buck and plunge and though somehow he managed to stay on, the young frontiersman (23 years old at this time) was badly gouged, scratched and bruised as the horse rammed into trees and plunged through brush, branches and brambles. This lasted until the horse wore itself out completely.

166. Straps this long and even longer were made by the Shawnees by first tanning a buffalo hide from which the hair had been leached away with application of a pasty mixture of wood ash and buffalo brains. Once the leached hair was able to be scraped away and the bare hide tanned until supple, then a strip of the desired width was carefully cut in a spiral from the outer edges of the hide until the center was reached. Depending upon the width selected, the final strap could be as long as seventy to one hundred feet. The twists would then be removed from the strap by soaking it well, pulling it to a moderate stretch (though not tight, or it would break in the drying process) and tying it between two trees to shrink as it dried. When fully cured it was a long straight leather strap with numerous utilitarian purposes. It could also be softened into a supple cord by then being "worked" over the edge of a tanning board.

167. The Delaware village known as Buckangehela's Town was located near the mouth of Stony Creek where it empties into the Great Miami River headwaters at the site of present De Graff in Logan Co., O. Stiahta's Town, more familiarly called Roundhead's Village after that chief's English name, was located on the site of the present town of Roundhead in Hardin Co., 15 miles north of Bellefontaine. Mingo Town was located in Champaign Co., ten miles northeast of present Urbana. Girty's Town was named after Simon Girty, who had taken up residence with the Shawnees in a village that was renamed in his honor and located on the site of present St. Marys, Auglaize Co. Upper Sandusky was located in present Wyandot Co. just east of the present city of Upper Sandusky.

168. That spring-fed stream is presently known as Macochee Creek, which empties into the Mad River one mile west of where Mackachack was located, the mouth of the creek situated within the town limits of the present village of West Liberty, Logan Co., O.

169. McKee's Town was where the British Indian agent had set up residence with his Shawnee wife and the town was renamed after him; it was located on a pleasant ridge close to a small stream now called McKee's Creek, the precise location of the village being exactly 2.5 miles southeast of the Logan Co. courthouse in Bellefontaine, Ohio, on the south bank of present McKee's Creek at almost exactly the point where County Road T-181 forms a "T" intersection with County Road T-179, and just short of the same distance northwest of Wapatomica.

170. Girty's Town was located on the west bank of the present St. Marys River at the eastern edge of the present city of St. Marys, Auglaize Co., O. Simon Girty and his brothers, James and George, had been captured by Indians as young boys and remained eight years with them— Simon with Senecas, James with the Shawnees, and George with the Delawares. All three were fluent in various Indian tongues, extremely well versed in Indian customs and valuable as interpreters.

171. Vincennes, also called Fort Sackville, Post St. Vincent and Fort St. Vincent in various accounts, was on the site of the present city of Vincennes, Knox Co., Ind. Hamilton, who had managed to gain back some of the Indian alliances Clark had winnowed away from the British— notably the Kickapoos—and had instructed Lemoult before leaving that he was to continue paying the annuities to the tribes on time and to make certain that no offense of any kind was given to the Indians by any of the Detroit garrison. Lemoult was to continue honoring the British obligation to pay the Indians $50 for each white scalp and $100 for each living white prisoner, adding that "Wherever it is possible, prisoners are to be bought in preference to scalps."

172. For the description of the frolic dance and the subsequent wedding dance as represented here the author is indebted to the late Arthur Rolette, principal chief (1973) of the Shawnees, and his late wife, Pearl, who explained to him in detail the action, purport, and dialogue of the dances.

What the author has indicated here as the dialogue that passed between Blue Jacket and Wabethe should not be construed as precisely the words they spoke, but they are representative of the wedding dance dialogue between partners and dialogue of a very similar nature was indeed exchanged by them.

173. The camp of Talgayetta—Chief Logan—was located approximately where the south end of the U.S. 68 bridge over the Scioto River is located, just south of the present city of Kenton, Hardin Co., O.

174. Solomon's Town was a small Shawnee village on or very near the site of the present town of Rushsylvania, Logan Co.

175. It was Girty's plan at this point to try to enlist the help of Talgayeeta (Chief Logan) in rescuing Kenton (Butler). The expatriate Cayuga chief agreed to do whatever he could to help, whereupon Girty returned to his own village.

176. Drouillard (whose name is spelled Drouilliard in some documents), who was long a trader among the Indians, had been contacted by his friend Talgayeeta and asked by him to appear in full uniform to impress the Indians and get them to let him take Bahd-ler (Kenton) to Detroit.

177. It was, of course, the plan of Talgayeeta and Drouillard that once Kenton (Butler) was safely in Detroit, to never return him to the Shawnees.

178. Ft. McIntosh, a stockaded installation enclosing about two acres, was built 25 miles down the Ohio River from Ft. Pitt and was only nine miles from the Ohio border. It was located on the point at the downstream side of the mouth of Beaver River on the site of the present city of Beaver in Beaver Co., Pa.

179. In a letter dated October 30, 1778, at Ft. McIntosh, Brig. Gen. Lachlan McIntosh wrote to the County Lieutenant of Botetourt County:

> *I have the pleasure to inform you that my plan of erecting posts in proper places, and securing as I go into the Indian Country, has its proper effect, and alarms the Savages much. Several Tribes have already applyed [sic] to me for peace, but I have given them no encouragement yet, until they give me Substantial proofs of their Sincerity, and untill [sic] I go to the Delaware Towns, where I propose setting off from here, in two or three days, and build a fort there to Secure these people in our Interest, from whence I may make Excursions to some of the Hostile Towns.*

180. It was the intent of Gen. McIntosh to march to the Sandusky Towns of the Wyandots and destroy them and then move on against Detroit, but lack of provisions caused him to halt at the Tuscarawas River (which he mistook to be the Muskingum River) and fortify. Ft. Laurens, the first American fort in the Ohio country, was built on the west bank of the Tuscarawas River 10 miles south of the present city of Canton, Ohio, and close to the present city of Bolivar. It was built on a slight rise above the river, the highest piece of ground in the area, and enclosed not quite an acre, but the river side (east) having no wall and the main gate situated in the west wall. The walls were of split hardwood timber, six inches thick, planted in a trench three feet deep and the pickets extending upward to a height of 15 feet above ground level. There was one blockhouse 20 feet square next to the gate and the interior side of the three walls were lined with cabins and soldiers' barracks. As soon as construction was finished, Gen. McIntosh placed Col. John Gibson in command, left him with a garrison of 150 men of his 13th Virginia Regiment and immediately returned to Ft. McIntosh.

181. Girty was fond of boasting that he could make it from Upper Sandusky to Ft. Pitt in three days and nights of traveling and that he often watched the movements in Ft. Pitt from nearby Coal Hill.

182. George Washington, in respect to the proposed invasion against the Iroquois, wrote: "The only certain way of preventing Indian ravages is to carry the war vigorously into their own country."

183. As much as the Shawnees, Wyandots, and other tribes suspected the Moravian missionaries and their Indian converts to be spying on them for the Americans, so too did many of the Americans believe that they were spying on them for the British and the western tribes. In point of fact, some of the Delaware converts were spying, as well as some of the missionaries, such as the Reverends John Heckewelder and David Zeisberger, and passing along to the Americans important intelligence concerning the activities of the British and Indians.

184. Moravian missionary David Zeisberger had established the mission he called Lichtenau (Pasture of Light) in May of 1776 less than three miles downstream from the Delaware village of Goschachgunk (Coshocton, Ohio), where, by the beginning of 1779, he had 250 converts. The Salem Mission was located 18 miles upstream from Lichtenau near the site of present Port Washington, Ohio. Gnadenhutten Mission was five miles upstream from there, at present Gnadenhutten, and the Schoenbrun Mission was on the site of present Schoenbrun, all three of the new missions in present Tuscarawas Co., O.

185. Six or eight weeks after this, George Washington was entertaining a number of guests at a dinner party. All were at the table and just ready to leave it when the express horn sounded from outside and in a few moments the butler brought Washington a dispatch. The guests, just rising from their chairs, stopped as Washington looked at the seal and said, "Keep your seats, gentlemen, keep your seats. Perhaps there may be some news for us." As they sat down again, Washington put on his spectacles, broke the seal and began to read the contents. Abruptly a great grin spread his lips and he became obviously more excited the farther he read. At last he refolded the letter, took off his spectacles and then held the folded paper up and said, "Gentlemen, this is a letter from Gov. Jefferson. He writes that he has just received intelligence that a Virginia colonel has conquered the Illinois country and that the Virginia flag now waves in triumph over Kaskaskia, Cahokia and Vincennes!" There was a tumultuous response from the guests and Washington ordered their glasses refilled and then stood up holding his own glass high before him. "Gentlemen," he said, "a toast." The others rose and held up their glasses similarly. Washington smiled and said, "To Colonel George Rogers Clark, the conqueror of the Illinois!" They all drained their glasses in enthusiastic approbation. Lt. Gov. Henry Hamilton, whom Clark had captured, was shackled and sent back to Williamsburg where he was imprisoned and kept in irons even in his cell.

186. The site Blue Jacket chose to establish his village is 2.5 miles west of present Campbell Hill, highest point in the State of Ohio. The village site is the site of the present city of Bellefontaine, seat of Logan Co., O., and is also the present home of the author.

187. The dish *takuwahnepi*—literally, bread water—was a tasty gruel made of pulverized corn from which the chaff had first been removed and then the corn mashed and boiled until it became a thick white fluid, not unlike hominy but with less substance. Then a quantity of seeping fluid was added (the seeping fluid made by allowing water to seep through clean wood ashes) and stirred in and cooked for a while. To this was then added walnut-sized chunks of meat—usually buffalo, elk, or deer, but occasionally *withsi,* which was dog meat—and the whole concoction stewed for a considerable while, with salt and other condiments or spices added at discretion. It was a favorite hearty at-home meal for warriors who had returned from forays on which they had existed for many days on only a few handfuls of parched corn and jerky carried in a pouch.

188. Apple Creek, in Cape Girardeau Co., Mo., has since been renamed Shawnee Creek.

189. The segment of the Shawnee tribe that broke away at this time ultimately became known as the Absentee Shawnees, who continued to retreat before the advancing tide of whites until finally being granted a reservation in Oklahoma Territory by the United States, where the remaining organized portion of the tribe still exists to this day.

190. One such flock of this abundant bird, which was almost twice the size of the mourning dove, was reported as having its front crossing the Ohio River while its rear was still in Mississippi, with the passage of the half-mile wide flock taking five full days! Further, there were a number of such flocks and it was estimated that at one time there were five times as many passenger pigeons in America as all other species of North American birds *combined.* For a detailed look at this bird, its natural history, abundance and ultimate extinction, see the author's book entitled *The Silent Sky: The Incredible Extinction of the Passenger Pigeon* (Little, Brown, 1965).

191. This first attack on Chalahgawtha was under command of the Continental Army officer Col. John Bowman who, stung by the successes of the backwoodsman Clark with his rag-tag militia army in the Illinois and Indiana country, had usurped troops raised for Clark and arranged this campaign to bring some glory to the regulars and, of course, to himself. His army consisted of 264 men, about half and half regulars and militia. That force outnumbered the Shawnee defenders at Chalahgawtha almost eight to one and Bowman had managed to bring this army to within rifle range of the village without detection. The element of surprise had been lost, however, through the carelessness and clumsiness of some of the men, the regulars blaming the militia and vice versa. One report, which the author discredits, states that the alarm was raised when a return-ing Shawnee hunter tried to slip through the lines of the whites and warn the villagers but that he was shot and scalped and that it was this commotion that alerted the Shawnees to impending attack.

192. No good reason, other than a simple loss of nerve, has been advanced for why Col. Bowman, with the Shawnees trapped in the very palm of his hand, abruptly ordered his troops to withdraw, gather up the Shawnee horses, and head for Kentucky. It was rumored—and probably accurately— he had suddenly begun to fear that the Shawnees who were absent from the village were about to burst upon the scene. It is also alleged, on patently ludicrous foundation, that while catching the horses, Bowman's men came upon a black woman, formerly a slave, who was residing with the Shawnees, who told them that a hundred warriors were approaching under leadership of Simon Girty and that by the time Bowman heard the story the figure was 500 warriors. There is also no foundation for the claim of some chroniclers that the precipitate withdrawal bordered on a panicky retreat. Bowman was not officially censured for his withdrawal but a great deal of private criticism was lodged against him by militia men after disbandment of the army.

193. Bowman's force had withdrawn the way they came, down the trail that more or less followed the course of the Little Miami River to its mouth. The Shawnees overtook them about two miles east of the present town of Bellbrook, in Greene Co., approximately where the present Sugar Creek Ski Hills resort area is located and continued southward for nearly another eight miles, to just north of present Waynesville in present Warren Co.

194. Militia Capt. James Harrod, founder of Harrodsburg, was the officer who, in exasperation at the stupidity of Col. Bowman's moves, acted on his own and without orders, got a hundred more than eager militiamen to follow him in a charge upon the Indians. It had its desired effect, but came somewhat late. The whites had a total of 31 men killed—ten at Chalahgawtha (some reports say nine) and 21 on the withdrawal—plus over sixty others who suffered wounds of varying degrees of severity, though none mortal. As soon as the army crossed the Ohio, Bowman stopped his force, declared they had accomplished a great victory, the plunder and horses taken from the Shawnees were gathered together and auctioned off on the spot, and the army imme-diately disbanded, the men returning to their homes each in his own way. Bowman, in his offi-cial report, stated that on the withdrawal his force had been attacked "by at least a hundred warriors."

195. One report states that the Kentuckians returned with 163 horses; another states that there were three Shawnee casualties.

196. Simon Kenton (Butler) was aided in his escape from Detroit by Capt. Peter Drouillard and the well-known trader John Edgar and his wife, Rachel, who provided him with clothing and weapons and suggested the escape route he could follow through Indiana to avoid passing through Shawnee territory. Two other prisoners had also made their escape with Kenton, Robert Bullock and Jesse Copher, and the three, staying under cover by day and traveling only at night, thirty days later had reached the new Ft. Nelson at the Falls of the Ohio (Louisville, Ky.) without any Indian trouble. Shortly afterwards John and Rachel Edgar and Peter Drouillard were arrested and charged with complicity in helping prisoners to escape. Drouillard escaped the next autumn, made his way to Kentucky and looked up Kenton who, in appreciation for the help Drouillard had given him, gave him 200 acres of prime bottom land from his own holdings.

197. Gaurie was a French trader who is the first known settler to plant roots on the site of what would become Chicago, Ill. His trading post was located on the west side of the North Branch of the present Chicago River.

198. The former trading post of Jean Baptiste Point du Sable was situated on the site of present Michigan City, Ind. The latter was on the Chicago River near its forks, on the site of the present Merchandise Mart in Chicago. Much greater detail in respect to the early settlement of the Chicago area may be found in the author's *Winning of America* series volume entitled *Gateway to Empire*.

199. The party attacked was under command of Capt. John Clarke and consisted of a sergeant and fourteen privates of the 8th Pennsylvania Regiment. Shortly after this time, Peter Parchment and several others were dispatched to Goschachgunk in an effort to get corn from missionary John Heckewelder at Lichtenau to bring back to the garrison, but they were attacked and Parchment was wounded, a rifle ball breaking his arm, which healed but was ever after crooked.

200. Maj. Gen. John Sullivan, 38, a New Hampshire native, was a lawyer at Dunham. In 1772 he had become major of the New Hampshire Regiment and in 1775–76 was a delegate to Congress. He was appointed Major General in July 1776.

201. The Battle of Minisink was fought about one mile from Laxawaxen Depot on the site of the present town of Highland in present Sullivan Co., N.Y.

202. Sullivan's loss of men slain by Indians was a mere 36. From the very onset of the planning stage of this expedition, George Washington left no doubt that annihilation of the Iroquois was to be the goal. In his directives to Gen. Sullivan in this respect, he wrote:

> The immediate objects are the total destruction of the hostile tribes of the Six Nations, and the devastation of their settlements, and the capture of as many prisoners of every age and sex as possible. . . . [You are] . . . to lay waste all the settlements around, so the country may not only be overrun but destroyed.

Day-by-day details of the entire expedition of Maj. Gen. John Sullivan may be found in the *Winning of America* series volume entitled *The Wilderness War* (Little, Brown, 1978; Bantam, 1982).

203. Washington wrote to Gen. Lafayette in regard to the campaign: "I am pleased with the entire destruction of the Country of the Six Nations and am convinced that the Indians are exceedingly disconcerted and humbled." Many of the Indian survivors of Sullivan's expedition fled to the vicinity of Ft. Niagara and appealed to the British commander for food because all theirs had been destroyed and they were starving. They blamed the British for their misfortune, telling the commander that they had struck the Americans only at British insistence and with the promise that they would be supplied with food, clothing, weapons, and ammunition. The commander, short on food for his own garrison, did give them some for a short time, but then received orders from Quebec to cease doing so, since no further provisions were expected from England until spring. As a result, a great many of the Indians, mostly Senecas, outside the walls of Ft. Niagara, became weakened from lack of food and froze to death during the winter.

204. Munsee is often spelled Muncie or Muncy. Some of the Munsees later settled in the Indiana country in the vicinity of the present city of Muncie.

205. The stream called Dagahshenodeago by the Delawares is the present Broken Straw Creek, its mouth located six miles below what was Conewago on the site of the present city of Warren in Warren Co., Pa.

206. Hutgueote, pronounced HOOT-gway-oat, means Arrow, but he was commonly called Red Eye by the whites. Natahgoah, pronounced NAH-tuh-GO-uh, meaning Crow, was usually called Captain Crow by the whites. Dehguswaygahent, pronounced day-gus-WAY-guh-hent, means Fallen Board. Dayoosta, pronounced duh-YOO-stuh, means Light in Weight or, more literally, It Is Light to Be Lifted. Dahgahswagaheh, pronounced DAH-guz-WAH-guh-heh, means Rifle Stock Dropped. Dahgahgahend, pronounced DAH-guh-GAY-hend, means White Eye. Gennehoon, pronounced JEN-uh-hoo-on, means Double Door. Both Crow and Red Eye, who eventually became a chief, later resided on the Allegheny Reservation at Cold Spring and both died there at about the same time in 1799.

207. Dunosahdahgah, pronounced due-NOSS-suh-duh-GAH, which means The Burnt House, was so named after an Indian dwelling there having burned accidentally a long time ago. The village was well known among the whites as Cornstalk's Town and was also often called Simon Girty's Town. Warhoyonehteh is pronounced war-hoe-YONE-uh-teh.

208. Gahgeote, pronounced GAH-jee-oat, means Half Town. He pursued the army to just below present Kittanning before giving up.

209. The Shawnee graveyard at Chalahgawtha was located on present Shawnee Creek, 200 yards upstream from where it is crossed by present Hawkins Road, just northwest of Xenia, seat of Greene Co. The Baltimore & Ohio Railroad line was built over a portion of the graveyard.

210. This was a party of 42 men under the general command of Maj. David Rogers, who had been sent downriver from Ft. Pitt to the Spanish governor in New Orleans the previous spring to procure a loan of funds and as much ammunition and other supplies as possible, as the money was needed for continuing the war against the Americans and the supplies were much needed by the troops in the upper Ohio River forts. Rogers's second in command was Capt. George Gibson, brother of Col. John Gibson of Ft. Pitt, and they were now on their return with the precious cargo of gunpowder, lead, new fusees (flintlock rifles), dry goods, rum, and a chest of Spanish silver dollars. The boats reached Ft. Nelson at the Falls of the Ohio (the settlement there soon to become Louisville) on August 29 and remained for about a month. When it left, it was augmented with a guard of 28 soldiers under Lt. Abraham Chaplin. The entire complement of men in the flotilla as it left the Falls of the Ohio was 70 men, which included hired men to work as pole men and guards, plus a few passengers from the Ft. Nelson area, who were largely civilians and retired officers wanting to get to Ft. Pitt and points east. Maj. Rogers also carried dispatches from George Rogers Clark and Col. John Todd to Gov. Thomas Jefferson, reporting on the weakness of Clark's command and that of the Kentucky settlements in general.

211. Some reports also place the third Girty brother, James, as having been here, but such reports are not reliable and available evidence indicates that James Girty was, at this time, involved with some Indian attacks occurring on the upper Ohio in the vicinity of Wheeling. The confusion probably results from the fact that all three Girty brothers were present as interpreters at the council held a fortnight later at Upper Sandusky.

212. The mouth of the Licking River is presently the dividing line between the cities of Covington and Newport, Ky., directly across the Ohio River from the present Riverfront Stadium ballpark in downtown Cincinnati, Ohio. This river mouth is 130 river miles upstream from present Louisville and 470 river miles downstream from Ft. Pitt.

213. The term "bark canoe" always seems to conjure up the picture of the picturesque birch bark canoe, but the Shawnees rarely, if ever, used birch, which was not indigenous to the Ohio country. Several different types of trees were used for making the standard bark canoe, but the most favored was elm, since it was very flexible and easy to work. Two experienced Shawnee men could make a bark canoe suitable for crossing the Ohio River in about two hours. An elm with a good straight trunk would be chosen that was a foot and a half to two feet in diameter. Using tomahawks, a line would be cut through the bark all the way around the tree just above ground level. Another line would be cut straight up the trunk for ten to twelve feet, one of the Shawnees standing on the shoulders of the other when it became too high to work otherwise. Then the man on top would cut a line around the tree similar to the one at the base. Elm bark separates from the base wood quite easily and they would pry it back, using the tomahawks as levers, until the bark came off in a single tube. One end of the tube would be flattened together so the cut lines met exactly and then, using sharpened wooden pegs, holes would be punched two or three inches apart about an inch or so inward from the ends of the tubular bark. The same thing would be done to the other end. Then long strands of tough wild grapevine would be used to lace each end very tightly. Finally, sections of sturdy branches would be cut just long enough to act as crossbars to prop the long cut apart to its fullest extent. Sometimes (not always) these crossbars would be also be snugged in place with pieces of grapevine through peg-holes. The result was a square-ended canoe that was not much for looks and could not make much speed, but which could very nicely carry a couple of men and their gear across the broad river. Paddles were made from tough stiff sections of oak bark. Such bark canoes always leaked at the ends, but not as much as might be expected, and if the load weight, including the paddlers, was positioned close enough to the center, the canoe would bow downward in the middle, lifting the ends high enough that they would barely come in contact with the water. When finished using such a canoe, the Indians usually found a secluded backwater up a creek, filled the canoe with water and then put large rocks in it to sink it for possible use another time. The elm bark resisted rotting for a considerable time and a canoe sunk in this manner in spring could be raised and used as late as the following fall, though they almost never survived undamaged through a winter.

214. The keelboats became visible from the mouth of the Licking about the time they began passing just below the present 11th District School in the Kenton Hills area of the city of Covington.

215. The single keelboat that had fallen behind some distance was the one under command of the upper Ohio frontiersman William Linn, which carried thirteen men, including Linn.

216. Maj. David Rogers was killed in the first volley of the firing and Simon Girty later boasted that it was he who had killed Rogers. Cap. George Gibson was also killed, although some accounts say he was among the captured and later killed by torture at Chalahgawtha. Lt. Robert Benham, who had been in command of one of the guard, managed to escape but had been shot through both hips and escaped by hiding among the branches of a fallen tree. Another who escaped was one of the boatmen, Basil Brown, wounded with a rifle ball that shattered his right arm (some accounts say both arms broken by the same rifle ball, but this appears to be fabrication). Unaware of each other on shore, the two wounded men survived for two days before finally discovering one another. For several weeks the pair helped one another survive and finally on November 27, still close to the mouth of the Licking River, they managed to attract the attention of a passing boat. Fearful of this being an Indian trick, the boat stayed well clear of them until downstream, then put out a canoe which came back and picked them up and carried them safely back to Ft. Nelson. Benham recovered from his wounds, although he walked with a limp the rest of his life due to the lead ball that had wedged in one hip after passing through the other and was never removed. Basil Brown's arm did not heal properly and his hand atrophied, the fingers curling up into a perpetual clawlike configuration. Benham later came back, claimed land at the mouth of the Licking and settled there until he was ousted by someone whose title to the land held up in court better than his. Only two of the men captured have been positively identified—one was Abraham Chaplin (called Chapline or Kaplan in some accounts) who was scheduled to be tortured to death at Chalahgawtha but who managed to escape, and Col. John Campbell, county lieutenant of Youghiogheny Co., a former friend of Simon Girty, who was recognized by Girty and saved from torture and death. Campbell was turned over to British authorities in Detroit, where he was kept in confinement for some time, then sent to Quebec, but finally exchanged and returned to the United States. (There is some substantial evidence that through all this period, Campbell was acting as a secret agent and spy for the British. Nevertheless, he was subsequently a Kentucky representative in the Virginia Legislature and became speaker of the Kentucky Senate in 1798, the year before his death.)

217. Capt. Arent de Peyster, commanding at Detroit, wrote to Canada Gov. Haldimand: "I have the pleasure to acquaint you that . . . Simon Girty, his brother and Matthew Elliott have defeated a Captain Rogers on the Ohio, a stroke which must greatly disconcert the rebels at Pittsburgh."

218. Contrary to some accounts, Lt. Abraham Chaplin was not one of those at the stake in Chalahgawtha. He had been condemned to death and painted black, but was in the custody of the Wyandots, not the Shawnees, and managed to escape from those Wyandots before the execution could take place. His report to authorities, along with that of a civilian named George Hendricks, who had been taken about two years earlier at a Kentucky salt lick and who escaped at the same time as Chaplin, comprised the first indication the western settlements had of a major invasion planned against them. The identity of the two put to the stake in Chalahgawtha is not known, nor that of the captive who was killed during the gauntlet run. The fourth man, Col.

John Campbell, was one of the two who reached the council house on the first gauntlet run, following which he was redeemed by Simon Girty to take to Detroit as a prisoner.

219. Capt. Henry Bird (often referred to incorrectly as colonel, a rank he earned considerably later) was an officer of the British 8th Regiment. His name has frequently been spelled Byrd.

220. The winter of 1779–80 was noted as being one of the coldest on record all over the country. Snow was on the ground unceasingly from mid-November through March and temperatures plummeted to far below zero. All the major rivers, including the Ohio, Mississippi, Susquehanna, Potomac, and Delaware froze solidly, and even New York harbor froze so hard for five weeks that the port was cut off from sea supply and heavy cannon were dragged across the ice from Staten Island to Manhattan. Numerous eastern journals recorded that the consistently reached low temperature for that five-week period was − 16°.

221. There are a number of reports that many of the Indians died of scurvy, but this is not true. Scurvy was a disease unknown to the Indians. This story had its foundation at Ft. Niagara, where many of the displaced Iroquois had gathered outside the fort walls and begged what supplies they could from the British throughout the winter. But the British in the fort were also short of supplies and it was they who suffered from a severe outbreak of scurvy.

222. Among the more prominent of the new stations or forts in Kentucky were Martin's, Bryan's, Ruddell's Mills (a few miles from Ruddell's Station), Ruddell's Station (which was the rebuilt Hinkson's Fort), Louisville adjacent to Ft. Nelson, Lexington, Georgetown, Crowe's Station, Ft. Jefferson (in far western Kentucky on Mayfield Creek, five miles below the mouth of the Ohio where it flows into the Mississippi, in present Ballard Co.), a new Hinkson's Station at the mouth of Limestone Creek (burned by Indians almost as soon as erected, in April 1780) and others.

223. Boonesboro settlers killed in 1779 included Frederick and Joseph Stams, Richard Hines, David Bundan, Michael Myers, John Dumferd, Joshua Barton, Thomas South, and John Baugh, while three were captured—Joab Barton, Moses McIlwain, and Ambrose White.

224. Some accounts claim Bird had with him 1,000 regulars, 300 Canadian Rangers and 1,000 Indians, but this is a considerable exaggeration.

225. The Maumee Rapids was a 16-mile sporadic stretch of shallow, rocky, swift waters extending upstream from its foot, located just above the present U.S. 20/25 bridge connecting the west end of present Perrysburg to the center of present Maumee, with the unnavigable rapids continuing sporadically upstream to its head at present Grand Rapids, Ohio, the entire course flanked by a portage trail along the northwest shoreline, formerly called the Maumee Trail but presently the Anthony Wayne Trail. One account states that the British Indian agent Matthew Elliott was also a member of Bird's force, but that is an error, since Elliott was at this time at (or en route to) Quebec.

226. The Auglaize River empties into the Maumee River at the site of the present city of Defiance, seat of Defiance Co., O.

227. The location called Wapaghkonetta later became the site of the principal Shawnee village under Chief Catahecassa—Black Hoof—and was named Wapakoneta, located on the site of the present city of Wapakoneta, Auglaize Co., O. The Great Miami headwaters were reached at the foot of a marshy glacial lake, present Indian Lake, at the site of the present village of Russell's Point, Logan Co., O.

228. This rendezvous point was in the center of the present city of Dayton, Montgomery Co., O., at the northeastern edge of the downtown area.

229. The Great Miami River empties into the Ohio River some 20 miles west of present downtown Cincinnati, Hamilton Co., O., at the point where the present states of Ohio, Indiana, and Kentucky converge.

230. Some writers have contended that Simon Girty was also involved in the agitation of the Indians by recalling to them their dead heroes, but subsequent events indicate this was not true and that Simon, as so frequently occurs in the accounts at the time, was blamed for acts of malice and brutality that were perpetrated by his brothers, especially Jim (James), who was a man virtually without scruples.

231. By this time the white population in Kentucky was greatly alarmed, as word had filtered to them of the invasion being launched against them. Most outlying cabins were abandoned and the residents had taken refuge in the nearest forts, fearfully awaiting what was to come. As word reached them of the certain advance against them of the combined British and Indian force, the county lieutenant of Kentucky Co., Col. John Bowman, wrote an urgent letter to Col. Daniel Brodhead, who was in command at Ft. Pitt:

Kentucky County
May 27th, 1780

Colonel Brodhead,
Sir:—At this most alarming period, I think it necessary to inform you of the designs of our cruel enemy, the British and Indians, against this part of the Western frontiers of Virginia. Lieutenant Abraham Chaplin, who was taken last November [October] at the time Colonel Rogers was defeated by the Indians on the Ohio, and George Hendricks, who was likewise taken at the Salt Springs on Licking in the year 1777 with Major Boone, made their escape from the Wyandotte [sic] Nation of Indians, living on the waters of Sandusky, the 27th and 28th ultimo, who bring intelligence that a large number of the different tribes of Indians in conjunction with some of the troops belonging to the King of Great Britain, to the amount of 2,000 in the whole, 600 of whom are green coat Rangers from Canada, were preparing to attack the garrison at the Falls of Ohio [Ft. Nelson] with cannon &c. And after reducing the same, their next destination is to Illinois in order to take that post. Likewise that Captain Matthew Elliott gave them information that the different tribes of Indians were gathering their horses in order to assist the enemy on their expedition over the carrying place from Omey [Omi, meaning Maumee River, but confused with the Auglaize tributary of the Maumee], and that the enemy will be at the Falls of Ohio in about four weeks from this time.

Though I have not had the honor of being personally acquainted with you, but from character am well assured of your great zeal for the welfare of the United States in general, and that you have always been ready to render them your services on all occasions—therefore, I am induced to request of you all assistance of men, ammunition, and provisions, together with artillery, in order to relieve us from the approaching danger, which seems to threaten this part of the world, as far as in your power, consistent with the line of your duty, which I am in hopes you will not deny. I am certain you are sensible, that should this country give away, the Illinois will fall, of course, which will enable our enemy, the Britons, to call all the Indians at the westward into their service, which would, I am persuaded, be of very bad consequence to the United States in general. Pray pardon the freedom I have taken, as I assure you it is from no other motive but the public good.

I am, with esteem, your most obt. and very humble servt.

John Bowman
County Lieutenant of Kentucky County

To Colonel Brodhead.

232. This camp was made at the site of present Falmouth, Pendleton Co., Ky.

233. Gray's Run was crossed close to its mouth where it empties into the South Fork of the Licking River at present Cynthiana, Harrison Co., Ky.

234. This crossing was made at the site of the present village of Lair, Harrison Co., Ky.

235. Isaac Ruddell had been hurt a few days before when a large rock he and others were moving had slipped and rolled onto his leg.

236. At least one account states that the whites in Ruddell's put up a three-day resistance, during which time the fort was repeatedly bombarded until breached, at which time the place was surrendered. This does not jibe with most other accounts, which indicate the surrender was almost immediate and after only one shot was fired from the 6-pounder. This same account states that during the attack someone in the fort made a long shot of some three or four hundred yards with his rifle and killed one of the British regulars, and that when the place was surrendered and the guns stacked, Bird asked Isaac Ruddell which gun it was that had performed the successful shot. When it was pointed out to him, so the account goes, Bird claimed the rifle as his own, took it back to Detroit and had it ornamented with silver. During an 1864 interview by historian Lyman Draper, Simon Girty's daughter, Mrs. Sarah Munger (who was born 11 years after this incident) related that her father said that at the surrender of Ruddell's he (Simon) was bearer of the white flag and entered the fort to demand the surrender of the place; that when he went in hundreds of rifles were trained on him; that he convinced them to surrender and that Girty "had hard work afterwards to save them from the Indians." The former part of the comment, that Girty was flag-bearer and demanded the surrender seems to be an exaggeration; the latter point, that he had hard work saving the prisoners from the Indians seems to be largely true.

237. Elizabeth Bowman Ruddell was the daughter of Col. John Bowman and the wife of Isaac Ruddell. One account states that the infant was killed by the Indian jerking it away from Mrs. Ruddell and dashing its brains out against a tree, but since they were inside the fort at the time and there were no trees there or in the immediate vicinity, this report is considered spurious. A similar story, entirely fictional, is that when the infant was jerked away from her and she leaped to its rescue, Mrs. Ruddell was tomahawked and she, too, fell into the flames and expired. In point of fact, she was taken prisoner, along with other members of her family, and was later redeemed from the Indians by Maj. Lemoult in Detroit, who helped Isaac Ruddell get some members of his family back when he, Lemoult, discovered that Ruddell was a fellow Mason. In addition to Elizabeth Ruddell, Lemoult was able to effect the redemption of Ruddell's daughter, Elizabeth, and his two youngest sons, John and Isaac, but they were unable to locate Stephen and Abram who, it was believed by them, had been killed.

238. One account states that Isaac Ruddell, because of the injury to his leg, was executed with the others who were elderly, ill or injured, but this was not true, as Isaac Ruddell was taken to Detroit and remained there for a considerable while, finally returning to Kentucky after the war. It was rumored that while he was in Detroit, Ruddell became an informer for the British and spied on his fellow captives, for which he was allegedly paid 900 guineas. When he returned to Kentucky he was tried for collusion with the enemy but acquitted, but an irate neighbor nevertheless whipped him badly with a hoop-pole for his rumored Tory activities. Ruddell survived the beating as well as the gossip that plagued him for many years and became a successful Kentucky dairy farmer. A large number of the captives taken to Detroit remained there after the war and became Canadian residents, never again returning to Kentucky.

239. Martin's Station was located five miles south of Ruddell's, on the bank of Stoner Creek, three miles below (north of) the site of present Paris, Bourbon Co., Ky.

240. Bryan's Station (often erroneously written as Bryant's) was established by William Bryan, an uncle of Rebecca Boone, wife of Daniel. The station was located on North Elkhorn Creek, five miles northeast of present Lexington, Fayette Co., adjacent to where present Bryan Station Pike (State Route 57) crosses North Elkhorn Creek. William Bryan was killed by Indians close to the station just a month before the surrender.

241. Accounts of the number captured at the two forts range from a low of 360 to as high as 600. The most prevalent number seems to be 470 actually taken into captivity and that is probably very nearly correct. No less than 20 and perhaps as many as 24 or 25 were killed during the initial attack.

242. Many accounts show the name of Stephen Ruddell's brother as Abraham, but that is an error; it was actually Abram, who was 7 years old when taken. He had been slightly wounded and had crawled behind a log and hidden. When discovered, he allegedly begged the Indians to kill him, but they did not. It is not known what Shawnee name he was given nor into whose family he was adopted, but he spent many years with the Shawnees and it seems likely he was adopted into the family of a medicine man, since he returned to the whites with a considerable knowledge of Indian doctoring and remedies. During his captivity he had his ear lobes cut so he could wear ear bobs and rings.

243. The two who escaped the Indians en route were John Sellers and John Hinkson. The latter was aided by Simon Girty in his escape, the two having been companions some time before in Pennsylvania. The other prisoners were marched all the way to Detroit, however. There, outside the fort, a number of small houses were built close together for the lodging of these prisoners and the place was dubbed Yankee Hall. A great many of the captives refused repatriation when the time came and elected to remain in the north as Canadian citizens.

244. The entire force under Capt. Bird, including the captives, had crossed the Ohio River in relays in the available canoes, but it had taken a considerable while and was not finished until dark. Among the last of the canoes to cross were those carrying the swivels and the heavy wheeled cannon. The swivels made it across all right but the canoe carrying the cannon never showed up. Several boatloads of Indians went back to look for it and finally found the empty, overturned canoe some distance downstream and the belief was that they had struck a floating log and overturned. No trace was found of either the cannon or the four soldiers who had been paddling it across. The fact of the matter was that Simon Kenton (who had now discarded the name Butler and resumed his true identity, having discovered that he hadn't actually killed a neighbor earlier, as he had thought) and a man named Charles Gatliff had followed the Bird force to the Ohio and watched the crossing from under cover. As it got dark and they saw their opportunity, they attacked the final boat carrying the cannon, dumping the gun and its ammunition in the water at the mouth of the Licking and killing all four of the soldiers. The cannon was later recovered by the Kentucky settlers. Greater details of these incidents may be found in *The Frontiersmen*.

245. As taken from the Shawnee Tribal Records and as related by the late Thomas Wildcat Alford, great-grandson of Tecumseh.

246. George Rogers Clark had appealed to Col. John Bowman for aid in the proposed campaign against the Shawnee villages, but was refused. However, Col. John Slaughter, with a force of 150 regulars, had received orders from Virginia "to guard and protect the people of Kentucky County" and chose to interpret these as giving aid to Clark, which he did, placing himself and his command under Clark's orders for the expedition. When Clark's force crossed the Ohio River at the mouth of the Licking they built a small blockhouse for their stores on the Ohio side, the first white construction on the site of present Cincinnati, Ohio, just about where the Riverside Stadium is located.

247. Red Snake and Girty had been spying on the advance of the Clark army when they spied Simon Kenton (Bahd-ler) scouting ahead and Red Snake had drawn a bead on him and was in the act of squeezing the trigger when he was stopped by Girty, making this the second time Girty had saved Simon Kenton's life.

248. The source of the Shawnee silver, of which there was a considerable abundance, has always been a matter of mystery and intrigue. There is no doubt whatever that the Shawnees did have access to a large and continuing supply of raw silver and there is no evidence of such ore ever having been transported into the Shawnee territory from elsewhere. There is much romantic folklore about the so-called "lost Shawnee silver mines," most of which is rather ridiculous, but enough truth exists in the record as to be intriguing. Such mines, if they existed, are believed to have been located in present Warren and Green Counties in Ohio, such reports based on the accounts of various white men who had been held captive at Chalahgawtha and were forced to carry ore to the village for smelting and working. These prisoners were marched, always blind-folded, for what seemed to them a few hours (but which was probably less) upstream along the course of Massies Creek to some location in the Clifton Gorge area, from just behind present Wilberforce University to "The Glen" in the present village of Yellow Springs. At a certain point the prisoners were ordered to sit and wait under guard until they were laden with heavy sacks of what they believed to be silver-bearing ore, which they were compelled to carry back to Chalahgawtha. Some attempts to slip the blindfolds were, to a limited extent, successful. With a map or two of "mine locations," this general area is well described by Dr. Roy S. King, University of Arizona, in an interesting paper entitled "Silver Mines of the Ohio Indians," in the *Ohio Archaeological and Historical Quarterly*, XXVI (1917), 114–116. For many years after their removal to the Auglaize Reservation, small parties of Shawnees returned every summer to Greene Co. and stopped for a few days of camping in "The Glen" at Yellow Springs, now a part of the campus of Antioch University. They then passed onward to the location given in Professor King's paper and from there to well-marked locations in Warren Co. along Caesar Creek near present Harveysburg, where excavations (made before the advent of white pioneers) were discovered by the earliest arriving settlers. Virtually all of this area has now been covered over by the U.S. Corps of Engineers impoundment called Caesar Creek Lake. Early excavations of two similar excavations found in the glen at Yellow Springs showed vertical shafts with evidence of timbering in one of them. Excavation evidence at one site is still vaguely apparent. Geological surveys state that the Clifton limestone formation outcropping in this glen as well as the nearby Clifton Gorge is not ore-bearing. Yet, William Albert Galloway (lineal descendent of James Galloway, first white settler in the Chalahgawtha area), while he was a student at Antioch College, did some blasting in the gorge and uncovered a half-inch vein near the falls on the east end of Yellow Springs Creek, which runs through these grounds. The residue of some specimens from this vein were submitted to a competent assayer in Cincinnati and were found to contain a very definite bead of high-grade silver. Some decades ago an exploratory shaft in Clifton Gorge but no heavy deposit of silver was located and the shaft was abandoned and sealed off when it showed signs of collapsing. Only a few years ago a geology student collecting rock samples in the gorge found several pieces of ore quite rich in silver content. The mother lode, if one exists, however, has never been located.

249. Due to the series of events that followed, even though Chalahgawtha was reoccupied by the Shawnees and the village rebuilt, the treasure of Shawnee goods was never recovered from the marsh. Years later this marsh was drained and became farmland, which it still is to the present day. A large barn sits atop the site that had been occupied by the council house and the spring was reported to have been located approximately 700 feet northwest of that council house and some 300 feet south of the Little Miami River. Draining of the marsh caused the spring to fail and its walls to eventually collapse. Extensive searches have been carried out by various individuals (including the author) and groups, including modern Shawnees, but the lost Shawnee treasure has never, so far as is recorded, been recovered, although occasional implements, utensils and weapons have been found. Greater details concerning the amount and type of silver and other goods and the circumstances involved in the caching of it, as well as details of the George Rogers Clark invasion, may be found in *The Frontiersmen.*

250. The artillery Clark used was the very 6-pounder cannon that had been used against Ruddell's Fort and which Simon Kenton and Charles Gatliffe had stolen from the Capt. Bird force as it crossed the Ohio River.

251. In his official report of August 22, 1780, to Gov. Jefferson, George Rogers Clark wrote:

> *Our loss was about 14 killed and 13 wounded; theirs at least triple that number. They carried off their dead during the night, except 12 or 14 that lay too near our lines for them to venture. . . . We destroyed upwards of 800 acres of corn, besides great quantities of vegetables.*

252. The Lower Peckuwe Town was located just a little over two miles upstream on the Great Miami River from where the old Miami village of Pickawillany had been situated on the site of the present city of Piqua, Miami Co., O., at the mouth of Loramie Creek, that village site located adjacent to where Lockington Dam has been constructed. Upper Peckuwe Town was located on Loramie Creek thirteen miles upstream from its mouth at the site of the present village of Ft. Loramie, Shelby Co., O. Some time later, when the Shawnees established yet another Chalahgawtha, on the Maumee River, the seventh of that name in Ohio, the former Lower Peckuwe Town was repopulated by Peckuwes and was renamed Peckuwe, a name later corrupted to the present Piqua.

253. Some accounts contend that Tecumseh (and/or Chiksika) were present at Chalahgawtha during the evacuation by Catahecassa and his people and at Piqua Town during the battle with Clark's force, but this is incorrect, as it was not till over a month later that the brothers returned from their extended northern and western trip.

254. William Burnett's trading post, one of the most important in the northwest, was located at the site of the present city of Niles, Berrien Co., Mich. Burnett was highly favored among the Potawatomies, especially because he had married Kawkeeme, sister of the tribe's powerful chief, Topenebe (Toe-PEN-uh-bee), whose name meant Sits Quietly. At least one account states that Burnett did not establish his post here until 1783, but that is incorrect; the post on the St. Joseph River was established in the spring of 1778.

255. Lower Sandusky was a major Wyandot village located close to 50 miles downstream on the Sandusky River from Upper Sandusky, and about 10 miles upstream from the western end of Sandusky Bay. The village was located on the site of the present city of Fremont, Sandusky Co., O. The well-used Indian trail from the mouth of the Auglaize ran directly east, practically along the line of present State Route 281 from present Defiance to about the site of the present village of Mermill on the Middle Branch of Portage River, then angling slightly northward through the present towns of Wayne and Millersville to present Fremont.

256. Pipe was also frequently referred to as Captain Pipe. He had recently formed a close association with the war chief of the Delawares, Wingenund, and together—often with the aid of Simon Girty and one or both of his brothers—they had been leading some devastating attacks against the settlements from Ft. Pitt down to Wheeling.

257. Only two of the three islands remain today, the third and smallest having long ago been washed away with floods. The two remaining are presently called Manchester Island Number One and Manchester Island Number Two. It was from the former that the attack was launched.

258. The twisting creek in question here is present Isaacs Creek which empties into the Ohio River only a half-mile downstream from the present city of Manchester in Adams Co., O. The small tributary of that stream, in which the canoes were hidden the previous fall, is present Williamson Hollow directly north of the center of Manchester.

259. There is no clear identification as to exactly who this group of 39 immigrants were, except that they had come from far to the east, presumably Philadelphia, had purchased their two keelboats at the boatyard located at the mouth of the Youghiogheny and had visited for two days in Wheeling on their way downriver. At Wheeling they had been warned about the river attacks that had been occurring, but they had expressed confidence in their numbers and their ability to defend themselves and equally expressed an unshakable faith that the Lord would see them through. They couldn't have been more incorrect. So far as the grisly "prank" of the Shawnee war party was concerned, it worked far beyond their expectations. The man who leaped from the cliff with a tomahawk in his back was not instantly killed. He swam a distance underwater and upon surfacing managed to grasp a floating log and clung to it as it floated all through the remainder of that day and the ensuing night until, the following morning, April 13, he was spotted as he drifted past the Limestone settlement some fourteen miles below where he had started and was brought to shore. One of his lungs had been punctured by the tomahawk, which had finally fallen free of his back somewhere along the way as he drifted, and he was dying, but he lived long enough to explain to his rescuers, which included Simon Kenton, what had occurred. Kenton mounted a rescue party and went to the scene, where they spied what they all thought to be an Indian on guard over a group of bodies, an Indian who had fallen asleep. Kenton had put the others in hiding and himself spent a considerable time creeping up, only to realize when he got very close that it was all a macabre illusion. They buried all the dead here in a common grave before returning to Limestone.

260. No signature was appended to the letter written to Gov. Haldimand, but the handwriting and other clues seem to indicate it was penned by Col. Guy Johnson, British superintendent of Indian Affairs and nephew of Sir William Johnson.

261. At this very time, missionary David Zeisberger, in his quarters at Tuppaking, was writing to Col. John Gibson about their presence here:

> *I acquaint you that a number of Indians, about 250 in all, are approaching towards you. As much as I could learn, it is their intention to go to Wheeling. They also said to Fort McIntosh and Fort*

Pitt. The first place I am apt to believe most where they will go. They will try to decoy the garrison out where they lie in ambush for them, or drive some cattle or horses that they shall be followed, and so cut them off. The party is headed by Matthew Elliott and a few English and French, but I believe some of them will turn back from Gnadenhutten, where they are at present and not go to war. We wish they were gone from us, for they are very troublesome to us. . . . You will be careful not to mention abroad that you had the intelligence from our towns, for it would prove dangerous for us if the Indians should get intelligence of it.

262. At Ft. Pitt early in February, Gen. Daniel Brodhead, progressively angrier over the continued attacks on the settlements in that vicinity, had ordered Col. David Williamson to lead a punitive expedition against the Delawares and Wyandots on the Tuscarawas and Sandusky, giving him a free hand in the matter of chastising them.

263. One account states that the two who escaped were a boy and a girl, both of whom had been scalped by the Americans, but survived.

264. More complete details of the Moravian Massacre—or Gnadenhutten Massacre, as it came to be known—as well as the events preceding and subsequent to it, may be found in *The Frontiersmen*.

265. Site of present Mingo Junction in present Jefferson Co., O., about 4 miles south of the present city of Steubenville.

266. There is much disparity in the reports concerning the number of Indians. Some accounts say as few as 250, others as many as 1,600. Girty himself, when he came to ask Crawford to surrender, told the colonel his army was surrounded by over three times his own number, which would be over 1,450 men. The consensus seems to be, however, that there were "around a thousand of the enemy."

267. Some accounts have contended that only 300 of the 489 whites made it back to the settlements.

268. Girty made considerable efforts to save Crawford, even offering $3,000 worth of goods for his life, but to no avail. The site where Crawford was burned at the stake was on the east side of Tymochtee Creek, some 200 yards east of the creek proper and four miles upstream from its mouth at the Upper Sandusky, placing it very close to where State Route 103 crosses Tymochtee Creek, two miles west by west-southwest of the village off Tymochtee and 7.5 miles north of the present city of Upper Sandusky, Wyandot Co., O. Greater details of the Crawford campaign, his capture and death can be found in *The Frontiersmen*.

269. The captive alluded to was Charles Beasley, brother of Capt. John Beasley, who was held by the Shawnees for a couple of weeks, during which time he was questioned by Girty about the strength of the fort. Beasley finally managed to escape and made his way back to Bryan's, arriving there only two days before the attack.

270. The fording place was located at the site where present old U.S. Highway 68 crosses the Licking River just less than a thousand feet downstream where the new (present) U.S. 68 crosses the river.

271. The two residents of Bryan's Station who had escaped to Lexington were John Bell and Richard Tomlin, who also came back with the rescuers and later fought at the Blue Licks Battle.

272. Aaron Reynolds was known to have killed one of the Indians as he was peering through a split rail fence.

273. These three who prevented the fire from spreading were Ellison Williams and two 16-year-olds named Michael Mitchell, Jr., and Robert Gayle.

274. The man shot in the head and killed inside the station was Michael Mitchell, Sr., father of the youth who helped prevent the fire from spreading. One account says the rifle ball struck him in the forehead; another says it struck him just below the left eye. The other man fatally shot was Lawrence Adkins, who was shot through the stomach and soon died. The third man, Nicholas Tomlin, had his arm broken by a ball.

275. Col. Levi Todd was in command at Lexington when the two men arrived with word of the attack on Bryan's Station. Instantly he sent messengers to Boonesboro, Harrodsburg, Danville, and Stanford to raise men and send them immediately to help. (Danville and Stanford were the new names for, respectively, what had been Crowe's Station and Logan's Fort.)

276. The detachment of 17 had been led by Capt. Robert Patterson. It was when they reached Lexington again that Col. Levi Todd sent messengers to his brother, Col. John Todd, and the Lincoln Co. Lieutenant, Col. Stephen Trigg, to come at once with reinforcements.

277. Colonels Stephen Trigg and John Todd, along with Maj. Hugh McGary and others, arrived at Lexington the evening of August 17 with 130 mounted men. With the men from Lexington and Boonesboro, this number was increased to 170 and by the following morning another dozen had arrived, making a total of 182 to ride out in defense of Bryan's, while only a handful would remain to defend Lexington. It was the hope and belief of all that they would quickly be followed up by additional men from Harrod's, Logan's, and Crowe's. They were not wrong in this; as soon as the word had reached Stanford of the attack, Benjamin Logan gathered 470 men, with Simon Kenton, who was there, as one of the company commanders, and set out at once for Lexington and Bryan's. But Logan's was some 50 miles farther south and it would take a good while to reach Bryan's.

278. The route followed through the ravine after crossing the Licking River was essentially the route of old U.S. 68 to where it joins with the new route of that number, a thousand feet south of the south entrance to the present Blue Licks Battlefield State Park, then continuing along that highway, following the ridge to the north boundary of the park, almost exactly one mile from the ford.

279. When the white force under Col. John Todd reached the south bank of the Licking, they found that the trail of the supposedly retreating Indian party was so fresh that mud was still swirling in the tracks they had made in the shallows where they crossed. Boone, who knew the terrain well, strongly advised against crossing, suspecting that there might be an ambush. He was backed up in this contention by both Col. Todd and Col. Trigg. However, Maj. Hugh McGary, noted for his stubborn hotheadedness, insisted they pursue, accused those who were hesitating of cowardice and said he was going to chase them down if he had to do it alone. He stormed at them: "All of you who are not damned cowards, follow me and I'll soon show you the Indians!" Stung by the words, a few followed McGary, then more, until even Boone, Todd, and Trigg finally gave in and followed.

280. Among the dead whites were their two principal commanders, Colonels John Todd and Stephen Trigg and most of their other officers, including Majors Edward Bulger, Silas Harlan, and James McBride, Captains John Beasley (captured and later executed), John Bulger, John Gordon, William McBride, Clough Overton, and Joe Kincaid (who is listed as a private in some accounts), Lieutenants William Givens (listed as McGivens in one account), Thomas Hinkson (listed as Hinson in some accounts), John Kennedy, Joseph Lindsay (listed as a private in some accounts), James McGuire, John McMurtry (listed as ensign in some accounts, who was captured and later executed), and Barnett Rogers. Killed among the privates were Charles Black, Samuel Black, Israel Bone, Samuel Brannon, James Brown (surveyor and listed as Mr. in some accounts), Esau Corn, Hugh Cunningham, John Doglass (listed as Douglas and Douglass in various accounts), William Eads (spelled Eadds in some accounts), Thomas Farrier, Charles Ferguson, Ezekiel Field, John Folley, Daniel Foster, John Fry, James Graham (also called Little Jim), Jervis Green, Daniel Greggs, Francis Harper, Matthew Harper, William Harris, John Jolly, James Ledgerwood (Lederwood in some accounts), Gilbert Marshall, Francis McBride, Andrew McConnell, Isaac McCracken, Henry Miller, John Nelson, John Nutt, John O'Neal, John Oikal, Joseph Oldfield, Drury Polley, John Price, William Robertson, Lewis Rose, Matthias Rose, William Shannon, James Smith, William Smith, John Stapleton, Valentine Stern, William Stevens, John Stevenson, William Stewart, Richard Tomlinson (in some accounts, the first name given as Rifhard, which is obviously a typographical error), Israel Wilson, John Wilson, a second man also named John Wilson, Archibald Woods, Matthew Wylie, and Jesse Yokum (also spelled Yocum or Yoacum in some accounts). Col. Daniel Boone was one of the few principal officers who was not killed, though his son Israel was. The site of this battle is now the Blue Licks Battlefield State Park, where a monumental obelisk has been raised upon which are engraved the names of all those slain among the whites.

281. Because Simon Girty has long been branded a despicable renegade by American historians, he has almost never been given the credit due him for his brilliance as a strategist. The Blue Licks campaign was one of virtually perfect planning and execution, as were many other operations he directed against the Americans. Although the disaster for the whites at Blue Licks was largely due to the hotheadedness of Maj. Hugh McGary in not exercising proper caution in the face of an enemy, the blame for the defeat was ultimately laid on George Rogers Clark, who was not even at the scene. Clark had been very lax in communicating with his superiors in Virginia and, because of shortages of men, supplies and ample protection, had not been able to build a series of forts that he had been directed to build by the governor of Virginia. Further, rumors were flying that most of the time Clark was so drunk he couldn't function properly in any capacity. In retrospect, it was deemed by authorities that had such forts been built, the attack that occurred against Bryan's Station and the ambush at Blue Licks would not have taken place.

282. The location alluded to was where present Cowan Creek empties into Todd Fork less than two miles northeast of present Clarksville, Clinton Co., O. Clark's army was principally volunteers from Kentucky and numbered, at the beginning, 1,050 men. It was guided by Simon Kenton, Daniel Boone, and Phil Waters, all three of whom had been prisoners of the Shawnees at Chalahgawtha.

283. The detachment that left George Rogers Clark's main army under command of Col. Benjamin Logan, second in command to Clark, was said, in some accounts, to have numbered as many as 300 horsemen, but 150 is the correct figure.

284. One of the volunteers in Clark's army on this occasion was a Scot named James Galloway, who was very impressed by the land in the Chalahgawtha area. When the Indian threat had ended and the land was thrown open to settlement, he was the first white to come there with his family and settle.

285. The man who had been shot was not Clark but rather Capt. Victor McCracken. His brother, Isaac, a private, had been among those who had been killed at the Blue Licks Battle. Capt. McCracken's wound was serious, the ball having shattered his arm bone just above the elbow. The injury was treated as well as could be done under their circumstances, but by the time the army was halfway back to the Ohio River, the wound had become gangrenous and it was obvious he was dying. He managed to hold on until they reached the spot on the north shore of the river where they had assembled after making their crossing and there he died and was buried.

286. As nearly as can be determined, this remarkable hunting feat by Tecumseh occurred about three miles north of present Urbana, Champaign Co., O., close to the area where U.S. 68 crosses King Creek. As a rule, the Shawnees never hunted buffalo until midautumn, so that if any females were killed in the hunt who had calves, those calves would be old enough to survive on their own.

287. The Pigeon Town destroyed was located at the mouth of present Greenville Creek where it empties into the Stillwater River close to the site of the present village of Covington, Miami Co., O. A village of the same name was then built by the refugees from there, along with some of the Maykujays on present Macochee Creek, three miles upstream from Mackachack Town, placing it four miles upstream of Macochee Creek where it empties into the Mad River at present West Liberty, Logan Co., O. One report states that Logan's detachment reached the French Store of Peter Loramie during the night and that Loramie, hearing them coming, blew out his candle and hid behind the door. When Logan's men entered and began milling around, Loramie mingled with them and slipped through the crowd and escaped, but his establishment was destroyed after being plundered of all goods that were wanted by the Americans.

288. The Delaware village known as Mingo Town, adjacent to which the Cherokees settled and into which they gradually became assimilated, was located on the site of the present village of Mingo, ten miles northeast of present Urbana, in Champaign Co., O.

289. The British commandant, Gen. Haldimand, had passed along his own instructions received from London, to De Peyster, adding his own comment that "Nothing is more natural than this desire [of the Shawnees to continue their offensive]. Yet under the express orders I have received, it is impossible I can comply with their Request."

290. It was just at this time, in the summer of 1783, that George Washington himself proposed to Congress what he called a plan—but which was nothing less than a monumental governmental conspiracy—by which the western lands belonging to the Indians could most easily, least expensively and least bloodlessly be wrested from them. Washington suggested that, in order to "induce them to relinquish *our* territories and remove to the illimitable regions of the West" that the Indians be maneuvered into positions where they had little choice but to sell their lands. Since the expense of a major Indian war could not be shouldered by the young government of the United States, all efforts should be made to implant as many new settlers as possible on Indian lands. In order to do this, there should be made grants of land that was either free, as bounty for previous services performed, or priced so low that few would be able to pass up the opportunity of buying. Washington made special note of suggesting that these settlers should consist largely of veterans of the war, since the presence of former soldiers might tend to awe the Indians or, if it didn't and the Indians rose up in arms, then such settlers would make excellent militia to protect the United States frontier. He also noted that in heavily settling the territory, the settlers would soon kill off all the game and make the land so unattractive to the Indians that they would be "as eager to sell as we are to buy." Washington laid out a blueprint of negotiation for such lands: first, government agents should point out to the Indians that as allies of the British, they had then become conquered when the British surrendered and, as a conquered people they had no land rights or rights of any other kind and therefore could not make demands. Yet, in its generosity, the United States would, if the Indians gave up their claims, pay them a certain amount and also provide them with new lands of their very own farther to the west. In such negotiations, Washington's plan went on, commissioners could promise them that the United States government "will endeavor to restrain our people from hunting or settling" on the new lands that had been so generously given to the tribes, yet at the same time the plan made it clear that despite the promises, the restrictions would be very temporary; that, as always occurred on the frontiers, the bolder of the settlers would begin penetrating and settling the Indian territory and when the Indians complained, new negotiations could proceed and the tribes again moved farther west. The commissioners who handled such treaties, Washington advised, should get the lands as cheaply as possible, but being sensible to try at any given time not to "grasp at too much" lest some form of unified resentment spring up and balk the westward expansion. This plan laid out to the Congress, Washington concluded, "is the cheapest and least distressing way of dealing with them." So logically and well, if not morally and ethically, was the proposal by George Washington laid out that the Congress immediately accepted it and began putting it into application.

291. This extensive tract of land called the Virginia Military Lands took in all the country bordered by the Ohio River to the south, the Scioto River to the east and also to the north in that area of central Ohio where the course of the river was east and west, and the Little Miami River to the west. The only portion of that tract not bounded by a stream was that between the headwaters of the Little Miami and the Scioto and so a diagonal connecting boundary line was drawn between them. The tract totaled 4,000,200 acres of highly fertile lands, which Virginia felt sure would satisfy her troops and veterans. Even though none of it had been surveyed into townships of regular form, the land was declared open for settlement to any individual who held a Virginia Military Land Warrant; such individual having the right to take land in any shape, to the total of his specified acreage on the warrant, so long as it did not overlap anyone else's previously located claim. And, of course, no one was paying much attention to the fact that *any* settling on such land was in direct violation of existing treaties with the tribes.

292. The Treaty of Paris was signed on September 3, 1783. John Adams acted as commissioner on behalf of the United States and he was a tough negotiator. Where the matter of the western boundary of the United States was concerned, the British intended for it to be the Ohio River. Adams declared it must be the Mississippi to the west and the Great Lakes to the north or the treaty would not be signed and the war would continue until the British lost their dominion in Canada as well. At last it was the British commissioner, Oswald, who acceded to the demand, including all Indian lands contained therein, with no stipulation whatsoever for the tribes. The Loyalists in America were, for the most part, ruined with this signing of the Treaty of Paris. During the war great numbers of them had fled to the frontier outposts at both ends of Lake Erie. Niagara and Detroit had been their stronghold and might, with both places remaining unmolested in their hands during the full course of the Revolutionary War. Now both strongly fortified stations were expected to be turned over peacefully to the Americans according to the terms of the treaty, but the treaty terms were remarkably nebulous as to when this should occur, merely saying it should occur "in due time and with all convenient speed," but that was a very dangerous nebulosity to have in such a treaty. Both places were crowded with British subjects— military, civilian, and Loyalist—and none were in any hurry to uproot themselves and retire to Canada and so far as the western Great Lakes was concerned, the Americans might be in control on paper, but as Alexander McKee had assured the Indians, paper was flimsy and it was possession that counted . . . and the British were still most decidedly in possession. The British had no intention whatever of giving up Niagara, Detroit, or any others of their western posts until actually forced to do so.

293. The crossing was made at the site of present Cairo, Alexander Co., Ill., and the Cherokee Trail they followed in Kentucky is the course presently followed by State Route 121.

294. The creek headwaters here was the present West Fork of Clarks Creek in the vicinity of the present village of Stella, Calloway Co., Ky.

295. This vow made by Tecumseh was solemnly made and never broken for the remainder of his life.

296. Though the Shawnees engaged in many strikes in subsequent years against the various stations in Kentucky, Simon Kenton's Station on Lawrence Creek, just east of the present village of Washington, Mason Co., Ky., though one of the nearest and most accessible to the Shawnees, was never touched.

297. Unfortunately, very little was ever recorded in respect to Chiksika's marriage to the Cherokee woman, not even her name—only that she and Chiksika had taken up residence together in the town of her birth, Running Water, that she bore him two daughters (and possibly a son) whose names were not recorded, and that she outlived him.

298. The second Treaty of Ft. Stanwix was signed on October 27, 1784. By it the residue Six Nations were allotted several small reservations in New York State and gave up all claim, if any remained, to any and all lands west of New York and Pennsylvania.

299. This was a very extensive parcel of land running from present Luther Lake near Orangeville and running southward through many present towns and the present cities of Orangeville, Elmira, Waterloo, Kichener, Cambridge, Paris, Brantford and Dunville, the mouth of the river adjacent to Rock Point Provincial Park and located 33 miles west of the head of the Niagara River at Buffalo, N.Y. The Mohawk leader Joseph Brant—Thayendanegea—had established his new residence at the site of what is the present city of Brantford, Ontario.

300. The boy captured and adopted by Michikiniqua—Little Turtle—was William Wells, who was captured near the mouth of Ohio Brush Creek while descending the Ohio River with his parents and siblings and several other families. He was later given another Miami Indian name, Epiconyare, meaning The Brave One.

301. Simon Girty, at this time still in the pay of the Indian Department of the British out of Detroit, was receiving as his salary $1 per day except when actively employed at treaties, at which time he received $3 per day. He was also entitled to rations and land—200 acres for himself and each of his children. Catherine Malotte, an uncommonly beautiful young woman about 18 years old with very long copper-colored hair, had been captured with a large party of immigrants on the Ohio River some 25 miles below Wheeling on March 15, 1780. A number were killed but a larger number captured, of which she was one. The capture was made by a band of the Muncees of the Delaware tribe. She was later, for reasons unknown, delivered by her captor, a warrior named Washnase, over to the Shawnees and came into the possession of a warrior named Leaning Tree. She and Simon Girty were married, presumably at Girty's home, near the mouth of the Detroit River in August, 1884.

302. The entire remaining Delaware faction called the Nanticokes had been for some years residing in the area of Wyoming, Pa., along the Susquehanna, but were originally from Maryland. At the time of this removal to Ohio, they numbered fewer than 100 individuals.

303. Ft. Harmar was built in the form of a regular pentagon and enclosed an area of three-quarters of an acre. The walls were constructed of large horizontal timbers and the bastions were large upright timbers buried deeply in the soil and projecting into the air to a height of fourteen feet, these uprights fastened to one another by strips of timber tree-nailed into each picket.

304. This line, in present terms, would be from present downtown lakefront Cleveland, southward through Akron and Massillon to just below Nevarre, then almost due west clear across the state to west of Indian Lake, then southward through Sidney, Piqua, Dayton, Middletown, Hamilton, and to some twenty miles west of downtown Cincinnati. All territory to the east and south of this line was claimed to be United States territory by right of conquest, which takes in roughly two-thirds of the entire State of Ohio.

305. Immediately following the signing of the Ft. McIntosh Treaty on January 21, 1785, the Congress of the United States ratified it and, with precipitation, introduced a bill proposing measures for the disposal of the Ohio lands to the east and south of the treaty line. Within three months from the signing of the treaty, an ordinance was passed by Congress under which the first segment of this land was to be surveyed. They were calling this first segment The Seven Ranges and it lay primarily within the far eastern Ohio territory where surveyors were apt to have little trouble with the Indians, although a certain amount of trouble was expected, since these would be the first lands governmentally surveyed north and west of the Ohio River. The boundaries of this new segment called The Seven Ranges were sharply drawn, beginning at the point where the western Pennsylvania boundary met the Ohio River 1,800 feet downstream from the mouth of Little Beaver Creek, from which point a line was drawn due west for 42 miles, then due south from here to the Ohio River almost at the mouth of the Little Muskingum River just east of present Marietta, with the eastern boundary following the Ohio River back upstream to the point of origin.

306. Kekewapilethy, pronounced KEK-ee-wop-pill-LETH-ee, has also been spelled Kekewe-pellethe in some accounts. He was a member of the Thawegila sept of the Shawnees and served for a brief period as third subchief of Wapatomica.

307. The treaty was attested to by the treaty commissioner's clerk, Alexander Campbell, as well as by Maj. William Finlay, Capt. Thomas Doyle, Nathan M. Donnell, James Montgomery, Daniel Elliott, John Boyce, James Rinkings, Nathaniel Smith, Isaac Teans, and James Sufferance. All the chiefs mentioned in the text signed the treaty with the exception of Blue Jacket, though some accounts (including *The Frontiersmen*) erroneously say that he did.

308. This letter, before being dispatched, was also signed by two Maykujay subchiefs, Painted Pole and Shade.

309. Maj. Robert Finney, commander of the fort bearing his name, had ordered the fort evacuated as the river began rising precipitately following several days of heavy rainfall. Taking all their most essential gear with them, the garrison had moved to the top of the ridge on the west side of the Great Miami and camped there, expecting there would be some minor flooding and a major cleanup in store as soon as they could reoccupy the place. Within two days, however, the fort had been all but wholly inundated and, even as they had watched, was damaged severely by the juggernaut logs and trees propelled along by the irresistible current. Only three hours before the Shawnee war party under Blue Jacket showed up, Maj. Finney gave the order to move out and the entire company headed west and south along the Ohio's north shore. When they reached the high ground opposite Louisville at the Falls of the Ohio, he ordered the construction of a new fort, this one, like the first, to be named Ft. Finney.

310. George Rogers Clark had been selected to lead a campaign against the tribes on the Wabash, most particularly the Miamis, who had recently been making many punishing raids into the Kentucky country, doing a great deal of killing, burning and horse stealing. By June more than 500 horses had been stolen from the Kentucky settlements. The campaign was to carry the war into their own country and cow them. Clark's men rendezvoused at Clarksville, just across the river from Louisville, on September 10, 1786, and his total force numbered some 1,800 men.

311. It has been stated that Blue Jacket's absence at this time was occasioned by his leading a war party against the new settlement of Marietta that had sprung up on the Ohio side of the Ohio River in the area surrounding Ft. Harmar at the mouth of the Muskingum River. No verification of this has been located and more conclusive evidence indicates that at this time both he and Shemeneto were leading separate raids against the Kentucky settlements.

312. The white man who was killed was a deserter from the army of Col. Benjamin Logan, a private named Willis Chadley.

313. The army was that of Col. Benjamin Logan who had initially been a part of Clark's move toward the Wabash villages. Clark, however, had correctly deduced that the Shawnee warriors would have gone to join the Wabash River Indians and that their villages would therefore be unprotected. He had detached Logan with orders to return to Kentucky, raise another force as quickly as possible and spear to the Shawnee towns and destroy them. Logan returned to Kentucky, had no trouble raising 790 mounted volunteers, who rendezvoused at Limestone (present Maysville, Mason Co., Ky.) and, guided by Simon Kenton, marched quickly to the Shawnee villages. When they discovered that Chadley had deserted, they had advanced the remaining distance at top speed, which was why they had arrived so soon after the deserter. The army attacked Mackachack in three wings: Col. Robert Patterson, backed by Maj. Hugh McGary, leading the left wing; Col. Thomas Kennedy, seconded by Capt. Christopher Irvine in the right wing; Colonels Henry Lee and Richard Trotter protecting the rear with its supply train and beef cattle; the main body of the army in the center under Logan and led by Col. Daniel Boone and seconded by Maj. Simon Kenton.

314. The officer who was killed was Capt. Christopher Irvine.

315. This man was Col. Thomas Kennedy.

316. The practice of polygamy, once very common among the Shawnee, had by this time all but disappeared, though some of the older chiefs, such as Moluntha, had two or three wives. One account states that Moluntha had raised an American flag on a pole over his wegiwa, that had been given to him by the American commissioners at the Great Miami Treaty, and that he was also wearing a large cocked hat when he surrendered.

317. These three were Maj. Hugh McGary and Privates Ignatius Ross and William Lytle.

318. This man who grabbed Spemica Lawba was Pvt. Ignatius Ross.

319. Hugh McGary was subsequently court-martialed in Kentucky on four indictments: One, murder of a Shawnee Indian, who was unarmed and under protection of Gen. Benjamin Logan at the time; two, disobedience of orders; three, disorderly conduct as an officer, in that the accused made threats to kill Col. James Trotter, his superior in rank and who did not approve McGary's act; four, abuse of other field officers for the same reason. On November 11, 1786, McGary was found guilty of indictments one and three, innocent of indictment two and part-guilty of indictment four. The sum total of his sentence was suspension from command for a period of one year.

320. One account states that two warriors were also taken prisoner, the first of which was allegedly stripped, smeared with gunpowder, and set afire. The second was allegedly a young Delaware who had come to the village to marry a Shawnee girl and who, the account says, was slowly strangled to death before being scalped. No other accounts mention such occurrences and since

Col. Logan would not have permitted such to occur, the account is considered to be entirely spurious. However, in the letter later written by Alexander McKee to Sir John Johnson, he states that the head chief of the Maykujays (Moluntha) "was burnt and blown up with gun powder set round him in small bags . . ." but this did not happen and the spurious story has apparently grown out of this remark.

321. Kisathoi and Tebethto—Margaret and Elizabeth McKinzie—had neither been captured or killed. They had long ago decided that if the time ever came when they could simply walk away, they would do so. Having escaped the initial attack, they had simply kept walking and some days later were rescued by the trader John Kinzie, who took them to Detroit and subsequently married Margaret. Full details of their capture, life in Detroit, marriages and families and ultimate reunion with their father, Moredock McKinzie, can be found in *Gateway to Empire*.

322. The total plunder gathered from the villages was relatively small, valued at $2,200 and, at the conclusion of the campaign, divided equally among the men who had participated. In his official letter to Virginia Gov. Randolph, Logan wrote:

> *May it Please Your Excellency:*
> *You will find by the enclosed paper, that on September 14th, 1786, I received orders to collect a sufficient number of men in the District of Kentucky to march against the Shawanese Towns. Agreeable to said orders, I collected 790 men, & on the 6th day of October I attacked the above mentioned towns, killed ten of the chiefs of that nation, captured thirty-two prisoners, burnt upwards of two hundred dwelling houses, & supposed to have burnt fifteen thousand bushels of corn, took some horses & cattle, killed a number of hogs, & took near one thousand pounds value of Indian furniture, & the quantity of furniture we burnt I cannot account for it. The militia who were under my command were not above twenty-seven days on duty, & I think not one-half of them were not twenty days on duty. Nearly five hundred of those men rode their own horses & carried their own provisions, & from my orders were not entitled to have any interest in the service of a public horse. The expedition was carried on in a rapid manner, & I would venture to say the expenses will be found to be very moderate.*
>
> *I have the honor to be, &c.*   *Benjamin Logan*
> *December 17th, 1786*   *C.L. of Lincoln*

323. Spemica Lawba, taken into captivity, was transported to Kentucky and there adopted into the family of Col. Benjamin Logan, who treated him in a very kindly way and whom he came to love. Col. Logan adopted him as his own son, giving him the name John Logan, though he was most often called Johnny Logan. Some accounts refer to him as Captain John, Captain Jim or Jimmy Logan. For added details of his captivity and later life, see also *The Frontiersmen*, *Gateway to Empire* and the author's young adult historical novel entitled *Johnny Logan* (Little, Brown, 1983).

324. Pronunciations of the names of these chiefs are: Sindathon (SIN-duh-thon), Monakaduto (MON-uh-kuh-DUE-toe), Topenebe (Toe-PEN-uh-bee), Nanimisea (Nan-nuh-MISS-ee-yuh), Nescotnemeg (Nee-SCOT-nee-meg), Nichinesica (Nitch-ee-NESS-sik-kuh), Oulamy (OOOH-luh-mee), Wafrugahquealied (Wuh-FROO-guh-QUEE-uh-leed), Sekahos (See-KAH-hoes), and Wabacumaga (WAH-buh-koo-MAH-guh).

325. Some accounts contend that Blue Jacket led an attack against the Americans at Vincennes on December 17. Undoubtedly, Shawnee attacks were occurring there and in Kentucky, but not on this occasion led by Blue Jacket, who was indisputably at the Grand Council at the mouth of the Detroit River.

326. The Weas and Piankeshaws later became recognized as full tribes in their own right. The Pepicokias, also called the Eel River Miamis, became absorbed into the Piankeshaw. The Kalatikas, the Mengakonias, and the Ouiatenons ceased to exist as subtribes by the mid-nineteenth century through both attrition and absorption into the main body of Miamis. Smaller, regional groupings such as those known as Mississinewas, Tippecanoes, Salamonies, and Mishawakas never did receive recognition even as subtribes and their designation was short lived.

327. The reference to Five Nations instead of Six was because the sixth nation, the Tuscaroras, had no voice or vote in such matters.

328. By this was meant that when and if the need arose, the residue Iroquois were prepared to cross over into New York at Buffalo from the British Ft. Erie located at the foot of Lake Erie and at the mouth of the Niagara River.

329. Very often the early references to the Auglaize River were made in their shortened form of 'Glaize, which caused many early writers to mistakenly assume the name of the river and its valley and portions of the Maumee was Glaze.

330. At practically this very moment, Robert Todd, at Lexington, was writing to Gov. Randolph: "There are now more Shawnee on the south side of the Ohio River than have been discovered at any one time for the past two years."

331. The site suggested is the site of present Aberdeen, O., specifically in the bottomland at the upstream point where present Fishing Gut Creek enters the Ohio River in Brown Co., O.

332. Gen. Benjamin Logan, writing the Virginia governor immediately following the exchange, made no mention of the theft of fourteen horses by the whites but instead wrote: "The Shawanoes have exchanged for their prisoners all but ten; I met them at Limestone, where they professed a great deal of friendship, but I fear it was only a deception."

333. The Northwest Territory took in all of present Ohio, Indiana, Illinois, Michigan, Wisconsin, and eastern Minnesota.

334. Among other things, the Ordinance of 1787 provided for the appointment of a governor, judges, and other territorial offices, for the establishment of both civil and criminal laws, for the laying out of counties, the setting up of a general assembly, and the authorization of a duly elected delegate to Congress who would have the right to debate but not to vote during the temporary government. The Ordinance of 1787 further prohibited the molestation of any man because of his mode of worship or his religion; it provided the benefits of the writs of *habeas corpus* and of trial by jury; prohibiting in this new Territory either slavery or involuntary servitude; and that "Religion, morality and knowledge being necessary to good government and the happiness of mankind, schools and the means of education shall forever be encouraged." The prohibition of slavery was, of course, an ideal, not an overnight accomplishment and, though constantly diminishing over the years, slavery continued in much of the Northwest Territory for another 63 years following enactment of the ordinance. This Ordinance also provided that whenever there were five thousand free males of full age in a specific region of territory, the people there should be authorized to elect representatives to a territorial legislature. These men, when chosen, were then empowered to nominate ten freeholders of five hundred acres each, from whom the president of the United States, not yet even chosen, would then appoint five to form a legislative council. These representatives were to serve two years in office, the councilmen five. Such territories, when established, were to be only temporary governments. As soon as a particular area in one was sufficiently populated and settled, application could be made for entry into the Union as a state, as a full and equal partner of the original thirteen colonies presently in the process of officially becoming states. Subsequently, Delaware became the first to ratify the United States Constitution and become a State—this occurring on December 7, 1787, followed by Pennsylvania on December 12 and New Jersey on December 18. Others followed in rapid succession in 1788.

335. One of the effects of the instructions of the Virginia executive prohibiting the people of Kentucky from going out of the state on offensive Indian actions unless in actual and immediate pursuit of an invading enemy, was a meeting of the various county lieutenants in which they sent a joint message to the Virginia governor saying, in regard to the rulings, that the restrictions "have placed us in so critical a situation as to oblige us to decline all offensive operations at present & can only act on the defensive." There were many other far-reaching effects to the Ordinance of 1787. The Ohio Company, under immediate application to the federal government by its agents, Dr. Manasseh Cutler and Winthrop Sargent in Salem, Massachusetts, contracted to purchase for no less than a dollar per acre a one-million-acre chunk of Ohio·and the deal was consummated only ten days after the ordinance was enacted, but with certain "deals" being made for discounts, and in the end the Ohio Company wound up having to pay only nine cents per acre for the gigantic tract. That piece of land was bounded by the Ohio River from the mouth of the Scioto upstream to the western boundary, then being surveyed, of the Seventh Range of Townships, then, by said boundary, northward to the northern boundary of the Tenth Range of Townships, then on a due west line back to the Scioto and down that stream to its beginning. Initially 1.5 million acres was petitioned for, but the final actual purchase amounted to 964,285 acres. In New York, sales of parts of the Seven Ranges amounting to $73,000 were made practically overnight. Judge John Cleve Symmes and his backers, who had become very interested in procuring the rich lands between the Great Miami and Little Miami Rivers, took immediate steps to make this a reality. Even before the sale was legally consummated, Symmes sold to Matthias Denman of Springfield, New Jersey, a tract of 740 acres directly opposite the mouth of the Licking River, for which Denman paid him five shillings per acre in Continental scrip, or about 15 pence per acre, which amounted to less than $125 for the entire plot that ultimately became downtown Cincinnati, Ohio.

336. Maysville remains the name of the city to this day. John May, at the same time, laid out another settlement ten miles south of the new Maysville on the eastern leg of the old Warrior Trail leading to Blue Licks, which he called May's Lick, and the town that grew there retains that name today.

337. An Army officer stationed at Ft. Harmar had been keeping track of the river traffic and he noted in his report: "From the 10th of October, 1786, until the twelfth of May, 1787, 177 boats, 2,689 souls, 1,333 horses, 766 cattle and 102 wagons have passed Muskingum, bound for Limestone and the Rapids."

338. This site of the new Chalahgawtha was three miles downstream from the confluence of the St. Marys and St. Joseph rivers where the Maumee is formed. Located on the north bank, it was situated just east of the expressway that is U.S. Highways 24 and 30, on land that is presently occupied by the Lakeside Golf Course on the east side of the city of Ft. Wayne, Ind.

339. Ft. Ouiatenon was on the north bank of the Wabash River a half mile downstream from the mouth of the Wea River which empties into the Wabash from the south. The fort itself was situated just west of the present Purdue University Airport, on the site of present Lafayette, Tippecanoe Co., Ind.

340. Pimitoui was a substantial Potawatomi village that was located on the site of the present city of Ottawa, in La Salle Co., Ill. On some maps this village is located farther downstream on the Illinois, across from the mouth of the Vermilion River at the site of present Utica, Ill., but that is an error.

341. A few accounts have stated that Chaubenee was "fully six feet tall" but he was not. His great bulk tended to make him look taller than he actually was. One of his names, Built Like a Bear, was bestowed upon him when he was still just a young man, due to his impressive bulk.

342. No record has been found of the name of Chaubenee's mother, although in some accounts she has been described as having been a Mohawk rather than a Seneca. However, since she was purportedly from a village on the Genesee River of western New York State, and that was the territory of the Senecas, it is most likely that she was indeed of the latter tribe. There is no doubt that Chaubenee's father, Opawana, was an Ottawa. Chaubenee's name presents a number of complications. Quite often the spellings of Indian names are given in a variety of ways, especially in the Indian language rendition, but the author has rarely encountered an individual with more different spellings of his Indian name or more different interpretations of that name into English. Just a few spellings of the Indian name include Shawbonee, Shabonee, Chaboner, Shabehnay, Shabehneh, Shabenai, Chamblee, Chaboneh, Shobonier, Cowabeenai, Shabbone, Chamblie, and Chambly. The English translation of his name has been given as follows: Field of Wheat, Built Like a Bear, Burly Shoulders, Fighter, He Has Pawed Through, and Coal Burner. Even on occasions when he signed his own name, Chaubenee did it differently on separate occasions—sometimes even spelled differently on different pages of the same document. In the treaty signed at Prairie du Chien in 1825, he signed it Chaboner; at another treaty there four years later, he signed it Shabehnay; on the Chicago Treaty of 1833, he signed with two different spellings, Shabehnah and Shabenai. Tecumseh wrote and spoke of him as Chaubenee and called him Coal Burner. In DeKalb Co., Ill., there are two towns allegedly named after him, called Shabbona and Shabbona Grove. The author, after considerable study of this matter, has elected to use the Indian form of Chaubenee (pronounced Show-BEE-nee) and the English form of Coal Burner, since these two variations have been the most frequently encountered in the documents of the period.

343. It should be mentioned here that in *The Frontiersmen,* the author erroneously identified Chaubenee as being a member of the Sac Tribe, but this error was corrected in *Gateway to Empire.*

344. Saukenuk (pronounced SAC-eh-nook) is sometimes erroneously shown on maps as being located on the south bank of the Rock River. Actually, it was on the north bank, three miles upstream from where the Rock River enters the Mississippi, and the entire village was situated within the limits of what is now the city of Rock Island, in Rock Island Co., Ill. The center of the village was at the foot of a small rapids on the site of present Black Hawk State Park, opposite Vandruff Island and directly across the Rock River from present Milan, Ill.

345. This grant of land to Julien Dubuque and the lead mines he further developed there were located on and near the site of the present city of Dubuque, Iowa.

346. Wabasha's Village was located near the site of the present town of the same name in Wabasha Co., Minn.

347. Site of present Madison, Dane Co., Wis.

348. Siggenauk's villages were located at present Milwaukee, Wis. Siggenauk (pronounced SIG-gee-nawk) was called Blackbird by the English.

349. Siggenauk (the elder) was one of the few prominent chiefs east of the Mississippi who saw clearly the power the Americans would one day have in this region. Few believed him and when he died, his own son, Siggenauk (the younger) was very anti-American.

350. Site of the present city of Chicago, Cook Co., Ill. Checagou meant, in the Indian language, "the place of onion smells," and was so named after the wild onion and leeks that grew so abundantly in the swampy terrain . . . and which smelled so badly when spring came and the frozen wild vegetables thawed and rotted.

351. At least two modern accounts, one no doubt influencing the other, have interpreted this to mean that Chiksika requested that he not be buried but that his body be left exposed for the birds to pick. That, of course, was not his meaning at all, which a careful reading of the comment shows.

352. Some recent accounts have stated that Chiksika was killed while participating with Cherokees in an attack against Buchanan's Station on the Cumberland River, site of present Nashville, Tenn., but it is believed this is an error, since Chiksika's death is listed in most contemporary accounts as having occurred on April 13, 1788, and the combined Shawnee and Cherokee attack upon Buchanan's Station occurred on September 30, 1792, four and a half years later.

353. There remains to this day a prevailing belief among the Cherokees that Tecumseh married one of their women on this visit and through her sired at least one daughter—and as many as three in some accounts. No solid verification has been discovered to support such claims. More than likely they confuse Tecumseh with Chiksika who did, indeed, have a Cherokee wife and daughter at this time. Cherokee tradition states that Tecumseh married one of their young women whose name was Tahneh, but that the name was later changed to Naomi when she became a Christian. This woman later allegedly married a white man identified only as Gen. Proctor (but *not* the Gen. Proctor of Ft. Malden and the War of 1812 infamy). The involved Cherokee tradition goes on to say that there are supposed to be two lines of descendants—the so-called "Fair-skinned Proctors," who are supposedly the descendants of Tecumseh, and the so-called "Dark-skinned Proctors," who are allegedly the descendants of Tecumseh's brother, Lowawluwaysica, later called Tenskwatawa or The Prophet. Since no substantial supportive evidence exists to back up these contentions, nor even any evidence that Lowawluwaysica ever accompanied Tecumseh or Chiksika to the Southern tribes, the traditions are looked upon as merely fanciful and a desire to claim relationship with the Shawnee warrior who came among them and so excelled and who then went on to become one of the greatest of all Indian warriors in American history.

354. Strode's Station was located two miles west of the present city of Winchester in Clark Co., Ky., on the west side of a small branch of present Strode's Creek, just north of present U.S. Route 60.

355. Site of present downtown Cincinnati, Ohio. The Losantiville settlement was begun with the erection of four cabins, the first of which was built on what is now Front Street, east of and close to Main Street. At this time the lower table of land was thick with sycamore and maple trees, while the upper was primarily beech, oak, and hickory. Through these dense forests the streets were laid out, their corners marked on various trees. This initial survey extended from Eastern Row (present Broadway) to Western Row (present Central Avenue) and from the Ohio River as far north as Northern Row (now Seventh Street).

356. Throughout 1788, more of the colonies had ratified the United States Constitution and been accepted as states of the Union, joining Delaware, Pennsylvania, and New Jersey, who had done so just as 1787 was closing. Georgia had become the fourth state on January 2, followed a week later by Connecticut. Massachusetts became the sixth state on February 6, Maryland the seventh on April 28 and South Carolina the eighth on May 23. New Hampshire became a state on June 21 and Virginia four days later. The eleventh to gain statehood was New York, on July 26 and the twelfth was North Carolina on November 21, 1789. Rhode Island was the last of the original thirteen colonies to become a state, this occurring on May 29, 1790.

357. Ft. Washington, built on the site of present Cincinnati, Ohio, was constructed beginning in June 1789 by an American detachment of 140 men under Maj. James Doughty, ordered out by Gen. Josiah Harmar from the fort which bore his name at present Marietta, Ohio. The specific site of Ft. Washington was just a little east of present Broadway where Third Street now crosses it.

358. Gen. Harmar, upon leaving Ft. Harmar, had left that installation under command of Capt. David Zeigler, with 20 men. The 70 soldiers stationed at Ft. Washington fell under Harmar's command immediately upon his arrival.

359. During the year 1789 alone, no less than 20,000 settlers had come down the Ohio River. Over the past seven years, 1,500 had been killed during the descent of the stream.

360. St. Clair had arrived at Ft. Washington on January 2, 1790, and created Hamilton Co.—named after his good friend, Gen. Alexander Hamilton—on January 3. Its boundaries took in all the territory of the Symmes Purchase, lying between the Great Miami and Little Miami Rivers. On that day as well, the Losantiville proprietors, Matthias Denman, Robert Patterson, and Israel Ludlow agreed to change the name of their settlement, in honor of St. Clair and his membership in the Society of Cincinnatus, to Cincinnati.

361. The man in question who made this incredible leap was named Ben Eulin. He was a storekeeper at Point Pleasant who had been out hunting. He was 25 years old, thin and wiry and weighed only 120 pounds. Eulin was a former trader among the Indians. At the time this incident occurred, on April 25, 1790, he was no longer trading with the Indians because of having run afoul of them due to some shady practices in which he was engaged. He had fled from them and was sure that if captured he would be killed, and so he took the risk of his incredible leap. As soon as he reached the woods and was out of sight of the Indians, he became sick and started vomiting blood and lay down beside a log, certain he was dying. Actually, he had only broken some internal blood vessels and the damage was not great. He had not even suffered a broken bone. Recovering somewhat in about an hour, he made his way downstream to the cabin of Peter Van Bibber. He was very much bruised and his system badly shocked, but he recovered fully. One account states that Eulin was wholly unarmed and was out with a bridle trying to catch a horse that had strayed, but this account is suspect, since it is most unlikely he would have been seeking a stray horse near the top of a high river bluff. Another account says the tree was intertwined with wild grapevines, which broke his fall. He finally settled on a farm at Greenupsburg where he lived with his wife, three sons and two daughters, until his death at age 51 in 1816.

362. This minor incursion, generally known as the Scott and Harmar Expedition, came about when Gen. Charles Scott of Kentucky, irate at the continued attacks by raiding parties, led 230 mounted Kentucky volunteers to Cincinnati and joined 100 regulars under Harmar.

363. Although Simon Kenton was along on this expedition, he was not with the detachment that found and killed the warriors. It was made up of fourteen soldiers under an ensign, plus sixteen of Scott's militia, and were guided by Kenton's fellow frontiersmen Joshua Baker and Alexander McIntire.

364. The New French Store was the name given to a new trading post close to Kekionga that had been established by the trader John Kinzie. That initial name did not last long and the post and little settlement that sprang up around it had become known as Miamitown and the open ground adjacent to the trading post had become a favored assembly place and staging ground for the Indians. Gen. Harmar's advance force under Col. John Hardin of the Kentucky Militia left Ft. Washington on September 26, 1790, with orders to proceed on Clark's trace for 25 miles and then to stop and await further orders. He did so, remaining in place at the designated spot until joined by Harmar's main force which left Ft. Washington four days later, at 10 A.M. on September 30, bringing with it artillery consisting of a 6-pounder, a 3-pounder and a 5½-inch howitzer. Harmar reported to Secretary of War Knox that: "My whole force was 1,453 (including two troops of cavalry) but from this number we may safely deduct 200 of the Militia as good for nothing."

365. Some accounts say the Ottawa reinforcement amounted to 200 warriors, but that is incorrect. The entire Indian force amounted to 150 warriors and chiefs, almost evenly divided at fifty each for the Shawnees, Miamis, and Ottawas.

366. As Harmar's army passed through the site where the Chalahgawtha on the Little Miami had been located, the general wrote in his log:

> All these Chillicothys are elegant situations—fine water near them and beautiful prairies. The savages know how to take a handsome position as well as any people on earth. When they leave a Chillicothy, they retire to another place and call it after the same name.

367. The army reached the Maumee River Chalahgawtha on the morning of September 19 and made camp there, destroying it and surrounding habitations when they left. The presence of Simon Girty had been observed and reported to Gen. Harmar who, some accounts contend, blanched when he heard this and thereafter seemed very nervous and upset.

368. This was done despite standing orders that had been issued prohibiting the destruction of any British property during the campaign.

369. In his report, Harmar said he burned a total of 190 buildings still standing in Kekionga and the contiguous towns.

370. Harmar stated in his report that the standing corn that was destroyed amounted to some 20,000 bushels.

371. The detachment, under command of Col. Hardin, with Lt. John Armstrong commanding the regulars, left the main army the morning of September 19. Its mission was to range outward to the northwest, engage any enemy encountered and destroy what towns they found. Almost all of the many accounts state that this detachment numbered around 200 men. One account, however, says that it numbered 310 men, but mistakes the Hardin detachment for one sent out by Harmar the previous day, numbering 300 men, which was under command of Lt. Col. James Trotter and consisted of 30 federal troops, 40 of Maj. Fontaine's light horse cavalry and 230 active riflemen; this detachment returning to the main army the same evening, having encountered, killed, and scalped two Indians. Some accounts say Hardin was disliked and that many of the militia deserted from his detachment after traveling only two miles, but Harmar makes no report of this.

372. Various accounts claim the American loss in this skirmish ranged from a high of 181 men to as few as 22 (this latter number undoubtedly referring only to the regulars). The most frequently quoted number by the more reliable sources is 70, which jibes with Gen. Harmar's report, which also states that all but 7 of the 30 regulars were killed and bitterly berates the militia, who were at the rear, for fleeing in panic and abandoning the regulars to their fate. This ambush took place where the Indian trail leading toward the Elkhart River crossed the Eel River, 6 miles northwest of present Ft. Wayne, at the place where present U.S. 33 crosses Eel River, 4 miles southeast of present Churubusco, Ind. One of the extraordinary incidents was that of a Maj. John Adams who was struck by five different rifle balls and yet survived, carrying the balls within his body for the rest of his life.

373. The soldiers were nonplussed that their commander should order a retreat and just leave all their dead lying on the ground at the scene of the attack. They complained so bitterly that after the retreat had reached a point eight miles distant from the Chalahgawtha on the Maumee, Harmar relented, established a camp and sent out another detachment during the night of October 21, which arrived back at Kekionga on the morning of September 22. This detachment was under command of Col. John Hardin and Maj. John P. Wyllys, consisting of 60 regulars and the remaining militia. One account, generally reliable, states that the army did not stop its first retreat until it reached the site of the remains of the old Chalahgawtha on the Little Miami River and that it was from this point that the second detachment was sent back. This is not possible, since the second ambush took place only three days after the first—on October 22—and old Chalahgawtha was at least 160 miles distant from the scene of the first ambush. Even if they had all been mounted, which they were not, the army could not have traveled such a great distance and then the detachment return the same distance, a total of at least 320 miles, in three days.

374. Once again the troops expected their general would lead the full army back in a massive retaliatory assault and once again Harmar put his force into full retreat, this time determined not to stop and fearful that if the Indians came again, the wounded and sick among them, as well as their artillery and stores would all fall to them—an apprehension shared by Harmar's adjutant, Capt. Ebenezer Denny. Harmar, in an early report, said "Our loss is about 160 killed," but in this he erred, the actual figure being 183. Harmar's official return of killed and wounded, written on November 4, 1790, at Ft. Washington, listed the following: Total federal troops killed, 75, including Maj. Wyllys and Lt. Frothingham; total militia killed, 108, including Maj. Fontaine, Captains Tharp, Scott, and McMurtry, Lieutenants Clark and Rogers, and Ensigns Sweet, Bridges, Higgens, and Therlkeld. Total of all military personnel killed, 183.

375. Gen. Harmar's army, which began its final retreat on October 23, arrived back at Ft. Washington on November 3, 1790.

376. Harmar claimed in his report that "the Indians killed is supposed to be 200." Other accounts say about 100 Indians were killed and wounded. Since the Indians had only a total force of 150 when they met the army, those figures are obviously considerably incorrect. Michikiniqua and Blue Jacket both later stated the same figures for the loss of the Indians in killed and wounded—a total of "30 dead and 15 who survived being wounded." The astounding thing of the whole matter is that Harmar termed the campaign a victory for his army, reporting to Secretary of War Knox that:

> No interruption whatever was offered by the enemy on our return; a convincing proof, this, of their having received a blow which they felt. I flatter myself good consequences will be the result. We have not, I conceive, lost much more than man for man with the savages. Our loss can be repaired; theirs is irreparable.

The reaction of Sgt. Ben Whiteman to Harmar's claim eloquently expressed the feeling of the greater majority of the army: "If that was victory," he said, "then I pray to God that I may never see defeat!"

377. Pskipahcah Ouiskelotha (pronounced Puh-SKIP-uh-kuh Whis-kee-LO-tha) was taken under the protection of Col. John Hardin and remained with his family until returned to the Shawnees at the Treaty of Greenville in 1795.

378. No less than five separate accounts mention in passing that Tecumseh was on hand for and took part in the defeat of Gen. Harmar's army, but that is incorrect, as reflected by the more reliable accounts of his whereabouts at this time.

379. The merchants of Montreal were every bit as alarmed over the American threat to their trading enterprises as those of Detroit and prepared a petition which was submitted to the governor-general of Canada, dated December 20, 1790, as follows:

> *To his Excellency . . . the memorial and petition of the merchants of Montreal trading to the Indian or upper country humbly showeth that your memorialists being ardently engaged in the Indian or upper country trade of the province are not a little alarmed for the safety of the property which they have entrusted to the Indian country by reason of the late attempt of the Americans to establish by force a post or posts on the frontiers of the province near Detroit. That should such attempt be attended by success, it is evident that the Indian trade to the south of Lake Erie must fall into their hands to the loss and prejudice of the province in the sum not short of £30,000 sterling. That from so near a vicinity to Detroit your memorialists cannot help suspecting that the views of obtaining that key to the west or the northwest are strongly entertained by our rival neighbors; and they consider with much pain that should they possess themselves of Detroit, they will have in their power the means of commanding the whole western and northwestern trade, which your memorialists esteem to produce returns for British manufactories, chiefly in furs, to the value of £150,000 sterling. Your memorialists might remark on the bad consequences which would follow in particular to the new settlement should our neighbors become masters of the post of Detroit, but knowing that your Lordship can better discern than they can point out, the political injuries which the province would sustain in such an event, they confine themselves solely to the Indian trade, of which from long expense and extensive dealings they can speak with certainty and precision. Your memorialists are aware that by the Treaty of Peace of 1783, a great part of the Indian country was ceded to the American states, but having carried on the trade of that country as was usual before and during the war under the protection and safeguard of the government; your memorialists not having since the peace encountered any difficulty from the subjects of the American states, have been led to extend the Indian trade farther west than formerly, from which circumstances their property and connections in that country being greater and more widely extended, any sudden check to their commercial pursuits would occasion their ruin.*

380. President George Washington, immediately upon learning the particulars of Harmar's abortive expedition, had remarked to his secretary of war, Henry Knox, "I expected little from it from the moment I heard he was a drunkard."

381. The settler who was burned and disemboweled while still alive was Abner Hunt, who had been captured while traveling between the new settlements of Symmes City and Colerain. Tecumseh's exact whereabouts at this time are not certainly known and several accounts have stated in passing that Tecumseh was "probably" with the war party that did this, but the evidence weighs against this, especially since he continued to stand strongly against torture of prisoners under any conditions.

382. The site of this attack is presently marked by the Big Bottom State Monument, one mile downstream on the Muskingum from the present village of Stockport, Morgan Co.

383. This was a party of men from Ft. Washington whose enlistments had expired and, under command of Capt. Elijah Strong, they were on their way back to more civilized Pennsylvania and Virginia. Twenty men were killed in that first vicious barrage and the two in the boat who had been killed were rowers on either side of Strong himself, and the sternsman was the one wounded. The bodies were discovered by a party under Simon Kenton, who buried them.

384. This was a party commanded by a Capt. Moore of Pittsburgh, who was himself killed in the onslaught that occurred on March 20, 1791. The three who escaped and reached Maysville were John Price, John Wilson and Robert Dunlap; the latter, severely wounded, died several days later.

385. This attack occurred on March 23, 1791. The two prisoners used as decoys in this case were David Thomas and Peter Devine. The boat was under command of John May, founder of Maysville and May's Lick, who had once before been captured on the river by Blue Jacket and released with the promise that he would leave the country and not return. This time he was killed.

386. The boats that managed to get away were those commanded by Captains William Hubbell and William Plaskett. The bodies of the Greathouse party, and most of the others who became victims of Indian attacks this spring of 1791, were found and buried by Simon Kenton and his party. Shortly after this, land companies began offering $50 apiece for Indian scalps. Kenton's party found some Indian canoes and set up an ambush of their own, killed and scalped five Indians and decapitated an Indian boy, whose head was stuck on a pole at the river's edge as a warning to other Indians. Shortly after this, on an expedition to the area of Paint Creek, Kenton's sixty men had come across the newly interred Shawnee chief named Meshepeshe, whose body was ravaged, clothes and goods taken, the head of the dead man scalped and the body itself tossed into the mud.

387. Although there is no way of proving such a supposition, it is not beyond the realm of possibility that this news-relaying system devised by Tecumseh was later adopted 59 years later, with some variation, by the famous Pony Express service from St. Joseph, Missouri, to Sacramento, California, and which remained in business for a year and a half until supplanted by the telegraph.

388. As nearly as can be determined, Tecumseh's base of operations for his spying ventures against St. Clair was located just a little over two miles north of Ft. Washington, on approximately the site of the present campus of the University of Cincinnati.

389. Kethlipecanunk, located at the mouth of the Eel River, was on the site presently occupied by Logansport, Cass Co., Ind.

390. "Pet" Indians was a term in wide use at this time, referring to those individual Indians who had separated from their own tribes, had come to the Americans and were living with them and working with them in various ways.

391. Detachments under Col. John Hardin, Maj. Barbee, and Captains McCoy, King, Longsdon, Brown, and Price struck the villages hard, finding them virtually devoid of warriors and having no great difficulty cowing the women, children, and elderly left behind. Scott's main army had halted at Ouiatenon—site of present Lafayette, Ind.—but a major detachment under Lt. Col. Wilkinson pushed on at high speed to the mouth of Eel River, marching 36 miles in 12 hours to do so, and destroyed the village. Scott, in his report of June 20 to Secretary of War Henry Knox, wrote:

> Many of the inhabitants of this village were French and lived in a state of civilization. By the books, letters and other documents found there, it is evident that the place was in close connection with and dependent on Detroit. A large quantity of corn, a variety of household goods, peltry and other articles were burned with this village, which consisted of about 70 houses, many of them well furnished.

392. Tayauendottoontraw (pronounced Tay-yaw-EN-dot-TOO-on-traw) was also known as Spliced Arrow; Tsoondoweno (pronounced Tuh-SEW-on-DOW-ee-no) was also called Gray Eyes. Some reports contend that Thayendanegea—Chief Joseph Brant—accompanied these two chiefs on their mission, but Lyman Draper showed conclusively that this was impossible, since he was elsewhere at the time. The emissaries were not well treated when they reached the South: the Cherokees gave the proposed alliance poor encouragement; the Creeks were opposed; the Choctaws stole the horses of the emissaries while they were in council and when they pursued and caught the thieves and killed one, the dead man turned out to be a man of great influence among the Choctaws and the Wyandot emissaries had to flee to the north to avoid retribution and nothing was accomplished. One account erroneously states that Tecumseh was part of the delegation of emissaries sent to the South at this time.

393. Kenapacomaqua was also known as L'Anguille, a town originally established around a French trading post but, at this time, harboring no trading post at all.

394. Actually, in building the fort, the devotions of John Graves Simcoe were exclusively to the Crown and he was far more interested in how the Indians could help the British than vice versa. Simcoe fully expected an early renewal of the war with the Americans and that their build-up of an army at Ft. Washington was primarily to take Detroit by force, since it had not been turned over to them by the British in accordance with the terms of the Treaty of Paris. Graves made no attempt to disabuse the Indians of their supposition that the Ft. Miamis construction implied direct aid. Fort Miamis is correctly pronounced my-AM-mees (but often incorrectly pronounced my-AM-miss) and was named after the old French fort close by which had originally been called Fort-of-the-Miamis. Quite a few different accounts give the name of the fort in the singular, as Fort Miami.

395. In addition to the draft of Kentucky Militia for his force, St. Clair had harbored the belief that he would have plenty of free-agent Kentuckians volunteering to serve under his banner. In this he was sadly mistaken, since all the frontiersmen knew the general who, though he had served competently in the Revolution, was now considerably overweight, suffered badly from both gout and asthma, and, worst of all, had virtually no experience in fighting Indians. Simon Kenton seemed to put the feelings of the populace in perspective when asked why he hadn't volunteered to serve under St. Clair. His response was: "St. Clair? Well sir, I'll tell you. St. Clair, he's a minister-looking man. He's well disciplined, too, but he has no brier look about him, no keenness."

396. A remark being passed on from person to person, which Tecumseh overheard and passed along to the Maumee, was a wry comment made by Judge John Cleve Symmes when he saw what sort of army St. Clair had, which appeared to Symmes to be a ragtag conglomerate of males who, "gotten from the prisons, wheel barrows and brothels of the nation at two dollars a month, will never answer our purpose of fighting Indians."

397. One of the principal profiteers of this situation was former Secretary of the Treasury William Duer, at this time in partnership with Secretary of War Henry Knox in a real estate scheme in New England and similarly a cohort of Alexander Hamilton. His maneuverings with the quartermastering that was supposed to supply St. Clair with necessary goods was actually preventing its accomplishment and at the same time lining his own pockets—a public thievery that was exposed much too late.

398. At least one source states that the army moved out of Cincinnati on September 5-6, but it appears this is an error.

399. Some sources have suggested that St. Clair left Ft. Washington with a total of 2,300 men, but that figure is incorrect and the actual number was 1,390 men.

400. One source states that the St. Clair army had with it 12 pieces of field artillery. This, upon comparison with Indian reports of the plunder taken, appears to be an error.

401. Ft. Hamilton was erected on the site of the present city of Hamilton, seat of Butler Co., O.

402. This site was in present Darke Co., O., three-quarters of a mile southeast of the confluence of Mud Creek and Prairie Outlet, and about a thousand feet due east of the group of small lakes known as Wayne Lakes, on the site of the present Fort Jefferson State Memorial in the southwest quadrant of the present village of Ft. Jefferson, five miles south of present Greenville, seat of Darke Co.

403. It was at this juncture that St. Clair sent a message to Secretary of War Henry Knox that no Indians had yet been seen except for a few wandering hunters at a distance, that he was sure the Indians were fleeing in front of his army and that he hoped to engage them in battle before long.

404. One modern source states that three deserters were captured almost immediately and brought back to St. Clair, who had them shot as a warning to others. The report, however, is of questionable authenticity.

405. A large number of the accounts of St. Clair's Defeat state that his force in the defeat amounted to 1,400 men or more. That, of course, as has been shown, is incorrect. When the battle broke out, St. Clair had a total of 920 effectives.

406. The stream encountered was, of course, the headwaters of the Wabash, not the St. Marys. The route traveled by the army from Ft. Jefferson to this point essentially followed the route of present State Route 121 five miles to present Greenville and then twenty-three miles on the route followed by present State Route 49 to the present village of Ft. Recovery in Mercer Co., three miles east of the Ohio-Indiana border.

407. Although this placement of the militia detachment north of the stream was later claimed by St. Clair to be a standard precautionary measure, there was considerable feeling among the militia that it was done to prevent their desertion during the night. There was probably an element of truth in both contentions.

408. No complete listing exists of all the Indians, or even all the chiefs,. who took part in St. Clair's Defeat, but a listing of some of the more notable Indians known to have participated may be of value. They included: Apekonit (William Wells)—adopted Miami warrior; Berry—Shawnee warrior; Black Beard—Shawnee chief; Black Fish—Shawnee warrior; Black Partridge—Potawatomi chief; Buckangehela—Delaware principal chief; Carrymaunee (Walking Turtle)—Winnebago chief; Catahecassa (Black Hoof)—Shawnee principal chief; Chaubenee (Coal Burner)—Potawatomi chief; Chiuxca—Shawnee chief; Coonahaw—Shawnee warrior; Gomo—Potawatomi chief; Kasahda—Ottawa chief; Main Poche—Potawatomi chief; Michikiniqua (Little Turtle)—Miami principal chief; Mtamins—Potawatomi chief; Otussa—Ottawa chief; Pipe—Delaware chief; Siggenauk (Blackbird)—Wyandot chief; Stiahta (Roundhead)—Wyandot chief; Tarhe (The Crane)—Wyandot principal chief; Tecumseh—Shawnee warrior; Topenebe—Potawatomi chief; Wasegoboah (Stand Firm)—Shawnee warrior; Wehyehpihehrsehnwah (Blue Jacket)—Shawnee war chief; White Loon—Wyandot chief; Wingenund—Delaware chief.

409. There is no known cause for this little incident of shooting in the midst of the night, nor who the soldiers were who were involved. Some white survivors recalled it happening but none with any knowledge of the details.

410. The unusual assembly was the result of the forward guards having sent a runner with word to the commanding general that sentries who had earlier fired their weapons had now discovered considerable footprints in the new snow and there was every reason to believe the enemy was moving into position to attack in the morning. When the troops were assembled, St. Clair addressed them, saying:

> *From intelligence delivered to me during the night I am led to believe that we will be attacked by Indians today. Perhaps very soon. All men will see to their weapons at once. Artillerymen will position and load the cannons. Emergency fortifications are to be erected beginning this moment.*

411. One account, believed apocryphal, states that:

> *Butler was much beloved by the Indians who were friendly to the United States. Among those who loved him most was Big Tree, a Seneca chief in the Genesee Valley. He vowed to avenge the death of Butler by killing three of the hostile Indians. Because the treaty of peace at Greenville in 1795 thwarted his bloody purpose, Big Tree committed suicide.*

Another fanciful account involving Butler states that two Shawnees found the wounded Butler propped against a tree and they killed and scalped him and a moment later Simon Girty supposedly came by, identified the corpse as Butler, "cut out Butler's still warm heart, diced it into fourteen pieces so that representatives of all the nations fighting there that day could eat of it and taste revenge."

412. There is reasonably good evidence to believe that one of the men Blue Jacket killed was his own brother, Capt. Charles Van Swearingen, as indicated in several contemporaneous accounts and also as presented in *The Frontiersmen;* by the same token, members of that family have also contended, using the family Bible as evidence, that Charles Van Swearingen actually died many years after this. Until stronger proof is uncovered one way or another; the author views this matter as an unresolved dichotomy.

413. One of the women who escaped was a Mrs. Catherine Miller, described as the extremely beautiful wife of a private, who was so fleet of foot that she outran just about everyone and was described as having long red hair that streamed out behind her like a flag when she was running. She died in Cincinnati 47 years later, in 1838.

414. Some accounts have said that Simon Girty led the Indian forces against the whites, but that is patently untrue.

415. An account stating that Blue Jacket attempted to organize a pursuit of the fleeing soldiers and that "only 20 of his Shawnee were willing to try" is wholly without foundation, as is the further statement in the same account that some kegs of whiskey were found and "the wild drunken victory celebration which followed ended any possibility of the warriors following and finishing off St. Clair's army."

416. One account states that the Indians pursued the retreating soldiers and that while the Indians: "were in eager chase of the unfortunate fugitives, they were thrown into such consternation by an eclipse of the moon that the pursuit was stopped, and a consultation held; and so long was the debate that an opportunity was afforded the scattered remnants of the Army to reach a place of security." Quite a phenomenon, since the retreat took place in full daylight. Unfortunately, not all such fictitious accounts are so flagrantly false and easily detectable as this. Those who were able to flee went directly to Ft. Jefferson, 28 miles distant, where they arrived in scattered clusters throughout the afternoon and into the night. The detachment of 140 regulars under Maj. John Hamtramck, having been unsuccessful in its pursuit of the deserters, arrived at Ft. Jefferson while the refugees of the defeat were still coming in. Hamtramck was subsequently put under arrest on charges that he had refused to march out and give succor to those still retreating, but in his court-martial he was honorably acquitted. With little pause, the retreating remnants continued all the way back to Cincinnati, arriving there at noon on November 8, returning in just four days from a march that had taken 48 days on the outgoing trip.

417. One of these cannon, a 6-pounder, was plowed up a number of years afterwards on the battleground by the farmer who then owned the field. It was taken by him to Cincinnati where he sold it for $60 to Capt. Joseph Jenkinson, who commanded the volunteer artillery corps there.

418. Included in this figure are the estimated two hundred wives, children, and prostitutes who were killed. The official American tally was shocking. Out of 52 officers in the battle, 39 had been killed, and of the remaining 13, seven were wounded. Of the 868 rank and file, regulars and militia alike, 593 were killed and 257 wounded. The final grim totals were almost beyond belief: a total of 632 officers and men had been killed and 264 wounded. Out of a total of 920 American officers and men who took part in the battle, only 24 men of St. Clair's army returned uninjured, while at the same time only 66 Indians were killed and nine wounded. Rather amazingly, since all accounts agree he was constantly in the thickest of the fighting, St. Clair was not wounded, though eight bullet holes were later found in his hat and clothing. St. Clair's Defeat was then, and remains today, the greatest Indian victory over any American military force, including George Armstrong Custer's famous defeat on June 25, 1876, at the hands of the Sioux at the Little Big Horn, in which the American loss was 264 men.

419. The scalped bodies of these two—Tobias Woods and Absalom Craig—were found by Simon Kenton who had been asked to look for them when they failed to return home.

420. Following the defeat, St. Clair had been generally condemned by practically everyone, not the least of whom was President George Washington himself. When his private secretary, Tobias Lear, informed him in his office of the staggering defeat, Washington first blanched and then became all but apoplectic with unbridled rage. He said to Tobias:

> Right here, yes here, on this very spot, I took leave of him. I wished him success and honor. "You have your instructions," I said, "from the Secretary of War. I had a strict eye to them and will add but one word—beware of a surprise!"—I repeated it—"BEWARE OF A SURPRISE!

You know how the Indians fight us!" He went off with that, as my last solemn warning thrown into his ears. And yet!—to suffer that army to be cut to pieces, hacked, butchered, tomahawked, by a surprise—the very thing I guarded him against! Oh, God! Oh, God, he is worse than a murderer! How can he answer it to his country? The blood of the slain is upon him—the curse of widows and orphans—the curse of Heaven!

Lear reported that Washington's tone was appallingly vehement and that more than once the president threw up his hands as he hurled imprecations upon the name of St. Clair. At last, Lear reported, Washington's rage abated somewhat and he sat down on a sofa, looked at his secretary and said in a more normal voice: "This must not go beyond this room." He then paused for a long while and when he spoke again, it was in a very low voice:

"General St. Clair shall have justice," he said. "I looked hastily through the dispatches—saw the whole disaster, but not the particulars. I will hear him without prejudice; he shall have full justice!"

St. Clair's case was subsequently thoroughly investigated by a committee of the House of Representatives and he was honorably acquitted, but public sentiment had set itself against him too strongly and St. Clair wound up resigning his commission, though retaining his office as governor.

421. Ft. St. Clair was erected on the site of the present city of Eaton, the Preble Co. seat.

422. The crossing of the Ohio River with the stolen horses was made at the site where the present town of Dover, Mason Co., Ky., is located.

423. This camp was set up midway between the present villages of Fayetteville and Chasetown in present Brown Co., O., at the point where the small tributary called Little Indian Creek enters the East Fork of the Little Miami River.

424. The man killed by Tecumseh was Samuel Barr, one of the men of Simon Kenton's party of twenty-four men, who had earlier discovered and killed Frog Hunter and then followed his trail to this camp, upon which the plan had been made to attack in the midst of night.

425. The big man who had so fortuitously escaped being killed by Sinnanatha was none other than Simon Kenton. Sinnanatha—Stephen Ruddell—just before the War of 1812, visited Kenton in Ohio, and Kenton showed Ruddell the ball that had struck him that night, cut into his clothes and buried itself there and bruised Kenton's chest. Kenton, later finding the ball still enmeshed in his clothing, kept it as a memento of his close call. Not until Kenton divulged the circumstances of where and how it occurred did Ruddell realize its significance and inform him that he was the one who had shoved his gun against Kenton's chest and fired.

426. In later recounting of this fight, Sinnanatha—Stephen Ruddell—said there were only ten warriors in the party, other than himself and Tecumseh, but he had this figure confused with the number who remained behind with Tecumseh to track the whites. Had there been only twelve, they would scarcely have required three huge marquee tents; nor could a dozen Indians have successfully stolen 56 horses and forced them to swim the Ohio River; finally, Kenton himself said the Indian party attacked was about three times larger than his own party of 24 men.

427. Sinnanatha—Stephen Ruddell—was very reluctant in later years, after returning to the whites, to speak much about the forays he went on against the whites in company with Tecumseh, fearing he would be branded a renegade. This case, where the whites were the initial attackers, was one of the exceptions. His younger brother, Abram, who had also been adopted by the Shawnees and whose Indian name has not been discovered, always bore a well-hidden hatred for his adopted tribe and was clever enough to use their own beliefs against them, as well as their belief in his honesty, of which there was precious little. The Shawnees believed that if one person killed another while under the influence of alcohol, the killer was morally unresponsible and should not be punished. Abram would get deliberately drunk (or feign drunkenness) and, while in this state, would kill some of his fellow Indians. He did this a number of times and was always held morally innocent and never punished. An example of the depth of his hatred and cunning may be seen in the case when, while with the Indians at a sugar camp in early spring, he cut a long hollow weed with large diameter and put one end of it into a kettle of boiling maple syrup.

When another young Indian came up he pretended to be drinking through the straw and enjoying it immensely. The other Indian youth asked him if it did not burn his mouth and he said no, that it cooled as it passed through the straw, but the secret was in getting the end of the straw far back into the throat. The other Indian cut a similar straw for himself, put it into the syrup and deep into his throat and sucked hard. He pulled in a large amount of the thick scalding fluid which continued to burn his throat tissues for a long while due to its heat-holding viscosity. The victim fell to the ground, rolling in pain and as others ran up to help, Abram Ruddell said, "I told him not to try to drink the melassa, that it was too hot and would burn his mouth!" The tissues in the mouth and throat of the young Indian swelled so rapidly that he could not speak or hardly even moan. Before long the swelling affected his breathing and got consistently worse until he died of suffocation. Abram was never found out and in after years used to laughingly boast about what he had done.

428. In regard to this mission, the report stated:

> A description of the spectacle which the field presented, tho' covered with twenty inches deep of snow, would be offensive to humanity . . . a fatigue party of 40 was ordered out to bury the dead—the rest being engaged in looking for the cannon and fitting up the carriages. The cannon could not be found—supposed to be thrown into a large creek hard by, which was froze over. Every possible search was made, but in vain. The party returned to Fort Jefferson, bringing with them one howit, one six-pound carriage, two three-pound ditto, and four sleds with double teams loaded with iron. The carriages which could not be brought away were destroyed. . . . [e]Ncamped on the field of battle during the night of the 4th February. Not a tree or bush, or scarcely a twig, could be found . . . which had not been marked by a ball.

429. The official report stated that St. Clair had conducted his campaign with skill and great personal bravery and that the defeat was chiefly owing to the want of discipline in the militia and to the negligence of the War Department, whose duty it was to procure and forward the provisions and military stores necessary for the expedition; that the army was weakened by short allowances and desertion and by the fact that its finest fighting unit had to be sent in pursuit of the deserters; that against a force greatly superior to his own in numbers, the general had held the battlefield for an uninterrupted conflict lasting three hours, nor did he order a retreat until the field was covered with bodies of his men and further efforts were unavailing; that the general himself was the last to leave the ground when the retreat was ordered; and that, finally, "General Arthur St. Clair still retains the undiminished esteem and good opinion of General Washington."

430. Sagoyewatha—Red Jacket—returned to the Americans but what he told them was a very greatly watered-down version of what had been said to him. He merely said the western tribes were seriously considering peace and were willing to talk to the Americans about it next summer. He made no mention whatever of the Shawnee demand for payment for American inroads into Ohio or reimbursement for the lost Kentucky lands, and only gave a bare mention to the fact that the western tribes would really like to maintain the Ohio River as the border between themselves and the Americans.

431. Site of present Ludlow's Springs just east of present Eaton, Preble Co., O.

432. One of Gen. Wayne's officers, Capt. Thomas T. Underwood, kept a very accurate and detailed journal during this period and throughout the Wayne Campaign and his observations provided a clear and concise picture of the type of force Wayne was molding. One such entry, in regard to the shooting of deserters, provides an example:

> Pittsburg. Oct. 26, 1792. I will name part of what took place the last few weeks. Captain Ballard Smith arrested for intemperance and tried by General Court Martial, sentenced to be suspended for six months and then to take command of his company. Sergeant Trotter deserted Saturday night; was brought to camp Sunday one o'clock. Tried by Court Martial and sentenced to be shot. He was shot the same evening on the Grand Parade. One of Captain Robert Campbell's troopers, by the name of Newman, deserted. Brought back the 3d day. Tried by Court Martial and sentenced to be hanged. He was hanged the 4th day after the sentence passed on him. 8 or 9 of the infantry

was tried for desertion and all condemned and shot, except four or five deserters; these was [sic]
pardoned by the Commander-in-Chief and joined their companies.

433. In one of his reports to Secretary of War Henry Knox, Wayne said:

*The Savage can be a very formidable opponent if allowed to fight in places and seasons of his
own choosing. In the Fall of the year he's strong, ferocious and full of spirits—corn is in plenty
and venison and other game everywhere to be met with; in Spring he is half-starved, weak and
dispirited. Their great weakness lies in that they are disorganized and neither equipped nor inclined
to conduct long compaigns . . . The worst thing an army can do, yet one which all have done in
the past, is to respond to their hit-and-run attacks, many of which are subterfuges meant to draw
seemingly larger military forces into positions where they may be suddenly overwhelmed by surprise
by forces much greater in number . . . Permit me to choose the season for operations. Give me
time to manoeuver and discipline the army, so as to inspire them with a confidence in their own
prowess, authorize me to direct ample and proper magazines of forage, stores and provisions to
be thrown into the advanced posts at the most favorable and convenient periods . . . Give me
authority to make these arrangements and I will pledge my reputation as an officer to establish
myself at the Miami villages, or at any other place that may be thought more proper, in the face
of all the savages of the wilderness.*

434. Such drills were not without hazard. Capt. Underwood, in his Journal, related that: "One
of Captain Moses Porter's artillery men had his right hand shot off and died this morning with
lock jaw."

435. Some sources have contended that Scott had with him 1,000 mounted volunteers when he
reported to Wayne on the evening of October 11, but that is an error and the correct number is
800.

436. Two days after the departure of Wayne's army from Ft. Washington, a severe smallpox
epidemic struck Ft. Washington and felled a third of the garrison that had been left there.

437. Even while back at Legionville, Wayne had planned on making Arthur St. Clair's most
advanced post, Ft. Jefferson, the facility from which he would launch his campaign against the
Maumee villages. To this end he had directed that an enormous amount of supplies and equipment
be forwarded there to be held in readiness for his arrival. His rage was extreme when he arrived
to find that hardly a quarter of what he had requisitioned to be sent there had arrived and equally
furious that he had not been informed of the deficiency. While he blamed corrupt civilian government contractors, the greater fault—not revealed until many years later—lay in his second-
in-command, Brig. Gen. James Wilkinson, who, as it turned out, was not only at the head of a
cabal of officers intentionally sabotaging Wayne's efforts, but was also a spy in the pay of Spain
and, possibly, Great Britain, and whose efforts at this time (though greatly expanded later) were
simply to cause his commander to be fired so that he himself could take over as commander-in-
chief. Wilkinson engaged in many plots and subplots to vilify Wayne in the eyes of Congress and
the public and was later described by historian Frederick J. Turner as "the most consummate
artist in treason that the nation ever possessed." Wilkinson's machinations were not fully revealed
until some seventy years after his death.

438. Wayne had been instructed by Secretary of War Henry Knox to make no concerted attack
against the Indians yet, not so long as there was a chance a warless peace could be effected, to
which end he should also exert himself with the tribes on behalf of the United States government.
In these instructions, Knox went on to say:

*The sentiments of the great mass of Citizens of the United States are adverse in the extreme to
an Indian War and although those sentiments would not be considered as sufficient cause for the
Government to conclude an infamous peace, yet they are of such a nature as to render it advisable
to embrace every expedient which may honorably terminate the conflict . . . the favorable opinion
and pity of the world is easily excited in favor of the oppressed. The Indians are considered in a
great degree of this description. If our modes of population and War destroy the tribes, the*

disinterested part of mankind and posterity will be apt to class the effects of our Conduct and that of the Spaniards in Mexico and Peru together.

439. McMahon wanted to attack at once and not risk the jibes of others back at Ft. Greenville if they returned without engaging the enemy. Kenton did not agree, but said if McMahon persisted, he and his spies would accompany them only until they were attacked, which would occur, and at that point would retreat and, being mounted, would leave the McMahon detachment far in the rear. McMahon at that point let common sense become the better part of valor and returned, for which wisdom both he and Kenton were congratulated by Wayne.

440. Guy Carleton, Lord Dorchester, had no authorization from the home office to make so inflammatory a speech and when word of it finally filtered back to the king, he was strongly rebuked.

441. The majority of modern accounts state that Ft. Miamis (properly pronounced My-am-mees, but most often improperly pronounced My-am-miss) was built by the British at the foot of the Maumee Rapids (see Note 225) in April 1794, but that is not the case. The fort was actually built in the late summer of 1791, but was, for the first two and a half years, little more than a small stockaded fortification in the wilderness. It did not become a significant installation until April of 1794 when its defenses were considerably strengthened on order of Lt. Gov. John Graves Simcoe.

442. It hadn't taken long for word of Lord Dorchester's inflammatory speech and Simcoe's strengthening of Ft. Miamis to reach Gen. Wayne at his headquarters in Greenville and instead of being upset over it, he was mildly pleased. It confirmed his often repeated contention that the Indian problem was woven of a whole piece of cloth of which the British were an integral part. He was now determined that if the British should make any attempt to intervene in behalf of the Indians, he would overrun and demolish them.

443. Kenton had, off and on over the years, suffered from recurring attacks of malaria, but this one during early 1794 was especially severe and incapacitated him for Wayne's entire campaign.

444. On April 14, Wayne ordered out a detachment from Greenville under Lt. Col. David Strong to return to Cincinnati and commandeer the supplies being held there that the contractors were haggling about and would not release. Wayne, in sending out the detachment (which successfully brought back the supplies), said, "I will no longer be imposed upon or trifled with, nor shall the army be starved to death."

445. The military escort was under command of Maj. Robert (William in some accounts) McMahon and consisted of eight riflemen under Capt. Ara Hartshorn and fifty dragoons under Capt. Philip Taylor, plus ten drovers.

446. The four officers killed at this time were Maj. Robert McMahon, Captains Philip Taylor and Ara Hartshorn, and Lt. William Craig.

447. Accounts of the number of casualties for both sides in this affair are greatly varied, ranging from as few as 14 whites killed to as many as 75; and equally ranging from as few as 17 Indians to as many as 80. The most accurate figures seem to be those given in the Journal of William Clark, who states that the Indians had a total of 40 casualties, including 20 killed and 20 wounded, and that the total American casualties were 63, which included 23 killed and 40 wounded. It has been stated in several accounts, evidently generated by a claim made by Gen. William Henry Harrison in a speech to the U.S. House of Representatives in April 1819, that a small number of British took part in the Ft. Recovery attack, including Simon Girty as well as a captain and six matrosses (gunner's mates) clad in Indian clothing and their faces blackened to avoid detection, but these accounts are open to question. In the *Western Star*, a newspaper published at Stockbridge, Massachusetts, and not particularly noted for its accuracy, an item datelined Philadelphia, November 21, 1794, states:

> At Fort Recovery, a great number of British soldiers, with their faces blacked, assisted in the attack. Three British officers kept at a distance behind the assailants and directed the operations.

Twenty-two Americans were killed, thirty wounded and three missing. If any circumstance could add to the atrocity of this behavior on the part of our grandam Mother Country, it is that these poor savages were led into the field with the greatest reluctance.

448. It has been reported that later it was discovered that the departing Ottawas and Chippewas had come across some Shawnee women working in the fields and robbed and raped them, but the author considers the allegations ill supported and unlikely.

449. The stretch of ground covered by the fallen timbers extended along the northwest bank of the Maumee from present Turkeyfoot Rock, just over a mile upstream from the present Interstate 475 bridge (this area presently called the Fallen Timbers State Memorial) to the narrow piece of ground between the head of present Silver Lake and the northern bulge of Blue Grass Island, 3,000 feet downstream from that same bridge; the lower (northeasternmost) portion of this Fallen Timbers area being exactly three miles upstream from the present Ft. Miamis State Memorial.

450. This first camp north of Greenville on Wayne's advance occurred where present State Route 49 crosses the upper Stillwater River about midway between the present villages of Ansonia and Lightsville in Darke Co. Wayne had left behind at Greenville a garrison of 150 soldiers under Maj. John Buell.

451. The bridge and Ft. Adams were built at the mouth of Beaver Creek less than a mile north of the present village of Wabash in Mercer Co., O.

452. This camp was made on the site of the present village of Wilshire, Van Wert Co., O., on the Indiana border.

453. Wayne thought at first this was merely an accident, but later became convinced, with considerable justification, that this had been a very nearly successful attempt on his life engineered by Gen. Wilkinson; an allegation he was never able to prove but, in view of Wilkinson's other treacheries, was very probably correct.

454. The newly arrived force was made up of 800 Kentucky volunteers under command of Col. Barbee, who joined Scott's volunteers with Wayne. Most accounts state that Wayne, when he clashed with the Indians, had a total of 3,500 men (citing 2,000 regulars and 1,500 Kentucky Militia) but this is incorrect. Wayne had 2,200 regulars and, initially, 1,600 volunteers, which gave him 3,800 when he left Greenville, and the addition of Col. Barbee's contingent, which is mainly overlooked, gave him a total of 4,400 troops.

455. Tecumseh, in his own words, remarked on this to one of Harrison's messengers, Joseph Barron, in 1811, saying, in regard to Harrison, "I remember him as a young man sitting by the side of General Wayne." Since Tecumseh did not attend the Wayne treaty in Greenville in 1795, after which Harrison was no longer aide to Wayne, it had to be while Harrison was still Wayne's aide and therefore immediately after the army left its Greenville headquarters on the march north.

456. The tributary they had encountered was present Flatrock Creek, which they followed to its mouth just over two miles north of the present village of Charloe, Paulding Co., O.

457. Roche de Boeuf was a collection point for cattle being moved past the 16-mile stretch of rapids on the old Maumee Rapids Trail (now called the Anthony Wayne Trail), located at the upstream edge of the present village of Waterville, Lucas Co., O.

458. From which the present city and county of Defiance get their names. The fort was located on the site of the present Old Fort Defiance City Park in Defiance.

459. All the sick and lame were left to garrison Ft. Defiance under Maj. Hunt. Chief Snake was a minor Shawnee village chief whose village was located on approximately the site of the present village of Florida, Henry Co., O.

460. The camp on the night of August 16 was on the north bank of the river at approximately the location where the present U.S. 6 bridge over the Maumee is located in Henry County.

461. The army encampment on the night of August 17 was at the site of the present town of Grand Rapids, in Lucas Co., O., probably where present Metropolitan Park is located.

462. As nearly as can be determined, the tribal breakdown of warriors taking part in this conflict are as follows: 100 Delawares, 100 Wyandots, 150 Miamis, 150 Ottawas, 200 Potawatomies, 500 Shawnees, 800 Chippewas; so reported Antoine Lanell, a Canadian trader captured by the Americans during the battle.

463. The American advance was led by Lt. Harry Towels, who was killed in the first fire from the Indians, along with his sergeant, Eli Edmundson.

464. The artillery fire came from the company of Capt. John Price, which was at that moment under command of Lt. Percy Pope, on the right of the army's advance.

465. Several accounts contend that Lowawluwaysica, "at the first firing, ran away from the Wayne fight and never stopped running until he reached Detroit." That, of course, is an exaggeration. He did run away, but he did not go to Detroit, although his whereabouts were unknown for several days and it was at first supposed by the Shawnees that he had been among the number killed.

466. Capt. Robert M. Campbell led the first wave of the main army to enter the wood and he was killed almost immediately with a shot through the breast. His command was taken over by Capt. John Arnold.

467. Sinnanatha—Stephen Ruddell—who admitted having fought on the side of the Indians in this battle, rather grandiosely claimed in an 1866 interview at his Quincy, Ill., home with historian Lyman Draper that his gun had gotten wet and he could not get it to go off; otherwise, as he stated it: "mine would have been the first gun of the battle, but because it was wet, I had to retreat."

468. Sinnanatha, in his interview with Dr. Draper, stated that Tecumseh and his followers, to make their escape, "attacked an American artillery squad, cut the horses loose and rode to safety." Since Stephen Ruddell was not terribly careful with his facts as he remembered them 72 years later, it is believed this account is fanciful, especially since it was never remarked upon by Chaubenee, who was beside Tecumseh throughout the battle.

469. One American soldier wrote that as the army came in sight of Ft. Miamis, "We beat our drums. Blowed our trumpets."

470. This act of Col. McKee's was extremely important in keeping the Indians linked to some degree with the British and helped restore a certain amount of the trust that had been demolished at the locked gates of Ft. Miamis. In his letter to the Detroit commander, Col. Richard England, ten days after the Battle of Fallen Timbers, McKee wrote:

> *Camp near Ft. Miamis, Aug. 30, '94*
> *Sir—I have been employed several days in endeavoring to fix the Indians (who have been driven from their villages and cornfields) between the Fort and the Bay. Swan Creek is generally agreed upon, and will be a very convenient place for the delivery of provisions, etc. . . .*

471. Some accounts say the Indian loss was in excess of 100 and Col. Alexander McKee, in his official report, claimed only 19 Indians had been killed and about the same number lost. Capt. William Clark, in his journal, said the Americans had only 24 killed and that the "loss of the enemy not precisely ascertained, but not more than thirty or forty were found dead, and a few Canadians." Several accounts have the Americans suffering over 100 killed. Wayne reported, most accurately, it appears that he had 44 men killed and 89 others wounded, and he claimed that the Indian loss was about double his own. In actuality, the Indians' loss, while not certainly known, was very close to the same amount as Wayne's.

472. Later, when Chief Kinjoino of the Ottawas was asked to explain why the Indians had been beaten at Fallen Timbers, he replied with a remark that seemed to echo the belief of many of the Indians who participated in the battle: "The Great Spirit was angry and She turned Her face away from Her red children."

473. Wayne started his army back toward Ft. Defiance on August 23, following the burial of his dead. Small parties of Indians continued dogging the army and firing on it when they could. In this pursuit several Indians were killed and the army got little rest at night as the Indians hooted and howled back and forth throughout the night like owls and wolves just beyond the perimeter of each night's camp. Pvt. John O'Brian was one of a number of soldiers who were shot and wounded or killed during the return march; a ball from an adjacent hill struck him low in the back, angled through the bottom part of his stomach and finally lodged in his penis.

474. Stephen Ruddell, who had for so long been the Shawnee named Sinnanatha, returned to Kentucky and in 1801 at the great Cane Ridge Meeting he became converted and joined the Baptist Church and commenced preaching this same year. For the rest of his life he remained an evangelist, as Lyman Draper reports,

> . . . laboring earnestly whenever an opportunity offered, preaching to the poor frontier settlers the Gospel "without money and without juice." He went off with Stone and others and labored with them ever after. In northern Missouri he formed several churches. He was quite successful as a preacher, seldom attempting a regular doctrinal or argumentative discourse; but was a warm-heart preacher—pathetic and personal in his appeals, and exhibiting fine oratorical powers. He evinced much of the Indian style of animated eloquence, learned doubtless from the great efforts of Tecumseh in his native appeals to his countrymen.

The final clause assumes that Ruddell heard Tecumseh making "his native appeals to his countrymen" but that, of course, is in error, since Tecumseh did not begin making such appeals until at least six years after Ruddell had returned to the whites.

475. Actually, the initial grant was for 24,000 acres, but this was increased by 1,200 acres in order to have enough to supply the demand. Greater details of the fraudulent land sales in France and the formation of the French Grant may be found in *The Frontiersmen*.

476. The exact number of Shawnees who threw in their lot with Tecumseh at this time is not known. Some sources have claimed as many as over 100, others as few as 16. From the size of the village ultimately established by Tecumseh at Deer Creek for himself and his followers, a reasonable guess would be that there were probably in the vicinity of 50 to 60.

477. The headwaters of Deer Creek were located close to the headwaters of the Mad River, but were in the Scioto River drainage and the area where Tecumseh established his Deer Creek Village was northwest of present London, Ohio, and close to the present boundary separating Champaign and Madison counties.

478. A good part of the reason why the British were finally willing to surrender these posts to the Americans had its basis in the fur trade. Due to various human conflicts and overharvesting of the fur animals in the Northwest Territory, less than one-fifth of the current British fur trade revenue in North America of £200,000, was being generated from there and the cost it was entailing to maintain these posts for that purpose and to maintain good relations with the tribes was really no longer worth the expense. New British trade routes to the far west, spearing far beyond the Mississippi and into the vast Northwestern Territory beyond, all the way to the Pacific, were opening far greater prospects for an unopposed continuation of the fur trade.

479. There is a great deal of confusion and misinformation in regard to Tecumseh and his wives. That he had three different wives at separate times is generally accepted as true, though the name of one of them has not even been recorded. Of the two about which a smattering of information is recorded—Mohnetohse and Mamate—the available data is hopelessly confused between the two with much overlapping and considerable attributing of the details about one to the other and vice versa. The resultant hodgepodge cannot be cleared up unless at some time in the future additional documentation is uncovered that can set the record straight. While the author cannot ignore the fact of the marriages and their resultant offspring, neither can he be absolutely positive of exactly what happened to whom and when. In this respect a concerted effort has been made to deduce, as far as it has been possible to do so with the known facts, what actually occurred in respect to Tecumseh's wives and offspring. The reader should bear this in mind and not accept as incontrovertible the information as presented here in these regards. If mistakes have been made, despite the efforts for accuracy, the author sincerely apologizes.

480. Sauganash (pronounced SAW-guh-nash) was the son of a Potawatomi woman, said to have been "of remarkable beauty and keen intelligence" but whose name is not known to be recorded, and a British officer of Detroit named Capt. William Caldwell, who was a sometimes trader and frequent liaison with the Indians in the company of McKee, Elliott and Girty. The name Sauganash was a nickname meaning "The Englishman" (which comes down in the Ottawa tongue as Sagonas). However, his real Potawatomi name was Tequitoh (teh-KWEE-toe) which, in English, means Straight Tree. One source, unverified by any other and discounted by the author, states that the mother of Sauganash was a Mohawk and the daughter of a chief named Rising Sun.

481. Conner's Trading Post was situated at or near present Connersville, Fayette Co., Ind.

482. Wampum strings (for minor points) and belts (for major issues) were always exchanged at such treaties as an important adjunct to record keeping. Although such belts were valuable, they were not (as many easterners thought, and as many people still think) a form of currency. Rather, they were a form of record-keeping developed among the tribes through the centuries and used to impress indelibly the desired points embodied in the message of the speaker delivering them. Most often made from tubular shell beads strung into strings and a foot and a half in length, the individual strands of the belt were skillfully woven together to form intricate variations of color and design, each significant in its own right and each imparting a special message. Even seasoned frontiersmen and traders who had been among the Indians for many years found it uncanny how an Indian could glance at such a belt and then recite verbatim the terms of a treaty or words of an agreement, as if he were reading from a printed page. Sometimes the strands woven together would form a belt as long as 10 or 12 feet, but most often they were only four or five inches wide and about three to four feet long. And, though the belts were originally constructed from freshwater or ocean shell pieces drilled through in a laborious process with a slender flint drill rolled between the palms, a revolution in wampum belt construction had occurred when traders began stocking variously colored clear and opaque glass beads. Easterners became fond of snickering over the passion of the Indians for the beads, believing them to be for ornamentation purposes only. Such, in fact, was rarely the case. Those beads fulfilled as important a function in Indian record keeping as did paper and pen for the whites; thus, beads became enormously profitable items in the Indian trade. In general terms (though there were variations) a black wampum belt signified war talk, while white was one of peace, prosperity and health. Violet signified tragedy, death, sorrow, and disaster, sometimes even war. To make the message of the belts plainer, stick figures would be woven into the belts or there would be geometric designs of various types—diamond shapes, stars, hexagons, parallel lines, wavy lines, intersecting line patterns, etc., each with its own significance. Metaphoric expressions transferred to beaded wampum belts required extreme care in preparation lest any wrong idea be relayed. Metaphors commonly used and transferred to wampum belts included a raised hatchet, signifying war, and a buried hatchet, signifying peace; kindling a fire, meaning deliberation and negotiations; covering the bones of the dead, meaning giving or receiving reparation and forgiveness for those killed; a black cloud signified a state of disaster or imminent war; brilliant sunshine or an unobstructed path between two nations signified peace; a black bird represented bad news, a white or yellow bird, good news. Indian speakers rarely spoke without lengths of wampum, either strings or belts or both, draped over their shoulders or arms, to which they referred frequently as they spoke and which were sporadically presented to dignitaries in attendance as points were made.

483. When the new Secretary of War, Timothy Pickering, received a copy of the completed treaty on September 27, he expressed grave concern to both Gen. Wayne and President Washington that too few Potawatomi chiefs had been present to negotiate and sign the treaty and cessions of certain lands without the concurrence of all the chiefs might result in further strife on the far Northwestern frontier. A listing of the names of the sixteen Potawatomi chiefs who signed the treaty, along with their alternative names and English translations of their names appears in James A. Clifton's *The Prairie People* (Lawrence, Kan., 1977) pp. 152-155.

484. Gen. Wayne had been given sole power to negotiate for the United States in all matters, but with very specific instructions received from President Washington through Secretary of War

Timothy Pickering, regarding what he should say and what his primary considerations should be—foremost of which being very large cessions of land.

485. Part of Wayne's specific instructions were to avoid making any such assertion, which would only serve to irritate and alienate those in attendance.

486. Although in the open council this is what Wayne told the chiefs that the treaty included, that treaty in its actual written form called for the Indians to turn over to white authorities any Indian guilty of killing a white person unjustly, but there is no mention whatever of whites turning over to the Indians any white person guilty of unjustly killing an Indian.

487. With those words, the Americans gained cession to more than half of the entire Ohio Territory without restriction. (See earlier map of the Partition of Ohio.)

488. Wayne was here doing a little improvising, since his instructions had authorized him to negotiate for only ten such tracts, but the attitude of the Indians in attendance made him feel he could push for the additional six and they would not question it, and in this he was quite correct and successful.

489. And, though Wayne did not say it, most importantly to cow the Indians and keep them in check in case of future unrest.

490. By the terms of the Greenville Treaty, the Indians ceded to the United States an area of territory comprising some 25,000 square miles, not even including those sixteen separate tracts, which were each about six miles square. For these cessions of such unbelievable value, economically, strategically, and territorially, the United States agreed to pay in goods the value of $1,666 for each of the 12 tribes there represented, plus an additional annuity of $825 worth of goods to each of the tribes. When averaged out, it meant that the United States was paying one cent for every six acres acquired!

491. The completed Greenville Treaty was immediately dispatched special express by Wayne to the secretary of war, who in turn presented it to the President. Heartily approving of it, the President presented it to the United States Senate on December 9, and on December 22, 1795, the Greenville Treaty was ratified.

492. Wayne, in respect to his arrival at Detroit, wrote to his son:

> *Here, in the center of a wilderness, you see ships or large Vessels of War and Merchantmen lying at the Wharf or sailing up and down a pleasant river of About One Mile wide, as is passing and repassing from the ocean.*

The General's condition, after arriving at Detroit, gradually degenerated, the gout that had affected his feet and legs expanding to attack liver, kidneys and heart. Late in the year he decided to try to get back to Philadelphia for better medical treatment and he was placed aboard a small schooner bound for Buffalo. On December 15, while en route and just off Presque Isle, at present Erie, Pa., his condition took so drastic a turn for the worse that the schooner put in and Wayne was taken inside Ft. Presque Isle, where he died before sunset. He was buried beneath the fort's flagpole.

493. The ceremony took place at the waterfront on what is presently Griswold Street. A bronze plaque affixed to the main entrance of the Detroit Post Office states that "Here, on July 11, 1796, at 12 o'clock noon, was performed the final act of the War of Independence."

494. Naythawaynah has also been referred to in early documents by the name of Pugeshashenwa or its diminutive form, Pachetha, but the author believes this was a nickname later applied and its meaning unclear.

495. This third village established by Tecumseh was located less than two miles west of the site of the present village of Brookville, Franklin Co., Ind., and just barely west of the boundary line established by the Greenville Treaty, which ran from Ft. Recovery in a direct line to the mouth of the Kentucky River.

496. The term "prairie island" was commonly in use at the time and referred to the isolated groves of dense forest that existed here and there in the vast prairie lands extending from northern Ohio westward through Indiana and especially in the northern half of Illinois. Such groves appeared from a distance to be great dark islands in a vast sea of grass. The town established by Chaubenee at this time was on the site of the present village of Shabonee Grove in De Kalb Co., Ill.

497. In regard to the alleged silver deposits close to Chalahgawtha, see Note 248.

498. There are still fortune hunters in Kentucky who persist in looking for the lost Shawnee silver mines in the valley of the Red River, the Kentucky, and other streams. To date no silver deposit has been found, but still they keep coming . . . and coming.

499. President John Adams had been very impressed with Michikiniqua and had remarked, "I find Chief Little Turtle to be a remarkable man. I only wish all the chiefs who visit here were so wise and so reasonable."

500. Word had not yet reached Tecumseh and his followers that the 24-year-old William Henry Harrison had just resigned his commission in the United States Army in order to accept the post of Secretary of the Northwest Territory under Gov. Arthur St. Clair.

501. The new Buckangehela's Town was located in present Madison Co., Ind., along the south shore of the White River just to the east of the present city of Anderson, either on or adjacent to present Mounds State Park.

502. Where these two trails crossed is the site of present Urbana, Champaign Co., O.

503. In addition to the shipyard at Buffalo, the Americans had established another at the mouth of the River Rouge near the King's Wharf in Detroit and were turning out sturdy sailing ships as rapidly as possible, including the new United States brig *Adams,* that had cost some £10,000 to construct.

504. In late March 1797, the family of James Galloway had moved into the Little Miami Valley and claimed land where Chalahgawtha had been. Tecumseh had met with them and visited with them frequently. Later the great grandson of Tecumseh, Thomas Wildcat Alford, aided William Albert Galloway in the production of a book entitled *Old Chillicothe* (Xenia, O., 1934), which provides many insights into the life of Tecumseh and Shawnee history and culture in general, but its merit is marred by certain inaccuracies and outright fictions, such as the alleged romance that occurred between Tecumseh and Rebecca Galloway. In his historical narrative, *The Frontiersmen,* the author presented details of this romance as reported by Galloway and Alford, only to discover to his chagrin, through years of continued study into the life of Tecumseh, that the supposed romance had no basis in fact and was a whole-cloth fabrication that evidently sprang from the vivid imagination of Rebecca Galloway in her later years and was related as truth.

505. The settlement referred to here by Tecumseh was the new settlement of Springfield established by Simon Kenton at the head of six families along with a dozen Negro slaves. The 1,000-acre claim by Kenton was located at the site of the present city of Springfield, seat of Clark Co., O.

506. The specific spring spoken of here still exists. It is located on the Hunt farm, named for its present owners, which fronts on old U.S. 68 three miles north of Springfield. The spring is now covered over with a spring house built of brick many years ago. The watercourse formed in part by this spring is presently called Kenton Creek.

507. A very prevalent belief exists in numerous accounts that the death of Alexander McKee occurred in 1794 shortly after the Battle of Fallen Timbers; that he had a pet deer believed by the Indians to be a physical manifestation of Moneto and that this deer one day charged McKee and struck him with his antlers in the behind, puncturing his femoral artery and he quickly bled to death; that it was more for this reason than for the Battle of Fallen timbers that the Indians believe Moneto was angry and frowning upon them and, by this act, telling them to sue for peace with the Americans. Unfortunately, the author, in *The Frontiersmen,* accepted this report as factual when, in fact, the whole story is apocryphal, as further research over the years has disclosed. The author apologizes for this error. In regard to the Indian death ritual described in this present segment, no clear explanation seems available for why the Indians waited 16 months before holding their Death Dance for Alexander McKee, who had died of tetanus in his home close to Amhertsburg on January 14, 1799, almost five years after the supposed death caused by the deer. Matthew Elliott had been immediately appointed to succeed McKee. The 66-year-old Elliott, however, was greatly disliked by the new commander at Ft. Malden, Capt. Hector McLean, who keenly resented the fact that Elliott, though illiterate, had amassed a small fortune that McLean knew could not have been legally acquired through his meager salary in the Indian Department. Elliott was an ugly, dark-skinned, pug-nosed black Irishman from Donegal, who had a large farm called The Point a mile downstream on the Detroit River from Amherstburg on which he had the finest cattle and a huge house lavishly furnished, along with 50 slaves to keep everything in top-notch shape. McLean was positive Elliott had to be embezzling and catching him at it became his aim and it hadn't taken long. When he discovered Elliott had officially requisitioned supplies for 534 Indians in a settlement where there were only 160 inhabitants, McLean filed charges and Elliott was dismissed from the Indian service and Thomas McKee, son of the former Indian agent, appointed (as McKee had requested in his will) as Elliott's successor. The young McKee was no improvement, being so constantly drunk he was all but incapable of properly presiding over delicate negotiations with the tribes.

508. One source, generally considered reliable, describes Lowawluwaysica's face as ugly, and that "his right eye was pierced and blinded, leaving that side of his face permanently and hideously twisted." That description, however, is incorrect. An excellent painting of Lowawluwaysica without his eye patch in later years (when his name had been changed to Tenskwatawa and when he was considerably heavier), rendered by artist Charles Bird King, does depict an empty socket that is only slightly sunken, and there is no trace whatever, apart from this, of distortion to the right side of his face. There is, incidentally, no known portrait of Tecumseh, and a pencil sketch allegedly done of him by a young French trader at Vincennes named Pierre Le Dru, is said to be a composite and highly inaccurate when viewed against the multitude of verbal descriptions of his physiognomy. Also, there is a portrait of the Cherokee chief Sequoyah that has quite frequently been misidentified in print as Tecumseh. A grandson of Tecumseh was said to have greatly resembled his grandfather and a drawing of that individual is sometimes falsely represented as Tecumseh. It is safe to say that no known representation of the actual Tecumseh exists.

509. Ft. Industry was constructed at the mouth of Swan Creek on the site of present Toledo, Lucas Co., O.

510. Harrison, member of the Jeffersonian Party, was elected territorial delegate to the United States Congress on September 24, 1799, at a meeting called in Cincinnati by Gov. St. Clair.

511. The presidential term of John Adams (1797–1801) was essentially free of Indian troubles as compared to that of his predecessor, George Washington, and successor, Thomas Jefferson. Washington had died at the age of 67 on the previous December 14 and had been buried at his Mount Vernon estate near Alexandria, Va.

512. Winnemac (pronounced WIN-nee-mack)—also known as Catfish—had a small village on the Tippecanoe River at the site of the present town of Winamac in Pulaski Co., Ind.

513. The reference here was to marijuana which, in recent years, had come into somewhat more prevalent use among the tribes, though still more ceremonially than addictively.

514. Kenton was at this time still recovering from another of his severe attacks of malaria, this one evidently the worst he had yet suffered. It was believed that the illness had largely deranged him for a considerable while and, though he eventually returned to his normal senses, he was assuredly not in his right mind on this occasion.

515. Kenton had lost the quarter-million acres of land he had purchased from John Cleve Symmes when the latter was forced to admit to the government that he was unable to pay for his long-pending purchase. Congress had at once canceled the sale and Symmes lost everything, including the money various buyers had paid him for lands within the purchase.

516. Exactly how much Kenton actually paid for the land in question was never fully recorded, but the available evidence seems to indicate a sum in the vicinity of $100,000. The tract bargained for included about three-fourths of the present State of Indiana, plus a sizeable wedge of western Ohio; this whole tract beginning at the mouth of the Great Miami and running northeastward upstream all the way to Indian Lake, then on a direct line from there to the Wabash River headwaters at Ft. Recovery, then down the Wabash for its full length, curving in a broad northern arc westward to present Lafayette and southward down the same river from there all the way to the mouth of the Wabash at the Ohio River and then back upstream on the Ohio to the point of origin—an area, in very rough figures, of some 3,200,000 acres.

517. There is no evidence to suggest that Tecumseh personally kept any of the money or goods involved in this deal, but that he passed everything on to the various villages and tribes, with special instructions that most of it be used to ease the burden of the elderly and the widows and children of the warriors slain by whites. Much later, when Kenton regained his senses and realized what he had done, he accepted his great loss philosophically and admitted that "I reckon I wasn't thinking too straight at the time."

518. Tecumseh had at this time taken a woman to live with him, whom he apparently eventually married, but very little is known about her apart from the fact that, while very attractive, she was also slovenly, lazy, and not particularly intelligent. It is reported that she remained with Tecumseh for two years and was sent away by him for "improperly preparing a turkey for dinner and disgracing him before his guests," although that story, which stems from Anthony Shane, appears to be apocryphal. There are also even hazier hints that she was supplanted by yet another woman who remained with him for five years, but the claims are not at all well substantiated.

519. William Henry Harrison, in regard to Indian policy, was being very closely directed by President Thomas Jefferson, who had been inaugurated on March 4, 1801. Jefferson, while publicly displaying a very benevolent attitude toward the Indians, was embarking upon a number of programs designed specifically to eradicate the tribes east of the Mississippi. Harrison was at this particular time being strongly encouraged by President Jefferson, in a very coldly calculated manner, to maneuver the Indians into a position in which they would have no recourse but to farm, in which pursuit they would gradually fall deeper and deeper into debt and thus be obliged to cede their lands in order to survive. As Jefferson wrote to Harrison:

> *When they withdraw themselves to the culture of a small piece of land, they will perceive how useless to them are the extensive forests and will be willing to pare them off in exchange for necessaries for their farms and families. To promote this, we shall push our trading houses, and be glad to see the good and influential individuals among them in debt, because we observe that when these debts go beyond what the individual can pay, they become willing to lop them off by a cession of lands. But should any tribe refuse the proffered hand and take up the hatchet, it will be driven across the Mississippi and the whole of its lands confiscated.*

520. Michikiniqua's requests met with a favorable response from both the secretary of war and the president because they felt having the distribution center at Ft. Wayne would help act as a curb in keeping the Indians away from the subversive British influence at Ft. Malden; and Harrison was also instructed to make efforts to curtail the trade in liquor.

521. Gov. Harrison, at Vincennes, reported abuses being made by traders who caused Indians to be "made drunk and cheated of their peltries . . ." but this was a decidedly sanctimonious stance, considering that one of Harrison's largest land acquisitions, involving the territory of the Sac and Fox tribes among others, was soon to be fraudulently made in St. Louis by getting some minor Sac chiefs drunk and causing them to sign over the enormous tract to him, which those chiefs involved did not even have a right to sell. Full details of this may be found in the author's *The Winning of America* Series volume entitled *Twilight of Empire* (Little, Brown, 1988; Bantam, 1989).

522. John McDonald, colonel of the newly formed Ohio Militia, who was on hand on this occasion, was extremely impressed by Tecumseh and wrote:

When Tecumseh rose to speak, as he cast his gaze over the vast multitude which the interesting occasion had drawn together, he appeared one of the most dignified men I ever beheld. While this orator of nature was speaking, the vast crowd preserved the most profound silence. From the confident manner in which he spoke of the Indians . . . he dispelled as if by magic the apprehensions of the whites—the settlers returned to their deserted farms and business was generally resumed throughout that region.

523. This was the first of six such treaties engineered by William Henry Harrison involving lands belonging to both the Miamis and Potawatomies along the Wabash River and this particular one was signed by eight minor Potawatomi village chiefs. Winnemac, secretly in the employ of Harrison, was closely involved in all of these transactions.

524. A few questionable accounts indicate that Tecumseh may have gone as far east on this trip as western Massachusetts and Vermont. This is possible, though not proven, since he crossed the St. Lawrence River just upstream from Montreal at Lachine, where he briefly visited the French trader Edouard Papineau.

525. Construction had begun on Ft. Dearborn on August 17, 1803, by a detachment led from Detroit to the present Chicago area by Capt. Zebulon Pike. Located to present landmarks, the fort was situated on the high bank above the south edge of the Chicago River at the place now occupied by the southern end of the Michigan Avenue Bridge and Wacker Drive.

526. Pineshow's Village, visited by Tecumseh on July 3, 1804, was located on the south bank of the St. Peter's River (present Minnesota River) in Scott Co., Minn., five miles downstream from the present town of Shakopee.

527. In 1800 the Louisiana Territory had passed into the hands of France from Spain, with the proviso that France would never sell it to any power other than Spain. France had immediately begun negotiations with the American government to sell it to them and the deal had been consummated in the vast Louisiana Purchase.

528. Immediately after obtaining the signatures of the five Sacs—who had no authority whatever to act on behalf of the tribe in such a matter—Harrison sent the treaty to Washington where, just over a month later, it was ratified by Congress. This deal ultimately resulted in the Black Hawk War. Full details of the colossal land fraud and its aftermath, including the entire text of the November 3, 1804, Treaty of St. Louis, may be found in the author's *Twilight of Empire*.

529. This epidemic was probably, though not certainly, an especially severe strain of influenza.

530. The author, in *The Frontiersmen*, erred in stating that the major speech of Lowawluwaysica occurred in the village of Tawa. The *secondary* speech occurred there, following the epidemic, but the major speech itself, as later discovered evidence disclosed, did indeed take place at Tecumseh's Village at Greenville, as indicated in the text following.

531. Although often referred to as a chief, Tecumseh never officially held this title, not even as the head of his own village, nor did he ever refer to himself as a chief. In fact, later, when he had established the huge village of Tippecanoe, he expressly stated that he was a warrior, not a chief, and that matters among him and his people were no longer under the jurisdiction of chiefs.

532. The triangular spit of land where Tecumseh's Village was situated was formed by the confluence of present Greenville Creek and Mud Creek, and the land itself on that site was immediately named Tecumseh Point, a name which it retains to the present day.

533. Greenville residents at this time estimated the permanent population of Tecumseh's Village at 400, but with a constant ebb and flow of from four hundred to six hundred others who were transient.

534. Oskesh, a Potawatomi, should not be mistaken for Oshkosh, the Menominee chief of Wisconsin, who came into prominence later.

535. A great deal of confusion exists in regard to just how many trips Tecumseh made to recruit followers to his plan, the actual tribes he visited, and the length of time he was gone. There are numerous claims of his visiting places and tribes where he never went, while, at the same time, extensive trips he *did* take are often only barely hinted at and poorly reported. Some biographers contend he never left the original Northwestern Territory. A report by John D. Hunter that Tecumseh visited the Osages in 1811 appears to be spurious and the whole-cloth invention of Hunter to enhance his own position. Yet, since Tecumseh himself declared his intention of visiting the Osages, the possibility that he might have done so should not be rejected out of hand simply on the basis of Hunter's falacious account. Tecumseh was clearly known to have visited the Illinois tribes as well as the Absentee Shawnees in Missouri during the summer of 1808 and there are numerous hints that he did, in fact, visit the Osages at this time, which it would only have been reasonable for him to do, since he was on the fringe of their territory at this point and the author is convinced that this was when he visited them, though evidently without any signal success, since no Osages were known to have joined his coalition. Another account, similar to Hunter's, written by one William Johnson (or Johnston), a long-time prisoner of the Crow Indians, that Tecumseh recruited among that tribe and the Blackfeet in 1809 appears to be entirely fictional. Some biographers consider as similarly fictitious Caleb Atwater's detailed account of his accompanying Tecumseh's party in an offical capacity as Tecumseh visited upper New York and Canada and the Iroquois tribes and yet, while there are aspects of that account which Atwater no doubt padded to improve his own stature, the author does not discount that the trip actually did take place. William Henry Harrison eventually became well aware of the journeys Tecumseh was taking and the recruiting he was doing and, writing of this to the secretary of war, remarked:

> The implicit obedience and respect which the followers of Tecumseh pay him are wonderful. If it were not for the vicinity of the United States, he would perhaps be the founder of an empire that would rival in glory Mexico or Peru. No difficulties deter him. For four years he has been in constant motion. You see him to-day on the Wabash, and in a short time hear of him on the shores of Lake Erie or Michigan, or on the banks of the Mississippi; and wherever he goes he makes an impression favorable to his purpose.

Taking the bits and pieces of information from a very wide variety of sources—some contributing only a key remark or two of substantive nature—the author has attempted to present as factually as possible an accurate accounting of where Tecumseh went and when and a similar reconstruction, as closely as possible, of what he said and to whom. The only recruiting trip taken by Tecumseh during this period from 1802 through 1811 that was reasonably well documented was his visit to the southern tribes in that latter year. If future researchers, through new material being discovered, should find error in this present reconstruction, the author apologizes and notes only that the reconstruction was done as carefully as possible with the known sources available at the time.

536. Tenskwatawa, sometimes spelled Tengskwatawa, is pronounced TENS-kwah-TAH-wuh, not Ten-SQUAT-uh-wuh. This name has also been said to mean The Open Door.

537. Among the Sac contingent present at this gathering was a warrior named Winnebea—Spinning Top—who was the brother of the Sac Chief Wabetejee—White Cedar. In an 1823 discussion with Maj. Stephen Harriman Long during that officer's second expedition, Winnebea stated:

> We value our medicine bags so highly that we would not part with them while life endures. True, some of us did, at one time, at the instigation of the Shawnee Prophet, throw them away; but this proved to us the source of many heavy calamities—it brought on the death of all who parted with their bags. . . . I told him he wished to impose upon us, that our bags had not lost their virtue, that still, in the hour of need, we applied to them and generally with success; that we kept them in our villages, and that when our friends were sick, we applied to them for relief, and that if we were not successful in all cases, at least we were in most instances. But he was very angry at me and offered to strike me, which he would have done had he not been prevented.

538. There are several accounts which contend that the preceding April Lowawluwaysica had fallen into a coma, was thought dead and was prepared for burial. Then, allegedly, he recovered consciousness and spoke at length of his journey in his trancelike state into the world of the

Shawnee gods, who gave him instructions on the directions he should follow and the reforms he should make among the Shawnees as their Prophet. The accounts are garbled, highly contradictive and do not at all fit into the scheme of known events, including the move of Tecumseh and his followers to Greenville, the epidemic at Tawa, the death of Penegashega, and the subsequent verbal declarations of Lowawluwaysica/Tenskwatawa at the great meeting in Greenville. Lowawluwaysica could not have been declared Shawnee Prophet so long as Penegashega was alive and held that title and Penegashega did not die until August, four months after the alleged "trance" and supposed elevation of Lowawluwaysica to Prophet.

539. Location of this site of Tecumseh's Stony Creek Village is in Logan Co. 1.5 straight-line miles south from the center of the present village of De Graff, exactly one mile up Stony Creek from its mouth and 1,000 feet west of the low Stony Creek valley on the higher benchland presently occupied by cornfields. The site, by road, is 1.7 miles south of De Graff just to the east of County Road 63.

540. The first Stony Creek Council had been accidentally discovered on the third or fourth day after it commenced by Kenton as he was passing through the area with a friend, Jim McPherson, of Urbana, 15 miles southeast. Kenton crept up and spied on it from hiding and observed the war dance and tomahawks being struck into the war posts, but was not close enough to hear what was being said. Kenton and McPherson warned all nearby residents, who forted up in the blockhouse at Springfield, waiting attack. When it had not occurred in four days, Kenton and McPherson returned to the site along with Charles McIlvain and Maj. Thomas Moore and approached openly under a white flag. They were at first turned away and then allowed a small council in a nearby cabin, at which the Indians stated that the council was a private Indian matter but there was no need for white residents to be alarmed. (One of the accounts, highly romanticized, states that at this point Kenton had a verbal altercation with Tecumseh which, if such altercation did occur, which is highly doubtful, could not have been with Tecumseh, since the quoted conversation indicates no recognition whatsoever of Kenton for Tecumseh or vice versa, and the same account has Kenton thrashing one of the warriors with a hickory stick and threatening others with his knife; the whole account, in the author's opinion, is unbelievable.) Gov. Tiffin was immediately notified by express. A considerable alarm was raised and an exchange of letters occurred between Maj. Moore and Gov. Tiffin, in one of which was enclosed the speech to the Indians from the governor.

541. Gov. Tiffin received the letter in the spirit it was meant to portray and at once called off any alarms and urged the settlers to go back to their homes and remain calm and peaceful and under no circumstances to do anything to harm the Indians at Stony Creek, who were obviously minding their own business and having their own private councils.

542. The white officer, who was part of the deputation of messengers from Harrison, was Capt. William Prince.

543. Harrison made a serious mistake here, in attributing to the Delawares the revered title of grandfathers, a title which was held among the Northwestern tribes by the Wyandots, offshoots of the Hurons, who were greatly venerated by their neighboring tribes. The simple error considerably undermined Harrison's effectiveness among the Indians for some time.

544. A great deal has been written by modern biographers in regard to this, the first truly significant, fully substantiated prediction by Tecumseh, via Tenskwatawa. Considerable effort is made to show that Tecumseh had access to many whites and could probably have come into possession, from one of them, an almanac giving the date and time of the next eclipse of the sun. Some sources state unequivocally that the prediction was made possible through information received from the Shakers, but the claim is unsubstantiated and the Shakers were not known to have visited Tecumseh and Tenskwatawa until sent to them almost a year later, in March 1807, as a deputation to assess the potential danger they posed. What is generally sloughed over is the fact that not only did the brothers not have prior knowledge that Harrison would levy such a challenge, neither could they have known that it would reach them while they were temporarily staying at Buckangehela's Town on the White River and not at their own quarters in Tecumseh's

Town at Greenville where, if Tecumseh did have access to such an almanac, the book would no doubt be. Granted, for whatever reason, Tecumseh may have, prior to this time, memorized when the next solar eclipse was to be, so as to utilize its occurrence in awing the tribes, but this seems to be grasping at straws. Whether or not he possessed such prior almanac knowledge is a matter that cannot be known now—there is as good a case against it as for it—but there is certainly no way he could have learned of the precise time when a large meteor would streak across the heavens and when an earthquake would occur and predict these things, and these are matters we will come to anon.

545. William Wells, in a letter written in June 1807 to William Henry Harrison at Vincennes, stated that no fewer than 1,500 Indians had passed through Ft. Wayne en route from the north to hear the preachings of The Prophet at Greenville.

546. The Potawatomi name of Main Poche has evidently been lost. In various documents of the British and Americans, Main Poche's name has been presented as Main Poc, Man Pock, Main Pock, Mar Pock, Marpoc, Mar Poc, and other variations. However, the greatest accuracy occurs with Main Poche, which is directly of French origin and means "Puckered Hand" or "Withered Hand," referring to the congenitally deformed left hand of Main Poche, which rendered it clubbed, though not wholly useless. Many of his tribesmen revered him because of it, elevating him to shaman, the deformity accepted as a mark of favor placed upon him by the Great Spirit.

547. Harrison, in reference to the *Chesapeake* affair and of British agents agitating among the Indians, stated to the legislature:

> *We are, indeed, from our situation, peculiarly interested in the contest which is likely to ensue; for who does not know that the tomahawk and scalping knife of the savage are always employed as the instruments of British vengeance? At this moment, fellow citizens, as I sincerely believe, their agents are organizing a combination amongst the Indians within our limits, for the purpose of assassination and murder.*

Harrison was not far wrong, albeit a bit premature. The new Canadian governor, James Craig, was reorganizing and strengthening the Indian Department in the west under Sir William Johnson's part-Mohawk grandson, William Claus, to whom he wrote:

> *I shall be very glad to receive some information as to the history of the Prophet, as he is called, and the extent of his influence among the Indians; if this is great and some of our Indian Department can enter into intercourse with him, it might be worthwhile to purchase it though at what might be a high price upon other circumstances.*

Craig had also just secretly reinstated the 70-year-old Matthew Elliott as deputy agent and chief of Indian field operations in the Northwest, since he was the man most apt to get reliable information about the Shawnees, particularly Tecumseh and Tenskwatawa. His instructions to Elliott stated that he was to

> *act as secret emissary to the various chiefs to sound them out in private, impressing upon them with delicacy and caution that England expects their aid in the event of war and being certain to remind them that the Americans are out to steal their lands.*

548. The Shaker delegation was comprised of three men—Ben S. Youngs, David Darrow and Richard McNemar, the latter a well-educated Presbyterian minister who had joined the Shaker Society after prominent leadership in a number of notable revival meetings in Tennessee and Kentucky during 1801 and 1802.

When the Shakers returned to Kirker with their report after an absence of a month, they were all sunshine and roses in their praise for what they had seen and heard. They had not seen much of Tecumseh, but Tenskwatawa had welcomed them and treated them very courteously and had conversed with them at great length through an interpreter about the sins of witchcraft, the beating of wives because they would not have children, stealing, adultery, prostitution, lying, and, most especially, drinking. The Prophet, they said, denounced Indian women marrying whites, advocated the return to use of ancient dress, weapons, cooking, and farming equipment, and stated in the strongest of terms that it was the duty of young Indians to love, honor, cherish, support, and respect the aged and infirm mothers and fathers among their people. Completely swayed by the impassioned comments of Tenskwatawa, the Shaker Committee had concluded its long and detailed report with such comments as:

> On this occasion our feelings were like Jacob's when he cried out "Surely the Lord is in this place, and I knew it not." . . . Although these poor Shawnees have had no particular instruction but what they received from the outpouring of the Spirit, yet in point of real light and understanding, as well as behavior, they shame the Christian world . . ."

At virtually the same time as he received the report from the Shakers, Gov. Kirker received a letter signed by Simon Kenton, James McPherson, James M. Reed and William Ward, which warned of activities occurring at Greenville, where the four whites had visited. They wrote:

> When we arrived there we found . . . that the Shawnee chiefs were all away from that place, mostly gone to Detroit, and that there was a number of Pottawottamies and other foreign Indians at that place . . . seen some parties coming in and some few returning so . . . could not tell what number was there . . . many spoke a language never before heard, nor was there an Ohio Indian at that place who understood them, except by their interpreter who was of the Sauky [Sac] nation. The Pottawottamies said they were of a nation called Wynapaas [Winnebagoes?] and that they had been three months and a half constantly traveling, coming from their homes. They all had rifles and were nearly naked. On parting they all gave us their left hand, resolutely refusing the right. The reason given by the Indians for coming to Greenville, is to listen to the Prophet.

Kirker took no alarm from this message, preferring to believe the "much closer study of the situation" performed by the Shakers.

549. Kekoonshartha (pronounced Ke-coon-SHAR-thuh) was also known by the French translation of his name, Le Maigouis. His village, called L'Arbre Croché, was located near Waugoshance Point, at the northwestern tip of the Lower Peninsula of Michigan. That Trout's evangelizing on behalf of Tenskwatawa was effective became apparent when American traders at Mackinac began complaining that suddenly the Indians were refusing liquor as payment for the furs and hides they were bringing in.

550. There is considerable disparity in the accounts as to the identity of the settler who was killed. His name is variously listed as Myer, Boyer, Myers, Boyers, Bayers, Mier, and Bowyer. The first name is variously given as John, Thomas, and William. The author, in *The Frontiersmen*, used the name Myer, but is now inclined to accept the finding of Lyman Draper, who delved into the matter at considerable length and concluded that the name should accurately be Thomas Bowyer. Also, the death of the settler is variously given in the accounts as June 6, September 3, and September 19. Actually, the nearest the act can be pinpointed is "toward the end of April." The incorrect dates stem from the fact that the first council as the result of this murder was the council held with Chief Stiahta (Roundhead), who appeared in behalf of Tecumseh, on June 6. With the white populace still fearful the Indians agreed, on September 3, to a council of Indians and whites to be held at Springfield on September 19, which was what occurred, this council lasting for three days.

551. Some sources contend that Blue Jacket was a resident at Tecumseh's Village at Greenville, but that is incorrect. Blue Jacket was still principal chief of the Maykujays, still war chief of the tribe and still residing at his own village, Blue Jacket's Town. His overt loyalties remained entirely with the tribe until his death. However, Bil Gilbert in his Tecumseh biography, *God Gave Us This Country* (Atheneum, 1989) is probably closest to the truth when he states, in regard to Blue Jacket after the Greenville Treaty, that:

> Though he did nothing openly that would jeopardize the pension he received from the Americans, he remained in touch with Tekamthi and was, at the very least, covertly in sympathy with the resistance movement which his former protégé organized.

552. Unfortunately, no copy was made of this grand speech given at Chillicothe and not even a worthwhile summation seems to exist; only a few descriptive comments in the broadest general sense. One witness said Tecumseh's speech was, "impassioned . . . rapid and vehement, his manner bold and commanding."

Another was the remark of William Remick, who was present as a boy, along with his father, and who wrote that:

> *His address was on the subject of a contemplated move against them [the whites] by his tribe, which it was his object to disprove, and also to show that he and his tribe entertained the kindest feelings, and proposed a renewal of pledges of good faith, which were accepted. His address was pretty, romantic and elegant, and produced a good effect. Tecumseh was popular, friendly and honest. Everybody respected and believed in him, and he had their good wishes.*

Not *all* the whites were convinced. Simon Kenton was so wholly convinced Tecumseh was a great and implacable enemy of the whites that he said at this time, very seriously, "I propose that we kill Tecumseh. He is getting too much power. If we let him live, he's going to raise the devil all over the Northwest."

Kenton's words went unheeded for the time being.

It was while traveling from Springfield to Chillicothe that Tecumseh specifically pointed out to Duncan McArthur the spot where he was born at the spring close to Old Town, near Xenia.

553. Thomas Worthington was enormously wealthy and closely tied to the political history of the State of Ohio, holding a variety of offices. He had arrived in Chillicothe in 1798 and was appointed major of militia and deputy surveyor-general of the Northwest Territory. He was elected to the first Ohio Constitutional Convention, the first United States senator from Ohio (1803) and was elected the State's fourth governor (1814–1818). His fine mansion, Adena, named (says one source) after the Hebrew word for Paradise, or (says another source) after the prehistoric Indian culture responsible for many intricate mounds in the area, remains a showplace and tourist attraction to this day.

554. These are the hills, especially Mount Logan, that are depicted on the present Great Seal of the State of Ohio, with that original painting from which the Great Seal was adapted having been rendered by an artist seated with his easel on the very grounds of Adena.

555. Thomas Worthington's daughter later remarked that: "We were strictly charged to take no notice of their eccentricities and to manifest no displeasure at any accident."

556. A more complete explanation of the humor and bantering associated with the *unsoma* may be found in Note 50. The author has seen and held this fine presentation tomahawk on several occasions.

557. The Northwest Trail from Greenville followed approximately the route of the present Ohio State Route 571 to the Indiana State Line at Union City and then Indiana State Route 28, encountering the Mississinewa River at the site of the present village of Deerfield in northcentral Randolph Co., Ind.

558. A mild controversy exists among historians as to who was actually in charge in regard to the two Shawnee brothers, some in all seriousness pointing to Tenskwatawa as the leader, largely because of his greater visibility and renown as The Prophet, and because Tecumseh more or less kept out of the limelight. The dispute is silly, since there can be no question that Tecumseh was absolutely in charge in all matters and relegated to Tenskwatawa what he wished him to do. This fact becomes most visible at the time of the move from Greenville to the Tippecanoe. Were Tenskwatawa in command, or even cocommand, he would, by right, tradition, and protocol, have traveled in front alongside Tecumseh and the group the elder brother led; he was, in fact, placed in the very subservient, almost demeaning, position of leading the contingent of women, children, elderly, and baggage. That alone resolves the dispute, which should never have been raised initially, as to where command lay.

559. This village is referred to by a variety of names, including Tippecanoe, The Tippecanoe Village, Prophetstown, The Prophet's Town, Tecumseh's Village, and Tecumseh's Town. To avoid confusion, the most commonly used name, Tippecanoe, will be used except in those instances of direct quote where it is referred to otherwise. The precise location of the village was initially just over 2.5 miles downstream from the mouth of the Tippecanoe River on the north bank of the Wabash at the point where State Route 225 crosses the Wabash River, 1.5 miles southeast of the present village of Battle Ground, Tippecanoe Co., Ind., and extending for .25 mile upstream toward the mouth of the Tippecanoe. Later, as increasing numbers of Indians assembled here, the village grew so large that it extended up the Wabash for two full miles, all the way to just south of the reservoir formed by the dam on present Harrison Creek and to within .75 mile of the mouth of the Tippecanoe River, and extended from the Wabash River bank away from the river for 500 to 1,000 feet. The cabins of Tecumseh and Tenskwatawa were located atop the benchland 70 feet above the level of the Wabash at almost exactly the place where the small unimproved road called 2R East Road crosses State Route 225.

560. Catahecassa had by this time allowed a Quaker mission under the Reverend William Kirk to be established at Wapakoneta and new American farming techniques to be inaugurated there, including the planting of orchards and the breeding of cattle and hogs. Most of the Indians there were now living in houses rather than wegiwas and had almost wholly adopted white man's clothing. A sawmill had been established and a grist mill was presently being erected. Kirk had recently described the inhabitants as being both "civilized and sober" but neglected to mention that the humor and laughter, the games and dances and competitions that were once the hallmark of Shawnee culture were now almost completely absent. Kirk had also neglected to file reports with officials in Washington who had sanctioned the project and just a month before, in December 1808, the government had terminated his project, leaving the Shawnees without the expert agrarian help and direction upon which they had become very dependent.

561. Harrison was neatly deluded by the message; so much so that he immediately ordered a sizeable supply of food supplies and farming equipment be given by the quartermaster to the delegation to be taken back to Tippecanoe. He also wrote to the secretary of war that he had been successful in causing The Prophet to become "a useful tool" in furthering the government's present Indian policy. Part of the duplicity was carried on by the subchief who was in charge of the delegation who, after delivering the message, told Harrison in a private conference:

> I have now listened to that man upward of three years and have never heard him give any but good advice. He tells us that we must pray to the Great Spirit who made the world and everything in it for our use. He tells us that no man could make the plants, the trees and the animals, but that they must be made by the Great Spirit, to whom we ought to pray and obey in all things. He tells us not to lie, to steal, nor to drink whiskey; not to go to war but to live in peace with all mankind. He tells us also to work and make corn.

One source states that Tecumseh himself visited Harrison at Vincennes in March 1808 for a two-week period, commenting that Harrison "discovered him to be possessed of considerable talents" and that the governor's "astonishment was excited by the address and art with which he managed the Indians" and, finally, that Harrison was "completely deceived by this fellow's profound subtilty [sic] notwithstanding both the special prejudice he had previously formed against him, and the general knowledge he possessed of Indian cunning and duplicity." That report is very much out of place, since the only times Harrison ever saw Tecumseh were at the two councils held at Vincennes, in 1810 and 1811. The account appears to be a mixture of Tenskwatawa's visit in the late summer of 1808 and Harrison's later image of Tecumseh.

562. Kenton at this time, having lost virtually all of his holdings in Kentucky and Illinois, had claimed some several thousands of acres in the area of present New Madrid, Mo., along the Mississippi River to the south of Cape Girardeau. An Ohio land speculator had heard of the Missouri land claims Kenton made and went to see them. Highly impressed with the richness of the land, he offered to buy Kenton's claims for "several thousand dollars in cash and sixteen hundred acres of choice land near the new village of Columbus, Ohio, in Franklin County, very rich" and would take over the payments still due on the New Madrid lands, but Kenton refused to sell.

563. Harrison, immediately after his meetings with Tenskwatawa, wrote to Secretary of War Henry Dearborn and expressed his belief that:

> *The celebrated Shawnese Prophet is rather possessed of considerable talents. . . . I was not able to ascertain whether he is, as I at first supposed, a tool of the British or not. His denial of being under any such influence was strong and apparently candid. . . . He frequently harangued his followers in my presence, and the evils attendant upon war and the use of ardent spirits was his constant theme. . . . Upon the whole, Sir, I am inclined to think that the influence which the Prophet has acquired will prove rather advantageous than otherwise to the United States. . . . At no anterior period have our relations with neighboring tribes been placed on a better footing. . . . Our Indian frontier will be free from those alarms and apprehensions which have had so much effect in retarding its settlement.*

564. Ft. Madison had been established late in 1808 by a detachment of soldiers under Lt. Alpha Kingsley that was sent up the Mississippi from St. Louis. It was erected on the west side of the Mississippi 15 miles upstream from the mouth of the Des Moines River, on the site of the present city of Ft. Madison, Lee Co., Iowa.

565. The new Secretary of War, William Eustis, had recently written to Harrison that there was a growing need for settler expansion and he had ordered the Indiana Territory governor to "take advantage of the most favorable moment for extinguishing the Indian title to lands lying east of the Wabash." Harrison had immediately arranged for a meeting with chiefs to be held at Greenville and, in his usual manner of stacking the deck in his own favor at such land-purchase councils, the only chiefs invited to attend this meeting were those presently beholden to the United States due to subsidies and annuities.

566. Though the preliminary treaty for this land, enacted at Greenville, involved chiefs of little significance, the final treaty concluded at Ft. Wayne on September 30, 1809, was also signed by more important chiefs whom Harrison bribed with lavish gifts to support the sale; among these latter chiefs were Anderson of the Delawares and Five Medals and Wapamanqua of the Potawatomies, along with the old and venerable Michikiniqua, who, some reports contend was very ill at this time, mentally as well as physically. A total of 1,396 Indians had been assembled at Ft. Wayne for the final negotiations, including 660 Potawatomies, 353 Miamis, 374 Delawares, and 8 Shawnees.

567. Even while Tenskwatawa was still at Vincennes, Harrison wrote to the Secretary of War about him, saying:

> *I must confess that my suspicions of his guilt have been rather strengthened than diminished at every interview I have had with him since his arrival. He acknowledges that he received an invitation to war against us from the British, last fall, and that he was apprised of the intention of the Sacs and Foxes, &c., early in the spring, and was warmly solicited to join their league. But he could give no satisfactory explanation of his neglecting to communicate to me circumstances so extremely interesting to us and towards which I had a few months before directed his attention, and received a solemn assurance of his cheerful compliance with the injunctions I had impressed upon him. The result of all my inquiries on the subject is that the late combination was produced by British intrigue and influence, premature and ill-judged. . . . The warlike and well-armed tribes of the Potawatomies, Ottawas, Chippewas, Delawares, and Miamis, I believe, neither had nor would have joined in the combination; and although the Kickapoos . . . are much under the influence of The Prophet, I am persuaded that they were never made acquainted with his intentions, if they were really hostile toward the United States.*

568. This is a liberal interpretation of the symbolism of the sacred slab, based upon the preachments of Tenskwatawa, the grand plan of Tecumseh and other events which subsequently transpired. Whether this interpretation is entirely accurate is subject to debate. One of these slabs is still known to exist and is presently part of the Milford G. Chandler loan collection in the Museum of Anthropology, Univ. of Mich. at Ann Arbor.

569. A great deal of controversy exists as to whether Tecumseh actually so accurately predicted the greatest earthquake ever recorded on the North American continent. Since earthquakes are not precisely predictable, even with the most sophisticated of modern technology, most historians tend to discount the alleged Tecumseh prediction entirely and contend that it is part of the mythology that has evolved over the years in regard to Tecumseh, or else they merely slide over the matter with bare mention, or else do not address the issue at all. Nevertheless, the facts that exist and considerably intertwine in this respect really do require that a closer look be given to the matter in as unbiased a manner as possible. It is known that Tecumseh first announced his grand plan at the beginning of 1801 and that at that time, while he was not, so far as the written record goes, specific about what his great sign would be, it is well established that he did say it would be a sign given to all of the tribes simultaneously. When he began visiting the various tribes that same year of 1801, and continued to do so through the end of 1811, he told each group he addressed of his plan for the great amalgamation of the tribes, and that all of these tribes would, at a prescribed time, be given a very specific sign by which they would know that the time had come for them all to converge and array themselves for a great confrontation with the whites. No record or account has ever turned up in regard to these early talks that specifically mentions either the great meteor or the subsequent earthquake. Yet it seems inconceivable that he could have fired these disparate tribes with the determination to cast aside their intertribal animosities as well as their own tribal identities and join him in such an amalgamation without giving them some sort of explanation as to *when* the great sign he spoke of would come and *what* that sign would be, especially when he kept saying that it was something that would be recognized immediately by all tribes simultaneously when it came. It also stands to reason he would have had to tell them *where* to converge. Nevertheless, there is no clear record or account that during these earlier years of organizing his amalgamation of tribes that he did, in fact, predict an earthquake, or when it would occur, or to what rendezvous point the Indians were to converge. When, in 1810, he had the sacred slabs carved and distributed, they pointed rather more directly to the specifics of his earthquake prediction, yet again there is no written account at this time that indisputably records such an earthquake prediction, although the time frame for its occurrence, to the very day, had now been laid out, through the sacred slabs and red sticks. One might argue that such a written account occurs in the very symbols of the slabs, yet that is tricky ground, since the literal translation of the symbolic message of the slabs was not made until well after the occurrence of the earthquake. The same argument can be used in respect to the great meteor that occurred precisely thirty days before the earthquake. The first actual *written* accounts of Tecumseh predicting an earthquake did not come *prior* to the earthquake, but afterwards by a few months, these accounts based on interviews of Indians and traders who were in attendance when Tecumseh made the alleged predictions. After leaving his council with William Henry Harrison at Vincennes at the end of July 1811, Tecumseh immediately went to the Southern tribes where, on a number of occasions during his visits with the various chiefs and warriors, it is finally stated that he told them clearly when he returned to the north he would stamp his foot and cause the earth to shake so terribly that water jugs would break, buildings and trees would fall, people and animals would be knocked down, rivers would run backwards, lakes would be swallowed up and others would appear where none had been known before. All this is very explicit, but nonetheless written *after* the earthquake had occurred, which makes it suspect, since this is the usual technique of mythology in attributing prior knowledge of a known fact. Still, to be fair, one must take into consideration that a good many people, Indians and whites alike, have all stated that they were on hand among the Southern tribes when Tecumseh made such predictions at different places and at different times; witnesses using virtually the same phraseology in their quoting of him, yet these witnesses largely unknown to one another, which seems a most improbable set of coincidences to account for unless Tecumseh had actually used the words ascribed to him. Tecumseh's father, Pucksinwah, was recorded as being able to predict future events, including his own death, with great accuracy. Such was the case, as well, with Tecumseh's elder brother, Chiksika. Tenskwatawa's rise to become the Shawnee Prophet and his continuance in that station were founded almost entirely upon accurate predictions which Tecumseh gave him to relay to the people. The weight of known evidence—the gathering together of the tribes, the promises of signs, the sacred slabs and the red sticks, the post-earthquake testimony of so many people in so startlingly similar a manner of his pre-earthquake predictions, the fact that Tecumseh was at the epicenter of the earthquake when it occurred, and Tecumseh's ultimate well-witnessed prediction of his own death—all these things, when combined, seem to indicate that Tecumseh did indeed have a certain prophetic ability and that he very likely did predict the gigantic earthquake that struck in an area where no other earthquake had ever been recorded prior to this time.

570. The Sacs and Foxes arrived at Amherstburg in mid-June and were extremely well treated and supplied from the British stores at Ft. Malden with more arms and ammunition than they had anticipated receiving and they returned home prepared to protect British interests at Prairie du Chien and elsewhere in their territory if such should be threatened.

571. Leatherlips's Village was located on the west bank of the Scioto River two miles south of the present Franklin County city of Dublin at approximately the location where present Dublin Road and Hayden Run Road intersect. Franklinton later became the eventual permanent capital of Ohio, Columbus.

572. Very little has been recorded in respect to the death of Blue Jacket, who was 55 years old at this time, although it is reported that the death was as the result of a fever and it is generally believed the causative agent was cholera. Various dates are given for his death, ranging from 1810 to 1824, although Thwaites and Kellogg in *The Revolution on the Upper Ohio* (Madison, 1904), and Lyman Draper in *Simon Kenton Papers* (DD-BB-4: 60) concur on the 1810 date. Since nothing further was ever recorded of Blue Jacket's activities after this date, the 1810 date is believed to be accurate.

573. Michael Brouillette, one of William Henry Harrison's most dependable and well-paid spies (earning the unusually high salary of $12 per month), had been outfitted and disguised as a trader by Harrison and sent about June 1 to Tippecanoe to spy on Tecumseh and Tenskwatawa.

574. Very little is known about Gimewane (pronounced, using a hard G, Gee-mee-WAH-nee), meaning Rain. She was sometimes referred to by others as The Queen, which is believed to have been a disparaging sobriquet. Stephen Ruddell described her as being "a low, heavy set, sour old squaw . . . with very little influence over The Prophet or anyone else."

575. In considering Barron's description of what had happened to him on his arrival at Tippecanoe and the intercession of Tecumseh on his behalf following The Prophet's threatening remark, Harrison correctly concluded that Tecumseh was the true power figure there or, as he put it, "the really efficient man—the Moses of the family . . ." as well as being a reasonable man who might carry on business in the manner of civilized men. However, as soon as Barron reported to Harrison that in coming to council at Vincennes, Tecumseh meant to bring some thirty of his principal men and about a hundred of his young warriors, Harrison sent another express to Tecumseh requesting earnestly that Tecumseh should come attended by only "a few of your young men."

576. The mansion and estate of William Henry Harrison, called Grouseland, was located in the center of the present city of Vincennes, Ind., just north of the old U & M Railroad near the bridge. The main house, a brick structure with mansard roof and four chimneys projecting nine feet above roof level, was comprised of 13 rooms well appointed with the very best of furnishings and accoutrements, from finely made overstuffed sofas and chairs to huge mirrors and chandeliers and the very finest imported rugs over burnished hardwood floors. A great curving staircase in the entry parlor swept graciously to the second floor, its balustrade and bannister uprights hand-carved and exquisite. There were similarly carved mantels and door frames. A beautiful hand-polished mahogany piano was in the drawing room and there was an abundance of items of silver and brass. The place was kept in splendid condition by a large staff of uniformed slaves, both men and women. Adjacent to the house was a large roofed portico for councils and on the grounds another large open-air council area had been laid out amid the well-landscaped gardens, with here and there extensive arbors that provided cooling shade beneath the intertwined grapevines that covered them. The name Grouseland had been used because of the many ruffed grouse that inhabited the woodlands surrounding the estate.

577. Captain George Rogers Clark Floyd, commanding officer of Ft. Knox, located on the river three miles above Grouseland, wrote on August 14, 1810, to his lady in Louisville, the following:

Nothing new has transpired since my last letter to you except that the Shawanoe Indians have come; they passed this garrison, which is three miles above Vincennes, on Sunday last in canoes, about eighty in number, all painted in the most terrific manner; they were stopped at the garrison by me, for a short time; I examined their canoes and found them well prepared for war in case of an attack. They were headed by the brother of The Prophet, who is perhaps one of the finest looking men I ever saw—about six feet high, straight, with large fine features and altogether a daring bold-looking fellow. The governor's council with them will commence tomorrow morning. He has directed me to attend. . . .

578. It was during this movement of the council site, when there was a lot of intermingling of the people in attendance, that Tecumseh was engaged in conversation by one of the civilian dignitaries in attendance, who asked him who his parents were. Tecumseh spoke of his father, Pucksinwah, to some extent and then told the gentleman that "My mother, Methotasa, was a Cherokee who was taken prisoner in a war between the Cherokees and the Shawnees and adopted into the Peckuwe sept of the Shawnees by a warrior named Oshashqua."

579. In his subsequent report to the War Department, Harrison stated that in Tecumseh's speech:

Every instance of injustice and injury which have been committed by our citizens upon the Indians from the commencement of the revolutionary war (There are unfortunately too many of them) was brought forward and exaggerated. . . .

580. At this point in his speech, Tecumseh said what has been recorded as ". . . It was me . . ." It is very difficult to say exactly what Tecumseh meant by that brief sentence. Possibly he was thinking of something else entirely. Possibly, too, the interpretation of his speech at this point was faulty. More likely, the subsequent transcription was either in error or inadvertently omitted something that gave this sentence significance. The author tends to believe the sentence should have read "It was ours," which was interpreted as "It was mine" and subsequently transcribed as "It was me."

581. The meaning of this comment was that they would accept gunpowder for purposes of hunting their game, but not the tomahawk for purposes of war against the Americans.

582. Cebebaqua is pronounced See-bee-BAH-kwa.

583. Makataimeshekiakiak (pronounced Mack-uh-TY-mee-shee-KEE-uh-kee-yak) and the uprising he led, called the Black Hawk War, is the subject of the author's *The Winning of America* series volume entitled *Twilight of Empire* (Little, Brown, 1988; Bantam, 1989).

584. A Detroit newspaper reported at this time:

It is noticed with concern in the Detroit area that more and more Indians from the Northwest Territory are coming to the British post at Malden (opposite Gibraltar) to be provided with arms, ammunition and supplies. Now the rumors that have been floating about since 1805 that Tecumseh is forming a great coalition of tribes to oppose the Americans take greater significance and fears [have] grown intense, especially in view of the critically deteriorating relations between the United States and the British.

Lewis Cass, who subsequently became governor of Michigan Territory, U.S. secretary of war and a presidential candidate, observed, after hearing Tecumseh speak:

It was the utterance of a great mind, roused by the strongest motives of which human nature is susceptible, and developing a power and labour of reason which commanded the admiration of the civilized as justly as the confidence and pride of the savage.

585. Harrison, despite his promises to the Indians that the Ft. Wayne Treaty was the last cession of land the United States would seek, realized that statehood was coming for Indiana eventually, which he would welcome because, as he had confided to President James Madison, "I am heartily tired of living in a territory. . . ." To this end he had asked the President for authority to secure more land to Indiana Territory before it was too late. Madison had agreed and it was then that Harrison summoned Main Poche to Vincennes.

586. Peesotum (pronounced Pee-SO-tum), meaning Big Fighter, had previously been named Quaquanese (pronounced Kwa-kwa-NEE-see), meaning Little Flying Creature, which was generally translated as Grasshopper. He is believed to have been a member of Topenebe's band on the St. Joseph River.

587. One account, unacceptable because of numerous inconsistencies and improbabilities, states that Joseph Barron accompanied Wilson on this visit to Tippecanoe.

588. The Long Knife Fire meant Virginia.

589. As soon as Capt. Wilson delivered Tecumseh's response to Gov. Harrison and gave him a concise verbal report of his mission, including the good treatment he had received, as well as a summation of what they had discussed, Harrison congratulated him on a good job well done, dismissed him and immediately penned a letter to Secretary of War Eustis in which, regarding Tecumseh, he wrote, in part:

> *Upon being told that I would not suffer him to come with so large a force, he promised to bring with him a few men only. I shall not, however, depend upon this promise, but shall have the river watched by a party of scouts after the descent of the chief, lest he should be followed by his warriors. I do not think this will be the case. The detection of the hostile designs of an Indian is generally, for that time, to defeat them. The hopes of an expedition, conducted through many hundred miles of toil and difficulty, are abandoned frequently upon the slightest suspicion; their painful steps retraced, and a more favorable moment expected. With them, the surprise of an enemy bestows more éclat upon a warrior than the most brilliant success obtained by other means. Tecumseh has taken for his model the celebrated Pontiac, and I am persuaded he will bear a favorable comparison in every respect to that far-famed warrior . . .*

590. In addition to having been reinforced by Col. Boyd's Fourth Regiment of 800 regulars from Pittsburgh, he had also been strengthened by the arrival of 65 seasoned Indian fighters, all mounted and well armed, from Kentucky.

591. Seekaboo is said in some accounts to have been proficient in the Southern tribal dialects because he was a halfbreed Creek-English who had been captured by the Shawnees and adopted into the tribe and had been living with them for over 20 years. One account states that among the select party of mounted Indians who accompanied Tecumseh to the Vincennes council and then to the Southern tribes was Alexander Elliott, the eldest son of Matthew Elliott, believed to be the son of the elder Elliott's Shawnee wife. It would not be altogether far-fetched to consider this as true, except for the fact that only one account makes mention of it at all and then only briefly; yet young Elliott had some degree of prominence and it seems unlikely that if he were along, other accounts would not have commented on it. For this reason, and unless future documentary evidence might come to light to substantiate it, the author discounts the report.

592. There is an account of an incident occurring at this time that, while apocryphal, has been so often repeated that it needs to be mentioned here and put to rest as being fictitious. It appears to stem from an interview Dr. Lyman Draper held in Detroit in August 1863 with Sauganash—Billy Caldwell—at which Dr. Draper quoted Sauganash as saying:

> *General Harrison asked Tecumseh what was the cause of his and the Indians' grief. Tecumseh said he could not write a word, but he could answer the question without the utterance of a word even. Harrison said he would like to know about it. Tecumseh then pointed Harrison to a seat beside him on a bench—giving Harrison the larger part of the seat—then he hitched upon Harrison till he got his hip fairly upon the general's, who moved away a little—and Tecumseh so repeated the process till Harrison exclaimed, "See, Tecumseh, you are crowding me off!" "Ah," said Tecumseh, "that exactly explains our grief—you whites are crowding us Indians a little by little, and we don't know where we shall in the end be crowded to."*

593. Tecumseh had made a serious tactical error in informing Harrison that he was leaving at once to see the Southern tribes and draw them into his amalgamation. In this utterance, Harrison found the key to breaking up the Indian union, causing great division among the tribes and, as a result, diminishing Tecumseh's influence and power. Immediately following the council's adjournment, Harrison wrote to Secretary of War William Eustis and stated his conviction that Tecumseh and Tenskwatawa were strong in their determinations against the Americans. From the very first the policy of the United States had been to keep the Indians divided and in this way, by dealing with individual chiefs or small groups, gradually whittle away the Indian land into American possession. Harrison accurately considered that, in Tecumseh's forming such a wide-scale pact between all the tribes, that:

A step of this sort would be of infinite prejudice to the United States. . . . It would shut the door against further extinguishment of Indian title upon the valuable tract of country south of the Wabash. . . . The establishment of tranquility between the neighboring tribes will always be a sure indication of war against us. . . .

He then discussed the trip Tecumseh was embarking upon to the Southern tribes, saying that Tecumseh had: "labored hard to convince me that he had no other intention by this journey than to prevail on all the Tribes to unite in bonds of peace." He said that Tecumseh had tried to make him think he would not return to Tippecanoe until next spring, but his spies had reported that all the signs were that something was to occur late in the fall, which meant that government action of some kind prior to that time was imperative. Tecumseh, he said, had sent the majority of his people back up the Wabash to Tippecanoe, but had himself, with a select group of horsemen, gone down the Wabash for that visit to the South, which, Harrison stressed,

. . . affords a most favorable opportunity for breaking up his Confederacy . . . He is now upon the last round to put a finishing stroke to his work. I hope, however, before his return, that that part of the fabrick which he considered complete will be demolished and even its foundation rooted up . . .

Harrison, strongly emphasizing the need for a very telling preemptive strike, asked permission to march against the Tippecanoe village, where Tenskwatawa was in charge and who, without the sagacity and influence of Tecumseh behind him, could be handily defeated and the Indians dispersed. In his reply, Secretary of War Eustis relayed the President's concern about the outbreak of a general Indian war, saying:

I have been particularly instructed by the President to communicate to your excellency his earnest desire that peace may, if possible, be preserved among the Indians, and that to this end every proper measure be adopted. But this is not intended . . . that the banditti under the Prophet should not be attacked and vanquished, provided such a measure should be rendered absolutely necessary.

It was precisely the sort of waiver Harrison had hoped for. He was convinced that something would occur, instigated by Tenskwatawa, that would justify his marching toward Tippecanoe and that, if he did so, Tenskwatawa would foolishly attack him and give Harrison that opportunity, as he stated it, to retaliate and render the Indian amalgamation "demolished and even its foundation rooted up. . . ."

594. The crossing was made in northwestern Alabama close to the present city of Florence, Colbert Co. George Colbert was the son of an English trader, also named George Colbert, and a Chickasaw woman whose identity remains unclear.

595. Red Pepper's Town was located on the north bank of the Oktibbeha (present Tibbee) River some 3 miles southwest of the present town of West Point, Clay Co., Miss.

596. Mashulatubbe's Village was located along the Noxubee River directly west of the present town of Brooksville and 8 miles upstream from present Macon, Noxubee Co., Miss.

597. There are numerous accounts that provide, from memory of participants, bits and snatches of the many speeches Tecumseh delivered to the Southern tribes. In large measure, these appear to have been basically identical, though skillfully tailored from speech to speech to meet the conditions and audience. The quotations of Tecumseh's remarks in these pages depicting his visit to the Southern tribes is a compilation of the recording of the salient points Tecumseh made in his speeches, but there are no known actual transcriptions of entire speeches as they were delivered.

The elemental similarity of the many accounts, however, lends considerable authenticity to what was uttered and these bits and pieces have been placed together, as much as possible, in the order in which Tecumseh delivered them, both in place and in content.

598. Whether or not Tecumseh meant this as a prediction is not known, but it was certainly prophetic, since the Choctaws were subsequently pushed off their lands in Alabama and Mississippi and required to relocate in Oklahoma.

599. Pushmataha is pronounced POOSH-muh-TAH-ha.

600. Tecumseh is known to have made seven major speeches while he was among the Choctaws and these were known to be in Mashulatubbe's Town, Yazoo Town, Mokalusha, Chishahoma, Cusha, Yahnubbee, and Chunky. Mokalusha was located on the Nanawaya River close to the present Choctaw Indian Reservation on that stream a few miles northeast of the present city of Philadelphia in Neshoba Co., Miss. Chunky, sometimes called Chunky's Town, was located on the west side of the Okahatta (present Chunky) River three miles northeast of the present town of Hickory and four miles upstream from the present town of Chunky in Newton Co., Miss.

601. Chief Stonahajo, also known as Stonie-hadjo, subsequently berated the Choctaws bitterly for not killing Tecumseh when he was in their country.

602. Among the Creek Indians present at Little Prince's Town when Tecumseh spoke there was a chief named Hopoithyarhohar, who was among the faction that opposed Tecumseh. Hopoith-yarhohar reported to G. W. Stedham, who wrote the information to Dr. Lyman Draper on Nov. 30, 1881, that the following was the speech (or part thereof) that Tecumseh made at that time:

> *My Grand Children. You have always been very stubborn children. Your ears were filled with trash, so that you could not hear and I desire you to listen attentively to what I have to say to you. I am now about ready to take up arms against the United States and when I strike them a blow, you will know it, as I will shake the whole earth. The ground will give way from under the white man's feet, and he will mire down. I will be on firm ground and I will kill them with my war club. My enemy may include you as an enemy and strike you a blow. If he should, remain quiet; and should he so far as to cut off your fingers that grip the gun, do not resist, as I will do the work myself. I am determined to exterminate them from the face of the continent.*

Note, again, the predictive reference to the earthquake. Hopoithyarhohar stated that Tecumseh gave them red sticks, which were the countdown to the war and which, among the Indians in the South therefore became known as the Red Stick War. These red sticks were called *Tugekahga Gunstah* by the Cherokees, who refused to accept them. During the War of 1812, when it broke out, Hopoithyarhohar acted as an express rider for the U.S. Army and he was also one of the Creek faction who remained loyal to the United States during the Civil War.

603. Tuckabatchee, principal village of the Tuckabatchee clan of the Muscogee Creeks, was located close to the present Fort Toulouse State Monument in present Elmore Co., Ala., where the Coosa and Tallapoosa rivers converge to form the Alabama. Tecumseh, just before or after this visit to Tuckabatchee, also spoke at the villages of Cusseta, Coweta, and Arpehkus.

604. George Washington Campbell wrote to H. S. Halbert who relayed the information to Dr. Lyman Draper (see DD-YY-10: 69, 69¹):

> *The speech of Tecumseh as he spoke it to the Creeks or Muscogees was very powerful, and the points were the very same to the Choctaws, Cherokees, Seminoles. It was told to me by Boles, the chief of a squad of Cherokees who split off from the Cherokees and finally settled in Eastern Texas, where Cherokee County is now. Stonahajo told of the speech to the Cherokees and the points were the same. Here is his speech to the Muscogees:*
>
> *"In defiance of the pale faced warriors of Ohio and Kentucky, we have traveled through these settlements, once our beloved hunting ground; no war whoop was heard, but there is blood on our knives. The pale faces felt the blow but knew not when it came. Accursed be the race that has seized on our country and made women of our warriors. Our fathers from their graves reproach us as slaves and cowards. I hear them now in the wailing winds. The Muscogees were once a mighty people. The Georgians tremble at their war hoop; and the maidens of my tribe on the*

distant Lakes sang the praises of your warriors and sighed for their embraces. Now your very blood is white, your tomahawks have no edge, your bows and arrows were buried with your fathers. Oh, Muscogee brothers, brush from your eyes the sleep of slavery. Once more strike for vengeance—once more for your country. The spirits of the mighty dead complain; their tears drop from their weeping skies. Let the white race perish! They seize your land, they corrupt your women, they trample on the grave of your dead. Back whence they came, on a trail of blood, they must be driven. Back! Back! Aye, into the great waters whose accursed waves brought them to our shores. Burn their houses! Destroy their stock! Slay their wives and children! The red man owns the country and the pale face must never enjoy it. War NOW! War FOREVER! War upon the living! War upon the dead! Dig their bones from the grave! Our country must give no rest to a white man's bones. This is the will of the Great Spirit, revealed to my brother, his familiar, the Prophet of the Lakes. The Great Spirit sends me to you. All the tribes of the North are dancing the War Dance. Two mighty warriors across the Great Waters will send us guns, powder and lead. Tecumseh will soon return to his country. My prophets shall tarry with you. They will stand between you and the bullets of your enemies. When the white men approach you, the yawning Earth shall swallow them up. Soon shall you see my arm of fire streaked across the sky. I will stamp my foot and the very Earth shall shake."

—*George Washington Campbell*

It is interesting to note that the speech alludes to some whites being killed by surprise by Tecumseh's party as it moved southward across Kentucky; also that predictive reference is made both to the meteor and the earthquake, neither of which occurred until after Tecumseh had left the South.

605. The crossing was made at about the place where the present Interstate 55 crosses the Mississippi with the limits of the present city of Memphis, Shelby Co., Tenn.

606. Tanwakanwakaghe was located at the mouth of the Grand River where it empties into the Osage River, about at the site of the present Benton County seat of Warsaw, Mo.

607. The theft of the settlers' horses had played directly into Harrison's plans, who had been watching and waiting for the justification he required to move his army in the direction of Tippecanoe. The horse theft alone could not, however, justify in the eyes of the secretary of war and president his actually attacking the Indians. There was nothing, however, prohibiting a show of strength and he hoped, by doing so, to egg Tenskwatawa into attacking him—something he knew Tecumseh, were he on hand, would never do.

608. Ft. Harrison was erected in October (completed October 28, 1811) on the east bank of the Wabash two miles from present downtown Terre Haute, Vigo Co., Ind. Three days later, at the mouth of the Vermilion, Harrison's force built a small advanced stockade called Ft. Boyd for supplies storage.

609. Harrison estimated the opposing Indian force as being 900 to 1,000 warriors. The British, in their reports, said the Indian force was from 250 to 300 warriors. Tecumseh himself later remarked that 350 warriors fought at the Battle of Tippecanoe.

610. The high rock Tenskwatawa described, where he subsequently took his post during the battle, is the present landmark known as Prophet Rock, on the west side of Northeast Road, three-quarters of a mile southwest of the present town of Battle Ground, Tippecanoe Co., Ind.

611. This campsite was located on the edge of present Burnett Creek at the southwestern edge of the present town of Battle Ground. At this point, even though the men had been given orders to sleep on their arms, many of the soldiers were disgruntled over the possibility that they might be cheated out of a battle with the Indians.

612. Accounts vary widely on the numbers of dead and injured. The figures given here represent the most accepted numbers. Gen. Lewis Cass later said that only one Shawnee Indian was killed and three others wounded and that the majority of the Indian casualties were among the Potawatomies, Kickapoos, and Winnebagoes. The British claimed only 25 Indians were killed, of which one was a Shawnee. One highly exaggerated source even claimed that there was great Indian loss, with 60 Winnebagoes among the slain.

613. Though Harrison's loss in killed and injured were by far the greater, he claimed, on the basis of holding the ground after the battle and burning Tippecanoe, that the battle was a victory for his force. It was a tragedy for the Indians, but cannot really be considered the defeat for them that Harrison claimed. The victory for Harrison lay in the destruction of Tenskwatawa's power and the loss, to a certain extent, of Tecumseh's prestige among the tribes. After Harrison's departure, many of the American dead were disinterred by the Indians and scalped, then left exposed to the elements. Their bones lay on the ground there until about 1830 when a company of young men under Capt. Huntington of Terre Haute went to the scene, gathered up the bones and reburied them in a common grave.

614. Tecumseh did indeed leave Tecumapese at the Apple Creek Village, but he was hardly out of sight before she slipped away and returned to Francis Maisonville and soon afterwards married him. A number of reports say they had six children together but the author discounts this as being entirely implausible, since at this time Tecumapese was 53 years old.

615. All of the extensive land claims of Simon Kenton in the New Madrid area disappeared in this earthquake.

616. The lake formed by this caving in of the land was the body of water presently known as Reelfoot Lake.

617. According to the National Earthquake Information Center, Denver, Colorado, with whom the author conferred on March 5, 1990, this great earthquake, now known as the New Madrid Earthquake, occurred at 12:15 A.M. local time (0815 UTC) and measured 8.0 on the Richter scale. (The most powerful earthquake ever recorded anywhere was that which struck Japan on March 2, 1933, and registered 8.9 on the Richter scale.) The New Madrid Earthquake at this time had immediate aftershocks that lasted for two days. These were followed by three more earthquakes in the same New Madrid area; the first on the succeeding January 23, another on January 27, and a final tremendous shock, said to have caused as much damage as the other three combined, on February 13 and lasting, at intervals, for an hour.

618. An extract of a letter from Chicago appeared in the *Louisiana Gazette* of St. Louis (later renamed the *Missouri Gazette*) on March 21, 1812, as follows:

> *The Potawatomies are all for war and are forming plans to sack this garrison [Ft. Dearborn] and the Winnebagoes are assembled at Millewakee, 90 miles northwest from this place, to the amount of 500, and breathe nothing but war and revenge. From every village nothing is heard but the song of war and it is expected to commence as soon as a few chiefs return who went to Vincennes to feel the pulse of Governor Harrison . . .*

Just over a fortnight later, a party of 11 roving Winnebagoes hit a farm just outside Chicago, killed two men and took a third into captivity, throwing the entire settlement into a panic.

619. An intriguing little snatch of information concerning this visit of Tecumseh to Amherstburg, for which there are apparently no further details, states in its entirety: "Tecumseh, before several persons, openly and keenly reproved an European of the Indian Department, for ill usage of his wife."

620. So virulent had grown the hatred of Catahecassa for Tecumseh that the Shawnee principal chief at this time went to see the Shawnee agent at Ft. Wayne, John Johnston, and stated that the Shawnees as a tribe were so opposed to Tecumseh and his troublemakers and so willing to demonstrate their friendship to the United States that if Johnston sanctioned it, they would send out a party of their best men to assassinate both Tecumseh and Tenskwatawa. Johnston put off giving them an answer until he spoke with his superiors and then wrote to the secretary of war saying, "I have been much embarrassed to know what to say to them on this head. I have however on reflection deferred the matter until Governor Harrison could be consulted."

The offer by Catahecassa was subsequently declined.

621. Though Hull had initially been ordered to raise twelve hundred men, so many volunteers flocked in that by the time he left Urbana his whole force consisted of 400 regulars taken from U.S. forts along the Ohio and 1,800 volunteer militia from Ohio, Kentucky and Michigan.

622. This fording place was at the point where present U.S. 68 crosses the river on the southern edge of the present town of West Liberty, Logan Co., Ohio.

623. This fort was built three miles southwest of present downtown Kenton, Hardin Co., O.

624. Peter Vassar, found guilty of drunkenness and dereliction of duty, suffered the sentence of having both ears chopped off short and the letter *M* branded on each cheek, signifying miscreant.

625. It is not known why Tecumseh had this long conference with Stickney at Ft. Wayne, but the assumption is that, having been secretly summoned by Matthew Elliott, he wished to leave the strong impression that his motives were pacific, so that Tippecanoe—where he had left Tenskwatawa and some 90 warriors, mainly Winnebagoes and Kickapoos, to protect the women and children—would not be attacked in his absence. While Tecumseh admitted to Stickney that he planned to visit the British, his principal reason for going to that area was to confer with the tribes near Detroit to help promote a lasting peace among the western tribes. Stickney reported to his superiors that he had considered detaining Tecumseh but, in view of the force the Shawnee had with him, had ultimately decided such a move would not be terribly prudent. Tecumseh had arrived in Ft. Wayne on June 17 and left there on June 21.

626. This council was held about two miles up the Wabash from the site of present Peru, Miami Co., Ind.

627. Isador Chaine (sometimes spelled Chene), who long ago had led the incursion against Boonesboro, was a double agent employed by Matthew Elliott and had come under the guise of antagonism toward Tecumseh, allegedly on behalf of the Michigan tribes that wished to remain neutral.

628. This bridge was built one-half mile up the Huron River from its mouth at the head of Lake Erie in Monroe Co., Mich., and seven miles below the present town of Flat Rock.

629. Brownstown is the site of the present city of Wyandotte and Maguaga is the site of the present town of Ecorse, both in Wayne Co., Mich.

630. Sandwich is the site of present Windsor, Ontario, Canada.

631. Hog Island was so named because of a large pig farm that had been established there many years before. The present name of the island is Belle Isle.

632. A more detailed account of the taking by the British of Ft. Mackinac may be found in the author's *The Frontiersmen*.

633. Some sources contend that McArthur had only 120 men on this movement.

634. By this time the American prisoners, taken aboard the *Cuyahoga* and kept under guard at Ft. Malden, who had been expecting rescue by Hull every day for nearly a month, now had just about given up hope. Quartermaster General William Beall, who had been writing letters of growing concern, wondering where Hull was and why he did not attack when he could do so very easily and with hardly any real risk, had plunged to the depths of despair by this time as he wrote:

> The British officers and soldiers begin to laugh at Hull. . . . He is now the object of their jest and ridicule instead of being, as he was formerly, their terror and greatest fear. . . . I can scarcely think that Gen. H. will be defeated, but appearances justify such a belief. I am confident that he will not take Malden, though 300 men could do it. . . . Why does he not, by taking Malden, silence and drive the Indians away who infest the Country and secure a safe Communication with the States, and safety to our Frontiers? Heaven only knows. I for a Harrison . . . !

635. In the subsequent court-martial of Gen. Hull on charges of cowardice and treason, it was charged that Capt. Brown had gone to Ft. Malden under secret orders from Gen. Hull for the purpose of arranging the details of a surrender by Hull of his army to the British. Events which followed Brown's secret meetings with the British tended to support this contention and later comments by Hull himself tended to authenticate the allegation. Hull, however, at the trial, emphatically denied the allegation and the charge was not proved.

636. The militia detachment that saved Denny's force was led by Robert Lucas. Later, because of reports being circulated impugning the honor and reputation of Maj. Denny, Col. McArthur, at Denny's request, ordered a court of inquiry to sit in the matter, with Col. Findley as president of the court and Col. Cass and Maj. Van Horne as the other two members. The court interviewed witnesses and participants and, after weighing the testimony, unanimously acquitted Maj. Denny with honor.

637. This supply train, forwarded by Ohio Gov. Return J. Meigs, was under command of Capt. Henry Brush, a Chillicothe lawyer who, on crossing the Maumee, saw so much Indian sign that he stopped and hastily wrote and dispatched the following letter to Gen. Hull by express rider:

> *Sir:—Your letter of the eleventh instant was received by Governor Meigs at Chillicothe on the 18th, who immediately issued a call for your requisite supplies and volunteers. Ninety-five citizens volunteered, of who I have been given the honor of command. Our brigade is composed of 150 packhorses loaded with flour and other provisions and a drove of beeves numbering about 300 animals, which have given us many problems in the driving. We left Chillicothe on the 20th inst and today we reached and crossed the Maumee Rapids. Due to the large number of Indians hovering about us, reported by my spies, it is considered altogether too dangerous for us to continue much farther toward Detroit without a strong escort being provided by you, since Indians control the road which follows the lake shore and the British control the waters. Our intention, therefore, is to continue only as far as the French town at River Raisin and then remain at that place to await said escort. I am, Sir,*
>
> > *Yr mst obdt yr mst humble svt,*
> > *H. Brush—Capt., commanding*
> > *the Ohio volunteers*

Frenchtown was a long-established French settlement several miles up the River Raisin from its mouth at Lake Erie, on the site of the present city of Monroe, Monroe Co., Mich.

638. The small advance party sent out by Maj. Van Horne was led by militia Captains Robert Lucas, who was in command, and William McCulloch as second officer.

639. Jim Blue Jacket, son of the war chief and a good warrior in his own right, was also frequently called Little Blue Jacket or Blue Jacket's Son. After his death at the Battle of Brownstown, several other warriors, in honor of his bravery and the courageous manner in which he died, assumed his name. Later accounts mentioning Jim Blue Jacket as accompanying Tecumseh on the retreat up the Thames mistakenly assume this to be the son of Blue Jacket, but such is not the case.

640. These three were Capt. McCulloch, his black slave, and a private, the latter two not identified beyond such description. One account states that at the point where the ambush took place, McCulloch had stopped at a small rivulet and while his horse was drinking the firing broke out and that McCulloch alone was struck by 9 bullets.

641. The civilians were from Frenchtown and had stopped to warn the column that there were many Indians near Brownstown and that they believed an ambush was being set up. Maj. Van Horne refused to believe it, especially since Capt. Lucas had already told him that McCulloch and his two men had been hit by only ten or twelve Indians at most.

642. Some accounts say Tecumseh's wound was caused by buckshot from a shotgun, but this seems unlikely; also, a few accounts say this wounding did not occur until the so-called second Battle of Brownstown, which was actually the Battle of Maguaga, but that is not the case.

643. Although almost all accounts tell of this incident of the execution of the young American soldier, none gives any identification of who the man was. Most accounts say he was a private, but two state that he was an officer, which is unlikely since, in such a case, the victim would probably have been more specifically identified.

644. One account states that Tecumseh was at this time reinforced by the arrival of 200 Indians under Stiahta—Roundhead—but this is incorrect, since Stiahta was still lying in ambush with his Indians just north of Frenchtown, awaiting the movement of the Brush supply convoy into the ambush he had set up.

645. Lt. Col. Miller had decided that these three dead at Maguaga and those at Brownstown would be buried by the detachment on its return from River Raisin with the Brush convoy.

646. John Whistler, Jr., survived the wound, though only with difficulty and a long convalescence. Just a little over a year later, in the autumn of 1813, he contracted a disease, probably cholera, and died.

647. Some accounts have contended that 60 Indians were killed, but that is a fabrication. One account claims there were 20 Americans killed and 50 wounded and that the loss to the British and Indians was about the same, but this is incorrect. Another account, closer to the truth, states that for the combined British and Indians, there were 15 killed and 30 wounded.

648. The majority of the American soldiers had discarded their knapsacks at the outbreak of the ambush and were without sufficient food to continue to their objective. Lt. Col. Miller had become sick and Militia Col. Cass also sent a message to Hull asking permission to take command and continue the mission, since the Brush convoy was only 22 miles distant and there would be plenty of food there. Hull, still headquartered at Sandwich, did not even respond to Cass but sent Miller an order to return to Detroit, which Miller did two days later.

649. Simon Girty's son, Thomas, was part of Muir's force. In the midst of the battle he encountered a Canadian officer who was wounded and could not walk and begged young Girty to carry him. They reached Muir's force safely enough, but young Girty suffered heat stroke from his exertion and died (although one account says they came to a puddle of water along the way, from which both Girty and the officer drank freely, but that Girty was immediately taken sick with a fever and died, though the officer did not). Young Girty's body was taken to his father's farm south of Amherstburg and buried there in the orchard.

650. The reaction of Hull's army at the order to retreat to Detroit was one of great dismay and anger among his troops. As Ohio Militia Sgt. James Foster put it in his journal:

> [W]hen, to our astonishment, we were ordered to strike our tents and cross over to Detroit!— To encamp in the rear of the fort, and to give up every pretention of a hostile nature.—Great God! what were our feelings now? A territory which we had invaded without opposition, we quit in disgrace. The laurels we had hoped to reap before the ramparts of Malden, were left ungathered— and we were doomed to bear the agonizing burden of dishonor.

Capt. Robert Lucas, writing to a friend of his in Ohio, was extremely bitter, saying there was never a more patriotic army than the one he was in, nor an army that had it more completely in its power to have accomplished every objective; an army, he added furiously, that had now sunk into disgrace because of the lack of a real general to lead it. He termed Hull imbecilic and treacherous and opposed to his colonels, who were strongly united in their patriotism, and yearned that one of these colonels could take command from Hull and wipe away the foul stain that Hull had brought upon the army.

651. Immediately after their first meeting, Brock wrote about Tecumseh in his official report: "A more sagacious or more gallant Warrior does not, I believe, exist. He has the admiration of everyone who conversed with him."

To his own general staff he described Tecumseh as being "the Wellington of the Indians," which was considerable praise, indeed.

652. It was from this comment by Brock, apparently, that the story sprang that Tecumseh was commissioned a British brigadier general. In point of fact, there is no record that Tecumseh was ever commissioned a brigadier general, honorary or otherwise, though the story persists in most accounts of his life and even in some contemporary documents he is referred to as General Tecumseh. Similar stories exist in regard to both Michikiniqua (Little Turtle) and Blue Jacket receiving commissions from the British as brigadier generals. No documentation exists that any of these three Indians were ever officially appointed to the rank of brigadier general and if there is any grain of truth to the assertions, which is most unlikely, it undoubtedly stems from a verbal honorary award of rank being bestowed.

653. On hand at this meeting was Gen. Brock's aide-de-camp, Capt. John B. Glegg, who later wrote:

> Tecumseh's appearance was very prepossessing; his figure light and finely proportioned; his age I imagined to be about five and thirty; in height, five feet nine or ten inches; his complexion, light copper; countenance oval, with bright hazel eyes, beaming cheerfulness, energy and decision. Three small silver crowns, or coronets, were suspended from the lower cartilage of his aquiline nose; and a large silver medallion of George the Third, which I believe his ancestor had received from Lord Dorchester, when governor-general of Canada, was attached to a mixed coloured wampum string, and hung around his neck. His dress consisted of a plain, neat uniform, tanned deer-skin jacket, with long trousers of the same material, the seams of both being covered with neatly cut fringe; and he had on his feet leather moccasins, much ornamented with work made from the dyed quills of the porcupine.

654. There is very strong reason to believe that shortly after the arrival of Brock, perhaps that first night he was in Amherstburg—August 13—Hull sent a secret messenger to Brock and began working out preliminaries to his ultimate surrender. Maj. Denney, who was left in command at Ft. Gowie in Sandwich when Hull retreated to Detroit, was given instructions to "defend your post to the last extremity," and yet Brock had no sooner begun his movement when Denney was ordered to evacuate. To further substantiate some sort of "deal" having been made between Hull and Brock, there is the matter of Lt. James Dalliba. An artillery officer, Dalliba, immediately upon returning to Detroit, established a very strong American battery consisting of 28 heavy cannon, including the devastating 24-pounders. As soon as Dalliba was able to deduce where the British batteries were being situated across the river from Detroit, he ordered his guns to be brought to bear upon those positions. Having accomplished this he asked Hull for permission to commence firing. Hull's response, recorded by Dalliba, was:

> Mr. Dalliba, I have made an agreement with the enemy that if they will never fire on me I will never fire on them. Those who live in glass houses must take care how they throw stones. The answer to your question, Mr. Dalliba, is no. Permission is denied.

Another version of this comment has the words "will make" substituted for "have made," which makes a considerable difference. The latter clearly indicates that Hull had made arrangements with the British previously, either through Capt. Brown or, more likely, through Capt. Rough. All the evidence, even though circumstantial, indicates that this is precisely what Gen. Hull did. About this time Col. Cass, in collusion with other militia officers, wrote to Ohio Gov. Return J. Meigs, saying:

> From causes not fit to put upon paper, but which I trust I shall one day live to communicate to you, this army has been reduced to a critical and alarming situation. We have wholly left the Canadian shore, and have left the miserable inhabitants, who depended upon our will and our power to protect them, to their fate. Unfortunately, the General and principal officers could not view our situation and our prospects in the same light. That Malden might easily have been reduced, I have no doubt. That the army were in force and spirits enough to have done it, no one doubts. But the precious opportunity has fled, and instead of looking back, we must now look forward.
>
> The letter from the Secretary of War to you, a copy of which I have seen, authorizes you to preserve and keep open the communication from the State of Ohio to Detroit. It is all important it should be kept open. Our very existence depends upon it. Our supplies must come from our State. This country does not furnish them. In the existing state of things, nothing but a large force of two thousand men at least, will effect the object. It is the unanimous wish of the army, that you should accompany them.
>
> Every exertion that can, must be made. If this reaches you safely by Murray, he will tell you more than I can or ought here to insert.

Hardly had Cass finished writing when Quartermaster Gen. James Taylor rushed to the militia officers with unbelievable news: a boat from Detroit, bearing an officer, was heading toward the British under a white flag. Colonels Cass, McArthur and Findley immediately presented themselves to Hull and demanded to know what was going on. Hull pretended incomprehension and said he would check on it, told them to wait, and left the office. In a few moments he returned saying that Capt. Hickman had had a conversation with Capt. Rough on the matter of capitulation. Hickman, he said, did not wish Capt. Rough to consider that he had permission to carry a flag to the enemy, but, Hull added, "evidently Captain Rough probably misunderstood and believed he had such permission. That's all I know, gentlemen." He dismissed them and immediately the militia officers, this time five of them signing (Cass, McArthur, Findley, James Taylor, and Ezekiel Brush), appended a note to the back of the letter previously written, the note saying:

> *Since the other side of this letter was written, new circumstances have arisen. The British force is opposite, and our situation has nearly reached its crisis. Believe all the bearer will tell you. Believe it, however it may astonish you, as much as if told you by one of us. Even a —— is talked of by the ——.* [The missing words in this addenda, which were to be filled in verbally to Gov. Meigs by the messenger, were "Capitulation" and "Commanding Officer."] *The bearer will supply the vacancy. On you we depend.*

The message was entrusted to an Ohio soldier named Murray, who was placed under the care and guidance of the trusted Indian messenger they knew as Johnny Logan—Spemica Lawba. Finally, because of this rise in mutinous feelings against him by officers of the militia, it was important for Hull to get the principal leaders of the cabal away until the surrender was a *fait accompli*; he thereupon reversed his earlier decision to send out no more detachments to meet and escort the Brush convoy and now sent his principal opponents, Colonels McArthur and Cass, with a detachment of over 350 men to go by a circuitous route (58 miles as opposed to 30 by direct route) and bring in the convoy. (The direct route from Detroit to Frenchtown—present Monroe—was along the road presently followed by Michigan State Route 56; Hull sent McArthur and Cass on a route that would take them along present Michigan State Route 112 westward to Ypsilanti, U.S. 23 southward to Dundee, and State Route 50 eastward to Monroe.) The journey would keep them away long enough, Hull knew, for him to effect the capitulation in their absence.

655. There is every reason to believe that the mutual bombardment was part of the "show" that Hull insisted upon prior to surrendering, to give the illusion that he was resisting as an able commander should; quite likely part of the "deal" that was arranged by Capt. Rough in his visit to Brock under the white flag.

656. That force, having failed in attempting to find Capt. Brush and his convoy, had been on its return for some time and was at this moment only three miles distant. Sending scouts forward to discover what the situation was, they learned of the inglorious surrender and were themselves forced to capitulate. Their fury and anguish were great and Col. McArthur jerked his sword from its scabbard and broke it in half across his knee, with other officers quickly following his example.

657. The exodus from Ft. Dearborn, apart from the escorting party of Miami Indians, consisted of 68 regular army officers and soldiers, 13 children below teen-age, 11 women, 4 civilian males, 12 members of the Chicago Militia, and one Indian agent, William Wells, on detached duty from Ft. Wayne.

658. A complete minute-by-minute reconstruction of the entire Fort Dearborn Massacre, with full identification and disposition of every known participant, killed or captured, may be found in the author's *Gateway to Empire*.

659. Chief Black Hawk (Makataimeshekiakiak) later stated in his autobiography that he was upset when he presented himself and his men to Tecumseh and was not accorded the pomp and ceremony he expected and felt befitted him and he was equally miffed that he was not asked to be taken into Tecumseh's inner council as a coleader.

660. Like Harrison, Zachary Taylor would one day become president of the United States.

661. Some accounts show Tecumseh as leading this attack, but he was neither there nor leading it, though he had planned it.

662. Some accounts say Tecumseh led the attack on Ft. Wayne, but this is incorrect. Although he did plan it, he was not present and was, at the time it occurred, at Ft. Malden trying to convince Col. Henry Proctor to supply soldiers and artillery for this very attack. A couple of accounts also say Tenskwatawa led this assault, but Tenskwatawa was at this time participating in the attack on Ft. Harrison, far down the Wabash.

663. Capt. Oscar Rhea was formally arrested as soon as Harrison arrived and he was given his choice of resigning his commission or undergoing court-martial. He chose resignation, left the fort and was never heard of again.

664. It was during this period that Tecumseh also developed a closer attachment to old Matthew Elliott, who often accompanied him to dinners with staff officers and their ladies at Gen. Brock's table. As one of those attending officers wrote in regard to Tecumseh's dinner manners:

> His habits and department [comportment] *were perfectly free from what could give offence to the most delicate female; he readily and cheerfully accommodated himself to all the novelties of the situation and seemed amused without being at all embarrassed by them. He could never be induced to drink spirituous liquor of any sort, though in other respects he fed like everyone else at the table. He said that in his early youth he had been greatly addicted to drunkenness—the common vice of the Indian—but he had found that it was bad for him, and had resolved never again to taste any liquid but water. That an uneducated being could deny himself an indulgence of which he was passionately fond, and to which no disgrace was attached in the opinion of his associates, proves, we think, that he had views and feelings to raise him above the level of an unenlightened savage.*

665. LaCroix, in some accounts, is spelled Le Croix. The former spelling appears to be correct.

666. The British and Indians were incorrect in believing that the American force coming down the Maumee was moving specifically against them; Winchester at this point had no knowledge of the force of Muir and Tecumseh so near and had merely been ordered to descend the Maumee to the foot of the Rapids, which was the contemplated point for assembling the army for its push in the spring against Proctor. The British and Indian detachment was also incorrect in regard to who was in command of the Northwestern army. Gen. James Winchester had indeed joined Harrison at Ft. Wayne, but did not take control. The War Department had finally realized, through a multitude of protests from frontier citizens, that making Winchester commander-in-chief had been a serious error; he was disliked, mistrusted, and had nowhere near the experience in frontier fighting that Harrison had. Top command was thereupon turned over to Harrison, along with the rank of major general, and Winchester was designated as his second in command, which considerably embittered him. Harrison at first decided on a winter campaign and had initiated it by detaching half the army under Winchester with instructions to go down the Maumee to its mouth and then follow the western shore of the lake into Michigan; Harrison's wing of the army would move directly north into western Michigan and then turn eastward and the two wings of the army would rejoin in the vicinity of Detroit. After Winchester's wing was in movement, however, Harrison had second thoughts, recognizing the difficulty of a winter campaign and of maintaining supply lines at such a season. Wisely, he canceled the plan and sent an express to Winchester to halt and go into winter quarters, which was what was occurring.

667. The temporary installation built by Winchester adjacent to the remains of old Ft. Defiance was named Ft. Winchester.

668. There does not seem to be any clear record of exactly where this new village was located in northwestern Indiana. However, it is possible that it was situated on the Kankakee River, perhaps somewhere between the present villages of Dunns Bridge in Jasper Co. and English Lake in Pulaski County, since the Indian trail leading from Winnemac's Village (present Winamac, Pulaski County) to the Potawatomi villages in the Chicago area crossed the Kankakee close to where present U.S. 421 crosses that stream. There is further reason to believe this in view of the fact that Tecumseh continued recruiting actively during February and March among the Potawatomies on the Kankakee and Illinois Rivers.

669. Spemica Lawba—Johnny Logan—was the only Indian in Ohio history to be buried with full United States military honors.

670. The actual number of men in the Lewis detachment is open to conjecture. Some accounts contend there were 600 men, others say 550. The more reliable, however, give the figure as 420 men, which was then increased to 520 men with the second detachment sent to join Lewis under Lt. Col. John Allen.

671. British Maj. Richardson, in his account, wrote:

> The different vessels being laid up for the season, parts of their crews were ordered to serve with the artillery, and the two companies of the Newfoundland Fencibles attached to the brigade. No sight could be more beautiful than the departure of this little Army from Amherstburg. It was the depth of winter; and the river at the point we crossed being four miles in breadth, the deep rumbling noise of the guns produced and prolonged their reverberations, like the roar of distant thunder, as they moved along the ice, mingled with the wild cries of the Indians, seemed to threaten convulsion of nature; while the appearance of the troops winding along, now lost behind some cliffs of rugged ice, now emerging into view, their polished arms glittering in the sunbeams, gave an air of romantic grandeur to the scene.

672. In this respect, Gen. Winchester later wrote:

> The troops could not be rallied. The Indians from the British right and left . . . overwhelmed us with numbers. Col. Allen fell; Col. Lewis and myself were captured. I immediately discovered that we were in the power of the noted Huron [Wyandot] chief, Roundhead [Stiahta] compared with whose valor, humanity and honor, the real character of Col. Proctor, if ever justice shall be done, will receive a passport to imperishable infamy . . .

673. The Americans who survived the massacre and were led to Detroit were eventually shipped to Ft. George on the Niagara River, held there for a time and finally taken across the river and released on American soil. Statistics regarding dead and wounded in the Frenchtown affair are numerous and highly contradictory, but the most accurate figures indicate that about 400 Americans were killed and about 500 captured. Of the many who attempted to escape, only 33 managed to make it to safety and spread the news.

674. Ben Graves had long before vowed to his concerned mother in Kentucky that he would never allow himself to be taken prisoner by the Indians.

675. The bullet fired at Catahecassa struck him in the cheek, glanced along the bone and lodged in the neck. Catahecassa was immediately operated upon by the camp surgeon, who removed the misshapen bullet. The Shawnee principal chief did survive but it was the better part of a year before he fully recovered. The assailant was never found.

676. Unknown to Proctor and the Indians at this point was that a large body of militia had been raised in Kentucky with Lexington as the assembly point and only two days before had crossed the Ohio River to Cincinnati under Gen. Green Clay.

677. Robert H. Barclay, a Scot, who was at this time 27 years old, had served with conspicuous bravery and honor in 1805 under Admiral Horatio Nelson at Trafalgar and had lost an arm in that battle, as Nelson himself had lost his right arm in the attempt to take Santa Cruz de Tenerife in 1797.

678. These three artillery emplacements—with a total of one 24-pounder cannon, three 6-pounder cannon and two howitzers—making up the battery on the north side of the river were located inside the present city of Maumee, the emplacement farthest west on the grounds of the present St. Josephs School, the one farthest east on the grounds of the present Union School, the middle one on present Conant Street about a hundred feet south of its intersection with Broadway. The battery on the south side of the river was located in present Perrysburg at about the northwest quadrant of the present Ft. Meigs Cemetery.

679. Gen. Harrison had himself arrived at Ft. Meigs on April 20, only eight days before the British and Indians arrived. It was at about this time that he sent out a detachment and had them erect a much smaller fortification on the Sandusky River eight miles above Sandusky Bay, called Ft. Stephenson, which was located on the site of the present city of Fremont, Sandusky Co., O. Another, even smaller outpost called Ft. Seneca, more a supply depot than anything else, was constructed eleven miles farther upstream on the Sandusky River from Ft. Stephenson, this one located at the site of the present town of Ft. Seneca in present Seneca County.

680. The actual size of Proctor's military force embarking from Amherstburg was 520 regular officers and men and 460 Canadian militia.

681. As soon as Harrison saw the British beginning to erect their batteries for bombardment, he put his corps of engineers and most of his troops to work in digging the network of intersecting traverses, working so rapidly that by the time the British batteries commenced firing, the men inside the fort were well protected in their need to move about in defense of the installation. (One report states Proctor did not learn about the presence of the trenches and traverses until the British bombardment began, but that is not correct, although it is true that Proctor was not fully aware of how effective they would be until the bombardment began.) The principal traverse thrown up by Harrison's men, called the Grand Traverse, was 12 feet high, 20 feet wide at the base and 900 feet long. The second traverse ran parallel to the first and was 700 feet long. Various rooms for protection were dug at angles at the bottom of these huge trenches and smaller slit trenches, just wide enough for the passage of a man, connected the two trenches in various places as well as running to the magazine, headquarters and various other important locations.

682. This encampment of the Indians was located on the plateau some fifty feet above the river level at the southern terminus of Michigan Avenue in present Maumee, Lucas Co., O.

683. Chiuxca, at this time acting as temporary principal chief of the Shawnees during the convalescence of Catahecassa following the assassination attempt, was being called Tom Chiuxca (or Chiuxco) by the Americans and also occasionally addressed or referred to as Captain Tommy.

684. It is reported that Gen. Harrison said he was tempted by the challenge, but finally decided against it, but he also forbade a suggestion from a subordinate officer that a lantern be swung and when Tecumseh approached that he be downed by a volley from the ramparts.

685. Willow Island is presently named Ewing Island. It lay in a direct northeast-southwest line between Ft. Meigs and the British encampment adjacent to old Ft. Miamis.

686. The American soldier whose head was blown off was Silas McCulloch of the Wheeling area. The volunteer recording events of the siege wrote in his log:

> We silenced one of their pieces several times, but did not fire as often as the enemy, as we surpassed them in shooting. Men were carried away from their batteries in blankets and other things, which proved we had done some execution . . . . A bullet struck the seat on which the general was sitting, and the writer of this article received a stroke from a bullet as he stood directly opposite the General, but sustained no injury.

687. Spotted Arm, also called Broken Arm, was one of the most powerful of the Winnebago chiefs. His village at Lake Mendota (present Madison, Wis.) was one of the largest Winnebago villages. He later played an important role in the Black Hawk War, details of which may be found in the author's *Twilight of Empire*. His Indian name was Manahkeetshumpkaw, pronounced Muh-NAH-keets-SHUMP-kaw.

688. Actually, while there was a sufficiency of cannon powder, it was the actual cannonballs that were in limited supply within Ft. Meigs. As the bombardment continued, Harrison encouraged his men to try to recover the spent British balls that had come into the fort or wedged in timbers, offering a gill of whiskey for every cannonball turned into him that had come from the British artillery. By the end of the third day of the bombardment, over a thousand gills of spirits had been earned by the soldiers. The volunteer who was keeping a log, wrote in it for the following dates:

[May 1] *"During the day they fired 256 times and four times in the night. (Not including 30 balls fired by the gunboat.) Our wounded amounted this day to about 8—1 mortally, 2 badly and 5 slightly."*

[May 2] *"We lost this day one man killed, and 10 wounded, besides several others slightly touched with Indian bullets. . . . They fired 457 times during the day, and four times at night."*

[May 3] *". . . The Indians shot one of our men through the head and killed him, and we had six men killed by the cannon and bombs, and three men wounded. The enemy fired 516 times during the day, and 47 times during the night."*

[May 4] *" . . . Several men were wounded and two soldiers killed by the bombs in the night. They fired in all 207 times in the day, and 15 times in the night."*

689. Gen. Harrison had all injured moved to a large and well-protected hospital tent immediately and all dead quickly and quietly buried in simple ceremonies near the rear wall of the fort.

690. This was the 1,200-man reinforcement of Kentucky Militia volunteers under Gen. Green Clay, which left Cincinnati on its march north on April 7, arrived at Ft. Amanda on the upper Auglaize on April 23 and arrived at Ft. Defiance on April 27, where several days were spent preparing the boats for transporting the troops the remaining 60 miles down the Maumee to Ft. Meigs.

691. That island, a quarter-mile wide and three-quarters of a mile long, is the present Blue Grass Island whose upper end is located some 500 yards downstream (east) of the present Interstate 475/U.S. 23 bridge on the Toledo by-pass.

692. Gen. Clay, having gone into camp on a broad sand bar along the southeast shore of the river about a mile above the old Fallen Timbers battlefield and two miles above where Tecumseh wished to stage the ambush, had sent a messenger to Gen. Harrison with word of his proximity and of his intention to arrive first thing in the morning. About the same time that Tecumseh was conferring with Proctor, Gen. Harrison sent an express—Capt. John Hamilton—to Gen. Clay with explicit instructions: he was to split his force, with one detachment to land on the north bank of the Maumee and move at once to spike the cannons in the British batteries on the heights across the river from the fort and, immediately upon the successful completion of this mission, they were to return to their boats, cross the river and come to the fort; the other detachment was to land on the south side of the river prior to reaching the fort, attack any Indians between them and the fort on the south side and drive them off and then themselves come to the fort. Harrison added that while this was occurring, he planned to lead a diversionary sortie against the British batteries pounding him from east of the fort, with the similar objective of spiking the guns and then returning to the fort. Harrison ended his orders by adding: "I take occasion to warn you against that rash bravery which is characteristic of the Kentucky troops, and if persisted in is as fatal in its results as cowardice."

Gen. Clay immediately held a conference with his staff officers and placed regimental commander Col. William Dudley in charge of an 800-man detachment that was to spike the British guns on the north side of the river and return at once, cross the river and get to the fort. Gen. Clay, himself, would lead the other detachment of 400 men on the south bank mission.

693. Col. William Dudley's detachment of 800 men had put ashore on the north side of the river before coming into sight of either the Americans in Ft. Meigs or the Indians and British on the north side at or near the gun emplacements. Some accounts say this landing was made two miles above the British battery, but that is not correct. The landing was made just below the downstream end of present Blue Grass Island and about three-quarters of a mile upstream from the British battery. Dudley had instructed his men that they were to spike the enemy's cannons, but he said nothing to them about the order that as soon as this was accomplished they were to fall back to the boats and immediately cross over to Ft. Meigs. Upon landing he split his force into three wings and placed them 100 yards apart. The right wing, closest to the river, was to march forward and charge the battery from below; the middle wing to strike it directly and the left wing to circle around it to the north and then move in at a right angle to cut off the retreat of the enemy and thus capturing the officers and men manning the guns. This did not work, however, as their advance was spotted by Tecumseh's Indians when they were just under a half mile from the emplacements and the alarm given.

694. As soon as the cannon were spiked, Col. Dudley ordered two companies to remain at the battery and the remainder to charge the retreating Indians. This pursuit ordered by Dudley was in direct disobedience of the orders he had received and there seems little doubt that he saw here what he thought was an opportunity to grasp a significant military plum and could not resist.

695. Dudley's men had moved forward in a series of small charges, routing the Indians from behind the trees and logs where they had taken cover and many Americans were killed or wounded in this maneuver. The Indians would fire from hiding, then leap up and dash toward their rear a distance, stop, take cover, and reload for another shot as the Americans appeared again. Over two hours were consumed in this sort of stop-and-start fighting, until the head of Dudley's force finally met odds it could not beat back, which was in the vicinity of the present Wayne Trail School.

696. These soldiers retreating in disorder to their boats were the members of the two companies that Dudley had left at the batteries who, becoming aware that a retreat was in progress and seeing Indians racing around on the north to cut them off from behind and a force of British closer to the river moving rapidly around them on the south to similarly cut them off, dropped their weapons and raced pell-mell back toward the boats. The weak and injured were left behind, most of which were overtaken and tomahawked where caught. The British force, regaining the battery, met and killed or captured the members of Dudley's main body of troops who were now themselves in full retreat. Many of these, seeing themselves cut off by the British, immediately surrendered.

697. No less than seven accounts mention in passing that cannibalism took place upon the bodies of the Americans, but this seems to be the only authenticated instance of it and this was not cannibalism per se but rather a ritualistic act of taking the courage of an enemy into one's own body.

698. Lt. Joseph R. Underwood, who was badly wounded by a bullet, then captured and stripped and forced to run this gauntlet, wrote in his statement:

> *I was flogged over the head and shoulders with whipping sticks, but escaped all injury from their war clubs, tomahawks and guns. . . . I suppose there were between 30 and 40 prisoners killed and wounded in running the gauntlet. It was here that Captain Lewis lost his life. After we got inside the old fort we were directed to sit down. Those suffering from wounds were kindly and affectionately permitted and requested by our companions to lie and rest in their laps . . .*

In the statement by Orderly Sgt. Samuel K. Stivers (later Colonel) he wrote that the American prisoners:

> *were taken through the gate-ways, and some thirty were killed by the Indians just outside of the fort as they were hurried through the gate, the Indians standing and shooting down such as they chose and then tomahawked and scalped them.*

699. Orderly Sgt. Stivers's statement continued:

> *Indians rushed in and with their war clubs, spike in end, would kill the prisoners and scalp them . . . six or seven dispatched near me, the blood and brains bespattering my naked body . . .*

Lt. Underwood's statement continued:

> *An Indian painted black accoutered with tomahawk, butcher knife, and rifle, mounted the dilapidated earthen embankment of the old Fort, which seemed to rise three or four feet higher than the ground on which the prisoners were sitting or lying, and by his infuriated look, manner and gesticulations, determined to commence a general massacre. His Indian dialect we did not understand, but it was manifest from the excited conduct of the British and Indians that something horrible was impending. [Several other sources commenting on this related that what the Indian said at this point was, "We will kill all these dogs!"] . . . The Indian raised his rifle and*

> *shot the man at the foot of the embankment through the body, killing him on the spot. He then loaded his gun and shot another prisoner who died immediately. He then laid his gun down and drew his tomahawk and jumped down from the embankment among the prisoners. Up to this point I saw all he did, but he jumped down with tomahawk in hand and began to drive it into the skulls of the prisoners next to him, which was followed by the rising up of the men in an effort to get away from the Indian by passing over those who continued to occupy a sitting posture. By this movement I was trampled in my own blood, as I lay in the lap of a fellow soldier named Gilphin . . . and I did not see the blows given with the tomahawk, but I distinctly heard the cracking of the skulls of the men who were killed by it. . . . During the massacre of these unarmed prisoners . . . the scene, in its conflicting passions of savage rage and human mercy, was indescribable . . .*

Underwood then continued with a detail of events after the arrival of Tecumseh and Col. Elliott.

700. Three accounts mention the Indians killing one of the British guards and Orderly Sgt. Stivers wrote of this occurrence in his statement:

> *One of the British sentinels, a tall grenadier, was trying with his bayonet to save a Kentuckian from the tomahawk of an Indian, when the latter drew a pistol from his leather hunting shirt, exclaiming, 'You damned Yankee, too!' and shot him down.*

Several other accounts mentioned that the British guards at first attempted to protect the prisoners, but were thrust back and threatened themselves.

701. A few accounts state that Proctor, who had arrived on the scene some time earlier, had viewed the captives with unveiled hatred and then gave the Indians guarding them leave to select any man each of them wanted and kill him in any manner desired, which permission was then acted upon with alacrity. William G. Ewing, in his statement, wrote:

> *They were huddled together in an old British garrison and the Indians around them selecting such as whom fancy dictated to great shares of inhuman stunts for murder, and although they had surrendered themselves prisoners of war, yet in violation of the customs of war, the inhuman Proctor did not yield them the least protection, nor attempt to screen them from the tomahawks of the Indians . . .*

Ewing then describes the arrival of Tecumseh and his chastisement of the Indians and denunciation of Proctor.

702. Several accounts mention the killing of the offending Indian by Tecumseh, but there still remains some doubt as to whether or not it actually occurred, as other reliable witnesses on hand do not mention it in their accounts. The author believes it probably occurred, since it is consistent with Tecumseh's previous warnings and his past record of opposition to mistreatment of prisoners.

703. Orderly Sgt. Stivers said in his statement in this regard:

> *The Indians quieted down with wonderful quickness and, under Tecumseh's withering rebukes, they slunk away like so many whipped puppies . . .*

Even Maj. John Richardson, an avowed Indian-hater, later wrote in his condescending and pompous report that of Tecumseh this day:

> *nought of the savage could be distinguished save the color and the garb . . . a savage such as civilization herself might not blush to acknowledge as her child . . .*

Capt. Leslie Combs of the 13th Regiment (later Gen. Combs), who had been appointed chief of spies by Gen. Green Clay a month earlier and who had been a survivor of the massacre at River Raisin as well as being among those of Dudley's force who were captured, wrote in a letter to Lyman Draper:

> *I was near Tecumseh when he made his speech . . . whereby the lives of some hundreds of prisoners were saved, of whom I was one . . . He was a truly great man and gallant warrior; then about 45 years old, I think.*

704. Orderly Sgt. Stivers, without going into details about it, stated that: "Colonel Elliott acted nobly in this humane work of stopping this horrid slaughter . . . ."

Several accounts mention Elliott striking the Indians with the flat of his sword, one stating that: "Elliott came, denounced the Indians, and with the side of his sword struck them beside and over their heads and they quickly scampered off . . ." Combs's account merely states that Elliott had his sword in hand and "waved it about."

705. Statistics in respect to the number killed in Dudley's Defeat vary, but "about 300" seems to be the most accepted figure. Of Dudley's detachment, 150 of those who retreated to the boats and were cut off by Tecumseh managed to get across and into the safety of Ft. Meigs; 195 were caught in the woods and gathered apart from those who were taken to old Ft. Miamis; 155 survived the massacre outside and inside old Ft. Miamis. Thus, with 500 surviving in captivity (many of whom were wounded) out of the total of 800 that were in Dudley's detachment, the figure of 300 dead seems reasonably accurate.

706. Site of the present town of Vermilion, Erie Co., O.

707. Including the 77 killed and 196 wounded in and around Ft. Meigs by the bombardment and enemy small-arms fire, the Americans lost a total of about 377 killed and about 250 wounded. Including regulars and militia, the British lost 15 killed and 41 wounded. The Indian losses were not recorded but believed to be less than the British. Gen. Harrison, on determining that the enemy had indeed withdrawn, put Ft. Meigs under command of Gen. Green Clay and himself returned to the Ohio Valley to recruit more men and reorganize his army.

708. Oppomishshah is pronounced OP-poe-MEESH-uh.

709. Harrison had been sending out numerous requests for volunteers to aid him in the coming struggle, applying not only to Gov. Meigs in Ohio and Gov. Shelby in Kentucky, but also to John Armstrong, the United States secretary of war. He held out a tempting offer to Isaac Shelby, writing:

> To make this last effort, why not, my dear sir, come in person? You would not be object to a command that would be nominal only. I have such confidence in your wisdom that you, in fact, should be "the guiding head and I the hand". [sic] The situation that you would be placed in would not be without its parallel. Scipio, the conqueror of Carthage, did not disdain to act as the Lieutenant of his younger and less experienced brother, Lucius.

Shelby, who had acquired considerable recognition as an officer during the American Revolution, wrote in response:

> No apology was necessary to invite me to your standard. Had I more age and much greater experience, I would not hesitate to fight under your banner for the honor and interest of my beloved country.

Gov. Shelby thereupon issued a proclamation inviting all able-bodied Kentuckians, with good rifles and horses of their own, to meet him in thirty days at Newport (across the Ohio from Cincinnati) and he would lead them to the headquarters of the Northwest wing of the army and share with them in its perils and triumphs.

Ohio's Gov. Meigs was no less fulfilling in his response and on July 2 issued the following rather exaggerated appeal:

FREEMEN OF OHIO

> Your state is again invaded by the British and their savage allies. The Indians have invested Lower Sandusky, and Fort Meigs is again in imminent danger of reduction. Cleveland has, perhaps, fallen, and your brethren in that quarter may have perished by the hands of a relentless foe!
>
> When your country is thus critically situated, we cannot for a moment believe that you will withhold your services. Our patriotism has heretofore been viewed with astonishment by other states:—Will you then hesitate at this important period to return to the field, where glory and honor await you—where your exertions for a few days will humble a proud and perfidious enemy? Will you not rather add lustre to your characters, by repelling the invaders of your state, and the murderers of your friends and connections? We know your anxiety to serve your country; and

while we regret that a call on your patriotism is indispensably requisite at this season, we repose unbounded confidence in your ability and will, to relieve the posts on the frontier, and to save from defeat and destruction the brave army of the illustrious Harrison.

Rally, then, fellow citizens, around the standard of your country, and unite in its defence.— While you have arms to guard and breasts to shield, let the enemy know your willingness to stem the storm of war, and share in all its dangers and privations.

We recommend mounted men to embody themselves without delay; and repair to Delaware, Franklinton [present Columbus] or Urbana, where companies and squads will be organised and then marched for the most contiguous posts which are besieged or annoyed by the enemy.

RETURN J. MEIGS
DUNCAN M'ARTHUR

P.S. Gov. Meigs goes, this day, to Franklinton and Delaware to make arrangements for arms, ammunition, provisions and forage; and Gen. M'Arthur goes to Lebanon, Xenia, and Urbana, to make similar arrangements.

Chillicothe, July 2d, 1813

710. In a daring raid against the British moorings at Ft. Erie near Niagara, a small force of Americans had managed to capture the two British ships *Caledonia* and *Detroit* and added them to the growing fleet under Commodore Perry. Five American ships had slipped past the British defenses and were moved from Buffalo to Presque Isle. These included the two schooners *Tigress* and *Somers*, which carried a total of seven guns, the supply ship *Ohio*, the 60-ton sloop *Trippe*, and the recaptured and refitted *Caledonia*. In addition, five other ships were presently under construction at the Presque Isle shipyard.

711. Immediately upon the appearance of the enemy, expecting that the British would begin a bombardment the next day, Gen. Clay quickly employed all hands in throwing up new traverses, covering up the magazines, clearing out the old trenches and making other preparations for what was anticipated would come. Orders were given for five hundred of the garrison to be constantly on guard duty and the remainder to abandon their tents and sleep alongside the walls with their weapons in their arms. During that night of July 20, Gen. Green Clay sent an express to Gen. Harrison, then at Ft. Stephenson, apprising him of the appearance of a great enemy force and the bottling up of Ft. Meigs in another siege, along with the defensive measures he had taken. The American artillery at this time was under command of a Lt. Henderson.

712. This was a detachment under the command of a Lt. Mountjoy.

713. A couple of sources claim Tecumseh took as many as a thousand warriors with him in this movement, but eight hundred appears to be the more correct number.

714. Once again Gen. Clay waited until darkness had fallen and sent an express to Gen. Harrison, outlining this movement by Tecumseh's Indians.

715. The detachment was under command of Lt. Col. William Gaines.

716. From this movement Gen. Clay deduced that the British meant to launch a direct attack against the fort and immediately issued additional weapons so that each man should have two guns to fire when the attack came. Nothing of the sort happened and the British were seen no more, which perplexed the Americans considerably. At this point Gen. Clay sent a third messenger to Harrison with the latest intelligence. Harrison sent back an express, saying that he was reasonably sure Tecumseh's move with his Indians toward Ft. Winchester was a feint. He was equally sure that the British move across the Maumee was actually the start of a movement to storm the virtually untenable little Ft. Stephenson which, at this time, had a garrison of 170 men under Maj. George Croghan, young nephew of the famed Indian fighter, George Rogers Clark. The fort itself, apart from the rifles of the garrison, had only one 6-pounder cannon for defense. Harrison, not wholly certain which of the three forts—Meigs, Stephenson or Winchester—was the real target on this campaign of Proctor's, decided to move his own headquarters to Ft. Seneca where he would be more centrally located to all three and better able to come to the defense of whichever was attacked. In leaving Ft. Stephenson, he told Maj. Croghan, "Should the British troops approach you in force with cannon and you can discover them in time to effect a retreat, you will do so immediately, destroying all public stores."

At the same time Harrison dispatched a message to the Ohio governor to send relief troops at once.

717. Gen. Clay had just received an express from Gen. Harrison in which the commanding general told Clay that he reposed entire confidence in his ability, with the troops under his command, to repulse the enemy should the fort itself be attacked in earnest, but that he was prepared to reinforce him should it become necessary.

718. Inside Ft. Meigs there was initially a great clamor among the soldiers and even many of the officers to send out immediately a reinforcement to help their fellow American soldiers, who were evidently those from Ft. Winchester or a separate reinforcement, who were driving the Indians before them. Gen. Clay, however, to numerous grumblings of protest, remembered only too well what had happened when the detachment under Col. Dudley had gone out and then chased a group of Indians who looked like easy prey. He now assured his men that it was merely a sham battle between the British and the Indians in an effort to lure them out and positively refused to allow such a rescue reinforcement to go out, directing that the fort gates remain closed. The soldiers, many of them anguished at the incomprehensible orders of their general, watched as the supposed body of soldiers outside chased the Indians, many of the "soldiers" waving toward the men in the fort and beckoning them with extravagant arm movements to join and help them, their cries in English of *"Come on! Help us!"* clearly audible.

719. A very sizeable reinforcement of some 5,000 men was at this moment en route to Gen. Harrison at his Ft. Seneca headquarters, 11 miles upstream, but could not possibly reach him for another four or five days.

720. Convinced that Ft. Stephenson was to be the focus of the next attack of Proctor's force, Gen. Harrison sent an express to Croghan, ordering him to abandon and fire the fort and join him at once at Ft. Seneca, eleven miles up the Sandusky River. Croghan, acting under previous instructions of Harrison that "if you cannot retreat with safety, you are to defend the post to the last extremity," wrote back in a way that was deliberately imperious and insubordinate in case his message fell into enemy hands, which was very likely:

> Sir, I have just received yours of yesterday, 10 o'clock p.m., ordering me to destroy this place and make good my retreat, was received too late to be carried into execution. We have determined to maintain this place, and by heavens we can.

Croghan's message got through, however, and Harrison, not understanding the circumstances, was furious. He immediately sent a detachment to relieve Croghan of command. Croghan himself rushed to Ft. Seneca and explained the situation to Harrison, resolving the misunderstanding and receiving from Harrison the return of his command, with orders to defend it.

721. Spotted Arm—also called Broken Arm—(Manahkeetshumpkaw) later had this wound tattooed on his arm, complete with blood, in a remarkably lifelike representation of what the wound looked like originally.

722. Even with this effort to recover their dead and wounded, the British left behind in the ditch, twenty-six dead (Lt. Col. Short and a lieutenant, along with 24 privates) and 14 wounded privates. Croghan's men buried the dead the following day and cared for the wounded.

723. Of the seven Americans wounded, only one was not back on duty at the end of six days. Maj. George Croghan's defense of Ft. Stephenson was deemed by a great many as the single most gallant military action of the War of 1812.

724. On the fifth day of August, three days after Proctor's defeat at Ft. Stephenson and immediate retreat to Amherstburg, Capt. Perry finally emerged with his small fleet of nine ships from the protection of the harbor at Presque Isle and sailed westward along the southern Lake Erie shoreline to Maumee Bay. Leaving his ships at anchor there, he had gone to Harrison's headquarters at Ft. Seneca, 35 miles distant, where the general's force had just been bolstered by a reinforcement of 5,000 men. (The old frontiersman, Simon Kenton, now 58, joined Shelby's army as it came through Urbana, to serve not as a combatant but as a counselor and advisor.) In the realization that the British fleet was anchored in the mouth of the Detroit River and having learned of Proctor's critical problem of supplies and men, along with Tecumseh having been abandoned by many of his Indians, the general and the commodore had quickly devised a course of action. Perry was to sail across Lake Erie and carefully study the situation prevailing near the mouth of the Detroit and, if possible, show himself enough to lure the enemy fleet out after him before it was really prepared for such an enterprise. If he was successful in so doing and if he did engage the enemy fleet and if he did, in fact, defeat them, it would place the American fleet in complete control of Lake Erie and, without any time wasted, Harrison would load his army aboard Perry's ships and move at once to invade Canada at Amherstburg.

725. Perry's ships had appeared off present Barclay's Point at the mouth of the Detroit River on August 24.

726. On July 13, Proctor had dispatched an urgent message to Sir George Prevost for reinforcements of regulars, arms, supplies, ammunition and additional artillery for his push against the Americans, at the same time requesting more support and supplies for Commodore Barclay's fleet on Lake Erie, writing in part:

> *Even 100 seamen pushed on here immediately would, in all probability, secure the superiority on this lake . . . I am already weakened on shore by my efforts to enable Captain Barclay to appear on the Lake; if he should not receive 100 seamen, I shall be under the necessity of sending more soldiers on board the vessels.*

That request having met with no favorable response after a wait of five weeks, Proctor had sent an even stronger message by express to Prevost on August 18, announcing that the enemy had abruptly appeared in superior force to Capt. Barclay and yet not one sailor had been supplied him, notwithstanding every solicitation. The matter, he added, was becoming desperate; western Canada was in very real jeopardy. Refurbishment of the warship *Detroit* was completed but of little use without a proper crew and Proctor added:

> *The Detroit is launched and if I had seamen, a few hours would place this District in security. I entreat your excellency to send me the means of continuing the contest . . .*

Prevost, however, instead of forwarding the requisite supplies and men, responded finally on August 22, commenting in regard to Proctor's situation:

> *Although it may be one of difficulty, you cannot fail of honourably surmounting it, notwithstanding the numerical superiority of the enemy's force, which I cannot but consider as overbalanced by the excellent description of your troops and seamen, valorous and well-disciplined. The experience obtained by Sir James Yeo's conduct towards a fleet infinitely superior to the one under his command will satisfy Captain Barclay that he has only to dare, and the enemy is discomfited.*

727. Gen. Proctor's August 26 response to the infuriating letter of Sir George Prevost on August 22 was as pointed as he dared let himself become to his superior and he wrote, in part:

> *Your Excellency speaks of seamen, valorous and well-disciplined. Except, I believe, the twenty-six whom Captain Barclay brought with him, there are none of that description on this Lake. On board of His Majesty's Squadron there are scarcely enough hands (and those of a miserable description) to work the vessels, some of which cannot be used, for want of men, even such as we have. . . . I entertain the highest opinion of Captain Barclay and have afforded him every aid I possibly could. We have set too strong an example of cordiality not to have it prevail through both services. We have but the one object in view, the good of His Majesty's Service and preservation of this District. Seamen should be pushed here by the dozens.*

728. The battle was occurring near present Put-In-Bay, among Ohio's Bass Islands (then called the Sister Islands) in Lake Erie, close to present South Bass Island, 15 miles north-northwest of present Sandusky, 10 miles north-northwest of present Marblehead and 5 miles almost due north of the northern end of the peninsula presently known as Catawba Island. Some accounts say that when the Indians heard the noise of the battle, they went to Point Pelee to see it, from which they could see smoke rising. The author finds this very unlikely, however, since Point Pelee was some 35 miles distant and the battle took only a little over three hours (from 11:45 A.M. to 2:50 P.M.) The two forces were fairly evenly matched, with Perry perhaps having the slight edge. Barclay's fleet had greater tonnage and guns with greater range, but Perry had three craft more than Barclay and 580 able seamen, plus marines, whereas Barclay had a total of 355 men, of whom no more than 60 were able seamen. In a very close contest, Perry won and sent his famous brief scribbled message on the back of an envelope to Harrison:

> *We have met the enemy and they are ours—two ships, two brigs, one schooner and a sloop.*

Upon receiving the message, Harrison almost immediately put his army into movement to invade Canada. Greater details of the Battle of Lake Erie may be found in a variety of sources, including the author's *The Frontiersmen.*

729. Word of Barclay's defeat reached Gen. Proctor (but not the Indians) on September 12 and he immediately decided to abandon Ft. Malden and Amherstburg and retreat eastward. However, fearful of what the Indian reactions would be, especially Tecumseh's, he did not tell them immediately and swore Matthew Elliott to secrecy in the matter as well, lest the knowledge make the Indians "uneasy." One report states that at this time (either on September 12 or 13) Tecumseh confronted Proctor and asked why the ships had not returned. Proctor is alleged to have responded:

> *My fleet has whipped the Americans, but the vessels have been heavily damaged. They have gone into Put-In-Bay in the islands to refit themselves. They will be back here in a few days.*

The author considers that report very dubious. Proctor had already been threatened by Tecumseh that if the Indian ever caught him in a lie, he and all his warriors would abandon him and Proctor could not afford such a possibility. He now needed the Indians more than ever and he would hardly jeopardize this with a flat lie that would be revealed as such in only a matter of days. Further, instructions Proctor received from his superior, Maj. Gen. Francis de Rottenburg, were to the point in regard to what he should do while he awaited as long as possible the approach of Harrison's army:

> *This interval you will employ by looking well at your situation in communication with Tecumseh, and the Indians, in ascertaining the impression which this* [Perry's victory] *has produced on them, and in concerting with them the measures best calculated to lessen the consequences of that disaster.*

To this end, Proctor ordered Matthew Elliott to notify the Indians to assemble for a major council.

730. Proctor had ordered his engineers early in the morning to begin the dismantling of Ft. Malden, but to "do so in a manner that will not alarm the Indians" and leaving those confused engineers to figure out how such a thing could be accomplished.

731. The following year, at Proctor's court-martial, his behavior on this particular day was examined in considerable detail by the prosecutor who commented, in regard to Tecumseh, that:

> *the indignation of that brave and superior man—and the suspicions of the Indians in general— arose entirely from a want of frankness and candor in Maj. General Proctor.*

Further testimony suggested strongly that Proctor was at this time extremely fearful of the reaction of Tecumseh and his warriors when they found out about the proposed retreat and simply wanted to postpone the eruption for as long as possible.

732. At this point, Matthew Elliott mounted up and rode the several miles south to the farm of old Simon Girty, now so blind he could see little more than to distinguish daylight from night, and told him that Harrison's army would soon be here, adding that Girty and anyone else connected with the British Indian Department had better be off at once, as they would most likely be killed if caught. Girty immediately packed up some things and was led eastward to the Grand River where he took refuge under the protection of his friends the Mohawks until the close of the war.

733. Having suspected what Tecumseh was going to say in response, Proctor had ordered an exact written copy be made of the Indian's speech in order to preserve it and later be able to show it to his superiors and colleagues so they could better understand "the insolence to which I was forced to submit in order to prevent that chieftain's withdrawing from the struggle."

734. Shelby's 4,000 mounted Kentucky volunteers had crossed the Ohio River at Newport on August 30 and arrived on September 11 at the mouth of the Portage River on Lake Erie where Harrison was assembling his force for the crossing of the lake (site of present Port Clinton, Ottawa Co., O.). However, Proctor was incorrect in his belief that all 4,000 of these horsemen were to follow the west shore of Lake Erie to Detroit and cross there. The greater majority of the horses were released in a great pasture of blue grass on the Catawba Peninsula, where an area one mile square was fenced to keep them in until the return of the troops from Canada. One mounted regiment consisting of 1,000 men, however (that of the U.S. congressman from Kentucky, Col. Richard M. Johnson), was indeed sent around the lake to Detroit to cross over there and rendezvous with Harrison at Sandwich (present Windsor).

735. British officials subsequently agreed with Tecumseh's assessment that it was cowardice to leave Amherstburg and Ft. Malden without making any attempt at its defense. Brig. Gen. Henry Proctor was tried by court-martial for disobedience of orders in retreating from Ft. Malden without fighting, was found guilty and cashiered from His Majesty's service and returned to England in disgrace.

736. Several accounts state that at this time Proctor expressly designated the place where he would halt and fight a battle with Harrison as being at the forks of the Thames in the area of the village of Chatham and a nearby Moravian town. Allegedly Tecumseh agreed to this. The author believes that to be entirely incorrect. Not only did Proctor have insufficient knowledge of that terrain to have selected so specific a site, but in those final days of the march up the Thames, Tecumseh persistently asked Proctor when he was going to stop and make his stand and Proctor kept promising this spot and that, but in the end always moved on. This led at last to the famous confrontation between Tecumseh and Proctor where Tecumseh strongly berated him for his constant retreating and demanded he make his stand or he would desert him and Proctor finally gave in to his wishes—none of which would have occurred had Proctor laid out the final battle location to Tecumseh while they were still at Ft. Malden.

737. William Henry Harrison had, late in August, met with Tarhe and other pro-American chiefs at Upper Sandusky and prevailed upon them to send a delegation to Brownstown to meet with Walk in the Water and deliver a final offer for him to make peace with the Americans. Their words and their descriptions to him of the strength of the American army were as much responsible for his final defection as were Tecumseh's at this time.

738. The invasionary fleet had put off from the Port Clinton area the previous day, but had come ashore and camped overnight at Put-In-Bay on South Sister Island and also on Middle Sister Island, those islands now known as South Bass Island and Middle Bass Island.

739. A journalist aboard the flagship wrote that as they:

> drew near the Canadian shore, an object was discernable flitting along the beach, now dashing with rapid movements down the entire front of the approaching fleet, and anon leisurely passing as if to reconnoitre. A nearby view revealed a trim and athletic horseman—Tecumseh—mounted on an Indian pony, dressed in a belted hunting frock of smoked deer skin, with the appendage of long gaiter strapped below the knee, and richly ornamented moccasins. Notwithstanding the flight of his ally, he had lingered behind to ascertain the force of the invading enemy. After singly confronting their floating batteries until satisfied of their numerical strength, he leisurely withdrew in dignified defiance from the shore . . .

One account states that Matthew Elliott was with Tecumseh for this vigil, but since the accounts of those aboard the ships describe only one horseman as being on hand, that report concerning Elliott is discounted.

Harrison's army came ashore several miles below Amherstburg at Bar Point and came first to the farm of Simon Girty, where they asked his whereabouts. They were told he had gone down the lake to get something of his fixed. One of the men allegedly said, "If he were here we would soon fix him so he wouldn't need any more fixing in this world." An older giant of a man is supposed to have remarked in return, "No you wouldn't." It was Simon Kenton, who had come along to make sure no harm befell his old friend. When some of the men threatened to burn down the farmhouse and its outbuildings, they were prevented from so doing by Kenton and some of the officers. (One account romantically has the old friends, Kenton and Girty, meeting again at this time, warmly embracing and then engaging in a fanciful conversation about old times together, which was impossible since Girty was by this time residing in the protection of the Mohawks on Grand River some 200 miles to the east.)

The army then moved northward toward the town and came to The Point, the rather opulent estate of Matthew Elliott, which did not fare so well at their hands. They plundered it of all its transportable goods, including a large supply of spirituous liquors on which they became roaringly drunk, then burned it before continuing into Amherstburg.

Harrison immediately sent out a detachment of 700 men under McArthur to take possession of Detroit, which he did without incident.

740. A few accounts claim that Stiahta—Roundhead—was killed on October 1 near the mouth of the Thames while he was spying on Harrison's movements. An Indian was killed, it is true, but he was simply a warrior who had adopted the name of the chief he idolized and was not the actual Roundhead himself, although these reports have caused much confusion among biographers.

741. Some accounts contend that Tecumapese, sister of Tecumseh, was with him during these last days, but that is not true; she was at this time living with her French trader husband, Francis Maisonville, in Missouri. She and Tecumseh never saw one another again after his departure from there following the 1811 earthquake.

742. Harrison, on his arrival at Amherstburg, finding Ft. Malden and other governmental structures in ashes, had immediately selected some 3,000 men of his army and led them in pursuit of the retreating British and Indians, and because his vanguard was made up of mounted Kentucky volunteers, they quickly drew up close to the retreating force. Commodore Perry, with a few of his vessels, paced the army on shore, sailing eastward along the Lake St. Clair shore to present Lighthouse Cove at the southeastern end of the lake, then up the Thames, but the navigation was tricky and strenuous and he did not ascend the river very far before halting. Perry continued on shore with Harrison.

743. The Americans had three men killed and six wounded in this skirmish. One account claims ten Indians were killed here and a great many wounded, but this appears to be an exaggeration.

744. Many of the eyewitness accounts coincide in their comments that in every such instance of encounter with the enemy, Tecumseh was unfailingly the last Indian to leave the field, making sure that all others had safely preceded him before moving along himself. Long after the death of Tecumseh numerous accounts were written about this last full day of Tecumseh's life and every account claims vivid and close anecdotal contact with Tecumseh on this day; here he saved a lost young boy and returned him to his mother, allegedly Tecumseh's niece; there he helped a youth preserve his cow and his father's home from destruction by the Indians; here he spent the night in the flour mill of an old trader friend to keep it from being burned down so the pursuing whites would not get any benefit from it; at another place he rescued one of his warriors who was allegedly caught and being tortured by a small group of Kentuckians, supposedly holding the offenders at bay with a brace of pistols jerked from his belt while he cut the warrior loose and let him run off. There are a multitude of other such stories, some of which may have some slight bearing in truth but which are at least largely exaggerated and more often than not created out of whole cloth and merely contribute to the Tecumseh mythology that has flourished ever since. A whole chapter could be devoted to these incidents alone and had Tecumseh done all the things attributed to him for this one day it would have taken several days at least. The author has therefore elected to disregard the majority of these anecdotes and adhere only to those incidents that seem most authentic and that coincide most properly with his known movements on this final day.

745. There are three distinct versions in regard to Tecumseh's giving Chaubenee the sword— the one, which seems most likely, as shown in the text; another that states he gave the sword to Chaubenee and said, "When my son becomes a noted warrior and able to wield this sword, give it to him"; and a final version, diametrically opposed to the second, to give it to his son even though he would never be a good leader because he had too much white blood in him (supposedly from Mamate, or perhaps out of a white woman whom history has failed to record as a part of Tecumseh's life). The son he was allegedly referring to here was 17-year-old Naythawaynah (better known by his nickname, Pachetha) who, according to some accounts, participated in the Battle of the Thames, though he was previously, at this time, and later, without distinction of his own. Since history does not indicate that Tecumseh ever evinced any particular parental devotion to him, it appears unlikely that Tecumseh would have made such a bequest and far more likely that, as indicated in the first instance, he gave his treasured gift from Brock to his closest friend, Chaubenee, as his own.

746. Exactly why Tecumseh gave this strange specific instruction is a puzzlement and there are numerous interpretations. That he actually believed he would rise "with my life renewed" and lead them to victory is highly unlikely; that he somehow knew Wasegoboah would never be able to fulfill the request is a possibility; that he simply wanted, at his own death, for his people to clear out and get away as quickly as possible is by far the greater likelihood and the one that, in fact, actually occurred. Perhaps he felt that if he had not given so explicit a command in conjunction with the prediction of his falling, they would simply have continued the battle beyond any hope of escape. Whether one chooses to believe or disbelieve Tecumseh's ability to predict future events is of little moment; whatever the case, the fact remains that the element of mysticism that accompanied Tecumseh throughout most of his life persisted to the very eve of his death.

747. Because of matters to follow in regard to Tecumseh's death, it is necessary at this point to recount an incident that occurred during Harrison's pursuit of the enemy this morning. Moving along the south bank of the Thames, the mounted Kentuckians were in the lead. Among them, riding a fine white horse, was a gray-haired, hawk-nosed old Indian fighter named William Whitley, age 64, with the honorary rank of colonel, who had arrived in Kentucky among the earliest of the settlers and had helped in the establishment of Boonesboro. It had always been a habit of his to load his rifle with two balls instead of one—a practice that had more than once saved his life when an attacking Indian was struck by one or both of the balls. As they proceeded on their march, Whitley glimpsed four Indians spying on them from the brush on the opposite side of the river and decided to stay behind as the column went on and see if he could get a shot at them. He went into hiding and, after the column passed out of sight, the Indians came into the open. Whitley threw up his rifle and shot. All the Indians disappeared but Whitley was sure he had downed one of them and thereupon plunged his horse into the river and swam it across, searched and found a dead Indian freshly killed by two balls, one having struck him in the collarbone and the other having passed through his throat and broken his spine. He scalped the Indian, remounted and swam back over the river. Soon catching up to his companions at the rear of the column, he waved the scalp in the air, saying "I told you I'd get one! This is the thirteenth Indian scalp I've taken and I'll have another before night or lose my own!" He then continued to the head of the column and showed the scalp to his company commander, Capt. James Davidson, who reprimanded him for the risk he took, at which Whitley responded, "Don't fear, Captain, the ball is not run nor the powder made that is to kill me."

It is interesting to note that a grandson of Whitley became one of the most famed of all the western mountain men—William Sublette. Whitley, though aged 64, was not the oldest soldier at the Battle of the Thames; that honor going to Pvt. Joel Cook, who was 90 years old.

748. Proctor had in his possession, on leaving Amherstburg, a total of 20 pieces of artillery; Harrison only two. Pressed as the British were by the Americans, however, and fearful their guns would be captured, fifteen cannon were deliberately destroyed and abandoned during the retreat.

749. Although some accounts say Matthew Elliott had by this time gone in advance of the army and was not anywhere near the vicinity of the battleground, at least one account states that Elliott was here and that Tecumseh, looking over the proposed battle site, remarked to him that he thought the area around the Moravian town was better suited for a battle, but at this point he was satisfied to let it be almost anywhere, just so the army would stop its retreat and dig in to fight.

750. The battleground was located 10 miles upstream on the Thames River from present Thamesville and 5 miles downstream from present Wardsville.

751. It appears that hardly had Tecumseh disappeared than Proctor and his principal field officers and aides, along with Matthew Elliott and some prominent civilians, withdrew a mile or more toward the Moravian Town to wait, certain that the Americans could not be stopped and wanting a good head start in their final flight away from them.

752. Matchemeneto was the Evil Spirit and greatly feared, especially when his presence was believed to be felt before an important fight. Quite often in Shawnee history, entire campaigns had been called off when a Matchemeneto sign similar to this occurred. Were it not for the numerous reliable witnesses to this ominous occurrence, it would have all the earmarks of a fancy later invented. Yet every Indian on hand at this time, individually and at different times and in different interviews, related this event in remarkably similar detail, so it seems it really did occur. None recalled hearing a shot but all remembered the brief ominous buzzing sound of the bullet.

753. Harrison, having received word from his scouts about how the enemy, British and Indians alike, had deployed themselves, decided that if he made a thrust at once at the British he might be able to quickly overrun them and then, having flanked the Indians, concentrate on them who, he had been told, were on the stretch of dry tangled timberland between the two swamps. Harrison ordered Col. Richard M. Johnson to lead his thousand mounted dragoons on an immediate charge against the British position. He did so and the engagement has to be considered one of the shortest in history. The British fired one volley from their rifles and then, without even firing the loaded and primed cannon, either fled precipitately or immediately surrendered. Estimates of the length of the battle ran from as short as one minute to a maximum of five minutes. A runner rushed to Proctor to tell him what occurred and Proctor and his people instantly galloped away. They paused only briefly in the Moravian Town, where Proctor, without dismounting, had a drink and gave orders to the guards there to do the best they could. Then Proctor and his officers and the remainder of the entourage thundered away to the east and did not stop except for brief rests until they reached safety a few days later upon joining with the main British army near York, in the area of present Toronto. Matthew Elliott joined the British force at Burlington Bay and died there the following year.

754. The initial advance squad of 20 horsemen was followed up by about half of the remaining horsemen in Col. Richard Johnson's regiment, led by himself and amounting to about 500 men, including the 144-man advance company led by Capt. James Davidson.

755. This was Col. Richard M. Johnson. Many of the Indians had mistaken him for Gen. Harrison and had shot simultaneously at him and there was a short-lived jubilation among the Indians when they believed they had brought down their dreaded foe, but word soon came that it had not been Harrison after all. Richard Johnson, though severely wounded (five bullet wounds, two of them very serious), recovered and was subsequently inaugurated (in 1837) as vice president of the United States under Martin Van Buren.

756. One of the most persistent of the romanticized accounts is the fiction that Johnson, after being severely wounded, downed and fallen upon and pinned by his dying horse, managed to get a pistol out of his saddlebag and shoot the Indian who was in the act of raising his tomahawk above Johnson's head for the coup de grâce. The fiction is further enlarged with the claim that the Indian so adroitly dispatched was Tecumseh. In point of fact, it was Wasegoboah who was killed here, not Tecumseh, and the shot came from someone else entirely, not Johnson, since not only were Johnson's wounds so severe (including one or both of his hands shattered by bullets through his knuckles) as to preclude use of a pistol, his two pistols, both still loaded and primed, were later recovered from the saddlebags of his horse. As noted, the body of Wasegoboah at this place was later misidentified as that of Tecumseh and Johnson was proclaimed as the hero who killed Tecumseh—a claim he himself did not initially make (nor deny) but a claim that his political allies subsequently did and that they developed into a carefully nurtured campaign slogan that helped him immensely in his bid for the vice presidency of the United States. (Much later, Johnson did say it was he who killed Tecumseh.) Further, had it been Tecumseh who was killed (irrespective of who killed him), the fighting would have ended instantly as the Indians had been previously instructed to flee at once if Tecumseh were killed. Not only did the Indians continue fighting furiously for over an hour after Johnson fell, the voice of Tecumseh was clearly heard throughout that time encouraging his warriors in their efforts.

757. Grievously wounded, Johnson's horse managed to carry him to the river bank where the tent of the surgeon, Dr. Samuel Theobald, was located. Johnson was lifted off the horse and taken into the tent and almost immediately thereafter Johnson's wounded horse fell over and died.

758. This gray-haired man who was killed here was William Whitley, who had earlier in the day killed the Indian with his cross-river shot. Abraham Scribner, in his account, states that Whitley was killed by two balls that passed through his head simultaneously.

759. Stiahta—Roundhead—fell close to where Tecumseh subsequently fell and was another of the dead Indians whose body was later mistaken for Tecumseh's. The officer who slashed at him with his sword was Capt. James Davidson and the soldier who shot under the belly of Davidson's horse and killed Stiahta was Pvt. Massey from Georgetown, Ky.

760. This soldier was the 18-year-old private named David King. As the lines of the Indians and Americans had separated somewhat and his own rifle having been discharged, King hurriedly attempted to reload and, in his excitement, rammed a ball into the barrel of the gun before realizing he had not first poured in a charge of powder. At this point he dropped his own useless weapon and crawled rapidly toward Whitley to get his gun, which was still loaded with two balls, since Whitley had been killed before he could shoot. Managing to get the gun and Whitley's shot pouch, he returned to his lines.

761. The soldier who shrieked the warning was identified only as Pvt. Clarke.

762. In this flurry of firing, Capt. Davidson was hit three times, the wounds serious but none of them fatal.

763. Warrior training was such among the tribes that a prebattle directive such as this was of extreme importance and was to be obeyed, at the proper time, without question and without delay.

764. Battle statistics indicate that the Americans had 12 killed and 22 wounded, with British losses about the same. The bodies of 33 Indians were found on the scene.

765. There exist no less than forty-five (perhaps considerably more!) accounts, all of them differing with one another in various points, of the death of Tecumseh, who killed him and under what circumstances. Most writers these days simply throw up their hands and simply say the details are contentious and therefore unable to be stated as history. Yet, in going over all these known accounts in a very painstaking manner and attempting to retain what fits with the known facts and discard those matters out of hand that could not possibly have been so, some interesting conclusions can be derived. The account just stated in this text is, the author feels, as close to what actually occurred as can be derived from known documentation. Such matters as the Battle of Tippecanoe, the Frenchtown (or River Raisin) Massacre, the first and second Siege of Fort Meigs, the Siege of Fort Stephenson and, most of all, the Battle of the Thames, became extremely prominent political matters in later years when participants in these events were running for elective offices. Two presidents-to-be—William Henry Harrison and Zachary Taylor—and one future vice president—Richard M. Johnson—played important roles in these matters and the heroism, leadership and sagacity (or lack of these things) became extremely important political jousting points. Facts were blown all out of proportion, stories were created out of whole cloth and soon what was the truth was buried under a mire of half-truths, partial truths and outright lies. This was most particularly true in regard to Tecumseh's death and Richard M. Johnson's involvement (or lack of it) in the matter. Unfortunately, most historians have accepted too much of the political hoopla as truth and have named Richard Johnson as the man who killed Tecumseh. Johnson's opponents fixed most strongly on the elderly frontiersman, William Whitley, as the one who squeezed off the fatal shot. Careful investigation, however, virtually eliminates both these gentlemen as prospects for this place in history and puts it in the lap of a political nobody, an ordinary individual undistinguished by anything else in his lifetime—Pvt. David King. The account that, under closest scrutiny, seems to come closest to the truth is that of Capt. James Davidson, which was published as a letter to the editor in the *Louisville Journal* in October, 1859, and, because of its accuracy, the germane portion of his account is appended here as follows:

Lincoln County, Ky., Oct 22, 1859

To the Editors of the Louisville Journal.

Gentlemen: I have read with much interest, the two very different accounts of the death of Tecumseh, recently copied into your paper. You say you do not propose to enter deeply into this discussion. Perhaps you do not know the amount of interest a number of your subscribers take in this question. I will give you some idea of it. I have been solicited by a number of gentlemen, to give you my opinion on the subject, and to put you in possession of facts which I know to be facts. This by way of explanation that I do not enter this arena to challenge any man's veracity— all men may be honestly mistaken, myself being as liable as others. You can judge whether my statements possess interest to a sufficient number of your subscribers to entitle them to a place in your columns or not.

In regard to Mr. Hamblin's account, I think he is totally mistaken in supposing that Colonel Johnson killed Tecumseh. He must have been mistaken in supposing the Indian Colonel Johnson killed to be Tecumseh. I will presently make it appear why I think so.

My account tallies somewhat with that of Capt. Ferguson. I believe him to be mistaken as to the man who killed Tecumseh, but the discrepancies between our statements are so nearly reconcilable, that the truth can be almost positively established. I commanded a company of 144 volunteers, in the Battle of the Thames, in Col. Johnson's Regiment; they were mounted riflemen. In enlisting my company, I had collected 133 men, when an old Indian fighter named Col. Whitley (miscalled Maj. Whistler in the above mentioned article), avowed his determination of going. In vain his friends attempted to deter him. He had acquired a taste for Indian fighting (having already figured in seventeen battles), and was determined to go. He accordingly enlisted, but being so old a man, the company voted him free of camp duty. This, connected with the fact that all discipline was slack among the volunteers, might erroneously lead a stranger to suppose that he was "fighting on his own hook." This man had few faults and many virtues, conspicuous among the latter was his dauntless bravery, amounting almost to recklessness.

After we forded the Thames, Whitley caught sight of four Indians on the opposite side and lingered behind, trying to get a shot at them. We went on, and when we had gotten about a mile on our road we were overtaken by Whitley, who rode up with a triumphant air, holding aloft the scalp of an Indian. He gave me the account of having killed the Indian, in a singularly venturesome manner. I reprimanded him for it, and received for an answer: "Don't fear, Captain, the ball is not run nor the powder made that is to kill me." This was a favorite saying of the old fellow. He was as complete a fatalist as either of the two Napoleons. This, I think, proves that Capt. Ferguson and I refer to the same man.

Capt. F. says: "Furthermore, there were no Indians in that part of the British line which was charged by Colonel Johnson and the Kentucky Mounted Volunteers; and he was wounded in the very commencement of the charge, before the two lines had come in close contact, and was immediately borne from the field, his brother, next in command, then leading the charge, and commanding the regiment the remainder of the day."

Capt. F. is mistaken in supposing that Colonel Johnson did not charge upon the Indians. They were the only foes we had, but they were enough, as they numbered us about three to one. [Error: this advance by Johnson, numbering about half (or near 500) of his regiment was met by approximately the same number of Indians, although Davidson was probably referring to his own company.] *The mistake rises from the fact that Colonel Johnson divided his men. He and Lt. Col. Johnson (his brother) arranged it that Colonel R. M. Johnson was to charge the Indians and Lieut. Col. Johnson the British. After Colonel J. was wounded, he was succeeded in the command (in our part of the field) by Major Thompson of Scott County (an uncle of Johnson's, I believe).*

We were posted at the extreme right, in a dense forest, with thick undergrowth. A short time after the charge commenced, and in the heat of the battle, I saw Johnson pass, supported on his horse, badly wounded. He was immediately borne from the field. It was so short a time from the commencement of the action, that it would have been a most fortunate chance if the first Indian he met was Tecumseh (for he had scarcely time to meet two), and he killed him. It is enough to make one a fatalist, and believe it was his manifest "destiny" to kill Tecumseh, and that he was "raised up" for that purpose.

I do not wish to be thought in any way to detract from Colonel Johnson's reputation. He was undoubtedly one of the bravest men I ever saw. I did not see him the moment he was wounded, and therefore cannot say he did not shoot Tecumseh; but I was not more than ten yards from him all the time he was on the field. I had held a conversation with him just before the charge was made, and I think it likely I would have seen or heard something of it. I think Mr. Hamblin is incorrect in saying that Johnson's horse fell on the field. The horse on which he was carried off was a white one, with a terrible-looking wound in his side, with the blood streaming at every step. I have always understood that he [the horse] *did not fall until he reached the river-bank, when (Johnson being taken off) he fell, and immediately died. Dr. Theobald (of the South, near Lake Providence), was one of Colonel Johnson's supporters, and can probably settle the question.* [An editorial note was added here by Gen. Leslie Combs, who edited Davidson's account, to the effect that:

> *Dr. Theobald states that he was surgeon's mate of Colonel Johnson's regiment; went with him in his charge, and saw him wounded in the first fire of the enemy. Afterward took his holsters and pistols from his saddle-bow when his horse fell and died, and carried them back to camp; both of the pistols being loaded. This being so, it is certain that Colonel J. did not shoot Tecumseh, or any other Indian, in the battle. Davidson and Theobald are men of unquestionable veracity, and are still alive. I know nothing myself of the facts. The Johnsons were both brave men.—Leslie Combs, June 7, 1860.* [Gen. Combs was himself a captain at the time of the Battle of the Thames.]

Soon after Johnson was carried off, the Indians charged on us and one of them shot and killed Col. Whitley, who fell near my horse's feet. The Indian sprang forward to scalp him, which I endeavored to prevent by striking at him with my sword, but he evaded the blows, and persisted in his attempt, until a man by the name of Massey [Lt. Massie], *from Georgetown, aimed at him under my horse's belly and shot him dead.*

I will now proceed to tell you who I think did kill Tecumseh. In my company was a private of the name of David King. He was a splendid specimen of backwoods man, brave as Caesar, an honest man, an unnerving marksman. Whilst we were awaiting another charge from the Indians, King, in loading his gun, put in his ball, forgetting the powder, and had no means of drawing the ball. He was much vexed and told me about it, saying: "Captain, what shall I do?" I told him Whitley had a fine gun, but it was hazardous to attempt to get it. He immediately crawled toward Whitley, keeping the body between him and the Indians, and succeeded in getting his gun and shot-pouch, and regaining his tree. The Indians peppered the spot with balls, but fortunately none hit him. He and some five or six of his comrades asked my permission to go a little further to the right, as they wished to prevent the Indians flanking us. They outnumbered us so far, that it was with great difficulty we could keep from being surrounded. I detached them a short distance to the right, but their eagerness to get to the Indians made them move faster than the left wing; on perceiving which, I started toward them to warn them. I was afraid they might be cut off from the rest of the company. When I got about half way to them, I heard a fellow named Clarke, exclaim: "Look out, King! An Indian is aiming at you!" Whereupon, the Indian turned to fire upon Clarke, thereby exposing his left breast to King's aim, who instantly fired, and as the Indian fell, King exclaimed: "I've killed one damned yaller Indian booger!"

(I should have mentioned above that it was Whitley's custom to load his gun with two bullets, and that when King got the gun, it was cocked, but not discharged. He therefore used the charge

that Whitley put in.) I got the men in the right place, and soon returned to my other men. I was soon after severely wounded three times, and saw no more of King and his comrades until after the battle.

That evening, I was lying on the field, feeling (like Charles Lamb) "ratherish unwell," when some of my men, among them King, came to hunt for me. Whilst they were getting ready to carry me off, King said to me: "Captain, I wish you would let us go by and see the Indian I killed; I wish to see if I made a good shot. If I did, two of old Whitley's balls went in at his left nipple. I took aim by it, and if the yaller devil has any knives, I want them." At first, being in great pain, I demurred, telling him I knew he could not find the Indian, and if he could, he couldn't identify him. "Oh!, yes, Captain," he replied. "My Indian is right behind that old dead tree," pointing to one about fifty yards off. It being on line of march to the camp, I consented. When we got there, we found the Indian behind the tree. They turned him over, and, sure enough, his left breast was pierced by two balls, about half an inch below the left nipple. The Indian was plainly, but more comfortably, dressed than the rest of the Indians, having on the finest wampum belt I ever saw . . . next day Mike (my brother) and Charles A. Wickliffe, of Bardstown, determined to have a look at "King's Indian." They went to the spot, and found the Indian. Whilst they were looking at him, Gen. Harrison and two British officers came up, and one of the latter exclaimed: 'I believe that is Tecumseh!' The other also thought it was him . . . They agreed that this was Tecumseh. . . . Because Tecumseh was killed where Johnson made his charge, Johnson got the credit of killing him, and as there was a great rivalry between Shelby's and Johnson's Corps, we were glad that the Colonel of our regiment got the credit for it. King never cared a cent for it, and I thought it made no difference who killed him. It is only at the request of friends that I make this public. King brought Whitley's gun home, and restored it to his family. Some of Whitley's descendants are living in this County. King moved to Tennessee, and died there about twelve years ago. All his comrades who were with him when he shot the Indian are dead, but there are a number of persons in this County who have heard it from their lips.

I have to employ an amanuensis, and it may be that some mistake has crept into this account; but I have heard it carefully read, and I believe it to be a true statement of what I know concerning the matter.

Respectfully, James Davidson

Among some of the many other accounts of the manner of Tecumseh's death are these:

—Black Hawk later said in his autobiography that Tecumseh was shot and killed by a ball that entered his body near the hip and that his body was not mutilated; that his skull was crushed by a rifle butt; that he wore a British medal; that during the night the Indians brought off the body of Tecumseh in sight of the fires of the American camp;

—Capt. George Sanderson said in his account:

That it was Tecumseh's body that was skinned I have no doubt. I knew him. . . . He was a man of huge frame, powerfully built, and was about six feet two inches in height. I saw his body on the Thames battlefield before it was cold. I saw the Kentucky troops in the very act of cutting the skin from the body of the chief.

—Samuel G. Drake states that Tecumseh was wounded in the arm and killed by a shot in the head.

—Col. Stewart said in his account that he cut the belt off that Tecumseh was wearing, which was stained with the blood of Tecumseh.

—D. K. Foster, nephew of Chaubenee, says in his account:

My uncle . . . was with Tecumseh on the day he was killed. [Tecumseh] was stooping, scalping a soldier. When he was in that position another soldier came on horse back with his musket and fired at him at the same time. He could almost touch him on his back. He then run his bayonet through him, so the great warrior was slain on the spot. The soldier who killed him was killed on the same spot. The brave warrior was hid under a brush heap . . . they [Indians] took his body and carried it away for burial . . . Chaubenee said they had skinned the wrong one instead of Tecumseh.

—Alfred Brunson, who was in the battle, said the body of Tecumseh: "was left to rot above ground with the other Indians."

—John P. Brown says Tecumseh was shot in the heart with one rifle ball and three buckshot.

—Pvt. Daniel Kenshald in his account says in the battle he secured Tecumseh's tomahawk, which he took home as a trophy; said Tecumseh swung at him with the tomahawk and missed his aim and hit him [Kenshald] on the arm and before he could strike again he was shot and fell against Kenshald, who took the ax from his hand.

—Pvt. James Knaggs, who fought in the battle, said in his account that:

> I saw Tecumseh . . . lying on his face dead and about fifteen or twenty feet from Johnson. He was shot through the body, I think through the heart. The ball went out through his back. His tomahawk, with a brass pipe on the head of it, was clutched in his right hand; his arm was extended as if striking, and the edge of the tomahawk was stuck in the ground. He was dressed in red-speckled leggins and a fringed hunting shirt.

—Col. James Coleman, in his account, stated Tecumseh was killed near Col. Whitley by two bullets in the left breast and that his body was not mutilated.

—Garrett Wall claims that Tecumseh was shot with rifle balls in both the head and left breast.

—Lt. Stephen Clever's account states that Johnson did not kill Tecumseh, who was killed some 300 yards distant from him; that Tecumseh was identified by a small trinket he wore, and that his body was skinned and mangled.

—Clark's *Potawatomi* states that Tecumseh was shot "above or in the eyes" and his *Indian* states that Tecumseh's thigh was mutilated by men who wanted strips of skin to make razor strops.

—Lt. Abraham Shane said in his account:

> Tecumseh was not a large man, for I helped to bury him and I ought to know. . . . We came to a small Indian dead. He lay upon his back. A pistol shot had disfigured his face . . . One Indian turned the body over on the face, tore away the calico shirt from the shoulders and raised a long plaintive howl as he pointed to a deep scar under the right shoulder of the corpse. This, he said, was Tecumseh. We carried the body to Gen. Harrison, who was well acquainted with Tecumseh. Harrison said it was Tecumseh and ordered it to be decently buried. I took my men and we buried the body in the clump of trees where he fell.

—Col. Richard M. Johnson showed Lyman Draper the pistols he had used in the battle and remarked, "with them I shot the chief who confronted and wounded me in the engagement."

Draper persisted in asking whether or not it was Tecumseh and Johnson defensively replied:

> They say I killed him! How could I tell? I was in too much of a hurry when he was advancing upon me to ask him his name or inquire after the health of his family. I fired as quick as convenient and he fell.

Johnson claimed to have Tecumseh's tomahawk. In 1842, while he was vice president, Johnson remarked that he had indeed killed Tecumseh.

—Sauganash, interviewed, stated that he was with Tecumseh when the fatal shot came; that the bullet came from behind and had been shot by one of the retreating British; that Tecumseh walked a distance, sat down on a log and then fell over dead.

—Tecumseh K. Holmes said he viewed bodies, but none were that of Tecumseh, whom he knew well; he was of the opinion the body had been taken by his friends, along with others who had fallen, and buried.

—Ordnance Sgt. William Gaines wrote in his account that Tecumseh

> had on no ornaments but a British Medal & three silver half Moons . . . he was shot about the hip . . . part of his hip was taken away . . . Col. Johnson's pistol ball broke his Skull . . . Tecumseh was buried by our troops.

In a subsequent account, however, Gaines said Tecumseh was killed 100 yards from Col. Johnson and that all his trophies were taken by the men.

—Ottawa Chief Noonday, interviewed by interpreter Leonard Slater, said he was directly on Tecumseh's right when he fell and that Col. Johnson killed him with a shot in the breast and that he and Chief Saginaw seized him at once and bore him from their field; that he, Noonday, had taken Tecumseh's tomahawk and hat.

—Peter Navarre stated in his account that Tecumseh:

> was standing behind a large tree that had been blown down, and was killed by a ball that passed diagonally through his chest. After death he was shot several times, but otherwise his body was not mutilated in the least, being buried in his regimentals, as the old chief desired, by myself and a companion, at the command of Gen. Harrison. All statements that he was scalped or skinned are absolutely false.

—Chiefs Carrymaunee and Four Legs, in a joint statement, claimed that:

> Tecumseh fell in the first fire, pierced by 30 bullets, and we carried him four or five miles into the thick woods and buried him.

—J. Scott Harrison, son of the general, wrote:

> I do not know that my father saw the bodies of either of these Indians [Tecumseh and Stiahta] after death. I am inclined to think that he did not, as he would otherwise have most probably alluded to his recognition of his old enemy, Tecumseh, who you are aware he knew very well.

—Dr. Samuel Theobald states that interpreter Anthony Shane, former adopted Shawnee and companion of Tecumseh, was unable to identify the body pointed out to him as Tecumseh's as being that of his adopted Shawnee brother; Theobald was convinced that the body of Tecumseh was carried off by fellow Indians, unmutilated.

—Andrew Clark, a white man who was an adopted Shawnee and one of Tecumseh's aides, himself was shot in the battle and found propped up against a tree and dying; in his final words he told questioners that he had seen Tecumseh killed and that Tecumseh's body had been borne off someplace by his companions.

—Col. Robert Anderson says in his account that Tecumseh was:

> engaged in a personal encounter with a soldier armed with a musket—he caught the bayonet of the soldier under his arm and was about to strike with his tomahawk when a horseman rode up and shot Tecumseh dead with a pistol

and that he saw Tecumseh's body a day or two after the battle and it was not mutilated.

—Maj. James Whitaker said the Indian whose thighs were skinned for razor strops "looked like Tecumseh, only shorter and smaller in every way . . ."

—Gen. William Henry Harrison, who, along with Commodore Perry, viewed a body that had been mutilated, admitted that:

> I first thought it was Tecumseh, but the body was too small—it must have been a nephew of his, who much resembled him, though smaller in size.

Harrison, however, though he wrote an extensive report to Secretary of War John Armstrong on October 9, made no mention whatever of Tecumseh's death, nor did he mention it in his letter of October 11 to Return J. Meigs.

—Chaubenee, who for many years refused to even discuss the subject, finally, in an interview some twenty years later "seemed to recall" that Tecumseh was mortally wounded in the neck by Col. Johnson and that his thigh was not mutilated; that the night following the battle he, Chaubenee, accompanied by a party of warriors, went to the fatal field and found Tecumseh's remains where he fell. A bullet had pierced his heart, and his skull was broken, probably by the butt of a gun, otherwise the body was untouched, and that they took him away and buried him.

—Pvt. John S. Herndon said in his account:

> I was in the heat of battle and when the second charge was made on us by the Indians, Edward Elloy, J. Harrod Holman and myself were close together and near the spot where Col. Whitley

was laying dead (say 30 or 40 steps) and an Indian advanced on Whitley and was scalping him, when Holman leveled his gun and fired and killed the Indian who was scalping Whitley, and Holman ran and obtained the two pistols of the Indian, which he kept until his death, and the British soldiers whom we had taken prisoners told us that was Tecumseh whom Holman had killed . . . it is but justice to the history of our country to say that J. Harrod Holman was the man who killed Tecumseh.

—Captain Parks, a Shawnee warrior, said Tecumseh was his old and greatly loved friend whom he was with in the battle, in which:

Tecumseh singled out a mounted officer, shot at and made a dash at him, and himself received a pistol shot at the hands of the officer, and Tecumseh, badly hurt, was carried off by his Indian friends and died that night.

—Simon Kenton said he recognized the body of Tecumseh immediately after the fight, but that he deliberately failed to identify it because he knew it would be mutilated by souvenir hunters; that he purposely misidentified the body of another chief, nearby, as that of Tecumseh and that this body was severely mutilated, and that when he went to look at the body of Tecumseh again the next day, it was gone; and that another one being pointed out as Tecumseh, was not and even though badly mutilated, he could tell it was not because the mutilated Indian did not have a fine set of teeth, which Tecumseh did have; that when he viewed the desecration that had been perpetrated on the body of the chief thought to be Tecumseh, he had commented to a companion that "There have been cowards here."

—Capt. Thomas P. Leathers's account said that when the dead body of Tecumseh was found:

it was pierced with about a dozen bullet wounds, several of which would certainly have proved fatal; Leathers had the powder horn he claimed to have been Tecumseh's.

—Gen. Henry Proctor at first discounted reports of Tecumseh's death and then, when convinced of the truth of them, did not inform his superiors of that fact for three weeks.

—Lewis Cass was the first American to *officially* report to Washington the death of Tecumseh and identification of his body, but this did not occur until October 28, 23 days after the battle.

—Isaac Hamblin stated in his account that:

Johnson's horse fell under him, he himself also being deeply wounded; in the fall he lost his sword, his large pistols were empty, and he was entangled with his horse on the ground. Tecumseh had fired his rifle at him, and when he saw him fall, he threw down his gun and bounded forward like a tiger, sure of his prey. Johnson had only a side pistol ready for use. He aimed at the chief, over the head of his horse, and shot near the centre of his forehead. When the ball struck, it seemed to me that the Indian jumped with his head full fifteen feet into the air; as soon as he struck the ground a little Frenchman ran his bayonet into him, and pinned him fast to the ground.

—Naythawaynah, better known as Pachetha, son of Tecumseh, interviewed a year later by Lewis Cass, related that he was near his father's side in the battle but that his uncle, The Prophet, was in the Creek country; he said he had no doubt Col. Johnson killed his father.

—William Conner, the trader and Indian agent, stated in his account that he was sent by Harrison to identify a body believed to be Tecumseh's; that he identified it as Tecumseh, whom he knew well; that close to the body of the chief lay an American officer and a lad and that the officer had been killed by a large bullet, the lad by a smaller one, and the chief by a very small one, which would just fit the light rifle carried by the officer's aide, as he was supposed to be. The chief, Conner thought, shot the officer, the boy shot the chief and was instantly shot in turn by one of Tecumseh's braves.

—Capt. James Davidson's account, by far the most accurate in personal observation, says Tecumseh was killed by two lead balls in the left breast and through the heart, that he wore no ornamentation or sign of rank, but he also adds the hearsay that the body was mutilated.

Through close study of the many varying accounts of what happened after Tecumseh was killed, the author has concluded to his own satisfaction that the body of Tecumseh was not mutilated and that sometime during the night of October 5–6 or possibly the following night, Indians slipped back to the battlefield, recovered and removed the body of Tecumseh and buried it.

In that respect, the following is an authentic Shawnee statement made by the late Head Committeeman and Custodian of the Tribal Records of the Absentee Shawnees, whose Indian name was written Ganwawpeaseka, but who was known to the whites as Thomas Wildcat Alford, great-grandson of Tecumseh:

> *Some years after the burial of Tecumseh, a band of Shawnees returned to the scene to disinter the body of Tecumseh and bear it back to their Oklahoma reservation for a reinterment suitable for the greatest leader of their race. This party, selected because it knew the precise spot of interment along a small creek, found that the creek at flood times had washed away all evidence of the great warrior's last resting place. Rather than dig haphazardly in an effort to find the bones, the remains were left in place and the Shawnees still maintain their vigil at this spot with racial fidelity, in sorrow and silence.*

Shawnee tradition states that:

> *No white man knows, or ever will know, where we took the body of our beloved Tecumseh and buried him. Tecumseh will come again!*

Tecumseh!

Index

Index